Wine Spectator's

CALIFORNIA WINE

by James Laube

A COMPREHENSIVE GUIDE TO THE WINERIES,
WINES, VINTAGES AND VINEYARDS OF AMERICA'S
PREMIER WINEGROWING STATE

WINE SPECTATOR PRESS • NEW YORK

Published by Wine Spectator Press
A division of M. Shanken Communications, Inc.
387 Park Avenue South
New York, New York 10016

Illustrations by Dorothy Reinhardt
Maps by Richard L. Thompson

ISBN 1-881659-25-9

THIS BOOK
IS DEDICATED TO MY FAMILY
AND WRITTEN IN MEMORY OF
ANDRÉ TCHELISTCHEFF
FOR HIS
INSPIRATIONAL POWER.

FOREWORD

❖

I wish this book had been available when I started drinking and collecting California wine 20 years ago. It would have saved me from a lot of false starts and frustrations.

Back then there was little information available about the fledgling California wine industry. Today, the problem is nearly the opposite: there are plenty of books about California wine, but few are opinionated enough, or comprehensive enough, or written in plain enough language, to make an all-around guide that you can trust when deciding which wines to buy.

California Wine fills that gap. If you could have only one book on this colorful, fascinating topic, this is the one to have. James Laube, who has been writing about California wine since 1978 and for *Wine Spectator* since 1980, has written the definitive guide. It is both broad in scope and precise in its critical approach. With painstaking care, *California Wine* presents nuts-and-bolts information about nearly 700 wineries—virtually every one in the state—including who owns each one, how many acres of vineyard each owns, who the winemakers are, and what wines are produced. Then—and this is where the book will make the biggest waves—Laube rates the wines and wineries.

James Laube is already known as the leading expert on California wine, and has authored two previous books on the subject, *California's Great Cabernets* (1989) and *California's Great Chardonnays* (1990). But here he looks at the big picture. This book provides blanket coverage of Cabernet Sauvignon and Chardonnay, updating what Laube has previously written, but it doesn't stop there. Who makes the best Pinot Noir from year to year? The best Zinfandel? Are any California Merlots or

Syrahs of outstanding quality? These questions and many more are answered.

The book is based on a huge volume of research and on Laube's proven ability as a wine taster and critic. It includes reviews of more than 7,000 wines, many of which he has tasted repeatedly over the years. But, for all the details that the serious student of wine will find invaluable, this book is not for snobs. It is written in a deliberately accessible style to help you learn as much as possible about California wine.

New and improved maps show where the wineries are located and where some of the best single-vineyard wines come from. Introductory chapters help you understand what the various types of wine taste like, how wine is made and how to build an intelligent wine collection, among other topics.

It's not surprising that no one has tried to write a book of this scope before. The task of researching it was monumental, the logistics of tasting 30,000 wines and choosing 7,000 to include were nightmarish, and the chores of editing and organizing this book were daunting. Such a project was waiting for a writer with the sweeping knowledge of California wine that James Laube has, and an organization with the people and resources that *Wine Spectator* has, to do it right.

I am proud to present this book. I am confident it will quickly become the Webster's of California wine.

MARVIN R. SHANKEN
Editor and Publisher, *Wine Spectator*

DISCOVERING CALIFORNIA WINE

❖

There are more than 800 wineries in California today and more than twice that many different wine brands. Each year nearly 4,000 new wines are released on the market. Even as I write there are new wineries being born and old ones closing. Vineyards are being bought, sold, planted and replanted. Winemakers are rethinking their wines and changing their techniques. New vintages are being released, other vintages are maturing, and others are fading. All of this adds up to a fast-paced business that gives us an amazing array of choices. Keeping abreast of this ever-changing market can be mind-boggling.

My intention in writing this book is to provide a comprehensive guide to California wines. In one sense, *California Wine* is a diary of wine notes, observations, recollections, analysis, opinion, and conjecture. It presents the results of 17 years of research, 30,000 tasting notes, hundreds of interviews with winemakers and many miles of travel in each of the state's main wine appellations.

This book's organization reflects the belief that our desire to learn more about wine is driven by our wine-drinking experiences. That is, when we find a wine that excites our taste buds, it triggers a greater curiosity. Thus the process of discovery for most wine lovers begins with the selection of a wine and whatever taste sensations it provides.

Your palate, and your palate alone, is the final judge of a wine's quality, for no one knows your tastes better than you do. However, at its most basic level, a wine is good or it isn't. It pleases or it doesn't. When a wine fails to please, it can easily be replaced by another. When a wine excites, then the questions quickly multiply: What

is its grape type? Where was it grown and in what kind of soil? How was it made? How long will it age?

Once begun, this process of discovery leads to an almost endless succession of steps backward. Even after you have tracked a wine back to its most specific origins, to the very plot of land where its grapes were grown, to the year they were picked and vinified and the climatic circumstances of that year, further mysteries remain. Exactly what is it that makes one wine so different from the next, or one vintage so different from another, even when the grapes are grown in seemingly identical sites under seemingly identical circumstances? Or why does one grape variety grow so well in one climate, yet so poorly in another? Why do some wines age so gloriously and others so miserably?

Fortunately, no one can answer all of those questions all the time, or much of the mystery of wine would be gone. A wine's character is the result of a complex set of circumstances involving grape type, soil, climate and vinification technique. Professionals who have studied wine their entire lives still seek answers to these puzzles. Researching these details can be fun. It's like detective work, gathering evidence and piecing together clues about a wine's origins and style.

I believe in this theory of the wine discovery process because it happened to me and I've seen it happen to literally hundreds of other wine lovers. Once you get the wine bug, your appetite for information, insight, analysis and opinion often becomes insatiable. This does not happen overnight. I had drunk fine wines on many occasions, but one dinner party in particular convinced me that wine was something special and I've been interested in it ever since. In 1974, the year my curiosity about wine turned to a greater fascination, choices were plentiful. I moved from drinking Wente's Le Blanc de Blancs, an off-dry Chenin Blanc that's still made, to Louis Martini's Zinfandels and Cabernets, multiplying my experiences and options. Then it was on to Heitz Chardonnay and Cabernet, and even an expensive ($9.50 then) Martha's Vineyard Cabernet.

When, like me, you have begun to find the choices intriguing, the next step is to visit the vineyards and wineries and their tasting rooms in Napa and Sonoma, Monterey or Santa Barbara, where you can step inside Beringer, Sebastiani, Meridian or Sanford and taste an entire spectrum of wines, from white Zinfandel to Riesling to Gewürztraminer to Pinot Noir to Merlot to Ports and dessert-style wines—all without leaving the room. At this point, your options really snowball, which can trigger greater curiosity.

Crisscrossing California's wine country leads to fascinating discoveries about geography and climate. You notice that it's cool, foggy and even chilly in Russian River at midday in the summer and scorching hot on Diamond Mountain 20 miles away. You discover the proximity of sandy soils to river beds, the clay flats and gusty winds of Carneros, the low-lying fog that clings to the floor of the Santa Ynez Valley. You notice the steep hillsides and rocky terrain of the mountains and later learn that hillside vines grow well there because the vines are naturally stressed, there's good drainage and the elevation helps protect against spring frosts. And as you descend to the valley below, you discover that it's cooler on the mountain top than on the valley floor. You experience the changes in temperature as you shed your sweatshirt in the morning, find your shorts and T-shirt for the afternoon, then wish you'd brought a jacket as you dine outdoors in the evening and the cool night air blows off the chilly waters of the Pacific Ocean.

This detective work, this process of discovery, has led to the growth in popularity of California wine and contributed to its rise in quality. As a fast-growing, well educated, upwardly mobile and financially able generation of wine lovers emerged in the 1960s, '70s and '80s, it quickly embraced wine, creating a nearly ideal market synergy between supply and demand, creativity and innovation, curiosity and education. At times there are imbalances, as nature intervenes to influence supply, making one year's crop larger or better than the next or previous year's. In much the same way the economy seems to stretch or shrink your buying power from year to year.

Today's California wine drinker is already well informed, educated, sophisticated and opinionated. Still, good advice always comes in handy.

This book is written for all California wine drinkers, whether young and inexperienced, seeking guidance in what can be a complex and intriguing subject, or older and wiser, with great wine collections and knowledge to match. In both the individual wine reviews and the winery profiles—which range from thumbnail sketches to more detailed analyses—I have tried to focus on what is most likely to interest you: the best wines and producers. There are discussions about different grape and wine types, appellations where different grapes are grown, vintages, how wine is made and the thought processes involved, along with my thoughts on how California's fine-wine industry emerged. I offer general overviews of these subjects, simply as food for thought, since there are many well written books that deal with them in far greater detail. I've also offered my advice on making the most of your wine collection, whether you're new to wine and can benefit from my experiences and recommendations, or you're already an expert but would like to read one writer's diary of tasting notes.

You won't find here a tasting note on every wine ever produced in California or a reference to every single winery or brand that's out there. Nor is this an attempt to tell all the stories behind the wineries and winemakers, or to analyze why and how the soils in Anderson Valley differ from those in Carmel Valley. What you *will* find here are a lot of useful reviews, ratings, comparisons and discussions about California wine. It is my hope that this book will make you a wiser and better-informed consumer—that it will leave you more and more pleased with each bottle of California wine you buy.

JAMES LAUBE
Napa, California
June 1995

ACKNOWLEDGMENTS

❖

No book is a solo act. I've had the support and cooperation of many of my *Wine Spectator* colleagues, family and friends this past year while writing *California Wine*.

I am most indebted to my book editor, Greg Walter, a close and valued friend and confidant, for all his thought, input, analysis, brain power and dedication to this our third book together. Greg has been involved in literally every phase of this book, from the earliest beginnings two years ago when we began to develop the concept and format, through the collection of data, analysis of wines and wineries, vintages and appellations, page and map designs, front line editing, more than a few harrowing deadlines, endless weeks, sleepless nights, night shifts (and working weekends) and a few good laughs along the way.

I'm fortunate to have had once again the sharp eyes and keen mind of Lisa King as my valued (and trusted) chief copy editor. This too is our third book together and her contributions to the final manuscript are greatly appreciated. I'm fortunate too to have had the enthusiastic help of Kathleen Marcks Hardesty and Mark Norris, who helped organize scores of tastings involving thousands of wines and collect, sort and organize winery and wine data and detail the maps.

My editor and publisher, Marvin R. Shanken, has been a passionate fan and collector of California wine for more than 20 years and he put all of his energy behind this book from day one. For that I'm especially grateful. All authors should be so fortunate as to have this kind of backing and support.

Thanks to the whole Wine Spectator Press team, headed by Michael Moaba, that worked diligently to meet many ultra-tight deadlines. This team includes Ann Berkhausen, Amy Lyons, Tara Collins, Julie Nord, Alan Richtmyer, Donna Marianno Morris, Kathy McGilvery, Ronald Sequeira, Jr., Laura Zandi, Christine Carroll, Connie McGilvray and Niki Singer. I would also like to single out my other colleagues at *Wine Spectator* who have helped me in one way or another, especially Jim Gordon. Many people in the wine industry, from growers to retailers to restaurateurs to consumers also have contributed to this book by sharing their knowledge about wine with me or giving me feedback about what in wine piques their interest.

Last, and never least, thanks to my wife, Cheryl, for all her loving support, my brother Tom for his advice and good thoughts and my children, Dwight and Margaux, who did what they could to make sure this book stayed on course.

TABLE OF CONTENTS

How to Use This Book

❖

This is an exciting era in the history of California wine. At no time has California wine been better or our wine-buying options greater. However, greater choice in the marketplace often means greater confusion for the buyer. No single source can give you all the answers you want about wine, but a good reference book can point you in the right direction. This book is my effort to provide such a reference.

Wine reviews form the heart of this book—more than 7,000 individual tasting notes, each of which is given a numerical rating on a scale of 50 to 100 points, are included. Many of these wines are still available on the market. Others may be harder to find, but you'll come across them at auctions, at fine wine stores and on the best restaurant wine lists. Still others are stored away in collectors' wine cellars. How are they aging? Are they still worth drinking? Or are they old and tired, headed over the hill? In researching this book over the past three years, I've tracked virtually all the major wines produced in California, from Alicante to Zinfandel, compiling detailed vertical tasting notes on the most important wines and on some very rare ones too.

In addition to the wine reviews, this book contains a wealth of information that will help shape your wine-buying decisions and steer you to the best wines, wineries, appellations and vintages. Even as this book ages and the wines listed here get harder to find, you'll still find it useful. The tasting notes will help when you need to look up an older wine. Information about the vintages and which grapes grow best in which appellations will continue to be valuable, as will the maps. In time, vineyards will be replanted, often to different grape varieties. New appellations will emerge and prominent vineyards will change owners. But the profiles found here will remain pertinent because vineyards like Martha's Vineyard, Rochioli Vineyard or Sanford & Benedict will still be talked about years from now, regardless of who owns them.

This book covers nearly 700 wineries, from the largest, which produce millions of cases, to the smallest family-owned ones, which put out just a few hundred cases. Each winery entry identifies the owner, when the winery was founded, where it is located, whether it owns its own vineyards or buys grapes, where the grapes are grown and who makes the wine. It also provides an overall winery performance rating of one to five stars, with five stars being outstanding, four stars excellent, three stars good to very good, two stars fair or mildly satisfying, and one star poor. The winery analysis is based on my tasting research, which I discuss later in the introduction.

RESEARCH, TASTING NOTES AND RATINGS

Statistical information about the wineries was obtained from the wineries themselves. Analysis of vintages, wine styles and appellations is based on my research as well as on interviews with winery owners, winemakers, grape growers and members of the wine trade. Figures and statistics relating to American Viticultural Areas, their boundaries and grape acreage come from state and federal agencies that monitor those statistics.

Most of the wine research comes from my 17 years of covering the California wine industry and from some 30,000 tasting notes compiled during the past decade; virtually all of the notes are based on tastings conducted in the past two years. Most of the tasting analysis, notes and ratings come from blind tastings, in which objectivity is preserved because the identity of the wine is not known. I try to taste each wine as many times as possible so as to form the most accurate profile of the wine. Virtually every wine reviewed in this book has been tasted at least twice; many have been tasted three or four times. In general, I give the wine the best review it has earned. I also try to retaste wines that have been inconsistent in tastings.

I try to taste the major red wines—Cabernet Sauvignon, Merlot, Pinot Noir and Zinfandel—of the major producers from the barrel as well as from the bottle. This gives me an early look at the wines and the vintage, which helps shape and reinforce later impressions. However, none of the tasting notes in this book are based on barrel samples of unbottled wine. I also taste wine at wineries in the company of their winemakers, which allows me to pick up small details about a vineyard or wine or the style of wine the winemaker is aiming for. I typically taste 40 to 60 wines in a single day, two to three times a week—an average of 5,000 wines a year, give or take a few hundred, for the past 10 years.

For my tastings, the wines are wrapped with paper to conceal their labels. Price, appellation, producer, vintage and wine type are not factors in evaluating the wines. Price is only a factor in determining whether a wine is a good value. White wines and sparkling wines are chilled to appropriate levels before tasting, 50 to 55 degrees Fahrenheit. Red wines are served at cool room temperature, usually 60 to 65 degrees.

ABOUT THE SCORING SYSTEM

After tasting a wine several times (and spitting it out into a bucket), I write a description of it and rate it from 50 to 100 points. I find the rating scale useful, simply because it clarifies how much (or how little) I liked the wine. I prefer the 100-point scale because it offers a wider range of scoring possibilities than a system of one to five stars. The latter might be adequate if there were only a few hundred wines to rate each year. But to successfully distinguish between several thousand wines each year, the 100-point scale is the better choice. I've come to think of the 100-point system as a pleasure scale, with the higher numbers representing the most pleasurable wines. However, no rating system is perfect. A number can't tell you everything you need to know. You will also want to study a wine's description, which will specify its style, its flavors, its degree of balance or perhaps a unique feature. But when sorting through thousands of wines, sometimes remembering a number helps, just as it helps remembering a producer's name or the best vintages for different wines. Another way of looking at the 100-point scale is to say that a wine that gets 90 to 100 points earns an A grade, 80 to 89 a B, 70 to 79 a C, and 60 to 69 a D. Below 60 is failing.

Wines that score between 95 and 100 points I consider classics. These are wines that display uncommon richness, depth and complexity and rank among the very finest wines in the world. Wines that rate 90 to 94 I consider excellent, wines you would be more than happy drinking every day. Wines that rate 85 to 89 I consider very good. These are well crafted wines that offer ripe, rich, complex flavors and true varietal character. They also often represent very good value, but a few are high-priced, so beware. Wines that rate 80 to 84 I consider good everyday wines. They may not be as fruity or complex as more highly rated wines and they may have one or more minor flaws. They might be too tannic, or have strong earthy flavors mingling with the fruit, but not enough of an off-putting character to warrant a lower score. Wines that rate 70 to 79 I consider fair, ordinary wines that may have noticeable flaws, such as too much tannin or a slight sour edge, or they may taste watery or diluted from lack of concentration. They may also be older wines that have started to decline in quality; it's important to remember that when looking at ratings for older wines. Wines that rate 60 to 69 are flawed or really old wines that are best avoided. These wines are marked by serious defects, such as moldiness, excessively high acidity (or volatile acidity), gamy flavors, sulfur or spoilage defects. Below 60, forget it. No winery would remain in business if it routinely produced wines that scored in the 60s. Even those that consistently rate in the 70s are in danger of losing their audience.

There are plenty of ordinary wines being produced in California, but few truly awful ones reach mainstream markets. This is an indication that producers have the proper quality control mechanisms in place to isolate and eliminate wines with obvious defects before they reach the market.

RATING THE WINES

For each bottling produced by a winery, I've given an overall rating between one and five stars, with five stars being outstanding, four stars being excellent, three stars being very good, two stars being fair or mildly satisfying and one star being poor. NR means not rated, an indication that the wine is either too new to rate or that I have no recent notes on which to base an informed opinion or honest advice. These wines may also no longer be in production.

The five-star (★★★★★) wines are the ones I consider the finest California has to offer. If you were to build a dream cellar, these are the wines you'd want to focus on. In general, wines that have earned this highest designation

• have long, consistent track records for style and excellence (reds such as Cabernet, Merlot, Pinot Noir or Zinfandel may also be ageworthy);

• come from vineyards with long, consistent track records for distinctive styles and excellent quality;

• are from winemakers who have long and distinguished track records for excellence.

Four-star (★★★★) and three-star (★★★) wines are also well above average and excellent choices. They too should be on your list of wines to look for. Four-star wines are often wines that are improving and reaching higher quality levels, and they may have just missed earning five stars. Many wines in this book fall into that category. In some instances these are wines that have been great in the past, but may have recently declined in quality. The same is true with three-star wines, which are, in general, good to very good. Bear in mind, that with many varietals such as Chenin Blanc, Gewürztraminer, Riesling and Sauvignon Blanc, a three-star entry may be the best available. These wines may also be less consistent than more highly rated ones, with a few lesser vintages mixed in among otherwise superb wines. In this category you may also find some higher-priced wines whose quality doesn't justify their expense.

Two-star (★★) wines are considered fair, average, serviceable wines that are pleasant enough, but lack the extra dimensions and distinctive qualities to merit a higher rating. Here too you may encounter some higher-priced wines that don't measure up in quality. One-star (★) wines are best avoided, not so much because they're awful, but because you have far better options available. These are wines of last resort. If you read this book carefully, you'll buy the right wines and dodge the dreary.

For serious collectors or those interested in obtaining the finest wines, the best place to start is with the four- and five-star wines. Three-star wines are often a mixed bag containing excellent values such as Zinfandel, Petite Sirah, Merlot and Pinot Noir, but also some wines with inflated reputations.

RATING THE PRODUCERS

For each winery, I've studied the overall quality of its wines and given it a one- to five-star rating, using the same criteria outlined above. When you're starting out, you need advice about which wineries consistently produce the highest-quality wines across the board. It's important to note that a winery that makes a spectacular Cabernet or Chardonnay might only get a three-star rating because its other wines are ordinary.

WHAT TO LOOK FOR IN A WINE

The simple answer is pleasure. For me, the world's great wines have several things in common. They are ripe, intense, well focused, richly flavored, deeply concentrated and impeccably balanced. They also have a sense of harmony, finesse and grace. Finally, they have long, lingering, complex aftertastes. These factors apply to wines that are young, middle-aged or old. If you can find four or five of these qualities in any given wine, you'll find pleasure. What should you avoid in a wine? The absence of those qualities. With experience, you'll learn to identify significant flaws: when a wine lacks ripe fruit flavors or concentration or is out of balance; when one characteristic, such as tannin or oak, dominates a wine; when a wine is too woody or too chewy from tannins, giving it a coarse texture; or when its flavors simply don't appeal to you.

HOW THE BOOK IS ORGANIZED

California Wine includes the following chapters:

• *Chapter 1: California Wine: Yesterday and Today.* This is an overview of the evolution of winegrowing in California. It presents the origins and early growth of California's wine culture, and the development of the commercial wine industry, leading to the current quest to make the finest wines in the world.

• *Chapter 2: Grapes and Wine Styles.* This chapter examines the different grape varieties, their characteristics, where they excel, how much of each is made in California, and the wine styles that have emerged. Particular emphasis is placed on the main varieties—Cabernet, Chardonnay, Merlot, Pinot Noir and Zinfandel—but Sauvignon Blanc, Syrah and Petite Sirah are discussed, as are their different styles; recommendations about which producers make the best of each wine are provided as well. This chapter also discusses which appellations are best for different grapes.

• *Chapter 3: Appellations and Vineyards.* This chapter focuses on the main winegrowing appellations, how climate and soil influence the grapes and wine styles and which grapes grow best (and worst) in each area. Included are vineyard acreage statistics and maps showing the wineries and vineyards within each appellation.

• *Chapter 4: How Wine Is Made.* This is a general discussion of how red, white, dessert and sparkling wines are made, and how appellation, varietal, barrel type and stylistic considerations combine to give a wine its unique personality.

• *Chapter 5: A Summary of the Vintages: 1933 to 1994.* Here I present a year-by-year analysis of the vintages for most major varietals, using a five-star rating system. This discussion addresses the growing season and harvest conditions as they affect the overall quality of wines. The main focus is on Cabernet, Chardonnay, Merlot, Pinot Noir and Zinfandel.

• *Chapter 6: Building Your Wine Collection.* This chapter talks about wine tasting and what you need to start a wine collection or cellar, offering some specific advice you'll want to consider, whether you're just starting out or already have a cellar full of wines.

• *Chapter 7: Winery Profiles and Tasting Notes.* This chapter forms the heart of the book. It lists alphabetically all the major and most of the minor wineries and brands, providing facts about each winery: who owns it, when it was founded, its acreage and the wines it produces, plus its overall ratings. Individual wine ratings, as well as a summary description of each wine and its style are also found here, along with tasting notes and the 50- to 100-point ratings.

CHAPTER 1

CALIFORNIA WINE: YESTERDAY AND TODAY

It is easy to view California wine as a new and fast-paced industry. We are seeing in this business new wines and wineries, new labels and appellations, new winemakers, new technology, new vintages—all a whirlwind of change. But the roots of California wine date back more than 200 years, to the time when the first European settlers arrived.

WINE AND CULTURE

The early settlers, led by Spanish missionaries, planted Mission grapes as they built a string of missions on the California coast along what is now Highway 1 and part of Highway 101. As important as the Mission grape was to early California wine, its origins remain a mystery. It likely came from Spain and proved a productive vine, better suited for sweet wines than dry, but versatile. With its red skin, it was capable of producing both red and white wines. Later it was used for fortified wines and also distilled into brandy. The Mission grape is still grown in California, although acreage has declined to 1,060. The first known vineyard was planted at Mission San Juan Capistrano in 1779, and it yielded its first wine—a sweet, fortified beverage—in 1782. After that,

small vineyards were planted with increasing regularity at missions and on larger ranches, but apparently not fast enough to satisfy everyone. Father Junipero Serra, whose vision guided the formation of the mission system, moved back and forth along the coast and inland, heading as far north as Sonoma. As he established missions, vineyards often followed. Historian Thomas Pinney, in his excellent book, *A History of Wine in America* (1989), recounts that Serra "regularly complained of the difficulty of obtaining a supply of wine for the celebration of mass"; indeed, the Catholic Church was one of the first markets in California for wine. "Plenty of good wine during supper," a member of explorer Jedediah Smith's party remarked in 1826 while in San Gabriel.

Mission San Gabriel, east of Los Angeles, grew into the largest and most prosperous of the missions and was also the largest winemaking operation, but, as Pinney notes, California winemaking at that time could not be described as any larger than a cottage industry. After the Spanish missionary period ended in about 1833, winegrowing continued to be centered in the greater Los Angeles area, and Southern California dominated California wine for the next 50 years. A prophetic observation was made by General Mariano Vallejo: that the wine from the Sonoma Mission, the northernmost of the missions, "was considered by the Padres the best wine raised in California."

As the Spanish were setting up missions, a wave of easterners, among them French, German, Italian and Hungarian immigrants, began to arrive in California. These new arrivals often came from countries where wine was an integral part of everyday living. For them, planting grapes, even a small vineyard, and making wines, even a few barrels, provided a direct link to their European heritage. Wine for these settlers had always been the mealtime beverage, drunk at lunch and dinner, after long days of hard work. Wine had also been part of festivals, parties, weddings and other celebrations, and of many religious ceremonies. One needed, even in a new land, to make enough wine for family and friends to last a year—until the next harvest.

COMMERCIAL WINE

Jean Louis Vignes, a Frenchman whose family hailed from Bordeaux, is credited with introducing fine wine to California and raising wine from a domestic craft to a commercial enterprise. The well-named Vignes (*vines* in French) imported and planted Cabernet Sauvignon vines from Bordeaux in what is now the heart of Los Angeles in the 1830s, and may have produced his first Cabernet around 1837, for in 1857 he advertised some of his wine as being 20 years old.

By the 1850s another prominent Frenchman, Charles LeFranc, had begun planting Cabernet and other varieties in the Santa Clara Valley, using Château Margaux, the famous estate in Bordeaux, as a model. The Bordeaux château model, a blend in which Cabernet dominates and wines are uncommonly long-lived, influenced many of the pioneering vintners of the mid- to late-1800s, both in their desire to create magnificent wines and also in their willingness to blend different grapes, à la Bordeaux.

Southern California continued to be the place where most of California's wine was grown, but San Francisco was where it was sold and drunk. Nevertheless, many winegrowing advances were being made farther north. Pinney makes references to wine in Santa Clara in 1824 and General Vallejo's mission vineyard in Sonoma in 1835. In 1838 George Yount planted the first vineyard in Napa Valley near what is now the town of Yountville, employing grapevine cuttings from Vallejo in Sonoma.

In 1846 a vineyard was planted at the foot of Mount Diablo in Contra Costa County by Dr. John Marsh. Winegrowing spread slowly throughout California, but when gold was discovered at Sutter's Mill in 1848, leading to the Gold Rush of 1849, California changed forever, becoming the destination for many more thousands of immigrants who came to pan for gold, work in mines and otherwise carve out a living for themselves and their families.

In 1857 the remarkable Count Agoston Harazsthy of Hungary, a leading importer of grapevine cuttings, founded Buena Vista Winery in Sonoma. Two years later the wine industry was large enough to be recognized by the state legislature, which passed an act that exempted new grapevines from taxation until they were four years old. Harazsthy, among others, observed that the California wine industry would never reach its potential as long as the Mission grape was the standard. Better grapes were needed to make superior wines. Vintners would have to rethink wine from theory to practice and learn how the great wines were made. They would also eventually have to learn how the great wines of the world were sold, but that would come much later.

THE NOTION OF FINE WINE

According to Pinney, the most ambitious and sustained application of California's early wealth and devotion to wine came from railroad baron Leland Stanford. In 1869 he bought land already planted to grapevines in what is now Alameda and was making wine by 1871. In 1881, following a visit to the great châteaux of Bordeaux, he began to buy large quantities of land along the Sacramento River in Tehama and Butte counties, between Red Bluff and Chico, with the aim of growing wines that would rival the great wines of France. In one year, 1,000 acres of vines were planted using an elaborate plan for irrigation and drainage. Among the many grapes rooted at Vina Ranch were Burger, Charbono and Zinfandel. By the time Stanford died, his Vina Ranch had 3,500 acres in vines and a wine cellar that could hold 2 million gallons. Unfortunately, despite all Stanford's ambition, his vineyards and wine had little impact on the industry as a whole, according to Pinney.

A vineyard he planted near Palo Alto is today the site of Stanford University.

Elsewhere more important progress was being made and better grapes planted. In 1861 Charles Krug founded a small winery in St. Helena, and in 1862 Jacob Schram started his winery in the hills west of Napa Valley, now home of Schramsberg. Many more wineries were founded in the 1870s that still exist today. Beringer Vineyards winery in St. Helena dates to 1876. Gustav Niebaum, a Finnish fur trader, founded the grand Inglenook chateau in Rutherford in 1879; it's now the Niebaum-Coppola Estate. The Christian Brothers founded a winery in 1882, as did whaling tycoon Alfred Tubbs, who built the handsome stone Chateau Montelena winery north of Calistoga. Still others planted their vineyards on the hills and mountains: Mayacamas was founded in 1889 on Mount Veeder, and Rossini, founded in 1885 on Howell Mountain, is now Burgess Cellars. Though difficult to plant and farm, mountain vineyards were above frost lines and often cooler than those on valley floors. Best of all, these vineyards yielded wines with dark colors and intense flavors.

In northern Sonoma County, all kinds of farm and agricultural endeavors were unfolding. Many European immigrants planted small vineyards to make their own wine. One Italian settlement named its community Asti after the city in Piedmont, Italy, and began making wine around 1882, calling itself Italian Swiss Colony. A year later, one of the largest vineyard estates, Fountain Grove, was planted, eventually expanding to 400 acres of vines and a winery capacity of 600,000 gallons. The Simi brothers were already making wine in Healdsburg by 1881.

There were many more. The original Ridge Vineyards winery in the Santa Cruz Mountains was built in 1885 high atop the coastal range at elevations reaching 2,600 feet. Actress Lillie Langtry pursued fine wine in Lake County north of Napa Valley from 1886 to 1906, the year of the great earthquake. Today her former property is known as Guenoc for its winery and appellation of the same name. Nichelini winery in Chiles Valley, an offshoot into the hills east of Napa Valley, was founded in 1890, as was Deer Park Winery on Howell Mountain.

The wineries of this era were small-scale, unspecialized and individually owned, according to Pinney. Charles Wetmore, the state's chief executive viticultural officer, says that "not a single bearing vineyard" was planted systematically with the grapes to produce the kinds of great wines being made in Bordeaux, Burgundy, Sauternes or Hermitage, or to make Port or Sherry. There was Cabernet, but mostly in small experimental vineyards. There was Pinot Noir too, apparently, but also in very small quantities. Chardonnay appears not to have been well known or planted until the 1930s, although Sémillon was. As those grapes were imported from Europe, California wineries named their wines after the appellations where they excelled, calling their wines Chambertin, Hermitage, Burgundy, even Chateau Yquem—named after, though spelled differently than, the famous Château d'Yquem.

Scores more wineries were built and abandoned in the next quarter century. Many were later to be rediscovered by a new wave of wine enthusiasts in the 1960s to 1990s, who bought land for a weekend retreat only to find an old overgrown vineyard with stumpy vines, or a weathered stone winery or cave. While these old wineries typically produced a wide variety of wines, most of ordinary quality and on a small scale, more and more vintners began to focus on higher-quality wines. They sought better grapes, the right soils, the best climates and improved techniques.

These pioneers made intelligent decisions about where to begin. Early vineyards planted in Rutherford, Oakville and St. Helena in Napa Valley are still prime wine real estate, as are parts of Livermore Valley, Russian River Valley, Alexander Valley and mountaintop areas from Santa Cruz to Mendocino. This is compelling evidence that vintners were aware of the role of soil and climate in seeking to create finer wines. Areas such as Santa Clara that later fell victim to urban sprawl were once choice locations for world-class wine grapes. Evidence of the quality of those early wines is less abundant today, but many of them were highly regarded and won medals in world competitions. Inglenook's "California Claret" and "Medoc-Type" Cabernets of the late 1800s aged well—often amazingly well—for 100 years. The failure to develop a market for wines outside California hurt the industry most of all, according to Pinney, "for it destroyed all incentive to take the trouble and run the risks required to grow the best varieties and to make the highest standard of wine."

In 1900 Frenchman Georges de Latour founded Beaulieu Vineyard in Rutherford, creating an elaborate home estate, vineyard and winery. The early wines at Beaulieu were not unlike those made elsewhere in California, a mixture of different grapes and styles, mostly sweet but many dry. But increasingly de Latour focused on Bordeaux and Cabernet, which he planted extensively, eventually growing several hundred acres. Nearby in Rutherford, the handsome stone Inglenook chateau would rival Beaulieu with its excellent wines.

TROUBLED TIMES

As the notion of fine wine was beginning to take shape, two disasters struck. Phylloxera, a louse that attacks the root system of grapevines, appeared in the late 1800s, and the infestation extended into the next century, eventually wiping out most of California's vineyards. According to one estimate, in Napa Valley alone 10,000 acres of vineyard were destroyed between 1889 and 1892; by 1900 there were only 2,000 acres of vineyard left there. Efforts to replant the vineyards were hampered not only by the costs, but also by the absence of phylloxera-resistant rootstock. By 1915, 250,000 acres of vineyard statewide had been ruined by phylloxera. According to Pinney,

> The symbolic high point of California winegrowing before Prohibition overwhelmed it came, as all well-made dramas, only shortly before the fall. In 1915, when the shadow of Prohibition was already moving rapidly over the country, California seized on the opportunity provided by the nearly opened Panama Canal to promote its climate, its industries, and its future through the great Panama-Pacific International Exposition in San Francisco; it was also a dramatic way for San Francisco to show the world how it had risen, phoenix-like, from the ashes of [the] 1906 [earthquake and fire]. California's wine men, now pretty well seasoned in the business of international exhibitions, were ready to make the most of their chance to show the best on their own ground.

When that time came, though, much of Europe was embroiled in World War I, and there was little attention paid to California wine; its chances for international publicity vanished. When the official history of the Panama-Pacific Exposition was published, in five large and pre-

tentious volumes, it gave California wine the briefest of descriptions, wrote Pinney: "This is history—closed by the Eighteenth Amendment."

Prohibition was passed, outlawing the manufacture, transportation, sale and possession of alcoholic beverages (although not the consumption thereof) from 1920 to 1933. It forced most of California's several hundred wineries to close. Their vineyards were left untended and susceptible to disease or were replanted to other cash-generating crops. Californians could still make wine for their own consumption. A few wineries, including Beaulieu, survived by producing altar wines. Not everyone quit, though. On the eve of Prohibition in 1919, a Frenchman named Tam founded what is now Chalone Vineyard in the Gavilan Mountains, planting Chenin Blanc vines, perhaps believing he was rooting Chardonnay. Nevertheless, at the very time when a broader, better organized and more sophisticated wine industry seemed likely to emerge from California, extending into a broader U.S. and perhaps even international market, it nearly vanished completely.

It's difficult to predict what might have happened if Prohibition had not become law. Phylloxera and World War I already had affected the California wine industry negatively. It is likely that the industry would have continued to grow and improve the quality of its wines, however slowly and unsurely. But clearly the industry would have faced arduous economic times. It might have flourished during the Roaring '20s, only to face the collapse of the stock market in 1929, the Great Depression of the 1930s and the global devastation of World War II. In all likelihood, whatever minor progress California wine might have made in this era would have been offset by domestic and global turmoil. Certainly Europe's great wine estates suffered from the ravages of the wars and depressed economies. A healthy wine industry would have given California a real advantage immediately after WW II, when there was little European competition and thousands of American military personnel were coming home after having been exposed to wine during their stay in Europe.

AFTER REPEAL

For many reasons, some quite obvious, Prohibition proved unpopular. Wine, although illegal everywhere, was nevertheless also available everywhere. Saloons were closed, but Americans persisted with wine, even on a very small scale. Those who viewed wine as part of their culture and heritage kept on nourishing their vines and making wine. Wine grapes continued to be shipped east in refrigerated railroad cars, where Americans of European descent would buy them and crush and ferment them into their own homemade wines. Enforcement of Prohibitionist laws proved difficult. When the depression hit, people needed jobs, and California's wine industry began to revive itself ever so slowly.

By 1932 indications were that Prohibition would be repealed in time for the 1933 vintage. Many would-be vintners anxiously prepared for the rebirth of the wine industry. Upon Repeal, Inglenook made a brilliant 1933 Cabernet, still uncommonly dark and intense 50 years after its release. That same year Louis M. Martini readied his new winery in St. Helena, and the great wine dynasty of Ernest and Julio Gallo was born in a small warehouse in Modesto. Shipping grapes east for home winemakers remained a viable industry, but it became apparent that the California wine industry needed to reestablish its credentials, make better wines and serve broader markets. It was obvious to some, including the Gallos, that one way to penetrate and capture Midwestern and Eastern markets was to provide better wines at more affordable prices, serving markets where European immigrants lived and drank wine daily. As long as immigrants could make homemade wine that was better than anything they could afford to buy, the demand for California wine would be minimal. In 1937 Alfred Fromm, a native German, came to California and visited several wineries, finding the Christian Brothers' Mont La Salle facility on Mount Veeder most attractive. The Christian Brothers was on the verge of bankruptcy but had lots of good wine, and Fromm, a marketing visionary, struck a deal to sell the wine, correctly figuring that if he put the Christian Brothers name on the bottle he could inspire a sense of confidence in the buyer through the wine's connection with a religious order.

In the aftermath of Repeal, California's wineries were in sad shape. According to Professor Harold Winkler, Napa's wineries were in no better condition in 1934 than in 1880. Many of the wines produced in the 1930s, 1940s and 1950s had serious bacterial defects. Sweet wines were more popular than dry wines, as their defects could easily be masked. The wine industry had to make the best of the grapes, vineyards and facilities it had before it could invest in the new equipment and technology that would raise quality. The University of California at Davis played a major role in this transition. The work done there was instrumental in defining the climatic zones for growing fine-wine grapes—identifying five regions and rating them from coolest to warmest—and in cleaning up California's wines, establishing strict sanitation guidelines for winery operations and for wine stability.

In the past decade, Davis has been criticized by many for its doctrine of sterile, filtered, highly processed, squeaky-clean wines, and many winemakers who studied there followed that doctrine carefully—perhaps to a fault. For while Davis was correct in identifying many of the stability and bacterial problems facing California wines, as well as many in Europe, its professors and graduates tended to approach wine as something that could be manipulated or corrected from within the cellar, more a laboratory product than an agricultural one. They knew that the best wines came from the best grapes and vineyards, but they also recognized how many wines—both domestic and European—suffered from serious and obvious defects. That scores of Europe's great winemakers, including Christian Moueix of Château Petrus, attended Davis and benefited from their educations is proof of the school's importance in technical matters.

In the period from 1940 to the 1960s, those at Davis and elsewhere recognized the need for a viable wine economy to serve the new American consumer—who had learned to love wine while in Europe during and after World War II—as well as wine drinkers who expected quality and consistency. Tools of mass production led to many commercial successes, perhaps none of them greater than Gallo Hearty Burgundy, a perfectly consistent, highly reliable, technically faultless, mass-produced wine that carried no vintage date or specific grape variety, could be found virtually everywhere and could be relied on to taste the same year after year after year.

By the 1950s, California vintners recognized the need to develop markets throughout the country. Producers such as the Gallos, the Sebastianis, Fromm and later Robert Mondavi studied the market more and more carefully. Some serviced it with ordinary table wines. Others looked ahead to greater possibilities.

The New Vision

In 1937 Georges de Latour traveled to Europe to find a classically trained French winemaker. He hired a Russian-born, French-educated enologist named André Tchelistcheff, a brilliant perfectionist who loved vineyards, wine and teaching. He immediately helped Beaulieu Vineyard improve its wines. The more California wine he tasted, the more impressed he was, even though the industry faced serious hurdles. When de Latour died in 1940, the 1936 vintage of BV Cabernet was still in small oak barrels. As a tribute to de Latour, Tchelistcheff suggested naming the wine Georges de Latour Private Reserve, setting a new standard for the finest wine California had to offer. At the time there were fewer than 100 acres of Cabernet in Napa Valley and BV Private Reserve 1936 sold for $1.50 a bottle, commanding the same price 15 years later. Vineyards were infested with diseases such as red leaf virus, which made for pretty red and orange grape leaves in the fall, but were in reality a sign that the vines were seriously ill. Hope and expectations for the future outpaced the reality that revitalizing the vineyards and crafting fine wines would take time.

In 1938 Inglenook's John Daniel, wine writer Frank Schoonmaker and their good friend John Gantner began their quest for the perfect Pinot Noir vineyard in Napa Valley. They finally settled on Spring Mountain, where they planted a vineyard and started making experimental wines in the 1940s, eventually choosing the name School House for their brand. In 1941 Jack and Mary Taylor revived Mayacamas on Mount Veeder and in the early 1940s Martin Ray left Paul Masson Vineyards to start his own winery in the Santa Cruz Mountains. In 1943 Frank Bartholomew revived the crumbling Buena Vista winery, and Lee Stewart was making wine in an old winery at the base of Howell Mountain that he called Souverain. In 1952 James Zellerbach began planting Chardonnay and later Pinot Noir in the hills above Sonoma for his Hanzell Vineyards, where he hoped one day to create wines that were the equals of fine red and white Burgundies. Fred and Eleanor McCrea bought property on Spring Mountain in the 1940s and planted Stony Hill Vineyard to Chardonnay, from which they began making small lots of wine in 1952. And so, slowly but surely, the quest for fine wine began to move forward.

The Pace Quickens

In the 1960s the California wine industry began to lay the foundation for a wine boom in the 1970s. In 1959 a trio of Stanford Research Institute engineers bought the old Ridge vineyard and began making small batches of wine on the weekends. In 1961 Joe and Alice Heitz founded Heitz Wine Cellar on Highway 29 and in 1966 Heitz bottled his first single-vineyard Cabernet from Tom and Martha May's Martha's Vineyard in Oakville. That same year, Robert Mondavi, who had encouraged his family to move from the Central Valley and buy the Charles Krug Winery in 1943 and who believed that Napa Valley wine had a great future, built his own winery in Oakville, Napa's first new winery since Prohibition.

Consumer tastes began to change; dry wines with varietal names became increasingly popular, replacing sweeter wines. At the time, many critics expected red wine sales to soar, and they did for a while. But what surprised everyone was that white wine quickly grew in popularity, taking over the lead. Suddenly, it seemed that wineries couldn't produce Chardonnay fast enough to meet consumer demand. Without a model for growing Chardonnay or Sauvignon Blanc, wineries planted them where they knew they would ripen—often right next to their Cabernet or Zinfandel vines. Without a model for vinifying these wines, they employed the same vinification techniques used for reds.

Studies conducted in the 1970s suggested that Americans were becoming more curious about wine. Articles in newspapers and magazines often painted a pretty picture of California's wine future and there were many predictions of a wine boom. Americans weren't great wine consumers then or now, but logic held that if average consumption doubled or tripled, to several gallons a year, there would be a tremendous demand for wine. If America ever became like France or Italy, where per capita wine consumption exceeded 20 gallons a year at that time, California wine would be a bonanza. In 1977, Coca-Cola bought Sterling Vineyards in Napa Valley while launching a media blitz promoting its Taylor California Cellars brand. Schlitz, the brewer, owned Geyser Peak in Sonoma. Nestlé, the food giant, owned Beringer Vineyards. All signs, it seemed, pointed to a great future for California wine.

FINE WINE AS ART AND LIFESTYLE

The late 1960s and early 1970s spawned new interest in country living. The rural lifestyle had an allure for many businessmen and professionals who had succeeded in one career but were looking for new challenges or something more fulfilling. Owning a vineyard or winery became a status symbol for many of them. Tom Jordan, the multimillionaire Colorado oilman, built a luxurious chateau in Alexander Valley in 1972, producing his first wine in 1976. In the Santa Ynez Valley, an heir to the Firestone tire company founded a winery, while other business executives pooled their money to build Zaca Mesa. In Napa Valley, big money continued to pour in. Multimillionaire nurseryman Gil Nickel revived a historic stone winery in Oakville, renaming it Far Niente, Italian for "without a care." The prospect of Americans drinking wine as Europeans did, combined with the romantic lure of lush green vineyards, country living and working the land, led to a wave of new wineries opening up in the 1970s and 1980s, many of whose owners held aspirations of making the world's greatest wines.

In 1976, when a Franco-Californian tasting was held in Paris to commemorate the United States Bicentennial, two upstart wineries from Napa Valley finished in first place, winning in both the red and white wine categories, with French critics serving as judges. It was the tasting heard around the world. Stag's Leap Wine Cellars 1973 Cabernet, the winery's second vintage, placed first ahead of Château Mouton-Rothschild 1970, Château Haut-Brion 1970 and Château Montrose 1970. In fifth place was Ridge Monte Bello 1971, followed by Château Leoville-Las Cases 1971, Mayacamas Cabernet Napa Valley 1971, Clos Du Val Cabernet Napa Valley 1972, Heitz Martha's Vineyard Cabernet Napa Valley 1970 and Freemark Abbey Cabernet Napa Valley 1969. In the white-wine category, Chateau Montelena Chardonnay 1973, a blend of Alexander Valley and Napa Valley grapes, placed first ahead of a group of highly regarded white Burgundies. The tasting triggered an avalanche of global publicity for California wine, as newspapers and magazines around the world heralded the story.

The allure of California wine so captured the world's imagination that the greatest French winemaker of the 20th century, Baron Philippe de Rothschild, owner of the great Mouton-Rothschild estate in Pauillac, decided to invest in California, forging a partnership in Napa Valley with Robert Mondavi. In 1979 they announced their joint venture for a wine to be called Opus One, a marriage of French and California winemaking know-how applied to Napa Valley Cabernet. Over the next decade, several dozen foreign wine companies, led by the great French Champagne houses, purchased land and built wineries in California, anticipating a wine boom. Money flowed from Germany, Belgium, Switzerland and Japan, with Sonoma's crown jewel, Chateau St. Jean, being purchased by Suntory. Christian Moueix, who had studied winemaking at Davis, and liked California wine and its possibilities, followed Baron Philippe's lead. He became a partner in a historic Napa vineyard with John Daniel's two daughters. Napanook, which Daniel planted in the 1930s, became home to Dominus Estate and by 1994, Moueix was sole proprietor, often phoning his Napa vineyard once a day from France.

By the late 1970s and early 1980s, several other important trends emerged and further shaped the market. Many of the assumptions about which grapes grew best in which areas proved true, while others did not. Cabernet was perfect for Oakville, Rutherford and the Stags Leap District in Napa, and pockets in Sonoma Valley and Alexander Valley. Chardonnay and Pinot Noir were better suited for the cooler climates of Carneros, Russian River Valley and Santa Barbara. Monterey Cabernet proved a colossal failure in most cases. The sites chosen were too cool to ripen the grapes, leaving them marked by pungent vegetal flavors. A new admiration for Zinfandel and century-old vines emerged, as white Zinfandel sales soared. Those gnarly old Zin vines planted around 1900 in the Dry Creek and Sonoma Valleys proved that the farmers who planted them understood where fine-wine grapes would excel and fully ripen. The move toward cooler climates for appropriate grapes proved as important as the recognition that controlling crop yields and using more natural winemaking techniques would lead to finer, more complex wines. Vintners began to rely heavily on toasty oak barrels and Burgundy's concept of *terroir:* matching the right grape type to the right soil and climate and thereby increasing one's chances for success.

By the late 1980s and early 1990s, many of the earlier assumptions about grape growing and winemaking in

California had come under full review, and innovations continued. Grapevines continued to be planted in much cooler climates, but with the right rootstock and clones to survive and prosper. Winemakers started taking more chances in hopes of crafting even finer, more detailed wines. They left Chardonnay in a barrel for up to two years. They used minimal filtering, if any at all, and tried natural yeast fermentations. The Gallo brothers, after decades of mass-producing modestly flavored wines, moved into northern Sonoma intending to make the highest-quality wines possible. Their Chardonnay grew in prime Russian River Valley soil, their Cabernet and Zinfandel in the hills of Dry Creek Valley; hundreds more acres were rooted in Alexander Valley. Gallo's investment in the production of fine wine demonstrated that this was the future for California wine.

The market for California wine has grown global. A small but keenly interested wine culture, closely allied with new trends in fine cuisine and restaurants, has solidified in the United States. A viable commercial wine industry has emerged and grown stable. Winemakers forge ahead with new styles based on Rhône and Italian varietals. Steadily, more and better low-priced varietal wines have appeared, replacing the generic table wines that had dominated the market since the 1960s. The state's largest fine-wine producers, Robert Mondavi, Beringer and Kendall-Jackson, have spread their interests throughout the state, buying land, planting vineyards and building wineries in Santa Maria Valley, Paso Robles and Monterey. Even smaller wineries have been expanding. Caymus, based in Napa, bought vineyard land and built a small winery in Monterey for Chardonnay, then considered planting Pinot Noir on the Sonoma Coast.

More money flowed into California wine. In 1995 William Jarvis completed a $20-million subterranean winery in Napa Valley to produce 5,000 cases of wine. Restaurateur Pat Kuleto spent millions, too, developing a rugged hillside vineyard in the hills east of Napa Valley, and talked of making wine. And when money didn't flow, wineries such as Robert Mondavi went public, raising millions to retire debt and expand business. California wine continued to attract more small artisans as well, whose passion for and love of fine wine inspired even greater quality.

Those who subscribe to theories about history repeating itself will note that phylloxera returned to Napa Valley in the 1980s, as well as to many other parts of the state. Its arrival forced a $1 billion replanting of vineyards in Napa alone. Optimists claimed this would hasten the matching of the right grape varieties to the proper soils and climates, the first and most important step toward even greater quality.

Anti-alcohol sentiments have appeared again, leading to warning labels and higher taxes, but also to a healthy debate about the benefits of moderate wine consumption. There is fierce competition in the wine industry; only the fittest and finest survive. But this much seems clear: American wine lovers are willing to pay for the best available wines—the strongest endorsement possible for California's fine-wine producers, some of whom are already making great wines, the kinds of wines that rival and often surpass the great wines of the world. Still, California's best wines are yet to come.

CHAPTER 2

GRAPES AND WINE STYLES

In order to appreciate wine, it's essential to understand the characteristics different grapes offer and how those characteristics should be expressed in wines. Cabernet, Merlot and Zinfandel are all red grapes, but as wines their personalities are quite different. Even when grown in different appellations and vinified using different techniques, a varietal wine displays qualities that are inherent to its personality. Muscat should always be spicy, Sauvignon Blanc a touch herbal. Zinfandel is zesty, with pepper and wild berry flavors. Cabernet is marked by plum, currant and black cherry flavors and firm tannins. Understanding what a grape should be as a wine is fundamental, and knowing what a grape can achieve at its greatest is the essence of fine-wine appreciation.

This chapter focuses on the major grape varieties and varietal wines in California. It discusses each grape's varietal character, how well it succeeds or fails as wine, where it grows best and how styles differ based on appellation, whether the wine is suited for blending or best on its own, when it reaches maturity and how it ages. There is also a statistical overview of where the grapes are planted and charts showing how the state's grape acreage has changed in the past few years. These charts are divided by county (not appellation) and show the favored spots for the major varietals, as well as which grapes are gaining favor and which are declining in popularity. Grapes and wine styles are also discussed in Chapter 3:

"Appellations and Vineyards," as is the question of which grapes perform best in the key growing areas.

In Europe, the finest wines are known primarily by geographic appellation (although this is changing; witness the occasional French and Italian use of varietal names). In California, however, most wines are labeled by their varietal names. To a large extent, this is because in California the process of sorting out which grapes grow best in which appellations is ongoing and Americans were first introduced to fine wine by varietal name. In Europe, with a longer history for matching grape types to soil and climate, the research is more conclusive: Chardonnay and Pinot Noir, for instance, are the major grapes of Burgundy. Cabernet Sauvignon, Merlot, Cabernet Franc, Malbec and Petite Verdot are the red grapes of Bordeaux. Syrah dominates Rhône reds, while Marsanne and Roussanne are used for Rhône whites. Barolo and Barbaresco are both made of Nebbiolo, but the different appellations produce different styles of wine. In Tuscany, Sangiovese provides the backbone of Chianti, but it's just one grape in a blend. A different clone of Sangiovese is used for Brunello di Montalcino.

In time, California's appellation system may well evolve into one more like Europe's. Already appellations such as Carneros and Santa Maria Valley are becoming synonymous with Chardonnay and Pinot Noir, while Rutherford, Oakville and the Stags Leap District are associated with Cabernet-based red table wines. Wineries with vested financial interests in these appellations and the marketing clout to emphasize the distinctive features of the wines grown in these areas will determine how the appellation system evolves and whether specific wine styles emerge. The appellations themselves will also determine which grapes excel and deserve special recognition.

This chapter also discusses when wines are at their peak for drinking and, in general, how they age. It's my view that virtually all California wines, regardless of their color, varietal character or history, are best consumed in their youth. Specifically, all whites and virtually all reds reach maturity and should be consumed within one to three years of their vintage dates. Wines with a 1995 vintage date should therefore be at or near their peak from 1996 to 1998. I know there are exceptions to this and that some California wines do age well. But I also think most wines, regardless of where they're grown, are best in their youth and that as a rule they don't benefit significantly from aging. I know that some wines do need to age and others have reputations for improving with age. But the simple fact is that most do not. Moreover, the trend around the world is to make wines that are more accessible earlier. Even in areas such as Bordeaux, Burgundy and the Rhône, where there's a history of long-lived wines, the vast majority of wines are not meant to be cellared for long periods. Vintners understand that most wines are consumed early on—usually within hours of purchase—and are styling their wines for more immediate pleasure. This doesn't mean that there aren't exceptions. Clearly wines grown at the great estates in great vintages are capable of aging and improving. These wines may need several years of cellaring, but given today's wine styles, most are very appealing much earlier than consumers often realize. To protect yourself from buying wines and aging them only to find they've lost their fruit or charm, it's wise to drink them earlier.

A second crucial element in deciding when to drink a given wine is your own taste. If you buy a wine, drink it and think it's delicious now, there's little reason to age it for several more years unless you strongly believe it's going to improve. If a wine tastes wonderful to you now, the odds are it will lose some or most of its fruit (and charm) and be less pleasing in four or five years. Moreover, the odds are that your tastes will change a little too; that the wines you think are great today may not always appeal to you. If, however, you know your tastes and like older, more mature-tasting wines, then you're aware of the risks, consequences and potential pleasure of drinking them. If you're new to wine and want to age wines and experience drinking older wines, there are several options. You can easily buy older wines at retail and off restaurant wine lists. You can also cellar a few bottles and taste how they evolve. But buying a case or two of expensive Cabernet or Pinot Noir and then not tasting it for 10 or 15 years can mean taking quite a risk. The most ageworthy wines I can recommend are the four- and five-star wines, but always follow your own taste preferences.

There are always exceptions. But I have tasted literally thousands of older wines—and I still recommend that you drink your wines young, when they are at their freshest, most vibrant and fruitiest, and that you age wines with great caution and care. There are collectors who say that money is no object in building their wine cellars, who buy as much fine wine as they can each year. They may impress their spouses or friends with a wonderful wine collection. But what happens when they begin to open up those bottles and realize the wines they paid large sums of money for have faded and lost their charm? These wine connoisseurs look much less savvy when they're stuck with several cases of expensive wine that is over the hill.

The remainder of this chapter looks at major the grape varieties and styles of wine they yield.

ALICANTE BOUSCHET

Alicante Bouschet is used primarily in blending, for its dark color and intense flavors. A few wineries still produce it as a wine, but it fails to excite. Acreage is now 1,600 and falling, having steadily declined from some 30,000 acres after Prohibition.

BARBERA

Plantings of this once popular grape have declined sharply, dropping from 19,267 acres in 1980 to 9,261 in 1994, with most of that grown in the Central Valley. A few wineries still produce it as a varietal wine, but those numbers too are dwindling. Its main attribute as a blending wine is its ability to maintain a naturally high acidity even in hot climates. Louis M. Martini made excellent, even ageworthy Barberas for years. I think the wine has more potential than is currently realized, with its bright, crisp berry flavors, and I suspect it may stage a modest comeback as Italian-style wines gain popularity.

BURGER

Wildly popular in California's jug wine era, this white vinifera grape outnumbered all other white varietals for years. It's known for its ability to produce a large crop, but quality is ordinary, ideal for jug wines. Acreage now stands at 1,931.

CABERNET FRANC

Increasingly popular as both stand-alone varietal and blending grape, Cabernet Franc is used primarily for blending in Bordeaux, although it can rise to great heights in quality, as seen in the grand wine Cheval Blanc. As a varietal wine, it usually benefits from small amounts of Cabernet and Merlot, and can be as intense and full-bodied as either of those wines. But it often strays away from currant and berry notes into stalky green flavors that become more pronounced with age. In France it's also made into a lighter wine called Chinon, but so far no one in California seems to be seriously considering that. Given its newness in California, it may just be a matter of time before Cabernet Franc gets more attention and rises in quality. Acreage is now 1,740.

CABERNET SAUVIGNON

The undisputed king of red wines, Cabernet Sauvignon has a long and distinguished history in California dating to the late 1800s. It is a remarkably steady and consistent performer throughout much of the state. In specific appellations, it is capable of rendering wines of uncommon depth, richness, concentration and longevity. While it grows well in many appellations, it rises to its greatest heights in Napa Valley and its smaller appellations such as Calistoga, Oakville, Rutherford and the Stags Leap District. It also performs exceptionally well in the mountains on both sides of the valley and in select vineyards in Alexander Valley, Dry Creek Valley, Sonoma Valley, Sonoma Mountain and Paso Robles. Beyond that, it grows well in pockets here and there, such as Ridge's Monte Bello Vineyard in the Santa Cruz Mountains and at Santa Cruz Mountain Vineyards. Even as Cabernet's popularity as a wine grows, it's unlikely any appellation will surpass Napa Valley's high-quality Cabernets and Cabernet blends. Year after year, the sheer number of excellent Cabernets produced in Napa dominates the market.

At its best, Cabernet produces wines of great intensity and depth of flavor. Its classic flavors are currant, plum, black cherry and spice. It can also be marked by herb, olive, mint, tobacco, cedar and anise flavors. Ripe, jammy notes are also often evident. In warmer areas, it can be supple and elegant. In cooler areas, such as Monterey or Carneros, it can be marked by pronounced vegetal, bell pepper, oregano and tar flavors. It can also be very tannic if that is a feature of the desired style. The best Cabernets start out dark purple-ruby in color, with firm acidity, a full body, great intensity, concentrated flavors and firm tannins. Cabernet has an affinity for oak and usually spends 15 to 30 months in new or used French or American barrels, a process that when properly executed imparts a woody, toasty cedar or vanilla flavor to the wine while slowly oxidizing it and softening the tannins. Through most of its history in California, the best Cabernets have been 100 percent Cabernet. Since the late 1970s, many vintners have turned to the Bordeaux model and blended smaller portions of Merlot, Cabernet Franc, Malbec and Petite Verdot into their Cabernets. The case for blending is still under review. Clearly there are successes. Yet many of the state's best Cabernets are still 100 percent Cabernet: Caymus Special Selection, Heitz Martha's Vineyard and Chateau Montelena, for instance. The Bordeaux model is built around not only the desire to craft complex wines, but also the need to ensure that different grape varieties ripen at different intervals or to give a wine color, tannin or backbone. Many other producers are shifting back to higher percentages of Cabernet, having found that blending doesn't add complexity and that Cabernet on its own has a stronger character.

Within Napa Valley, microclimates are a major factor in the weight and intensity of the Cabernets. Winemakers also influence the style as they can extract high levels of tannin and heavily oak their wines. Rutherford-grown Cabernets, for instance, are marked by deep, complex currant, plum and cherry flavors and firm but fine tannins. In Oakville the wines share a similar weight and intensity, but are also often marked by more herb, mint and cedar flavors. In Yountville, the coolest area, the wines sometimes have substantial tannins. In the Stags Leap District the Cabernets tend to be more supple, with black cherry, herb and olive notes and polished tannins. In St. Helena, a small area, the wines are remarkably well focused, with dark currant and black cherry flavors and firm but fine tannins. Many Calistoga vineyards yield bold, intense, deeply flavored wines, while those on Diamond Mountain produce wines that share an earthy austerity and firm tannins. On Howell Mountain the wines are quite dense and tannic, with an earthy edge.

Sonoma Valley Cabernets are often quite hard and tannic, with a green herb and olive edge to the flavors. In Dry Creek Valley they are lighter, less concentrated and less intense than in Napa Valley, although when grown in the hills, the wines generally show more depth and richness. In Russian River, a cool area for Cabernet, certain vineyards can get ripe enough for Cabernet, but usually the wines are not as heavy and dense as they are in Napa Valley and there is often a green, hard edge to their tannins. In the Santa Cruz Mountains, another cool appellation, the Cabernets are often marked by hard, intense, gritty tannins. In Paso Robles the wines are medium-bodied, with supple textures and elegant fruit flavors. (Further discussions about Cabernet as it relates to different appellations appear in Chapter 3).

With 32,595 acres in vines, Cabernet is second only to Zinfandel in red-wine acreage. Napa County, with 8,850 acres in vines, and Sonoma County, with 6,357 acres spread out among its districts, are the most popular sites. Mendocino (1,285 acres), Monterey (3,582), Sacramento (1,138), San Joaquin (3,439) and San Luis Obispo (2,596) also have significant Cabernet plantings.

CARIGNANE

Once a major blending grape for jug wines, Carignane's popularity has diminished, and plantings have dropped from 25,111 acres in 1980 to 8,883 in 1994. It still appears in some blends, and old vineyards are sought after for the intensity of their grapes. But the likelihood is that other grapes with even more intensity and flavor will replace it in the future.

CHARBONO

This grape has dwindled in acreage. Its stature as a wine was supported mainly by Inglenook-Napa Valley, which bottled a Charbono on a regular basis. Occasionally it made for interesting drinking and it aged well. But more often it was lean and tannic, a better story than bottle of wine. A few wineries still produce it, but none with any success.

CHARDONNAY

As Cabernet is the king of reds, so is Chardonnay the king of white wines, for it makes the state's most consistently excellent, rich and complex white. This is an amazingly versatile grape that grows well in a variety of locations up and down the state's coastal areas. Compared to Cabernet, which dates to the 1800s, Chardonnay is much newer to California, introduced in the 1930s but not popular until the 1970s. In the 1950s to 1970s, most of the state's Chardonnay was planted in areas now considered far too warm for it to reach its full potential. Warmer areas in Napa Valley, for instance, have been abandoned, while areas such as Anderson Valley, Carneros, Monterey, Russian River, Santa Barbara and Santa Maria Valley, all closer to cooler maritime influences, are now producing wines far superior to those made a decade ago.

When well made, Chardonnay offers bold, ripe, rich and intense fruit flavors of apple, fig, melon, pear, peach, pineapple, lemon and grapefruit, along with spice, honey, butter, butterscotch and hazelnut flavors. Winemakers build more complexity into this easy-to-manipulate wine using common vinification techniques: barrel fermentation, *sur lie* aging during which the wine is left on its natural sediment, and malolactic fermentation (a process which converts tart malic acid to softer lactic acid). No other white table wine benefits as much from oak aging or barrel fermentation. Chardonnay grapes have a fairly neutral flavor, and because they are usually crushed or pressed and not fermented with their skins the way red wines are, whatever flavors emerge from the grape are extracted almost instantly after crushing. Red wines that soak with their skins for days or weeks through fermentation extract their flavors quite differently.

Because Chardonnay is also a prolific producer that can easily yield 4 to 5 tons of high-quality grapes per acre, it is a cash cow for producers. Many Chardonnays are very showy, well oaked and appealing on release, but they lack the richness, depth and concentration to age and have in fact evolved rather quickly, often losing their intensity and concentration within a year or two. Many vintners, having studied and recognized this, are now sharply reducing crop yields, holding tonnage down to 2 to 3 tons per acre in the belief that this will lead to greater concentration. The only downside to this strategy is that lower crop loads lead to significantly less wine to sell, therefore higher prices as well. It appears likely that in the next decade, a new tier of high-quality Chardonnays from California's coolest appellations will emerge, showing even greater depth, richness and concentration, but probably they will be made in much smaller case lots and sell for higher prices. Consumers appear willing to finance this trend, which is likely to affect all the major varietal wines in California.

Chardonnay's popularity has also led to a huge market of ordinary wines, so there's a broad range of quality to choose from in this varietal. There are a substantial number of California-appellation Chardonnays, which can range from simple and off-dry to more complex and sophisticated. The producer's name on the wine, and often its price, are indicators of the level of quality.

Sonoma County, with its vast Chardonnay plantings in Alexander Valley, Russian River Valley, Sonoma Valley and the Sonoma portion of Carneros, leads in plantings with 11,308 acres, followed by Monterey County (9,859 acres), Napa Valley (8,591 acres, including Carneros), Santa Barbara County (5,300), San Joaquin (5,281), Mendocino (3,921) and San Luis Obispo (3,013). Total state plantings of Chardonnay have reached 56,255 acres—a figure which exceeds French Colombard's (at 49,498 acres) for the first time in history, and which makes it the most widely planted wine grape in the state.

CHENIN BLANC

Currently used primarily as a blending grape for generic table wines, Chenin Blanc should perform better in California, and someday it may. In 1980 it trailed only French Colombard in total acres, but now it's in third place behind Chardonnay and French Colombard. It can yield a pleasant enough wine, with subtle melon, peach, spice and citrus notes. Chalone and Chappellet have both made excellent wines from this grape. Most of the 26,157 total acres planted are in the Central Valley.

FRENCH COLOMBARD

The king of jug wine white grapes, French Colombard is the second most widely planted in the state. Virtually all of it goes into jug wines; its value is that it produces an abundant crop, averaging 11 tons per acre, and makes clean and simple wines with firm acidity. There are now 49,498 acres of this grape in the state.

GAMAY

Fading in popularity, and the subject of some debate as to its real identity, Gamay in California is really a grape called Valdigue, which produces a simple, ordinary, somewhat fruity wine. It is used primarily for blending. Plantings are now 1,329 acres and dropping.

GAMAY BEAUJOLAIS

This grape is a high-yield clone of Pinot Noir that makes undistinguished wines in most places where it's grown. Used primarily for blending, it now covers 1,073 acres and is declining, as those serious about Pinot Noir are using superior clones and planting in cooler areas.

GEWÜRZTRAMINER

Gewürztraminer can yield magnificent wines, as is best demonstrated in Alsace, France, where it is made in to a variety of styles from dry to off-dry to sweet. In California this wine has always been an afterthought, although the late harvest version can be excellent and among the very best in the world. The grape needs a cool climate that allows it to get ripe; areas such as Anderson Valley and Russian River Valley appear well suited to it. It's a temperamental grape to grow and vinify, as its potent spiciness can be overbearing when unchecked. At its best, it produces a floral and refreshing wine with crisp acidity that pairs well with spicy dishes. When left for late harvest, it's uncommonly rich and complex, a tremendous dessert wine. Acreage has dropped to 1,602 acres.

GRENACHE

The second most widely planted grape in the world, Grenache is a workhorse blending grape, with 12,107 acres in vines in California, mostly in the Central Valley, where it yields a fruity, spicy, medium-bodied wine with supple tannins. Occasionally an old vineyard is found and its grapes made into a varietal wine, which at its best can be good. It may make a comeback as Rhône-style enthusiasts seek cooler areas and an appropriate blending grape.

GRIGNOLINO

This grape, which can yield a pleasant rosé wine,

has all but vanished from the landscape, with current state figures indicating no significant acreage.

JOHANNISBERG RIESLING

In California this grape is also known, simply, as Riesling or, occasionally, White Riesling. It has been declining in acreage the past few years and quality rarely rises above the good category. As a dessert wine, though, it can be exceptional, with its characteristic floral, spice and grapey pear flavors. Arrowood, Navarro, Joseph Phelps and Chateau St. Jean are among its leading producers. Grows best in cool coastal areas that allow the grapes to ripen slowly. There are now 3,194 acres statewide.

MALBEC

Malbec is a blending grape only, and an insignificant one at that with only 68 acres, but a few wineries use it, the most obvious reason being that it's considered part of the Bordeaux-blend recipe.

MARSANNE

A few California wineries are experimenting with this white grape, which is popular in the Rhône (along with Roussanne and Viognier), but so far the acreage is minimal. At its best, Marsanne can be a full-bodied, moderately intense wine with spice, pear and citrus notes. But it is not likely to be a major factor, even as Rhône-style wines gain popularity.

MERLOT

Merlot is the red-wine success of the 1990s: its popularity has soared along with its acreage. It now totals 9,605 acres in vines, more than double its 1990 acreage, and it seems wine lovers can't drink enough of it. Despite its popularity, its quality ranges only from good to very good most of the time, though there are a few stellar producers—Beringer Bancroft Vineyard, Duckhorn and Matanzas Creek, for instance.

Several styles have emerged. One is a Cabernet-style Merlot, which includes a high percentage (up to 25 percent) of Cabernet, similar currant and cherry flavors and firm tannins. A second style is less reliant on Cabernet, softer, more supple, medium-weight, less tannic and features more herb, cherry and chocolate flavors. A third style is a very light and simple wine; this type's sales are fueling Merlot's overall growth.

Like Cabernet, Merlot can benefit from some blending, as Cabernet can give it backbone, color and tannic strength. It also marries well with oak. It's important to remember that Merlot is relatively new in California, dating to the early 1970s, and is a difficult grape to grow, as it sets and ripens unevenly. Many critics believe Washington State has a slight quality edge with this wine. By the year 2000, vintners should have a better idea of which areas are best suited to this grape variety.

As a wine, Merlot's aging potential is fair to good. I think it's better in its youth than with four or five years' cellaring, but there are some Merlots that age well and surprise. It may be softer with age, but often the fruit flavors fade and the herbal flavors dominate. Napa County, with 2,721 acres, has the largest plantings, followed by Sonoma County at 2,530 acres, San Joaquin at 893 acres and Monterey with 833 acres.

MOURVÈDRE

This grape is also known as Mataro, and with only 301 acres it's a minor factor now, pursued by a few wineries that specialize in Rhône-style wines. The wine can be pleasing, with medium-weight, spicy cherry and berry flavors and mild tannins.

MUSCAT

Known as Muscat, Muscat Blanc and Muscat Canelli, this grape's acreage now totals 1,185. As a wine it is marked by strong spice and floral notes and can be used in blending.

NEBBIOLO

The great grape of Northern Italy, which excels there in Barolo and Barbaresco, Nebbiolo now has a small foothold in California, with 74 acres. So far the wines are light and uncomplicated, bearing no resemblance to the Italian types. But given the grape's potential for complex and ageworthy wines, and California's multitude of microclimates, it has potential.

PETITE SIRAH

Long favored as a blending grape, giving otherwise simple, light-colored wines more color, depth, intensity and tannin, Petite Sirah's acreage continues to dwindle, and now numbers only 2,351 acres, down from 11,061 in 1980. As tastes changed, Petite Sirah, with its ripe berry flavors and crisp, chewy tannins, fell out of favor. Moreover, the dense, inky wines that showed promise failed to improve with age, only becoming more tannic and earthy. Stags' Leap Winery continues to excel with a Petite Sirah made from very old vines.

PINOT BLANC

Often referred to as a poor man's Chardonnay because of its similar flavor and texture profile, Pinot Blanc measures 1,243 acres in California and can make a terrific wine, as it does with the Chalone, Chateau St. Jean and Steele bottlings. When well made, it is intense, concentrated and complex, with ripe pear, spice, citrus and honey notes. Can age well, but is best early on while its fruit shines through.

PINOT NOIR

Pinot Noir, the great grape of red Burgundy, excelled in California in the late 1980s and early 1990s and seems poised for further progress. Once producers stopped vinifying it as if it were Cabernet, planted vineyards in cooler climates and paid closer attention to tonnage, quality increased substantially, particularly in areas such as Carneros, Russian River Valley and Santa Barbara County. It's fair to say that California has a legitimate claim to producing world-class Pinot Noir. The best examples offer the classic black cherry, spice, raspberry and currant flavors, and an aroma that can resemble wilted roses, along with earth, tar, herb and cola notes. It can also be rather ordinary, light, simple, herbal, vegetal and occasionally weedy. It can even be downright funky, with pungent barnyard aromas. In fact, Pinot Noir is the most fickle of all grapes to grow: it reacts strongly to environmental changes such as heat and cold spells, and is notoriously fussy to work with once picked, since its thin skins are easily bruised and broken, setting the juice free. Even after fermentation, Pinot Noir can hide its weaknesses and strengths, making it a most difficult wine to evaluate out

of barrel. In the bottle too it is often a chameleon, showing poorly one day, brilliantly the next.

The emphasis on cooler climates coincides with more rigorous clonal selection, eliminating those clones suited for sparkling wine, which have even thinner skins. These days there is also a greater understanding of and appreciation for different styles of Pinot Noir wine, even if there is less agreement about those styles—should it be rich, concentrated and loaded with flavor, or a wine of elegance, finesse and delicacy? Or can it, in classic Pinot Noir sense, be both? Even varietal character remains subject to debate. Pinot Noir can certainly be tannic, especially when it is fermented with some of its stems, a practice that many vintners around the world believe contributes to the wine's backbone and longevity. Pinot Noir can also be long-lived, but predicting with any precision which wines or vintages will age is often the ultimate challenge in forecasting.

In the 1980s Carneros, which covers the southern portions of Napa and Sonoma, experienced tremendous growth in plantings; the grapes were to be used both for table wine and for sparkling wine, the best cuvées becoming highly reliant on Pinot Noir. This caused some concern, as the well financed sparkling wine houses snapped up Pinot Noir wherever they could find it. In the process, many vineyards that might have yielded superb table wines were lost and prices for the grapes escalated. But Carneros is also the home of the wineries with the most money, which gives it a significant edge when it comes to marketing and promoting their huge investments. Carneros Pinot Noirs are spicy, with red cherry and earth nuances, but the wines so far have not shown extra dimensions of richness and depth. Moreover, for all their early appeal, they mature rather quickly. Still, Carneros Creek, Robert Mondavi, Acacia and Saintsbury, among others, occasionally produce brilliant wines, so it may be just a matter of time before Carneros Pinot Noirs come into their own.

While it's close, I give a slight quality edge to Russian River and Santa Barbara County. Russian River wineries have less money and marketing clout than those in Carneros, but the quality of Pinot Noir from Rochioli, Williams & Selyem (with Rochioli and Allen vineyards), Gary Farrell and Dehlinger, among others, has quickly risen. The wines feature bold, ripe, bright black cherry, raspberry and spice flavors, and they're a shade more delicate and floral, even while maintaining their intensity and finesse.

Wines from Santa Barbara and the Central Coast can offer distinctive vegetal and herbaceous flavors, but when things go right and the grapes fully ripen, cherry, spice and earth nuances rise above the vegetal notes and can render wines of tremendous depth, intensity, focus and finesse. Coolness alone is not always a virtue, as it can lead to grapes with thick skins and firm if not chewy tannins. Monterey's progress with Chardonnay should be a good harbinger of things to come with Pinot Noir. In this area, both Chalone and Calera have made excellent wines, and since the best soil and exposure sites have been identified, there's every reason to believe quality will rise higher.

Sonoma has the largest plantings, with 2,905 acres in vines, followed by Napa (2,464), Monterey (1,369) and Santa Barbara (759). Carneros, which has 1,440 acres in Pinot Noir, is not broken out as a district by the state.

SANGIOVESE

This grape appears to have a bright future in California, both as a stand-alone varietal wine and for use in blends with Cabernet, Merlot and maybe even Zinfandel. Sangiovese is best known for providing the backbone for many superb Italian red wines from Tuscany, Chianti and Brunello di Montalcino, as well as the so-called Super Tuscan blends. It is somewhat surprising that Sangiovese wasn't more popular in California given the strong role Italian immigrants have played in the state's winemaking heritage. Until the mid-1980s, acreage was minimal and even now there are fewer than 400 bearing acres. Atlas Peak Vineyards in Napa Valley made an early commitment to this grape, planting 120 acres, with the early wines showing good but light varietal character. Also among the early entries: Robert Pepi, under the Colline di Sassi label; Ferrari-Carano, with both a Sangiovese and a blend called Siena, a wine that includes Cabernet and Merlot; Swanson; Flora Springs and Robert Mondavi Winery.

Sangiovese is distinctive for its supple texture and medium-to full-bodied spice, raspberry, cherry and anise flavors. When blended with a grape such as Cabernet, it gives that wine a smoother texture and lightens up the tannins. In that regard, Ferrari-Carano's Siena is the current trendsetter, but expect sweeping stylistic changes as winemakers learn more about how the grape performs in different locales as well as how it marries with different grapes. Worth watching.

SAUVIGNON BLANC

Among varietal white wines, Sauvignon Blanc, or Fumé Blanc as it's often labeled, comes in second behind Chardonnay in terms of quality and popularity, but by a good distance. The fundamental taste difference between the two is that leading Chardonnays rely on rich fruit—pear, apple, fig and grapefruit—and Sauvignon Blanc relies more on a spectrum of herbal and grassy flavors. Robert Mondavi rescued the variety by labeling it Fumé Blanc in the 1970s and he and others have enjoyed success with it. The key to its success seems to be in taming its overt varietal intensity, which at its extreme leads to pungent grassy, vegetal and herbaceous flavors. Many winemakers treat it like Chardonnay, employing barrel fermentation, *sur lie* aging and malolactic fermentation, resulting in a sort of poor man's Chardonnay, which I think works well. But its popularity comes as well from the fact that it is a prodigious producer and a highly profitable wine to make. It can be crisp and refreshing, matches well with foods, costs less to produce and grow than Chardonnay and sells for less. It also gets less respect from vintners than perhaps it should. Its popularity ebbs and flows, at times appearing to challenge Chardonnay and at other times appearing to be a cash-flow afterthought. But even at its best, it does not achieve the kind of richness, depth or complexity Chardonnay does and in the end that alone may be the defining difference.

With 11,345 acres in vines—compared to 56,255 acres of Chardonnay—Sauvignon Blanc is still a distant second in plantings (among grapes used primarily in varietal wines). To its credit, it grows well in a variety of appellations, ranging from Lake and Mendocino Counties to Sonoma and Napa and farther south in Santa Barbara. It marries well with oak and Sémillon, and many vintners are adding a touch of Chardonnay for extra body. The wines drinks best in its youth, but sometimes will benefit from short-term cellaring. As a late-harvest wine, it's often fantastic, capable of yielding amazingly complex and richly flavored wines. Napa County still has the largest acreage, with 2,165 acres in vines, followed by Sonoma (1,418 acres), Monterey (1,403 acres) and San Joaquin (1,289 acres).

SÉMILLON

Sémillon, which enjoys modest success as a varietal wine, continues to lose ground in acreage, dropping to

1,482 acres statewide. It can make a wonderful late-harvest wine, and those wineries that do focus on it can make well balanced wines with complex fig, pear, tobacco and honey notes. When blended into Sauvignon Blanc, it adds body, flavor and texture. When Sauvignon Blanc is added to Sémillon, the latter gains grassy herbal notes.

SYMPHONY

A new grape variety that crosses Muscat of Alexandria and Grenache Gris, Symphony can be vinified in a wide variety of styles, from dry to dessert. Its signature is its spiciness, gaining more peach, honey and apricot flavors when fermented as a dessert wine. Chateau de Baun has pursued this grape enthusiastically in a variety of styles from dry to dessert, with mixed results.

SYRAH

By the year 2000, this should be one of the most exciting new wines in California. Already its rise in quality is most impressive, as the grape seems to grow well in a number of areas and is capable of rendering rich, complex and distinctive wines, with pronounced pepper, spice, black cherry, tar, leather and roasted nut flavors, a smooth, supple texture and smooth tannins. Syrah appears to have the early-drinking appeal of Pinot Noir and Zinfandel and few of the eccentricities of Merlot, and may well prove far easier to grow and vinify than any other red wine aside from Cabernet. Plantings have grown steadily to 596 acres, most in ideal locations along coastal valleys, so their future should be bright. It would not surprise me if Syrah eventually rivals Pinot Noir and Zinfandel for second place after Cabernet.

VIOGNIER

Viognier, an early 1990s darling of Rhône lovers, totals only 115 acres in vines. It is also one of the most difficult grapes to grow as it struggles to produce. But fans of the floral, spicy wine are thrilled by its prospects. So far most of the Viogniers are rather one-dimensional, with an abundance of spiciness but less complexity than they should have. Still, there are a few bright spots.

ZINFANDEL

This tremendously versatile and popular grape is still tops in acreage for red grapes, with 32,704 acres of vines statewide. Much of that is grown in the state's San Joaquin Valley (12,523 acres), where it's vinified into white Zinfandel, a blush-colored, slightly sweet wine. Real Zinfandel, the red wine, is the quintessential California wine. Its roots are not known for certain, although it is thought to have originated in Southern Italy as a cousin of Primitivo. In California it has served many masters. It has been used for blending with other grapes, including Cabernet and Petite Sirah. It has been made in a claret style, with berry and cherry flavors, mild tannins and pretty oak shadings. It has been made into a full-bodied, ultraripe, intensely flavored and firmly tannic wine designed to age. And it has been made into late-harvest and Port-style wines that feature very ripe, raisiny flavors, alcohol above 15 percent and chewy tannins.

Zinfandel's popularity among consumers fluctuates. By the early 1990s Zinfandel was enjoying another groundswell of popularity, as winemakers took renewed interest, focusing on higher-quality vineyards in areas well suited to Zinfandel. Styles aimed more for the mainstream and less for extremes, emphasizing the grape's zesty, spicy pepper, raspberry, cherry, wild berry and plum flavors, and its complex range of tar, earth and leather notes. Zinfandel lends itself to blending. Many of the best are so-called field blends planted years ago with small amounts of Alicante, Petite Sirah and Carignane. The classic is Ridge Geyserville, which doesn't indicate a varietal on the label, as it is about 60 percent Zinfandel, less than the 75 percent required for varietal labeling.

Zinfandel is a challenging grape to grow: its berry size varies significantly within a bunch, which leads to uneven ripening. Because of that, Zinfandel often needs to hang on the vine longer to ripen as many berries as possible. Closer attention to viticulture and an appreciation for older vines, which tend to produce smaller crops of uniformly higher quality, account for better-balanced wines. Zinfandel fares well in a variety of appellations, but seems to have an edge as it moves closer to the coast in warm valleys such as Dry Creek. It also performs well in the hills and mountains of Napa, Sonoma and Mendocino, as well as farther south in Paso Robles. After San Joaquin, Sonoma leads in acreage with 3,769 acres, followed by Napa (1,989) and Mendocino (1,715).

ACREAGE BY GRAPE: **RED VARIETALS**

NUMBER OF ACRES

GRAPE	1980	1985	Percent Change 1980-85	1990	Percent Change 1980-90	1993	Percent Change 1990-93	1994	Percent Change 1990-94
Aleatico	169	53	-69%	0	-100%	0	0%	0	0%
Alicante Bouschet	4,901	3,162	-35%	2,042	-58%	1,614	-21%	1,600	-22%
Aramon	71	0	-100%	0	-100%	0	0%	0	0%
Barbera	19,267	14,804	-23%	10,646	-45%	9,870	-7%	9,261	-13%
Beclan	76	0	-100%	0	-100%	0	0%	0	0%
Black Malvoisie	509	219	-57%	87	-83%	80	-8%	92	6%
Cabernet Franc	76	294	287%	1,130	1,387%	1,639	45%	1,740	54%
Cabernet Sauvignon	21,759	20,430	-6%	24,115	11%	31,650	31%	32,595	35%
Calzin	0	0	0%	0	0%	78	-100%	0	0%
Carignane	25,111	16,300	-35%	11,033	-56%	9,145	-17%	8,883	-19%
Carnelian	2,749	1,592	-42%	1,250	-55%	1,045	-16%	1,047	-16%
Centurian	1,035	592	-43%	580	-44%	662	14%	571	-2%
Charbono	46	84	83%	0	-100%	51	-100%	0	0%
Early Burgundy	572	214	-63%	143	-75%	60	-58%	0	-100%
Gamay	4,657	2,447	-47%	1,517	-67%	1,244	-18%	1,329	-12%
Gamay Beaujolais	3,980	2,520	-37%	1,424	-64%	1,231	-14%	1,073	-25%
Grand Noir	91	0	-100%	0	-100%	0	0%	0	0%
Grenache	16,764	14,047	-16%	12,418	-26%	12,359	0%	12,107	-3%
Grignolino	55	52	-5%	0	-100%	0	0%	0	0%
Lambrusco	0	0	0%	10	100%	111	1,010%	111	1,010%
Malbec	56	56	0%	91	63%	99	9%	68	-25%
Mataro (Mourvèdre)	930	491	-47%	210	-77%	270	29%	301	43%
Merlot	2,592	1,955	-25%	4,010	55%	7,944	98%	9,605	140%
Meunier	0	0	0%	160	100%	231	44%	228	43%
Mission	3,654	2,310	-37%	1,118	-69%	1,047	-6%	1,060	-5%
Muscat Hamburg	66	63	-5%	62	-6%	0	-100%	0	-100%
Nebbiolo	500	0	-100%	0	-100%	51	100%	74	100%
Perelli 101	128	0	-100%	0	-100%	0	0%	0	0%
Petite Sirah	11,061	5,093	-54%	3,023	-73%	2,439	-19%	2,351	-22%
Petite Verdot	0	0	0%	46	100%	101	120%	132	187%

NUMBER OF ACRES

GRAPE	1980	1985	Percent Change 1980-85	1990	Percent Change 1980-90	1993	Percent Change 1990-93	1994	Percent Change 1990-94
Pinot Noir	9,224	7,429	-19%	8,554	-7%	8,576	0%	8,727	2%
Pinot St. George	634	143	-77%	0	-100%	0	0%	0	0%
Red Veltliner	65	0	-100%	0	-100%	0	0%	0	0%
Refosco	103	0	-100%	0	-100%	0	0%	0	0%
Royalty	2,246	1,169	-48%	818	-64%	818	0%	773	-6%
Rubired	10,561	7,975	-24%	6,948	-34%	7,541	9%	7,312	5%
Ruby Cabernet	16,926	10,577	-38%	6,881	-59%	6,454	-6%	5,916	-14%
Salvador	2,502	1,262	-50%	749	-70%	772	3%	845	13%
Sangiovese	0	0	0%	39	100%	228	485%	358	818%
Souzao	197	0	-100%	0	-100%	0	0%	0	0%
St. Macaire	144	50	-65%	0	-100%	0	0%	0	0%
Syrah	60	86	43%	144	140%	471	227%	596	314%
Tinta Madeira	649	172	-73%	52	-92%	52	0%	0	-100%
Valdepenas	1,872	966	-48%	540	-71%	536	-1%	496	-8%
Zinfandel	27,652	24,775	-10%	27,989	1%	32,729	17%	32,704	17%
Other Red	0	344	100%	302	100%	333	10%	477	58%
TOTAL RED GRAPES	193,710	141,726	-27%	128,131	-34%	141,531	10%	142,432	11%

ACREAGE BY GRAPE: **WHITE VARIETALS**

NUMBER OF ACRES

GRAPE	1980	1985	Percent Change 1980-85	1990	Percent Change 1980-90	1993	Percent Change 1990-93	1994	Percent Change 1990-94
Burger	1,651	1,701	3%	2,293	39%	2,227	-3%	1,931	-16%
Chardonnay	12,245	22,847	87%	37,714	208%	53,309	41%	56,255	49%
Chasselas Dore	0	59	100%	0	0%	0	0%	0	0%
Chenin Blanc	21,129	38,980	84%	32,666	55%	27,945	-14%	26,157	-20%
Emerald Reisling	2,583	2,892	12%	1,304	-50%	1,116	-14%	814	-38%
Feher Szagos	300	130	-57%	54	-82%	0	-100%	0	-100%
Flora	372	343	-8%	0	-100%	0	0%	0	0%
Folle Blanche	351	226	-36%	0	-100%	0	0%	0	0%
French Colombard	27,384	68,313	149%	58,655	114%	54,187	-8%	49,498	-16%
Gewürztraminer	2,688	3,974	48%	1,838	-32%	1,687	-8%	1,602	-13%
Gray Reisling	1,817	2,407	32%	491	-73%	267	-46%	243	-51%
Green Hungarian	352	351	0%	162	-54%	107	-34%	86	-47%
Malvaisa Bianca	754	1,331	77%	2,099	178%	2,381	13%	2,408	15%
Muscat Blanc	1,033	1,532	48%	1,332	29%	1,182	-11%	1,185	-11%
Muscat Orange	0	0	0%	36	100%	49	36%	68	89%
Palomino	3,702	2,697	-27%	1,484	-60%	1,119	-25%	1,032	-30%
Pedro Ximenes	208	64	-69%	0	-100%	0	0%	0	0%
Peverella	420	409	-3%	0	-100%	0	0%	0	0%
Pinot Blanc	1,520	2,136	41%	1,829	20%	1,619	-11%	1,243	-32%
Sauvignon Blanc	4,171	13,299	219%	12,597	202%	11,920	-5%	11,345	-10%
Sauvignon Vert	526	234	-56%	102	-81%	72	-29%	68	-33%
Sémillon	2,709	2,827	4%	2,176	-20%	1,843	-15%	1,482	-32%
St. Emilion	1,173	1,091	-7%	774	-34%	590	-24%	560	-28%
Sylvaner	1,219	1,221	0%	193	-84%	163	-16%	117	-39%
Symphony	0	0	0%	75	100%	245	227%	170	127%
Viognier	0	0	0%	11	100%	79	618%	115	945%
White Reisling	7,945	9,732	22%	4,946	-38%	3,654	-26%	3,194	-35%
Other White Wine	0	260	100%	139	100%	183	32%	200	44%
TOTAL WHITE GRAPES	**96,252**	**179,056**	**86%**	**162,430**	**69%**	**165,944**	**2%**	**159,773**	**-2%**

SOURCE: CALIFORNIA AGRICULTURAL STATISTICS SERVICE

CHAPTER 3

APPELLATIONS AND VINEYARDS

Where a wine's grapes are grown ultimately determines its style, character and personality. Cabernet planted in too cool a climate fails to ripen and will have green tannins. Pinot Noir grown in too warm a climate overripens and is robbed of its varietal character. Correctly matching grapes to soil and climate is a precise exercise that is often carried out by trial and error. As we will see in the next chapter, "How Wine Is Made," the decisions that are most crucial to a wine's quality and style are which grapes to grow and where to plant them. Many vintners are successful right from the start in planting the proper grapes in the proper place. But many more try to force their will on nature, learning the hard way which combinations work and which don't.

In Europe, after several hundred years of matching grape types to soil and climate, a disciplined system of appellations has evolved. In California, vintners are still learning, although since the late 1970s there has been tremendous progress in identifying which appellations best accommodate which grape types. As early as the late 1800s, vintners in Napa Valley and other parts of the state began to pinpoint areas well suited for Cabernet. In Napa, Rutherford emerged as a favored site. In Sonoma County, vintners found that Dry Creek Valley produced wonderful Zinfandel and Petite Sirah. During the 1940s, Pinot Noir's potential in Carneros became evident, though it was another 40 years before that potential was realized. The pace today is much quicker and our knowl-

edge much greater, but there is still much to be learned. For instance, Santa Maria Valley has now been recognized as natural for Chardonnay, yet it may also be ideal for Sangiovese and Syrah.

When you buy a bottle of wine, the producer's name, grape variety and vintage date can help you assess its style and quality. A wine's appellation should also be a clue as to its style and quality, as particular grapes and appellations show an affinity for each other: Cabernet for Rutherford, Pinot Noir for Russian River Valley, Sauvignon Blanc for Lake County and Chardonnay for Santa Barbara, for instance.

Great wines are distinctive and they have a sense of the place where they're grown. The French call this *terroir*; it's the way in which soil and climate influence the biology of the vinestock and grape. *Terroir* is the interaction of an infinite number of variables that include temperatures by day and night, rainfall distribution by season and year, exposure, soil acidity, soil depth and so on. In short, it's anything natural that influences the growth of a vine. Distinctive wines can polarize consumers; a wine with too strong a personality may be overbearing, yet it may be the perfect example of a wine from its appellation, a true reflection of its *terroir*.

In California there are no restrictions that limit which grapes can be grown in an appellation. But common sense, experience and economics influence the choices. A vintner who owns expensive hillside property where Cabernet excels probably won't grow Gewürztraminer there for two reasons: Gewürztraminer likes cooler weather than Cabernet and it sells for less. The dual forces of *terroir* and economics combine to influence where grapes are grown.

U.S. APPELLATION SYSTEM

In the United States, appellations have been formalized as American Viticultural Areas (AVAs), which determine the wording that is permitted on a wine label. In order for a wine to carry an AVA, it must be 85 percent from that appellation. In the case of varietal wines, 75 percent of the named variety must be from that appellation. If a vineyard name is used, 95 percent of that wine must come from that source. To use the term "estate bottled," both the winery and vineyard or vineyards must fall within the AVA used on the label and the producing winery must own or control, through a long-term lease, all vineyards used in the wine.

The AVAs are new and far from perfect. AVAs are requested by petitioners, usually vintners and growers who own land in or buy grapes from an area they believe is distinctive and merits greater recognition. They apply to the U.S. Bureau of Alcohol, Tobacco and Firearms, which holds hearings where evidence is introduced to support or oppose an appellation, usually on the basis of boundary (but sometimes based on the name too, in the case of Stags Leap and Dry Creek). The basic outline for an AVA includes specific geographic features such as soil, but also climate, temperature, elevation and rainfall, as well as whether the area is known locally or nationally (there are many Dry Creeks). The boundaries must also be readily identifiable on a U.S. Geologic Survey Map. Historic and geographic evidence of a name (Rutherford, Howell Mountain) weighs in as a factor, as do distinctive geographic boundaries and features (such as mountains, ridges and elevations), and to some extent winegrowing history, however brief.

AVAs do not follow political boundaries, such as county lines, except where the political boundary follows a natural one like a river, a bay or a ridge line. The boundaries are usually drawn to include the largest area under consideration rather than the smallest. For example, Napa Valley is a narrow valley through which the Napa River flows, bordered on the west and east by two mountain ranges. Yet the Napa Valley AVA covers most of the county, extending far beyond the real valley and well into northern and eastern valleys that really are separate. This is because growers in outlying areas historically sold grapes to prominent Napa wineries for bottling of "Napa Valley" wines. Depriving them of the right to sell their grapes as "Napa Valley" Cabernet would have caused them financial hardship. Conversely, wineries buying grapes from vineyards outside a narrower Napa Valley appellation might have been forced to change their labels to Napa County—a less prestigious name.

There are obvious differences between Calistoga in the north and Yountville, or even Carneros, farther south. Clearly, these areas have different soils and climates. How does the AVA system distinguish between them? Part of the answer lies in the smaller appellations within Napa Valley. Rutherford, Oakville and the Stags Leap District are now appellations that designate wines with distinctive styles. Spring Mountain, Mount Veeder and Howell Mountain are also AVAs, and soon St. Helena and Calistoga will join them. It's also likely that Diamond Mountain, Yountville and Coombsville will eventually be AVAs, as might the Oak Knoll area, which lies south of Yountville and north of Napa.

Sonoma County, too, has its share of problems with multiple overlapping AVAs. A vineyard in Windsor could label its wine any number of ways, from California, the broadest possible, to North Coast, Sonoma County, Northern Sonoma, Sonoma Coast, Russian River Valley or Chalk Hill, and still comply with the spirit of the appellation system.

Glamour and marketing clout have a lot to do with which appellations are used. California has more appeal than San Joaquin Valley. Growers in Pope Valley, northeast of Napa Valley, could have their own AVA (and probably will someday), but Napa Valley has a far greater national and international reputation. It would take years to establish any similar reknown for the name Pope Valley. This may be the most important lesson about appellations: Many vintners who make ordinary Napa Valley wines benefit from the use of the name, in effect riding on the coattails of the region's great wines. AVAs are no guarantee of quality—style, perhaps, but not quality. Names and reputations sell wine.

THE INFLUENCE OF CLIMATE AND SOIL

The greatest single influence on California's climate is the Pacific Ocean. Were it not for the cooling effect of the ocean, most of the coastal valleys that form the state's finest winegrowing areas would simply be too warm for producing fine wine. Each of the key coastal appellations—from Temecula to Anderson Valley—owes its moderate temperatures to the ocean (in the case of Carneros and Livermore Valley, the San Pablo Bay plays a role, too). The regular occurrence, especially during the summer months, of coastal fog and its movement inland in the late afternoon and evening is California's natural air conditioning system. The most dramatic presentation of this phenomenon can be viewed while standing on the Golden Gate Bridge on a summer afternoon when the cold fog whips in under the bridge, with gusting winds of 20 to 40 miles per hour. It is in this way that the Pacific Ocean shapes and defines the main coastal valleys, most of which run north-south. But each of these valleys is different in size and faces the ocean at a slightly different angle. Some have higher mountains and elevations than others. All of these and other factors contribute to the unique features of the appellation.

Soil is the other major factor influencing how a grapevine grows. Compared to Europe's, California's soils are "young," rich in minerals and fertile—sometimes to a fault. California's soils also vary greatly, from the sandy benches that line rivers to the limestone beneath Calera or Chalone. A walk through Rutherford in August will leave your boots caked with a unique, very fine dust. Even within a vineyard, soils can vary significantly. There is skill involved in matching rootstock to soil type, as certain stocks perform better in rich soils and others are better suited to sparse or shallow soils. Clay soils hold water better than stony vineyards that were once river bottom. An iron-rich red soil will hold the day's heat longer than a chalky white soil. Mountain vineyards are mostly rocky and well drained. The major valleys—such as Napa and Sonoma—are complex geographic entities. But the alluvial fans that form as the mountains shift and crumble are highly regarded for their rich soils, sun exposure and drainage. While there is no one soil that is best suited for all grapes, some sites are clearly better, as reflected by their expression of *terroir* and the quality of the wines they yield.

Here, alphabetically, are the major appellations, including AVAs and counties. I have also listed what I call "Reference Wines" for the major appellations. These are wines that year in and year out display the best regional character that each appellation has to offer.

ALEXANDER VALLEY
AVA 1984, 66,000 acres, 6,500 acres in vines

This northern Sonoma County appellation straddles the Russian River Valley. Cabernet and Chardonnay are its leading wines. It is now home to several wineries; among the better known are Simi, Jordan, Clos du Bois, Alexander Valley Vineyards, Chateau Souverain and Geyser Peak. Curiously, Silver Oak, based in Napa Valley, helped build this appellation's Cabernet credentials as much as Simi, Clos du Bois' Marlstone and Briarcrest, Rodney Strong's Alexander's Crown or Jordan did. And after all is said and done, Silver Oak Cabernet still dominates, though for how long is unclear, as Simi and others are intent on making better wines. Despite its proximity to the Pacific Ocean, Alexander Valley is a warm appellation with the valley floor a mix of gravelly loam soils. Grapes grow well here—sometimes too well, as vine vigor has been a major problem. One of the area's real stars is Robert Young Vineyard, known for the superb Chardonnays it yields for Chateau St. Jean, in addition to dessert-style wines. This vineyard can easily produce 5 to 6 tons of Chardonnay per acre without sacrificing quality.

Over the years the Cabernets, while supple and elegant, have often been marked by herb and bell pepper notes. Replanting vineyards with new rootstock and clones and the use of new trellising systems are changing the wine styles. Chardonnays tend to be ripe and full-blown, with juicy tropical fruit flavors, but they can also be lean and one-dimensional. Clearly it's a diversified appellation, with wineries such as Marcassin using Gauer Ranch grapes for its "Upper Barn" bottling of Chardonnay, and Ridge relying on Geyserville at the northernmost edge of the appellation for its Zinfandel-based table wine. The wild card for the future is Gallo, which has planted nearly 1,000 acres in and around Asti to a variety of reds, including Zinfandel, Syrah and Sangiovese. Of note: the Northern Sonoma appellation was drawn, at Gallo's request, to encompass its 2,000 acres in vines reaching from Russian River (for Chardonnay) to Asti and including its Frei Ranch in Dry Creek.

REFERENCE WINES

Cabernet Sauvignon: Clos du Bois Marlstone and Briarcrest, Geyser Peak Reserve Alexandre and Geyser Peak Reserve, Jordan, Silver Oak, Simi Reserve, Stonestreet Legacy
Chardonnay: Chateau St. Jean Belle Terre and Robert

Young Vineyards, Ferrari-Carano, Landmark Damaris Reserve, Marcassin Gauer Ranch Upper Barn
Merlot: Alexander Valley Vineyards, Chateau Souverain, Stonestreet
Zinfandel: Joseph Phelps, Ridge Geyserville, Sausal, Scherrer

AMADOR COUNTY

Not an AVA, but important for its Zinfandel, which occupies two-thirds of its Sierra foothills acreage, at an elevation of 1,500 to 2,500 feet. This area has been made popular by Sutter Home, the white (and red) Zin producer. Sutter Home has some 1,800 acres here. More than half of it is Zinfandel, which produces a hearty if rustic and earthy wine with wild berry flavors and often substantial tannins. Progress with quality has been slow, but often good values emerge. Both the Fiddletown (310 acres in vine) and Shenandoah Valley (1,200 acres) AVAs are within Amador County, although a portion of the latter stretches into El Dorado County.

REFERENCE WINES

Barbera: Renwood
Zinfandel: Karly, Renwood, Santino, Sutter Home Reserve

ANDERSON VALLEY
AVA 1983, 57,000 acres, 1,100 acres in vines

This slender valley in Mendocino County stretches inland from close to the Pacific Ocean and is home to both mainstream and off-beat wine styles. Chardonnay, Pinot Noir and Zinfandel are often excellent, but it's the Gewürztraminers and Rieslings—dry, off-dry and dessert-style—and sparkling wines that make an interesting mix. Moreover, in some spots Cabernet does well; Merlot might have a future here too. The Villa Mt. Eden Signature Series Cabernet 1992 from Greenwood Ridge Vineyard proved uncommonly rich and concentrated. Riesling and Gewürztraminer plantings are more than 100 acres each, not much in size, but the quality is often excellent, led by Navarro's bottlings. Chardonnay tends to be crisp, with apple and spice notes, although again Navarro often gets the most flavor into its Premiere Reserve Chardonnay. Pinot Noir continues to improve, adding depth and richness to Roederer Estate's and Scharffenberger's sparkling wines, not to mention table wines, the best being Williams & Selyem's

Ferrington Vineyard, which made its debut in 1992. In the hills, which rise above the fog lines and get more sun, Zinfandel from DuPratt Vineyard can be excellent.

REFERENCE WINES

Cabernet Sauvignon: Villa Mt. Eden Signature Series
Chardonnay: Navarro, Steele Dennison
Pinot Noir: Edmeades Dennison, Navarro, Greenwood Ridge, Roederer Vineyard, Steele DuPratt Vineyard, Williams & Selyem Ferrington Vineyard
Zinfandel: Edmeades Ciapusci and Zeni Vineyards

ARROYO GRANDE
AVA 1990, 42,880 acres, 420 acres in vines

This new AVA in southern San Luis Obispo County is home to Maison Deutz, Talley Vineyards and Saucelito Canyon wineries, and has a climate similar to its neighbor to the north, Edna Valley. So far Chardonnay and Pinot Noir are the early leaders, with high hopes for the Talley Vineyards Pinot Noir. Saucelito Canyon's Zinfandels, grown at the eastern edge of the appellation, have been impressive.

ARROYO SECO
AVA 1983, 18,240 acres, 2,200 acres in vines

Jekel and Ventana are the two lone wineries in this Monterey County appellation which rests on the eastern side of the coastal range and is best known for Chardonnay and Riesling. Jekel's Sanctuary Vineyard is the only notable one rooted to red grapes here. This appellation is of little importance so far.

ATLAS PEAK
AVA 1992, 11,400 acres, 656 acres in vines

High above the Stags Leap outcropping in the Napa Valley is Foss Valley, which sits like a shallow bowl surrounded by hills. William Hill bought the property and planted the first vines, believing it ideally suited for Cabernet. He eventually sold it to a group headed by Tuscany's Piero Antinori that also included Bollinger and Whitbread. Today Atlas Peak Vineyards (see listing) is part of the Wine Alliance family of wineries, and is best known for its efforts with Sangiovese, including a Cabernet-Sangiovese blend called Consenso; the wines have ranged from fair to good. Cabernet is a new part of the product mix and is very good in its first vintage.

Chardonnay also is untested. The bottom line is that the Sangiovese and Chardonnay are still young and unproven; however, Cabernet appears well suited and another half dozen varieties may yet prove themselves.

CALAVERAS COUNTY

This county lies southeast of Sacramento in the Sierra Foothills. It's not an AVA, but it is home to some 200 acres in vines, including Chardonnay, Sauvignon Blanc and Zinfandel. It's of little importance as a viticultural area.

CALIFORNIA

This is the all-encompassing appellation. California has more than 330,000 acres in vines and produces 85 percent of the country's wine. On wine labels, California means the grapes have come from a variety of appellations. The California appellation includes a range of products from expensive wines such as Kendall-Jackson's Cardinale to the most inexpensive wines. Depending on the producer, it can represent good quality.

CALIFORNIA SHENANDOAH VALLEY
AVA 1983, 10,000 acres, 1,200 acres in vines

Shenandoah Valley in Virginia is the other Shenandoah, hence the use of California in the name of this Sierra Foothills appellation. Zinfandel is the major grape, with many decades-old vines that yield ripe, intense wines featuring firm tannins, earthy berry and tar flavors and a rustic edge. Rhône- and Italian-style reds are also joining the mix.

REFERENCE WINES

Syrah: Sobon
Zinfandel: Amador Foothill, Renwood Grandpère, Santino, Story, Sobon

CALISTOGA

Not an AVA, but sure to be one eventually as Napa Valley is further subdivided. This northernmost city in the valley is warm and excels with many grapes, but Cabernet is the star. A number of important wineries are based here, among them Sterling Vineyard, Clos Pegase and Cuvaison. Sauvignon Blanc is also favored here.

REFERENCE WINES

Cabernet Sauvignon: Araujo Estate Eisele Vineyard, Chateau Montelena, Robert Pecota Kara's Vineyard

Merlot: Duckhorn, Three Palms Vineyard, Robert Pecota Steven Andre Vineyard

CARMEL VALLEY
AVA 1983, 19,200 acres, 150 acres in vines

Southeast of the famous town of Carmel, this Monterey County appellation rises up from sea level and gets substantial rainfall. Durney is the major winery here and its Cabernets can be good, but more often are hard and tannic and even with age they fail to impress. Chardonnay is a better bet. Georis Merlot is distinctive, but tannic too.

CARNEROS
AVA 1983, 36,900 acres, 6,200 acres in vines

This AVA straddles the southernmost portions of Napa and Sonoma Valleys. Its soils vary, but in general are thin (usually less than 3 to 4 feet deep), especially when compared with the rich, loamy soils in the heart of Napa Valley. Nor is the soil very fertile, since it was once part of the bottom of San Pablo Bay, a mix of clay and loamy deposits. Rainfall is sparse, the growing season long and the climate shaped by the bay and whipping winds that blow through the area almost daily. Because it is cooler than Napa or Sonoma Valleys proper, and because vintners could use the names Napa Valley or Sonoma Valley if they chose, it emerged as Napa and Sonoma vintners' best choice for Chardonnay and Pinot Noir. Both those grapes have had their successes here. The Chardonnays are bright and lively, with earthy apple, pineapple and crisp lemon flavors. Pinot Noir is marked by spicy cherry and berry flavors and is crisp and tight in structure, much like the Chardonnay. As for aging, neither of the wines so far ages exceptionally well, but this is still a new area with its best sites yet to be exploited. Most often Carneros is synonymous with consistently high-quality Chardonnays and Pinot Noirs.

Méthode champenoise sparkling wine is the other major product of Carneros' Chardonnay and Pinot Noir plantings, led by Codorniu Napa, Domaine Carneros, Domaine Chandon and Gloria Ferrer. Cabernet, which fared so well for so long at Buena Vista with its excellent Special Selection and Private Reserve bottlings, has faltered of late, with wines that increasingly display an herbal, weedy edge and lack tart cherry and berry notes. Merlot, however, shows potential; Cuvaison's is first-class. The Syrah from Truchard, grown at the northernmost edge of Carneros-Napa, is so rich and authentic, with classic toasty cherry and berry flavors, that it too may be a strong presence in the future. Grown in the dark, warm soils, Syrah and other red varieties may be a good match.

REFERENCE WINES

Cabernet Sauvignon: Buena Vista, Paul Hobbs Hyde Vineyard

Chardonnay: Acacia, Gloria Ferrer, Grgich Hills Carneros, Marcassin Hudson Vineyard, Robert Mondavi, Ravenswood Sangiacomo Vineyard, Saintsbury, Robert Sinskey, Truchard

Merlot: Buena Vista, Cuvaison, Havens, Robert Sinskey, Truchard, Ravenswood

Pinot Noir: Acacia, Carneros Creek, El Molino, Étude, Robert Mondavi, Saintsbury, Truchard

Others: Truchard (Syrah), Beringer (Viognier Hudson Vineyard)

CENTRAL COAST

This appellation covers coastal counties from the San Francisco Bay Area in the north to Santa Barbara County in the south. It includes the following AVAs: Arroyo Grande, Arroyo Seco, Carmel Valley, Chalone, Edna Valley, Livermore Valley, Mount Harlan, Paso Robles, San Lucas, San Ysidro, Santa Cruz Mountains, Santa Lucia Highlands, Santa Maria Valley, Santa Ynez Valley and York Mountain.

CHALK HILL

AVA 1983, 21,100 acres, 1,000 acres in vines

Chalk Hill covers the easternmost portion of Russian River Valley in northern Sonoma, taking its name from the area's chalky, volcanic dust soils. Chardonnay is the predominant grape grown here, with Rodney Strong's Chalk Hill Chardonnay and Chalk Hill Winery carrying the name to market. Chalk Hill Winery, with nearly 300 acres in vines, does well with Chardonnay and Sauvignon Blanc. Its Cabernet has been more variable, but has been excellent on occasion.

CHALONE

AVA 1982, 8,640 acres, 120 acres in vines

A single-winery appellation in the Gavilan Mountains that straddles the Monterey and San Benito county borders, near Pinnacles National Monument.

These mountains rise up from the Salinas Valley, and the vineyard is 1,800 feet above sea level in rugged, parched, windswept terrain. And it's been home to Chalone's excellent Chardonnays, Chenin Blancs, Pinot Blancs and Pinot Noirs for nearly four decades. Many of the vines date to the 1940s. All four of the main wines are excellent and long-lived, marked by a youthful austerity and a capacity to develop complex nuances, often with flinty mineral flavors. The Chardonnay is the most consistently excellent performer, capable of rendering uncommonly complex and long-lived wines. Pinot Noir also fares well here, but as a grape it's more variable and through the 1980s it produced a leaner, more tannic, less interesting wine than it did the decade before. The Pinot Blanc is simply California's finest, at times sharing the focus, intensity and discipline of the Chardonnay. The Chenin Blanc, too, merits special attention, as it often renders a remarkably complex and enduring wine.

CHILES VALLEY

Not an AVA, but part of the Napa Valley, Chiles Valley lies east of the main valley floor and is home to several vineyards.

CLARKSBURG

AVA 1984, 65,000 acres, 5,500 acres in vines

Best known for its Chenin Blancs made by Kenwood, Hacienda and Grand Cru, this appellation is home to Bogle Vineyards but no other wineries. Chardonnay, Merlot, Petite Sirah and Cabernet are also grown here, just outside of Sacramento.

CLEAR LAKE

AVA 1984, 168,900 acres, 3,200 acres in vines

Years ago most grapes gave way to pears in this Lake County AVA, but Sauvignon Blanc still excels and the Cabernet, Chardonnay and Zinfandel can make very appealing, lighter wines. Steele's Catfish Vineyard Zinfandel carries this appellation.

DIAMOND MOUNTAIN

This region of northwestern Napa is not an AVA, but is likely to become one. The most famous property here is Diamond Creek Vineyards (see listing), which bottles three (and sometimes four) separate vineyard-designated Cabernets from its 20 acres in vines. These are uncommonly complex and long-lived wines, from as distinctive a vineyard as exists in California. Others, including Sterling Vineyards' Diamond Mountain Ranch, have had less success with both Cabernet and Chardonnay, while von Strasser appears to have found a groove with its Cabernets. Cabernet and other Bordeaux-style reds will likely dominate.

REFERENCE WINES

Cabernet Sauvignon: Diamond Creek, Sterling Diamond Mountain Ranch, von Strasser

DRY CREEK VALLEY
AVA 1983, 80,000 acres, 5,500 acres in vines

This narrow valley in Northern Sonoma is home to many first-class Zinfandels; this grape seems to excel in this area which, during the growing season, starts with cool mornings and warms sufficiently in the afternoons to give the tricky Zinfandel grape the right amount of heat without overdoing it. Ridge Lytton Springs, Rafanelli, Quivira, Ferrari-Carano, Nalle, Preston, Lytton Springs, Dry Creek Vineyards and Gallo Sonoma are all crafting superb Zins marked by spicy raspberry and black cherry flavors. Cabernet is slowly making inroads and seems to perform best in the hills—witness the excellent Gallo Northern Sonoma, which is estate bottled, and Rafanelli—but can be lighter and lacking the richness, depth and concentration of the best from Napa Valley. Among whites, Sauvignon Blanc leads in acreage and can yield good wines marked by grassy, herbal notes. Clos du Bois' Flintwood Chardonnay is the best known of that variety, grown farther south.

REFERENCE WINES

Cabernet Sauvignon: Gallo Northern Sonoma, Rafanelli
Merlot: Dry Creek Vineyard, Mazzocco
Sauvignon Blanc: Preston, Quivira
Zinfandel: Chateau Souverain, Dry Creek Vineyard, Ferrari-Carano, Gallo Frei Ranch, Lytton Springs, Meeker, Nalle, Quivira, Preston, Rabbit Ridge, Rafanelli, Ridge, White Oak Saunders Vineyard

EDNA VALLEY
AVA 1982, 22,400 acres, 1,550 acres in vines

Edna Valley's fame begins and ends with Chardonnay, led by Edna Valley Vineyard and to a lesser extent Meridian

and Chamisal. This South Central Coast AVA is very close to the ocean and quite cool, so much so that Edna Valley Vineyards' efforts with Pinot Noir, which failed to ripen in too many years and frequently led to pungently vegetal wines, have largely faded. In warm years, the Edna Valley Chardonnay is bold, rich and intensely flavored.

REFERENCE WINES

Chardonnay: Carmenet, Chamisal Special Reserve, Edna Valley Vineyards, Meridian, Mount Eden MacGregor Vineyard

EL DORADO
AVA 1983, 414,000 acres, 442 acres in vines

The few vineyards in this Sierra Foothills appellation northeast of Sacramento rise to between 2,200 and 3,000 feet of elevation. Most of the major varieties are grown here, with Zinfandel the leader among reds and Chardonnay the leader among whites. The Zinfandels have a distinctive presence, often marked by very ripe berry and tar flavors, with firm and chewy tannins that give them a rustic edge.

REFERENCE WINES

Zinfandel: Boeger Walker Vineyard

FIDDLETOWN
AVA 1983, 11,500 acres, 310 acres in vines

Fiddletown borders the Shenandoah Valley in the Sierra Foothills and its Zinfandel, the main grape grown, shows a similar style, with very ripe, sometimes raisiny flavors and an earthy tarry edge.

GREEN VALLEY-SONOMA
AVA 1983, 32,000 acres, 1,000 acres in vines

West of the Russian River Valley appellation, Green Valley-Sonoma is closer to the ocean, therefore even cooler and best suited for cool-climate grapes such as Chardonnay and Pinot Noir and the sparkling wines made from them. Iron Horse excels with both grapes, yet it is often a struggle to fully ripen the Pinot Noir. Marimar Torres Estate produces both wines too, building more richness and depth into the Chardonnay and a bit more flavor and finesse into the Pinot. Still, the Pinot Noirs are often marked by herb, tea and cherry notes. Kistler's Dutton Ranch bottling remains the benchmark for quality, yet carries the broader Russian River Valley Kistler Dutton Ranch appellation.

REFERENCE WINES

Chardonnay: Iron Horse
Pinot Noir: Iron Horse

GUENOC VALLEY

AVA 1981, 3,000 acres, 270 acres in vines

This is a single-winery appellation that bears the name of its only winery, Guenoc (see listing), which is succeeding with many varieties. Cabernet and Chardonnay (Genevieve Magoon Vineyard) are the early quality leaders; Zinfandel, Sauvignon Blanc and Petite Sirah show promise.

HOWELL MOUNTAIN

AVA 1984, 14,080 acres, 198 acres in vines

Howell Mountain, in northeastern Napa, is an old winegrowing area with vineyards and wineries dating to the late 1800s, but what really put this appellation on the map was the Dunn Cabernets, enormously rich, complex and earthy wines that have quickly established themselves among California's élite. Other vineyards, namely La Jota, Bancroft Ranch (for stunning Merlot made by Beringer), Lamborn and Park-Muscadine (now part of Dunn, but long used by Ridge) have also focused on red grapes, with styles that reflect the earthy austerity of the appellation. Still others, most notably Chateau Woltner, have gone in the opposite direction, favoring Chardonnay. Wineries at the base of the mountain (Burgess, Forman) don't meet elevation qualifications for inclusion in the appellation. Curiously, Angwin, the only town on the mountain, is a hamlet founded by Seventh Day Adventists, who are teetotalers.

REFERENCE WINES

Cabernet Sauvignon: Cornerstone, Duckhorn Vineyards, Dunn Vineyards, La Jota
Chardonnay: Chateau Woltner, Liparita, Peter Michael
Merlot: Beringer Bancroft Ranch, Liparita
Zinfandel: Lamborn Family Vineyard, Rocking Horse Lamborn Family Vineyard

KNIGHTS VALLEY

AVA 1983, 36,240 acres, 1,000 acres in vines

Beringer Vineyards is the major landowner and pacesetter in this northeastern Sonoma AVA, with two varieties: Cabernet, which dates to 1976, and Sauvignon Blanc. Peter Michael Winery, at the south of the valley near Napa Valley, is the lone winery and is making strides with its Cabernet. Beringer's Cabernet and red Meritage are medium-bodied, moderately tannic and very flavorful wines that reach a pleasant drinking plateau early on.

LAKE COUNTY

Not an AVA, but a political boundary used occasionally in wine labelling. With nearly 3,500 acres in vines, it is part of the North Coast appellation, even though, like Napa Valley, it doesn't touch the coast.

REFERENCE WINES

Cabernet Sauvignon: Guenoc Langtry
Chardonnay: Guenoc Genevieve Magoon Vineyard
Sauvignon Blanc: Buena Vista, Lakewood
Zinfandel: Steele Catfish Vineyard

LIVERMORE VALLEY

AVA 1982, 96,000 acres, 1,600 acres in vines

Historically important as the home of Wente Bros. and Concannon, this appellation east of San Francisco is marked by lean, stony soils and encroaching suburbs. Its best wines are Sauvignon Blanc, Sémillon (and blends thereof), Chardonnay and Cabernet, even if the latter two don't show the depth and complexities of the state's best. Concannon's Petite Sirah, among the first bottled as a varietal wine, can be complex, with dried fruit and spice flavors and chewy tannins.

REFERENCE WINES

Chardonnay: Fenestra, Wente
Petite Sirah: Concannon
Sauvignon Blanc: Concannon, Wente

LODI

AVA 1986, 458,000 acres, 45,000 acres in vines

Lodi is home to Guild, Robert Mondavi's Woodbridge winery and Sebastiani's California-appellation wines. This Central Valley area south of Sacramento can make good table wines, but most of the grapes are used in blends that end up carrying the larger and higher-profile California appellation.

McDOWELL VALLEY
AVA 1983, 2,300 acres, 540 acres in vines

This is a single-winery appellation in Mendocino County east of Hopland. McDowell Valley Vineyards has followed the varietal trends of the era, focusing first on Cabernet and Chardonnay with modest success and many wines of uneven quality. Since redirecting attention to Rhône-style wines, the success ratio has risen significantly, with appealing Syrah and Grenache among the newcomers.

MENDOCINO COUNTY

Not an AVA, but a political boundary that takes in the northernmost appellations of the North Coast and includes as AVAs Anderson Valley, McDowell Valley, (a single-vineyard and winery AVA), and Potter Valley. Long dedicated to Colombard and Carignane for use as blending grapes in jug wines, Parducci and later Fetzer pioneered varietal wines through trial-and-error winemaking. They determined that grapes such as Sauvignon Blanc and Zinfandel thrived best inland in warmer areas and that Chardonnay, Pinot Noir and Riesling were better suited to the cooler climate of Anderson Valley to the west of the county's major city, Ukiah. Today, some 12,000 acres are planted to vines and winegrowing is important (as is logging in the densely forested areas), but is still considered the county's number-two cash crop—number one being the well tended, well protected and highly clandestine marijuana gardens, according to the county's agricultural commissioner. Many of the best wines still carry the broader Mendocino County appellation rather than a more specific area, notably Kendall-Jackson's Ciapusci and Zeni Vineyard Zinfandels and Villa Mt. Eden's Signature Series Cabernet Sauvignon, which comes from Greenwood Ridge Vineyard in Anderson Valley. In the reference wines that follow, I've grouped some wines in their more specific appellations even though their labels may indicate the broader county area.

REFERENCE WINES
Chardonnay: Fetzer, Hidden Cellars, Parducci
Sauvignon Blanc: Fetzer, Hidden Cellars, Parducci
Zinfandel: Edmeades Ciapusci and Zeni Vineyards, Gabrielli, Hidden Cellars, Kendall-Jackson Zeni Vineyard, Lolonis, Parducci, Steele Pacini

MONTEREY COUNTY

Monterey County is not an AVA, but a political boundary used when a wine fails to meet more specific appellation requirements. Arroyo Seco, Santa Lucia Highlands, Chalone, San Lucas and Carmel Valley are AVAs within the county. Many wineries use the broader Monterey appellation with excellent results.

REFERENCE WINES
Cabernet Sauvignon: Durney, Lockwood, Mirassou
Chardonnay: Chalone, Cronin Ventana Vineyard, Estancia, J. Lohr Riverstone Vineyard, Mer et Soleil, Morgan, Talbott
Merlot: Chateau Julian, Georis, Lockwood
Pinot Noir: Chalone, Estancia Pinnacles Vineyard, Morgan

MOUNT HARLAN
AVA 1990, 7,440 acres, 47 acres in vines

A single-winery appellation that features Calera's vineyards in lime-rich soils 2,000 feet above sea level in the Gavilan range east of Salinas. Calera (see listing) bottles four separate vineyard-designated Pinot Noirs—Jensen, Mills, Reed and Selleck—all marked by ultra-ripe, very complex and occasionally funky flavors—but all Pinot Noir nonetheless. A small vineyard of Viognier is also rooted.

MOUNT VEEDER
AVA 1990, 15,000 acres, 1,000 acres in vines

For years, the venerable Mayacamas Vineyards carried the torch for this rugged mountain appellation in southwestern Napa County, producing distinctive and age-worthy Cabernets and Chardonnays. Mount Veeder Winery joined later and the old Christian Brothers Mont La Salle winery dates back years, although it is now home to The Hess Collection. Red wines dominate, with Cabernets that are characteristically earthy, concentrated, tannic and chewy. Hess manages to polish the edges a bit more than Mayacamas, whose wines have been lighter and more herbal of late. Mount Veeder Winery blends in grapes from the valley floor to soften its Cabernets. Zinfandel is the other big wine, with wineries such as Chateau Potelle, Franus and Sky making impressive wines. Chardonnay is austere, with a tight, flinty edge to it. Jade Mountain likes

Syrah grown near the peak. The appellation rises up to 2,500 feet and gets drenched with rainfall, with nearly double the city of Napa's 24 inches annually.

REFERENCE WINES

Cabernet Sauvignon: Chateau Potelle, The Hess Collection, Mayacamas
Chardonnay: Chateau Potelle, The Hess Collection, Mayacamas
Zinfandel: Chateau Potelle, Franus Brandlin Vineyard, Sky

NAPA VALLEY
AVA 1983, 300,000 acres, 33,200 acres in vines

Napa Valley is far and away California's most famous winegrowing district. It owes much of its fame to pioneers who settled in the Rutherford area and established such important winery estates as Beaulieu Vineyard and Inglenook. Those two wineries created many fine wines, but it was always Cabernet Sauvignon that led in quality—much as it still does today. By the late 1940s and early 1950s, BV and Inglenook were joined by Charles Krug and Louis M. Martini to form the Big Four Cabernet producers, which slowly carried Napa's high-quality Cabernet message to the broader domestic market. The list of leading Cabernet and Meritage producers is still long and impressive. By the 1960s Heitz Cellar, Robert Mondavi, Freemark Abbey, Mayacamas and Sterling Vineyards were crafting excellent Cabernets. In the 1970s, Caymus, Diamond Creek, Clos Du Val, Stag's Leap Wine Cellars, Joseph Phelps and Chateau Montelena joined the group.

From the 1960s through the 1980s, the valley gradually shifted to more site-specific wines with the realization that the places where Cabernet flourished, in rich soil with warm temperatures, were not ideal for other varieties. This led to the steady march of Chardonnay and Pinot Noir to Carneros, to the uprooting of less popular Petite Sirah and Gamay, among others, and to the planting of more Merlot and Sauvignon Blanc. By the 1980s, the valley began to be divided into smaller appellations. Areas such as Carneros, the Stags Leap District, Oakville, Rutherford, Mount Veeder, Howell Mountain and Spring Mountain are now all AVAs (they are covered elsewhere in this chapter in more specific detail), and there are plans to add St. Helena, Calistoga, Diamond Mountain, Yountville, Coombsville (east of Napa) and Oak Knoll, an area between Napa and Yountville well regarded for Chardonnay, to the list. The trend toward smaller appellations will help define which grapes excel in different areas. It will also help clean up the overly large Napa Valley appellation, which should be limited to the Napa River watershed, but because of historical uses includes remote areas such as Pope Valley, Chiles Valley and Wooden Valley—virtually the entire county.

By 1995 nearly half of Napa Valley was planted to Cabernet and Chardonnay, with smaller amounts of Zinfandel, Merlot and Pinot Noir, the latter mostly in Carneros. Clearly Cabernet is king of Napa's reds, but other varieties also grow well in this appellation. Economics plays a role here too, as Cabernet or Cabernet blends that sell for $30, $40, $50 or more a bottle provide a greater incentive than Zinfandel or Syrah at a fraction of the price. Merlot is off to a good start in many areas, but is more site-specific than any red grape other than Pinot Noir. Stags' Leap Winery Petite Sirah remains one of the state's finest. Sangiovese plantings, still at just a few hundred acres, are beginning to show promise.

REFERENCE WINES

Cabernet Sauvignon: Beringer Private Reserve, Cafaro, Caymus, Duckhorn, Forman, Robert Mondavi, Sequoia Grove, Sterling Reserve, St. Clement and St. Clement Oroppas
Chardonnay: Beringer Vineyards Private Reserve, Chateau Montelena, Far Niente, Flora Springs Barrel Fermented, Franciscan, Forman, Grgich Hills, Long, Merryvale, Patz & Hall, Silverado, Stag's Leap Wine Cellars
Merlot: Duckhorn, Markham, Robert Mondavi, Newton, Shafer, St. Clement, Sterling Vineyards, Swanson
Pinot Noir: Robert Mondavi and Robert Mondavi Reserve, Monticello
Syrah: Jade Mountain, Phelps Vin du Mistral, Swanson
Zinfandel: Biale Aldo's Vineyard, Caymus, Dickerson Vineyard, Green & Red Rancho, Hogue, Ravenswood Dickerson Vineyard, Storybook Mountain, The Terrace; Turley Wine Cellars Aida, Hayne and Moore Vineyards
Others: Beringer (Nightingale dessert wine), Far Niente (Dolce), Stags' Leap Winery (Petite Sirah)

NORTH YUBA
AVA 1985, 17,500 acres, 365 acres in vines

Renaissance Winery is the lone winery here and there's a full assortment of the major varieties planted in these hills above the Sacramento Valley. While the winery has its fans, no one wine has yet to emerge as a star. Still, the vineyard is young and enthusiasm high for its potential.

NORTHERN SONOMA
AVA 1985, no official record of acres in vines

Drawn at the request of Gallo to include all of its Sonoma County vineyards, it includes portions of Dry Creek, Alexander Valley, Russian River and Knights Valley.

OAKVILLE
AVA 1994, 5,800 acres, 4,200 acres in vines

As in Rutherford, Cabernet rules in this Napa district, although here it offers more diversity. Once again the names tell the story: Robert Mondavi Reserve, Opus One, Heitz Martha's Vineyard, Groth Reserve and Far Niente are all here. Oakville Cabernets share with Rutherford's the right to be called rich and complex wines. They are also similar in structure, intensity and weight. The most marked difference is that Oakville Cabernets, from grapes grown in a slightly cooler area, are often marked by mint, herb, and sage notes. Representing the extremes are Heitz Martha's Vineyard, famous for its minty currant notes, and Groth Reserve, which often struggles to ripen beyond coffee, sage and tobacco notes. Turnbull (formerly Johnson-Turnbull) too is often quite minty, while Silver Oak's Bonny's Vineyard (no longer produced as a separate bottling) was often marked by weedy, herbal notes. In the case of Groth and Bonny's Vineyard, their proximity to the Napa River accounts for their vines' vigorous growth and need for a long growing season to ripen fully. Chardonnay, Sauvignon Blanc and Zinfandel also do well in pockets. The district extends into the foothills and includes about half of Dalla Valle Vineyards to the east, stopping short of Napanook Vineyard, home to Dominus Estate.

REFERENCE WINES
Cabernet Sauvignon: Dalla Valle and Dalla Valle Maya, Far Niente, Franciscan, Groth and Groth Reserve, Harlan Estate, Heitz Martha's Vineyard, Oakville Ranch, Opus One
Chardonnay: Lewis Cellars, Oakville Ranch

PASO ROBLES
AVA 1983, 614,000 acres, 6,300 acres in vines

This area is gaining a reputation for a number of red varieties, with Syrah, Zinfandel and Cabernet the leaders. Most of the vineyards are planted east of Highway 101, with the major wineries being Meridian, Arciero, J. Lohr, Wild Horse and Eberle. Cabernets from Meridian and Eberle are medium- to full-bodied and mature early, with good depth and flavor, but not the richness and concentration found in Napa Valley's best. Zinfandel is bright and intense, with Peachy Canyon a leader. Syrah from Meridian can be spicy and complex. Wild Horse excels with Chardonnay, Pinot Noir and Merlot. The owners of Chateau de Beaucastel in France have vineyards in the eastern portion of the AVA, with a Rhône-style blend in mind. The best wines lie ahead.

REFERENCE WINES
Cabernet Sauvignon: Eberle, Justin, Meridian, Peachy Canyon, Wild Horse
Chardonnay: Wild Horse
Syrah: Eberle Fralich Vineyard, Tobin James, Meridian
Zinfandel: Adelaida, Eberle, Peachy Canyon, Ridge, Rosenblum, Wild Horse

POPE VALLEY

Part of the broad Napa Valley AVA, Pope Valley is in reality a separate and distinct area northeast of Napa Valley, with several hundred acres in vines. Early indications are that it's a very good area for Sauvignon Blanc, Cabernet, Chardonnay and Merlot. In time, it will probably become an AVA that can carry both the Pope Valley and the Napa Valley names.

POTTER VALLEY
AVA 1983, 27,500 acres, 1,000 acres in vines

Potter Valley, in northeastern Mendocino County, is insignificant as appellations go. Sauvignon Blanc appears the favored grape at this stage, although some Chardonnay is grown there, liking the cool climate.

RUSSIAN RIVER VALLEY
AVA 1983, 96,000 acres, 8,375 acres in vines

Because of its proximity to the ocean and its cool, damp climate, this central Sonoma County appellation has been slow to develop. Early Italian settlers planted red grape varieties farther inland, but as the Chardonnay boom took hold, more vintners focused on this area, realizing its potential for both Chardonnay and Pinot Noir. In terms of acreage, Chardonnay rules supreme, with names such as DeLoach, Rochioli, Kistler, Sonoma-Cutrer, Gallo (Estate-Bottled Chardonnay), Dehlinger and dozens more that buy grapes from here and blend them with Chardonnay grown elsewhere. Meanwhile, Pinot Noir is gaining by leaps and bounds. Led by J. Rochioli Reserve, Gary Farrell, Williams & Selyem (Rochioli, Allen, Olivet Lane and a generic Russian River Valley bottling) and Dehlinger, Pinot Noir can be bright, rich, lush and complex, combining delicacy and finesse with intensity and concentration. Several other varieties, namely Zinfandel, Sauvignon Blanc, Gewürztraminer and Merlot, also shine in warmer areas. The next decade should better define the appellation, but figure on Chardonnay and Pinot Noir as major players either way.

REFERENCE WINES

Chardonnay: Dehlinger, DeLoach O.F.S., Gary Farrell Allen Vineyard, Iron Horse, Kistler Dutton Ranch and Vine Hill Vineyards, Marimar Torres Estate, J. Rochioli and J. Rochioli Reserve, Williams & Selyem Allen Vineyard
Merlot: DeLoach
Pinot Noir: Dehlinger, Gary Farrell Allen Vineyard, Williams & Selyem Allen and J. Rochioli Vineyard, J. Rochioli and J. Rochioli Reserve
Sauvignon Blanc: Chateau St. Jean La Petite Étoile, DeLoach, J. Rochioli and J. Rochioli Reserve
Zinfandel: DeLoach Barbieri Ranch, Papera Ranch, Pelletti Ranch, Gary Farrell Collins Ranch, Hop Kiln, Limerick Lane, Martinelli, Joseph Swan Frati Ranch and V.H.S.R Vineyard, J. Rochioli Sodini Vineyard, Williams & Selyem

RUTHERFORD
AVA 1994, 6,500 acres, 5,000 acres in vines

Pioneers Beaulieu and Inglenook set the pace here early on with Cabernet, and it is still the finest wine from this appellation in the heart of Napa Valley. The names alone tell the story: BV Private Reserve, Caymus Special Selection, Flora Springs Reserve, Freemark Abbey Bosche, Niebaum-Coppola Estate Rubicon, Livingston

Moffett Vineyard and Heitz Bella Oaks, to name the important wines. Rutherford soils are rich and loamy, largely alluvial fans that have been formed from the mountains that line both sides of the valley. Cabernet performs exceptionally well here, as there is an ideal mixture of cool mornings and evenings and warm, sunny days, usually ripening the grapes fully and quite easily; an abundance of rich currant, plum and cherry flavors, with herb, mint and spice notes and fine but substantial tannins is the result. Because of those supple tannins most Rutherford wines are showy early on. But they often have the richness, depth and concentration to age well for 15 to 30 years, sometimes even longer. Zinfandel is a minor player here, but Niebaum-Coppola, with its Edizione Pennino bottling from its vineyard, and Elyse from Morisoli Vineyard, produce lovely wines.

It would not surprise me if at some future date an effort is made to claim a Rutherford Bench appellation that would focus on the western vineyards. While the Rutherford Bench is a modern term, many believe it best describes the gentle slope from the western foothills. An early effort to have both a Rutherford and a Rutherford Bench appellation failed, as drawing the lines proved too political. The same is true for the once-proposed Oakville and Oakville Bench appellations.

REFERENCE WINES

Cabernet Sauvignon: Beaulieu Private Reserve, Caymus Special Selection, Flora Springs Reserve, Freemark Abbey Bosche Vineyard, Livingston Moffett, Niebaum-Coppola Rubicon, Whitehall Lane Morisoli Vineyard
Chardonnay: El Molino
Merlot: Sullivan
Zinfandel: Edizione Pennino (Niebaum-Coppola), Elyse Morisoli Vineyard

ST. HELENA

St. Helena's AVA application was recently still pending with federal officials. This Napa district is home to many wineries and is excellent for Cabernet Sauvignon, notably from Spottswoode, Grace Family Vineyard and Abreu Vineyard.

REFERENCE WINES

Cabernet Sauvignon: Grace Family Vineyard, Spottswoode

SAN BENITO COUNTY
AVA 1987, 45,000 acres, 1,800 acres in vines

This county east of Monterey is rarely used as an AVA, but Calera uses it for its vineyard-designated Pinot Noirs, all of which are excellent, ultraripe and juicy.

SAN LUCAS
AVA 1987, 32,000 acres, 5,000 acres in vines

Rarely used on labels, since many of the grapes grown in this southernmost Monterey County district go into wines that carry the California appellation. Grapes grown include Cabernet, Chardonnay and Sauvignon Blanc. Lockwood is the lone winery.

SAN LUIS OBISPO COUNTY

This county is not an AVA, but a South Central Coast political boundary that includes the Paso Robles, York Mountain, Edna Valley and Arroyo Grande AVAs.

REFERENCE WINES

Cabernet Sauvignon: Justin, Wild Horse
Chardonnay: Au Bon Climat Talley Reserve, Ojai, Wild Horse
Merlot: Tobin James
Pinot Noir: Au Bon Climat Talley Vineyard (Arroyo Grande), Talley Vineyards (Arroyo Grande)
Zinfandel: Santa Barbara Winery, Saucelito Canyon

SANTA BARBARA COUNTY

Not an AVA, but a political boundary that includes the Santa Ynez Valley and Santa Maria Valley appellations within. Many of the Chardonnay and Pinot Noir blends made here are excellent.

REFERENCE WINES

Cabernet Sauvignon: Foxen, Gainey Limited Selection
Chardonnay: Au Bon Climat, Byron and Byron Reserve, Camelot, Cottonwood Canyon Barrel Select, Sanford Barrel Select, Steele Bien Nacido
Merlot: Foxen
Pinot Noir: Au Bon Climat, Byron, Foxen, Hitching Post, Longoria, Sanford, Lane Tanner, Wild Horse, Whitcraft
Syrah: Qupe, Fess Parker, Zaca Mesa

SANTA CRUZ MOUNTAINS
AVA 1982, 110,000 acres, 200 acres in vines

Small in vineyard acreage, rugged and mountainous in physical geography, but rich in distinctive wines, the Santa Cruz Mountains AVA is home to Ridge Vineyards, its Monte Bello vineyard, David Bruce and Bonny Doon and their eccentric wines, Santa Cruz Mountain Vineyards, Mount Eden, and Cronin Vineyards. Because of the area's various microclimates, Cabernet, Chardonnay, Pinot Noir and Zinfandel all achieve successes and failures. The generally cool climate can make it ideal for Chardonnay or Pinot Noir one year, but tough on Cabernet—and vice versa when it's hotter. Clearly Monte Bello, at 2,000 feet of elevation, is a great site for Cabernet. Bruce's Pinot Noirs have strayed all over the course, but the past few vintages have yielded exceptional wines, deep and complex. Bruce and Ridge also hit the mark with Chardonnay regularly. Ken Burnap's Santa Cruz Mountain Vineyards produces ultraripe and deeply concentrated Cabernets and Pinot Noirs. Kathryn Kennedy's Cabernets are also well crafted.

REFERENCE WINES

Cabernet Sauvignon: Cinnabar, Cronin, Kathryn Kennedy, Ridge Monte Bello, Santa Cruz Mountain Vineyards Bates Ranch
Chardonnay: David Bruce, Cinnabar, Cronin, Ridge, Storrs
Pinot Noir: David Bruce, Mount Eden, Sarah's Vineyard

SANTA LUCIA HIGHLANDS
AVA 1992, 22,000 acres, 1,850 acres in vines

Smith & Hook is the major proponent of this appellation in central Monterey County and uses it for its Cabernet, but Talbott's estate vineyard, planted to Chardonnay, also lies in the slender appellation. So far, Chardonnay, as evidenced by Talbott's fine offerings, is the quality leader. Cabernet and Merlot are promising.

SANTA MARIA VALLEY
AVA 1981, 82,180 acres, 4,800 in vines

Increasingly important for its high-quality Chardonnays and Pinot Noirs, Santa Maria Valley, in northern Santa Barbara County, is home to Au Bon Climat, Byron, Cambria, Foxen Vineyard and Rancho

Sisquoc, along with two important, independently owned vineyards, Bien Nacido and Sierra Madre. Santa Maria's popularity as a winegrowing area developed around the success of the former Tepesquet Vineyard, which supplied Chardonnay to dozens of wineries, many from Napa and Sonoma. The vineyard was sold and divided by Kendall-Jackson and Robert Mondavi Winery, the former founding Cambria and the latter buying Byron. Nestle's Wine World, owner of Beringer and Meridian, is the other major landowner; it owns Riverbench Vineyard near Byron. The stars of this AVA are Chardonnay, which is bright, rich and intensely flavored, and Pinot Noir, which is marked by rich cherry and cola flavors and herb and spice notes. Syrah, from Qupe and Cambria, is also excellent.

REFERENCE WINES

Cabernet Sauvignon: Rancho Sisquoc Red Cellar Select
Chardonnay: Au Bon Climat, Cambria, Foxen, Whitcraft
Pinot Noir: Au Bon Climat, Byron and Byron Reserve, Whitcraft Bien Nacido, Wild Horse

SANTA YNEZ VALLEY
AVA 1983, 154,000 acres, 1,200 acres in vines

This narrow valley in Santa Barbara County stretches eastward from near the Pacific Ocean to farther inland, where it's considerably warmer. A debate has arisen as to whether the appellation is better suited for cooler-climate varieties such as Chardonnay and Pinot Noir or warm-weather grapes such as Cabernet and Merlot. Sanford & Benedict Vineyard in the western portion is the best known, and it is the source for some of Sanford's Chardonnays and Pinot Noirs. To the east lie Zaca Mesa, Fess Parker, Firestone, The Gainey Vineyard and Buttonwood Farm. Firestone, with 227 acres in vines, is the largest vineyard. Syrah, Gewürztraminer and Riesling fare well in parts, while Cabernet, Merlot and Sauvignon Blanc are often marked by strong vegetal flavors.

REFERENCE WINES

Cabernet Sauvignon: Santa Barbara Winery
Chardonnay: Gainey Limited Selection, Firestone, Santa Barbara Winery Lafond and Santa Barbara Reserve, Sanford Sanford & Benedict
Pinot Noir: Au Bon Climat, Foxen, Gainey Limited

Selection, Hitching Post Sanford & Benedict, Sanford Sanford & Benedict, Lane Tanner
Others: Firestone (Merlot, Gewürztraminer, Riesling)

SIERRA FOOTHILLS
AVA 1987, 3,200 acres in vines

An umbrella AVA that covers Amador, Calaveras, El Dorado, Mariposa, Nevada, Placer, Tuolomne and Yuba Counties. Several wineries use this designation, and Zinfandel is the quality leader.

SONOMA COAST
AVA 1987, 480,000 acres, no official record of acres in vines available.

This is an unwieldy and largely unnecessary AVA formed primarily to suit Sonoma-Cutrer's desire to include all of its major Chardonnay districts within one boundary for use in its "estate-bottled" label, in much the same way Northern Sonoma was created to encompass the Gallo vineyards. It stretches from north of the Green Valley-Russian River area to Carneros.

SONOMA COUNTY

The Sonoma County designation is not an AVA but is based on the political boundary and commonly used as a catch-all for many excellent wines that do not qualify for a more specific appellation or that benefit from blending with wines from more than one area within the county. Sonoma's diverse winegrowing appellations encompass several prominent AVAs; among the most important are Alexander Valley, Dry Creek Valley, Russian River Valley and Sonoma Valley. Sonoma County is also home to many smaller AVAs, including Chalk Hill, Green Valley-Sonoma, Knights Valley, Sonoma Mountain and Sonoma Coast. Carneros, which lies partly within Sonoma County, is usually treated as a separate appellation.

As a general rule, the most westerly areas are too cool for wine grapes to ripen, but vines are being planted within several miles of the ocean on south-facing hills protected from the winds. Moving eastward and inland, the temperatures get increasingly warm and then hot. The soils in each of the areas can also vary significantly, from rocky volcanic ones to sandy loam soils found, for example, along the Russian River.

CALIFORNIA WINE REGION MAPS

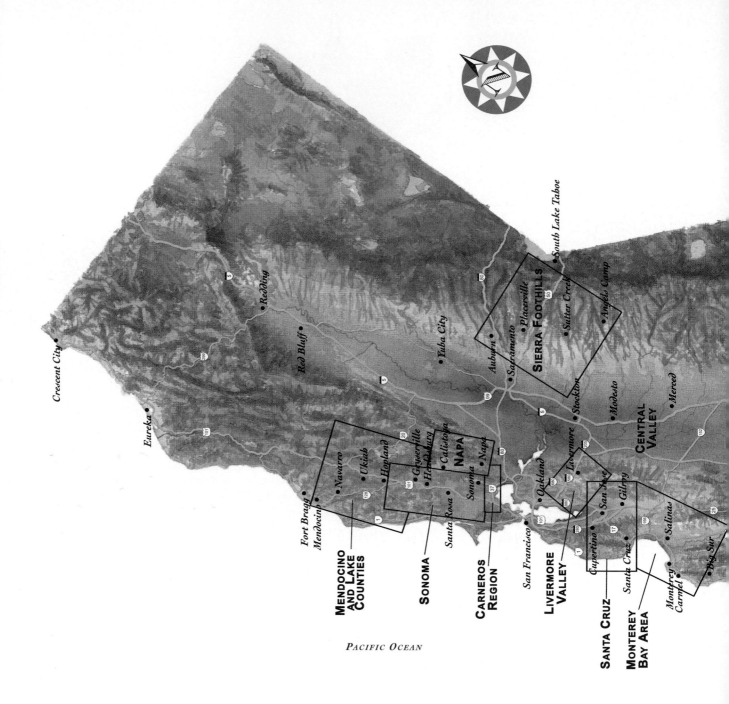

Crescent City

Eureka

Redding

Red Bluff

Fort Bragg
Mendocino

Navarro

Ukiah

Hopland

Santa Rosa

Guerneville
Healdsburg

Calistoga
Sonoma

NAPA

Napa

Yuba City

Auburn

Sacramento

Placerville

SIERRA FOOTHILLS

Sutter Creek

South Lake Tahoe

Angels Camp

Stockton

Modesto

Merced

CENTRAL
VALLEY

Oakland

Livermore

San Jose

Gilroy

San Francisco

Cupertino

Santa Cruz

Salinas

Monterey
Carmel

Big Sur

MENDOCINO
AND LAKE
COUNTIES

SONOMA

CARNEROS
REGION

LIVERMORE
VALLEY

SANTA CRUZ

MONTEREY
BAY AREA

PACIFIC OCEAN

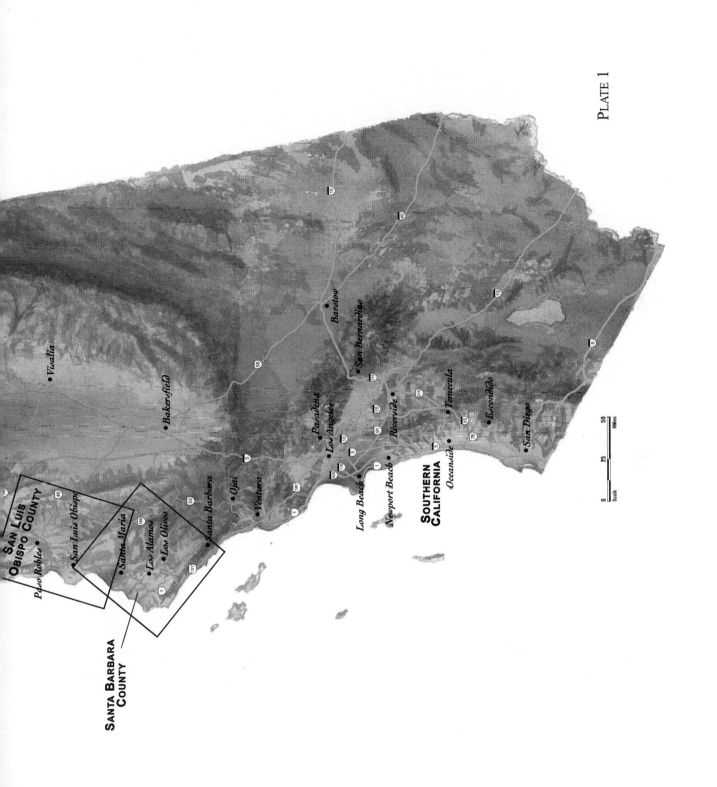

PLATE 1

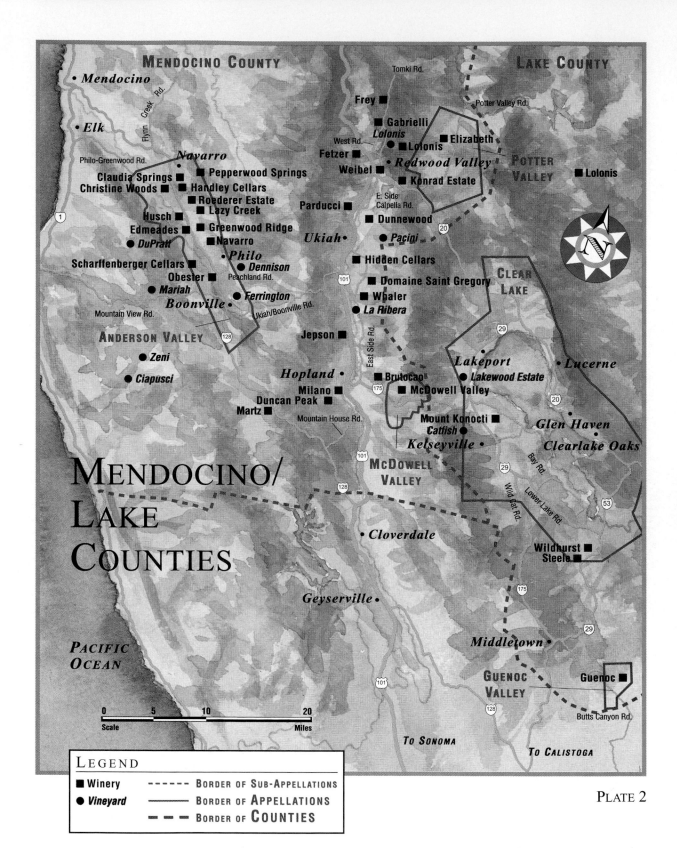

MENDOCINO COUNTY

LAKE COUNTY

Tomki Rd.

• *Mendocino*

Frey ■

Potter Valley Rd.

Gabrielli ■
Lolonis

• *Elk*

West Rd.

Fetzer ■

Lolonis ■ Elizabeth ■

POTTER
VALLEY

■ Lolonis

Philo-Greenwood Rd.

Navarro

Weibel ■

• *Redwood Valley*

Claudia Springs ■
Christine Woods ■
Husch ■
Edmeades ■
● *DuPratt*

■ Pepperwood Springs
■ Handley Cellars
■ Roederer Estate
■ Lazy Creek
■ Greenwood Ridge
■ Navarro

Konrad Estate ■

Parducci ■

E. Side
Calpella Rd.

■ Dunnewood

Ukiah •

● *Pacini*

Scharffenberger Cellars ■
Obester ■
● *Mariah*
Boonville

Philo
● *Dennison*
Peachland Rd.
● *Ferrington*

■ Hidden Cellars

CLEAR
LAKE

■ Domaine Saint Gregory

Mountain View Rd.

Ukiah/Boonville Rd.

■ Whaler
● *La Ribera*

ANDERSON VALLEY

Jepson ■

East Side Rd.

Lakeport
● *Lakewood Estate*

• *Lucerne*

● *Zeni*

● *Ciapusci*

Hopland •

Brutocao ■
McDowell Valley ■

Milano ■
Duncan Peak ■
Martz ■

Mountain House Rd.

Mount Konocti ■
Catfish ●
Kelseyville •

Glen Haven

Bay Rd.

Clearlake Oaks

McDOWELL
VALLEY

Lower Lake Rd.

MENDOCINO/
LAKE
COUNTIES

Wild Cat Rd.

• *Cloverdale*

Wildhurst ■
Steele ■

Geyserville •

PACIFIC
OCEAN

Middletown •

0   5   10   20
Scale   Miles

GUENOC
VALLEY

Guenoc ■

Butts Canyon Rd.

TO SONOMA

TO CALISTOGA

LEGEND

■ Winery   - - - - - BORDER OF SUB-APPELLATIONS
● Vineyard   ───── BORDER OF APPELLATIONS
                — — — BORDER OF COUNTIES

PLATE 2

To Yorkville   **To Ukiah**

Cloverdale •   Crocker Rd.

Bandiera ■

SONOMA COUNTY NORTH

River Rd.

Asti Rd.

• Asti

Dutcher Creek Rd.

Silver Oak ■

J. Fritz ■

Lake Sonoma ■   ● Gallo Sonoma

ALEXANDER VALLEY

Ferrari-Carano ■   Dry Creek Rd.   ■ Frick

0   1   2   4
Scale   Miles

Meeker ■
■ Duxoup
Preston ■
Preston ●

■ Geyser Peak
■ Chauffe-Eau
■ J. Pedroncelli

● Gauer Ranch

Canyon Rd.

Yoaklm Bridge Rd.

Chateau Diana ■

Michel-Schlumberger ■

Dry Creek Rd.

• Geyserville
■ DeLorimier
Geyserville ●   128

● Gauer Ranch

DRY CREEK VALLEY

Quivira ■
A. Rafanelli ■
Robert Stemmler ■
■ Dry Creek

Lambert Bridge Rd.

Chateau Souverain ■

■ Clos du Bois
■ Trentadue
■ Weinstock

● Robert Young

● Murphy Ranch

● Canepa

■ Murphy-Goode Estate

■ Alexander Valley Fruit & Trading Co.

W. Dry Creek Rd.

Peterson ■

Lytton Springs Rd.

● Calcaire
● Briarcrest   ■ Hafner

Pine Flat Rd.

Lambert Bridge ■

■ Lytton Springs
■ Mazzocco

● Hawley

Nalle ■
● Flintwood

■ Simi
● Vinwood Estate
Jimtown Ranch

● Marlstone   ● Scherrer
■ Sausal

Bellerose ■

101

Healdsburg Ave.

Jordan

● Alexander's Crown
■ Johnson's Alexander Valley
■ Alexander Valley

Seghesio ■   ■ Optima
Robert Mueller ■

Wallace Creek Rd.

Healdsburg

Powell Ave.

Belle Terre ●   ■ Hanna

Wheeler ■
■ White Oak

■ Field Stone
■ Melim

Mill Creek ■

Alderbrook ■

Grant Ave.

● Stuhlmuller

Armida ■

Foppiano ■

■ Wild Hog Hill
■ Domaine St. George

Chalk Hill Rd.

KNIGHTS VALLEY

Mietz ■

■ Limerick Lane

■ Stonestreet

Christopher Creek

RUSSIAN RIVER VALLEY   128

● Frank Johnson

LEGEND

■ **Winery**   ------ **BORDER OF SUB-APPELLATIONS**
● *Vineyard*   ──── **BORDER OF APPELLATIONS**
              --- **BORDER OF COUNTIES**

PLATE 3

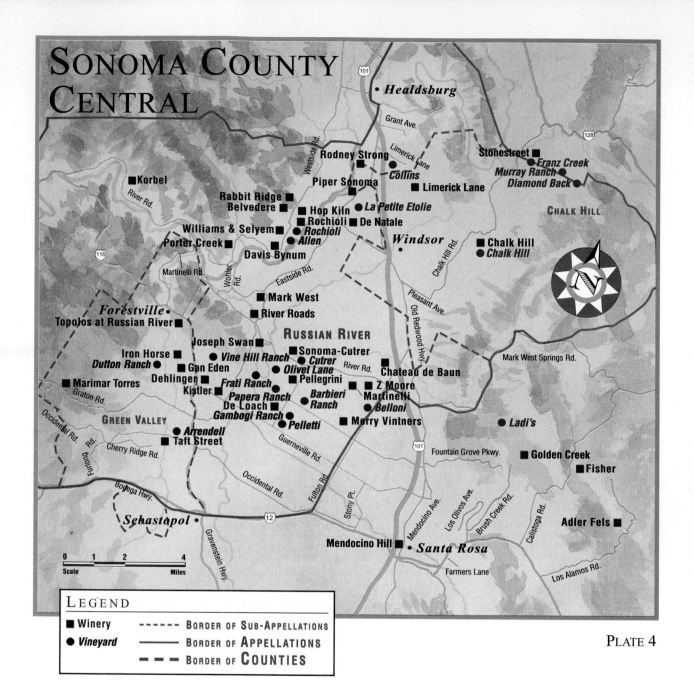

SONOMA COUNTY CENTRAL

• *Healdsburg*

Grant Ave.

Rodney Strong ■
Limerick Lane
● *Collins*

Piper Sonoma ■
■ Limerick Lane

Stonestreet ■
● *Franz Creek*
Murray Ranch ●
Diamond Back ●

Korbel ■

River Rd.

Rabbit Ridge ■
Belvedere ■
■ Hop Kiln
■ Rochioli
● *La Petite Etolie*
● De Natale

CHALK HILL

Williams & Selyem ■
● *Rochioli*
● *Allen*

Windsor
•

Chalk Hill Rd.

■ Chalk Hill
● *Chalk Hill*

Porter Creek ■

Davis Bynum ■

Martinelli Rd.

Wohler Rd.

Eastside Rd.

Pleasant Ave.

■ Mark West
■ River Roads

Forestville •
Topolos at Russian River ■

Mark West Springs Rd.

RUSSIAN RIVER

Joseph Swan ■

Old Redwood Hwy.

Iron Horse ■
● *Vine Hill Ranch*
Dutton Ranch ●

■ Sonoma-Cutrer
● *Cutrer*
● *Olivet Lane*

River Rd.

■ Chateau de Baun

Gan Eden ■
Dehlinger ■
Frati Ranch
Kistler ■

■ Pellegrini

■ Z Moore
● Martinelli

Marimar Torres ■

Papera Ranch
De Loach ●
Gambogi Ranch ●

Barbieri Ranch

● *Belloni*

Graton Rd.

● *Pelletti*

■ Merry Vintners

GREEN VALLEY

● Ladi's

Occidental Rd.

Furlong Rd.

● *Arrendell*
■ Taft Street

Guerneville Rd.

Fountain Grove Pkwy.

Cherry Ridge Rd.

■ Golden Creek
■ Fisher

Occidental Rd.

Bodega Hwy.

Sebastopol •

Fulton Rd.

Stony Pt.

Mendocino Ave.

Los Olivos Ave.

Brush Creek Rd.

Calistoga Rd.

■ Adler Fels

0 1 2 4
Scale   Miles

Gravenstein Hwy.

Mendocino Hill ■
● *Santa Rosa*

Farmers Lane

Los Alamos Rd.

LEGEND

■ **Winery**
● *Vineyard*

------ BORDER OF SUB-APPELLATIONS
———— BORDER OF APPELLATIONS
- - - BORDER OF COUNTIES

PLATE 4

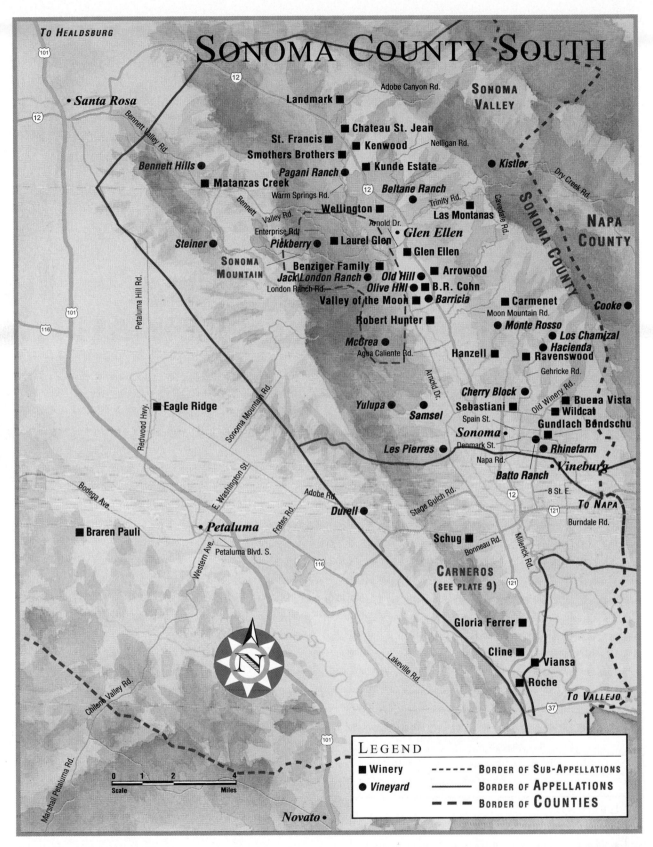

SONOMA COUNTY SOUTH

TO HEALDSBURG

SONOMA VALLEY

• Santa Rosa

Landmark ■

Adobe Canyon Rd.

Chateau St. Jean ■

St. Francis ■
Kenwood ■

Nelligan Rd.

Smothers Brothers ■

• Kistler

Bennett Hills •

Kunde Estate ■

Pagani Ranch •

Matanzas Creek ■

Beltane Ranch •

Trinity Rd.

Warm Springs Rd.

Wellington ■

Las Montanas

Arnold Dr.

Enterprise Rd.

Steiner •

Glen Ellen

Pickberry •

Laurel Glen ■

Glen Ellen ■

SONOMA
MOUNTAIN

Benziger Family ■

Arrowood ■

Jack London Ranch •

Old Hill ■

London Ranch Rd.

Olive Hill ■

B.R. Cohn ■

Valley of the Moon ■

Barricia •

Carmenet ■

Moon Mountain Rd.

Robert Hunter ■

Monte Rosso •

Cooke •

Los Chamizal •

McCrea •

Hacienda •

Agua Caliente Rd.

Hanzell ■

Ravenswood ■

Gehricke Rd.

Eagle Ridge ■

Cherry Block •

Buena Vista ■

Yulupa •

Samsel •

Sebastiani ■

Wildcat ■

Spain St.

Gundlach Bundschu ■

Sonoma •

Les Pierres •

Denmark St.

Rhinefarm ■

Napa Rd.

Vineburg •

Batto Ranch •

Durell •

8 St. E.

TO NAPA

Braren Pauli ■

• Petaluma

Burndale Rd.

Schug ■

Bonneau Rd.

CARNEROS
(SEE PLATE 9)

Gloria Ferrer ■

Cline ■

Viansa ■

Roche ■

TO VALLEJO

NAPA
COUNTY

SONOMA COUNTY

Dry Creek Rd.

Cavedale Rd.

Old Winery Rd.

Millerick Rd.

Bennett Valley Rd.

Bennett Valley Rd.

Petaluma Hill Rd.

Sonoma Mountain Rd.

Redwood Hwy.

Bodega Ave.

E. Washington St.

Frates Rd.

Adobe Rd.

Stage Gulch Rd.

Western Ave.

Petaluma Blvd. S.

Lakeville Rd.

Chileno Valley Rd.

Marshall Petaluma Rd.

Novato •

LEGEND

■ Winery
• Vineyard

----- BORDER OF SUB-APPELLATIONS
——— BORDER OF APPELLATIONS
– – – BORDER OF COUNTIES

0 1 2 4
Scale   Miles

PLATE 5

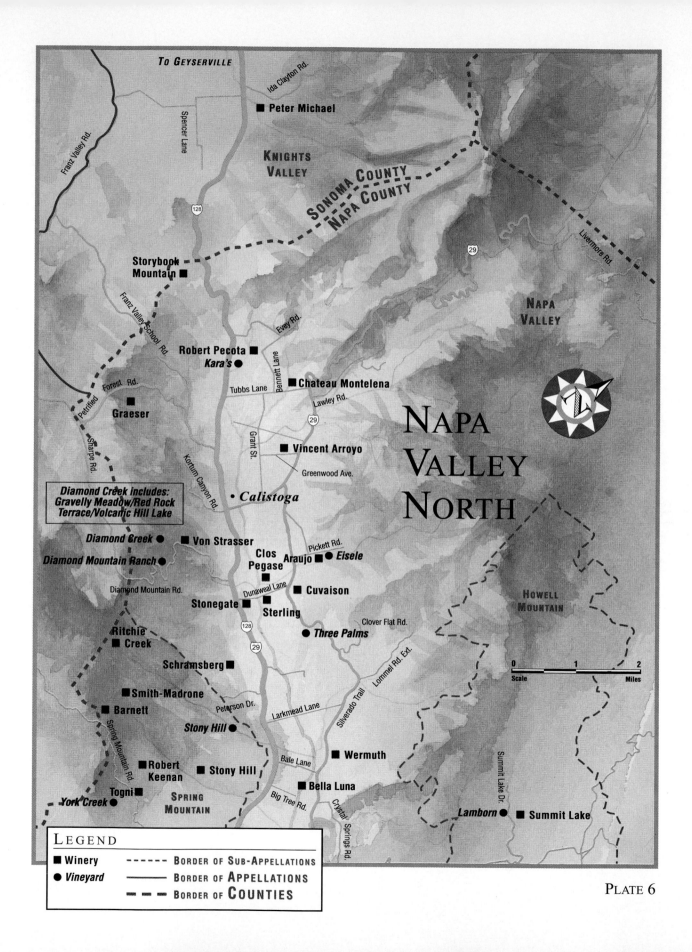

To Geyserville

Ida Clayton Rd.

■ Peter Michael

KNIGHTS
VALLEY

Spencer Lane

Franz Valley Rd.

SONOMA COUNTY
NAPA COUNTY

Livermore Rd.

128

29

NAPA
VALLEY

Storybook
Mountain ■

Franz Valley School Rd.

Evey Rd.

Robert Pecota ■

Kara's ●

Bennett Lane

Forest Rd.

Tubbs Lane

■ Chateau Montelena

Lawley Rd.

Petrified

Graeser ■

29

Sharpe Rd.

■ Vincent Arroyo

Grant St.

Greenwood Ave.

Kortum Canyon Rd.

Diamond Creek includes:
Gravelly Meadow/Red Rock
Terrace/Volcanic Hill Lake

• Calistoga

NAPA
VALLEY
NORTH

Diamond Creek ● ■ Von Strasser

Diamond Mountain Ranch ●

Clos
Pegase
■

Pickett Rd.

Araujo ■ *Eisele* ●

Diamond Mountain Rd.

Dunaweal Lane

■ Cuvaison

HOWELL
MOUNTAIN

Stonegate ■

Sterling

Ritchie
■ Creek

128

● *Three Palms*

Clover Flat Rd.

29

Lommel Rd. Ext.

0   1   2
Scale   Miles

Schramsberg ■

Silverado Trail

■ Smith-Madrone

■ Barnett

Peterson Dr.

Larkmead Lane

Summit Lake Dr.

Spring Mountain Rd.

Stony Hill ●

■ Robert
Keenan

● *Stony Hill*

Bale Lane

■ Wermuth

Togni ■

York Creek ●

SPRING
MOUNTAIN

Big Tree Rd.

■ Bella Luna

Crystal Springs Rd.

Lamborn ● ■ Summit Lake

LEGEND

■ Winery   - - - - - BORDER OF SUB-APPELLATIONS
● *Vineyard*   ——— BORDER OF APPELLATIONS
              - - - BORDER OF COUNTIES

PLATE 6

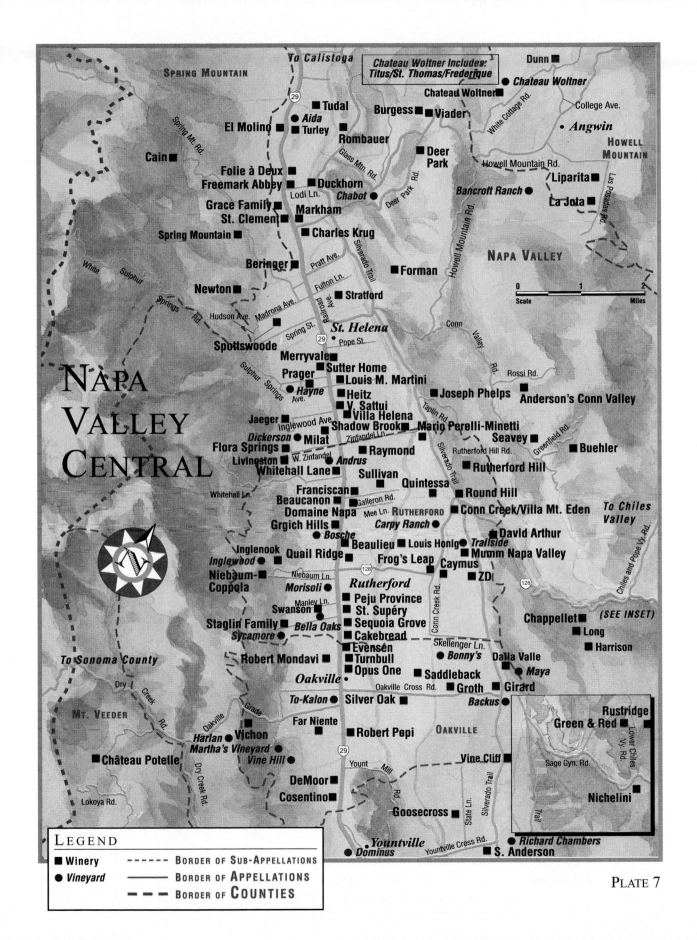

To Calistoga

SPRING MOUNTAIN

Chateau Woltner Includes:
Titus/St. Thomas/Frederique

Dunn ■

● *Chateau Woltner*

29

Tudal ■

● *Aida*

El Molino ■   ■ Turley

Rombauer ■

Burgess ■   ■ Viader

Chateau Woltner ■

White Cottage Rd.

College Ave.

● *Angwin*

HOWELL
MOUNTAIN

Cain ■

Deer
Park ■

Howell Mountain Rd.

Liparita ■

Folie à Deux ■
Freemark Abbey ■   ■ Duckhorn

Lodi Ln.   *Chabot* ●

Deer Park Rd.

Bancroft Ranch ●

Glass Mtn. Rd.

La Jota ■

Las Posadas Rd.

Grace Family ■
St. Clement ■   ■ Markham

Charles Krug ■

NAPA VALLEY

Spring Mountain ■

Beringer ■

Pratt Ave.

Silverado Trail

Forman ■

Scale
0   1   2
Miles

Newton ■

Fulton Ln.

Railroad Ave.

■ Stratford

Conn

Hudson Ave.   Madrona Ave.

Spring St.

St. Helena

Pope St.

Valley Rd.

Rossi Rd.

Spottswoode ■

Merryvale ■

**NAPA
VALLEY
CENTRAL**

Sulphur Springs

Prager ■

● *Hayne*

Sutter Home ■

Louis M. Martini ■

Heitz ■

V. Sattui ■

Villa Helena ■

Joseph Phelps ■

Anderson's Conn Valley ■

Jaeger ■

Inglewood Ave.

Shadow Brook ■

Mario Perelli-Minetti ■

Taplin Rd.

Greenfield Rd.

Dickerson ■ Milat ●

Zinfandel Ln.

Seavey ■

Buehler ■

Flora Springs ■

Livingston ■   W. Zinfandel

● *Andrus*

Raymond ■

Rutherford Hill Rd.

Rutherford Hill ■

Whitehall Lane ■

Sullivan ■

Silverado Trail

Whitehall Ln.

Franciscan ■
Beaucanon ■

Galleron Rd.

Quintessa ■

Round Hill ■

Domaine Napa ■

Mee Ln.   RUTHERFORD

Conn Creek/Villa Mt. Eden ■

To Chiles
Valley

Grgich Hills ■

Carpy Ranch ●

● *Bosche*

Beaulieu ■   Louis Honig ●

David Arthur ■

Chiles and Pope Vy. Rd.

Inglenook ■

Inglewood ●

Quail Ridge ■

Frog's Leap ■

128

Trailside ●
Mumm Napa Valley ■

Caymus ■

Niebaum-
Coppola ■

Niebaum Ln.

Morisoli ●

Rutherford

Peju Province ■

ZD ■

128

Manley Ln.

Swanson ■

St. Supéry ■

Chappellet ■

(SEE INSET)

Staglin Family ■   *Bella Oaks* ●

Sycamore ●

Sequoia Grove ■

Cakebread ■

Long ■

Skellenger Ln.

Harrison ■

Evensen ■

Robert Mondavi ■

Turnbull ■

Opus One ■

Bonny's ●

Dalla Valle ■

Maya ●

Oakville ●

Saddleback ■

Oakville Cross Rd.

Groth ■   Girard ■

To-Kalon ●

Silver Oak ■

Backus ●

Conn Creek Rd.

RUTHERFORD

Rustridge ■
Green & Red ■

Far Niente ■

Harlan ● Vichon ■
Martha's Vineyard ●

OAKVILLE

Oakville Grade

Robert Pepi ■

OAKVILLE

Lower Chiles Vy. Rd.

■ Château Potelle

MT. VEEDER

Vine Hill ●

Vine Cliff ■

Sage Cyn. Rd.

Nichelini ■

To Sonoma County

Dry   Creek   Rd.

DeMoor ■

Yount   Mill   Rd.

Cosentino ■

Lokoya Rd.

Dry Creek Rd.

29

Goosecross ■

State Ln.

Silverado Trail

Yountville ●   Yountville Cross Rd.

● *Richard Chambers*

Dominus ●

S. Anderson ■

Trail

LEGEND

■ Winery   - - - - - BORDER OF SUB-APPELLATIONS

● *Vineyard*   ———— BORDER OF APPELLATIONS

– – – BORDER OF COUNTIES

PLATE 7

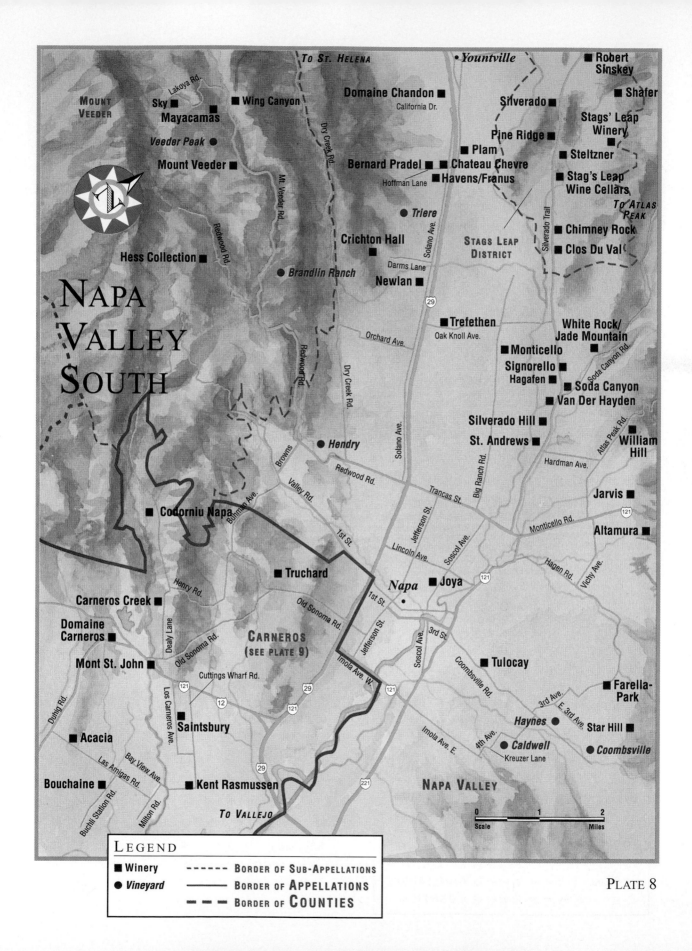

Napa Valley South

To St. Helena

• *Yountville*

■ Robert Sinskey

■ Shafer

Mount Veeder

■ Sky
■ Mayacamas
Veeder Peak ●
■ Mount Veeder

■ Wing Canyon

Lakoya Rd.

Dry Creek Rd.

Mt. Veeder Rd.

Redwood Rd.

■ Hess Collection

Brandlin Ranch ●

Domaine Chandon ■
California Dr.

Silverado ■

Pine Ridge ■

Stags' Leap Winery ■

■ Plam
Bernard Pradel ■
■ Chateau Chevre
Hoffman Lane
■ Havens/Franus

■ Steltzner

■ Stag's Leap Wine Cellars

To Atlas Peak

● *Triere*

Crichton Hall ■

Solano Ave.

Darms Lane

Newlan ■

STAGS LEAP DISTRICT

Silverado Trail

■ Chimney Rock
■ Clos Du Val

29

■ Trefethen
Oak Knoll Ave.

Orchard Ave.

Dry Creek Rd.

Solano Ave.

White Rock/ Jade Mountain

■ Monticello
Signorello ■
Hagafen ■

Soda Canyon Rd.

■ Soda Canyon
■ Van Der Hayden

Silverado Hill ■
St. Andrews ■

Big Ranch Rd.

Hardman Ave.

Atlas Peak Rd.

■ William Hill

● *Hendry*

Browns

Valley Rd.

Redwood Rd.

Trancas St.

Jarvis ■

121

■ Codorniu Napa

Bonina Ave.

1st St.

Jefferson St.

Lincoln Ave.

Soscol Ave.

Monticello Rd.

Hagen Rd.

Vichy Ave.

Altamura ■

■ Truchard

Henry Rd.

Old Sonoma Rd.

1st St.

Napa ● Joya ■

121

Carneros Creek ■

Dealy Lane

Old Sonoma Rd.

CARNEROS
(SEE PLATE 9)

Jefferson St.

Soscol Ave.

3rd St.

Coombsville Rd.

■ Tulocay

3rd Ave.

E. 3rd Ave.

■ Farella-Park

Domaine Carneros ■

Mont St. John ■

Los Carneros Ave.

Cuttings Wharf Rd.

121

12

121

Imola Ave. W.

121

Imola Ave. E.

Haynes ●

4th Ave.

Star Hill ■

● *Caldwell*
Kreuzer Lane

Coombsville

Saintsbury

Dutng Rd.

■ Acacia

Bay View Ave.

Las Amigas Rd.

Buchli Station Rd.

Milton Rd.

■ Bouchaine

■ Kent Rasmussen

29

221

NAPA VALLEY

To Vallejo

Scale 0 1 2 Miles

Legend

■ Winery
● *Vineyard*

- - - - BORDER OF SUB-APPELLATIONS
——— BORDER OF APPELLATIONS
– – – BORDER OF COUNTIES

PLATE 8

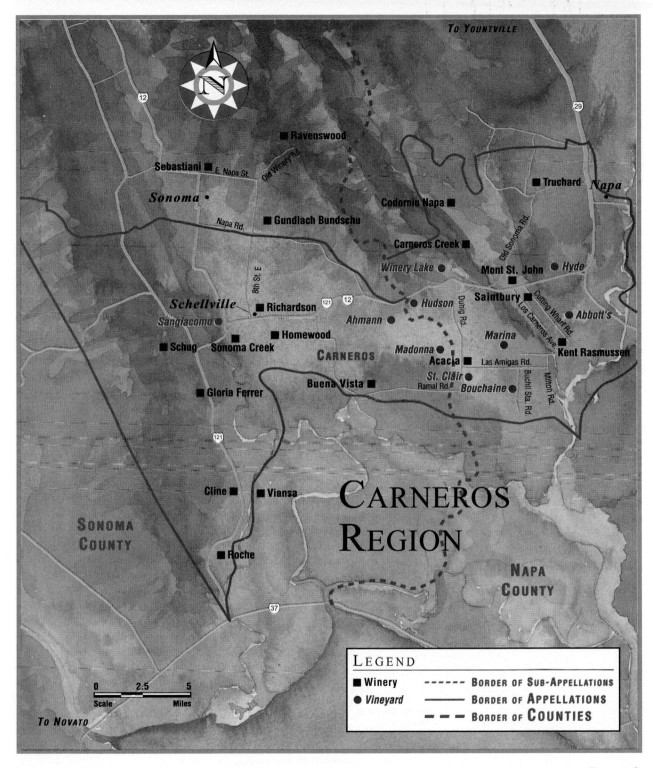

To YOUNTVILLE

Ravenswood

Sebastiani E. Napa St.
Old Winery Rd.

Sonoma

Truchard Napa

Codorniu Napa

Napa Rd. Gundlach Bundschu

Carneros Creek

Old Sonoma Rd.

Winery Lake Mont St. John Hyde

8th St. E

Schellville Richardson
Sangiacomo

Hudson Saintbury

Ahmann Dunig Rd. Los Carneros Ave. Cutting Wharf Rd. Abbott's

Marina

Schug Homewood
Sonoma Creek

Madonna Acacia Las Amigas Rd. Kent Rasmussen

CARNEROS

Buena Vista

St. Clair
Ramal Rd. Bouchaine Buchli Sta. Rd. Milton Rd.

Gloria Ferrer

Cline Viansa

SONOMA
COUNTY

Roche

CARNEROS
REGION

NAPA
COUNTY

To NOVATO

0   2.5   5
Scale   Miles

LEGEND

■ Winery   ------ BORDER OF SUB-APPELLATIONS

● Vineyard ——— BORDER OF APPELLATIONS

– – – BORDER OF COUNTIES

PLATE 9

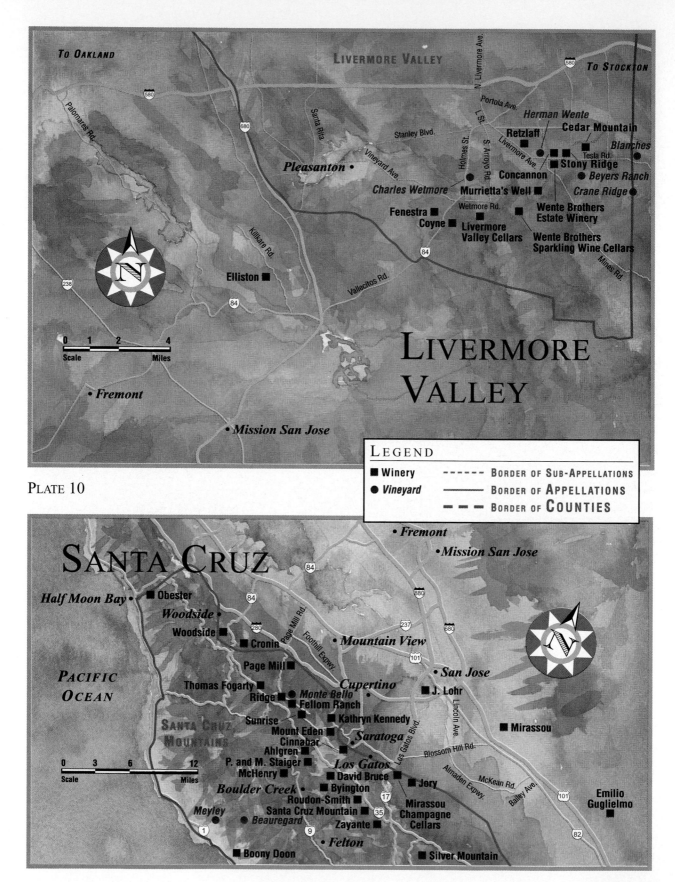

PLATE 10

PLATE 11

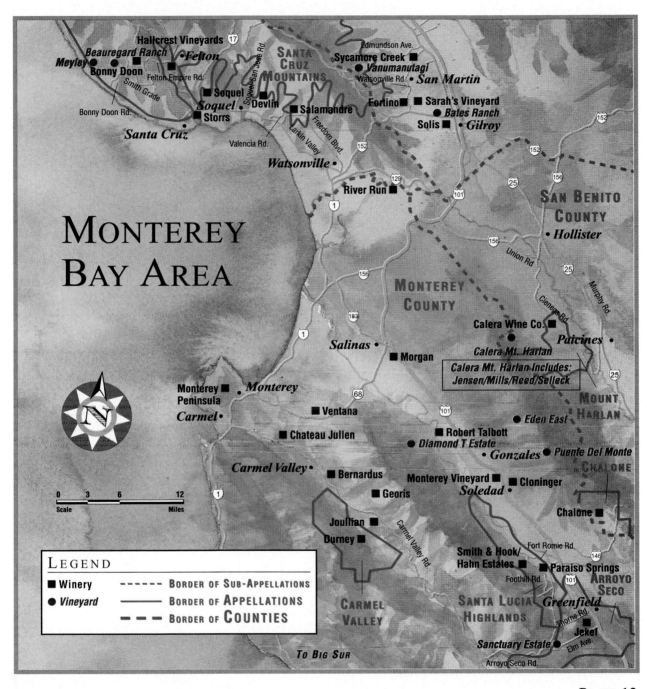

MONTEREY BAY AREA

Hallcrest Vineyards
Beauregard Ranch • Felton
Meyley • Bonny Doon
Felton Empire Rd.
Smith Grade
Bonny Doon Rd.
Soquel
Soquel • Devlin
Storrs
Santa Cruz
Valencia Rd.

SANTA CRUZ MOUNTAINS

Squel-San Jose Rd.

Salamandre
Larkin Valley
Freedom Blvd.
Watsonville •

Edmundson Ave.
Sycamore Creek ■
Vanumanutagi •
Watsonville Rd. • San Martin

Fortino ■ ■ Sarah's Vineyard
• Bates Ranch
Solis ■ • Gilroy

River Run ■

SAN BENITO COUNTY
• Hollister

Union Rd.

MONTEREY COUNTY

Calera Wine Co. ■
• Paicines •
Calera Mt. Harlan •

Calera Mt. Harlan Includes:
Jensen/Mills/Reed/Selleck

Salinas •
■ Morgan

Monterey ■ • Monterey
Peninsula
Carmel •

Ventana

Chateau Jullen

• Eden East

Robert Talbott ■
• Diamond T Estate
• Gonzales • Puente Del Monte

MOUNT HARLAN

CHALONE

Carmel Valley •
■ Bernardus
■ Georis

Monterey Vineyard ■
Soledad • ■ Cloninger

Chalone ■

Joullian ■
Durney ■

Carmel Valley Rd.

Fort Romie Rd.

Smith & Hook/
Hahn Estates ■ ■ Paraiso Springs
Foothill Rd.

ARROYO SECO

CARMEL VALLEY

SANTA LUCIA HIGHLANDS
Greenfield
Thorne Rd.
Jekel
Sanctuary Estate ■ Elm Ave.
Arroyo Seco Rd.

TO BIG SUR

0 3 6 12
Scale   Miles

N

LEGEND

■ Winery   - - - - - BORDER OF SUB-APPELLATIONS
● Vineyard   ———— BORDER OF APPELLATIONS
                  — — — BORDER OF COUNTIES

PLATE 12

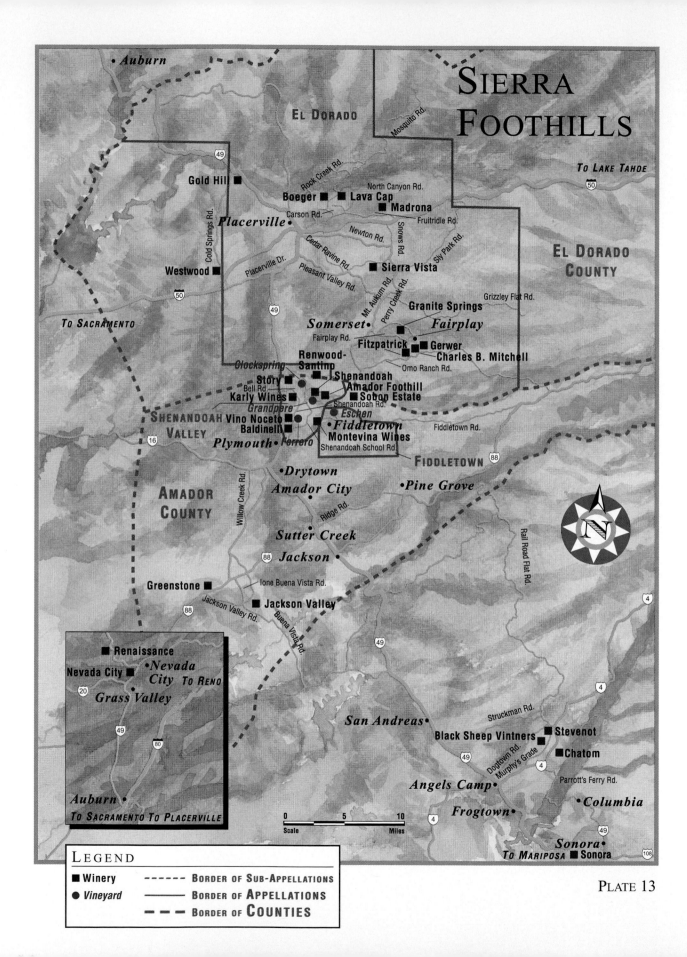

SIERRA FOOTHILLS

- Auburn

EL DORADO

TO LAKE TAHOE

50

Rock Creek Rd.

North Canyon Rd.

Gold Hill ■

Boeger ■   ■ Lava Cap

■ Madrona

Carson Rd.   Fruitridle Rd.

Placerville •

EL DORADO
COUNTY

Cold Springs Rd.

Newton Rd.   Shows Rd.

Cedar Ravine Rd.   Sly Park Rd.

Westwood ■   Placerville Dr.   ■ Sierra Vista

Pleasant Valley Rd.

50   Grizzley Flat Rd.

49   Granite Springs

TO SACRAMENTO   Somerset •   Fairplay

Fairplay Rd.   Fitzpatrick ■ ■ Gerwer

■ Charles B. Mitchell

Renwood-   Omo Ranch Rd.
Santino

Clockspring   ● Shenandoah

Story ■   ● Amador Foothill
Bell Rd.   Soboan Estate
Karly Wines ■   ● Shenandoah Rd.

Grandpere   ● Eschen   Fiddletown Rd.
Vino Noceto ●
SHENANDOAH   Baldinelli ● Fiddletown
VALLEY   ● Ferrero Montevina Wines
16   Plymouth •   Shenandoah School Rd.

FIDDLETOWN   88

• Drytown

Amador City •   • Pine Grove

AMADOR
COUNTY

Ridge Rd.

Willow Creek Rd.

• Sutter Creek

88   Jackson •

Rail Road Flat Rd.

Greenstone ■   Ione Buena Vista Rd.

88   Jackson Valley Rd.   ■ Jackson Valley

Buena Vista Rd.

49

4

4

Struckman Rd.

San Andreas •

Black Sheep Vintners ■ Stevenot

49   Dogtown Rd. ■ Chatom
Murphy's Grade   4

Parrott's Ferry Rd.

Angels Camp •

• Columbia

4   Frogtown •

49

Sonora •
TO MARIPOSA ■ Sonora

108

Scale 0   5   10   Miles

LEGEND

■ **Winery**	- - - - - **BORDER OF SUB-APPELLATIONS**
● *Vineyard*	——— **BORDER OF APPELLATIONS**
	– – – **BORDER OF COUNTIES**

PLATE 13

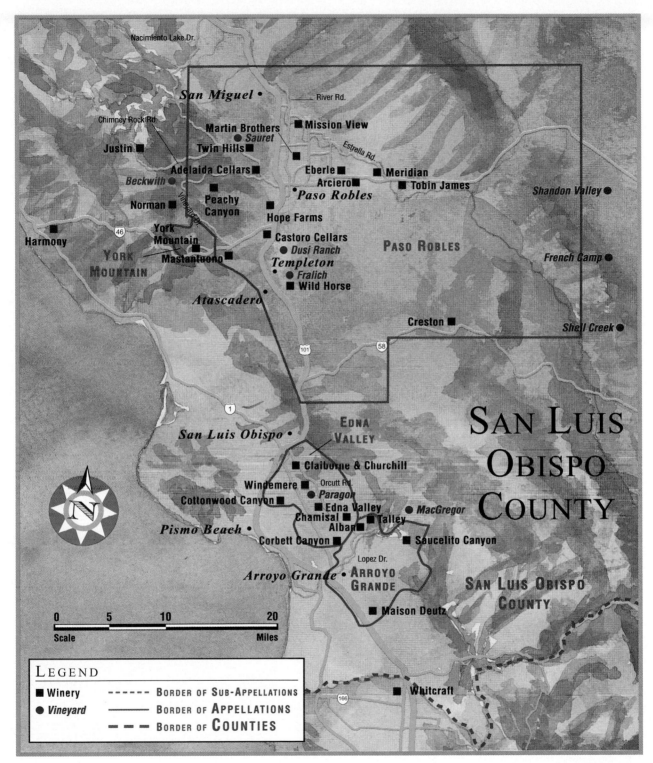

Nacimiento Lake Dr.

San Miguel •   River Rd.

Chimney Rock Rd.

■ Mission View

Martin Brothers ■
• Sauret
Justin ■   Twin Hills ■

Adelaida Cellars ■

Beckwith •   Eberle ■   Meridian ■
Arciero ■   ■ Tobin James

Norman ■   Peachy   • Paso Robles   Shandon Valley •
Canyon

(46)   York   Hope Farms ■   PASO ROBLES
Mountain
Harmony ■   Castoro Cellars ■   French Camp •
YORK   • Dusi Ranch
MOUNTAIN   Mastantuono ■   Templeton
• Fralich
Atascadero •   ■ Wild Horse

Creston ■   Shell Creek •

(101)   (58)

(1)   EDNA   SAN LUIS
VALLEY
San Luis Obispo •   OBISPO
■ Claiborne & Churchill   COUNTY

Windemere ■   Orcutt Rd.
• Paragon
Cottonwood Canyon ■   ■ Edna Valley   • MacGregor
Chamisal ■   ■ Talley
Alban ■
Pismo Beach •   ■ Saucelito Canyon
Corbett Canyon ■
Lopez Dr.
Arroyo Grande •   ARROYO   SAN LUIS OBISPO
GRANDE   COUNTY

■ Maison Deutz

0   5   10   20
Scale   Miles

■ Whitcraft

(166)

LEGEND
■ Winery   - - - - - BORDER OF SUB-APPELLATIONS
• Vineyard   —————— BORDER OF APPELLATIONS
             – – – –   BORDER OF COUNTIES

PLATE 14

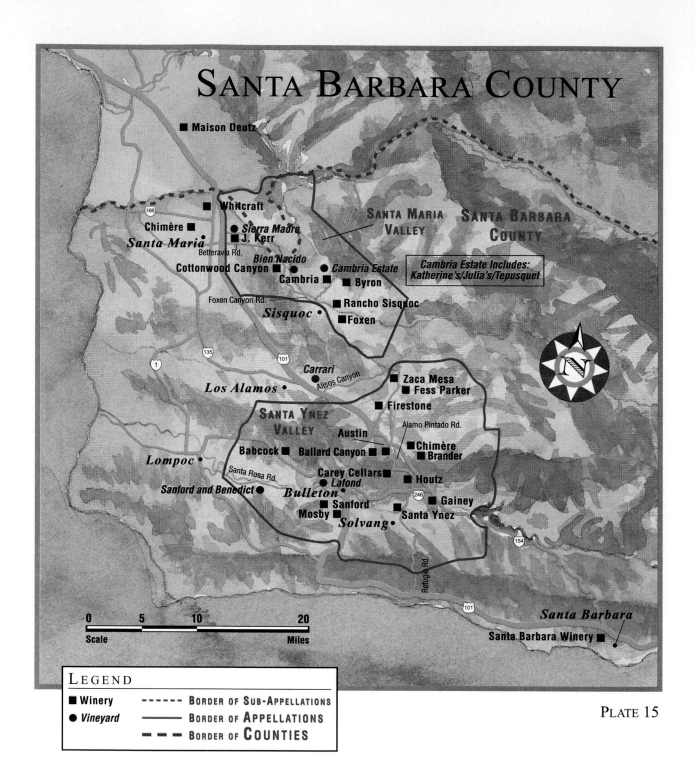

SANTA BARBARA COUNTY

■ Maison Deutz

(166) Whitcraft ■

Chimère ■

Santa Maria

● *Sierra Madre*
■ J. Kerr

Betteravia Rd.

Bien Nacido
Cottonwood Canyon ■ ● ● *Cambria Estate*
Cambria ■ ■ Byron

SANTA MARIA VALLEY

SANTA BARBARA COUNTY

Cambria Estate Includes:
Katherine's/Julia's/Tepusquet

Foxen Canyon Rd.

Sisquoc ● ■ Rancho Sisquoc
■ Foxen

(135) (101)

Carrari ●

Los Alamos ● Alisos Canyon

(1)

■ Zaca Mesa
■ Fess Parker

■ Firestone

SANTA YNEZ VALLEY

Alamo Pintado Rd.

Austin

Lompoc ●

Babcock ■ Ballard Canyon ■ ■

■ Chimère
■ Brander

Santa Rosa Rd.

Carey Cellars ■
● *Lafond*

■ Houtz

Sanford and Benedict ●

Bulleton ●

(246) ● Gainey

■ Sanford
Mosby ■ ■ Santa Ynez

Solvang ●

Refugio Rd.

(154)

(101)

Santa Barbara

Santa Barbara Winery ■

0   5   10   20
Scale   Miles

PLATE 15

LEGEND

■ Winery   ----- BORDER OF SUB-APPELLATIONS
● *Vineyard*   ——— BORDER OF APPELLATIONS
                   – – – BORDER OF COUNTIES

Clear patterns are developing regarding the best matches between grapes and appellations, each of which is discussed under the specific AVA, but Zinfandel in Dry Creek, Cabernet in Alexander Valley and Chardonnay and Pinot Noir in Russian River are working best. Indeed, Russian River Chardonnays and Pinot Noirs are among the best in the state. This county's Cabernet, while often excellent in Alexander Valley and Sonoma Valley, lags well behind Napa Valley's. Zinfandel rises to its greatest heights in Sonoma County's Dry Creek and Sonoma Valleys. Sauvignon Blanc, Merlot and sparkling wines also excel here.

REFERENCE WINES

Cabernet Sauvignon: Arrowood, Chateau St. Jean, St. Francis Reserve
Chardonnay: Arrowood, Fisher Coach Insignia, Sonoma-Loeb, Stonestreet
Merlot: Arrowood, St. Francis, Stonestreet
Zinfandel: Greenwood Ridge, Grgich Hills, Mazzocco, Rabbit Ridge, Ravenswood, Ridge

SONOMA MOUNTAIN
AVA 1985, 5,000 acres, 633 acres in vines

Laurel Glen's superb Cabernet is the star of this mountain appellation. Owner Patrick Campbell's excellent vineyard typically yields dark, intense and complex wines from a sloping, eastward-facing vineyard. Also of note are Benziger's estate vineyard; Jack London Ranch, a source of Cabernet, Merlot, Pinot Noir and Zinfandel for Kenwood; McCrea Vineyard and Steiner Vineyard.

REFERENCE WINES

Cabernet Sauvignon: Laurel Glen
Chardonnay: Kistler McCrea Vineyard

SONOMA VALLEY
AVA 1982, 103,200 acres, 5,950 acres in vines

Sonoma County's oldest winegrowing area is one mountain range west of Napa Valley and has a similar—but much smaller—narrow north-south shape. Buena Vista and the old Bundschu winery (now Gundlach Bundschu) date to the 1800s, but this appellation has yet to define itself with one wine—not that that's bad. So far Cabernet from Laurel Glen (on Sonoma Mountain), Kenwood Artist Series, B.R. Cohn Olive Hill Vineyard,

Carmenet, Gundlach Bundschu Rhinefarm and Louis M. Martini's Monte Rosso hold an edge among reds. Zinfandel also does well in several vineyard-designated wines but isn't widely planted. Chardonnay, led by Hanzell, Sonoma-Cutrer's Les Pierres, McCrea Vineyard, Kistler Estate and Durell Vineyard, fares well in the southern part of the valley where it borders on Carneros. Pinot Noir, after a glorious run at Hanzell from the 1960s through the 1970s, fares less well in warmer areas but does better when it hits Carneros. St. Francis is producing excellent Merlot, which represents a most intriguing possibility for the future.

Gundlach Bundschu's Rhinefarm Vineyard at the southernmost part of the appellation challenges all the rules: it is a mixture of all the major varieties—Cabernet, Chardonnay, Gewürztraminer, Merlot, Pinot Noir and Zinfandel—most of them capable of yielding fine wines. Kunde, long the major source of Sonoma Valley grapes for Sebastiani but now a winery of its own, is the biggest vineyard, covering several hundred acres with a wide variety of grapes.

REFERENCE WINES

Cabernet Sauvignon: Carmenet, B.R. Cohn Olive Hill Vineyard, Kenwood Artist Series, Kenwood Jack London Vineyard, Kistler Estate, Louis M. Martini Monte Rosso
Chardonnay: Hanzell, Kistler Estate and Durell Vineyard, Matanzas Creek, St. Francis Reserve
Merlot: Kenwood Jack London Vineyard, Matanzas Creek, St. Francis Reserve
Pinot Noir: Hanzell, Joseph Swan Steiner Vineyard
Syrah: Kendall-Jackson Durell Vineyard
Zinfandel: Gundlach Bundschu Rhinefarm Vineyards, Haywood Chamisal Vineyard, Ravenswood Old Vine, Ridge Pagani Vineyard, Rosenblum Samsel Vineyard Maggie's Reserve, St. Francis Old Vines

SPRING MOUNTAIN DISTRICT
AVA 1993, 8,600 acres, 800 acres in vines

This is an old winegrowing area in the hills west of St. Helena, rising up to nearly 2,500 feet. Grapes have been grown here for more than a century. If you count Stony Hill and its amazing Chardonnay as part of the appellation, then there's a track record for great wines. If you count Newton, also at a lower elevation, the Cabernets and Merlots are impressive. Higher up, Cain, with its excellent Cain Five, merits attention; Keenan and Smith-Madrone have done well on occasion, but are uneven in quality.

REFERENCE WINES

Cabernet Sauvignon: Barnett, Cain Five, Pride Mountain

STAGS LEAP DISTRICT
AVA 1989, 2,700 acres, 1,300 acres in vines

Best known for its supple Cabernets, its many excellent wineries, and the rivalry of the two Stags Leap wineries, the Stags Leap District is proof of how the appellation system works for consumers in defining styles and as a marketing tool. Because it won AVA approval ahead of Oakville and Rutherford, it had a head start in marketing. The Cabernets in particular impress, led by Stag's Leap Wine Cellars with its Cask 23, Fay and SLV bottlings; Silverado Vineyards with its estate and Limited Reserve; Shafer Hillside Select, Clos Du Val Reserve, Pine Ridge and its Stags Leap Vineyard, Steltzner, S. Anderson with its Richard Chambers Vineyard and Chimney Rock with its Elevage and Reserve bottling. Each of these wineries produces very fine wines across the board, from Merlot to Chardonnay, although in the end the reds are best. Many of the whites, while appearing to come from this area, are in fact made from grapes grown elsewhere, so reading the label carefully is important.

Nathan Fay planted the area's first Cabernet vines in the Stags Leap area in the 1960s, realizing that at the time there were only a few hundred acres of Cabernet in Napa and many wineries wanted it. Vintners Warren Winiarski of Stag's Leap Wine Cellars and Bernard Portet of Clos Du Val both decided Stags Leap was slightly cooler than upvalley and therefore conducive to planting Cabernet. It is also an absolutely beautiful area, with its huge rock outcropping. In 1972 both wineries produced their first Cabernets and in 1976 Winiarski's 1973 vintage won the Paris Tasting. Portet's 1972, while from a lesser year, also made an impression in that tasting. The district may be cooler than Rutherford, St. Helena or Calistoga, but it is warm enough to ripen Cabernet, and these wines are typically marked by smooth, polished textures and soft tannins. The range of flavors includes black cherry, olive, herb, tobacco and currant, but the winemaker's hand greatly influences the style—witness the difference between Cask 23 and Silverado Limited Reserve. Despite being showy and appealing early on, the Cabernets can age exceptionally well—Stag's Leap Wine Cellars Cask 23 1974 was amazingly complex and vibrant on its 20th anniversary.

REFERENCE WINES

Cabernet Sauvignon: S. Anderson Richard Chambers Vineyard, Clos Du Val Reserve, Shafer and Shafer Hillside Select, Silverado Vineyards and Silverado Vineyards Limited Reserve, Stag's Leap Wine Cellars Cask 23, Fay and SLV Vineyards, Vichon SLD
Merlot: Clos Du Val, Shafer, Silverado, Robert Sinskey
Zinfandel: Clos Du Val

TEMECULA
AVA 1984, 100,000 acres, 1,700 acres in vines

This appellation, near the border of Riverside and San Diego counties, is built around the fortunes of Callaway Vineyard & Winery. Early experiments with standards such as Cabernet, Petite Sirah and Chardonnay drew mixed results and today many early assumptions are under reconsideration. Whites, led by Sauvignon Blanc, Chardonnay and some Viognier, have an edge over the reds, but that may change as winemakers study Sangiovese and Syrah. While inland and warm here, the Rainbow Gap allows the afternoon breezes through enough to cool the area off by late afternoon and evening.

YORK MOUNTAIN
AVA 1983, 5,200 acres, 30 acres in vines

A single-winery appellation that lies west of Paso Robles in a cool area. York Mountain, the single winery, fails to inspire across the board.

YOUNTVILLE

Yountville is not yet an AVA, but it may be some day and could easily include Dominus Estate, Charles Krug Winery's Slinsen Vineyard and Trefethen's estate. This area could also be included in an Oak Knoll appellation, which might roughly cover the Napa Valley floor from Napa's city limits to Yountville. Another area that could be included is Soda Canyon, although this might also become a separate AVA. The district is well suited for Chardonnay, led by Trefethen.

CHAPTER 4

HOW WINE IS MADE

Wine is simply fermented grape juice. You could make wine in your hand if you could hold squeezed grape juice long enough. The natural yeasts on the grape skins would convert the sugar in the juice to alcohol, giving you wine.

As your appreciation for wine grows, so may your curiosity about the winemaking process. The basic chemistry is simple, but making fine, complex wines is far more involved, and there are significant differences in how wines are made when different styles are the goal. These involve such basics as the ripeness of the grapes when harvested, whether the wine undergoes a secondary fermentation, called malolactic fermentation (ML), and whether it's aged in new or used oak barrels and for how long—or whether it's aged in oak at all. This chapter will highlight some of the important winemaking steps involved in making great wine.

THE ROOTS OF GREAT WINES

The notion of fine wine begins with the most basic decisions: what kind of grapes to grow and where to plant them. A wine's potential quality is determined by where it's grown; great wines start in the vineyard.

Factors that influence a vine's health include the soil's texture, drainage, depth and color. Areas that receive lots of rainfall benefit from rocky soils that drain easily. Cool areas benefit from soils that collect and hold heat. Exposures influence how much or how little sun a vine receives; a north-facing vineyard would receive less sunlight than a south-facing vineyard. Yet, grapevines are amazingly hardy plants that actually grow well in most soils. This is why there are often many different grape varieties planted in one area—why you'll find a Chardonnay or Pinot Noir vineyard flourishing in an area considered perfect for Cabernet or Zinfandel. So any given area may in fact be well suited for a variety of grapes.

While there is a wide variety of soils and climates that suits some grape varieties, the finest wine grapes need fairly specific soils and climatic conditions to excel. When grape and soil are properly matched, the resulting wines reflect the place where they're grown, what the French call *terroir*. As discussed in Chapter 3, *terroir* expresses the interaction of many factors with the grapevines: temperatures by day and night, rainfall distribution by season and year, exposure, soil acidity, soil depth and so on; in short, anything natural that influences the growth of a vine.

This is perhaps the most important trend in winegrowing today—matching the right grape to the right soil and climate, or microclimate—a vineyard's immediate surroundings. Thus, many vintners are currently seeking cooler coastal climates, such as Carneros, Russian River, Santa Barbara and Santa Maria, for grapes such as Chardonnay and Pinot Noir. The jury is still out on varietals such as Merlot and Syrah, but in the next decade vintners should have more experience and better ideas about where these grapes have the best chances for success. There's a far better understanding of why Cabernet ripens so well in areas such as Oakville, Rutherford and the Stags Leap District and Zinfandel blossoms in Dry Creek and Sonoma Valleys. Chapter 3, "Appellations and Vineyards," and Chapter 2, "Grapes and Wine Styles," touch on this subject.

There are also important economic considerations that determine where grapes are grown and what kinds of wines they produce. While it makes good sense to plant Cabernet in Napa Valley, where it has flourished for nearly a century, planting Gamay there makes less sense. Great Napa Cabernet vineyards are expensive and the finest Napa Cabernets command high prices—in the $25 to $100 a bottle range in 1995. But there aren't any great Napa Gamays, and even the finest bottlings only command modest prices. For the same reasons growing Cabernet in cool areas of Monterey County in the 1970s proved disastrous. Many of those vineyards were planted as investments by large agribusiness concerns more interested in growing grapes for profit than in making quality wines. Looking at the prices commanded by Napa Valley Cabernets, investors believed that planting Cabernet would bring them the highest monetary return. But these Cabernets were marked by strong vegetal flavors, because the grapes didn't fully ripen even in hot years. The result was a steady stream of mediocre wines that hurt the reputation of Monterey wines more than it helped.

ROOTSTOCK AND CLONES

Having decided what kinds of grapes to grow and where to grow them, vintners can choose from a variety of rootstocks, grape clones and vine trellising systems, all of which contribute to the vine's health and ultimately to the wine's quality.

Vigorous rootstock can lead to vines that are very productive—productive enough for areas where five to ten tons of fruit per acre is the desired yield and ordinary table wines are the end result. Conversely, devigorating rootstock leads to less vigorous vines, and is better suited for vintners seeking a smaller crop and superior quality. Differing grape clones can lead to different sized berries and flavor profiles; they will also ripen at different times. A winery might use two or three different clones of Pinot

Noir or Chardonnay in a vineyard in hopes of creating wines with more complex flavors. If those clones ripen at different stages, it can be a real challenge to harvest all the grapes at optimum maturity.

Trellising systems influence how vigorous a grapevine becomes and how much sun exposure it receives, factors which in turn influence how grape berries and clusters ripen. The basic fact to keep in mind is this: crop yield is crucial to a wine's quality. The lower the grape yield per acre, the more concentrated the juice will be and the more complex and intensely flavored the resulting wine. That's why there's such an emphasis today on reducing or limiting crop loads and why growers thin large crops once the grape clusters have formed. A vine tries to ripen all its berries. If it's carrying many clusters, it has to work harder and longer to supply the nutrients to ripen all the berries. If the vine is bearing too many grapes—overcropping—often it will nearly ripen all the berries but stop short of full maturation.

Where a vine is grown will also help determine its ability to produce. Mountain-grown vines are notorious for their meager crops. Getting two to three tons per acre off a mountainside vineyard is an achievement. But those berries may be smaller and have a lower juice-to-skin ratio, and thus be more intensely flavored (and tannic) than berries from vines grown in more hospitable soils. Valley-floor vines rooted in rich soils can produce a much larger crop and in fact don't limit their crops as well as mountain-grown vines do.

Again, economics plays a role in these decisions. Large-scale wineries need enough grapes to produce the thousands of cases of wine they sell each year. They want vineyards and grapevines that yield sufficiently large crops on a consistent basis. A vineyard that typically yields five or six tons of Chardonnay grapes a year may be ideal for a winery producing a good Chardonnay that sells for $10 a bottle. Cutting that vineyard's yield in half might produce a richer, more concentrated wine, but it would also cut production in half, driving the wine's price tag up as well. That winery might not be able to sell as many $20 bottles of wine as $10 bottles of wine. But a winery that needs to sell 50,000 or 100,000 cases of Chardonnay or Cabernet to meet marketing goals can't afford to have its production cut in half, and since supply, demand and quality are closely interrelated, large-volume wines have price ceilings. High-quality, small-production wines can often charge what the market will bear.

GROWING, PICKING AND CRUSHING GRAPES

Climatic conditions and weather patterns—rain, hail, frosts, droughts, windstorms and cold—influence how a grape cluster forms and what kind of quality it will produce. When grape clusters bloom in spring, the number of berries a cluster will produce is determined. If there's frost at the wrong time, young berries can be damaged. Heavy winds at bloom can affect flowering. California has experienced a series of droughts in the past 10 years, but for the most part established vines with deep roots survive droughts just fine, though they may yield smaller crops. Younger, developing vines, however, are likely to be affected, as they require more water.

Vintners prefer years when there is plenty of rain in the fall after harvest and during the winter months—but not enough to flood or seriously erode vineyards. They prefer mild springs, so their grapes set healthy grape clusters. They prefer mild to warm summers, which favor even ripening patterns, to heat waves or cold spells. They prefer their grapes to ripen fully and to be harvested when they have optimum flavor. No vintner likes rain at harvest. While some rain is usual and won't necessarily harm the grapes, persistent rain can break the ripening pattern, temporarily lower sugar levels and lead to mold, grape shatter and mildew. The rain will have less impact on the grapes if the weather turns dry and warm immediately thereafter, rather than remaining cool.

Vintners must determine, as best they can, the optimal time to harvest their grapes. Often the decision is influenced by the weather, the size of the crop, the number of days it might take to harvest, the threat of rain or prolonged heat or a cooling pattern. Once harvest approaches, a vintage is on the line. Picking dates can make or break an entire year, directly influencing a wine's flavor and shaping its style, character and aging potential. Young, immature grapes yield wines with less depth, richness and flavor in both reds and whites. Immature white wines are marked by crisp acidity and flinty or lemony flavors. With some styles of Sauvignon Blanc or Chenin Blanc this can be desirable. With reds, immature grapes lead to lighter colors and more green herb and tea flavors. Overripe grapes, both red and white, often make wine with jammy flavors, thicker textures and higher alcohol levels. The trend today among fine-wine producers is to pick the grapes based on flavor rather than on statistical measurements such as sugar level or acidity.

Once picked, the grapes are crushed and fermented as cleanly as possible, avoiding any leaves, bugs, stems, rot or raisins. Red and white wines go through different fermentation processes, so we will discuss them separately.

FERMENTATION OF RED WINES

Because they get their flavor from the grape skins, most red wines—Cabernet, Merlot, Pinot Noir, Syrah and Zinfandel—are fermented with natural yeasts that grow on the grape skins or with yeasts that work especially well with the grape variety and desired wine style. The grapes ferment with their skins, often at varying temperatures, until the fermentation is complete and the yeasts have converted the sugar to alcohol. Sometimes a small number of stems are left in with Pinot Noir or Syrah grapes during fermentation for added tannin—at the risk of adding unwanted astringency. Now the wine is usually "worked" or manipulated to maximize or minimize color and flavor extraction during fermentation. One technique is "pumping over": wine is pumped from the bottom of the tank to the top with hoses. Or the grape cap, which is formed when crushed grape skins float to the top of the vat riding carbon dioxide bubbles, is punched down into the juice, either by foot or by plunger, in effect mixing the grape skins with the juice. Either way, the grape skin cap is periodically broken up to encourage flavor extraction, allow more air in and encourage the yeasts to complete the fermentation.

Certain grapes, such as Gamay or Pinot Noir, are often fermented by a process called carbonic maceration, or whole-berry fermentation: the grapes are poured into a closed, carbon dioxide-filled vat and ferment on their natural yeasts until their skins soften and eventually break, freeing the juice, which is then gently squeezed out. Some Pinot Noir producers will set aside a portion of their grapes for this technique, because it captures bright, fresh fruit flavors and gives the wine a healthy red berry color.

After fermentation, the free-run juice is separated from the grape solids. Most fine red wines are aged short-term either in upright tanks (made sometimes of wood but usually of temperature-controlled stainless steel) or put directly into a combination of American and French, new and used, small oak barrels. The remaining grape juice is pressed out of the grape solids, and a portion of this "press juice" is sometimes added back to the

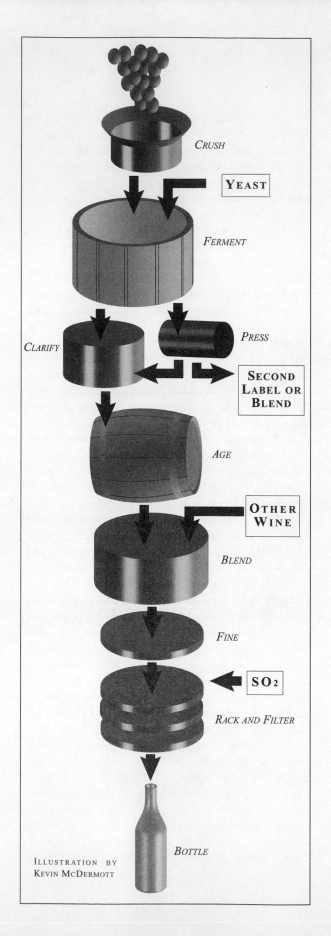

CRUSH

YEAST

FERMENT

CLARIFY

PRESS

SECOND LABEL OR BLEND

AGE

OTHER WINE

BLEND

FINE

SO₂

RACK AND FILTER

BOTTLE

ILLUSTRATION BY KEVIN McDERMOTT

MAKING RED WINES

This chart shows the more common steps and methods used for making Cabernet, Merlot, Pinot Noir, Sangiovese, Syrah and Zinfandel. The options and individual style permutations are too numerous to cover here, although I have indicated the more common differences below.

1. HARVEST: Ripe grapes are harvested at between 22 and 25 degrees Brix, leading to wines of 12 to 14 percent alcohol. To get an alcohol conversion level, multiply the stated Brix by .55.

2. CRUSH: Grapes are crushed and destemmed. The resulting unfermented juice, known as "must," remains in contact with skins and sometimes stems. The juice is inoculated with yeast or begins fermentation with natural (wild) yeasts living on grape skins. Red wines can spend from 5 to 25 days or longer fermenting on the skins, depending on the winemaker's desired style. During this phase, the must is "pumped over" the floating grape skins or otherwise manipulated to extract color and flavor and allow in sufficient air for fermentation. Fermentation usually continues until it is complete and all the sugar has been converted to alcohol, leaving the wine "dry".

3. PRESS AND CLARIFY: "Free run" wine is separated from the must and allowed to settle, often going directly into barrel. The remaining grape skins are then pressed, which squeezes out the remaining wine and leaves the pomace.

4. AGING AND BLENDING: Most red wines are aged in oak barrels for 10 to 36 months. With the exception of Pinot Noir (which is rarely blended with other grapes), they may or may not be blended. Some winemakers prefer to make their blends early on; others choose to wait longer to evaluate possible blends.

5. RACKING AND CLARIFICATION: For most reds, the wines are moved from barrel to barrel, a process called "racking," which aerates and clarifies the wine. During this process, a small amount of lees, or sediment, may remain at the bottom of the barrel or tank. Several rackings usually leave the wine clear. Occasionally fining or filtration is required to remove unwanted sediment or bacteria. Many wines are unfined and unfiltered. At some point after fermentation and prior to bottling, a small amount of sulfur dioxide is added.

6. BOTTLING: After the wines have aged in oak and have been racked and clarified, they are ready to be bottled. Depending on the wine, the finished bottle is either ready to be sold or aged at the winery for one to three years.

main wine depending on the grape variety and wine style. The press juice is usually more tannic, and sometimes more bitter. At some point, either before or after going into barrel, virtually all red wines undergo a secondary fermentation called malolactic (ML), which converts crisper malic acid into softer lactic acid. Occasionally a red wine will have a difficult time undergoing ML or may not undergo it at all. The resulting wine will be crisper and slightly higher in malic acid and may require more barrel aging to soften it. The greater danger is that the wine might undergo ML in the bottle—a disaster that can lead to a spritzy wine or even push the cork out of a bottle.

BARRELS

Aging wine in small oak barrels accomplishes several things. It allows a tiny amount of oxygen through the barrel staves to slowly oxidize the wine and soften the tannins. It also imparts a flavor, which varies with the wood type and its age. Oak can impart strong aromas and flavors of toasty, smoky, charred wood or vanilla. If mishandled or not kept clean, barrels can impart a dirty, dank, earthy or musty edge and spoil a wine's flavor. The major reds that receive oak aging include Cabernet, Cabernet blends, Merlot, Pinot Noir, Sangiovese, Syrah and Zinfandel. Depending on the wine's weight and intensity, it will spend from 10 months to three years in oak. Lighter reds such as Pinot Noir spend less time in oak than full-bodied Cabernets.

There are many different kinds of oak and many different ways to treat them. Some oaks are selected and treated specifically for Cabernet and others for Pinot Noir or Zinfandel. The decision is influenced by two factors: a desired oak flavor and wine style and the cost of the barrels. In 1995 the best French oak barrels cost about $550 each, with American oak costing about half that. One barrel holds enough wine for about 25 cases. Good barrels can be used several times, especially for white wines, and are often passed on for use with heavier reds. In barrel, reds are periodically racked, or moved from one barrel to another. This process exposes the wine to oxygen and helps clean it up by separating it from solids remaining from fermentation. After several rackings a wine will be sufficiently clear for bottling.

FINING AND FILTRATION

Unfined or unfiltered wines often have a hazy edge to their color. These wines usually have more richness, complexity and flavor, because nothing's been taken away from them. But they can look less appealing—like cloudy water—to those unaccustomed to natural wine. Unfined and unfiltered wines also run the risk of bacterial growth occurring in the bottle, which can ruin the taste of the wine. Most red wines are fined, usually by adding whipped egg whites, gelatin, isinglass (fish glue) or other coagulants that combine with the sediment particles and then settle out; others are separated in centrifuges. The purpose of the process is to give the wine clarity and brilliance, to remove any unnecessary particles that are too light to sink to the bottom and to eliminate spoilage bacteria. Brettanomyces, one of the worst of these, is a yeast bacterium that when left unchecked can induce a strong, dry, horsy, leathery flavor in wines.

Filtration, when overdone, can rob a wine of its character. It can not only strip away the aroma, textural nuances and body, but occasionally impart a sterile, filter-pad flavor. The whole issue of filtration is controversial. Clearly the best wines are those that are "made" in the vineyard through precision farming techniques, and handled as little as possible thereafter—filtration is significant handling. Many winemakers, however, believe a fine, or polish, filtration is an insurance policy against having a wine go bad in the bottle, which not only destroys the wine but has an immeasurable long-term negative impact on their businesses. If a high-profile winery that specializes in small case lots of several wines loses one lot of wine to spoilage, consumers might be forgiving. If a winery loses 20,000 cases of a nationally distributed brand it could be fatal. I believe in the minimalist or non-interventionist school of winemaking, where as little as possible is done to the wine in shepherding it from the vine to the bottle. But if a winemaker discovers a bacterial problem, fining or filtering to remove that problem is essential to the wine's quality and to the vintner's financial well-being.

BLENDING

Wines such as Cabernet, Merlot, Zinfandel and Sangiovese often benefit from blending. Pinot Noir is usually left alone, although occasionally a vintner might

CRUSH

DRAIN

PRESS

SECOND
LABEL

Oak Barrels

CLARIFY

Stainless Steel
Tank

YEAST

FERMENT
AND AGE

FERMENT

FINE

SO₂

RACK AND
FILTER

BOTTLE

ILLUSTRATION BY
KEVIN McDERMOTT

MAKING WHITE WINES

This chart shows common steps and methods used for making the major white wines of California. The options and style permutations vary greatly. Chardonnay and Sauvignon Blanc are often either fermented in or aged in oak barrels. Chenin Blanc, Gewürztraminer and Riesling most often age in stainless steel to preserve their freshness; they are very rarely aged in oak, except when made as a dessert-style wine.

1. HARVEST: Ripe grapes are harvested at between 21 and 25 degrees Brix, leading to wines of 11.5 to 14 percent alcohol. Dessert-style wines can be picked at up to 25 to 40 degrees Brix, but are not fermented dry.

2. CRUSH, PRESS AND CLARIFY: Grapes are crushed and destemmed; the resulting unfermented grape juice is known as must. The free run juice is quickly drained away from grape skins (to minimize contact) into either oak or stainless steel for fermentation, and is chilled. The remaining material is then gently pressed; the additional must is either added back to the free run juice or used in other wines, such as second labels. Wines are clarified by letting solids settle at the bottom of the tank or barrel.

3. FERMENTATION AND AGING: Juice is inoculated with yeast or allowed to ferment with its own natural yeasts. Fermentation converts sugar to alcohol; many whites have a trace of residual sugar after fermentation. Chardonnay and Sauvignon Blanc then age for six to 14 months in oak barrels, often on the lees (i.e. with the sediment that results from fermentation left in); Chenin Blanc. Gewürztraminer and Riesling age in stainless steel tanks. Malolactic fermentation for all or a part of the wine is an option.

4. BLENDING: Chenin Blanc, Gewürztraminer and Riesling are aged briefly and released for sale while they are young and fresh; they are rarely blended. Sauvignon Blanc and/or Sémillon are often blended with each other. Chardonnay is rarely blended.

5. FINING AND COLD STABILIZATION (optional): Most whites are fined by adding bentonite, a powdery clay, which removes excess proteins and clarifies the wine. Cold stabilization at 30 degrees Fahrenheit removes excess potassium bitartrate.

6. RACKING AND FILTRATION: In racking, the wine is clarified by being pumped off its lees. Sulfur dioxide is generally added at this point, but it can be added at most stages of winemaking. Filtration (optional) can range from a very fine polish filter to a coarser one. Many Chardonnays are unfined and unfiltered.

7. BOTTLING: Most white wines are bottled and go directly to market within six months to a year.

blend a very small portion of another wine with it for color or backbone. Cabernet and Merlot are well suited for each other and are often paired with Malbec, Petite Verdot and Cabernet Franc; Merlot can soften Cabernet, while Cabernet can add flavor and tannin to Merlot. Zinfandel is occasionally blended with small portions of Petite Sirah, Carignane and Sangiovese. Sangiovese often blends well with Cabernet, as either the dominant or the secondary flavor.

FERMENTATION OF WHITE WINES

White-wine production differs from red-wine production beginning at the time the grapes are crushed. Until then, most of the same principles regarding ripeness and clean grapes apply. White wines are crushed and separated from their skins almost immediately. Often the "crush" is a gentle squeeze—just enough pressure to break open the skins and let the juice run free without smashing the skins. Then the grapes are pressed—again, more gently than red grapes. The press juice may be added back to the wine, or it may be used for lower-priced or different-style wine. At this stage, control of oxidation is crucial to the freshness and vitality of the unfermented grape juice. Many wineries chill the juice to preserve freshness prior to fermentation. Those that prefer to barrel-ferment their Chardonnay or Sauvignon Blanc may pump it directly into barrels.

This process differs markedly from the techniques used in the 1960s through 1980s, when white wines were made more like reds and were often allowed one to two days of skin contact to extract flavor and were fermented in vats or stainless-steel tanks. At that time, also, there was widespread avoidance of malolactic fermentation for whites. Because the Chardonnays of the era were often grown in warm areas, they were harvested at lower acidity levels than today. Putting a wine through ML would have reduced the acid level even further. It was also common then to add acidity to wines as needed. Putting a wine through ML and then adding back acidity would have created two seemingly unnecessary steps.

Winemaker-controlled cold fermentation is considered revolutionary in winemaking circles. In Burgundy, a Chardonnay wine can be barrel-fermented in a naturally cool cellar. But in California, winemakers must combat warmer weather. The introduction of temperature-controlled stainless steel was welcomed as a way to do so.

For whites such as Gewürztraminer or Riesling, neither of which is normally aged in oak, temperature-controlled stainless steel helps preserve the freshness and vitality of the young wine—and these wines are best when they are at their fruitiest.

A wine's style is also affected by whether its fermentation is allowed to finish, leaving a dry wine, or stopped, leaving an off-dry wine with a trace of residual sugar. Both styles are common in wines such as Gewürztraminer and Riesling. A touch of sweetness is appealing to many wine drinkers, and it can take the edge off a wine such as Gewürztraminer, which by nature may have a slight bitter taste. Many wineries deliberately leave a trace of residual sugar in their Chardonnays for flavor, sweetness and body. Most of the finest Chardonnays are fermented until dry, then aged in contact with their lees (the sediment from dead yeast cells expired after fermentation), a process called *sur lie* aging. The lees continue to interact with the wine while it ages, usually for eight months to a year or more.

After fermentation, either in barrel or stainless steel, the wine is allowed to settle and clarify. While in barrel, the wine may be racked off its sediment, or lees, into a different barrel or it may be left in its original barrel until time for bottling. As with reds, a white wine is either left unfined and unfiltered, or is lightly filtered in one or more of these ways: with a centrifuge, with a powdery clay called bentonite or with filter pads. Many whites are then cold stabilized, in a process that eliminates all or most of the tartaric acid crystals which are created when tartaric acid combines with potassium or calcium. The crystals are not harmful, but they can be an annoyance to consumers, just as sediment or a cloudy haze raises questions about a wine's cleanliness or stability.

Most white wines are not blended. Chardonnay, Gewürztraminer, Riesling and Viognier, for example, are usually left 100 percent varietal. However, Sauvignon Blanc and Sémillon are often blended with each other in different proportions to achieve a desired style and flavor profile.

SPARKLING WINES

Legally, California sparkling wines can be called Champagne, a name that the French Champagne trade would prefer was restricted to only those wines produced in the Champagne region. The French Champagne houses who make many of the leading sparkling wines in California honor the name and don't use it. Several California wineries, however, do call their wines Champagne, including Schramsberg.

The finest sparkling wines are made by the process known as *méthode champenoise,* a labor-intensive process that turns the still wine into a bubbly or sparkling one. The essence of *méthode champenoise* is that the wine undergoes a secondary fermentation inside the bottle. In general, California sparkling wines employ Chardonnay, Pinot Noir, Pinot Meunier and blends thereof. These grapes are harvested at slightly lower sugar and ripeness levels than those used for table wines. This is changing slightly, however, as vintners re-examine their earlier efforts, many of which were overly crisp and tart. Sparkling-wine producers want to begin with a fairly neutral-flavored wine that is naturally high in acidity, because sparkling wine is highly manipulated. Through the *méthode champenoise,* complexity is built into the wine. After the primary fermentation, which can occur in stainless steel or oak barrels, (and sometimes ML as well) the cuvée is either kept separate for a vintage-dated wine (rare in both California and Champagne) or used for blending with several vintages. The cuvée is then bottled with a little fresh yeast and a precise amount of sugar that will referment in the bottle, add about 1 percent alcohol and produce a gas pressure of six atmospheres.

The second fermentation takes a few months, during which time the yeast adds other flavor dimensions to the cuvée. When the wine has aged the desired time, the yeast must be removed. To concentrate the yeast cells in the neck of the bottle for easy removal, the bottles are stored in racks facing downward at an angle and rotated periodically, a process called riddling. When all the sediment is resting in the neck of the bottle, the bottle necks are placed in an icy solution that freezes the sediment. The bottle cap (or cork) is then disgorged, allowing the pressure to "pop out" the solid sediment. The wine is, next, immediately topped up with more wine (called *dosage;* this may include a trace more sugar or a dash of brandy) and recorked and wrapped with a wire cage to hold the cork in place. Finally, the wine may be aged further, depending on the winery's desired style.

Most sparkling wines and Champagnes are non-vintage—the goal being a consistent house style year after year. In exceptional years, vintage-dated wines are made, usually for wines that should benefit from aging. Rosés are created by adding a small percentage of Pinot Noir to the cuvée to give it color and flavor. Blanc de blancs are made with Chardonnay. Blanc de noirs are made from Pinot Noir grapes and can have a slightly pink hue, but are often indistinguishable in color from other sparklers. Crémant is a lighter, less pressurized, less gassy style that's also more elegant and often creamy in texture.

DESSERT WINES

California makes wonderful dessert wines from Riesling, Gewürztraminer, Sauvignon Blanc and Sémillon grapes. With these white dessert wines, the most common production method is a natural—and curious—one, employing botrytis cinerea, the noble rot, a mold that forms on grape clusters under certain autumn weather conditions. When misty mornings and sunny afternoons lead to the spread of botrytis, the clusters of mature grapes shrivel, concentrating both sugar and acid. As the rot spreads, the berries shrink and their juice evaporates. When harvested, the berries are very gently squeezed, and the resulting juice is intensely sweet, rich and honeyed. Fermentation must be warm and lasts for several weeks, often taking place in barrels, until the yeasts stop working, leaving both alcohol and sugar, with honey, pear, nectarine and apricot flavors. Often these dessert wines carry the words "selected late harvest," which indicates the grapes were picked especially late, making a wine that's even sweeter than a "late harvest"— a term that can apply to white or red wines, as in late-harvest Zinfandel.

Port is a sweet, fortified, usually red wine that is made with modest success in several styles, often with Zinfandel and Petite Sirah. The wine's fermentation is stopped at about 6 percent alcohol, with residual sugar, at which time brandy is added. The Port is then aged in barrels for two to three years, with an alcohol level of about 16 to 20 percent. Several wineries are beginning to experiment with the grape varieties used in Portugal— Tinta Madeira, Touriga, Tinta Cao and Souzao, among others. But for now, California Port remains mostly a curiosity, with a few good, and no great, examples.

CHAPTER 5

A SUMMARY OF THE VINTAGES: 1933 TO 1994

A vintage date is like a snapshot. It reflects the year's growing conditions in a given appellation and is often an important indicator of a wine's quality. Growing conditions include many factors—whether the weather was warm, hot, cool or rainy, when those climatic conditions occurred and how they might have affected the quality of the grape crop and subsequent wines. In analyzing a vintage we also take into account such factors as the size of the harvest.

A vintage date becomes a more precise quality indicator when it is combined with a producer's name, a grape or wine style and an appellation. When all that information is presented together, it gives you a solid basis for making your buying decisions and anticipating the wine's quality and style. Is there such a thing as a perfect vintage? In theory, yes. It would go something like this: normal rainfall from late fall through winter, no frost and light (if any) rain in spring, an average to slightly below average-sized grape crop, mild, dry weather in the spring through summer months followed by a steady warming pattern in September—allowing a well balanced grape crop to ripen fully without the hindrance of rain.

This chapter offers a general assessment of California's vintages and how they have been expressed in the major wine types. The wines covered are Cabernet, Chardonnay, Merlot, Pinot Noir and Zinfandel; the primary vintages covered are 1980 through 1994. The vintages before 1980 are discussed in more general terms, focusing primarily on Napa Valley Cabernet and tracing the years back to 1933. A one- to five-star rating is provided for each year overall as well as a similar rating for each of the major varietals.

Chapters 2 and 3, "Grapes and Wine Styles," and "Appellations and Vineyards," discussed which grapes and wines tend to excel in different appellations. This chapter summarizes how each grape did in the major areas in any given year. But clearly there are important distinctions to be made within most vintages on the basis of appellation and wine style. In the case of Cabernet, the vintage rating is weighted heavily toward Napa Valley, which produces more than triple the number of superb Cabernets than the entire rest of the state combined. However, when they're of note, Alexander Valley, Sonoma Valley and Dry Creek Valley Cabernets are also discussed. For Chardonnay the major areas are Napa Valley, Carneros, Russian River, Monterey and the South Central Coast appellations of Santa Barbara and Santa Maria Valley. For Merlot, the major areas considered are

Napa Valley, Carneros, Sonoma Valley, Alexander Valley and Sonoma County. For Pinot Noir, Carneros, Russian River Valley and the Santa Maria-Santa Barbara areas are the ones considered. For Zinfandel, it's Napa and Sonoma Counties and the appellations within them. Note also that the vintage ratings are weighted to the most important wines and to wineries that specialize in the finest wines. They are not weighted to California-appellation wines that are blends of wines and/or grapes from several appellations.

Five stars (★★★★★) indicate an outstanding vintage with many classic wines. These are vintages that give you the best odds of buying great and ageworthy wines. In California, Cabernet has the best and longest track record for excellence, followed very closely by Chardonnay. These two wines have higher ratings than either Merlot, Pinot Noir or Zinfandel, which are more difficult grapes to grow and which make more temperamental and variable wines.

Four stars (★★★★) indicate a very good to excellent year that falls just short of outstanding and may well have many outstanding wines. This rating could also indicate a particularly outstanding year in just one appellation.

Three stars (★★★) indicate an above-average to good vintage which may include a few outstanding wines, but will show more variable quality.

Two stars (★★) indicate a fair to average year. In these vintages, there will be few truly outstanding wines.

One star (★) indicates a poor vintage that is best avoided. California's vintages vary significantly, especially given the diversity of the state's appellations. On the other hand it rarely has disastrous vintages, as Europe does; there, it's not uncommon for an entire appellation to have an off year.

To assess the more recent vintages, I monitored the year's climatic patterns and growing season and interviewed dozens of winemakers during and immediately after harvest. There are years when rain at harvest does not affect the wines. Other times a little rain can cause significant damage. So weather records alone can't enable you to judge a vintage. The best way to judge a vintage is simply to taste the wines on a regular basis. I often taste the major wines four to six months after harvest, which gives an early indication about quality. A vintage's character may well be readily apparent at harvest time. But sometimes it can take years for a vintage to fully reveal its personality.

In discussing the different varietals, bear in mind that most wines—primarily Chardonnay, Merlot, Pinot Noir and Zinfandel—are usually at their best early in their lives. Most of the best Cabernets reach a mature and appealing drinking age five to seven years after the vintage and surely are ready to drink at eight to ten years. Many can age and continue to improve much longer, especially if stored properly (see Chapter 6: "Building Your Wine Collection"). There are also ageworthy Chardonnays, Merlots, Pinot Noirs and Zinfandels. The key in deciding when to drink the wines lies in your tastes. Once you decide whether you like young, fruity, fresh and vibrant wines, or more mature wines with softer textures and perhaps more complex flavors, you'll make the most of your buying decisions. The point is that if you age your wines, you're accepting the risk that the wine might change and lose its appeal, or that your tastes might change and you'll find yourself less enthused by wines you once liked.

See Appendix 4 for a chart summarizing the following discussion of vintages:

1994	★★★★
Cabernet Sauvignon	★★★★★
Chardonnay	★★★★
Merlot	★★★
Pinot Noir	★★★★
Zinfandel	★★★★

A long, moderate growing season throughout the state was interrupted by several heavy rainstorms in the North Coast that affected Carneros Chardonnay, but this is still generally regarded as a very good to outstanding year for Cabernet, Zinfandel and Pinot Noir, and good to excellent good for Merlot and Chardonnay. Throughout most of the state, climatic conditions were very good through the harvest. Many vintners predicted the Cabernets and Pinot Noirs would be among the best ever made. Barrel samples of the 1994 vintage indicated a very good to outstanding crop; the wines were dark in color, rich in flavor and well proportioned. At this point, it rates as very good to excellent overall, with Cabernet and Pinot Noir worth watching carefully. This is a conservative rating; 1994 could easily merit a five-star ranking eventually.

1993	★★★
Cabernet Sauvignon	★★★
Chardonnay	★★★★
Merlot	★★★
Pinot Noir	★★★
Zinfandel	★★★

Across the board, this vintage produced lighter colored, medium-bodied and in some instances thin wines in all the major varieties. Vintners reported generally good climatic conditions throughout the year but noted uneven ripening patterns with red wines, which led to variable quality. Expect some superb wines, particularly Cabernets, but also some rather ordinary, lighter, early-maturing wines. Zinfandel proved a sleeper, with many well balanced and appealing wines that were lower in alcohol than the 1990 through 1992 vintages. Pinot Noir in Santa Barbara and Santa Maria was very good as well.

1992	★★★★★
Cabernet Sauvignon	★★★★★
Chardonnay	★★★★★
Merlot	★★★★
Pinot Noir	★★★★
Zinfandel	★★★★

This vintage was excellent to outstanding for the major varieties, in part because the growing season came off without the interference of rain. Cabernets from Napa and the North Coast were ripe, complex and well balanced, not quite as deep and complex as either the 1990s or 1991s, but supple and appealing. The Cabernets were well balanced and should drink well early on. Chardonnay was first-rate in all the major districts, with rich, full-bodied and very complex wines. Merlot was very good to excellent, and Pinot Noir was most impressive in Russian River and Santa Barbara. Zinfandel yielded very ripe and full-bodied wines.

1991	★★★★★
Cabernet Sauvignon	★★★★★
Chardonnay	★★★★★
Merlot	★★★★
Pinot Noir	★★★★
Zinfandel	★★★★★

This is a first-class vintage across the board for all the major varieties except Merlot, which was nevertheless well above average and not far off the pace. There was a very long growing season throughout most of the state and also a large crop, which led to some wines having green tannins and slightly unripe flavors. But quality was still very high. Cabernets from Napa in particular were intense, tannic and well balanced, a shade less opulent than the 1990 vintage, but with the potential for long lives. Chardonnays were ripe, rich, intense and flavorful, with scores of top-flight wines. Pinot Noirs from Russian River, Carneros, Santa Barbara and Santa Maria were intense and complex, well above average and well structured for cellaring. Zinfandel hung on the vines a long time, producing an excellent crop of wines.

1990	★★★★★
Cabernet Sauvignon	★★★★★
Chardonnay	★★★★★
Merlot	★★★★
Pinot Noir	★★★★★
Zinfandel	★★★★★

An outstanding vintage all around, 1990 has been the best of the 1990s decade so far. This drought year produced a smaller than normal crop, and each of the major varieties was impressive in each of the key growing areas. Cabernet experienced the best vintage since its star run 1985, 1986 and 1987, with the 1990 vintage most closely resembling 1985 for its ripe, opulent flavors and supple, fleshy textures. These wines were appealing to drink early on and have the intensity, depth and concentration to age well for 10 to 15 years—and in some instances much longer. Chardonnays, too, were ripe and full-bodied, complex and concentrated, delicious to drink. Merlot also came through in fine fashion, showing a style similar to the Cabernets, with ripe, fleshy flavors and good concentration. A small crop and warm weather combined to render this Pinot Noir vintage the best since 1986, as the best producers made ripe, full-bodied and enormously complex wines that are still developing quite well. Low yields played to Zinfandel's favor as well, allowing the grapes to ripen to their fullest, making this the best vintage since 1985 for most wines and the best since 1987 for many others.

1989	★★
Cabernet Sauvignon	★★
Chardonnay	★★★
Merlot	★★★
Pinot Noir	★★
Zinfandel	★★

This year was dubbed "the vintage from hell" by many vintners, as rain wreaked havoc at harvest time, especially in the North Coast growing areas, with all major varietals showing the effects. The 1989 crop was also larger than normal, which often means grapevines struggle to ripen all their grapes. When rain fell it led to botrytis in the white wines and earthy, diluted flavors in many of the reds. Hillside vineyards planted to red varieties fared the best. Cabernet, Pinot Noir and Zinfandel tended to be lean and austere, with modest flavors and a hollowness at mid-palate, showing more crisp, earthy tannins than needed. Chardonnays too were highly variable, with a few impressive wines picked before the rains, but many more with earthy, diluted flavors and a lack of concentration. Merlot fared better, with many very good and well balanced wines. It was a better year all around south of San Francisco, as the South Central Coast Pinot Noirs in particular were ripe and full-bodied.

1988	★★
Cabernet Sauvignon	★★
Chardonnay	★★★★
Merlot	★★
Pinot Noir	★★
Zinfandel	★★

In this drought year with a smaller than average crop, Chardonnay fared better than the reds, which were crisp and lean with modest depth. A heat wave in May led to significant berry shatter and uneven ripening. While the growing season was otherwise good, some rain in October affected late-ripening vineyards. Most of the wines were medium-bodied, with modest fruit intensity, lacking richness and concentration. Chardonnay, however, produced a good crop of ripe and flavorful wines that were marked by delicate flavors. Merlot, Pinot Noir and Zinfandel all had spots of success but overall quality was below normal.

1987	★★★★
Cabernet Sauvignon	★★★★
Chardonnay	★★★★
Merlot	★★★★
Pinot Noir	★★
Zinfandel	★★★★

A drought year with a much smaller than average crop, 1987 had a growing season that ranged from warm to hot, which worked well for Cabernet, Chardonnay, Merlot and Zinfandel, but less well for Pinot Noir. Chardonnays tended to be tight and concentrated, and turned out very well, while Pinot Noirs were light- to medium-bodied, with modest color and depth. Cabernet was clearly the star, especially in Napa Valley, followed closely by Merlot in Napa and Sonoma Counties, even though the Merlot crop was off 30 to 40 percent. Both Cabernet and Merlot were early maturing, showing ripe, plush and complex flavors with excellent depth and fine balance. Zinfandel had its crop severely reduced, but that can often be a good thing for heavy-bearing vines, as it ensures all the berries will ripen—a key to the grape's success.

1986	★★★★★
Cabernet Sauvignon	★★★★★
Chardonnay	★★★★★
Merlot	★★★
Pinot Noir	★★★★
Zinfandel	★★★★

This was an excellent vintage across the board despite an unusually large crop. Cabernet followed its superb 1985 vintage with many ripe, intense and firmly tannic wines that were well structured. There were also a large number of rich, intense and well focused Chardonnays made in the major growing areas. Merlot fared less well with the large crop, experiencing variable quality, while Zinfandel enjoyed another above-average year, although many wines were enormously tannic. Carneros and Russian River-grown Pinot Noirs were superb and ageworthy.

1985	★★★★★
Cabernet Sauvignon	★★★★★
Chardonnay	★★★★★
Merlot	★★★★
Pinot Noir	★★★★
Zinfandel	★★★★★

Largely due to the success of the Cabernet Sauvignon crop, which yielded a broad range of supple, complex and impeccably well balanced wines, 1985 is generally considered the best of the many fine vintages of the decade. A long, mild growing season and slightly below average crop size contributed to the wines' fine balance. At harvest the temperatures remained mild without heat waves, which allowed the grapes to reach ideal maturity. The red wines, for example, were uniform in their excellent colors, rich fruit flavors and very fine, gentle tannins. Chardonnay too was very complex and concentrated, perhaps the best vintage since 1975. Merlot, Pinot Noir and Zinfandel were also well above average, with many finely balanced, seductive and appealing wines. Few wineries missed capturing the excellence of the year and all of the wines are now mature. The Cabernets have generally aged very well, perhaps not as well as some of the early forecasts, but one of the appealing factors of the vintage was the wines' early-drinking allure. Many collectors waited too long on these wines; most have already peaked and the number of truly outstanding wines will soon begin to dwindle.

1984	★★★★
Cabernet Sauvignon	★★★★★
Chardonnay	★★★★
Merlot	★★★
Pinot Noir	★★★★
Zinfandel	★★★★

A very warm to hot and relatively compact growing season in 1984 yielded an unusually high number of ripe, plump and showy red wines. Cabernet led the way with its best vintage since 1978, and were it not for the excellent 1985 and 1986 vintages, it would receive even higher acclaim. While these were enormously complex and effusively fruity wines, their tannins were soft and fleshy. Most of the 1984 Cabernets reached an early plateau and

many are already declining. Chardonnays were ripe and intense too, with early-drinking allure. Pinot Noirs and Zinfandels were also excellent, especially in the North Coast, with Merlot just off the pace.

1983	★★
Cabernet Sauvignon	★★
Chardonnay	★★
Merlot	★★★★
Pinot Noir	★★
Zinfandel	★★★

A troubled vintage, 1983 saw a huge crop, uneven weather patterns, heat waves that dehydrated grapes and rain at harvest. It all added up to an assortment of clumsy, unbalanced and often unappealing wines. The saving grace was Merlot, which beat the odds; it tops Cabernet in only about one year out of five. Cabernets were intense, but marked by earthy, diluted flavors and harsh tannins that left them dry and uninteresting by age ten. Chardonnays lacked finesse and harmony; many were crisp and austere, made from grapes that were not ripe. Others showed evidence of botrytis. Zinfandel fared slightly better than Cabernet—vintners whose grapes ripened early made balanced wines, while many others were crisp and tannic. Pinot Noir fared well given the odd weather.

1982	★★
Cabernet Sauvignon	★★
Chardonnay	★★
Merlot	★★★
Pinot Noir	★★
Zinfandel	★★★

This was a difficult year, with a large crop, uneven weather patterns and rain at harvest all contributing to a curious mix of wines. Early on, the Cabernets tasted fine, but with each passing year they showed more earthy, diluted flavors. Chardonnay, too, rendered a few appealing wines, but many showed earthy botrytis flavors, especially in cool areas of Sonoma. The small amount of Merlot that was made fared well. Pinot Noir was good but variable and Zinfandel was slightly above average, but in this transitional year its popularity as a red table wine dropped in the face of rising white Zinfandel production.

1981	★★★
Cabernet Sauvignon	★★★
Chardonnay	★★★★
Merlot	★★★
Pinot Noir	★★★
Zinfandel	★★

A drought year with a short, warm to hot growing season and no rain at harvest, 1981 yielded a crop of supple, well balanced wines that were showy early on. Cabernets were ripe and balanced, medium-bodied and very pleasing to drink in their youth; they have aged fairly well. Chardonnay was very fruity and well balanced, with many excellent offerings. The Merlots were supple and forward, with soft tannins. Pinot Noir, especially from Carneros, was excellent. Zinfandel was average.

1980	★★
Cabernet Sauvignon	★★
Chardonnay	★★★
Merlot	★★
Pinot Noir	★★★
Zinfandel	★★

This was a warm to hot vintage with many heat waves and a very large crop, yielding wines of average quality, with many reds marked by very ripe and earthy flavors but modest concentration. Cabernet proved especially variable, with the best being bold, ripe and fruity, with supple tannins. Chardonnay was above average, with many good wines. Merlot was good, with several appealing wines, but from a small sampling. Pinot Noir was above average, from a small sampling. Heat played havoc with Zinfandel's ripening patterns.

1979	★★★★

This vintage was very good to excellent for Cabernet, Chardonnay, Merlot and Pinot Noir, but less so for Zinfandel. It was also markedly different from 1978, which offered very ripe and rich wines; the 1979s were more austere and elegant, but well structured. The top Cabernets aged well and many are still holding.

1978	★★★★★

This was a watershed year for Cabernet, with many ripe, rich and full-bodied wines produced in the wake of the breakthrough 1974 vintage and the famous Paris Tasting of 1976. The vintage was first class for Chardonnay, Merlot and Zinfandel, but a shade too hot for Pinot Noir, which was grown in far warmer areas than today. The 1978 Cabernets have aged very well, although by now most have peaked or declined.

1977	★★★

The second year of a two-year drought, 1977 produced a very small crop of pleasantly balanced wines. Especially successful for Cabernet and Chardonnay, both of which were early-maturing. A few stars remain.

1976	★★

This was the first of two drought years and it yielded a very small crop of intensely flavored wines, with many reds that dried out because the berries were shriveled at harvest.

1975	★★★★

Coming after the monumental 1974 vintage, 1975 lived in its shadow. But this was a very good year for Cabernet and Chardonnay, both of which were elegant and well balanced.

1974	★★★★★

A big crop of bold, ripe and complex wines were made in 1974, especially by many of the new Napa Cabernet producers. The Paris Tasting of 1976 focused global attention on California Cabernet and Chardonnay, which outperformed expensive French wines from Bordeaux and Burgundy; when these wines came to market in 1977 and 1978 they were a huge hit. The Cabernets in particular were intense and full-blown. They have aged well, but most are past their primes.

1973 ★★★

This was a very good year all around, with a clean, well balanced grape crop and generally elegant, subtle, well proportioned and harmonious Cabernets and Chardonnays. This vintage was generally underrated, as it immediately preceded the 1974 vintage, which won most of the headlines.

1972 ★

One of the few vintages to be hurt by harvest rains, the 1972 vintage was notable mainly for the number of new producers who went on to make an impact. Among the newcomers that year were Caymus, Diamond Creek, Silver Oak, Clos Du Val, Stag's Leap Wine Cellars and Burgess. The wines are now well past their primes.

1971 ★

Another wet harvest, remarkably back to back with 1972, 1971 left a crop of largely uninspiring wines with earthy, diluted flavors.

1970 ★★★★★

Severe spring frosts reduced the crop size by nearly half in 1970, but the wines, Cabernet in particular, were spectacular and among the longest-lived in the past 30 years. The top wines, such Beaulieu Private Reserve, Ridge Monte Bello, Mayacamas and Heitz Martha's Vineyard, remain in superb condition. This is the last in a string of great vintages starting with 1968.

1969 ★★★★

Considered the least of the 1968 through 1970 vintages, 1969 nonetheless provided its share of great wines, led again by Heitz Martha's Vineyard, Mayacamas, Beaulieu Private Reserve, Ridge Monte Bello and Robert Mondavi Unfined Cabernets. Supple, harmonious and elegant, they aged exceptionally well and still provide fine drinking moments. Hanzell Pinot Noir remains excellent as well.

1968 ★★★★★

This was a great vintage of ripe, complex and ageworthy wines, the best of which—the Beaulieu Private Reserve, Heitz Martha's Vineyard, Mayacamas, Ridge Monte Bello and Robert Mondavi Cabernets are still in amazingly good condition. Hanzell Pinot Noir was brilliant.

1967 ★★

Considered good, with early-maturing wines, but 1967 is nowhere near the class of 1966 or 1968.

1966 ★★★★

This vintage is first-class for ripe, supple and complex Cabernets, with Heitz Martha's Vineyard, Mondavi and Beaulieu Private Reserve the best bets.

1965 ★★★

It was a good vintage of early-drinking wines, but 1965 is nothing memorable now.

1964 ★★★★

This year's was an extremely short crop reduced by spring frosts, but so good that all 24,000 cases of Beaulieu Cabernet were bottled under the Private Reserve label—the only time in history that has occurred.

1963 ★

Another vintage hard hit by spring frosts, 1963's quality is considered only fair.

1962 ★

Spring frosts took their toll again in 1962, a vintage of poor to ordinary quality.

1961 ★★

Springs frosts were a factor in reducing the 1961 crop size by 50 to 75 percent, but the wines were ordinary to good.

1960	★★★

The wines from this vintage were widely admired by winemakers of the era, with Charles Krug and Inglenook the leaders.

1959	★★★

In a year well regarded by winemakers, the Inglenook and Beaulieu Vineyard Private Reserve bottlings were particularly excellent.

1958	★★★★★

This has long been considered a great vintage, with impressive Cabernets from Beaulieu Vineyard, Charles Krug, Inglenook and Louis M. Martini, all of which aged exceptionally well.

1957	★★

Considered a fair to good vintage, but the Louis M. Martini Cabernet was extraordinary for years.

1956	★★★

Considered good by vintners of the era.

1955	★★★

This year got high marks from vintners of the era, and many of its wines aged well.

1954	★★★

A year viewed as very good by vintners of the era.

1953	★

Remembered for the "Freeze of '53," spring frosts that wiped out most of the year's crop, but the first windmill—windmills prevent freezing by keeping the air moving—was installed near Calistoga, saving one vineyard.

1952	★★★

Hard hit by spring frosts and record-breaking cold weather, but the Louis M. Martini and Charles Krug Cabernets were superb.

1951	★★★★★

Along with 1958, 1951 is considered the best vintage of the decade, with mild weather and a good crop of fully ripened grapes. Beaulieu Vineyard Private Reserve, Charles Krug and Louis M. Martini Cabernets were all excellent into the 1990s.

1950	★★★★

Considered an excellent year by vintners of the era.

1949	★★★

Heavy frosts cut 1949's crop size, but the Cabernets were well structured and aged well.

1948	★

Plagued by adversity, 1948 included a drought into March followed by 14 days of rain in Napa Valley, which delayed development of the vines. Grapes were harvested under cool conditions and the wines were considered only fair.

1947	★★★

Frosts were again a factor in reducing 1947's grape crop, but warm weather led to a ripe and well balanced group of Cabernets.

1946	★★★★

Viewed as a great vintage at harvest time and for several years thereafter, although its quality was later debated.

1945	★★★★

Heavy rains led to a potentially large crop, but spring frosts cut its size.

1944	★★

Heavy frosts cut 1944's crop size, and vintners of the era rated the vintage as good.

1943	★★

Winemakers of the era considered 1943 only good.

1942	★★★

Few wines, but vintners rated the 1942 vintage very good.

1941	★★★★

Memorable for the magnificent Inglenook Cabernet, a profoundly complex and amazingly long-lived wine that I've rated a perfect 100 on several occasions.

1940	★★★★

Winemakers of the era thought 1940 an excellent year. Few notes.

1939	★★★

Rated as good by winemakers.

1938	★★

I have no notes on the 1938 vintage; a few winemakers liked it.

1937	★★★

Considered very good by winemakers of the time.

1936	★★★★

Memorably, this vintage produced the first Beaulieu Vineyard Private Reserve bottling, which aged exceptionally well for 40-plus years.

1935	★★

Simi's 1935 Cabernet was memorable for its vitality into the 1980s.

1934	★★★

Collectors and winemakers recall this as an excellent year.

1933	★★★

The year of Repeal boasted an Inglenook Cabernet that remained amazingly dark, rich and complex in 1989.

CHAPTER 6

BUILDING YOUR WINE COLLECTION

What is a wine collection? It can be as simple as a case or two stashed in an unused corner for daily consumption. Or it can constitute a serious hobby—an enjoyable obsession, for some. This chapter is written to help you make the most of your wine-buying dollars, whatever level of wine interest you might have.

As you get started, it's best to let your curiosity and tastes lead you to discoveries. You've probably already tasted a great many wines; you've read the reviews others have given them, you've followed the producers, styles and vintages. You're already following the market and know which wines you like and drink the most often. The next step is stocking your cellar.

Once you catch the wine bug and start buying wine, you'll want to consider building or buying a cellar. In this book, "wine cellar" means nothing more than a place to store your wine. The most important considerations are that it be cool (ideally no warmer than 65° F), dark and vibration-free. "Wine cellars" come in all shapes and sizes, from a few bottles in a rack above the refrigerator (the kitchen, however, is not a great place to store wine) to elaborate, barn-sized underground cellars that can cost more than most new homes.

I've seen spectacular cellars that look like shrines to Bacchus and I've seen stacks of cardboard wine boxes

wedged in a hallway closet. One of California's greatest winemakers, André Tchelistcheff, used to keep his modest wine collection under his bed. Ingenuity has a way of creating a cellar that works. The best cellars I've seen are the ones that are well thought out, organized, easy to use and used on a regular basis. They're not mausoleums, filled with dead or dying trophy wines, owned by someone who has no idea what he has or when he will ever drink it. If money is no object in building your collection, that's fine. But if you stockpile your cellar with the most expensive and sought-after California wines and let them age too long, you've wasted your money. Opening up rare, old and dead wines won't impress your closest friends any more than will burning money in your fireplace to keep warm, or serving three-day-old leftovers for that special occasion dinner. Buying fine wines and not drinking them before they fade is a waste of money and wine. Above all, the wines you collect or cellar should reflect your personal tastes and the kinds of wines you like to drink or serve to friends.

THE BASICS

Because wine has become so popular in the past decade, many new and clever ideas have cropped up about how to build a cellar. Several companies sell temperature-controlled wine cellars that plug into electrical outlets and can store hundreds of bottles. You can buy books on build-it-yourself cellars that include details on insulation, air conditioning and building bins to store single bottles or cases of wine. You can also rent wine cellar space. Wine stores often have lockers where you can keep your wine. (The only drawback is that your access is limited to store hours.)

Since wine is a living thing, it is constantly changing. Wine reacts most adversely to heat and direct light, which is why traditional cellars are cool and dark. A cellar does need to be dark. It needs to be moderately cool, ideally between 55° and 65°, and to maintain an even temperature that doesn't rise or fall dramatically within a few hours or days. If your cellar is 55° from November to March, and gradually warms to 65° in June or July, that is a steady progression that won't adversely affect your wine. Many European winemakers I've interviewed say it is healthy for a wine cellar to undergo modest temperature changes with the seasons, as they believe it helps ageworthy wines develop.

If your cellar area stays above 65°, your wines will mature more quickly. Whites and lighter reds, such as Pinot Noir and Gamay, are particularly susceptible to heat. Heartier reds will also mature faster—which isn't always such a bad thing, depending on your age. If the temperature stays above 70° to 75° for weeks and months, your wine may well get cooked. Excessive heat all but eliminates a wine's fruity flavors, leaving it flat and dull. Humidity isn't a factor in home wine cellars. Humidity is desirable inside a winery's barrel-aging room because it minimizes the amount of wine that can evaporate from a barrel. But once wine is in a bottle, sealed with a cork and, usually, a tin foil around the neck, the humidity level shouldn't affect it.

WHAT TO BUY

Once you've settled on storage conditions, the focus turns to what, and how much, to collect. Again, your personal tastes in wine should guide you. I've dwelled on personal taste throughout this book, because it's the essence of enjoying fine wine. No one knows your taste preferences better than you and the sooner you become comfortable knowing which wines you like, when you like to drink them and how much money you're willing to spend, the sooner you will feel comfortable with your cellar.

I like to drink most of my wines when they are very young, rich, fruity, complex and concentrated, and I think this is true of many wine critics. I taste more than 4,000 new releases each year, the vast majority being young wines (and some barrel samples). My palate is attuned to young wines. I drink most whites—Chardonnays, Sauvignon Blancs, Rieslings and Gewürztraminers—within a year of their release. I drink most Pinot Noirs and Zinfandels within a year or two of release, Merlots and Syrahs within two to four years of release, Cabernets at five to seven years after release.

I'd rather drink a wine a year or two too early than one week too late. I age a few wines, ones I think will develop with additional bottle time or that have a track record for improving with age. But I'm often disappointed with older wines, sometimes because I really liked the wine when it was young, and it has merely changed with aging, other times because the wine has not improved with age, or worse, it has deteriorated. I've spent a lot of money on certain wines that I've aged too long. Since coming to this realization a few years ago, I've bought wines more carefully. I often buy three or four bottles of a wine I like instead of a case. I drink the wines whenever I (or my friends) feel like it and I'm not worried when my supplies dwindle. I hate to see the last bottle of my favorite Pinot Noir sitting there empty. But it's a much worse feeling to open an expensive wine I've aged for 10 years and find that it's no longer delicious, but merely an old wine whose time has come and gone and I'm there to administer its last rites.

Coming to grips with when you like to drink your wines will be an important factor in determining the size and scope of your collection. If you like to age and drink more mature wines and are good at picking the right ones and keeping them properly stored, then you'll need to make accommodations to store those wines. If you drink them earlier, then your turnover will be faster and you'll need less cellar space.

If you're new to wine, I would encourage you to age a few wines to see how they develop. Or spend a few dollars ordering old wine off a restaurant wine list. This will help you decide whether you do or don't like older wines. One easy taste test is to buy a case each of a very good or outstanding Chardonnay, Pinot Noir, Merlot, Zinfandel and Cabernet. Drink a few bottles within the first few months and then try a bottle every four to six months, saving a few bottles for further aging. If you find that you still like the wines at four or five years, that's fine. If they seem young and intense, then cellar them longer. Try and keep one or two bottles for six to eight or ten years, and see how you like them then. But if you open the Chardonnay in a year and find it's less appealing than it was the day you bought it, then you've learned a valuable lesson. Drink up the rest. Reds will age longer most of the time, so if you find the Cabernet is still tough and chewy at age five or six, it will probably make it to year ten or twelve in good shape. Wines go through developmental phases, so it's not uncommon for a wine to hit what's called a "dumb" phase where it tastes closed or awkward. Once a wine loses its fruit, though, it's not going to regain it at some later date.

Bear in mind that bottles can vary in quality, so don't be surprised if you open two bottles from the same case and find one's more pleasing than the next. It happens. I'd also recommend you buy a few very expensive wines and put them in a blind tasting against some lower-priced wines. Cover all the bottles with paper and taste the wines. Then try them with dinner. See which you like the best. See which bottles empty the fastest. Then take the paper off. If you liked the least expensive wines, you've learned another good lesson. High price doesn't always equal quality. It's more a factor of supply and demand. If you like less expensive wines, you'll save lots of money over the years.

WHOSE ADVICE SHOULD YOU TRUST?

How you obtain wine buying advice is another important link to a successful cellar. I hope you'll read *Wine Spectator's* coverage of California wine, which is comprehensive, timely and more thorough than that of any other publication I know. You can also tap other resources: critics, wine merchants, books and friends. And don't forget the most important critic of all—you.

You'll get your most objective advice from independent critics and friends as they can easily tell you what they like with no strings attached. You'll get more biased advice from the wineries and winemakers, as they're keenly interested in selling their wine. This is why you often hear a winery or winemaker claim that their current release—the wine they're selling right now—is the best wine they've ever made. The truth is no one hits a home run every time. Winemakers may be trying to be honest

and objective when they say this wine is their best wine ever, but most of the time, they're too close to their work to be very objective. Besides, they have a lot riding on a wine's sales success. Your wine merchant can also be a good source of information. Knowledgeable wine merchants can help steer you to the wine styles you like and can afford. But sometimes merchants overbuy a wine, find it's not as good as they thought (or as the winemaker or critics said) and then start looking for ways to unload it. After all, making and selling wine is a business.

What about wine critics? There are many out there. Most take wine seriously. Some take wine (and themselves) too seriously. Some aren't serious enough. A good critic should be someone you trust, whose tastes usually coincide with yours. Good critics should be able to describe which wines please them the most and why, as well as which ones disappoint the most, and why—and say so in terms you can comprehend. They should have several years' experience (the more the better) with the wines they're recommending. They should taste all or most of the major wines released each year and most importantly they should be consistent; that is, if they like a wine or wine style one time, they should still like it the next time they critique it. On the other hand, I wouldn't expect a critic to be "right" all the time and I certainly wouldn't want a critic to ignore a wine's flaw simply because that winery or wine has earned praise in the past.

How often are critics correct in their advice? How often is anyone right about anything? How often do you agree with your friends about movies, books, music or the new restaurant in town? In my view, if a critic is correct 60 to 75 percent of the time, that's a pretty good average. If your stockbroker beat the stock market by that average, you'd be ecstatic. In this case being "correct" means that the critic's view of the wine is borne out by your own impressions. If you rarely agree with a critic, or don't like his style of writing, descriptions, or rating system, then seek different advice. I'd be especially cautious (no, downright suspicious) of critics who think they're always right and everyone else is always wrong, or who assume everyone's tastes should be identical to theirs. Critics who can admit their faults—when they misjudged a wine or vintage or style—and point out where they went wrong, are credible and in tune with reality. They can generally be counted on to give you a straight answer.

Be suspicious of critics who:

• Are reluctant to take stands or defend their descriptions of wines they like or dislike.

• Claim (or think) they're always right and that other critics are always wrong.

• Think they're experts on all wines from all over the world all the time.

• Never visit the appellations or countries they profess to know so well.

• Overgeneralize (or wing it) when finding fault with a style they don't like (or perhaps don't understand).

• Are unwilling to admit they might have been wrong and unwilling to change their minds.

• Only taste the high-profile wines. I know many tasting groups who select a critic's top 10 or 12 wines from a report, buy those wines and then critique them in a blind tasting. Then they criticize the critic for over- or underrating this or that wine or vintage. What they haven't done is taste the other 499 wines that comprise the market. That experience is essential in forming a broad market view.

• Boast they taste hundreds of wines a day. We each have different capacities to taste and comprehend what we're tasting. I can remember when tasting 12 wines seemed like a lot. I've also been in situations where I've tasted more than 100 wines in a day (and usually regretted it). It is possible to taste that many wines. But at some point you lose your ability to concentrate and the margin for error increases. Even when spitting, you absorb some alcohol and it affects your ability to concentrate. Simple fatigue takes its toll.

• Routinely only taste a wine once and pronounce judgment. I try to taste a wine two to three times, especially wines I give high ratings to or wines that have excellent reputations for high standards.

• Never go out on a limb for wines they feel strongly about.

• Don't taste blind—that is, without knowing a wine's identity. Blind tasting isn't the only way to judge wines, but it is the most objective.

• Rate wines out of barrel and don't tell you. I've seen this trend increase of late as critics scramble to be the first in print with a review. Critics who rate barrel samples and then write reviews implying it was a bottled wine are deceiving their readers. I've visited wineries shortly after reading glowing reviews of a wine, only to discover the wine reviewed was a barrel sample and is still several weeks (or months) away from bottling.

• Decry wines of elegance, grace, finesse, delicacy or wines that are "too fruity." Or, conversely, those who describe wines that are pickley, gamy, dirty, leathery, horsey or have fecal aromas as complex. (Sorry, you've got to draw the line somewhere.)

• Have a conflict of interest, either as a part-owner of, investor in or as a consultant to wineries they write about. A critic who has a financial interest in a winery may refrain from writing directly about his wine, but still promote his own interests merely through criticism of the competition.

• Identify with the wine trade rather than with you, the consumer.

• Appear to like all wines and dislike none.

Put more faith in critics who:

• Have experience: at least five and preferably ten years covering the topic they're writing about. As the California wine industry has grown to nearly 800 wineries—with thousands of new wines released each year—it's increasingly more complex to cover than it was in the 1970s and 1980s, when there were one-fifth or one-quarter as many wineries as well as a fraction of the number of wines.

• Have an open mind about wines and are willing to rethink their views.

• Taste often and cover the whole spectrum of wines.

• Reexamine older vintages in the same serious manner as they review new releases.

• Admit they haven't tried every wine and don't know everything there is to know about wine.

• Speak a language you can understand and offer advice you find useful.

MAKING YOUR BUYING DECISIONS

Having determined your wine needs, assembling a wine collection still presents challenges. Wine can be expensive and many of the best wines are difficult to obtain as well. Cabernet and Chardonnay are popular because they not only have strong personalities, but are usually made in large quantities, which makes them available to a broad audience.

RELATIVE AGEABILITY CHART

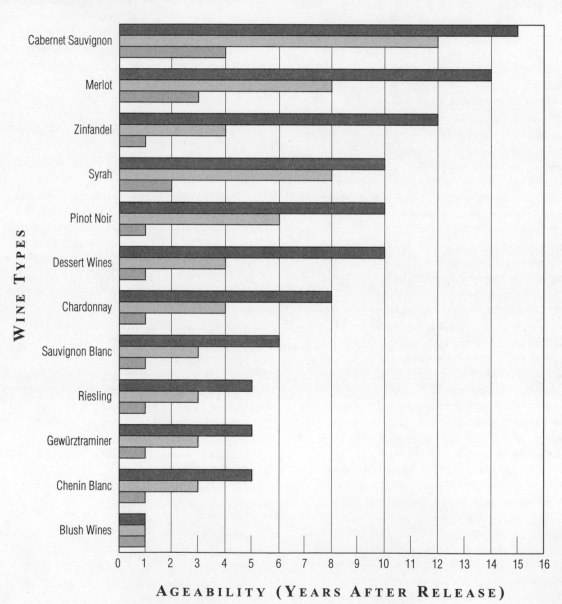

- Age Potential
- Peak Drink
- Begin Drink

WINE TYPES

- Cabernet Sauvignon
- Merlot
- Zinfandel
- Syrah
- Pinot Noir
- Dessert Wines
- Chardonnay
- Sauvignon Blanc
- Riesling
- Gewürztraminer
- Chenin Blanc
- Blush Wines

0 1 2 3 4 5 6 7 8 9 10 11 12 13 14 15 16

AGEABILITY (YEARS AFTER RELEASE)

Wine bottle designations include, from left, half-bottle, bottle, magnum and double magnum, and imperial.

HARRY AUNG

In this book I've reviewed and rated more than 7,000 individual wines. I've also rated each winery's overall performance on a one- to five-star scale and each of its wines on a one- to five-star scale. The four- and five-star wines are the ones I think are the best. In building a wine collection, that's where I'd start. (For more about the 100-point and star ratings see "How To Use This Book").

With Cabernet and Chardonnay, you'll have the broadest choice of outstanding wines. California winemakers have more experience and success with these two varieties and in a great year it's not unusual to find 50 or more outstanding wines to choose from. It's much harder on a year-to-year basis to find outstanding Pinot Noir, Zinfandel and Merlot, and even harder to find great Sangiovese or Syrah. A great year for Pinot Noir might yield 15 or 20 stellar wines, most of which have fewer than 500 cases for the world. That's changing slowly, as more fine wines of these types are made. But you'll often have to work harder at finding these wines. As a bottom line, I'd recommend focusing on the wines California excels at—and which are the primary focus of this book: Cabernet and Cabernet blends, Chardonnay, Merlot, Pinot Noir, Sangiovese, Sauvignon Blanc, Syrah and Zinfandel. With these wines, I'd diversify, focusing on what you like to drink most often, without ignoring other alternatives, as you may find your tastes change with time.

INVESTING IN WINE

I'm amazed by how many people associate (or confuse) collecting wine with investing. Even neophytes who've just bought their first few cases of Cabernet from a great vintage start talking about their "investment" in wine and how much more the wine will be worth in 10 years. I suppose part of this is rationalization. It sounds much better to tell your spouse that the $5,000 or $10,000 you just spent on wine for your cellar (that you'll drink in five to ten years) represents a great investment. But you shouldn't confuse collecting with investing. You collect wines to drink them. You invest in wines to earn a profit. Great wines from great producers in great vintages do appreciate in value, but the market is highly unpredictable. Often a wine's value is greatly distorted by the sale of one bottle of wine at a charity auction for an astronomical price. In general, I don't recommend using wine as an investment tool. If you're looking to earn a return on your capital, to make money, there are better ways to do it. Put your $5,000 or $10,000 in growth-oriented mutual funds and watch it grow. I certainly wouldn't forgo your IRA contribution or stop funding your 401(k) plan and put that money into wine instead.

If, however, you have diversified investments and decide you'd like to invest in wine as well, here are some guidelines.

• Make sure you have a cool, dark cellar and an inventory of stock. (Keeping records of what wines you own is a good idea anyway, even for a collector's cellar).

• Make sure you have a specific insurance policy in case of fire, theft or earthquake.

• Focus on wines that have the greatest chance for price appreciation and wines that will be in demand in five to ten years—or longer. This is where it gets tricky, because a wine that sells for $50 or $100 a bottle today may be in great demand. But it may not appreciate in value as fast as a $25 or $35 bottle of wine.

• Buy low and sell high as often as possible. Reread the general rules for investing and recognize that when a wine you paid $25 for starts selling for $50 or $75, it's a good time to sell. Why? You've doubled or tripled your money. If there are buyers willing to pay, be prepared to sell. That same wine may appear in a tasting and get panned. What's it worth then? Maybe far less.

• Pay close attention to the market. I don't know many wine investors. I know many people who claim they invest in wine, but I've never seen their financial books, so I can't say whether they're making a profit or wise investment. My guess is that if they are right 60 to 70 percent of the time—picking the right wine and selling it at a good profit—then they're happy. But I expect many collectors make bad investments in wine, occasionally (or often) sustaining losses, and that others end up drinking their investments, realizing that that was the real reason they bought the wine in the first place.

• Remember that wine really isn't a liquid investment if you need cash in a hurry. It can take months to sell 50 or 100 cases of wine. And what if you have to move? Transporting a thousand bottles of wine is expensive and risky—especially during the summer months.

• Remember that despite the cozy black market where wines are sold and traded without paperwork, any profits you earn are taxable.

• Focus on the best vintages. In years such as 1984, 1985, 1986 and 1987, there were many excellent Cabernets produced, but the one year that sticks out in collectors' minds is 1985. The other vintages may be just as good for certain wines, but 1985 has the cachet.

• Consider oversized bottles, such as magnums or double magnums. They're rarer and are sometimes prized by other collectors.

• Keep an eye out for the new stars. Often new producers' wines sell at lower prices than the competition and, once discovered, they will become more expensive.

• Consider buying futures in great years, as you will pay a discounted price in advance of the wine's release.

WINE FUTURES

Collecting or investing in wine futures involves buying a wine, at a discounted price, in advance of its release—usually a year or two. This option has its risks: the wine may not live up to its advance billing; the winery or retailer who took your money may go out of business. Also, since so often you cannot taste a wine before buying futures in it, how can you know for sure whether it's a wine you'll like? Unfortunately, because many of the best wines are in limited supply and sell quickly, we have to buy some wines without tasting them—or we don't get a crack at them at all. I'd have most confidence in the wines from an established producer who has a track record for excellence. Also, if you live in an area where it's difficult to obtain certain wines, buying futures can be beneficial. Another good reason to consider futures is you can often ask a winery to set aside several magnums or double magnums of the wine you want.

CHAPTER 7

WINERY PROFILES AND
TASTING NOTES

In this chapter each of the wineries chosen for this book is profiled and tasting notes are provided for their noteworthy wines. Use this section as a guide for your wine-buying strategy, or as a reference guide to check up on the wines in your cellar.

Wineries are listed alphabetically. The typical listing has the following features:

• The winery name is listed, followed by the winery's location (the city and/or appellation), ownership and winemaker information.

• Overall Rating: This rating on the five-star scale denotes the winery's overall quality.

• Wine Ratings: These ratings on the five-star scale indicate the quality of each of the winery's featured wines.

• Winery Data: This section contains data on case production, vineyards' holdings and produce and grape purchases.

• Winery Profile: This is a brief description of the winery with an evaluation of its overall strengths, weaknesses and notable features.

• Tasting Notes: These are presented for selected wines. In many cases, a wine summary will precede the actual tasting notes. This summary gives you a general look at the wine's style and other characteristics common to the wine regardless of vintage. The individual tasting notes focus on each vintage of that wine and what makes it distinct.

In the interest of saving space, I have used several abbreviations in this chapter. Below is a list of those abbreviations, in the order that they follow in each profile:

F: The year the winery was founded.
O: The winery's owner(s).
W: The winery's winemaker(s).
S: The winery's secondary label(s).
$: The price range for the wines produced.
C: The winery's annual production in cases.
V: Vineyards the winery owns in acres.
G: Grape varieties grown in winery-owned vineyards.
P: Grapes purchased from outside vineyards.

For detailed explanations of the 100-point and five-star rating scales, please see "How To Use This Book" or the bookmark included with this book.

ABREU VINEYARDS
Napa Valley
F: 1987. O: David Abreu. W: David Abreu, Ric Forman.
S: None.

OVERALL	$25	★★★

WINE RATINGS

Cabernet Sauvignon Napa Valley	★★★

WINERY DATA
C: 400. V: None. G: None. P: Cabernet Sauvignon
(Napa Valley).

Dave Abreu operates a vineyard management firm in Napa Valley, overseeing the farming and vineyard operations of many wineries, including Staglin, Araujo and Spottswoode. In 1987 he began bottling wine from Madrona Vineyard in St. Helena near Spottswoode. The 1987 was made by long-time friend Ric Forman at his winery and offered rich, complex, spicy currant and mineral flavors. The 1989 was similar in style, but less concentrated. Most of the 400 cases are sold through a mailing list.

TASTING NOTES

CABERNET SAUVIGNON NAPA VALLEY (★★★):
Very good so far, with ripe, plush harmonious wines. No 1988 was produced.
1989: Less complex and concentrated, but appealing for its ripe fruit flavors. **86**
1987: Complex with rich, currant, spice, mineral and anise notes, finishing with plush tannins. **89**

ACACIA WINERY
Carneros
F: 1979. O: Chalone Wine Group. W: David Lattin.
S: Caviste.

OVERALL	$11-25	★★★

WINE RATINGS

Chardonnay Carneros	★★★
Chardonnay Carneros Reserve	★★★
Pinot Noir Carneros	★★
Pinot Noir Carneros St. Clair Vineyard Reserve	★★★
Sparkling Wine Carneros	★★★
Caviste Zinfandel Napa Valley	★★★

WINERY DATA
C: 50,000. V: 43 acres in Carneros. G: Chardonnay (41 acres), Viognier (1), Malbec (1). P: Chardonnay (Carneros), Pinot Noir (Carneros), Zinfandel (Napa Valley).

A pioneer of Carneros-grown, vineyard-designated Chardonnays and Pinot Noirs, Acacia had early success with these two varietals, sparking interest in the Carneros appellation and demonstrating the unique personalities of different vineyard microclimates. At one point in the mid-1980s, founders Mike Richmond and Jerry Goldstein and winemaker Larry Brooks bottled six different Pinot Noirs—from Iund, Lee, Madonna, St. Clair, Winery Lake Vineyards and Carneros—along with Chardonnays from Marina, Winery Lake, Napa Valley and Carneros. While Chardonnay always comprised the largest production, Acacia's single-vineyard Pinot Noirs captured the imagination of Burgundy lovers. In 1984 the managing partners attempted to branch into Bordeaux-style wines in an ill-fated venture with Joe Cafaro. Acacia-Cafaro produced one vintage of a Cabernet, a Merlot and a Sauvignon Blanc. None of the wines saw widespread distribution. Meanwhile, Acacia's investors were divided over winery management decisions, expansion plans and profits and decided to sell the winery and its only vineyard, the 43-acre Marina Vineyard. In 1986 Acacia was acquired by the Chalone Wine Group.

The new owners trimmed Acacia's lineup to two Chardonnays, Marina and Carneros, and two Pinot Noirs, St. Clair and Carneros, while adding a vintage-dated Brut sparkling wine and a Zinfandel under its Caviste label. By 1993, the winery planned to further narrow its focus for Chardonnay and Pinot Noir, keeping a Carneros and a Reserve wine for each variety while adding a lower-priced Chardonnay with a California appellation to the Caviste line. Total production is 50,000 cases, with Chardonnay comprising about 35,000 cases, including 4,000 cases of Reserve. Pinot Noir production hovers around 13,000 cases, with 2,000 cases of Reserve. Caviste Zinfandel totals about 1,200 cases and sparkling wine about 1,000 cases.

TASTING NOTES

CHARDONNAY CARNEROS (★★★), RESERVE (★★★): Captures the essence of Carneros with its crisp, bright pear, apple, pineapple and citrus flavors. Oak adds another dimension but never dominates.

1993: Lightly fruity with an earthy edge to the pear and citrus notes. Good but nothing more. **84**

1992: Crisp and flinty, with a core of austere citrus and pineapple flavors. **87**

1991: Smooth and silky, with hints of pear, apple and nutmeg. **83**

Reserve 1992: Crisp and flinty, with tart citrus, pear, apple and pineapple flavors that are tightly reined in. Can stand short-term cellaring. Acacia's first Reserve. **89**

CHARDONNAY VARIOUS BOTTLINGS:

Carneros Marina Vineyard 1991: Strikes a nice balance between rich, toasty, buttery oak and spicy pear and hazelnut flavors. **89**

Napa Valley 1991: Elegant and stylish, with ripe, spicy pear, apple and citrus flavors and light oak shadings. **85**

PINOT NOIR CARNEROS (★★): Typically elegant, with ripe, spicy cherry and raspberry flavors and firm tannins.

1993: A touch earthy, with modest berry and cherry fruit and light oak shadings, picking up a green tannic edge on the finish. **83**

1991: Tight and firm, with a narrow band of cherry and herb flavors that finish on the tannic side. **83**

1990: Spicy, with forward plum, cherry and strawberry flavors that finish with a peppery note. **86**

1989: Funky, with earthy, gamy Pinot Noir flavors that lack focus. **75**

1988: Clean and supple, with ripe cherry, spice and strawberry notes. **85**

1987: Spicy, with earthy cherry and currant flavors that turn complex on the finish. **86**

1986: Intense and focused, with spicy black cherry and raspberry flavors that are complex and concentrated. **86**

1985: Simple and dried out, with light, spicy cherry notes. **80**

1984: Charming on release, it's now dried out, having dropped its fruit. **80**

PINOT NOIR CARNEROS ST. CLAIR VINEYARD RESERVE (★★★): The St. Clair bottling usually provides more

richness, intensity and depth, with distinctive berry and mineral flavors.

1992: Firm and a touch tannic, but the core of ripe cherry, berry and toasty oak folds together nicely on the finish. **87**

1991: Austere, but the cherry and berry flavors sneak through past the tannins. **83**

1990: Firm and ripe, with a tight core of plum and cherry flavors. **88**

1989: The best of the 1989 Acacia Pinots, it is light, with silky, delicate cherry, tea and berry notes. **85**

1988: Firm, rich and intense, with a tight band of cherry, spice and strawberry flavors. **87**

1987: A light St. Clair, with a lean, narrow band of spicy cherry flavors. **84**

1986: Deep, ripe, rich and intense, packed with dense, chewy, earthy currant and cherry flavors, finishing with pepper notes. **91**

1985: Elegant and spicy, with sage, cherry and currant flavors leading to a tight, tannic finish. **86**

1984: Very ripe, with bright black cherry and spice flavors that are elegant and lively. **87**

1983: Drying, with a gamy, meaty edge to the Pinot Noir flavors. Opens with aeration. **85**

1982: Lean and tart, with crisp, focused black cherry and spice flavors that turn tannic. **84**

1980: Minty and herbal, turning dry and tannic; the fruit has faded. **79**

1979: Sleek and elegant, with spicy cherry, earth and anise notes, framed by light oak shadings. **86**

PINOT NOIR VARIOUS BOTTLINGS:

Carneros Iund Vineyard 1991: Lean, spicy and minty, with earthy cola flavors that turn tannic on the finish. **82**

Carneros Iund Vineyard 1986: Young and vibrant, elegant and graceful, with sweet cherry and currant flavors that linger on the finish. **91**

Carneros Iund Vineyard 1985: Supple and elegant, with spicy toffee, cherry and cedar flavors. **87**

Carneros Iund Vineyard 1984: Supple and forward, a harmonious and complex Iund, with spice, dried cherry and orange peel flavors. **88**

Carneros Iund Vineyard 1983: Dense, with a gamy, volatile edge to the ripe cherry and wild berry aromas and flavors. **83**

Carneros Iund Vineyard 1981: Gamy and funky, a walk through the barnyard. **79**

Carneros Iund Vineyard 1980: Earthy and tannic, an odd wine. **70**

Carneros Lee Vineyard 1982: Mature and complex, with gamy, smoky spice, plum and dried cherry flavors. **88**

Carneros Lee Vineyard 1981: Tannic, thin and drying out, with just a trace of cherry flavor. **79**

Carneros Lee Vineyard 1979: Ripe and spicy, firmly tannic still, but displaying enough plum and cherry notes to hold your interest. **85**

Carneros Madonna Vineyard 1986: Silky and elegant, with spicy cherry, currant and anise flavors that are deep and complex. **87**

Carneros Madonna Vineyard 1985: Ripe and intense, rich and concentrated, with layers of herb, plum and spice; firmly tannic. **87**

Carneros Madonna Vineyard 1984: Mature, with tarry, earthy, gamy notes and only a trace of black cherry on the finish. **82**

Carneros Madonna Vineyard 1982: Mature and drying out, leaving a strong tannic aftertaste. **79**

Carneros Madonna Vineyard 1980: The focused plum flavors fan out on the palate, with a silky texture and smoky nuances. **87**

Carneros Winery Lake Vineyard 1982: Minty and herbal, with a sage edge to the ripe currant and dried cherry flavors. Still tannic. **85**

Carneros Winery Lake Vineyard 1981: Oaky, blunt and tannic, with an odd array of sage, menthol and plum flavors. **78**

Caviste Zinfandel Napa Valley (★★★): Early efforts aim for balance and supple texture, with light berry and spicy oak shadings.

1992: Captures the essence of Zin with its bright wild berry and cherry notes. **85**

1991: Pleasant cherry and raspberry flavors make it appealing. **86**

1990: Thick and concentrated, with plum, blueberry and black cherry flavors shaded by toast and tar notes. **86**

Adelaida Cellars
Paso Robles

F: 1981. **O:** John & Adree Munch, Don & Elizabeth Van Steenwyk. **W:** John Munch, Neil Collins. **S:** None.

Overall	$14-28	★★★

Wine Ratings

Cabernet Sauvignon Paso Robles	★★★
Chardonnay San Luis Obispo County	★★★
Chardonnay San Luis Obispo County Reserve	★★★
Zinfandel San Luis Obispo County	★★★

Winery Data

C: 6,000. **V:** 17 acres in Paso Robles. **G:** Cabernet Sauvignon (9 acres), Syrah (2). **P:** Cabernet Sauvignon (San Luis Obispo County), Chardonnay (San Luis Obispo County), Zinfandel (Paso Robles), Sangiovese (Paso Robles).

After operating out of leased space at several wineries, Adelaida Cellars is now a joint venture between founder-winemaker John Munch and his wife, Adree, and Don and Elizabeth Van Steenwyk. The winery is now on the Van Steenwyk's property in Paso Robles. Munch oversees production of the 6,000-case winery, which focuses on Cabernet, Chardonnay and Zinfandel, primarly from purchased grapes from San Luis Obispo and Paso Robles. The winery owns 17 acres and plans to produce Syrah.

Tasting Notes

Cabernet Sauvignon Paso Robles (★★★): While early efforts with Cabernet were erratic, the most recent vintages are superior, showing better focus and more finesse.

1988: Ripe and spicy, with a pretty core of rich currant and berry flavors that gain a touch of spicy oak before thinning out on the finish. A tasty wine that's crisp and elegant. **87**

1987: Very flavorful, rich and fruity, with beautifully articulated berry, currant and cherry flavors that emerge with the aromas of wildflowers and continue through the finish. Delicately laced with oak, firmly tannic, well balanced and complex. **89**

Chardonnay Various Bottlings (★★★): Recent vintages show harmony, richness and polish.

San Luis Obispo County 1991: Ripe, round, rich in texture and harmonious, with well defined honey, butterscotch and pear aromas and flavors that persist on the long finish. Has a definite style and remains graceful. **88**

Paso Robles 1990: Ripe and lively, with smooth, elegant pear, apple, spice and vanilla flavors that are well focused and persistent. Could use a little more richness and concentration, but overall it's a solid wine with character. **87**

San Luis Obispo County Reserve 1991: Serves up rich and complex honey, pear and butterscotch flavors, with hints of nutmeg, vanilla and spice. A big, full-blown wine that packs in lots of flavor; could use a little more finesse. **87**

ZINFANDEL VARIOUS BOTTLINGS (★★★):
San Luis Obispo County 1991: An oaky wine dominated by toasty, buttery flavors and a firm tannic edge, but the ripe cherry, tar and plum flavors peek through on the finish. **87**

San Luis Obispo County 1990: Has ripe, floral aromas, and cherry and berry flavors, but it takes on a slightly earthy, metallic flavor that detracts from the quality. Not too tannic. **82**

Paso Robles 1989: Tart and lively, with ripe berry, spice and oak notes that turn a bit rough and tannic on the finish. **83**

Paso Robles 1988: Very ripe and rich, with big, concentrated cherry, plum and spice flavors. Its high alcohol and deep color are reminiscent of a late-harvest wine, but it manages to stay in balance. **88**

ADLER FELS
Sonoma County
F: 1979. O: Ayn Ryan & David Coleman. W: David Coleman. S: None.

OVERALL	$9-14	★★
WINE RATINGS		
Chardonnay Sonoma County		★★
Chardonnay Sonoma County Coleman Reserve		★★
Gewürztraminer Sonoma County		★★
Sauvignon Blanc Sonoma County		★

WINERY DATA
C: 12,000. V: None. G: None. P: Chardonnay (Carneros), Chardonnay (Sonoma County), Chardonnay, Gewürztraminer, Sauvignon Blanc (Russian River Valley).

Owner-winemaker David Coleman, a graphic designer, is the free-thinking, free-spirited force behind Adler Fels, a winery in the mountains overlooking Sonoma Valley that he owns with his wife, Ayn Ryan. Despite Coleman's creativity, the winery has a checkered history, occasionally making sound wines but more often producing erratic or even bizarre styles. The winery's 12,000-case production, from purchased grapes, is divided more or less equally among Chardonnay, Sauvignon Blanc and Gewürztraminer. The Coleman Reserve Chardonnay has emerged as the best wine, with the 1991 offering intense, complex flavors and good balance. The 1991 Gewürztraminer is spicy, with a sweet grapefruit edge, and the 1991 Sauvignon Blanc (or Fumé Blanc as it's sometimes called) can be pungently varietal in the extreme.

TASTING NOTES

VARIOUS BOTTLINGS:
Chardonnay Sonoma County 1992: Marked by a strong muscat and spice edge, but it holds together with ripe pear and light oak shadings. **84**

Chardonnay Sonoma County Coleman Reserve 1992: Earthy, with a slight bitter oak edge which detracts from the ripe fruit flavors. **81**

Chardonnay Sonoma County Coleman Reserve 1991: A big, ripe and juicy Chardonnay with intense pear, spice, apple and grapefruit notes that take on an earthy, grassy edge on the finish. Serves up lots of flavor; one of the better recent Adler Fels Chardonnays. **86**

Gewürztraminer Sonoma County 1992: Smooth and refreshing, with modest grapefruit and spice aromas and flavors; the finish is slightly sweet. **84**

Sauvignon Blanc Sonoma County 1992: So floral it could pass as a Riesling, it's an appealing wine with nice fruit, too. **83**

ADOBE CANYON
This is a second label for Landmark Vineyards (see listing).

AHLGREN VINEYARD
Santa Cruz Mountains
F: 1976. O: Ahlgren Vineyard Inc. W: Dexter Ahlgren. S: D. Ahlgren.

OVERALL	$14-18	★

WINE RATINGS

Cabernet Sauvignon Santa Cruz		
Mountains Bates Ranch		★
Chardonnay Santa Cruz Mountains		
Buerge Vineyard		★
Chardonnay Santa Cruz Mountains		
Mayers Vineyard		★

WINERY DATA

C: 2,000. **V:** 0.5. **G:** None. **P:** Cabernet Sauvignon, Chardonnay, Sémillon (Santa Cruz Mountains and Monterey County).

This tiny, 2,000-case, family-owned and operated winery specializes in small lots of Cabernet, Chardonnay, Merlot, Sémillon and Zinfandel primarily from purchased grapes from the Santa Cruz Mountains, including Cabernet and Merlot from Bates Ranch, Monterey and Santa Clara Valley. In my limited tastings, the wines have been below average in quality. The Cabernets are tough and tannic, built for cellaring, but I wonder if they will ever outgrow their rugged personalities. The Chardonnays, which carry vineyard designations from Buerge Vineyard and Mayers Vineyard in 1991, are both earthy to a fault. A 1992 Zinfandel was planned.

TASTING NOTES

VARIOUS BOTTLINGS:

Cabernet Sauvignon Santa Cruz Mountains Bates Ranch 1988: Tannic and tough, with a moderate level of oak, cherry and spice aromas and flavors struggling to get past the layers of astringency. Might be fine after 1996. **76**

Chardonnay Santa Cruz Mountains Buerge Vineyard 1991: Crisp and earthy, a lean wine with modest peach and mineral flavors. **79**

Chardonnay Santa Cruz Mountains Mayers Vineyard 1991: Earthy mineral aromas and sweet pineapple flavors are a little jarring. **73**

ALBAN VINEYARDS
Arroyo Grande, San Luis Obispo County
F: 1986. **O:** Alban Vineyards Inc. **W:** John Alban. **S:** None.

OVERALL	$18-32	★★

WINE RATINGS

Roussanne San Luis Obispo County	★★
Viognier San Luis Obispo County	★★

WINERY DATA

C: 2,000. **V:** 65 acres in Edna Valley. **G:** Viognier (32 acres), Syrah (15), Roussanne (15), Grenache (3). **P:** Viognier (Central Coast).

Winemaker John Alban is an enthusiastic Rhône Ranger. His 65-acre vineyard in Edna Valley is planted to Viognier (32 acres), Syrah (15 acres), Roussanne (15 acres) and Grenache (3 acres). The first vintages of Viognier are good, tart and spicy, while the Roussanne shows riper pear and peach flavors. A 1992 Syrah was in the works and may have the most potential. Total production is about 2,000 cases.

TASTING NOTES

ROUSSANNE SAN LUIS OBISPO COUNTY (★★): Variable, but first vintages captures the grape's varietal character.
1992: Lean and flinty, with hints of peach and pear flavors that stay with you. Well balanced and crisp, with a fruity finish. **84**
1991: A ripe and complex Roussanne, with pretty toast, pear and honey flavors that are spicy and linger on the finish. **86**

VIOGNIER SAN LUIS OBISPO COUNTY (★★): Shows off the grape's aroma, but is lean and trim in body.
1992: Aromatic and spicy, but it turns lean and crisp on the palate, with tropical fruit, pear and citrus notes. The finish is crisp and clean. **84**
1991: Tight, lean and simple, with a narrow band of tart apple and spicy notes. Good but lacks richness and depth. Tastes like young vines. **82**

ALDERBROOK WINERY
Dry Creek Valley
F: 1981. **O:** George & Dorothy Gillemot. **W:** Bob Cabral. **S:** None.

OVERALL $9-15   ★★

WINE RATINGS

Chardonnay Dry Creek Valley	★★
Meritage White Dry Creek Valley Duet	★★
Sauvignon Blanc Dry Creek Valley	★★
Sémillon Dry Creek Valley	★★
Zinfandel Dry Creek Valley	★★

WINERY DATA

C: 22,000. **V:** 63 acres in Dry Creek Valley. **G:** Chardonnay (50 acres), Sauvignon Blanc (13). **P:** Cabernet Sauvignon (Dry Creek Valley), Chardonnay (Dry Creek Valley), Merlot (Sonoma Valley), Mourvèdre (Russian River Valley), Muscat Canelli (Sonoma Valley), Sémillon (Dry Creek Valley), Syrah (Russian River Valley), Zinfandel (Russian River Valley).

This Healdsburg-based winery changed ownership in 1991, when it was purchased by George and Dorothy Gillemot. Previously it was owned by Mark Rafanelli (cousin of David Rafanelli of A. Rafanelli Winery), John Grace, the vineyard manager, and Philip Staley, a dentist who oversaw winemaking. The initial focus was on white varietals grown in western Sonoma County, but the winery plans to add Russian River Pinot Noir and Syrah along with Zinfandel from Teldeschi Ranch to its lineup. So far the wines have been sound and well made, but have not risen above average in quality. The 1990 Dry Creek Chardonnay is firm and intense, with modest oak and pear flavors. The 1990 Duet, a blend of Sémillon and Sauvignon Blanc, is light and grassy. The 1990 Sauvignon Blanc is crisp, with herb and apple notes, while the 1990 Sémillon shows the most depth and flavor, with peach, pear and buttery oak flavors. Production in 1994 was 22,000 cases.

TASTING NOTES

CHARDONNAY DRY CREEK VALLEY (★★): Made in an understated style that could use more generosity.
1993: Marked by an herbal edge, with just a hint of pear and spice coming through. **83**
1992: Appealing for nectarine and tangerine edge flavors and spicy nuances. **85**
1990: Hard, firm and intense, with oaky pear, honey and melon flavors that stay with you. **82**

MERITAGE WHITE DRY CREEK VALLEY DUET (★★): No consistent style, but Sauvignon Blanc-based wines can be that way.

1992: Smooth and flavorful, silky at the core and jumping with green berry, citrus and anise flavors. Finishes lively. **87**
1990: Light, fruity, grassy and fresh, this soft, simple wine, based on Sauvignon Blanc, seems almost sweet, or at least exuberantly fruity. **81**

SAUVIGNON BLANC DRY CREEK VALLEY (★★): Variable, with no discernable stylistic pattern.
1994: Plays its lively pear and green apple fruit against a nice thread of spicy oak, weaving a touch of green herb through it all. **85**
1993: Soft and fruity, generous with its spicy orange and pear fruit. **82**
1990: A crisp, straightforward wine, with apple and herb flavors and good balance. **80**

SÉMILLON DRY CREEK VALLEY (★★): Variable, in a simple style.
1993: Bright and fruity, a friendly wine with melon and tobacco flavors. **83**
1992: Crisp in texture, with tobacco and slightly weedy notes dominating the fruit. **78**
1990: Fruity, round and aromatic, with buttery vanilla overtones to the basic peach and pear flavors. Nicely balanced and flavorful. **85**

ZINFANDEL DRY CREEK VALLEY (★★):
1993: Tight and intense, with a sharp edge to the earthy raspberry and currant flavors. A big and rambunctious style that can stand short-term cellaring in hopes it will soften. **85**

ALEXANDER VALLEY FRUIT & TRADING CO.
Alexander Valley

F: 1984. **O:** Steve & Candace Sommer. **W:** Steve Sommer, Mike Duffy. **S:** Clavage.

OVERALL $9-12   ★

WINE RATINGS

Dessert Wine Alexander Valley	NR
Zinfandel Dry Creek Valley	NR

WINERY DATA

C: 8,000. **V:** 60 acres in Alexander Valley, Dry Creek Valley. **G:** Chardonnay (10 acres), Zinfandel (30), Carignane (10), Merlot (5), Gamay (5). **P:** None.

This Alexander Valley winery, not to be confused with nearby Alexander Valley Vineyards, produces 8,000 cases of Carignane, Chardonnay, a red table wine called Clavage (a blend of Merlot, Carignane and Zinfandel) and Zinfandel. So far the wines have been of ordinary quality. The 1992 Dry Creek Zinfandel is lean and tannic, with a narrow band of fruit flavors.

TASTING NOTES

VARIOUS BOTTLINGS (NR):

Dessert Wine Alexander Valley 1990: Ripe and sweet, with hints of ripe cherry and plum jam flavors. Supple and medium-bodied. **82**

Zinfandel Dry Creek Valley 1992: Lean and tannic, this wine has a narrow band of spicy strawberry flavors, but it turns diluted on the finish, where the tannins win out. **81**

ALEXANDER VALLEY VINEYARDS
Alexander Valley
F: 1975. **O:** Harry Wetzel. **W:** Hank Wetzel. **S:** None.

OVERALL	$8-15	★★★

WINE RATINGS

Cabernet Sauvignon Alexander Valley	★★★
Cabernet Sauvignon Alexander Valley Wetzel Family Estate	★★★
Chardonnay Alexander Valley	★★
Chardonnay Alexander Valley Wetzel Family Estate	★★
Gewürztraminer Alexander Valley	★★
Merlot Alexander Valley	★★★
Merlot Alexander Valley Wetzel Family Estate	★★
Pinot Noir Alexander Valley	★★
Pinot Noir Alexander Valley Wetzel Family Estate	★★
Riesling Alexander Valley	★★
Zinfandel Alexander Valley Sin Zin	★

WINERY DATA
C: 40,000. **V:** 120 acres in Alexander Valley. **G:** Chardonnay (45 acres), Cabernet Sauvignon (45), Merlot (25), Zinfandel (5). **P:** None.

Alexander Valley Vineyards owes much of its reputation to its well crafted, affordable wines. The Wetzel family came to the valley in 1962 and planted 120 acres of estate vineyards over the next decade. They built the handsome winery in time for the 1975 harvest. Today the Wetzels produce 40,000 cases a year from vineyards planted to Cabernet (45 acres), Chardonnay (45 acres), Merlot (25 acres) and Zinfandel (5 acres).

The winery's Cabernet is its best wine. The Chardonnay usually is pleasantly fruity, but not especially complex. The 1990 features subtle pear, oak and honey notes. Merlot has been highly variable; it can be earthy and funky, but the 1990 and 1991 are solid, with ripe, bright berry and currant flavors flanked by spicy oak. Pinot Noir too has radical stylistic and quality swings, with some vintages tasting simple, grapey and tannic, while others are riper, with herb and cherry notes. The Sin Zin Zinfandel carries a bizarre label and is almost always rustic and tannic, and can be astringent and overly mature even on release. The winery produces an occasional Chenin Blanc, Gewürztraminer and Riesling of modest proportions in an off-dry style; these wines are appealing for their pure fruitiness.

TASTING NOTES

CABERNET SAUVIGNON ALEXANDER VALLEY (★★★), WETZEL FAMILY ESTATE (★★★): The winery was a rising star in the mid-1980s on the basis of its rich, complex 1984, 1985 and 1986 vintages, but the wines of late have been more elegant and refined, less flavorful and, to my taste, less exciting. These wines are best on release and for five to eight years, although the 1984 remains a big and potent wine.

1993: Made in a lighter style, with simple berry and cherry notes. Good but lacking the depth and flavor of the best. **80**

1992: Firm and well focused, with a medium-weight band of herb-laced currant and cherry fruit, finishing with mild tannins. **87**

1991: Elegant, with herb, blackberry and spice flavors and soft, mild tannins. **85**

1989: Firm, with vibrant currant and berry flavors shaded by toast and spice notes and well integrated tannins. **86**

1988: Smooth and flavorful, with well defined plum and currant aromas and flavors. **88**

1987: Elegant, with herb, cedar and currant flavors, echoing plum and coffee on the finish. **87**

1986: Firm and lean, with good depth to the black cherry and plum flavors. **86**

1985: Sleek and elegant, with complex herb, cedar, mineral and ripe plum flavors that are sharply focused. **87**

1984: Rich, thick and exotic, with meaty currant, spice and mineral flavors. This plush wine remains the best of this producer's early efforts. **93**

1983: Solid, with concentrated black cherry, currant, herb and cigar box nuances. Finishes with firm tannins. **88**

1982: Mature, but holding its ripe plum, cherry and cedar flavors. Still complex. **87**

1981: Mature but still displaying plum, spice, cedar and anise notes that are pleasing. **85**

1980: Fading, but it still has appealing cigar box, plum and herb flavors. **82**

1979: Rich and full-bodied, past its peak but still very flavorful, with dried plum, cherry and herb flavors. **84**

1978: Herbal, vegetal flavors dominate this mature, fading wine. **78**

1976: In two recent tastings, this wine showed unpleasant, odd, pungent, earthy, overripe flavors. **60**

1975: Despite some pretty aromas, it's thin, tart and fading, with faint hints of ripe plum and spicy herb flavors that linger on the palate. **75**

Wetzel Family Estate 1992: Lean and earthy, with a cedar and tobacco edge to the plum and berry notes. Needs short-term cellaring until 1997. **86**

Wetzel Family Estate 1991: Ripe and fruity, with appealing spice, mint, cherry and currant flavors. **84**

Wetzel Family Estate 1990: There's a tinge of bell pepper to the currant flavors. Turns supple on the finish. **88**

CHARDONNAY ALEXANDER VALLEY (★★), WETZEL FAMILY ESTATE (★★): Pleasantly fruity if consistently simple in style, easy drinking but not distinctive.

1990: Crisp and elegant, with subtle oak, pear and honey notes that stay with you. **83**

Wetzel Family Estate 1992: Pleasantly fruity with tart green apple and subtle grassy notes. **84**

Wetzel Family Estate 1991: This fresh, citrusy wine shows a lively streak of grapefruit flavor at the center, plus grace notes of vanilla and pear. Has a nice sense of balance without excess weight and the finish is smooth. **88**

GEWÜRZTRAMINER ALEXANDER VALLEY (★★): Ranges from fair to good, usually quite simple with spicy flavors and a touch of sweetness.

1992: Light, fresh and spicy, with appealing green apple and spice aromas and flavors. **80**

MERLOT ALEXANDER VALLEY (★★★), WETZEL FAMILY ESTATE (★★): Solid with a good core of ripe fruit, but it lacks the extra dimensions one might hope for.

1992: Intense and focused, with a supple core of berry, cherry and anise flavors and mild tannins. **87**

1991: Youthful and vibrant, with wild blackberry and blueberry flavors that turn rich and earthy, picking up an anise note. **86**

1990: A lovely, balanced wine that's ripe, rich and fleshy, with a pretty core of spicy black cherry and currant flavors framed by toasty, buttery oak notes. **87**

1989: Pleasantly ripe and fruity, with hints of herb, cherry and currant flavors. Also has a distinct oaky edge but isn't too tannic. **84**

Wetzel Family Estate 1992: Dark, tight and compact, with a firm core of currant, cedar and tobacco. Needs time to soften a bit and let the tannins subside. **86**

Wetzel Family Estate 1991: Earthy, mulchy flavors take most of the charm out of this sturdy, chunky wine. **77**

PINOT NOIR ALEXANDER VALLEY (★★), WETZEL FAMILY ESTATE (★★): Varies in quality from simple and ordinary to simple and fruity.

1989: Very firm and almost harsh, with earthy flavors and little fruit to rescue it. Tasted twice, with consistent notes. **65**

1987: Grapey in flavor, this wine is tannic and blunt. Woody and tannic on the finish. **74**

Wetzel Family Estate 1990: Simple and fruity, with wild blackberry and spice notes. **83**

RIESLING ALEXANDER VALLEY (★★): Emphasizes the grape's fruitiness, but often lacks the structure and acidity needed for backbone.

1991: Generous apple, peach and floral aromas and flavors are fresh and lively in this soft, modestly sweet Riesling. There is enough of an acidic backbone to keep it in balance this time. **86**

ZINFANDEL ALEXANDER VALLEY SIN ZIN (★): A curiosity for a winery that makes mostly reliable, well crafted wines. This one's often overly mature, earthy and leathery, absent the bright lively fruit that makes this varietal so exciting at its best.

1989: Tough and astringent, with a modicum of berry and spice flavors fighting through the haze of tannin. **76**

ROBERT ALLISON
This is a second label of Estate William Baccala (see listing).

ALTAMURA WINERY AND VINEYARDS
Napa Valley
F: 1985. **O:** Frank & Karen Altamura. **W:** Frank Altamura. **S:** None.

OVERALL	$25	★★★

WINE RATINGS

Cabernet Sauvignon Napa Valley	★★★
Chardonnay Napa Valley	★★★

WINERY DATA
C: 2,000. **V:** 61 acres in Napa Valley. **G:** Cabernet Sauvignon (15 acres), Merlot (10), Sangiovese (6), Italian Types (6), Sauvignon Blanc (20), Chardonnay (6). **P:** None.

After a solid start in 1985, with complex, concentrated Chardonnays grown in family-owned estate vineyards north of Napa, Frank Altamura is heading in a new direction. In 1994 he and his wife, Karen, ended a business relationship with Altamura's father, George, who initially financed the 2,000-case winery, and began planting a new vineyard in the Wooden Valley area east of Napa near the Solano County line. There they plan to focus more on red wines, including Cabernet, Sangiovese and other varieties. The early Altamura Chardonnays were tight and concentrated, designed to age, but eventually the vintages fell behind the market and sales slowed. The winery released three Cabernet Sauvignons, the 1988, 1989 and 1990, all of which feature ripe cherry and plum flavors wrapped in spicy, toasty oak.

TASTING NOTES

CABERNET SAUVIGNON NAPA VALLEY (★★★):
1990: Showy and elegant, with ripe, smooth supple black cherry, currant and vanilla-tinged oak shadings, finishing with mild, polished tannins. **88**
1989: Light and simple, with coffee, currant and plum notes. **83**
1988: Ripe plum and cherry flavors dressed in pretty, spicy oak. **85**

CHARDONNAY NAPA VALLEY (★★★):
1990: Packs in lots of flavor, with ripe pear and pineapple notes shaded by toasty buttery oak and a long, flavorful finish. Complex and concentrated. **88**

AMADOR FOOTHILL WINERY
Shenandoah Valley
F: 1980. **O:** Ben Zeitman & Katie Quinn. **W:** Katie Quinn. **S:** None.

OVERALL	$8-12	★★

WINE RATINGS

Sauvignon Blanc Shenandoah Valley Amador Fumé	★
Zinfandel Fiddletown Eschen Vineyard	★★
Zinfandel Shenandoah Valley Ferrero Vineyard	★
Zinfandel Shenandoah Valley Grandpère Vineyard	★

WINERY DATA
C: 10,000. **V:** 10 acres in Shenandoah Valley. **G:** Sauvignon Blanc (4 acres), Sémillon (2), Sangiovese (4). **P:** Zinfandel (Shenandoah Valley), Zinfandel (Fiddletown).

East of Plymouth in the Sierra foothills, Ben Zeitman and Katie Quinn operate Amador Foothill Winery, a 10,000-case business that specializes in Zinfandel, including vineyard-designated wines that reflect Zinfandel's austerity in the Sierra. The best is the Eschen Vineyard 1990, which is rustic and earthy, while the 1991 magnifies those earthy, rustic features. The Ferrero Vineyard 1990 is more floral, with berry notes, and a Grandpère Vineyard 1990 is tart, lean and earthy. A 1992 Fumé Blanc is tart and earthy, and the winery planned to bottle a Sangiovese with the 1992 vintage.

TASTING NOTES

VARIOUS BOTTLINGS:

Sauvignon Blanc Shenandoah Valley Amador Fumé 1992: Crisp and refreshing, a solid wine with an earthy edge to the decent pear fruit. **82**

Zinfandel Fiddletown Eschen Vineyard 1991: A solid if rustic Zin with earthy wild berry and spice notes, but it lacks finesse and polish. **78**

Zinfandel Fiddletown Eschen Vineyard 1990: This wine is austere and earthy, but a glimmer of berry and cherry aromas and flavors sneaks past the tannins on the tarry finish. **82**

Zinfandel Shenandoah Valley Ferrero Vineyard 1990: Ripe, warm and spicy, with floral and berry flavors that are balanced and lingering. **82**

Zinfandel Shenandoah Valley Grandpère Vineyard 1990: Tart, lean and earthy, but with a hint of cherry and cranberry flavors showing through the tannins. **83**

S. ANDERSON VINEYARD

Stags Leap District, Napa Valley

F: 1971. **O:** Carl G. Anderson. **W:** Jac Cole, Carol Anderson. **S:** None.

OVERALL	$18-46	★★★

WINE RATINGS

Cabernet Sauvignon Stags Leap District Richard Chambers Vineyard	★★★★
Chardonnay Carneros	★★★
Chardonnay Stags Leap District	★★★
Chardonnay Stags Leap District Proprietor's Reserve	★★★
Sparkling Wine Napa Valley	★★★

WINERY DATA

C: 10,000. **V:** 100 acres in Stags Leap District, Carneros. **G:** Chardonnay (60 acres), Pinot Noir (40). **P:** Cabernet Sauvignon, Cabernet Franc, Merlot (Stags Leap District).

The evolution of S. Anderson Vineyard reflects the strengths and character of its vineyards. This Stags Leap District winery is best known as a sparkling wine producer, but it also makes excellent Cabernet Sauvignon from Richard Chambers Vineyard and well crafted Chardonnays from its own vineyards. Dentist Stanley Anderson, who died in 1994, and his wife, Carol, started S. Anderson Vineyard in the 1970s. On weekends they commuted from their home in Pasadena to work on the vineyard. By 1979 they were making small lots of Chardonnay from their Yountville vineyard. Production of Chardonnay (1,850 cases) and Cabernet (600) is still small-scale compared to sparkling wine (7,500 cases), which the Andersons make in three styles—Brut, Blanc de noirs and rosé—all of which are consistently well made. The Andersons own 32 acres in Stags Leap, most of it planted to Chardonnay, with the grapes for their sparkling wines coming from their 68 acres in Carneros, planted to Pinot Noir and Chardonnay. Cabernet, however, is the star. The Andersons' son John is now president, while Carol still oversees the sparkling wines.

TASTING NOTES

CABERNET SAUVIGNON STAGS LEAP DISTRICT RICHARD CHAMBERS VINEYARD (★★★★): Supple and stylish, with rich flavors, smooth tannins, lots of buttery oak and a wonderful sense of harmony and finesse. The first five vintages are remarkably consistent in style. Very appealing to drink on release.

1991: Compact and vibrant, with an herbaceous edge to the rich vanilla, currant and wild berry flavors, finishing with firm tannins. **91**

1990: Tightly wound, but the currant, berry and spice flavors run deep, rich and supple, gaining complexity on the finish. **91**

1989: A deep, densely flavored 1989 that delivers intense black cherry, plum and currant flavors, shaded by vanilla, nutmeg and chocolate notes. **90**

CHARDONNAY VARIOUS BOTTLINGS (★★★): The most recent vintages have been leaner and trimmer and not as impressive as those from the late 1980s, which are not only rich and concentrated but ageworthy.

Carneros 1993: Young and vibrant, with a citrus-grapefruit edge to the pear and spice flavors. **86**

Stags Leap District 1992: Lean and firm, with a coarse, earthy edge to the ripe pear and pineapple flavors. **85**

Stags Leap District 1990: Crisp and light, with a decidedly floral edge to the peach and pear aromas and flavors. **82**

Stags Leap District Proprietor's Reserve 1991: Smooth and supple, with a pretty range of vanilla, nutmeg and pear flavors, turning silky on the finish. **89**

Anderson's Conn Valley Vineyards
St. Helena, Napa Valley
F: 1983. **O:** Gus & Phyllis Anderson, Todd & Dana Anderson. **W:** Todd Anderson. **S:** None.

OVERALL	$25-30	★★★★

WINE RATINGS

Cabernet Sauvignon Napa Valley	
Estate Reserve	★★★★
Pinot Noir Napa Valley	★★
Pinot Noir Napa Valley	
Valhalla Vineyards	★★

WINERY DATA
C: 5,300. **V:** 28 acres in Napa Valley. **G:** Cabernet Sauvignon (21 acres), Merlot (3), Cabernet Franc (1), Petite Verdot (1), Malbec (1), Sangiovese (1). **P:** Pinot Noir (Napa Valley).

This is definitely a winery to watch for Cabernet lovers. Founded in 1983 by Gus Anderson in Conn Valley, a narrow valley east of Napa Valley, this family-owned and operated winery specializes in complex and sumptuous Cabernets grown in a 28-acre vineyard. Legally Conn Valley is part of the larger Napa Valley appellation, but this is a distinctive vineyard yielding distinctive wines. Production is about 5,000 cases, including a Pinot Noir from purchased grapes. Anderson's son Todd is the winemaker.

Tasting Notes

Cabernet Sauvignon Napa Valley Estate Reserve (★★★★): Dark, rich and well oaked, with supple herb, black currant and spice notes and firm but polished tannins. Should age well, but they're very approachable early on. Both the 1988 and 1989 are better than the vintage, while the 1990 and 1991 are backward and unevolved, with their best yet to come.
1991: Tannic and earthy, with a leathery edge to the currant and cherry flavors, but it softens on the finish. Best after 1997. **88**
1990: Firm and intense, with rich, chewy cherry, chocolate and buttery oak flavors. Packs in lots of flavor, picking up mineral notes on the finish. Best after 1997. **90**
1989: Smooth and ripe, with generous plum and currant aromas and flavors that finish with toast, spice and fruit notes. **88**

1988: Rich and supple, with velvety tannins and warm currant, chocolate, anise, cherry and nutmeg flavors. Very appealing. **90**

Pinot Noir Napa Valley (★★): Also well oaked, it's more variable than the Cabernet, but it has a sense of style. Reminiscent of the Caymus Pinot Noir.
1992: Smoky and meaty, with a spicy, peppery edge to the ripe plum and cherry flavors. **85**
1989: Big, ripe and tannic, packing in lots of plum and currant flavors up front, but it fades on the finish. **84**

Antelope Valley Winery
Lancaster, Los Angeles County
F: 1979. **O:** Frank S. Donato. **W:** Cecil McLester. **S:** None.

OVERALL	$8-9	★

WINE RATINGS

Chardonnay Central Coast	★
Merlot California	
Bien Nacido Vineyards	★

WINERY DATA
C: 5,000. **V:** 6 acres in Los Angeles County. **G:** Merlot (3 acres), Cabernet Sauvignon (3). **P:** None.

This small, 5,000-case winery in Lancaster was founded in 1979 and is now owned by Frank S. Donato. My most recent experience is with two 1990 wines, a Merlot marked by earthy, gamy flavors and a Chardonnay that lacked appeal. The winery also makes a Dante's Reserve Cabernet and dessert wines.

Araujo Estate Wines
Calistoga, Napa Valley
F: 1990. **O:** Bart & Daphne Araujo. **W:** Tony Soter. **S:** None.

OVERALL	$40	★★★★★

WINE RATINGS

Cabernet Sauvignon Napa Valley	
Eisele Vineyard	★★★★★

WINERY DATA

C: 4,500. V: 36 acres in Napa Valley. G: Cabernet Sauvignon, Petite Verdot, Sangiovese, Sauvignon Musque, Viognier (Napa Valley). P: None.

Since the 1970s, Eisele Vineyard has proven to be one of California's greatest vineyards. Cabernet lovers have come to expect grand wines from this famous property at the foot of the Palisades mountain southeast of Calistoga. Through the years this vineyard has been the source of many stunning wines, primarily from the Joseph Phelps Vineyards (see listing). Along with the likes of Caymus Vineyard, Martha's Vineyard and Diamond Creek's three vineyards, Eisele Vineyard has a distinguished track record for consistently excellent, distinctive and ageworthy wines. In years such as 1974 (under the Conn Creek label), 1975, 1978, 1979, and 1985, these wines show uncommon richness, with thick, chewy, earthy tannins and a complex core of currant, berry and mineral flavors. They are also amazingly ageworthy, keeping their youthful, vibrant personalities for up to two decades.

In 1989, founders Milt and Barbara Eisele sold the vineyard to financier William Farley at a time when the vineyard needed replanting. In 1990, Farley decided not to pursue wine, and sold it to Bart and Daphne Araujo for $3 million. Bart Araujo, a former home builder, intends to build on the vineyard's ability to produce deeply concentrated and enormously complex wines. Upon acquiring the vineyard, the Araujos began a major overhaul of the vineyard, replanting many vines, adding new grape varieties (Petite Verdot, Syrah, Sangiovese, Sauvignon Musque and Viognier), building a handsome new winery and hiring well respected winemaking consultant Tony Soter to oversee the wine. The first vintage under the Araujo Estate label, the 1991 showed more finesse and polish than the 1991 Phelps Eisele (the winery's last bottling), but also the signature dark color, wonderful perfumed aromas and layers of currant, mineral and earthy nuances. Through several tastings, from barrel to bottle, it continues to show more depth and complexity. Plans are to build production to 4,500 cases

and may include a proprietary white wine as well as other varietals such as Sangiovese and Syrah.

TASTING NOTES

CABERNET SAUVIGNON NAPA VALLEY EISELE VINEYARD (★★★★★): Magnificent debut, with dark, rich, complex fruit and supple, polished tannins, marked by the characteristic mineral edge.

1991: A rich, concentrated, deeply perfumed wine, packed with currant and mineral flavors and framed by light oak notes. Finishes with a long, full, broad aftertaste and its color is very dark. Best from 1997 to 2004. **93**

ARCIERO WINERY
Paso Robles

F: 1985. O: Frank Arciero Sr., Phil Arciero, Frank Arciero Jr., & Kerry H. Vix. W: Malcolm Seibley. S: Monte Verde, Candlewood Cellars.

OVERALL	$7-14	★★

WINE RATINGS	
Cabernet Sauvignon Paso Robles	★
Chardonnay Paso Robles	★★
Monte Verde Cabernet Sauvignon California Proprietor's Reserve	NR
Monte Verde Chardonnay Central Coast Proprietor's Reserve	NR
Nebbiolo Paso Robles	★★
Zinfandel Paso Robles	★★

WINERY DATA

C: 110,000. V: 502 acres in Paso Robles. G: Chardonnay (193 acres), Merlot (58), Sangiovese (5), Cabernet Franc (2), Chenin Blanc (38), Muscat Canelli (16), Italian Type (30), Petite Sirah (39), Sauvignon Blanc (16), Zinfandel (105). P: None.

This is a big, ambitious vineyard and winery operation in Paso Robles, with some 502 acres in vines and producing more than 100,000 cases, but so far the wines, while modestly priced, have been rather ordinary, inconsistent and uninspiring. The Arciero family, large cement contractors in Southern California, own the winery and vineyard, which is planted primarily to Chardonnay (193 acres and the best wine so far), Merlot (58 acres), Chenin Blanc (38 acres), Petite Sirah (39 acres) and Zinfandel

(105 acres). Perhaps as the vines mature, better wine-making will lead to superior wines.

TASTING NOTES

VARIOUS BOTTLINGS:

Cabernet Sauvignon Paso Robles 1990: Lightly fruity, but surprisingly big, dry tannins dominate. Has a hollowness in the middle. **78**

Chardonnay Paso Robles 1992: Crisp and flinty, with simple citrus and pineapple flavors. **79**

Chardonnay Paso Robles 1991: Ripe and complex, showing real character, balancing green apple, spice and leesy aromas and flavors into a nice mouthful. Finish is solid and inviting. **86**

Chardonnay Paso Robles 1990: Light and bright, with pleasant green apple and delicate butter aromas and flavors and a racy, fresh finish. **84**

Nebbiolo Paso Robles 1991: Soft, simple and fruity, an easy-going red wine that bears little resemblance to an Italian Nebbiolo. **79**

Zinfandel Paso Robles 1992: Intense with jammy aromas but not the richness on the palate, where the earthy wild berry flavors are pleasant enough. **83**

Zinfandel Paso Robles 1988: The ripe aromas smell good, but the flavors turn watery, with hints of berry and earth. **77**

Monte Verde Cabernet Sauvignon California Proprietor's Reserve 1988: Aromatic, crisp and flavorful, with modest currant, black cherry, spice and cedar aromas and flavors up front, but it thins out on the finish. **79**

Monte Verde Cabernet Sauvignon California Proprietor's Reserve 1987: A simple wine with fresh, very fruity and direct flavors of berries and black cherries, intense enough to leave a fruity aftertaste. The texture is supple and soft. **80**

Monte Verde Chardonnay Central Coast Proprietor's Reserve 1990: Simple and sturdy, with modest, appealing green apple and earth aromas and flavors. **78**

ARIES

This is a second label for Robert Sinskey Vineyards (see listing).

ARMIDA WINERY
Russian River Valley
F: 1990. O: Robert Frugoli. W: Frank Churchill
S: None.

OVERALL	$10-13	★★

WINE RATINGS
Chardonnay Russian River Valley	★★
Merlot Russian River Valley	★★
Pinot Noir Russian River Valley	★

WINERY DATA
C: 6,000. V: 70 acres in Russian River Valley. G: Chardonnay (20 acres), Pinot Noir (35), Merlot (15). P: None.

Owner Robert Frugoli is a long-time Russian River Valley grape grower who turned winemaker in 1990, when he established Armida using grapes from his 70 acres of vines. He has released three wines, the best being a 1991 Chardonnay that shows promise, with its subtlety and finesse, but the 1992 is overly reliant on oak. Pinot Noir follows a similar pattern: the 1991 shows tight currant and cherry notes, but the 1992 is a gamy, earthy wine. The Merlot 1990 is smooth and elegant, with herb and currant flavors. Production is 6,000 cases, with plans to expand.

TASTING NOTES

VARIOUS BOTTLINGS:

Chardonnay Russian River Valley 1992: Relies a little too heavily on coarse oak, which overshadows the pear and nectarine flavors. **82**

Chardonnay Russian River Valley 1991: A subtle and polished wine, intense and flavorful, with spicy pear, honey and butter notes that are supple and complex. The finish is smooth and elegant, with a spicy edge. **88**

Chardonnay Russian River Valley 1990: Soft and generous, with appealing green apple, orange and spice aromas and flavors. The finish is simple and pleasant. **81**

Merlot Russian River Valley 1990: Smooth and elegant, with medium-bodied currant, spice and plum notes, light oak shadings and fine tannins. Balanced and ready to drink, but may age well too, because it's intense and the flavors have depth. **86**

Pinot Noir Russian River Valley 1992: Earthy, hollow and gamy, it lacks richness and substance, turning dry and tannic on the finish. **72**

Pinot Noir Russian River Valley 1991: Tight and oaky, but with a crisp core of currant and cherry flavors underneath. **84**

ARMSTRONG RIDGE

This is a second label for Korbel Champagne Cellars (see listing).

ARROWOOD VINEYARDS & WINERY

Sonoma Valley

F: 1986. **O:** Arrowood Vineyards & Winery Inc. **W:** Richard L. Arrowood, Michel Berthoud. **S:** Domaine Du Grand Archer.

OVERALL	$9-35	★★★★★

WINE RATINGS

Cabernet Sauvignon Sonoma County	★★★★
Cabernet Sauvignon Sonoma County Réserve Spéciale	★★★
Chardonnay Sonoma County	★★★★
Chardonnay Sonoma County Cuvée Michel Berthoud	★★★★
Chardonnay Sonoma County Réserve Spéciale	★★★★★
Merlot Sonoma County	★★★★
Viognier Russian River Valley Saralee's Vineyard	★★★
White Riesling Russian River Valley Oak Meadow Vineyard Select Late Harvest	★★★★
Domaine du Grand Archer Cabernet Sauvignon Sonoma County	★★
Domaine du Grand Archer Merlot Sonoma County	★★

WINERY DATA

C: 20,000. **V:** 5 acres in Sonoma Valley. **G:** N/A. **P:** Cabernet Sauvignon (Dry Creek Valley, Sonoma Valley, Alexander Valley, Knights Valley), Chardonnay (Sonoma Valley, Russian River Valley), Riesling and Viognier (Russian River Valley).

Veteran winemaker Richard Arrowood and his wife, Alis, established this winery in 1986, after Richard spent 12 years as winemaker at Chateau St. Jean. Today,

Arrowood Vineyards & Winery lies a few miles south of St. Jean in Sonoma Valley. Arrowood oversaw winemaking at both wineries before severing his ties with St. Jean in 1990. Not surprisingly, Arrowood has built on his strengths: his keen knowledge of Sonoma County vineyards (he's a native of Santa Rosa); a long association with St. Jean (where he made nearly a dozen vineyard-designated Chardonnays, Fumé Blancs, Rieslings and extraordinary dessert wines); and a knack for producing complex and engaging Chardonnays, primarily from Robert Young and Belle Terre vineyards.

After a decade on his own, this much is clear: he hasn't lost his touch. The 20,000-case Arrowood winery is diversified, but focuses on Chardonnay (6,000 cases), Cabernet (10,000 cases) and Merlot (3,000 cases), along with Réserve Spéciale bottlings (about 200 cases of each). These three varietals are typically blends of grapes grown in Sonoma County. The Arrowood Sonoma County Chardonnay and Réserve Spéciale are ripe and fruity, with complex flavors and light oak shadings, relying on grapes grown in the cooler climes of western Sonoma, including Russian River and Sonoma valleys. Arrowood has a good handle on Cabernet and Merlot as well. These two wines also carry the Sonoma County appellation, and usually feature grapes from Knights Valley, Alexander Valley and Sonoma Valley. Smaller lots of Viognier, Pinot Blanc and a late-harvest Riesling are also produced.

TASTING NOTES

CABERNET SAUVIGNON SONOMA COUNTY (★★★★): Supple and elegant, with polished currant, herb, coffee and cedary oak flavors followed by smooth tannins. A blend of Alexander Valley (Hoot Owl Creek and Belle Terre), Dry Creek (William Wheeler and Peter Balbi, two hillside vineyards, the latter of which sells to Rafanelli), Knights Valley (Peter Newman), and Sonoma Valley (the Smothers brothers' Remick Ridge Ranch). Merlot and Malbec grapes come from Rosewood vineyard in Russian River Valley, which gives the wine its tartness. It ages well but is best early on.

1991: Supple and elegant, with layers of herb, currant, wild berry, coffee and cedary oak flavors and smooth tannins. **91**

1990: Smooth and elegant, a generous wine with supple currant and blackberry flavors, spicy herbal overtones and a lively berry finish. **91**

1989: Supple and generous, with a nice core of currant, black cherry and plum flavors. **88**

1988: Appealing, with layers of raspberry, currant, black cherry and spice flavors, packing in plenty of intensity for the vintage. **87**

1987: Supple, ripe, smooth and complex, with flavors of anise, cedary oak, plum, cherry and currant. Tannins are soft. **89**

1986: The toasty oak notes fold into the ripe, supple currant and plum flavors. **90**

1985: Elegant and stylish, loaded with strawberry, cherry and spicy plum flavors and supple tannins. **90**

Cabernet Sauvignon Sonoma County Réserve Spéciale (★★★):

So far there's been only one wine, a 1989, which was solid for the vintage.

1989: Ripe and fleshy, with supple plum, cherry and currant flavors that are elegant and framed by pretty oak. **88**

Chardonnay Sonoma County (★★★★):

Intense and spicy, with rich pear and apple flavors. Can age, but drinks well at two years after it unwinds.

1993: Well focused, with a nice balance between ripe pear, spice and toasty oak flavors that picks up a ginger edge. **87**

1992: Bright and lively, with pretty pear, peach and nectarine flavors, picking up smoky, toasty oak on the finish. **91**

1991: Crisp and spicy, with ripe apple and pear flavors that fan out, turning complex on the finish. **88**

1990: Mature, with ripe pear, wood, spice and butterscotch flavors that turn complex on a long finish. **88**

Chardonnay Sonoma County Cuvée Michel Berthoud (★★★★):

1993: Rich and well focused, with complex and concentrated pear, fig, honey and toasty vanilla shadings, finishing long and smoky. **92**

1992: Crisp, with a tight band of tobacco, spice and pear flavors and light oak shadings. A bold, toasty wine. **85**

Chardonnay Sonoma County Réserve Spéciale (★★★★★):

A shade fuller and richer than the regular Chardonnay, with creamy oak playing a bigger role; available only in magnums.

1991: Supple, with generous spice, tangerine, pear and vanilla flavors that linger on a long and elegant finish. **90**

1990: Delicious and complex, with layers of honey, pear, apple and toast, shaded by smoky, buttery oak. **93**

Merlot Sonoma County (★★★★):

Shows complex, supple coffee, herb, currant and spice notes, with a texture like a red Burgundy.

1991: Complex and flavorful, with a rich, supple core of currant, cherry and spice flavors. **91**

1990: Complex, with beautifully integrated plum, currant and spice flavors framed by toasty, buttery oak. **91**

1988: Bright and concentrated, offering fresh berry and currant flavors shaded by anise and toast. **88**

Viognier Russian River Valley Saralee's Vineyard (★★★):

Captures the essence of this spicy varietal. The 1992 is a touch better than the 1991.

1993: Captures the essence of Viognier with its focused spiciness and concentration. **85**

1992: Ripe and intense, with pear, apricot, spice and almond flavors, but they fade on the finish. Clean and well balanced. **83**

White Riesling Russian River Valley Oak Meadow Vineyard Select Late Harvest (★★★★):

Sweet and delicate, with exotic guava, nectarine and apricot flavors.

1993: Gloriously sweet, rich, supple and complex, a many-layered swirl of honey, caramel, apricot, pear and exotic tropical fruit and spices, all balanced gorgeously on a fine thread of acidity. Wonderful now, but should be fine through 1998-2000. **96**

1991: Light, sweet and delicate, with exotic guava, nectarine and apricot aromas and flavors. The finish is sweet but balanced. Not an unctuous style, but a lovely dessert wine. **87**

Domaine du Grand Archer Various Bottlings (★★):

Cabernet Sauvignon Sonoma County 1992: Firm and intense, with a good dose of smoky, toasty oak up front, but the currant and cherry flavors rise to the occasion and hang on through the finish. **87**

Cabernet Sauvignon Sonoma County 1991: A gentle, youthful Cabernet with a sense of elegance and finesse. The ripe plum, currant and spice flavors are well integrated and balanced, finishing with just the right touch of tannin. Best in 1996. **89**

Merlot Sonoma County 1991: Lean and firm, with a tight band of currant and cherry flavors, but it turns hard and tannic on the finish. **82**

VINCENT ARROYO WINERY

Calistoga, Napa Valley
F: 1984. **O:** Vincent Arroyo Winery. **W:** Vincent Arroyo. **S:** None.

OVERALL	$15	★★★

WINE RATINGS		
Cabernet Sauvignon Napa Valley		★★★

WINERY DATA
C: 3,000. **V:** 50 acres in Napa Valley. **G:** Cabernet Sauvignon (15 acres), Petite Sirah (15), Chardonnay (3), Gamay Beaujolais (12), Merlot (5). **P:** None.

This small, 3,000-case winery in Calistoga has 50 acres of vineyards. Owner Vincent Arroyo produces smaller lots of Chardonnay and Petite Sirah, but his best wine is Cabernet, of which he makes about 750 cases.

TASTING NOTES

CABERNET SAUVIGNON NAPA VALLEY (★★★): The wines have improved with recent vintages. They were overly tannic early on but now show a nice balance between oak and black cherry, currant and spice notes. Best to drink early on.
1990: Strikes a nice balance between oak and black cherry, raspberry and currant flavors, finishing with spicy anise notes. **88**
1989: A peppery-smelling, full-bodied Cabernet, with earthy notes on the finish. **81**
1988: Ripe and very tannic, with currant, raisin and plum flavors that pick up oak and anise on the finish. **85**
1987: Extremely tannic, but packed with deeply perfumed black cherry, currant, herb and spice flavors. **88**

DAVID ARTHUR VINEYARDS

St. Helena, Napa Valley
F: 1985. **O:** David, Robert, Joye & Marilyn Long. **W:** David Long, Heidi Peterson Barrett. **S:** None.

OVERALL	$13-15	★★

WINE RATINGS		
Chardonnay Napa Valley		★★

WINERY DATA
C: 3,000. **V:** 55 acres in Rutherford. **G:** Chardonnay (30 acres), Cabernet Sauvignon (25). **P:** None.

This is a small, 3,000-case, family winery in the hills east of St. Helena near Chappellet. The family owns several hundred acres, including 55 acres in vines. The 1991 Chardonnay is crisp, with modest pear and apple flavors, and a Cabernet is in the works. Founder David Arthur Long has hired consultant Heidi Peterson Barrett, who has worked with several wineries in this area (Buehler, Dalla Valle and Chateau Montelena), so perhaps the quality will soon improve.

ATLAS PEAK VINEYARDS

Atlas Peak, Napa Valley
F: 1986. **O:** The Wine Alliance, Antinori. **W:** John Falcone. **S:** None.

OVERALL	$16-24	★★★

WINE RATINGS		
Cabernet Sauvignon Napa Valley		★★★
Chardonnay Atlas Peak		★★★
Atlas Peak Consenso		★★
Sangiovese Atlas Peak		★★
Sangiovese Atlas Peak Reserve		★★★

WINERY DATA
C: 7,000. **V:** 395 acres in Atlas Peak. **G:** Sangiovese (120 acres), Cabernet Sauvignon (105), Chardonnay (130), Merlot (40). **P:** None.

One of the most ambitious, high profile, capital intensive undertakings of the 1980s decade, Atlas Peak Vineyards brought together the great Tuscan vintner Piero Antinori, Champagne master Christian Bizot and Whitbread with the goal of creating a Super Tuscan line of wines using Sangiovese, Cabernet and blends thereof, along with anything else that developed from this then untested property that rises more than 1,000 feet above the Napa Valley floor. In 1985, the trio bought 800 acres and a partially developed vineyard from William Hill. They now have some 395 acres under vines, planting it primarily to Sangiovese (120 acres), Cabernet (105 acres), Chardonnay (130 acres) and Merlot (40 acres).

But the overall strategy has not gone as planned. The wines have failed to live up to expectations, cost overruns have limited expansion and enthusiasm has waned. The Sangiovese, dating back to 1989, has been light and thin, although the 1992 (84) showed a bit more depth with spice, smoke and strawberry flavors. Consenso, a Cabernet with 20 percent Sangiovese, shared a similar style, lean and light without much depth or concentration. Even the 1992 Reserve (85) failed to break out of that mold. Curiously, the best wines I've tasted were a sparkling wine made by Bizot that was rich, toasty and reminiscent of a fine Bollinger Champagne, and a Chardonnay. But only the latter wine was scheduled for commercial release.

In 1994, a reorganization of the partnership looked like this: Antinori acquired the winery and vineyards from the partners. Wine Alliance, Hiram Walker's California wine company that also owns William Hill, Clos du Bois and Callaway, became the sales and marketing unit while also managing the vineyards. As of early 1995, a winery on the property was still planned although now the showcase once envisioned and optimism about the wines and this property's future seemed on hold. This seems like an ideal place to grow red wines, given the excellent quality of the eastern hillside vineyards of Dalla Valle and Oakville Ranch further to the north, along with others. And clearly it's too early to count Antinori out; his family's been in the wine business more than 600 years, and it too may have begun with a slow start. Production in 1994 was about 8,000 cases, with talk of expanding to 60,000 cases within the decade.

TASTING NOTES

CABERNET SAUVIGNON NAPA VALLEY (★★★): Shows more focus and depth than the other Atlas Peak reds, which is why William Hill was so enthusiastic about its potential when he first planted vines there.
1991: The debut Cabernet is dark, supple, plush and flavorful, with ripe cherry, currant and cedary oak flavors that fold together. **87**

CHARDONNAY ATLAS PEAK (★★★):
1993: A touch earthy and oaky, but enough ripe pear and apple flavors come through to hold your interest. **85**

CONSENSO ATLAS PEAK (★★): A Cabernet-Sangiovese blend that doesn't serve either grape very well. Quality has been variable, with a trim band of flavor that lacks focus.
1990: Modestly flavorful, with stalky berry flavors that turn tannic on the finish. **83**
1989: Mature and drying, with an earth, cedar and coffee edge to the currant and berry flavors; turns leathery on the finish. **83**

SANGIOVESE ATLAS PEAK (★★), RESERVE (★★★): The 1992 Reserve is the best, but earlier bottlings failed to excite and they have been lean and trim, with modest fruit levels.
1992: Earthy, spicy aromas lead to medium-bodied strawberry and cherry flavors that turn smoky. **84**
1991: Light and fruity, with simple cherry and plum flavors that are pleasant enough. **82**
1990: Lean, tart and earthy, with spicy currant and raspberry flavors. **80**
1989: An earthy wine with modest varietal character, offering ripe plum and cherry notes and picking up oak on the finish. **82**
Reserve 1992: Firm in texture, more tannic than most California Sangiovese, with fairly intense blackberry and black cherry flavors. **85**

AU BON CLIMAT
Santa Ynez Valley
F: 1982. **O:** James Clendenen. **W:** James Clendenen, Jim Adelman. **S:** Il Podere Dell' Olivos.

OVERALL	$12-40	★★★★★

WINE RATINGS	
Chardonnay Arroyo Grande Valley Talley Reserve	★★★★
Chardonnay Santa Barbara County	★★★★
Chardonnay Santa Barbara County Le Bouge D'à Côté	★★★★★
Chardonnay Santa Barbara County Reserve	★★★★★
Chardonnay Santa Barbara County Bien Nacido Vineyard Reserve	★★★★
Chardonnay Santa Maria Valley Gold Coast Vineyard	NR
Pinot Blanc Santa Barbara County	★★★
Pinot Noir Arroyo Grande Valley Talley and Paragon Vineyards	NR

Pinot Noir Santa Barbara County
  Bien Nacido Vineyard
    La Bauge Au-Dessus   ★★★★
Pinot Noir Santa Maria Valley
  Rancho Vinedo Vineyard   ★★★
Pinot Noir Santa Ynez Valley
  Sanford & Benedict Vineyard   ★★★★

WINERY DATA
C: 10,000. V: None. G: None. P: Chardonnay, Pinot Blanc, Pinot Noir (Santa Barbara and San Luis Obispo Counties).

Aₜ this writing, Jim Clendenen is on top of the Chardonnay and Pinot Noir world in California, riding the crest of the best wave of wines he has ever produced. With Chardonnay, that lofty position can be a place of comfort, as it is California's most consistently excellent white wine. With finicky Pinot Noir, it's always precarious. My notes on Au Bon Climat's wines over the years show wild swings from highly manipulated, sometimes downright funky wines in difficult years to highly stylized, barrel-fermented, zesty, explosive wines in others. At their best these are some brilliant, complex, truly intriguing and totally exciting Pinot Noirs and Chardonnays.

Clendenen is an unabashed lover of Burgundian wines and his passion and dedication to these wines goes unchallenged. His winemaking career dates to the 1970s, when he worked as a winemaker at Zaca Mesa. In 1982 he and Adam Tolmach (also a Zaca Mesa grad) started Au Bon Climat and, after making wine at several rented locations, settled in 1988 in a portion of Bien Nacido Vineyard's facilities in Santa Maria Valley. Clendenen is also a partner in Vita Nova (see listing).

Clendenen doesn't own any vineyards, but he's skilled at picking grape sources and has a remarkable track record for excellence given that his sources are often pulled out from under him when vineyards are sold and contracts ended. Until recently his wines have enjoyed cult status, winning the highest praise in some corners and drawing raised eyebrows of doubt in others. ABC's best efforts, small 200- to 300-case lots of vineyard-designated wines, are often difficult to obtain, snapped up by devotees, and they are usually vastly supe-

rior to the generic wines of the same type made in 1,000-case lots. It's not surprising that those who only taste the regular wines have no appreciation for what happens when it all comes together in one of ABC's bold and distinctive Reserve or vineyard-designated bottlings. Today production is about 10,000 cases, and while there are times when it appears ABC is settling into a groove with its line of wines, things almost always change.

TASTING NOTES

CHARDONNAY ARROYO GRANDE VALLEY TALLEY RESERVE (★★★★):
1993: Medium-bodied but well focused and flavorful, with toasty oak, ripe pear, honey and spicy citrus notes, turning complex and elegant on the finish. **90**
1992: Serves up a pretty array of tropical fruit, with guava, pineapple, honey and pear flavors that remain spicy and long on the finish. **91**
1990: Hard and toasty, with a firm oak edge overshadowing the taut pear, peach and citrus flavors. **87**

CHARDONNAY SANTA BARBARA COUNTY (★★★★), RESERVE (★★★★★): Bold, ripe and intense, rich and tightly wound, often earthy, leesy and marked by toasty oak, but also tremendously complex and full-bodied. The best is the Reserve, usually carrying a Santa Barbara County appellation, although it can also carry a special winemaker designation, such as Le Bouge D'a Cote.
1993: Well focused with appealing fruit flavors, combining ripe pineapple, citrus and spicy oak flavors, folding together on the finish. **87**
1990: Crisp and clean, with tart green apple and spice flavors that are straightforward and easy to drink. **84**
Le Bouge D'à Côté 1993: Tight and medium-bodied, with flinty pear, cedar and vanilla notes of modest depth. Not quite the depth and complexity of the other ABC bottlings. **87**
Le Bouge D'à Côté 1992: Rich and earthy, with complex, concentrated pear, pineapple, oak and spice notes that pick up honey and pear flavors on the finish. **92**
Reserve 1990: Tremendously ripe, rich, complex fruit flavors, with tiers of pear, lemon, pineapple and toasty oak. Delicious. **95**
Reserve 1989: Very ripe and intense honey, pear, spice and butterscotch flavors, with zippy acidity and a butterscotch aftertaste. **91**
Reserve 1988: Ripe and exotic, with intense, concentrated tropical fruit, pineapple, guava, citrus and spice flavors and a touch of toasty oak. **91**

Reserve 1987: One fantastic wine. Tremendous richness, intensity, depth and complexity, with tiers of honey, pear, pineapple and citrus flavors. **96**

Los Alamos Vineyard Reserve 1987: A stylish Chardonnay that emphasizes toasty, oaky, buttery flavors over modest fruit. Clean and well made, with great aromas, it's a good choice for fans of this style. **82**

Reserve 1986: Mature, with intense and concentrated citrus, pear and butterscotch flavors with subtle oak shadings. **92**

CHARDONNAY SANTA BARBARA COUNTY BIEN NACIDO VINEYARD (★★★★):

1991: Deftly balanced and richly flavored, with layers of spicy pear, honey, fig and butterscotch flavors in a complex and lively style. Has wonderful harmony and finesse. **93**

Reserve 1990: Broad, rich butterscotch and earth notes around a core of pear and lemon flavors. The finish is smooth and elegant. **91**

CHARDONNAY SANTA MARIA VALLEY GOLD COAST VINEYARD (NR):

1993: Bold and oaky, with a rich leesy edge to the ripe pear and pineapple flavors, gaining intensity and depth on the finish, where it turns complex. **89**

PINOT BLANC SANTA BARBARA COUNTY (★★★):

1990: Appealing caramel and honey overtones to the ripe pear and melon aromas and flavors. **83**

PINOT NOIR ARROYO GRANDE VALLEY TALLEY AND PARAGON VINEYARDS (NR):

1993: Medium-bodied, firmly tannic, with spicy cherry and leathery notes that are tightly wound. Can stand cellaring to soften a bit, but it lacks the extra richness found in great vintages. **87**

PINOT NOIR SANTA BARBARA COUNTY BIEN NACIDO VINEYARD LA BAUGE AU-DESSUS (★★★★): Showcases the character of this vineyard, often leaning toward the herb, cola, earth and leather end of the spectrum, but these wines can also be quite rich, dense and concentrated, with black cherry, spice and berry flavors and firm tannins.

1993: Very ripe with dried cherry and berry notes, picking up a pleasant tea leaf and anise edge, holding its flavor while finishing with firm tannins. **85**

1991: Tight and focused, with complex cherry, spice, earth and oak flavors that turn meaty on the finish. Beautifully crafted. **92**

1990: Intense and lively, with a tight, rich core of cola, rhubarb, cherry and spice flavors, framed by toasty, buttery oak. **91**

Santa Barbara County 1989: Ripe and complex, with a supple core of earthy cherry, anise, cola, plum and oak flavors that turn racy on the finish. **87**

Santa Barbara County 1988: Rich, earthy and generous, with lavish black cherry, cola and smoke flavors. **80**

Santa Barbara County 1987: Firm and concentrated, with rose and cherry aromas, crisp acidity and smoky plum flavors. **84**

Santa Barbara County 1985: Pronounced vegetal and spicy aromas along with some earthy nuances in this lean, juicy wine. **73**

PINOT NOIR SANTA MARIA VALLEY RANCHO VINEDO VINEYARD (★★★):

1993: Well oaked, with herb, cola and black cherry fruit that turns supple in texture despite firm tannins. **86**

1992: Lean, elegant and youthful, showing tart black cherry, smoke and meat flavors and an earthy, vegetal edge. **86**

1990: Complex and aromatic, with cola, berry, earth and leather notes that are rich and concentrated. **86**

1988: A vibrant, fruity wine that serves up appealing strawberry and cherry flavors. **83**

PINOT NOIR SANTA YNEZ VALLEY SANFORD & BENEDICT VINEYARD (★★★★):

1991: Rich, smooth and elegant, with intense spice, cherry, raspberry and earth notes that glide across the palate. Part of the Sanford Signature Series. **91**

Benedict Vineyard 1989: Fresh and crisp, with an earthy, leathery edge to the cherry and spice notes. **87**

Benedict Vineyard 1987: Intense, with earthy cola, tar and fruit flavors accented by slightly smoky, peppery aromas. **88**

AUSTIN CELLARS

Los Olivos, Santa Barbara County
F: 1983. **O:** Santa Ynez Wine Inc. **W:** Claiborne Thompson. **S:** Alisos Canyon.

OVERALL   **$10-20**   ★

WINE RATINGS

Cabernet Sauvignon Santa Barbara County Mille Délices	★
Cabernet Sauvignon Santa Barbara County Perry's Reserve	★
Pinot Noir Santa Barbara County Reserve	★
Sauvignon Blanc Santa Barbara County Reserve	★
Sauvignon Blanc Santa Barbara County Lucas Vineyard	★

WINERY DATA

C: 7,000. **V:** None. **G:** None. **P:** Chardonnay, Pinot Noir, Riesling (Santa Barbara County), Cabernet Sauvignon, Muscat Canelli (Santa Ynez Valley).

Former Firestone winemaker Tony Austin started his winery in Santa Ynez Valley in 1981, producing Cabernet, Chardonnay and Pinot Noir while adding a white Meritage called Cumulus. The winery now lists Santa Ynez Wine, Inc. as its owner, with production at 7,000 cases. My most recent notes show the Cabernets as austere and marked by herbal notes, a 1991 Pinot Noir that stepped out of bounds with its vegetal, earthy flavors and a 1991 Sauvignon Blanc marred by earthy flavors. All three wines carried the Santa Barbara County appellation.

TASTING NOTES

VARIOUS BOTTLINGS (★):
Cabernet Sauvignon Santa Barbara County Mille Délices 1991: Ripe, supple and fleshy, with toasty, buttery oak and smooth cherry and plum flavors. **84**
Cabernet Sauvignon Santa Barbara County Perry's Reserve 1991: Austere, with spicy herbal notes, but not quite the rich fruit concentration to stand up to the tannins. Finishes with a spicy cola edge. **80**
Pinot Noir Santa Barbara County Reserve 1991: Steps out of bounds with its vegetal, earthy flavors. **79**
Sauvignon Blanc Santa Barbara County Reserve 1991: Mature, round and unusually earthy. The pineapple flavor shows a caramel edge and it has a definite tinny tinge to the finish. Drinkable, but why bother? **72**
Sauvignon Blanc Santa Barbara County Lucas Vineyard 1991: Soft, flabby and unexpectedly mature, with a caramel edge to the flavors. **70**

AZALEA SPRINGS

Napa Valley
F: 1991. **O:** Norman & Norah Stone. **W:** Kent Rasmussen. **S:** None.

OVERALL	$22	★★★

WINE RATINGS

Merlot Napa Valley	★★★

WINERY DATA

C: 1,200. **V:** 6 acres on Diamond Mountain, Napa Valley. **G:** Merlot. **P:** None.

This winery's debut, the 1991 Napa Valley Merlot offered smooth, plush and elegant currant, black cherry and plum flavors that were very appealing. The 6-acre Merlot vineyard, owned by Norman and Norah Stone, is in northern Napa Valley on the west side near the base of Diamond Mountain. Kent Rasmussen is overseeing winemaking at the Napa Wine Co. cooperative winery in Oakville. Newton Vineyards purchased grapes in 1991, but the owners intend to expand to 1,200 cases.

TASTING NOTES

MERLOT NAPA VALLEY (★★★):
1991: Smooth, plush and elegant, with a core of ripe, spicy currant, black cherry and plum flavors. **88**

BABCOCK VINEYARDS

Santa Ynez Valley
F: 1984. **O:** Walter, Mona & Bryan Babcock. **W:** Bryan Babcock. **S:** None.

OVERALL	$14-30	★★

WINE RATINGS

Chardonnay Santa Barbara County	★★
Chardonnay Santa Ynez Valley Mt. Carmel Vineyard	★★
Pinot Noir Santa Ynez Valley	★★
Pinot Noir Santa Ynez Valley Sanford & Benedict Vineyard	★★
Sauvignon Blanc Santa Ynez Valley 11 Oaks Ranch	★★★

WINERY DATA
C: 9,000. V: 48 acres in Santa Ynez Valley. G: Chardonnay (30 acres), Gewürztraminer (3), Johannisberg Riesling (3), Sauvignon Blanc (3) and Syrah (3). P: None.

While stylistic swings have plagued this winery in the past, there are signs that Babcock is on the verge of breaking through with more focus and consistency in its wines. Owners Walt and Mona Babcock and their son Bryan own 48 acres of vineyard in Santa Ynez Valley planted primarily to Chardonnay (30 acres), with 3-acre lots of Sauvignon Blanc, Johannisberg Riesling, Gewürztraminer and Syrah. Production is 9,000 cases.

Babcock's best wine to my taste is the 11 Oaks Sauvignon Blanc, made in a crisp, ripe and concentrated style, brimming with bright, lively fruit. The 1992 features layers of delicious pear, orange, spice and herb notes. The Chardonnays, including the lavishly oaked Grand Cuvée, vary greatly in quality, with some off-putting bottles marred by funky flavors and others capturing the essence of Santa Ynez Valley fruit. The 1993 Santa Barbara County is ripe and spicy, but lacking complexity. The 1990 Grand Cuvée is tight and hard, with strong oak flavors. The 1992 Pinot Noir is dark and intense, but also tannic and vegetal, as earlier vintages were. But among the most recent offerings, the 1991 Sanford & Benedict is impressive, tight and compact, with bright cherry and berry flavors, while the 1992 is a bit tart and green, with hints of cherry and spice. A dessert-style Riesling can also be excellent. A little more refinement in winemaking could upgrade these wines a notch or two.

TASTING NOTES

CHARDONNAY VARIOUS BOTTLINGS (★★):
Santa Barbara County 1993: Ripe and spicy, with fresh pear and apple notes. A fruity wine that's solid but lacking the extra dimensions you might expect. **85**
Santa Barbara County 1990: Attractive for its intense pear, citrus and spice flavors and lean focus. Crisp and balanced. **82**
Santa Barbara County Grand Cuvée 1990: Tight and hard in structure, but the flavors are appealing, displaying honey, apple and pear notes that extend into a solid finish. **83**

Santa Ynez Valley 1991: Smells off, but the flavors aren't bad, offering green apple, spice and honey notes. Ultimately it should be fine. **78**
Santa Ynez Valley Mt. Carmel Vineyard 1993: A slight bitter edge detracts from the modest pear and spice notes, but it lingers on the finish. The $25 price is out of line. **83**

PINOT NOIR VARIOUS BOTTLINGS (★★):
Santa Ynez Valley 1992: Dark and intense, with spicy herb, black cherry and earth flavors that finish on the austere and tannic side. Needs time to soften; try in 1997. **85**
Santa Ynez Valley 1991: Fragrant, with appealing floral, raspberry and red cherry aromas, but tight and unyielding on the palate, turning tannic and short. **79**
Santa Ynez Valley Benedict Vineyard 1991: Tight and compact. The bright cherry and berry flavors are lean and focused, finishing with firm, earthy tannins. Needs time to soften. Part of the Sanford Signature Series. **87**
Santa Ynez Valley Sanford & Benedict Vineyard 1992: Young and a bit green, with fruit that's barely ripe. Hints of cherry and currant come through with the herb and spice notes. Tannic enough to cellar until 1997. **85**
Santa Ynez Valley Selected Barrels Reserve 1989: Tastes and smells like cooked beets and menthol, which isn't my idea of Pinot Noir. **70**

SAUVIGNON BLANC SANTA YNEZ VALLEY 11 OAKS RANCH (★★★):
1992: Bright and lively, with delicious pear, orange, spice and herb flavors that extend into a deftly balanced finish. Elegant and distinctive. **89**
1991: Just misses the mark. Ripe, smooth and concentrated, crisp and lemony at the core, with honey, pineapple and butter overtones, making for a flavorful wine that doesn't quite strike a balance. **83**

BAILEYANA
San Luis Obispo County
F: 1971. O: Paragon Vineyard Co. Inc. W: Gary Mosby. S: None.

OVERALL	$14-15	★★

WINE RATINGS
Chardonnay Edna Valley
   Paragon Vineyard   ★★

WINERY DATA
C: 2,500. V: 705 acres in Edna Valley. G: Cabernet Sauvignon (100), Chardonnay (500 acres), Pinot Noir (60), Sauvignon Blanc (40). P: None.

This is one of the largest vineyards in Edna Valley, with 705 acres planted to Chardonnay (500), Cabernet (100), Pinot Noir (60) and Sauvignon Blanc (40). It is owned by Paragon Vineyard Co., a part-owner of the Chalone Wine Group and Edna Valley Vineyards. Since 1989, 2,500 cases of Chardonnay have been produced per year. The 1991 is simple and watery, but the 1992 and 1993 are vast improvements, offering ripe, juicy pear, pineapple and butterscotch flavors that are rich and harmonious. Worth watching.

TASTING NOTES

CHARDONNAY EDNA VALLEY PARAGON VINEYARD (★★):
1993: Serves up a ripe, well focused beam of pear and pineapple, with complex oak shadings that fold together neatly on the finish. Long aftertaste. **88**
1992: It exhibits ripe, juicy pear, pineapple, honey and butterscotch flavors that are rich and harmonious. Turns smooth and silky on the finish. **88**
1991: Light and lean, with simple grape and apple aromas and flavors that have a watery edge. **76**

BALDINELLI VINEYARDS
Shenandoah Valley
F: 1979. O: Ed & Kay Baldinelli, John Miller. W: Ed Baldinelli. S: None.

OVERALL	$8-10	★

WINE RATINGS

Cabernet Sauvignon Amador County	NR
Zinfandel Shenandoah Valley	NR

WINERY DATA
C: 15,000. V: 70 acres in Amador County. G: Cabernet Sauvignon, Zinfandel. P: None.

This Amador-based winery is owned by Ed and Kay Baldinelli, who own some 70 acres of vineyard, including the Dickson vineyard, which was planted in the 1920s. They produce about 15,000 cases a year of a light, crisp Shenandoah Valley Zinfandel and an Amador Cabernet, which in 1989 was rustic, earthy and tannic. The winery's bond lapsed in 1994 and a new owner, William Easton, rented the facility with plans to start a new brand called Domaine de la Terre Rouge.

BANCROFT VINEYARDS
Howell Mountain
F: 1983. O: James R. Bancroft. W: Gregory Graham. S: None.

OVERALL	$16	★★★

WINE RATINGS

Chardonnay Howell Mountain	★★★

WINERY DATA
C: 1,500. V: 90 acres in Howell Mountain. G: Cabernet Sauvignon (31 acres), Merlot (31), Cabernet Franc (5), Chardonnay (23). P: None.

San Francisco attorney Jim Bancroft owns this beautiful Howell Mountain vineyard, best known as the source of Beringer's exceptional Merlot, which carries the Bancroft Ranch designation. In 1988 Bancroft, who spends weekends and holidays at his ranch, began making Chardonnay in a tight, flinty, concentrated style. Bancroft's 90 acres of vines are made up of Merlot (31 acres), Cabernet (31), Cabernet Franc (5) and Chardonnay (23). Beringer uses the Cabernet in its Private Reserve, while Stony Hill buys Chardonnay for its SHV bottling.

TASTING NOTES

CHARDONNAY HOWELL MOUNTAIN (★★★): Tight, lean, intense and marked by mineral notes.
1992: Intense and flinty, with a focused core of earthy citrus, pear and light oak shadings. **86**
1990: Lively fruit, with hints of pear, citrus and vanilla. A crisp, focused wine. **84**
1989: Tart, tight and crisp, with firm peach, mineral and oak shadings that are complex and lingering. **89**

BANDIERA WINERY
Cloverdale, Sonoma County
F: 1937. **O:** California Wine Company Inc. **W:** Robert Keeble. **S:** None.

OVERALL	$6-12	★★

WINE RATINGS

Cabernet Sauvignon Napa Valley	★★
Chardonnay Napa Valley	★★
Fumé Blanc Napa Valley	★★

WINERY DATA
C: 100,000. **V:** 201 acres in Napa Valley. **G:** Cabernet Sauvignon (79 acres), Merlot (6), Malbec (3), Petite Verdot (3), Cabernet Franc (3), Chardonnay (41), Sauvignon Blanc (26), Zinfandel (39). **P:** None.

This 100,000-case winery focuses on a line of value-oriented wines, including Cabernet, Chardonnay, white Zinfandel and Fumé Blanc. The best two are the Cabernet, which in 1990 and 1991 carried a Napa Valley appellation and delivers generous currant, berry, herb and spice notes, and the Fumé Blanc, also from Napa. The winery, based in Cloverdale, owns more than 200 acres, most of which is planted to Cabernet (79 acres), but also includes Chardonnay, Sauvignon Blanc and Zinfandel.

TASTING NOTES

CABERNET SAUVIGNON NAPA VALLEY (★★):
1992: Pleasant, fruity, easy to drink style that features cherry and berry flavors. **83**
1991: Marked by herb and light oak shadings, this is another excellent Bandiera Cabernet. It delivers plenty of currant and cherry flavors at a price that's hard to beat. **85**
1990: Broad, supple and flavorful, a fine-textured wine with generous berry, currant and plum flavors echoing on the long finish. **87**

CHARDONNAY NAPA VALLEY (★★):
1993: A little broader than most 1993s, with toasty pear and vanilla flavors that work in a touch of honey on the finish. **84**
1992: Fruity and generous, offering a bright beam of nectarine and apricot flavors that linger on the finish. **85**
1991: Smooth and lively, with vanilla-scented apple and spice flavors, balanced and harmonious. **85**

FUMÉ BLANC NAPA VALLEY (★★):
1993: A very pretty wine with rose petal aromas, soft pear and floral flavors and a gentle finish. **86**

BANNISTER WINERY
Russian River Valley
F: 1989. **O:** Marty Bannister. **W:** Marty Bannister. **S:** None.

OVERALL	$12-18	★★★

WINE RATINGS

Chardonnay Russian River Valley	
Allen Vineyard	★★★
Zinfandel Dry Creek Valley	★★

WINERY DATA
C: 1,200. **V:** None. **G:** None. **P:** Chardonnay (Russian River Valley), Zinfandel (Dry Creek Valley), Zinfandel (Russian River Valley).

Considering its grape sources and winemaking experience, this winery has the potential to be a real star. After years of operating VinQuiry, an independent wine laboratory, Marty Bannister launched her own small wine brand in 1989, focusing on small-case lots of Chardonnay from Allen Vineyard (Russian River), and Zinfandel (early vintages from Dry Creek Valley, Russian River beginning with the 1993). So far the Chardonnay is the better of the two wines, although the Zinfandel, made in a claret style, with spicy and tarry notes merits attention. Production is 1,200 cases.

TASTING NOTES

CHARDONNAY RUSSIAN RIVER VALLEY ALLEN VINEYARD (★★★):
1993: Medium-weight with an appealing core of apple, spice and hazelnut flavors that turn elegant and delicate on the finish. Well crafted. **89**
1992: Serves up a lot of ripe pear, apple and spice flavors, with light vanilla notes on the finish. Elegant and balanced. **86**
1991: Ripe and generous, with focused, leesy apple and spice aromas and flavors. Echoes fruit on the finish. **84**
1990: Smooth and ripe, with layers of broad, rich pear, spice, honey and toast flavors. Offers plenty of flavor and depth, yet it's round, creamy and delicious. **88**

ZINFANDEL DRY CREEK VALLEY (★★):
1992: A spicy, cedary wine that turns tight and austere on the palate, echoing tar and caramel on the finish. **84**

1991: A balanced, claret-style wine with cedary oak flavors and ripe cherry notes. Easy to drink, but lacks flair. **83**

BARGETTO WINERY
Santa Cruz Mountains
F: 1933. **O:** Bargetto Santa Cruz Winery. **W:** Paul Wofford. **S:** Chaucer.

OVERALL	$8-18	★★

WINE RATINGS

Chardonnay Central Coast Cypress	★★
Chardonnay Santa Cruz Mountains	★★
Gewürztraminer Monterey County	NR
Merlot Central Coast	NR
Pinot Noir Santa Cruz Mountains	NR
Sparkling Wine Santa Maria Valley	
Blanc de Noirs	NR

WINERY DATA
C: 25,000. **V:** 28 acres in Santa Cruz Mountains. **G:** Chardonnay (11 acres), Merlot (7), Pinot Noir (5), Italian Type (5). **P:** None.

One of the oldest wineries in the Santa Cruz Mountains, Bargetto is known locally for its berry and fruit wines under the Chaucer label. But the winery is slowly upgrading the quality of its wines, moving from rustic to more supple. The Cabernet and Chardonnay under the Cypress label are the best, although at times I've also liked the Fumé Blanc. Gewürztraminer and Pinot Noir also are part of the product mix, which is now about 25,000 cases.

TASTING NOTES

CABERNET SAUVIGNON VARIOUS BOTTLINGS (★★):
Napa Valley Komes Ranch 1988: Supple and fruity, with ripe plum and cherry notes that pick up a trace of tar and spice on the finish. Firmly tannic. **84**
Santa Cruz Mountains Bates Ranch 1987: Intense and herbaceous, with weedy black currant and bell pepper notes that stay focused, finishing with an earthy edge and firm tannins. **83**

CHARDONNAY VARIOUS BOTTLINGS (★★):
Central Coast Cypress 1993: Simple and easy to drink, with a crisp edge of green apple to the basic flavors. **80**
Central Coast Cypress 1992: A ripe, fruity wine with spicy pear and apple notes. **82**

Central Coast Cypress 1991: Starts out elegant and spicy, but gains depth and complexity, with tiers of spice, honey, pear and mango flavors. Clean and refreshing. **85**
Central Coast Cypress 1990: Forward, fruity and easy to drink, with pleasant, soft apple and pear flavors. **82**
Santa Cruz Mountains 1993: Straightforward, fruity and spicy, apple and oak flavors nicely wrapped together to balance. **84**
Santa Cruz Mountains 1992: Lean and leesy, with an earthy citrus edge to the pear and spice notes. **83**
Santa Cruz Mountains 1990: This will appeal to Sauvignon Blanc lovers. Offers plenty of herb, spice and apple notes that are fresh and lively, with hints of grapefruit and melon on the finish. **85**

VARIOUS BOTTLINGS (NR):
Gewürztraminer Monterey County 1992: Soft and refreshing, with generous peach flavors and a nice overlay of rose petal and spice. A well mannered wine. **83**
Merlot Central Coast 1989: Firm and tart, with crisp black cherry, anise and currant notes. Well balanced. **80**
Pinot Noir Santa Cruz Mountains 1989: Mature in color and flavor, with drying tannins. **78**
Sparkling Wine Santa Maria Valley Blanc de Noir 60th Anniversary 1991: Earthy and gamy, but there's a hint of black cherry and spice that sneaks through on the finish. **79**

BARNETT VINEYARDS
Spring Mountain, Napa Valley
F: 1983. **O:** Fiona & Hal Barnett. **W:** Kent Rasmussen. **S:** None.

OVERALL	$15-32	★★★

WINE RATINGS

Cabernet Sauvignon Spring Mountain	★★★

WINERY DATA
C: 1,500. **V:** 15 acres in Napa Valley. **G:** Cabernet Sauvignon (11 acres), Chardonnay (2), Merlot (1), Cabernet Franc (2). **P:** Chardonnay (Napa Valley), Pinot Noir (Carneros).

I'm impressed by the first offerings from this 15-acre vineyard high atop Spring Mountain. Estate-grown Cabernet, including a 25-case Rattlesnake Hill bottling, leads the way, with a Napa Valley Chardonnay and a Carneros Pinot Noir also part of the lineup. Kent

Rasmussen is overseeing the 1,500-case production, and it looks like a good matchup.

TASTING NOTES

CABERNET SAUVIGNON SPRING MOUNTAIN (★★★): Early signs are positive, with ripe, firm fruit flavors that are supple and not overly tannic. The oak is in the background. The Rattlesnake Hill shows real potential.
1992: Chunky with spicy, toasty oak edge and a chewy core of cherry and currant flavors that finish with a strong tannic note. Best to hold until 1997. **87**
Rattlesnake Hill 1991: Firm, intense and spicy, with ripe currant, mineral, oak and pepper notes that are focused and concentrated. The long, fruity finish shows a supple texture and tight tannins. **90**
1990: Deep-colored, with peppery, herbal, vegetal notes. Tastes like a Rhône wine. **83**
1989: Firm and flavorful, with blackberry, cherry and currant flavors dressed up with spice, vanilla and chocolate. **86**

BAYVIEW CELLARS
Napa Valley
F: 1992. O: Ken Laird & John Richburg. W: John Richburg. S: None.

OVERALL	$7-14	★★

WINE RATINGS	
Cabernet Sauvignon Napa Valley	★★
Chardonnay Carneros	★★
Gewürztraminer Napa Valley	★★

WINERY DATA
C: 10,000. V: N/A. G: N/A. P: N/A.

This partnership brings together long-time Inglenook winemaker John Richburg and vineyard owner and manager Ken Laird, who oversees some 1,400 acres in vines from Carneros to St. Helena. So far the first wines include a moderately varietal, off-dry 1993 Gewürztraminer and a well crafted 1992 Carneros Chardonnay marked by smooth, creamy pear, honey, toast and apricot flavors. But the possibilities are many given Laird's access to grapes and Richburg's winemaking skills. Plans call for a Cabernet, with production

headed toward 10,000 cases, but it's unclear what the future holds, since Richburg is still a winemaking consultant with Inglenook.

TASTING NOTES

VARIOUS BOTTLINGS (★★):
Cabernet Sauvignon Napa Valley 1991: An earthy style with a leathery edge to the currant, spice and cedary oak flavors. Needs time to soften, but may always be on the tannic side. Best after 1997. **83**
Chardonnay Carneros 1992: Ripe, smooth and creamy, with pretty pear, honey, toast and apricot flavors that are rich and complex. **88**
Gewürztraminer Napa Valley 1993: Fruity and slightly sweet, with little spice or floral character to identify it as Gewürz. **77**

BEARBOAT
This is a second label for Piper Sonoma Cellars (see listing).

BEAUCANON WINERY
St. Helena, Napa Valley
F: 1986. O: Jacques de Coninck. W: Louis de Coninck. S: La Crosse.

OVERALL	$11-14	★★

WINE RATINGS	
Cabernet Sauvignon Napa Valley	★★
Chardonnay Napa Valley	★★
Merlot Napa Valley	★
La Crosse Cabernet Sauvignon Napa Valley	★
La Crosse Chardonnay Napa Valley	★
La Crosse Merlot Napa Valley	★

WINERY DATA
C: 30,000. V: 244 acres in Napa Valley. G: Cabernet Sauvignon (82 acres), Chardonnay (85), Merlot (67), Cabernet Franc (5), Chenin Blanc (5). P: None.

Owner Jacques de Coninck, who heads a large French negociant house, J. Lebegue in Bordeaux, owns some 244 acres spread throughout Napa Valley, but so far the wines have ranged from weak and unbalanced to modestly pleasing. After some dismal efforts, the 1990 Cabernet shows polish and finesse, with smoky oak and black currant flavors, much like the successful 1986, and the 1992 Chardonnay provides spicy pear and toasty oak flavors. The Merlot (10,000 cases) has ranged from pickley to serviceable, so perhaps things are beginning to turn around. Production is about 30,000 cases but should increase to more than 50,000 cases. The winery is located on the west side of Highway 29 in Rutherford.

TASTING NOTES

CABERNET SAUVIGNON NAPA VALLEY (★★):
1990: Smooth and flavorful, with appealing smoke, oak, currant and spice nuances. **86**

CHARDONNAY NAPA VALLEY (★★), ENVIE (NR):
1992: There are distinctive toasty oak and butter flavors up front, with pear and spice notes to keep it interesting. Balanced, with a sweet, smoky aftertaste. **85**
1991: Spicy, toasty and focused, with lively pear and nutmeg aromas and flavors. Crisp on the finish, with just a hint of bitterness. **83**
Envie 1991: Sweet and cloying, with more bubble gum aromas and flavors than fruit. Not much excitement in this unbalanced effort. **76**
1990: Nice butter and vanilla flavors are wrapped around grapefruit and citrus components. Smooth, well balanced and easy to enjoy. **83**

MERLOT NAPA VALLEY (★):
1991: Marked by a weedy, dill edge that turns earthy and funky. **77**
1990: Tight and more than a little tannic, with a green bean edge to the modest currant and black cherry flavors. The finish is a bit tough. **81**
1989: Offers a strange concoction of pickle, herb and stale, spicy Merlot flavors that are dull. **73**
1988: Very firm and focused, with moderately intense smoke, berry and currant flavors. The tannins are well integrated. **84**

LA CROSSE VARIOUS BOTTLINGS (★):
Cabernet Sauvignon Napa Valley 1991: Offers modest currant and berry notes. **77**
Cabernet Sauvignon Napa Valley 1989: A firm-textured, simple Cabernet with modest pepper, cherry and herb aromas and flavors. **77**

Chardonnay Napa Valley 1993: Well oaked, with subdued pear and apple flavors that turn soft on the finish. **83**
Chardonnay Napa Valley 1992: There's nice tension between oak and fruit in this medium-weight, smooth-textured wine, echoing peach and spice on the finish. **84**
Chardonnay Napa Valley 1991: Lean and focused, with a pleasant, smoky edge to the green apple, butter and spice aromas and flavors. **85**
Merlot Napa Valley 1993: Supple and fruity, with a pleasant band of herb, black cherry, spicy notes and mild tannins that turn smooth on the finish. **85**

BEAUCASTEL ESTATE
Paso Robles
F: 1990. **O:** Perrin Family & Robert Haas.

This is an ambitious new venture that brings together the Perrin family, owners of Chateau de Beaucastel of Chateauneuf-du-Pape in the Rhône Valley, and Robert Haas, owner of Vineyard Brands, a wine importer and wholesaler, with the goal of creating a line of Rhône-style wines 10 miles west of Paso Robles. The Perrin family purchased a 120-acre property and planted it to Rhône reds (Syrah, Grenache and Mourvèdre) and whites (Marsanne, Roussanne and Viognier). The first wines are planned for 1998 or 1999, depending on quality, but the winery does not appear to be in a hurry.

BEAULIEU VINEYARD
Rutherford, Napa Valley
F: 1900. **O:** Heublein Inc. **W:** Joel Aiken. **S:** None.

OVERALL	$7-40	★★★

WINE RATINGS

Cabernet Sauvignon Napa Valley Beau Tour	★★
Cabernet Sauvignon Napa Valley Claret Special Release	NR
Cabernet Sauvignon Napa Valley Georges de Latour Private Reserve	★★★★★
Cabernet Sauvignon Napa Valley Rutherford	★★
Chardonnay Carneros	★★
Chardonnay Carneros Reserve	★★★

Chardonnay Napa Valley Beau Tour	★★
Chardonnay Napa Valley Beaufort	★★
Meritage Red Napa Valley	★★
Merlot Napa Valley Beau Tour	★★
Pinot Noir Carneros	★★
Pinot Noir Carneros Reserve	★★★
Pinot Noir Napa Valley Beau Tour	★★
Sauvignon Blanc California Beau Tour	★★
Sauvignon Blanc Napa Valley Dry	★★

WINERY DATA

C: 420,000. **V:** 644 acres in Carneros, Rutherford. **G:** Cabernet Sauvignon (262 acres), Pinot Noir (157), Chardonnay (182), Sauvignon Blanc (8), Merlot (35). **P:** Cabernet Sauvignon (Rutherford, Napa Valley), Cabernet Sauvignon (Pope Valley), Merlot (Pope Valley, Rutherford), Chardonnay (Carneros, Napa Valley), Chardonnay (Rutherford), Chenin Blanc (Napa Valley, Rutherford), Sauvignon Blanc (Rutherford, Napa Valley), Cabernet Franc (Napa Valley), Gamay Beaujolais (Napa Valley), Pinot Noir (Napa Valley, Carneros).

For most of this century, Beaulieu Vineyard's Georges de Latour Private Reserve Cabernet Sauvignon has been the most famous and prestigious wine produced in California. This richly flavored, elegantly crafted wine has proven time and again to be a consistently excellent and amazingly ageworthy Cabernet, as well as one of California's top collectibles.

One could easily write a book chronicling the history of Beaulieu, its vineyards, wines and cast of characters, led by the legendary winemaster André Tchelistcheff, who shaped the style of most of BV's greatest wines.

Beaulieu is French for "beautiful place," and today it remains a magnificent estate. Founded in 1900 by Frenchman Georges de Latour and modeled after the great French chateaux he admired, the winery, vineyards and grounds are spectacular. His splendid estate, across the highway from the winery, is still beautifully kept, with its towering trees, scenic gardens and panoramic views of the western foothills.

BV's Private Reserve has a long and distinguished reputation dating to its first vintage in 1936. Through more than 50 vintages there have been many peaks and only a few low points for this wine. The great vintages from the 1930s and 1940s, made under the direction of Tchelistcheff, the Russian-born, French-trained winemaker, helped establish Napa Valley's reputation for world-class Cabernet. Through the 1950s and 1960s,

Tchelistcheff built on BV's greatness, continuing to refine its style and inspiring others to pursue fine wine in Napa Valley and elsewhere in California. Through his careful teachings, Tchelistcheff influenced an entire school of winemakers from the 1950s to the present day, among them August Sebastiani (Sebastiani Vineyards), John Daniel Jr. (Inglenook), Robert Mondavi (Charles Krug and now Robert Mondavi), Peter Mondavi (Charles Krug Winery), Joe Heitz (Heitz Wine Cellar), Mike Grgich (Grgich Hills), Rob Davis (Jordan), Jill Davis (Buena Vista and William Hill) and Tom Selfridge (Beaulieu and now Kendall-Jackson).

Georges de Latour had grand wines in mind when he selected property in Rutherford, the heart of Napa Valley. He began planting his first vineyard at the turn of the century with BV No. 1, and followed seven years later with BV No. 2. Each of the vineyards, on the west side of Highway 29, measured nearly 100 acres. The winery focused on sweet wines, so Cabernet Sauvignon vines made up only a small portion of the vineyards. Prohibition in the 1920s and early 1930s restricted the winery's sales to sacramental wines. While Prohibition forced most Napa Valley wineries to close, leaving vineyards untended or uprooted and replanted to prune trees, Beaulieu thrived. When repeal of Prohibition came in 1933, BV had a big head start in its re-entry into commercial wine.

Leon Bonnet produced the first Private Reserve in 1936, but retired a year later. Searching for a successor, de Latour met Tchelistcheff in Paris and wisely hired him as his new winemaker. Tchelistcheff arrived in Napa in 1938, bringing a sophisticated, worldly view of wine at a time when California wine was in disarray. That year, Tchelistcheff made BV's first Chardonnay and later excelled with his favorite wine, Pinot Noir. BV's 1946 and 1947 vintages from Carneros-grown grapes are reminders of how grand Carneros Pinot Noir can be. Those wines stand as two of the greatest wines ever made in California.

Under Tchelistcheff's direction, BV's wines steadily improved, production increased and new wines were added, but the winery's strength remained Cabernet, including a Rutherford bottling and a Beau Tour line of lower-priced wines. By the late 1960s BV needed a cash infusion and a winery overhaul, and the de Latour family could no longer afford to keep it.

In 1969 the de Latours sold the winery to Heublein Inc., based in Farmington, Conn. By the time Tchelistcheff left BV in 1973, the winery had taken on a more corporate style; where earnings and profits for shareholders shaped winemaking decisions. The winery's volume grew in subsequent years, reaching 450,000 cases by the 1990s, and BV remained a red wine house despite increased production of Chardonnay and Sauvignon Blanc. Clearly its Private Reserve Cabernet remains a first-class wine, but the rest of the lineup has been erratic and behind the times, especially its Chardonnay, Sauvignon Blanc and Pinot Noir. In 1994 BV introduced its first Meritage (called Tapestry) and a Merlot, and even tampered with its long-standing tradition for BV Private Reserve: for the first time, the 1990 was aged in both new French oak and   American oak, and included 3 percent Merlot, not 100 percent Cabernet. Still, the integrity of the vineyards and the house style were maintained, as the 1990 was elegant and stylish.

Today BV owns 644 acres, down from 800 in 1988, with Cabernet still the largest portion with 262 acres, followed by Pinot Noir (157 acres), Chardonnay (182) and Merlot (35). The vineyards are divided between Carneros and Rutherford, with the former appellation a key to the winery's future with Chardonnay and Pinot Noir, and the latter its anchor with Cabernet. In 1994 I tasted several experimental wines from beyond the Napa Valley appellation that indicated winemaker Joel Aiken is rethinking BV's Napa Valley and Carneros heritage. I considered it a healthy experiment, regardless of whether BV decides to move beyond Napa for its grapes. With the emergence of a Rutherford appellation and radical new stylistic changes both driven by consumer demand and winemaking technique, some change at BV seems imminent.

TASTING NOTES

CABERNET SAUVIGNON NAPA VALLEY BEAU TOUR (★★): This wine can be a good value, but it often leans toward the herb and bell pepper side of Cabernet.

1991: Crisp and austere, with an herb and bell pepper edge to the ripe Cabernet flavors. Close to maturity now, but better in 1996. **82**

CABERNET SAUVIGNON NAPA VALLEY CLARET SPECIAL RELEASE (NR):
1990: Weedy and herbal. This is labeled "Special Release" Claret, but it tastes more like the old Beau Tour Cabernet. A fair price for a ripe, balanced Cabernet. **79**

CABERNET SAUVIGNON NAPA VALLEY GEORGES DE LATOUR PRIVATE RESERVE (★★★★★): I have tasted all

the BV Private Reserves, and have tried most of the recent vintages on numerous occasions, and it's evident this wine is still worthy of the accolades it receives. Its signature is purity of Cabernet flavor, elegance, grace and finesse. It's never overly tannic and almost always impeccably balanced. It also ages exceptionally well. The greatest years are 1951, 1958, 1968 and 1970.

1990: Ripe and spicy, with rich plum and cherry flavors that hold together nicely, finishing with fleshy tannins and good length. Impressive for its subtlety and finesse. **89**

1989: Crisp and austere, with a green edge to the tobacco and currant notes. **83**

1988: Lean, tart and simple, with a narrow band of cranberry and anise flavors and a green, stemmy edge. **81**

1987: Sharply focused, with rich, plush black cherry, plum and currant flavors and smooth, wellintegrated tannins. Picks up a seasoned, spicy oak edge, but the fruit pours through on the finish. **92**

1986: Tight, compact and concentrated, with sharply focused currant and black cherry flavors, finishing with firm tannins. Should age well for years. **92**

1985: Elegant and stylish, with layers of silky black cherry and currant aromas and flavors, a long, supple, lingering finish and fine, smooth tannins. Wonderful balance, with the depth and richness to age. **95**

1984: Ripe, smooth and elegant, with warm, rich and seductive currant and black cherry flavors, finishing with soft, fleshy tannins and fine depth. **92**

1983: Crisp, lean and tannic, but better balanced than most 1983s. **82**

1982: Mouthfilling and rich, with gorgeous fruit flavors. A well knit wine on a firm framework. **93**

1981: A good but unexceptional wine, showing more gritty tannins than supple fruit. Well structured and balanced, but isn't a stand-out as a BV Private Reserve. **84**

1980: Bold and concentrated, a star of the 1980 vintage. Delicious, with ripe, massively rich and thickly concentrated layers of plum, cherry, currant and spicy oak flavors. **94**

1979: Smooth, complex and concentrated, a wine of enormous depth and finesse, with tiers of currant, black cherry and cedary oak flavors. **92**

1978: Has improved with age, revealing more depth and polish, with ripe plum, spice and cedar notes, finishing with fine tannins and good length. **89**

1977: A light and elegant wine in its youth, it has peaked and is now in decline, with diluted Cabernet flavors. **77**

1976: Very ripe and oaky, an unusually concentrated bottling with plum, cherry and raisin flavors, finishing with a chewy aftertaste. Despite its very ripe flavors and powerful personality, it hangs together quite well. **89**

1975: Smooth, elegant and harmonious, with smoky coffee and currant flavors and gentle tannins. **84**

1974: Despite bottle variation, at its best it reveals ripe, spicy currant and cherry flavors with a slightly nutty edge. **86**

1973: Once elegant and supple, this is a very good 1973 that has peaked. **85**

1972: A decent wine from a poor vintage, this one's past its prime. **72**

1971: Past its prime but holding, with light herb and currant notes. **78**

1970: A grand wine that's fully mature and still wonderfully complex, deep and intriguing, with layers of spice, currant, plum, cedar and herb flavors that turn rich, smooth and supple on the finish. **96**

1969: A graceful, elegant wine that continues to drink and age exceptionally well, with sweet, ripe, intense black cherry, plum and currant flavors framed by toasty oak. Great finesse and balance, with a long finish. This wine never underwent malolactic fermentation, which may account for its vibrant, youthful fruit profile. **94**

1968: The best wine of the decade at BV, with the 1969 its lone challenger, it's ripe, complex and enormously concentrated, with rich, focused plum, currant and black cherry flavors and a long, fruity aftertaste. **96**

1967: Tastes its age, but still has finesse and spicy black cherry flavors. **83**

1966: It's still a great drinking experience, with ripe black cherry, plum, anise and spice notes and a pretty touch of floral oak on the finish. Very persistent from start to finish. **92**

1965: Past its prime, this once very good wine is drying out. **78**

1964: My last note indicates this wine has dried out, with earthy, stemmy tea flavors. **70**

1963: The last time I tried this wine it offered a brief hint of dried cherry flavors, but quickly faded. It was good in its prime. **70**

1962: Fading, with anise and brown sugar flavors, but persistent on the finish. A good wine from a mediocre year. **73**

1961: Still elegant, with spicy tea and plum notes that fade and dry out. **76**

1960: In surprisingly good shape when I last tasted it. Fully evolved, with spicy herb, tea and plum flavors that dry out, but the flavors linger. Impressive color for a wine this age. **84**

1959: Long impressive for its elegance, grace and finesse. Fully mature, with ripe, rich, focused flavors, echoing spice, black cherry, currant and cedar notes on a long, lingering finish. Tastes as if it will age forever. **93**

1958: For me, this is the greatest Private Reserve produced in BV's first 30 years. It remains an incredibly delicious, wonderfully complex, delicate, deep and flavorful wine that is graced with layers of black cherry and spice flavors. Wine doesn't get much better. **98**

1957: Dried out and faded. Perhaps there is life in some bottles, but not in the ones I've tried, including several from the winery's cellars. **70**

1956: In its heyday a very fine wine, it's now fading, with tea, olive, plum and spice flavors. Worth the experience if you can find it. **87**

1955: Past its prime but still wonderful, with elegant, mature black cherry and olive flavors. **84**

1954: Aging well and still displaying a distinctive peppery edge to the dried cherry and plum flavors. **86**

1953: One of several great BV Private Reserves of the 1950s. This wine is aging amazingly well, with fresh, perfumed fruit aromas and elegant, supple black cherry, plum, herb and spice flavors. Long and complex on the finish. **92**

1952: A wine of great harmony, depth and complexity, delivering tiers of warm, rich, silky currant, black cherry, plum and spice flavors. An absolutely delicious wine with a long, full finish. **93**

1951: Considered by many the finest California Cabernet of this era. I've tried it more than a dozen times and it always shows very well. It's packed with rich, full-bodied plum, anise and black cherry flavors that are intense, concentrated and persistent. Recently I've tasted a dryness on the finish, so drink up. Worth going out of your way to try. **95**

1950: This wine has always reminded me of a Pinot Noir, with its lighter color, smooth, supple texture and rose petal aroma. It's a delicious wine, full of ripe plum, spice and cherry flavors and hints of rose on the finish. **89**

1949: This wine still displays a rich, intense personality with surprisingly firm tannins. The earthy black cherry and plum aromas and flavors are complex and lively for a wine this is age. **88**

1948: Every time I've tried this wine it has shown its age, with earthy, green, mature flavors. **73**

1947: From an excellent vintage, it shows incredible richness, complexity and harmony for a wine approaching its 50th birthday. There is still much to admire in this amazing wine that seems suspended in time. **93**

1946: Ripe, supple and generous even at this age, with plenty of black cherry, plum and spice nuances. **87**

1945: Oxidized. Could be enjoyed as a taste of history. **70**

1944: It's not the Private Reserve bottling, but the regular '44 still possesses plenty of character for a wine this old. Tarry, earthy flavors show its maturity, but it's still enjoyable. **75**

1943: Very deep color, with spice, brown sugar and stewed plum flavors that offer fine depth, complexity and persistence. The texture is thick; the finish is the best part. **87**

1942: Dark color, with mature floral and fruit aromas and tight black cherry and earthy plum flavors. There's a metallic note on the finish, but otherwise it's quite complete and balanced. **85**

1941: Considered a fine year in Napa Valley, and this '41 remains an elegant, deep, rich wine with earthy black cherry and cedar flavors, gentle tannins and excellent length. **89**

1940: Dark in color, with deep cherry, currant and cedar flavors that are warm and spicy. The tannins are supple and there's plenty of fruit on the finish. **89**

1939: Dark in color, deep, rich and complex, with intriguing plum and black cherry flavors and subtle oak seasoning. Balanced and complex, better now than in previous tastings. Can still endure. **91**

1936: Smooth and elegant, with smoke, dry black cherry and spice notes. A timeless wine that's past its prime but not fatigued. **86**

CABERNET SAUVIGNON NAPA VALLEY RUTHERFORD (★★): This bottling often shares the bright cherry and currant flavors of the Reserve and is sometimes exceptional, although recent vintages have been off the mark and less complex.

1991: Firm and compact, with pretty currant and cherry flavors that pick up spicy, cedary oak notes on the finish. **85**

1990: Firm in texture, with wide-open, spicy currant and black cherry aromas and flavors, not at all heavy. **85**

CHARDONNAY CARNEROS (★★), RESERVE (★★★): Intense and concentrated, with ripe pear and pineapple flavors, but 1990 and 1991 are crisp and tight.

1992: Strikes a nice balance between ripe pear and apple flavors and spicy, toasty oak, finishing with good length and pretty, complex flavors. A solid value. **86**

Carneros Reserve 1992: Ripe and spicy, with appealing pear, peach and pineapple flavors that turn elegant and refined, with an earthy edge. **88**

Carneros Reserve 1991: Ripe, smooth and buttery, with spicy pear, honey and butterscotch flavors that are rich and intense. **88**

Carneros Reserve 1990: Tight and compact, with subtle toast and pear notes that fan out on the finish, revealing more oak nuances. **83**

CHARDONNAY NAPA VALLEY BEAU TOUR (★★), BEAUFORT (★★):

Beau Tour 1993: Strikes a nice balance between apple and pear-laced fruit and subtle creamy oak flavors, turning elegant and refined on the finish. **86**

Beau Tour 1992: Crisp and focused, with ripe apple and pear flavors that are concentrated and a touch coarse, turning spicy on the finish. A good value. **83**

Beaufort 1991: Crisp and tasty, almost tart, with lemon and green apple flavors and a citrus bite on the finish. **82**

MERITAGE RED NAPA VALLEY (★★):

1990: An elegant wine with supple herb, plum and cherry notes, finishing with light tannins. **85**

MERLOT NAPA VALLEY BEAU TOUR (★★):

1991: Tough and chewy, with firm tannins that override the berry, herb and cherry flavors. **82**

PINOT NOIR CARNEROS (★★), RESERVE (★★★): Lean and spicy, often with minty notes to the ripe plum and black cherry flavors. Built to age, although the winery is intent on making a more supple and fruity style and letting aging take care of itself.

1992: Simple, with a spicy menthol edge to its light cherry flavors. **78**

Reserve 1992: Marked by minty plum and cherry notes, it's ripe and supple with good balance. **86**

Reserve 1991: Spicy and minty, ripe and intense, offering pretty plum and black cherry flavors. Finishes with firm tannins. **85**

Reserve 1990: This solid Pinot Noir displays chunky cherry, plum and currant notes that are straightforward and rich, but doesn't show much finesse or grace. Has potential, though. **84**

Reserve 1989: Tart and lively, with nicely focused raspberry and blueberry aromas and flavors shaded by herb and oak overtones. Snappy and crisp, a good wine to wash down a plate of roast chicken. **85**

Reserve 1987: Rich and smooth, with ripe strawberry, cherry and vanilla flavors that follow through. **87**

Reserve 1986: Crisp, lean and elegant, with spicy cherry, strawberry and herb notes. Well crafted. **87**

PINOT NOIR VARIOUS BOTTLINGS (★★):

Napa Valley 1947: Not quite the richness and vibrancy of the 1946, but another masterpiece, warm, ripe, supple and complex, with tiers of anise and cherry, turning silky and smooth. Carneros-grown. **95**

Napa Valley 1946: A fabulous wine with deep garnet color and smoky, meaty cherry, orange and stewed plum flavors that are smooth, crisp and lively. A delicious wine that shows no sign of tiring. Give it high marks for aging this long and this gracefully. **97**

Napa Valley Beau Tour 1992: Lightly fruity, with simple cherry and plum notes. **79**

SAUVIGNON BLANC VARIOUS BOTTLINGS (★★):

California Beau Tour 1994: Lean and harmonious, showing lots of nice pear and herb flavors that zip through the finish. **83**

Napa Valley Dry 1992: Light and fragrant, a perfumed wine with a citrus tang. **83**

BEAUREGARD RANCH
Napa Valley
F: 1989. **O:** Jim Beauregard. **W:** Jim Beauregard. **S:** None.

A new brand from Napa owned by grape grower Jim Beauregard. The first vintage was 1989, but I have not tasted any wines from this producer yet. Intentions are to make 3,000 cases of Cabernet and Chardonnay.

BEL ARBORS
This is a second label for Fetzer Vineyards (see listing).

BELLA LUNA WINERY
St. Helena, Napa Valley
F: 1994. **O:** Bella Luna Wine Co. **W:** Tom Eddy. **S:** None.

OVERALL	$NR	NR

WINERY DATA
C: 5.000. **V:** 35 acres in Napa Valley. **G:** Gamay (7 acres), Chardonnay (11), Merlot (14). **P:** Cabernet Sauvignon (Napa Valley).

In 1995, Charles and Ellen Benish of Chicago purchased the former Charles F. Shaw Winery in St. Helena for $1.6 million, renaming it Bella Luna and hiring Tom Eddy as winemaker. The Benishes own Cook Illinois Corp., a company that leases school buses, but plan to move to Napa and focus on their 35-acre vineyard which was replanted. The initial focus was Merlot with the first harvest planned for 1995. Initial production was expected to reach 5,000 cases.

BELLEROSE VINEYARD
Healdsburg, Sonoma County
F: 1978. **O:** Charles & Nancy Richard. **W:** Charles Richard. **S:** None.

OVERALL	$12-20	★★

WINE RATINGS
Cabernet Blend Sonoma County	
Cuvée Bellerose	★★
Merlot Sonoma County	★★
Sauvignon Blanc Dry Creek Valley	
Barrel Fermented Reserve	NR

WINERY DATA
C: 6,000. **V:** 20 acres in Dry Creek Valley. **G:** Cabernet Sauvignon, Merlot, Sauvignon Blanc (Dry Creek Valley). **P:** None.

Owner Charles Richard has used Bordeaux as a model for his rustic Cabernets grown in his 20-acre vineyard in Dry Creek Valley, which is planted to Bordeaux varieties. His main wine, Cuvée Bellerose, carries a Sonoma County appellation and is very ripe, often quite tannic, and nearly as often marked by earthy, leathery flavors that are drying and not appealing to me. I question whether these wines will ever come into balance. Bellerose makes a Merlot in the same chewy style, while a barrel-fermented Sauvignon Blanc is also part of the 6,000-case production.

TASTING NOTES

CABERNET BLEND SONOMA COUNTY CUVÉE BELLE-ROSE (★★):
1986: Soft and velvety, with generous cassis and toast aromas and flavors and sufficient tannins to suggest it may be an elegant wine after a few years. **83**
1985: Concentrated, woody and tannic, with a core of cherry flavors, but it's very hard and closed now, not showing much. May not have the fruit to outlast the oak and tannins. **82**
1984: Pungently earthy and leathery. **77**

MERLOT VARIOUS BOTTLINGS (★★):
Dry Creek Valley Reserve 1988: Intense raspberry, cherry and strawberry flavors enliven this crisp, medium-bodied wine that's straightforward, charming and easy to drink. **84**
Sonoma County 1986: Dry, leathery and tannic, not showing much in the way of fruit and finishing on the dry, oaky side. Avoid. **69**
Sonoma County 1985: Very woody and tough, with hard-nosed cherry and berry flavors buried beneath the prickly exterior. Has a tart balance and a woody finish. **73**

SAUVIGNON BLANC DRY CREEK VALLEY BARREL FERMENTED RESERVE (NR):
1990: Soft and floral, with lemony flavors that hint at rose petal on the finish. A plain wine with a slightly bitter finish. **77**

BELVEDERE WINERY
Healdsburg, Sonoma County
F: 1979. **O:** Bill & Sally Hambrecht. **W:** Kevin Warren. **S:** None.

OVERALL	$9-18	★★★

WINE RATINGS
Cabernet Sauvignon Sonoma County	★★
Chardonnay Alexander Valley	★★
Chardonnay Sonoma County Preferred Stock	★★★
Merlot Sonoma County	★★
Muscat Canelli Alexander Valley Late Harvest	NR
Zinfandel Dry Creek Valley	★★

WINERY DATA
C: 50,000. **V:** 546 acres in Alexander Valley, Russian River Valley, Dry Creek Valley, Anderson Valley. **G:** Chardonnay (160 acres), Zinfandel (78), Merlot (62), Cabernet Sauvignon (75), Other (171). **P:** Chardonnay (Russian River Valley).

Peter Friedman, a founder of Sonoma Vineyards (now Rodney Strong Vineyards), started Belvedere Winery with a diversified winemaking and marketing scheme: he offered both a high-end line and a value line. Early on, Belvedere produced wines that featured the vineyard as the brand, showcasing Pinot Noir and Chardonnay from Winery Lake Vineyard and Cabernet and Merlot from Robert Young Vineyard, among others. The 1981 Winery Lake Pinot Noir (95) is one of the greatest Pinot Noirs ever made in California, an amazingly supple and complex wine that's a dead ringer for a red Burgundy. The 1982 Winery Lake Pinot is almost the opposite, a bizarre, dense, herbal and weedy wine. The 1982 Robert Young Cabernet and Merlot were showy on release, but the magic was short-lived: at an early age they took on strong herbal and weedy flavors. Belvedere also developed a line of lower-priced wines bottled under the Discovery Series label, which grew to nearly 200,000 cases.

In 1989 Bill Hambrecht, a venture capitalist who helped finance Belvedere as a minority partner, assumed controlling interest of the winery, and it has since shifted emphasis to estate-bottled wines using Hambrecht's 546 acres of vineyard, including 250 acres in Alexander Valley, 235 acres in Dry Creek and 56 acres in Anderson Valley. Chardonnay plantings dominate (160 acres), with Zinfandel, Merlot and Cabernet the other major varieties.

So far Chardonnay has been the best wine, with the Sonoma County Preferred Stock bottling featuring spicy vanilla oak and smooth, rich pear and honey notes. Also impressive is the 1991 Russian River Chardonnay, made in the same oaky style with appealing fruit to match. The Dry Creek Zinfandel 1991 is good but not among the best. It is made in a claret style and features appealing anise and raspberry flavors, but the 1990 is tannic and bitter. The 1991 Merlot Sonoma County is clean, with simple berry and plum notes. The 1991 Cabernet Sonoma County is tart and green, with plum and berry notes. Production is about 50,000 cases, but expected to rise.

TASTING NOTES

CABERNET SAUVIGNON VARIOUS BOTTLINGS (★★):
Alexander Valley Robert Young Vineyard Gifts of the Land 1985: Very flavorful and serious in structure, with tannins that are still too harsh. The flavors are ripe and pruny, with herb and pickle accents. It's a toss-up whether the fruit will last until the tannins subside. **81**
Sonoma County 1991: Lean and a bit green, with cedar, tart plum and black cherry notes that pick up a tobacco and light oak flavor on the finish. **82**
Sonoma County Preferred Stock 1988: Complex and enticing for a 1988, with cedar, cherry, herb and spice flavors and firm tannins; it thins out on the finish. Pleasant and low-key. **84**

CHARDONNAY SONOMA COUNTY PREFERRED STOCK (★★★):
1993: Medium-weight with a spicy, nutty edge to the ripe pear flavors. **84**
1992: Ripe and supple pear, vanilla and spice flavors and light, toasty oak shadings. **90**
1991: Smooth, rich and complex, with tiers of smoky pear, spice, butter and honey notes. **89**
1990: Ripe, buttery, smoky and mature, this round-textured wine has generous fig, butter and oak flavors. **88**

CHARDONNAY VARIOUS BOTTLINGS (★★):
Alexander Valley 1993: Well oaked, with toasty buttery flavors, but also enough rich pear and apple-laced flavors to keep it in balance. **87**
Alexander Valley 1992: Serves up attractive pear, apple and spice notes that gain a honey edge on the finish. Light oak adds complexity. **87**
Alexander Valley 1991: Intense, concentrated and spicy, with an anise note showing through the strong apple and vanilla aromas and flavors. **86**
Alexander Valley 1990: A pleasant wine with bold, creamy apple, oak and pear flavors that are decent, but fail to go beyond simplicity. **80**
Russian River Valley 1991: Strikes a fine balance between ripe, supple, creamy fruit flavors and spicy, buttery oak. Finishes with bright fig and pear notes. An elegant wine that's pleasing to drink. **88**

Russian River Valley 1990: Ripe, smooth and creamy, with elegant pear, vanilla, honey and caramel flavors that are well proportioned. **85**

ZINFANDEL DRY CREEK VALLEY (★★):
1991: Appealing, with up-front anise and raspberry flavors that taper off on the finish. **86**
1990: Tart and tannic, with a bitter edge to the woody aromas and black cherry flavors. **74**
1989: Intense and oaky, but with a solid core of cherry and raspberry flavors. **85**

VARIOUS BOTTLINGS:
Merlot Sonoma County 1991: Crisp and lean, with simple cherry and plum aromas and flavors. **82**
Muscat Canelli Alexander Valley Late Harvest 1990: Rich, unctuous and smooth, with pungent orange, spice and grapefruit aromas and flavors. Tasted twice. **80**

BENZIGER FAMILY WINERY
Sonoma Valley
F: 1980. O: Benziger Family. W: Joe Benziger. S: Benziger Estate, Benziger Imagery.

OVERALL	$10-27	★★★

WINE RATINGS

Cabernet Blend Sonoma	
Mountain A Tribute	★★★
Cabernet Franc Alexander Valley	
Blue Rock Vineyard Imagery Series	★★
Cabernet Sauvignon Knights Valley	★★
Cabernet Sauvignon Sonoma County	★★★
Chardonnay Carneros	
Premiere Vineyard	★★★
Chardonnay Sonoma County	★★
Fumé Blanc Sonoma County	★★
Merlot Sonoma County	★★
Pinot Blanc Sonoma Mountain	
Skinner Vineyard Imagery Series	★★
Pinot Noir Sonoma County	★★
Sauvignon Blend Sonoma	
Mountain A Tribute	★★★
Sémillon Sonoma Mountain	★★
Sparkling Wine Carneros	
Brut Imagery Series	NR

Syrah Paso Robles ★★
Zinfandel Sonoma County ★★
Zinfandel Port Dry Creek Valley
  Mayo Family & Carreras Vineyard
  Imagery Series ★★★

WINERY DATA
C: 140,000. **V:** 85 acres in Sonoma Mountain. **G:** N/A.
P: Cabernet Sauvignon, Chardonnay, Merlot, Sauvignon Blanc, Zinfandel (Sonoma County), Chardonnay (Carneros), Chardonnay, Pinot Blanc (Napa Valley), Cabernet Franc, Petite Verdot, Malbec (Alexander Valley).

Benziger Family Winery started as a small-scale operation in Glen Ellen headed by Bruno Benziger and his family. By the early 1980s sales of its low-priced line of Glen Ellen Proprietor's Reserve and M.G. Vallejo wines had rocketed past 3 million cases, making them two of the hottest brands of the decade. These wines—Cabernet, Merlot, Chardonnay, Sauvignon Blanc and white Zinfandel—were sound values and often best buys. The Benzigers showed a knack for finding high-quality bulk wines and good grape sources, and an ability to market their wares. In 1993 the Glen Ellen and M.G. Vallejo brands were sold to Heublein, Inc.

Long before the sale to Heublein—by the mid-1980s—the Benzigers began their return to fine wines. Riding the wave of the success of its brands, today the winery is still adjusting its new lineup and makes about 140,000 cases, including several wines from its 85-acre estate vineyard. Most of these bottlings are solid, middle-of-the-road wines that are well made but rarely excite or offend. The top-of-the-line wines are called A Tribute, a red and a white Meritage that both carry a Sonoma Mountain appellation. The Carneros Premiere Vineyard Chardonnay shows more depth and complexity, while the Sonoma County Merlot, Pinot Blanc, Pinot Noir and Zinfandel display modest varietal character and are marked by creamy oak shadings. The Imagery Series features small lots of vineyard-designated wines that the winery dubbs the winemaker's Field of Dreams.

TASTING NOTES

CABERNET BLEND SONOMA MOUNTAIN A TRIBUTE (★★★): A crisp, reined-in wine with appealing flavors and modest tannins but it could use more rich fruit.
1990: Pleasant enough, with spicy herb and currant notes, but it lacks richness and depth. **84**

1989: Firm tannins, but enough mint and currant flavors come through to make it interesting. **86**
1988: Supple, with generous plum, nutmeg, currant, tobacco and raspberry flavors and mild tannins. **86**
1987: Elegant, with delicate, ripe plum, herb and chocolate flavors and cedar and cherry on the finish. **85**

CABERNET FRANC ALEXANDER VALLEY BLUE ROCK VINEYARD IMAGERY SERIES (★★): Good but lacks varietal distinction.
1992: Well oaked, with just enough weedy black currant flavors to stand up to it. **83**
1989: Ripe and intense, with spicy cherry and currant flavors that are framed by toasty oak. Finishes with firm tannins and a hint of tobacco. Avoids the green edge found in most California Cabernet Francs. **85**

CABERNET SAUVIGNON SONOMA COUNTY (★★★): Graceful, with rich, supple fruit and oak flavors made for early drinking.
1992: Medium-bodied, with spicy, toasty oak and supple cherry and currant fruit underneath. Well balanced and pleasant to drink. **87**
1991: Complex, with a nice core of currant and cherry aromas and flavors and pretty, toasty, buttery oak notes. **88**
1990: Supple, light and oaky, with herb and currant flavors underneath. **84**
1989: Light and herbal, with vanilla, oak and berry flavors. **81**
1988: Light in color and flavor, with pleasant strawberry, spice and vanilla flavors. **84**
1987: Rich, supple and generous, with plum, cherry, spice and nutmeg flavors combining to make a complex, elegant wine. **90**
1986: Supple and medium-bodied, showing fresh berry aromas, smooth flavors and a soft texture. **82**

CABERNET SAUVIGNON VARIOUS BOTTLINGS (★★):
Knights Valley 1992: Solid with a chunky core of currant and berry fruit, finishing with firm tannins and a good dose of oak. **87**
Sonoma Mountain 1989: Crisp and firm, with a narrow band of mint, currant and black cherry flavors. **84**
Sonoma Mountain 1988: A heavy dose of menthol, herb and bay leaf dominates the rich currant and cherry flavors. **85**
Sonoma Valley 1987: Distinctively minty and herbal, with intense, ripe plum and strawberry flavors. **85**

Sonoma Valley 1986: Marked by herb and mint aromas, with currant, plum and vegetal flavors. **78**

Sonoma Valley 1985: Smells great but turns austere on the palate, with mint, herb and cherry notes. **83**

Chardonnay Carneros Premiere Vineyard (★★★): Intense and polished, with fine balance.

1993: Smoky, toasty oak flavors lead to a medium-bodied core of ripe pear and spice flavors that hang with you. **85**

1992: Smooth and polished, a nicely balanced wine that offers plenty of pear and pineapple flavors. **88**

1991: Smooth, ripe, silky and complex, with pear, honey, toast and vanilla flavors, all in elegant proportions. **89**

1990: Bold, ripe and spicy, with a core of rich pear and vanilla flavors. **87**

Chardonnay Sonoma County (★★):

1992: Bright and spicy, a generous wine with lots of apple and nutmeg flavors. **85**

Fumé Blanc Sonoma County (★★): Quality varies as does style.

1994: Lean and nicely focused, centering around spice, pear and herb flavors. **84**

1993: Simple and refreshing, a citrusy wine with pear and herb notes that finishes a bit short. **80**

1992: Smooth, ripe and creamy, with pretty fig, pear, vanilla and spice flavors that turn complex and supple on the finish. **87**

Merlot Sonoma County (★★): Variable quality could use more richness.

1992: Firm and tannic, but enough cherry, herb and oak flavors come through on the finish to hold your interest. Can stand short-term cellaring into 1996 for it to soften. **87**

1991: Tastes unripe, with a green, tea-like edge. **80**

1990: A supple, fleshy, oaky, easy-drinking wine with soft herb, currant and spice flavors. **84**

1989: Light and elegant, with pleasant cherry and spice notes. **81**

1988: Pleasant, with a core of pretty cherry and plum flavors balanced by moderate tannins. **87**

Pinot Blanc Various Bottlings (★★):

Sonoma County 1992: Smooth and spicy, a toasty wine with nice pear and vanilla flavors that keep echoing on the finish. **85**

Sonoma County 1991: Simple, round and fruity, with a melony edge to the pear and toast flavors. **82**

Sonoma Mountain Skinner Vineyard Imagery Series 1993: Elegant and fruity, with soft pear and apple notes that linger, picking up a hint of citrus. **84**

Pinot Noir Sonoma County (★★): Medium-weight and lacks distinction.

1991: Medium-bodied, with smoky cherry, herb and plum notes. **84**

1990: Crisp, with herb and cherry flavors that turn light and cedary on the finish. **84**

1989: Smooth and elegant, with spicy currant and toasty oak shadings that complement the herb and butter notes. **85**

Sauvignon Blend Sonoma Mountain A Tribute White (★★★): Smooth and polished, with rich fig flavors. Complex.

1992: Crisp in texture, nicely harmonious in the way it weaves its spicy, toasty-onion nuances through the fig and lemon fruit. **86**

1990: A smooth-textured blend with nice butter and vanilla accents complementing the modest melon and fig flavors. **83**

Sémillon Sonoma Mountain (★★):

1991: Lean and austere, with green citrus and fig flavors. **83**

Sparkling Wine Various Bottlings (NR):

California Lagomarsino Vineyard Aleatico Blanc de Noirs Imagery Series 1991: Golden in color, not at all pink. A distinctively dry wine, unusually sturdy and scented with honey and spice, finishing with pear and berry flavors. A blanc de noir of the Italian grape Aleatico. **83**

Carneros Brut Imagery Series 1990: Spicy, with ripe pear and subtle hazelnut flavors that turn complex, lingering on the finish. Appealing. **87**

Syrah Paso Robles (★★):

1990: Intense and spicy, with pepper and cherry notes that turn herbal and cedary on the finish. **84**

Zinfandel Sonoma County (★★): Clean and correct but lacks distinction.

1992: Lean and spicy, a peppery wine with enough blackberry flavor to keep it balanced. **86**

1991: A supple wine with smooth, ripe berry and black cherry flavors that turn elegant and spicy. **87**

1990: Elegant and spicy, with ripe cherry and plum flavors that turn bittersweet on the finish. **84**

1989: Ripe and fruity, with crisp raspberry, cherry and pepper notes. **83**

ZINFANDEL PORT DRY CREEK VALLEY MAYO FAMILY & CARRERAS VINEYARD IMAGERY SERIES (★★★):

1990: A refreshing late-harvest Zin that's complex and well balanced, with jammy plum, black cherry and juniper berry flavors. Not too tannic or alcoholic, it's a complete and harmonious wine that's capable of cellaring. **87**

BERGFELD WINERY

St. Helena, Napa Valley
F: 1986. **O:** Bergfeld Winery. **W:** Rick Schuetz. **S:** None.

OVERALL	$15	★★

WINE RATINGS

Cabernet Sauvignon Napa Valley	★★
Chardonnay Napa Valley	★
Merlot Napa Valley	★★

WINERY DATA
C: 60,000. **V:** None. **G:** None. **P:** Cabernet Sauvignon, Chardonnay, Merlot (Napa Valley).

This winery traces its history back to 1855, and since 1934 it has operated as a cooperative winery, crushing member's grapes and making wines that were sold in bulk to clients such as E. & J. Gallo. In 1986, after Gallo established its own crushing facilities in Sonoma County, the cooperative's owners, more than 100 Napa growers, began marketing Chardonnay, Sauvignon Blanc, Cabernet and Merlot primarily from a tasting room adjacent to the winery. In 1990 Bergfeld acquired the J. Wile & Sons brand. So far the quality is ordinary to good.

TASTING NOTES

VARIOUS BOTTLINGS:
Cabernet Sauvignon Napa Valley 1988: Has nice flavors and texture, offering a balance of currant and berry flavors and spicy oak notes. A bit tannic, but soft at the center. **83**

Chardonnay Napa Valley 1990: Firm and tight, with correct but simple oaky pear, spice and nutmeg flavors. **78**

Merlot Napa Valley 1989: A clean single into center field. Fresh, lively and fruity, with moderate tannins and a finish that lingers. **87**

BERINGER VINEYARDS

St. Helena, Napa Valley
F: 1876. **O:** Wine World Estates. **W:** Edward G. Sbragia. **S:** None.

OVERALL	$8-45	★★★★★

WINE RATINGS

Cabernet Sauvignon Knights Valley	★★★
Cabernet Sauvignon Napa Valley	
Private Reserve	★★★★★
Cabernet Sauvignon	
Napa Valley Chabot Vineyard	★★★★★
Chardonnay Napa Valley	★★★
Chardonnay Napa Valley	
Private Reserve	★★★★★
Chardonnay Napa Valley	
Proprietor Grown	★★★
Chardonnay Napa Valley	
Sbragia Limited Release	★★★★★
Fumé Blanc Napa Valley	★★
Gamay Beaujolais	
Nouveau North Coast	★★★
Meritage Red Knights Valley	★★★
Meritage White Knights Valley	★★
Merlot Howell Mountain	
Bancroft Ranch	★★★★★
Nightingale Napa Valley	★★★★★
Viognier Napa Valley Hudson Vineyard	★★★
Zinfandel Napa Valley	★★★

WINERY DATA
C: 1,300,000. **V:** 1,942 acres in Napa Valley, Knights Valley, Lake County. **G:** Cabernet Sauvignon, Chardonnay, Chenin Blanc, Merlot, Sauvignon Blanc, Sémillon, Zinfandel. **P:** Cabernet Sauvignon, Chardonnay, Merlot, Sauvignon Blanc, Zinfandel (Napa Valley).

All things considered, Beringer Vineyards is a candidate for California's best all-around winery. It is doing many things exceptionally well—from its classy Reserve

Chardonnays and Cabernets to its Howell Mountain Merlot and delicious Nightingale dessert wines—and nothing poorly. Beringer has a long, proud history in Napa Valley, dating to its founding in 1876, when brothers Frederick and Jacob Beringer first began making

wines. Today a retooled and modernized Beringer Vineyards is one of Napa Valley's leading tourist attractions. The historic Rhine House, an ornate Victorian structure, has been fully restored and the grounds are immaculate. Visitors can see the old stone caves where wines and barrels were once stored. The winemaking takes place across the street and features a huge barrel-aging *chai*.

Since 1972 Beringer has been a whole new institution under the ownership of Nestlé, the Swiss food conglomerate, and the Labruyere family of Mâcon, France. By then Beringer had fallen on hard times and the quality of its wines had steadily declined. The turnaround started with the hiring of Myron Nightingale, a savvy and talented winemaker who began to monitor quality more carefully, discarding offbeat, non-vintage wines and dramatically upgrading others. Moreover, Wine World Estates, a division of Nestle and Beringer's corporate owner, lent considerable financial support, providing the winery with just about anything it needed to succeed, including hiring top professionals and letting them manage the business.

The breakthrough vintage was 1977, when Beringer introduced its first Private Reserve Cabernet, entirely produced from the Lemmon Ranch (now called Chabot) Vineyard in the hills east of St. Helena. That bottling signaled the dawn of a new era. Beringer has since built an impressive line of Reserve and vineyard-designated wines. Beringer also has substantial Chardonnay vineyards, and made a wonderful 1974 from Santa Barbara. Its first Knights Valley Cabernet was the 1976 vintage. While Nightingale established the bottom line on quality, his apprentice, Ed Sbragia, proved more than his equal as winemaster, and the wines continue to improve. Even when the wines miss—which is rare—it seems to inspire Sbragia to greater heights. In 1993 Sbragia had most of his wines well under control and was moving on to Carneros Pinot Noir with much anticipation.

TASTING NOTES

CABERNET SAUVIGNON KNIGHTS VALLEY (★★★): This medium-bodied wine is not in the same league as the Private Reserve or Chabot, but it's well crafted, with attractive cherry and herb notes.

1992: Solid with a chunky core of currant and berry fruit, finishing with firm tannins and a good dose of oak. Can stand short-term cellaring. **87**

1991: Offers pretty, rich currant, berry and spice flavors that turn elegant on the finish. **87**

1990: A flashy wine with pretty, toasty butter and oak notes up front, but also a nice core of berry, herb and currant flavors underneath. **88**

1989: Firm and tannic, with aromas of cedar and tobacco over the currant, plum and blackberry flavors. **85**

1988: Fresh and lively, with ripe plum, black cherry, spice and tea flavors. **86**

1987: Ripe, intense and tightly knit, with rich cherry, plum, herb and currant notes, packing lots of flavor on the finish. **90**

1985: Lots of concentration, with plum and cherry flavors and a touch of herb. **87**

CABERNET SAUVIGNON NAPA VALLEY PRIVATE RESERVE (★★★★★): Winemaker Sbragia emphasizes bold, rich high-extract flavors laced with plenty of toasty oak and huge, polished tannins, but the wines display a sense of harmony and grace. It's a dramatic style that reaches its peak at five to seven years after the vintage and can age up to twenty.

1991: Bright and lively, with a core of ripe, rich, juicy black cherry, currant, plum and anise flavors. Deep and complex, it finishes with strong fruit flavors and plush tannins. **95**

1990: Bold, rich and concentrated, with layers of ripe, spicy currant, black cherry and anise notes framed by toasty, buttery oak. Beautifully balanced, a wonderfully harmonious wine. **95**

1989: Rich and supple, with solid cherry, currant, plum and spice flavors that turn smooth and silky before the fine tannins kick in. **90**

1988: Ripe and flavorful, with generous currant, toast, chocolate and anise aromas and flavors and hints of leather on the finish. **88**

1987: Complex, fascinating and beautifully built. Deep currant, cherry, anise, leather, earth and herb notes vie for attention. It shows a different facet with every sip. The tannins are firm and powerful without being overwhelming. **94**

1986: Deliciously rich and concentrated, the layers of herb, mint, cherry and plum flavors are tightly wound together and framed by toasty oak and firm tannins. Elegant and stylish, this beautifully proportioned wine echoes fruit and oak. **97**

1985: Enormously deep, rich and concentrated, with layers of currant, cherry, plum, coffee and spice notes set off by toasty oak. A remarkably complex wine that echoes fruit flavors on the finish, where the tannins turn smooth and polished. **97**

1984: A blockbuster, massively proportioned, extremely rich and powerful, packed with ripe fruit and layers of cherry, cedar, chocolate and toasty vanilla. It's a mouthful of Cabernet that has a silky texture to stand up to the tannins. **94**

1983: A tribute to concentrated fruit, it is now mature but still intense, with plenty of ripe, concentrated currant, herb and spice flavors. **89**

1982: Richly flavored and deftly balanced, with lush cedar, chocolate, plum and currant flavors that are long and full on the finish. **91**

1981: Thoroughly delicious, with its broad, rich, supple currant and anise notes and delicate tannins, it continues to improve with age and shows no sign of losing its charm. **91**

1980: Ripe, rich, lush and supple, fully mature, with cedar, currant, herb and mint flavors that are well integrated and complex. **89**

1978: Rich, deep and powerful, with complex, concentrated currant, berry and cherry flavors and pretty oak shadings. Youthful and assertive when last tasted, as strong a showing as I've seen in years. **95**

1977: Fully mature, with complex chocolate, herb, cedar and currant flavors that are rich and smooth, picking up a trace of tannin on the finish. **88**

CABERNET SAUVIGNON NAPA VALLEY CHABOT VINEYARD (★★★★★): Comparing the Private Reserve with Chabot contrasts a vineyard's personality with a winemaker's style. The Chabot is tighter, more compact and tannic, emphasizing the vineyard, but with a similar flavor profile of black cherry, currant and spice.

1991: Dark and intense, with floral and fruity aromas that turn elegant and supple, with a pretty core of black cherry, currant and plum, gaining a firm tannic edge. **93**

1990: Tight and deeply complex, with a core of rich, chewy currant, black cherry and cedary oak flavors, turning tannic on the finish. **92**

1989: Well crafted, bright and lively, with a wonderful integration of lush, elegant cherry, currant and spice notes. Tannins are firm but in check. **90**

1988: A ligher Chabot with a shallow nose and a narrow band of fruit flavor that has a raisiny edge, turning earthy and tarry on the finish. **84**

1987: Supple and elegant, very complex, with ripe black cherry and currant flavors that linger on the finish, turning spicy. **94**

1986: Smooth and rich, with thick black cherry and currant flavors. Impeccably balanced, with a long, full finish. Amazingly complex; the best Chabot to date. **95**

1985: Mature, with herb, tar and earthy currant flavors that firm up on the finish. **86**

1984: A fine example of the rich, supple charm of the 1984 vintage, not as intense and backward as most bottlings from this vineyard. The bright plum, cherry and smoky anise flavors are attractive. **87**

1983: Austere, with drying tannins and a core of ample herb, currant, cherry and cedar flavors. Needs time to unfold. **85**

1982: Intense yet elegant, packed with fresh, ripe, juicy currant and cherry flavors, accented with a touch of mint, it's firm, lean and tannic. **89**

1981: Fully mature, with pure currant and berry flavors, ripe and full, with fine balance and plenty of mint and spice nuances. The tannins are deceptively soft; this wine has a fine backbone. **87**

CABERNET SAUVIGNON NAPA VALLEY STATE LANE VINEYARD (NR):
Reserve 1980: Decidedly herbal, with cedar, tea and chocolate notes. High in extract, true to style, but somewhat less appealing than the Lemmon-Chabot; that's the real Private Reserve. **85**

Reserve 1979: Supple, with ripe currant and spicy plum flavors that pick up a touch of anise and oak. The texture is smooth and polished, finishing with a smoky aftertaste. **89**

CHARDONNAY NAPA VALLEY (★★★), PROPRIETOR GROWN (★★★): Lighter and fruitier than the Reserve bottlings, with less oak and depth, but still well crafted.
1993: Lean and trim, with a narrow, earthy band of pear- and citrus-laced fruit. **84**

1992: Crisp, firm and focused, with a tight band of spicy pear, hazelnut and herb flavors. **87**

1991: Lean and silky, with hints of fig, pear and spice flavors that border on vegetal, but it hangs together. **84**

Proprietor Grown 1992: Firm, ripe and intense, with spicy pear, peach and light oak shadings. **87**

CHARDONNAY NAPA VALLEY PRIVATE RESERVE (★★★★), SBRAGIA LIMITED RELEASE (★★★★★): Both the Reserve and the Sbragia are bold, ripe and richly complex wines that with recent vintages rate among California's best.

Private Reserve 1993: Marked by a leesy edge, but it stretches the band of flavors, offering a strong core of rich fig, pear and honeyed notes that pick up a flinty edge. **92**

Private Reserve 1992: Bold, ripe and deftly balanced, with rich fig, pear, citrus and melon notes that finish with a pretty, toasty oak edge. Complex and concentrated. **92**

Private Reserve 1991: Offers a rich core of spicy pear and apple aromas and flavors and toastiness from oak, but it's firm and tight now, picking up honey and spice notes on the long finish. **90**

Private Reserve 1990: A fully ripe, lush Chardonnay that got the complete oak treatment, resulting in a buttery, toasty, honey-textured character that's delicious. The fruit and oak nuances linger on the finish. **90**

Sbragia Limited Release 1992: Tight, rich and dramatic, with sharply focused nectarine, peach, pear and toast nuances, picking up a toasty earthiness on the well balanced, elegant, spicy finish. **93**

Sbragia Limited Release 1991: Beautifully crafted, a rich and seamless wine with creamy pear, honey, toast and spice flavors of uncommon depth and finesse. **92**

FUMÉ BLANC NAPA VALLEY (★★): Inconsistent and as variable as this grape can be, but recent vintages show more balance and purity of flavor.

1991: Smooth and well balanced, with a honey component echoing on the finish to wrap up the solid pear, tobacco and spice aromas and flavors. **84**

GAMAY BEAUJOLAIS NOUVEAU NORTH COAST (★★★): Bright and fruity, among the best.

1994: Light and grapey, floral around the edges, pleasant all around, with a smooth finish. **82**

MERITAGE RED KNIGHTS VALLEY (★★★):
1991: Ripe and firmly tannic, with spicy currant and plum flavors. Tight and compact, it will benefit from short-term cellaring. **88**

MERITAGE WHITE KNIGHTS VALLEY (★★):
1992: Crisp, smooth and elegant, with refreshing lemon, fig and spice notes. **84**

MERLOT HOWELL MOUNTAIN BANCROFT RANCH (★★★★★): A big, ripe, intense and tannic wine, but the tannins are smooth and polished. Best to drink early on and up to age 10 to 12.

1991: Complex and intriguing, with layers of cherry, currant, chocolate and buttery oak flavors that all fold together neatly. The flavors fan out on the finish, where it picks up a pretty vanilla edge. **90**

1990: Big, ripe, rich and tannic, packing in lots of currant, herb, cedar and spice notes and adding a toasty, smoky, woody overlay. **90**

1989: Enormously concentrated, smelling of smoke and coffee and tasting of chocolate and black cherry, with a long, toasty finish. **91**

1988: Rich and complex, lavishly spread with buttery oak and bursting with berry and currant flavors underneath. The tannins are well integrated. **90**

1987: Warm, ripe and generous, with plush, concentrated herb, plum, chocolate and toasty oak flavors and a finish that echoes the plum and herb notes. **91**

NIGHTINGALE NAPA VALLEY (★★★★★): One of the best and most ageworthy dessert wines, capable of achieving uncommon richness, complexity and depth of flavor. Three bottlings are produced but not always in each vintage, a varietal Sauvignon Blanc and a Sémillon as well as a Sauvignon/Sémillon blend.

Sauvignon Blanc Napa Valley 1990: Grassy, with sweet pear and candied fruit flavors that turn to dried apricot and nectarine on the finish. Impressive. **90**

Sauvignon Blend Napa Valley 1990: Bold, ripe, smooth and creamy, with layers of lush fig, honey, pear, toast and tobacco flavors folding together on a rich, complex aftertaste. Delicious. **95**

Sémillon Napa Valley 1990: Ripe, smooth and supple, with rich, intense pear, fig and spice flavors that are deep and complex. **91**

Sauvignon Blend Napa Valley 1989: Racy and concentrated, with ripe, lush grass, fig, herb, butter and honey notes that turn complex and linger on the finish. **93**

Sauvignon Blend Napa Valley 1988: Complex, with an herbaceous edge to the ripe fig, honey, pear and toasty oak flavors. Turns elegant and refined on the finish. **91**

Sauvignon Blend Napa Valley 1987: Elegant and spicy, with sweet, ripe honey, pear, fig and toast notes. Finishes with a long, rich aftertaste that turns smoky and buttery. **92**

Sémillon Napa Valley 1987: Lush and creamy, with layers of honey, pear, fig and vanilla flavors that are complex and concentrated and a long, full finish. **93**

Sauvignon Blend Napa Valley 1986: Ripe and lush, with mint, butter, pear and fig flavors. Comes up short on the finish, but it's still impressive. **88**

Sauvignon Blanc Napa Valley 1985: Grassy, with ripe, lush fig and spice flavors that turn candied on the finish. Holds together, gaining complexity on the finish. **89**

Sauvignon Blend Napa Valley 1985: A blend of Sauvignon Blanc and Sémillon, it has a minty edge, with ripe fig and apricot notes that turn spicy. **88**

Sémillon Napa Valley 1985: Decadent and smoky, a rich, lush, creamy wine with ripe fig, apricot and spice flavors. **89**

Sauvignon Blanc Napa Valley 1983: A racy, grassy wine that exaggerates the Sauvignon Blanc character, making for an intriguing range of flavors. Turns bitter on the finish, but still serves up lots of flavor. **87**

Sémillon Napa Valley 1983: It's a mature gold, with a smoky, charred edge to the ripe fig and apricot flavors. The finish is short. **84**

Sauvignon Blend Napa Valley 1982: Mature, with sweet, earthy fig, dried apricot and honey flavors. **87**

Sauvignon Blanc Napa Valley 1981: Complex, with roasted coffee, caramel and fig flavors. Very rich and opulent, showing a true Sauvignon Blanc character. **91**

Sémillon Napa Valley 1981: Ripe, plush and oily, with buttery fig and spice flavors that turn complex and earthy on the finish. **92**

Sauvignon Blend Napa Valley 1980: Deep gold, amazingly complex and supple, with smooth, rich apricot, butter, pear and toast flavors that turn to butterscotch and honey on the finish. Sensational. **99**

VIOGNIER NAPA VALLEY HUDSON VINEYARD (★★★): New but already a leader, with more depth and focus.
1993: Elegant with delicate pear, spice and melon notes, avoiding the ultra-spiciness this wine can produce. **89**
1992: Displays ripe and creamy pear, honey and spice notes that hold together on the finish. **87**

ZINFANDEL NAPA VALLEY (★★★): Medium-bodied, with the emphasis on varietal character. The quality keeps improving.
1991: A solid, well balanced, youthful Zin with a tight core of cherry, wild berry and spice flavors. **86**
1990: Firm and tight, with modest fruit flavors and spice components that seem bound up in the generous tannins and acidity. **83**

BERNARDUS VINEYARDS & WINERY
Carmel Valley
F: 1990. O: Berk Holdings. W: Don Blackburn. S: None.

OVERALL	$9-25	★★★

WINE RATINGS

Chardonnay Monterey County	★★★
Pinot Noir Santa Barbara County Bien Nacido Vineyard	★★
Sauvignon Blanc Monterey County	★★★

WINERY DATA
C: 40,000. V: 45 acres in Carmel Valley. G: Cabernet Sauvignon (23 acres), Merlot (12), Cabernet Franc (2), Petite Verdot (1), Other (7). P: Chardonnay, Sauvignon Blanc (Monterey), Chardonnay (Edna Valley), Pinot Noir (Santa Maria Valley).

The first wines from this Carmel Valley winery are impressive. Through his Berk Holdings, proprietor Bernardus (Ben) Pom owns 45 acres in Carmel Valley, planted primarily to Cabernet (23 acres) and Merlot (12). He buys Chardonnay and Pinot Noir, the latter from Bien Nacido Vineyard. The Chardonnays feature rich, complex, buttery flavors. The 1993 Sauvignon Blanc is complex and well crafted. The 1992 Pinot Noir Bien Nacido is dark and richly flavored, with herb, tea, cola and berry flavors framed by toasty oak. Production in 1994 was 40,000 cases, of which two-thirds was Chardonnay, with an estate-grown Cabernet-Merlot blend in the works. The wines are now made in the old Domaine de Clarck winery, which Pom has purchased.

TASTING NOTES

CHARDONNAY VARIOUS BOTTLINGS (★★★):
1993: Solid with an appealing range of apple, pear, spice and light oak shadings, turning complex on the finish. **87**
1992: Ripe, smooth and buttery, with spicy pear, pineapple and hazelnut flavors that are rich and focused, complex and concentrated. **91**

California 1991: Smooth, ripe and round, with lots of spicy, buttery green apple flavors that turn toward pear and honey on the long, smooth finish. **89**

PINOT NOIR SANTA BARBARA COUNTY BIEN NACIDO VINEYARD (★★):
1992: Dark and richly flavored, with layers of herb, tea, cola and berry flavors and smoky, meaty notes on the finish. **86**

SAUVIGNON BLANC MONTEREY COUNTY (★★★):
1993: Broad, ripe and spicy, a toasty, honey-scented wine with oaky notes to its pear and apple flavors. **87**
1992: Smooth, rich and creamy, with hints of herb, citrus and spice, delivering ripe fig flavors on the finish. **87**

ROBERT BIALE VINEYARDS
Napa Valley
F: 1991. **O:** A. Biale, R. Biale, A. Perry & D. Pramuk. **W:** A. Perry. **S:** None.

OVERALL	$14-18	★★★★

WINE RATINGS
Zinfandel Napa Valley Aldo's Vineyard   ★★★★

WINERY DATA
C: 1,000. **V:** 17 acres in Napa Valley. **G:** Zinfandel (13 acres), Sauvignon Blanc (3), Sangiovese (1). **P:** Zinfandel, Cabernet Sauvignon, Petite Sirah, Refosco (Napa Valley).

This new winery is owned by long-time grape grower turned vintner Aldo Biale, whose son Robert is making small lots of vineyard-designated red wines with an emphasis on old-vine Zinfandel. Biale's northern Napa Zinfandel vineyard was planted in 1937 by Aldo's parents, Pietro and Christina Biale. The 1,000-case winery intends to stay small, but the Biales are looking for more old Zinfandel and Petite Sirah vineyards for vineyard-designated wines. Aldo's Vineyard recently expanded by 10 acres, adding Sangiovese. A 1992 Zinfandel and 1992 Refosco from D.E. Dyers Farm in Browns Valley, west of Napa, were in the works, along with 25 cases of 1991 Napa Valley Cabernet grown by H. Posert & Sons Vineyard in Rutherford.

TASTING NOTES

ZINFANDEL NAPA VALLEY ALDO'S VINEYARD (★★★★):
Appealing, with supple raspberry and cherry notes and mild tannins. The 1993 is right on the mark.
1993: Ripe and complex, with a seam of elegant cherry, plum and wild berry fruit. A wine of finesse and grace. **91**
1992: Supple and fruity, with spicy strawberry and cherry notes that turn smooth and elegant on the finish. **84**
1991: Effusively fruity, with ripe, supple cherry and raspberry flavors that are spicy and elegant, finishing with soft tannins. **91**

BLACK MOUNTAIN
Healdsburg, Sonoma County
F: 1975. **O:** Kenneth J. Toth. **W:** M. Dean Cox. **S:** J.W. Morris.

OVERALL	$9-20	★★

WINE RATINGS

Cabernet Sauvignon Alexander Valley Fat Cat	★★
Chardonnay Alexander Valley Douglass Hill	★★
Chardonnay Alexander Valley Gravel Bar	★★
Petite Sirah Alexander Valley Bosun Crest	★
Zinfandel Alexander Valley Cramer Ridge	★

WINERY DATA
C: 10,000. **V:** 100 acres in Alexander Valley. **G:** Cabernet Sauvignon. **P:** Chardonnay, Petite Sirah, Zinfandel (Alexander Valley).

Ken Toth, a former president of Sonoma Vineyards, owns more than 100 acres of vineyards in Alexander Valley, where he produces a Cabernet Sauvignon called Fat Cat, Chardonnays from Douglass Hill and Gravel Bar, and Petite Sirah and Zinfandel from Cramer Ridge. Quality has been highly variable, with the Chardonnays occasionally well made. The 1990 Cabernet is lean and tannic, while the 1991 Chardonnay Douglass Hill features nice green apple flavors. The 1991 Chardonnay Gravel Bar is austere but appealing for its crisp fruit flavors. The 1990 Petite Sirah Bosun Crest is overly tannic with little flavor, while the 1990 Zinfandel Cramer Ridge is funky, tannic and oaky. Production is about 10,000 cases; most of Toth's grapes are used for the J.W. Morris line of lower-priced wines.

TASTING NOTES

CABERNET SAUVIGNON ALEXANDER VALLEY FAT CAT (★★): Steady if unexciting, with ample flavors but not much finesse.

1990: Tight and tannic, an astringent wine with lean earth and berry aromas and flavors. Finishes tough. Needs until 2000 to begin to sort itself out. **80**

1988: Smooth and spicy, with minty, herbal edges to the ripe currant and berry flavors. A distinctive wine. Finishes with smooth tannins. **85**

1986: Wonderfully rich currant, plum and cherry flavors are smooth and lush up front, but the tannins and oak dominate the finish. **86**

1985: Has plenty of flavor, intensity and depth, but also a sense of elegance and finesse, with well defined herb, bell pepper, chocolate and currant flavors that are complex and long on the finish. **87**

CHARDONNAY ALEXANDER VALLEY VARIOUS BOTTLINGS (★★): Crisp and medium-bodied.

Douglass Hill 1991: Crisp and focused, with nice green apple, vanilla and spice aromas and flavors. A solid wine on a lean frame that keeps pumping out the flavor on the finish. **87**

Gravel Bar 1990: Austere and spicy, with hard-edged nutmeg and vanilla aromas and green apple flavors that broaden out a bit on the finish, ending up spicy. **86**

PETITE SIRAH ALEXANDER VALLEY BOSUN CREST (★): Austere and lacks charm.

1990: Lean, austere, steely dry and tannic, with surprisingly little flavor. Has a frame, but no stuffing. **77**

1987: Full-bodied, soft and generous, oozing with plum and currant flavors that persist on the finish. Well integrated tannins wouldn't get in the way of a hearty dish. **87**

ZINFANDEL ALEXANDER VALLEY CRAMER RIDGE (★): Usually lacks finesse or polish.

1990: A full-bodied, tannic, oaky Zin that's harsh and powerful. May develop into something, but would take until 1998, if the modest fruit flavor doesn't drop out. **78**

1987: Smells musty but tastes fruity, with plenty of blackberry flavor, but the drying texture is troubling. Seems too tannic for the fruit. **77**

BLACK SHEEP VINTNERS
Murphys, Sierra Foothills
F: 1986. **O:** David & Janis Olson. **W:** David Olson. **S:** True Frogs.

OVERALL	$7-13	★★

WINE RATINGS	
Zinfandel Sierra Foothills	★★

WINERY DATA
C: 2,500. **V:** None. **G:** None. **P:** Zinfandel (Sierra Foothills), Cabernet Sauvignon (Sierra Foothills), Sauvignon Blanc (Sierra Foothills), Chenin Blanc (Sierra Foothills).

David and Janis Olson bought this 2,500-case winery in Calaveras County in 1986. The winery, formerly known as Chipsa Cellars, now produces Sierra Foothills-grown Cabernet, Zinfandel, Sauvignon Blanc and Chenin Blanc.

TASTING NOTES

ZINFANDEL SIERRA FOOTHILLS (★★):
1991: Impressive for its elegance and graceful berry and pepper notes. **84**

BLOCKHEADIA RINGNOSII
Napa Valley
F: 1992. **O:** Michael Ouellette. **W:** Michael Ouellette. **S:** None.

OVERALL	$15	★★★

WINE RATINGS	
Zinfandel Napa Valley	★★★

WINERY DATA
C: 300. **V:** None. **G:** None. **P:** Zinfandel (Napa Valley).

This is a new brand owned by Michael Ouellette, manager of Mustard's Grill in Yountville. The first wine, a 1992 Zinfandel captures the essence of Rutherford-grown Zinfandel, with its richness and peppery flavors. The grapes are purchased from Niebaum-Coppola Estate.

TASTING NOTES

ZINFANDEL RUTHERFORD (★★★): Limited production, but well crafted, with classy Zinfandel flavors.
1993: Light but with appealing earthy raspberry and peppermint, spicy nuances. Finishes with mild tannins. **85**
1992: Ripe, smooth and polished, with a pretty core of peppery black cherry flavors. Mild tannins make it easy to enjoy. **88**

BLUE HERON LAKE WINERY
Napa Valley
F: 1985. **O:** John Newmeyer. **W:** David Mahaffey. **S:** None.

OVERALL	$14	★★

WINE RATINGS

Chardonnay Wild Horse Valley	★★

WINERY DATA
C: 600. **V:** 24 acres in Wild Horse Valley. **G:** Chardonnay (16 acres), Pinot Noir (7), Gewürztraminer (1). **P:** None.

Owner John Newmeyer sells most of the grapes from his 24-acre vineyard in Wild Horse Valley, but he produces 200 cases of Pinot Noir and 400 cases of Chardonnay.

TASTING NOTES

CHARDONNAY WILD HORSE VALLEY (★★):
1992: Crisp and nicely focused, a mouthful of bright pear, apple and nectarine fruit that lingers on the finish. **87**

BOCAGE
This is a second label for San Saba Vineyards (see listing).

BOEGER WINERY
Placerville, El Dorado County
F: 1972. **O:** Greg Boeger. **W:** Greg Boeger. **S:** Hangtown Red.

OVERALL	$8-15	★★

WINE RATINGS

Barbera El Dorado County	★★
Cabernet Sauvignon El Dorado County	★★
Chardonnay El Dorado County	★★
Johannisberg Riesling El Dorado County	NR
Meritage Red El Dorado County	NR
Merlot El Dorado County	★★
Sauvignon Blanc El Dorado County	★★
Zinfandel El Dorado County	★★
Zinfandel El Dorado County Walker Vineyard	★★★
Zinfandel Napa Valley Joseph A. Nichelini Vineyards	NR

WINERY DATA
C: 14,000. **V:** 31 acres in El Dorado County. **G:** Italian Type (2 acres), Rhône Type (5), Merlot (4), Muscat Canelli (1), Cabernet Franc (2), Cabernet Sauvignon (5), Chardonnay (2), Sauvignon Blanc (2), Zinfandel (5), Other (1). **P:** Sauvignon Blanc (El Dorado County), Barbera (El Dorado County).

Boeger's wines continue to improve, especially the Barbera and Walker Vineyard Zinfandel. The 14,000-case winery, the first to emerge in El Dorado County after Prohibition, has 31 acres of vineyards and grows small parcels of many varieties, none more than six acres. Greg Boeger, a Napa Valley native, is the owner and winemaker. He has family ties to the old Nichelini Winery, and he uses Nichelini grapes for a vineyard-designated Zinfandel.

The Barbera can be tarry and earthy, but the 1991 features lively berry and spice notes. The 1990 Cabernet displays cedar, herb and fruit flavors. The 1991 Chardonnay shows more complexity than previous vintages, with its attractive melon, pear and spice notes and toasty oak shadings. Usually it is simpler and less complex. The Merlot has been inconsistent, but the 1991 was ripe and intense, with supple currant, herb and cherry notes. The Sauvignon Blanc is light, with the 1993 displaying floral and green apple notes. The Nichelini Vineyard Zinfandel has been mixed, often running toward earthy, leathery flavors.

TASTING NOTES

BARBERA EL DORADO COUNTY (★★):
1992: Smooth and spicy, with low-key black cherry fruit rounded out with spicy oak. **84**
1991: Firm in texture, a lean wine with lively berry and currant flavors that echo on the finish. **84**
1990: Spicy, peppery, earthy, tarry overtones make this solid wine a bit more interesting than most Barberas. The finish is ripe and a little raw, with a touch of dill. **81**

1989: Crisp, flavorful and distinctive, offering lots of wild berry and plum aromas and flavors that hint at sage and spices on the finish. **85**

CABERNET SAUVIGNON EL DORADO COUNTY (★★):
1990: Mature in color, with cedar, herb and fruit flavors. A good wine that's a bit tannic. **83**
1989: A pleasant, fruity, fairly priced Cabernet offering ripe currant, berry and spice flavors framed by toasty oak. **83**
1987: Very ripe, fruity and generous, with plum, spice and cherry jam notes. Not too tannic and a bit fat around the edges. Picks up attractive smoky oak flavors on the finish. **85**
1985: A mature-tasting Cabernet that's ready to drink. Simple, with some decent cherry flavors. **77**
1984: Very nicely balanced between fruit, tannins and oak, it comes across as simple at first, but then you begin to notice the subtle plum, chocolate and cedar complexities. **81**

CABERNET SAUVIGNON NAPA VALLEY JOSEPH A. NICHELINI VINEYARDS (NR):
1989: Sharp and coarse, with light berry aromas and flavors and dry, gripping tannins. Has the classic 1989 hollowness in the mid-palate. **77**

CHARDONNAY EL DORADO COUNTY (★★): A good value with attractive fruit and flavors.
1991: Ripe and perfumed, offering intense, elegant, focused melon, pear and spice flavors that are clean and complex, picking up a toasty, earthy edge on the finish. **87**
1990: Butterscotch and vanilla flavors dominate this attractively oaky Chardonnay, and it offers enough pear and apricot flavors to give it substance and a bit of a finish. Quite enjoyable. **85**

JOHANNISBERG RIESLING EL DORADO COUNTY (NR):
1992: Light and fragrant, with bright apple and floral aromas and flavors, slightly sweet and appealing. **84**

MERITAGE RED EL DORADO COUNTY (NR):
1989: Straightforward, firm and tight, with ripe currant, plum and earthy oak flavors that linger on the finish. Tannic and well balanced, with lots of character. A blend of 46 percent Cabernet Franc, 27 percent Merlot, 26 percent Cabernet Sauvignon and 1 percent Petite Verdot. **83**

MERLOT EL DORADO COUNTY (★★): Usually quite good, with appealing fruit.
1992: Marked by smoky, toasty oak and a supple texture, it delivers enough cherry and raspberry-laced fruit to complement the wood. **86**
1991: Ripe and intense, with rich, supple currant, herb and cherry flavors that are complex and engaging, and cedar and anise notes on the finish. Very impressive for its bright flavors, depth and length. **86**
1990: Tough and tart, with simple, earthy flavors that never quite take off. **78**
1989: Fruity, fairly tight and well balanced, with tart raspberry and plum flavors, moderate tannins and a crisp, fruity finish. **86**

SAUVIGNON BLANC EL DORADO COUNTY (★★):
1993: Light, floral and lively, with green apple and pear flavors that echo through the finish. **83**
1992: Light and spicy, with zingy peach and pear flavors, finishing with a floral flourish. **84**

ZINFANDEL EL DORADO COUNTY (★★):
1992: Lots of buttery oak, spice, tar and raspberry flavors come through, making this a complex and intriguing wine despite some rough edges. **84**

ZINFANDEL EL DORADO COUNTY WALKER VINEYARD (★★★): Typically bold and ripe, and now showing more oak, it's one of the best from the Sierra Foothills.
1992: An oaky wine that's toasty and buttery, but there are plenty of pretty cherry and raspberry flavors to give it complexity. **87**
1991: Earthy, but it reveals enough ripe, spicy prune flavors to keep your interest. **87**
1990: Round and ripe, with fine, sweet currant and plum aromas and flavors. **90**
1989: A lighter wine that's fresh and fruity, with lots of spicy raspberry flavors. **84**
1988: Big and firm, with loads of delicious plummy Zin flavors. **85**
1987: A ripe, jammy wine that's well balanced, with full, supple plum and raspberry flavors and firm tannins. **86**

ZINFANDEL NAPA VALLEY JOSEPH A. NICHELINI VINEYARDS (NR):
1990: Leathery aromas and flavors add up to a mixed bag. The sweet plum flavor is overpowering, though enjoyable, and nice spicy notes give it character. **81**

1989: Ripe, tarry and oaky, with flavors that turn slightly bitter on the finish, showing a glimpse of cherry and raspberry nuances in between. **80**

1988: Ripe, smooth and fruity, with generous blackberry and vanilla aromas and flavors. A stylish wine with focused fruit and plenty of extract. **85**

Bogle Vineyards
Clarksburg
F: 1979. **O:** Chris & Patty Bogle. **W:** Christopher Smith. **S:** None.

Overall	$6-10	★★

Wine Ratings

Cabernet Sauvignon California	★★
Chardonnay California	★★
Chardonnay California Reserve	★★
Fumé Blanc Lake County Dry	★★
Merlot California	★★
Petite Sirah California	★★
Zinfandel California	★★

Winery Data
C: 70,000. **V:** 875 acres in Clarksburg. **G:** Chardonnay (488 acres), Merlot (119), Petite Sirah (38), Chenin Blanc (92), Zinfandel (103), Sauvignon Blanc (35). **P:** Chardonnay (Napa Valley), Chardonnay (Sonoma Mountain), Chardonnay (Arroyo Seco), Chardonnay (Clarksburg), Sauvignon Blanc (Lake County), Cabernet Sauvignon (Paso Robles), Cabernet Sauvignon (El Dorado), Zinfandel (Sierra Foothills), Petite Sirah (Clarksburg and Monterey), Merlot (Clarksburg and Monterey).

The Bogles have been farming in the Delta area for several generations. Their family winery dates to 1979 and the focus is on sound, well made, value-oriented wines, nearly all of which carry the California appellation. The Bogles own 875 acres of vineyards, with Chardonnay (488 acres) the dominant grape, followed by Merlot (119) and Zinfandel (103). The reds usually offer more character than the whites. My favorite is the Petite Sirah; the 1991 serves up generous plum and blackberry flavors wrapped in a light blanket of vanilla oak. Production is 70,000 cases.

Tasting Notes

Cabernet Sauvignon California (★★):
1992: Smooth and appealing, a youthful wine with modest red cherry and spice flavors. **81**
1990: Soft and fruity, with ripe black cherry aromas and flavors, turning a bit watery on the palate but finishing with a solid chord of spicy oak. **83**

Chardonnay California (★★), Reserve (★★):
1993: Crisp and fruity, lively, simple and appealing for its nectarine fruit. **82**
1992: A simple wine with tart pear and spice notes that finish with a slight citrus bite. **81**
Reserve 1992: Ripe and full-bodied, with intense pear, apple and spice notes, finishing with a light oak edge. Well crafted. **86**

Fumé Blanc Lake County Dry (★★):
1993: Crisp and citrusy, with a light herbal edge that adds a touch of complexity. **83**
1992: Light and refreshing, offering nice sweet pea and spice nuances along with the delicate grapefruit and apple flavors. Fruit echoes on the lean finish. A stylish, restrained wine. **85**

Merlot California (★★):
1992: Supple and fruity, nicely balanced and contained, a wine that shows some reserve and polish. **83**
1991: Light and fruity, offering exuberant plum and currant aromas and flavors that keep lighting up the finish. A lively wine. **85**
1990: Refreshingly fruity and lively, with pretty, ripe cherry, plum and berry notes. It's priced right. **82**

Petite Sirah California (★★):
1992: Spicy, earthy, barnyard notes add a little extra to the soft plum and berry flavors. **85**
1991: Generous plum and blackberry flavors are wrapped in a light blanket of vanilla in this smooth, supple wine. The tannins are beautifully integrated, so its finish is polished, soft and distinctive. **88**

Zinfandel California (★★):
1992: Dense and chewy, but the ripe plum and berry jam notes rise to the forefront, giving it balance and depth. **84**

Bon Marché
This is a second label for Buehler Vineyards (see listing).

Bonny Doon Vineyard
Santa Cruz Mountains
F: 1983. **O:** Grahm Family. **W:** Randall Grahm. **S:** Ca' del Solo.

OVERALL	$8-25	★★★

WINE RATINGS

Blush California Vin Gris de Cigare	★★
Chenin Blanc California Pacific Rim	NR
Grenache California Clos de Gilroy	★★★
Mourvèdre California Old Telegram	★★★
Muscat Canelli Monterey County	
Vin de Glaciere	★★★★
Red Table Wine California Le Gaucher	NR
Rhône Blend California	
Le Cigare Volant	★★★
Rhône Blend Santa Cruz Mountains	
Le Sophiste	★★★
Sparkling Wine California	
Le Canard Froid Pinot Meunier	NR
White Riesling California Pacific Rim	NR
Ca' del Solo Muscat Monterey County	
Moscato del Solo	NR
Ca' del Solo Rhône Blend	
American Il Pescatore	NR
Ca' del Solo Rhône Blend California	
Big House Red	★★
Ca' del Solo White Table Wine	
California Il Pescatore	NR
Ca' del Solo White Table Wine	
Monterey County Malvasia Bianca	★★

WINERY DATA

C: 60,000. **V:** 80 acres in Monterey, Santa Cruz Mountains. **G:** Syrah (10 acres), Roussanne (10), Malbec (5), Cinsault (10), Barbera (10), Nebbiolo (5), Muscat (10), Pinot Gris (10), Viognier (1). **P:** N/A.

While Randall Grahm's image is that of the head Rhône Ranger, he began as an advocate of Burgundian varieties (including an Oregon Pinot Noir), tinkered with Bordeaux-style wines (briefly making a Cabernet Sauvignon) and is now quite interested in Italian varieties (Nebbiolo, Barbera and Sangiovese). Production from his winery is now approaching 60,000 cases of nearly 30 different wines, from table wines to blush wines to fine grappas and eaux de vie, which he makes for himself and other producers such as Sebastiani. Most of the wines are sound and well made, and a few, such as Le Cigare Volant, Muscat Canelli Vin de Glaciere (made from frozen, concentrated Muscat juice), Grenache and Mourvèdre, demonstrate why his wines have such a devoted cult following. Bonny Doon owns 80 acres, 50 in Monterey and 30 in the Santa Cruz Mountains, and most of the acreage is planted to 10-acre plots of Syrah, Barbera, Muscat, Nebbiolo and Malbec. Many of the vineyards that he discovered in his early days of exploring Rhône varieties have since been purchased by others, drying up his sources. Still, he persists with a maverick style, making a Sangiovese in 1992.

TASTING NOTES

BLUSH CALIFORNIA VIN GRIS DE CIGARE (★★):
1992: Simple and fruity, showing fresh apple and strawberry flavors that turn soft. Drink chilled. **82**

CHARDONNAY MONTEREY COUNTY LA REINA VINEYARD (★★★): Early vintages were richer and more complex.
1990: Light and simple, with watery pear and apple notes. Could use more richness and concentration, but it's a decent drink. **78**

CHARDONNAY SANTA CRUZ MOUNTAINS (★★):
1990: Firm and earthy, with toasty pear, spice and oak flavors that are tight and unevolved. **83**

CHENIN BLANC CALIFORNIA PACIFIC RIM (NR):
1993: Simple, earthy, off-dry white with only modest apple fruit. **78**

GRENACHE CALIFORNIA CLOS DE GILROY (★★★): Marked by spicy, peppery notes that are supple and distinctive.
1993: Light, bright and fruity, with spicy berry and plum flavors. **87**
1992: Overwhelming pepper aromas and flavors dominate this exuberantly fresh and fruity wine with lively cherry flavors. **84**
1991: Light and supple, bursting with fruit, offering plenty of pepper, strawberry and raspberry flavors. **84**
1990: Vibrantly fruity, crisp in texture and broad enough in flavor to let the plum, cherry, strawberry and black pepper flavors roll on. **87**
1989: A vibrant, jammy, effusively fruity wine with great blackberry flavors. **88**

MOURVÈDRE CALIFORNIA OLD TELEGRAM (★★★): Strikes a nice balance between smooth, supple tannins and a range of Mourvèdre flavors.
1991: Shows a deft balance between ripe, supple, spicy fruit flavors and gentle, polished tannins. **87**

1990: Crisp and snappy, with tart, tight plum, currant and cherry flavors that are firmly tannic. **84**
1988: Vibrant cherry, blackberry and rose petal aromas and flavors that turn slightly tannic. **85**
1986: Ripe and rich, packed with blackberry flavors mixed with lots of black pepper and a touch of smoke. **90**

RHÔNE BLEND CALIFORNIA LE CIGARE VOLANT (★★★): A plush and supple Rhône blend with wild berry, cherry and currant flavors and polished tannins.
1991: Tight and firm but focused, with ripe, intense wild berry, cherry, spice and leather notes that are deep and complex. **88**
1990: Firm in texture, with focused blackberry and cherry flavors and an exotic edge of spice and black pepper notes. **87**
1989: A firm, tightly tannic wine with a lean beam of earthy cherry and plum aromas and flavors and hints of pepper on the nose. **80**
1988: Blackberry and currant aromas jump out of the glass at first whiff, joined by hints of leather and smoke on the palate. **86**
1987: Warm and generous, with nicely focused plum and black pepper aromas and flavors plus a welcome touch of spice on the finish. **85**
1986: Big and rich, with incredibly deep cherry and blackberry flavors, massive concentration, and a long, spicy finish. **90**
1985: Has lots of blackberry, black pepper and cherry flavors that are concentrated and attractive. **88**

RHÔNE BLEND SANTA CRUZ MOUNTAINS LE SOPHISTE (★★★):
1992: Bright and flavorful, a generous mouthful of floral, grapefruit, pear and apple flavors. **89**
1991: Ripe, round and spicy, with appealing herb notes around a core of peach, apple and cream flavors. Finishes solid and concentrated. Made from 73 percent Roussanne and 27 percent Marsanne. **88**
1989: Complex and flavorful, with oodles of rich pear, honey, vanilla and citrus flavors that are framed by oak. Echoes pineapple and orange notes on the finish. A tasty concoction. **86**

VIN DE GLACIERE VARIOUS BOTTLINGS (★★★★):
Malvasia Bianca Monterey County 1991: Ripe and sweet, with buttery pear, apricot and honey aromas and

flavors and a rich, creamy finish. A touch of vinegar helps balance the sweetness, but takes a bit of the richness away. **85**
Muscat Canelli Monterey County 1992: Brilliantly spicy, fruity and generous, showing its flavors with digital clarity—nutmeg, cinnamon, pear, apple and honey. The finish is sweet, rich and amazingly balanced. **92**
Muscat Canelli California 1990: Rich, perfumed, concentrated and sweet, with delicious, delicately spiced pear and orange blossom aromas and flavors that extend into a long, lovely finish. A wonderful after-dinner sipper. **91**

VARIOUS BOTTLINGS:
Framboise Santa Cruz Mountains NV: Delicious ripe fruit and plenty of it in this lightly sweet, rich fruit wine. A mouthful of raspberries. **90**
Red Table Wine California Le Gaucher 1992: A sturdy red table wine that shows off tart, ripe berry and cherry flavors. A blend of Mourvèdre and Barbera. **82**
Red Table Wine California Pinot Meunier 1991: Smooth in texture, lively in flavor, with plum and berry notes on a lean, crisp frame. Has intensity and length; worth holding until 1996 or 1997. **87**
Sparkling Wine California Le Canard Froid Pinot Meunier 1993: Soft and fruity, a little sweet and floral, but the berry flavors make this Pinot Meunier sparkler enjoyable. **83**
White Riesling California Pacific Rim 1992: Bone dry, lean and flavorful, with well focused peach, nectarine and floral aromas and flavors. **87**
White Riesling California Pacific Rim 1991: An eye-opener. Ripe but dry, with beautifully articulated Riesling aromas and flavors. **88**
White Table Wine California Grahm Crew Vin Blanc 1990: Fresh, light and sweet, with hints of cherry and strawberry flavors. **76**

CA' DEL SOLO: Ca' del Solo is a second label, with a variety of wines, the best being the Pacific Rim Riesling and the Rhône Blend Big House Red. The former captures the spicy elegance of Riesling, while the latter captures the spicy peppery qualities often found in Rhône-style reds.
Muscat Monterey County Moscato del Solo 1992: Slightly sweet and lightly sparkling, a delicate and delicious example of the sort of super-fruity dessert wine Muscat can make. **85**

Muscat Monterey County Moscato del Solo 1991: Light, sweet, fruity, spicy and delicately sparkling, with appealing peach and grapefruit flavors. **83**

Rhône Blend American Il Pescatore NV: Offers generous pear and berry aromas and flavors and a round and appealing finish. **86**

Rhône Blend California Big House Red 1992: Crisp and fruity, with abundant boysenberry, plum and spice aromas and flavors, clean and lively on the palate, with a slight tannic bite. **84**

Rhône Blend California Big House Red 1991: A brilliant purple color and effusive berry flavors give this a raffish appeal. **84**

Rhône Blend California Big House Red 1990: A peppery red wine—from the aroma to the finish this medium-bodied, lively wine is dominated by black pepper, but it's backed by enough ripe cherry flavor to keep it fruity. **85**

White Table Wine California Il Pescatore 1993: Soft and fragrant, a supple wine with generous, spicy pear and almond flavors and a silky texture. A blend of Pinot Noir, Pinot Meunier, Chardonnay and Riesling. **85**

White Table Wine Monterey County Malvasia Bianca 1992: Fresh and fruity, with spicy apple, peach and floral aromas and flavors and a dry, slightly soft finish. **85**

White Table Wine Monterey County Malvasia Bianca 1990: Fragrant, with seductive spice, litchi and pear aromas that carry through on the light-bodied, soft-textured finish. **84**

BONVERRE

This is a second label for St. Supéry Vineyard & Winery (see listing).

BOUCHAINE VINEYARDS

Carneros

F: 1980. **O:** Gerret Van S. Copeland. **W:** John Montero. **S:** Q. C. Fly.

OVERALL	$9-20	★★★

WINE RATINGS

Cabernet Franc Sonoma Valley	
Limited Release	★★
Chardonnay Carneros	★★
Chardonnay Carneros Estate Reserve	★★★
Gewürztraminer	
Russian River Valley Dry	★★
Pinot Noir Carneros	★★
Pinot Noir Carneros Reserve	★★★
Pinot Noir Russian River Valley	
Limited Release	★★
Q.C. Fly Chardonnay California	★★
Q.C. Fly Pinot Noir California	★★

WINERY DATA

C: 25,000. **V:** 31 acres in Carneros. **G:** Chardonnay, Pinot Noir. **P:** Chardonnay (Napa Valley), Gerwürztraminer (Russian River), Cabernet Franc (Sonoma Valley).

This Carneros winery, which started as Chateau Bouchaine with a focus on Burgundian varieties, has never lived up to expectations. Through the years its wines have been well made but rarely exciting, providing modest varietal fruit but rarely the extra depth and complexity one hopes for from Chardonnay and Pinot Noir.

Founded in 1981 by a trio of investors—Gerret Copeland, an heir to the Du Pont estate; Richard Sutton; and Austin Kiplinger, publisher of the *Kiplinger Washington* newsletters and *Changing Times* magazine—it is now owned solely by Copeland. Bouchaine's first winemaker was Jerry Luper, and though his first wines were good on release, they were inconsistent, which was not surprising since they came from disparate vineyard sources and bore appellations ranging from Alexander Valley to Winery Lake. A reorganization and Luper's departure to Rutherford Hill in 1986 led to the beginning of John Montero's regime and a decision to concentrate more on Chardonnay and less on Pinot Noir. The focus is now on Carneros Chardonnay, including Bouchaine's 31-acre vineyard near the winery. Cabernet Franc from Sonoma Valley was added in 1990, along with Russian River Gewürztraminer. Both the Pinot Noir and Pinot Noir Reserve are light in color with modest flavors and little to distinguish the two, although on occasion the Reserve is richer and more complex. The Chardonnays are styled like the Pinot Noirs, crisp and lean, although the Carneros Reserve has at times been fuller and richer. Q.C. Fly is a second label for Chardonnay and Pinot Noir of simple varietal character.

TASTING NOTES

CABERNET FRANC SONOMA VALLEY LIMITED RELEASE (★★):

1991: Lean and stalky, with a green tea edge to the currant flavors. **79**

1990: A clean, simple Cabernet Franc that's correct and balanced, but of little distinction. Most of what you taste now is oak, but hints of plum and spice lurk underneath. It's hard to say where this one's headed. **83**

CHARDONNAY CARNEROS (★★), ESTATE RESERVE (★★★):

1992: Fresh and lively, with zingy acidity to the pear, apple and spice notes. **86**

1991: Crisp, firm and a touch earthy, but the spicy pear and butterscotch flavors come through and the texture is smooth and supple. **87**

Estate Reserve 1991: Ripe, smooth and creamy, with mature, spicy pear and toasty oak flavors that linger on the finish. **88**

Estate Reserve 1990: Firm and spicy, with floral and apple notes that are crisp and tight. **84**

CHARDONNAY VARIOUS BOTTLINGS (★★):

Carneros Limited Release 1991: Elegant and refined, with spicy apple, pear and light oak shadings. **86**

Carneros Sangiacomo Vineyard Limited Release 1990: Butter and pear flavors dominate this wine, finishing with honey and spice notes. **87**

Napa Valley 1990: Elegant and fresh, with perfumed pear, apple and spice flavors. **85**

GEWÜRZTRAMINER RUSSIAN RIVER VALLEY DRY (★★):

1993: Bright and floral, a generous wine with a spicy edge to the pear and cream flavors. **85**

PINOT NOIR CARNEROS (★★), RESERVE (★★★): The reserve has more depth than the lighter regular bottlings.

1992: Smooth and polished, with attractive cherry, herb, toast and berry notes, turning elegant on the finish. **86**

1991: Earthy and tannic, with an herb, cola and wild berry edge that thins out. **82**

1990: Firm and tight, with a nicely focused beam of raspberry and red cherry flavors. **86**

1989: Light and simple, with modest cherry, herb and spice notes that turn smooth. **82**

Carneros Reserve 1991: Smooth and supple in texture, with an earthy, berry and cherry flavor profile that picks up a pleasant mushroomy edge. **88**

Carneros Reserve 1990: Crisp and elegant, with earthy black cherry and plum flavors, but ultimately it's simple. **82**

PINOT NOIR RUSSIAN RIVER VALLEY LIMITED RELEASE (★★):

1991: Crisp with an herbal, earthy edge that stretches into barnyardy flavors. A hint of black cherry sneaks through, but it turns dry and leathery on the finish. **82**

Q.C. FLY VARIOUS BOTTLINGS (★★):

Chardonnay California 1992: A spicy wine with appealing pear, apple and light oak shadings. **84**

Pinot Noir California 1992: Lean and simple, with a narrow band of spice and plum notes. Turns tannic on the finish. **81**

BRANDBORG CELLARS
Fairfax, Marin County
F: 1986. **O:** Terry & Susan Brandborg. **W:** Terry Brandborg. **S:** None.

OVERALL	$13-15	★★

WINE RATINGS	
Pinot Noir Mendocino County	★★
Pinot Noir Santa Maria Valley	
Bien Nacido Vineyard	★★
Zinfandel Napa Valley	★★

WINERY DATA
C: 3,500. **V:** None. **G:** None. **P:** Pinot Noir (Santa Maria Valley), Pinot Noir (Anderson Valley), Pinot Noir (Russian River Valley), Charbono (Mt. Veeder), Zinfandel (El Dorado), Zinfandel (Dry Creek Valley), Zinfandel (Mt. Veeder).

This small winery is a 3,500-case operation based in Fairfax in Marin County that is owned by Terry Brandborg. The quality of the wines, made from purchased grapes, has not risen above average, although Brandborg is working seriously with Pinot Noir from Bien Nacido Vineyard. The 1989 features attractive cherry, currant and spice notes and a plush texture. A 1989 Zinfandel Napa Valley offers delicate raspberry and strawberry flavors in a lighter style. Mendocino Pinot Noir has been more variable in two vintages, lean and narrow in 1990, but better in 1991, with simple but ripe fruit flavors. A Mount Veeder Charbono was in the works in 1994, while the Zinfandel now bears a California appellation.

TASTING NOTES

PINOT NOIR MENDOCINO COUNTY (★★):

1991: A good value in a simple, correct, fruity wine with light oak shadings. Spicy cherry and plum flavors linger on the finish. **84**
1990: Lean and narrow, with herb, tea and spice flavors and only modest fruit shadings. Tasted twice, with consistent notes. **73**

PINOT NOIR SANTA MARIA VALLEY BIEN NACIDO VINEYARD (★★):

1992: Laced with herb and tart black cherry flavors, this young and compact wine is tightly wound, so short-term cellaring should help. **86**
1991: Has the signature earth, cola and herb edge of this fine vineyard, along with its intensity and tannins. **84**
1990: Tight, with spicy tea, plum, raisin and oak shadings in a lean, compact style. **78**

PINOT NOIR SANTA BARBARA COUNTY (★★):

1989: A pretty, fruit-packed wine showing plenty of cherry, currant and spice flavors, moderate tannins, a plush texture and a polished finish. **87**

ZINFANDEL NAPA VALLEY (★★):

1989: Light and fruity, with pleasant, almost delicate raspberry and strawberry aromas and flavors. Might be nice slightly chilled. **84**

THE BRANDER VINEYARD
Los Olivos, Santa Ynez Valley
F: 1975. **O:** The Brander Vineyard. **W:** Fred Brander.
S: None.

OVERALL	$10-35	★★★

WINE RATINGS

Cabernet Blend Santa Ynez Valley Bouchet Tete de Cuvée	★
Chardonnay Santa Ynez Valley Teté de Cuvée	★★
Merlot Santa Ynez Valley Three Flags	NR
Sauvignon Blanc Santa Ynez Valley	★★★
Sauvignon Blanc Santa Ynez Valley Cuvée Nicolas	★★★
Sauvignon Blend Santa Ynez Valley Cuvée Natalie	★★★

WINERY DATA
C: 7,000. **V:** 40 acres in Santa Ynez Valley. **G:** Sauvignon Blanc. **P:** Cabernet Sauvignon, Chardonnay, Merlot, Sauvignon Blanc (Santa Ynez Valley).

Owner and winemaker Fred Brander focuses on Sauvignon Blanc at his 7,000-case winery. He owns some 40 acres in Santa Ynez Valley, and his Sauvignons can be intensely varietal though highly variable in style and quality. One of the best, the 1992, serves up distinctive rose petal aromas with spice, pear and citrus notes. A Bouchet Tête de Cuvée Cabernet blend runs toward the intensely herbal and vegetal spectrum that often characterizes red wines from this area.

TASTING NOTES

CABERNET BLEND SANTA YNEZ VALLEY BOUCHET TÊTE DE CUVÉE (★):

1990: Intense vegetal and herb-scented fruit flavors, with dry, slightly coarse tannins on the finish. Strives for complexity with its blend (14 percent Merlot, 16 percent Cabernet Franc), but in the end the vegetal notes win out. **79**
1989: A flash of smoky oak adds class to the plum and cherry flavors for a supple, spicy wine that's medium-bodied and not too tannic. **84**

CHARDONNAY SANTA YNEZ VALLEY TÊTE DE CUVÉE (★★):

1993: Distinctive for its citrus and nectarine flavors, it picks up a pleasant earthy edge on the finish. **84**
1992: Intense, with tinny grapefruit and pineapple flavors that stretch a bit too far. **78**
1990: Dirty, stale and earthy, this is a Chardonnay gone bad, with vinegary flavors that are hard to look past. Not recommended. **64**

MERLOT SANTA YNEZ VALLEY THREE FLAGS (NR):
1989: A stylish, plummy, herbal wine wrapped in a robe of toasty oak. Vanilla, spice and maple aromas lead to decent fruit flavors and good balance. **82**

SAUVIGNON BLANC SANTA YNEZ VALLEY (★★★):
1994: Lean and even a little austere, herbal flavors edging past the modest apple fruit, finishing with a green leafy edge. **84**
1993: Distinctly herbal, with an almost oniony edge to the fig and honey flavors. A substantial wine with strong flavors. **86**
1992: Ripe and generous, a distinctive wine that layers its pear, spice and floral aromas and flavors artfully, echoing sweet fruit on the finish. **87**

SAUVIGNON BLANC SANTA YNEZ VALLEY CUVÉE NICOLAS (★★★):
1993: Lithe and vibrant with tropical fruit, passion fruit and citrus competing for attention. Exciting flavors, bright and appealing from start to finish. **89**
1992: Soft, ripe and round, so generous and spicy that it resembles a Chardonnay more than a Sauvignon. A little herbal citrus character comes through on the finish. **87**

SAUVIGNON BLANC SANTA YNEZ VALLEY CUVÉE NATALIE (★★★):
1994: Light and floral, a nice mouthful of peach, pear and rose petal flavors that stay lively on the soft, extended finish. **89**
1993: Lean and crisp, with a narrow band of bright pear, citrus and grapefruit flavors, turning a touch coarse. **86**

BRAREN PAULI WINERY
Petaluma, Sonoma County
F: 1979. **O:** Larry Braren & Bill Pauli. **W:** Larry Braren. **S:** None.

OVERALL	$12-13	★★

WINE RATINGS

Cabernet Sauvignon Dry Creek Valley		★★
Merlot Alexander Valley		★★

WINERY DATA
C: 9,000. **V:** 102 acres in Dry Creek Valley, Mendocino. **G:** Cabernet Sauvignon, Merlot. **P:** None.

This winery is a partnership between friends Bill Pauli (owner of Richetti Vineyard in Mendocino, a fine Zinfandel producer) and winemaker Larry Braren. The most recent wines I've tried include a solid 1990 Cabernet Dry Creek Valley that is smooth and elegant, with juicy raspberry, cherry and spice notes, and a 1991 Merlot Alexander Valley with smooth, polished currant and cherry flavors. Production is about 9,000 cases and includes Chardonnay.

TASTING NOTES

VARIOUS BOTTLINGS (★★):
Cabernet Sauvignon Dry Creek Valley 1990: Smooth and elegant, with lots of juicy raspberry, anise, cherry and spice aromas and flavors, finishing with a light bite of tannin. Appealing for its beautifully realized fruit flavors and silky texture. **89**
Cabernet Sauvignon Dry Creek Valley Mauritson Vineyard 1989: Pungently herbal and mulchy, with beet and plum notes, all of which add up to an oddball wine. Drinkable, but there are far better. **78**
Cabernet Sauvignon Mendocino County 1987: Lavishly oaked, with a strong dill and slight pickle flavor, but plenty of ripe currant, plum and berry flavors stand up to it. An exotic style that some may find too oaky, but there's much to admire in the flavors. **84**
Merlot Alexander Valley 1991: A seamless wine that's elegant and polished, with pretty currant and cherry flavors. There are modest tannins on the finish. **85**

BRICELAND VINEYARDS
Humboldt County
F: 1985. **O:** Maggie Carey, Jack & Lee Maguire, Allan DeForno. **W:** Joe Collins. **S:** None.

OVERALL	$7-16	★★

WINE RATINGS

Pinot Noir Humboldt County		★★
Sauvignon Blanc Humboldt County		★★

WINERY DATA
C: 1,200. **V:** None. **G:** None. **P:** Chardonnay, Pinot Noir, Sauvignon Blanc (Humboldt County), Riesling, Chardonnay (Mendocino).

This 1,200-case winery features Humboldt-grown Pinot Noir and Sauvignon Blanc in light, pleasant styles and is the only winery I know of that makes commercial wines from this appellation. The 1991and 1992 Pinot Noir vintages are good, with modest varietal fruit.

TASTING NOTES

PINOT NOIR HUMBOLDT COUNTY (★★):
1992: A little less fruity and concentrated than the 1991, but it hits the right notes for Pinot Noir with its light, fresh berry and earth notes. Modestly tannic. **81**
1991: A light wine that serves up pretty rose petal and plum aromas and fresh cherry, earth and berry flavors, finishing with light tannins. First Pinot Noir I've tasted from this producer or Humboldt County. Could be the beginning of something exciting. **83**

SAUVIGNON BLANC HUMBOLDT COUNTY (★★):
1992: Crisp, vibrant and refreshing, with intense grape-fruit, lemon and citrus flavors that are rich and focused, long and lingering. **86**

BRINDIAMO
TEMECULA
F: 1988. **O:** John M. & Sally B. Thornton. **W:** Jon C. McPherson. **S:** None.

OVERALL	$6-18	★★

WINE RATINGS

Cabernet Sauvignon California	
Limited Bottling	★
Chardonnay California	★★
Pinot Noir Santa Barbara	
County Santa Maria Hills Vineyard	
Limited Bottling	★
Red Table Wine South Coast Gioveto	
Limited Bottling	★★
Rhône Blend South Coast	
Rosso Vecchio Limited Bottling	★★

This wine line including the 1991 Cabernet California, a Chardonnay California, the 1990 Pinot Noir Santa Barbara Santa Maria Hills Vineyard and a Rhône Blend South Coast Rosso Vecchio showed improvement and good value, although the quality is variable.

TASTING NOTES

VARIOUS BOTTLINGS :
Cabernet Sauvignon California Limited Bottling 1991: Weedy, with an herbal, earthy edge. **76**
Chardonnay California 1992: Fresh and lively, with a clove edge to the buttery oak and spicy pear flavors that turn elegant. **81**
Pinot Noir Santa Barbara County Santa Maria Hills Vineyard Limited Bottling 1990: Lean and austere, with more herb and tea flavors than fruit. A tough wine to warm up to. **77**
Red Table Wine South Coast Gioveto Limited Bottling 1993: Very well oaked with toasty vanilla flavors, but some appealing black cherry, strawberry and raspberry fruit flavors that fold together nicely. **86**
Rhône Blend South Coast Rosso Vecchio Limited Bottling 1993: Combines intensity and finesse with a solid core of currant, anise and cedary oak flavors that fold together nicely. **86**
Rhône Blend South Coast Rosso Vecchio Limited Bottling 1992: Crisp and spicy, tasting more mature than expected, with berry and orange peel notes on the finish. A blend of Mourvèdre, Grenache and Petite Sirah. **80**

DAVID BRUCE WINERY
Santa Cruz Mountains
F: 1964. **O:** David Bruce Winery Inc. **W:** David Bruce. **S:** None.

OVERALL	$12-100	★★★★

WINE RATINGS

Chardonnay Santa Cruz Mountains	
Estate Reserve	★★★
Chardonnay Santa Cruz Mountains	
Meyley Vineyard	★★★
Chardonnay Santa Cruz Mountains	
Split Rail Vineyard	★★★
Pinot Noir Santa Cruz Mountains	★★★★
Pinot Noir Santa Cruz Mountains	
Estate Reserve	★★★★
Zinfandel San Luis Obispo County	★★★

WINERY DATA

C: 25,000. V: 15 acres in Santa Cruz Mountains. G: Chardonnay (7 acres), Pinot Noir (7). P: Chardonnay, Pinot Noir (Santa Cruz Mountains), Chardonnay (San Ysidro), Chardonnay, Petite Sirah (California), Pinot Noir (Sonoma), Zinfandel (San Luis Obispo County), Pinot Noir (Russian River).

David Bruce's wines have zigzagged all over the course in his 30-year career. For most of that time the wines have been as varied and unpredictable as any in California, often bizarre or flawed yet also often brilliant and well crafted. Today, after a long period in the 1980s when his wines were off the wall, David Bruce is back on target, focusing on Santa Cruz Mountain-grown Chardonnay and Pinot Noir, the latter from his estate vineyard.

A dermatologist by profession, Bruce began as a home winemaker in the late 1950s and deserves credit for many pioneering efforts with grapes grown in different appellations. Bruce's experiments were hands-on; he worked at Martin Ray's winery and crushed grapes at Ridge Vineyards, helping with the 1961 vintage of the Monte Bello Vineyard. Bruce is known for his innovative wines, including a white Zinfandel made in the early 1960s; ultraripe, late-harvest Zinfandels; and downright funky Pinot Noirs. He began planting his vineyard in 1961, and the 15 acres are divided evenly between Chardonnay and Pinot Noir, the latter now his best wine.

Bruce focuses on two vineyard-designated Chardonnays (Meyley and Split Rail), both variable in quality but usually marked by bold fruit and oak flavors. The Meyley 1990 is offbeat, with earthy, candied flavors, but the 1991 is better, although not without a potent leesy edge. The Split Rail 1991 is rich, with an appealing Burgundian earthiness. The Estate and Reserve Pinot Noirs follow this Burgundian pattern, but a Vintner's Blend, made from purchased grapes from Mendocino, can be very good, with a range of spicy cherry, herb and wild berry flavors. Bruce makes no apologies for his wild stylistic swings. He has gone through different phases, testing different styles, and is now dedicated to his Burgundian pursuits. He still dabbles in other wines: Mr. Baggins, a Rhône blend, appears occasionally, as does a San Luis Obispo Zinfandel, which in 1990 was big and rangy, with complex, concentrated flavors. When drinking David Bruce's wines, keep the word "unpredictable" in mind, but don't be surprised when he gets it right.

TASTING NOTES

CHARDONNAY SAN YSIDRO (★★★):
1991: An oaky wine that turns bitter and funky, with smoky flavors on the finish, but no real fruit to speak of. For wood-lovers only. **74**

CHARDONNAY SANTA CRUZ MOUNTAINS (★★★), ESTATE RESERVE (★★★):
1990: Strives for complexity with its bold, ripe, oaky profile. The buttery pear and spice flavors come through, but it could use a little more finesse. **85**
Estate Reserve 1990: A bold, ripe wine that throws a lot of oak and ripe fruit at you. **84**

CHARDONNAY SANTA CRUZ MOUNTAINS VINEYARD SELECTION (★★★):
1990: Bitter, earthy and funky, with ripe, peppery pear and oak flavors. An oddball wine that turns vegetal on the aftertaste. **74**

CHARDONNAY SANTA CRUZ MOUNTAINS MEYLEY VINEYARD (★★★):
1991: Lean and tart, with a sour, leesy edge to the spice and pineapple flavors. **82**
1990: Grassy, herbal, candied aromas and flavors turn bitter on the finish. **69**

CHARDONNAY SANTA CRUZ MOUNTAINS SPLIT RAIL VINEYARD (★★★):
1991: Burgundian in style, rich and full-bodied, with complex layers of honey, pear, toast and butter, finishing with a long, creamy aftertaste. **89**

PINOT NOIR MENDOCINO COUNTY VINTNER'S SELECT (★★):
1990: Toasty oak aromas and spicy cherry flavors make this wine an excellent value. **85**

PINOT NOIR SANTA CRUZ MOUNTAINS (★★★★): Dark in color, supple and fleshy, with ripe berry flavors, earthy nuances and firm tannins from solid wood aging. Cellar for five to eight years.
1992: Peppery and leathery, turning smooth and plush, with hints of cherry, herb and anise. **88**
1991: Ripe, rich, smooth and creamy, with smoky oak, black cherry and spice notes that are complex and concentrated. **87**

1990: Smoky, smooth and complex, with rich black cherry, herb, cola and strawberry flavors that turn silky smooth. **91**

1989: Soft and almost syrupy in texture, with a strange maple or honey overtone. **75**

PINOT NOIR SANTA CRUZ MOUNTAINS ESTATE RESERVE (★★★★): Similar in color and flavors to the Estate, but the Reserve is more tannic and compact. Can also stand cellaring for five to eight years.

1992: Dense and chewy, with compact spice and pepper flavors that echo black cherry, herb, mineral and anise. Turns earthy and tannic on the finish. **91**

1991: Rich, intense and spicy, with delicious, smoky chocolate, berry and cherry flavors that turn smooth and complex. **90**

1990: Bold, ripe and complex, with spicy cherry, anise, tar and cola flavors that pick up a nice, earthy mushroom note. The texture is smooth and supple. **91**

RHÔNE BLEND CALIFORNIA MR. BAGGINS (NR):
1990: Light and fruity, with strawberry jam flavors that are clean and refreshing. Can be served slightly chilled. **80**

ZINFANDEL SAN LUIS OBISPO COUNTY (★★★):
1990: Big and rangy, with attractive, concentrated berry and spice aromas and flavors that persist through the finish. **90**

BRUTOCAO CELLARS
Hopland, Mendocino County
F: 1980. **O:** Leonard J. Brutocao. **W:** Nancy B. Walker. **S:** None.

OVERALL	$9-35	★★

WINE RATINGS

Cabernet Sauvignon Mendocino County Proprietor's Special Reserve	★★
Cabernet Sauvignon Mendocino County Albert Vineyard	★★
Chardonnay Mendocino County	★★
Chardonnay Mendocino County Bliss Vineyard	★★
Merlot Mendocino County	★★
Sauvignon Blanc Mendocino County	★★★
Zinfandel Mendocino County	★★
Zinfandel Mendocino County Hopland Ranch	★★

WINERY DATA
C: 11,000. **V:** 187 acres in Mendocino. **G:** Merlot (26 acres), Sémillon (4), Cabernet Sauvignon (50), Chardonnay (69), Sauvignon Blanc (17), Zinfandel (21). **P:** Pinot Noir, Chardonnay (Anderson Valley).

Long-time grape grower Leonard Brutocao launched his winery in 1986 in Hopland and today farms 187 acres, mostly Chardonnay (69 acres), Cabernet (50), Merlot (26), Zinfandel (21) and Sauvignon Blanc (17), producing 11,000 cases. The Sauvignon Blanc is to my taste the best and most refined in this lineup. The 1991 is rich and buttery, with exotic flavors, while the 1992 is smooth and polished. Early Cabernets were on the lean side, but more recently the Cabernet, Zinfandel and Merlot were ultraripe and unbalanced, stretched beyond varietal identification. Given the ripeness of the grapes, I assume better wines can be made.

TASTING NOTES

CABERNET SAUVIGNON MENDOCINO COUNTY (★★):
1990: Lean and crisp for a 1990, with medium-bodied herb, tea and tart black cherry flavors, finishing with fine tannins. **82**

1988: An appealing, straightforward wine with currant and strawberry flavors and moderate tannins. On the light side in texture. **83**

1986: Age has mellowed this smoky, cranberry-flavored wine, but it's still stiff on the finish. The spare flavors don't measure up to the nicely developing aromas. Good, but fairly tannic and lean. **82**

CABERNET SAUVIGNON MENDOCINO COUNTY PROPRIETOR'S SPECIAL RESERVE (★★):
1991: Ripe and smooth, with bright black cherry, anise and wild berry flavors that while distinctive don't remind us much of Cabernet. **83**

CABERNET SAUVIGNON MENDOCINO COUNTY ALBERT VINEYARD (★★):
1992: A bit funky, with tart berry and spicy notes that taste disjointed. **82**

CHARDONNAY MENDOCINO COUNTY (★★):
1991: Smooth, spicy, generous and lively, showing a bright beam of pear, nutmeg and vanilla aromas and flavors along with a touch of butter on the finish. **88**

1988: Ripe, intense and full-bodied but a touch alcoholic, with pear, spice and citrus notes that thin out on the finish. A fair price. **81**

CHARDONNAY MENDOCINO COUNTY BLISS VINEYARD (★★):

1993: Spicy with a perfumed aroma, it's elegant and subtle with pear and apple notes. **83**

1992: Intense and lively, with ripe, spicy pear and buttery oak flavors that turn smooth and elegant on the finish. **84**

MERLOT MENDOCINO COUNTY (★★):

1992: A big, ripe, oaky wine that doesn't have the fruit to stand up to the wood. It's tough and gnarly, with firm, drying tannins. **78**

1991: Supple and dark in color, with ripe plum, currant, spice and vanilla notes. **87**

1988: A light but flavorful red with plenty of plum and strawberry flavors and mild tannins. The fruit lasts nicely on the finish. **84**

SAUVIGNON BLANC MENDOCINO COUNTY (★★★):

1992: Smooth in texture, with almond, butter and floral aromas and flavors, finishing with a touch of toast or smoke. Although it lacks fruit, it's distinctive. **83**

1991: Buttery, spicy aromas and flavors turn rich on the palate, and some nice pineapple, vanilla and grapefruit notes make for a delicious wine. It's not especially characteristic of Sauvignon Blanc, but it offers plenty of pleasure. **90**

ZINFANDEL MENDOCINO COUNTY (★★):

1992: Firm and tight, with pretty, spicy cherry and wild berry flavors that stay with you. **84**

ZINFANDEL MENDOCINO COUNTY PROPRIETOR'S RESERVE (★★):

1991: Nice raspberry and blackberry flavors accented by a touch of toasty oak make for an attractive, easy-to-drink, softly tannic Zinfandel. Generous and rich. **85**

ZINFANDEL MENDOCINO COUNTY HOPLAND RANCH (★★):

1993: Ripe and juicy, with pretty wild berry and black cherry flavors that turn elegant. **84**

BRYANT FAMILY VINEYARD
Napa Valley
F: 1991. O: John Bryant. W: John Bryant, Helen Turley. S: None.

OVERALL	$N/A	NR

WINERY DATA
C: 1,000. V: 10 acres in Napa Valley. G: Cabernet Sauvignon. P: None.

Bryant Family Vineyard is a 10-acre vineyard devoted exclusively to Cabernet at the 1,500-foot elevation on Pritchard Hill in the hills east of St. Helena near Chappellet. With Helen Turley (Marcassin) in charge of winemaking, the focus is on low-yield (2 tons per acre), dense and concentrated wines, with the first wines from 1992 and 1993 impressive out of barrel. Production is targeted for 1,000 cases, with the first wines due in 1995. Worth watching.

BUEHLER VINEYARDS
St. Helena, Napa Valley
F: 1978. O: John Buehler Jr. W: David Cronin. S: Bon Marché.

OVERALL	$9-25	★★

WINE RATINGS

Cabernet Sauvignon Napa Valley	★★
Cabernet Sauvignon Napa Valley Reserve	★★★
Chardonnay Russian River Valley	★★
Pinot Noir Central Coast	NR
Zinfandel Napa Valley	★★
Bon Marché Cabernet Sauvignon Napa Valley	★★
Bon Marché Chardonnay Sonoma County	★
Bon Marché Pinot Noir Sonoma County	★

WINERY DATA
C: 50,000. V: 65 acres in Napa Valley. G: Cabernet Sauvignon (30 acres), Zinfandel (35). P: Chardonnay (Russian River Valley), Zinfandel (Napa Valley).

Bechtel Corp. executive John Buehler Sr. purchased property for Buehler Vineyards in a narrow fold of hills east of St. Helena. After planting vineyards, he and his son

John Jr. built a winery and began making wine in 1978. The early Buehler Cabernets were bold, ripe and distinctive, but with recent vintages the wines have been leaner, trimmer and less complex. The Buehlers own 65 acres planted to Zinfandel (35 acres) and Cabernet (30), both of which are made into wines marked by rustic, earthy, tarry flavors. The winery also has made Pinot Blanc, but in the early 1990s began buying Russian River Chardonnay. In 1993 the Buehlers hired former Far Niente assistant winemaker David Cronin to oversee winemaking and upgrade quality. Given the early promise of its vineyards, Buehler should be poised for a comeback, but it needs to tame the earthiness of its wines while providing more depth and complexity. Production is about 50,000 cases, a good portion of which is white Zinfandel.

TASTING NOTES

CABERNET SAUVIGNON NAPA VALLEY (★★), RESERVE (★★★): At first these wines were ripe and flamboyant, high in extract and alcohol and marked by tarry, earthy flavors. Even the best wines of the 1980s have turned earthy and weedy, aging poorly.
1991: Youthful and compact, this tightly wound wine is oaky and loaded with ripe berry and plum flavors. **86**
1990: Sleek, ripe and fruity, with spicy berry and mineral notes, finishing with soft tannins. **86**
1989: The flavors ring true, with cherry and plum nuances, but they turn thin and crisp on the finish. **82**
1987: Disjointed, with earthy currant and berry flavors; better after 1996. **85**
Reserve 1991: The best Buehler in years. Bold, ripe and complex, with attractive plum, currant and black cherry fruit that's rich and lively, with hints of mineral and earth. Best after 1996. **91**

CHARDONNAY RUSSIAN RIVER VALLEY (★★):
1993: Youthful and vibrant, with crisp, tart pear, peach and citrus notes. **85**

PINOT NOIR CENTRAL COAST (NR):
1993: A bit smoky and oaky, with a tannic, bitter edge. **79**

ZINFANDEL NAPA VALLEY (★★): Ripe and intense through most of the 1980s, with a high in 1987, but recent efforts are uneven in quality, often with unusual, non-Zinfandel flavors.

1993: Austere, with an earthy, gamy edge to the spice and wild berry flavors. **81**
1992: Elegant and spicy, with modest cherry, plum and raspberry flavors. **86**
1990: An odd wine with a strange Muscat edge to the earthy Zin flavors. **77**
1989: A rough-cut red with earthy, peppery flavors and a little hint of raspberry and anise. Straightforward and easy to drink. **83**
1987: Ripe and concentrated, with distinctive, intense blueberry and raspberry flavors, a polished texture and a welcome hint of smoke and pepper on the finish. A stylish wine with flavor to burn. **89**

BON MARCHÉ VARIOUS BOTTLINGS:
Cabernet Sauvignon Napa Valley 1992: Light and fruity, with a leathery oak edge to the flavors. **82**
Cabernet Sauvignon Sonoma County 1991: Bright and flavorful, with fresh currant, plum and blackberry aromas and flavors vying for attention. A vibrant wine. **84**
Chardonnay Sonoma County 1992: Fresh and fruity, a soft, simple wine with appealing apple and vanilla flavors. A hint of bitterness detracts on the finish. **79**
Pinot Noir Napa Valley 1990: Firm and crisp, with modest cherry and toast aromas and flavors that are simple and direct. A decent value. **79**
Pinot Noir Sonoma County 1991: Fresh and lively, with ripe plum, strawberry and cherry notes. An attractive, fleshy, easy-to-drink wine that's quite appealing. A terrific value. **86**

BUENA VISTA WINERY
Sonoma Valley
F: 1857. **O:** Racke USA. **W:** Judy Matulich-Weitz. **S:** None.

OVERALL	$8-20	★★

WINE RATINGS

Cabernet Sauvignon Carneros	★★
Cabernet Sauvignon Carneros Grand Reserve	★★
Chardonnay Carneros	★★
Chardonnay Carneros Grand Reserve	★★
Gewürztraminer Carneros	★★
Merlot Carneros	★★
Merlot Carneros Grand Reserve	★★

Pinot Noir Carneros	★★
Pinot Noir Carneros Grand Reserve	★★
Sauvignon Blanc Lake County	★★★

WINERY DATA

C: 200,000. **V:** 935 acres in Carneros. **G:** Gewürztraminer (36 acres), Johannisberg Riesling (38), Sauvignon Blanc (21), Zinfandel (9), Sémillon (5). **P:** None.

Buena Vista Winery was founded in 1857 by Agoston Haraszthy of Hungary and is California's oldest premium winery. The winery has undergone numerous changes, closing after the 1906 earthquake and reopening in the late 1950s. But it wasn't until the late 1970s, when the winery was acquired by A. Racke of Germany, that the turnaround began. Buena Vista built a large winery in the cool, windswept Carneros district and now owns 935 acres there. From 1978 to 1986 the winery made very successful Cabernets under its Special Selection and Private Reserve designations, and also made fine Chardonnays and Merlots.

Since the late 1980s, however, when the winery's vineyards came into full production and case volume grew to 250,000 cases, Buena Vista's fortunes have taken a sharp turn for the worse. Across the board, its wines have become lean, shallow and largely uninteresting. It's difficult to pinpoint a single cause, but it appears the winery has outgrown its ability to maintain quality.

Buena Vista's two main lines of wines are the Carneros and Grand Reserve bottlings, but there is little to distinguish the two. The Chardonnays are light, fruity and appealing but lack depth. The Merlots are lean and marked by herb and vegetal notes. The Pinot Noirs are tart and simple. The best wine has been the Lake County Sauvignon Blanc, which can be ripe and intense, rich and elegant, although the 1993 was disappointingly thin. In 1994 long-time winemaker Jill Davis departed for William Hill Winery in Napa and was replaced by former Inglenook winemaker Judy Matulich-Weitz.

TASTING NOTES

CABERNET SAUVIGNON VARIOUS BOTTLINGS (★★): In the late 1970s and into the early 1980s these were ripe, intense and concentrated, with rich currant, berry, herb and tar notes. Both the 1978 and 1979 Special Selections are excellent, but later vintages such as 1985 and 1986 have not aged well.

Carneros 1991: Lean and tannic, this tightly wound, youthful wine offers a narrow band of herb, currant and spicy oak flavors. **87**

Carneros 1990: Despite a barnyardy edge, the modest berry and cherry notes come through. **82**

Carneros Grand Reserve 1990: Earthy and vegetal, marked more by herb and bell pepper than classic Cabernet fruit flavors. **83**

Carneros Grand Reserve 1988: Firm and fleshy, with earthy notes that hint at currant and mint on the finish. **86**

Carneros Private Reserve 1986: At its peak, with a stalky, herbal edge to the black cherry and anise flavors. Turns firm and tannic on the finish, but it's in danger of turning earthier. **88**

Carneros Private Reserve 1985: With time, this wine will surpass the very fine 1984 with its intensity and depth of fresh, ripe, rich black cherry and cedar flavors that are just beginning to emerge from their tight coil. Tannins are integrated, and the finish is crisp. **87**

Carneros Private Reserve 1984: This wine is rich and mature with ripe, well focused black cherry, currant and spicy oak flavors. It is smooth and supple, elegant and lively. **87**

Carneros Private Reserve 1983: The 1983 is impressive for its crisp, lively cherry aromas and flavors and absence of dry, hard tannins. Well balanced, with plenty of complexity and hints of anise and cedar, this wine is perfectly enjoyable now and should hold for a few more years. **87**

Carneros Private Reserve 1982: A mature, elegant, Cabernet that is well developed. **85**

Sonoma Valley Special Selection 1979: Mature and showing its age now after a long run of excellent drinking. The dark, ripe currant and berry flavors are taking on a decadent edge and the oak stands apart from the fruit. **84**

Sonoma Valley Special Selection 1978: Showing its age now, with an earthy herb and green bean edge, this wine has crested and no longer delivers the rich, ripe currant and wild berry flavors it did for so many years. Drink up. **85**

CHARDONNAY CARNEROS (★★), GRAND RESERVE (★★): Lightly fruity, although the Grand Reserve 1991 is a clear attempt to put more richness and depth in the bottle.

1992: Lightly fruity, with simple pear, apple and pineapple notes that finish with a soft aftertaste. **83**

1991: Intense and snappy, with fresh, ripe pear and apple notes that are fresh and lively. Turns a little bitter on the finish, but stays in bounds. Tasted twice. **84**

Grand Reserve 1991: Tastes mature, with earthy, toasty flavors framing the ripe, spicy pear and pineapple notes. **86**

GEWÜRZTRAMINER CARNEROS (★★):

1993: Soft and fruity, simple in flavor, and the apricot finish is a little sweet. **80**

MERLOT CARNEROS (★★), GRAND RESERVE (★★): Crisp and tart, often weedy and herbal.

1992: Marked by thin herbal and vegetal notes, which overshadow the berry flavors. **82**

1991: Lean and herbal, with tea and tobacco overtones to the basic blackberry flavors. **82**

1990: Crisp and tart, with sharply focused berry and currant flavors, hinting at olives on the finish. **86**

Grand Reserve 1989: Lean and simple, with sharp acidity and hard tannins that override the berry flavors. **82**

PINOT NOIR CARNEROS (★★), GRAND RESERVE (★★): Simple, with modest cherry and spice notes, but lacking richness and depth.

1992: Lean, thin and earthy, with barely ripe fruit, an ordinary and uninspiring effort. **77**

1991: Simple and uninspired, with earthy berry notes that are flat. **80**

1990: Tart and clean, with crisp, simple cherry and spice flavors. **81**

Grand Reserve 1991: Lean and earthy, it strives for complexity with its buttery oak flavors, but the plum and berry flavors thin out. **83**

Grand Reserve 1990: Intense and focused, with ample currant, blackberry and cherry flavors plus a nice edge of toast and spice. **86**

SAUVIGNON BLANC LAKE COUNTY (★★★): Can be one of California's best, with pure and enticing varietal flavors that are elegant and refined; the 1993 is an off vintage for this wine.

1993: Bright and almost sweet, a fruity wine with a candied edge to the pear flavors. Lacks subtlety. **79**

BURGESS CELLARS
Napa Valley
F: 1972. **O:** Burgess Cellars Inc. **W:** Bill Sorenson. **S:** Bell Canyon Cellars.

OVERALL	$11-20	★★★

WINE RATINGS

Cabernet Sauvignon Napa Valley Vintage Selection	★★★
Chardonnay Napa Valley Debourbage Barrel Fermented	★★★
Chardonnay Napa Valley Triere Vineyard	★★★
Zinfandel Napa Valley	★★★

WINERY DATA
C: 30,000. **V:** 105 acres in Napa Valley. **G:** Merlot (15 acres), Chardonnay (35), Petite Sirah (10), Cabernet Sauvignon (25), Cabernet Franc (5), Zinfandel (15). **P:** None.

Burgess Cellars operates out of an 1880 winery at the foot of Howell Mountain. It was once home to Lee Stewart's Souverain winery in the 1940's, but in 1972 Tom Burgess, a former pilot, bought the winery and began making wine there. The winery is a few hundred feet above the Napa Valley floor but below the 1,400-foot elevation necessary to be part of the Howell Mountain appellation.

The 30,000-case winery specializes in Cabernet, Chardonnay and Zinfandel under the direction of Bill Sorenson, who has been with the winery since 1973. Burgess owns 105 acres of grapes, 35 of which are planted to Chardonnay, including the Triere Vineyard in Yountville, which it uses for a vineyard-designated wine. There are smaller parcels of Cabernet (25 acres), Merlot (15), Zinfandel (15), Petite Sirah (10) and Cabernet Franc (5). Each of its three wines is well crafted and age-worthy, but quality in the 1990s has dipped a bit with Chardonnay and Zinfandel. Recent Cabernets are also leaner than wines from the 1970s and 1980s.

TASTING NOTES

CABERNET SAUVIGNON NAPA VALLEY VINTAGE SELECTION (★★★): Typically tight and trim, with compact currant, earth and light oak shadings and firm tannins. Ages well for up to 10 years, but recent vintages have lacked the flair of earlier efforts.

1990: Balanced between ripe, spicy, supple fruit flavors and light oak shadings. **88**

1989: Light in aroma, but currant, berry and oak flavors come through. **86**

1988: Despite sharp edges, this wine offers a tight core of herb, currant, cherry and plum flavors. **85**

1987: Has a tough, woody edge to the currant and plum flavors, leaving a harsh, biting, tannic sensation. **85**

1986: Hard and tannic, with intense currant, coffee and cherry flavors that are tightly wound. **88**

1985: Mature, but still showing plenty of flavor, with a minty currant edge. **89**

1984: Lean, rich and intense, with layers of plum, spice, currant and black cherry flavors offset by toasty oak. **90**

1983: Crisp and firm, with lean, concentrated plum, currant and cedary oak flavors. **87**

1974: Dry and earthy; the fruit is gone, leaving a metallic edge. **74**

Chardonnay Napa Valley Debourbage Barrel Fermented (★★★):
1993: Supple and fruity, with appealing apple and pear notes of modest proportion. Picks up a light note on an elegant finish. **86**

Chardonnay Napa Valley Triere Vineyard (★★★): Recent vintages have lacked the complexity and concentration found in the 1980s vintages, which were underrated and ageworthy.
1992: Lean and smooth, a peachy, spicy wine with a caramel edge. **83**
1991: Tight and firm, with pear, apple and spice flavors that turn smooth and supple on the finish. **86**

Zinfandel Napa Valley (★★★): Elegant and well balanced, marked by spicy, peppery wild berry flavors. Has aged well in the past.
1991: Earthy and gamy, it shows just enough peppery Zinfandel flavors to hold your interest. **81**
1990: Elegant and spicy, with berry and cherry flavors that pick up anise and cedar notes. **84**
1989: Has a spicy, peppery edge to the raspberry flavors. **80**

Byington Winery & Vineyards
Santa Cruz Mountains
F: 1987. **O:** Byington Family. **W:** Alan Phillips. **S:** None.

Overall	$8-25	★★

Wine Ratings

Cabernet Sauvignon Napa Valley	★★
Chardonnay Mount Veeder	★★
Chardonnay Napa Valley	★★
Chardonnay Santa Cruz Mountains	★★★
Chardonnay Santa Cruz Mountains	
Redwood Hill Vineyard	★★
Merlot Sonoma County	
Bradford Mountain Vineyard	★★
Pinot Noir Santa Barbara County	
Bien Nacido Vineyard	★
Sauvignon Blanc San Luis Obispo County	
French Camp Vineyard Dry	★★
Zinfandel Santa Clara County	
Calle Cielo Vineyard	★★

Winery Data
C: 10,000. **V:** 8 acres in Santa Cruz Mountains. **G:** Pinot Noir (8). **P:** Cabernet Sauvignon, Chardonnay, Pinot Noir (Santa Cruz Mountains), Cabernet Sauvignon (Alexander Valley), Chardonnay (Napa Valley), Pinot Noir (Santa Barbara County), Merlot (Sonoma County).

Bill Byington, owner of Byington Steel, built a chateau-style winery on a hillside above Los Gatos in 1990, three years after starting his winery in rented space. There is an 8-acre Pinot Noir vineyard on the property, and Byington buys most of his grapes from vineyards spread throughout California, including Merlot from Bradford Mountain in Sonoma. The early wines were largely unimpressive, often overly mature, with thin flavors. The 1991 Chardonnay Santa Cruz Mountain Redwood Hill Vineyard shows more promise with its complex pear, honey and citrus notes. Production is 10,000 cases.

Tasting Notes

Cabernet Sauvignon Napa Valley (★★):
1987: Smells rich and fruity, then tightens up and turns tannic on the palate, but the forceful currant and black cherry flavors triumph on the finish. **86**

Chardonnay Various Bottlings :
Mount Veeder 1993: A touch earthy with a bitter seam, but enough pear, hazelnut and spice to make it palatable. **83**
Napa Valley 1990: Simple and watery, with ripe pear and melon notes that taste sweet on the finish. **78**

Santa Cruz Mountains 1993: Better balanced than most 1993s, with supple pear, citrus and light oak shadings, finishing with a pleasant aftertaste. **84**

Santa Cruz Mountains Redwood Hill Vineyard 1993: Medium-bodied with modest pear and oak shadings, picking up subtle nuances on the finish. **84**

Santa Cruz Mountains Redwood Hill Vineyard 1991: Broad, ripe and complex, with pretty pear, honey, grapefruit and vanilla flavors that are well proportioned and turn silky and elegant on the long, lingering finish. **89**

MERLOT SONOMA COUNTY BRADFORD MOUNTAIN VINEYARD (★★):

1991: Tart and flavorful, a raucous, juicy wine that echoes plum and berry on the finish. Rough enough to need until 1997 or 1998 to gain some polish. **83**

PINOT NOIR SANTA BARBARA COUNTY BIEN NACIDO VINEYARD (★):

1991: Pungent and earthy, with a dry leathery streak to the herb and berry flavors. **78**

SAUVIGNON BLANC SAN LUIS OBISPO COUNTY FRENCH CAMP VINEYARD DRY (★★):

1992: A pleasant wine, soft and a little sweet, with an herbal edge to the pear flavors. **80**

ZINFANDEL SANTA CLARA COUNTY CALLE CIELO VINEYARD (★★):

1992: An awkward Zin with a green, unripe edge to the berry flavors. Holds together well, but the greenness lingers on the finish. **82**

DAVIS BYNUM WINERY
Russian River Valley
F: 1965. **O:** Davis Bynum Winery Inc. **W:** Gary Farrell. **S:** None.

OVERALL	$9-21	★★

WINE RATINGS

Cabernet Sauvignon Sonoma County	★
Chardonnay Russian River Valley Allen-Griffin Vineyards Limited Release	★★
Chardonnay Sonoma County	★★
Fumé Blanc Russian River Valley Shone Farm	★★
Gewürztraminer Russian River Valley	★★
Merlot Russian River Valley Laureles Vineyard	NR
Pinot Noir Russian River Valley	★
Pinot Noir Russian River Valley Limited Release	★★
Zinfandel Russian River Valley	★★

WINERY DATA
C: 22,000. **V:** 12 acres in Russian River Valley. **G:** Merlot (7 acres), Cabernet Sauvignon (1), Pinot Noir (4). **P:** Sauvignon Blanc, Chardonnay, Pinot Noir, Cabernet Sauvignon (Russian River Valley), Merlot (Rincon Valley).

Davis Bynum joined the California wine industry in 1965, after more than a decade of making wines at home. Through the years his winery has produced many good wines, although they are rarely exceptional. Bynum has turned over many of the winemaking decisions to his sons, and to his winemaker Gary Farrell, who remains a loyal employee despite having a highly successful brand of his own (see Gary Farrell). Having been in the business for three decades, Davis Bynum Winery has made just about every kind of wine imaginable, but its focus the past few years has been on Sonoma County and Russian River Valley Pinot Noir, Chardonnay, Merlot and Zinfandel. Bynum's best wines are his delicate Pinot Noirs, but they pale in comparison with the best from this area even though the winery's vineyard sources, Rochioli and Allen vineyards, are first rate. The winery bottles an Allen-Griffin Vineyards Chardonnay, but it lacks the richness and flavor of the area's best.

The Cabernet is simple, with herb and spice notes, but not much depth or richness. The Chardonnays, including the Allen-Griffin Vineyards Limited Release, are simple and straightforward, but often a bit overdone with oak. Gewürztraminer is made in an off-dry style. Merlot is lean and crisp, with modest varietal character. The Fumé Blanc offers more intensity, while recent Zinfandels show more character, the 1991 featuring jammy pepper and plum flavors that are smooth and polished. Perhaps that's a sign of better wines to come.

TASTING NOTES

CABERNET SAUVIGNON SONOMA COUNTY (★):
1989: A simple, pleasant Cabernet with currant and blackberry flavors and a slightly herbal edge, but the firm tannins make this wine worth waiting out. Try after 1996. **81**

1987: Herbal, toasty flavors dominate in this lean, austere wine, offering plenty of tannin and not much fruit concentration to back it up. **79**

CHARDONNAY RUSSIAN RIVER VALLEY ALLEN-GRIFFIN VINEYARDS LIMITED RELEASE (★★):
1992: Clean, ripe and fruity, with creamy apple, pear and spice flavors that stay with you. **84**
1991: Simple, straightforward, spicy and refreshing, with citrus and apple aromas and flavors that echo lemon on the finish. **81**

CHARDONNAY SONOMA COUNTY (★★):
1991: Lean and excessively toasty, tasting like ash, with little fruit to redeem it on the finish. Tasted twice, with consistent notes. **69**

FUMÉ BLANC RUSSIAN RIVER VALLEY SHONE FARM (★★):
1994: Simple and fruity, appealing for its pear and gooseberry flavors. **82**
1992: Crisp and lively, an herbal wine with a nice core of pear and apple flavors. **85**

GEWÜRZTRAMINER RUSSIAN RIVER VALLEY (★★):
1992: Simple, slightly sweet, lacking in character. **74**

MERLOT RUSSIAN RIVER VALLEY LAURELES VINEYARD (NR):
1991: Lean and crisp, with a modest level of berry and herb flavors and an earthy finish. **81**

PINOT NOIR RUSSIAN RIVER VALLEY (★), LIMITED RELEASE (★★): The limited release is a shade more complex.
1991: Soft and silky, yet curiously lacking in intensity. A bit rough on the finish, but the plum flavor shows through. **84**
1990: Very light and watery, a thin wine with little to offer. **72**
Limited Release 1991: An elegant, refined, harmonious wine with pretty black cherry, spice and raspberry notes. Finishes with a delicate touch. **88**
Limited Release 1990: Elegant and lively, with pretty spice and cherry flavors. **85**

ZINFANDEL RUSSIAN RIVER VALLEY (★★): Improving as it offers more fruit and better focus.
1991: Ripe and jammy, with pretty black cherry, plum and raspberry flavors that turn smooth and plush. **87**
1990: A tasty, youthful Zinfandel with ripe, peppery plum and raspberry aromas and flavors that are a bit sweet and turn fruity and gamy on the finish. Offers plenty of flavor. **84**

BYRON VINEYARDS & WINERY
Santa Maria Valley
F: 1984. **O:** Robert Mondavi Inc. **W:** Byron "Ken" Brown, John Kerr. **S:** None.

OVERALL	$11-25	★★★★

WINE RATINGS

Cabernet Sauvignon	
Santa Barbara County	★★
Chardonnay Santa Barbara County	★★★★
Chardonnay Santa Barbara County	
Reserve	★★★★
Chardonnay Santa Maria Valley	★★★★
Pinot Blanc Santa Barbara County	★★★
Pinot Noir Santa Barbara County	★★★
Pinot Noir Santa Barbara County	
Reserve	★★★
Sauvignon Blanc Santa Barbara County	★★★

WINERY DATA
C: 30,000. **V:** 568 acres in Santa Maria Valley. **G:** Chardonnay (255 acres), Pinot Noir (90), Pinot Blanc (4), Rhône Type (20), Cabernet Franc (33), Cabernet Sauvignon (160), Pinot Gris (6). **P:** Sauvignon Blanc (Santa Ynez Valley).

After working for Zaca Mesa from 1978 to 1983, Byron "Ken" Brown founded his own winery in 1984. After a slow start, Byron has significantly improved the quality of its wines, with an amazingly complex string of Chardonnays that rank among the state's best. In 1990 the winery needed a cash infusion and was acquired by Robert Mondavi Winery. Brown remains involved in the winemaking, and Mondavi's financial backing has led to the winery's overseeing 568 acres (including acreage from the Tepusquet Vineyard, which Mondavi bought in 1987). The focus remains on Burgundian varietals, with

Chardonnay making up nearly half the winery's 30,000 cases. Byron has phased out Cabernet, which never did well in Santa Barbara, often displaying pungent vegetal notes, but still makes a rich and flavorful Sauvignon Blanc, the 1992 providing an array of spice, toast, herb, pear and citrus notes. Pinot Blanc and Pinot Gris are also part of the lineup.

TASTING NOTES

CABERNET SAUVIGNON SANTA BARBARA COUNTY (★★):
1990: Youthful and tight, with lean, rough-hewn cherry, plum and currant notes. It's also quite tannic and a touch earthy on the finish. **85**
1989: A funky wine with muddled herb and olive aromas. There are hints of plum and currant, but the flavors are mostly herbaceous. There are smooth and supple tannins on the finish. **82**

CHARDONNAY SANTA BARBARA COUNTY (★★★★),
RESERVE (★★★★): Beautifully crafted, ripe and elegant, with a rich, complex core of fruit flavors shaded by light toasty oak.
1993: Well oaked, with toasty vanilla and buttery notes, but lots of pretty ripe pear, apple, spice and honeyed notes. Turns complex and fruity. **90**
1992: Complex and concentrated, with hints of pear, spice, butterscotch and honey on the finish. **88**
1991: Complex, packing in lots of ripe, spicy honey, pear, citrus and buttery oak flavors that turn rich and smooth. **92**
Reserve 1993: Good richness, depth and intensity, a well focused and complex wine with tiers of honey, pear and smoky oak. Remarkably complex and concentrated. **91**
Reserve 1992: Builds richness and complexity, with tight green apple and spice flavors that soften and swirl into honey and cream notes on the long finish. **92**
Reserve 1991: Serves up ripe pear, apricot and honey notes, finishing with a rich, complex earthiness. **88**
Reserve 1990: Ripe, intense, rich and creamy, with wonderful spice, pear, hazelnut, vanilla and honey notes that are complex and concentrated. **92**

CHARDONNAY SANTA MARIA VALLEY (★★★★):
1992: Well focused, with intense pear, spice, nutmeg and toasty oak, all folding together in a rich and complex package. Holds its flavors on the finish. **91**

1991: Complex, with broad, creamy pear, peach and vanilla flavors and toasty oak shadings. **91**

PINOT BLANC SANTA BARBARA COUNTY (★★★):
1991: Byron's first Pinot Blanc. Smooth and creamy, with spicy vanilla and pear aromas and flavors. Nice balance, depth and richness. **88**

PINOT NOIR SANTA BARBARA COUNTY (★★★),
RESERVE (★★★): The Reserve is a shade fuller and oakier, it shows spicy cherry, cola, rhubarb and earth notes, finishing with fine tannins. Best to drink young.
1992: This crisp, focused, thick-textured wine has a leathery edge to the basic berry flavor. **83**
1990: Elegant and spicy, with black cherry, cola and rhubarb notes that turn silky and smooth. **87**
Reserve 1992: Firm and crisp, with an earthy, leathery herb and cola edge to the spicy black cherry flavors. **86**
Reserve 1991: Firm and intense, with rich, focused cola, cherry, herb and strawberry flavors. **88**
Reserve 1990: Firm in texture, with a broad range of plum, currant, spice, earth and leather flavors. **87**
Reserve 1989: Tight and firm, with an earthy rhubarb edge to the cherry and spice notes, turning silky on the finish. **87**
Reserve 1988: Remarkably supple, smooth and complex, with layers of black cherry, spice, cola and oak shadings. Elegant and refined. **88**

SAUVIGNON BLANC SANTA BARBARA COUNTY (★★★):
Delivers a wide range of flavors but keeps its focus and doesn't veer off into pungent vegetal flavors.
1993: Firm and nicely focused, modest fruit and a nice touch of herb sneaking in on the finish. **82**
1992: Firm and flavorful, with a nice array of spicy, toasty, slightly herbal pear, honey and grapefruit aromas and flavors. **90**

CA' DEL SOLO

This is a second label for Bonny Doon Vineyard (see listing).

CACHE CELLARS
Davis
F: 1978. O: Charles & Elizabeth Lowe. W: Charles Lowe. S: Teal Lake Cellars.

OVERALL	$10-24	NR
WINE RATINGS		
Chardonnay Napa Valley		NR
Meritage Red Napa Valley		NR
Merlot Napa Valley		NR

WINERY DATA
C: 5,000. V: None. G: None. P: Cabernet Sauvignon, Merlot, Chardonnay, Cabernet Franc, Petite Verdot, Malbec (Napa Valley).

One-time Inglenook winemaker Charles Lowe hauls organically grown Napa Valley grapes to Davis, where he vinifies them into 5,000 cases a year of Cabernet, Chardonnay, Merlot and red Meritage. Distribution is very limited and the wines have been in the fair to good range.

CAFARO CELLARS
St. Helena, Napa Valley
F: 1986. O: Joe Cafaro. W: Joe Cafaro. S: None.

OVERALL	$26-28	★★★
WINE RATINGS		
Cabernet Sauvignon Napa Valley		★★★
Merlot Napa Valley		★★★

WINERY DATA
C: 1,800. V: None. G: None. P: Cabernet Sauvignon (Carneros), Cabernet Sauvignon (Spring Mountain), Cabernet Sauvignon (Stags Leap District), Merlot (Carneros, Spring Mountain), Merlot (Stags Leap District).

Joe Cafaro is a well known Napa Valley winemaker, having worked for Chappellet, Keenan, Acacia and Robert Sinskey as well as consulting for several other brands. In 1986 he began making small lots of Cabernet (950 cases) and Merlot (850 cases) from grapes purchased in different sub-appellations of Napa. Both wines are 100 percent varietal and well crafted, with a deliberate style. Both the Cabernet and Merlot are blends of grapes grown in Carneros, Spring Mountain and the Stags Leap District. Given his dedication to these two wines, Cafaro remains worth watching.

TASTING NOTES

CABERNET SAUVIGNON NAPA VALLEY (★★★): The early vintages are more impressive: the 1986 showcases the style with its elegance and sharply focused flavors that are harmonious and supple. Recent vintages have been on the lean side, with less richness.
1991: Smooth and supple, with an attractive spicy currant and plum edge before the cedary oak and tannins kick in. Typical of the 1991 vintage with its understated flavors. Best to cellar into 1997. Tasted out of magnum. **88**
1990: Lean and elegant, modestly concentrated and mildly tannic, with a spicy, peppery edge to the cherry and currant notes. **84**
1989: Crisp and firm, with ripe currant and cherry flavors that are bright and lively, but also quite tannic. **85**
1988: Hard and tannic, this lean-textured wine manages to show appealing currant and berry flavors behind a wall of tannin. **81**
1987: Deep, dark, rich and plush, packed with currant, herb, black cherry and plum flavors. Wonderful harmony and finesse. **90**
1986: Elegant, with well defined, supple currant, plum and violet flavors that are quite harmonious. The delicious flavors sneak up on you. **93**

MERLOT NAPA VALLEY (★★★): Supple, elegant and well crafted, with classic herb, currant and tobacco notes. Best to drink early but can age.
1990: Supple and elegant, with focused currant, plum and cherry flavors that turn smooth and fleshy. **87**
1988: Rich, lively and concentrated, packed with herb, cherry, plum and currant flavors that are a bit tight and tannic now, but show a sense of harmony and finesse. **89**
1987: Tight, with firm herb and currant flavors that turn earthy and tannic. **85**
1986: Lean and tannic, with an elegant core of tobacco, cherry and currant flavors that dry out. **84**

CAIN CELLARS
St. Helena, Napa Valley
F: 1980. O: Jim & Nancy Meadlock. W: Christopher Howell. S: None.

OVERALL	$14-40	★★★★

WINE RATINGS

Cabernet Blend Napa Valley Cuvée	★★
Cabernet Sauvignon Napa Valley	★★
Meritage Red Napa Valley Cain Five	★★★★
Sauvignon Blanc	
Monterey County Musqué	★★

WINERY DATA

C: 13,500. **V:** 84 acres in Napa Valley. **G:** Cabernet Sauvignon (49 acres), Merlot (18), Cabernet Franc (9), Malbec (4), Petit Verdot (4). **P:** Sauvignon Blanc (Monterey).

Jerry and Joyce Cain spared no expense when they bought their vineyard at the top of Spring Mountain and built a large, stone-faced winery. The vineyards they terraced into the hillside are spectacular, but by the late 1980s the winery was experiencing financial difficulties, and in 1991 investor-partner Jim Meadlock bought out their interest and became the sole owner.

Cain Five is the star, a blend of the five Bordeaux varieties grown in Cain's 84 acres of vineyard. Some 8,000 cases of a Cabernet blend called Cuvée were made from the leftover wines and can be solid if leaner and more herbal. A Sauvignon Blanc called Musqué was solid in 1992, with bright fig and apple flavors and herb seasoning. Having decided to stick with Cain Five and refine its style, this winery is worth watching. About 6,000 cases of the 1991 Cain Five were produced.

TASTING NOTES

CABERNET BLEND NAPA VALLEY CUVÉE (★★):
1992: Lean, with a cedar and tobacco edge to the currant and cherry flavors, finishing with supple tannins and a spicy anise edge. **88**
1991: A bit green, with herb, cedar and simple currant flavors. **81**
1989: A crisp and spicy Cabernet blend with a definite earthy streak. **84**
1988: Smooth and cedary, with an earthy, tarry edge to the currant and plum flavors. **85**

CABERNET SAUVIGNON NAPA VALLEY (★★):
1987: Herbal and oaky at first, but also very rich and ripe, with layers of plum, currant, oak and cherry flavors that are elegantly styled. **88**

MERITAGE RED NAPA VALLEY CAIN FIVE (★★★★): Intense, complex and well oaked, packed with rich, lush currant, herb and spice flavors, finishing with smooth, polished tannins. Aging well so far, but appealing to drink early on too.
1991: Supple and complex, with a cedar and tobacco edge to the currant and spicy flavors, finishing with toasty oak and good length. **89**
1990: Big, ripe and fleshy, packed with juicy currant, tobacco, anise and spice flavors that are framed by toasty, buttery oak and firm but fleshy tannins. **91**
1989: Impressive for a 1989, with a focused, lively band of ripe, complex currant, cedar, tobacco and spice flavors. **87**
1987: Rich, smooth, plush and complex, with pretty toasty oak notes and layers of sweet currant, plum, anise and black cherry flavors that are elegant and supple. **92**
1986: Classy, with complex, focused oak, currant, cassis and spice flavors, blending in nicely with the buttery oak flavors. **90**
1985: An austere wine that leans toward the cedar-cigar box end of the Cabernet spectrum, with plum and currant flavors. **87**

SAUVIGNON BLANC MONTEREY COUNTY MUSQUÉ (★★):
1993: Crisp and flinty, with a core of citrus and grapefruit flavors. **85**
1992: Bright and flavorful, a nicely polished example of how to balance ripe fig and apple flavors with a modest touch of herbs and spicy oak. **87**

CAKEBREAD CELLARS
Rutherford, Napa Valley
F: 1973. **O:** Jack & Dolores Cakebread. **W:** Bruce Cakebread. **S:** None.

OVERALL	$13-42	★★★

WINE RATINGS

Cabernet Sauvignon Napa Valley	★★★
Chardonnay Napa Valley	★★★
Chardonnay Napa Valley Reserve	★★★
Sauvignon Blanc Napa Valley	★★★
Zinfandel Howell Mountain	★★★

Winery Data

C: 45,000. **V:** 77 acres in Napa Valley. **G:** Sauvignon Blanc (25 acres), Cabernet Sauvignon (50), Cabernet Franc (2).
P: Cabernet Sauvignon (Stags Leap), Cabernet Sauvignon, Chardonnay, Sauvignon Blanc (Napa Valley), Chardonnay (Carneros), Zinfandel (Howell Mountain), Merlot (Rutherford).

In the 1960s Jack Cakebread was operating an auto repair business in Oakland and working as a free-lance photographer when he discovered Napa Valley while on a photo assignment for a Napa wine book. In 1971 he and his wife, Dolores, purchased a 22-acre vineyard in Rutherford, where the winery is now, and began commuting from Oakland to Napa on weekends, starting a winery in 1973. Cakebread Cellars owns 77 acres, mostly Cabernet Sauvignon (50 acres) and Sauvignon Blanc (25), while purchasing Cabernet from the Stags Leap District, Chardonnay from Carneros, Zinfandel from Howell Mountain and Merlot from Rutherford. The winery currently produces 45,000 cases under the direction of the Cakebreads' son Bruce. Chardonnay, at 25,000 cases, makes up more than half the production, with Cabernet and Sauvignon Blanc both in the 10,000-case range.

Through more than a decade, the winery has had its ups and downs, but overall it's been a steady performer, at times excelling at all four of the major wines it makes, including 400-case Reserve bottlings of Chardonnay and Cabernet. Zinfandel is back in the fold; it's Dolores's favorite wine, but the winery dropped it in 1983, only to reinstate it in 1992 using grapes from Howell Mountain.

Tasting Notes

Cabernet Sauvignon Napa Valley (★★★): Usually intense and firmly tannic, but it can be lean and hard (1990) as well as a touch bitter. Other times it's lush and concentrated (1987).

1991: Serves up crisp, ripe black cherry and plum flavors before the tannins kick in. **88**

1990: Spicy and herbal, with an elegant core of currant and cherry flavors. **83**

1989: Firm and generous, with a tight core of plum and spice notes. **87**

1988: Crisp and focused, with a solid core of red currant and plum flavors. Mildly tannic. **86**

1987: Big, rich and lush, with intense, concentrated black cherry, currant and plum flavors that are broad and complex. **89**

1986: Fresh, clean and lively, with plenty of black cherry, mint, currant and plum flavors. **88**

1985: Lean and crisp, with medium-weight plum, currant, spice, cedar and tobacco notes. **84**

1984: Well focused vanilla, chocolate and black cherry flavors are framed by supple tannins and a pretty aftertaste. **87**

1983: A good 1983, but Cakebread's weakest vintage. Lean, thin and tannic; with ripe currant flavors that cannot match the tannins. **77**

Lot 2 1974: Deep, rich and plush, with mature but pleasing cedar, coffee, chocolate and currant flavors. One of the better 1974s, it is fully mature, complex and flavorful. The tannins turn smooth on the finish, with just a trace of dryness. Drink up. **91**

Cabernet Sauvignon Napa Valley Rutherford Reserve (★★★): Not dramatically different from the regular bottling, but the winery thinks it's special. Holding the wine for extended cellaring doesn't seem to add much.

1988: An odd range of flavors taste alternately of plum brandy and ash. **81**

1987: Ripe, rich, plush currant, black cherry and spice notes turn intense and concentrated, finishing with fine depth and finesse. **88**

1986: Lean and tannic, with crisp plum and currant notes, a hard-edged wine. **80**

1985: Lean yet rich, with crisp acidity and fresh, ripe plum flavors of medium depth. **85**

1984: Generous and supple, with broad cherry and chocolate aromas and flavors. **85**

1983: Lean and firm, with a pretty core of black cherry and currant flavors and fine tannins. **88**

Chardonnay Napa Valley (★★★), Reserve (★★★): Flinty and austere, with crisp citrus, pear and spice notes.

1993: A bit on the green side, with tart, zesty green apple flavors that are one-dimensional but focused. **84**

1992: Austere, with firm acidity and crisp lemon, pineapple, pear and pine flavors that linger. **87**

1991: Coarse and simple, with tart pear and apple notes. **81**

Reserve 1992: Clean and correct, with ripe pear, spice and cedary oak of moderate proportions, finishing with a pleasant fruity edge. **87**

SAUVIGNON BLANC NAPA VALLEY (★★★): Variable in quality, ranging from grassy notes to well defined varietal fruit flavors.

1992: Fresh and lively, with apricot and grapefruit flavors that sustain themselves through a clean finish. **87**

ZINFANDEL HOWELL MOUNTAIN (★★★): Long a strength at Cakebread, the 1992 is packed with peppery flavors.

1992: Intense and spicy, with loads of peppery fruit flavors that pick up wild berry notes. **90**

CALE CELLARS
Sonoma Valley
F: 1990. O: Michael & Jeanie Cale. W: Erich Russell. S: None.

OVERALL	$18-25	★★★

WINE RATINGS	
Chardonnay Carneros	
Sangiacomo Vineyard	★★★

WINERY DATA
C: 4,000. V: None. G: None. P: Chardonnay (Carneros).

Michael and Jeanie Cale founded this 4,000-case winery in Kenwood in 1990, focusing on Chardonnay grown at Sangiacomo Vineyard in the Sonoma County part of Carneros. Erich Russell is the winemaker, having joined the winery after working at Belvedere and Rabbit Ridge. The first vintages are well made and show promise.

TASTING NOTES

CHARDONNAY CARNEROS SANGIACOMO VINEYARD (★★★): Rich, full-bodied and complex, well oaked and creamy.

1993: Intense and spicy, with a sweetish lichee nut edge to the ripe pear and buttery oak flavors. **88**

1992: Creamy and complex, with pretty honey, pear, toast and butter flavors that pick up a smoky, toasty edge from oak barrels. Forward and easy to drink. **90**

CALERA WINE CO.
Mount Harlan, San Benito County
F: 1974. O: Josh Jensen. W: Sara Steiner. S: None.

OVERALL	$15-35	★★★★

WINE RATINGS	
Chardonnay Central Coast	★★★
Chardonnay Mount Harlan	★★★
Pinot Noir Central Coast	★★
Pinot Noir Mount Harlan Jensen	★★★★★
Pinot Noir Mount Harlan Mills	★★★★
Pinot Noir Mount Harlan Reed	★★★
Pinot Noir Mount Harlan Selleck	★★★★

WINERY DATA
C: 25,000. V: 47 acres in Mount Harlan. G: Pinot Noir (36 acres), Chardonnay (6), Viognier (5). P: Pinot Noir (Central Coast), Chardonnay (Central Coast).

While touring France as a student at Oxford, Josh Jensen became fascinated by Burgundy, worked several harvests there and decided to grow Chardonnay and Pinot Noir in California. To that end, he began a statewide search for thin soils laced with limestone, finally settling in 1974 in the rugged Mount Harlan area of San Benito County, where he found a property with an old lime kiln. Today Calera farms 47 acres, mostly Pinot Noir. He makes vineyard-designated Pinots from four vineyards: Jensen (14 acres), Selleck (5), Reed (5) and Mills (11). In Pinot Noir, Jensen strives for complexity in a dark, ultraripe, often jammy style full of intense flavors. Can be funky and decadent, with flavors stretched too far, but lately the wines have been dramatic and well crafted, capable of aging for five to seven years. Jensen Vineyard is usually the darkest and most complex. Calera also produces wine from Viognier (5 acres) and Chardonnay (6 acres) that are also rooted there. Jensen buys Chardonnay and Pinot Noir from the Central Coast. Production is 25,000 cases.

TASTING NOTES

CHARDONNAY CENTRAL COAST (★★★):
1993: Earthy, with a juniper berry edge, but also a pretty core of smooth, creamy pear and vanilla flavors. **88**
1992: Smooth, ripe and creamy, with vanilla, pear and spice flavors that turn silky and elegant. **89**
1991: Ripe and buttery, showing off spicy oak shadings, but there's a nice core of ripe pear, tart peach and pineapple flavors. **89**
1990: Rich and Burgundian in style, with earthy pear, spice, vanilla and hazelnut flavors that are broad and complex. **88**

CHARDONNAY MOUNT HARLAN (★★★):
1992: Compact and concentrated, with ripe pear, pineapple, butterscotch and toasty oak flavors. **89**
1990: Ripe, fat and buttery, with creamy pear, earth and spice flavors that are smooth and fleshy, finishing with a rich, thick aftertaste. **89**

PINOT NOIR CENTRAL COAST (★★): More vegetal than the Mount Harlan Pinot Noirs.
1992: Green and vegetal, with ashy flavors on the finish. **73**
1991: Displays spicy cherry, dill and plum flavors that are focused, lively and intense. **84**
1990: Ripe and perfumed, with pretty cherry, plum, herb and spice notes that are elegant. **87**
1989: An assertive, cherry-flavored wine with minty menthol aromas. **85**
1987: Has a pleasant balance of toast, cherry and gamy nuances and finishes with a leafy green flavor. **82**

PINOT NOIR MOUNT HARLAN JENSEN (★★★★★): The best and most consistent, often very ripe and complex.
1991: Aromatic with ripe, exotic wild berry and raspberry flavors that turn elegant and silky. **88**
1990: Bold and ripe, with a decadent edge of cherry and plum aromas and flavors. **87**
1989: Very dark and rich, packing a wallop of decadent and concentrated plum and cherry aromas and flavors. **89**
1988: Packed with rich, ultraripe black cherry, currant, herb and spicy earth flavors. Deeply flavored and very concentrated, with smooth, supple tannins. **92**
1987: Deep, rich, enormously complex and concentrated, with intense, sharply focused plum, currant, black cherry, raspberry, mineral and spice flavors. **93**
1986: A deliciously complex wine, with a magnificent interplay of plum, currant, nutmeg and vanilla flavors, a supple texture and vibrant acidity. **91**
1985: Effusively fruity, almost jammy, loaded with ripe, complex plum, cherry and raspberry flavors in a full-bodied, firmly structured wine. **92**

PINOT NOIR MOUNT HARLAN MILLS (★★★★):
Excellent fruit intensity, but not as deep as Jensen.
1989: A dramatic and complex Pinot Noir, rich, concentrated and effusively fruity, with tiers of black cherry, currant, anise and plum flavors that are broad and deep. **93**

1988: Dense and austere but has plenty of stuffing, with black cherry and currant flavors tightly wrapped in tannins. **89**

PINOT NOIR MOUNT HARLAN REED (★★★): Serves up a broad range of complex flavors.
1992: Elegant and fragrant, with a ripe, supple core of spicy cherry, raspberry and subtle earth notes. **91**
1989: A lean yet very ripe wine with jammy cherry flavors and a strong volatile edge. It's concentrated and earthy, finishing with potent berry flavors. **88**
1988: Ripe and intense, with pepper, stewed plum, herb and black cherry flavors that come with some alcoholic heat. **85**
1987: Spicy and slightly cooked, with cherry and beet flavors that are concentrated and rich, but also a bit earthy. **80**

PINOT NOIR MOUNT HARLAN SELLECK (★★★★):
1988: Ripe, with a complex raisiny edge, but also lots of spicy cherry and raspberry jam flavors that pick up a tarry edge. **89**
1987: Hard and tight now, but with a solid core of rich, concentrated, deeply perfumed black cherry, currant, plum and spice flavors. **92**
1986: Plenty of fresh, ripe berry and cherry aromas and flavors, full-bodied and tannic. **85**

CALISTOGA VINEYARDS
This is a second label of Cuvaison Winery (see listing).

CALLAWAY VINEYARD AND WINERY
Temecula
F: 1974. **O:** The Wine Alliance. **W:** Dwayne Helmuth. **S:** None.

OVERALL	$6-25	★★

WINE RATINGS

Cabernet Sauvignon California	★
Chardonnay Temecula Calla-Lees	★★
Chenin Blanc Temecula	
Sweet Nancy Late Harvest	★★★
Sauvignon Blanc Temecula	★★
Viognier Temecula	★★
White Riesling Temecula	★

WINERY DATA

C: 240,000. **V:** 720 acres in Temecula. **G:** Chardonnay (560 acres), Sauvignon Blanc (60), Pinot Blanc (30), Viognier (10), Other (60). **P:** Cabernet Sauvignon, Merlot, Cabernet Franc (Sonoma County), Cabernet Sauvignon, Petite Verdot (Napa Valley).

Industrialist Ely Callaway, one-time president of Burlington Industries and now a golf club manufacturer, founded this winery in Temecula in 1974, claiming he knew nothing about wine but considered that an asset. The early years were rough going for this winery, as its trial-and-error experiments with different varietals led to some downright funky red wines characterized by earthy, rubbery flavors, and whites that were often oxidized. Callaway tired of the wine business and realized Southern California's affection for his wines had its limits. He sold the winery to Hiram Walker in 1981, marking that company's first entry into the California wine business (it also owns Clos du Bois and William Hill and markets the Atlas Peak Vineyards wines under its Wine Alliance umbrella). Wine Alliance set Callaway on a fast-paced growth cycle, expanding the vineyards to 720 acres, dropping reds, lees-aging its Chardonnay in stainless steel and adopting the motto "White Wine. It's All We Make."

Production is nearly 240,000 cases. The top-selling wine is the Calla-Lees Chardonnay (100,000 cases), which at its best is fresh and fruity, without any oak flavors, but at times is overly leesy, bordering on sour. In 1994 Callaway sold its vineyards but signed a long-term agreement to buy the grapes. Other wines produced are a Viognier and white Riesling, and in 1989 Callaway returned to reds with a California-appellation Cabernet. Sweet Nancy, a botrytis-style Chenin Blanc, can be very good. Early trials with Pinot Gris, Mourvèdre, Dolcetto and Nebbiolo are ongoing.

TASTING NOTES

CABERNET SAUVIGNON CALIFORNIA VARIOUS BOTTLINGS (★):

1990: A full-bodied, tannic wine with modest fruit and herb flavors. Has the outline of a good Cabernet, but could use more stuffing. **79**
Hawk Watch 1991: Simple, with grapey Cabernet flavors; a servicable red. **79**

CHARDONNAY TEMECULA CALLA-LEES (★★):

1993: Crisp and simple, a lively wine with gentle pear and vanilla flavors that linger on the finish. **84**
1992: Ripe and fruity, with complex apple, pear and spice flavors that turn elegant and supple. **83**
1990: Intense and spicy, with pretty pear, pineapple, earth and oak flavors that are sharply focused, with good richness and depth. There's lots of fruit on the long and lingering finish. **88**

CHENIN BLANC TEMECULA SWEET NANCY LATE HARVEST (★★★):

1991: Sweet and vaguely floral, a little touch of honey and a wisp of vinegar on the finish. **79**

SAUVIGNON BLANC TEMECULA (★★):

1993: Soft, a little sweet, with apple and spice flavors that linger. **80**

VIOGNIER TEMECULA (★★):

1993: Soft and fruity, with mild but exotic tropical fruit overtones. **81**

WHITE RIESLING TEMECULA (★):

1991: Simple, sweet and slightly bitter, showing a strong pine character more than fruit flavor, although nice, modest apple notes emerge on the finish. **77**

CAMBRIA WINERY & VINEYARD
Santa Maria Valley
F: 1986. **O:** Jess Jackson & Barbara Banke. **W:** David Guffy. **S:** None.

OVERALL	$16-30	★★★★

WINE RATINGS

Chardonnay Santa Maria Valley	
Katherine's Vineyard Reserve	★★★★
Chardonnay Santa Maria Valley Reserve	★★★★
Pinot Noir Santa Maria Valley	
Julia's Vineyard	★★★
Pinot Noir Santa Maria Valley Reserve	★★★
Sangiovese Santa Maria Valley	
Tepusquet Vineyard	★★★
Syrah Santa Maria Valley	
Tepusquet Vineyard	★★★

WINERY DATA

C: 60,000. **V:** 775 acres in Santa Maria Valley. **G:** Chardonnay (670 acres), Pinot Noir (80), Syrah (10), Sangiovese (17). **P:** None.

As Kendall-Jackson's demand for Chardonnay soared in the 1980s, it sought grapes throughout California. One of the best sources proved to be Santa Maria Valley and the highly regarded, 2,000-acre Tepusquet Vineyard. In 1986 Jess Jackson began producing Cambria Chardonnay from Tepusquet. In 1987 Kendall-Jackson and Robert Mondavi Winery each bought part of the vineyard, with Kendall-Jackson acquiring nearly 1,000 acres, most of it in Chardonnay.

Today Cambria owns 775 acres, including 80 acres of Pinot Noir, produces 60,000 cases and is making delicious wines. Chardonnay has the edge now, but the Pinot Noirs are impressive for their texture and range of flavor and early experiments with Syrah are also encouraging. Katherine's Vineyard, a 350-acre section of Cambria's vineyard named after one of Jackson's daughters, is a 50,000-case brand. Julia's Vineyard, named after another of Jackson's daughters, is about 80 acres in size, yielding 10,000 cases of Pinot Noir. The 1992 vintage added 500-case lots of Syrah and Sangiovese carrying the Tepusquet vineyard designation. A Camelot Vineyard Chardonnay has also been produced, but Kendall-Jackson has designated Camelot as its own brand and plans to build a winery (see listing).

TASTING NOTES

CHARDONNAY SANTA MARIA VALLEY KATHERINE'S VINEYARD RESERVE (★★★★): Bold, ripe and intense, with bright, complex flavors and bracing acidity.
1993: Bright and lively, with vivid, medium-weight pear, spice, honey and hazelnut notes that turn elegant. **87**
1991: Soft, supple and low-key, showing simple pear and spice notes that are pleasant enough. **85**
1990: Smooth, creamy and rich, with complex apple, pineapple, nutmeg and fig aromas and flavors. **90**
Reserve 1991: Bold, ripe, rich and creamy, with deeply concentrated pear, pineapple and toasty, smoky oak flavors that are complex and mouth-filling. **91**

CHARDONNAY SANTA MARIA VALLEY RESERVE (★★★★): Oakier and heavier than the Katherine's Vineyard bottling. Best on release, but ages well for three years.
1993: Bold, ripe and harmonious, with rich pear, honey, butterscotch and spicy nuances, picking up a smoky leesy edge on the finish. Wonderful aftertaste. **91**
1992: Bold, ripe and complex, with tiers of fig, spice, oak, pineapple and citrus flavors that are rich and focused, picking up hints of honey and butterscotch on the finish. **91**
1991: Dense and compact, with spicy pear, citrus and nutmeg flavors that are tightly wound. **85**
1990: Fresh, bright and lively, with layers of apple, spice, honey and butter notes that turn smooth and elegant, picking up hints of pineapple and toast. **90**
1989: Complex and rich, with ripe pear, honey, butterscotch and spice flavors that are deep and compelling. **89**
1988: A ripe, unctuous, mouth-filling wine, brimming with peach, pear and toast aromas and flavors. **85**

PINOT NOIR SANTA MARIA VALLEY JULIA'S VINEYARD (★★★): Remarkably consistent, smooth-textured, with supple flavors that range from herb to dark cherry. Well crafted.
1993: Exotic in its spiciness, with plush cherry, herb, tea and cedary oak flavors. **87**
1992: Tight and firm, with sharply focused spice, black cherry, herb and cola flavors that are rich and concentrated. **87**
1991: Supple and elegant, with a smooth, fleshy texture and a core of rich, spicy herb and black cherry aromas and flavors. **87**
1989: Earthy, tarry and gamy, but has a nice core of cola and berry flavors, too. **80**
1988: Ripe, generous, silky and complex, with raspberry and plum flavors and hints of coffee, toast and chocolate on the long, complex finish. **88**

PINOT NOIR SANTA MARIA VALLEY RESERVE (★★★):
1992: Pleasantly fruity, with herb and black cherry flavors. Finishes with firm tannins and a cola edge. **86**

SANGIOVESE SANTA MARIA VALLEY TEPUSQUET VINEYARD (★★★):
1993: Light in texture and flavor, showing a nice thread

of persistent raspberry and spice flavors that linger on the finish. Best from 1996. **86**

SYRAH SANTA MARIA VALLEY TEPUSQUET VINEYARD (★★★): Deep in color, impressive for its intensity and purity of flavors. Worth watching.
1992: Supple, rich and fruity, with a wild berry edge to the smooth cedar, spice and leathery tobacco notes. **88**

CAMELOT
Santa Barbara County
F: 1993. **O:** Jess Jackson. **W:** Randy Ullom. **S:** None.

OVERALL	$11-20	★★★

WINE RATINGS	
Cabernet Sauvignon Central Coast	★★
Chardonnay Santa Barbara County	★★★
Pinot Noir Central Coast	NR

WINERY DATA
C: N/A. **V:** 490 acres in Santa Maria Valley. **G:** Chardonnay (470 acres), Merlot (10), Pinot Noir (10). **P:** Cabernet Sauvignon, Chardonnay, Pinot Noir (Central Coast), Cabernet Sauvignon, Merlot (North Coast).

This new brand from Kendall-Jackson Winery was introduced in 1993, and there are plans to build a new winery to produce Chardonnay, Cabernet and Pinot Noir, the latter two carrying Central Coast appellations. Camelot Vineyard first appeared as a vineyard-designated Chardonnay from Cambria. The 1993 Chardonnay featured the region's bright, crisp, intense flavors, with tart green apple and spice nuances. The 1992 Cabernet was made in a light style, with hints of currant and cherry flavors. The 1993 Pinot Noir featured smooth cherry, herb and vanilla notes. Randy Ullom, former winemaker for De Loach, is the winemaker. Given Kendall-Jackson's success with Chardonnay and Pinot Noir in this area, Camelot is worth watching.

TASTING NOTES

CABERNET SAUVIGNON CENTRAL COAST (★★):
1992: A lighter style, it still delivers enough spicy oak, currant and cherry flavors to keep your interest. **83**

CHARDONNAY SANTA BARBARA COUNTY (★★★):
1993: Crisp and focused, a stylish wine with zingy green

apple and spice aromas and flavors that extend into a lively, complex finish. **90**

PINOT NOIR CENTRAL COAST (NR):
1993: Supple and focused, with smooth cherry, herb and vanilla flavors that are elegant. **85**

CANDLEWOOD CELLARS
This is a second label of Arciero Winery (see listing).

CANEPA CELLARS
Alexander Valley
F: 1991. **O:** Canepa Family. **W:** Jim Canepa, Helen Turley. **S:** None.

OVERALL	$20	★★★

WINE RATINGS	
Chardonnay Alexander Valley	★★★

WINERY DATA
C: 2,500. **V:** 16 acres in Alexander Valley. **G:** Chardonnay. **P:** None.

This 16-acre vineyard in Alexander Valley was once the source of a vineyard-designated Chardonnay from Robert Pecota, who encouraged the vineyard's owner to make wine. A 1991 Chardonnay, made by Helen Turley of Marcassin Winery, showcases the vineyard's quality. It is an elegant and harmonious wine that features subtle toast, butter, pear and pineapple flavors.

TASTING NOTES

CHARDONNAY ALEXANDER VALLEY (★★★):
1991: Smooth, light, elegant and harmonious, with subtle toast and butter edges to the pear and pineapple aromas and flavors. Finishes with focused fruit flavors. **88**

J. CAREY CELLARS
Solvang
F: 1978. **O:** Firestone Vineyard. **W:** Alison Green. **S:** None.

OVERALL	$9-18	★★

WINE RATINGS

Chardonnay Santa Ynez Valley	NR
Pinot Noir Santa Ynez Valley	NR
Sauvignon Blanc Santa Ynez Valley	NR

WINERY DATA

C: 4,800. V: 24 acres in Santa Ynez Valley. G: Cabernet Sauvignon (18 acres), Merlot (3), Sauvignon Blanc (3). P: Chardonnay (Santa Ynez Valley), Pinot Noir (Santa Ynez Valley), Cabernet Franc (Santa Ynez Valley), Muscat (Santa Barbara County).

J. Carey Cellars, named after its founder, James Carey, is a 5,000-case brand that since 1987 has been owned by Firestone Vineyards. The winery is run independently from Firestone, but shares Firestone's winemaker, Alison Green. The winery owns some 24 acres of vineyards, including the 12-acre La Cuesta Vineyard, which is planted to Cabernet and Merlot. In recent vintages, the winery has made Chardonnay, Sauvignon Blanc and Pinot Noir. Given Santa Barbara's strength with Chardonnay and difficulties with Cabernet, the former is the wine to watch.

CARMENET VINEYARD

Sonoma Valley

F: 1981. O: Chalone Wine Group. W: Jeffrey Baker. S: None.

OVERALL	$12-25	★★★

WINE RATINGS

Cabernet Sauvignon Sonoma County Dynamite Cabernet	★★★
Cabernet Sauvignon Sonoma Valley Moon Mountain Estate Vineyard	★★★
Chardonnay Carneros Sangiacomo Vineyard	★★
Meritage Red Sonoma Valley	★★★
Meritage White Edna Valley Paragon Vineyard	★★

WINERY DATA

C: 31,000. V: 66 acres in Sonoma Valley. G: Cabernet Sauvignon (47 acres), Merlot (4), Cabernet Franc (13), Petite Verdot (2). P: Chardonnay (Carneros), Sauvignon Blanc, Sémillon (Edna Valley), Cabernet Sauvignon (Sonoma Valley), French Colombard (Napa Valley).

Carmenet, situated in the sloping mountains that form the eastern border of Sonoma Valley, is part of the Chalone Wine Group, which also owns Chalone Vineyards, Acacia and Edna Valley Vineyards. The winery initially focused on Bordeaux-style reds (Cabernet and Merlot blends) from its 66-acre estate vineyard that sits 1,600 feet above the valley floor, and whites (Sauvignon Blanc and Sémillon) from Edna Valley and Sonoma. The winery also makes a very fine Chenin Blanc from Saviez Vineyard in Napa Valley and in 1990 added Sangiacomo Chardonnay to its product mix. Production is 31,000 cases.

The winery now produces a Bordeaux-style blend that features mostly Cabernet Sauvignon with varying proportions of Merlot and Cabernet Franc. Parts of the 47-acre Cabernet vineyard, which is next to Louis Martini Winery's Monte Rosso vineyard, were planted in the early 1970s when it was known as Glen Ellen Vineyard. Cabernets from the vineyard were produced by Ridge, Kistler and Chateau St. Jean.

Carmenet's reds are sturdy, rough-hewn, chunky, oaky and coarse, but the flavors even out to become remarkably ripe, deep and complex.

TASTING NOTES

CABERNET SAUVIGNON SONOMA COUNTY DYNAMITE CABERNET (★★★):

1992: Smooth and polished, with a pretty core of cherry, currant and spicy flavors, picking up a nice light toasty oak edge on the finish. Has a nice sense of balance and proportion. **87**

1991: Ripe and spicy, with pretty earth and black cherry flavors that are shaded by toasty oak notes. **85**

CABERNET SAUVIGNON SONOMA VALLEY MOON MOUNTAIN ESTATE VINEYARD (★★★): Dark, intense and tannic, slow to evolve.

1990: Marked by herb, bell pepper and a green bean edge. Just enough soft cherry and berry notes come through to make it interesting. Finishes with firm tannins. **84**

1989: A solid, deep-colored, youthful wine with rich, ripe currant and herb flavors and firm tannins. **86**

Reserve 1989: Herbal and earthy, a lean, austere wine with modest fruit intensity, finishing with cedar and chocolate nuances. **83**

CARNEROS CREEK WINERY 137

CHARDONNAY CARNEROS SANGIACOMO VINEYARD (★★): The 1991 is a hit, laced with complex flavors, but the 1992 is a so-so follow-up, straying into earthy flavors.
1992: Tight and taut, with flinty grapefruit, citrus and spicy pear flavors that turn earthy. **82**
1991: Appealing, with a ripe, rich streak of lemon, grapefruit and apple flavors. **90**

MERITAGE RED SONOMA VALLEY (★★★): Tightly reined in and firmly tannic, sometimes to a fault, with crisp currant, cedar, tobacco and fruit flavors. Well oaked and capable of aging, although the early vintages are still tough, unevolved and in danger of drying out.
1989: Offers cedar, cigar box and spicy black currant flavors that are intense, focused and concentrated. **88**
1988: Lavish, buttery oak notes dominating the currant and black cherry flavors. **87**
1987: Firm and intense, with well knit cherry, coffee, cedar, herb and currant flavors. **89**
1986: Well crafted, with toasty vanilla and spicy plum aromas adding complexity to the elegant, refined, sharply focused black cherry flavors. **90**
1985: Elegant and stylish, with ripe plum and cherry flavors, accented by vanilla and tobacco nuances. **88**
1984: Mature, but the black cherry, currant and spice flavors are complex. **88**
1983: Tight and lean, mature and drying, leaving a hint of mint and plum. **83**
1982: Mature and turning earthy, with tannic currant and cedar flavors. **84**

MERITAGE WHITE EDNA VALLEY PARAGON VINEYARD (★★): Made from Edna Valley grapes, it's distinctive, tart and intense, but strays into the vegetal end of the spectrum. It can be a pungent, heavy-handed, highly stylized wine.
1993: Lean and crisp, a spicy wine with a toasted onion edge and a touch of melon that livens the finish. **83**
1992: Goes beyond herbal into vegetal flavors, but a fig and tobacco character emerges on the finish. **85**

CARNEROS CREEK WINERY
Napa Valley
F: 1972. **O:** Francis Mahoney. **W:** Melissa Moravec. **S:** Mahoney Estate.

OVERALL	$9-28	★★★

WINE RATINGS

Chardonnay California Fleur de Carneros	★★
Chardonnay Carneros	★★★
Grenache Reserve	★★★
Pinot Noir Carneros	★★★
Pinot Noir Carneros Fleur de Carneros	★★
Pinot Noir Carneros Signature Reserve	★★★
Mahoney Estate Pinot Noir Carneros Las Piedras Vineyard	★★★

WINERY DATA
C: 27,000. **V:** 75 acres in Carneros. **G:** Pinot Noir (65 acres), Chardonnay (10). **P:** Pinot Noir (Carneros), Chardonnay (Carneros), Chardonnay (Calaveras County).

Owner-winemaker Francis Mahoney has been at the forefront of Pinot Noir clonal research as well as an early advocate of the Carneros appellation. Dissatisfied with the Pinot Noir clones available when he started making wine, Mahoney embarked on an ambitious program to identify and test some 20 different clones. Mahoney's interest in winemaking grew out of an appreciation for wine that began when he worked as a wine retailer in San Francisco. In 1972, he and financial backer Balfour Gibson bought 30 acres in Carneros and planted 10 acres to vines, producing their first Pinot Noir in 1976. Early on, Carneros Creek made a wide assortment of wines, such as Zinfandel from Napa and Amador Counties and Cabernet from the Stags Leap District, including a vineyard-designated Fay Vineyard bottling. But Pinot Noir has always been Mahoney's passion and his best wine. The winery owns 75 acres, 65 of Pinot Noir and 10 of Chardonnay, and produces 27,000 cases, with a light and simple Fleur de Carneros Pinot Noir (12,000 cases) and Carneros Pinot Noir (7,000 cases) the mainstays. A vineyard-designated Pinot Noir came on line with the 1991 vintage.

TASTING NOTES

CHARDONNAY CALIFORNIA FLEUR DE CARNEROS (★★):
1992: Simple and correct, with ripe, earthy pear and toasty oak flavors that stay with you. A good value in everyday Chardonnay. **82**

CHARDONNAY CARNEROS (★★★): Inconsistent but often quite Burgundian; the 1990, for instance, serves up lots of rich flavors. But the past few vintages have been thinner and less interesting.

1992: Lean and austere, with a narrow band of smoky pear flavors. **84**

1991: Starts out with a fresh burst of spicy citrus and pear flavors, but thins out and turns simple on the finish. **84**

PINOT NOIR CARNEROS (★★★): When it's good, it's very, very good and when it misses it isn't by much. The oldest vintages, from the mid-1970s, have aged exceptionally well. The 1983 remains a rich, Burgundian-style wine. Recent vintages have been very good but short of outstanding, marked by ripe, intense fruit and spicy oak, often displaying an earthy, decadent side. The Signature Reserves from 1987 and 1988 are superb, but the following two vintages are less exciting.

1991: Ripe and intense, with an earthy, decadent, smoky edge. Just a hint of fruit emerges on the finish, where the flavors fan out. **88**

1990: Firm and focused, with a lively streak of blueberry, raspberry and currant flavors zinging through the earthy notes. **86**

1989: A solid wine with a nice tension among the plum, toast, smoke and sassafras flavors and a hint of tea on the finish. **85**

1988: Ripe and rich, with supple black cherry, spice and oak flavors that are youthful, intense and concentrated. **85**

1987: Plenty of ripe, spicy cherry and raspberry flavors up front, fine balance and good length. **85**

1986: Smooth and silky, elegant and complex, with delicate, spicy cherry, herb and cedary oak flavors that glide across the palate. The finish is long and lively. **91**

1985: Elegant and spicy, with mature black cherry, anise and cedar notes. **85**

1984: Extremely well made, tight and firm, packed with complex Burgundian fruit flavors. **88**

1983: Stunning, rich and Burgundian, earthy and complex. **90**

1978: Long superb, past its prime but still very fine, with ripe, rich, complex herb, currant, cola and spicy dried fruit flavors that turn supple. **89**

1977: Ripe, smooth and elegant, with fine, polished, mature cherry and plum flavors. **87**

1976: Holding its color and intensity, with ripe, spicy plum and currant aromas and flavors that are concentrated and tannic. **85**

Signature Reserve 1991: Smells ripe and generous, but turns smoky and gamy before you get a hint of cherry and herb flavors. **81**

Signature Reserve 1989: Soft and fleshy, with an herbal edge to the currant, cola and berry flavors. **80**

Signature Reserve 1988: Intense and elegant, with chocolate and toasty oak aromas and rich, concentrated, complex black cherry and plum flavors. **89**

Signature Reserve First Release 1987: A rich, supple wine with intense, concentrated spice, cola and cherry flavors rounded out by a touch of toasty oak. **87**

PINOT NOIR CARNEROS FLEUR DE CARNEROS (★★): This wine started out with attractive fruit flavors, made in the style of Saintsbury's Garnet, but the past few vintages have been very light, thin and stemmy.

1993: The light, simple cherry, herb and strawberry flavors are a bit cloying. **82**

1992: Light and simple. A narrow band of flavors turns tannic on the finish. **79**

1991: Thin and stemmy, with hints of plum and cherry, but ultimately it's a very simple wine that may offer some appeal. **77**

1990: Lean, tight and tough in texture, with solid if uninspiring black cherry, toast and anise aromas and flavors. **80**

MAHONEY ESTATE PINOT NOIR CARNEROS LAS PIEDRAS VINEYARD (★★★):

1992: Elegant with spicy herb, earth, cherry and cola flavors that turn elegant and supple. First from the Mahoney Estate. (Las Piedras Vineyard is on the Mahoney Estate. **87**

MAURICE CARRIE VINEYARDS AND WINERY
Temecula

F: 1986. O: Van Roekel Family. W: Steve Hagata. S: None.

OVERALL	$7-10	★

WINE RATINGS

Chardonnay Temecula	★
Chardonnay Temecula Private Reserve	★
Pinot Noir Santa Barbara County	★

WINERY DATA

C: 30,000. V: 45 acres in Temecula. G: N/A. P: Pinot Noir (Central Coast), Gewürztraminer (Napa, Sonoma).

So far the wines from this Temecula-based winery have ranged from ordinary to awful. The Van Roekels own some 45 acres and produce 30,000 cases. The wines I've tried were a simple, herb-laced 1991 Chardonnay Temecula, a 1991 Chardonnay Temecula Private Reserve that wasn't any better and an earthy, funky 1990 Pinot Noir from Santa Barbara. Some 40 percent of the wines are blush and another 40 percent are white varietals.

TASTING NOTES

VARIOUS BOTTLINGS (★):
Chardonnay Temecula 1991: Light and simple, with herb and pear flavors. **77**
Chardonnay Temecula Private Reserve 1991: A good white with spice, pear and light nutmeg flavors. **77**
Pinot Noir Santa Barbara County 1990: A bizarre wine with earthy, gamy cola and rhubarb flavors that are coarse and prickly. Misses the mark. Tasted twice, with consistent notes. **67**

CASA DALLA VALLE

This is a second label of Dalla Valle Vineyards (see listing).

CASTELLETO

This is a second label for Mount Palomar Winery (see listing).

CASTLE ROCK

Rancho Palos Verdes, Los Angeles County
F: 1994. **O:** South Bay Wine Group. **W:** Joe Briggs. **S:** None.

OVERALL	$10-13	★★

WINE RATINGS

Chardonnay Napa Valley Barrel Fermented	★★

WINERY DATA
C: 5,000. **V:** None. **G:** None. **P:** Chardonnay (Sonoma Valley), Chardonnay (Napa Valley).

Using purchased grapes from Napa and Sonoma Valleys, Castle Rock released its first Chardonnay in 1993, and has already built production to 5,000 cases. Joe Briggs oversees winemaking, and the winemaking operations are headquartered in Rancho Palos Verdes, in Southern California.

TASTING NOTES

CHARDONNAY NAPA VALLEY BARREL FERMENTED (★★):
1993: Subtle with polished pear and apple flavors, finishing with a spicy nutmeg edge. **84**

CASTORO CELLARS

Paso Robles
F: 1981. **O:** Niels & Berit Udsen. **W:** Niels Udsen, Tom Myers. **S:** None.

OVERALL	$6-16	★★

WINE RATINGS

Cabernet Blend Paso Robles Dieci Anni	★★
Cabernet Sauvignon Paso Robles Reserve	★★
Cabernet Sauvignon Paso Robles The Wine	★★
Chardonnay Paso Robles Reserve	★★
Chardonnay San Luis Obispo County	★★
Chardonnay San Luis Obispo County The Wine	★★
Pinot Noir Santa Barbara County	★
Zinfandel Paso Robles The Wine	★★★

WINERY DATA
C: 12,000. **V:** 15 acres in Paso Robles. **G:** Zinfandel (14 acres). **P:** Chardonnay, Sauvignon Blanc, Chenin Blanc, Muscat Canelli, Zinfandel, Cabernet Sauvignon, Merlot, Cabernet Franc, Petite Sirah, Gamay (Paso Robles), Pinot Noir (Santa Barbara).

Owner-winemaker Niels Udsen worked at J. Lohr Winery before starting his own brand in 1983. Today Castoro Cellars bottles some 12,000 cases, focusing on Cabernet (Paso Robles), Chardonnay (San Luis Obispo and Paso Robles Reserve), Pinot Noir (Santa Barbara) and Zinfandel (Paso Robles). The Cabernets are made in a lean, firm style. The 1990 Reserve and 1991 Reserve are both firmly tannic, but lack the extra depth and complexity Reserves usually deliver. The Chardonnay is made in a light and refreshing style, while the Reserve is oakier but still of average quality. The 1991 Pinot Noir Santa Barbara was marked by gamy flavors. The best wine is the Zinfandel Paso Robles.

TASTING NOTES

CABERNET BLEND PASO ROBLES DIECI ANNI (★★):
1991: A solid but high-priced Cabernet blend that features 14 percent Zinfandel and 44 percent Cabernet Franc. Spicy, with moderate fruit intensity. **79**

CABERNET SAUVIGNON VARIOUS BOTTLINGS (★★):
Paso Robles 1989: Has more character, richness and depth than most $10 Cabernets, offering ripe currant, plum and berry flavors, firm tannins and a touch of oak. The finish echoes berries and oak. **84**
Paso Robles Reserve 1991: Lean and compact, with hints of spice, currant and berry peeking through. Finishes with firm tannins; best after 1996. **82**
Paso Robles Reserve 1990: Firm, intense and tannic, but on the finish currant and berry flavors come through before the tannins clamp down. **82**
Paso Robles The Wine 1991: Spicy and simple, with herb and earth notes, but also a touch of currant and berry on the finish. **78**

CHARDONNAY VARIOUS BOTTLINGS (★★):
Paso Robles Reserve 1992: Firm and oaky, with light pear and spice flavors. **80**
San Luis Obispo County 1992: Light, refreshing and charming, with appealing vanilla, pear and floral aromas and flavors. Remains lively and fresh on the finish. **84**
San Luis Obispo County 1991: A smooth, spicy, oak-scented wine that remains fresh and full-flavored, echoing pear, pineapple and spice through the long finish. **84**
San Luis Obispo County The Wine 1992: Thin, with a tart, sour edge to the pear and citrus notes. **78**

PINOT NOIR SANTA BARBARA COUNTY (★):
1991: Earthy and sweaty, with a peppery edge. Lacks focus and pure Pinot flavor. **77**
1990: Oaky, gamy flavors override the cherry notes underneath. Unexciting. **73**

ZINFANDEL PASO ROBLES (★★★):
1990: Floral, fruity aromas give way to tart, fresh berry and cherry flavors. **82**

ZINFANDEL PASO ROBLES THE WINE (★★★):
1991: Crisp and intense, with earthy spice, tar and wild berry flavors, finishing with firm tannins. **84**

CATACULA
This is a second label of Green and Red Vineyard (see listing).

CAVISTE
This is a second label of Acacia Winery (see listing).

CAYMUS VINEYARDS
Rutherford, Napa Valley
F: 1972. **O:** Caymus Vineyards Inc. **W:** Chuck Wagner. **S:** Liberty School.

OVERALL	$13-100	★★★★★

WINE RATINGS

Cabernet Sauvignon Napa Valley	★★★★
Cabernet Sauvignon Napa Valley Special Selection	★★★★★
Pinot Noir Napa Valley Special Selection	★★★
Sauvignon Blanc Napa Valley Barrel Fermented	★★★★
White Table Wine California Conundrum	★★★★
Zinfandel Napa Valley	★★★
Liberty School Cabernet Sauvignon California Vintner Select Series Three	★★
Liberty School White Table Wine California Three Valley Select	★★

WINERY DATA
C: 60,000. **V:** 73 acres in Napa Valley. **G:** Cabernet Sauvignon (50 acres), Sauvignon Blanc (12), Others (11). **P:** Cabernet Sauvignon (Napa Valley), Cabernet Franc (Napa Valley), Sauvignon Blanc (Napa Valley), Chardonnay (Central Coast), Viognier (Marin County), Muscat (Tulare County).

Caymus Vineyards Special Selection Cabernet Sauvignon is synonymous with classically proportioned, richly flavored Rutherford-grown Cabernet. Owner Charlie Wagner, who was born and raised on this Rutherford estate, considers Caymus to be California's most consistent producer of great Cabernet. Given this winery's superb track record, it is a difficult point to debate.

The Wagners are first and foremost farmers and know their vineyards well. Their family began farming in Rutherford in 1906, planting vineyards in the late 1940s. After years of selling grapes to area wineries, the Wagners decided to try their hand at winemaking, naming their winery after the Caymus Indians. In 1972 Wagner and his son Chuck made their first wines, including a Cabernet, with the help of Randy Dunn (Dunn Vineyards), who supervised winemaking. Beginning in 1975, Caymus chose its best barrels of Cabernet for its limited-bottling Special Selection, a 100 percent Cabernet that's been made every year since except 1977. Caymus Special Selection is an amazing line of distinctive, richly concentrated, wonderfully flavorful and ageworthy Cabernets. While Dunn is often credited with crafting the great Caymus Cabernets, he is the first to point out that the strength of Caymus' wines lies in its vineyard and the quality of its grapes. Since Dunn left in 1984, Chuck Wagner has deftly demonstrated his ability to fine-tune these wines to near perfection.

Through the years, the Caymus lineup has almost always featured Zinfandel, Pinot Noir and Sauvignon Blanc, all from purchased grapes. On occasion Caymus has dabbled with other wines, including a blush wine, an occasional Chardonnay and a late-harvest, dessert-style wine made from Sauvignon Blanc. In the late 1970s the Wagners started a highly successful second label called Liberty School, which for years was a negociant brand that blended bulk wines. Recently the grape sources have been more specific, with the Liberty School Cabernet coming from Paso Robles and a white table wine from Central Coast vineyards. With recent vintages, both the Caymus Zinfandel and Sauvignon Blanc have been first-rate and among the state's best. In 1989 Caymus added a white table wine called Conundrum that is a blend of Chardonnay, Sauvignon Blanc and Muscat from all over California; the result is a sort of *sur lie*, barrel-fermented Chardonnay meets lavishly oaked

Sauvignon Blanc. Caymus Pinot Noir is made in a Cabernet style, featuring very ripe fruit, dark colors and lots of oak, but it too is distinctive and fun to drink. After much debate, Caymus is dropping both Pinot Noir and Zinfandel, but don't be surprised by a Sangiovese-Cabernet blend in the near future.

While the Special Selection Cabernet reigns supreme, with the 1991 selling for $100 a bottle, the standard Caymus Cabernet Sauvignon Napa Valley is a beautifully crafted wine, made from the Wagners' great connections with Rutherford and mountain-grown Cabernet vineyards. Through 1986 Caymus produced both an Estate and Special Selection Cabernet, but in 1984 added a Napa Valley Cuvée for a third wine before dropping the Estate bottling, expanding the Special Selection from 600 cases to nearly 2,000 today, and building the Napa Valley Cabernet to 20,000 cases.

TASTING NOTES

CABERNET SAUVIGNON NAPA VALLEY (★★★★): No longer from estate grapes, it nonetheless reflects the Caymus house style, as the Wagners' knowledge of the area's best vineyards comes into play. Well oaked, elegant and flavorful, it too can age well, but peaks at about five years. In the notes that follow, vintages from 1972 to 1986 are the Estate bottling.

1991: Deep, rich and plush, with a core of ripe, seductive currant and black cherry flavors framed by pretty, toasty, buttery oak. One delicious mouthful of Cabernet. **91**

1990: Firm and focused, with spicy tobacco and chocolate overtones to the ripe prune and currant aromas and flavors. **90**

1989: Elegant and forward, well balanced and easy to drink, serving up a pretty array of currant, tea and oak flavors. **88**

1988: Smooth and velvety, a medium-weight wine with complex, subtle tobacco, chocolate, plum and currant aromas and flavors. **87**

1987: Cedar, vanilla, spice and currant aromas give way to similar flavors that are full-bodied and rich; a wonderful dose of oak and tannin balances the solid core of supple fruit. **92**

1986: Complex and elegant, with smoky chocolate, plum and cherry aromas and flavors, supple, smooth and amazingly long on the finish. **94**

1985: A beautifully defined Rutherford Cabernet, rich, lean and elegant, with layers of spice, cedar, plum and black cherry flavors that echo on the palate. **92**

1984: Richly flavored and supple, with ripe plum, herb and currant flavors. The tannins, while thick, are smooth and fleshy. **91**

1983: Showing its age, with mature cedar, tar and plum flavors. **84**

1982: This wine peaked in 1991, but in its youth it was one of the best 1982s. Now the currant, plum and herb flavors show their maturity, with dried fruit, anise and spice flavors on the finish. Can age longer, but won't improve. **87**

1981: Ripe, forward and supple, with generous, fleshy plum, black cherry and cedar flavors, crisp acidity and smooth, polished tannins. **88**

1980: A deep, rich, concentrated wine with plenty of black cherry, currant and plum flavors, crisp acidity and tannins that are softening. Mature and at its peak. **90**

1979: Still youthful, dark and complex, with pretty spice, currant, herb, cherry and earth notes that are intense and elegant and a polished, supple texture. Aging exceptionally well. **91**

1978: Fully mature, with black cherry, herb, earth and cedar flavors that are soft and elegant. The tannins have softened. **87**

1977: Light in body, with modest mint and cedar flavors that are simple and fading. **77**

1976: Mature, but holding its ripe, supple plum and black cherry flavors. **85**

1975: An elegant yet generous wine with black cherry, plum and spice flavors that offer depth, complexity and elegance. **89**

1974: Very ripe and fruity on the nose, but with less flavor coming through. The fruit tastes hollow and less concentrated than in the past. **84**

1973: Mature but still very complex, with a full bouquet of fruit and deep, rich flavors of black cherry, currant and anise. All silk and polish on the palate. **93**

1972: Fully mature now but holding its own, this is a ripe, supple, elegantly balanced wine. **83**

CABERNET SAUVIGNON NAPA VALLEY SPECIAL SELECTION (★★★★★): Uncommonly rich and complex, darkly colored, offering ripe cherry, plum, herb, spice and tea flavors supported by firm, thick and polished tan-

nins. It spends three years in oak. Drinkable early on, reaching its peak at about age 10, it holds its fruit amazingly well and often outperforms the competition in lesser years: witness the very fine 1988 and 1989 vintages.

1991: Another tremendous wine, with enormous richness, depth and complexities, with classic layers of currant, plum, cherry and spice. Young and compact at this stage, tasted nearly a year before release and just after bottling. **99**

1990: Beautifully proportioned, rich and concentrated, with tiers of complex cherry, plum, currant and spice flavors and sweet tannins. There are pretty, toasty, buttery oak and vanilla flavors on the long, full finish. **98**

1989: Tight, tough and chewy, intense and tannic, but graced with a wealth of fruit flavors. The rich cherry, berry, prune and plum notes turn smoky and complex on the long, full finish. **93**

1988: The best 1988? Loaded with plum, prune and black cherry flavors, with hints of spicy vanilla and chocolate. Shows remarkable clarity and a supple texture that should get silkier and smoother with age. **94**

1987: Massive, rich and powerfully concentrated, dark in color and packed with currant, chocolate, black cherry and plum flavors, picking up a mint and mineral edge on the finish and developing a smooth, plush texture. **98**

1986: Wonderfully complex and forward, elegant and sharply focused, with tiers of ripe, rich and concentrated black cherry, plum, currant, anise and buttery oak flavors, with fine tannins that are well integrated. **98**

1985: An extraordinary wine, enormously rich, complex and lively, with layers of cedar, plum, cassis and black cherry that gracefully unfold on the palate. The tannins are lean, fine and mouthwatering, giving the wine a steely backbone and great length. **99**

1984: A magnificent wine, tight, lean and concentrated, with deeply perfumed ripe plum, black cherry, anise and currant flavors. Turning supple and generous on the finish, this is one terrific wine that defines complexity. **98**

1983: Rich and intense, complex and concentrated, loaded with plum, currant, spice and toasty oak flavors. **91**

1982: Massively structured, intense, firm and compact, with ripe plum, currant, anise and oak flavors and a pretty chocolate and caramel aftertaste. **92**

1981: Tight, firm and concentrated, with ripe plum, currant and black cherry flavors that are rich and compact, elegant and focused. **93**

CECCHETTI SEBASTIANI CELLARS

1980: Loaded with ripe plum, cherry, currant and anise flavors that are elegant and stylish, finishing with a pretty aftertaste and great length. **92**

1979: A gorgeous wine, rich, supple and complex, packed with ripe, vibrant currant, spice, cedar and anise flavors that are crisp, lively and long. **94**

1978: Rich, bold and dramatic, mature now, with complex layers of currant, earth, cedar, cherry and plum flavors that display uncommon depth and character. **93**

1976: Rich and tannic, with a fair amount of oak and plenty of plum, currant and anise flavors. It's rather coarse. **90**

1975: A magnificent wine, loaded with fresh, ripe plum, cedar, currant and chocolate flavors that are supple and elegant. **92**

CONUNDRUM CALIFORNIA (★★★★): Ripe and exotic, a distinctive, spicy wine that's rich and oaky; a blend of Chardonnay, Sauvignon Blanc and Muscat.

1992: Ripe and exotic, with spicy Muscat aromas, this wine tastes sweet, with ripe fig, melon and vanilla flavors. **88**

1991: Pours out lots of well-balanced pear, spice, vanilla, apple and peach flavors. **92**

PINOT NOIR NAPA VALLEY SPECIAL SELECTION (★★★): Typically dark, oaky and complex, with cherry and ripe plum flavors. Best early, but can age for five years. Now discontinued.

1990: Shows a good dose of toasty, buttery oak along with complex cherry and spice flavors. **84**

1989: Heavily oaked, with smoky, gamy notes and a trace of bitterness on the cherry and currant flavors. **78**

1988: An earthy wine with bark and cedar notes, but there's also a nice core of supple black cherry flavors. **82**

1987: Very firm and tannic, with flavors that lean toward smoke, toast, meat and cherry. **86**

1986: Modest but appealing, with cherry and plum flavors. **82**

1985: Mature, with cedar and toast flavors, turning to raspberry and chocolate on the finish. **88**

SAUVIGNON BLANC NAPA VALLEY BARREL FERMENTED (★★★★): Barrel fermented and lavishly oaked, but with lots of intense Sauvignon Blanc fruit flavors.

1993: Marked by herb and vegetal notes, it's smooth and supple, marked by a spicy aftertaste. **85**

1992: Intense and flavorful, with a band of complex, buttery pear, hazelnut and spice flavors. **91**

ZINFANDEL NAPA VALLEY (★★★): Well balanced, with spicy pepper and berry flavors and mild tannins. Ages well.

1992: Combines ripe, spicy, intense berry and cherry flavors with firm tannins and a pretty vanilla and oak overlay. **89**

1990: Dark, deep, ripe and concentrated, redolent of plum, raspberry and vanilla, turning earthy. **82**

1989: Tight and austere, with pretty raspberry and currant flavors and a whiff of barnyard. **83**

1988: Distinctive dill and anise overtones color the dark cherry and berry flavors. **80**

1987: A delicious claret-style Zinfandel with fresh, toasty oak notes to complement the raspberry and spicy cherry flavors. **85**

1986: Very stylish and elegant, with rich aromas of chocolate, toast and plum. **89**

LIBERTY SCHOOL VARIOUS BOTTLINGS (★★):
Cabernet Sauvignon California Vintner Select Series Three 1990: A fresh, lively Cabernet that's light and straightforward, with cola and cherry flavors that verge on jamminess and a hint of vanilla and spice on the finish. **83**
White Table Wine California Three Valley Select 1991: Fruity, floral, generous and a bit sweet, with almond and cream overtones. Smooth and appealing right through the spicy finish. A blend of Sauvignon Blanc, Chardonnay and Muscat. **85**

CECCHETTI SEBASTIANI CELLARS
Sonoma Valley
F: 1985. **O:** Cecchetti Sebastiani Cellars Inc. **W:** Don Sebastiani. **S:** Pepperwood Grove.

OVERALL	$8-10	★

WINE RATINGS

Cabernet Sauvignon Alexander Valley	★
Pepperwood Grove Cabernet Sauvignon California	★
Pepperwood Grove Chardonnay California	★
Pepperwood Grove Gamay Beaujolais California Nouveau	NR
Pepperwood Grove Pinot Noir California	★★

WINERY DATA
C: 30,000. V: None. G: None. P: None.

A negociant brand owned by Don Sebastiani and his brother-in-law Roy Cecchetti, started before Sebastiani became involved with his family's winery. He is now president of Sebastiani Vineyards and he and Cecchetti remain involved in winemaking, the most successful wine being a Pinot Noir bottled under the Pepperwood Grove label. Some 30,000 cases are produced, including Cabernet and Chardonnay, made from purchased bulk wine.

TASTING NOTES

VARIOUS BOTTLINGS:

Cabernet Sauvignon Alexander Valley 1989 (★): Firm, tannic, gamy and leathery, with modest black cherry flavors that try to squeeze past the wall of tannins. **74**

Pepperwood Grove Cabernet Sauvignon California 1990 (★): A simple, rustic red with beet and green bean flavors that are pretty basic. **74**

Pepperwood Grove Chardonnay California 1992 (★): This light, simple wine offers basic apple flavors and a watery texture. **76**

Pepperwood Grove Gamay Beaujolais California Nouveau 1994 (NR): Very light and soft, a little sweet, lacking backbone. **74**

Pepperwood Grove Pinot Noir California 1993 (★★): Simple with fleshy herb and cedary notes, finishing with spicy cherry flavors. **83**

Pepperwood Grove Pinot Noir California Cask Lot 1 1992: Light and simple. Shows more oak than Pinot character, giving it a smoky, cedary edge. **78**

Pepperwood Grove Pinot Noir California Cask Lot 2 1992: Much better than Cask Lot 1. A ripe, flavorful, concentrated, youthful wine, offering black cherry, cola and herb flavors and firm tannins on the finish. **86**

Pepperwood Grove Pinot Noir California Cask Lot 3 1992: Lightly fruity, with herb, tar and spice notes that add complexity to the plum and berry notes. **84**

CEDAR MOUNTAIN WINERY
Livermore Valley
F: 1990. **O:** Linda & Earl Ault. **W:** Earl Ault. **S:** None.

OVERALL	$15	★★

WINE RATINGS

Cabernet Sauvignon Livermore Valley Blanches Vineyard	★★
Chardonnay Livermore Valley Blanches Vineyard	★★

WINERY DATA
C: 1,200. V: 14 acres in Livermore Valley. G: Cabernet, Chardonnay. P: None.

A new winery based in Livermore Valley making Chardonnay and Cabernet from Blanches Vineyard. The first wines have ranged from fair to very good. The 1990 Cabernet is rich and focused, with supple currant, plum, spice and black cherry flavors, while the 1991 is openly fruity, with supple berry and cherry notes. The 1990 Chardonnay is earthy and metallic, but the 1991 and 1992 are improvements, made in an elegant, delicate style.

TASTING NOTES

CABERNET SAUVIGNON LIVERMORE VALLEY BLANCHES VINEYARD (★★): Elegant and fruity. Best to drink early on.
1991: Openly fruity, with supple floral and black cherry notes and soft tannins. **86**
1990: Rich and focused, with supple currant, plum, spice and black cherry flavors. The emphasis is on the purity of the fruit. **89**

CHARDONNAY LIVERMORE VALLEY BLANCHES VINEYARD (★★): Medium-weight with simple fruit flavors.
1992: A delicate wine, elegant and crisp, with subtle oak, pear and apple notes. **84**
1991: Fruity and elegant, with layers of honey, pear, toast and vanilla, finishing with a hint of nutmeg and spice. **86**
1990: An earthy, metallic edge detracts from the ripe pear and spice notes. **79**

CEPAGE
This is a second label for Joullian Vineyards (see listing).

CHALK HILL WINERY
Chalk Hill, Sonoma County
F: 1972. **O:** Frederick P. & Peggy J. Furth. **W:** David Ramey. **S:** None.

OVERALL	$16-21	★★★

WINE RATINGS

Cabernet Sauvignon Chalk Hill	★★★
Chardonnay Chalk Hill	★★★
Sauvignon Blanc Chalk Hill	★★★
Sémillon Chalk Hill Dessert Wine	★★★

WINERY DATA

C: 60,000. **V:** 235 acres in Chalk Hill. **G:** Chardonnay (127 acres), Sauvignon Blanc (21), Sémillon (6), Pinot Grigio (3), Cabernet Sauvignon (37), Merlot (32), Cabernet Franc (4), Malbec (2), Petite Verdot (1). **P:** Chardonnay (Chalk Hill).

Despite a checkered start, Chalk Hill Winery's wines took a turn for the better with the arrival of winemaker Dave Ramey in 1990. Owners Fred and Peggy Furth own a vast estate in the Chalk Hill appellation, with 235 acres in vines, most of which are Chardonnay (127 acres) Cabernet (37) and Merlot (32). Fred Furth, a highly successful San Francisco anti-trust and class action lawyer who began planting his vineyards in the 1970s, has spent millions developing his vineyards and winery, but to date the results are mixed. Early wines were often flawed. The 1987 Cabernet was so tart and bizarre it was finally declassified. The 1989 was thin, even for the vintage. But both the 1990 and 1991 Cabernets are improvements, rich and chewy. The Chardonnays too have been inconsistent. The 1990 is deep and complex, but the subsequent vintages are far less interesting. The winery makes nearly 60,000 cases—37,000 cases of Chardonnay, 10,000 cases of Sauvignon Blanc and 9,000 cases of Cabernet. A late-harvest Sémillon is made occasionally; the 1986 is delicious. Given Ramey's track record at Simi and Matanzas Creek and his knowledge of winemaking, this should be a winery to watch. But so far the vineyards have yet to prove their greatness.

TASTING NOTES

CABERNET SAUVIGNON CHALK HILL (★★★): Highly variable, although recent vintages show more richness, with earthy currant and leather flavors, along with high-extract tannins. The wines have no track record for improving with age.

1991: Tight and compact, with rich, complex currant, earth, tar and mineral flavors. Firmly tannic. **89**

1990: Dense, ripe, rich and concentrated, with focused currant, earth and black cherry flavors, picking up a touch of anise and spice on the finish. **89**

1989: Hard, tannic and barnyardy, and so earthy it's hard to like. **75**

1988: Smooth and silky, with well modulated cherry and plum flavors. **87**

1987: A bizarre wine that is stripped of character. **70**

CHARDONNAY CHALK HILL (★★★): The 1990 set the standard, with its finesse and tiers of complex flavors; the next two bottlings failed to meet that standard.

1993: Bold, ripe and spicy, with an earthy edge to the rich, creamy fig and apple flavors, with a vanilla and toast edge, and a complex aftertaste. **91**

1992: A blunt and coarse wine that's intense and concentrated, but lacking focus and finesse. **84**

1991: Taut and firm, with ripe pear and peach flavors that are focused but lacking grace. **83**

1990: Complex and engaging, with ripe, buttery pear, apple, spice and hazelnut flavors that are rich and deep. **91**

SAUVIGNON BLANC CHALK HILL (★★★): Austere but well made, with a band of pretty flavors.

1993: Ripe, round and generous, beautifully proportioned to show off the spicy, lemony pear and honey flavors that linger enticingly on the finish. **88**

1992: Lean and lemony, a dry, austere wine with a pleasantly bitter edge to the lively citrus, pear and vanilla flavors. **87**

SÉMILLON CHALK HILL DESSERT WINE (★★★):

1986: Would give most Sauternes a run for their money. The salty, nutty tobacco aromas and rich, ripe flavors are full and satisfying. **91**

CHALONE VINEYARD

Chalone

F: 1965. **O:** Chalone Wine Group. **W:** Michael Michaud. **S:** Gavilan Vineyards.

OVERALL	$14-48	★★★★

WINE RATINGS

Chardonnay Chalone	★★★★★
Chardonnay Chalone Reserve	★★★★★
Chenin Blanc Chalone	★★★

Pinot Blanc Chalone	★★★★
Pinot Noir Chalone	★★★
Pinot Noir Chalone Reserve	★★★
Gavilan Vineyards Chardonnay Chalone	★★
Gavilan Vineyards Pinot Blanc Chalone	★★
Gavilan Vineyards Pinot Noir Chalone	★★

WINERY DATA

C: 37,000. **V:** 184 acres in Chalone. **G:** Chardonnay (107 acres), Pinot Noir (35), Pinot Blanc (33), Chenin Blanc (9). **P:** None.

Chalone Vineyard is a highly regarded single-vineyard appellation in the Gavilan Mountains near Pinnacles National Monument. It traces its history to 1919, when a Frenchman named Tam began planting grapes in soils laced with limestone. The vineyard, high on a barren, windswept plateau 1,800 feet above sea level, changed hands several times before Richard Graff borrowed money from his mother to buy the property in 1965. The vineyard had suffered from neglect, but grapevines are amazingly resilient and Graff nourished them back to health. Rainfall is sparse in this arid climate, with 12 to 15 inches in a good year, but often much less, and Graff hauled water by truck to irrigate the vines. In 1960, 300 cases of Chalone Chardonnay were produced in a converted chicken coop that housed 40 barrels. The next year Graff made a 1961 sparkling wine, but it wasn't until 1966 that he started making small commercial lots of wine.

The commercial breakthrough came with the 1969 vintage of Chardonnay and Pinot Noir, which won critical acclaim, allowing Graff and his partner Philip Woodward to attract new investors. From there Chalone began making small case lots of Chardonnay, Pinot Noir and Chenin Blanc, the latter from vines planted by Tam around 1920, and later Pinot Blanc. In the 1970s the vineyards were gradually expanded and production grew, although the winery didn't have electricity or a modern facility until the 1980s. The vineyard is now 184 acres planted to Chardonnay (107 acres), Pinot Noir (35), Pinot Blanc (33) and Chenin Blanc (9). Production is 37,000 cases, with three bottlings each of Chardonnay and Pinot Noir—an Estate, a Reserve and a second label called Gavilan, the Reserve wines coming from the oldest vines. A Pinot Blanc and a Pinot Blanc Reserve also are made.

Chalone's wines owe their distinctive style not only to the unique soils and climate, but also to Graff's fascination with Burgundian vinification tech-

niques. All of the white wines are barrel fermented, aged *sur lie* and deftly balanced with oak. The Pinot Noir is fermented with a mixture of whole berries, wild yeast and some stem retention, although the winery is working hard at minimizing tannins in its Pinot Noir, with winemaker Michael Michaud aiming for less astringency and more finesse.

TASTING NOTES

CHARDONNAY CHALONE (★★★★★): Uncommonly rich and flavorful, deep in color, with tiers of complex flavors, bracing acidity, a broad, smooth texture and a flinty mineral aftertaste.

1993: Smooth and polished, with spicy pear, fig and light toasty oak shadings, more complete than most 1993s. **87**

1992: Tight, firm and focused, with pretty pear, spice, honey and butter notes that pick up an oaky edge on a long full finish. **91**

1991: Soft, spicy and generous, with pear and lemon flavors at the core and all sorts of vanilla, hazelnut and nutmeg notes to make it complex. **91**

1990: Crisp and concentrated, with well defined apple, honey and spice aromas and flavors that fan out. **89**

1989: Earthy, smoky aromas lead to fig and grapefruit flavors, making for a very distinctive wine. **88**

1988: More forward and fruity now than the Reserve, rich and complex, with firm fig, lemon, pear and spice flavors. **90**

1987: Earthy, rich and satiny, very smooth and distinctive, showing hints of toast, butterscotch, pear and lemon. **90**

1986: Amazingly delicious, rich, firm and complex, oozing with fresh, concentrated lemon, butterscotch, honey and toasty oak flavors. **94**

CHARDONNAY CHALONE RESERVE (★★★★★): These wines are selected from the oldest vines—they age exceptionally well, and often need three to five years to develop, very unusual for a California Chardonnay.

1992: Ripe, smooth and creamy, with a pretty array of earthy pear, spice, honey and butterscotch flavors, picking up vanilla and toasty notes on a long, full finish. **93**

1991: The bright and lively pear, spice, citrus and pineapple flavors are ripe, rich and focused, with light, buttery oak shadings and a silky finish. **91**

1990: Firm, tight and complex, with spicy, earthy pear, pineapple and butter notes that are focused and elegant. **89**

1989: Pungent and earthy, with mature Chardonnay flavors that reflect ripe pear and honey notes. **82**

1988: Hints of smoke, flint, lime, pear and fig slowly come together on the finish. **89**

1985: Enormously rich and complex, deep and concentrated, with intense cream, fig, honey, pear and vanilla flavors that spread out and saturate the palate. **94**

CHENIN BLANC CHALONE (★★★): Well oaked, capable of achieving complexities found in many Chardonnays.

1992: Round and spicy, definitely touched by oak, a smooth, polished wine that wears its toasty oak flavors lightly over a core of apple and melon. It's like a Chardonnay. **86**

PINOT BLANC CHALONE (★★★★): Hands down the best Pinot Blanc in California and the best I've tasted from anywhere. Shares the richness, depth and intensity of the Chardonnay, often with similar flavors and weight. Ages amazingly well.

1992: Intense and spicy, with ripe pear and apple flavors and a coarse texture. Short-term cellaring won't hurt. **86**

1991: Deep, rich and concentrated, packed with ripe pear, peach, mineral and spicy oak shadings and graced with crisp, lively acidity. **92**

1990: Intense and lively, with rich pear and citrus notes that turn earthy and bitter. **80**

1989: Ripe and buttery, with pear and butterscotch flavors and enough elegance and suppleness to keep it from being ponderous. **88**

PINOT NOIR CHALONE (★★★): There's no disputing these can be great wines, capable of long aging and more importantly gaining with age, but they are also austere and often tannic to a fault, marked by earthy plum and cherry notes that take on dried fruit qualities with age. In the 1980s the wines were thinner and more restrained than in the 1970s, but the 1990 shows more polish and finesse.

1991: Smooth and supple, well focused, with a pleasant core of cherry, earth and spice flavors that gains nuance and depth on the finish. **88**

1990: Crisp and elegant, featuring layers of plum, spice, vanilla and toast rolling smoothly across the palate. Shows restraint and plenty of polish. **90**

1989: A funky, earthy wine that has hints of lean raspberry and cherry flavors, turning bitter. **77**

1988: Pleasant enough, with floral and plum notes of modest depth. **83**

1987: Provides a core of decent spice, cherry and plum aromas and flavors, turning firm and tannic. **85**

1986: Tight and astringent, with oaky spice and plum flavors. **84**

1985: Crisp and elegant, with spicy plum and anise notes of modest proportions. **84**

1984: Shows rich, spicy plum and mint flavors that are lean and focused, finishing with firm tannins, but also some fruit. **85**

1983: Elegant and well proportioned, it picks up a pleasant anise and earth aftertaste. **86**

1982: Intense and earthy, with ripe prune notes that are firm and tannic. **84**

1981: Aging well; a crisp, lean wine with hints of plum and anise, turning tannic and stemmy. **83**

1980: Rich and smooth, with spicy dried cherry and plum flavors and fine tannins, picking up a trace of oak. **88**

1979: Lean and trim, with tightly focused spice, black cherry, anise and earth notes that are intense and lively. **88**

1977: Fully mature but aging well, with none of the tannic edge that often plagues Chalone Pinot Noirs. Complex and smooth, with earthy, gamy, sweet plum and cherry flavors, finishing with a spicy anise aftertaste. **92**

PINOT NOIR CHALONE RESERVE (★★★): The Reserve wines, made from vines planted in 1946, are sold primarily to Chalone Wine Group shareholders and have been uniformly hard and unyielding, not to my taste.

1990: Tight and hard-edged, lacking generosity, with tough plum and spice notes that are ruggedly tannic. **85**

1989: Tight and unyielding, with firm, hard-edged plum and spice flavors that turn tannic and drying. **83**

1988: Mature, with an earthy, smoky, leathery edge to the cherry and berry notes, but it's rough and tannic. **84**

1987: Broad and complex, with mineral and earth overtones to the ripe cherry and berry flavors. **86**

1986: Lean, hard and oaky, this is a curious wine that does not have the flavor or richness to match earlier Reserves. **79**

1985: Hard, flat and oaky, a simple and disappointing wine that fails to excite. **75**

1984: A disjointed wine that has ripe, floral plum flavors but tastes lean and simple. **82**

1983: Age has been kind to this one, taking away some of the rough edges, but it remains curious, with funky, pungent, earthy flavors. **80**

1982: A funky, earthy, bitter wine that has seen better days. **70**

1981: Warm, ripe and supple, with a silky texture and complex flavors that echo ripe plum, earth, tar and anise, finishing with delicacy and finesse. **88**

1980: Holding but not gaining, with astringent, tannic, smoky anise, tar, dried plum and cherry flavors. **82**

Gavilan Vineyards Various Bottlings (★★):
Chardonnay California 1989: Pleasantly fruity, with lively melon, pear, vanilla and butter flavors that are clean and well balanced. It's full-bodied, but the finish has begun to soften. **85**

Chardonnay Chalone 1993: Serves up a modest core of ripe pear, apple and vanilla notes that are well balanced for what's there. **84**

Chardonnay Chalone 1992: Crisp and fruity, with correct pear and spice notes, and the finish is clean and simple but missing those extra dimensions. **86**

Pinot Blanc Chalone 1992: Broad and spicy, a round wine with unfocused fruit and earth flavors. **81**

Pinot Noir Chalone 1992: Light but pleasant, with ripe, spicy cherry, oak and earth notes that stay with you. But it's not a grand wine. **82**

Pinot Noir Chalone 1991: Light and thin, showing mushroom and cherry notes. Not much there. **78**

CHAMISAL VINEYARD
San Luis Obispo County
F: 1980. **O:** Norman L. Gross. **W:** Clay Thompson. **S:** None.

OVERALL	$10-18	★★★

WINE RATINGS

Chardonnay Edna Valley	★★★

WINERY DATA
C: 3,000. **V:** 57 acres in Edna Valley. **G:** Chardonnay. **P:** None.

This is the oldest vineyard in Edna Valley, with 57 acres that were planted primarily to Chardonnay in the 1970s. Owned by restaurateur Norman Gross, the winery makes 3,000 cases of Chardonnay in a bold, ripe and intense style that aptly reflects this appellation. The wines have been on solid ground since 1986.

TASTING NOTES

Chardonnay Edna Valley (★★★), Special Reserve (★★★): Well oaked, with toasty, buttery flavors and intense pear, pineapple and spice notes. Can be pungently vegetal in cooler years and is occasionally marked by earthy honey and botrytis notes, as in 1990 and 1989.

1991: Toasty and buttery, with ample oak nuances and pretty, tart pineapple, citrus and herb aromas and flavors. **86**

Special Reserve 1989: Harmonious and delicious, with toasty, spicy butter and soft pear flavors. **91**

CHANSA CELLARS
Santa Maria Valley
F: 1988. **O:** Kim McPherson. **W:** Kim McPherson. **S:** None.

OVERALL	$10	★

WINE RATINGS

Chardonnay Santa Barbara County	★

WINERY DATA
C: 1,500. **V:** None. **G:** None. **P:** Chardonnay, Pinot Blanc (Santa Barbara County).

Chansa is a 1,500-case winery in Santa Maria owned by Kim McPherson that produced a crisp, odd-flavored 1989 Chardonnay from grapes grown at Bien Nacido Vineyard in Santa Barbara.

TASTING NOTES

Chardonnay Santa Barbara County (★):
1989: Crisp in texture but the flavors are unfocused, hinting at soy sauce and apple rather than the fresh fruit one would hope for. **77**

CHAPPELLET VINEYARD
St. Helena, Napa Valley
F: 1967. **O:** Donn & Molly Chappellet. **W:** Phillip Corallo-Titus. **S:** None.

OVERALL	$8-20	★★★

WINE RATINGS

Cabernet Sauvignon Napa Valley	★★★
Cabernet Sauvignon Napa Valley Pritchard Hill Estates	★★★
Chardonnay Napa Valley	★★★
Chenin Blanc Napa Valley Dry	★★★★
Merlot Napa Valley	★★

WINERY DATA

C: 25,000. **V:** 100 acres in Napa Valley. **G:** Cabernet Sauvignon (30 acres), Chardonnay (20), Chenin Blanc (25), Cabernet Franc (5), Sangiovese (10), Merlot (10). **P:** None.

Chappellet Vineyard sits on a rugged, forested slope of Pritchard Hill east of St. Helena. In 1967 Donn and Molly Chappellet moved here from Los Angeles, where Donn ran a successful industrial food vending business. The Chappellets' mountain-grown wines have had their moments of glory, rising to prominence in the late 1960s on the merit of the 1968, 1969 and 1970 Cabernets, wines that were remarkable for their depth and complexity. Since then the wines, including a Chardonnay, a Merlot and a well crafted Chenin Blanc, have been marked by inconsistencies and stylistic swings. A succession of winemakers has overseen winegrowing at Chappellet: Philip Togni (of Philip Togni Vineyard), Joe Cafaro (of Cafaro Cellars), Tony Soter (of Spottswoode Vineyard and Étude), Cathy Corison (of Corison Wines and Staglin Family Vineyards) and now Phillip Corallo-Titus. It seems apparent that the 100-acre vineyard, for all its terraced beauty, dictates the austere style and character all four wines share. Cabernet, with 30 acres, is the most widely planted variety, followed by Chenin Blanc (25 acres) and Chardonnay (20). Merlot and Sangiovese (10 acres each) are also grown. The winery produces about 7,000 cases of Cabernet, 5,000 of Chardonnay, 10,000 of Chenin Blanc and 800 of Merlot.

TASTING NOTES

CABERNET SAUVIGNON NAPA VALLEY (★★★): Always on the lean and tannic side, highly variable in quality. In some years it can be rich, with earthy currant, herb and spice notes, while retaining its austerity. Time does little to soften it.

Pritchard Hill Estates 1992: Firm and tannic, with a cedary edge to the tightly wound currant, tobacco and earthy notes. Will need time to soften, but it may not outgrow its tannins, which are substantial. **86**

1991: Firm and compact, with tight, earthy currant and herb flavors that fan out on the finish. Picks up hints of oak and spice along the way, making the flavors more interesting. Hold this one until 1999 or so. **89**

1990: A bizarre wine with earthy, minty overtones that dominate the cedary currant flavors underneath. **80**

Signature 1989: Firm and focused but not very flavorful, with more mineral and earth flavors than fruit. **82**

Reserve 1988: Toasty, spicy aromas and light fruit flavors indicate this is best for drinking in the near term. It's tasty and charming. **85**

Reserve 1987: Dark and intense, packed with rich, earthy currant and mineral flavors, finishing with firm, plush tannins. **89**

Reserve 1986: Sharply focused, with tart black cherry, anise and cedar flavors that are lean and elegant. Firmly tannic. **89**

Reserve 1985: Youthful and vibrant, tight and compact, with currant and black cherry flavors that are complex and concentrated. **88**

Reserve 1984: Earthy and decadent, with drying fruit flavors that are losing their charm. **84**

1983: Lean and simple, disproportionately tannic and drying out. **77**

1982: Light and herbal, with cherry flavor, this is a simple wine that's fading. **80**

1981: Mature, showing cherry and plum flavors tempered by age. **85**

1980: Distinctive and flavorful, with meaty mineral aromas and solid fruit flavors that last into the long, minty finish. **88**

1979: Hard and tannic, with a slightly green edge of unripe fruit. **79**

1977: Mature and drying out, with the ripe flavors fading. **80**

1976: Fading, with dried-out oak and Cabernet flavors. **76**

1975: Fully mature, with cedar, bark and black currant flavors. **77**

1974: Dry and bitter, with green, earthy flavors. **68**

1973: On the downward side and fading fast. **69**

1972: Faded now, with mature flavors of cedar and bark. **67**

1971: Fading fast, drying out. **78**

1970: Bold and ripe in its youth, it is drying out now and fading, with oak and dried fruit flavors. **84**

1969: In its prime a great wine, but losing its fruit now, with hints of dried-out currant and oak flavors. **85**

1968: Past its prime and drying out, with hints of dried fruit. **82**

CHARDONNAY NAPA VALLEY (★★★): Shares the austerity of the Cabernet with its crisp, flinty, understated style. Avoids the heavy oak and malolactic character evident in so many Napa Chardonnays, but often comes across as simple. Holds its fruit well but rarely evolves into anything special.

1992: Ripe and smoky, with spicy pear and light oak shadings. It's an understated wine with modest richness and intensity. **85**

CHENIN BLANC NAPA VALLEY DRY (★★★★): One of California's best; tart, lean, dry and flinty, with crisp melon and citrus notes. Ages amazingly well.

1992: Bright and fruity, dry and spicy enough to weave some nice nuances around the delicate apple fruit. **85**

1991: Crisp and appley, a brightly focused wine with piney, leafy overtones. Graceful and lively on the finish. **85**

MERLOT NAPA VALLEY (★★): Struggles to move beyond earthy, herbal flavors while sharing the Cabernet's austerity and tannic edge.

1992: Supple and elegant, with spicy plum and cedary oak flavors. **84**

1989: Earthy and strongly mossy, showing little fruit and mostly leafy aromas and flavors. **68**

1988: Ripe, lively and intense, with raspberry and cherry flavors, moderate tannins and a good shot of spicy oak. **85**

1987: Lean and mature, with an herb and tobacco edge to the earthy currant flavors. **85**

1986: Firm and tannic, with full-bodied, tart cherry and cranberry flavors. **83**

1985: Austere, with muted flavors so the tannin stands out. **78**

CHATEAU CHEVRE WINERY
Yountville, Napa Valley
F: 1979. O: Gerald P. & Betty L. Hazen. W: Gerald Hazen. S: None.

OVERALL	$11-25	★★
WINE RATINGS		
Chardonnay Napa Valley		★★
Merlot Napa Valley		★★

WINERY DATA
C: 1,000. V: 8 acres in Napa Valley. G: Merlot (7 acres), Cabernet Franc (0.5). P: Chardonnay (Napa Valley).

This small winery in Yountville is owned by former airline pilot Gerald Hazen and his wife, Betty. They have been making wines since the late 1970s, with the early focus on Merlots grown in their 8-acre vineyard; some of these are good, while others are flawed by earthy, funky flavors. A 1992 Chardonnay offers light pear, apple and toasty oak notes. Production is 1,000 cases, 500 of that being Merlot.

TASTING NOTES

CHARDONNAY NAPA VALLEY (★★):
1992: Offers light and elegant pear, apple and toasty oak notes that pick up a spicy edge on the finish. **83**

CHATEAU DE BAUN
Santa Rosa, Sonoma County
F: 1985. O: Ken & Grace de Baun. W: Jamie Meves. S: None.

OVERALL	$5-12	★★
WINE RATINGS		
Chardonnay Russian River Valley		★★
Pinot Noir Sonoma County		★★
Sparkling Wine Sonoma County Brut		NR
Symphony Russian River Valley Finale Late Harvest		★★★

WINERY DATA
C: 28,000. V: 105 acres in Russian River Valley. G: Chardonnay (48 acres), Pinot Noir (35), Symphony (17), Italian Type (5). P: Pinot Noir (Sonoma County).

Chateau de Baun made its mark with Symphony, a grape developed at U.C. Davis by crossing Muscat with Grenache Gris. The winery made this hybrid grape into as many as six different wines, each of which carried a proprietary name based on a musical term. The winery has since branched out, adding Chardonnay, Pinot Noir and sparkling wines. Owners Ken and Grace de Baun own 105 acres, planted primarily to Chardonnay (48 acres), Pinot Noir (35) and Symphony (17), from which they make some 28,000 cases.

De Baun appears to be on steady ground with its Chardonnay and Pinot Noir, both made in a light style using Russian River grapes. The 1992 Chardonnay serves up ripe, spicy pear and apple flavors, while the 1991 Pinot Noir is light and pleasant, with spicy cherry, earth and herb notes. The 1989 Symphony Finale Late Harvest combines sweet fruit flavors with a measure of delicacy and finesse. But often the potent spiciness of the Muscat dominates and even overwhelms the Symphony wines, a style that apparently has its following, although the winery's move to more conventional table wines suggests its appeal is limited.

TASTING NOTES

CHARDONNAY RUSSIAN RIVER VALLEY (★★):
1993: Appealing for its tangerine and nectarine flavors, it turns smooth and creamy, picking up a buttery edge on the finish. **87**
1992: Serves up ripe, spicy pear and apple flavors with a nice buttery oak edge. **85**
1991: Fresh and flavorful, with appealing green apple, lemon and butterscotch aromas. **86**

PINOT NOIR SONOMA COUNTY (★★):
1991: Light but pleasing, showing spicy cherry, earth and herb notes and firm tannins. **82**

SPARKLING WINE SONOMA COUNTY BRUT (NR):
Brut NV: Off-dry, simple and spicy, rather like a Muscat, with a slightly bitter finish. **77**

SYMPHONY RUSSIAN RIVER VALLEY FINALE LATE HARVEST (★★★):
1993: Aromatic and smooth, a little simple at first, but the floral, honey and pear flavors swirl around nicely as they grow on the finish. **88**
1989: Sweet and unctuous, although the finish is light enough qualify as delicate, with spicy floral notes to liven up the honey and apricot flavors. **87**

CHATEAU DE LEU WINERY
Green Valley-Solano
F: 1980. **O:** King Brewing USA Inc. **W:** Alessio Carli. **S:** None.

OVERALL	**$7-12**	★★

WINE RATINGS

Chardonnay Green Valley-Solano	★★
Pinot Noir Napa Valley	★

WINERY DATA
C: 10,000. **V:** 31 acres in Solano County Green Valley. **G:** Chardonnay (7 acres), Merlot (8), Petite Sirah (2), Sangiovese (4), Rhône Type (4), Cabernet Sauvignon (1), Cabernet Franc (1), Italian Type (2), Other (2). **P:** Cabernet Sauvignon (Napa Valley), Pinot Noir (Napa Valley, Sonoma County), Merlot (Napa Valley), Carignane (Solano County Green Valley).

In 1981 Ben Volkardt built Chateau de Leu in the hills of Green Valley in Solano County, making wines from family-owned vineyards and purchased grapes. Early wines were fair to good, but by the late 1980s the winery was on the market. It was purchased in 1989 by King Brewing USA Inc. The winery owns 31 acres and produces 10,000 cases, with a product mix that includes Chardonnay, Merlot, Pinot Noir, Sauvignon Blanc and Cabernet. Chardonnay is usually the best wine, with the 1992 showing earthy, tart grapefruit notes, although the 1991 Napa Valley Pinot Noir is better, marked by spicy oak flavors.

TASTING NOTES

CHARDONNAY GREEN VALLEY-SOLANO (★★):
1992: Earthy, with tart grapefruit flavors that turn lemony on the finish. **78**

PINOT NOIR NAPA VALLEY (★):
1991: This oaky wine features buttery, toasty notes, but has enough berry flavor to keep it interesting. **83**

CHATEAU JULIEN WINERY
Carmel Valley
F: 1982. **O:** Chateau Julien Inc. **W:** Bill Anderson. **S:** Emerald Bay Winery, Garland Ranch.

OVERALL	$7-15	★★

WINE RATINGS

Chardonnay Monterey County	
Barrel Fermented	★★
Chardonnay Monterey County	
Private Reserve	★★
Merlot Monterey County	★★
Merlot Monterey County	
Private Reserve	★★

WINERY DATA

C: 80,000. V: None. G: None. P: Chardonnay (Monterey), Cabernet Sauvignon (Monterey), Merlot (Monterey), Sauvignon Blanc (Monterey), Sémillon (Monterey), Gewürztraminer (Monterey), Johannisberg Riesling (Monterey).

Chateau Julien in Carmel Valley lies several miles east of the Pacific Coast Highway. Modeled after a French chateau, it carries the name of a famous Bordeaux appellation and is tourist oriented. It owns no vineyards, but makes 10,000 cases a year with a product mix that includes Merlot, Chardonnay, Cabernet and Sauvignon Blanc, all carrying the Monterey appellation. Another 70,000 cases are bottled under second labels, Emerald Bay and Garland Ranch. Merlot is its best wine; it's on the tannic side but does deliver dark, chocolaty flavors. The Chardonnay has been more variable, usually a touch earthy.

TASTING NOTES

CHARDONNAY MONTEREY COUNTY BARREL FERMENTED (★★), PRIVATE RESERVE (★★):
Barrel Fermented 1991: Soft and appley, offering more cider than Chardonnay characteristics, but it's pleasant and drinkable. **79**
Barrel Fermented 1990: A touch earthy, with a juniper berry edge to the spicy pear and citrus flavors, but a drinkable wine that's priced right. **81**
Private Reserve 1991: Mature with ripe apricot flavors that take on a rich but earthy edge, picking up a honeyed edge on the finish. Tastes overly mature. **80**

MERLOT MONTEREY COUNTY (★★), PRIVATE RESERVE (★★):
1991: Hard, tight and tannic, with a weedy, herbal edge to the fruit flavors. **82**
1989: Deeply colored, with ripe, rich chocolate flavors backed by firm tannins. **86**

1988: An average-quality Merlot with vegetal aromas and flavors. **72**
Private Reserve 1991: Supple and elegant, with a core of ripe cherry, currant and cedary oak flavors. **85**

GARLAND RANCH VARIOUS BOTTLINGS:
Chardonnay California 1991: Shows simple fruit flavors that could pass for Chenin Blanc, and at this price it's a decent white wine. **72**

CHATEAU MONTELENA WINERY
Calistoga, Napa Valley

F: 1972. O: James L. & Laura B. Barrett. W: Bo Barrett. S: None.

OVERALL	$12-30	★★★★

WINE RATINGS

Cabernet Sauvignon Napa Valley	
Calistoga Cuvée	★★★
Cabernet Sauvignon Napa Valley	
The Montelena Estate	★★★★★
Chardonnay Napa Valley	★★★★
Johannisberg Riesling Napa Valley	★★
Zinfandel Napa Valley	★★

WINERY DATA

C: 35,000. V: 115 acres in Napa Valley. G: Cabernet Sauvignon (81 acres), Cabernet Franc (7), Zinfandel (14), Merlot (5), Sangiovese (7). P: Chardonnay (Napa Valley), Johannisberg Riesling (Potter Valley), Cabernet Sauvignon (Napa Valley), Merlot (Napa Valley).

Chateau Montelena, a medieval-looking stone winery, dates back to 1882, but there's a gap of several decades between its first era and the modern one. In 1969 attorney Jim Barrett led a group of investors in buying the abandoned chateau. Their first wines appeared in 1972, made from purchased grapes by Mike Grgich, who had worked at Beaulieu Vineyard. The early wines were impressive; Grgich showed a deft hand with Chardonnay and Cabernet. The winery made headlines when its 1973 Chardonnay took first place in a famous blind tasting in Paris in 1976, where French wine critics judged it superior to a group of prestigious white Burgundies and other California Chardonnays.

Upon buying the winery, the new owners began planting Cabernet, producing the first estate-bottled Cabernet in 1978. The vineyards now cover 115 acres planted primarily to Cabernet (81 acres), with smaller amounts of Zinfandel (14), Cabernet Franc (7), Sangiovese (7) and Merlot (5). The winery's Chardonnay (Napa Valley) and Johannisberg Riesling (Potter Valley in Mendocino) are made from purchased grapes. Cabernet dominates, with 10,000 cases each of estate-grown (now called The Montelena Estate) and Calistoga Cuvée, another 10,000 cases of Chardonnay and smaller lots of Riesling (1,000 cases) and Zinfandel (2,000).

All the wines are good, but lately the Cabernet has been the most impressive. Montelena remains one of the most consistently excellent and remarkable Cabernet producers in California, making rich, concentrated, elegant and ageworthy wines year after year. That the style has remained so deliberate and constant is a tribute to the winery and to its three winemakers, Mike Grgich (now of Grgich Hills), Jerry Luper (of Freemark Abbey and Rutherford Hill) and current winemaker Bo Barrett, who has taken the wines to even greater heights. The Chardonnay grapes have been from both Alexander Valley and Napa Valley, although the former has been dropped. Through two decades, these were impeccably well-made wines, disappointing only in the past few years, when the wines have been less showy and on the lighter side. The Zinfandel too has gone through a tough phase in recent vintages.

TASTING NOTES

CABERNET SAUVIGNON NAPA VALLEY CALISTOGA CUVÉE (★★★): The Calistoga Cuvée is a new addition, but the first vintage showed how well Bo knows Cabernet.
1992: Bold, ripe and supple, with rich, focused currant, black cherry, plum and exotic spice flavors. Builds richness, intensity and depth on a long, complex finish. **90**

CABERNET SAUVIGNON NAPA VALLEY THE MONTELENA ESTATE (★★★★★): Unusually dark, complex and tannic, a bold and assertive wine that packs in lots of rich currant, mineral, earth and cedary oak flavors while maintaining a sense of elegance and balance. Tannin management is the big challenge in some years, but in others these dense and chewy wines age magnificently, reaching

a peak at about 10 years and capable of lasting 20.
1991: Uncommonly dark and intense, even for this vintage, with a rich core of leathery currant, spice, cedar and anise flavors that are young and rambunctious. Massive and in need of cellaring through 1999. **92**
1990: A less tannic and more elegant Montelena with focused currant and black cherry flavors that turn supple on the finish. **90**
1989: A hard, tough, rugged wine that's dense and tannic, but the raw materials of mineral and currant flavors are there. **85**
1988: Dark, dense and oaky, packed with currant, spice and earth flavors that are blunt, tannic and rugged at this stage. **87**
1987: Deep, ripe and powerful, with muscular currant, plum, anise and cherry flavors that are complex and concentrated, finishing with thick, tight tannins that may require cellaring until 1998. **95**
1986: Packed with fruit and tannins, this has a massive concentration of ripe, rich currant and plum flavors and an edge of leathery, smoky oak. **93**
1985: Amazingly rich and concentrated, packed with black cherry, currant, cedar and spice flavors and wrapped in thick tannins that promise a long life. It's massive but elegant. **95**
1984: An enormous wine that combines power and finesse with deep, rich, concentrated currant, black cherry and spicy plum flavors that are tight and closed now. **94**
1983: Still big and tannic but drying out, leaving more tannin and less currant and berry flavor to admire. **86**
1982: Elegant, with mature black cherry, plum and currant aromas and flavors, backed with toasty oak. **89**
1981: Simple by Montelena standards, with a narrow band of currant and spice flavors. **80**
1980: Mature, with generous ripe currant and berry notes that are beginning to fade and dry out. **86**
1979: Lean and elegant, fully mature, with black currant, mineral and cedar nuances that are rich and mature. **87**
1978: A striking wine with a broad, complex flavor spectrum. The currant, cedar, plum and cherry flavors are deeply concentrated and powerful, finishing with great length and firm tannins. **96**
1977: Bold, ripe and still quite appealing, but it's showing its age and the fruit is beginning to dry out. Still, you get nice currant and berry flavors with earthy mineral nuances. **90**
1974: A bold, rich and fruity 1974 with gutsy tannins,

still tightly closed and evolving. The ripe black cherry, currant and spice flavors are youthful and fresh but overshadowed now by the tannins. **90**

Cabernet Sauvignon Various Bottlings (NR):
North Coast 1976: Mature and drying, but the fruit that is left is appealing for its currant and mineral notes. **88**
North Coast 1975: Austere, with earthy currant and mineral flavors that are fully mature and showing signs of drying out. **86**
Sonoma County 1979: A shade leaner and sleeker than the 1978 Sonoma but with similar spicy black cherry, anise and mineral flavors. **88**
Sonoma County 1978: Fully mature now, with pretty floral, black cherry and spice aromas, a gentle, rich, elegant texture and tannins that are soft and supple. The finish offers hints of mineral and anise. Complex and charming. **87**
Sonoma County 1977: Smooth and polished, fully mature, with supple, earthy currant, mineral and spice notes and tannins that have softened. **91**
Sonoma County 1974: Mature and complex, with spicy cedar, herb, currant and anise notes, this full-bodied wine is beginning to dry out and the high tannin level makes for a chewy, gritty finish. **88**
Sonoma County 1973: Youthful and full of flavor the last time I tried it, with supple currant, anise and mineral notes framed by light oak. **87**

Chardonnay Alexander Valley (NR):
1987: Bold but harmonious, rich and fruity, with loads of grapefruit, spice and pineapple flavors. **90**
1986: Fruity, well balanced and complex, showing pineapple, lemon and vanilla flavors and a slightly leafy aroma. **89**
1985: Remarkably rich and elegant, graced with fresh, ripe, clean honey, pear and butter flavors that glide across the palate. **91**

Chardonnay Napa Valley (★★★★): Until recently among California's elite, made in a complex and openly fruity style that eschewed oak and was able to age for 10 years and longer. The most recent vintages failed to impress on release, but perhaps they simply need more time. Older vintages are well worth the experience, turning rich and creamy, totally satisfying and exciting. The grapes are from the Dry Creek area of Napa Valley,

northwest of the city of Napa. This area has a cool, mild, breezy climate that is ideally suited for Chardonnay.
1993: Marked by a tart, crisp, green edge but it holds together, with tart apple and citrus notes. **84**
1992: 1972-1992 Anniversary Bottling: Ripe and fruity, with rich pear, apple, melon and spice notes, turning smooth and polished on the finish, where the oak folds in. **88**
1991: A spicy wine with a tart Muscat edge and light pear and apple notes, but the flavors taper off on the finish. **83**
1990: Tastes like an overripe, late-harvest Chardonnay, with heavy notes of honey and pear. **81**
1989: Starts out with a burst of apple, pear, melon and toast flavors, then turns light and simple. **83**
1987: Intense, with vegetal flavors and a slightly sour finish. **72**
1986: Well defined and elegant, with spicy pear, apple and melon flavors. **90**
1985: Captures rich, ripe flavors of apple, pear and spice that play off each other. **90**

Zinfandel Napa Valley (★★): Up until the past few vintages this intense and peppery Zinfandel almost always ranked among California's best, but lately its been tannic and earthy. The 1992 marked an improvement.
1992: An improvement, with ripe cherry and peppery notes that turn elegant and refined, with firm tannins. **87**
1991: Earthy and coarse, with a tarry edge, but hints of stewed plum and pepper come through on the finish. **84**
1989: Very tough, tannic and hard, with a muted plum flavor. **80**
1987: Tough and earthy, with hard-edged oak and leaf flavors. **70**

Chateau Potelle
Mount Veeder, Napa Valley
F: 1983. O: Jean-Noel & Marketta Fourmeaux. W: Marketta Fourmeaux. S: None.

Overall	$9-32	★★★★

Wine Ratings

Cabernet Sauvignon Mount Veeder V.G.S.	★★★★
Cabernet Sauvignon Napa Valley Cuvée 95	★★★
Chardonnay Mount Veeder V.G.S.	★★★★

Chardonnay Napa Valley	★★
Sauvignon Blanc Napa Valley	★★
Zinfandel Mount Veeder V.G.S.	★★★★

WINERY DATA

C: 25,000. **V:** 47 acres in Mount Veeder. **G:** Cabernet Sauvignon (10 acres), Chardonnay (21), Zinfandel (16). **P:** Sauvignon Blanc, Sémillon, Chardonnay, Cabernet Sauvignon (Napa Valley).

Bordeaux residents Jean-Noel and Marketta Fourmeaux came to Napa Valley in 1983 after studying the California wine business as emissaries of the French government. Chateau Potelle's early wines came from purchased grapes and often carried both the Napa and Alexander Valley appellations, but since the late 1980s the 25,000-case winery, home of the former Vose winery, has narrowed its focus to two excellent, Mount Veeder-grown wines bottled under the V.G.S. designation (for Very Good Shit—really!): a superb Zinfandel (1,200 cases) and a classy Chardonnay (1,200 cases), augmented by Cabernet, Chardonnay and Sauvignon Blanc made from purchased Napa grapes. A V.G.S. Cabernet is also impressive. The Fourmeaux family owns 47 acres on Mt. Veeder, divided among Chardonnay (21 acres), Zinfandel (16) and Cabernet (10). Since shifting the focus to estate-grown wines, the quality has soared, and the Zinfandel is one of California's finest. Lower prices for the other wines have put the winery in the good-value arena.

TASTING NOTES

CABERNET SAUVIGNON MOUNT VEEDER V.G.S. (★★★★): The first two vintages, 1990 and 1992, reveal rich, complex, earthy currant flavors and tame tannins for Mount Veeder. Worth watching.
1992: Well oaked, with toasty buttery flavors, but also a supple core of complex currant, mineral, earth and tar notes and tame tannins. **92**
1990: Dark and rich, with an earthy currant, oak and mineral edge that's deep and intense, finishing with firm tannins. **91**

CABERNET SAUVIGNON NAPA VALLEY CUVÉE 95 (★★★): Pleasant, with mild berry and spice notes, ready on release.
1990: Pleasant but tight, with a core of currant, berry and cherry flavors, framed by firm tannins and light oak. **86**

CHARDONNAY MOUNT VEEDER V.G.S. (★★★★): The success of recent vintages is most impressive, with rich, intense, complex and well oaked wines that serve up lots of flavor.
1991: Ripe and vibrant with a pretty array of creamy pear, spice, honey and peach notes that finishes with a long, rich aftertaste. **91**

CHARDONNAY NAPA VALLEY (★★): Lighter than the V.G.S. but attractive enough, with subtle fruit flavors.
1991: Ripe and juicy, with pear, apple, spice and oak flavors. **88**
1990: Tart and earthy, with a canned pineapple edge to the chunky fruit and spice flavors, finishing abruptly, but on balance pleasant enough. **80**
1989: Fully mature, with honey, pear, pineapple and earth notes, picking up a smoky, buttery edge. **87**

SAUVIGNON BLANC NAPA VALLEY (★★): Bright and lively, with citrus and pear flavors.
1993: Bright and fruity, a lively, exuberant wine that echoes citrus and pear flavors. **86**

ZINFANDEL MOUNT VEEDER V.G.S. (★★★★): Amazingly supple and complex given the tannin level in most Mount Veeder reds, but this is a first-class effort with pretty raspberry, anise and buttery oak shadings. High-priced, but beautifully crafted. No 1991 was made, but 1993 was showy early on.
1992: Beautifully crafted, with layers of ripe, rich, supple raspberry, cherry and plum flavors. Turns smooth and polished on the finish, where the toasty, buttery oak adds depth. **92**
1990: Makes a statement with everything from the bottle shape to the bright, racy style. Plenty of plum, black cherry and raspberry aromas and flavors that turn elegant and smooth on the finish despite the ample tannins. **90**

CHATEAU ST. JEAN
Sonoma Valley
F: 1973. **O:** Suntory International. **W:** Don Van Staaveren. **S:** None.

OVERALL	$8-40	★★★★

WINE RATINGS
Cabernet Sauvignon Sonoma County	★★

Cabernet Sauvignon	
Sonoma County Cinq Cépages	★★★
Cabernet Sauvignon	
Sonoma County Reserve	★★★★
Chardonnay Alexander Valley	
Belle Terre Vineyard	★★★★
Chardonnay Alexander Valley	
Belle Terre Vineyard Reserve	★★★★
Chardonnay Alexander Valley	
Robert Young Vineyard	★★★★★
Chardonnay Alexander Valley	
Robert Young Vineyard Reserve	★★★★★
Chardonnay Sonoma County	★★
Fumé Blanc Russian River Valley	
La Petite Étoile	★★★
Fumé Blanc Sonoma County Dry	★★
Gewürztraminer Sonoma County	★★
Johannisberg Riesling Alexander Valley	
Hoot Owl Creek Vineyards	
Late Harvest Special Select	★★★★★
Merlot Sonoma County	★★
Mourvèdre Sonoma Valley	NR
Pinot Noir Sonoma County	★★
Sparkling Wine Sonoma County	★★★

WINERY DATA

C: 225,000. **V:** 150 acres in Sonoma Valley, Russian River Valley. **G:** Chardonnay (61 acres), Sauvignon Blanc (44), Merlot (21), Cabernet Sauvignon (8), Cabernet Franc (4), Pinot Blanc (4), Muscat Canelli (3), Malbec (2), Viognier (2), Petite Verdot (1). **P:** None.

From the outset, Chateau St. Jean set impeccably high standards for its wines. This beautiful chateau-style winery moved to the forefront of California wine in the 1970s with a series of vineyard-designated Chardonnays, Fumé Blancs, Rieslings and dessert wines, all of which ranked among the California elite. With Chardonnay in particular, St. Jean went to extremes. At one point its talented winemaker, Richard Arrowood (See Arrowood Vineyards & Winery), had nine different Chardonnays from one vintage on the market. The winery was like an experimental lab for Arrowood's research with Sonoma County's finest Chardonnay vineyards. Names like Robert Young, Belle Terre, Les Pierres (owned by Sonoma-Cutrer), McCrea Vineyard, Beltane Ranch (Kenwood), Frank Johnson Vineyard, Jimtown Ranch

and Wildwood Ranch were regulars in the St. Jean line-up, along with lesser-known names like Gauer Ranch (later Gauer Estate winery), Hunter Farms, Bacigalupi and Riverview Vineyards. The research paid off handsomely, and St. Jean (pronounced the American way, "jeen") emerged as California's foremost Chardonnay specialist. Two bottlings in particular, Robert Young Vineyard and Belle Terre Vineyard, served as reference points for Alexander Valley Chardonnay.

St. Jean founders and Central Valley table-grape growers Robert and Edward Merzoian and Ken Sheffield sold the winery to Suntory International for $40 million in 1984. After the 1990 vintage, Arrowood, the winemaker from day one, left to work full-time at his winery. There is much debate about whether the winery, which has grown to 225,000 cases, has maintained its standards. For me the answer is yes, although there have been signficant changes and there's no disputing that the competition has caught up with St. Jean. Still, the Robert Young and Belle Terre Chardonnays are classy wines, as are the late-harvest dessert Rieslings and Gewürztraminers. La Petite Étoile Fumé Blanc remains distinctive and the Cabernet Reserve is complex and well made. A Merlot and a Sonoma County Cabernet are appealing too, while the sparkling wines offer exceptional value. What's different is that there are now more than 125 wineries in Sonoma County, 700-plus in California, and the winery's personality has changed with Arrowood's leaving, in much the same way that Robert Mondavi Winery has changed since Robert Mondavi retired.

The goal now is to continue to expand into other varietals, particularly reds, including Rhône-style wines. The winery is producing 500-case lots of these new wines and hopes to expand to 3,000-case lots. St. Jean owns 150 acres, divided nearly evenly between Sonoma Valley and Russian River.

TASTING NOTES

CABERNET FRANC SONOMA VALLEY JEANETTE VINEYARD (★★): Serves up modest currant and cherry flavors, but is rather ordinary, as this varietal tends to be in California.
1989: Tight, firm and oaky, with a narrow band of currant and cedar flavors. **83**

CABERNET SAUVIGNON SONOMA COUNTY (★★): Well crafted, with medium-bodied currant, herb and cherry flavors and fine tannins. Best to drink on release.

1990: Ripe and chunky, it delivers rich currant and cherry flavors but is closed and tight. **86**

1989: A shade more juicy berry and cherry flavors showing than in the 1988, but it turns austere and tannic. **84**

1988: Smells nice, with attractive berry and cherry notes, but not as complex on the palate. **83**

1987: Strikes a nice balance between fruit and oak, with currant, black cherry, herb and prune notes. **88**

1986: Rich and supple, with good extract, and the herb, currant and cherry flavors are framed by toasty vanilla, oak, mineral and spice notes. **90**

1985: A good concentration of flavor, with toasty, buttery oak and spicy cassis flavors. **86**

CABERNET SAUVIGNON SONOMA COUNTY CINQ CÉPAGES (★★★): A blend of the five Bordeaux varieties that lacks distinction, but is a well crafted wine.

1990: Big, rich and dense, with rustic, chunky currant and oak flavors. **87**

CABERNET SAUVIGNON SONOMA COUNTY RESERVE (★★★★): Bold and dramatic in the best years, lavishly oaked and packed with flavor, with vintages such as 1987 aging very well.

1990: A dramatic Reserve that's rich and complex, with deep, penetrating currant, anise, black cherry, plum and toasty, buttery oak flavors. Tremendous depth and concentration. **93**

1989: Austere and tannic, with a narrow band of black cherry, earth and spice flavors, picking up a leathery edge on the finish. **85**

1988: Tight and closed, with hints of black cherry and currant that are light and simple. **84**

1987: Wonderfully rich, complex and compelling, with ripe, deep, plush black cherry, herb and currant flavors and sweet, toasty, buttery oak notes. **93**

CHARDONNAY ALEXANDER VALLEY BELLE TERRE VINEYARD (★★★★), RESERVE (★★★★): Rivals the Robert Young most years, surpasses it occasionally and shares its elegance and finesse. Often features tart apple and pineapple flavors.

1993: Ripe and spicy, with medium-weight pear, apple and light oak shadings. **86**

1992: Strikes a lovely balance between the ripe pear and peach flavors and pretty, toasty, buttery oak notes. **90**

1991: Focused and well proportioned, with toasty, buttery, ripe pear and honey notes. First Belle Terre to undergo malolactic fermentation. **88**

1990: Ripe and crisp, with tasty green apple and pineapple flavors. **87**

Reserve 1991: Disjointed now, but remarkably youthful with pine, spice and apple flavors that give way to smoky, toasty oak. Strives for complexity, turning a bit coarse and woody on the finish. **88**

CHARDONNAY ALEXANDER VALLEY ROBERT YOUNG VINEYARD (★★★★★), RESERVE (★★★★★): Exemplifies the pure spicy and elegant character of Alexander Valley Chardonnay with its tiers of honey, pear and apple flavors. Ages exceptionally well and often needs a year or two after release to blossom. Look for delicacy and finesse rather than sheer power. The Reserve is similar to the regular bottling but is aged longer, produced only in magnum and marked by toastier oak flavors.

1992: A showy wine with toasty, buttery oak, pear, spice and nutmeg flavors. Combines harmony, intensity and finesse. **91**

1991: Elegant and intense, with spice, pear and fig flavors that stay focused through the finish. Balanced and lively. **89**

1990: Starts out slow, but the flavors build to a rich, complex finish. Serves up spicy pear, smoke, butter and fig flavors, with a long, full finish. **90**

Reserve 1991: Ripe and fruity, with a core of complex, supple pear, peach and toasty oak flavors that fold together nicely. **91**

Reserve 1990: Youthful, rich and complex, with deeply concentrated pear, toast and spice flavors that are intense and lively. Packs in lots of flavor, with a long, full finish. **92**

CHARDONNAY SONOMA COUNTY (★★): A medium-weight, middle-of-the-road style that's well done, striking a balance between ripe fruit flavors and light oak shadings. A good value.

1992: A fruity, spicy wine with racy peach and honey notes of modest depth and intensity. **84**

1991: A crisp, citrusy wine offering basic grapefruit and pineapple flavors and a tangerine edge. **85**

FUMÉ BLANC RUSSIAN RIVER VALLEY LA PETITE ÉTOILE (★★★): This bottling exaggerates the intensity and personality of the varietal, often straying into grassy onion flavors.

1993: Light, simple and vaguely fruity, not much definition but pleasant and mildly herbal. **84**

1991: An earthy wine with grapefruit and lemon flavors that turn murky. **80**

FUMÉ BLANC SONOMA COUNTY DRY (★★): Leans toward the citrus and herb side of Sauvignon Blanc.

1993: Straightforward, a sturdy wine with simple pear fruit and hints of spice on the finish. **82**

1992: Crisp and citrusy, with herbal overtones that add a nice complexity to the lemon flavors. **85**

GEWÜRZTRAMINER SONOMA COUNTY (★★): Captures the essence of this spicy grape, but through no fault of its own can have a bitter grapefruit edge.

1992: Fruity and refreshing, a crisp, slightly sweet wine with modest grapefruit and spice flavors. **82**

JOHANNISBERG RIESLING ALEXANDER VALLEY HOOT OWL CREEK VINEYARDS (★★★★★): As delicious as late-harvest wine gets anywhere; sweet, rich and complex, with loads of flavor.

Late Harvest Special Select 1989: Deep, dark, ripe and rich, a gorgeous, unctuous wine that offers cascades of honey, floral, caramel, apricot, pear and ginger aromas and flavors, finishing almost delicately for such a rich wine. Fabulous to drink now and may still improve through 1998. **95**

Late Harvest Select 1988: Fresh and lively, with generous grapefruit, apple and pear aromas and flavors. The finish is sweet but balanced, with a tang of lemony acidity. **88**

MERLOT SONOMA COUNTY (★★): Has the right weight and balance, but the currant and herb flavors are muted, making it best to drink early on.

1992: Firm, with a supple beam of black cherry, blackberry and plum notes, finishing with a tannic edge. **86**

1991: Young and intense, tough and chewy. Difficult to judge, but surely it has gritty tannins. **84**

1990: Ripe and fruity, with complex plum, currant and black cherry flavors that turn supple, with anise and tar notes. **88**

1989: Austere and earthy, with just a trace of plum flavor. **80**

MOURVÈDRE SONOMA VALLEY (NR):

1990: Light in texture, with pleasing plum, cherry, leaf and spice aromas and flavors. **83**

PINOT NOIR SONOMA COUNTY (★★): The weakest of the reds, made in a simple, modestly varietal style.

1991: Well balanced and elegant, with pretty black cherry flavor. **86**

1990: Lean and a bit tough, with simple black cherry and cola flavors. **80**

CHATEAU SOUVERAIN
Alexander Valley
F: 1944. **O:** Wine World Estates. **W:** Tom Peterson. **S:** None.

OVERALL	$8-16	★★★

WINE RATINGS

Cabernet Sauvignon Alexander Valley	★★★
Cabernet Sauvignon Alexander Valley Winemaker's Reserve	★★★
Chardonnay Russian River Valley Allen Vineyard	★★★★
Chardonnay Russian River Valley Allen Vineyard Reserve	★★★
Chardonnay Russian River Valley Rochioli Vineyard Reserve	★★★
Chardonnay Sonoma County Barrel Fermented	★★★
Merlot Alexander Valley	★★★
Pinot Noir Carneros Winemaker's Reserve	★★
Sauvignon Blanc Alexander Valley Barrel Fermented	★★★
Zinfandel Dry Creek Valley Bradford Mountain Vineyard	★★★

WINERY DATA

C: 120,000. **V:** 212 acres in Alexander Valley. **G:** Cabernet Sauvignon (90 acres), Merlot (70), Sauvignon Blanc (17), Cabernet Franc (12), Zinfandel (7), Syrah (6), Petite Verdot (0.3), Sangiovese (0.3), Gamay Noir (6), Viognier (0.7).
P: Chardonnay (Carneros, Russian River Valley), Chardonnay (Alexander Valley), Cabernet Sauvignon (Alexander Valley), Merlot (Alexander Valley), Sauvignon Blanc (Alexander Valley).

Chateau Souverain's future has never looked brighter. For most of its history, the winery has been undercapitalized and has made wines of variable quality. The original Souverain Winery was in Napa Valley, founded by J. Leeland "Lee" Stewart in 1943 in the old Rossini winery (now Burgess Cellars). After years of making highly regarded Cabernets known for their elegance and finesse, Stewart sold the brand to Pillsbury, which in turn built a winery (now Rutherford Hill) before building a second winery at the current location in Alexander Valley in 1973, where the brand languished for more than a decade. In 1986 Wine World Inc. (Nestle) bought the winery, renamed it Chateau Souverain, and spent millions upgrading the facility, buying new oak, securing top-quality grape sources and planting new vineyards. Today Chateau Souverain's production is 120,000 cases, with high quality and solid values across the board, including vineyard-designated Chardonnays from J. Rochioli Vineyard, Howard Allen Vineyard, Durell Vineyard and Sangiacomo Vineyard, along with Zinfandel from Bradford Mountain. All of the wines show winemaker Tom Peterson's deft hand for polish and finesse. While well oaked, each of the wines is balanced and none is overdone.

TASTING NOTES

CABERNET SAUVIGNON ALEXANDER VALLEY (★★★): Supple and appealing, with herb, currant and spice notes and smooth, polished tannins. Made for early consumption, but well balanced and may surprise you.
1992: Oak dominates, but underneath the currant, cherry and spice flavors are elegant and polished, finishing with a coffee and toasty oak aftertaste. **85**
1991: Dense and chocolaty, with spicy currant, vanilla and toasty oak flavors. **85**
1990: Solidly built and packed with complex, concentrated currant, plum, toast and tobacco flavors. **90**
1989: Firm and focused, with moderately concentrated plum, spice and currant flavors. **85**
1988: Rich and full, with well focused currant, black cherry and spicy oak notes. **85**
1987: Has firm tannins, but it's balanced and velvety enough to allow the spicy black cherry and currant flavors to emerge. **87**

CABERNET SAUVIGNON ALEXANDER VALLEY WINEMAKER'S RESERVE (★★★): Marginally richer and more complex, although expect this line to get better as vineyard sources become more predictable.
1991: A big, ripe and chewy wine with black cherry, plum and currant flavors framed by toasty, buttery oak. **91**
1990: Solid, rich and focused, with supple currant, spice and cedary oak flavors, picking up a peppery, tannic edge on the finish. **87**
1988: Firm in texture, with coarse tannins surrounding a core of ripe berry and cedar flavors. **83**

CHARDONNAY CARNEROS SANGIACOMO VINEYARD (★★★): Very complex and well balanced.
1990: Spicy, smoky and complex, with a polished texture and generous pear and apple flavors at the core. **90**

CHARDONNAY RUSSIAN RIVER VALLEY ALLEN VINEYARD (★★★★), RESERVE (★★★): Steadily improving with richer flavors.
1992: Bold, ripe and buttery, with rich, spicy pear, hazelnut and creamy vanilla flavors that are plush and silky, finishing with a long, complex aftertaste. **91**
1990: Crisp and flavorful, with lovely peach, nectarine and apple aromas and flavors that turn toward spice and vanilla on the long finish. **88**
Reserve 1992: Complex and spicy, with a core of rich, concentrated, buttery pear, vanilla and honey flavors and a long, smooth finish. **90**
Reserve 1991: A ripe, round, full, Burgundian-style wine that offers butterscotch and honey overtones to the generous pear and apple flavors. A good value. **90**

CHARDONNAY RUSSIAN RIVER VALLEY ROCHIOLI VINEYARD RESERVE (★★★):
1993: Marked by creamy oak, it turns rich and smoky with ripe, fleshy pear and spicy vanilla notes, finishing with a complex aftertaste. **89**

CHARDONNAY SONOMA COUNTY BARREL FERMENTED (★★★):
1992: The spicy pear and apple flavors are simple and direct, with light, toasty oak shadings. **84**
1991: A simple, easy-to-drink wine with spicy apple, pear and melon notes. **85**

CHARDONNAY SONOMA VALLEY DURELL VINEYARD (★★★):
1991: Firm and focused, showing generous nutmeg, pear and caramel aromas and flavors. **88**

MERLOT ALEXANDER VALLEY (★★★): Smooth and elegant, not just an attempt to make a lighter Cabernet. Marked by herb, plum and cedary oak flavors, impressive for its delicacy and soft tannins.
1992: Relies heavily on cedary oak for its flavor and structure, then the tannic plum, currant and cherry notes come through. **85**
1991: Smooth and round, bordering on opulent. The currant and berry flavors are shaded nicely by spice, caramel and tobacco notes. **87**
1990: Broad and full-bodied, with ripe plum and cherry flavors and hints of herbs and leather. **86**
1989: Ripe, full and generous, with focused plum, cherry and currant flavors that are supple and tasty. **89**

MERLOT SONOMA COUNTY (★★★):
1990: Smooth and elegant, with supple cherry, currant, herb and spice flavors and subtle oak shadings that finish with a pretty, smoky plum edge. **87**

PINOT NOIR CARNEROS WINEMAKER'S RESERVE (★★): Light and spicy, with delicate cherry, herb and strawberry notes that are elegant. Could be richer, but it's better to err on this side than being too tannic. Look for quality to improve.
1993: Supple and refined, with modest herb, cherry, spice and light toasty oak shadings. **84**
1992: Elegant and focused, with spicy wild berry, cherry and blueberry flavors that are crisp and refreshing, finishing with light tannins. **85**
1991: A delicate wine with supple cherry, herb and spice flavors of modest depth and richness. **84**

SAUVIGNON BLANC ALEXANDER VALLEY BARREL FERMENTED (★★★): Fresh and lively, with a good mixture of fruit, herbs and oak.
1994: Lean and lively, flavors centered around nectarine, grapefruit and a touch of grass. **85**
1993: Fresh and lively, with snappy pear, sweet pea, fig and citrus notes. Medium-bodied, with good depth and richness. **87**

1992: Smooth and silky, a pretty wine with pear, melon and spice aromas and flavors, barely varietal but pleasant to drink. **86**

ZINFANDEL DRY CREEK VALLEY BRADFORD MOUNTAIN VINEYARD (★★★): Reflects the house style of polish and finesse, and the pepper and wild berry flavors give it character.
1992: Smooth and smoky, with a core of spicy raspberry and black cherry flavors. **87**
1991: Smooth, ripe and fleshy, with a core of pretty plum, cherry and berry flavors. **87**
1990: Tight and compact, with firm berry and cherry aromas and flavors framed by subtle oak shadings and a raisiny edge on the finish. **84**
1989: Firm and flavorful, with pleasant, bright berry and cherry flavors that bounce through the finish. **82**
1987: Fresh and unpolished, with lush raspberry, cherry and vanilla aromas and flavors and a plush texture. **85**

CHATEAU WOLTNER
Howell Mountain
F: 1980. **O:** Woltner Estates Ltd. **W:** John Schilter, Edward Lemon. **S:** None.

OVERALL	$15-60	★★★

WINE RATINGS

Chardonnay Howell Mountain	★★
Chardonnay Howell Mountain Estate Reserve	★★★
Chardonnay Howell Mountain Frederique Vineyard	★★★
Chardonnay Howell Mountain St. Thomas Vineyard	★★★
Chardonnay Howell Mountain Titus Vineyard	★★★

WINERY DATA
C: 10,000. **V:** 56 acres in Howell Mountain. **G:** Chardonnay. **P:** None.

Howell Mountain is hearty red wine country to most, but not to Francis and Françoise DeWavrin-Woltner. Despite hefty red-wine credentials, the former owners of Bordeaux's great Château La Mission-Haut Brion focus on mountain-grown Chardonnay. In 1980 the DeWavrin-Woltners sold La Mission, which had been in their family since 1919, and became partners at Conn Creek Winery in Napa Valley before planting their own vineyard. Their 56 acres of vineyard, 1,800 feet above the Napa Valley floor, produce five wines, three with vineyard designations. Today the 10,000 cases are made up of five bottlings: Titus, St. Thomas and Frederique Vineyards, a Reserve and a generic Howell Mountain bottling.

The Woltner style is unmistakably Burgundian, with a heavy emphasis on crisp acidity, austere, tightly concentrated flavors and the generous use of oak, all designed to create wines with long-term aging potential. I have found the vineyard-designated wines more similar than not—austere and flinty, with lemon, pear and vanilla notes. I give the wines good marks for their deliberate style. At the same time, they will not appeal to everyone, or to everyone's wine budget, with the Titus 1987 priced at $56, $3 more than the 1986 Opus One. Clearly these are luxury Chardonnays designed for collectors who fully appreciate nuances and are willing to wait as these wines evolve.

TASTING NOTES

CHARDONNAY HOWELL MOUNTAIN (★★):

1993: Light and fruity, with fresh pear and apple notes that pick up a spicy citrus edge on the finish. **86**
1992: Serves up pleasing spice, pear, citrus and honey notes that are lively and fruity. **84**
1991: Fresh, ripe and fruity, with crisp apple, pear and melon flavors and a pretty, spicy edge. **84**
1989: Tart and simple, with hints of nutmeg to liven up the basic lemon and pineapple aromas and flavors. Finishes well. **82**

CHARDONNAY HOWELL MOUNTAIN ESTATE RESERVE (★★★):

1993: Offers modest pear and spice notes with a flinty edge, but little more as the flavors are simple. **84**
1992: Tight and focused, with firm, rich, spicy pear and toasty oak flavors that linger on the finish. **90**
1991: This tart, lean, lemony wine shows crisp apple, pear and spice notes that are tight and focused. **87**

CHARDONNAY HOWELL MOUNTAIN FREDERIQUE VINEYARD (★★★):

1993: Lean and tart, with a strong citrus edge to the crisp apple and pear notes. Comes across as disjointed. **82**
1992: Tart and tightly wound, with spicy pear and mineral shadings, picking up light, toasty oak and nutmeg flavors that are crisp and persistent. **90**
1991: Crisp and lean, showing a coarse edge to the citrus and pear flavors. **85**

CHARDONNAY HOWELL MOUNTAIN ST. THOMAS VINEYARD (★★★):

1993: Marked by tart, flinty pear and citrus flavors. Simple at best. **83**
1992: Tart and intense, with a tightly wound core of grapefruit, pineapple and light oak flavors. **88**
1990: Tight and taut, with crisp lemon, apple, nectarine and pear flavors and subtle oak shadings. **90**

CHARDONNAY HOWELL MOUNTAIN TITUS VINEYARD (★★★):

1993: Tart and flinty, with an earthy citrus edge, but not much more in the way of fruit. **82**
1992: A lean, crisp wine with tart citrus and pear flavors, finishing with a hint of nutmeg and clove. **88**
1991: Lean and tight, with hints of pear and spice and light oak shadings that blend together nicely, finishing with delicate fruit nuances and buttery honey notes. **90**

CHATOM VINEYARDS
Calaveras County
F: 1989. O: Chatom Cellars Inc. W: Chuck Hovey. S: None.

OVERALL	$6-14	★★

WINE RATINGS
Cabernet Sauvignon Calaveras County	★★
Chardonnay Calaveras County	★★
Merlot Calaveras County	★★
Sangiovese Calaveras County	★★
Sauvignon Blanc Calaveras County	★★
Sémillon Calaveras County	★★
Zinfandel Calaveras County	★★

Winery Data

C: 6,000. **V:** 65 acres in Sierra Foothills. **G:** Chardonnay (12 acres), Merlot (6), Sangiovese (5), Brunello (3), Syrah (1), Sauvignon Blanc (9), Cabernet Sauvignon (12), Zinfandel (11), Sémillon (2), Other (2). **P:** None.

Since 1989 Chatom Vineyards has been making 6,000 cases of wine from Calaveras County grapes. Its own 65 acres of vines are planted to a variety of grapes, including Chardonnay (12 acres), Zinfandel (11), Cabernet (12), Merlot (6), Sangiovese (5) and Syrah (1). Early efforts show a well made Sauvignon Blanc, along with Cabernet, Chardonnay and Merlot that were medium-weight, with pleasant flavors. The Sangiovese was off the mark.

Tasting Notes

Cabernet Sauvignon Calaveras County (★★):
1992: Well oaked, with an odd toasted grain edge, but the fruit is ripe and supple, albeit a bit dry and tannic. Best to cellar into 1996 and see what happens. **84**
1991: Supple and generous, with pretty, toasty vanilla and oak nuances and a crisp band of spicy cherry flavors. **83**

Chardonnay Calaveras County (★★):
1993: Intense and spicy, with a grassy edge to the pear and apple flavors. **82**
1991: Fresh and appealing, offering nice tropical fruit aromas and flavors at the core. A blast of spiciness and a whiff of honey come through on the finish. **83**

Merlot Calaveras County (★★):
1992: Light with modest varietal character and a strong woody component that turns earthy and rubbery. **74**
1991: An oaky wine with toasty, buttery wood flavors. Fruit purists will find this a bit overdone, but it's smooth and flavorful, with currant and herb notes. **85**

Sangiovese Calaveras County (★):
1992: Lean and awfully woody, with a fresh-sawn character that obliterates the modest fruit. **70**

Sauvignon Blanc Various Bottlings (★★):
Calaveras County 1993: Smooth and generous, showing nicely defined pear and floral flavors that just keep coming and coming on the finish. A terrific Sauvignon Blanc that tones down the varietal character. **90**

Calaveras County Select 1991: Ripe and generous, a broadly built wine with honey and fig overtones. **86**
Calaveras Fumé 1991: Lean, simple and refreshing, a lighter style of Sauvignon with some floral overtones and a hint of honey on the finish. **80**

Sémillon Calaveras County (★★):
1993: Bright, focused and layered with appealing fruit aromas and flavors, centering around peach, pear and pineapple. **87**

Zinfandel Calaveras County (★★):
1992: Well oaked with smoky buttery flavors, but an elegant core of wild berry and cherry fruit adds a nice dimension. **84**
1991: A well mannered Zin with toasty, buttery, intense wild berry flavors, but it's also quite gritty and tannic on the finish. **81**

Chauffe-eau Cellars
Alexander Valley
F: 1990. **O:** Keith Nelson & William R. Hunter. **W:** William R. Hunter. **S:** Cirri.

Overall	$17-20	★★★

Wine Ratings

Cabernet Sauvignon Alexander Valley	★★
Chardonnay Carneros Sangiacomo Vineyard Sans Filtrage	★★★
Chardonnay Russian River Valley Dutton Ranch Sans Filtrage	★★★

Winery Data

C: 1,000. **V:** 2 acres in Alexander Valley. **G:** Syrah.
P: Chardonnay, Merlot (Carneros), Merlot, Cabernet Franc (Sonoma Valley), Chardonnay, Merlot (Green Valley), Cabernet Sauvignon (Alexander Valley).

Keith Nelson and William Hunter oversee Chauffe-eau in Geyserville, formerly Vina Vista Winery, where they produce 1,000 cases of Cabernet, Chardonnay (from Dutton Ranch and Sangiacomo) and Merlot. The 1987 Cabernet Alexander Valley is marked by herbal flavors and chewy tannins and the 1992 Chardonnay Sangiacomo offers smooth, polished, pretty honey and apple flavors.

TASTING NOTES

VARIOUS BOTTLINGS :

Cabernet Sauvignon Alexander Valley 1987: Tannic and chewy, with lots of herb, toast, cherry and currant aromas and flavors coming through. Has intensity and personality. Better after 1996. **85**

Chardonnay Carneros Sangiacomo Vineyard Sans Filtrage 1993: Moderately rich, with light honey, pear and butterscotch flavors that build on the finish. Flavors linger on the finish. **87**

Chardonnay Carneros Sangiacomo Vineyard Sans Filtrage 1992: Smooth and polished, a brightly spicy wine with honey and apple echoing on the finish. Has elegance and lovely balance. **89**

Chardonnay Carneros Sangiacomo Vineyard Sans Filtrage 1990: Crisp and refined, with tart citrus, honey and pineapple notes that are clean and refreshing. Elegant and balanced, with a kiss of oak on the finish. **86**

Chardonnay Russian River Valley Dutton Ranch Sans Filtrage 1993: Ripe and floral, with pear, spice and apple notes that are medium weight, with smoky toasty oak notes, turning a bit coarse on the finish. **86**

CHIMERE WINERY

Santa Maria Valley

F: 1989. **O:** Gary Mosby. **W:** Gary Mosby. **S:** None.

OVERALL	$10-18	★★

WINE RATINGS

Chardonnay Edna Valley	★★
Merlot Santa Barbara County	★★
Pinot Blanc Santa Barbara County	★

WINERY DATA

C: 2,500. **V:** None. **G:** None. **P:** Merlot (Santa Barbara County), Pinot Noir (Santa Barbara County), Chardonnay (Santa Barbara County), Pinot Blanc (Santa Barbara County), Nebbiolo (Santa Barbara County), Pinot Noir (Edna Valley).

The 1989 Chimere Edna Valley yielded 247 cases of an intensely flavored, varietally true Chardonnay that offered a spectrum of citrus, pear, melon and spice flavors. Owner Gary Mosby plans to expand into Merlot, Pinot Noir, Pinot Blanc and Nebbiolo, all from purchased grapes from Santa Barbara County, reaching 2,500 cases.

TASTING NOTES

VARIOUS BOTTLINGS:

Chardonnay Edna Valley 1989: Intense and varietal, with plenty of citrus, pear, melon and spice flavors that are rich and well focused. The finish gets a touch coarse, but with a few months' aging the rough edges may round out. **83**

Merlot Santa Barbara County 1992: Smooth and supple, silky-textured and fine-grained, nicely focused berry and spice flavors lingering on the finish. Best from 1996. **83**

Pinot Blanc Santa Barbara County 1993: Earthy, with a tinny edge to the canny pineapple and honey notes. Awkward. **76**

CHIMNEY ROCK WINERY

Stags Leap District, Napa Valley

F: 1981. **O:** Chimney Rock Winery Inc. **W:** Douglas Fletcher. **S:** None.

OVERALL	$10-30	★★

WINE RATINGS

Cabernet Sauvignon Stags Leap District	★★
Chardonnay Carneros	★★
Fumé Blanc Napa Valley	★★
Meritage Red Stags Leap District Élevage	★★★
Sauvignon Blanc Napa Valley	★★

WINERY DATA

C: 20,000. **V:** 66 acres in Stags Leap District. **G:** Cabernet Sauvignon (55 acres), Merlot (7), Cabernet Franc (3). **P:** Sauvignon Blanc (Napa Valley), Chardonnay (Carneros).

Former Pepsi International executive Sheldon "Hack" Wilson and his wife, Stella, bulldozed half the Chimney Rock Golf Course in the Stags Leap District to make way for their 66-acre vineyard and handsome Cape Dutch-style winery. The winery focuses on Stags Leap Cabernet, Chardonnay (from Carneros and Stags Leap) and Fumé Blanc. Both the white wines have been erratic and on the lean and simple side. The Cabernets are made in a delicate, understated style, often to a fault, as they too come across light and lacking the richness and depth found in so many other Stags Leap Cabernets. Recognizing that,

Wilson and winemaker Douglas Fletcher have added a Reserve wine they call Élevage (good breeding), aiming to pack more punch into their Cabernet. Both the 1990 and 1991 show more depth and flavor, a good sign.

TASTING NOTES

CABERNET SAUVIGNON STAGS LEAP DISTRICT (★★):
1991: The modest currant, berry, pepper and cherry flavors are well defined for a wine of this age. **84**
1990: An earthy, herbal wine with rugged tannins and a band of tight, closed currant and oak flavors. **85**

CHARDONNAY VARIOUS BOTTLINGS (★★):
Carneros 1993: Blunt and a touch earthy, with a muted grapefruit edge to the Chardonnay flavors. **82**
Stags Leap District 1992: Leans a little too heavily on wood flavors, which gives it a dry, oaky mouthfeel. **82**
Stags Leap District 1991: Lean and crisp, with a dull, brackish edge to the spice and pear flavors. **79**

FUMÉ BLANC NAPA VALLEY (★★):
1992: Simple and slightly sweet, a modestly appealing wine with gentle pear and vanilla flavors. **77**

MERITAGE RED STAGS LEAP DISTRICT ÉLEVAGE (★★★):
A little more of everything, from higher extract fruit to toastier oak, clearly an improvement over previous Cabernet vintages, which ran from simple to diluted.
1991: Strives for complexity with its smoky oak aromas and rich black cherry, currant and butter flavors. **88**
1990: Ripe and flavorful, with generous currant and blueberry aromas and flavors, finishing spicy and fresh. **88**

SAUVIGNON BLANC NAPA VALLEY (★★):
1993: Lean and herbal, and the citrus flavors keep it lively. **82**

CHRISTIAN BROTHERS

The Christian Brothers, long a landmark in Napa Valley with its grand Greystone Cellars north of St. Helena, was once one of California's largest generic table wine producers. Founded in 1882, this venerable winery owned several other wineries throughout the state, including the Mont La Salle facility on Mount Veeder, now home of The Hess

Collection. By the 1980s The Christian Brothers owned some 1,500 acres of Napa Valley vineyards, making it one of the largest vineyard owners in Napa. Efforts to improve the quality of its wines, under the direction of winemaker Tom Eddy (see listing) showed steady progress; the winery produced excellent Napa Valley Cabernets in 1984, 1985 and 1987 and a barrel-fermented Chardonnay that was rich and creamy. In 1989, however, the Christian Brothers' order tired of the wine business and decided to pursue other interests, and the winery and brands, including a lucrative brandy business, were sold to Heublein Inc., who refocused the brand back to generic table wines.

CHRISTOPHE
Napa Valley
F: 1984. **O:** Boisset U.S.A. **W:** Ginny Mills. **S:** Joliesse.

OVERALL	$8-9	★★

WINE RATINGS	
Cabernet Sauvignon Napa Valley	★★
Chardonnay Napa County	★★
Pinot Noir Carneros	★

WINERY DATA
C: 58,000. **V:** None. **G:** None. **P:** Sauvignon Blanc, Pinot Noir (Napa Valley), Cabernet Sauvignon, Chardonnay, Cabernet Franc, Merlot (Napa County), Sauvignon Blanc, Zinfandel, Cabernet Sauvignon, Chardonnay (California).

This is a négociant brand founded by French négociant Jean-Claude Boisset after he sold his winegrowing venture in Napa Valley (see St. Supéry). He kept Ginny Mills, the talented winemaker who blends wines primarily from Napa and Sonoma Counties and oversees a lineup that focuses mainly on Chardonnay but also includes Cabernet, Sauvignon Blanc and Pinot Noir. Quality is variable, depending on what bulk wines are on the market, but often the wines are very good, offering more character and flavor than wines two to three times their price. Production is 58,000 cases.

CHRISTOPHER CREEK
Russian River Valley
F: 1972. **O:** John & Susan Mitchell. **W:** Paul Brasset. **S:** None.

OVERALL $13-14   ★★

WINE RATINGS
Syrah Russian River Valley   ★★

WINERY DATA
C: 2,500. V: 10 acres in Russian River Valley. G: Chardonnay
(2 acres), Petite Sirah (3), Syrah (5). P: None.

This 2,500-case winery is the former Sotoyome
Winery and now focuses on Chardonnay, Petite Sirah and
Syrah from estate-grown vineyards in Russian River
Valley. The 1990 Syrah was tight and firm, with rich,
earthy plum and cherry flavors, the 1992 a shade
more elegant

TASTING NOTES

SYRAH RUSSIAN RIVER VALLEY (★★):
1992: Elegant and spicy with an appealing core of
currant, cherry and spice, but it could use a shade more
richness. **84**
1990: Firm and tight, with rich, concentrated, earthy flavors that blend nicely with the plum and cherry notes.
Complex and long on the finish, it won't shortchange
you on flavor. **86**

CILURZO VINEYARD AND WINERY
Temecula
F: 1978. **O:** Vincenzo & Audrey Cilurzo. **W:** Larry
Evilsizer. **S:** None.

OVERALL $8-12   ★

WINE RATINGS
Chardonnay Temecula
    Barrel Fermented Reserve   ★

WINERY DATA
C: 10,000. V: N/A. G: N/A. P: None.

This 10,000-case winery produces a wide range of
wines from the Temecula appellation, but quality is variable, rarely above average and often below it. The product mix includes Petite Sirah, Chardonnay, Chenin Blanc,
white Zinfandel and Chenin Blanc. Cilurzo's vineyards
were planted in 1968, making them the oldest in this
area. Most of the wines are sold from the tasting room.

CINNABAR VINEYARD & WINERY
Santa Cruz Mountains
F: 1983. **O:** Tom Mudd & Melissa Frank. **W:** Tom Mudd,
George Troquato. **S:** None.

OVERALL $20-25   ★★★

WINE RATINGS
Cabernet Sauvignon
    Santa Cruz Mountains   ★★
Chardonnay Santa Cruz Mountains   ★★★

WINERY DATA
C: 5,000. V: 30 acres in Santa Cruz Mountains. G: Chardonnay
(13 acres), Cabernet Sauvignon (10), Pinot Noir (4), Merlot (1),
Cabernet Franc (1). P: None.

Cinnabar sits on a hilltop overlooking Saratoga.
Former Stanford research engineer Tom Mudd and his
wife, Melissa Frank, purchased the property in 1983 and
planted Cabernet and Chardonnay, adding a modern winery in 1987. Production has grown to 5,000 cases, split
roughly between the two estate-grown wines.

TASTING NOTES

CABERNET SAUVIGNON SANTA CRUZ MOUNTAINS (★★):
Made in an elegant style marked by herb and pepper
notes, but it can be full and rich, as the 1986 shows.
Quality is improving.
1990: Distinct for its spicy, peppery edge and firm
tannins, this is tightly wound, finishing with chewy
tannins. **85**
1989: Tight, tannic and earthy, with peppery Cabernet
flavors that are youthful, firm and tannic. **82**
1988: Tight and firm, with tart currant and black cherry
flavors, but also a smoky ash note that intrudes. **82**
1986: The best of the Cinnabar Cabernets, it's ripe and
tasty, with rich, pretty currant, plum and blackberry flavors that are tight and focused. Impressive for its intensity and depth, this should be a lovely wine to drink
through the decade and beyond. **87**

CHARDONNAY SANTA CRUZ MOUNTAINS (★★★):
1993: Serves up a modest core of ripe pear and apple-
laced flavors, turning spicy with a light oak edge. **85**
1992: Young and tight, with a leafy green edge to the
pear, fig and spice notes. **86**

1991: Rich and focused, with complex honey, pear and butterscotch flavors that are deep and persistent. **91**

CLAIBORNE & CHURCHILL
San Luis Obispo County
F: 1983. **O:** Claiborne & Churchill Inc. **W:** Claiborne W. Thompson. **S:** None.

OVERALL	$10-17	★★

WINE RATINGS

Chardonnay Edna Valley MacGregor Vineyard	★★
Gewürztraminer Central Coast Dry Alsatian Style	★★
Pinot Noir Edna Valley MacGregor Vineyard	★★
Riesling Central Coast Dry Alsatian Style	★★

WINERY DATA
C: 4,000. **V:** 6 acres in Edna Valley. **G:** N/A. **P:** Riesling (Central Coast), Gewürztraminer (Central Coast), Chardonnay (Edna Valley), Pinot Noir (Edna Valley).

Claiborne Thompson and his wife, Fredericka Churchill, started their winery focusing on white wines made from Edna Valley and Central Coast grapes. Thompson was a college lecturer in old Norse and Scandinavian languages in Michigan before remarrying and moving to California, where he worked in the cellar at Edna Valley Vineyards. Early results with Chardonnay, Gewürztraminer and Riesling are mixed but encouraging. Both wines are made in a dry Alsatian style. Recent Pinot Noirs are better than early attempts. Production is 4,000 cases.

TASTING NOTES

CHARDONNAY EDNA VALLEY MACGREGOR VINEYARD (★★):
1993: Medium-bodied, but with enough pear, spice and lemony flavors to keep your interest, as the flavors fan out on the finish. **87**
1991: Firm in texture, offering floral flavors that are more reminiscent of Riesling than Chardonnay. The finish is spicy and solid. **80**

GEWÜRZTRAMINER CENTRAL COAST DRY ALSATIAN STYLE (★★): Showcases the grape's spicy, floral attributes, with lean citrus and grapefruit flavors.
1993: Crisp and austere, with a dry, spicy edge. **85**
1991: Generous floral aromas and lean grapefruit flavors make this dry wine interesting and enjoyable. Clean, focused and true to type. **82**

PINOT NOIR EDNA VALLEY MACGREGOR VINEYARD (★★): After modest attempts in 1990 and 1991, the 1992 MacGregor Vineyard is a marked improvement, with tart berry and cherry flavors framed by smoky, toasty oak.
1992: Strives for complexity with its smoky, toasty oak, and there are enough tart berry and cherry flavors underneath to hold your interest. **88**
1991: Pungent and earthy, but picks up ripe black cherry and spice flavors with a barnyard edge. **82**
1990: A lighter Pinot Noir with spicy strawberry, earth and nutmeg flavors. **78**

RIESLING CENTRAL COAST DRY ALSATIAN STYLE (★★):
1993: Sharply focused pear and peach fruit on a light, simple frame. Could use a smoother texture. **82**
1991: Softer and less racy than most dry Rieslings, with generous peach, apricot and almond aromas and flavors shaded by vanilla and spice notes on the finish. Unusual but appealing. **85**

CLAUDIA SPRINGS WINERY
Anderson Valley
F: 1989. **O:** C. & B. Klindt, C. & W. Hein. **W:** Bob Klindt. **S:** None.

OVERALL	$10-16	★★

WINE RATINGS

Chardonnay Anderson Valley	★★
Pinot Noir Anderson Valley	★★
Zinfandel Mendocino County	★★

WINERY DATA
C: 1,200. **V:** None. **G:** None. **P:** Chardonnay, Pinot Noir, Zinfandel (Mendocino County).

This 1,200-case winery in Anderson Valley produces Pinot Noir, Chardonnay and Zinfandel from purchased grapes. The 1991 Pinot Noir was appealing for its juicy plum, currant and cherry flavors, while the 1992 Zinfandel Mendocino was firm and tannic, laced with earthy berry flavors.

TASTING NOTES

CHARDONNAY ANDERSON VALLEY (★★):
1993: Well balanced, with vanilla-tinged oak flavors and ripe pear and spice notes. **83**

PINOT NOIR ANDERSON VALLEY (★★):
1991: Firm, ripe and juicy, with intense, complex plum, currant, cherry and spice flavors. **86**

ZINFANDEL MENDOCINO COUNTY (★★):
1992: Firm and tannic, with lean, earthy, tarry fruit flavors that turn dry. **81**

CLINE CELLARS
Carneros
F: 1982. **O:** Cline Cellars Inc. **W:** Matthew A. Cline. **S:** None.

OVERALL	$9-20	★★★

WINE RATINGS

Carignane Contra Costa County	★★
Merlot California	★
Mourvèdre Contra Costa County	★★★
Mourvèdre Contra Costa County Reserve	★★★
Muscat Contra Costa County	★
Rhône Blend Contra Costa County Côtes d'Oakley	★★
Rhône Blend Contra Costa County Oakley Cuvée	★★★
Sémillon California Barrel Fermented	★★
Syrah Contra Costa County	★★
Zinfandel Contra Costa County	★★★
Zinfandel Contra Costa County Big Break	★★★
Zinfandel Contra Costa County Bridgehead	★★★
Zinfandel Contra Costa County Reserve	★★★

WINERY DATA
C: 25,000. **V:** 251 acres in Carneros, Contra Costa County. **G:** Mourvèdre (140 acres), Carignane (20), Alicante Bouschet (5), Syrah (22), Viognier (6), Malbec (4), Roussanne (4), Cinsault (2), Zinfandel (45), Sémillon (3). **P:** Sauvignon Blanc, Sémillon (Sonoma Valley).

Brothers Fred and Matt Cline are grandsons of Valeriano Jacuzzi, founder of the device and company that bears his name. In 1982 Fred Cline decided to enter the wine business using family-owned vineyards in Oakley, a rural area in Contra Costa County. Not many people think of Oakley as wine country, but a variety of Rhône-style grapes grow exceptionally well there. The family's 251 acres are planted to a wide range of varieties, including Mourvèdre (140 acres), Syrah (22), Zinfandel (45) and Carignane (20), providing Bonny Doon, Joseph Phelps, Edmunds St. John and others with grapes. In 1982 the Clines purchased the old Fripo Winery in Oakley, but moved to Carneros in 1991, where the family bought a horse ranch and some 40 acres of vineyard across the highway from Viansa. Production is 25,000 cases, including many small lots of designer wines. The main lineup features a Côtes d'Oakley (a Carignane-Mourvèdre-Zinfandel blend), Oakley Cuvée (Mourvèdre and Carignane), Mourvèdre and Zinfandel, all from Contra Costa County.

TASTING NOTES

CARIGNANE CONTRA COSTA COUNTY (★★): Supple and elegant, with earthy raspberry flavors.
1991: Supple and elegant, with spicy earth and raspberry flavors that pick up a wild berry edge on the finish. Not too tannic. **83**
1990: Supple, generous and flavorful, with spicy plum, blackberry and vanilla aromas and flavors. Remains smooth and fruity through the lingering finish. **86**

MERLOT CALIFORNIA (★):
1989: An average-quality red that's medium-bodied and mostly vegetal in flavor. **75**

MOURVÈDRE CONTRA COSTA COUNTY (★★★), RESERVE (★★★): Marked by distinctive, medium-weight tar, earth and raspberry flavors and firm but supple tannins. A Reserve appears occasionally.

1989: Combines a forward, tarry raspberry flavor that's tight and focused with firm tannins and an earthy aftertaste. **85**

Reserve 1989: A clumsy wine with ripe plum and mint flavors, it comes across as disjointed and out of focus. **78**

Muscat Contra Costa County (★):
1990: Sweet, simple and a little sticky on the finish, with perfumed after-shave aromas and flavors that are none too subtle. **72**

Rhône Blend Contra Costa County Côtes d'Oakley (★★): Simple and sturdy, with lots of flavor; a good value. A blend of Carignane, Mourvèdre, Zinfandel and Alicante Bouschet.
1991: A simple, sturdy red with black cherry and charred oak aromas and flavors. **82**

Rhône Blend Contra Costa County Oakley Cuvée (★★★): Serves up an attractive range of complex flavors at a very affordable price.
1990: Rich and complex, it gushes with ripe currant, berry, spice and cedar flavors. **89**
1989: Brilliantly fresh, fruity and concentrated, offering all sorts of berry and cherry flavors. **88**
1988: Well knit and supple, with vivid black cherry, spice and blackberry flavors that turn elegant. **90**

Sémillon California Barrel Fermented (★★):
1990: Ripe, soft and generous, with tropical fruit aromas and flavors that pump up the volume through a generous finish. Has a tang of citrus on the finish to balance it. **86**

Syrah Contra Costa County (★★): Carries the same dusty berry flavors as the other wines, but so far is not as distinguished.
1991: Ripe and concentrated, with minty, meaty aromas and berry and cherry flavors. There are mild tannins on the finish. **84**
1990: Elegant and fruity, with earthy, tarry raspberry and spice notes. **84**

Zinfandel Contra Costa County (★★★): Rustic, with wild berry and raspberry flavors. Can be leathery.
1993: Well proportioned, with crisp berry and earthy notes that become muddled on the finish. Solid but lacking finesse. **85**

1992: Zesty, with spicy, chunky oregano flavors, but not much in the way of fruit. **84**
1991: A tight, solid, youthful Zin with currant and raspberry flavors that turn leathery and earthy. **84**
1990: A wonderful balance of hearty, earthy raspberry, spice and tar notes. **86**
1989: Big and generous, with a nice tension between the ripe blackberry and plum flavors. **86**
1987: Ripe, fruity and generous, with a deep color and nicely focused raspberry and cherry flavors. **89**

Zinfandel Contra Costa County Big Break (★★★):
1993: Distinct for its ripe chunky plum, berry and tarry flavors and chewy tannins. Best to cellar it short-term to soften. **87**

Zinfandel Contra Costa County Bridgehead (★★★):
1993: Appealing for its ripe, bright cherry and raspberry fruit that turns vibrant and complex, finishing with firm tannins. **87**

Zinfandel Contra Costa County Reserve (★★★): Vibrant, mouthfilling and well balanced, with plenty of that dusty berry flavor found in the Rhône reds.
1993: Dense and chewy, with an intense core of tar, plum, spice and nutmeg, turning complex and tannic on the finish. Needs short-term cellaring. **88**
1992: Bright and vibrant, a firm and compact Zin that's weighted toward tarry berry and jam notes. **89**
1991: Tight, firm and focused, offering rich currant and raspberry aromas and flavors that are lively. **86**
1990: A mouth filling red with a minty edge to the concentrated plum and berry flavors. **82**
1989: A bit tannic and oaky, but ripe berry and currant flavors emerge on the finish. **84**
1987: Classic, old-fashioned Zinfandel with briary aromas and ripe raspberry and cherry flavors. **87**

Cloninger Cellars
Monterey County
F: 1988. **O:** Loren Cloninger. **W:** John Estell. **S:** None.

OVERALL	$15	★★

WINE RATINGS

Cabernet Sauvignon Monterey County	★★
Chardonnay Monterey County	★★

WINERY DATA

C: 2,500. V: None. G: None. P: None.

A partnership of four families in Monterey, this 2,500-case winery focuses on Chardonnay and Cabernet, both of average quality so far. The 1990 Cabernet is smooth and supple, with ripe berry and currant flavors. The 1991 Chardonnay is coarse, with hard apple and lemon flavors.

TASTING NOTES

VARIOUS BOTTLINGS (★★):

Cabernet Sauvignon Monterey County 1990: Smooth, supple and generous, with a solid core of ripe berry and currant flavors. **82**

Chardonnay Monterey County 1991: Coarse, with a hard edge to the apple peel and lemon aromas and flavors. **79**

CLOS DU BOIS

Alexander Valley

F: 1974. O: The Wine Alliance. W: Margaret Davenport. S: None.

OVERALL	$8-21	★★★

WINE RATINGS

Cabernet Franc Alexander Valley Reserve L'Étranger	★★
Cabernet Sauvignon Alexander Valley	★★
Cabernet Sauvignon Alexander Valley Winemaker's Reserve	★★★
Cabernet Sauvignon Alexander Valley Briarcrest Vineyard	★★★
Cabernet Sauvignon Alexander Valley Marlstone Vineyard	★★★
Chardonnay Alexander Valley Barrel Fermented	★★
Chardonnay Dry Creek Valley Calcaire Vineyard	★★★
Chardonnay Dry Creek Valley Flintwood Vineyard	★★★
Gewürztraminer Alexander Valley Early Harvest	★★
Malbec Alexander Valley Reserve L'Étranger	★★
Merlot Sonoma County	★★★
Pinot Noir Sonoma County	★★
Sauvignon Blanc Sonoma County	★★★
Zinfandel Sonoma County	★★★

WINERY DATA

C: 400,000. V: 480 acres in Alexander Valley. G: Chardonnay (240 acres), Cabernet Sauvignon (100), Merlot (100), Other (40). P: Chardonnay, Cabernet Sauvignon, Merlot, Sauvignon Blanc, Sémillon (Alexander Valley), Chardonnay, Cabernet Sauvignon, Merlot (Dry Creek Valley).

With 480 acres in vineyards and a new, modern winery, Clos du Bois is a dominant force in Sonoma County wine. It was founded in 1974 by businessman Frank Woods and a group of investors who placed acquisition of vineyards ahead of building a winery. Winemaking was done out of a large warehouse in Healdsburg. In 1988 Clos du Bois was sold to Hiram Walker's Wine Alliance, which also owns Callaway and William Hill and markets Atlas Peak's wines.

Clos du Bois' 400,000-case output is focused on high-volume (and generally high-quality) wines. Its biggest sellers are Alexander Valley Cabernet (50,000 cases), Alexander Valley Barrel Fermented Chardonnay (150,000 cases), Sonoma County Merlot (80,000 cases) and Alexander Valley Barrel Fermented Sauvignon Blanc (50,000 cases). This lineup is augmented by smaller lots of vineyard-designated Chardonnays (Calcaire in Dry Creek Valley and Flintwood in Alexander Valley), a Briarcrest Vineyard Cabernet (Alexander Valley), a Marlstone Vineyard Bordeaux-style red (Alexander Valley), a Winemaker's Reserve Cabernet, a Gewürztraminer (Alexander Valley), a Pinot Noir (Sonoma County) and a Zinfandel (Sonoma County). All in all, it's a solid lineup, with the large-volume wines usually outshining the competition, but the high-end wines, while often very good, are not quite up to the best in their league. Still, the winery's substantial vineyard properties could yield better wines, and the winery seems to be moving in that direction.

TASTING NOTES

CABERNET FRANC ALEXANDER VALLEY RESERVE L'ÉTRANGER (★★): "The stranger"; not made every year.
1991: Tight and firm, with a narrow band of cherry, plum, herb and tobacco flavors. **85**

CABERNET SAUVIGNON ALEXANDER VALLEY (★★), WINEMAKER'S RESERVE (★★★): Supple and elegant, with fine balance, cherry flavors, light oak shadings and mild tannins. Ages well over the short term. Can include up to 25 percent Cabernet Franc. Reserve is worth watching
1991: Supple and elegant, easy to drink, with pretty currant, toast and berry flavors. **86**
1990: Surprisingly rich, concentrated and complex, offering ripe currant, berry and spice flavors and a nice dose of toasty oak. **87**
Winemaker's Reserve 1991: Intense and concentrated, with layers of complex currant, black cherry and herb flavors. Finishes with a nice touch of oak. **92**

CABERNET SAUVIGNON ALEXANDER VALLEY BRIARCREST VINEYARD (★★★): The darkest and most concentrated of the wines, this 100 percent Cabernet is marked by intense berry, cherry and mineral flavors and often chewy tannins. Very consistent, with good but not great aging capability. Worth watching.
1991: A pleasant, well balanced wine with pretty plum and currant flavors that stay with you. **87**
1990: Broad, ripe and supple, with complex currant, anise, cherry and mineral flavors and soft tannins. **88**
1989: An unusual red with strawberry and honey flavors and a sense of sweetness, perhaps from botrytis. **80**
1987: Pretty currant, vanilla, herb and spice flavors take on a chocolate edge, finishing with supple tannins. **88**
1986: Soft, velvety and broad, with appealing herbal and floral aromas and flavors. **87**
1985: Herbal and lavishly oaked, this is a good but unexciting 1985, as the flavors are muted by oak. **82**
1984: Exhibits ripe plum and cherry flavors and is laced with lavish oak and gritty tannins. **87**

CABERNET SAUVIGNON ALEXANDER VALLEY MARLSTONE VINEYARD (★★★): A blend of Cabernet, Merlot and Cabernet Franc, it is supple and elegant, well oaked and marked by herb and cherry flavors and fleshy tannins. Appealing early on, it too ages well but is never great. Has room for improvement, but worth watching.
1991: Shows ripe plum, cranberry, cherry and cedary oak flavors that are well focused. **88**
1990: Forward and fleshy, with lots of appealing berry and plum flavors dressed up with spicy oak. **88**
1989: Crisp, firm and elegant, with lively black cherry, anise, herb and currant flavors. **84**
1987: A tightly knit, harmonious wine with rich, intense currant, herb, spice, chocolate and berry flavors that are neatly woven together. **90**
1986: Soft and supple, with modest herb, vanilla and cherry flavors and hints of beets and dill on the finish. **85**
1985: Lavishly oaked, rich and supple, with pronounced herb and cedar notes and concentrated olive, black cherry, anise and spice flavors. **88**
1984: Offers rich, supple plum, anise, cherry and chocolate flavors flanked by firm tannins, ample oak and a measure of elegance. **89**

CHARDONNAY ALEXANDER VALLEY BARREL FERMENTED (★★): Given its 150,000-case volume it's a well made wine, although recent vintages have been leaner, crisper and less satisfying.
1993: Crisp and fruity, with a leafy edge to the appealing, slightly sappy apple and pear flavors. **84**
1992: A successful wine in a light, elegant style. Pear, vanilla, spice and toast notes are focused and bright. **84**

CHARDONNAY DRY CREEK VALLEY CALCAIRE VINEYARD (★★★): Consistent but rarely outstanding, made in a tight, firm style that accents pear, peach and spice notes.
1993: Crisp and clean, with an intense band of honey, pear and spice notes. **88**
1992: Strikes a nice balance between ripe pear, spice and citrus notes and toasty oak flavors. **89**
1991: Tight, firm and fruity, with spicy apple and melon notes. Well balanced, intense and lively. **88**
1990: Lean and simple, with earthy, smoky pear flavors, a crisp texture and a bit of astringency on the finish. **83**

CHARDONNAY DRY CREEK VALLEY FLINTWOOD VINEYARD (★★★): Bolder and riper than Calcaire, usually very well made, but variable.
1993: Marked by nut and honey notes; well oaked, with a slight toasty bitter edge that may dissipate with time. **86**

1991: Ripe and spicy, with pretty citrus and pear flavors that linger on the finish. **87**

1990: Light, watery and lacking concentration, with ripe pear and citrus notes that are tasty but lack persistence. **81**

GEWÜRZTRAMINER ALEXANDER VALLEY EARLY HARVEST (★★): Quality has dipped, and the most recent efforts are lighter and simpler.

1993: Soft and simple, with nice pear flavors echoing on the finish. **79**

MALBEC ALEXANDER VALLEY RESERVE L'ÉTRANGER (★★): Like the Cabernet Franc, this wine is made when the grapes warrant it, but it's less interesting than either the Briarcrest or Marlstone.

1991: Fruity and lively, a simple wine with grapey, slightly spicy flavors. **82**

1987: Wildly aromatic, with floral notes and warm, ripe, soft plum, currant, berry and cherry flavors that are bright and vivid. **87**

MERLOT SONOMA COUNTY (★★★): The most consistent and well balanced of the Clos du Bois reds, even though its case volume has doubled in recent years. Shows deft oak shadings and supple currant and berry flavors. Ages well for short- to mid-term.

1992: Ripe and intense with a tight, focused beam of wild berry and cherry flavors. **88**

1991: Supple, ripe and balanced, with pretty black cherry, currant, spice and cedary oak flavors. It's delicious, with richness, depth and length. **87**

1990: Combines fresh, ripe currant and cherry flavors with toasty oak shadings, finishing with gentle tannins. **87**

1989: Light in color and flavor, its modest cherry and cola notes compete with oak. **82**

1988: Leans toward the herbal, vegetal spectrum of Merlot, with mint, olive and vegetable notes. **81**

1987: Offers wonderful aromas and plenty of ripe plum, currant, smoke and spice flavors that are rich and elegant. **89**

PINOT NOIR SONOMA COUNTY (★★): A weak link, it's thin and vegetal with tealike flavors, and it's often overly mature on release. Can only improve.

1990: Delivers toasty oak flavors with modest depth and intensity. **82**

SAUVIGNON BLANC VARIOUS BOTTLINGS (★★★): Smooth and polished, well oaked, with a nice balance of herb, pear and spice notes.

Alexander Valley Barrel Fermented 1993: Simple and subdued, a pleasant wine with pear and modest spice flavors. **80**

Sonoma County 1994: Very fresh and lively, bright with apple and floral flavors. **84**

ZINFANDEL SONOMA COUNTY (★★★): The winery's newest wine features spicy pepper and wild berry flavors in an elegant, supple style.

1992: Firm, intense and lively, with spicy cherry, raspberry and cedary oak flavors. **87**

1991: Ripe, intense and spicy, with a core of elegant wild berry, black cherry, earth and anise flavors. **87**

CLOS DU VAL

Stags Leap District, Napa Valley
F: 1972. **O:** John Goelet & Bernard Portet. **W:** Krino Souilah. **S:** None.

OVERALL	$12-45	★★★

WINE RATINGS

Cabernet Sauvignon Napa Valley	★★★
Cabernet Sauvignon Stags Leap District	★★★
Cabernet Sauvignon Stags Leap District Reserve	★★★★
Chardonnay Carneros Carneros Estate	★★★
Merlot Stags Leap District	★★★
Pinot Noir Carneros	★★
Sémillon Stags Leap District	★★
Zinfandel Stags Leap District	★★★

WINERY DATA
C: 80,000. **V:** 255 acres in Stags Leap Distict, Carneros. **G:** Cabernet Sauvignon (89 acres), Merlot (25), Cabernet Franc (14), Pinot Noir (15), Zinfandel (10), Chardonnay (96), Sémillon (6). **P:** None.

In 1970 John Goelet, a wealthy New York businessman, hired Frenchman Bernard Portet to devise a strategy for starting a wine company in California. After traveling throughout California, Portet settled on a site in the Stags Leap District because it was cooler than areas farther up the valley and because local growers such as Nathan Fay (of Fay Vineyard) made excellent homemade Cabernets with more polish and finesse than many others in Napa. From the outset, Portet sought to establish Clos Du Val as a Bordeaux-style chateau known better for understated wines of complexity and finesse than for wines of intense varietal character. The initial focus was on Cabernet, followed by Merlot and Zinfandel and then Carneros-grown Chardonnay and Pinot Noir. Sémillon is also made in small quantites. The winery owns 255 acres, with 145 in the Stags Leap District and 110 in Carneros.

A Stags Leap Cabernet (14,000 cases) and Carneros Chardonnay (15,000 cases) are the major wines in the 80,000-case output. The winery's strength has always been reds, especially Cabernet. The Chardonnay is made in a crisp, lean style, while the Sémillon features rich fig and citrus notes. The Carneros Pinot Noir is the weak link. At times in its first 20 years, Clos Du Val Cabernets were considered part of the Napa elite, but the wines have all taken a turn toward lighter, simpler flavors. A 1994 shakeup of winery personnel seemed to acknowledge that the wines need more pizzazz.

TASTING NOTES

CABERNET SAUVIGNON NAPA VALLEY (★★★):
1990: Ripe with supple cherry, currant, herb and anise notes, finishing with firm earthy tannins. **87**
1989: Tough with chewy tannins and an earthy core of coffee, currant and spice notes. **82**

CABERNET SAUVIGNON STAGS LEAP DISTRICT (★★★): True to the house style, these wines are supple and polished, often rich and complex, but recent efforts are less satisfying. Ages well for up to seven years.
1990: Austere and tannic, with just a glimpse of fruit peeking through. **84**
1989: Lean and firm, with a narrow band of currant and cedar notes. **83**
1988: Tight, with currant, cherry and plum flavors and mild tannins. **86**
1987: Ripe and supple, with rich, generous plum, currant, black cherry, chocolate and spicy vanilla notes that are elegant and concentrated. **90**
1986: A spicy, exotic wine with a supple, fleshy texture, showcasing plum, currant, chocolate and cedar flavors. **91**
1985: Elegant and refined, with sharply focused black

cherry, currant and cedar flavors, finishing with fine tannins. **91**
1984: Ripe, open and generous, with firm currant and black cherry flavors and hints of tobacco on the finish. **92**

CABERNET SAUVIGNON STAGS LEAP DISTRICT RESERVE (★★★★): Clos Du Val's best wine, period. Deftly balanced, with a tight, narrow beam of supple currant and herb flavors, a nice touch of oak and firm but polished tannins. Can age well, but is best at six to ten years.
1990: Light for a 1990 Reserve; has elegant cherry, currant and earthy notes and a sense of finesse, but it lacks richess. **88**
1988: Firm and tight, it serves up focused currant and cedar flavors with a smooth, polished texture. **87**
1987: Dense, chewy and concentrated, a wine with depth and complexity, offering chocolate, earth, ripe plum and currant flavors. **92**
1985: Rich and elegant, tightly wound, with bright cherry, cedar, anise and plum flavors that are long and satisfying. Has excellent structure and depth. **94**
1982: Showing attractive bottle bouquet and some maturity and development, with cedar, chocolate, plum and tobacco flavors. It's a rich, tannic, full-bodied wine. **88**
1979: Mature now, it is supple and generous, with cedar, tobacco, cherry and currant flavors that pick up an anise edge. Past its prime but very appealing. **90**
1978: Ripe and intense, with vibrant currant, black cherry and cedar notes that are complex and concentrated. Still impressive for its depth of flavor. **91**

CHARDONNAY CARNEROS NAPA VALLEY CARNEROS ESTATE (★★★): Crisp, clean and lean, with tart, understated citrus, pear and apple notes and light oak. Good but never great.
Special Select 1993: Marked by earthy, funky flavors that override the ripe pear and buttery oak flavors. Tastes better on the aftertaste. **86**
1992: Ripe, with a band of simple pear, spice and light oak flavors of moderate depth. **85**
1991: Tight and youthful, with a green edge to the tart apple and pear flavors. **87**

MERLOT STAGS LEAP DISTRICT (★★★): Often rich and complex, marked by a supple texture and pure varietal expression, but variable.

1992: Tart and austere, with a lean band of wild berry and cherry, but the flavors build. **84**
1991: Complex and elegant, with ripe herb, currant and smoky oak flavors and a supple, silky texture. **89**
1990: Solid, full-bodied and fruity, with a slightly oaky or stemmy edge that toughens up the texture, but the berry and plum flavors are focused. **86**
1989: Supple and earthy but elegant, with focused currant, earth, cedar and herb flavors. **86**
1988: Wonderfully rich and complex, with deep, focused currant, black cherry, cedar and herb flavors that fan out. **90**
1987: Firm yet supple, with smoky currant, sage and oak flavors, but it's as tight as a drum. **85**
1986: Tight and firm, yet with a supple texture that lets the currant, herb and cedar flavors glide across the palate. **86**
1985: Harmonious, with ripe, complex black cherry, herb, currant and spice notes. **89**
1984: Graceful in its balance of ripe plum and currant flavors, it gains complexity with smoke, herb and anise notes. **87**

PINOT NOIR CARNEROS (★★): It's been a long time since this wine offered any drama. Recent bottlings have been light and thin.
1990: Light and thin, with a narrow band of tea, herb and fruit flavors. **78**
1989: A light, lean, austere wine that shows modest, earthy tea and herb flavors. **81**

SÉMILLON STAGS LEAP DISTRICT (★★):
1991: Goes beyond floral into florid, with aromas of rotting flowers making this a decadent, unpleasant Sémillon. **73**

ZINFANDEL STAGS LEAP DISTRICT (★★★): Like the Merlot, it's often solid, with deft balance and attractive flavors, but more variable of late.
1991: An earthy style with modest berry and spice flavors that are elegant. **84**
1990: Light and vegetal, with more herb than fruit flavors, very uncharacteristic of this winery. **74**
1989: Presents a fine balance of flavor and finesse, with tarry, earthy pepper and berry flavors and a sense of elegance. **87**

1988: Hearty and complex, combining ripe blackberry, tar, anise and earth notes. **85**
1987: Has Zinfandel character in spades, from the effusively fruity, herbal aromas to the slightly pickley flavor. **83**
1986: A bit tannic, but the spicy raspberry aromas ride through. **87**
1985: Big, tight, tannic and concentrated, with jammy currant and blackberry flavors. **90**

CLOS LA CHANCE
Santa Cruz Mountains
F: 1992. **O:** Bill & Brenda Murphy. **W:** Eddy Szyiewicz, Steve Lagier. **S:** None.

OVERALL	$18-20	★★★

WINE RATINGS
Cabernet Sauvignon	
Santa Cruz Mountains	★★★
Chardonnay Santa Cruz Mountains	★★★

WINERY DATA
C: 2,000. **V:** 0.75 acres in Santa Cruz Mountains. **G:** Chardonnay (0.75 acres). **P:** Chardonnay, Pinot Noir, Cabernet Sauvignon, Cabernet Franc, Merlot (Santa Cruz Mountains).

In 1992 Bill and Brenda Murphy founded this 2,000-case winery in Saratoga and focused on Chardonnay (1,350 cases) and lesser amounts of Cabernet and Pinot Noir, all carrying the Santa Cruz appellation. The 1992 Chardonnay hit a nice balance between toasty oak and ripe pear and apple notes.

TASTING NOTES

VARIOUS BOTTLINGS (★★★):
Cabernet Sauvignon Santa Cruz Mountains 1992: Good intensity and depth, with ripe cherry, currant and wild berry flavors that are focused and complex, finishing with firm tannins. **88**
Chardonnay Santa Cruz Mountains 1993: Ripe, smooth and creamy, with pear, hazelnut, and toasty buttery oak, turning rich and complex on the finish, where the flavors fan out. **89**
Chardonnay Santa Cruz Mountains 1992: Strikes a nice balance between spicy, toasty oak and ripe pear and

apple notes. Gains complexity on the finish, where the flavors are most interesting, fanning out with toasty pear notes. **87**

CLOS PEGASE
Calistoga, Napa Valley
F: 1984. **O:** Jan I. Shrem. **W:** John Quinones. **S:** None.

OVERALL	$18-25	★★★

WINE RATINGS

Cabernet Blend Napa Valley Hommage	★★
Cabernet Sauvignon Napa Valley	★★★
Chardonnay Carneros	★★★
Merlot Napa Valley	★★
Sauvignon Blanc Napa Valley	★★

WINERY DATA
C: 38,000. **V:** 247 acres in Napa Valley, Carneros.
G: Chardonnay (131 acres), Merlot (68), Cabernet Sauvignon (41), Cabernet Franc (3), Petite Verdot (4). **P:** None.

With Clos Pegase, Jan Shrem poured millions of dollars into the construction of one of Napa Valley's showcase wineries. The controversial post-modernist architect Michael Graves designed this elaborate estate. But after buying grapes for several years and making mainstream wines, Shrem learned that the key to great wines lies in obtaining great grapes. Often that means owning great vineyards, and Shrem has made a commitment to do that. He now owns 247 acres, including 205 in Carneros planted primarily to Chardonnay. Shrem also grows Cabernet (41 acres) and Merlot (68 acres). Recent efforts with Cabernet have shown more depth and complexity, but the Chardonnay, Merlot, Sauvignon Blanc and Hommage—a blend of Cabernet and Petite Sirah—are middle-of-the road wines.

TASTING NOTES

CABERNET BLEND NAPA VALLEY HOMMAGE (★★): A curious blend of Cabernet and smaller amounts of Merlot and Cabernet Franc. It's a rustic, tannic wine that so far lacks focus.
1991: A good wine with ripe currant and plum flavors, but it comes across as awkward and hollow in the middle, finishing with crisp tannins. **85**

1990: Crisp and harmonious, gaining some flesh and silkiness as it unfolds its cherry, prune and spice flavors. Approachable now, but better from 1997. **86**

CABERNET SAUVIGNON NAPA VALLEY (★★★): The superb, Bordeaux-style 1990 was a big breakthrough, but the 1991 is leaner and tannic, so quality is still variable.
1991: While this is a firmly austere and tannic wine, it's also quite flavorful, with layers of currant, cedar, spice and tobacco. **87**
1990: Firm and intense with solid cherry, currant and plum flavors that gently unfold into a spicy, concentrated wine. **91**
1987: Crisp and tart, not very rich in texture or flavor, with modest tobacco, currant and vanilla aromas and flavors. **82**
1986: Smells attractive, with lots of cherry, plum and herb flavors lingering on the finish. **88**
1985: Soft, buttery and elegant, a harmonious wine of modest proportions, with currant, plum and nutmeg flavors. **86**

CHARDONNAY CARNEROS (★★★): Medium-bodied, emphasizing ripe fruit and light oak.
Pegase Circle Reserve 1993: Marked by ripe fruit and spicy nuances, with spicy apple and pear notes that pick up a nectarine edge on the finish. **87**
1992: Strikes a nice balance between spicy vanilla-tinged oak and ripe pear flavor. **83**
1991: Lean, tight and concentrated, with pear and apple flavors at the core, shaded by earthy mineral flavors. **87**

MERLOT NAPA VALLEY (★★): Fails to excite. It's variable in quality, often tannic and lean.
1991: Tough and tannic, a chunky wine with a smoky, stalky edge to the modest cherry and tea flavors. **80**
1990: Elegant and focused, with rich, ripe currant, berry, spice and cedary oak flavors . **86**

SAUVIGNON BLANC NAPA VALLEY (★★):
1992: A toasty, oaky wine, leaning a little toward the bitter side. **79**

CLOVERDALE RANCH
This is a second label for Pellegrini Winery (see listing).

CODORNIU NAPA
Carneros
F: 1989. **O:** Codorniu S.A. **W:** Janet Pagano. **S:** None.

OVERALL	$15	★★★

WINE RATINGS
Sparkling Wine Napa Valley Brut Cuvée ★★★

WINERY DATA
C: 15,000. **V:** 170 acres in Carneros. **G:** Chardonnay (85 acres), Pinot Noir (85). **P:** Chardonnay (Carneros), Chardonnay (Napa Valley), Pinot Noir (Carneros), Pinot Noir (Napa Valley).

Spanish sparkling wine giant Codorniu, which has been making wine since 1872, followed the foreign investment trail to California in the late 1980s, settling in Carneros. The company built a handsome, modern winery into a hillside so as to blend in with the rural area. Codorniu owns 170 acres in Carneros, divided evenly between Chardonnay and Pinot Noir, and also buys those two varieties from growers in Carneros and Napa Valley. The non-vintage Brut Cuvée that made its debut in 1992 is a 50-50 blend of Chardonnay and Pinot Noir, with 75 percent of the grapes coming from Napa Valley. A Carneros Cuvée and Reserve are in the works. The winery plans to build from its current base of 15,000 cases to 160,000 cases. Winemaker and general manager Janet Pagano has a deft hand with *méthode champenoise* sparkling wine and owner Codorniu has a long-term commitment to excellence, making this a winery to watch.

TASTING NOTES

SPARKLING WINE NAPA VALLEY BRUT CUVÉE (★★★): Intense, elegant and well crafted, with complex pear, cream and spice notes.
NV: Intense and concentrated, with a band of ripe cherry, strawberry and spice notes and a lingering finish. **87**

B. R. COHN WINERY
Sonoma Valley
F: 1984. **O:** Bruce R. Cohn. **W:** Charlie Tolbert. **S:** None.

OVERALL	$12-32	★★★

WINE RATINGS

Cabernet Sauvignon	
Napa County Silver Label	★★
Cabernet Sauvignon Sonoma Valley	
Olive Hill Vineyard	★★★★
Chardonnay Carneros	★★★
Chardonnay Carneros	
Joseph Herman Vineyard Reserve	★★
Chardonnay Napa Valley Silver Label	★★
Merlot Napa Valley Silver Label	★★
Merlot Napa-Sonoma Counties	★★

WINERY DATA
C: 15,000. **V:** 61 acres in Sonoma Valley. **G:** Cabernet Sauvignon (48 acres), Merlot (13). **P:** Chardonnay (Sonoma Valley Carneros), Cabernet Sauvignon (Sonoma Valley), Merlot (Napa Valley).

Owner Bruce Cohn managed rock and roll bands in the 1970s and 1980s before buying the Olive Hill Vineyard in Sonoma Valley. For years the manager of the Doobie Brothers and Night Ranger sold grapes to Kenwood, Ravenswood and Gundlach Bundschu, but in 1984 Cohn began producing his own estate-grown Cabernet, with Helen Turley (Marcassin) overseeing winemaking. The wine features bold, ripe, seductive fruit flavors, toasty, buttery oak and supple tannins. The Olive Hill Cabernet remains the star, coming from Cohn's 61-acre vineyard. By the late 1980s, the winery had added Chardonnay, Merlot and a Silver Label Cabernet that carries a Napa appellation. Production is 15,000 cases, 4,000 of which is the Olive Hill Cabernet.

TASTING NOTES

CABERNET SAUVIGNON NAPA COUNTY SILVER LABEL (★★): Made from purchased grapes and bulk wines, this wine carries the Napa appellation and can be a good value. It's intense and compact, more rustic and tannic than the Olive Hill.
1989: Smooth and inviting, with supple currant and plum flavors. **82**
1988: Intense, with complex plum, currant, black cherry and herb notes. **87**

CABERNET SAUVIGNON SONOMA VALLEY OLIVE HILL VINEYARD (★★★★): Well oaked, supple and seductive, with ripe, juicy currant, anise and spice flavors, very appealing early on. Ages well, but is best on release.

1991: Ripe and juicy, with rich, supple black cherry, anise and cedary notes, finishing with fine tannins. **90**

1990: Ripe, smooth, rich and complex, with pretty, toasty, buttery oak and layers of cherry, currant, anise and plum flavors. **90**

1989: Smooth and generous, with ample plum, currant, vanilla and toast flavors. **84**

1988: Rich and oaky, with pretty, smooth, polished currant, herb, plum and vanilla flavors. **86**

1987: Well oaked, with rich, ripe, intense cherry and currant flavors that turn elegant, firm yet integrated tannins and a smoky, meaty edge. **92**

1986: Enormous concentration of rich, ripe fruit, combining power and grace with intense black cherry and currant flavors, flanked by spice and rich cedar notes from oak. **92**

1985: Complex and enticing, with bold, ripe, juicy currant, black cherry and anise flavors that fan out, finishing with firm tannins and subtle nuances. **94**

1984: Fully mature, with a decadent, earthy, dry tannic edge to the ripe currant and spicy berry flavors. Finishes with a dry, oaky aftertaste. **85**

CHARDONNAY CARNEROS (★★★): Intense and concentrated, but needs short-term cellaring to soften.

1993: Offers a range of citrus and apricot flavors, but turns a little earthy on the finish. **84**

1992: Rough and raw in texture and flavor, packed with peach aromas and apple and pear flavors, picking up oak on the finish. **87**

CHARDONNAY CARNEROS JOSEPH HERMAN VINEYARD RESERVE (★★):

1993: Tight with a narrow band of pear and green nectarine flavors. **82**

CHARDONNAY NAPA VALLEY SILVER LABEL (★★): Made from purchased grapes, it can be a good value.

1991: Creamy and complex, offering honey, pear and hazelnut flavors that are elegant and lively. **88**

MERLOT VARIOUS BOTTLINGS (★★): Quality and grape sources vary; it's solid if unexciting. Not in the same league as the Olive Hill Cabernet.

Napa Valley Silver Label 1989: Definitely herbal, with heavy dill and pine overtones to the basic currant flavor. **82**

Napa-Sonoma Counties 1992: Smooth and supple, but with gamy overtones to the basic berry flavors, turning tough on the finish. **80**

Napa-Sonoma Counties 1990: Youthful and lively, with distinctive raspberry and spice flavors. **84**

COLGIN
Napa Valley
F: 1992. **O:** Ann Colgin & Fred Schrader. **W:** Helen Turley. **S:** None.

OVERALL	$29	★★★

WINE RATINGS

Cabernet Sauvignon Napa Valley	
Herb Lamb Vineyard	★★★

WINERY DATA
C: 400. **V:** N/A. **G:** None. **P:** Cabernet Sauvignon (Howell Mountain).

Florida art dealers Ann Colgin and Fred Schrader use the Cabernet-only 7-acre Herb Lamb Vineyard, at the base of Howell Mountain to produce wines made by Helen Turley (Marcassin). Only 400 cases will be produced and sold via a winery mailing list. Early indications based on barrel samples are that the quality is very high. The first commercial release was the 1992 vintage. Worth watching.

TASTING NOTES

CABERNET SAUVIGNON NAPA VALLEY HERB LAMB VINEYARD (★★★):

1992: Dark, intense and compact, rich and focused, with pretty black cherry and currant fruit, finishing with a spicy anise edge and supple tannins. **92**

COLOMA GOLD
This is a second label for Gold Hill Vineyard (see listing).

CONCANNON VINEYARD

Livermore Valley
F: 1883. O: Tesla Vineyards, L.P. W: Tom Lane.
S: None.

OVERALL	$8-15	★★★

WINE RATINGS

Cabernet Blend	
Livermore Valley Assemblage	★
Cabernet Sauvignon Central Coast	
Selected Vineyards	★
Chardonnay Central Coast	
Selected Vineyards	★★
Chardonnay Livermore Valley Reserve	★★
Petite Sirah Livermore Valley	★★★
Petite Sirah Central Coast	
Selected Vineyards	★★★
Sauvignon Blanc Livermore Valley	★★
Sauvignon Blend	
Livermore Valley Assemblage	★★

WINERY DATA

C: 80,000. V: 194 acres in Livermore Valley. G: Petite Sirah (67 acres), Cabernet Sauvignon (42), Merlot (4), Muscat Canelli (4), Syrah (3), Sauvignon Blanc (54), Sémillon (12), Petite Verdot (4), Cabernet Franc (4). P: Chardonnay (Livermore Valley), Chardonnay, Petite Sirah, Cabernet Sauvignon, Riesling (Central Coast), Cabernet Franc (Napa Valley), Sangiovese (Napa Valley).

Irish entrepreneur James Concannon founded this winery in Livermore Valley in 1883, some 18 years after arriving in the U.S. at the age of 18. Concannon remained family-owned, producing a wide range of wines, until the 1980s, when ownership changed hands several times. The property passed from Distillers Co. to a partnership headed by Sergio Traverso and Deinhard, to Deinhard by itself, and now to Wente, which took over ownership in 1992. Through the years Concannon's wines have been consistently good but never great, its lone star being its dark, rich and peppery Petite Sirah, which ranks among the best in the state. The winery owns 194 acres in Livermore Valley and produces 80,000 cases, including Cabernet, Chardonnay, Petite Sirah and Sauvignon Blanc.

TASTING NOTES

CABERNET BLEND LIVERMORE VALLEY ASSEMBLAGE (★):
1991: Earthy and herbal, with murky, muddled, chalky fruit flavors. **78**

CABERNET SAUVIGNON VARIOUS BOTTLINGS (★): Lean and simple, usually marked by herb and bell pepper flavors.
Central Coast Selected Vineyards 1992: Supple and spicy, with an herb and cedar edge to the Cabernet flavors. **84**
Livermore Valley Concannon Estate Vineyard 1991: Smoke, herb and bell pepper flavors dominate. **79**

CHARDONNAY CENTRAL COAST SELECTED VINEYARDS (★★):
1993: Well crafted, striking a nice balance between the ripe pear and apple notes and light oak flavors, finishing with a grassy edge. **84**
1992: Nicely balanced between ripe, bright peach and apple flavors and light oak shadings. **86**
1991: This firm, spicy wine offers nice nutmeg and apple flavors that echo on the finish. **82**

CHARDONNAY LIVERMORE VALLEY RESERVE (★★): The Reserve is richer and fuller than the Central Coast bottling.
1993: Offers attractive ripe pear, apple and spice notes with light toasty oak shadings, turning complex on the finish. Well crafted. **87**
1991: Strikes a wonderful balance between intense, ripe fig and melon flavors and subtle oak notes. **89**

PETITE SIRAH CENTRAL COAST (★★★): This wine has been less satisfying, a touch earthier and less flavorful than the Livermore Valley bottlings.
1991: Rich and hearty, with peppery plum, spice and currant notes and mild tannins. **83**

PETITE SIRAH LIVERMORE VALLEY SELECTED VINEYARDS (★★★): The estate-bottled Petite Sirah is often excellent, rich, spicy, peppery and tannic, but quality varies.
1991: An earthy barnyard edge colors the basic black cherry flavor, and the finish is soft and short. **81**

SAUVIGNON BLANC LIVERMORE VALLEY (★★): Crisp and sturdy, with bright citrus and lemon flavors.
1992: Crisp and simple, a sturdy wine with bright, lemony flavors. **81**

SAUVIGNON BLEND LIVERMORE VALLEY ASSEMBLAGE (★★):
1993: Soft and appealing, with a touch of spice and honey sneaking in on the light finish. **80**

CONN CREEK WINERY
St. Helena, Napa Valley
F: 1973. **O:** Stimson Lane Vineyards & Estates. **W:** N/A. **S:** None.

OVERALL	$14-30	★★★

WINE RATINGS

Cabernet Blend	
Napa Valley Anthology	★★★
Cabernet Sauvignon Napa Valley	
Barrel Select	★★
Cabernet Sauvignon Napa Valley	
Limited Release	★★
Merlot Napa Valley Barrel Select	★★

WINERY DATA
C: 2,700. **V:** 3 acres in Napa Valley. **G:** Cabernet Sauvignon. **P:** Cabernet Sauvignon (Napa Valley), Merlot (Napa Valley), Cabernet Franc (Napa Valley), Sangiovese (Napa Valley).

Conn Creek Winery is in the midst of reestablishing itself. Bill Collins founded the winery in 1973 and produced a number of memorable Cabernets, particularly the magnificent 1973 from Steltzner Vineyard and a monumental 1974 from Eisele Vineyard. Both wines were produced by Lyncrest Winery before it went out of business. Collins expanded into Chardonnay and built a modern winery on the Silverado Trail in 1980, but by 1986 production outpaced sales and the winery was sold to Stimson Lane, a unit of U.S. Tobacco Co. Today Conn Creek's production is 2,700 cases, and the goal is to upgrade quality and rebuild the winery's reputation. The new Meritage-style red, Anthology, was tremendous in 1991. The rest of the lineup needs work.

TASTING NOTES

CABERNET BLEND NAPA VALLEY ANTHOLOGY (★★★): Amazingly complex and well crafted; the challenge now is to maintain quality. The Triomphe bottling is no longer produced.
1991: Complex and elegant, with supple, polished currant, black cherry, plum and vanilla flavors that fold together nicely, finishing with a long, full aftertaste and pretty fruit flavors. A wine of harmony and grace. Better after 1998 or 1999. **93**

CABERNET SAUVIGNON NAPA VALLEY (★★): Solid, middle-of-the-road Cabernets with cherry and currant flavors, but none of the extra dimensions you might expect. Various bottlings have been used over the years.
Barrel Select 1991: Firm and tight, with a narrow, compact band of cherry and currant flavors. Firmly tannic. **85**
Limited Release 1991: Well focused, with supple currant and black cherry flavors that turn smooth and polished, finishing with spice and anise notes. **88**
Barrel Select 1988: Firm and flavorful, with nicely focused black cherry and currant flavors, gaining a trace of tobacco on the finish. **84**
Barrel Select 1987: Modest cherry, tobacco and currant flavors that get richer on the finish, hinting at prune, cedar and spice. **87**
Reserve 1987: Crisp and elegant, with fine cedar and tobacco aromas and cherry, plum and currant flavors. **87**
Barrel Select 1985: An elegant, lean, fruity wine with ample black cherry and currant flavors. **84**

MERLOT NAPA VALLEY BARREL SELECT (★★): Crisp and lean, good but nothing more.
1990: A lighter style, but with ample cherry, currant and berry notes that turn smooth and supple. **87**
1989: Soft in texture, with earthy, smoky flavors that turn a bit gamy. **80**
1988: Offers bright, lively black cherry, currant, plum and spice flavors. **86**
1987: A strong minty quality dominates the rich, concentrated currant and cherry flavors. **87**

R. & J. COOK
Clarksburg
F: 1979. **O:** Roger & Joanne Cook. **W:** Steve Birtwhistle. **S:** Chestnut Hill.

OVERALL	$7-10	★★

WINE RATINGS

Merlot Clarksburg	★
Chestnut Hill Winery	
Cabernet Sauvignon California	
Coastal Cuvée	★★
Chestnut Hill Winery	
Chardonnay California	★★
Chestnut Hill Winery Merlot	
North Coast Coastal Cuvée	★

WINERY DATA
C: 60,000. V: 160 acres in Clarksburg. G: Merlot, Cabernet, Chardonnay, Petite Sirah. P: None.

Owners Roger and Joanne Cook come from farming backgrounds in the Delta region. In the late 1960s they began planting a vineyard in Clarksburg that now totals 160 acres. In 1979 they started making wine from their own grapes. Their product line of value-oriented varietals includes Cabernet, Chardonnay, Merlot and Petite Sirah, along with generic table wines. Production is about 60,000 cases. Chestnut Hill is a second label.

TASTING NOTES

VARIOUS BOTTLINGS :
Merlot Clarksburg 1989: Supple, firm and fruity, with pretty oak shadings adding complexity to the ripe plum and currant notes. **82**
Chestnut Hill Winery Cabernet Sauvignon California Coastal Cuvée 1991: Smells tired and a bit stale, and the fruit bears the mark of coastal Cabernet with its herbal and vegetal notes. Still, its texture is smooth and it picks up focused currant and berry flavors. **82**
Chestnut Hill Winery Cabernet Sauvignon California Coastal Cuvée 1990: An appealing, herbal wine that's ripe and robust. The dominant olive and cherry flavors have just enough smoke and spice nuances to take on a nice roasted character. Gutsy and flavorful. **84**
Chestnut Hill Winery Chardonnay California 1991: Simple, earthy, tired and woody, but drinkable. **74**
Chestnut Hill Winery Merlot North Coast Coastal Cuvée 1992: Chunky, with a narrow band of earthy currant and oak flavors. May be more forthcoming with time in the bottle. **78**
Chestnut Hill Winery Merlot North Coast Coastal Cuvée 1991: A tart wine with modest cherry and cranberry flavors. The color is deep and the aromas are appealing, but it's tough and thin. **78**

CORBETT CANYON VINEYARDS
Arroyo Grande, San Luis Obispo County
F: 1978. O: The Wine Group. W: John Clark. S: None.

OVERALL	$5-9	★★

WINE RATINGS

Cabernet Sauvignon	
California Coastal Classic	★★
Cabernet Sauvignon	
Napa Valley Reserve	★★
Chardonnay Central	
Coast Coastal Classic	★
Chardonnay Santa Barbara	
County Reserve	★★
Merlot California Coastal Classic	★
Pinot Noir Santa Barbara	
County Reserve	★
Sauvignon Blanc Central Coast	
Coastal Classic	★

WINERY DATA
C: 300,000. V: None. G: None. P: Cabernet Sauvignon (Napa Valley), Cabernet Sauvignon, Merlot (California), Chardonnay, Pinot Noir (Santa Barbara County).

The largest winery in San Luis Obispo County turns out 300,000 cases of mainstream varietals that range in quality from ordinary to good, even though the winery stretches to Napa Valley for some of its Cabernet. Corbett Canyon was founded in 1978 as Lawrence Winery by Jim Lawrence, who purchased grapes from throughout California. The winery struggled financially and was sold to Glenmore Distillers in 1982, and by 1988 the winery was back on the market, finally purchased by its current owner The Wine Group, which also owns the Franzia and Summit generic wine brands.

TASTING NOTES

CABERNET SAUVIGNON CALIFORNIA COASTAL CLASSIC (★★):
1991: Generous blackberry and currant flavors streak through this light, simple, fruity wine, and its finish is lively and refreshing. **80**

CABERNET SAUVIGNON NAPA VALLEY RESERVE (★★):
1991: A grapey Cabernet with a coarse, tannic edge. Packs intense flavors, but is short on finesse. **82**
1990: Deftly balanced and easy to drink, this full-flavored Cabernet is soft on tannins and long on fruit flavors. **84**
1989: Ripe and lush, with supple, focused cherry and currant flavors that pick up a tasty anise and spice aftertaste. Smooth, generous and not too tannic. **85**

CHARDONNAY CENTRAL COAST COASTAL CLASSIC (★):
1993: Light and fruity with a bit of a metallic edge to the peach and pear fruit. **80**
1992: Has an ashy, spoiled fruit edge to the flavors. **75**

CHARDONNAY SANTA BARBARA COUNTY RESERVE (★★):
1993: Simple and fruity, rather like canned pears in flavor, finishing fresh. **81**
1992: Moderate intensity and depth, with spice, pear and light oak shadings. **82**

MERLOT CALIFORNIA COASTAL CLASSIC (★):
1992: Simple and fruity, more like a light Zinfandel than a Merlot. **82**

PINOT NOIR SANTA BARBARA COUNTY RESERVE (★):
1992: Simple but pleasant, with light cherry, earth and spice notes. **82**

SAUVIGNON BLANC CENTRAL COAST COASTAL CLASSIC (★):
1992: Light, fragrant and appealing, showing spicy anise, pear and citrus aromas and flavors and a soft, flavorful finish. **82**

CORISON
Napa Valley
F: 1987. **O:** Cathy Corison. **W:** Cathy Corison. **S:** None.

OVERALL	$28	★★★

WINE RATINGS

Cabernet Sauvignon Napa Valley		★★★

WINERY DATA
C: 2,500. **V:** None. **G:** None. **P:** Cabernet Sauvignon (Napa Valley), Cabernet Franc (Napa Valley).

Long-time Napa Valley winemaker Cathy Corison worked at Freemark Abbey, Chappellet (for 10 years) and Yverdon before starting her Cabernet-only label with the 1987 vintage. Corison buys all her grapes from growers throughout Napa Valley (Vine Hill Ranch, Morisoli Vineyard, Garvey Vineyard) and believes her blended wine is more complex than any of the vineyards on their own. Production is 2,500 cases a year and quality has been high. Corison made the early Staglin Family Vineyards wines, but now works with just two other wineries, Fritz Maytag's York Creek Ranch (long a source of grapes for Ridge) and Long Meadow Ranch, another new venture in St. Helena.

TASTING NOTES

CABERNET SAUVIGNON NAPA VALLEY (★★★): Deftly balanced between ripe, supple currant flavors and toasty oak, a graceful and polished style. Drinks well early, with no track record for aging.
1991: Strives for complexity with its leathery coffee and currant flavors, but it turns dry and tannic on the finish. **89**
1990: Smooth and generous, with ripe currant, cherry and chocolate aromas and flavors, all of it holding together in elegance and harmony. **90**
1989: Firm and focused, with strong herbal aromas and flavors and a nice core of ripe currant and black cherry flavors. **86**
1988: Ripe and supple, with currant, plum and black cherry flavors and subtle oak shadings. **87**
1987: A seductive wine with toasty, buttery oak and solid, rich, complex black cherry, plum, currant and anise flavors that turn chunky and tannic. **90**

CORNERSTONE CELLARS
Napa Valley
F: 1991. **O:** Bruce Scotland. **W:** Bruce Scotland. **S:** None.

OVERALL	$33	★★★

WINE RATINGS

Cabernet Sauvignon Howell Mountain		★★★

WINERY DATA
C: 1,000. **V:** None. **G:** None. **P:** Cabernet Sauvignon (Howell Mountain).

Former wine retailer Bruce Scotland worked for several wineries before launching Cornerstone with the 1991 vintage. Through a friendship with Randy Dunn, Scotland buys Howell Mountain Cabernet from Beatty Ranch, one of Dunn's Cabernet sources, and makes his wines at Chappellet. The 1991 yielded 1,000 cases. It's ripe and generous, with focused currant, plum and black cherry flavors, tannic but polished, a good candidate for cellaring. Scotland is also involved with School House Pinot Noir and a new Pinot Noir brand called Vignette, using grapes from the highly regarded Rochioli Vineyard. Worth watching.

TASTING NOTES

CABERNET SAUVIGNON HOWELL MOUNTAIN (★★★):
1991: Ripe and generous, with tight, focused currant, plum and black cherry flavors that are plush and concentrated, finishing with a long, complex, tannic aftertaste. **93**

COSENTINO WINERY
Yountville, Napa Valley
F: 1980. O: Vintage Grapevine Inc. W: Mitch Cosentino. S: Crystal Valley Cellars.

OVERALL	$18-45	★★★

WINE RATINGS	
Cabernet Franc North Coast	★★
Cabernet Sauvignon Napa Valley	★★
Cabernet Sauvignon Napa Valley Reserve	★★★
Chardonnay Napa Valley	★★
Chardonnay Napa Valley The Sculptor	★★★
Meritage Red California The Poet	★★
Meritage Red Napa Valley M. Coz	★★★
Merlot Napa Valley	★★★
Pinot Noir Carneros	★★
Sauvignon Blend Napa Valley The Novelist	★★
Zinfandel Sonoma County The Zin	★★★
Crystal Valley Cellars Various Bottlings	NR

WINERY DATA
C: 15,000. V: 5 acres in Napa Valley. G: Merlot (4 acres), Cabernet Franc, Petite Sirah, Chardonnay, Viognier, Nebbiolo (0.5). P: Chardonnay, Cabernet Sauvignon, Cabernet Franc, Merlot, Pinot Noir, Sauvignon Blanc (Napa Valley), Cabernet Sauvignon, Nebbiolo (Sonoma Valley), Zinfandel, Sangiovese (Alexander Valley), Pinot Noir (Russian River Valley).

Mitch Cosentino's wines zigzag all over the course: they are occasionally brilliant, complex and well crafted, and almost as often are missing the ingredients that make his best wines so appealing. Cosentino is a former wine wholesaler who started a winery in Modesto, which he once could claim to be the second-largest winery in that Central Valley city (Gallo, the world's largest winery, is headquartered there too); he bottled wines there under the Crystal Valley Cellars brand. Beginning in the early 1980s, Cosentino began focusing on North Coast wines, and in 1990 he built a winery in Yountville next door to Mustard's Grill. Cosentino still buys virtually all his grapes, except for the 4 acres of Merlot planted near his winery. In 1992 Cosentino took on partners, and Vintage Grapevine Inc. is now the owner.

The 15,000-case product line is mostly small case lots and still a mix of exotic brand names: The Poet (a red Meritage), The Sculptor (a *sur lie* Chardonnay), The Zin (a Zin from Alexander Valley) and M. Coz (another Cabernet blend) that riled the owner of Chateau Cos-d'Estournel when it debuted as "Cos," leading to a legal dispute. Recent efforts show a marked improvement across the board, including smooth and polished Merlots and Pinot Noirs. In 1993 a Sangiovese, Il Tesoro, was produced, and occasionally a Sémillon called The Sem is made, along with The Novelist, a Sémillon-Sauvignon Blanc blend. Worth watching.

TASTING NOTES

CABERNET FRANC NORTH COAST (★★): Quality varies, as it often shows off the varietal's stalkiness.
1990: Firm and tight yet supple, with weedy herb and currant flavors that are light and pleasant. **83**
1989: Offers gamy barnyard aromas, sweet currant flavors and an earthy vanilla note. **78**
1988: Stalky, herbal, vegetal notes interrupt the currant and berry flavors. **80**

CABERNET SAUVIGNON VARIOUS BOTTLINGS (★★): At times it carries both the Napa Valley and Napa County appellations. It's a middle-of-the-road style that features ripe Cabernet flavors but no extra dimensions.
Napa County 1990: Ripe and jammy, with straightforward Cabernet flavors that show hints of plum, cherry and spicy oak. Tannic. **81**

Napa County 1989: Firm and balanced, with an attractive component of plum and currant that softens the tannic edge. **86**

Napa Valley 1992: Medium weight, with a pleasant band of currant, cherry and light oak shadings and mild tannins. **87**

Napa Valley 1991: Tight, with narrow, compact spice, herb, mineral and currant flavors that are well focused and tannic. **86**

Napa Valley 1990: Austere, with chewy currant and cedar notes, but the flavors hang on. **84**

Napa Valley Punched Cap Fermented 1992: Offers a pretty array of ripe plum and cherry-laced fruit before the tannins step in, leaving the finish with cedar and tobacco edge. Best after 1997. **88**

North Coast 1988: Crisp but harmonious and elegant, offering well focused currant, cherry and coffee flavors. **86**

North Coast 1987: Tough and tannic, with rich, ripe cherry and currant flavors. **80**

North Coast 1985: Light, with a velvety texture, smooth vanilla and cherry flavors, soft tannins and a lingering finish. **84**

CABERNET SAUVIGNON RESERVE VARIOUS BOTTLINGS (★★★): Improving of late, with ripe, complex fruit flavors and a sense of elegance missing in earlier efforts.

Napa Valley Reserve 1990: Very ripe, with a cherry jam and raspberry edge, it turns elegant and supple, with mild tannins. **87**

Napa Valley The Winemaster 1989: Modest but flavorful, with earthy plum and currant flavors. **80**

North Coast Reserve 1988: Crisp and austere, with modest cherry and plum flavors. **81**

North Coast Reserve 1987: Despite a tough, tannic edge, this is a ripe, rich, full-bodied wine with ample currant, cherry and plum flavors and a nice touch of herb. **86**

North Coast Reserve 1986: Rich and broad, with lush oak and dill notes to the black cherry and currant flavors. **88**

North Coast Reserve 1985: Simple but pleasant plum, cherry and spice notes. **81**

CHARDONNAY NAPA VALLEY (★★):

1993: Tart with a lemony edge to the pear and spice notes. Medium-weight and well balanced. **83**

1992: Ripe and creamy, with an elegant framework and spicy pear, vanilla, fig and melon notes. **86**

1991: Soft, broad and flavorful, with rich nutmeg, pear and vanilla flavors. **87**

CHARDONNAY NAPA VALLEY THE SCULPTOR (★★★): Solid, mainstream Napa Valley Chardonnay that's flavorful but uninspiring.

1993: Lean and trim, with an earthy edge to the ripe pear and apple flavors. **86**

1992: Crisp and fruity, a simple wine with appealing apple and nectarine flavors. **81**

1991: A highly stylistic wine showing lots of toasty, buttery oak flavors that have shades of pear, spice and vanilla. **85**

MERITAGE RED CALIFORNIA THE POET (★★): A Meritage red that's usually on the lean side.

1990: Tightly wound, with blunt, chunky cedar, currant and oaky flavors. Needs time; best after 1998. **86**

1989: Simple but pleasing, with firm oak and ripe currant flavors that gain a touch of spice. **81**

1988: Lean, dry and austere, with firm tannins and modestly intense plum, currant and cherry flavors. **85**

1987: Firmly textured and tightly wrapped in tannin, this has a solid but not very intense core of nutmeg, vanilla, currant and plum aromas. **85**

MERITAGE RED NAPA VALLEY M. COZ (★★★): Appears on the verge of greatness with recent efforts, well oaked and richly flavored, with past efforts more variable.

1991: Strikes a nice balance between ripe, spicy fruit flavors and buttery oak, but it needs time. **89**

1990: Elegant and richly fruity, with wonderful currant, black cherry, vanilla and cedar flavors gently unfolding, finishing with excellent length and fine tannins. **92**

1989: Has hints of seasoned oak and focused currant and black cherry aromas and flavors, finishing with a touch of anise and plenty of tannins. **88**

1988: Tight and firm, with ripe, rich, concentrated black cherry, currant, raspberry, chocolate and vanilla flavors. **87**

MERLOT NAPA VALLEY (★★★): Wines of grace and finesse, with polished tannins and rich flavors.

1992: Supple, elegant and complex, it serves up pretty, silky currant, coffee, vanilla and spice notes that glide across the palate. **89**

1991: Tight and firm, with cedary cherry flavors that are wrapped in drying tannins. **77**

1990: Tight and woody, with cedary oak notes showing over the ripe currant and black cherry flavors. **84**

1989: Lean and earthy, with currant and cherry flavors peeking through. **83**

PINOT NOIR CARNEROS (★★): Uneven quality through the years, but the 1992 is excellent, ripe and generous. Unfined and unfiltered.

1993: Modest herb, cola and fruit flavors are framed by toasty, buttery oak. **84**

Punched Cap Fermented 1993: Marked by herb, oak and cola flavors, enough black cherry and plum flavor comes through to hold your interest, but the herbs hang with you. **86**

1992: Ripe, generous and broad, showing lots of plum, berry and oak character. Impressive. **89**

1991: Austere and tannic, with spicy, minty cherry flavors that turn to cola on the finish. **82**

PINOT NOIR VARIOUS BOTTLINGS (★★):

Napa Valley 1990: Lavishly oaked, with pretty spice and butter notes and beefy Pinot Noir flavors that are interesting, but could use more fruit. **83**

Sonoma County 1990: Oaky, firm and tannic, a big Pinot Noir with broad earth, plum, anise and toasty, buttery oak nuances. **83**

Sonoma County 1989: Light and elegant, with complex aromas of cherry, spice, brown sugar and oak and a trace of tea and spice. **82**

SAUVIGNON BLEND NAPA VALLEY THE NOVELIST (★★): Another middle-of-the-road wine that's often too oaky.

1992: Strives for complexity with its overt oaky notes, but you have to hunt for the true Sauvignon Blanc flavors. **85**

ZINFANDEL SONOMA COUNTY THE ZIN (★★★): A solid wine, very ripe and jammy, with the tannins in check.

1993: Earthy and tannic, with chewy, peppery berry and plum flavors that pack a wallop. Short-term cellaring may give it a little finesse. **87**

1992: A pretty and harmonious wine with toasty oak notes adding complexity and richness to the core of spicy cherry and raspberry flavors. **88**

1991: Ripe and generous, with rich, spicy raspberry, cherry, plum and oak shadings. Packs in lots of flavor. **89**

1990: Very ripe and jammy, with intense, focused raspberry, plum and cherry flavors that are rich and plush. **88**

CRYSTAL VALLEY CELLARS VARIOUS BOTTLINGS (NR):

Cabernet Sauvignon Napa Valley Unfined 1989: Ripe and spicy, with a firm, chewy, tannic edge and a leathery flavor that borders on horsey. Fine if you don't mind a barnyard edge to your Cabernet. **80**

Pinot Blanc Napa Valley 1991: An earthy, almost decadent wine that's dark and smoky, offering little charm but plenty of character. **77**

Sauvignon Blanc Napa Valley 1992: Simple and a bit austere, a citrusy wine with herb and vanilla overtones. **82**

CÔTES DE SONOMA

This is a second label for Pellegrini Winery (see listing).

COTTONWOOD CANYON

San Luis Obispo County

F: 1988. **O:** Norman J. Beko. **W:** Norman J. Beko. **S:** None.

OVERALL	$20-38	★★

WINE RATINGS

Chardonnay Santa Barbara County	★★
Chardonnay Santa Barbara County Barrel Select	★★
Pinot Noir Santa Barbara County	★★
Pinot Noir Santa Barbara County Barrel Select	★★

WINERY DATA

C: 7,000. **V:** 53 acres in Santa Barbara County. **G:** Chardonnay (44 acres), Pinot Noir (9). **P:** Cabernet Sauvignon (Paso Robles), Pinot Noir (Santa Barbara).

In 1988 Norman Beko shifted careers from wine wholesaler and distributor to winemaker with the founding of Cottonwood Canyon. With 53 acres of vineyards (44 of Chardonnay), Beko focuses on Santa Barbara County Chardonnay (6,000 cases) and Pinot Noir (600 to 1,000 cases). So far the wines have been variable in quality, although the 1989 Chardonnay Barrel Select (90 cases) is fat, ripe and oily, with intense tropical fruit flavors. The 1989 Pinot Noir is solid, but the 1990 is earthy and vegetal.

TASTING NOTES

CHARDONNAY SANTA BARBARA COUNTY (★★), BARREL SELECT (★★):
1991: Extremely dark color and sherrylike aromas and flavors just turn woody on the finish. **70**
1990: The honey, fig and pineapple aromas and flavors are more reminiscent of Sauternes than Chardonnay. The finish is ripe and solid. Tasty, if unusual in character. **80**
Barrel Select 1990: Looks and smells more like a Sauternes than a Chardonnay, with honey, tobacco and fig flavors. Strange, but drinkable and definitely distinctive. **79**
Barrel Select 1989: Fat, ripe and oily, with intense tropical fruit flavors and loads of rich banana, honey, pear and butter notes that are long and full. A delicious mouthful of wine. **90**

PINOT NOIR SANTA BARBARA COUNTY (★★), BARREL SELECT (★★):
1990: Earthy and vegetal, with chili pepper and spicy tomato flavors and a cherry note on the finish. **79**
1989: A rich and exotic wine that offers smoky, toasty notes and ripe cherry, earth and cola flavors. Finishes with complexity and depth. Not too tannic. **86**
Barrel Select 1989: Rough around the edges, but has a core of ripe, focused plum, cherry, oak and spice notes. **82**

H. COTURRI AND SONS
Sonoma Valley
F: 1979. **O:** The Coturri Family. **W:** Tony Coturri. **S:** None.

OVERALL	$15-20	★★

WINE RATINGS

Zinfandel Sonoma Valley	
Chauvet Vineyards	★★

WINERY DATA
C: 3,000. **V:** N/A. **G:** N/A. **P:** N/A.

Few wineries have divided critics as Coturri has. This 3,000-case winery in Glen Ellen was among the first—if not the first—to take organic farming and winemaking to the limit, using everything from organic fertilizers to wild yeast fermentations. Over the years a number of bizarre wines have emerged, marked by earthy, funky, sometimes dirty and volatile flavors, but then along comes a wine like the 1990 Zinfandel Chauvet Vineyards, a ripe, hot, sweet and raisiny sort of junior Port which, while extreme in style, has no defects. Cabernet, Chardonnay and Sauvignon Blanc are also part of the product mix. Although I have not been a big fan in the past, recent efforts have given me cause to reexamine the entire lineup. It appears as if the winemaking has improved.

COUNTERPOINT
This is a second label for Laurel Glen Vineyard (see listing).

THOMAS COYNE WINERY
Livermore Valley
F: 1990. **O:** Thomas S. & Emilie A. Coyne. **W:** Thomas S. Coyne. **S:** Thomas Coyne Wines.

OVERALL	$12-15	★★

WINE RATINGS

Merlot El Dorado County	
Quartz Hill Vineyard	★★
Merlot Sonoma County	★★

WINERY DATA
C: 1,000. **V:** None. **G:** None. **P:** Merlot (El Dorado, Sonoma), Merlot (Livermore Valley), Cabernet Sauvignon (Livermore Valley), Cabernet Sauvignon (Sonoma), Rhône Type (Contra Costa County).

This is a new winery in Livermore that with the 1990 vintage introduced two Merlots, one from Sonoma and a second from Quartz Hill Vineyard in El Dorado County. The Sonoma bottling is dense and chewy, with attractive herb, cherry and cedar notes, while the Quartz Hill bottling features bright cranberry and cherry notes. A Rhône-style red is also produced. Production is just about at 1,000 cases.

TASTING NOTES

MERLOT VARIOUS BOTTLINGS (★★):
El Dorado County Quartz Hill Vineyard 1990: Lively and fruity, with bright cranberry, black cherry, anise and tar notes that are tasty. **84**
Sonoma County 1990: A dense, chewy, rich Merlot showing herb, cherry and cedar notes that turn oaky and a bit earthy on the finish. Balanced and tannic. **84**

ROBERT CRAIG WINE CELLARS

Napa Valley

F: 1992. O: Robert Craig. W: Robert Craig. S: None.

Overall	$25	★★★
WINE RATINGS		
Cabernet Howell Mountain		★★★
Cabernet Mount Veeder		★★★
Affinity Cabernet Blend		★★★

WINERY DATA
C: 3,000. V: 7 acres in Napa Valley. G: Cabernet Sauvignon. P: Cabernet Sauvignon (Howell Mountain, Mount Veeder) and Merlot (Howell Mountain, Mount Veeder, Carneros).

Robert Craig was one of William Hill's partners in the 1970s when Hill began developing mountain vineyard products. From 1981 through 1990 he was general manager for The Hess Collection and in 1992 he started his own wine brand, focusing on Cabernet and Cabernet blends, using grapes from Howell Mountain (from Dennis John's White Cottage Road Vineyard) and Mount Veeder (PymRay Vineyards owned by comedian/actor Robin Williams). In 1995, he bought a 7-acre vineyard north of Napa, which is also planted to Cabernet. The first wines from the 1992 vintage were made in a lean, austere style. The 1993s were similar but showing a shade more depth and richness. Affinity is a Bordeaux-style blend, made from Rutherford and Carneros-grown grapes.

CRESTON VINEYARDS & WINERY

Paso Robles

F: 1981. O: Creston Manor Associates Ltd. W: Victor H. Roberts. S: None.

Overall	$9-17	★★
WINE RATINGS		
Cabernet Sauvignon Paso Robles		★★
Cabernet Sauvignon Paso Robles		
Winemaker's Selection		★★
Chardonnay Paso Robles		★
Merlot Paso Robles		★★
Pinot Noir Paso Robles		★
White Table Wine Paso Robles		
Chevrier Blanc		★★
Zinfandel Paso Robles		★★

WINERY DATA
C: 40,000. V: 121 acres in Paso Robles. G: Cabernet Sauvignon (33 acres), Cabernet Franc (1), Sémillon (5), Chenin Blanc (3), Zinfandel (17), Chardonnay (28), Sauvignon Blanc (18), Merlot (2), Pinot Noir (14). P: Chardonnay, Pinot Noir, Merlot, Zinfandel (Paso Robles).

Creston was founded by a group of Los Angeles investors headed by Christina Crawford, daughter of Joan Crawford. The 121-acre vineyard is high atop a remote hill at 1,700 feet of elevation. Ownership changed hands in 1987, with Larry and Stephanie Rosenblum now in control and doing business as Creston Manor Associates Ltd., with Alex Trebek (of "Jeopardy" fame) as a partner. Production is 40,000 cases, including Cabernet from Paso Robles and San Luis Obispo, Chardonnay, Merlot, Pinot Noir and Zinfandel. The wines are uniformly well made but none stands out or excites. The Cabernet, including a Winemaker's Selection, offers spicy currant and herb flavors, bordering on vegetal. The Chardonnay is inconsistent, ranging from overly oaky to light and simple. The Merlot is oaky too, but with appealing cherry and berry notes. The 1992 Pinot Noir is an improvement, with cherry and spice notes folded together nicely with the oak flavors. The 1990 Zinfandel is rich and distinctive, but the 1991 is lean and simple.

TASTING NOTES

CABERNET SAUVIGNON VARIOUS BOTTLINGS (★★):
Paso Robles 1989: Young and firm, with intense, bright cherry and currant notes that turn tannic on the finish, where it gains an herbal edge. **85**
Paso Robles Winemaker's Selection 1989: Elegant and oaky, with supple herb and currant notes. Fits the Creston style, but not as rich and complex as earlier bottlings. **83**

Paso Robles Winemaker's Selection 1988: Firm and fruity, with generous raspberry and vanilla flavors, turning toward herb on the finish, which becomes tough and astringent. **80**

San Luis Obispo County 1990: Firm and intense, with focused cranberry flavors that bow to the tannins. **81**

CHARDONNAY PASO ROBLES (★):
1992: Relies a little too heavily on oak for its flavor and structure, which gives it a woody, astringent edge. **77**
1991: Soft and round, but pulls itself together with nice, spicy apple and honey aromas and flavors. **83**

MERLOT PASO ROBLES (★★):
1991: Smooth and simple with cedary oak, toast and spicy currant flavors of modest proportion. **84**

PINOT NOIR PASO ROBLES (★):
1992: Shows off toasty, buttery oak and delivers enough spice, cherry and herb notes to keep it interesting. **83**
1991: Has a decent core of plum and cherry flavors, but turns simple and limey on the finish. Drinkable, but there are far better wines available. **74**

WHITE TABLE WINE PASO ROBLES CHEVRIER BLANC (★★):
1994: Smooth and lavishly perfumed, a brightly appealing wine that shows a nice touch of pear on the finish. **86**

ZINFANDEL PASO ROBLES (★★):
1991: Lean, earthy and oaky, showing modest berry and cherry flavors that don't quite stand up to the wood and earthiness. **78**
1990: Ripe and rich, with distinctive plum, spice and cherry aromas and flavors that stay with you on the finish. **87**

CRICHTON HALL
Napa Valley
F: 1983. O: Richard & Judith Crichton. W: Richard Crichton. S: None.

OVERALL	$18	★★

WINE RATINGS
Chardonnay Napa Valley	★★

WINERY DATA
C: 6,000. V: 17 acres in Napa Valley. G: Chardonnay.
P: Merlot, Cabernet Sauvignon, Pinot Noir (Napa Valley).

Owners Judith and Richard Crichton produce 6,000 cases of Chardonnay, Merlot and Pinot Noir from their 17-acre vineyard. The star is their Chardonnay; the 1990 is well oaked and chunky, with spicy pear, almond and citrus notes.

TASTING NOTES

CHARDONNAY NAPA VALLEY (★★):
1990: Rich, smooth and toasty, with ripe pear, almond and citrus flavors that are thick and bold. Could use a little more finesse on the aftertaste. **84**

CRONIN VINEYARDS
Woodside, San Mateo County
F: 1980. O: Duane & Nancy Cronin. W: Duane Cronin. S: Portola Hills.

OVERALL	$10-22	★★★

WINE RATINGS
Cabernet Blend California Joe's Cuvée	★★
Cabernet Sauvignon Santa Cruz Mountains	★★
Cabernet Sauvignon Stags Leap District Robinson Vineyard	★★★
Chardonnay Alexander Valley Stuhlmuller Vineyard	★★★
Chardonnay California Nancy's Cuvée	NR
Chardonnay Monterey County Ventana Vineyard	★★
Chardonnay Napa Valley	★★★
Chardonnay Santa Cruz Mountains	★★★★
Meritage Red Stags Leap District Robinson Vineyard Concerto	★★
Pinot Noir Santa Cruz Mountains Peter Martin Ray Vineyard	★★
Sauvignon Blend Napa Valley	★★★

WINERY DATA

C: 2,000. V: 1 acre in Santa Cruz Mountains. G: Chardonnay.
P: Chardonnay, Cabernet Sauvignon (Santa Cruz Mountains),
Chardonnay (Alexander Valley), Chardonnay (Napa Valley),
Cabernet Sauvignon (Stags Leap District).

Former Silicon Valley computer programmer Duane Cronin began making wine in the basement of his home in Woodside (south of San Francisco) as a sideline, initially focusing on small lots of Chardonnay. Cronin Vineyards is still small-scale, making 2,000 cases. Chardonnay is still its strength, although the Cabernet can be exceptional and on rare occasions the Sauvignon Blanc has been rich and buttery. The Pinot Noir from Peter Martin Ray Vineyard in the Santa Cruz Mountains is the only wine that has failed to soar like his Chardonnays, as it was on the lean, thin side in 1988, 1990 and 1991.

Cronin purchases grapes from key appellations throughout California and utilizes Burgundian vinification techniques. In most years he produces three to four Chardonnays, the best coming from the Santa Cruz Mountains, but bottlings from Ventana in Monterey and Stuhlmuller in Alexander Valley often rival it in quality. The Cabernets listed below typically come from Robinson Vineyard in the Stags Leap District and from the Santa Cruz Mountains, a good study in comparing appellations as each is reflective of its source. Concerto is the new Meritage blend that's mostly Cabernet and made entirely from Robinson Vineyard in Stags Leap District. It replaces the Cabernet in the lineup.

TASTING NOTES

CABERNET BLEND CALIFORNIA JOE'S CUVÉE (★★):
1990: Heavy-handed, with cedary oak flavors, but it picks up hints of currant, green olive, herb and tobacco. **86**

CABERNET SAUVIGNON SANTA CRUZ MOUNTAINS (★★):
Quality varies in this cooler climate. The wine is often ripe and exotic, with cherry and chocolate flavors, but can be tannic and leathery.
1990: Lean and earthy, with currant and cherry flavors struggling to break loose. **84**
1989: Crisp and sharply focused, offering a nice range of cedar, currant and coffee flavors. **88**

1988: A fruity, exotic wine with ripe black cherry, anise and toast flavors on a structure that's not overly tannic. **83**
1987: Intense and flavorful, with heaps of spicy currant, herb and sour cherry flavors and a crisp finish. **84**

CABERNET SAUVIGNON STAGS LEAP DISTRICT ROBINSON VINEYARD (★★★):
Variable too, with recent wines tasting lean and tough, but from 1986 to 1988 they showed polish and finesse.
1990: Lean and a bit green, with firm tannins and a tight oak overlay, but enough currant and cherry flavors emerge; patience required. **82**
1989: Shows off ripe, tart, bright black cherry and currant flavors up front, but turns austere and thins out on the finish. **85**
1988: Plenty of supple cherry and currant flavors in this appealing wine. **86**
1987: Offers bright, pure currant and cherry flavors accented with nutmeg, cedar and vanilla. **89**
1986: Alluring, with wild berry and currant flavors, turning supple, with fine tannins and fruit echoing on the finish. **88**

CHARDONNAY ALEXANDER VALLEY STUHLMULLER VINEYARD (★★★):
1993: Spicy with a cedary oak edge to the modest pear and citrus notes. Well balanced for the fruit it has. **85**
1992: Pleasantly balanced between ripe, spicy pear flavors and light, buttery oak shadings. **88**
1990: Tight and focused, with rich, complex honey, pear and toast flavors that are intense and lively. **88**

CHARDONNAY CALIFORNIA NANCY'S CUVÉE (NR):
1991: Crisp and intense, with spicy pear and apple flavors. **82**

CHARDONNAY MONTEREY COUNTY VENTANA VINEYARD (★★):
1992: Well oaked but smooth and creamy, with a cidery edge to the ripe pear and apple flavors. **86**
1991: An earthy wine displaying toasty mineral flavors that turn astringent. **83**
1990: Intense and buttery, with ripe, round pear, citrus and melon flavors that hang together nicely. **88**

CHARDONNAY NAPA VALLEY (★★★):

1993: Ripe and spicy, with apple, pear, honey and toasty oak flavors of modest proportions. **85**

1992: Intense and earthy, with firm pear, nutmeg and spice notes that pick up on the finish. **88**

1991: Provides interesting, spicy wood, honey, pear and butterscotch flavors that turn rich and tasty. **87**

1990: Ripe, round and generous, smooth and creamy, with bold pear, honey, butter and vanilla flavors. **90**

CHARDONNAY SANTA CRUZ MOUNTAINS (★★★★):

Intense and earthy, all well oaked and marked by rich, complex flavors, finishing with elegance and grace.

1993: Pleasant enough, but lacking richness and depth, with spicy pear, toasty oak and light honey notes. Medium-bodied. **84**

1992: Tight and compact, with an earthy edge to the ripe pear and oak notes, turning complex on the finish. **89**

1991: Bold, ripe and generous, with tiers of spice, honey, pear and toasty oaky flavors that turn elegant. **91**

1990: Showing maturity in color and flavor, this is a big, toasty wine with honey, nut and pear flavors that are rich and smoky. **91**

MERITAGE RED STAGS LEAP DISTRICT ROBINSON VINEYARD CONCERTO (★★):

1991: Firm and tannic, with ripe cherry and currant flavors flanked by anise and cedary oak. **87**

PINOT NOIR SANTA CRUZ MOUNTAINS PETER MARTIN RAY VINEYARD (★★):

Thin and earthy so far, lacking generosity and flavor.

1991: Lean, thin and tannic, with a narrow beam of cherry, earth and juniper berry flavors. **81**

1990: Mature, with earth and tar flavors that pick up a mushroom edge on the finish. **83**

1988: Ripe, bold and exotic, with tiers of plum, currant, herb and rhubarb flavors. **81**

SAUVIGNON BLEND NAPA VALLEY (★★★):

1992: Very ripe and buttery, a spicy wine with mouthfilling pear and oak flavors and a touch of mineral. **88**

1991: Crisp in texture and ripe in flavor, with overtones of vanilla, spice and butter to go with the pineapple and herb flavors. The finish is firm and spicy. **84**

CRYSTAL VALLEY CELLARS

This is a second label of Cosentino Winery (see listing).

CULBERTSON WINERY
Temecula
F: 1981. **O:** John M. & Sally B. Thornton. **W:** Jon C. McPherson. **S:** None.

OVERALL	$10-20	★★

WINE RATINGS

Sparkling Wines	★★

WINERY DATA
C: 35,000. **V:** 6 acres in Temecula. **G:** N/A. **P:** N/A.

The stately Culbertson Winery is the one to see in Temecula, with its fine restaurant and tasting room. Founder John Culbertson owned Martech International in Houston, providing diving and exploration services for the oil industry, when he took up home winemaking. Eventually he purchased an avocado ranch in northern San Diego County where he made his first commercial wine. In 1981 he began to make *méthode champenoise* sparkling wine, and in 1988 he built a winery in Temecula next door to Callaway, with production rising to 80,000 cases, all from purchased grapes. Progress over the first decade was steady, with recent offerings showing more depth and flavor.

In 1991 John and Sally Thornton took over ownership from Culbertson following a dispute among partners. Production is now 35,000 cases, with sparkling wine still the main focus. A Blanc de Noir (16,000 cases) and a Brut NV (16,000 cases) are the largest sellers. Table wine, including Cabernet, Chardonnay, Muscat Canelli, Pinot Noir, Sangiovese and a Rhône-style red are in the works, the former two carrying a California appellation, the latter made from South Coast grapes. A Thornton label for vintage-dated sparkling wines is in the works.

TASTING NOTES

VARIOUS BOTTLINGS (★★):
Artist Series Cuvée de Frontignan 1994: Sweet, with just enough ripe pear and apple flavors to ward off the slight bitterness that creeps in on the finish. **78**

Artist Series Cuvée Rouge 1994: The dark ruby color may throw you, but this is a sparkling wine for red wine drinkers, with grape, cherry, strawberry and plum notes. **84**

RICHARD CUNEO

This is a second label for Sebastiani Vineyards (see listing).

CUTLER CELLARS
Sonoma Valley
F: 1990. **O:** The Cutler Cellar Inc. **W:** Lance Cutler.
S: None.

OVERALL	$19-20	★★★

WINE RATINGS

Cabernet Sauvignon	
Sonoma Valley Batto Ranch	★★★
Meritage Red Sonoma Valley Satyre	★★★

WINERY DATA
C: 1,500. **V:** None. **G:** None. **P:** Cabernet Sauvignon, Merlot, Cabernet Franc (Sonoma Valley).

Longtime Gundlach Bundschu winemaker and author Lance Cutler (a.k.a. Jake Lorenzo) makes small lots of Cabernet, including a bottling from Batto Ranch in Sonoma and a blend called Satyre. For years Gundlach Bundschu bottled a very fine Batto Ranch Cabernet, but by the mid-1980s the winery began to focus more on estate-grown wines and Cutler began using the grapes in 1985 for his 100 percent Cabernet. Satyre is a blend of Cabernet, Merlot and Cabernet Franc. Production is about 1,500 cases.

TASTING NOTES

CABERNET SAUVIGNON SONOMA VALLEY BATTO RANCH (★★★): Consistently very elegant and refined, from an excellent vineyard and showing a deft hand at winemaking; reaches its peak at about five years.
1990: Ripe and fruity, with an herb and bell pepper edge to the currant and cherry flavors. **88**
1987: Mature, with generous blackberry, oak and herb flavors that glide smoothly across the palate. **88**
1986: Ripe, rich, deep and intense, with currant, cherry and plum flavors, firm tannins and spicy oak nuances. **86**

1985: Very firm and rich, with smoky, tarry currant and black cherry accents, elegantly packed into a generous frame. **91**

MERITAGE RED SONOMA VALLEY SATYRE (★★★): A Cabernet blend of finesse and complexity, with tiers of flavor and supple tannins. Appealing on release.
1987: Ripe and plush, with tiers of herb, plum, anise and cherry flavors that are deep, rich and complex. **89**
1986: Ripe and full-bodied, with herb, currant and cedar flavors, a lush texture, firm tannins and a spicy, woody finish. **85**

CUVAISON WINERY
Calistoga, Napa Valley
F: 1969. **O:** Schmidheiny Family. **W:** John Thacher.
S: Calistoga Vineyards.

OVERALL	$15-28	★★★★

WINE RATINGS

Cabernet Sauvignon Napa Valley	★★★
Chardonnay Carneros	★★★★
Chardonnay Carneros Reserve	★★★★
Merlot Carneros	★★★
Pinot Noir Carneros	★★★
Calistoga Vineyards	
Chardonnay Napa Valley	★★

WINERY DATA
C: 50,000. **V:** 289 acres in Carneros. **G:** Chardonnay (191 acres), Pinot Noir (62), Merlot (35). **P:** Cabernet Sauvignon, Cabernet Franc (Napa Valley).

Cuvaison makes all its wines well, a few exceptionally well and none poorly, and appears on the verge of making truly fantastic wines. Since its founding in 1970, the winery has gone through a succession of owners and styles. Its early wines, made by Philip Togni, were eccentric to a fault, with Cabernet and Zinfandels marked by high extract, high alcohol, heavy oak and gritty tannins, and Chardonnays that were bold and assertive, reflective of the style of the era. Since John Thacher took over in 1983, quality has been on a steady upswing and production has leveled off at 50,000 cases. The Schmidheiny family of Switzerland bought Cuvaison in 1986 and invested heavily in vineyards, the most ambitious being a

289-acre estate in Carneros where Cuvaison grows all its Chardonnay (more than 40,000 cases, including a Reserve), Merlot and Pinot Noir. Cabernet is the only grape that's purchased. All of the wines share a distinctive house style, with ripe, focused, supple fruit flavors, good intensity, fine balance and a sense of harmony and finesse. Each of the varietals also is made under a second label, Calistoga Vineyards.

TASTING NOTES

CABERNET SAUVIGNON NAPA VALLEY (★★★): Typically firm and intense, with a solid core of currant, herb and oak flavors, usually well balanced and capable of aging up to 10 years. Vintages from the late 1970s and early 1980s were tannic monsters that didn't come around.
1991: Firm and intense, with a core of ripe, rich currant, cherry and spicy oak flavors. **88**
1990: Tight and a little on the tough side, with a beam of cherry, currant and berry flavors pushing through on the finish, picking up a trace of tobacco. **88**
1989: Austere and hollow, with currant, smoke and toast flavors that turn dry and tannic. **82**
1988: Lean and crisp, with simple plum, spice and tobacco notes. **82**
1987: Has a great sense of balance and proportion, with layers of rich, intense cherry, chocolate, currant and spice flavors. **89**
1986: Combines deep, rich, concentrated black currant and cherry aromas and flavors with delicate herb and oak nuances, a firm structure, crisp acidity and firm tannins. **90**
1985: Complex, with toasty oak flavors to complement the ripe plum and cherry notes. The tannins are fine and elegant. **88**
1984: Rich and complex, with cedar, currant and spicy cherry flavors that are lean and well focused. **88**

CHARDONNAY CARNEROS (★★★★): Deftly balanced, complex and intense, with rich fruit and pretty oak shadings.
1993: Pleasantly fruity with ripe, medium-weight apple, pear, spice and citrus notes that stay focused. **86**
1992: Plenty of bright pear and spicy pineapple flavors that are moderately rich and intense, but the wood flavors stand out. **89**
1991: Crisp and lean, with tart apple and pineapple flavors that turn elegant and harmonious. **89**

1990: Tart and crisp, with pretty tropical fruit flavors that turn smooth and elegant. Has a creamy texture. **88**

CHARDONNAY CARNEROS RESERVE (★★★★): Deeper than the regular bottling, these are elegant wines that improve for three to four years.
1993: Well mannered, ripe and fruity with pear, citrus and light oak shadings that fold together nicely on the finish. **88**
1992: Tight with a firm band of citrus, pear, spice and light oak shadings, this vibrant young wine will benefit from short-term cellaring. **88**
1990: Straightforward, ripe and rich, with honey, pear and fig notes that are intense and focused. **88**

MERLOT CARNEROS (★★★): All Carneros-grown, despite some bottlings' Napa Valley appellation, it's a full bodied wine that's well balanced, with herb, cherry and spice flavors, but in recent vintages shows a green, cedary wood edge that's less appealing. The 1984 remains stunning.
1991: A touch on the green side, with cedary wood and herb flavors and just enough currant flavor to stand up to it. **85**
1990: Tight and herbal, with a green edge to the plum, tea and currant flavors, finishing with mild tannins. **88**
1989: Pleasant, with herb, olive and strawberry flavors, but lacking complexity. **84**
1988: A delicate wine that's bright and lively, with crisp currant and cherry notes and fine, subtle tannins. **87**
1987: Sharply focused, with tight cherry, currant and earth notes and fine but firm tannins. **86**
1986: Tight, firm and focused, with earthy black cherry and currant notes and fine tannins. **86**
1985: Lean and crisp, with ripe cherry, earth and currant notes and fine tannins. **85**
1984: Impressive for its richness and depth, with cherry, currant, anise and earth flavors that offer harmony and complexity, soft, thick tannins and toasty oak on the finish. **92**

PINOT NOIR CARNEROS (★★★): Shows delicacy and finesse in a medium-weight style; could use a little more richness.
1992: Spicy, with a smoky oak edge to the cherry and plum flavors. Thins out on the finish. **85**

1991: Ripe and spicy, with fresh, crisp and elegant black cherry, nutmeg and wild berry notes that turn delicate. **87**

Calistoga Vineyards Chardonnay Napa Valley (★★): **1992:** A fruity style with ripe apple, pear and melon notes that finishes with a cedary edge. **82**

Dalla Valle Vineyards
Oakville, Napa Valley
F: 1986. **O:** Oakville Hills Cellar Inc. **W:** Heidi Peterson Barrett, Richard Peterson. **S:** Casa Dalla Valle.

Overall	$30-75	★★★★★

Wine Ratings

Cabernet Blend Napa Valley Maya	★★★★★
Cabernet Sauvignon Napa Valley	★★★★★

Winery Data
C: 5,000. **V:** 25 acres in Napa Valley. **G:** Cabernet Sauvignon (21 acres), Cabernet Franc (2), Merlot (1), Sangiovese (1). **P:** Cabernet Franc (Napa Valley).

Dalla Valle is an exciting new winery that has hit full stride with its two mountain-grown reds, a rich and dense Cabernet Sauvignon and a vineyard-designated blend of Cabernet and Cabernet Franc called Maya. Maya is the daughter of owners Gustave and Naoko Dalla Valle, who moved to Napa in 1982 and built a spectacular Mediterranean-style home and winery in the hills above the Silverado Trail in the Rutherford district. These are indeed very distinctive wines, grown on a sloping hillside with reddish-brown soil, and while it remains to be seen how well the wines age, right now they are impressive for their flavor and style. From the 25-acre estate vineyard, Cabernet is the main wine, with 2,200 cases; Maya is a 500-case brand from a 4-acre plot. Pietre Rosse is a non-vintage blend of Tuscan Sangiovese and Napa Sangiovese, but so far it has failed to impress me as much as some other Sangioveses. Credit Heidi Peterson Barrett, the winemaker, with recent refinements.

Tasting Notes

Cabernet Blend Napa Valley Maya (★★★★★): Uncommonly dark and potent, with tiers of flavor and firm tannins. Seems well built to age, but it's enjoyable now. The 1992 was $75 a bottle.
1992: Beautifully balanced, dark, rich and supple, with brilliant, complex currant, plum, herb and mineral flavors that run deep and concentrated, turning elegant. **94**
1991: Bold and ripe, showing delicious currant, black cherry and plum flavors before the firm tannins kick in. This tightly wound wine finishes on the short side, but cellaring until 1998 should make it more appealing. **90**
1990: Dark and inky, with ripe, rich, complex currant, plum, cherry and spice flavors that turn smoky and buttery on the finish, with mineral, herb and coffee notes. **90**
1989: Smooth and polished, with generous, spicy vanilla aromas and black cherry, plum and currant flavors that linger on the solid finish. Has lots of personality. **91**
1988: Rich and elegant, with tight currant, plum and cherry flavors that hang in there on the finish, where the tannins firm up. **86**

Cabernet Sauvignon Napa Valley (★★★★★): Early vintages were hard and austere and didn't undergo malolactic fermentation, but the wine's full potential is realized with the 1990, a deep, dense and richly flavored wine.
1992: Dark, dense and chewy, with ripe currant, mineral and cedary oak flavors and a tannic finish. **92**
1991: An exotic wine with ripe, spicy black cherry and wild berry flavors that add an intriguing flavor profile. Well balanced, with richness, depth and concentration, finishing with firm tannins. **91**
1990: Deep, dense and delicious, bursting with plum, currant, chocolate and spice aromas and flavors, generous and concentrated, an elegant wine with power. **93**
1989: Crisp and intense, a lean, austere 1989 that offers a tight, compact core of cherry and currant flavors. **84**
1988: Tight and closed, with a nice core of plum and currant flavors. **88**
1987: Shows polish and finesse, with complex, concentrated currant, mint and mineral flavors. **89**
1986: Hard, tannic, austere, even stemmy in texture, a tough wine to warm up to, with firm currant, herb and beefy flavors. **84**

DE LOACH VINEYARDS
Russian River Valley
F: 1975. O: Cecil & Christine De Loach. W: Max Gasiewicz. S: None.

OVERALL	$9-25	★★★

WINE RATINGS

Cabernet Sauvignon Russian River Valley	★★
Chardonnay Russian River Valley	★★★★
Chardonnay Russian River Valley O.F.S.	★★★★★
Chardonnay Sonoma County Sonoma Cuvée	★★
Fumé Blanc Russian River Valley	★★
Gewürztraminer Russian River Valley Early Harvest	★★
Gewürztraminer Russian River Valley Late Harvest	★★★
Merlot Russian River Valley	★★★
Pinot Noir Russian River Valley	★★
Pinot Noir Russian River Valley O.F.S.	★★
Sauvignon Blanc Russian River Valley Dry	★★
Zinfandel Russian River Valley	★★★
Zinfandel Russian River Valley Barbieri Ranch	★★★
Zinfandel Russian River Valley Papera Ranch	★★★
Zinfandel Russian River Valley Pelletti Ranch	★★★

WINERY DATA
C: 110,000. V: 272 acres in Russian River Valley.
G: Chardonnay (50 acres), Pinot Noir (21), Zinfandel (119), Cabernet Sauvignon (41), Sauvignon Blanc (4), Merlot (18), Gewürztraminer (13), Cabernet Franc (5). P: Chardonnay (Russian River Valley), Sauvignon Blanc (Russian River Valley).

With its varied wine lineup, De Loach Vineyards has become one of California's steadiest performers. Owners Christine and Cecil De Loach founded their winery in 1975, six years after they bought a property on Olivet Lane in the Russian River area that had 24 acres planted to Zinfandel from as far back as 1905. Two years later they added another 27-acre vineyard nearby, where the winery now sits. By 1975 Cecil had taken an early retirement from the San Francisco Fire Department and wine became the couple's full-time profession.

All of the wines are well made, but Chardonnay has been the star, an uncommonly rich, elegant and flavorful wine that ranks among California's best. White Zinfandel, accounting for 28,000 of the winery's 110,000 cases, helps pay the bills. Chardonnay, with nearly 30,000 cases (including the O.F.S. bottling) is the other big line, and the product mix also includes smaller case lots of Cabernet, Gewürztraminer, Merlot, Pinot Noir, Sauvignon and Fumé Blanc, and a series of vineyard-designated Zinfandels. The best wines carry the O.F.S. designation, for Our Finest Selection. The Cabernet and Pinot Noir are for me the least interesting. The De Loaches now farm 272 acres, which lets them control most of their grapes.

TASTING NOTES

CABERNET SAUVIGNON RUSSIAN RIVER VALLEY (★★): Both 1990 and 1991 are lean, tannic and on the green side, in years when almost everyone got their Cabernets ripe.
1991: Lean, with an herbal, green bean edge to the tannic Cabernet flavors. **78**
1990: Young and tight, with an earthy, oaky edge to the currant and raspberry flavors. Needs time for the tannins to soften, but it may always be earthy. **84**

CHARDONNAY RUSSIAN RIVER VALLEY (★★★★): Rich and creamy, with a wide spectrum of tropical fruit flavors. Ages well, but is best early on.
1992: Smooth and focused, a lively wine with a polished texture, offering lots of nice apple and pear flavors that persist impressively on the finish. **88**
1991: Complex and lively, with intense flavors that zing across the palate, showing layers of pear, honey, grapefruit and spice. **88**

CHARDONNAY RUSSIAN RIVER VALLEY O.F.S. (★★★★★): Close in style to the regular bottling, but the O.F.S. carries a bit more oak and is more opulent.
1992: Brimming with fresh, ripe, juicy tropical fruit, spicy pear and tart peach flavors, this is another delicious wine that shows off the winery's opulent, elegant style. **91**
1991: Vibrant, lively and complex, with grapefruit, pear and nectarine aromas and flavors that are crisp and focused through the spicy finish. **91**

1990: Ripe and intense, with crisp, clean, sharply focused grapefruit and pear flavors that are fresh and lively. **90**

CHARDONNAY SONOMA COUNTY SONOMA CUVÉE (★★): **1992:** Firm and fruity, with a solid core of nectarine and spice shining through to the finish. **85**

GEWÜRZTRAMINER RUSSIAN RIVER VALLEY EARLY HARVEST (★★): **1992:** Crisp and flavorful, with focused grapefruit and rose petal aromas and flavors coursing through the wine to a dry, lively finish. **88**

GEWÜRZTRAMINER RUSSIAN RIVER VALLEY LATE HARVEST (★★★): Sweet and rich without being cloying. **1991:** Very sweet and spicy, with a strong resin flavor running through the dominant honey and apricot characteristics. **86**

MERLOT RUSSIAN RIVER VALLEY (★★★): Variable in quality, often a bit green, but the 1992 was wonderful, rich and complex.
1992: Ripe and supple, with pretty herb, wild berry, chocolate and vanilla flavors that unfold with a silky smooth texture. **89**
1991: The distinctive herb, olive and vegetal flavors are quite pungent, dominating the flavor spectrum. **78**

PINOT NOIR RUSSIAN RIVER VALLEY (★★), O.F.S. (★★): Lean and rustic, with green, tea and herb notes, not in the same league as the best from this area.
1992: A rustic wine with tart, earthy, gamy Pinot Noir flavors that are tightly reined in. **82**
1991: Green, herbal flavors characterize this lean, spicy wine. **74**
O.F.S. 1990: Broad and flavorful, offering tea, herb, cola and cherry flavors that pick up an earthy, leathery edge. **82**

SAUVIGNON BLANC RUSSIAN RIVER VALLEY (★★): Bottled as either Sauvignon Blanc or Fumé Blanc, these wines have strong varietal flavors that stray into vegetal and floral areas, but the wine generally lacks focus.
Fumé Blanc Russian River Valley 1993: Lean in texture, a floral wine with a sweet edge to the modest pear flavors. **81**

Sauvignon Blanc Russian River Valley Dry 1993: Strongly varietal, with herbal, vegetal flavors that keep playing on the finish. **84**

ZINFANDEL RUSSIAN RIVER VALLEY (★★★): **1992:** Effusively fruity, brimming with fresh, ripe cherry, raspberry, cedar and anise flavors. Classic Zinfandel. **89**
1991: Ripe, racy and rambunctious, this wild berry and herb-scented wine has distinctive flavors. **83**
1990: Ripe, rich, polished and robust, with plenty of berry, plum and vanilla flavors and hints of toast and anise. **89**
1989: A lighter wine, but there are peppery raspberry and strawberry flavors. **82**
1988: The drying oak overpowers the simple pepper and raspberry flavors. **78**
1987: Bursting with blackberry and raspberry flavors and a seasoning of black pepper, all on a framework of tart, lean intensity. **90**
1986: Black pepper aromas and flavors give this a Rhône-like character, with appealing floral and raspberry flavors. **88**

ZINFANDEL RUSSIAN RIVER VALLEY BARBIERI RANCH (★★★): **1991:** Intense and concentrated, but a gamy flavor runs through this wine. **82**
1990: Youthful, exuberant flavors lean toward wild berry, cherry and smoky oak, with a touch of gaminess. **82**

ZINFANDEL RUSSIAN RIVER VALLEY PAPERA RANCH (★★★): **1991:** Lean, tart and earthy but also well focused, with austere, peppery raspberry, cherry and plum notes. **85**
1990: Earthy flavors flit in and out as the ripe plum and cherry notes try to get focused on the palate. **81**

ZINFANDEL RUSSIAN RIVER VALLEY PELLETTI RANCH (★★★): **1991:** Tart, crisp and lively, with a narrow, focused band of rich raspberry and wild berry flavors. **86**
1990: Tight and tannic, with a solid core of blackberry and black cherry aromas and flavors. **87**

DE LORIMIER WINERY
Alexander Valley
F: 1985. O: Alfred & Sandra de Lorimier. W: Donald H. Frazer. S: None.

OVERALL	$10-20	★★

WINE RATINGS

Chardonnay Alexander Valley Clonal Select	★★
Chardonnay Alexander Valley Prism	★★
Meritage Red Alexander Valley Mosaic	★★
Meritage White Alexander Valley Spectrum	★★

WINERY DATA
C: 5,500. V: 54 acres in Alexander Valley. G: Chardonnay (14 acres), Sauvignon Blanc (9), Sémillon (4), Cabernet Sauvignon (7), Merlot (15), Cabernet Franc (3), Malbec (0.6), Petite Verdot (0.5), Sangiovese (0.7). P: None.

This winery, owned by surgeon Alfred de Lorimier, is near Geyserville at the northern end of Alexander Valley, where a 54-acre vineyard is the source of grapes for a Chardonnay called Prism, a Meritage red called Mosaic and a Sauvignon Blanc blend called Spectrum. Chardonnay stands above the other two wines, showing more depth and flavor. Mosaic has been marked by gamy, vegetal flavors that are more complex than appealing. Spectrum is lean and thin, with citrus and apple notes. Production is in the 5,500-case range with plans to grow to 25,000 by the year 2000 or so.

TASTING NOTES

CHARDONNAY ALEXANDER VALLEY CLONAL SELECT (★★):
1992: Intense and oaky, but the ripe pear, apple and fig flavors emerge, finishing with a complex range of toasty oak flavors. **87**

CHARDONNAY ALEXANDER VALLEY PRISM (★★):
1991: Lean and crisp, with tart pear and lemon flavors, but also an earthy edge. **84**
1990: Spicy, floral and perfumed notes are attractive on the nose, but they are less interesting on the palate. **80**

MERITAGE RED ALEXANDER VALLEY MOSAIC (★★):
1991: Well balanced, with a supple core of plum and cherry offsetting the cedary oak and mild tannins. Young and vibrant, it can stand cellaring into 1997. **85**
1990: Lean and simple, with plum and vegetal notes that turn thin and bland. **77**
1988: An earthy, gamy wine that strives for complexity but comes across as muddled. The herb, currant and cedar flavors taste blurred instead of focused and lively. **81**

MERITAGE WHITE ALEXANDER VALLEY SPECTRUM (★★):
1992: Delicate with understated fig, melon, cigar box and butterscotch flavors that fold together nicely. **89**
1991: Lean and herbal, with a greenish edge to the citrus and apple flavors. **82**

DECOY
This is a second label for Duckhorn Vineyards (see listing).

DEER PARK WINERY
Howell Mountain
F: 1979. O: David & Carol Clark, Lila & Robert Knapp. W: David Clark. S: None.

OVERALL	$14-24	★★

WINE RATINGS

Cabernet Sauvignon Howell Mountain Beatty Ranch Reserve	★★
Petite Sirah Howell Mountain	★★
Zinfandel Howell Mountain Beatty Ranch	★★
Zinfandel Howell Mountain Beatty Ranch Reserve	★★

WINERY DATA
C: 3,000. V: 3.5 acres in Napa Valley. G: Zinfandel (1 acre), Petite Sirah (0.5), Sauvignon Blanc (2). P: Zinfandel (Howell Mountain), Petite Sirah (Howell Mountain), Cabernet Sauvignon (Howell Mountain).

This beautiful old stone winery dates to 1891, making it one of the oldest on Howell Mountain. Owners David and Carol Clark and Lila and Robert Knapp refurbished it in time for the 1979 vintage and they've produced up to 3,500 cases of mostly red wines, including hearty, high-extract Zinfandel, Petite Sirah and Cabernet. My limited experiences with the Chardonnays have not been memorable. The winery owns 3.5 acres of vines, most of it planted to Sauvignon Blanc, relying on Beatty Ranch for its Zinfandel and on Randy Dunn, who now owns the former Park-Muscadine Vineyard, for old-vine Petite Sirah.

TASTING NOTES

CABERNET SAUVIGNON HOWELL MOUNTAIN BEATTY RANCH RESERVE (★★): Recent efforts show improvement, with a distinctive spicy, peppery edge to the full-throttle fruit flavors, and strong tannins.

1990: Distinctive for its spicy pepper flavors and austere tannins, this ripe and full-bodied Cabernet turns lean and crisp on the finish. Cellar until 1997 or 1998 to allow it to soften. Even then it will be on the tannic side. **88**

1988: Firm and leathery, with a tight core of berry, cherry, cedar and oak flavors. **87**

PETITE SIRAH HOWELL MOUNTAIN (★★):
1987: Crisp in texture, with firm tannins and lively acidity supporting a range of flavors that include berry, plum, chocolate and spice. **82**

ZINFANDEL HOWELL MOUNTAIN BEATTY RANCH (★★), RESERVE (★★): Less to my liking than others; the austerity of the fruit fails to stand up to the tannins.

1990: Tight, with earthy pepper and tar notes and just a hint of prune flavor. **81**

1988: Mature for an '88, but aging well, showing pepper, caramel and raspberry flavors. **83**

Reserve 1987: Still firm and tannic but generous, with ripe blackberry, cherry and tar flavors. **85**

DEHLINGER WINERY
Russian River Valley
F: 1975. **O:** Tom Dehlinger. **W:** Tom Dehlinger. **S:** None.

OVERALL	$15-25	★★★★

WINE RATINGS

Cabernet Franc Russian River Valley	★
Cabernet Sauvignon Russian River Valley	★★
Chardonnay Russian River Valley	★★★
Chardonnay Russian River Valley Montrachet Cuvée	★★★★
Pinot Noir Russian River Valley	★★★
Pinot Noir Russian River Valley Reserve	★★★★
Syrah Russian River Valley	★★★★

WINERY DATA
C: 9,000. **V:** 45 acres in Russian River Valley. **G:** Chardonnay (13 acres), Pinot Noir (15), Cabernet Sauvignon (7), Cabernet Franc (4), Merlot (3), Syrah (3). **P:** None.

Tom Dehlinger quietly plies his winemaking skills with grapes grown on a 45-acre, family-owned vineyard in Russian River Valley near Sebastopol. His wines have included Cabernet, Zinfandel and Merlot, but the real stars are the Burgundian varietals, where he's shown a master's hand in crafting intensely flavored, richly concentrated wines. His vineyard is best suited for Chardonnay (13 acres) and Pinot Noir (15 acres), which ripen fully, while his Cabernet and Cabernet Franc struggle, the wines often being marked by green herb and bell pepper notes and gritty tannins. Syrah was added with the 1992 vintage. Merlot and Zinfandel have been dropped. The regular Chardonnay (2,500 cases) and Pinot Noir (1,500 cases) are the biggest sellers from this 9,000-case winery.

TASTING NOTES

CABERNET FRANC RUSSIAN RIVER VALLEY (★):
1989: A lean, tough texture and cooked plum and currant flavors compete with strong herbal notes. **75**

CABERNET SAUVIGNON RUSSIAN RIVER VALLEY (★★): The style is consistent, but less to my taste, especially in years when unripe flavors appear. In this cool climate, quality is more variable.

1991: Ripe, supple and elegant, with a rich core of currant, herb, mineral and toasty oak, all well proportioned, finishing with rich tannins and fine length. **88**

1990: Firm and tannic, an austere wine with crisp, lean, herbal fruit flavors that finish with a dry, tannic edge. **80**

1989: Lean in texture, with gamy, funky aromas and flavors that show hints of plum or chocolate on the finish. Tannic and tight; needs until about 1997 to soften. **79**

1988: Tannic but light, with pleasant greenish plum and currant aromas and flavors. Needs time to soften those tannins. **83**

1987: An elegant, balanced style, with concentrated cherry, raspberry, currant and earthy herb notes, but they're well proportioned. The tannins, while fine, are very firm, and the finish is drying. **88**

1986: A tough but impressively concentrated wine, with delicious currant and plum aromas and flavors that extend well into the long finish. **90**

Chardonnay Russian River Valley (★★★): Distinct for its crisp, intense and deeply concentrated flavors as well its complexity and finesse.

1993: Intense and lively, with a focused band of pear, citrus, spice and light oak shadings. **88**

1992: Relies heavily on wood and toasty oak, but has a rich core of spicy pear flavors underneath. **84**

1991: Intense and lively, with rich, sharply focused pineapple, butterscotch, spice and honey notes. **89**

Chardonnay Russian River Valley Montrachet Cuvée (★★★★): Adds another tier of complexity and definition to an already fine Chardonnay.

1992: Serves up lots of ripe fruit, with elegant pear, spice and honey flavors, and the finish turns rich and smoky, with vanilla notes that add complexity. **92**

1990: Ripe and full, with pretty pear, nectarine, tangerine and honey notes and subtle oak shadings. **89**

Pinot Noir Russian River Valley (★★★): Tightly wound and richly flavored, very consistent given the vagaries of this variety.

1992: Tight and chewy, but the black cherry and cedary oak flavors that do emerge are pleasing if tannic. **88**

1991: Less rich and concentrated than the Reserve, but very fine nonetheless, with supple herb, cherry and spice notes. **87**

1990: A ripe, oaky wine that packs in lots of toast, currant, plum and spice notes that are firmly tannic. **85**

1989: This smoky, woody-tasting wine has modest plum flavors underneath. **80**

1987: Tasty, with complex, toasty oak, fresh, ripe cherry and deep smoke flavors that gain suppleness and intensity on the palate. **89**

1986: Very ripe and supple, with spicy currant, plum and cherry flavors, finishing with smoky toast and floral notes. **88**

1985: Aging well, holding its core of spicy black cherry flavors and picking up earthy anise and cedar nuances. **88**

1984: Elegant and medium-bodied, with some complexity to the cherry and strawberry flavors. **87**

Pinot Noir Russian River Valley Reserve (★★★★): The Reserve is quickly joining the elite of California, with uncommonly dark color and depth of flavor. Ages well.

1992: Intense and tightly wound, remarkable for its depth and flavor, with mineral, black cherry and cedary oak aromas and firm tannins. **91**

1991: Dark, rich, complex and spicy, this is a delicious Pinot packed with cherry, raspberry and plum flavors, finishing with a smooth, supple texture. **91**

1990: Lean and spicy, with juicy raspberry and spice flavors and a coarse texture. **81**

Syrah Russian River Valley (★★★★): Enormous depth and richness from the first offerings. Definitely worth watching.

1992: Uncommonly dark with deep purple hues and a rich, plush core of plum, cherry, currant and mineral flavors. Serves up a big, bold mouthful of Syrah. Ready now but worthy of cellaring short-term. **93**

DeMoor Winery
Oakville, Napa Valley
F: 1978. **O:** Sky Court Napa Inc. **W:** Michael Cox.
S: None.

Overall	**$9-15**	★★

Wine Ratings	
Cabernet Sauvignon Napa Valley	★★
Chardonnay Napa Valley	★★
Sauvignon Blanc Napa Valley	★★
Zinfandel Napa Valley	★★

Winery Data
C: 15,000. **V:** None. **G:** None. **P:** Chenin Blanc (Napa Valley), Cabernet Sauvignon, Cabernet Franc (Oakville), Chardonnay (Carneros), Zinfandel (Howell Mountain).

The DeMoor Winery in Oakville began as Napa Cellars in 1978, and has always been a low-key operation despite its highly visible location on Highway 29 north of Yountville. Over the years the wines have lacked consistency, ranging in quality from fair to good, not surprisingly since the winery doesn't own any vineyards and its grape sources have often changed. The one thread of continuity through most of the winery's existence was winemaker Aaron Mosley. In 1983 the deSchepper family of Belgium bought the winery, selling it in turn to Sky Court Napa Inc. in 1990. The 15,000-case winery, with winemaker Michael Cox on board, now focuses on mainstream Cabernet, Chardonnay, Sauvignon Blanc and Zinfandel, with wines at times carrying both a Napa Valley and California appellation.

TASTING NOTES

CABERNET SAUVIGNON NAPA VALLEY (★★): Ripe and oaky, better early on. Recent efforts are dry, lean, hollow and tannic.
1990: Green and herbal, with pungent bell pepper and earthy Cabernet flavors. Turns dry and tannic on the finish. Better after 1996, but it may never outgrow its herbal profile. **78**
1989: An oaky wine with lots of toasty, buttery flavors, but the currant and plum flavors hang on. **86**

CHARDONNAY NAPA VALLEY (★★):
1993: Marked by a grassy edge, with a lean band of pear and citrus notes. **80**
1992: Simple and fruity, with spicy pear and pineapple flavors. **83**
1991: Tart and bordering on sour, with leesy apple and pear aromas and flavors tightly wrapped in a lean package. **82**

SAUVIGNON BLANC NAPA VALLEY (★★):
1992: Haylike aromas plus a whiff of barnyard make this a distinctive wine that not everyone can warm up to. **76**

ZINFANDEL NAPA VALLEY (★★): Intense and spicy in 1991, with Rhône-like overtones.
1991: Intense and spicy, with heady, complex, Rhône-like aromas, picking up plum and prune notes that have a distinctive peppery edge. **87**

DENATALE VINEYARDS
Russian River Valley
F: 1985. **O:** Ron & Sandy DeNatale. **W:** Ron DeNatale. **S:** None.

OVERALL	$10	NR

WINE RATINGS

Pinot Noir Russian River Valley	NR

WINERY DATA
C: 1,000. **V:** 7 acres in Russian River Valley. **G:** N/A. **P:** None.

With 7 acres in vines and 1,000 cases of wine, DeNatale is a small family run winery in Healdsburg with most of its Chardonnay, Cabernet, Zinfandel and Pinot Noir sold in Sonoma County. I have tasted their wines only once but have no recent notes as they have limited commercial availability. The 1991 Pinot Noir was so heavily oaked that it was undrinkable.

DEUX AMIS WINERY
Dry Creek Valley
F: 1987. **O:** James Penpraze & Phyllis Zouzounis. **W:** Phyllis Zouzounis. **S:** None.

OVERALL	$12	★★

WINE RATINGS

Cabernet Sauvignon Dry Creek Valley	★★

WINERY DATA
C: 1,400. **V:** None. **G:** None. **P:** Zinfandel, Petite Sirah (Dry Creek Valley), Zinfandel (Alexander Valley).

In 1987 Phyllis Zouzounis, winemaker at Mazzocco, and James Penpraze started this small winery using purchased grapes. The 1,400-case winery makes 900 cases of Zinfandel from Dry Creek and Alexander Valleys, with smaller lots of Cabernet. The 1987 Cabernet was firmly tannic, but with a solid core of fruit flavors.

DEVLIN WINE CELLARS
Santa Cruz Mountains
F: 1978. **O:** Charles & Cheryl Devlin. **W:** Charles Devlin. **S:** Soquel Cellars, Capitola Cellars.

OVERALL	$10	★

WINE RATINGS

Cabernet Sauvignon Santa Cruz Mountains Beauregard Ranch	★
Chardonnay Santa Cruz Mountains Meyley Vineyard	★

WINERY DATA
C: 10,000. **V:** None. **G:** None. **P:** Chardonnay (Santa Cruz Mountains), Merlot (Central Coast), Sauvignon Blanc (Central

Coast), Zinfandel (Santa Cruz Mountains, Central Coast), Cabernet Sauvignon (Santa Cruz Mountains, Central Coast).

Most of Devlin's 10,000 cases are sold from its sales and tasting room in Soquel, south of Santa Cruz. My most recent notes are for the 1991 Cabernet Santa Cruz Mountains Beauregard Ranch, which was marred by funky, tanky flavors, and an equally flawed Chardonnay from Meyley Vineyard in Santa Cruz that tasted oxidized. The product mix also includes Chenin Blanc, Gamay, Merlot, Muscat, Sauvignon Blanc, Syrah and Zinfandel along with a red table wine.

DIAMOND CREEK VINEYARDS
Diamond Mountain, Napa Valley
F: 1968. **O:** Al & Adelle Brounstein. **W:** Phil Steinschriber, Jerry Luper. **S:** None.

OVERALL	$50-200	★★★★★

WINE RATINGS

Cabernet Sauvignon Napa Valley Gravelly Meadow	★★★★★
Cabernet Sauvignon Napa Valley Gravelly Meadow Lake Blend	★★★★★
Cabernet Sauvignon Napa Valley Lake Vineyard	★★★★★
Cabernet Sauvignon Napa Valley Red Rock Terrace	★★★★★
Cabernet Sauvignon Napa Valley Three Vineyard Blend	★★★
Cabernet Sauvignon Napa Valley Volcanic Hill	★★★★★

WINERY DATA
C: 3,500. **V:** 20 acres in Napa Valley. **G:** Cabernet Sauvignon (18 acres), Merlot (1), Cabernet Franc (0.8). **P:** None.

In 1968, a year after buying a 79-acre parcel in the narrow Diamond Creek canyon, Al Brounstein began clearing the hillsides and discovered he had three distinctly different soil types and exposures. He planted the three sites to Bordeaux varieties, using budwood from Bordeaux's first growths. After making his first Cabernets in 1972, he wondered whether the vineyards would yield distinctively different wines. He found that

each of the vineyards, named after their soil composition, had a unique personality. Volcanic Hill is 8 acres of volcanic ash on a south-facing slope. Red Rock Terrace is 7 acres of iron-rich, reddish clay on a steeper grade with a northerly exposure. Gravelly Meadow is a flatter 5 acres of rocky gravel soil. Brounstein planted a fourth vineyard, a three-quarter-acre parcel called Lake Vineyard, and since 1978 its grapes have been bottled separately in years when it's distinctive. Otherwise it becomes part of the Gravelly Meadow blend.

Brounstein and his wife, Adelle, have stuck to their plan: being California's first Cabernet-only estate. The three main wines, grown at the 600-foot elevation, share a rustic, mountain-grown austerity, a result of small berries and low crop yields. Intense and tannic when young, Diamond Creek's Cabernets are also deeply colored and enormously concentrated, capable of aging and gaining for up to two decades. Production peaks at 3,500 cases in a good year. Because of their distinctive qualities and limited production—often just a few hundred cases of each wine—prices have soared. The three main bottlings sell for $50, and the 1992 Lake sold out quickly at $200 a bottle, making it California's most expensive wine. Periodically Brounstein bottles a three-vineyard blend, which he uses for charity wine auction donations, and there have been wines labeled Special Selection (in lighter years) and First and Second Pick (designating wines picked before or after rains). In 1991 Brounstein bottled six different sections of his vineyards under a microclimate series to further demonstrate the vineyards' unique features. From the outset, Jerry Luper has been the behind-the-scenes winemaker. Curiously, other Diamond Mountain-grown Cabernets from Sterling, von Strasser, Pine Ridge and Roddis Cellar have not achieved similar richness and depth.

TASTING NOTES

CABERNET SAUVIGNON NAPA VALLEY GRAVELLY MEADOW (★★★★★): Gravelly Meadow tends toward more herb and mineral flavors. Ages exceptionally well for up to 20 years.

1992: Firm and compact, with a tight band of currant, earth, spice and cherry flavors. **93**

1991: Chewy in texture, but brightly focused currant and plum flavors shine through the layer of fine tannins. **92**

Gravelly Meadow Lake Blend 1991: Bright and chewy, with a solid core of currant and berry flavors. It's almost floral at the edges, an elegant wine behind the layer of tannins. **92**

1990: High in extract, with concentrated currant, cedar and herb flavors and hints of cola and tea on a long, smooth finish. **90**

1989: Earthy and herbal, with more tannins than the modest currant and spice flavors seem able to support. **83**

1988: Lean and tannic but well focused, with spicy cedar aromas and flavors and cranberry and black cherry notes. **87**

1987: Intense and decidedly herbal, with layers of currant, cherry, cedar, toast and tobacco notes that are firm and structured. **90**

1986: Very tight and compact, with concentrated earth, cedar and plum flavors that are very intense and deep, lurking behind dense tannins. **94**

1985: Hard, tart and tannic, a very austere Gravelly Meadow that serves up a firm core of cedar and black cherry flavors. A long ager. **92**

1984: Very rich and concentrated, with a supple texture and lavish cedar, plum, currant and spice flavors that go on and on. **94**

1983: Austere and compact, with lean earth, currant, spice and cherry flavors that are very well structured. **88**

1982: Mature but still tight and austere, with plenty of cedar, earth, anise and black cherry flavors that are intense and lively. **89**

1981: Earthy but turning supple, with complex cedar, black cherry, currant and spice flavors that are still firm and evolving. **89**

1980: A rich, complex wine that displays layers of black cherry, currant and cedar flavors that are well integrated, finishing with a touch of coffee and anise. **92**

1979: Elegant, with a spicy, earthy, cedary edge that blends in nicely with the herb and black cherry flavors. **92**

1978: Dense and powerful, packed with minty currant, earth and spice flavors and subtle oak shadings. Deeply concentrated, with a tannic aftertaste. **95**

1977: A durable 1977, it is rich, thick and earthy, with mineral, earth, currant and black cherry flavors that are austere. **89**

1976: Mature and a shade past its prime, it is still very appealing, with ripe, concentrated cherry, earth and mineral flavors up front and ample tannins at the rear. **85**

1975: Fully mature and deeply colored, a sturdy, muscular wine with narrowly focused fruit, earth and mineral flavors. **85**

1974: Rich and earthy, deeply colored and very concentrated, with currant and berry flavors and uncommon depth and intensity for a Cabernet this old. Can age another decade, although it's drinking exceptionally well now. **94**

CABERNET SAUVIGNON NAPA VALLEY LAKE VINEYARD

(★★★★★): Usually the most supple and richly flavored, but it is too dense, complex and ageworthy.

1992: Showy early, with more buttery oak than usual, and also more supple with tiers of currant, herb, spice and chocolate notes. **94**

1990: Bright and lively, packed with broad currant, herb, mineral, tobacco and prune flavors that gain complexity and depth from oak shadings. **91**

1987: Tightly tannic and youthful, but full of ripe black currant, black cherry and plum flavors. Cedary and sophisticated in aroma, big in structure and full-bodied, but still years away from maturity. **92**

1984: Rich, concentrated and elegant, with complex cedar, currant, herb, plum and vanilla flavors that are well integrated and very harmonious. The tannins are moderate. **90**

1978: Massive and intense, with tightly concentrated currant, cherry, herb and spice flavors that finish with tight, firm tannins. Impressive for its depth and complexity. **98**

CABERNET SAUVIGNON NAPA VALLEY RED ROCK

TERRACE (★★★★★): Red Rock Terrace is usually more elegant and refined, but it ages very well.

1992: Ripe and spicy, with rich black cherry, currant, anise and cedary oak flavors that are focused and lively. **91**

1991: Earthy, herbal and chewy, with a solid, chunky cherry flavor that carries onto a long finish and a cedar-tobacco character that makes it distinctive. **91**

MicroClimate 3 1991: Spicy and peppery, bursting with currant and jammy blackberry flavors, marvelously dense and deep, flashing all sorts of nuances to make it interesting, all of it centered around the concentrated fruit. **94**

1990: A rustic wine that's chunky, chewy and tannic, with a solid core of black cherry and currant flavors. **89**

1989: Tough and tannic, with concentrated red cherry, currant and black pepper aromas and flavors that persist onto a long finish. **88**

1988: Very firm and concentrated, but not as tannic and dense as this wine can often be, featuring black cherry and currant aromas and flavors that extend well onto a long, supple finish. **88**

1987: Enormous richness, depth and complexity, with currant, cherry, tobacco and spice flavors that display great intensity and length. **94**

1986: Classic California Cabernet. Beautifully focused, firm and flavorful, with delicious currant and black cherry notes, full tannins, great balance and long, tannic finish. **95**

1985: Dense, earthy and concentrated, with herb, juniper berry and spicy pepper notes to complement the currant and cedar flavors that turn tannic. **93**

1984: Generous, with supple, concentrated black cherry, currant, anise and vanilla flavors that linger long and full on the finish. An amazing wine that ranks among the very finest Diamond Creeks. **96**

1983: Offers pretty, complex aromas of cedar, berries and spice but is still closed, with hints of black cherry and earth on the finish. **88**

1982: Tight and austere but mature now, with hints of cedar, cherry, earth and spice flavors. **87**

1981: Elegant and concentrated, with ripe cherry, currant, earth and cedar flavors that are moderately tannic and well balanced. **91**

1980: Firm and herbaceous, lacking the fruitiness it usually offers. Still, the cedar, berry and tobacco notes are complex. **86**

1979: Lean and compact, yet well endowed with ripe, spicy currant, anise and cherry flavors that linger. **92**

1978: Dark and intense, with potent herb, currant, earth and cherry flavors that are complex and concentrated. Firm and tight on the finish, with plenty of depth and concentration. **95**

First Pick 1977: Still dark and firmly tannic, but the rich, earthy currant, anise and mineral flavors are complex and concentrated, pumping out lots of flavor on a long, full finish. **88**

1976: This has evolved into a delicious wine. No longer just tight and tannic, it is amazingly complex, smooth and supple, with layers of currant, anise, cedar and spice flavors. The tannins are soft and rich. **94**

1975: Deep and concentrated, with mature currant, cherry and cedar aromas and a complex earthiness. **88**

1974: Deeply colored, with wonderfully complex and youthful aromas. The spicy, grapey currant flavors pick up an anise note on a long, full finish. **92**

1972: Past its prime, with frail, mature fruit, cedar and spice flavors. **74**

CABERNET SAUVIGNON NAPA VALLEY THREE VINEYARD BLEND (★★★): Unique because it's a blend but not in the same class as the other wines.

1992: A rare blend of the three Diamond Creek vineyards, it is also the least distinctive. Tight, firm and tannic, with an earthy currant edge. **87**

1990: Austere, but laced with herb, currant, tobacco and plum flavors framed by spicy, toasty oak notes. **87**

1989: Herb, toast and currant flavors are evident in this medium-bodied wine, but the flavors are diluted, turning murky. **81**

1985: Ripe and compact, with layers of plum, cedar, currant and spice flavors and firm tannins. **89**

1984: Ripe, with sumptuous plum and black cherry flavors, but not quite the expected tannic bite. **89**

1981: Complex, with layers of cherry and currant flavors supported by firm, dry tannins and cedar notes. **90**

CABERNET SAUVIGNON NAPA VALLEY VOLCANIC HILL (★★★★★): Volcanic Hill is usually the earthiest and most tannic. Uncommonly dark and long lived.

1992: Supple and elegant, with polished currant, black cherry and plum flavors. Finishes with good length and firm tannins. **91**

1991: Lean and trim, a harmonious wine offering a burst of currant, cherry and berry flavors, although the tannins are raw. **91**

MicroClimate 4 1991: Firm and brilliantly focused, a dense wine with concentrated plum, currant and raspberry flavors shaded by more than a hint of cedar. A real mouthful of Cabernet, lithe and muscular. **93**

1990: Solid and flavorful, with raspberry and currant flavors bursting through the fine veil of tannins, echoing fruit and spice on the finish. **90**

1989: Hard-edged and solidly built, with tightly wound currant, plum and cherry flavors, well integrated tannins and nice hints of cedar on the finish. **86**

1988: Tight and lean, an austere wine with tough tannins overshadowing the currant and cassis flavors, with hints of toast and cedar on the finish. **88**

1987: Very intense and concentrated, deep and perfumed, firm and tannic, with rich currant, herb and cherry aromas and flavors that promise a long life in the bottle. **95**

1986: Deep, rich and unusually concentrated, packed with ripe plum, currant, cedar and vanilla flavors that are amazingly complex and structured. **96**

1985: Fresh and young, with tart, clean black cherry and currant flavors that are supple and elegant. While this wine has a long way to go, the tannins are turning soft and fleshy now, more typical of the vintage. **93**

1984: Softening a bit yet typically austere, with tight, ripe plum, currant and vanilla flavors that are very complex, deep and concentrated. **94**

1983: Firm and austere, yet loaded with vanilla, currant and berry flavors. May always be on the tannic side. **89**

1982: Still austere and tannic, a dense, tight, concentrated wine whose tart cherry, cedar, earth and cranberry flavors are just beginning to emerge and soften. **89**

1981: Big, ripe and densely structured, still tight and concentrated, with hints of currant and cherry flavors and a touch of spice and earth on the finish. The tannins are softening. **92**

1980: A touch herbaceous, but with plenty of cedar, bell pepper and black cherry flavors. Turns austere and tannic on the finish. **90**

First Pick 1979: Enormously deep, complex, rich and concentrated, packed with black cherry, earth, cedar and coffee flavors that are assertive and amazingly long-lasting. **95**

1978: Deep in color and austere in style, with dense, powerful currant, earth, spice and oak flavors that are sharply focused, long and full on the finish. An awesome, youthful wine that should hold another decade. **94**

1977: Austere and with some bottle variation, it is fully mature but still deeply colored, with an earthy mineral and currant edge and drying tannins on the finish. **85**

1976: Mature, drying and still tannic, it displays ripe fruit that is hard and firm but aging well. **87**

1975: Amazingly rich, elegant and concentrated, just now emerging from its tannic slumber. Its complex cedar, cherry and currant flavors are long and full on the finish. **92**

1974: Aging very well, with tight, complex cedar, currant, mineral and spice flavors that turn smooth and supple. This is still an intense and flavorful wine that has years of life ahead of it. **89**

1973: Mature, with austere fruit flavors, it's fading but still offers enough flavor to drink. **80**

1972: Mature, with ripe plum, cherry and earth flavors and firm tannins. **83**

DICKERSON VINEYARD
Napa Valley
F: 1985. **O:** William J. Dickerson. **W:** Joel Peterson. **S:** None.

OVERALL	$9-16	★★★★

WINE RATINGS

Cabernet Blend Napa Valley	
Ruby Cabernet Limited Reserve	★★★
Merlot Napa Valley Limited Reserve	★★★★
Zinfandel Napa Valley Limited Reserve	★★★★★

WINERY DATA

C: 400. **V:** 16 acres in Napa Valley. **G:** Zinfandel (9 acres), Merlot (4), Cabernet Blend (2). **P:** None.

Dickerson Vineyard in Napa Valley, long a source of superb Zinfandel for Ravenswood, is now a brand too, with Ravenswood's Joel Peterson making small lots of Zinfandel, Merlot and Cabernet from the 16-acre vineyard in Rutherford. The Zinfandel grown here is marked by minty overtones and black cherry flavors in both bottlings. Total production is 400 cases, and given this vineyard's track record for superb grapes it's no wonder the Dickerson wines are excellent. The Cabernet Blend is mostly Ruby Cabernet. The wine is made at Ravenswood in Sonoma Valley.

TASTING NOTES

CABERNET BLEND NAPA VALLEY RUBY CABERNET LIMITED RESERVE (★★★):

1992: Ripe and chunky, with spicy black cherry, currant and plum flavors that finish with a firm tannic grip. **85**

1991: This rich, high-extract wine combines classic Cabernet flavors with a hint of Zinfandel-like fruit, offering a burst of cherry and spice. **87**

MERLOT NAPA VALLEY LIMITED RESERVE (★★★★):

1992: Intense and lively, with solid currant, cherry and light toasty oak shadings that give it richness, depth and complexity. Delicious. **90**

ZINFANDEL NAPA VALLEY LIMITED RESERVE (★★★★★):
1991: Very ripe, with a spicy, minty edge, this one packs in the essence of Zinfandel and then some. Loaded with complex black cherry and raspberry flavors. **92**

DION
Sonoma Valley
F: 1986. **O:** Jerry Dion. **W:** Jerry Dion. **S:** None.

OVERALL	$10	NR

WINE RATINGS	
Chardonnay Sonoma Valley	NR
Zinfandel Sonoma Valley	NR

WINERY DATA
C: 2,000. **V:** 7 acres in Sonoma Valley. **G:** Chardonnay (7 acres). **P:** Zinfandel (Sonoma Valley).

The Dion family owns this vineyard in the western hills of Sonoma Valley, where it grows Chardonnay (7 acres) and buys Zinfandel for its 2,000-case production. The early wines were made by Bob Ellis at Mark West Vineyards.

DOLCE
This is a second label for Far Niente Winery (see listing).

DOMAIN HILL & MAYES
Napa Valley
F: 1993. **O:** Hill & Partners. **W:** William Hill. **S:** Clos Fontaine du Mont.

OVERALL	$20-32	★★★

WINE RATINGS	
Cabernet Sauvignon Napa Valley	
Clos Fontaine du Mont Reserve	★★★
Chardonnay Napa Valley	
Clos Fontaine du Mont	★★★

WINERY DATA
C: 30,000. **V:** 334 acres in Carneros, Napa Valley.
G: Chardonnay (241 acres), Cabernet Sauvignon (93).
P: Chardonnay, Cabernet Sauvignon, Chardonnay (Mount Veeder).

Since the early 1970s, William Hill has bought, developed, and sold more mountain vineyards than anyone else I know—and he's still at it. Sterling's Diamond Mountain Ranch, The Hess Collection Mount Veeder estate, Hill's own Mount Veeder property and Atlas Peak Vineyards are the main properties he has planted and sold. By 1990, the William Hill Winery needed cash and Hill decided to sell his winery and name and some of his vineyards (Mount Veeder went to Kendall-Jackson). He leased others long-term, primarily to Wine Alliance, the firm that also bought his winery and name for $36 million. Hill stayed on briefly as a consultant with William Hill Winery, but then shifted gears and launched Domain Hill & Mayes with John Mayes, a longtime business associate.

Domain Hill & Mayes is the umbrella company for a series of small vineyard-oriented wines: Hill's Van Duzer Oregon venture, which makes Chardonnay, Pinot Noir, Riesling and sparkling wine; Clos Fontaine du Mont, a Cabernet and Chardonnay brand using mountain-grown grapes and grapes from Hill's Soda Canyon property below Atlas Peak; Carneros Bighorn Ranch, which has 241 acres of Chardonnay; Kreuse Creek, a 93-acre Cabernet vineyard in Coombsville, east of Napa; and an as yet unnamed Anderson Valley brand with a 40-acre Merlot and Chardonnay vineyard. The goal is to build volume to 55,000 cases by decade's end. The 1991 Hill & Mayes Clos Fontaine Cabernet is lean and tart, with earthy herb, oak, currant and berry flavors. The 1992 Chardonnay is ripe and supple, with rich pear, honey and spice notes.

TASTING NOTES

VARIOUS BOTTLINGS (★★★):
Cabernet Sauvignon Napa Valley Clos Fontaine du Mont Reserve 1991: Lean and tart, with a narrow band of earthy herb, oak, currant and wild berry flavors. Better after 1997, but may always be austere. **85**
Chardonnay Napa Valley Clos Fontaine du Mont 1992: The first wine under Hill's new label, it is ripe and supple, with moderately rich pear, honey and spice notes. **87**

DOMAINE BRETON
This is a second label for Guenoc Winery (see listing).

DOMAINE CARNEROS
Carneros
F: 1987. O: Domaine Carneros Inc. W: Eileen Crane.
S: None.

OVERALL	$20-30	★★★

WINE RATINGS

Sparkling Wine Carneros Brut	
Sparkling Wine Carneros	★★★
Brut Blanc de Blancs	
Sparkling Wine Carneros	★★★
Cuvée Taittinger	★★★

WINERY DATA
C: 35,000. V: 110 acres in Carneros. G: Chardonnay (66 acres), Pinot Noir (33), Pinot Blanc (5), Pinot Meunier (6). P: Pinot Noir, Chardonnay (Carneros).

This beautiful chateau's primary owner is Taittinger, the prestigious French Champagne producer. From its stately locale on Highway 121, Domaine Carneros is home to some of California's most delicate and elegant sparkling wines, made under the direction of Eileen Crane, who first worked at Domaine Chandon and then helped build Gloria Ferrer, where she made the first wines. Domaine Carneros owns 110 acres, with Chardonnay and Pinot Noir (a new addition) the principal grapes, plus smaller amounts of Pinot Blanc and Pinot Meunier. Worth watching.

TASTING NOTES

SPARKLING WINE CARNEROS VARIOUS BOTTLINGS (★★★): All are elegant and delicate, with green apple and pear flavors. The vintage-dated Blanc de blancs is the best so far.
Brut NV: Lean and lemony, with tart, flinty green apple and pear flavors. **80**
Brut Blanc de Blancs 1988: Brightly focused through and through, with rich lemon, pineapple and pear flavors. **88**
Cuvée Taittinger 1989: Ripe and intense, with a core of earthy pineapple and black cherry flavors that linger on the finish. **88**
Cuvée Taittinger NV: A touch coarse and earthy, but enough rich pear, honey and toast notes pour through to keep it interesting. **87**

DOMAINE CHANDON
Yountville, Napa Valley
F: 1973. O: Moët-Hennessey, Luis Vuitton. W: Dawnine Sample Dyer, Richard Geoffroy. S: Shadow Creek.

OVERALL	$12-22	★★★

WINE RATINGS

Sparkling Wine Carneros Blanc de Noirs	★★★
Sparkling Wine Napa County Brut Cuvée	★★★
Sparkling Wine Napa-Sonoma Counties	
Brut Reserve	★★★★

WINERY DATA
C: 450,000. V: 1,510 acres in Mendocino, Napa Valley, Sonoma County, Carneros. G: Cabernet Franc (16 acres), Chardonnay (410), Cabernet Sauvignon (63), Merlot (30), Pinot Blanc (49), Pinot Meunier (90), Pinot Noir (602), Petite Sirah (30), Sauvignon Blanc (12) P: Pinot Noir (Napa Valley, Carneros), Chardonnay (Napa Valley, Carneros), Pinot Blanc (Napa Valley, Carneros), Pinot Meunier (Napa Valley).

In 1973 Moët & Chandon became the first French Champagne-maker to set its sights on a large-scale sparkling wine operation in California, settling in Napa Valley near the Veteran's Home in Yountville. The first vintages were made at Trefethen, but in 1977 a beautiful winery and grounds were completed and by the 1980s Chandon was making 100,000 cases. Since then another half dozen Champagne houses have followed Moët's lead and built sparkling wine facilities in California, as have the two major Spanish cava makers, the Ferrer family (Freixenet in Spain, Gloria Ferrer in Carneros) and Codorniu (Codorniu Napa).

In more than two decades, Domaine Chandon has come to symbolize Moët's long-term commitment to international investment and uniformly high standards. Consistency of style is Chandon's strength even as case production hovers around 450,000 cases. It is a steady, dependable brand whose only fault may be that it rarely takes chances with its Cuvées. Much of the consistency is due to the winemaking skills of Dawnine Dyer, who joined the winery in 1976 and has been well trained by her French counterparts. Chandon's 1,510 acres are spread throughout the North Coast, with Carneros (776 acres) the largest, but also substantial holdings in Napa Valley (332), Mendocino (300) and Sonoma County (101). Pinot

Noir, with 602 acres, is the largest variety, followed by Chardonnay (410), Pinot Meunier (90), Cabernet (63), which it sells, and Pinot Blanc (49 acres). The product mix features non-vintage Brut, Brut Cuvée, Blanc de Noirs, Étoile and Reserve, although some surprises are in the works, including a rosé marked by complex strawberry, cherry and vanilla notes.

TASTING NOTES

BLANC DE NOIRS CARNEROS NV (★★★): Crisp, intense and earthy, with hints of black cherry and spice. This bottling shows off Pinot Noir, which is 89 percent of the blend, mostly from the 1990 vintage. Also contains 11 percent Pinot Meunier.
NV: Crisp and earthy, with a vague overlay of cherry flavor echoing in the background. The finish is soft and cedary. **80**

BRUT CUVÉE NAPA COUNTY NV (★★★): A blend of Pinot Noir and Chardonnay, it too is ripe and intense, with a floral, spicy edge to the citrus and pineapple flavors.
NV: Ripe and intense, with a floral, spicy edge to the pear and pineapple flavors. **85**

BRUT RESERVE NAPA-SONOMA COUNTIES NV (★★★★): Mostly Pinot Noir (68 percent) with smaller amounts of Chardonnay and Pinot Meunier, it can be rich and toasty, with complexity and finesse, having aged four years *sur lie*.
NV: Mature, with earthy, yeasty flavors that pick up pear, black cherry and spice notes. **87**

DOMAINE DU GRAND ARCHER

This is a second label for Arrowood Vineyards & Winery (see listing).

DOMAINE NAPA WINERY

St. Helena, Napa Valley
F: 1985. **O:** Michel Perret. **W:** Grant Taylor. **S:** None.

OVERALL	$10-15	★★

WINE RATINGS	
Chardonnay Napa Valley	★★
Merlot Napa Valley	★★

Sauvignon Blanc Napa Valley	
Michel A. Perret	★

WINERY DATA
C: 10,000. **V:** 10 acres in Napa Valley. **G:** Sauvignon Blanc (6 acres), Merlot (4). **P:** Cabernet Sauvignon, Chardonnay, Merlot (Napa Valley).

Frenchman Michel Perret made a number of foreign investment real estate deals while building his small winery off Highway 29 in Rutherford, where he makes bland, medium-weight Cabernet, Chardonnay and Sauvignon Blanc. Production is about 10,000 cases.

TASTING NOTES

VARIOUS BOTTLINGS:
Chardonnay Napa Valley 1991: Crisp and lively, offering a beam of generous green apple, citrus and vanilla flavors. **82**
Merlot Napa Valley 1990: Simple, fruity and light, an amiable wine with modest berry and currant flavors. **84**
Sauvignon Blanc Napa Valley Michel A. Perret 1992: Lean and a bit austere, with an earthy edge to the modest vanilla and pear flavors. **81**

DOMAINE SAINT GREGORY

Mendocino County
F: 1988. **O:** Gregory Graziano & Lowell Stone. **W:** Gregory Graziano. **S:** None.

OVERALL	$12-14	★★

WINE RATINGS	
Chardonnay Mendocino County	★★
Pinot Noir Mendocino County	★★

WINERY DATA
C: 10,000. **V:** 140 acres in Mendocino County. **G:** N/A. **P:** N/A.

Gregory Graziano founded this winery in Ukiah in 1988, producing 10,000 cases of wine from 140 acres of vineyard. It's an eclectic lineup, including standards Chardonnay and Zinfandel but also an assortment of Italian-style wines such as Moscato, Nebbiolo, Pinot Bianco and Sangiovese; these are bottled under the Monte Volpe brand (see listing). So far the 1991

Chardonnay has been marked by toasty, buttery oak and attractive Chardonnay flavors. The Pinot Noirs from 1990 and 1991 are appealing for their straightforward fruitiness.

TASTING NOTES

CHARDONNAY MENDOCINO COUNTY (★★):
1992: Medium-weight with ripe pear, spice and apple notes, finishing with a slight carmel edge. Ready. **85**
1991: Serves up a lot of toasty, buttery oak, plus layers of ripe, spicy pear, fig and nutmeg flavors. A solid 1991 that hangs together nicely. **86**

PINOT NOIR MENDOCINO COUNTY (★★):
1992: Lean and crisp, with a range of wild berry and cherry flavors. **81**
1991: Ripe and floral, with supple plum and raspberry flavors. **84**
1990: Firm and tight, with pretty raspberry and cherry flavors and a nice toasty edge adding complexity to the finish. **86**

DOMAINE ST. GEORGE WINERY
Sonoma County
F: 1934. **O:** Pan Magna Group. **W:** Bob Fredson. **S:** Oak Vineyards, Cambiaso.

OVERALL	$6-10	★★

WINE RATINGS
Cabernet Sauvignon California	
Vintage Reserve	★★
Cabernet Sauvignon Sonoma County	
Premier Cuvée Reserve	★★
Chardonnay California Vintage Reserve	★

WINERY DATA
C: 350,000. **V:** 22 acres in Russian River Valley. **G:** Cabernet Sauvignon (12 acres), Merlot (10). **P:** Chardonnay (Dry Creek Valley, Chalk Hill), Chardonnay (Monterey, Alexander Valley), Cabernet Sauvignon (Dry Creek, Alexander Valley), Merlot (Alexander Valley).

Domaine St. George produces Cabernet, Chardonnay and Merlot in the old Cambiaso winery in Russian River. A Vintage Reserve Chardonnay, carrying a California appellation, is also produced but it's very ordinary, often sweet and nothing to get excited about. The Cabernet can at times be decent.

TASTING NOTES

CABERNET SAUVIGNON VARIOUS BOTTLINGS (★★):
California Vintage Reserve 1992: Supple and generous, with ripe, bright, fleshy cherry and plum flavors. Very appealing and easy to drink. **85**
Sonoma County Premier Cuvée Reserve 1989: Spicy, with a cedary oak frame and chewy tannins, it delivers just enough ripe fruit flavors to keep it in balance. **83**
Sonoma County Premier Cuvée Reserve 1988: Earthy, spicy and firmly tannic, the fruit is dropping out of this wine, leaving the tannic framework behind. **77**

CHARDONNAY CALIFORNIA VINTAGE RESERVE (★):
1993: Tastes sweet beyond ripeness, with cloying pear and apple flavors. For those who like their Chardonnays sweet. **78**

DOMINUS ESTATE
Yountville, Napa Valley
F: 1982. **O:** Christian Moueix. **W:** Chris Phelps, Jean-Claude Berrouet.

OVERALL	$55	★★★★★

WINE RATINGS
Cabernet Sauvignon Napa Valley	★★★★★

WINERY DATA
C: 7,000. **V:** 112 acres in Napa Valley. **G:** Merlot (20 acres), Petite Verdot (3), Cabernet Sauvignon (53), Cabernet Franc (15), Chardonnay (19), Malbec (0.88). **P:** None.

Dominus Estate began in 1982 as a highly publicized joint venture between Christian Moueix of Chateau Petrus and John Daniel's daughters, Robin Lail and Marcia Smith. The partnership came in the wake of the even higher-profile Mondavi-Rothschild Opus One venture three years earlier. Dominus brought together Moueix's winemaking talents—honed and refined in

Pomerol, where his family owns several esteemed châteaux—with Lail and Smith's famous Napanook vineyard in Yountville, which they inherited from their father (John Daniel owned Inglenook through 1964). Long a source of fine Cabernet grapes used by Daniel during his glory days at Inglenook, the vineyard is known for producing dense and tannic wines, and for years it provided the backbone for many grand Inglenook Cask Cabernets. Yet few California wines have divided the critics like Dominus, with its rich, earthy flavors and massive tannins. Without a doubt, it was a rugged first decade for Dominus as Moueix and his staff wrestled with a vineyard that yields rustic, tannic wines. Beginning with the debut 1983 vintage, an unusually tannic year in Napa, Dominus showed the signature of the vineyard. In the years 1984 through 1986, efforts were made to refine the style and tame the tannins, with varying degrees of success. By 1987 Dominus showed even more precision in its balance and flavor and in years such as 1989, a difficult year for most Napa Cabernets, Dominus proved amazingly complex and well crafted. The 1990 and 1991 vintages show that Moueix and his winemaker, Chris Phelps, have a better handle on the vineyard and the wine.

In 1994 Lail and Smith bowed out of the Dominus venture, selling their interest to Moueix, leaving him as sole proprietor of the 112-acre Napanook property and the Dominus brand. Lail retained ownership of the Daniel Estate name, which was used periodically as a second label by the partners. Production has ranged from 3,000 to 7,000 cases, with the blend including small portions of Merlot and Cabernet Franc.

TASTING NOTES

CABERNET SAUVIGNON NAPA VALLEY (★★★★★): As distinctive and divisive a wine as is produced in Napa, but a true reflection of terroir and what a vineyard has to offer. Dense, dark, chewy and tannic, often with earthy, leathery notes, but also with a core of rich currant and berry flavors. Best to decant. Ages well but not yet to greatness, as the early vintages have peaked and are not gaining. The vintages to follow are 1989 through 1991, the best efforts so far.
1991: The best Dominus to date, brimming with bright, rich, supple and complex herb, currant, cedar and cherry

flavors, picking up a mineral and spice edge on the finish, which runs deep and long. A tremendous effort. **95**
1990: Big, rich and chewy, a high-extract wine packed with currant, mineral, earth and spice flavors of remarkable depth and breadth. It finishes with firm tannins, but is impeccably balanced. **93**
1989: Rich, dense and leathery, with a core of tight currant, earth, coffee, cedar and anise flavors, it's deeply concentrated and firmly tannic. The texture is smooth and silky. Has more balance and finesse than most 1989s. **92**
1988: Earthy, gamy flavors dominate this solid, silky wine, but it picks up hints of leather, currant and tobacco on the finish. **88**
1987: Dense, rich, tannic and concentrated, with a core of solid currant, oak, spice and earthy cedar flavors, picking up a gamy, meaty quality on the finish. Admirable for its power and strength. **92**
1986: Elegant and understated, with fine balance and softening tannins. Offers a core of supple currant, anise, leather and spice flavors, with light oak shadings and firm tannins. Delicate for Dominus. **88**
1985: A complex and harmonious wine that shows subtlety and finesse, with earthy currant, tar, cedar and tobacco flavors that are focused, finishing with smooth tannins. **92**
1984: Mature, with appealing currant, spice and cedar flavors, but also a firm dose of tannin. **85**
1983: Has developed nicely, with rich, earthy, tannic currant and tar flavors. Lively acidity keeps the flavors alive and the texture is softening. **85**

DRY CREEK VINEYARD
Dry Creek Valley
F: 1972. **O:** David S. Stare. **W:** Larry Levin. **S:** None.

OVERALL	$7-20	★★★

WINE RATINGS	
Cabernet Franc Dry Creek Valley	★★
Cabernet Sauvignon Dry Creek Valley	★★★
Cabernet Sauvignon Dry Creek Valley Reserve	★★★
Cabernet Sauvignon Sonoma County	★★★
Chardonnay Sonoma County	★★

Chardonnay Sonoma County Reserve	★★
Chenin Blanc California Dry	★★
Fumé Blanc Sonoma County	★★
Fumé Blanc Sonoma County Reserve	★★
Meritage Red Dry Creek Valley	★★★
Merlot Dry Creek Valley	★★
Merlot Dry Creek Valley Reserve	★★
Merlot Dry Creek Valley Bullock House Vineyard	★★
Zinfandel Dry Creek Valley Old Vines	★★★
Zinfandel Dry Creek Valley Reserve	★★★

WINERY DATA

C: 110,000. **V:** 95 acres in Alexander Valley, Dry Creek Valley. **G:** Chardonnay (33 acres), Sauvignon Blanc (32), Cabernet Sauvignon (5), Merlot (15), Zinfandel (10). **P:** Chenin Blanc (Clarksburg), Chardonnay, Sauvignon Blanc (Sonoma County), Merlot, Cabernet Sauvignon, Zinfandel (Dry Creek Valley).

In 1972, when David Stare set up the first new winery in Dry Creek Valley since the end of Prohibition, he focused on Loire Valley whites, Chenin Blanc from the Delta and Sauvignon Blanc from Sonoma. Stare, along with Robert Mondavi, deserves credit for championing Sauvignon Blanc through the 1970s and 1980s, raising its quality and bringing it the recognition it deserves. Dry Creek Vineyard still relies heavily on its Sonoma County Fumé Blanc and standard Sonoma County Chardonnay for nearly half its 110,000-case output, but recently the reds have been more interesting. Sonoma County Cabernet (9,000 cases), Merlot (10,000 cases) and Zinfandel Dry Creek (8,000 cases) dominate the reds. The winery owns 30 acres in Alexander Valley and 65 more in Dry Creek, most of it planted to Chardonnay and Sauvignon Blanc, with smaller parcels of Cabernet, Merlot and Zinfandel.

TASTING NOTES

CABERNET FRANC DRY CREEK VALLEY (★★):

1990: Tough and woody, with tight tannins, smoky aromas and herb and dill flavors. **83**

CABERNET SAUVIGNON DRY CREEK VALLEY (★★★), RESERVE (★★★):

Pleasantly fruity, with bright berry and raspberry flavors, a supple texture and mild tannins. Best on release. Ages fairly well. The appellation switches back and forth from Sonoma County to Dry Creek.

1991: Ripe, intense and spicy, with high-extract, jammy currant, raspberry and plum flavors that pack a wallop. **87**

1990: Elegant, with ripe, intense currant, black cherry, herb and cedar flavors that are well focused. **88**

1989: Tough but focused, with tasty currant, plum and berry flavors. **86**

1988: Ripe raspberry and currant flavors are framed by tight, stemmy tannins. **81**

1987: Firm and concentrated, packed with jammy currant, cherry and mint flavors. Tannic. **84**

1986: A soft, smooth, supple Cabernet with ripe cherry, herb and tobacco flavors. **88**

1985: Lean and elegant, with stylish, ripe cherry and raspberry flavors and spicy oak nuances that fill out on the finish. **89**

Reserve 1991: Firm, tight and tannic, but with enough rich currant and plum flavors to hold your interest. **89**

CHARDONNAY SONOMA COUNTY (★★), RESERVE (★★):

1993: Marked by spicy pear and apple notes of modest proportion. Pleasant if on the light side. **84**

1992: Herbal and leafy, with a lean edge to the pear and apple notes. May be more appealing with time in the bottle. **80**

1991: Intense and lively, with elegant pear, spice, nutmeg and anise flavors that fade on the finish. **85**

1990: A spicy wine with ripe, mellow apple, pear and citrus notes that are clean and pleasant, finishing with a fruity aftertaste. **82**

Reserve 1992: A touch racy with pear, nectarine and honey notes of modest proportion, although the flavors fan out on the finish. **86**

Reserve 20th Anniversary 1991: Tastes smooth and mature, with honey, pear and toast notes of moderate richness. **87**

CHENIN BLANC CALIFORNIA DRY (★★):

1993: Smooth, off-dry, a generous wine with nicely compact pear and melon fruit. **82**

FUMÉ BLANC SONOMA COUNTY (★★), RESERVE (★★):

Recent bottlings lack the varietal intensity of earlier vintages; it is now tamer and softer, but capable of straying into pungent, vegetal flavors.

1993: Simple, sturdy and nicely focused, with pear and green leafy notes. **84**

1992: Light and fresh, a simple wine with melon and sweet pea aromas and flavors and a sweet finish. **82**

Reserve 1992: Fresh, citrusy and modestly herbal, a sturdy wine with simple flavors. **82**

Reserve 1991: Round and generous, showing a honey edge to the fig and herb flavors. **85**

MERITAGE RED DRY CREEK VALLEY (★★★): The finest of the red wines. Complex and refined.

1990: An herbal, oaky wine with ripe, chunky currant, plum and wild berry flavors. **89**

1988: Smooth and tasty, with a smoky, gamy edge to the well defined cherry and spice flavors. **86**

1987: Attractive for its balance of ripe currant, plum, anise and cherry flavors and toasty oak shadings. Still tannic, but shows a suppleness on the finish. **87**

1986: A ripe, jammy, moderately distinctive wine that has well integrated and pleasant soy, cherry, cedar and coffee flavors. **80**

1985: Herb-scented red cherry and strawberry flavors compete with spicy oak for attention in this silky, concentrated wine. **88**

David S. Stare Vintner's Reserve 1984: Shows ripe fruit galore, with minty and grapey flavors wrapped in solid tannins. **88**

MERLOT DRY CREEK VALLEY VARIOUS BOTTLINGS (★★): Marked by supple herb and berry notes, a medium-bodied wine that lacks focus.

1992: Marked by a cedary oak edge to the herb and cherry flavors, finishing with crisp tannins. **84**

1991: Alluring for its wild berry and cherry flavors, it's also firmly tannic and tight. **84**

1990: Ripe, supple and tasty, with spicy plum and currant notes and hints of anise, coffee, cedar and oak. **87**

1989: Soft and supple, with elegant currant and raspberry flavors framed by spicy, buttery oak. **86**

1988: Simple, pleasant, fruity and fresh, with toasty cherry and plum flavors. **83**

Reserve 1991: Supple and generous, with ripe currant and black cherry flavors that are bright and vivid. **87**

Bullock House Vineyard 1991: Crisp and focused, a spicy wine with enough berry flavors to keep it lively. **83**

ZINFANDEL DRY CREEK VALLEY OLD VINES (★★★), RESERVE (★★★): Very ripe and jammy, with tarry cherry and raspberry flavors and fine tannins. Improving.

Old Vines 1992: Lean, with a band of modest, tannic wild berry and raspberry flavors, but not the depth or richness you might expect from old vines. **83**

Old Vines 1991: A classy wine that serves up generous plum, cranberry and spice flavors that are supple and fleshy. **87**

Old Vines 1990: A ripe, dark, Port-like wine with jammy plum flavors that border on raisiny. **85**

Old Vines 1989: Ripe and a little raisiny, with a strong chorus of raspberry and black currant flavors. **85**

Old Vines 1988: Delicious raspberry and strawberry flavors make this immediately appealing. **86**

Old Vines 1986: Very deep, concentrated and complex, loaded with ripe berry and cherry flavors. **85**

Reserve 1991: Ripe and spicy, with tarry black cherry and raspberry jam flavors. **88**

DUCKHORN VINEYARDS

St. Helena, Napa Valley

F: 1976. **O:** St. Helena Wine Co. **W:** Thomas Rinaldi. **S:** Decoy.

OVERALL	$12-25	★★★★

WINE RATINGS	
Cabernet Blend Howell Mountain	★★★
Cabernet Sauvignon Napa Valley	★★★★★
Merlot Napa Valley	★★★★★
Merlot Napa Valley Three Palms Vineyard	★★★
Merlot Napa Valley Vine Hill Ranch	★★★
Sauvignon Blanc Napa Valley	★★★

WINERY DATA

C: 30,000. **V:** 69 acres in Napa Valley. **G:** Sauvignon Blanc (18 acres), Sémillon (5), Merlot (21), Cabernet Franc (4), Cabernet Sauvignon (16), Petite Verdot (3), Viognier (2). **P:** Sémillon, Sauvignon Blanc, Merlot, Cabernet Sauvignon, Cabernet Franc (Napa Valley), Sauvignon Blanc, Merlot, Cabernet Sauvignon, Cabernet Franc (Howell Mountain), Sauvignon Blanc, Merlot, Cabernet Sauvignon, Cabernet Franc (Carneros), Sauvignon Blanc, Merlot, Cabernet Sauvignon, Cabernet Franc (Rutherford).

Duckhorn Vineyards specializes in hearty, rich and tannic red wines, notably Cabernet, Merlot and a proprietary Howell Mountain Bordeaux-style blend. Each is well crafted and among Napa's finest, but Duckhorn is best known as a champion of Merlot, a wine that first captured Dan Duckhorn's imagination in the early 1970s and led him to seek investors and start this winery, which first produced wine in 1978. Until recently, Duckhorn's three main red wines—Napa Valley Cabernet, Merlot and a Three Palms Vineyard Merlot—were made entirely from purchased grapes grown from Carneros to Howell Mountain, and included such prizes as Spottswoode-grown Cabernet. It is Duckhorn's belief that given the right mixture of vineyards, grapes and final wine selection, one can craft a complex and consistent wine each year. To that extent, he and Tom Rinaldi, the winemaker since 1978, have been exceedingly successful. But Duckhorn also realized that control of grape sources is essential to quality, and the winery has since purchased property. It has 69 acres in vines, divided among Cabernet Sauvignon (16), Sauvignon Blanc (18), Merlot (21), and with smaller amounts of Cabernet Franc, Sémillon, Petite Verdot and Viognier.

The goal is to buy vineyards as properties become available. Despite Duckhorn's success with Merlot, the Cabernet is its best red wine, although Merlot runs a close second. The Howell Mountain Cabernet Blend is quite impressive for its expression of that appellation. The Three Palms Vineyard Merlot, while good and distinctive, has of late been the least impressive of the four reds. The vineyard is a victim of phylloxera and is now being replanted, which may interrupt Duckhorn's production of that wine. Sauvignon Blanc is the lone white in the winery's 30,000-case output.

TASTING NOTES

CABERNET BLEND HOWELL MOUNTAIN (★★★): Austere and tightly wound, true to its source, with a solid core of earthy currant flavors. It has no track record for aging.
1991: Serves up lots of ripe, spicy black cherry, currant and anise flavors before the chewy tannins kick in. Needs cellaring until 1998 or so, when the fruit may be more forthcoming. **88**
1990: Tight, tannic and firm, a youthful and intense wine with spicy, cedary currant, earth and berry flavors. **88**
1989: Deep, dark and complex, with rich Cabernet flavors and hints of earthiness that add complexity and intrigue. **87**

CABERNET SAUVIGNON NAPA VALLEY (★★★★★): Hits all the right notes, with consistently fine, complex and concentrated wines that are deftly balanced and improve with age.
1990: Young, firm and intense, with a core of rich, complex, concentrated currant, cherry, anise and toasty, buttery oak flavors. A wine of great harmony and finesse. **93**
1989: Firm and spicy, with lots of minty, earthy tobacco overtones to the ripe currant, cherry and raisin flavors. **83**
1988: Medium-bodied, with strong tannins on the finish, but enough currant and cherry flavors come through. **85**
1987: Delicious, with intense, concentrated, rich and sharply focused black cherry, currant and chocolate flavors. Despite the abundant flavors and tannins, the texture is still smooth and seductive. **95**
1986: Big, ripe and intense, turning smooth in texture, with deep plum, cherry, tar and vanilla flavors, long and perfumed. **94**
1985: Serves up a massive concentration of rich, deep fruit and tannin. The compact black currant, cedar and plum flavors are dense and structured. **92**
1984: Deep and powerful, tightly structured, with plum, black currant, cedar and earth flavors tightly woven together. **91**
1983: Mature, with cedar, plum, cherry and anise flavors that are ripe, supple and elegant. **86**
1982: Very impressive considering the vintage, displaying generous, ripe, supple, elegant plum, black cherry and currant flavors and a touch of chocolate. Not quite the depth of 1978 and 1980, but still well balanced. **88**
1981: Lean and mature, drinking well, with ample currant and spice flavors that are very attractive. **86**
1980: Impressive for its deep currant, mint and earth notes. **91**
1978: Tight, firm and tannic but aging nicely, with a solid core of spicy currant and cedar flavors and a long, full, focused finish. **92**

MERLOT NAPA VALLEY (★★★★★): While a less consistent wine than the Cabernet, it is still among California's finest, very well crafted if at times heavy-handed and highly reliant on Cabernet for its tannic backbone. Ages well for up to 10 years.
1992: Tart and grapey, with herb, spice, currant and cherry flavors that finish with a cedary oak edge. **88**
1990: Alluring, rich and complex, with currant, plum and

herb characteristics. Tight and tannic, with strong oak and leather flavors. **89**

1989: Brimming with ripe, rich currant and black cherry flavors, this wine exhibits the vitality of youth and sustains it through the finish. **86**

1988: Bright and lively, medium-bodied, with pretty currant, cherry, herb and spice flavors that turn tannic. **86**

1987: Enormously deep, gutsy and complex, with rich, earthy currant, herb, toast and cedar flavors that are sharply focused, rich and long on the finish. **93**

1986: Tight and lean, with austere cherry and currant flavors and gripping tannins. **85**

1985: Duckhorn's finest to date, it possesses deep, rich, intense, powerful, complex currant, black cherry, anise and herb flavors that are tight, focused and long on the finish. **95**

1984: Tight, firm and tannic, with earthy currant, cedar, herb and spice notes. Youthful, powerful and just reaching maturity. **92**

1983: Deep, rich, complex and earthy, but the tightly focused currant, berry, anise and herb flavors pour through. Still a bit tannic. **90**

1982: Rich, complex and focused, with ripe currant, earth, cedar and cherry flavors that are neatly woven together and a long, complex finish. **92**

1981: Intense and focused, with earthy, meaty currant and anise flavors backed by firm, tight tannins. **87**

1980: Ripe and fruity, with supple currant, cranberry, cedar and anise flavors that are bright and focused. The tannins are softening. **91**

1979: Elegant and supple, fully mature, with herb, olive, currant and black cherry flavors that are focused and lively. Impressive for its length and finesse. **91**

MERLOT NAPA VALLEY THREE PALMS VINEYARD (★★★): Three Palms renders an austere wine that often shows more tannin than fruit, but the style is distinctive and consistent.

1991: An elegant and spicy Merlot that seems a bit out of balance, with flavors that range from ripe cherry to greener notes. **84**

1990: Dense, meaty and leathery, with a tart edge to the earthy currant flavors. Turns chewy and tannic. **83**

1989: Rich and earthy, with tight, firm, tannic currant and cherry flavors underneath. **87**

1988: Tight and firm, with pretty currant, cranberry, tea and spice flavors that are well integrated and supported by firm tannins. Finishes with an earthy note. **87**

1987: Rich, concentrated and sharply focused, the currant, plum, chocolate, anise and vanilla flavors are bright and lively, with firm but smooth tannins. **90**

1986: Tough, dry and earthy, with barnyard flavors competing with the currant and berry notes. Backward and unevolved. **84**

1985: Sharply focused, deftly balanced, youthful and tight, with firm currant and black cherry flavors. A seam of elegance runs through this tight, tannic wine. **91**

1984: Ripe and supple, with pretty currant, berry and cherry notes, finishing with firm, dry tannins and oaky vanilla shadings. **87**

1983: Rich, complex and smoky, with tight, sharply focused currant, tar, anise and black cherry flavors. Enormously complex, earthy and concentrated. **92**

1981: An earthy wine, lean and focused, with oaky currant, spice, cedar and tobacco notes and firm tannins. **87**

1978: Ripe and fruity, with concentrated currant, plum and cherry flavors, finishing with firm tannins and good length. **88**

MERLOT NAPA VALLEY VINE HILL RANCH (★★★): Duckhorn produced a few Vine Hill Ranch Merlots and they too are austere, earthy and tannic, but very consistent in that style.

1987: Offers a pretty green olive note to the currant, herb and spice flavors. **88**

1986: Distinctly earthy and leathery, with coffee and cedar notes that overshadow the currant and berry flavors. **83**

1985: Ripe and focused, with elegant currant, cedar and vanilla flavors that pick up a touch of leather on the finish. **86**

SAUVIGNON BLANC NAPA VALLEY (★★★): Manages to be rich and complex, with fig and grapefruit notes, while taming the varietal's herbaceous tendencies.

1993: Bright and straightforward, distinctly herbal on the smooth, generous finish. **85**

1992: Crisp and firm, with focused pear, vanilla and grapefruit flavors that stay with you from start to finish. Picks up fig and honey notes. **89**

DUNCAN PEAK VINEYARDS
Mendocino County
F: 1986. **O:** Hubert Lenczowski. **W:** Hubert Lenczowski.
S: None.

OVERALL	$16	★★

WINE RATINGS
Cabernet Sauvignon Mendocino County ★★

WINERY DATA
C: 300. **V:** 4 acres in Mendocino County. **G:** Cabernet
Sauvignon, Cabernet Franc, Merlot. **P:** None.

Attorney Hubert Lenczowski produces several hundred cases of Cabernet from a family-owned ranch near Hopland. A 4-acre vineyard is planted to Cabernet, Merlot and Cabernet Franc. Both the 1991 and 1992 were well made, with appealing flavors.

TASTING NOTES

CABERNET SAUVIGNON MENDOCINO COUNTY (★★): The first two vintages offer plenty of appealing fruit flavors.
1992: The ripe cherry and currant flavors are bright and lively, but somewhat one-dimensional. Approachable now but will probably be smoother in 1996. **85**
1991: Packs in lots of ripe, rich plum, cherry and herb flavors that turn lighter and simpler on the finish. Well balanced but very young. Needs time. **88**

DUNN VINEYARDS
Howell Mountain
F: 1979. **O:** Randy & Lori Dunn. **W:** Randy Dunn.
S: None.

OVERALL	$33-39	★★★★★

WINE RATINGS
Cabernet Sauvignon Howell Mountain ★★★★★
Cabernet Sauvignon Napa Valley ★★★★

WINERY DATA
C: 5,000. **V:** 20 acres in Howell Mountain. **G:** Cabernet Sauvignon (6 acres). **P:** Cabernet Sauvignon (Napa Valley).

Randy Dunn worked at Caymus Vineyards from 1975 to 1984 and helped Caymus refine the style of its Special

Selection Cabernet. In 1978, with the help of Charlie and Lorna Wagner, Dunn and his wife, Lori, bought and revived an old 5-acre Cabernet vineyard on Howell Mountain that became the anchor for their archetypal Howell Mountain Cabernets. The Dunns made 660 cases of their 1979, buying about half their grapes from a neighboring vineyard that they leased and Dunn managed. Dunn worked at Caymus on weekdays and at Dunn Vineyards on weekends, gradually building production to 4,000 to 5,000 cases, roughly divided between an inky Howell Mountain Cabernet and an almost-as-inky Napa Valley bottling made from purchased grapes and bulk wines. After the 1984 vintage, Dunn left Caymus and signed on as a consultant with several other wineries (La Jota, Livingston and Pahlmeyer), but by 1993 he had severed his ties with all of these clients.

Dunn's Cabernets are massive, complex and enormously concentrated. Both the Napa Valley and Howell Mountain have been amazingly consistent over the years (a strength with Caymus too), the Napa Valley owing part of its intensity to the healthy portion of his Howell Mountain that Dunn blends in for color and backbone. Even in off years, the strength of the Howell Mountain vineyard's personality comes through. Older vintages, dating to 1979 and 1980, are still deeply colored, youthful and vibrant and appear to have the stuffing to age 25 to 30 years—and maybe even longer. In 1991 the Dunns bought the old Park-Muscadine vineyard, a 47-acre parcel with 15 acres in vines, mostly Zinfandel and Petite Sirah long sold to Ridge and others. Over time Dunn intends to replant the vineyard to Cabernet.

TASTING NOTES

CABERNET SAUVIGNON HOWELL MOUNTAIN (★★★★★): Uncommonly dark and immense, with tiers of earthy currant, mineral, spice and cedar flavors. While tannic, it's also richly fruity, built for the long haul. Ages well.
1990: Dark in color, with very ripe, opulent and fleshy fruit flavors and an oaky edge, but it's tightly wound and compact now, finishing with chewy tannins and a burst of cherry and mineral. **92**

1989: Youthful, dark, tart and potent, showing layers of intense currant, anise, black cherry and cedar flavors. Has an earthy, oaky edge and is uncommonly tight and focused for an '89. **89**

1988: Deep in color, with a wealth of currant, cherry and spice flavors and a touch of earthiness. Very complex and complete for an '88, with tannins adding backbone. **90**

1987: Another masterpiece from this producer, with intense and deeply concentrated fruit flavors and a core of pretty, elegant, well integrated plum, cherry, currant and spice notes. Picks up a touch of earthiness on a tannic finish. **95**

1986: Bold, deep, rich and concentrated, tight and sharply focused, with layers of ripe plum, black cherry, earth and spice flavors. High in extract, thick and powerful. **96**

1985: Still the least impressive Dunn I've tasted, mainly because oak plays such a strong role in the flavor. Perhaps with time it will taste more balanced, but this wine spent more time in new French oak than most Dunns, and it shows. **88**

1984: A bold, rich, dramatic wine, packed with dense, chewy, deeply concentrated plum, currant and anise flavors. Fruit pours through on the finish. **96**

1983: Tart and earthy, also quite tannic, but loaded with currant, spice and cherry flavors. The finish is tannic too, but the fruit hangs in there. **91**

1982: Remains the star of the vintage, with its core of rich fruit and earthiness. Packed with complex currant and black cherry flavors. **94**

1981: Tight and compact, with deep, powerful, chewy currant and black cherry flavors. The tannins are thick but elegant and the finish picks up a touch of earthiness. Youthful and impressive. **93**

1980: Massive and inky, this wine is packed with ripe plum, currant and black cherry flavors and pretty spice and cinnamon scents. Won't shortchange you on tannin either. **95**

1979: Sharply focused, with deep, rich, thick layers of fruit that echo plum, cassis and black currant flavors. Firm but polished, it's mature and drinkable now but should hold up through the next decade with ease. **94**

CABERNET SAUVIGNON NAPA VALLEY (★★★★): Shares many of the Howell Mountain characteristics and can rival it in some years, but it's a shade lighter and matures more quickly.

1991: Despite its deep color, firm tannins and fruit concentration, this wine is still rough and tumble, with earthy, oaky flavors that override the backward berry and currant notes. In two tastings, this wine showed more like a barrel sample than a finished wine. **90**

1990: Dense, ripe and concentrated, with a tough edge of tannin but plenty of berry, currant and plum flavors showing through. A massive wine that holds together nicely. **92**

1989: Deep, dark and tannic, an enormously concentrated and intense wine that packs in more power and flavor than most 1989s. It has rich currant, herb, mineral and spicy berry flavors and firm tannins. **89**

1988: Youthful and unevolved but showing the same strength of character found in other Dunn Napa Valley bottlings. Packs in plenty of black cherry, currant and raspberry flavors, finishing with firm tannins. **90**

1987: A bold, rich, dramatic wine with loads of raspberry, plum and black cherry flavors. Elegant and refined, beautifully balanced. **94**

1986: Remarkably elegant and concentrated, with pure, ripe plum and currant flavors. Picks up a touch of mint and bay leaf on the finish, and it's tannic, but the fruit comes through on the finish. **93**

1985: Tough and tannic in this tasting, but with a core of rich, firm plum and currant flavors. Packed with flavor but tight as a drum. The finish is long and tannic. **93**

1984: Broad, rich and complex, with tiers of plum, black cherry, currant and spice flavors. Wonderful balance and depth of flavor. The fruit intensity builds on the finish. **97**

1983: A very complete '83 with tart, ripe black cherry and currant flavors. Has the vintage's tannic edge and may always be a bit tannic, but overall it's complex and intriguing. **91**

1982: The earthy tar and rose petal aromas are mature, with soft tannins, but there are plenty of deep, rich plum and black cherry aromas and flavors to back it up. Nearing its peak. **91**

DUNNEWOOD VINEYARDS
Mendocino County
F: 1943. **O:** Canandaigua Wine Co. **W:** George Phelan. **S:** None.

OVERALL	$7-10	★★

WINE RATINGS

Cabernet Sauvignon North Coast	
Barrel Select	★★
Chardonnay Carneros Gold Label Select	★★
Chardonnay North Coast Barrel Select	★★
Merlot North Coast Barrel Select	★★
Sauvignon Blanc North Coast	
Barrel Select	★
Zinfandel Sonoma Valley Barrel Select	★

WINERY DATA

C: 170,000. V: 10 acres in Mendocino. G: Chardonnay (10 acres). P: Cabernet Sauvignon (Alexander Valley), Cabernet Sauvignon, Chardonnay, Pinot Noir, Merlot, Sauvignon Blanc, Zinfandel (North Coast), Chardonnay, Pinot Noir (Carneros).

Not a joint venture between Dunn and Spottswoode, but a brand introduced in 1988 by Guild Wineries and now part of the Canandaigua Wine Co. The quality of its wines—Cabernet, Chardonnay, Merlot and Zinfandel—has slowly eroded over the years. The Cabernet, for instance, has gone from a Napa Valley appellation in 1984 to a North Coast appellation. All the wines are made in Mendocino. Sauvignon Blanc and Pinot Noir are also part of the 170,000-case production, which could easily get larger or smaller. A 1992 Carneros Chardonnay is the best wine in years under this label, but the Merlot and Zinfandel are marked by muddled flavors.

TASTING NOTES

CABERNET SAUVIGNON NORTH COAST BARREL SELECT (★★):
1991: Firm, austere and tannic, with rough edges, but there are enough plum and currant flavors to admire. **84**

CHARDONNAY CARNEROS GOLD LABEL SELECT (★★):
1993: Medium-weight, with a modest smoky pear edge. **83**
1992: Serves up lots of honey, pear, butter and vanilla flavors that are rich and complex. Retains its elegance and finesse, with a long, full finish that keeps echoing the flavors. **88**

CHARDONNAY NORTH COAST BARREL SELECT (★★):
1993: Simple and fruity, with hints of pear, apple and spice, turning grassy on the finish. **80**

1992: Fresh and lively, with spicy nectarine, peach and pear flavors that are elegant and floral on the finish. **83**

MERLOT NORTH COAST BARREL SELECT (★★):
1992: Very ripe, almost pruny, with gobs of currant and blackberry flavors and a soft but persistent finish. **82**

SAUVIGNON BLANC NORTH COAST BARREL SELECT (★):
1992: The herbal, weedy flavors never quite let go so the fruit can emerge. **78**

ZINFANDEL SONOMA VALLEY BARREL SELECT (★):
1992: Austere, with an earthy, cedary edge to the muted berry flavors. **80**

DURNEY VINEYARD
Carmel Valley
F: 1977. O: Robert Freeman. W: Peter Watson-Graff. S: None.

OVERALL	$9-31	★★

WINE RATINGS

Cabernet Sauvignon Carmel Valley	★★
Cabernet Sauvignon Carmel Valley	
Reserve	★★
Chardonnay Carmel Valley	★★
Chenin Blanc Carmel Valley	★★
Pinot Noir Carmel Valley	★★

WINERY DATA

C: 15,000. V: 92 acres in Carmel Valley. G: Cabernet Sauvignon (27.6), Chardonnay (27.6), Chenin Blanc (27.6), Merlot (9.2). P: None.

Durney Vineyard was the long-time dream of William (who died in 1989) and Dorothy Durney, who in 1968 were among the first to plant grapes in Carmel Valley on property they bought in 1954. The vineyard rises to 1,200 feet and is now planted mostly to Cabernet, and Chardonnay, Chenin Blanc. While the style of the Cabernet is deliberate and consistent, the wines are to my taste overly tannic. I've tasted these Cabernets on many occasions, and I am not frightened by tannins, but the wines have simply been too chewy and rustic to ever come into balance. In 1994, the winery was sold to a new group of investors headed by Robert Freeman, who is based in Miami.

Tasting Notes

Cabernet Sauvignon Carmel Valley (★★), Reserve (★★):
Dark in color, dense and chewy, almost always wearing more tannin than fruit. Ages poorly, with unevolved flavors and hard tannins.

1990: Dense and chewy, this is a tannic wine that will need years to soften. Its core is tight and firm, with hard-edged currant, herb and oak flavors that are deep and concentrated. **86**

Reserve 1989: Simple, with spicy herb and currant notes and gritty, drying tannins. Lacking the substance you would expect from a Reserve wine. **83**

Reserve 1988: Intense and fruity up front, with ripe, jammy cherry and plum flavors that are rich and concentrated, finishing with firm tannins and a burst of fruit. **84**

Reserve 1985: Dark, intense and tannic, this is a youthful and unevolved wine with rich, chewy currant, anise and plum flavors that turn dry, earthy and tannic on the finish. **84**

Reserve 1983: Ripe, aromatic and flavorful, offering plenty of currant and plum flavors and tough tannins. **86**

Reserve 1982: Better than the regular bottling, but still a rough, chewy customer that offers more earthy, leathery flavors than fruit. **76**

Reserve 1978: A slightly musty edge suggests it's corked, but it's much like the 1978 regular bottling, with an earthy mushroom flavor that covers up the fruit. Some bottles are pungently vegetal. **74**

Chardonnay Carmel Valley (★★):
Light and simple, decent but unexceptional.

1990: Smooth and generous, showing an unusual character reminiscent of kiwi fruit. The finish is light and soft. **84**

Chenin Blanc Carmel Valley (★★):

1993: Light, simple and fruity, off-dry but nicely balanced to show off the melon and apple fruit. Ready now. **85**

Pinot Noir Carmel Valley (★★):

1990: Showing mature Pinot Noir flavors, with an herb, tea and mint edge to the black cherry notes. Picks up an earthy flavor on the finish. **80**

1989: Fruity, almost grapey, but ultimately simple and sturdy, showing little grace or finesse. **80**

1988: Firm and concentrated, with a tannic edge and mildly earthy cherry and beet flavors. **80**

Duxoup
Dry Creek Valley
F: 1981. **O:** Andy & Debra Cutter. **W:** Debra Cutter. **S:** None.

Overall	$10-16	★★

Wine Ratings	
Charbono Napa Valley	★★
Gamay Dry Creek Valley	★★
Syrah Dry Creek Valley	★★

Winery Data
C: 2,000. **V:** None. **G:** None. **P:** Gamay (Napa), Syrah, Chardonnay (Dry Creek).

Owners Andy and Debra Cutter keep a very low profile, selling their wines only to selected markets. They named their winery in Healdsburg after the Marx Brothers' movie Duck Soup. All their wines, made from purchased grapes, share a rustic style. Production is about 2,000 cases and now includes Charbono from Calistoga, Gamay and Syrah from Dry Creek Valley and Zinfandel from Sonoma. In my last tasting of their wines, the 1987 Charbono was about as fruity and complex as that varietal gets, while the Gamay was a wine to sink your teeth into. The 1986 and 1987 Syrahs also showed merit, with deep colors, attractive floral aromas and berry flavors.

Tasting Notes

Various Bottlings (★★):

Charbono Napa Valley 1987: An unusual wine for the cellar. Extremely deep color and concentrated aromas of blackberry and spice, with intense berry flavors and a tangy, lingering finish. **88**

Gamay Dry Creek Valley 1990-1991 NV: Well rounded and fruity, medium-bodied, with luscious, grapey aromas, good plum, currant and spice flavors and a pleasant backbone of tannins. **85**

Gamay Dry Creek Valley 1988: Effusively fruity and fresh in aroma, but heavier on the palate, with tart, grapey flavors and a short, dry finish. **76**

Gamay Dry Creek Valley 1987: One to sink your teeth into. A lively, flavorful red with a bright purple color, berry and pepper flavors and a firm structure. **86**

Syrah Dry Creek Valley 1987: Very youthful color, vibrantly fruity and nicely focused, showing raspberry and floral aromas and flavors and an underlying gentle tannin structure. **87**

Syrah Dry Creek Valley 1986: Very fragrant and flavorful, showing a good concentration of berry and slightly floral aromas and flavors supported by soft tannins. **85**

EAGLE RIDGE WINERY
Penngrove, Sonoma County
F: 1986. **O:** Barry Lawrence. **W:** Kevin McGuire. **S:** None.

OVERALL	$12	NR

WINE RATINGS

Zinfandel Amador County	
Grandpère Vineyard	NR

WINERY DATA
C: 5,000. **V:** 3.5 acres in Petaluma. **G:** Ehrenfelser (3.5 acres). **P:** Zinfandel (Amador County).

Eagle Ridge Winery claims to be the largest winery in Penngrove, simply because it's the only one. It produces 5,000 cases of an eclectic mix of reds and whites under the brand names Eagle Ridge, Quail Creek, A Class Act and Cardinal Zin. Owner Barry Lawrence converted an old family dairy into a winery and owns the largest Ehrenfelser vineyard (3.5 acres) in California, and makes a wine from that grape. A 1989 Zinfandel from Grandpère Vineyard (Amador) was yet another addition to the lineup.

EBERLE WINERY
Paso Robles
F: 1983. **O:** W. Gary Eberle. **W:** W. Gary Eberle, Daniel Panico. **S:** None.

OVERALL	$9-28	★★★

WINE RATINGS

Cabernet Sauvignon Paso Robles	★★
Cabernet Sauvignon Paso Robles Reserve	★★
Chardonnay Paso Robles	★★
Muscat Canelli Paso Robles	★★
Syrah Paso Robles Fralich Vineyard	★★★
Viognier Paso Robles Fralich Vineyard	NR
Zinfandel Paso Robles Sauret Vineyard	★★★

WINERY DATA
C: 12,000. **V:** 35 acres in Paso Robles. **G:** Cabernet Sauvignon (17 acres), Chardonnay (14), Muscat Canelli (4). **P:** Zinfandel, Syrah, Viognier, Barbera (Paso Robles).

Former Penn State defensive tackle Gary Eberle became involved in Paso Robles winemaking in 1977 with the founding of Estrella River Winery (now home to Meridian). After some success with several varieties, Eberle departed following a family dispute and started his 12,000-case winery in 1981, producing Paso Robles-grown Cabernet, Chardonnay, Muscat, Syrah, Viognier, Zinfandel, Syrah and Barbera. The dark, rich Zinfandel from Sauret Vineyard and the supple Syrah stand out as Eberle's strengths. His Cabernet has shown promise at times but is variable in quality. The Chardonnay is the least interesting, while the off-dry Muscat and Viognier appear to be tasting-room wines aimed at visitors rather than serious wines for the future. Eberle's 35 acres of vineyard are planted primary to Cabernet (17 acres) and Chardonnay (14 acres).

TASTING NOTES

CABERNET SAUVIGNON PASO ROBLES (★★), RESERVE (★★): Early promise is unfulfilled in these medium-weight, moderately varietal wines. To their credit, they are supple and easy-going, but not especially complex.

1991: Marked by weedy herb, black olive and currant flavors, picking up a touch of cedar and toasty oak, impressive for its supple texture. Best Eberle in several vintages. **88**

1990: Light, with an earthy, leathery edge to the spicy cherry and currant notes, but ultimately simple. **84**

1989: Soft and fleshy, with herb, currant, anise and cedar flavors that trail off on the finish. **83**

1988: Fresh and lively, with pretty cherry, raspberry and currant flavors that turn spicy and plush on the finish. Modest tannins. **86**

1987: Has a burnt taste that overshadows the ripe currant and berry notes. Lean, tough and tannic, too. **76**

1986: Rich, smooth and complex, with cedar, black cherry, spice and currant flavors framed by firm, supple tannins. **85**

Reserve 1987: Herbal, with bell pepper and black olive notes. It turns tannic and gritty on the finish, with most of the fruit having dropped out already. **78**

CHARDONNAY PASO ROBLES (★★): Eberle doesn't seem to have his heart in this wine, which is soft and simple, lacking flair and complexity.

1993: Funky and earthy, with a bitter edge to the buttery pear and oak notes. **78**

1992: Serves up simple, spicy pear and nectarine flavors. **83**

MUSCAT CANELLI PASO ROBLES (★★): Light and spicy, but at times dull.

1994: Light, sweet and simple, a solid wine with delicate litchi flavors that needs a light dessert to balance it. **82**

1993: Light and spicy, offering plenty of fruit in a soft, gentle style. **81**

SYRAH PASO ROBLES FRALICH VINEYARD (★★★): Dark and complex, showing more flavor and promise than most of the lineup.

1992: Firm and supple, with generous plum and berry flavors that get spicy on the finish. **86**

1991: Lean in texture but very flavorful, with raspberry and plum flavors at the center; leathery, floral nuances and an earthy finish. **85**

VIOGNIER PASO ROBLES FRALICH VINEYARD (NR):

1993: Dark in color and soft in texture, spicy wine with simple flavors that are not very fresh. **78**

ZINFANDEL PASO ROBLES SAURET VINEYARD (★★★): The best wine overall, very ripe and complex, loaded with flavor and character.

1993: Rough and tumble now, with sharp, edgy tannins, but appealing wild berry and cherry flavors that persist. **86**

1992: Coarse and tannic, with a thin band of earthy raspberry flavors. Tannins turn gritty on the finish. **82**

1990: Ripe and opulent, with rich raspberry, currant, plum and cherry flavors framed by spicy, toasty oak notes. **88**

TOM EDDY
Napa Valley
F: 1991. **O:** Tom & Kerry Eddy. **W:** Tom Eddy. **S:** None.

OVERALL	$32	★★★

WINE RATINGS	
Cabernet Sauvignon Napa Valley	★★★

WINERY DATA
C: 300. **V:** None. **G:** None. **P:** Cabernet Sauvignon (Napa Valley), Cabernet Sauvignon (Howell Mountain), Cabernet Sauvignon (Mount Veeder), Cabernet Sauvignon (Oakville).

Tom Eddy, one-time winemaker for The Christian Brothers and Souverain, started his own wine brand with the 1991 vintage, producing 240 cases of Cabernet Sauvignon from three vineyards—Bella Vista on Diamond Mountain, Vyborny Ranch in Oakville and Beatty Ranch on Howell Mountain—with about 10 percent Merlot from Vyborny Ranch. The first Cabernet showed a core of rich, complex fruit flavors, and a Napa Chardonnay is set to follow. Production is expected to grow to 2,500 cases by 2000.

TASTING NOTES

CABERNET SAUVIGNON NAPA VALLEY (★★★):

1991: Rich, supple and complex, with an array of pretty plum, currant, black cherry, anise and mineral flavors, finishing with smooth, polished tannins. **91**

EDMEADES WINERY
Anderson Valley
F: 1972. **O:** Jess Jackson. **W:** Van Williamson. **S:** None.

OVERALL	$12-20	★★★

WINE RATINGS	
Chardonnay Anderson Valley	
Dennison Vineyard	★★★
Chardonnay Mendocino County	★★
Pinot Noir Anderson Valley	
Dennison Vineyard	★★★
Zinfandel Mendocino County	
Ciapusci Vineyard	★★★
Zinfandel Mendocino County	
Zeni Vineyard	★★★

Zinfandel North Coast ★★★

WINERY DATA
C: 9,000. V: 64 acres in Anderson Valley. G: Chardonnay (34 acres), Pinot Noir (28), Pinot Grigio (0.26), Sangiovese (0.17). P: Chardonnay, Pinot Noir, Gewürztraminer (Anderson Valley), Zinfandel (Mendocino).

Donald Edmeades planted several varieties of grapes in Anderson Valley in the late 1960s, but it wasn't until after his death that his son Deron started a winery, in 1972. Jed Steele, who went on to greater fame with Kendall-Jackson and now his own Steele Wines, was one of the first winemakers. This small winery focused on vineyard-designated Zinfandels, among other wines, creating names for Zeni, DuPratt and Pacini vineyards as fine Zin sources. In 1988 Jess Jackson, proprietor of Kendall-Jackson, bought the winery and has since replanted most of its 64 acres of vines to Chardonnay and Pinot Noir. The wine lineup also includes Zinfandel (carrying the Zeni and Ciapusci vineyards designations), and Gewürztraminer. There is also talk of making sparkling wine there, but not under the Edmeades brand. Plans are to build production to 24,000 cases.

TASTING NOTES

CHARDONNAY ANDERSON VALLEY DENNISON VINEYARD (★★★):
1993: Direct and fruity, with bright pear, spice, hazelnut and light toasty oak shadings, turning elegant. **88**

CHARDONNAY MENDOCINO COUNTY (★★):
1993: A touch spritzy, with earthy pear and apple notes of modest depth. **82**

PINOT NOIR ANDERSON VALLEY DENNISON VINEYARD (★★★):
1993: Firm and a bit oaky now, but the ripe plum and cherry flavors pick up a spice and anise edge on the finish. Can stand short-term cellaring. **86**

ZINFANDEL MENDOCINO COUNTY CIAPUSCI VINEYARD (★★★):
1990: This rough-and-tumble, chewy, tannic Zinfandel doesn't shortchange you on flavor, offering plenty of plum, berry and smoky oak notes. **86**

ZINFANDEL MENDOCINO COUNTY ZENI VINEYARD (★★★):
1993: Tight and firm, with a hard tannic edge. The chewy core of earthy raspberry and spice takes a while to work through, but it turns more palatable on the finish, where it picks up oak and peppery notes. **88**

ZINFANDEL NORTH COAST (★★★):
1992: A solid, chunky Zin with pepper, wild berry and spice notes that are fresh and vibrant. **86**

EDMUNDS ST. JOHN
Emeryville, Alameda County
F: 1985. O: Steve Edmunds & Cornelia St. John. W: Steve Edmunds. S: New World Red.

OVERALL $11-20 ★★★

WINE RATINGS

Grenache El Dorado County Marchini Bianco	NR
Pinot Grigio El Dorado County	
Rhône Blend California El Nino	NR
Rhône Blend California Les Côtes Sauvages	★★★
Syrah Sonoma Valley	★★★
Syrah Sonoma Valley Durell Vineyard	★★★★
Viognier Knights Valley	★★★
Zinfandel California	★★★
Zinfandel Mount Veeder	★★★

WINERY DATA
C: 5,000. V: 5 acres in El Dorado. G: Syrah (2.67 acres), Grenache (1), Cinsault (1), Mourvèdre (0.33). P: Grenache (Mendocino), Mourvèdre (Mt. Veeder), Mourvèdre, Syrah (El Dorado Knights Valley), Cinsault (Dry Creek), Carignane (Mt. Veeder), Viognier (Knights Valley), Pinot Grigio (El Dorado), Zinfandel (Amador County).

Rhône Ranger Steve Edmunds has doggedly pursued old-vine vineyards throughout California. His search has led him to Placerville in the Sierra Nevada foothills, Knights Valley, Sonoma Valley, Mount Veeder and Oakley in Contra Costa County. In the process he has crafted many exciting wines using Syrah from Durell Vineyard, Grenache, Zinfandel, Carignane, Mourvèdre,

Viognier and others. The downside to his vineyard discoveries is that other wineries often move in on his grape sources once they taste how good his wines are. His best wines have been the Durell Syrah, a Zinfandel and a Rhône blend he calls Les Côtes Sauvages. His eclectic product mix varies each year and there are often surprises when he finds a small batch of grapes and vinifies them into an exciting wine, exemplified by rich and complex bottlings of Pinot Grigio and Viognier. Edmunds St. John is housed in a warehouse between Berkeley and Oakland. Production hovers around 5,000 cases, with most of the wines numbering fewer than 500 cases. Don't be surprised by anything that shows up under his label—even the 1987 Napa Valley Cabernet was rich and complex, with its Rhône-like, earthy nuances.

TASTING NOTES

RHÔNE BLEND CALIFORNIA LES CÔTES SAUVAGES (★★★): Typically broad, rich and supple, with a spicy, peppery edge to the currant and cherry flavors. Ages well.

1992: Intense and spicy, with a distinct peppery edge to the grapey currant flavors, turning tannic and leathery on the finish. **88**

1991: Broad, rich and spicy, with black cherry, raspberry and blueberry flavors that are complex and long on the finish, with a lingering aftertaste. **89**

1989: The best of the early Côtes Sauvages, it's bright and vivid, with black cherry flavors that turn smooth and delicate. **88**

1988: Delicate and balanced, with cherry, currant and spice notes. **83**

1987: Lean, with a gamy edge to the currant and black cherry flavors. Sound, but lacks depth and focus. **83**

1986: Smells complex, with mature, spicy, smoky aromas that are kept alive by crisp acidity. Plum and cherry notes peek through on the finish. **87**

Reserve 1987: A shade richer and fuller than the regular 1987, but still marked by a gamy currant flavor. **85**

SYRAH SONOMA VALLEY (★★★): Deeply colored and packed with rich, supple flavors. The appellation varies with the grape source.

Sonoma Valley 1988: Very firm and tannic, with a wonderful concentration of cherry, blackberry and chocolate flavors beating out the tannins. **85**

California 1987: Vegetal notes tend to shoulder past the generous plum and berry flavors. **81**

Sonoma County 1986: Beautifully concentrated and long, with enough fine tannins to hold it for years in the cellar. After a touch of earthiness on the nose, blueberry, plum and anise flavors emerge. **91**

SYRAH SONOMA VALLEY DURELL VINEYARD (★★★★): Ranks among California's best Syrahs. Grapes are from the Durell and now Fenaughty vineyards.

1991: Another superb Syrah that combines tight, firm, rich and opulent currant and raspberry flavors with pretty oak and toast shadings. **91**

1990: Bold, rich and compelling, with ripe, opulent currant and raspberry flavors, finishing with a spicy and complex aftertaste. Very impressive. **90**

1989: Firm and focused, with rich, spicy currant and plum aromas and flavors that are deep and concentrated, finishing with power and finesse. **89**

1988: Tight and lean, with currant, spice, earth and cedar flavors. **87**

1987: Fleshy and rich, with harmonious plum and black cherry flavors. A lovely wine with depth and complexity. **89**

1986: Mature and drying out, but you get a nice taste of black cherry and spice. **85**

VIOGNIER KNIGHTS VALLEY (★★★): Captures the essense of this spicy grape and shows more complexity than most.

1992: Ripe, rich, smooth and distinctive, with complex, concentrated spice, hazelnut and pear flavors. **88**

ZINFANDEL VARIOUS BOTTLINGS (★★★): Consistently very well made, ripe, spicy and peppery, with supple berry flavors. Can carry the Mount Veeder or California appellation.

California 1991: Ripe, lush and fruity, with broad, enticing black cherry aromas and flavors. Has depth, intensity and richness. **88**

Mount Veeder 1990: Ripe and fleshy, with spicy anise, raspberry and black cherry flavors that turn smooth and polished on the finish. **88**

VARIOUS BOTTLINGS (NR):

Cabernet Blend Napa Valley Les Fleurs du Chaparral 1987: With earthy flavors reminiscent of a good northern Rhône, it's big and luscious, with a core of plum and blackberry flavors and attractive accents of game and smoke. **90**

Grenache El Dorado County Marchini Bianco 1991: Fruity and delicate, pleasing and easy to drink. It's 100 percent Grenache. **83**

Mourvèdre California 1986: Spicy and peppery, with a Zinfandel-like edge that turns broad and fruity on the finish. **88**

Pinot Grigio El Dorado County 1991: Very appealing and true to its varietal character, with creamy, delicate, floral flavors that show harmony and finesse. **86**

Rhône Blend California El Nino 1992: Lean, firm and tannic, with a narrow band of leather, berry and tarry flavors that are appealing. **84**

Rhône Blend California Port O'Call New World Red Table Wine 1989: Ripe and exotic, with a leathery edge to the plum, spice and tobacco aromas and flavors. Hints at tropical spices; firmly tannic. **84**

Rhône Blend Napa Valley Cuvée Wahluke 1990: Bright and lively plum and black cherry flavors are supple and complex through the finish. **87**

EDNA VALLEY VINEYARD

San Luis Obispo County
F: 1980. **O:** Paragon Vineyard Co. & Chalone Wine Group. **W:** Eric Laumann, Larry Brooks. **S:** None.

OVERALL	$15-25	★★★

WINE RATINGS

Chardonnay Edna Valley	★★★
Chardonnay Edna Valley Paragon Vineyard Reserve	★★★
Pinot Noir Edna Valley	★★
Pinot Noir Edna Valley Paragon Vineyard Reserve	★★

WINERY DATA

C: 60,000. **V:** 796 acres in Edna Valley. **G:** Chardonnay (475 acres), Pinot Noir (60), Sauvignon Blanc (50), Sémillon (5), Cabernet Sauvignon (106). **P:** None.

Edna Valley Vineyards grew out of the Niven family's Paragon Vineyards, which they began planting in the early 1970s, developing several hundred acres, most of it Chardonnay. In 1980 Chalone Vineyards began buying this Chardonnay and bottling it under the Edna Valley label. Later the two interests formed a joint venture and by 1990 Paragon was closely tied to the Chalone Wine Group; they own 796 acres of vineyard, with Chardonnay still the leader at 475 acres, but also large holdings of Cabernet (106 acres), Pinot Noir (60) and Sauvignon Blanc (50), which is used in the Carmenet Bordeaux-style white. Chardonnay remains the star, with annual production topping 60,000 cases, all of it barrel fermented. The Pinot Noir (2,000 cases) has been variable.

TASTING NOTES

CHARDONNAY EDNA VALLEY (★★★): Bold, rich, intense and sometimes exotic, usually well oaked too, but it can get earthy and vegetal. It's almost always a big, muscular wine.

1993: Ripe, smooth and polished, with pleasant honey, pear and citrus flavors that fold together nicely on the finish. Has more depth and richness than most 1993s. **88**

1992: This is a dense, rich, earthy wine with a lean streak of citrus and pear flavors. There's noticeable bottle variation. **84**

1991: This exotic wine displays plenty of honey, orange, pear and pineapple aromas and flavors and the finish is crisp and tart. **88**

CHARDONNAY EDNA VALLEY PARAGON VINEYARD RESERVE (★★★):

1991: Stretches to the extremes, with funky, earthy peach and apple flavors. Best on the finish, where the flavors fold into a butterscotch aftertaste. **85**

PINOT NOIR EDNA VALLEY (★★): Struggles to ripen, often resulting in an earthy wine marked by herb, cola and rhubarb flavors and chewy tannins. Sometimes it's lighter and marked by black cherry and spice flavors. Variable quality has given its owners cause to rethink their strategy with this grape.

1992: Ripe and supple, with herb, cherry, spice and cedar notes. **83**

1990: Lean in texture but ripe in aroma and flavor, with a core of black cherry flavors and a hint of soap on the finish that may bother some. **84**

PINOT NOIR EDNA VALLEY PARAGON VINEYARD RESERVE (★★):

1992: Firm and compact, with herb, black cherry and plum notes that pick up a sweet edge. **86**

EL MOLINO

St. Helena, Napa Valley
F: 1871. O: Reginald B. & Marie Mason Oliver.
W: Reginald B. Oliver, Scott McLeod. S: None.

OVERALL	$30	★★★★★

WINE RATINGS

Chardonnay Napa Valley	★★★★★
Pinot Noir Napa Valley	★★★★

WINERY DATA
C: 1,100. V: 67 acres in Rutherford. G: Pinot Noir (2 acres), Chardonnay (32), Cabernet Sauvignon (26). P: Pinot Noir (Carneros).

El Molino is a restored winery north of St. Helena, originally built in 1871 but refurbished and reintroduced as a brand by Reg Oliver in 1981. El Molino's Chardonnays and Pinot Noirs have moved to the forefront of the California scene even though the winery keeps a low profile and the wines are difficult to obtain, as most are sold to restaurants and mailing-list customers. But they are worth the extra search. Production runs about 1,100 cases, 600 of that Pinot Noir. At first the Pinot came from Abbott's Vineyard in Carneros, but in 1990 the source changed to two other vineyards, Hyde Vineyards and one owned by Carneros Valley Investors (CVI), and beginning with 1993 a small amount of Oliver's Rutherford-grown Pinot Noir will go into the blend. The Chardonnay is 100 percent Rutherford from Oliver's Star Vineyard. Until recently, the appellation on the label read St. Helena, Napa County, as that was what was on the original label. The current label simply reads Napa Valley. Oliver owns 67 acres in Rutherford divided between Chardonnay (32 acres) and Cabernet (26 acres), plus 2 acres of Pinot Noir. The wines are given minimal handling and display rich, complex flavors.

TASTING NOTES

CHARDONAY NAPA VALLEY (★★★★★): Uncommonly rich, deep and complex, with tiers of flavor and a wonderful sense of harmony and finesse. Does not undergo malolactic fermentation and ages very well.

1993: Complex with an appealing core of ripe pear and apple notes with just the right amount of oak shading. **88**
1992: Elegant and refined, with layers of complex pear, fig and spice flavors. Youthful and tight now, but the flavors run deep and long. **91**
1991: Silky and elegant, youthful and tight, with pretty, fresh, ripe pear and spice flavors that linger. **92**
1990: Big, ripe and concentrated, with layers of complex fig, pear, spice and honey flavors that turn to smoky butterscotch and vanilla on the finish. Delicious. **95**

PINOT NOIR VARIOUS BOTTLINGS (★★★★): Steadily improving, marked by ripe cherry and spice flavors with deft oak shadings. Ages well. Appellation has changed over the years with vineyard sources.
Napa Valley 1992: Bold, ripe, rich and complex, with cherry, plum and spice flavors that linger. Supple yet tannic. **91**
Napa Valley 1991: Firmly tannic, an austere wine with a tight band of smoky cherry, leather and spice flavors. Needs short-term cellaring. **89**
Napa County 1990: Bold, ripe and assertive, brimming with intense black cherry, plum and spice notes that are firm and focused. Has the tannins to cellar, but don't miss the gorgeous fruit. El Molino's finest. **92**
Napa County 1989: Young and tight, with a lean band of spicy cherry, cedar and earth notes and a light tannic grip. **86**
Napa County 1988: Trim and firm, with a spicy orange peel edge to the cherry and cedar flavors. **83**
Napa County 1987: Very mature, chocolaty and spicy, with little fruit but plenty of nutmeg and earth notes and a hint of cherry. **85**
Carneros Abbott's Vineyard 1986: Intense and tannic, with a spicy, peppery edge to the black cherry flavors. **86**
Carneros Abbott's Vineyard 1985: Aging well, with a leathery edge to the ripe cherry and spice notes. The fruit dries up on the finish. **88**
Carneros Abbott's Vineyard 1984: Turning dry and leathery, with a decadent edge. Fading. **83**

ELIZABETH VINEYARDS

Redwood Valley, Mendocino County
F: 1982. O: Betty Foster. W: Alan Green. S: None.

| OVERALL | $10 | ★★★ |

WINE RATINGS

| Zinfandel Mendocino County | ★★★ |

WINERY DATA

C: 8,000. V: 50 acres in Mendocino County. G: Chardonnay (5 acres), Sauvignon Blanc (15), Zinfandel (30). P: None.

This family-owned vineyard in Redwood Valley began as a vineyard operation, selling grapes to Mendocino wineries, but since 1987 has made about 8,000 cases of wine from its 50 acres of vines, most of which are Zinfandel.

TASTING NOTES

ZINFANDEL MENDOCINO COUNTY (★★★): Impressive for its varietal character and balance, marked by attractive berry flavors.
1992: Smooth, ripe and complex, with layers of supple black cherry, plum and wild berry flavors and thick tannins. **86**
1990: Fruity and elegant, with attractive berry and cherry notes, but they're only moderately rich and could be more focused. **85**

ELKHORN PEAK CELLARS
Napa Valley
F: 1991. O: Ken Nerlove, Greg Gahagan & John Kryzanowski. W: Kent Rasmussen. S: None.

| OVERALL | $15-21 | ★★ |

WINE RATINGS

Chardonnay Napa Valley	
Fagan Creek Vineyards	★★
Pinot Noir Napa Valley	
Fagan Creek Vineyards	★

WINERY DATA

C: 1,700. V: 8 acres in Napa Valley. G: Chardonnay (4 acres), Pinot Noir (4). P: None.

Elkhorn Peak produces two wines from its 8-acre vineyard, which is divided between Chardonnay and Pinot Noir. A 1992 Chardonnay offers ripe fruit and smoky oak flavors, and a 1992 Pinot Noir is light and simple. Both carry the Fagan Creek Vineyards designation.

TASTING NOTES

CHARDONNAY NAPA VALLEY FAGAN CREEK VINEYARDS (★★):
1993: Complex with toasty, smoky oak and ripe pear, spice and hazelnut notes that gain intensity and nuance on the finish. **85**
1992: For fans of ultraripe, woody, smoky Chardonnay. For all its excesses, there are enough ripe pear and apple flavors to keep it in balance, if only barely. **87**

PINOT NOIR NAPA VALLEY FAGAN CREEK VINEYARDS (★):
1992: Light and simple, with barely ripe fruit flavors that offer hints of unripe strawberries. **79**

ELLISTON VINEYARDS
Sunol, Alameda County
F: 1983. O: Elliston Vineyards Inc. W: Adam LaZarre. S: None.

| OVERALL | $10-22 | ★★ |

WINE RATINGS

Cabernet Blend Napa Valley	
Captain's Claret	★★
Chardonnay Central Coast	
Sunol Valley Vineyard	★★
Pinot Blanc Central Coast	
Sunol Valley Vineyard	★★

WINERY DATA

C: 4,000. V: 23 acres in Santa Cruz Mountains, Sunol Valley. G: Pinot Gris (5 acres), Chardonnay (10), Pinot Blanc (5), Pinot Noir (3). P: Cabernet Sauvignon (Central Coast).

Elliston is a 4,000-case winery in Sunol that was among the first in California to focus on Pinot Gris. Today the product mix relies mostly on Central Coast Chardonnay (1,400 cases), but also includes a California Cabernet called Captain's Claret, a Santa Cruz Chardonnay, a Pinot Blanc from Sunol Valley, and a Central Coast Pinot Gris and Pinot Noir, the latter beginning with the 1992 vintage. The 1991 Chardonnay Sunol

Valley Vineyards was bright and fruity, while the 1991 Pinot Blanc was tart, with peach and mineral flavors. The winery owns 23 acres of vineyard, with 10 acres of Chardonnay, 5 acres each of Pinot Blanc and Pinot Gris and a bit of Pinot Noir. All of the Cabernet is purchased.

T*ASTING* N*OTES*

V*ARIOUS* B*OTTLINGS* (★★):
Cabernet Blend Napa Valley Captain's Claret 1992: Shows off its pretty wild berry, cherry and currant flavors in a medium-bodied style, with firm but mild tannins and good length. **84**
Chardonnay Central Coast Sunol Valley Vineyard 1991: Fruity, with tiers of ripe pear, apple, citrus and spice flavors that are bright and lively. **85**
Pinot Blanc Central Coast Sunol Valley Vineyard 1991: Ripe and creamy, with peach and mineral flavors supported by tart acidity. **82**

E*LYSE* V*INEYARDS*
Rutherford, Napa Valley
F: 1987. **O:** Nancy & Ray Courson. **W:** Ray Courson. **S:** None.

O*VERALL*	$14-16	★★★

W*INE* R*ATINGS*
Red Table Wine Napa Valley Nero Misto	★★★
Zinfandel Howell Mountain	★★★
Zinfandel Napa Valley Coeur du Val	★★★
Zinfandel Napa Valley Morisoli Vineyard	★★★

W*INERY* D*ATA*
C: 4,300. **V:** None. **G:** None. **P:** Zinfandel (Howell Mountain), Petite Sirah (Howell Mountain), Cabernet Sauvignon (Napa Valley), Zinfandel (Napa Valley).

N*ancy* and Ray Courson started Elyse in 1987, intially focusing on Zinfandel from Morisoli Vineyard in Rutherford, which was planted in 1915. They then added a red table wine called Nero Misto ("mixed black," a blend of Petite Sirah, Zinfandel, Alicante, Grenache, Grand Noir, Carignane and Mondeuse), a Howell Mountain Zinfandel, and a Zinfandel blend called Coeur du Val. All grapes are purchased. Plans are to add a Morisoli Cabernet and a Rhône-style red (a blend of

Syrah, Grenache, Cinsault and Mourvèdre), bringing production to 4,300 cases. Quality so far has been impressive. Worth watching.

T*ASTING* N*OTES*

R*ED* T*ABLE* W*INE* N*APA* V*ALLEY* N*ERO* M*ISTO* (★★★): Hearty, with deep flavors and chewy tannins.
1992: A hearty red with firm, chewy tannins and ample raspberry and spice notes that finish with drying tannins. **84**
1991: Deep, dark, dense and ripe, with generous plum, blackberry and slightly toasty flavors that soften up on the finish. **86**
1990: Rich and almost jammy, with lots of grapey, plummy flavors, moderate tannins and a good accent of vanilla from oak aging. **86**

Z*INFANDEL* H*OWELL* M*OUNTAIN* (★★★): More austere, tannic and peppery than the Morisoli.
1992: Pure Zinfandel from start to finish, with spicy pepper, wild berry and raspberry notes that pick up a pleasant earthy nuance on the finish, where the crisp, dry tannins come through. **87**
1991: Firm, ripe and focused, offering generous blackberry and spice aromas and flavors. The finish is firm and tannic, with plenty of flavor. **85**

Z*INFANDEL* N*APA* V*ALLEY* C*OEUR DU* V*AL* (★★★): A blend of Zinfandel grown throughout the valley.
1992: Firm and tight, this crisp and flavorful wine serves up spicy cherry and raspberry flavors before the tannins clamp down. **85**

Z*INFANDEL* N*APA* V*ALLEY* M*ORISOLI* V*INEYARD* (★★★): Fruitier than the Howell Mountain, this Rutherford-area vineyard shows black cherry and raspberry flavors that are rich and focused.
1992: The black cherry and raspberry flavors are bright and lively, well focused and spicy, turning firm and tannic on the finish. **88**
1991: Tart, tight and focused, with bright cherry, plum and raspberry flavors that turn vivid and lively, with mild tannins. **87**
1990: Ripe, generous and flavorful, with plum, blackberry and vanilla aromas and flavors that remain rich and fruity through the finish. **88**

1989: Lean and sharply focused, with bright raspberry and spice aromas and flavors that are tart and lively on the finish. **85**

EMERALD BAY WINERY
This is a second label of Chateau Julien Winery (see listing).

EPOCH
This is a second label for Justin Vineyards & Winery (see listing).

ESTANCIA
Rutherford, Napa Valley
F: 1986. **O:** Franciscan Estates. **W:** Alan Tenscher. **S:** Pinnacles.

OVERALL	$7-20	★★★

WINE RATINGS

Cabernet Sauvignon Alexander Valley	★★
Chardonnay Monterey County	★★★
Chardonnay Monterey County Reserve	★★★
Meritage Red Alexander Valley	★★★
Meritage White Monterey County	★★★
Merlot Alexander Valley	★★★
Pinot Noir Monterey County	★★
Sangiovese Alexander Valley	★★
Sauvignon Blanc Monterey County	★★
Pinnacles Vineyard Chardonnay Monterey County	★★★
Pinnacles Vineyard Pinot Noir Monterey County	★★

WINERY DATA
C: 140,000. **V:** 740 acres in Alexander Valley, Monterey County. **G:** Cabernet Sauvignon (156 acres), Cabernet Franc (21), Merlot (19), Sauvignon Blanc (25), Gewürztraminer (25), Pinot Noir (72), Chardonnay (422). **P:** None.

Estancia, a brand produced at Napa's Franciscan Vineyards, offers some of the best values in California from its considerable vineyard holdings in Monterey, where 500 acres are planted mostly to Chardonnay, and in Alexander Valley, where 240 acres are planted to Bordeaux varieties (primarily Cabernet) and Sangiovese.

Across the board, the wines, especially the Chardonnay, are well crafted, with bright flavors, elegant structures and supple textures. They are ideal for everyday drinking and restaurants. The brand grew out of Franciscan's desire to shift its focus to estate-grown Napa Valley wines while continuing to utilize its considerable vineyard acreage in Alexander Valley. In 1986 Agustin Huneeus, president of Franciscan, launched the brand and its volume has quickly risen to 140,000 cases, with further growth potential. The lineup includes Cabernet, Chardonnay, Meritage (red and white), Merlot, Sauvignon Blanc and Sangiovese. Both the Merlot and Sangiovese are new. Plans call for building a winery in Monterey for white wine production, while the reds will continue to be made at Franciscan. Also, the former Pinnacles vineyard and brand, owned by Franciscan, will become part of the Estancia line, with the Chardonnay and Pinot Noir headed toward reserve designations.

TASTING NOTES

CABERNET SAUVIGNON ALEXANDER VALLEY (★★): A wine of delicacy and finesse, with supple fruit flavors and light tannins.
1992: Earthy, dry and tannic, with modest currant flavors coming through. **82**
1991: Ripe, fruity and supple, with pretty blackberry, plum and cherry aromas and flavors and mild tannins. **85**
1990: Lean and hard-edged, with an ashy component that tends to overpower the ripe blackberry and currant flavors. **86**
1989: Ripe currant and cherry flavors turn crisp, with modest intensity. **85**
1988: Firm and somewhat tannic for the level of flavor intensity, but generally well put together. **81**

CHARDONNAY MONTEREY COUNTY (★★★), RESERVE (★★★): Bold, ripe and creamy, yet elegant and refined. Packs in lots of flavor without weight.
1993: Pleasantly fruity with elegant pear, toast and spice flavors that fan out and turn complex on the finish. **87**
1992: Complex and well balanced, with ripe, creamy pear, vanilla, spice and toast flavors that turn silky and elegant on the finish. **88**
1991: A smooth, level-headed wine that's ripe, spicy and round in texture, picking up pear, apple and light toast notes. **86**
Reserve 1993: Clean and well balanced, with light pear, apple, honey and toast notes that turn elegant. **87**

MERITAGE RED ALEXANDER VALLEY (★★★): More complex than the Cabernet, yet it shares that wine's weight and flavor profile, with a shade more richness and depth.

1991: An oaky wine with an herbal, gamy edge to the fruit flavors. Finishes with hints of currant and mint and firm tannins. **85**

1990: Ripe and distinctive, with a toffee and spice edge to the supple currant and blackberry flavors. The finish is rich and elegant. **89**

1989: Ripe and chewy, with plenty of currant, cherry, herb and oak flavors that are well proportioned, with mild tannins. **85**

1988: A unique toast and caramel edge to the currant and cherry flavors makes this appealing up-front, but it loses intensity. **83**

1987: Offers spicy, peppery aromas and a lean texture, broadening into finely focused cherry and currant flavors, with mild tannins. **88**

MERITAGE WHITE MONTEREY COUNTY (★★★):

1993: Rich, spicy and round, starting off like a barrel-fermented Chardonnay, hinting at herb and butter on the generous finish. Goes for depth and achieves most of it. **87**

1992: Elegant and fleshy, with pretty fig, spice and melon notes that linger. Soft and easy to drink. **84**

MERLOT ALEXANDER VALLEY (★★★):

1992: Supple and complex, with pretty herb, currant and cedary oak flavors that are well focused and long on the finish. **88**

PINOT NOIR MONTEREY COUNTY (★★):

1993: A lighter style with strawberry jam and spicy flavors made in a fruity, delicate style. **84**

SANGIOVESE ALEXANDER VALLEY (★★):

1991: Pleasantly fruity, a youthful wine that shows some cola and herb notes to the basic berry flavors. **83**

SAUVIGNON BLANC MONTEREY COUNTY (★★):

1994: Broad and spicy, with an undertone of vegetal flavors that sneak through the modest pear and toast on the finish. **82**

1993: Soft and fruity, a nicely balanced wine for drinking while it's fresh. **82**

PINNACLES VINEYARD CHARDONNAY MONTEREY COUNTY (★★★):

1992: Ripe and rich, with earthy pear, mineral, spice and butterscotch flavors that are complex. **89**

1991: Strives for complexity with its smoky, toasty aromas, picking up modest pear and pineapple flavors. **84**

PINNACLES VINEYARD PINOT NOIR MONTEREY COUNTY (★★):

1991: Rich, focused and lively, with a bright, complex core of cherry, cola and earth notes. **89**

1990: Light and simple, with hints of plum, earth and spice flavors. **79**

1988: Earthy, tealike with funky flavors on the finish. **74**

ESTATE WILLIAM BACCALA
Mendocino County

F: 1970. **O:** William & Bob Baccala & Steve Situm. | **W:** William Baccala. **S:** Stephen Zellerbach, Robert Allison.

OVERALL	$10-15	★★
WINE RATINGS		
Chardonnay Sonoma County		★★
Merlot Napa Valley		★★★
Stephen Zellerbach		
Cabernet Sauvignon California		★
Stephen Zellerbach		
Chardonnay California		★★
Stephen Zellerbach		
Sauvignon Blanc California		★

WINERY DATA
C: 5,000. **V:** None. **G:** None. **P:** Cabernet Sauvignon, Chardonnay (Sonoma County), Merlot, Chardonnay, Zinfandel (Napa Valley), Sauvignon Blanc (California).

William Baccala started his first winery in Mendocino County before selling the facility (now Jepson) and moving to Sonoma County, where he bought the Zellerbach brand but not the winery. Zellerbach has become his second label. Through most of this time he has focused on well made Merlots, with the 1990 and 1991 vintages under the Baccala label carrying the Napa Valley appellation. In 1993 Baccala bought the former Tijsseling Winery in Hopland, where he now makes his wines.

TASTING NOTES

CHARDONNAY SONOMA COUNTY (★★):
1992: Ripe and spicy, with lively pear and peach notes that turn simple and fruity on the finish. **82**
1991: A pleasant wine with cream, vanilla, pear and spice notes, finishing with a subtle, delicate edge. **86**

MERLOT NAPA VALLEY (★★★): This wine is usually well crafted, with a solid core of fruit flavors and smooth tannins.
1991: Bright and lively, with vivid currant and cherry notes, picking up a spicy edge on a mildly tannic finish. **86**
1990: Full-bodied, with ripe, spicy flavors, a deep color and a lingering finish that echoes plum, currant and cherry notes. **88**

STEPHEN ZELLERBACH VARIOUS BOTTLINGS:
Cabernet Sauvignon California 1991: Oaky and herbaceous, with a drying, spicy, leathery edge. **78**
Chardonnay California 1993: A lightly fruity wine with ripe pear, apple and melon flavors, finishing with a trace of oak. **83**
Sauvignon Blanc California 1992: Veers strongly toward the herbal-vegetal end of the scale. **78**

ESTRELLA RIVER WINERY
San Luis Obispo County
F: 1977. **O:** Bronco Wine Co. **W:** N/A. **S:** None.

OVERALL	$6	★★

WINE RATINGS
Chardonnay California Proprietor's Reserve	★★
Sauvignon Blanc California Proprietor's Reserve	★

WINERY DATA
C: N/A. **V:** N/A. **G:** N/A. **P:** N/A.

Estrella River became the first major winery in San Luis Obispo County in 1977, when Gary Eberle, his family and a group of investors planted several hundred acres to vines, built a winery and launched this brand. Despite commercial success, a rift among partners led to its being sold. Eberle departed to start his own winery (see Eberle Winery), and Wine World Estates (owner of Beringer, Chateau Souverain, Napa Ridge and Maison Deutz) bought the Estrella winery in 1988, renaming it Meridian. The brand name has since been revived by the Bronco Wine Co. and now produces California-appellation Chardonnay and Sauvignon Blanc.

TASTING NOTES

VARIOUS BOTTLINGS:
Chardonnay California Proprietor's Reserve 1992: Tastes sweet beyond ripeness, but delivers pretty peach and pineapple flavors that linger, turning slightly cloying. **82**
Sauvignon Blanc California Proprietor's Reserve 1993: Soft and fragrant, spicy enough to make the slightly buttery pear flavors interesting. **80**

ÉTUDE WINES
Napa Valley
F: 1982. **O:** Tony Soter. **W:** Tony Soter. **S:** None.

OVERALL	$24	★★★★

WINE RATINGS
Cabernet Sauvignon Napa Valley	★★★★
Pinot Blanc Napa Valley	★★★
Pinot Noir Carneros	★★★
Pinot Noir Rosé Napa Valley	★★★

WINERY DATA
C: 6,000. **V:** None. **G:** None. **P:** Pinot Noir (Carneros), Pinot Blanc (Carneros), Cabernet Sauvignon (Napa Valley).

Winemaker Tony Soter first made wine at Chappellet with some success in the 1970s, but he built his name and reputation at Spottswoode, where he served as winemaker through its first decade (1982-1991). Along the way he started his own company and brand, Étude Wines, buying Cabernet Sauvignon from several mid-Napa Valley growers and Pinot Noir from Carneros vineyards. There is little question about his talent as a winemaker; witness the excellent string of Spottswoode Cabernets. But Soter is the first to credit Spottswoode's vineyard for the character of that wine. The grapes he's buying are very good, but not in the same class as Spottswoode's.

Quality has generally been very high, but inconsistent. With Pinot Noir there has been a steep learning curve, although he's getting a better handle on that wine every year. Pinot Blanc and a refreshing rosé of Pinot Noir are also part of the 6,000-case product mix. Soter's consulting clients include Niebaum-Coppola Estate, Araujo Estate and Moraga in Beverly Hills.

TASTING NOTES

CABERNET SAUVIGNON NAPA VALLEY (★★★★): Typically dark, rich, complex and supple, high in extract, with firm tannins and minty, herbal currant flavors. Can be variable; witness the very ripe 1990 and the leaner, trimmer 1991. These wines have no track record for aging yet.

1991: Smooth and elegant, with a focused band of spice, currant and cedary oak that gently unfolds, turning supple and polished. **90**

1990: Bold and ultra-ripe, bordering on jammy, with supple black cherry and plum flavors, framed by spicy oak, but the fruit pours through and the texture is polished. **91**

1989: Tight, firm and focused, deftly balancing the ripe, spicy currant flavors and cedary oak shadings. **87**

1987: Distinctive for its tobacco, herb and cedar notes, and the currant and black cherry flavors underneath add complexity to this warm, ripe and supple wine. **88**

1986: Deep, rich, intense and fruity, with cedar, currant, plum and spice flavors that are tightly wound and compact. Needs to shed some tannin. **92**

1985: Packed with plum, cherry, anise and spice flavors and firm with tannins and oak, it offers deeply concentrated flavors that are just beginning to reveal their potential. **90**

PINOT NOIR CARNEROS (★★★): These wines have steadily improved since the first vintage in 1984, with recent efforts showing a measure of delicacy and finesse, with complex cherry and plum flavors and a silky texture. Best on release.

1992: Smooth and elegant, with a pretty beam of ripe black cherry, currant and light oak shadings. Finishes with a delicate edge. **89**

1991: Spicy and floral, with a touch of mint, this is a firm, closed wine that slowly reveals a core of earthy black cherry and plum flavors. **89**

1990: Ripe and flavorful up front, with plum, cola, black cherry and spice notes. Firm and tight, it is nearing its peak. **87**

1989: Smooth, ripe and plush, with complex spice, cola and black cherry flavors that are focused and elegant, finishing with a creamy texture. **87**

1988: Mature and complex, with supple black cherry, mushroom, smoke, spice and dried flower aromas and flavors. **87**

1987: From a lighter vintage, this wine has peaked and now shows earthy dried fruit flavors. **79**

1986: Fully mature, the spice, plum and dried cherry flavors have taken on a pleasantly decadent, earthy edge. **84**

1985: A shade past its prime but holding, it shows mature cherry, spice and plum flavors. **80**

1984: Fully mature and past its prime but still drinkable, with light plum and cherry notes. **77**

EVENSEN VINEYARDS & WINERY
Oakville, Napa Valley
F: 1979. **O:** Sharon Evensen. **W:** Greg Evensen. **S:** None.

OVERALL	$7-10	★★

WINE RATINGS

Chardonnay Napa Valley	NR
Gewürztraminer Napa Valley	NR

WINERY DATA
C: 800. **V:** 6 acres in Napa Valley. **G:** Gewürztraminer (5 acres), Chardonnay (1). **P:** None.

The Evensen family owns 6 acres of vineyard near Oakville, 5 planted to Gewürztraminer, their main wine, and 1 to Chardonnay. The winery makes 800 cases a year of mostly Gewürztraminer in an off-dry style, and distribution is very limited.

FALLENLEAF VINEYARD
Sonoma Valley
F: 1982. **O:** Fallenleaf Winery Inc. **W:** John Montero. **S:** None.

OVERALL	$9-12	★★

WINE RATINGS

Chardonnay Carneros	★★
Sauvignon Blanc Sonoma Valley	★★

WINERY DATA

C: 5,000. **V:** 16 acres in Sonoma Valley. **G:** Chardonnay (8 acres), Sauvignon Blanc (8). **P:** None.

Fallenleaf began as a vineyard on the Carneros-Sonoma border. By the late 1980s, small lots of Chardonnay and Sauvignon Blanc were being made at Bouchaine Vineyards. Production from the 16-acre vineyard is 5,000 cases of a light and tinny Chardonnay and a vegetal Sauvignon Blanc. John Montero is the winemaker.

TASTING NOTES

VARIOUS BOTTLINGS (★★):
Chardonnay Carneros 1991: Light and crisp, with a tinny edge to the modest pear and apple flavors. **77**
Sauvignon Blanc Sonoma Valley 1991: Frankly vegetal, with more celery and pepper than fruit, but the finish is crisp and refreshing. **80**

FAR NIENTE WINERY

Oakville, Napa Valley
F: 1979. **O:** Far Niente Winery, Inc. **W:** Dirk Hampson. **S:** Dolce.

OVERALL	$32-50	★★★★

WINE RATINGS

Cabernet Sauvignon Napa Valley	★★★★
Chardonnay Napa Valley	★★★★
Dolce Sémillon Napa Valley	★★★★★

WINERY DATA

C: 36,500. **V:** 167 acres in Napa Valley. **G:** Cabernet Sauvignon (58 acres), Merlot (7), Cabernet Franc (6), Chardonnay (76), Sémillon (14), Sauvignon Blanc (4). **P:** None.

Oklahoma nurseryman Gil Nickel outbid Robert Mondavi and others to buy this prized property in Oakville, west of Highway 29. The vineyard is next door to Martha's Vineyard (Heitz Cellars) and Mondavi's To-Kalon Vineyard, two great Cabernet sites, and Nickel and partner Richard Stelling have spent a small fortune restoring the 1885 winery, tunneling barrel-aging caves and replanting the vineyards. The winery's strength has always been Chardonnay (24,000 cases), which ages exceptionally well, followed by a Sémillon-based dessert wine called Dolce (500 cases) and a Cabernet (12,000 cases) that is variable but steadily improving. The winery draws from 167 acres of vineyard, led by Chardonnay (76 acres, mostly in the Coombsville area east of Napa), Cabernet (58 acres) and Sémillon (14 acres).

TASTING NOTES

CABERNET SAUVIGNON NAPA VALLEY (★★★): Plagued by uneven quality. The 1984 to 1986 vintages show better depth and balance and are true to the years, but they lack the complexity that the best from this area have. Ages well and is improving.
1992: Exciting and full-bodied, with a rich, complex core of cherry and currant flavors, finishing with mild tannins. **93**
1991: Supple and elegant, with a band of spicy currant, black cherry, cedar, anise and light oak flavors. Impressive for its balance, delicacy and fine tannins. **88**
1990: Youthful, firm, tannic and leathery, showing toasty new oak notes, but also nice currant and spice flavors that stay with you on the finish. **89**
1989: Smoky, with smooth, supple cedar, tobacco and currant flavors that are well balanced and well mannered for an '89. Hints of herb and chocolate emerge on the aftertaste. **86**
1988: Well balanced for an '88, with ripe, intense currant and cherry aromas and flavors, hints of herb and spice and firm tannins. **86**
1987: Earthy, spicy and supple, with some barnyardy, leathery overtones that the solid core of currant and plum flavors can easily handle. **88**
1986: Firm and structured, with tight, focused black cherry, cedar, pepper and anise flavors coming through to give it depth and complexity. **91**
1985: Rich and concentrated, with coffee, cedar, black cherry and spicy oak flavors, finishing with a hint of earthiness. **90**
1984: Bold, ripe, rich and supple, with opulent, sharply focused black cherry, plum and currant flavors and soft tannins. Plenty of depth and intensity behind the fruit. **92**
1983: Austere and dry as 1983s go, but with some attractive Cabernet flavors as well, with hints of berries, cherries and plums framed by cedary oak. **84**
1982: Mature and past its prime, with dry cedar, currant and earth notes. **81**

CHARDONNAY NAPA VALLEY (★★★★): Superb from the outset, well oaked, with pure, ripe, intense fruit flavors. Does not undergo malolactic fermentation and ages very well, although the winery is considering putting a portion of the wine through malolactic fermentation. A shade less complex of late.

1993: Crisp and flinty, less complex of late, with a tart citrus edge to the pear and lemony notes. Finishes with crisp acidity, but comes up short on flavor. **87**

1992: Broad and ripe, with spicy toast and pear flavors that are a bit on the green side. **89**

1991: Crisp, lean and intense, with spicy pear, pineapple and citrus notes that are complex and concentrated, finishing with a clean, grapefruit-skin edge. **89**

1990: Youthful and very tight, with honey, pear, spice and apple flavors held in by crisp acidity. **90**

DOLCE SÉMILLON NAPA VALLEY (★★★★★): Uncommonly complex and flavorful, with brilliant fruit flavors and amazing length.

1992: Sweet with a ripe sugary edge, turning to apricot, pear, honey and spice, but also with a green tobacco edge. **89**

1991: Brilliant yellow, rich with fig, apricot, honey, pear and spice, with toasty buttery oak on the finish. **91**

1990: Wonderfully complex, with tiers of honey, spice and fig aromas and flavors, picking up nectarine and anise notes that turn smooth and fleshy on a long, full finish. **95**

1989: Bold, ripe and complex, with intense, rich pear, spice, butter, nutmeg and honey flavors that fan out on the palate. Harmonious and elegant, with layers of apricot and butterscotch emerging on the finish. **93**

FARELLA-PARK VINEYARDS
Napa Valley
F: 1985. **O:** Frank & Anne Park Farella. **W:** Tom Farella. **S:** None.

OVERALL	$9-25	★★

WINE RATINGS

Cabernet Sauvignon Napa Valley	★★
Chardonnay Napa Valley	
Barrel Fermented	★★
Merlot Napa Valley	★★

Sauvignon Blanc Napa Valley	★

WINERY DATA
C: 1,200. **V:** 25 acres in Napa Valley. **G:** Merlot (8 acres), Cabernet Sauvignon (5), Chardonnay (8), Sauvignon Blanc (3). **P:** None.

Anne and Frank Farella own 25 acres in Napa Valley from which they make 1,200 cases of Cabernet, Chardonnay, Merlot and Sauvignon Blanc. Quality has slowly improved since their first vintage in 1985, but the wines are still ordinary for Napa Valley. The heavily oaked Merlot is the best wine so far. The Sauvignon Blanc is light and grassy.

TASTING NOTES

VARIOUS BOTTLINGS:
Cabernet Sauvignon Napa Valley 1991: Supple and smooth, with herb, currant, cedar and anise flavors that come together nicely. **85**
Chardonnay Napa Valley Barrel Fermented 1992: Earthy, with a funky edge to the mature pear and spice flavors, although it straightens out on the finish. **83**
Merlot Napa Valley 1990: Laced with herb and currant flavors, this is still a tightly knit and tannic wine. **84**
Merlot Napa Valley 1988: An oaky wine that offers decent currant and cherry flavors to stand up to the wood. **84**
Sauvignon Blanc Napa Valley 1991: Light and soft, with a grassy edge to the simple apple flavors. **75**

GARY FARRELL WINES
Russian River Valley
F: 1982. **O:** Gary Farrell Wines. **W:** Gary Farrell. **S:** None.

OVERALL	$15-32	★★★★★

WINE RATINGS

Cabernet Sauvignon Sonoma County	
Ladi's Vineyard	★★★
Chardonnay Russian River Valley	★★★★
Chardonnay Russian River Valley	
Allen Vineyard	★★★★★
Chardonnay Russian River Valley	
Westside Farms	★★★★

Merlot Sonoma County Ladi's Vineyard	★★★
Pinot Noir Russian River Valley	★★★★
Pinot Noir Russian River Valley	
Allen Vineyard	★★★★★
Pinot Noir Santa Barbara County	
Bien Nacido Vineyard	★★★★
Sauvignon Blanc Russian River Valley	
Rochioli Vineyard	★★★★
Zinfandel Russian River Valley	★★★★

WINERY DATA

C: 6,000. **V:** None. **G:** None. **P:** Chardonnay (Russian River Valley), Chardonnay (Santa Barbara County), Pinot Noir (Russian River Valley), Pinot Noir (Santa Barbara County), Merlot (Sonoma County), Cabernet Sauvignon (Sonoma County), Zinfandel (Russian River Valley).

Since the late 1980s, Gary Farrell's wines have quickly risen to the top in California. Farrell began his career as the winemaker for Davis Bynum Winery, where he still works, but in 1982 he began making small lots of wine under his own label. The quality, particularly of the Chardonnay and Pinot Noir from Allen Vineyard, places his wines among the best; the Sauvignon Blanc and Zinfandel run close behind, slightly ahead of the Cabernet and Merlot. Regardless of how one judges them, there's a definite sense of style that runs through these finely crafted wines. While Farrell doesn't own any vineyards, his contacts are first-rate: he buys Allen Vineyard Chardonnay and Pinot Noir, Rochioli Sauvignon Blanc, Bien Nacido Pinot Noir and Ladi's Vineyard Cabernet and Merlot. Production is about 6,000 cases.

TASTING NOTES

CABERNET SAUVIGNON SONOMA COUNTY LADI'S VINEYARD (★★★): Has yet to reach the complexity of Farrell's best wines, but this sharply focused, deeply colored, plush-textured Cabernet is very impressive and consistent.
1992: Full-bodied, with well focused ripe cherry and currant fruit that slowly unfolds, showing more depth, detail and richness on the finish. Just showing its potential; should be excellent after 1997. **89**

1991: Deeply colored, firm and intense, with spicy black cherry, currant and plum notes that pick up nice cedary oak flavors on the finish. Has a crisp tannic edge. **87**
1990: A beautifully crafted wine with ripe, rich currant, mineral and plum flavors framed by toasty, cedary oak shadings that add complexity. **89**
1989: A successful, focused and lively 1989 that offers ripe, crisp currant, toasty oak and mineral flavors. **85**
1988: Lean and focused, with sharp-edged currant aromas and flavors shaded by floral notes. **85**

CHARDONNAY RUSSIAN RIVER VALLEY (★★★★):
1991: Deftly balanced, with spicy, smoky, buttery oak flavors that add complexity to the ripe, rich and crisp apple and pear notes. Finishes with a lovely, spicy nutmeg aftertaste. **92**

CHARDONNAY RUSSIAN RIVER VALLEY ALLEN VINEYARD (★★★★★): Intense and lively, rich and complex, with bright, focused flavors and supreme balance. Ages well.
1993: Tight and compact, with a nice toasty oak edge to the pear, apple and spice notes, fanning out on a complex aftertaste, where the butterscotch flavors gain richness. **92**
1992: Firm and tight, with a compact band of pear, honey, spice and cedary oak flavors; complex and concentrated. **88**
1991: A big, bold, rich and intensely flavored wine that's concentrated and packed with spice, lemon, fig and pear flavors that are tight and complex. **92**

CHARDONNAY RUSSIAN RIVER VALLEY WESTSIDE FARMS (★★★★):
1993: Medium-weight, with ripe pear, peach and apple notes picking up a spicy, toasty oak edge on the finish, where the flavors fan out and turn complex. **89**

MERLOT SONOMA COUNTY LADI'S VINEYARD (★★★): Shy of greatness but getting close, uniformly dark, plush and concentrated.
1992: A touch earthy, with leather, currant and cedary notes that turn dry and tannic. **83**
1991: Firm and compact, a dark and richly flavored wine with pretty black cherry, plum and mineral flavors, turning smooth and polished on the finish. **88**
1990: This wine could pass for a Pomerol with its rich smoke and plum aromas and smooth, plush texture. Pumps out lots of flavor, with cherry and spice notes, but

retains its elegant mouth-feel, finishing with fine, polished tannins. **89**

PINOT NOIR RUSSIAN RIVER VALLEY (★★★★): Bright and lively, with rich, concentrated fruit flavors, supple and complex.

1991: Smooth, ripe and generous, with spicy cherry, raspberry and earth flavors that are intense, concentrated, rich and delicate. Finishes with a broad array of flavors. **88**

1990: Supple, generous and fruity, with pretty cherry, strawberry and raspberry flavors that are delicate and elegant. **89**

1989: Aromatic and rich, with lovely berry and currant aromas and flavors that persist through the crisp, lively finish. **87**

1988: Ripe and bright, with lively, intense and spicy black cherry, herb and raspberry flavors that are focused and concentrated. **90**

1987: Light and delicate, with spicy cherry and currant notes that are elegant and tasty. **85**

1986: Lots of complex fruit and oak, with ripe cherry, strawberry and plum flavors that are broad and rich. **90**

PINOT NOIR RUSSIAN RIVER VALLEY ALLEN VINEYARD (★★★★★): A shade deeper, with broad, amazingly complex flavors. The 1990 remains stunning.

1992: Serves up ripe plum and raspberry flavors of moderate richness and intensity, but it turns tight, tannic and compact on the finish. **88**

1991: Bright, ripe, intense and focused, the rich fruit notes turn elegant and graceful, finishing with moderate tannins. **87**

1990: Amazingly complex, with broad, elegant, spicy blackberry, cherry, tea and spice flavors, picking up smoky, cedary oak on the finish. **95**

1988: A charming Pinot Noir that's bold, rich and complex, brimming with plum, black cherry, herb and spice notes. Long, rich and concentrated, with wonderful depth. **91**

1987: A complex little wine with plenty of plum and cherry flavors and a touch of earth and hay. **84**

1986: Light in color and weight, with earthy cherry and plum flavors that are lively but not especially rich or complex. **84**

1985: Elegant and balanced, with mature, earthy plum and berry flavors that stay with you. **85**

1984: Ripe and fleshy, showing mature plum jam, herb and spice notes that dry out on the finish. **86**

1982: Fully mature and aging gracefully, with herb, spice and plum notes that dry out on the finish. **87**

PINOT NOIR SANTA BARBARA COUNTY BIEN NACIDO VINEYARD (★★★★): Showcases the vineyard's character—impressive so far.

1992: Intense and spicy, with peppery notes and a firm tannic backbone. The herb, tea and berry flavors barely sneak past the tannins. **85**

1990: Tight, firm, rich and concentrated, with sharply focused black cherry, beet, cola, herb and spice flavors that are deep and compelling. Youthful and tight, it finishes with a long, full aftertaste. **91**

SAUVIGNON BLANC RUSSIAN RIVER VALLEY ROCHIOLI VINEYARD (★★★★): Not made every year, but it's intense and concentrated, among the very best in California.

1992: Enormously rich, intense and concentrated, with a wealth of complex flavors ranging from ripe fig, grapefruit and pear to sweet pea and spice, finishing with a touch of honey. The finish is long and complex; a stunning Sauvignon Blanc. **93**

ZINFANDEL RUSSIAN RIVER VALLEY (★★★★): Beautifully crafted, with ripe fruit flavors at the forefront. Sometimes carries the Collins Vineyard designation.

Collins Vineyard 1993: Dark, tight and intensely wound, this young wine needs short-term cellaring to soften its rough edges. The chunky currant and raspberry flavors, though, are appealing, rich and well focused. **89**

1992: A beautifully crafted wine with amazing fruit complexity. The tiers of cherry, raspberry and boysenberry are bright, intense and lively until the tannins clamp down on the finish, where the tar and cedary oak flavors fold in. **92**

1991: Fresh and lively, with generous blueberry, raspberry and floral aromas and flavors that wrap around the palate like a spoonful of fresh fruit. **88**

Collins Vineyard 1990: Lean and focused, with impressive plum and berry flavors and hints of mineral and tar on the finish. **88**

FELLOM RANCH VINEYARDS
Santa Clara County
F: 1983. O: Roy S. & Roy E. Fellom. W: Mike Daggett.
S: None.

OVERALL	$6-18	NR

WINE RATINGS
Cabernet Sauvignon
   Santa Cruz Mountains   NR
Zinfandel Santa Clara County   NR

WINERY DATA
C: 1,500. V: 12 acres in Santa Cruz Mountains. G: Cabernet
Sauvignon. P: Zinfandel (Santa Clara Valley).

Fellom Ranch is a 12-acre Cabernet vineyard on
Montebello Road not far from Ridge Vineyards. The win-
ery makes 800 cases each of Santa Cruz Mountains
Cabernet and, from purchased grapes, Santa Clara
Zinfandel.

FENESTRA WINERY
Livermore Valley
F: 1976. O: Fenestra Winery. W: Lanny Replogle.
S: None.

OVERALL	$9-35	★★

WINE RATINGS
Cabernet Sauvignon Livermore Valley   NR
Chardonnay Livermore Valley
   Toy Vineyard   ★
Merlot Livermore Valley   ★★
Sémillon Livermore Valley   ★★
White Table Wine
   Livermore Valley Semonnay   NR
Zinfandel Livermore Valley   ★★

WINERY DATA
C: 4,000. V: None. G: None. P: Cabernet Sauvignon, Merlot,
Chardonnay, Zinfandel, Sémillon, Pinot Noir (Livermore
Valley), Cabernet Sauvignon, Merlot, Chardonnay, Zinfandel,
Sémillon, Pinot Noir (Santa Lucia Highlands).

Lanny Replogle was a chemistry professor at San Jose
State University when he started making wine under the
Fenestra label. He made his wines at Stony Ridge Winery
and Ruby Hill Winery before settling into an 1889-era winery in Livermore Valley. The 4,000-case product mix, all
made from purchased Livermore grapes (except one
Cabernet bottling), includes Cabernet (Livermore and Santa
Lucia), Chardonnay (Toy Vineyard), Merlot, Sémillon and
Zinfandel, all made in lots of 500 cases or less. Smaller lots
of Pinot Blanc, Sauvignon Blanc, white Zinfandel and late-
harvest Riesling and Sémillon are made occasionally. The
wines are sound but rustic and merely average. The Merlot,
with ripe, bright flavors, and the Zinfandel are the best.

TASTING NOTES

CABERNET BLEND LIVERMORE VALLEY (NR):
1990: Light and simple with a modest core of currant
and cherry-laced fruit. **78**

CABERNET SAUVIGNON VARIOUS BOTTLINGS (NR):
Livermore Valley 1991: Leans toward the herb and vegetal side of Cabernet, with just enough berry fruit to keep
it interesting. Firmly tannic. **79**
Livermore Valley 1990: Better than the 1989, but it's
still tough and tannic, with just a hint of currant and
berry flavors. **82**
Monterey County Smith and Hook Vineyard 1989:
Tight, tannic and chewy, with wood and tannin overriding the modest plum and cherry flavors. **79**

CHARDONNAY LIVERMORE VALLEY TOY VINEYARD (★):
1993: Lean and earthy, with a leesy edge to the pear and
pineapple flavors. **82**
1992: Tastes awkward and disjointed, with earthy
Chardonnay and oak flavors. **75**

MERLOT LIVERMORE VALLEY (★★):
1991: Light, bright and crisp, offering pleasant berry and
currant flavors that linger. **83**
Special Reserve 1989: Lush, plush and flavorful. A stiff
dose of spicy French oak blends well with the ample cassis and black cherry flavors. **89**

SÉMILLON LIVERMORE VALLEY (★★):
1992: Round and generous, very pretty for its honey-
scented pear and apricot fruit. **86**

**WHITE TABLE WINE LIVERMORE VALLEY
SEMONNAY (NR):**
1992: Broad, spicy and generously scented with oak, this
one has a nice core of citrusy flavor. **85**

ZINFANDEL LIVERMORE VALLEY (★★):
Special Reserve 1991: Dry and earthy, with chewy tannins and a waxy berry flavor. **78**
1990: Light in color, with earthy rhubarb flavors. **80**
1989: Smooth and refined, with pretty aromas and wild berry, oak and raspberry flavors. **87**

FERRARI-CARANO WINERY
Dry Creek Valley
F: 1981. **O:** Don & Rhonda Carano. **W:** George Bursick.
S: None.

OVERALL	$11-48	★★★★

WINE RATINGS

Cabernet Sauvignon Sonoma County	★★★
Cabernet Sauvignon Sonoma County Reserve	★★★
Chardonnay Alexander Valley	★★★★★
Chardonnay California Reserve	★★★★★
Fumé Blanc Sonoma County	★★★
Fumé Blanc Sonoma County Reserve	★★★
Merlot Alexander Valley	★★★
Pinot Noir Napa-Sonoma Counties Rhonda's Reserve	NR
Sangiovese Alexander Valley	★★★
Sauvignon Blanc Sonoma County El Dorado Gold	★★★
Siena Sonoma County	★★★★
Zinfandel Dry Creek Valley	★★★★

WINERY DATA
C: 88,000. **V:** 529 acres in Alexander Valley, Dry Creek Valley, Carneros. **G:** Chardonnay (208 acres), Sauvignon Blanc (91), Merlot (67), Cabernet Sauvignon (42), Sangiovese (60), Bordeaux Red Varieties (30), Zinfandel (14), Pinot Noir (5), Other Red (7), Sémillon (5). **P:** Chardonnay (Carneros), Zinfandel (Dry Creek Valley), Sauvignon Blanc (Alexander Valley, Chalk Hill), Sauvignon Blanc (Sonoma Valley, Dry Creek Valley), Cabernet Sauvignon (Sonoma Mountains), Cabernet Sauvignon (Alexander Valley), Malbec (Alexander Valley).

Ferrari-Carano is the ambitious, fast-paced and highly successful undertaking of hoteliers Don and Rhonda Carano, owners of the Eldorado Hotel and Casino and partners in the new Silver Legacy casino, both in Reno. Beginning in 1979, the Caranos began buying vineyard property in northern Sonoma County and have since expanded their holdings, investing millions acquiring and planting vineyards. Today they own 529 acres in more than a dozen locations, from Alexander Valley to Dry Creek to Carneros. Their beautiful, state-of-the-art winery, barrel-aging *chai* and showcase Villa Fiore estate are in Dry Creek Valley.

Ferrari-Carano first made its mark with Chardonnay and Fumé Blanc; having mastered those wines as well as any producer in California, the winery is now moving into an impressive array of reds, with classy Cabernet, Merlot and Zinfandel, exciting Reserve Cabernet, Sangiovese and Syrah, and the absolutely delicious Sangiovese-Cabernet-Merlot blend called Siena. Recently all the reds have shown more depth, richness and complexity, a factor Carano and winemaker George Bursick attribute to their mountain-grown grapes. The most important mountain vineyard has nearly 100 acres in vines in an area where Chalk Hill, Alexander Valley and Knights Valley meet. By 2000, the winery may well be producing 100 percent mountain-grown reds (except Pinot Noir). To top things off, the winery also produces a plush dessert wine called Eldorado Gold. About the only wine Bursick has tried and not yet mastered is Pinot Noir, but in 1994 he was enthusiastic about the winery's first attempt with their new vineyard in Russian River Valley. The entire lineup is on solid ground.

TASTING NOTES

CABERNET SAUVIGNON SONOMA COUNTY (★★★):
Supple and fruity, with soft tannins and moderate depth, but getting richer. Earlier wines were made under the Alexander Valley appellation.
1991: Well oaked, with the currant, herb and berry flavors just able to balance out, finishing with a subtle tobacco edge. **86**
1990: Bright and vibrant, with an array of lively, ripe currant and black cherry flavors, adding cedar and toasty oak on the finish. **89**
1988: Tart, crisp and focused, with generous currant and blackberry flavors and hints of cedar and tobacco on the finish. **84**
1987: Tightly wound, with ripe plum, cranberry and smoky oak flavors that pick up firm tannins. **84**

1986: A pleasant wine with mint, currant and herb flavors of moderate depth. **80**

CABERNET SAUVIGNON SONOMA COUNTY RESERVE (★★★): Early attempts were dark and plush, better than the vintage in general, but expect even grander wines in 1990 to 1992, as the mountain-grown grapes add more intensity and depth.
1989: Austere, with firm, gritty tannins, a core of intense, very ripe fruit flavors and hints of plum and prune, finishing with crisp tannins. **85**
1988: Dark in color, with a pretty bouquet of mint, currant and plum aromas and intense chocolate, berry and oak flavors that turn tight and narrow on the finish. **86**
1987: Crisp, tart and tannic, with modest black cherry and toast aromas and flavors. **83**

CHARDONNAY ALEXANDER VALLEY (★★★★★): A shade richer and fuller than the Reserve, with bright, lively flavors.
1993: Deliciously fruity with a solid core of spice, pear and apple, framed smoky, toasty oak, with a long lingering finish. **91**
1992: Serves up a lot of ripe, generous fruit, with pear, pineapple, honey, vanilla and almond flavors that are deftly balanced, finishing with an amazingly long and complex finish. **93**
1991: Packs in lots of flavor, with intense, ripe pear, grapefruit, lemon and honey notes framed by creamy, toasty, buttery oak. Juicy and complex; keeps pumping out flavor on the finish. **91**

CHARDONNAY CALIFORNIA RESERVE (★★★★★): A touch leaner and more refined than the Alexander Valley, well oaked, exceptionally well made and amazingly consistent. The Reserve includes Carneros Chardonnay.
1992: Complex, with ripe pear and apple flavors and a rich creamy texture that picks up an exotic tangerine edge that lingers. **91**
1991: Has lots of ripe, exotic pineapple, spice and tropical fruit flavors with light honey and toasty, buttery oak notes that add richness and complexity on the finish. **92**
1990: Bold, ripe, rich and intense, this is a complex and deeply concentrated wine that packs in lots of honey, pear, toast and butterscotch flavors. **92**

FUMÉ BLANC SONOMA COUNTY (★★★), **RESERVE** (★★★): Well oaked, but rich and fruity with herb, pear and citrus notes.
1993: Fruity and citrusy, showing some nice orange and cream flavors and a smooth touch of oak. **88**
Reserve 1993: Bright and fruity, tart enough to lend some zing to the concentrated apricot and apple flavors. **87**

MERLOT ALEXANDER VALLEY (★★★): Elegant and fruity, but like the Cabernet gaining depth and richness with recent efforts.
1991: Beautifully articulated fruit and oak flavors, with ripe currant, cherry and spice notes that pick up toasty, buttery oak on the finish. The texture is smooth and supple. **89**
1990: Elegant, lean and complex, with focused herb, currant, spice and cedary oak flavors. **87**
1989: Straightforward, with ripe, sturdy cherry and berry flavors and firm tannins. **85**
1988: A fresh, fruity, exuberant wine with modest tannins and crisp acidity supporting the strawberry and cherry flavors. **85**
1987: Distinctively herbal, with a core of supple, elegant black currant flavor. **84**
1986: Sharply focused, with a fleshy texture, firm, tight tannins and bright cherry, currant and cedar flavors. **87**

PINOT NOIR NAPA-SONOMA COUNTIES RHONDA'S RESERVE (NR): The focus shifts to Russian River with 1994. Rhonda's Reserve has been dropped.
1990: Tastes more like Beaujolais than Pinot, but has crisp raspberry and tar flavors. **82**

SANGIOVESE ALEXANDER VALLEY (★★★):
1991: Vibrant and fruity, with spicy plum and raspberry fruit that's bright and vivid. **85**

SAUVIGNON BLANC SONOMA COUNTY ELDORADO GOLD (★★★):
1991: A smooth and appealing wine that's ripe and rich, showing fig, pear, apricot and honey flavors. **83**
1989: A very focused, rich and fruity dessert wine, with clean, vivid apricot, fig and honey flavors. **88**

SIENA SONOMA COUNTY (★★★★): A blend, roughly Sangiovese 40 percent, Cabernet (50 percent) and Merlot (10 percent), a complex and intriguing wine that combines rich raspberry and spice flavors with a supple elegance. Leads the pack in California.

1992: Stretches the flavor range from blackberry and currant to tar and anise, then turns elegant, finishing with a cedary oak edge. Needs short-term cellaring. **89**

1991: Bright, crisp and complex, with compelling, spicy black cherry and raspberry flavors that are well balanced, focused and lively. **90**

ZINFANDEL DRY CREEK VALLEY (★★★★): Vibrant and well oaked, but the fresh fruit pops out and is supple and round.

1992: Fresh, lively and vibrant, with a core of pretty, spicy black cherry, wild berry and light oak flavors. Rich and complex. **89**

1991: Wonderful harmony of peppery, spicy, zesty fruit flavors and pretty oak shadings. **90**

1990: An oaky wine with lots of smooth, buttery wood shadings, but also rich, lively currant and raspberry aromas and flavors, adding up to a plush mouthful of Zinfandel. **90**

GLORIA FERRER CHAMPAGNE CAVES
Carneros
F: 1982. **O:** Freixenet Sonoma Caves Inc. **W:** Robert Iantosca. **S:** None.

OVERALL	$14-25	★★★

WINE RATINGS	
Chardonnay Carneros	★★★★
Pinot Noir Carneros	★★
Sparkling Wine Carneros	
Late Disgorged Cuvée	★★★
Sparkling Wine Sonoma County Brut	★★★

WINERY DATA
C: 70,000. **V:** 230 acres in Carneros. **G:** Pinot Noir (180 acres), Chardonnay (50). **P:** Pinot Noir (Carneros), Pinot Noir (Alexander Valley).

Afber watching the success of Domaine Chandon and a handful of other French Champagne houses, Freixenet, the giant Spanish sparkling wine firm, moved into California in 1986, planting 230 acres of vineyards and constructing a large winery along the western edge of Carneros. The sparkling wines have been on solid footing from the start—well made, very consistent and highly reliant on Pinot Noir, which accounts for 180 acres of the vineyard. In the early 1990s the winery began making excellent Chardonnay and very good Pinot Noir table wines. The winery's 70,000-case output is dominated by 50,000 cases of the Sonoma Brut (mostly Pinot Noir), with smaller lots of Brut Rosé, Carneros Cuvée, Royal Cuvée and a Blanc de Noirs. The big surprise is the Chardonnay, which is rich, toasty and elegant.

TASTING NOTES

CHARDONNAY CARNEROS (★★★★): Strikes a fine balance between ripe, elegant fruit flavors and moderately toasty, spicy oak. More complex than the sparkling wines.

1993: Combines delicacy and finesse, with creamy pear, honey, spice and nutmeg shadings, with a complex aftertaste that folds together nicely. **91**

1992: Rich and fruity, a generous wine that keeps pumping out apple, pear and pineapple flavors, all the while remaining balanced and smooth. **91**

1991: Tight and intense, with pear and smoky oak flavors that are complex and concentrated. **90**

PINOT NOIR CARNEROS (★★): Lighter, as if it is from a Champagne clone of Pinot Noir.

1991: Light in color and texture, with delicate, spicy tea leaf, raspberry and rhubarb aromas and flavors. **85**

SPARKLING WINES (★★★):
Carneros Late Disgorged Cuvée 1987: Serves up ripe, rich spice and pineapple flavors up front. **86**
Sonoma County Brut NV: Fresh and lively, with a modest dose of black cherry, rose petal and spice flavors. **86**

FETZER VINEYARDS
Mendocino County
F: 1968. **O:** Brown-Forman Inc. **W:** Dennis Martin. **S:** Bel Arbors.

OVERALL	$7-24	★★★

WINE RATINGS	
Cabernet Sauvignon	
California Valley Oaks	★★
Cabernet Sauvignon North Coast	
Barrel Select	★★

Cabernet Sauvignon

Sonoma County Reserve	★★★
Chardonnay California Sundial	★★
Chardonnay Mendocino County	
Barrel Select	★★
Chardonnay Mendocino County	
Bonterra Organically Grown	★★
Chardonnay Mendocino	
County Reserve	★★★
Fumé Blanc Mendocino County	★★
Gewürztraminer California	★★
Johannisberg Riesling California	★★
Johannisberg Riesling	
Sonoma County Late Harvest Reserve	★★★
Merlot California Eagle Peak	NR
Petite Sirah Mendocino County Reserve	★★
Pinot Noir California	★★
Pinot Noir North Coast Barrel Select	★★
Pinot Noir Santa Barbara County	
Bien Nacido Vineyards	★★
Pinot Noir Sonoma County	
Olivet Lane Vineyard	★★
Red Table Wine Mendocino County	
Bonterra Organically Grown	★★
Sauvignon Blanc Mendocino County	
Barrel Select	★★
Zinfandel Mendocino County	
Barrel Select	★★
Zinfandel Mendocino County Reserve	★★★
Bel Arbors Chardonnay California	
Founder's Selection	NR

WINERY DATA

C: 2,400,000. **V:** 320 acres in Mendocino County. **G:** Cabernet Sauvignon, Chardonnay, Merlot, Sauvignon Blanc, Zinfandel. **P:** Cabernet Sauvignon, Chardonnay, Merlot, Sauvignon Blanc, Zinfandel.

Lumberman Barney Fetzer and his family settled into grape growing in Mendocino in the 1960s, making their first wines in 1968. By 1980 Fetzer was growing rapidly and had passed Parducci in case volume, offering a wide range of well crafted, value-oriented wines, including large volumes of white Zinfandel, Gewürztraminer, Fumé Blanc, Chardonnay, Zinfandel, Petite Sirah, Cabernet and Pinot Noir. A second label, Bel Arbors, was added for a line of lower-priced wines. Fetzer Vineyards enjoyed many successes: brands such as the Sundial Chardonnay soared to 100,000 cases with ease. By the end of the 1980s, Fetzer was one of the fastest growing and most profitable wineries in California, and today sells 2.4 million cases.

Under the direction of president (and former winemaker) Paul Dolan, the Reserve Cabernets and Chardonnays have improved significantly. A second tier of Barrel Select wines have also maintained high standards of quality at affordable prices. By 1992 the Fetzer family decided to sell the winery to Brown Forman, a national marketing firm that handles large beer, wine and spirits accounts. The Fetzers retained most of their vineyards, agreeing to sell the grapes back to their former winery.

TASTING NOTES

CABERNET SAUVIGNON CALIFORNIA VALLEY OAKS (★★):
1990: Smooth and correct, a good, easy-to-drink wine with modest fruit and herb flavors and moderate tannins. Fine for everyday drinking. **83**

CABERNET SAUVIGNON NORTH COAST BARREL SELECT (★★):
Well crafted and intense, with herb, currant and spice notes.
1991: Sturdy, with tight currant and oak flavors that turn dry and tannic on the finish. **83**
1990: Spicy and complex, with pretty, ripe and supple currant and cherry aromas and flavors that are framed by light, cedary oak. **86**

CABERNET SAUVIGNON SONOMA COUNTY RESERVE (★★★):
Big, rich, intense and well oaked, with chunky currant and cherry flavors. Approaching major-league status. Ages fairly well.
1988: Crisp and austere, with a lean band of herb, currant and cedary oak flavors, finishing with dry tannins. **83**
1987: Another big-scale wine packing in lots of richness, flavor and tannin along with an earthy streak. **85**
1986: Lean and tight, but packed with plum, currant and smoky oak aromas and flavors that persist on the finish, where it turns a bit gamy. **88**
1985: A dense, rich, concentrated wine with intense herb, chocolate, currant and black cherry flavors and a tannic finish. **86**

CHARDONNAY CALIFORNIA SUNDIAL (★★): Lighter and less complex than earlier efforts.
1993: Smooth and fruity, a generous wine with simple flavors that taper on the finish. **81**
1992: Light and fruity, with ripe pear and spice notes. **83**

CHARDONNAY MENDOCINO COUNTY BARREL SELECT (★★), BONTERRA ORGANICALLY GROWN (★★): Solid fruit flavors with less oak and finesse. The Bonterra is organically grown.
Barrel Select 1993: Appealing for its ripe apple, pear and spice notes and light oak shadings, with flavors that hang with you. Well made. **87**
Barrel Select 1992: An oaky wine that has the fruit intensity to match, with spice, pear, toast and honey notes. **85**
Bonterra Organically Grown 1993: Smooth and spicy, generous with its pear and nutmeg flavors, gliding gently into the finish. **84**
Bonterra Organically Grown 1992: Bold and ripe, with spicy apple, pear and oak flavors that are full-bodied, finishing with a touch of coarseness. **84**
Bonterra Organically Grown 1991: Lean and focused, a light-textured wine with appealing vanilla and spice aromas and pear and apple flavors. **88**

CHARDONNAY MENDOCINO COUNTY RESERVE (★★★): Offers good intensity and finesse, with complex flavors but no signature style.
1993: Complex, with attractive flavors, ranging from ripe pear, spice, honey and toasty oak, all folding together on the finish, where the flavors linger. **88**
1991: Lush and silky, with pretty pear, vanilla and honey notes that finish with hints of nutmeg, butter and melon. **87**

FUMÉ BLANC MENDOCINO COUNTY (★★): Moderate varietal character, clean and balanced.
1993: Bright and appealing, its pear and apple flavors shaded nicely with touches of herb and celery. The fruit wins on the finish. **87**
1992: Smooth, perhaps a little bit sweet, with an herbal citrus edge to the pear and vanilla flavors. **83**

GEWÜRZTRAMINER CALIFORNIA (★★): Spicy, fruity and off-dry.
1992: Sweet and spicy, with floral overtones to the slightly sugary pear and honey aromas and flavors. **81**

JOHANNISBERG RIESLING CALIFORNIA (★★): Off-dry and fruity.
1992: Soft and appealing, with bright apple, peach and apricot flavors that linger, nicely balanced and focused. **86**

JOHANNISBERG RIESLING SONOMA COUNTY LATE HARVEST (★★★):
1988: Very ripe, lush and opulent, with rich apricot, spice and honey flavors. **91**

MERLOT CALIFORNIA EAGLE PEAK (NR):
1992: Lean and crisp, a chewy wine with modest berry and plum flavors and firm tannins. **81**

PETITE SIRAH MENDOCINO COUNTY RESERVE (★★): Big, dark, tannic and rustic, with lots of chunky flavors.
1990: Big and dark, and the tannins pack a wallop, but enough wild berry, plum and cherry flavors emerge; it will always be tannic. **85**

PINOT NOIR VARIOUS BOTTLINGS (★★): Well oaked, with ample flavor, but lacks delicacy and finesse. Steadily improving, though. Appellation varies from California to North Coast.
California 1991: Smells ripe and spicy, with concentrated black cherry and raspberry flavors, but the finish is short, with firm tannins. **84**
California Barrel Select 1991: Bold and ripe, with intense cherry and plum flavors that turn spicy and oaky. **88**
California Reserve 1990: Lean, crisp and tart, with a narrow band of pleasant ripe cherry and plum flavors. **84**
Mendocino County Reserve 1986: Very ripe, plummy and supple, with a smooth texture and pretty spice, oak, cherry and anise notes; firmly tannic. **87**
North Coast Barrel Select 1992: Light and simple, with thin herb and cherry notes. **80**
Santa Barbara County Bien Nacido Vineyards 1992: A sound Pinot Noir with buttery oak shadings that dominate the earthy cola, herb and cherry flavors. **86**
Sonoma County Olivet Lane Vineyard 1992: Strikes a nice balance between buttery oak and firm, spicy cherry flavors. **87**

RED TABLE WINE MENDOCINO COUNTY BONTERRA ORGANICALLY GROWN (★★):
1991: Intense and spicy, with ripe cherry and pepper

notes that turn dry and tannic on the finish. **83**

1990: Firm and chunky, with lots of black cherry and berry flavors, deep color and lively acidity. **83**

SAUVIGNON BLANC MENDOCINO COUNTY BARREL SELECT (★★):

1993: Soft and simple, a little citrusy and a little spicy, not much intensity. **79**

1992: Light and clean, a harmonious wine that shows some restraint, offering well modulated pear and herb flavors. **85**

1991: Subtle melon and spice flavors and a light overlay of buttery oak make this an interesting wine. **85**

ZINFANDEL MENDOCINO COUNTY BARREL SELECT (★★): Hits all the right notes, with spicy berry flavors.

1992: Firm and compact, with spicy cherry, earth and raspberry flavors, picking up a buttery note. **86**

1989: Firm and fruity, with generous spice and plum flavors and a dried orange edge. **84**

ZINFANDEL MENDOCINO COUNTY RESERVE (★★★):
Big, ripe and intense but balanced, with complex flavors.

1991: Lavishly oaked, with toasty, buttery wood flavors dominating, but hints of cherry, spice and pepper seep through. **87**

1986: Big and tough, but rich raspberry flavors and a supple texture kick in, and the finish is smooth and chocolaty. **88**

BEL ARBORS CHARDONNAY CALIFORNIA FOUNDER'S SELECTION (★★):

1992: Soft, simple and appealing, with generous vanilla and spice notes adding to the pear flavor. **80**

FICKLIN VINEYARD
Madera, Fresno County
F: 1946. **O:** Ficklin Family. **W:** Peter Ficklin. **S:** None.

OVERALL	$10-25	★★

WINE RATINGS	
Port California Special Bottling	★★
Tinta Port California	★★

WINERY DATA
C: 9,000. **V:** 30 acres in Madera. **G:** Other (30 acres). **P:** None.

Ficklin has been making Port-style dessert wines in the Central Valley since 1948, when Walter Ficklin determined that traditional Port varieties—Tinta Madeira, Touriga, Tinta Cao and Souzao—were the best bets for this hot climate. The family-owned winery has 30 acres in Madera and makes about 9,000 cases a year, the main wine being the non-vintage Tinta Port. A vintage-dated bottling appears in select years. The Tinta Port can be very good, with sweet plum and spice nuances. It is mature on release, falling short of greatness, and is not in the same league as true vintage Port from Portugal.

TASTING NOTES

VARIOUS BOTTLINGS (★★):

Port California Special Bottling No. 6 1983: Rich and complex, already acquiring a definite sense of maturity, offering interesting chocolate, walnut and smoke overtones to the basic ripe plum and prune flavors. **87**

Port California Special Bottling No. 5 1980: Light in texture, spicy and elegant, with appealing cherry, toast and walnut aromas and flavors. **84**

Tinta Port California NV: Light in texture and not as sweet as some California Ports, but it's a flavorful dessert wine offering modest cherry and walnut aromas and flavors. **78**

FIDDLEHEAD CELLARS
Davis, Yolo County
F: 1989. **O:** Kathy Joseph. **W:** Kathy Joseph. **S:** None.

OVERALL	$25-29	★★★

WINE RATINGS	
Pinot Noir Santa Maria Valley	★★★

WINERY DATA
C: 2,000. **V:** None. **G:** None. **P:** Pinot Noir (Santa Maria Valley), Sauvignon Blanc (Santa Ynez Valley).

Kathy Joseph, former winemaker for Robert Pecota Winery, founded her own brand in 1989, focusing on Pinot Noir from the Sierra Madre Vineyard (in Santa

Maria Valley) and Oregon, and Sauvignon Blanc from the Santa Ynez Valley. Using purchased grapes, Joseph produces up to 2,000 cases a year from her winery in Davis. Her initial efforts with Pinot Noir are impressive for their finesse and delicacy.

TASTING NOTES

PINOT NOIR SANTA MARIA VALLEY (★★★): Captures the essence of Santa Maria Valley, yet tames the herbal, earthy flavors that often appear in these wines.
1992: Attractive for its supple, delicate texture and alluring black cherry, cola, herb and spice flavors. Unfolds gently, turning supple and complex. **88**
1990: A bright, lively Pinot that offers complexity in a ready-to-drink style. The flavors extend from spicy berry to vegetal and it finishes with hints of herb and raspberry. **82**

FIELD STONE WINERY
Alexander Valley
F: 1977. **O:** John & Katrina Staten. **W:** Michael Duffy. **S:** None.

OVERALL	$9-20	★★

WINE RATINGS

Cabernet Sauvignon Alexander Valley	★★
Cabernet Sauvignon Alexander Valley Staten Family Reserve	★★
Cabernet Sauvignon Alexander Valley Vineyard Blend	★★
Cabernet Sauvignon Alexander Valley Hoot Owl Creek Vineyards	★★
Cabernet Sauvignon Alexander Valley Turkey Hill Vineyard	★★
Chardonnay Sonoma County	★★
Gewürztraminer Sonoma County	★
Petite Sirah Alexander Valley	★★
Sauvignon Blanc Mendocino County Quillen Vineyard	★★★

WINERY DATA
C: 10,000. **V:** 15 acres in Alexander Valley. **G:** Cabernet Sauvignon (5 acres), Petite Sirah (6), Viognier (1), Merlot (3). **P:** Gewürztraminer (Sonoma County), Sauvignon Blanc (Dry Creek Valley), Chardonnay (Carneros, Russian River Valley), Chardonnay, Cabernet Sauvignon (Alexander Valley), Cabernet Sauvignon (Alexander Valley).

Owners John and Katrina Staten planted Field Stone's vineyards in the 1960s, a full decade before building an underground winery. The Statens made their first wines in 1977. The focus is on small case lots of Cabernet (2,000 cases), Chardonnay (1,000), Sauvignon Blanc (1,000) and Petite Sirah (800), all sharing a rustic style, which is somewhat surprising given that Field Stone's winemaker, Michael Duffy, crafts such supple and polished Cabernets and Chardonnays under his Optima label, and his Cabernet comes from the same vineyards as Field Stone's. There are 15 acres of vines at the winery, but the Statens also own 100 more acres of vines, most of which they sell. The Petite Sirah is memorable for its massive tannins and inky color; a portion of the vineyard dates to 1894. After a dispute among partners in 1995 the vineyards were divided, and the future of vineyard-designated names such as Turkey Hill remains unresolved.

TASTING NOTES

CABERNET SAUVIGNON VARIOUS BOTTLINGS (★★): The various bottlings include Staten Family Reserve, Hoot Owl Vineyards and Turkey Hill, each good but not great. Quality varies considerably, from lightweight to heavily oaked to vegetal, austere and tannic.
1991: Light-bodied, with currant and plum flavors that pick up a cedary oak edge. **84**
1989: Firm and tannic, a tight, unyielding, youthful Cabernet that offers a nice array of plum and cherry aromas and flavors. **85**
1987: Moderately tannic, with olive, cassis and tobacco flavors, a velvety texture and a finish that tapers off. **85**
Hoot Owl Creek Vineyards 1990: Dominated by drying tannins that overpower the simple cherry and plum flavors. **80**
Hoot Owl Creek Vineyards 1986: Supple, fruity, distinctively herbal and less hearty than usual, offering moderate blackberry and currant flavors scented by pleasant herbal notes. **85**
Hoot Owl Creek Vineyards 1985: Has massive tannins and very ripe, full-bodied, jammy black cherry and currant flavors and a very dry finish. **87**
Staten Family Reserve 1990: Firm and intense, with a core of crisp, lean currant, coffee and herb flavors, turning austere. **84**
Staten Family Reserve 1989: Hard and backward, with tannic flavors that hint at cherry and currant. **82**

Staten Family Reserve 1987: The extremely toasty flavors border on burnt, and turn vegetal and lean. **72**

Turkey Hill Vineyard 1985: With attractive, mature aromas and flavors on a firm framework of tannin, this wine is a bit harsh, with spice and ripe cherry flavors. **84**

Turkey Hill Vineyard 1984: Firm and concentrated, wrapping its currant, black cherry and spice flavors in a velvety blanket of soft tannin. **88**

Vineyard Blend 1990: Ripe, intense and spicy, with a good dose of cedary oak, but the cherry and currant aromas and flavors measure up. **84**

CHARDONNAY SONOMA COUNTY (★★): Just as inconsistent as the Cabernet: ripe and generous one year, flat and dull the next.

1993: Ripe and perfumed, with a dash of honey and pear notes, turning earthy on the finish. **82**

1992: Comes across as flat and one-dimensional, with spicy pear and oak flavors. **80**

1991: Fresh and spicy, with generous pear, almond and vanilla aromas and flavors that become broad and generous. **89**

GEWÜRZTRAMINER SONOMA COUNTY (★):

1992: Simple and fruity, with a perfumy edge to the otherwise refreshing apple and spice aromas and flavors. Comes off as dry. **81**

PETITE SIRAH ALEXANDER VALLEY (★★): Would get four stars for color and tannin. It's typically dense, chewy and peppery.

Old Vines 1990: Firm, tannic and chewy, with blackberry and plum flavors racing through it. **83**

1988: Ripe, generous and not wanting for tannin, but mellow enough to let the black pepper and cherry flavors slide through. **85**

1987: Firm in texture but generous, offering blueberry and cherry aromas and flavors. **84**

SAUVIGNON BLANC MENDOCINO COUNTY QUILLEN VINEYARD (★★★):

1992: Fresh and juicy, with a beam of nice pear, grapefruit and spice flavors. **89**

FIELDBROOK VALLEY WINERY
Arcata, Humboldt County
F: 1976. **O:** Bob & Judy Hodgson. **W:** Bob Hodgson. **S:** None.

OVERALL	$9-18	★★

WINE RATINGS

Chardonnay Mendocino County	
Redwood Valley Vineyard	★★
Merlot Napa Valley Frediani Vineyard	★★
Pinot Noir Napa Valley Beard Vineyard	★★
Sauvignon Blanc	
California Meredith Vineyard	★★
Sauvignon Blanc Mendocino County	
Webb Vineyard	★★
Zinfandel Mendocino County	
Pacini Vineyard	★★

WINERY DATA
C: 1,000. **V:** None. **G:** None. **P:** Zinfandel, Sauvignon Blanc (Mendocino County), Pinot Noir (Napa), Merlot (Trinity).

Fieldbrook operates out of Arcata in Humboldt County—in far Northern California—producing 1,000 cases of wine from purchased grapes, mostly Sauvignon Blanc (400 cases) and Zinfandel (300). Chardonnay grapes are purchased from Redwood Valley in Mendocino County and the wine shares the grassy herb and pear flavors often found in Sauvignon Blanc. Merlot comes from Frediani Vineyard in Napa Valley, and Pinot Noir from Beard Vineyard in Napa Valley. The Sauvignon Blanc carries several appellations, from California to different vineyards (Webb in Mendocino County and Meredith in Trinity County), while the Zinfandel comes from the well regarded Pacini Vineyard in Mendocino County.

TASTING NOTES

CHARDONNAY MENDOCINO COUNTY REDWOOD VALLEY VINEYARD (★★):
1992: Marked by a tart, grassy edge and hints of pear and herb flavors. **81**

MERLOT NAPA VALLEY FREDIANI VINEYARD (★★):
1991: Supple and elegant, with ripe, spicy cherry, wild berry and plum flavors. **84**

PINOT NOIR NAPA VALLEY BEARD VINEYARD (★★):
1992: Delicate and spicy, with pretty herb, tea, plum and cherry flavors that are ripe and focused. **87**

SAUVIGNON BLANC CALIFORNIA MEREDITH VINEYARD (★★):
1992: Modestly varietal, soft and appealing, echoing pear and spice flavors. **83**

SAUVIGNON BLANC MENDOCINO COUNTY WEBB VINEYARD (★★):
1994: Light and juicy, a crisp-textured wine with sappy citrus and pear flavors. **83**
1993: Bright and fruity, its flavors are centered around grapefruit and sweet vanilla. **87**

ZINFANDEL MENDOCINO COUNTY PACINI VINEYARD (★★):
1993: Deeply colored, serving up plenty of pure, ripe cherry, wild berry and spicy raspberry flavors. **87**
1992: Firm, gritty and tannic, but the wild berry flavors sneak past the tannins. **86**
1991: Firm and flavorful, with distinctive wild berry, plum and orange rind flavors. **84**

FIFE VINEYARDS
Napa Valley
F: 1989. **O:** Dennis Fife. **W:** Dennis Fife. **S:** None.

OVERALL	$16-20	★★★

WINE RATINGS

Petite Sirah Napa Valley	★★
Petite Sirah Napa Valley	
Les Vieilles Vignes	★★★
Zinfandel Napa Valley	★★★
Zinfandel Napa Valley	
Les Vieilles Vignes	★★★

WINERY DATA
C: 800. **V:** 40. **G:** None. **P:** None.

Former Inglenook-Napa Valley winery president and general manager Dennis Fife started his own small Zinfandel and Petite Sirah brand in 1989, producing a few hundred cases of each from his 40-acre Fife Vineyard north of St. Helena, including a Vielles Vignes

(old vines) bottling for each. His wines are made in rented space in Oakville. Plans are to keep production at 600 to 800 cases. So far the Zinfandel has a narrow quality lead over the Sirah.

TASTING NOTES

PETITE SIRAH NAPA VALLEY VARIOUS BOTTLINGS (★★):
1991: Tight and lean, with a narrow band of fruit flavors. **81**
Les Vieilles Vignes 1991: Solid and firm in texture, with soft edges and generous berry and plum aromas and flavors. **87**

ZINFANDEL NAPA VALLEY (★★★):
1991: A classy wine, spicy, vibrant and elegant, with intense tar, raspberry and earth notes, finishing with smooth tannins. **88**
Les Vieilles Vignes 1991: A distinctive wine that's ripe and racy, with ample plum and berry flavors on a lean frame. **85**

JOSEPH FILIPPI VINTAGE CO.
Fontana, San Bernardino County
F: 1922. **O:** Joseph Filippi Family. **W:** J.P. Filippi, Nick Karavidas. **S:** Filippi, Joseph.

OVERALL	$4-18	★

WINE RATINGS

Chardonnay Monterey County	
Limited Release Winemaker's Reserve	NR
Sauvignon Blanc Monterey County	
Limited Release Winemaker's Reserve	NR

WINERY DATA
C: 90,000. **V:** 20 acres in San Bernardino County. **G:** Grenache (10 acres), Mission (5), Chasselas (5). **P:** Zinfandel, Mission (California), Zinfandel (Central Coast), Cabernet Sauvignon (Monterey), Carignane (San Diego County).

Joseph Filippi Vintage Co. was founded in 1922 in Fontana, and makes some 90,000 cases of generic table wines. The winery crushes mostly Grenache and Mission grapes, but recently added a Chardonnay and Sauvignon Blanc, both from Monterey.

FIRESTONE VINEYARD

Santa Ynez Valley

F: 1972. **O:** Firestone Family Partnership. **W:** Alison Green. **S:** Prosperity.

OVERALL	$18-28	★★★

WINE RATINGS

Cabernet Sauvignon Santa Ynez Valley	★★
Cabernet Sauvignon Santa Ynez Valley Vintage Reserve	★★
Chardonnay Santa Ynez Valley Barrel Fermented	★★★
Gewürztraminer California	★★★
Johannisberg Riesling Santa Barbara County Selected Harvest	★★★
Merlot Santa Ynez Valley	★★
Sauvignon Blanc Santa Ynez Valley	★

WINERY DATA

C: 75,000. **V:** 228 acres in Santa Ynez Valley. **G:** Chardonnay (60 acres), Sauvignon Blanc (12), Cabernet Sauvignon (31), Syrah (19), Cabernet Franc (10), Riesling (40), Gewürztraminer (14), Merlot (36), Pinot Noir (6). **P:** Chardonnay, Merlot, Sauvignon Blanc (Santa Ynez Valley), Gewürztraminer (Santa Barbara County).

Brooks Firestone (he's an heir to the Firestone tire company fortune) and his wife Kate pioneered wine-growing in Santa Ynez Valley in 1972, when they planted a vineyard that now covers 228 acres and is home to a picturesque winery. Chardonnay (60 acres), Riesling (40), Merlot (36) and Cabernet (31) dominate the plantings, but Cabernet is on its way out, with Syrah (now 19 acres) due to expand. Across the board, the wines are well made, sharing a house style of light to medium fruit intensity, and while they do not overpower, they offer enough delicacy and finesse to succeed. Lately each of the main wines has shown a shade more depth of flavor. The Cabernet and Merlot are often strongly marked by herb, tobacco and vegetal notes, but they also have smooth, supple textures. Production has reached 75,000 cases, with Riesling accounting for 20,000 cases.

TASTING NOTES

CABERNET SAUVIGNON SANTA YNEZ VALLEY (★★), VINTAGE RESERVE (★★):
1991: Firm and compact, with medium-weight currant, cherry and toasty wood flavors. **84**

1990: Light and supple, with soft herb, cedar and cherry notes, finishing with modest tannins. **83**
1989: Earthy and vegetal, with pungent aromas and strong dill and herb flavors that override the currant notes. **78**
Vintage Reserve 1990: Firm and spicy, with pleasant oak and vanilla notes to round out the modest blackberry and currant flavors. **84**

CHARDONNAY SANTA YNEZ VALLEY BARREL FERMENTED (★★★): Shows more oak, depth and texture of late, with pretty fruit flavors.
1993: A fruity wine with pretty pear, spice and honey notes framed by light oak shadings. Elegant and refined. **87**
1992: Ripe and elegant, with beautifully defined pineapple, pear and slightly herbal spice flavors. **86**
1991: Graceful, with spicy, toasty apple, pear and vanilla aromas and flavors that swirl around on the finish. **89**

GEWÜRZTRAMINER CALIFORNIA (★★): Dry, with spicy flavors and a delicate texture.
1992: Fresh, dry and spicy, with distinctive grapefruit and floral aromas and flavors, finishing with an extra burst of flavor. **84**

JOHANNISBERG RIESLING SANTA BARBARA COUNTY SELECTED HARVEST (★★★): Ripe and fruity, with spicy pear and peach notes.
1991: Rich, sweet and golden, with pineapple, honey and lemon aromas and flavors. **84**

MERLOT SANTA YNEZ VALLEY (★★): Light and smooth-textured, but often vegetal and herbal.
1992: A spicy, herbal wine with green pepper and racy vegetable flavors. **81**
1991: Supple and well proportioned, with cherry, berry and herb flavors that are elegant and lively. **83**
1990: Herbal, earthy and tarry in a light, uncomplicated style. **78**

SAUVIGNON BLANC SANTA YNEZ VALLEY (★): Rarely overcomes its earthy, weedy qualities.
1992: Soft and fruity, with a strong earthy and weedy streak. **81**

FISHER VINEYARDS
Sonoma County
F: 1973. **O:** Fred & Juelle Fisher. **W:** Mitch Firestone-Gillis, Paul Hobbs. **S:** None.

OVERALL	$28	★★★

WINE RATINGS

Cabernet Sauvignon Napa Valley	
Coach Insignia	★★★
Cabernet Sauvignon Sonoma County	
Wedding Vineyard	★★★
Chardonnay Sonoma County	
Coach Insignia	★★★
Chardonnay Sonoma County	
Whitney's Vineyard	★★★★
Merlot Napa Valley	★★

WINERY DATA

C: 8,000. **V:** 75 acres in Sonoma County, Napa Valley. **G:** Chardonnay (49 acres), Cabernet Sauvignon (20), Merlot (4), Cabernet Franc (2). **P:** Chardonnay (Sonoma County), Cabernet Sauvignon (Napa Valley).

Fred and Juelle Fisher (he's from the "Body by Fisher" family) planted their 20-acre vineyard on the ridge that separates Napa and Sonoma, where they've also built a beautiful winery from trees cut on their property. The Fishers produce Chardonnay from their estate vineyard and from purchased grapes, but their 55-acre Cabernet vineyard is in Napa off Silverado Trail, hence the Napa-Sonoma designation on many of their wines. Recently Napa Valley has been the appellation for the Coach Insignia Cabernet and Merlot, while the Coach Insignia and Whitney's Vineyard Chardonnays carry a Sonoma County appellation.

TASTING NOTES

CABERNET SAUVIGNON NAPA VALLEY COACH INSIGNIA (★★★): Intense and muscular with tannin control the main issue. Has carried several appellations over the years: Napa Valley, Napa-Sonoma Counties, and Sonoma County. A Wedding Vineyard bottling appeared in 1991.
1991: The tight, rich, intense plum and currant flavors are framed by toasty, cedary oak. **84**
Wedding Vineyard 1991: A gamy wine with dry, plush tannins and an earthy streak, but also currant and chocolate flavors that are appealing. **88**

1990: Rich, dark, complex and concentrated, packed with dense currant, anise, cedar and spice flavors. **90**
1989: Hard and tannic, a strapping wine with a solid core of currant and chocolate flavors and a bit of leather. **82**
1987: Woody and tough around the edges, with a solid core of ripe cherry and currant flavors, heavily toasted oak and drying tannins. **85**
1986: Mature, with a tannic edge to the currant and herb flavors. **88**
1985: Mature and marked by ripe black currant and plum flavors that are deep and long-lasting. **90**
1984: A very tight and sharply focused wine with tart black cherry, raspberry and currant flavors, supported by fine, lean tannins. **89**

CHARDONNAY SONOMA COUNTY COACH INSIGNIA (★★★): Solid, intense and flavorful.
1993: Strikes a nice balance between toasty, smoky oak and spicy pear flavors. Medium-weight, but pleasant as the flavors linger on the finish. **88**
1992: Light and spicy, a well crafted wine with a nice vanilla-clove streak running through the fresh apple flavors. **86**
1991: Marked by ripe, rich fruit that's intense and flavorful, with smooth pear, spice, butter and toast flavors all neatly woven together. **91**

CHARDONNAY SONOMA COUNTY WHITNEY'S VINEYARD (★★★★): This bottling is the star, very rich, smooth, complex and ageworthy, although less intense recently.
1993: Medium-weight with herb, pear, spice and citrus notes, but not the richness and concentration this wine achieves in top years. Finishes with smoky oak. **85**
1992: Elegant and showy, with creamy pear, vanilla and nutmeg notes that are pure and well defined. **88**
1991: Bold, ripe and buttery oak aromas lead to rich, concentrated, complex pear, honey and spice flavors. **90**

MERLOT NAPA VALLEY (★★): Not in the same class as the other wines, it's leaner, less ripe and less complicated.
1991: Despite a green cedary edge from wood, this is a ripe, supple and polished Merlot with pretty black cherry and plum aromas and flavors. **87**

FITZPATRICK WINERY
El Dorado County
F: 1980. **O:** Brian & Diana Fitzpatrick. **W:** Brian Fitzpatrick. **S:** None.

OVERALL	$6-13	NR

WINE RATINGS

Cabernet Sauvignon Coloma Canyon	NR
Sauvignon Blanc El Dorado County	NR
Zinfandel Shenandoah Valley	NR

WINERY DATA
C: 4,000. **V:** 10 acres in El Dorado County. **G:** Cabernet Sauvignon (3 acres), Merlot (2), Chardonnay (1), Syrah (1), Grenache (1). **P:** Cabernet Sauvignon, Chenin Blanc, Chardonnay (El Dorado County), Zinfandel (Shenandoah Valley), Petite Sirah, Cabernet Sauvignon (Sierra Foothill).

This 4,000-case winery in El Dorado County makes Cabernet from the Coloma Canyon vineyard, Sauvignon Blanc from El Dorado, Zinfandel from Shenandoah Valley and a red table wine. A portion of the grapes are estate-grown.

FLORA SPRINGS WINE CO.
St. Helena, Napa Valley
F: 1978. **O:** Flora Springs Wine Co. **W:** Ken Deis. **S:** None.

OVERALL	$8-40	★★★★

WINE RATINGS

Cabernet Sauvignon Napa Valley	★★★
Cabernet Sauvignon Napa Valley Reserve	★★★★★
Chardonnay Napa Valley Barrel Fermented	★★★★★
Meritage Red Napa Valley Trilogy	★★★★
Sangiovese Napa Valley	★★★
Sauvignon Blanc Napa Valley	★★★
Sauvignon Blanc Napa Valley Soliloquy	★★★

WINERY DATA
C: 35,000. **V:** 450 acres in Napa Valley. **G:** Sauvignon Blanc (44 acres), Sangiovese (14), Malbec (1), Pinot Noir (3), Zinfandel (60), Chardonnay (101), Merlot (64), Cabernet Sauvignon (148), Petite Verdot (2), Cabernet Franc (8). **P:** None.

After retiring from Bechtel Corp. in 1977, Jerry Komes and his wife, Flora, purchased the old Louis M. Martini Winery (ca. 1888) on Zinfandel Lane south of St. Helena with plans to ease into retirement. But their grown children soon joined them and their plans were revised: the family bought vineyard land that now totals 450 acres, making them one of the largest vineyard owners in Napa Valley. In 1978 Flora Springs began making wine, with Ken Deis, a former Heitz Cellars winemaker, overseeing production since 1980. Plantings of Rutherford Cabernet dominate, with 148 acres, followed by significant acreage of Chardonnay, Merlot, Zinfandel and Sauvignon Blanc. Sangiovese (14 acres) is also part of the mix. The 35,000-case production is diverse, with Chardonnay (6,000 cases) leading, followed by Merlot (4,500), Trilogy (a red Meritage, 2,500), Sangiovese (1,800) and Soliloquy (a Sauvignon Blanc, 1,000). The whites have been excellent from the start, led by the extremely rich and complex Barrel Fermented Chardonnay, but now the reds too are increasingly well made, with the 1991 Reserve Cabernet a star of the vintage. Trilogy, a blend of equal parts of Merlot, Cabernet and Cabernet Franc, is elegant and flavorful. Sangiovese appears right on the mark and poised for excellence, while in 1993 the winery set its sights on Pinot Noir. A second line of wines aimed at value, Floreal, was dropped in 1994.

TASTING NOTES

CABERNET SAUVIGNON NAPA VALLEY (★★★): Ripe and intensely flavorful, with firm tannins.
1987: Firm and intense, with black cherry, currant and plum flavors that are plush and concentrated until the tannins sneak up. **89**
1986: Earthy, with a lean texture, herbal flavors and a tart finish with simple cherry notes. **85**
1985: Ripe and rich, with well defined black cherry, currant, spice and cedary oak flavors. **88**

CABERNET SAUVIGNON NAPA VALLEY RESERVE (★★★★★): Steadily improving as the winery isolates the best grapes for this wine. The 1991 and 1992 vintages show enormous richness and depth, vast improvements.
1992: Sharply focused, with a bright, rich core of plum, currant and black cherry fruit that turns supple and elegant. Wonderful depth. **96**

1991: A stylish wine that packs in lots of ripe, rich flavors and then polishes them with toasty, buttery oak. The currant, plum and cherry flavors are bright and lively, picking up spicy herb and tobacco notes on a long, full finish. **97**

1990: Shows depth and substance, with compact currant and spice flavors. **88**

1989: Ripe, with a solid beam of smoky tobacco aromas and currant and plum flavors. **85**

CHARDONNAY NAPA VALLEY BARREL FERMENTED (★★★★★): Almost always a star, bold, ripe, rich and creamy, packed with flavor and finesse. Ages exceptionally well.

1993: Marked by earthy, woody flavors that dominate the spicy pear and grapefruit notes. Comes across as a bit coarse and disjointed, atypical of this wine in the past. **84**

1992: Bold, rich and flavorful, a plush and supple wine with layers of pear, spice and hazelnut flavors framed by toasty, buttery oak notes that linger. **90**

1991: Ripe and spicy, with honey, apple, vanilla and pear flavors that take on a peachy nutmeg edge. The flavors echo on a long finish. **91**

1990: Smooth, ripe and generous, with rich, complex, polished pear, spice, hazelnut and honey notes. **92**

1989: An extremely rich, luxuriously textured Chardonnay with orange blossom aromas, ripe pear and honey flavors and a full, fruity finish that just keeps going. **91**

1988: Smells toasty, with oaky, buttery accents and tight, concentrated lemon, pear and honey flavors. **91**

1987: Remarkably smooth and rich, with intense pear, pineapple and spicy oak flavors that are complex and intriguing, finishing with honey and vanilla notes. **93**

1986: This wine continues to improve, though it's still oaky. Underneath that toasty veneer are pear, pineapple and spice flavors that are very well balanced. **87**

1985: Just misses the mark. It has consistently shown more dry oakiness than fruit on the palate. There are plenty of concentrated pear and spice flavors, and with further aging the wood may soften, giving the wine more harmony and finesse. **85**

MERITAGE RED NAPA VALLEY TRILOGY (★★★★): Can be brilliant, but some efforts have been lighter. The best capture ripe, rich, supple fruit flavors, with mild tannins and lots of finesse. Ages well.

1991: A racy Trilogy with distinctive earthy, leathery flavors that override the currant, cherry and cedary oak notes. **89**

1990: Lean and austere, with a tight band of complex currant, berry and cedary oak flavors. **85**

1989: Ripe, with perfumed currant, berry and cassis notes and buttery, toasty oak shadings. **85**

1988: Tight and firm, with currant and berry flavors, but like most 1988s it loses intensity on the finish, where it turns austere. **85**

1987: Pretty currant, cherry, plum and toast flavors are rich, lively and well integrated, with soft, round tannins and a silky-smooth texture. **90**

1986: Lean, firm and tannic, this is a tightly knit wine with herb, currant and anise flavors. It's more closed and austere now than on release. **88**

1985: Appealing, with its ripe, rich, supple currant, black cherry and plum flavors and smooth tannins. **88**

1984: The first bottling of this proprietary wine is fully mature, ripe and supple, with earthy spice, currant, plum and cedar flavors, finishing with a drying, oaky aftertaste. **84**

SANGIOVESE NAPA VALLEY (★★★): An impressive start, with bright fruit flavors and a supple texture.

1993: Marked by tart, crisp wild berry, herb and spicy oak flavors, turning tannic and compact. **86**

1992: Ripe, rich and focused, with pretty spice, strawberry and anise flavors that turn complex. **89**

SAUVIGNON BLANC NAPA VALLEY (★★★):
1993: Straightforward, soft and fruity, pleasant with pear flavors and a flash of spice on the finish. **85**

SAUVIGNON BLANC NAPA VALLEY SOLILOQUY (★★★): An elegant and understated Sauvignon Blanc.

1993: Earthy, tired flavors detract from this simple, straightforward white. **77**

1991: So dressed up with earthy, butter and vanilla flavors, that the fruit and character of the grapes gets lost. Still, it makes for a pleasant drink, if only for a glass or two. **82**

1990: Fresh, polished and complex, its sharply focused orange, pear and vanilla aromas and flavors turn opulent and generous on the creamy finish. Has style and richness, but never gets too heavy. **88**

1989: A lively, light wine, showing finesse and subtlety to the lemon and vanilla-tinged grapefruit flavors. Has better length than most '89s. **88**

THOMAS FOGARTY WINERY
Portola Valley, San Mateo County
F: 1981. **O:** Thomas Fogarty. **W:** Michael Martella.
S: None.

OVERALL	$12-22	★★

WINE RATINGS
Chardonnay Santa Cruz Mountains	★★
Pinot Noir Napa Valley	★★
Pinot Noir Santa Cruz Mountains	★★

WINERY DATA
C: 10,000. **V:** 22 acres in Santa Cruz Mountains.
G: Chardonnay (16 acres), Pinot Noir (6). **P:** Gewürztraminer (Monterey).

Cardiovascular surgeon Thomas Fogarty founded his 10,000-case winery in 1981 in the San Francisco Peninsula area known as Portola Valley. He planted Chardonnay (16 acres) and Pinot Noir (6) between 1978 and 1980. The focus is on estate-grown wines, but through the years wines have been made from many different grapes and appellations, with mixed results. The one wine that is the most consistently appealing is the Gewürztraminer, made from grapes grown at Ventana Vineyard in Monterey.

TASTING NOTES

CHARDONNAY SANTA CRUZ MOUNTAINS (★★): Well oaked but often lacking the fruit to stand up to it.
1992: Smooth and silky, showing pleasant spice and pear flavors that finish gently. **82**

PINOT NOIR VARIOUS BOTTLINGS (★★): Inconsistent: it's tough and tannic one year, spicy and fruity the next.
Napa Valley 1988: Woody tannins make it rough, but cherry and strawberry flavors emerge. **86**
Santa Cruz Mountains 1989: A tough, chewy, tannic wine with a gamy, leathery edge. **74**
Santa Cruz Mountains 1988: Full of attractive spice, plum and berry flavors on a medium-bodied frame. **83**

FOLIE À DEUX WINERY
St. Helena, Napa Valley
F: 1981. **O:** Richard Peterson. **W:** Richard Peterson.
S: None.

OVERALL	$10-20	★★

WINE RATINGS
Cabernet Sauvignon Napa Valley	★★★
Chardonnay Napa Valley	★★
Chenin Blanc Napa Valley	★★
Sparkling Wine Napa Valley	NR
Zinfandel Napa Valley	NR

WINERY DATA
C: 12,000. **V:** 14 acres in Napa Valley. **G:** Cabernet Sauvignon (5 acres), Chardonnay (9). **P:** Chenin Blanc, Cabernet Sauvignon, Muscat Canelli, Chardonnay (Napa Valley), Chardonnay (Carneros).

Folie à Deux ("a shared fantasy") in St. Helena was founded in 1981 by Larry and Evie Dizmang, two mental health professionals (the label is a parody of the Rorschach test). Nearly half the 12,000-case production is Chardonnay, with Cabernet, Chenin Blanc, Zinfandel, a sparkling wine and a white table wine also part of the mix. The winery does well with both Chardonnay and Cabernet, but ran into financial difficulties in the early 1990s and by 1993 was under federal protection undergoing a financial reorganization. In 1995 a group of investors headed by Richard Peterson purchased the winery for a reported $1.4 million, which included the inventory and brand name.

FOPPIANO VINEYARDS
Dry Creek Valley
F: 1896. **O:** L. Foppiano Wine Co. **W:** Bill Regan.
S: Riverside Farms, Fox Mountain.

OVERALL	$8-20	★★

WINE RATINGS
Cabernet Sauvignon Russian River Valley	★
Fox Mountain Cabernet Sauvignon Sonoma County Reserve	★★
Merlot Russian River Valley	★★
Petite Sirah Napa Valley La Grande Petite	★★★

Petite Sirah Sonoma County	★★★
Sauvignon Blanc Dry Creek Valley	★★
Zinfandel Dry Creek Valley	★★

WINERY DATA

C: 200,000. **V:** 135 acres in Russian River Valley.
G: Chardonnay (29 acres), Cabernet Sauvignon (24), Petite Sirah (26), Gamay (9), French Colombard (15), Early Burgundy (5), Merlot (11), Sauvignon Blanc (15), Cabernet Franc (6).
P: Zinfandel, Sauvignon Blanc (Dry Creek Valley).

Foppiano Vineyards is approaching its 100th anniversary, having been founded in 1896 southwest of Healdsburg. Today it is a highly modernized winery, producing 200,000 cases of wine under three labels: the Fox Mountain Reserve Cabernet and Chardonnay from Russian River; Foppiano Cabernet, Chardonnay, Petite Sirah, Sauvignon Blanc and Zinfandel; and Riverside Farm white Zinfandel, Cabernet, Chardonnay and Zinfandel. Many of the grapes come from the winery's 135 acres of vines in Russian River. The Fox Mountain Reserves indicate Foppiano's determination to make great wines, even if they've yet to achieve it (and may not with Cabernet from Russian River). The Petite Sirah is the best Foppiano wine, although a 1991 Zinfandel Dry Creek (the first made) impressed me with its spice, earth and raspberry notes.

TASTING NOTES

CABERNET SAUVIGNON RUSSIAN RIVER VALLEY (★):
1990: Looks and tastes mature for a wine this young, with stewed plum and spice notes. **80**

MERLOT RUSSIAN RIVER VALLEY (★★):
1992: Firm and compact, with cherry and currant flavors that pick up herb and spice notes. **83**

PETITE SIRAH VARIOUS BOTTLINGS (★★★): Dark and intense, very ripe and flavorful, but can be tannic and variable.
Napa Valley Reserve La Grande Petite 1991: Inky in color and a little earthy around the edges, but with solid berry flavors carrying through on the finish. **80**
Russian River Valley 1988: Jammy berry notes and ripe, fresh fruit flavors dominate this broad, tannic wine. **86**

Russian River Valley Reserve La Grande Petite 1987: Somewhat harsh and tannic despite the black cherry flavor. Lacks focus. **79**
Russian River Valley 1986: Big and full-bodied, quite oaky, with blueberry, pepper and cherry flavors. **83**
Sonoma County 1991: Firm in texture, with bright black cherry and toast flavors that echo on the tannic finish. **82**
Sonoma County 1990: Dark in color, full-bodied, very concentrated and tannic, with ripe blackberry flavors accented by vanilla and spice notes. **87**

SAUVIGNON BLANC DRY CREEK VALLEY (★★):
1992: Crisp and straightforward, a simple wine with bright fruit. **81**

ZINFANDEL DRY CREEK VALLEY (★★):
1993: Spritzy with earthy berry and spice notes that are light and elegant. **81**
1991: Crisp and fruity, with a spicy, earthy raspberry edge that's appealing. **87**

FOX MOUNTAIN CABERNET SAUVIGNON SONOMA COUNTY RESERVE (★★):
1987: Simple, with earthy, tarry, mature Cabernet flavors that dry out on the finish. **79**
1986: A correct wine that's lean and tightly wrapped, with appealing, mature aromas of herbs, dried cherry, rose petal and spice. **87**
1985: Dense, earthy and vegetal, with some plum flavor, but it's also quite tannic. **75**
1984: Firm and concentrated, yet supple enough to display its bright berry and currant flavors in a smooth style. **85**

FOREST GLEN
Sonoma County
F: 1990. **O:** Bronco Wine Co. **W:** Ed Moody, Merry Edwards. **S:** None.

OVERALL	$10-12	★★

WINE RATINGS

Cabernet Sauvignon Sonoma County	
Barrel Select	★★
Chardonnay Sonoma County	
Barrel Fermented	★★

WINERY DATA
C: 50,000. V: None. G: None. P: Cabernet Sauvignon (Alexander Valley), Cabernet Sauvignon (Sonoma County), Chardonnay, Merlot (California).

This 50,000-case brand is owned by the Franzia family, owners of Bronco Wine Co., which went on a wine brand buying spree beginning in the 1990s, acquiring eight labels in addition to Forest Glen: Estrella River, Grand Cru, Hacienda Wine Cellars, Laurier Vineyards, J.W. Morris, Napa Creek Winery, Rutherford Vintners and Salmon Creek Cellars. With Merry Edwards consulting, the quality of the Chardonnay has reached outstanding (1992), but otherwise the wines are in the good to very good range. The focus is on Cabernet and Chardonnay, from grapes grown throughout Sonoma County.

TASTING NOTES

CABERNET SAUVIGNON SONOMA COUNTY BARREL SELECT (★★): Good but nothing more, with modest flavors, made in an early drinking style.
1992: Earthy, with a narrow range of spicy currant flavors, turning tannic on the finish. **83**
1991: This wine offers bright, lively cherry and plum flavors that are crisp and pleasing. **85**
1990: Firm and austere, offering spicy currant, cedar and herb flavors that pick up a trace of tobacco. **83**

CHARDONNAY SONOMA COUNTY BARREL FERMENTED (★★): One high note with the excellent 1992 bottling, but otherwise merely good.
1993: Clean and lightly fruity, with pear, spice and vanilla notes. **83**
1992: Bold, ripe and richly flavored, offering ripe pear, spice, honey and toasty oak flavors that linger. **90**

FOREST HILL VINEYARD
Napa Valley
F: 1987. O: Forest Hill Vineyard Inc. W: Bob Levy. S: None.

OVERALL	$28	★★

WINE RATINGS
Chardonnay Napa Valley Private Reserve ★★★

WINERY DATA
C: 1,000. V: None. G: None. P: Chardonnay (Napa Valley).

Plastic surgeon David Manace expanded his home winemaking hobby in 1987 by starting Forest Hill, where he now makes 1,000 cases a year of Reserve Chardonnay with winemaker Bob Levy (of Merryvale and Harlan Estate). Not surprisingly, the wines are excellent, rich and complex.

TASTING NOTES

CHARDONNAY NAPA VALLEY PRIVATE RESERVE (★★★): Impressive start; the first two vintages are very appealing.
1993: Crisp and narrow, with ripe pear and spicy oak flavors that fan out a bit, but it could use a little more richness and depth. **85**
1992: Tight and flinty, with citrus, pear and spicy, toasty oak flavors that fan out on the finish, gaining depth and complexity. **90**
1991: Intense, rich and lively, with tight, focused pear, vanilla, smoke and toast flavors that are concentrated and deep. **90**

FORMAN VINEYARD
St. Helena, Napa Valley
F: 1983. O: Richard Forman. W: Richard Forman. S: Chateau La Grande Roche.

OVERALL	$23-30	★★★★★

WINE RATINGS
Cabernet Sauvignon Napa Valley	★★★★★
Chardonnay Napa Valley	★★★★★
Chateau La Grande Roche Pinot Noir Napa Valley	★★

WINERY DATA
C: 4,000. V: 86 acres in St. Helena, Napa Valley, Rutherford. G: Chardonnay (43 acres), Cabernet Sauvignon (30), Merlot (7), Cabernet Franc (3), Petite Verdot (2). P: None.

Ric Forman has filled his life wall to wall with Napa Valley wine and has had a hand in developing many important wines. While a student at U.C. Davis, he worked at Stony Hill, the famous Chardonnay estate.

After school he worked briefly at Robert Mondavi Winery. In 1968 he was hired at age 24 to be winemaker for the new Sterling Vineyards winery, where he worked until 1978, in the process developing new

wines such as Sauvignon Blanc and Merlot while defining the Sterling Reserve Cabernets. After Sterling he had a brief stint at Newton before starting his own winery in the hills east of St. Helena near the Meadowood Resort.

Forman has acquired 86 acres of vineyard, mostly Chardonnay and Cabernet, and his focus is on those two wines. His Cabernet (2,200 cases) is a Bordeaux-style blend containing Merlot and Cabernet Franc. He makes 1,800 cases of his estate-grown Chardonnay. Both wines show a definite house style that's very consistent. The Cabernet aims for finesse and understated flavors, rarely overwhelms but charms with its subtlety and grace. His Chardonnay is one of the few left in Napa that doesn't undergo malolactic fermentation, the goal (which he achieves) being a longer-lived wine that develops character and complexity in the bottle.

Tasting Notes

Cabernet Sauvignon Napa Valley (★★★★★): Packs in lots of complex flavors, but finesse and grace are its signature. Ages very well.

1992: Weaves together a pretty array of ripe cherry, currant and spicy oak flavors, with an earthy edge. Very well focused, young and vibrant, but in need of cellaring until 1999 or so. **92**

1991: Inky and raw like a barrel sample, but it serves up lots of concentrated currant, spice and cherry flavors, finishing with a peppery, tannic edge. **89**

1990: Sleek and elegant, with tight, firm, focused herb, currant, cedar and spice flavors. This youthful and concentrated wine finishes with fine tannins, but needs short-term cellaring to soften and develop. **90**

1989: Ripe and supple, a fleshy wine with a soft texture and enough backbone to carry the currant and spice flavors. It hints at anise and herbs, but remains fruity. **88**

1988: Solid tea, black cherry and currant flavors are backed by strong, rich tannins; shows more depth and concentration than most '88s. Picks up an herbal, oaky note on the aftertaste. **88**

1987: Ripe and intense, with concentrated currant, cherry, cedar and spice flavors that are tightly wound, firm and tannic. Has a supple, smooth texture before the tannins build up. **93**

1986: A beautifully sculpted wine, rich and cedary, with vibrant currant, plum and spice flavors that are lean and concentrated, finishing with firm tannins. **93**

1985: Very rich and cedary, with a touch of elegance and finesse and deep currant, spice and plum flavors. Finishes with fine, smooth tannins; it's focused, long and complex. **93**

1984: Rich, forward and delicious, a splendid Cabernet with supple, layered black cherry, currant and anise flavors framed by toasty oak and smooth tannins. **92**

1983: Mature and drinking well, holding its core of rich, complex currant, berry and spice flavors. **90**

Chardonnay Napa Valley (★★★★★): Starts out crisp and tight, but blossoms in the bottle, showing flinty apple and citrus notes.

1992: Crisp and lean, with lots of spice notes, but also sharply focused apple, pear and nectarine flavors. **89**

1991: Tart, lean and crisp, with spicy lemon, honey, pear and toast notes. Youthful, concentrated and full of flavor, but will require time to open and be more generous. **89**

1990: Tight, firm and crisp, with intense, focused pear, pineapple, peach and citrus flavors and a pretty overlay of toasty, buttery oak notes. **90**

1989: Tight and tart, with melon, pear, citrus and butterscotch flavors that are ripe and attractive, finishing with good length. **88**

1988: Intense, concentrated and complex, with pear, pineapple, spicy oak, peach and vanilla notes that gain prominence on the finish. **92**

1987: Plenty of fresh, ripe pear, spice, butter and toast notes that are long and tasty. **89**

1986: Toasty and smoky, with richness, depth and intensity and a smooth, silky texture to the ripe lemon, pear, butterscotch and smoke notes. **92**

1985: Amazing for its depth, intensity and sheer elegance, offering great complexity, with tiers of rich, toasty butterscotch, honey, citrus and spice flavors. **93**

Chateau La Grande Roche Pinot Noir Napa Valley (★★):

1991: Rich, full-bodied, complex and flavorful. The spicy, smoky cherry and plum flavors are long on the finish. Supple enough to drink now, but has the depth to cellar through 1998. **85**

FORTINO WINERY
Gilroy
F: 1948. **O:** Fortino Winery Inc. **W:** Gino Fortino. **S:** None.

OVERALL	$6	★★

WINERY DATA
C: 25,000. **V:** 52 acres in Hecker Pass. **G:** N/A. **P:** N/A.

Founded in 1948, Fortino in the Hecker Pass area near Gilroy produces a rustic mix of wines from its own 52 acres of vineyards and purchased grapes. The lineup includes Cabernet, Chardonnay, white Zinfandel, Riesling, Ruby Cabernet, Petite Sirah and Charbono, among others. These old-style wines can be pleasant enough, although they're far from the cutting edge. Production is 25,000 cases, much of it sold from the tasting room.

FOSS CREEK CELLARS
This is a second label for Robert Mueller Cellars (see listing).

FOX MOUNTAIN
This is a second label for Foppiano Vineyards (see listing).

FOXEN VINEYARD
Santa Maria Valley
F: 1987. **O:** Foxen Vineyard Inc. **W:** Bill Wathen. **S:** None.

OVERALL	$12-30	★★★

WINE RATINGS
Cabernet Sauvignon Santa Barbara County	★★★
Cabernet Sauvignon Santa Maria Valley	★★
Chardonnay Santa Maria Valley	★★
Chardonnay Santa Maria Valley Tinaquaic Vineyard	★★★
Chenin Blanc Santa Barbara County	★★★
Merlot Santa Barbara County	★★★
Pinot Noir Santa Maria Valley	★★★
Pinot Noir Santa Ynez Valley Sanford & Benedict Vineyard	★★★

WINERY DATA
C: 6,000. **V:** 15 acres in Santa Maria Valley. **G:** Chardonnay (5 acres), Merlot (2), Cabernet Sauvignon (2), Cabernet Franc (1). **P:** Pinot Noir, Chardonnay (Santa Maria Valley), Pinot Noir, Syrah, Viognier (Santa Ynez Valley), Cabernet Sauvignon, Merlot, Chenin Blanc (Santa Barbara County).

Richard Dore, a member of the Foxen family, longtime cattle ranchers in Santa Maria, and Bill Walthen, former vineyard manager of Rancho Sisquoc and Chalone, started Foxen Vineyard in 1987. The wines have gone from good to better, with each vintage showing more promise. The winery produces only 6,000 cases, with a lineup that includes Cabernet, Chardonnay, Chenin Blanc, Merlot, Pinot Noir (two bottlings) and Syrah. All of the reds are solid, but the most striking is perhaps the Santa Barbara Cabernet, which of late has been right on the mark even though it's from an area where this varietal is often marred by vegetal flavors. The Chardonnay has been hit or miss.

TASTING NOTES

CABERNET SAUVIGNON SANTA BARBARA COUNTY (★★★): Ripe and plush, with bright, lively fruit flavors, supple and elegant, steadily improving after lackluster bottlings from 1987 to 1988.
1992: Firm and intense, with a core of spicy currant, herb and cedary oak flavors. Finishes with a supple texture and good length. **87**
1991: Smooth and generous, offering mouthwatering black cherry, plum, anise and other spice flavors, all lingering nicely on the finish. **89**
1990: Smells fruity and forward, but turns simple on the palate, with plum, black cherry and a trace of oak on the finish. **84**
1989: Rich and vibrant, jam-packed with ripe currant, black cherry, plum and spice flavors that are sharply focused and backed by smooth tannins and plenty of depth. **91**

1988: Deliciously fruity and focused, with generous blackberry, currant and plum aromas and flavors that extend into a long finish. A wine with personality. **89**

CABERNET SAUVIGNON SANTA MARIA VALLEY (★★):
Not in the same class as the Santa Barbara bottling.
1990: Another good vintage for Foxen, this is a firm, compact wine with crisp currant, mint and cola notes, finishing with firm, dry tannins. **83**
1989: A dramatic improvement over previous vintages, this is a crisp, lean wine with minty currant notes that avoids the pronounced vegetal characteristics found in earlier efforts. **86**
1988: Lean and crisp, with intensity and depth, but showing a vegetal edge that dries out. **75**
1987: Dense and vegetal, with potent asparagus and bell pepper flavors. **74**

CHARDONNAY SANTA MARIA VALLEY (★★), TINAQUAIC VINEYARD (★★★): Inconsistent, but the 1992 Tinaquaic Vineyard is loaded with flavor.
1993: Complex and concentrated, with tiers of honey, pear, apple spice and toasty oak shadings, finishing with a complex aftertaste. **90**
1992: Strives for complexity with its earthy, toasty notes and creamy texture, but it comes up short on depth, turning simple. **84**
1991: Lean, crisp and simple, with tart pear and apple notes. **79**
Tinaquaic Vineyard 1993: Earthy, with a strong leesy edge to the pear and pineapple flavors, but offers more depth and intensity than many 1993's. **85**
Tinaquaic Vineyard 1992: Spicy and toasty, with crisp, rich nectarine, peach, pear and nutmeg flavors that are complex and concentrated. Finishes with a burst of fruit that stays rich and focused. **92**

CHENIN BLANC SANTA BARBARA COUNTY (★★★):
Follows the Chalone model of barrel fermentation, and keeps the fruit up front.
1993: Smells and tastes like a barrel-fermented Chardonnay at first, kicking in its bright apple and melon flavors. Sacrifices charm for flavor and seems a little sweet on the finish. **83**
1992: Has all the earmarks of a barrel-fermented Chardonnay—spicy, toasty overtones, polished texture, buttery fruit at the fore—but it carries them all lightly and with a sense of elegance. **87**

MERLOT SANTA BARBARA COUNTY (★★★):
1991: Tight and firm, with sharply focused black cherry and currant flavors that pick up pretty floral and spice notes on the finish. **88**

PINOT NOIR SANTA MARIA VALLEY (★★★), SANTA YNEZ VALLEY SANFORD & BENEDICT VINEYARD (★★★): Brilliantly fruity and complex, moving to the forefront of the Santa Maria-Santa Ynez Pinot Noir class. Worth watching.
1992: Intense and focused, with a narrow beam of herb, cola and black cherry flavors. Finishes with firm tannins. **87**
1991: Intense and lively, with spicy cherry, herb and cola flavors that have a gamy edge. **88**
1990: Brilliantly fruity and rich, with spicy oak notes seamlessly melded into the cherry and currant flavors at the core. Smooth and generous without being heavy. **89**
1989: Distinct for its cola-sassafras edge, this is an intense wine that turns earthy and meaty on the finish. **84**
1988: A tart, lean wine with earthy cola and berry flavors that have a pleasant but distinct gamy edge. **85**
1987: Crisp, lean and firm, with tart earth, cherry and spice flavors that are intense and focused, finishing with tight, dry tannins. **86**
Sanford & Benedict Vineyard 1992: Intense and tightly wound, with a narrow band of herb, tea, cola and black cherry flavors. **86**
Sanford & Benedict Vineyard 1991: Dark, intense, tannic and concentrated, in that order. Needs to soften, but the cherry and raspberry flavors are rich and potent. **89**

FRANCISCAN VINEYARDS
Rutherford, Napa Valley
F: 1972. **O:** Eckes Family & Agustin Huneeus. **W:** Alan Tenscher. **S:** None.

OVERALL	$11-30	★★★

WINE RATINGS

Cabernet Sauvignon Napa Valley Oakville Estate	★★★
Cabernet Sauvignon Napa Valley Oakville Estate Reserve	★★★
Chardonnay Napa Valley Oakville Estate Barrel Fermented	★★★

Chardonnay Napa Valley
  Oakville Estate Cuvée Sauvage ★★★★
Meritage Red Napa Valley Magnificat ★★★
Merlot Napa Valley Oakville Estate ★★★
Merlot Napa Valley Oakville Estate
  Reserve ★★★
Zinfandel Napa Valley Oakville Estate ★★★

WINERY DATA
C: 54,000. **V:** 218 acres in Oakville. **G:** Cabernet Sauvignon (93 acres), Chardonnay (44), Cabernet Franc (18), Merlot (32), Zinfandel (31). **P:** None.

In its first period, from 1972 to 1985, Franciscan appeared headed for disaster, as its product mix included low-priced Burgundies, weedy Cabernets and oxidized Chardonnays. This is all the more curious since one of its early owners (1975-1979) was Justin Meyer, whose Silver Oak Cellars produces well focused Cabernets. Despite many shortcomings, the winery had vineyards in good if not great locations in both Napa and Alexander Valleys. In 1979 the Eckes family of Germany bought Franciscan and in 1985 Agustin Huneeus (of Seagram, Concannon and Souverain) joined as president, redirecting the winery with a skilled staff, centralizing winemaking in Rutherford and separating the vineyards by brands: Napa Valley grapes were used for Franciscan and Alexander Valley grapes for Estancia, both with good success.

Franciscan owns 218 acres, with Cabernet (93 acres), Chardonnay (44), Merlot (32) and Zinfandel (31) the focus. Production is 54,000 cases and holding, with each of the aforementioned grapes made into varietal wines, along with a Meritage called Magnificat. The standard Cabernet and Chardonnay (18,000 cases each) dominate, with lesser amounts of Merlot (10,000) and Zinfandel (7,500).

TASTING NOTES

CABERNET SAUVIGNON NAPA VALLEY OAKVILLE ESTATE (★★★), RESERVE (★★★): Elegant and medium-weight, a good, early-drinking, restaurant-style wine with herb, spice and currant notes.
1991: Ripe and fleshy, with modest herb, cherry and toasty oak flavors. **82**
1990: Dense and chewy, with tough-textured tannins up front that make it hard to pick out all the flavors, but the currant, berry and plum notes are bright and compact. **88**

1989: Shows wonderful balance for an '89, with ripe, spicy cherry, mineral, earth and tobacco notes. **87**
1988: Firm in texture but unfocused, with modest cherry and currant aromas and flavors and hints of herbs on the finish. **81**
1987: Tart, herbal and tightly focused, with ripe cherry and bay leaf flavors, turning generous on the finish. **87**
1986: Forward and open, this wine has juicy currant, herb and spicy oak flavors that are full-bodied and deceptively tannic. **84**
Reserve 1988: Light, crisp and pleasant, with appealing strawberry and spice aromas and flavors but little depth or style. **81**
Reserve 1985: Garnet in color, with mature, supple herb and spice notes adding to the currant and cherry flavors. **84**

CHARDONNAY NAPA VALLEY OAKVILLE ESTATE BARREL FERMENTED (★★★): Rich and oaky.
1993: Marked by smoky, toasty oak and a ripe core of pear, apple and spice, it turns complex and concentrated on the finish. **90**
1992: Elegant and complex, with layers of spicy pear, hazelnut and smoke notes turning smooth and silky. **91**

CHARDONNAY NAPA VALLEY OAKVILLE ESTATE CUVÉE SAUVAGE (★★★★): Similar to the Barrel Fermented bottling, but this one stretches the band of flavors, turning creamy and complex. Ages well.
1993: Ripe and oaky, with an elegant core of pear, hazelnut, toasty oak and spicy flavors, turning elegant and complex on the finish, where the flavors linger. **89**
1992: Youthful, tight and unevolved, displaying toasty oak and ripe pear flavors that are compact and concentrated, especially pleasing on the finish. **90**
1991: Ripe, tight and focused, with pretty pear, spice, citrus and apple flavors that are framed by toasty, buttery oak. Complex and concentrated. **91**

MERITAGE RED NAPA VALLEY MAGNIFICAT (★★★): Elegant and understated, with Merlot and Cabernet Franc in the blend.
1990: Lean and crisp, with a tight, narrow band of spice, currant and herb flavors, finishing with firm tannins. **87**
1989: Lean and cedary, a tight, compact wine with solid currant and cola aromas and flavors that remain solid at the finish. **86**

1988: Firm and tannic, but it has rich cedar, tobacco, currant and anise flavors that are quite appealing. Complex and balanced. **87**

1987: Has plenty of herb, plum, cedar and chocolate flavors that are high in extract, but it's a rough-hewn wine with a somewhat coarse texture and firm, drying tannins. **88**

1986: Mature and ready to drink, it offers supple currant and cherry flavors along with a touch of herb and oak. **79**

1985: Very firm and tannic, but with generous fruit flavors and a real sense of elegance, turning smooth and long on the finish, echoing cherry and chocolate. **90**

MERLOT NAPA VALLEY OAKVILLE ESTATE (★★★), RESERVE (★★★): Supple and harmonious, with soft tannins and herb and currant flavors. A new Reserve is rich and decadent, with greater depth and concentration.

1991: Tight and firm, with a narrow band of herb, earth and currant flavors. **85**

1990: Ripe, fleshy and focused, with nicely articulated raspberry, currant and vanilla aromas and flavors that keep echoing on the spicy finish. **87**

Reserve 1991: Well oaked, with a toasty vanilla edge, it delivers solid herb, currant and cherry flavors that turn deliciously decadent on the finish, where the tannins firm up. **89**

ZINFANDEL NAPA VALLEY OAKVILLE ESTATE (★★★): Appealing for its spicy, peppery flavors and up-front fruit flavors.

1993: Strikes a nice balance between toasty buttery oak and pepper and berry-laced Zinfandel fruit. **86**

1992: Strives for complexity with its range of flavors, but it's hard to look past the earthiness, which dominates the berry flavor. **80**

1991: An elegant, claret-style wine marked by toasty oak and ripe cherry and currant notes. Balanced and supple. **85**

1990: Firm and focused, with a strong oak frame around the intense plum and blackberry aromas and flavors. **87**

1989: Tough and concentrated, with powerful plum and cherry aromas and flavors that hint at herbs and cedar at the edge. **88**

1988: Raspberry, cherry and chocolate aromas and flavors pervade this lively, focused, effusive, sharply defined wine. **87**

FRANUS WINERY
Napa Valley
F: 1987. **O:** Peter Franus. **W:** Peter Franus. **S:** None.

OVERALL	$14-22	★★★

WINE RATINGS

Zinfandel Mount Veeder Brandlin Vineyard	★★★
Zinfandel Napa Valley Hendry Vineyard	★★★★

WINERY DATA
C: 1,000. **V:** None. **G:** None. **P:** Zinfandel (Mount Veeder and Napa Valley).

Peter Franus left a career as a journalist for winemaking, working briefly at Chalone and William Hill Winery before settling in as winemaker at Mount Veeder Winery from 1981 to 1992. In 1987 Franus began making small lots of Zinfandel in a rented Napa warehouse that he shared with Mike Havens. Part of Franus's fascination with Zinfandel stems from the excellent vineyards on Mount Veeder. He has settled on two key vineyards, George Hendry Vineyard and Brandlin Vineyard, which he bottles separately with vineyard designations. Production has climbed to 1,000 cases of each wine with the 1992 vintage. He has also added a Hendry Vineyard Cabernet, which is spicy and elegant. Future growth will come as Franus finds additional vineyards worthy of being bottled as vineyard-designated wines.

TASTING NOTES

ZINFANDEL MOUNT VEEDER BRANDLIN VINEYARD (★★★): Austere but well focused, with tight fruit flavors and ample tannins.

1992: Serves up classic Zinfandel flavors, with its well focused spice, pepper and wild berry notes. **88**

1991: Tight and austere, with firm, chewy tannins, but enough cherry and raspberry flavors underneath to merit attention. **86**

Late Picked 1991: Lots of ripe, juicy berry and cherry flavors that don't turn jammy or raisiny. It carries its 17 percent alcohol without getting hot. **89**

ZINFANDEL NAPA VALLEY HENDRY VINEYARD (★★★★): Ripe and intense, with more depth and complexity than the Brandlin.

1992: Ripe and spicy, with bright, rich, lively raspberry, anise and black cherry flavors that are firmly tannic and framed by light oak. **89**

1991: Ripe and intense, with tart, vivid, concentrated, sharply focused berry, pepper, cherry and floral aromas and flavors that turn rich and complex. **90**

1990: Bold, ripe and flavorful, with rich, intense cherry, plum and raspberry flavors that are long and peppery on the palate. **89**

1989: Intense and complex, with crisp berry, cherry and raspberry flavors that take on a pleasant earthy edge. **86**

1988: Dark, ripe and concentrated, with ripe berry and pepper flavors that are intense and lively, finishing with firm, chewy tannins. **88**

1987: Tart, firm and crisp, with cherry and berry flavors that are bright and lively, picking up a toasty, buttery note on the finish. **88**

FREEMARK ABBEY WINERY
St. Helena, Napa Valley
F: 1886. **O:** M. Warren, D. Heggie, C. Carpy, J. Bryan, L. Wood, T. Edwards, B. Webb, W. Jaeger. **W:** Ted Edwards, Brad Webb. **S:** None.

OVERALL	$15-35	★★★

WINE RATINGS

Cabernet Sauvignon Napa Valley	★★
Cabernet Sauvignon Napa Valley Bosche Vineyard	★★★★
Cabernet Sauvignon Napa Valley Sycamore Vineyard	★★★
Chardonnay Napa Valley	★★★
Chardonnay Napa Valley Carpy Ranch	★★★
Johannisberg Riesling Napa Valley	★★★
Johannisberg Riesling Napa Valley Edelwein Gold	★★★★
Merlot Napa Valley	★★

WINERY DATA
C: 38,000. **V:** 126 acres in Napa Valley. **G:** Chardonnay (35 acres), Sauvignon Blanc (14), Johannisberg Riesling (8), Merlot (54), Cabernet Sauvignon (6). **P:** Chardonnay, Riesling, Merlot, Cabernet Sauvignon, Cabernet Franc, Petite Verdot (Napa Valley).

The re-birth of Freemark Abbey Winery in 1967 preceeded the 1970s wine boom, and this winery set high standards with several of its wines, notably the Bosche Cabernet and the late-harvest Edelwein dessert wine. A group of seven partners, including longtime winegrower Chuck Carpy and legendary winemaker Brad Webb, founded the winery. Through its cellars have passed many fine winemakers (Jerry Luper, Mike Richmond and Ted Edwards, the currant steward, among others). Freemark Abbey had a big advantage because its partners knew the best areas in the valley for grapes; witness their recognition of the Bosche Vineyard in Rutherford. For years the grapes from that property went into the Beaulieu Vineyard Private Reserves, and BV set aside special lots bottled especially for proprietor John Bosche. But in 1968 Bosche asked Carpy to make wine from his vineyard. Carpy did, and by 1969 Cabernet Bosche became part of Freemark Abbey's lineup. The winery's Chardonnay, Riesling and Merlot, along with vineyard-designated Carpy Ranch Chardonnay and Sycamore Vineyard Cabernet (also in Rutherford), have more often than not been solid, well made and pleasant wines. Production hovers around 38,000 cases, and most of the grapes are from the winery's 126 acres of vineyards, with Merlot (54 acres) the largest planting, overshadowing Cabernet (6 acres) and Chardonnay (35). Both Bosche and Sycamore remain privately owned.

TASTING NOTES

CABERNET SAUVIGNON NAPA VALLEY (★★): Clean, correct and well balanced, with earthy currant and spice flavors, but pales by comparison with the other wines. Best on release.

1991: Correct and well balanced, with a firm band of earthy currant flavors and light oak shadings. **85**

1990: Tight, lean and compact, with currant and spice flavors that pick up an oaky edge. **83**

1989: An earthy wine with spicy, leathery currant, tar and cedar notes that turn firm and tannic on the finish. **81**

CABERNET SAUVIGNON NAPA VALLEY BOSCHE VINEYARD (★★★★): Among the most elegant and refined of the great Rutherford Cabs, a classy, supple, well integrated wine that is very consistent and ageworthy.

1991: Firm, rich and focused, with complex cherry, currant and anise flavors that linger. Beautifully balanced; better after 1997. **90**

1990: Young and chunky, but classic Bosche with its core of ripe, supple currant and black cherry flavors. Unevolved now, but complex and concentrated; better after 1997. **90**

1989: Lean and crisp, with a narrow range of earthy currant, black cherry and cedary oak flavors. **87**

1987: Laced with herb, olive, currant, mint and spice notes, but it's austere and the tannins are a bit crisp and tight. **87**

1986: Tight and firm, with a core of nice currant and cedar flavors, finishing with crisp tannins. **86**

1985: Lean, tight and concentrated, with firm black cherry, plum, currant, earth and cedar flavors that are intense and lively. The finish is narrow and focused. **90**

1984: Chunky, showing mature currant, black cherry, cedar and spice notes before firm tannins kick in. **87**

1983: A little rough around the edges now, this is a serious, intense wine with high acid, lots of tannins and loads of complex plum, cherry and anise flavors that are very well focused. Needs cellaring. **80**

1982: Tough, lean and tannic, with herb, cherry, spice and currant flavors, but it's still elegant. **88**

1981: Has pretty black cherry flavors and is leaner and more compact on the palate than the nose suggests. **86**

1980: Rich and ripe, with sharply defined fruit flavors and a touch of herb, cherry and anise. **88**

1979: Mature but still dense and concentrated, with compact currant, anise and cedar notes, finishing with firm tannins. Still excellent. **88**

1978: Mature and fading, with drying cedar and currant flavors. After a long run in prime condition, it has passed its peak. **87**

1976: Ripe, jammy and chunky, turning dry and austere on the finish. **84**

1975: Deeply colored but fading, with pleasant dried cherry and currant flavors. **85**

1974: Showing its age but retaining its elegant personality, it's drying out and losing its fruit, but there are just enough complexity and finesse to hold your interest. Drink up if you still have a bottle. **85**

1973: Smooth and polished, with a core of pretty, mature currant, anise and smoky cedar notes. Still delicious. **89**

1971: From a difficult vintage, this 1971 is an extraordinary wine that has aged extremely well. It's fully mature and elegant, with complex, mature toast, cedar, plum and currant flavors. **86**

1970: Amazingly rich and elegant, with supple cedar, black cherry and currant flavors, smooth tannins and a long, delicious finish. Complex and enticing. **91**

CABERNET SAUVIGNON NAPA VALLEY SYCAMORE VINEYARD (★★★): Lacks the depth of Bosche, but can be very good. It's marked by herb, currant and cedar flavors.

1990: Supple and polished, with ripe, rich, complex currant, herb, anise and cedar flavors that linger. **89**

1989: Deep in color, with an earthy, herbal edge to the currant and berry notes. **86**

1988: A good 1988, with lean, tannic and earthy Cabernet flavors that pick up a spicy vanilla edge on the finish. **84**

1987: A wonderful expression of ripe, supple Cabernet, with currant, berry, cherry and anise flavors that turn smooth and supple on the finish. **90**

1986: Turning herbaceous, with weedy black currant flavors and cedary oak underneath. Deeply colored, with an elegant framework. **88**

1985: Lean, with a narrow beam of currant and cherry flavors. Not up to the best '85s. **85**

CHARDONNAY NAPA VALLEY (★★★): Accentuates ripe fruit and typifies a Napa Valley Chardonnay, as it brings together several mid-valley sources. Off pace lately.

1992: Has just enough ripe pear, spice and light oak shadings to hold together. Simple but pleasant. **83**

1991: Bright and fruity, a simple wine with nice pineapple and spice aromas and flavors. **81**

CHARDONNAY NAPA VALLEY CARPY RANCH (★★★): This bottling is aged *sur lie* and has been overdone, but usually is crisp and spicy.

1991: Firm and compact, with a slight leesy edge to the ripe pear and apple flavors. Picks up a pretty, toasty oak edge on the finish, and the flavors linger. **88**

JOHANNISBERG RIESLING NAPA VALLEY (★★★): Appealing for its forward fruitiness, with grapefruit, peach and pine notes.

1990: On the dry side, showing focused grapefruit, peach and pine aromas and flavors that are harmonious and balanced toward smoothness. Refreshing, with beautifully realized fruit. **85**

JOHANNISBERG RIESLING NAPA VALLEY EDELWEIN GOLD (★★★★): Among the best in California of this type, it ages well and gains depth, with rich, complex apricot and honey notes.

1991: Ripe, buttery, rich and sweet, with all kinds of

spice, honey and butter notes gracing the sweet pineapple, fig and pear flavors. **92**

1989: With its golden color and honey, apricot and spice aromas and flavors, this is a knockout from the first whiff to the last echo of the long finish. A rich, sweet, seductive wine. **92**

MERLOT NAPA VALLEY (★★): Succeeds with its supple texture and mild tannins, but tends to be dominated by weedy, herbaceous qualities.

1992: Medium-weight with a narrow band of herb and currant flavors, finishing with a light tobacco edge. **83**

1991: A solid wine with currant and berry flavors, finishing with the slightest tannic bite. **84**

1989: Smells excessively weedy and earthy, but comes through with strong blackberry and black currant flavors that linger on the finish. **80**

FREMONT CREEK WINERY
St. Helena, Napa Valley
F: 1988. **O:** Beckstoffer Vineyards. **W:** Erin Green, Dimitri Tchelistcheff. **S:** None.

OVERALL	$6-9	★★

WINE RATINGS

Cabernet Sauvignon	
Mendocino/Napa Counties	★★
Chardonnay	
Mendocino/Napa Counties	★★
Sauvignon Blanc	
Mendocino/Napa Counties	★★

WINERY DATA
C: 5,000. **V:** 1830 acres in Rutherford, Oakville, St. Helena, Carneros, Mendocino. **G:** Chardonnay (650 acres), Cabernet Sauvignon (540), Merlot (210), Sauvignon Blanc (120), Pinot Noir (90), Zinfandel (50), Gewürztraminer (95), Chenin Blanc (75). **P:** None.

Andy Beckstoffer is one of the largest independent grape growers in the North Coast—with 1,830 acres in vines, he has tremendous resources available, but his Fremont Creek wines don't reflect that. Guenoc, for instance, makes a great Cabernet from Beckstoffer's St. Helena Vineyard, but for whatever reason Beckstoffer sells his best grapes to others (which makes him popular)

and produces rather ordinary wines under his 5,000-case label. It is almost as if he makes wines from his youngest and least interesting grapes, leaving the best for sale. His acreage includes 880 acres in Mendocino, 430 in Rutherford (mostly Cabernet, including a former BV vineyard south of the Robert Mondavi Winery), 89 in Oakville and 410 in Carneros, most of that Chardonnay.

FREY WINERY
Redwood Valley
F: 1980. **O:** Frey Vineyards Ltd. **W:** Jon Frey. **S:** None.

OVERALL	$7-14	★★

WINE RATINGS

Zinfandel Mendocino County	★★

WINERY DATA
C: 20,000. **V:** 43 acres in Mendocino. **G:** Chardonnay (10 acres), Sauvignon Blanc (10), Cabernet Sauvignon (12), Zinfandel (8), Merlot (3). **P:** None.

Physician Paul Frey started this winery in 1980 after buying a vineyard at the northern end of Redwood Valley. Today the 20,000-case winery is best known for its organic wines, which are made in a rustic (and risky) style without sulfur dioxide, which has led to a number of bizarre and overly oxidized wines (mostly whites, but reds too). I've had poor luck with the whites, but the reds are somewhat better. The best is a Zinfandel, followed by a Cabernet, a Syrah and a Petite Sirah.

TASTING NOTES

ZINFANDEL MENDOCINO COUNTY (★★):
1992: Very ripe and fruity, with layers of cherry, raspberry and plum flavors; the tannins are in check. **84**

1990: Ripe in flavor, with a firm underpinning of tannin and a streak of menthol adding complexity to the meaty berry flavors. **84**

FRICK WINERY
Alexander Valley
F: 1976. **O:** William R. Frick & Judith M. Gannon. **W:** William R. Frick. **S:** None.

OVERALL $13 ★★

WINE RATINGS
Zinfandel Dry Creek Valley ★★

WINERY DATA
C: 2,000. V: 6 acres in Dry Creek Valley. G: Syrah (4 acres), Viognier (2). P: Cinsault, Zinfandel, Petite Sirah, Merlot, Cabernet Sauvignon (Dry Creek Valley).

The Frick Winery has moved almost as often as its grape sources have changed. It began in an abandoned gas station in Bonny Doon in the Santa Cruz Mountains, moved to a warehouse in Santa Cruz (now Storrs) and since 1988 has been situated in Geyserville. The label looks as if it were penned by Ralph Steadman and the wines are ripe, bold and full-blown but inconsistent. Production is around 2,000 cases, with Zinfandel (500 cases) the leader over Cinsault Rosé, Petite Sirah and Syrah, all four wines carrying the Dry Creek appellation.

J. FRITZ CELLARS
Alexander Valley
F: 1979. O: Arthur J. Fritz Jr. & Barbara Fritz. W: David Hastings. S: None.

OVERALL $10-18 ★★

WINE RATINGS
Chardonnay Russian River Valley
   Barrel Select ★★
Chardonnay Sonoma County ★★
Sauvignon Blanc Dry Creek Valley ★★
Zinfandel Dry Creek Valley
   80-Year-Old Vines ★★

WINERY DATA
C: 30,000. V: 48 acres in Dry Creek Valley. G: Sauvignon Blanc (21 acres), Chardonnay (17), Zinfandel (6), Merlot (2), Cabernet Sauvignon (1), Cabernet Franc (1). P: Zinfandel, Petite Sirah (Dry Creek Valley), Melon, Chardonnay (Russian River), Chardonnay (Monterey), Petite Sirah (Pope Valley).

Arthur and Barbara Fritz founded this 30,000-case winery in Cloverdale in 1979. Through the years the wines have lacked consistency: they're good on some occasions, less good on others, sometimes even bizarre. The three main wines—Chardonnay (10,000 cases), Sauvignon Blanc (2,900 cases) and Zinfandel from 80-year-old vines (1,500 cases)—are supplemented by smaller lots of Cabernet, Melon and late-harvest Zinfandel.

TASTING NOTES

CHARDONNAY VARIOUS BOTTLINGS (★★):
Russian River Valley Barrel Select 1992: Appealing for its complex blend of spicy, toasty oak and ripe pear and fig flavors. **85**
Sonoma County 1992: Despite an earthy, grassy edge it hangs together, with spicy pear and apple notes that are simple but pleasant enough. A fair price. **83**

SAUVIGNON BLANC DRY CREEK VALLEY (★★):
1994: Solid, flavorful, generous with its pear, spice and slightly herbal flavors. **83**
1993: Light and fragrant, balancing spicy pear flavors with a nice touch of sweet peas. **86**

ZINFANDEL DRY CREEK VALLEY 80-YEAR-OLD VINES (★★):
1992: Firm and intense, with wild cherry, raspberry and spice notes. **83**
1991: Tart and spicy, with light berry and raspberry flavors that thin out on the finish. **82**
1990: Smells earthy, but has nice, tart raspberry and strawberry flavors and hints of spice and earth. **82**

FROG'S LEAP WINERY
Rutherford, Napa Valley
F: 1981. O: John & Julie Williams. W: John Williams. S: None.

OVERALL $11-19 ★★★

WINE RATINGS
Cabernet Sauvignon Napa Valley ★★★
Chardonnay Carneros ★★★
Merlot Napa Valley ★★
Sauvignon Blanc Napa Valley ★★
Zinfandel Napa Valley ★★

WINERY DATA
C: 44,000. V: 73 acres in Napa Valley. G: Cabernet Sauvignon (23 acres), Zinfandel (12), Sauvignon Blanc (16), Merlot (22). P: Sauvignon Blanc, Chardonnay, Zinfandel, Merlot, Cabernet Sauvignon (Napa Valley), Chardonnay (Carneros).

In 1981 Larry Turley, his former wife, Jeannine, and John and Julie Williams struck a deal to make wine together on Turley's property, which was once used to raise frogs whose legs were destined for fine restaurants. Frog's Leap began with John Williams, then at Spring Mountain Vineyards, as winemaker, focusing on Sauvignon Blanc (still the winery's biggest seller with 15,000 cases). As the winery grew it added Cabernet, Chardonnay, Merlot and Zinfandel, making 5,000 to 6,000 case of each, and occasionally a late-harvest wine called Late Leap. Production has risen to 44,000 cases, a portion of that coming from 73 acres of winery-owned vineyards, but quality has suffered in the process. In 1994 Frog's Leap's size prompted Turley to break apart the partnership and start his own winery, Turley Wine Cellar, and the Williamses took on new partners, building a winery in Rutherford.

TASTING NOTES

CABERNET SAUVIGNON NAPA VALLEY (★★★): After a strong period in the mid-1980s, recent vintages have been varied and less concentrated, coinciding with a doubling of production since 1986.

1991: Firm and compact, with spice, herb and currant notes, finishing with firm tannins and concentrated flavors. **86**

1990: Firm in texture, a tightly wound wine with generous ripe plum, blackberry and spice aromas and flavors. **88**

1989: Tough, tight, lean and tannic, with weedy herb, cedar and chocolate flavors that tend to override the currant notes. **79**

1988: Has lovely, ripe raspberry, plum and cherry flavors of moderate depth, concentration and intensity. **86**

1987: Offering enormous depth and richness, a massively concentrated wine with a silky texture and intense currant, plum and cassis flavors framed by toasty oak. **91**

1986: Ripe and expansive, with a fragrant, complex bouquet of fruit and flowers and rich, concentrated, elegant flavors that echo black currant, cherry, plum and spice. **91**

1985: Unusual green pepper and herbaceous notes run through the peppery black cherry flavors, adding another dimension. **85**

1984: A wonderfully delicious wine, rich, smooth and supple, with tiers of currant, black cherry, cinnamon and cedar flavors. **92**

CHARDONNAY CARNEROS (★★★): The Carneros-grown grapes produce an intense and lively wine that lacks extra dimensions. More variable in quality recently.

1992: Firm and spicy, with compact pear, pineapple and toasty apple flavors. **87**

1991: Firm, youthful and complex, a tightly wound wine offering spice, pear and toasty oak flavors that take on an earthy edge. **89**

MERLOT NAPA VALLEY (★★): Good but nothing more, medium-weight, offering ripe fruit flavors but also herb and tea notes.

1991: Supple and generous, with sweet currant and herb flavors that are focused and well proportioned, finishing with soft tannins. **86**

1990: Hard, tight and smoky, with green, tealike tannins and oak notes that override the ripe plum flavors. **84**

SAUVIGNON BLANC NAPA VALLEY (★★): Once a leader, it's now middle-of-the-pack, marked by grassy citrus and spice notes.

1992: Tart, lean and grassy, with lemon and grapefruit flavors that fan out to spice and pear notes. Clean and refreshing. **85**

ZINFANDEL NAPA VALLEY (★★): Has also shown a steady decline, although most vintages are medium-bodied with spicy berry flavors.

1992: Earthy and a bit funky, with an odd woody streak to the flavors. **74**

1991: Despite a strong buttery oak flavor, the spicy, peppery Zinfandel flavors shine through, giving this wine a smooth texture. **85**

1990: Big and ripe, with a strong floral edge to the spicy plum flavors, but it tastes simple. **80**

1989: Starts off fruity and plummy, but the texture turns simple. **83**

1988: Supple, smooth and generous, with plenty of velvety cherry, plum and raspberry flavors that fill the mouth. **88**

GABRIELLI WINERY
Redwood Valley, Mendocino County

F: 1989. **O:** Gabrielli Winery Inc. **W:** Jefferson Hinchliffe. **S:** None.

OVERALL	$12-22	★★

WINE RATINGS

Chardonnay Mendocino County	★★
Chardonnay Mendocino County Reserve	★★
White Table Wine	
Mendocino County Ascenza	★★
Zinfandel Mendocino County	★★
Zinfandel Mendocino County Reserve	★★

WINERY DATA

C: 8,000. V: 14 acres in Redwood Valley. G: Sangiovese (7 acres), Syrah (7). P: Chardonnay, Pinot Noir, Riesling, Sémillon (Potter Valley), Chardonnay, Pinot Noir, Riesling, (Anderson Valley), Chardonnay, Zinfandel (Redwood Valley), Zinfandel (Talmage), Zinfandel, Chenin Blanc, Sémillon (Ukiah Valley), Zinfandel, Sémillon (Napa Valley).

This Mendocino-based winery is owned by a partnership of several families and produces 8,000 cases of wine, with the focus on Chardonnay and Zinfandel and smaller lots of Pinot Noir, Riesling and Sangiovese. Quality is average but improving.

TASTING NOTES

CHARDONNAY MENDOCINO COUNTY (★★), RESERVE (★★): Ranges from simple to moderately complex, with smooth, toasty oak and spice flavors.

1992: Lean and simple, with a narrow band of pear and oak flavors. **80**

1991: A rich, round wine with beautiful spice-scented pear, butter and vanilla flavors. **87**

Reserve 1992: Simple and fruity, with spicy pear, herb and grass notes that are elegant and understated. Not up to Reserve status. **83**

Reserve 1991: Crisp and earthy, with a mineral edge to the basic apple and lemon peel aromas and flavors. **78**

WHITE TABLE WINE MENDOCINO COUNTY ASCENZA (★★): A blend of Chenin Blanc, Riesling and Chardonnay.

1991: Smooth and silky, with Chardonnay-like aromas and flavors that focus on spice, vanilla, apple and melon. An elegant wine. Made from Chenin Blanc, Riesling and Chardonnay. **84**

ZINFANDEL MENDOCINO COUNTY (★★), RESERVE (★★): The best of the lineup, tight and firm, with spicy berry notes, often quite tannic.

1993: Ripe but not overdone, with hints of plum and cherry jam turning spicy and tannic. **86**

1992: Lean and compact, with a tight band of spicy cherry, raspberry and tar notes. **85**

1991: Firm and flavorful, pumping out the berry and spice flavors. **85**

1990: Firm and more than a little tannic, but has a beam of nice blackberry, plum and spice flavors. **85**

Reserve 1992: Firm and tannic, with a core of spicy cherry, raspberry and gamy oak flavors. **84**

Reserve 1991: Firmly tannic, with light cherry and strawberry flavors. **84**

Reserve 1990: Tough and tannic, with more oak than black cherry and blackberry flavors. **82**

THE GAINEY VINEYARD
Santa Ynez Valley

F: 1984. O: Daniel J. Gainey. W: Richard Longoria. S: None.

OVERALL	$9-30	★★★

WINE RATINGS

Cabernet Franc Santa Ynez Valley	
Limited Selection	★★★
Cabernet Sauvignon Santa Barbara	
County Limited Selection	★★
Cabernet Sauvignon Santa Ynez Valley	★
Chardonnay Santa Barbara County	★★
Chardonnay Santa Ynez Valley	
Limited Selection	★★★★
Merlot Santa Ynez Valley	
Limited Selection	★★
Pinot Noir Santa Barbara County	★★
Pinot Noir Santa Ynez Valley	
Limited Selection	★★★
Riesling Santa Ynez Valley	★★
Sauvignon Blanc Santa Ynez Valley	
Limited Selection	★★

WINERY DATA

C: 12,000. V: 62 acres in Santa Ynez Valley. G: Chardonnay (17 acres), Sauvignon Blanc (13), Johannisberg Riesling (9), Cabernet Sauvignon (7), Merlot (10), Cabernet Franc (4), Sémillon (1). P: Chardonnay, Pinot Noir, Riesling (Santa Ynez Valley), Chardonnay, Pinot Noir (Santa Maria Valley).

The Gainey Vineyard is 62 acres of vineyard carved out of a much larger 1,800-acre ranch devoted to farm animals and a variety of crops. The winery, headed by winemaker Richard Longoria (see Longoria listing) makes 12,000 cases, with Chardonnay, Riesling and Sauvignon Blanc the leaders, and Cabernet, Cabernet Franc, Merlot and Pinot Noir also part of the picture. Of the reds, the Cabernet Franc Limited Edition, Merlot and Pinot Noir show the most promise. The Cabernet Sauvignon struggles with vegetal flavors.

TASTING NOTES

CABERNET FRANC SANTA YNEZ VALLEY LIMITED SELECTION (★★★):

1990: Dark, intense and juicy, with ripe cherry and currant flavors that are framed by spicy, cedary oak. The impressive finish shows off depth and complexity. **88**

CABERNET SAUVIGNON VARIOUS BOTTLINGS (★): Marked by stemmy, vegetal flavors that lack ripeness.

Santa Maria Valley 1988: An earthy, leathery wine with muddled herb and metallic flavors. **77**
Santa Ynez Valley 1989: Lean and narrow, with tight, tannic, vegetal coffee and currant flavors that turn dry. **77**

CABERNET SAUVIGNON LIMITED SELECTION VARIOUS BOTTLINGS (★★): Can be richer and fuller, but it shares the vegetal qualities of the regular bottling.

Santa Barbara County Limited Selection 1989: Smooth and graceful, with spicy, toasty vanilla notes around a core of supple currant and mint flavors. **83**
Santa Barbara County Limited Selection 1986: Pungently earthy and vegetal flavors turn dense. Not very appealing. **75**
Santa Ynez Valley Limited Selection 1988: Full-bodied and thick with tannins, picking up smoky dried cherry flavors and a dry, tannic finish. **75**

CHARDONNAY SANTA BARBARA COUNTY (★★):

1993: Has enough of a core of pear, spice and honey to hold your interest. Medium-weight and well focused. **86**
1991: Firm and flavorful, with well defined apple, earth, honey and spice flavors. **84**

CHARDONNAY SANTA YNEZ VALLEY LIMITED SELECTION (★★★★): Ripe, racy and concentrated.

1993: Tight and intense, with a sharply focused core of pear, nectarine, honey and smoky, toasty oak, all folding together neatly on the finish, where the flavors linger. **91**
1992: A racy wine with lots of spice, oak, ripe pear and pineapple flavors that are rich, intense, complex and concentrated, finishing with a honey edge. **91**

MERLOT SANTA YNEZ VALLEY LIMITED SELECTION (★★): Quality varies significantly, but in years such as 1988 it is complex and impressive.

1990: Clean, crisp and correct, with cedar, herb and berry notes and fine tannins. **83**
1988: Very supple, elegant and silky, with plenty of vanilla, butter and spice notes from oak on top of ample plum and currant flavors. **89**
1987: Despite its dark color, it's a lean, tight wine with a narrow band of herb, tar and currant notes. May be more forthcoming with time. Firmly tannic. **81**

PINOT NOIR SANTA YNEZ VALLEY LIMITED SELECTION (★★★): Improving; can be rich and flavorful, well oaked and earthy, but alluring.

1991: Alluring, with a rich, smooth texture, complex flavors and a well focused, elegant finish. Part of the Sanford & Benedict Vineyard Signature Series. **88**
1990: Strives for complexity with its dark color, ripe fruit and toasty oak flavors, but smoky wood notes win out on the firmly tannic finish. **85**
1989: Despite a strong leathery edge, this wine has its appeal, with cola and rhubarb flavors and earthy cherry notes. **83**
1988: Ripe and decadent, with a distinctive earthy, leathery streak that adds character to the basic black cherry and currant flavors. Turns a bit smoky and peppery on the finish. **86**

PINOT NOIR VARIOUS BOTTLINGS (★★):

Santa Barbara County 1990: Ripe, rich and intense, with spicy herb and cherry flavors, taking on an earthy raspberry edge on the finish, where it's meaty and a bit funky. **87**
Santa Barbara County 1986: Full-bodied, complex and oaky, with aromas and flavors of leather, spices and cherries, firm tannins and lively acidity. **88**
Santa Maria Valley 1989: Light and herbal, almost like a rosé, with faint cherry and spice notes. **74**

RIESLING SANTA YNEZ VALLEY (★★): Delicate and spicy.
1992: Light, delicate, gently fruity and off-dry, offering appealing apple, peach and apricot aromas and flavors in modest proportions. A light dose of bubbles makes it refreshing. **85**

SAUVIGNON BLANC SANTA YNEZ VALLEY LIMITED SELECTION (★★): Intense and herbaceous, but has appealing fruit too.
1993: Definitely on the oaky side, spicy, toasty and woody through the finish, but not harshly so. **83**
1992: Crisp and lively, with generous pear and spice aromas and flavors, hinting at herbs on the finish. **82**

E. & J. GALLO WINERY
Sonoma County
F: 1933. **O:** Gallo Family. **W:** N/A. **S:** E. & J. Gallo Sonoma.

OVERALL	$5-50	★★★★

WINE RATINGS

Cabernet Sauvignon Northern Sonoma	★★★★
Cabernet Sauvignon Sonoma County	
Gallo Sonoma	★★★
Chardonnay Northern Sonoma	★★★★
Chardonnay Sonoma County	
Gallo Sonoma	★★★
Merlot Dry Creek Valley	
Frei Ranch Vineyard	★★
Zinfandel Dry Creek Valley	
Frei Ranch Vineyard	★★★★

WINERY DATA
C: 70,000,000. **V:** 2,000 acres in Sonoma County. **G:** Cabernet Sauvignon, Chardonnay, Merlot, Sangiovese, Syrah, Zinfandel (Sonoma County). **P:** None.

After decades of mass-producing value-oriented wines, from Hearty Burgundy to Bartles & Jaymes wine coolers, the world's largest winery (70 million cases and $1 billion in sales annually) is focusing on super-premium wines from its considerable Sonoma County vineyard holdings and further emphasizing its estate-grown Cabernet, Chardonnay and Zinfandel. The shift to the high end of the wine market came late in the distinguished winemaking careers of Ernest and Julio Gallo.

Both brothers were in their 80s when the $60 Northern Sonoma Cabernet and $30 Chardonnay were released, nearly 60 years after they founded their winery in Modesto in 1933. Plans to enter this market were in the works for decades, as wine drinkers shifted from sweet wines to dry generic table wines to varietal wines.

The Gallos were longtime buyers of top-quality Napa and Sonoma grapes, at times purchasing anywhere from 25 percent to 40 percent of the grapes and bulk wines from those areas. In the 1970s the Gallos decided to put their money in Sonoma County, buying the old Frei Ranch, 625 acres of Cabernet, Merlot and Zinfandel in Dry Creek Valley where a giant winery is under construction; the Laguna Ranch, 360 acres of Chardonnay in a cool spot in Russian River Valley; 200 acres at Canyon Creek in Dry Creek; and another 800 acres in Alexander Valley, 600 of that in sweeping vineyards around the hamlet of Asti. The Asti area vineyards are planted to a wide assortment of mostly red-wine grapes—Syrah, Sangiovese, Zinfandel and the like—most of which Gallo will eventually make into wines.

Just about anything's possible, given the quality of Gallo's vineyards, winemaking know-how, research capabilities and determination to rise to the top of the quality charts. My notes focus on the Sonoma County (Gallo Sonoma) and estate-bottled (Northern Sonoma) wines. Most of Gallo's other bottlings are clean, well made and easy to drink, even if they do not excite as the new wines do. The first serious attempt with Cabernet in 1978 aged very well for the first decade of its life, but vintages thereafter have been leaner and trimmer. The breakthrough is the 1990 Northern Sonoma Cabernet. Sadly, Julio Gallo died in 1993, but his clear vision of quality lives on in these new wines.

TASTING NOTES

CABERNET SAUVIGNON NORTHERN SONOMA (★★★★): This wine could carry the Dry Creek appellation, as it is entirely from the Gallos' Frei Ranch. Introduced with the 1990 vintage, it combines rich, complex fruit flavors with a sense of elegance and finesse, showing off a nice array of toasty oak flavors. No track record for aging, but it drank well on release.
1991: Youthful and vibrant, with ripe, rich, supple spice, cherry and berry flavors that run deep. Concentrated, and the finish is long and full. **91**

1990: Ripe and spicy, supple and complex, with concentrated currant, spice, cedar and black cherry flavors that are beautifully focused and rich. Combines a wealth of flavor with elegance and finesse. **93**

CABERNET SAUVIGNON SONOMA COUNTY GALLO SONOMA (★★★): Lacks the finesse of the Northern Sonoma, but has attractive herb and currant flavors.
1991: Lavishly oaked, with heavy toasty wood flavors, but the fruit is elegant and polished, focused with wild berry and black cherry fruit that emerges on the finish. **90**
1990: An herbal wine with spicy red pepper flavors adding complexity to the currant and berry notes. **86**

CHARDONNAY NORTHERN SONOMA (★★★★): Elegant and complex, with rich, focused flavors and deft oak shadings. Entirely from the Laguna Ranch in Russian River Valley.
1993: Serves up attractive ripe pear, peach, honey and spice, all in a delicate style. **88**
1992: Complex and enticing, with a rich core of toasty, buttery oak and ripe, spicy pear flavors that are focused and long on the finish. Has style and finesse. **91**
1991: Elegant, rich and flavorful, with complex spice, pear, apricot, honey and toast flavors. Has a wonderful sense of balance and finesse. **92**

CHARDONNAY SONOMA COUNTY GALLO SONOMA (★★★): A shade fruitier than the Northern Sonoma, but also simpler with ripe, spicy fruit flavors.
1993: Serves up lots of flavor, with ripe apple, pear, citrus and honey notes in an elegant package. Finishes with a clean fruity aftertaste. **87**
1992: Another brilliant effort, combines ripe, intense well focused pear, spice, citrus and buttery oak with a sense of elegance and finesse. **89**
1991: Smooth and polished, with ripe, rich, spicy melon, pear and apple notes that gain complexity. **89**

MERLOT DRY CREEK VALLEY FREI RANCH VINEYARD (★★): The least impressive in the new lineup, not surprising given Merlot's tendencies. Marked by herb and currant flavors, but lacking the depth and extra dimensions of the other wines. Worth watching.
1992: Crisp and lean, with a tart, trim band of cherry and plum-laced fruit. **82**
1991: Firm and compact, with cherry and currant flavors that turn spicy on the finish. **87**

ZINFANDEL DRY CREEK VALLEY FREI RANCH VINEYARD (★★★★): Julio Gallo's favorite wine was Zinfandel, and this is a lovely rendition, bold, ripe, complex and spicy, a fine-tuned wine that ranks among the state's best already.
1992: A touch leathery, but enough wild berry and cherry fruit hangs in to keep in balance. **86**
1991: Rich, smooth and supple, with complex raspberry, anise, earth and tar notes that gently unfold, revealing even greater depth on the finish. **91**
1990: A bright and lively Zin with spicy black cherry, raspberry and pepper notes that are deep and complex, finishing with a long, lingering aftertaste. **90**

GAN EDEN
Sonoma County
F: 1985. **O:** Yayin Inc. **W:** Craig Winchell. **S:** None.

OVERALL	$8-14	★★

WINE RATINGS	
Black Muscat San Joaquin County	★★
Cabernet Sauvignon Alexander Valley	★★
Chardonnay Sonoma County	★★
Gewürztraminer Monterey County Late Harvest	★★
Sauvignon Blanc Sonoma County	★★
Sémillon Sonoma County	★★

WINERY DATA
C: 25,000. **V:** None. **G:** None. **P:** Chardonnay, Sauvignon Blanc, Sémillon (Sonoma County), Cabernet Sauvignon (Alexander Valley), Muscat (San Joaquin County).

Gan Eden makes the best kosher wines in California. The 25,000-case lineup includes Cabernet, Chardonnay, Black Muscat, Gewürztraminer and Sauvignon Blanc, all from purchased grapes. The main problem has been consistency; the 1987 Cabernet is rich and supple, with impressive depth and polish, but the 1988 and 1989 were far less interesting. Chardonnay too has fluctuated in quality.

TASTING NOTES

BLACK MUSCAT SAN JOAQUIN COUNTY (★★):
1993: Soft, sweet, with plum and spice flavors that linger lightly on the finish. **80**

CABERNET SAUVIGNON ALEXANDER VALLEY (★★):
1989: Well oaked, with a gamy edge, but enough rustic earthy currant flavors pull through to keep it interesting. Firmly tannic; best after 1996. **83**
1988: An odd Cabernet that turn turns tough and coarse on the finish despite its plum flavor. **77**

CHARDONNAY SONOMA COUNTY (★★):
1993: Tart with a green, leesy edge to the apple, pear and melon flavors, but it holds together nicely through the finish. **88**

GEWÜRZTRAMINER MONTEREY COUNTY LATE HARVEST (★★):
1993: Frankly sweet, with peach and apricot flavors that fade a little on the finish. **81**

SAUVIGNON BLANC SONOMA COUNTY (★★):
1993: Crisp and lively, a fruity wine with green apple flavors and distinctive nuances of celery and sweet peas. **83**

SÉMILLON SONOMA COUNTY (★★):
1993: Light and lively, a brightly fruity example of early-drinking Sémillon. **83**

GARLAND RANCH
This is a second label for Chateau Julien Winery (see listing).

GAVILAN VINEYARDS
This is a second label for Chalone Vineyard (see listing).

DANIEL GEHRS
Los Olivos, Santa Barbara County
F: 1991. **O:** Daniel Gehrs. **W:** Daniel Gehrs. **S:** None.

OVERALL	$8-10	★★

WINE RATING

Chardonnay Monterey County	★★
Chenin Blanc Monterey County Le Chenay	★★
Chenin Blanc Santa Barbara County Le Cheniere	★★
Pinot Blanc Monterey County	★★
Sauvignon Blanc Monterey County Fumé En Vogue	★★
White Table Wine Monterey County Muscadet	★★

WINERY DATA
C: N/A. **V:** None. **G:** None. **P:** Zinfandel (Sonoma), Chardonnay, Muscat (Monterey), Rhône Varieties (Paicines).

Daniel Gehrs had a long and successful winemaking career at Congress Springs before it fell victim to financial difficulties and his partners (a British conglomerate) decided to sell it. From there he worked as a consultant at Retzlaff Vineyards before joining Zaca Mesa. His fascination with Loire Valley wines like Chenin Blanc, Pinot Blanc and Muscadet led to his founding his own brand in 1991, using purchased grapes from Santa Barbara and Monterey Counties. The first wines are well made, with pure varietal character.

TASTING NOTES

VARIOUS BOTTLINGS (★★):
Chardonnay Monterey County 1991: Smooth, spicy and fruity, with polished pear and apple aromas and flavors, a touch of nutmeg and a Muscat-like edge. **84**
Chenin Blanc Monterey County Le Chenay 1993: Gehrs adds 20 percent Chardonnay to this cuvée, which gives it a little more body, but it's still a trim, compact wine with tart apricot and pear flavors. **84**
Chenin Blanc Santa Barbara County Le Cheniere 1993: This barrel-fermented wine strives for complexity, and its toasty oak notes make for an interesting wine. Serves up spicy pear and apple flavors that ring true for Chenin Blanc. **83**
Pinot Blanc Monterey County 1993: Simple, with pear and herb notes; the least interesting of the new Gehrs wines. **81**
Sauvignon Blanc Monterey County Fumé En Vogue 1993: Another Loire-style wine, this Sauvignon Blanc has grapey, racy flavors that pick up honey and pear nuances on the finish. **83**
White Table Wine Monterey County Muscadet 1993: One of Gehrs' Loire-style wines, this is crisp and flinty, with a narrow band of spice, tart pear and mineral tones. **84**

GEORIS WINERY
Carmel Valley
F: 1988. **O:** Walter Georis. **W:** Walter Georis, Dan Lee.
S: None.

OVERALL	$25	★★★

WINE RATINGS	
Merlot Carmel Valley	★★★

WINERY DATA
C: 1,800. **V:** 22 acres in Carmel Valley. **G:** Merlot (18 acres), Cabernet Sauvignon (3), Cabernet Franc (1). **P:** None.

Walter Georis has gone from surf rock (*Endless Summer* soundtrack) to Birkenstock salesman to restaurateur (Casanova in Carmel) to wine. He now makes a dense and chewy Merlot from estate-grown vines in Carmel Valley. Production has risen from a few hundred cases to 1,800 as the vineyard has grown to 22 acres, 18 of that Merlot. The goal is to produce a long-lived Merlot and soon a Cabernet. The Merlot certainly has the tannin and concentration to endure, but the question is whether it will ever soften up and evolve into something more complex. The jury is still out.

TASTING NOTES

MERLOT CARMEL VALLEY (★★★): Dark, intense and usually quite tannic, but there's a solid core of fruit flavors.
1989: Impressive for its richness and chewy concentration, with currant, mineral, herb and cedar notes. **87**
1987: Full, warm and inviting, with lots of spicy, rich accents from oak aging piled on top of ripe plum, cherry and herb flavors. Has fine tannins, a plush texture and a lingering, spicy finish. **89**
1986: A distinctly weedy, tannic wine that clamps down on the palate. **77**
1985: Lean but concentrated, with ripe berry and black cherry flavors nestled into a background of sweet oak. **83**

GERWER WINERY
El Dorado County
F: 1982. **O:** Gerwer Family. **W:** Vernon Gerwer. **S:** None.

OVERALL	$N/A	NR

WINE RATINGS	
Blush El Dorado County White Zinfandel	NR
Petite Sirah El Dorado County	NR
Sauvignon Blanc El Dorado County	NR

WINERY DATA
C: 5,000. **V:** 20 acres in El Dorado County. **G:** Sauvignon Blanc, Petite Sirah, Zinfandel. **P:** None.

Vernon Gerwer and his family founded this 5,000-case winery in El Dorado County in 1982 after a U.C. Davis experimental vineyard proved encouraging. Using grapes from their 20-acre vineyard and buying other grapes in the area, Gerwer makes Sauvignon Blanc, Petite Sirah and white Zinfandel, among other wines. The winery was once known as Stony Creek.

GEYSER PEAK WINERY
Alexander Valley
F: 1880. **O:** Henry, Mark & Victor Trione. **W:** Daryl Groom, Mick Schroeter. **S:** Canyon Road, Venezia.

OVERALL	$6-20	★★★★

WINE RATINGS	
Cabernet Sauvignon Alexander Valley	
Estate Reserve	★★★★
Cabernet Sauvignon Sonoma County	★★
Chardonnay Alexander Valley Reserve	★★★★
Chardonnay Sonoma County	★★
Gewürztraminer Sonoma County	★★
Johannisberg Riesling Mendocino County	
Late Harvest Selected Dried Berry	★★★★
Malbec Alexander Valley	★★
Meritage Red Alexander Valley	
Reserve Alexandre	★★★
Merlot Alexander Valley	★★★
Petite Sirah Alexander Valley	NR
Petite Verdot Alexander Valley	★★
Port Alexander Valley Henry's	
Reserve Vintage Port	★★★
Riesling Sonoma County Trione	
Vineyards Late Harvest Reserve	NR
Sauvignon Blanc Sonoma County	★★
Syrah Alexander Valley	★★★★
Syrah Alexander Valley Reserve	★★★★

White Table Wine California Semchard ★★
Canyon Road Chardonnay California ★★
Canyon Road Sauvignon
    Blanc California ★★

WINERY DATA

C: 300,000. **V:** 1,037 acres in Sonoma County, Lake County, Mendocino County. **G:** Chardonnay (536 acres), Cabernet Sauvignon (198), Sauvignon Blanc (59), Merlot (65), Red Bordeaux Varieties (50), Syrah (33), Zinfandel (23), Sangiovese (2), Petite Sirah (2), Other White Varieties (60). **P:** Cabernet Sauvignon (Napa Valley), Sauvignon Blanc, Merlot, Gamay, Sémillon, Chardonnay, Cabernet Sauvignon (Alexander Valley), Cabernet Sauvignon, Sauvignon Blanc, Merlot (Dry Creek Valley), Sauvignon Blanc, Merlot (Knights Valley), Sauvignon Blanc, Gewürztraminer, Riesling (Monterey).

Few wineries have undergone as dramatic a transformation as Geyser Peak. This winery was founded in 1880 and for most of its existence its wines were mired in mediocrity. Schlitz, the Milwaukee brewer, tried to revive the winery beginning in 1972 by remodeling it and modernizing the equipment, retooling it for mass production. But by 1982 Schlitz decided to get out of wine and sold Geyser Peak to Santa Rosa businessman Henry Trione, who bought the winery with hopes of making fine wines. Trione had one big advantage: he owned a source of grapes for fine wine: nearly 1,000 acres of vineyard in the Alexander and Russian River Valleys. But still the winery struggled, finally selling off its Summit line of jug wines and then slowly upgrading the quality of its estate-grown wines. In 1989 Penfolds, the Australian wine company, bought a 50 percent interest (which it later sold back to the Triones) and sent its talented winemaker, Daryl Groom, to work with the vineyards and winery. After his arrival (and even a bit before) quality surged, with an across-the-board improvement; reds are rich and supple and whites are bright and fruity.

The winery today owns 1,037 acres of vineyard, mostly in Sonoma, but also in Mendocino and Lake Counties, with Chardonnay (536 acres) and Cabernet (198) the leaders. Production hovers around 300,000 cases, led by Chardonnay and Johannisberg Riesling (40,000 cases each), with another 100,000 cases bottled under the Canyon Road label. The best wines are clearly the Reserves and the small-case-production designer varietals. The dessert wines also are excellent.

TASTING NOTES

CABERNET SAUVIGNON ALEXANDER VALLEY ESTATE RESERVE (★★★★): Poised for greatness, with recent vintages showing richness and finesse, complex flavors and supple tannins.
1991: Ripe and generous, a smooth-textured wine with broad currant, black cherry and berry flavors shaded with spicy oak and a touch of herb. **90**
1990: Strives for complexity and elegance, offering bright, ripe currant and raspberry flavors that are intense, yet it's crisp and spicy, with pretty oak seasoning. **90**
1989: Youthful, firm and chewy, with a solid dose of spicy wood flavors that complement the chunky currant, earth, tar and tobacco notes. Very tannic. **87**
1987: Ripe, rich and focused, with a broad texture, generous black currant, blackberry and chocolate flavors that echo on the long finish and nice spice and vanilla notes from oak. **89**
1986: Mature and firmly tannic, but the cedar and currant flavors are nice. **82**
1985: A lighter 1985 with modest cedar, currant and spice notes. **83**

CABERNET SAUVIGNON SONOMA COUNTY (★★): Medium-weight and well balanced, with adequate fruit flavors. Ready on release. Has sometimes carried the Alexander Valley appellation.
1991: Appealing for its balance and flavor, it serves up pretty, focused berry and cherry flavors and has a spicy oak and herb edge. **84**
1990: Ripe, round and spicy, with generous cherry, raspberry and clove flavors and hints of herb and vanilla. **81**
1989: Light and simple, with a pronounced earthy, leathery edge to the currant flavors. **80**
1987: Appealing for its ripe, bright raspberry and currant flavors. **88**
1984: Grapey, tarry, dense and chocolatey. **77**
1983: Mature, with complex currant, herb, earth and oak flavors. **85**

CHARDONNAY ALEXANDER VALLEY RESERVE (★★★★): Steadily improving, showing more oak and depth.
1993: Strikes a nice balance between ripe pear and pineapple with light toasty oak shadings. **90**
1992: Rich and smoky, with layers of complex pear,

spice, honey and vanilla flavors that are focused and lively. The flavors linger on the finish. **87**

CHARDONNAY SONOMA COUNTY (★★): Straightforward, with attractive pear and apple flavors.
1993: Ripe and juicy, with spicy pear, apple and nutmeg flavors that smooth out on the finish. **85**

GEWÜRZTRAMINER SONOMA COUNTY (★★): Soft and spicy, with simple fruit flavors.
1992: Soft and slightly sweet, with a perfumed edge to the appealing pear and apricot flavors, finishing sweet and simple. **80**

JOHANNISBERG RIESLING MENDOCINO COUNTY LATE HARVEST SELECTED DRIED BERRY (★★★★):
1990: Ripe, spicy and balanced, an elegant dessert wine just oozing with grapefruit, honey, apricot and spice aromas and flavors that keep echoing on the long, generous finish. **93**

MALBEC ALEXANDER VALLEY (★★):
1991: Crisp, fruity and distinctive, a small-scale wine with appealing vanilla, raspberry and spice aromas and flavors. **85**

MERITAGE RED ALEXANDER VALLEY RESERVE ALEXANDRE (★★★★): Ripe, intense and complex, like the Reserve Cabernet, and steadily improving. Worth watching.
1991: Ripe and intense, this elegantly crafted wine serves up an array of pretty plum, currant, herb and cherry notes, finishing with an earthy edge and crisp tannins. **91**
1990: Smooth, plush and elegant, with tiers of spicy currant, black cherry, anise and cedar flavors, this is an invitingly complex and vibrant wine. **90**
1987: Ripe and complex but sharply focused, with elegant, intense blackberry and black currant aromas and flavors and hints of nutmeg and cedar on the finish. **88**
1986: This austere wine has plenty of herb, dill and oak notes graced by pretty plum and currant flavors that are elegant. **89**
1985: Soft, velvety and aromatic, boasting olive, herb and plum aromas and flavors, spicy and cedary on the finish, complex and artfully balanced. **87**
1984: Smooth and supple, with ripe plum, earth and tar notes. Mature. **84**

1983: Elegant and fully mature, with a good dose of spicy oak and currant, herb and tar notes. Tannins are softening. **83**

MERLOT ALEXANDER VALLEY (★★★): Smooth and supple, with bright, ripe flavors and soft tannins.
1992: Combines smoky, toasty oak with ripe cherry and berry flavors. Finishes with a peppery edge, thanks to 9 percent Syrah. **85**
1991: Soft, smooth and supple, with generous blackberry and vanilla flavors. **87**

PETITE SIRAH ALEXANDER VALLEY (NR):
1989: A wall of tannin blocks entry to this deep, dark wine, overshadowing the tart black cherry and berry flavors. **79**

PETITE VERDOT ALEXANDER VALLEY (★★):
1991: Firm and tight, with herbal currant notes. This varietal is still best for blending. **82**

PORT ALEXANDER VALLEY HENRY'S RESERVE (★★★):
1992: Dark, rich and peppery, with layers of plum, prune and black cherry flavors that turn spicy and earthy. **87**

RIESLING SONOMA COUNTY TRIONE VINEYARDS LATE HARVEST RESERVE (NR):
1993: Very sweet and rich, smooth and syrupy, with spicy, floral overtones to the modest honey and apricot flavors. Best from 1997. **87**

SAUVIGNON BLANC SONOMA COUNTY (★★):
1994: Lean and lively, distinctive for its anise and herbal overtones to the basic apple and kiwi flavors. **85**
1993: An elegant, grassy wine that's appealing for its freshness and vibrancy. **85**

SYRAH ALEXANDER VALLEY (★★★★), RESERVE (★★★★): Impressive for its rich, spicy flavors and broad, supple texture.
1991: An impressive Syrah, ripe and spicy, with toasty cherry and currant notes that turn elegant and supple on the finish, where the tannins are mild. **90**
Reserve 1991: Smooth and supple, with rambunctious flavors of berry, spice, vanilla and chocolate rattling around underneath. **91**

WHITE TABLE WINE CALIFORNIA SEMCHARD (★★): A Sémillon-Chardonnay blend made in the Australian style. **1993:** Herbal, almost vegetal flavors sneak in around the edges of the mostly apple and leaf flavors, and the finish is crisp. **81**

CANYON ROAD VARIOUS BOTTLINGS (★★):
Chardonnay California 1993: Light and fruity, a little lean, simple on the finish. **78**
Chardonnay California 1992: Guilelessly refreshing, offering plenty of spicy apple and grapefruit aromas and flavors that extend into a lively finish. Not especially complex, but has plenty of appeal. **84**
Sauvignon Blanc California 1993: Lively and citrusy, a mouth-filling wine showing exuberant fruit and bright acidity. Delicious. **85**

GIRARD WINERY
Oakville, Napa Valley
F: 1980. **O:** Girard Winery Inc. **W:** Mark A. Smith.
S: Stephens Winery, Ol' Blue Jay.

OVERALL	**$9-40**	★★★

WINE RATINGS

Cabernet Sauvignon Napa Valley	★★★
Cabernet Sauvignon Napa Valley Reserve	★★★
Chardonnay Napa Valley	★★★★
Chardonnay Napa Valley Reserve	★★★★
Chenin Blanc Napa Valley Dry	★★

WINERY DATA
C: 20,000. **V:** 85 acres in Napa Valley. **G:** Chardonnay (42 acres), Cabernet Sauvignon (32), Cabernet Franc (2), Merlot (1), Sémillon (8). **P:** Chenin Blanc (Napa Valley).

Former Kaiser Industries vice president Stephen Girard Sr. bought property in Oakville on the Silverado Trail in 1974 and established a vineyard and later a winery, which is run by his son Steve Jr. A few years later, the Girards added a second, 40-acre property, Viridian Vineyard, in the hills west of Yountville behind the Napanook Vineyard. The Girards make 20,000 cases a year from their 85 acres, with Chardonnay the leader at 8,000 cases. All the wines are estate-grown except the Chenin Blanc, which comes from purchased grapes.

Overall the quality of the wines has been high, but has dipped in recent years as the wines have gotten lighter.

TASTING NOTES

CABERNET SAUVIGNON NAPA VALLEY (★★★), RESERVE (★★★): Intense, lean and crisp, with firm tannins and pleasant fruit flavors, but it could use more richness and depth. Ages well, maintaining its tannic edge. Recent vintages are more austere.
1991: Serves up pretty floral, plum and cherry notes before the tannins clamp down. **86**
1990: Intense and flavorful, with ripe, spicy cherry and currant flavors that turn crisp and tannic. **87**
1989: Tough and tannic, with more minty, herbal aromas and flavors than fruit. The finish is astringent and tight. **82**
1988: Hard-edged and tannic, with very dry fruit flavors. It takes time to find the currant and berry flavors. **85**
1987: Intense, concentrated and tannic, with solid austere currant, black cherry and spice flavors that are drying. **86**
1986: Decidedly minty and herbal, with layers of firm, concentrated currant, plum and cherry flavors. **88**
1985: Sleek and elegant, with spicy cedar and cigar box aromas, ripe plum and black cherry flavors and firm, drying tannins. **88**
1984: Mature, with cedary oak overtones and supple, complex cherry and spice flavors. **85**
1982: Mature but still displaying its big size, with rich, chewy flavors and tannins that are dry and firm. **87**
Reserve 1991: Youthful and austere, with dry, gripping tannins, but also plenty of ripe cherry and currant notes. Awkward now. **87**
Reserve 1990: Firm, chunky and herbal, with aromas that include earthy, along with currant and spice, notes. **86**
Reserve 1989: A lean, tight wine with a narrow band of fruit that fades away. **82**
Reserve 1987: Pleasantly fruity, with intense, ripe black cherry and currant flavors that have a spicy oak edge. Tannic, but with good depth of flavor. **88**
Reserve 1986: Mature but still firm and tightly structured, with intense anise, cherry, black currant and plum flavors. **91**
Reserve 1985: Elegant and complex, with firm, dry tannins and plenty of delicious plum, currant, spice and oak flavors. **89**
Reserve 1984: A big, ripe, mature wine with generous plum, black cherry and anise flavors. **89**

CHARDONNAY NAPA VALLEY (★★★★), RESERVE (★★★★): A shade lighter of late, but it can be rich, creamy, smoky and complex, with good aging potential. The Reserve is well oaked.

1992: Smooth and creamy, with ripe, spicy pear, vanilla and toast notes that are rich and focused, finishing with good length and flavor. **88**

1991: Ripe, round and earthy, with toasty vanilla, pear, lemon and nutmeg aromas and flavors. **90**

Reserve 1992: A spicy wine with creamy pear, vanilla and nutmeg flavors that hang together nicely, finishing with a complex aftertaste. **89**

CHENIN BLANC NAPA VALLEY DRY (★★): Crisp and dry, with appealing fruit flavors.

1992: Crisp and fruity, with ripe pear, apple and spice notes. An ideal wine for lighter fare or casual sipping. **83**

GLASS MOUNTAIN QUARRY

This is a second label for Markham Vineyards (see listing).

GLEN ELLEN WINERY

Sonoma Valley

F: 1980. **O:** Heublein Inc. **W:** Peter McCullough. **S:** M.G. Vallejo.

OVERALL	$4-7	★★

WINE RATINGS	
Chardonnay California Proprietor's Reserve	★★
M. G. Vallejo Chardonnay California Harvest Select	★★
M. G. Vallejo Sauvignon Blanc California	★★

WINERY DATA
C: 4,000,000. **V:** None. **G:** None. **P:** N/A.

Glen Ellen Winery was founded in 1980 by the Benziger family (see Benziger Family Winery) and became one of the most successful "fighting varietal" brands ever, with production reaching nearly 4 million cases by the time the Benzigers sold it to Heublein.

Quality across the board was good, with a full range of popular varietals from Cabernet to white Zinfandel, all carrying the California appellation and labeled "Proprietor's Reserve." The winery discovered vineyard sources throughout California and developed a sophisticated network for buying, blending and bottling bulk wines. Its success helped fuel the so-called fighting varietals class of wines, usually priced at $4 to $7.

TASTING NOTES

VARIOUS BOTTLINGS (★★):

Chardonnay California Proprietor's Reserve 1993: Features ripe, lively pineapple and grapefruit flavors that hang with you. Well made. **85**

M. G. Vallejo Chardonnay California Harvest Select 1992: Light and fruity, with a spicy edge that gives it some extra zing. **84**

M. G. Vallejo Sauvignon Blanc California 1992: Still fresh and floral, with a rose petal edge to the modest pear fruit. **83**

GOLD HILL VINEYARD

El Dorado County

F: 1985. **O:** Hank Battjes. **W:** Hank Battjes, Dimitri Tchelistcheff. **S:** Coloma Gold.

OVERALL	$8-11	NR

WINE RATINGS	
Merlot El Dorado County	NR

WINERY DATA
C: 2,000. **V:** 35 acres in El Dorado County. **G:** Chardonnay (20 acres), Merlot (2), Cabernet Franc (1), Cabernet Sauvignon (10). **P:** None.

Gold Hill Vineyard is about a mile south of Sutter's Mill, where gold was discovered in 1849, leading to the great California gold rush. The winery owns some 35 acres of vineyard and makes about 2,000 cases of wine from El Dorado-grown grapes, with Cabernet Franc, Cabernet, Chardonnay and Merlot the dominant wines.

GOLDEN CREEK VINEYARD

Santa Rosa, Sonoma County

F: 1983. **O:** Ladi Danielik. **W:** Ladi Danielik. **S:** None.

OVERALL	$12-16	★★

WINE RATINGS

Cabernet Blend Sonoma County	
Caberlot Reserve	NR
Cabernet Sauvignon Sonoma County	NR
Merlot Sonoma County Reserve	★★

WINERY DATA

C: 1,000. V: 12 acres in Russian River Valley. G: Cabernet Sauvignon and Merlot. P: None.

Czechoslovakian-born Ladi Danielik founded this winery northwest of Santa Rosa in 1983, planting some 12 acres to Merlot and Cabernet, from which he makes three wines—two of them varietal and one a blend called Caberlot Reserve. He also sells grapes to Gary Farrell.

TASTING NOTES

VARIOUS BOTTLINGS:

Cabernet Blend Sonoma County Caberlot Reserve 1991: Ripe and spicy, with solid plum and currant flavors, finishing with herb and light oak shadings. A 50-50 blend of Cabernet and Merlot. **83**

Cabernet Sauvignon Sonoma County 1990: Simple, with light plum and cherry notes. **80**

Merlot Sonoma County Reserve 1991: Ripe and grapey, with spicy cherry, currant and wild berry flavors that turn crisp and leathery on the finish. Better after 1997. **84**

Merlot Sonoma County Reserve 1990: Lean and earthy, with a leathery edge to the fruit flavors. Finishes with chewy tannins; needs until 1996 to soften. **82**

GOOSECROSS CELLARS

Yountville, Napa Valley
F: 1985. **O:** David Topper & Geoff Gorsuch. **W:** Geoff Gorsuch, Tom Eddy. **S:** None.

OVERALL	$15-20	★★

WINE RATINGS

Chardonnay Napa Valley	★★

WINERY DATA

C: 5,400. V: 10 acres in Napa Valley. G: Chardonnay (10 acres). P: Chardonnay (Napa Valley).

A Chardonnay specialist based in Yountville, Geoff Gorsuch heads this family-owned winery that makes 5,400 cases a year from both estate-grown and purchased grapes. Quality has varied, but in 1994 the winery appeared to be on solid footing again, and planned to introduce its first Cabernet, a 1992 from Napa.

GRACE FAMILY VINEYARDS

St. Helena, Napa Valley
F: 1976. **O:** Richard & Anne Grace. **W:** Gary Galleron. **S:** None.

OVERALL	$75	★★★★★

WINE RATINGS

Cabernet Sauvignon Napa Valley	★★★★★

WINERY DATA

C: 200. V: 2 acres in Napa Valley. G: Cabernet Sauvignon 2 acres). P: None.

Stockbroker Richard Grace moved to St. Helena in the 1970s seeking a more countrified lifestyle. In 1976 he planted a 1-acre vineyard in front of his home, using budwood from Bosche Vineyard, and two years later he got his first real crop. The ripening grapes looked so appealing that he asked Charlie Wagner of Caymus Vineyard to examine them and possibly make wine. Wagner took a look, then crushed the grapes and kept them separate. Once it was apparent that the wine stood on its own, Wagner made a special vineyard-designated bottling of Grace Family Vineyard under the Caymus label. That arrangement continued through the 1982 vintage. Beginning with 1983, Grace sold his wine under his own label and added a second acre to his vineyard, also building a beautiful miniature winery. He now makes 200 cases a year. The wines are 100 percent Cabernet, ripe, supple and beautifully crafted, with bright, opulent flavors. The winemaking style has changed over the years, shifting from Caymus's long barrel aging to less time in the barrel, but quality remains exceptionally high and the wine is scarce even at $75 a bottle.

TASTING NOTES

CABERNET SAUVIGNON NAPA VALLEY (★★★★★): Rich and elegant in style, loaded with fruit flavors and marked by soft, fleshy tannins. Ages very well, but peaks at three to five years. Only the 1991 failed to earn an outstanding score, as it seems unusually tight and tannic on release.

1991: Lean and earthy, with firm tannins that dominate the spicy currant and cedar flavors. **88**

1990: Wonderfully complex, showing a toasty, smoky, buttery oak overlay to the ripe currant and cherry flavors underneath. The tannins are chewy and firm, but softening. **92**

1989: Plush and opulent, with supple currant, cherry and spice notes framed by light oak shadings. **90**

1988: Dense in color and flavor, rich and concentrated, with tiers of ripe black cherry, plum and currant flavors and spicy, toasty oak notes. **90**

1987: Deep, rich and perfumed, with intense, concentrated currant, cherry, anise, earth and smoky oak flavors that are amazingly fresh, lively and elegant. Best Grace ever. **97**

1986: Firm, rich and elegant, with chocolate, plum, currant and black cherry flavors that are well structured and impeccably balanced. **93**

1985: Amazingly complex, supple and elegant, offering rich, concentrated, beautifully defined cassis, currant and plum flavors and a touch of anise and toasty oak on the finish. **95**

1984: Enticingly generous and forward, mature now, with deep, rich, lush plum, cassis and cherry flavors that are framed by toasty French oak. The tannins are soft and fleshy. **92**

1983: Absolutely delicious, ripe, rich, round and deep, with complex plum, black cherry and currant flavors that are plush and elegant, finishing with fine tannins. Wonderful complexity, harmony and finesse. **93**

1982: Lean, tight and delicate, with plenty of sharply focused plum, cassis and currant flavors and a good dose of oak. **89**

1981: Effusively fruity and forward, with elegant, supple cherry and plum aromas and flavors. Mature now. **88**

1980: Mature but still showing rich, concentrated and focused black cherry and plum flavors, with layers of cedar and vanilla. **92**

1979: Defines the Grace vineyard's richness, suppleness and elegance, with rich chocolate, plum and cherry flavors that are delicately balanced. Mature. **92**

1978: Mature, with drying flavors, but there's still much to admire in the elegant spice, cassis, currant and black cherry flavors. **86**

GRAESER WINERY
Calistoga, Napa Valley
F: 1985. O: Richard L. Graeser. W: Richard L. Graeser, James Yerkes. S: None.

OVERALL	$13-25	★★

WINE RATINGS

Cabernet Sauvignon Napa Valley	★★
Chardonnay Napa Valley Silverado	
Summers Vineyard	★★

WINERY DATA
C: 2,300. V: 9.5 acres in Napa Valley. G: Cabernet Sauvignon (6 acres), Cabernet Franc (2), Merlot (1). P: Chardonnay (Napa Valley).

Richard Graeser founded this winery on Petrified Forest Road west of Calistoga on property his parents purchased in 1958. In 1984 he began clearing part of the forested hillside for vineyard, planting 10 acres of vines to Bordeaux varieties. From the estate vineyards come Cabernet, Merlot and Cabernet Franc, with Chardonnay and Sémillon made from purchased grapes. More than half the winery's 2,300-case output is Cabernet.

TASTING NOTES

VARIOUS BOTTLINGS (★★):

Cabernet Sauvignon Napa Valley 1991: Austere, tannic and earthy, with chewy tannins and a leathery streak to the Cabernet flavors. Finishes with a dry stalky, green bean edge. **79**

Chardonnay Napa Valley Silverado Summers Vineyard 1992: Lean and thin with lemony citrus flavors but not much ripe fruit. **78**

GRAND CRU VINEYARDS
F: 1970. O: Bronco Wine Co.. S: None.

OVERALL	$7-14	★★

Wine Ratings

Gewürztraminer California	
Premium Selection	NR
Johannisberg Riesling California	
Premium Selection	NR
Merlot California Premium Selection	NR

Winery Data

C: N/A. V: None. G: None. P: N/A.

This 50,000-case winery in sleepy Glen Ellen had a good reputation from the 1970s through the 1980s for off-dry Gewürztraminer and medium-weight Chardonnay, Chenin Blanc and Cabernet. But the winery had financial troubles, and Walt and Tina Dreyer, one-time owners of Orowheat Bread, were the last to pump money into it before selling the brand and inventory to Fred Franzia's Bronco Wine Co. in 1993.

Granite Springs Winery

El Dorado County
F: 1981. O: Lester & Lynne Russell. W: Lester Russell. S: None.

Overall $9   ★★

Wine Ratings

Zinfandel El Dorado County	★★

Winery Data

C: 10,000. V: 24 acres in El Dorado County. G: N/A. P: N/A.

Granite Springs Winery takes its name from the granite soils where its vineyards are rooted. Owners Les and Lynne Russell produce up to 10,000 cases a year of a variety of wines, but for me the reds, led by Zinfandel and Petite Sirah, are the best values. Cabernet, Sauvignon Blanc, Chenin Blanc and white Zinfandel have also been part of the product mix.

Tasting Notes

Zinfandel El Dorado County (★★): Can be intriguing for its array of flavors.
1990: Interesting array of toast, berry, cherry and leather flavors. **82**

Green and Red Vineyard

St. Helena, Napa Valley
F: 1977. O: Jay & Pam Heminway. W: Jay Heminway, Helen Turley. S: Catacula.

Overall $15-16   ★★★

Wine Ratings

Chardonnay Napa Valley Catacula	
Vineyard	★★
Zinfandel Napa Valley Chiles Mill	
Vineyard	★★★

Winery Data

C: 3,000. V: 16 acres in Napa Valley. G: Chardonnay (7 acres), Zinfandel (9). P: Zinfandel (Napa Valley).

I've become a big fan of Green and Red Zinfandel, owner Jay Heminway's best wine to date. With the hiring of Helen Turley as consultant, however, one can expect the Chardonnay (and Zin too) to show more depth and richness in the future. In the late 1970s and early '80s Heminway planted his 16-acre vineyard in Chiles Valley, which is really separate from Napa but is included in the Napa Valley boundary. The 3,000-case output is roughly divided between the two varietals.

Tasting Notes

Chardonnay Napa Valley Catacula Vineyard (★★): Variable, although the 1991 was complex, with earthy pear and spice flavors.
1993: Pleasant enough, with a core of ripe pear, vanilla and earthy notes on the finish. Lacks focus. **84**
1992: An odd wine with a gluey edge to the pear flavors. **80**
1991: Round and complex, with lots of interesting earth, spice and toast nuances to the silky pear and apple flavors. **88**

Zinfandel Napa Valley Chiles Mill Vineyard (★★★): Very consistent, medium weight and color, but with appealing tart berry, spice and pronounced pepper notes and mild but firm tannins.
1992: A big brawny wine, intense and chewy, with firm, dry tannins and a wallop of oak, but there's a lot of fruit too. **88**
1991: A peppery, firm, classic wine that's nicely balanced, fresh and fruity, offering enough complex, spicy raspberry and blackberry flavors to perk it up. **85**

1990: A spicy, peppery wine with cherry and raspberry flavors that are fresh and lively, even delicate. The oak is smooth and buttery, and it's not too tannic. **90**

GREENSTONE WINERY
Amador County
F: 1981. **O:** Fowler & Van Spanje Families. **W:** Stan Van Spanje. **S:** None.

OVERALL	$10-13	★★

WINE RATINGS	
Zinfandel Amador County	★★
Zinfandel Amador County Special Release	★★

WINERY DATA
C: 12,000. **V:** 30 acres in Amador County. **G:** Cabernet Sauvignon, Chenin Blanc, French Colombard, Sauvignon Blanc, Zinfandel. **P:** N/A.

Greenstone Winery is owned by the Fowler and Van Spanje families, who produce some 12,000 cases of wine from their estate vineyard in Ione in Amador County. The lineup of wines includes French Colombard, Chenin Blanc, Sauvignon Blanc, Cabernet and Zinfandel, the latter being the best of the lot to my taste.

TASTING NOTES

ZINFANDEL AMADOR COUNTY (★★): Solid, marked by intense, spicy berry and plum flavors, but it can have an earthy, tarry edge.
1990: Clean, ripe and spicy, with a tarry, leathery edge to the cherry and raspberry flavors. Turns smooth and fleshy on the finish. **84**
1987: Tight, firm and intense but well proportioned too, with spicy berry and plum notes that linger. Not too tannic. **84**

GREENWOOD RIDGE VINEYARDS
Anderson Valley
F: 1980. **O:** Allen Green. **W:** Allen Green, Jed Steele. **S:** None.

OVERALL	$9-20	★★★

WINE RATINGS	
Cabernet Sauvignon Anderson Valley	★★
Cabernet Sauvignon Anderson Valley Estate Reserve	★★
Chardonnay Anderson Valley Du Pratt Vineyard	★★
Chardonnay Anderson Valley Late Harvest	NR
Chardonnay Mendocino County	★★
Merlot Anderson Valley	★★
Pinot Noir Anderson Valley Roederer Estate Vineyards	★★★
Pinot Noir Mendocino County	★★★
Sauvignon Blanc Anderson Valley	★★
White Riesling Anderson Valley	★★
White Riesling Mendocino County Late Harvest	★★★
Zinfandel Sonoma County	★★★
Zinfandel Sonoma County Scherrer Vineyards	★★★

WINERY DATA
C: 6,000. **V:** 12 acres in Anderson Valley. **G:** Cabernet Sauvignon (4 acres), Merlot (4), Riesling (4). **P:** Chardonnay, Sauvignon Blanc, Pinot Noir, Zinfandel (Anderson Valley), Zinfandel (Sonoma County).

Greenwood Ridge Vineyards rests at the 1,200-foot elevation above Anderson Valley. Owner Allen Green founded this winery in 1980 and produces some 6,000 cases of wine a year from his 12-acre vineyard and purchased grapes. The wines have shown a steady improvement in recent vintages, especially the Pinot Noir and Zinfandel, and a 1992 Cabernet Sauvignon from Villa Mt. Eden is ample evidence of the ripeness achievable at this location. Production is more or less evenly divided among Cabernet, Chardonnay (Du Pratt Vineyard), Merlot, Pinot Noir (Roederer), Sauvignon Blanc (Ferrington Vineyard), Riesling (including a late harvest) and Zinfandel.

TASTING NOTES

CABERNET SAUVIGNON ANDERSON VALLEY (★★), ESTATE RESERVE (★★): Struggles to ripen most years, often marked by herb and olive notes, but it can get ripe, as it did in 1992.

1992: Dark, thick and plush, with rich, chunky earthy currant, toasty oak and black cherry flavors that are intense and concentrated. Packs in lots of flavor. **89**

1991: Lean, earthy and oaky, and the wood dominates the currant and berry flavors. **82**

1989: Marked by strong herb, olive and wood flavors that miss the mark. **74**

1988: A solid wine with pretty currant, cherry, mint and herb notes. **83**

Estate Reserve 1990: Firm and flavorful, with tannic black currant and plum aromas and flavors that fade on the finish. **81**

Estate Reserve 1989: Ripe and aromatic, with rich, plush currant, anise, cedar and cherry flavors that are sharply focused, broad and complex. **87**

CHARDONNAY VARIOUS BOTTLINGS (★★): Variable, but the 1992 Du Pratt is rich and complex.

Anderson Valley Du Pratt Vineyard 1992: Smooth and generous, a mouthful of pear, peach and spice flavors that balance elegantly on a crisp structure. **90**

Anderson Valley Late Harvest 1993: Sweet and syrupy, a generous wine that echoes honey and caramel. **85**

Mendocino County 1991: Light and fruity, with definite floral overtones and crisp apple on the finish. **83**

MERLOT ANDERSON VALLEY (★★): Variable; austere and tannic when unripe, but it can be fresh and fruity, with vibrant flavors.

1992: Firm and compact, with a core of lean, chunky currant and wild berry flavors. Turns tannic on the finish. **86**

1991: Firm, tight and tannic, this austere wine shows a narrow beam of cherry aromas and flavors, but the tannins are gripping. **78**

1989: Fresh and fruity, with lively black cherry, spice, currant and herb notes that are crisp and smooth. **85**

PINOT NOIR VARIOUS BOTTLINGS (★★★): Consistently ripe and fruity, with the Roederer Estate 1992 bottling a dark and remarkably complex wine.

Anderson Valley 1990: Youthful and firm, framed by oak, and a nice touch of cherry and raspberry flavor comes through on a tannic finish. **87**

Anderson Valley 1989: Bright and fruity, with lots of

cherry and currant aromas and flavors and hints of toast on the finish. **87**

Anderson Valley Roederer Estate Vineyards 1993: Ripe, smooth and polished, with an elegant core of black cherry, currant and wild berry, finishing with a plush aftertaste, fine tannins and a grapey edge. **89**

Anderson Valley Roederer Estate Vineyards 1992: Deeply colored, with ripe, rich, well focused black cherry, wild berry and raspberry flavors that are complex and concentrated. **90**

Mendocino County 1991: Ripe, intense and juicy, with rich raspberry, cherry and spice flavors that are focused and polished. **87**

SAUVIGNON BLANC ANDERSON VALLEY (★★): Variable, but can be pleasant enough, with spice and fig flavors.

1993: Earthy, minty flavors dominate this toasty wine; a little sharp with oak flavor on the finish. **80**

1992: Fresh and spicy, with pleasant fig and butterscotch aromas and flavors, hinting at herbs on the finish. **84**

WHITE RIESLING ANDERSON VALLEY (★★): Off-dry and spicy, with pear and peach notes.

1993: Bright and fruity, a light wine that's a little spritzy, which balances the sweet peach and nectarine flavors. **85**

WHITE RIESLING MENDOCINO COUNTY LATE HARVEST (★★★): Ripe, sweet and delicious, with honey-scented pear and apricot flavors.

1989: Very ripe, sweet and generous, with nutmeg, honey, apricot and pear aromas and flavors. Gets very rich and unctuous on the finish. **89**

ZINFANDEL SONOMA COUNTY (★★★), SCHERRER VINEYARDS (★★★): Ripe, with bright, showy Zin flavors.

1991: A fresh, fruity wine with modest tannins and plenty of body and likable blackberry, raspberry and plum flavors. **85**

1990: Firm in texture and generous in flavor, with ripe berry, plum and spice aromas and flavors that become plush and mouth-filling on the finish. **86**

1989: Supple and fruity, with fresh, smooth strawberry and cherry flavors. **81**

1988: Firm and fruity, with lots of appealing plum, raspberry and vanilla aromas and flavors on a medium frame, turning peppery on the finish. **86**

Scherrer Vineyards 1993: Bright and youthful, with dark cherry flavors at the core and some nice vanilla, toast and bitter almond notes on the finish. Firmly tannic. **87**

Scherrer Vineyards 1992: Tight and compact, with wonderful wild berry and plum flavors that are wrapped in chewy tannins. **88**

GRGICH HILLS CELLAR
Rutherford, Napa Valley
F: 1977. **O:** Miljenko Grgich & Austin Hills. **W:** Miljenko Grgich. **S:** None.

OVERALL	$13-50	★★★

WINE RATINGS

Cabernet Sauvignon Napa Valley	★★★
Chardonnay Carneros Selection	★★★★
Chardonnay Napa Valley	★★★★★
Fumé Blanc Napa Valley	★★★
Johannisberg Riesling Napa Valley	
Late Harvest	★★★
Zinfandel Sonoma County	★★

WINERY DATA
C: 60,000. **V:** 233 acres in Napa Valley. **G:** Chardonnay (165 acres), Cabernet Sauvignon (45), Sauvignon Blanc (20), Merlot (3). **P:** Zinfandel (Sonoma County).

Croatian-born winemaker Miljenko "Mike" Grgich had impeccable credentials by the time he and Hills Bros. Coffee heir Austin Hills founded Grgich Hills Cellar in 1977. Grgich came to California in 1958, having earned a degree in wine science from Zagreb University in Croatia. He worked with Lee Stewart at Souverain, Robert Mondavi and André Tchelistcheff at Beaulieu, before being hired by Chateau Montelena for the 1972 vintage. His second vintage of Chardonnay at Montelena, the 1973, wowed the wine world, placing first in the famous Paris Tasting of 1976, when French critics judged it superior to the finest white Burgundies in a blind tasting.

At Grgich Hills the Chardonnays have always been brilliantly crafted, and the rest of the wines—including Fumé Blanc, Cabernet and Zinfandel, the latter from grapes grown—have been impressive, in Sonoma. The winery has substantial vineyard holdings in Napa and Carneros, with Chardonnay the leader at 165 acres. The winery output has been about 60,000 cases, and while I'm still a big fan of the Chardonnay, the Cabernet and Zinfandel have been less inspiring of late.

TASTING NOTES

CABERNET SAUVIGNON NAPA VALLEY (★★★): Less impressive recently, leaner and thinner, lacking richness and depth. Wines from the early and mid-1980s were superior.

1990: Deeply colored, with cedary oak and currant flavors that turn elegant and supple, with a modest tannic bite. **87**

1989: Austere and oaky, awkward and showing more wood and tannins than fruit. **81**

1988: Firm and earthy, with a gamy edge to the basic Cabernet fruit flavors, finishing short but solid. **84**

1987: Crisp, ripe and elegant, with currant and black cherry flavors that are typically understated. **86**

1986: Firm and tightly structured but a bit awkward, with muted black cherry, currant and spice flavors that are concentrated. **88**

1985: Rich and fruity, with lively raspberry, cherry, currant and anise flavors that are nicely seasoned by spicy, toasty oak notes. **90**

1984: Dark, with complex and exotic blackberry and black cherry flavors that turn spicy and tannic. Distinctive. **89**

1983: Ripe, full and fairly tannic, with bright plum and black cherry flavors that finish with a tannic edge. **88**

1982: Still firm and trim but mature, with fleshy plum, currant and anise flavors. **87**

1981: Lean and supple, with herb, bell pepper and ripe plum flavors. Mature. **86**

1980: Mature, very ripe, smooth and complex, oozing with rich, fleshy plum and black cherry flavors, supple tannins and a tasty finish. **90**

CHARDONNAY CARNEROS SELECTION (★★★★): New as the shift to Carneros grapes becomes more evident. Impressive.

1992: Deftly balanced, wtih complex, concentrated pear, honey, vanilla and spice flavors that gently unfold, picking up a butterscotch edge. **90**

CHARDONNAY NAPA VALLEY (★★★★★): Intense and tightly wound, with a compact core of fruit flavors and a long, lingering finish, built to age but often less showy on release. For years this has been a blend of vineyards from Rutherford to Coombsville to Carneros.

1992: Supple, with elegant pear, honey and apple flavors that pick up a citrus edge on the finish. **88**

1991: Serves up plenty of ripe, spicy pear and apple flavors along with a touch of peach and citrus. **88**

1990: Continues to improve after being shy and reticent on release, showing more polish and harmony. Focused, concentrated and flavorful. **89**

1989: Fresh and lively, with plenty of focused grapefruit, pineapple and nutmeg aromas and flavors that stay fresh and crisp on the finish. **88**

1987: Clean, with fresh apple, pear and spicy nutmeg flavors. **90**

1986: Lively and fruity, with ripe pear and spice flavors and a touch of smokiness propped up with firm acidity that gives it depth and complexity. **92**

1985: Plenty of generous ripe fig, oak, spice and pear aromas and flavors, but the finish trails off, leaving a pleasant smoky, oaky aftertaste. **92**

FUMÉ BLANC NAPA VALLEY (★★★): Can be very complex, with herb, pear and spice flavors and a long, lingering finish. It can also be herbaceous.

1993: Crisp, with a flinty grapefruit and citrus edge and lingering flavors. **85**

1992: Tart and a bit green, with crisp grapefruit, fig and lemon notes that turn biting on the finish. **84**

JOHANNISBERG RIESLING NAPA VALLEY LATE HARVEST (★★☆):

1993: Sweet and deeply honeyed, with a floral character that keeps echoing on the smooth and elegant finish. **88**

ZINFANDEL SONOMA COUNTY (★★): Solid, with very ripe fruit flavors and firm tannins, but lacks the extra polish and dimensions achieved with Zinfandel these days. Grapes from Martini's Monte RossoVineyard are part of the blend now.

1992: Oaky and earthy, with a mature, cedary edge to the cherry and berry notes. Works out better on the finish, where the flavors turn to pepper and berry, but lacks focus. **84**

1991: Ripe and chunky, with rich, tannic raspberry and tart cherry flavors and cedary oak notes on the finish. **84**

1990: Light for a 1990 but the good with the spicy, peppery strawberry flavors ring true for Zinfandel. The tannins are modest. **84**

1989: Firm and tannic, with nice, spicy raspberry, cranberry and vanilla flavors that are modest. **83**

1988: Elegant and peppery, with spicy plum and cedar notes, finishing with fine, light tannins. **85**

1987: Dried out and earthy, this wine is marked by strong American oak flavors and has not evolved beyond youthful austerity. **78**

1986: Plump, concentrated and smooth, with lots of blueberry and raspberry flavors, light oak and mild tannins. **85**

GROTH VINEYARDS & WINERY
Oakville, Napa Valley
F: 1982. **O:** Dennis D. & Judith M. Groth. **W:** Michael Weis. **S:** None.

OVERALL	$13-50	★★★★

WINE RATINGS

Cabernet Sauvignon Napa Valley	★★★★
Cabernet Sauvignon Napa Valley Reserve	★★★★★
Chardonnay Napa Valley	★★
Merlot Napa Valley	★★
Sauvignon Blanc Napa Valley	★★

WINERY DATA
C: 40,000. **V:** 165 acres in Napa Valley. **G:** Cabernet Sauvignon (54 acres), Chardonnay (36), Sauvignon Blanc (27), Merlot (22). **P:** Sauvignon Blanc (Napa Valley).

Dennis Groth left the high-tech life at Atari Computer for Napa wine, buying a large property in Oakville in 1982 and promptly hiring Nils Venge, then winemaker at Villa Mt. Eden Winery, Groth's neighbor to the east. The winery now makes five wines, all estate-grown except the Sauvignon Blanc, with the Cabernet and Reserve Cabernet the big stars. Groth owns 165 acres in Napa, with 54 of them around the winery devoted to Cabernet. Chardonnay (36 acres), Merlot (22) and Sauvignon Blanc (27) are also grown.

Because the Cabernet ripens late in this cool spot in the valley, it is often among the last picked in the Oakville area. When it ripens fully, it makes a thick, dense, enormously complex wine that offers an uncommonly wide range of succulent flavors, from currant to mineral to herb and spice, with firm but fleshy tannins and ample oak shadings. In cooler years, when the grapes are less ripe at harvest, the wines are clearly marked by green vegetal flavors that echo coffee, tobacco and green beans. Groth has decided it's wiser to wait and hope the grapes reach 24 degrees Brix in sugar content rather than pick early. The other wines are good, occasionally very good, but sometimes off the mark. Groth acknowledges as much and is determined to raise quality across the board. Production has leveled off at 40,000 cases. In 1994 Groth and Venge parted ways, with Venge focusing on his Saddleback Cellars brand; Michael Weis, late of Vichon, is the new winemaker as of 1995.

TASTING NOTES

CABERNET SAUVIGNON NAPA VALLEY (★★★★): The standard estate bottling usually mirrors the Reserve and can be rich and supple, although not as grand and concentrated.

1991: The currant and coffee flavors are rich and intense, laced with cedary oak and herbal notes, finishing with a weedy black currant and chocolate edge. Firmly tannic. **90**

1990: Dense and concentrated, a dark, chunky wine that has plenty of flavor, running from plum and currant to herb and tobacco, echoing coffee and spice on the finish. **90**

1989: Pleasant but not especially rich or concentrated, with light herb, currant and cedar notes that turn light and simple, with very light tannins. **82**

1988: A lean, tannic wine with unripe green bean and ash flavors. Weakest Groth ever, with biting tannins. **79**

1987: Intense and concentrated, with ripe, supple currant, herb, cedar and tea flavors. Balanced and harmonious. **88**

1986: Smooth, complex and silky, with currant, herb, cedar and coffee flavors that turn rich and spicy and a pleasing mineral flavor on the aftertaste. The tannins are supple. **90**

1985: Ripe, supple, complex and generous, with tiers of currant, plum, spice and cedary oak flavors. Harmonious,

intense and beautifully balanced, with firm yet fine tannins. The finish goes on and on. Still has years of life ahead. **94**

1984: Ripe and supple, fully mature, with lots of cedar, chocolate, currant and mineral flavors. Well balanced, complex and moderately tannic. **88**

1983: Lean and tart, typical of 1983s, with a narrow band of cedar, spice and leafy fruit flavors. A bit past its peak. **85**

1982: Fully mature and drinking very well, with cedar, currant, coffee and spice flavors that are rich yet supple, picking up a trace of earth on the finish. There's just a trace of tannin remaining. **88**

CABERNET SAUVIGNON NAPA VALLEY RESERVE (★★★★★): The Reserve in ripe years can be stunning, amazingly complex and jam-packed with rich flavors.

1991: Distinctive for its richness and depth, but marked by herb, bell pepper and racy currant flavors that offer uncommon depth and complexity in a distinct style. **95**

1990: A supple and seductive wine that's silky and complex, with tiers of currant, cherry, cedar, herb and mineral flavors that stay with you on a long, full, rich finish. Beautiful harmony of flavors. **94**

1989: Distinctive for its coffee, olive and cedar nuances, it also serves up ripe, rich, concentrated currant, chocolate and black cherry flavors, picking up a prune note on the finish. **87**

1988: Smooth and supple, vastly superior to the regular bottling, with creamy vanilla, currant and herb flavors and smooth tannins. Could be cellared for a few years, but 1988 is not a keeper vintage. **87**

1987: A big, ripe and intensely flavored wine that packs in herb, currant, mineral and spice flavors. There's a wonderful sense of harmony and finesse; it's firmly tannic and oaky on the finish, with a long, potent aftertaste. **93**

1986: Tight and austere, with firm tannins that are tightly wrapped around the currant and herb flavors. Shows more oak and tannins than the regular bottling and is more typical of the 1986 vintage. **89**

1985: Dark in color, with wonderful, perfumed aromas of currant, cherry, mineral and spice and a broad, rich, supple, silky texture that carries the flavors on a long, full, delicious aftertaste. Picks up herb, tea, cocoa and vanilla nuances. A tremendous wine, pure and simple. **97**

1984: A wonderful rich and complex mouthful of Cabernet. Typical weedy currant, cedar, coffee and spice

flavors turn smooth and silky, with soft, fleshy tannins on the finish, where it picks up a pretty vanilla taste. **92**
1983: Fuller and richer than the regular bottling but showing a similar stage of maturity, with the cedar, earth, green olive, tar and currant flavors turning leafy and tannic. **88**

CHARDONNAY NAPA VALLEY (★★): Improving but still behind the pack, it's well oaked, with spicy apricot flavors.
1993: Tart and earthy, with a pungent, grassy edge to the spicy pear flavors. **84**
1992: Coarse and simple, with earthy fig, pear and spice flavors that turn chunky on the finish. **83**
1991: Supple and creamy, with spicy pear, apple and oak flavors that are focused and well knit, but they taper off on the finish. **86**

MERLOT NAPA VALLEY (★★): New to the lineup, displaying herb, cherry and cedar notes. Worth watching.
1991: Tart and earthy, with cedary oak dominating the cherry and herb flavors underneath. **82**
1990: Supple and elegant, with earthy currant, tea and cedar flavors. Has fine balance, firm tannins and good length. **85**

SAUVIGNON BLANC NAPA VALLEY (★★): The least interesting, a medium-weight wine marked by herbal and grassy notes.
1994: Lean and definitely herbal, showing an onion-skin edge to the peppery pear flavors. **83**
1992: Crisp in texture, fruity at the core and generous with its leafy pear flavors. **83**

GROVE STREET WINERY
Sonoma County
F: 1991. **O:** Bill & Sally Hambrecht. **W:** Kevin Warren. **S:** None.

OVERALL	$7	★

WINE RATINGS

Cabernet Sauvignon California	
Vineyard Select	NR
Chardonnay Sonoma County	NR
Chardonnay Sonoma County	
Healdsburg Vineyard Select	NR

Chardonnay Sonoma County	
Vintage Select	NR

WINERY DATA
C: 75,000. **V:** 175 acres in Alexander Valley, Russian River Valley. **G:** Chardonnay (145 acres), Cabernet Sauvignon (30). **P:** Chardonnay, Cabernet Sauvignon (Alexander Valley), Chardonnay (Russian River Valley).

Owned by Bill Hambrecht of Belvedere Winery, Grove Street is a new, 75,000-case winery and wine brand that specializes in California-appellation, value-oriented Cabernet, Chardonnay, white Zinfandel and red and white table wine.

TASTING NOTES

VARIOUS BOTTLINGS (NR):
Cabernet Sauvignon California Vineyard Select 1992: Lean and tannic; the fruit just barely sneaks past. **75**
Chardonnay Sonoma County 1992: Tastes sweet and simple, with light fruit notes. **75**
Chardonnay Sonoma County Healdsburg Vineyard Select 1993: Simple and flavorful, with an unfortunate rubbery edge to the pear fruit. **77**
Chardonnay Sonoma County Vintage Select 1992: Intense and a bit earthy, with a grassy edge to the pear and pineapple flavors. **84**

GUENOC WINERY
Guenoc Valley
F: 1976. **O:** Magoon Estate Ltd.. **W:** Derek K. Holstein. **S:** Domaine Breton.

OVERALL	$11-35	★★★★

WINE RATINGS

Cabernet Franc Lake County	★★★
Cabernet Sauvignon Lake County	★★
Cabernet Sauvignon Napa Valley	
Beckstoffer Vineyard Reserve	★★★★
Cabernet Sauvignon North Coast	★★
Chardonnay Guenoc Valley	★★★
Chardonnay Guenoc Valley	
Genevieve Magoon Vineyard Reserve	★★★★
Meritage Red Lake County	
Langtry Estate	★★★

Meritage White Guenoc Valley
Langtry Estate ★★★
Merlot Lake-Napa Counties NR
Petite Sirah North Coast ★★★
Port California ★★
Sauvignon Blanc Guenoc Valley ★★★
Zinfandel California ★★

WINERY DATA

C: 95,000. **V:** 307 acres in Napa Valley, Guenoc Valley.
G: Cabernet Sauvignon (45 acres), Chardonnay (139),
Sauvignon Blanc (37), Petite Sirah (36), Cabernet Franc (8).
P: Cabernet Sauvignon, Chardonnay, Cabernet Franc, Merlot
(Lake County), Cabernet Sauvignon, Chardonnay (Napa Valley),
Chardonnay (Sonoma County).

In an unusual land swap, in 1963 the Magoon family
traded 23 acres of prime Hawaiian real estate for 23,000
acres in rural Lake County. This land, which dips into
Napa County, is the foundation for Guenoc, the winery,
and Guenoc Valley, the nation's first single-proprietor
American Viticultural Area, covering 1,200 acres. Grapes
had been grown in the area since 1854, and this scenic
estate was once home to the famous Victorian actress
Lillie Langtry, who settled there in 1888 with the intention of making the greatest claret in the country. Langtry
took her wine seriously, producing wine until 1906, when
she returned to France.

At Genevieve Magoon's urging, her sons Orville and
Eaton decided to try something "more romantic" than
running cattle and mowing hay, and they began studying
wine-grape growing. In the late 1960s they began to
plant an extensive vineyard, utilizing Orville's passion
for precision and the wine know-how of Roy and Walt
Raymond of Raymond Vineyards, who helped in the
vineyard design and who oversaw production of the early
wines, beginning in 1976. The Magoons restored the
Langtry house and proceeded to build a modern winery.
By the mid-1980s their efforts began to pay off with
increasingly better wines.

Today the winery farms more than 300 acres, with
Chardonnay (139 acres) the dominant grape, followed
by Cabernet (45), Sauvignon Blanc (37) and Petite
Sirah (36). Production is 95,000 cases, including a second label, Domaine Breton. All the wines are well
made, clean and balanced, but a few stand out: the
Beckstoffer Napa Valley Reserve Cabernet, Genevieve

Magoon Reserve Chardonnay and Langtry Estate
Meritage Red and White.

TASTING NOTES

CABERNET FRANC LAKE COUNTY (★★★):
1990: Complex and inviting, with layers of ripe, supple
currant, berry and cherry flavors framed by toasty, buttery oak. **88**
1985: The weedy and vegetal flavors are intense and
pungent, straightforward and blunt. **70**

CABERNET SAUVIGNON LAKE COUNTY (★★): Medium-
weight and appealing for its supple flavors.
1991: Tight, with a supple band of currant, cedar and
spice flavors that finish with a firm, tannic edge. **87**
1990: Lean and firmly tannic, but with a pleasant core of
currant and cedary oak flavors. Turns tannic. **84**
1989: Lean and lively, but the flavors run toward the vegetable end of the spectrum, with green bean and bell pepper notes sliding past the red cherry flavors. **77**
1987: Lively and well balanced, with pretty plum, cherry,
currant and spice flavors that echo fruit from start to finish. **89**
1986: Lean, tannic and vegetal, with unfocused fruit and
beet flavors. Modest in scope. **78**

**CABERNET SAUVIGNON NAPA VALLEY BECKSTOFFER
VINEYARD RESERVE (★★★★):** From grapes grown in a
5-acre vineyard near Spottswoode in St. Helena. Each of
the vintages has been superb, with ripe, rich, complex
fruit flavors, polished tannins and a sense of harmony
and finesse.
1991: Young and tight but well focused and concentrated,
serving up complex herb, currant and black cherry flavors that turn supple and elegant on the finish. Shows a
measure of finesse and restraint. **94**
1990: Ripe and aromatic, rich and flavorful, with a tight, solid
core of black cherry, cedar, currant and spice flavors that fan
out. Supple and generous, yet with a firm backbone. **92**
1989: Ripe and rich, with generous loganberry and
blackberry flavors that keep bubbling up on the finish.
Shades of coffee, smoke and spice make it interesting.
Has tannin to lose. **90**
1987: Very fruity and lively, with gorgeous black cherry,
currant and plum flavors supported by crisp acidity and
firm tannins. **92**

CABERNET SAUVIGNON NORTH COAST (★★):
1991: Simple, with earthy, tannic dill and herbal flavors. There's a tannic edge on the finish and the fruit is only modestly rich. **82**

CHARDONNAY GUENOC VALLEY (★★★): Improving, with a tight core of pear and spice flavors and pretty oak shadings.
1993: Crisp, with a tight, juicy beam of pear, apple and spice flavors. **85**
1992: Elegant and spicy, with pretty pear and toasty oak notes that finish with honey and buttery oak flavors. **89**
1991: Tight and lean, with spicy oak dominating the pear and fig flavors. **85**

CHARDONNAY GUENOC VALLEY GENEVIEVE MAGOON VINEYARD RESERVE (★★★★): Deep and complex, with rich flavors and toasty oak nuances.
1993: Marked by smoky, toasty notes, but with juicy pear and apple fruit to match, turning elegant and lively on the finish, where a quince edge emerges. **90**
1992: Complex and concentrated, elegant and graceful, with a rich core of spicy pear, honey, hazelnut and buttery oak flavors. **89**
1991: Its smoky, toasty oak shadings give it complexity, and the fruit is ripe and concentrated, echoing pear and vanilla notes. **88**

MERITAGE RED LAKE COUNTY LANGTRY ESTATE (★★★): Elegant and refined, supple and polished, with rich, complex flavors.
1991: A stylish wine with layers of plum, red cherry, raspberry and herb flavors that stay focused and linger on a long finish. Picks up cedary oak on the aftertaste and the tannins are firm and polished. **90**
1990: Firm and focused, with a tight core of currant, spice and cedar flavors that finish with fine tannins and good length. **89**
1989: Strikes a nice balance between ripe currant and black cherry aromas and flavors and spicy, toasty, buttery oak notes. Finishes with firm, chewy tannins. **87**
1988: Fresh, lively and well balanced, with pretty cherry, raspberry, plum and oak flavors that hang together fairly well. **86**
1987: Supple, smooth and complex, with ripe, rich currant, plum and cherry flavors and a nice touch of tobacco and oak on the finish. **89**

MERITAGE WHITE GUENOC VALLEY LANGTRY ESTATE (★★★): Classy, with rich, spicy flavors on an elegant framework.
1993: Classy, with aromatic spice, herb and honey notes around a core of pear and melon flavors. **88**
1992: Rich and complex, with herb, honey, citrus and fig flavors. **90**

MERLOT NAPA-LAKE COUNTIES (NR):
1987: Firm and focused, with well articulated berry and currant aromas and flavors and hints of plum on the finish. **86**

PETITE SIRAH NORTH COAST (★★★): Sturdy, with firm tannins and a peppery edge.
1990: Rich and peppery, with wild berry and currant notes that are fresh and lively. **87**
1989: Ripe and peppery, but the finish is short. Lacks depth and richness. **83**
1988: Sturdy and fruity, with plenty of plum and oak aromas and flavors. Generous, stylish and well balanced. **86**

PORT CALIFORNIA (★★):
1992: Sweet and decidedly plummy, showing a distinctive range of spice and fruit flavors that echo plum on the solid finish. Tempting now, better from 1998. **89**

SAUVIGNON BLANC GUENOC VALLEY (★★★): Beautifully crafted, with a range of appealing flavors and a soft, fleshy texture.
1994: Snappy and fruity, a wine with a lot of zip and character, echoing peach, vanilla and herb on the lively finish. **87**
1993: Light and earthy, a smooth-textured wine that's a dead ringer for Chardonnay. **82**
1992: A wonderfully crafted wine with bright lemon, citrus, fig and spice flavors. Elegant and lively, with a crisp, mouth-watering finish. Has intensity without weight. **86**

ZINFANDEL CALIFORNIA (★★): Light, with berry and spice notes.
1991: Light in style, with ripe berry flavor, it picks up a pleasant, earthy tar note on the finish. **83**
1990: Crisp and lively, showing nicely turned plum, berry and spice flavors. **84**
1989: Firm and tight, packing in plenty of spicy, minty berry aromas and flavors. **85**

EMILIO GUGLIELMO WINERY
Morgan Hill, Santa Clara County
F: 1925. **O:** Emilio Guglielmo Winery, Inc. **W:** George E. Guglielmo. **S:** Emile's.

OVERALL	$8-12	★

WINE RATINGS	
Chardonnay Monterey County	NR
Merlot Napa Valley	NR
Pinot Noir Santa Clara Valley	
Private Reserve	NR
Red Table Wine Santa Clara County	
Claret	NR
Zinfandel Santa Clara Valley	
Private Reserve	NR

WINERY DATA
C: 60,000. **V:** 65 acres in Santa Clara Valley. **G:** Petite Sirah (20 acres), Zinfandel (25), Pinot Noir (6), Merlot (4), Grignolino (10). **P:** Cabernet Sauvignon (Santa Clara Valley), Chardonnay, Cabernet Sauvignon (Monterey).

The family-owned Emilio Guglielmo Winery in Morgan Hill is now run by the third generation of winemakers, producing 60,000 cases of wine primarily from its 65 acres of vines and grapes purchased in the Santa Clara area, but it has also branched out to Napa Merlot and Monterey Chardonnay. Quality is ordinary, with the rustic reds, such as Zinfandel and Petite Sirah, the best bets. Old-time California wine drinkers may recall sipping Emile's Private Stock jug wines.

TASTING NOTES

VARIOUS BOTTLINGS (NR):
Chardonnay Monterey County 1992: Light and spicy, appealing for its apple and peach flavors and bright finish. **82**
Merlot Napa Valley 1990: Lean and a little astringent, but the toasty tobacco and grape flavors come through. **78**
Pinot Noir Santa Clara Valley Private Reserve 1990: Dull, flat and gamy, with hints of cherry and plum flavors. A simple wine. **75**
Red Table Wine Santa Clara County Claret 13th Limited Bottling 1989: A dry, tannic, earthy and rustic wine that dries out. Marginal. **70**

Zinfandel Santa Clara Valley Private Reserve 1989: Earthy and gamy, with a ripe, raisiny edge to the flavors. Finishes with crisp, dry tannins and cedary oak. **79**

GUILLIAMS VINEYARDS
St. Helena, Napa Valley
F: 1983. **O:** John & Sandy Guilliams. **W:** John Guilliams. **S:** None.

OVERALL	$17-20	★★

WINE RATINGS	
Cabernet Sauvignon Spring Mountain	★★

WINERY DATA
C: 1,000. **V:** 7 acres in Spring Mountain. **G:** Cabernet Sauvignon (5.6 acres), Cabernet Franc (0.7), Merlot (0.7). **P:** None.

John and Sandy Guilliams produce some 500 cases of Cabernet from their 7-acre vineyard. The wine also includes some Merlot and Cabernet Franc, and the 1990 is supple and understated, with herb, spice, currant and oak notes.

TASTING NOTES

VARIOUS BOTTLINGS:
Cabernet Sauvignon Spring Mountain 1990: Supple and elegant, with herb, spice, light oak and ripe currant flavors. This is a well crafted, understated wine that's pleasant to drink now but should hold well through 1998. **86**
La Vieille Montagne Cabernet Sauvignon Napa Valley 1988: Leans toward the weedy, herbal, earthy side of Cabernet, turning thin. **80**
La Vieille Montagne Cabernet Sauvignon Napa Valley 1987: Firm in texture, with focused nutmeg, cherry and prune aromas and flavors and green tannins. **81**
La Vieille Montagne Cabernet Sauvignon Napa Valley 1986: Attractive for its balance of fresh, ripe, rich herb and fruit flavors and oaky vanilla notes. **84**

GUNDLACH BUNDSCHU WINERY
Sonoma Valley
F: 1858. **O:** Vineburg Wine Co. **W:** Linda Trotta. **S:** None.

Overall   **$9-18**   ★★★

Wine Ratings

Cabernet Franc Sonoma Valley Rhinefarm Vineyards	★★★
Cabernet Sauvignon Sonoma Valley Rhinefarm Vineyards	★★★
Cabernet Sauvignon Sonoma Valley Rhinefarm Vineyards Vintage Reserve	★★★
Chardonnay Sonoma Valley	★★
Chardonnay Carneros Sangiacomo Vineyard Special Selection	★★
Gewürztraminer Sonoma Valley Rhinefarm Vineyards	★★
Meritage Red Sonoma Valley Bearitage	★★
Merlot Sonoma Valley	★★★
Merlot Sonoma Valley Rhinefarm Vineyards	★★★
Pinot Noir Sonoma Valley Rhinefarm Vineyards	★★
White Riesling Sonoma Valley Dresel's Sonoma Riesling	★★
Zinfandel Sonoma Valley	★★★
Zinfandel Sonoma Valley Rhinefarm Vineyards	★★★

Winery Data

C: 50,000. **V:** 400 acres in Sonoma Valley. **G:** Cabernet Sauvignon, Chardonnay, Merlot, Gewürztraminer, Riesling, Pinot Noir, Zinfandel. **P:** Zinfandel (Sonoma Valley), Chardonnay (Sonoma Valley).

Jacob Gundlach and Charles Bundschu founded this winery east of Sonoma in 1858, producing wines under the Bacchus Wines label. Following Gundlach's death, Bundschu operated the winery and the 400-acre Rhinefarm Vineyard until 1906, when the great San Francisco earthquake destroyed the stone winery. Prohibition put an end to Bundschu's winemaking, but the vineyard survived and remained a source of grapes to area wineries. Bundschu's grandson Jim Bundschu inherited the winery and in 1969 decided to reopen it, with the first wines appearing after the 1973 vintage. Through the next decade, Bundschu added wines, mostly estate-grown, including Cabernet, Chardonnay, Gamay Beaujolais, Gewürztraminer, Merlot, Pinot Noir, Riesling and Zinfandel (both Rhinefarm and Sonoma Valley). The lineup is solid across the board, with wines fairly priced

and a few that rank among the state's best. Production is 50,000 cases.

Tasting Notes

Cabernet Franc Sonoma Valley Rhinefarm Vineyards (★★★):
1989: A fresh, fruity, broad wine with blueberry and blackberry flavors and firm tannins. **87**
1987: Soft, ripe and generous, with floral nuances in the ripe plum and cherry flavors and firm tannins. **89**

Cabernet Sauvignon Sonoma Valley Rhinefarm Vineyards (★★★): From a cool spot for Cabernet, this vineyard yields consistent if unspectacular wines marked by bright fruit flavors that occasionally lean toward herbaceous.
1992: Ripe and juicy, with pretty cherry and plum flavors that turn supple and polished. Finishes with a pretty aftertaste that echoes fruit. Has the tannic structure to cellar into 1997. **87**
1991: Laced with herb, green olive and spicy bell pepper notes, this is a supple and polished wine that picks up complexity on the finish. **88**
1990: Firm and chunky, an austere wine that never quite shows enough flavor to beat the tannins. The flavors edge toward green olive and tobacco rather than fruit. **83**
1989: Simple and unfocused, with a bell pepper edge to the basic currant flavor. Moderately tannic. **80**
1987: A herbaceous wine with spice, herb and bell pepper notes, but supple currant, plum and cherry flavors come through. **85**
1986: Delicious, with beautifully focused fruit and lots of currant, black cherry, spice and vanilla flavors that are intense and lively. **89**
1985: A smooth, sumptuous wine offering layers of vanilla, chocolate, currant and spicy berry flavors and smooth, supple tannins. **91**
1984: Has attractive, ripe, forward plum and black cherry flavors and a lean, firm structure. **85**

Cabernet Sauvignon Sonoma Valley Rhinefarm Vineyards Vintage Reserve (★★★): Similar to the Rhinefarm bottling but more intense, showing off more new oak.
1989: Austere, with a decent band of cherry and plum flavors, but on the finish it loses focus. **84**

1987: Bold, ripe, rich and tannic, this a mouthful of Cabernet, with ripe plum, currant, chocolate and vanilla flavors that are dense and concentrated. **89**

1986: Intense and concentrated, with rich, ripe currant, cherry, plum and spice notes and a good dose of tannin. **83**

CHARDONNAY CARNEROS SANGIACOMO VINEYARD SPECIAL SELECTION (★★):
1991: Lean and racy, with a definite grapefruit flavor running through it. **85**

CHARDONNAY SONOMA VALLEY (★★): Crisp and clean, with modest fruit flavors.
1991: A crisp, clean and correct wine with modest hints of pear and vanilla that fade. **83**

GEWÜRZTRAMINER SONOMA VALLEY RHINEFARM VINEYARDS (★★):
1992: Soft and watery, a simple wine with modest fruit flavors and vague mineral nuances on the finish. **77**

MERITAGE RED SONOMA VALLEY BEARITAGE (★★):
1990: Fruity but sharp and aggressive, dominated by raspberry and strong herbal flavors. **81**

MERLOT SONOMA VALLEY (★★★): Can be supple and complex, with rich, focused flavors, but it is also variable and sometimes has a lean, green edge.
1988: Lean and a bit green, with thin plum and berry notes. Firmly tannic, but it could use a little flesh. **84**
1986: Firm and tight but well focused, with ripe cherry, plum and currant flavors. There are subtle oak shadings and tight tannins on the finish. **87**
1985: Ripe, rich and polished, with focused currant and cherry flavors and firm, fine tannins. **88**
1984: Tight and firm, but not showing much fruit. Hints of berry and currant, but they fade on the finish. **82**
1983: Lean and tight, with berry and cherry flavors that turn dry and tannic on the finish. **80**
1982: Tight and firm, with smoky currant and spicy vanilla flavors from oak. It's also quite tannic. **83**
1981: Ripe and plummy, with pretty rose petal, berry and currant notes, but the finish turns dry and oaky and there's still plenty of tannin. **84**

MERLOT SONOMA VALLEY RHINEFARM VINEYARDS (★★★): This bottling offers more depth and complexity than the regular, but is also variable.

1992: Ripe and intense, with a wild berry and black cherry edge that picks up nice oak shadings on the finish. **88**
1990: Intense and grainy, with ripe raisin, cedar and herb flavors that are chewy and tannic, and have the potential to improve. **85**
1989: A sturdy, tannic wine that needs time. **80**
1988: Firm and tight, with modest, ripe plum, currant, herb and spice notes that are compact and firmly tannic. **81**
1987: Rich and focused, with concentrated, complex currant, cedar, coffee, herb and anise notes. Intense and firmly tannic. **87**
1986: Pretty, supple and elegant, with cinnamon, herb, tobacco and ripe plum flavors tempered with integrated tannins. **91**
1985: Firm, silky and beautifully focused, with delicious currant and cherry flavors, harmonious already, finishing with smooth tannins. **92**

PINOT NOIR SONOMA VALLEY RHINEFARM VINEYARDS (★★): Inconsistent: it's light and simple one year, bright and fruity the next.
1992: Lean and trim, with a crisp, narrow band of spice and cherry flavors. **82**
1991: Smooth in texture but weak and tealike in flavor. **78**
1989: Light in color, offering pretty strawberry, cherry and plum jam flavors. **83**
1988: Smooth and supple, with gently unfolding cherry, strawberry and spice aromas and flavors. Focused and flavorful. **88**
1986: Smooth, silky and elegant, with a velvety texture and ripe strawberry, cherry, spice and smoke flavors. **87**

WHITE RIESLING SONOMA VALLEY DRESEL'S SONOMA RIESLING (★★):
1993: Light and fruity, showing nice pear and nectarine flavors that linger softly on the finish. **83**
1992: A sweet, rather full-bodied Riesling with a nice, smooth texture but simple apple and grapefruit flavors. Has a nice feel, but doesn't dazzle. **82**

ZINFANDEL SONOMA VALLEY (★★★):
1992: A claret-style Zin that's fresh and vibrant, with pretty black cherry, plum and toasty, buttery oak flavors, all folded neatly together in a complex and enticing wine. **92**
1991: Jammy and exuberant, showing strawberry and raspberry flavors and moderate tannins. **85**

1989: Fresh and flavorful, leaning more toward rhubarb than the typical raspberry flavor. **84**

1988: A claret-style Zin offering delicious berry, plum, violet and toast aromas and flavors plus a frank dose of tannin. **88**

1987: Charming from the youthful color through the delicate finish, bursting with fresh, appealing strawberry and cherry aromas and flavors. **87**

ZINFANDEL SONOMA VALLEY RHINEFARM VINEYARDS (★★★): Another steady performer that is usually good but is capable of rising to the top of its class with uncommon complexity.

1990: Firm and focused, with lots of ripe berry, cherry, tobacco and vanilla aromas and flavors that extend into a long finish. **87**

1989: Rough and ready, with generous, ripe plum and pepper aromas and flavors, full-bodied and concentrated. **87**

1988: Lovely black cherry and black pepper aromas and flavors seem to jump out of the glass in this smooth-textured, firmly structured wine. **88**

1987: Oak overtones detract from the quality. The flavors are simple and decent but unexciting. **71**

1986: Zinfandel meets Chateauneuf-du-Pape; a real find. Extremely peppery and full-bodied, with ripe berry flavors, firm tannins and lively acidity. **90**

1985: Very peppery and Rhône-like. Shows tasty fruit, cinnamon and pepper flavors. **84**

HACIENDA WINE CELLARS
Sonoma Valley
F: 1973. **O:** Bronco Wine Co. **W:** N/A. **S:** None.

OVERALL	$6-8	★★

WINE RATINGS

Cabernet Sauvignon California Clair de Lune	★★
Chardonnay California Clair de Lune	★★★
Meritage Red Sonoma County Antares	NR
Merlot California Clair de Lune	★★
Pinot Noir Sonoma Valley Estate Reserve	★★

WINERY DATA
C: N/A. **V:** N/A. **G:** N/A. **P:** N/A.

Newspaperman and UPI war correspondent Frank Bartholomew bought, sight unseen, several old stone buildings in Sonoma Valley that had been abandoned and in ruins for decades. It turned out he had discovered Agoston Haraszthy's original Buena Vista Winery, founded in 1857 and one of the first wineries in California. Bartholomew and his wife, Antonia, revived the winery and vineyards, but when he became president of United Press International and was based on the East Coast, he had little time for the wine business. In 1968 Bartholomew sold the winery property but kept the estate's vineyard. In 1973 he refitted an old hacienda-style building and started Hacienda Winery. Crawford Cooley joined the business in 1976 and ran the winery until 1992, when he sold it to Fred Franzia's Bronco Wine Co. At that time Hacienda had grown to a 30,000-case winery producing Cabernet, Chardonnay (under the Clair de Lune designation), Chenin Blanc from Clarksburg, Pinot Noir and Antares, a Bordeaux-style blend. By the time Franzia took over, all the wines were well made but none were exceptional. The label's future is unclear.

HAFNER VINEYARD
Alexander Valley
F: 1967. **O:** Mary, Dick, Parke, Scott & Betsy Hafner, Julie H. Farrell. **W:** Parke Hafner. **S:** Wilson-Cole Cellars.

OVERALL	$10-18	NR

WINE RATINGS

Cabernet Sauvignon Alexander Valley	NR
Chardonnay Alexander Valley	NR

WINERY DATA
C: 10,000. **V:** 98 acres in Alexander Valley. **G:** Chardonnay (70 acres), Cabernet Sauvignon (28). **P:** None.

The Hafners are primarily grape growers in Alexander Valley and have counted Gary Farrell as one of their clients. The winery makes about 10,000 cases of Cabernet and Chardonnay each year from its 98-acre vineyard, nearly all of it sold through direct marketing.

HAGAFEN CELLARS
Napa Valley
F: 1980. **O:** Hagafen Cellars Inc. **W:** Ernie Weir.
S: None.

OVERALL	$8-28	★★

WINE RATINGS

Cabernet Sauvignon Napa Valley	★★
Cabernet Sauvignon Napa Valley Reserve	★★
Chardonnay Napa Valley	★★
Chardonnay Napa Valley Reserve	★★
Johannisberg Riesling Napa Valley	★★
Pinot Noir Napa Valley	NR

WINERY DATA
C: 3,000. **V:** 13 acres in Napa Valley. **G:** Pinot Noir (9 acres), Cabernet Franc (4). **P:** Chardonnay (Napa Valley), Johannisberg Riesling (Napa Valley), Cabernet Sauvignon (Napa Valley).

Hagafen in Hebrew means "the vine," and in 1980 this winery became the first kosher-wine producer in the North Coast appellation. It was founded by Zach Berkowitz, Domaine Chandon's viticulturalist, and Ernie Weir, along with silent partner Rene di Rosa, the original owner of Winery Lake Vineyard in Carneros. The product mix has varied over the years, and recently has included Cabernet (the best wine), Chardonnay, Pinot Noir, a Pinot Noir Blanc and Riesling. Production has hovered around 3,000 cases.

TASTING NOTES

CABERNET SAUVIGNON NAPA VALLEY (★★), RESERVE (★★): Highly variable, hitting a high with a wonderful 1987 but missing in 1989 and 1990.
1990: Heavy-handed, with dusty, woody oak flavors. The fruit struggles to reach the surface, but it's a one-dimensional wine dominated by oak. **77**
1989: A normally good winery stumbled with this one. Dull, earthy and gamy, lacking any liveliness or richness. **68**
1987: Offers lots of yummy, seductive, ripe plum, currant, jam and toasty oak flavors that are rich and complex yet firmly structured, with smooth, thick tannins. **88**
Reserve 1988: Supple and balanced, with smooth currant and spice flavors. **83**

CHARDONNAY NAPA VALLEY (★★), RESERVE (★★): Variable too, but with fewer stylistic swings, it is generally solid.
1992: Crisp, spicy and fruity, a simple wine with nice peach, pear, honey and vanilla aromas and flavors, all in a lean package. **85**
1991: Smooth and spicy, with a nice beam of apple and pear flavors that carry through to the finish. **86**
Reserve 1991: Soft and generous, a ripe wine with appealing pear and spice flavors. **82**

JOHANNISBERG RIESLING NAPA VALLEY (★★): Soft and fruity, with appealing apple and floral notes.
1994: Fresh, fruity and appealing, lightly sweet and loaded with peach, nectarine and floral flavors. Drink it young. **86**
1991: Soft and fruity, with fresh, appealing apple and floral aromas and flavors that turn slightly spicy on the finish. **84**

PINOT NOIR NAPA VALLEY (NR):
1991: Ripe and oaky smelling, turning tight and astringent on the palate. The fruit is tempting, but the balance is off. **77**

HAHN ESTATES
Monterey County
F: 1988. **O:** Smith and Hook. **W:** Art Nathan. **S:** None.

OVERALL	$10	★★

WINE RATINGS

Cabernet Sauvignon Santa Lucia Highlands	★★
Chardonnay Monterey County	★★
Merlot Monterey County	★★

This brand is owned by Smith and Hook. The Cabernets demonstrate the woes of cool-climate Cabernet, as they are often marked by Monterey's herb and vegetal notes and gritty tannins. The Chardonnay, Monterey-grown too, is a shade more appealing, with apple and pear flavors. The Merlot fits in between the two, as it is well oaked but also well mannered.

TASTING NOTES

CABERNET SAUVIGNON SANTA LUCIA HIGHLANDS (★★): Leans too heavily on herbaceous flavors.

1992: Austere with firm tannins and a rustic, cedary edge to the cherry and plum-laced Cabernet fruit. **83**

1991: A herbaceous wine with modest fruit and gritty tannins. **80**

1990: Simple and correct, with herb, wood and currant notes that turn tannic and spicy on the finish. A good value. **80**

1989: Thick, tough and coarse, lacking in charm, with earthy flavors. **73**

1988: Ripe, dense and vegetal, with a wall of tannin surrounding the currant and berry aromas and flavors. Not a style that will appeal to everyone, but within bounds for Monterey Cabernet. **80**

CHARDONNAY MONTEREY COUNTY (★★): Well oaked, but with pretty fruit flavors too.

1993: Youthful and fruity, with ripe pear and apple notes that turn spicy. **85**

1992: Ripe, spicy and generous, a nicely polished, smooth-textured wine with layers of pineapple, pear and honey flavors. **89**

MERLOT MONTEREY COUNTY (★★): Also well oaked, but with a solid core of fruit flavors.

1992: Chewy, tannic and hard, with modest currant flavors. **81**

1991: An oaky wine with buttery, toasty flavors dominating, but the spicy cherry and herb notes stand up to the wood. **84**

1990: Concentrated and full-bodied, with dense black cherry and herb flavors framed by rough oak. **83**

1989: Tight and firm, with a rich, smooth core of currant and cherry flavors and firm tannins and oak on the finish. **86**

HALLCREST VINEYARDS
Santa Cruz Mountains
F: 1964. **O:** John, Lorraine & Shirin Schumacher. **W:** John Schumacher. **S:** Organic Wine Works.

OVERALL	$10-19	★★

WINE RATINGS

Barbera El Dorado County	
Ritchie Vineyard	NR
Cabernet Sauvignon El Dorado County	
Covington Vineyard	★★
Cabernet Sauvignon El Dorado County	
De Cascabel Vineyard	
Proprietors Reserve	★★
Cabernet Sauvignon Santa Cruz	
Mountains Beauregard Ranch	
Proprietors Reserve	★★
Chardonnay California Fortuyn Cuvée	NR
Chardonnay Santa Cruz Mountains	
Meyley Vineyard	NR
Merlot El Dorado County	
De Cascabel Vineyard	★★
Merlot El Dorado County	
De Cascabel Vineyard	
Proprietors Reserve	★★
Zinfandel California	
Doe Mill Vineyard	★★
Organic Wine Works	
Chardonnay Mendocino County	
Redwood Valley Vineyards	NR
Organic Wine Works	
Fumé Blanc Napa Valley	NR
Organic Wine Works	
Merlot Butte County	NR
Organic Wine Works	
Pinot Noir Mendocino County	NR
Organic Wine Works Red Table	
Wine California A Notre Terre	NR
Organic Wine Works	
Sémillon Napa Valley	NR
Organic Wine Works	
Zinfandel Napa County	★★

WINERY DATA
C: 14,000. **V:** 5 acres in Santa Cruz Mountains. **G:** Riesling. **P:** Sauvignon Blanc, Sémillon, Merlot, Zinfandel (Napa Valley), Chardonnay, Pinot Noir, Gewürztraminer (Mendocino County), Chardonnay, Cabernet Sauvignon (Santa Cruz Mountains), Barbera, Cabernet Sauvignon, Merlot (El Dorado).

Chaffee Hall founded the original Hallcrest Vineyards in the 1940s, establishing a sound reputation for long-lived, estate-bottled Cabernet. The winery closed in 1969 and the grapes were sold to Concannon. In 1976 the winery reopened under the name Felton Empire, which produced Cabernet and Riesling before expanding operations. By the late 1980s the winery had run into financial trouble and was sold to the Schumacher family, which had made wine under the Davis Wine Cellars and Schumacher Cellars labels. John Schumacher received permission to use the Hallcrest Vineyards label, thus keeping it alive. Today the 14,000-case lineup includes Barbera from El Dorado County, Cabernet from El Dorado and Santa Cruz, Chardonnay from several appellations, Merlot and Zinfandel, along with a line of organic wines bottled under the Organic Wine Works label. Like most organic wines, they are funky and because they are made without sulfites, should be consumed early on.

TASTING NOTES

BARBERA EL DORADO COUNTY RITCHIE VINEYARD (NR):
1990: Crisp and very tart, bursting with raspberry, strawberry and black cherry aromas and flavors. **80**

CABERNET SAUVIGNON VARIOUS BOTTLINGS (★★):
El Dorado County Covington Vineyard 1990: Ripe and vibrant, with rich, spicy black cherry, currant and earth notes. Firmly tannic. **86**
El Dorado County De Cascabel Vineyard Proprietors Reserve 1990: Distinctive for its ripe berry and cherry flavors, it is firm and compact, with ample tannins. **85**
Santa Cruz Mountains Beauregard Ranch Proprietors Reserve 1990: A rustic wine with an earthy streak to the cherry and raspberry flavors. **84**

CHARDONNAY VARIOUS BOTTLINGS (NR):
California Fortuyn Cuvée 1991: Earthy and bordering on sour, this is a funky wine that misses the mark. **72**
Santa Cruz Mountains Meyley Vineyard 1991: Takes a walk on the wild side, with firm, compact and exotic—almost funky—caramel, pineapple, pear and earth flavors. **77**

MERLOT EL DORADO COUNTY DE CASCABEL VINEYARD (★★), PROPRIETORS RESERVE (★★):
1991: Firm and fruity, showing a band of focused plum, blackberry and spice flavors. **83**
Proprietors Reserve 1991: Firm and compact, but with pretty plum and currant flavors that peek through and linger on a long, full finish. Firmly tannic. **87**

ZINFANDEL CALIFORNIA DOE MILL VINEYARD (★★):
1990: Ripe and lively, with generous blackberry and spice aromas and flavors that fade on the finish. **83**

ORGANIC WINE WORKS VARIOUS BOTTLINGS:
Chardonnay Mendocino County Redwood Valley Vineyards 1992: Fresh apple and pear aromas and buttery apple-cider flavors make this wine unusual but palatable. A candied streak runs through it, too. It's a controversial style. **77**
Fumé Blanc Napa Valley 1992: Strongly buttery, with an overwhelmingly butterscotch character that flattens the fruit flavors. Thick, candied flavors make it heavy on the finish. **71**
Merlot Butte County 1992: Spicy, strongly herbal tobacco aromas and flavors hint a bit at berries on the finish in this medium-weight Merlot. Not for everyone. **80**
Pinot Noir Mendocino County 1992: Light, with hints of tea and strawberry flavors and a tart-sweet balance that ends up watery. Simple. **73**
Red Table Wine California A Notre Terre 1992: Youthful, colorful and flavorful, with the sort of floral, peppery berry flavors typical of Rhône reds. Finishes jammy and fresh, but has a smoky, almost ashy edge. **79**
Red Table Wine California A Notre Terre 1991: A vivid purple rim to the color and bright plum flavors make this a fresh, youthful wine to drink soon, while it retains its charm. Equivalent to a good Beaujolais. **83**
Sémillon Napa Valley 1992: This bizarre wine smells and tastes more like grappa, but turns flat and soft on the palate. **67**
Zinfandel California 1991: Youthful and exuberant, with nicely modulated blackberry and vanilla aromas and flavors that persist on the plump, generous finish. **86**
Zinfandel Napa County 1992: Extremely ripe and young, with vivid raisin, blackberry and prune flavors that are sweet and grapey. Unusual but tasty, like supercharged grape juice. **80**

HANDLEY CELLARS
Anderson Valley
F: 1982. O: Milla & Raymond Handley, Rex McClellan. W: Milla Handley. S: None.

OVERALL   **$8-18**   ★★

WINE RATINGS

Chardonnay Anderson Valley ★★
Chardonnay Dry Creek Valley ★★
Pinot Noir Anderson Valley ★★
Sauvignon Blanc Dry Creek Valley ★★

WINERY DATA

C: 14,000. V: 45 acres in Anderson Valley and Dry Creek Valley. G: Pinot Noir (10 acres), Chardonnay (26), Sauvignon Blanc (9). P: Gewürztraminer, Riesling (Anderson Valley).

Milla Handley worked at Chateau St. Jean and Edmeades before starting Handley Cellars in 1982, focusing on Chardonnay (Anderson and Dry Creek bottlings), Gewürztraminer, Pinot Noir and Sauvignon Blanc, largely from the winery's 45 acres of vines. These wines share a house style that is simple, fruity and easy to drink. Handley also produces a line of sparkling wines that are worth seeking out.

TASTING NOTES

CHARDONNAY ANDERSON VALLEY (★★): Simple, light and fruity.
1992: Crisp and elegant, with ripe apple and citrus notes, finishing with a grapefruit edge. **83**
1991: Lightly fruity, with simple spice and pear flavors. **80**

CHARDONNAY DRY CREEK VALLEY (★★):
1992: Tart, with crisp grapefruit, citrus and spicy pear notes on the finish. **84**

PINOT NOIR ANDERSON VALLEY (★★): Light and fruity, on the delicate side.
1992: Laced with herb, cola and cherry flavors, this medium-bodied wine has an alluring, supple texture. **84**
1991: Light and flavorful, offering appealing currant and spice aromas and flavors on a delicate frame. **84**

SAUVIGNON BLANC DRY CREEK VALLEY (★★): Shows pleasant citrus and pear notes.
1993: Ripe and spicy, nicely focused pear, spice and a touch of herb, a beautifully balanced style that centers around fruit. **87**
1992: Soft, fruity and pleasant, and its slightly citrusy overtones add a nice extra touch. **85**

HANNA WINERY
Sonoma County
F: 1985. O: Elias S. Hanna. W: Douglas Wilson, Merry Edwards. S: None.

| OVERALL | $10-16 | ★★ |

WINE RATINGS

Cabernet Sauvignon Alexander Valley ★★★
Chardonnay Russian River Valley
  Reserve ★★
Chardonnay Sonoma County ★★
Merlot Alexander Valley ★★
Pinot Noir Russian River Valley NR
Sauvignon Blanc Sonoma County ★★★

WINERY DATA

C: 22,000. V: 267 acres in Sonoma County. G: Malbec (1 acre), Petite Verdot (1), Zinfandel (5), Sangiovese (6), Nebbiolo (7), Pinot Noir (10), Syrah (10). P: None.

Elias Hanna, a heart surgeon, has substantial vineyard holdings, with 265 acres in vines spread throughout Alexander Valley (82 acres), Russian River (80) and Sonoma Valley (105). He produces Cabernet, Chardonnay, Merlot and Sauvignon Blanc, and a Russian River Pinot Noir joined the lineup in 1992. The 22,000-case winery is located west of Santa Rosa and so far the wines have been above average, with Cabernet and Chardonnay the quality leaders.

TASTING NOTES

CABERNET SAUVIGNON ALEXANDER VALLEY (★★★): Has carried both the Alexander Valley and broader Sonoma County appellations. It's intensely fruity, with appealing cherry and currant flavors of moderate depth.
1991: Ripe and firmly tannic, with a tight core of black cherry and cedary oak flavors. **85**
1990: Soft and supple, with underlying, intense currant and blackberry flavors. **87**
1988: Firm in texture, with nice black cherry and currant flavors running through it, shaded by tar and toast notes. **86**
1987: Ripe, rich currant notes blend with a touch of austere tannin and plenty of smoky, toasty oak flavors. It's balanced, but the flavors lack harmony and finesse. Perhaps with time it will be more graceful. **80**

1986: Deeply colored and impressive, with tart plum and cherry flavors, a touch of vanilla from oak aging and firm but not harsh tannins. **87**

1985: Mature, with hints of cassis, blackberry and blueberry flavors and tannins that are firm but softening. **86**

CHARDONNAY VARIOUS BOTTLINGS (★★): Medium-weight and well balanced, with spicy, toasty oak shadings.

Russian River Valley Reserve 1992: Supple and fruity, with a spicy, toasty edge to the ripe pear and creamy vanilla flavors. **85**

Sonoma County 1991: Smooth, ripe and creamy, with spicy pear, nectarine and vanilla flavors. A good wine that lacks the extra dimension to be great. **86**

MERLOT ALEXANDER VALLEY (★★): Tends to be crisp and a touch green, with herb and currant flavors.

1991: Hard and a bit green, a lean, austere, modestly fruity wine with hints of plum and herb. **82**

1990: Crisp and focused, with cherry, plum and bell pepper flavors that are firm and well proportioned. **85**

PINOT NOIR RUSSIAN RIVER VALLEY (NR):

1992: Smooth, polished and noticeably oaky. The elegant cherry and raspberry aromas and flavors make it appealing. **85**

SAUVIGNON BLANC SONOMA COUNTY (★★★): Crisp, with a citrus edge to the spicy oak flavors.

1993: Crisp and lemony, a spicy wine with a polished texture and a finish that's light but persistent. **85**

HANZELL VINEYARDS
Sonoma Valley
F: 1957. **O:** Hanzell Vineyards. **W:** Robert Sessions. **S:** None.

OVERALL	$20-25	★★★★

WINE RATINGS

Cabernet Sauvignon	
Sonoma Valley	★★
Chardonnay Sonoma Valley	★★★★★
Pinot Noir Sonoma Valley	★★★

WINERY DATA
C: 3,000. **V:** 33 acres in Sonoma Valley. **G:** Chardonnay (17 acres), Pinot Noir (16). **P:** None.

Drinking great Burgundies like Montrachet and Romanée-Conti inspired James D. Zellerbach to build Hanzell Vineyards on a hill that overlooks the city of Sonoma. Zellerbach honed his appreciation for fine wine while serving as U.S. ambassador to Italy. A wealthy member of the family that owned the paper products firm Crown Zellerbach Corp., he decided to duplicate Burgundian winemaking techniques with hopes of making California-style red and white "Burgundies." Zellerbach spared no expense to build this tiny jewel of a winery, a miniature replica of the famous Clos de Vougeot in Burgundy. In 1952 he began planting his vineyard, followed four years later by the winery, named after himself and his wife, Hanna, combining her first name with his last.

The first Chardonnay vintage in 1956 produced enough wine to fill one large bottle. There followed a 30-year-plus string of superb Chardonnays, which were among the first (if not the first) in California to age in new French oak barrels. Later came equally attractive and compelling Pinot Noirs; Brad Webb, a highly respected winemaker, oversaw production, utilizing advanced techniques such as temperature-controlled stainless steel tanks for fermentation. This grand experiment ended rather abruptly when Zellerbach died in 1963 and his wife sold the winery. The entire inventory of wines was sold at auction, including two vintages of Chardonnay and one of Pinot Noir that were purchased by Heitz Wine Cellars in Napa Valley.

No wines were made in 1963 or 1964, but new owners Douglas and Mary Day resumed winemaking in 1965. In 1973 Robert Sessions became winemaker and general manager after working at Mayacamas, and in 1976 Barbara de Brye of Great Britain purchased Hanzell. Being a claret drinker, she had some 5 acres of Bordeaux grape varieties rooted in a separate vineyard, and from 1979 to 1992 Hanzell produced a Cabernet. Following de Brye's death in 1991, a decision was made to discontinue Cabernet and the vines were grafted over to Pinot Noir.

The success with Chardonnay and Pinot Noir secured Hanzell's reputation. The Chardonnay, though barrel-aged, is not made with strict Burgundian techniques despite Zellerbach's intentions; it is fermented in stainless steel and is not lees aged, nor does it undergo a full malolactic fermentation. Still, it has proved an unusually long-lived and distinctly complex Chardonnay, both by Californian and European standards. Pinot Noir has been more variable, as it almost always is, although the string of vintages from 1961 to 1981 reveals a number of truly remarkable wines with tremendous depth, complexity and aging capacity. Since 1982 the Pinot Noir has been in a slump, lacking focus and often marred by weedy, herbal flavors. Winemaker Sessions is at a loss to explain why the style shifted so dramatically, since no winemaking or vineyard practices changed, but by the end of the 1980s Hanzell Pinot Noir had lost most of its luster, sales were slow and the winery decided to rethink its style, aiming for riper fruit, lighter tannins and a little more toasty oak.

Cabernet never really blossomed the way de Brye hoped. While the vineyard seemed to be in a good location, the wines were unusually austere and tannic, with earthy herb and currant flavors. I have tasted the Cabernets on several occasions, and it appears Hanzell made the right decision dropping it and refocusing on what made it famous in the first place. Production is about 3,000 cases from 33 acres of vineyard.

Tasting Notes

Cabernet Sauvignon Sonoma Valley (★★): Austere and marked by earthy tannins, with herb and currant flavors. Very consistent over the years, although it never lived up to expectations. Discontinued in 1992.

1990: A racy wine with weedy bell pepper, olive and earth flavors. Firmly tannic. **83**

1989: The aromas are mildly interesting, but on the palate the flavors are lean and austere, with a narrow band of currant, cedar and spice. **82**

1988: A chewy wine with enough ripe currant flavor to balance the rough tannins. **82**

1987: Firmly tannic and tight, with a hard core of currant and earth notes. An unevolved wine that's closed and backward but quite concentrated. **84**

1986: Big, chewy and complex, with lots of ripe currant, plum and weedy herbal flavors and a wallop of tannins on the finish. **88**

Chardonnay Sonoma Valley (★★★★★): Tight and flinty early on, with citrus and pear notes, but remarkably concentrated and ageworthy, gaining depth and richness with time. Peaks after most Chardonnays have faded.

1991: Big, ripe and assertive, with ripe nectarine, pear and spice notes that stay focused on the finish. **91**

1990: Broad, ripe, lively and intensely fruity, with rich, concentrated pear, pineapple and citrus notes that are sharply focused. **89**

1988: Fresh and aromatic, with tight pear, lemon, fig and melon flavors that are rich, elegant and very well balanced. **90**

1987: Has plenty of fresh, clean, ripe pear and citrus aromas and flavors that turn elegant and subtle on the finish. With fine fruit definition, it has more elegance than most Hanzells and good length on the finish. **89**

1986: Very ripe and forward, quite woody, with pretty pineapple, pear, apple and spice flavors of great intensity and depth. **87**

1985: Excellent balance, intensity and depth; may become a classic. It combines ripe, rich pineapple, pear, spice and citrus notes that show remarkable finesse and elegance, and there's a smoky aftertaste. **90**

1984: Very ripe and fruity, a forward wine that has good intensity and depth, with pear, honey and citrus notes that build on the finish. **84**

1983: Light and simple by Hanzell standards, with less flavor and intensity, but still well made. It has pretty pine, pear and pineapple flavors that are perhaps more elegant than most Hanzells. **84**

1982: Elegant and stylish, with pretty honey, lemon, pear and spice flavors and a wonderful balance of fruit and oak. More subtle than many Hanzells. **89**

1981: Forward and fruity, with fresh, lively lemon, pear and pineapple flavors and good intensity and depth. **86**

1980: Enormous depth and concentration, very ripe and rich, with fig, pear and honey flavors. Big and full-blown. **90**

1979: Elegant and spicy, with the pear and melon flavors beginning to dry out, becoming somewhat coarse. Still, there's plenty to like in this wine. **85**

1978: Incredibly rich, ripe, smooth and buttery, with intense fig, pear, spice and lemon flavors, finishing with lovely honey notes and a long, creamy aftertaste. **95**

Pinot Noir Sonoma Valley (★★★): Until the 1982 vintage, this was the most ageworthy Pinot Noir in

California, an amazingly complex, intricate and durable wine. Quality since has varied, with many wines marked by weedy, herbal and earthy flavors.

1991: Earthy with spicy stewed plum and anise flavors and firm, intense tannins. Best to cellar this until 1997 for it to soften a bit. **86**

1990: Rustic, with chunky, earthy plum and black cherry flavors that are in an awkward phase, but the core of complex tar and rose petal notes should be more compelling with time. **85**

1989: Light and fruity, with toasty strawberry, plum and currant flavors that are intense and lively. **88**

1988: Ripe and flavorful, with intense cherry, currant, plum and spice flavors that are full, rich and supple, intense and concentrated. Tannins are firm. **88**

1987: Charming in its own way, with fresh, ripe, intense and sharply focused strawberry, cherry and tarry anise notes. **87**

1986: Earthy and muddy flavors turn weedy and vegetal in one of the least satisfying Hanzells. **79**

1985: Austere, with a narrow band of anise, cherry and strawberry notes and good depth and intensity. **85**

1984: Austere and thin in flavor, but the tannins and dry oak flavors are substantial. **80**

1983: Light and simple, with spicy anise and cedar notes and coarse tannins. **83**

1982: Weedy and earthy, with chewy tannins. **77**

1981: Ripe and forward, with cherry and plum flavors that are bright and lively. **83**

1980: Earthy and herbal, with weedy currant and spice flavors that turn tarry. **84**

1979: Another stunning Hanzell, with bold, ripe, complex flavors that echo plum, raisin, currant and black cherry. Youthful and vibrant, with great length. **95**

1978: Ultraripe and raisiny, with roasted plum and currant flavors. A big, potent wine that's tight and lacking the extra complexity found in most Hanzells. **87**

1977: Elegant and intense, with currant and plum flavors. **87**

1976: Ripe and chewy, enormously concentrated, with chunky plum, prune and currant flavors. Tells the story of the vintage. **91**

1975: Supple and fruity, round and fleshy, with spicy plum, currant and tar notes. **92**

1974: Ultraripe and flavorful, not unlike the 1974 Cabernets. Tiers of black cherry, plum, currant, tar and anise flavors unfold into an elegant finish, where a touch of cedar and spice add extra complexity. **91**

1973: Smooth and elegant for Hanzell. This wine combines ripe, spicy cherry and plum aromas and flavors with a measure of elegance and finesse, finishing with firm, drying tannins that let the flavors pour through. **89**

1972: Ripe and vibrant, with deep, rich, intense plum, currant and cherry flavors that are lively and potent, finishing with a burst of spice. A powerful, amazing wine that's held its youthful personality. Could be the best wine of the entire '72 vintage. **93**

1971: Bold, ripe and intense, deeply concentrated and full of spicy plum, currant, anise and rose petal flavors, with firm, dry tannins and plenty of length. Showing a trace of oxidation on the finish, but this wine has the depth and richness to age on. **92**

1970: Fully mature and at a fine drinking stage. Less opulent and ripe than either 1968 or 1969, it is more refined, with delicate plum, anise and dried cherry notes. What's most striking is the long, smooth, elegant finish. **90**

1969: Firm and tight, with ripe plum and currant flavors that are reminiscent of the 1969 except on a smaller scale. Appealing in its austerity, with tar and rose petal notes that come through on the finish. **87**

1968: Ultraripe and raisiny, this comes from a famous vintage of ripe wines. While it's deep and concentrated and Port-like, the plum, currant and cherry flavors manage to retain their balance and appeal. A distinctive, long-lived, potent wine that's firmly tannic. **89**

1967: A hard, tight wine that shows more tannin and oak than most Hanzells this age. Despite its austerity there are nice cherry and currant aromas and flavors that stay with you. **86**

1966: Mature but holding, it has a soft texture and ripe, polished, earthy plum and cherry flavors framed by cedary oak. **87**

1965: In fantastic condition, much like the 1961. The fruit is ripe and sweet, with layers of plum, cherry, currant and vanilla flavors that are intense, focused and lively, finishing with a sweet plum, smoke and rose petal edge. **93**

Heitz Bottling 1962: Bottled under the Heitz Wine Cellars label. Tart, crisp and gamy, with volatile fruit flavors that are fading, picking up cedary notes on the finish. A wine that still shows decent fruit, but doesn't have the stellar quality of the 1961. Worth the experience, though. **78**

Heitz Bottling 1961: Bottled under the Heitz Wine Cellars label. In absolutely fantastic condition, ripe, rich, sweet and concentrated, with intense tar, plum, currant and cherry flavors that run deep and complex. Despite a good dose of alcohol, it's smooth and focused. The finish is long and wonderfully complex, with tiers of dried fruit flavors. **97**

HARBOR WINERY
West Sacramento, Sacramento County
F: 1972. **O:** Charles H. Myers. **W:** Charles H. Myers. **S:** None.

OVERALL	$8-15	★

WINE RATINGS

Merlot Napa Valley	
Narsai David Vineyard	NR

WINERY DATA
C: 1,000. **V:** None. **G:** None. **P:** Cabernet Sauvignon, Merlot (Napa Valley), Zinfandel, Mission (Amador County).

I've only tasted one wine from this small Sacramento-based winery, the 1991 Merlot Napa Valley Narsai David Vineyard, which was lean and earthy, with modest flavors.

TASTING NOTES

MERLOT NAPA VALLEY NARSAI DAVID VINEYARD (NR):
1991: Lean and earthy, a crisp wine with modest flavors. **78**

HARLAN ESTATE
Oakville, Napa Valley
F: 1992. **O:** William Harlan. **W:** Bob Levy, Michel Rolland. **S:** None.

OVERALL	$65	★★★★

WINE RATINGS

Cabernet Sauvignon Napa Valley	★★★★

WINERY DATA
C: 1,000. **V:** 25 acres in Oakville. **G:** Cabernet Sauvignon, Merlot. **P:** None.

William Harlan built a lucrative real estate development firm in San Francisco before turning his sights to winemaking in Napa Valley, where he is part owner of the Meadowood Resort and Merryvale Vineyards, both in St. Helena. For his own winery, he zeroed in on the Oakville area, where he now has a 25-acre hillside vineyard high above Martha's Vineyard planted primarily to Bordeaux varieties, led by Cabernet Sauvignon. He plans to add another eight acres of vines. In 1987, Harlan began making small lots of wine from his vineyard and it is now proving its worth with extraordinary Cabernet-based red wines; his first commercial release, the 1990 vintage, came on the market in 1995. Bordeaux enologist Michel Rolland (of Château Le Bon Pasteur and others) and Bob Levy, winemaker for Merryvale, oversee winemaking. Quality is very high with production expected to rise slowly from 1,000 cases in 1994 to 2,500 cases. Worth watching.

TASTING NOTES

CABERNET SAUVIGNON NAPA VALLEY (★★★★): Early indications are that these are stunning wines with uncommon richness, depth and complexity, plush, concentrated flavors and thick, polished tannins.
1992: Delicious, with ripe, rich, supple layers of toasty oak, cherry and currant. Well focused, with polished tannins that are long on the finish. **93**
1991: Intense and elegant, with a sharply focused core of currant, black cherry, cedar and spice, finishing with a long aftertaste. **92**
1990: Deep, rich, dark and harmonious, with bold, round, supple and complex tiers of black cherry, currant and plum flavors and with thick, plush tannins. **93**

HARMONY CELLARS
Paso Robles
F: 1989. **O:** Chuck Mulligan. **W:** Chuck Mulligan. **S:** None.

OVERALL	$6-13	★★

WINE RATINGS

Cabernet Sauvignon Paso Robles	★★
Chardonnay Paso Robles	★★
Pinot Noir Paso Robles	★★

WINERY DATA
C: N/A. **V:** None. **G:** None. **P:** Cabernet Sauvignon, Pinot Noir, Zinfandel, Chenin Blanc (Paso Robles), Chardonnay (Edna Valley), Chardonnay (Templeton).

This winery has released three wines, all Paso Robles-grown: Cabernet 1989 and 1990, Chardonnay 1992, and a most intriguing Pinot Noir 1990, which is marked by rich plum, blueberry and pepper flavors that give it a Syrah-like edge.

TASTING NOTES

CABERNET SAUVIGNON PASO ROBLES (★★):
1990: Mature, with earthy, cedary, tarry flavors that turn to tea and tobacco on the finish. **77**
1989: A fruity, firm, crisp, palate-cleansing Cabernet with pretty cherry and raspberry flavors that linger. **85**

CHARDONNAY PASO ROBLES (★★):
1992: An oaky wine with toasty butter and vanilla flavors and also nice pear and peach notes. **82**

PINOT NOIR PASO ROBLES (★★):
1990: A distinctive wine that has a Syrah-like edge, with flavors that center on plum, blueberry and black pepper and a definite spicy edge. **88**

HARRISON VINEYARDS
St. Helena, Napa Valley
F: 1988. **O:** Michael & Lyndsey Harrison. **W:** Lyndsey Harrison, Helen Turley. **S:** None.

OVERALL	$26-40	★★★

WINE RATINGS
Cabernet Sauvignon Napa Valley ★★★
Cabernet Sauvignon Napa Valley Reserve ★★★
Chardonnay Napa Valley ★★★

WINERY DATA
C: 1,800. **V:** 17 acres in Napa Valley. **G:** Chardonnay (7 acres), Cabernet Sauvignon (10). **P:** None.

Michael and Lyndsey Harrison bought an established 17-acre vineyard on Pritchard Hill along the eastern hills of Napa Valley in 1987, making their first wine, a Cabernet, two years later, followed by a Chardonnay, both estate-grown. Helen Turley (of Marcassin Winery) has been retained as a consultant. The early wines were solid, complex and rich in varietal fruit. Production hovers around 1,800 cases, divided more or less equally between the two wines.

TASTING NOTES

CABERNET SAUVIGNON NAPA VALLEY (★★★), RESERVE (★★★): Variable in quality. The 1989 and 1990 Reserves are rich and dark, but subsequent vintages are tighter and more austere.
1992: Smooth and elegant, with supple currant and spicy notes that finish with a cedary oak flavor. **88**
1991: A dark, tight, intense and tannic wine with sharply focused currant, plum and tart berry flavors. **86**
1990: Young, ripe and intense, with a tight, firm core of currant, cherry and spicy oak flavors. Raw and unevolved now, but shows intensity and depth. **87**
1989: Bold, dark, ripe and concentrated, with sharply focused currant, black cherry, plum and spice flavors that have just the right touch of tannin and oak. Intense and powerful. **91**
Reserve 1990: Ripe, rich, smooth and supple, with polished currant, oak and spice flavors. This full-bodied wine is compact and tightly wound, finishing with chewy tannins. **91**

CHARDONNAY NAPA VALLEY (★★★): Appealing for its ripe fruit and complex flavors.
1993: Smoky, cedary oak leads to a rich core of pear, spice and earthy flavors that are complex and concentrated. **90**
1992: Elegant, with ripe pear, hazelnut and spice flavors, picking up pretty, toasty oak flavors that turn creamy and smooth on the finish. **89**
1991: A ripe, smooth, buttery wine with hints of spice and pear that spread out on the palate. **88**

HART WINERY
Temecula
F: 1980. **O:** Travis & Nancy Hart. **W:** Travis Hart. **S:** None.

OVERALL	$7-20	★★

WINE RATINGS

Cabernet Sauvignon

Temecula Hansen Vineyard	NR
Merlot Temecula	NR
Sauvignon Blanc Temecula	NR

WINERY DATA

C: 3,800. **V:** 8 acres in Temecula. **G:** Syrah (2 acres), Viognier (2), Sauvignon Blanc (2), Sémillon (0.5), Cabernet Franc (1). **P:** Merlot, Cabernet Sauvignon (Temecula), Merlot (San Diego County), Grenache, Mourvèdre, Cinsault, Aleatico (San Bernardino).

Carlsbad school teachers Travis and Nancy Hart planted a vineyard in Temecula in the early 1970s and sold grapes before starting a winery in 1980. Their 3,800-case operation includes Cabernet, Chardonnay, Sauvignon Blanc (blended with Sémillon) and Merlot, and the winery is exploring Rhône-style wines as well, with Syrah and Viognier under production.

TASTING NOTES

VARIOUS BOTTLINGS:

Cabernet Sauvignon Temecula Hansen Vineyard 1989: Shows decent, up-front fruit flavors, with cherry and currant notes that fade on the finish. A pleasing, easy-to-drink wine. **82**

Merlot Temecula 1989: Full-bodied and flavorful, with plenty of raspberry and apple-skin flavors, tart acidity and moderate tannins. Overall, a simple, straightforward wine. **80**

HARTWELL VINEYARDS

Napa Valley

F: 1990. **O:** Bob Hartwell. **W:** Heidi Peterson Barrett. **S:** None.

OVERALL	**$55**	★★★★

WINE RATINGS

Cabernet Sauvignon Stags Leap District	★★★★

WINERY DATA

C: 200. **V:** 2 acres in Stags Leap District. **G:** Cabernet Sauvignon. **P:** None.

This is a 2-acre Cabernet Sauvignon vineyard in the Stags Leap District owned by Bob Hartwell that produces 200 cases a year. The wines are made at and marketed by Grace Family Vineyard in St. Helena. The debut wine, a 1991, is remarkably complex, but it's difficult to find. Phylloxera forced replanting in 1995.

TASTING NOTES

CABERNET SAUVIGNON STAGS LEAP DISTRICT (★★★★): 1991: Ripe, round, smooth and supple, this wine delivers a pretty core of currant, cedar and spice flavors, finishing with smooth tannins and toasty oak nuances. **92**

HAVENS WINE CELLARS

Napa Valley

F: 1984. **O:** Michael & Kathryn Havens, Jonathan Scott, S. Russell Lane. **W:** Michael Havens. **S:** Uptown Wine.

OVERALL	**$10-20**	★★★

WINE RATINGS

Merlot Carneros

Truchard Vineyard Reserve	★★★
Merlot Napa Valley	★★★

WINERY DATA

C: 6,500. **V:** 3 acres in Carneros. **G:** Sauvignon Blanc (3.5 acres). **P:** Merlot, Cabernet Franc (Napa Valley), Merlot, Syrah, Cabernet Franc (Carneros).

Michael Havens earned a doctorate in humanities and became a college professor before turning his hobby of home-winemaking into a full-time vocation. In 1983 Havens purchased a 3-acre parcel in Carneros next to Truchard Vineyard and bought grapes from Truchard for his Merlot. He later joined Truchard as winemaker when the Truchard family started its winery in 1989. In 1994 he left Truchard to focus on his own brand, which has grown to 6,500 cases, with Merlot (4,000 cases) the leader. A Reserve Merlot from Carneros, a Napa Valley Sauvignon Blanc and a Carneros Syrah are also part of the lineup.

TASTING NOTES

MERLOT CARNEROS TRUCHARD VINEYARD RESERVE (★★★): Similar to, though a shade richer than, the Napa Valley, but it has yet to establish a consistent style.

1990: Crisp, focused and smooth in texture, with vibrant currant, blackberry and spice aromas and flavors. Finishes with a burst of flavor and ample tannins. **88**

1989: Lean and tough, with a strong tannic backbone, cedary, earthy flavors and a hint of berry and currant. **82**

1988: The ripe, jammy, floral aromas don't follow through on the palate, where it's tight and biting, with hard-edged tannins. **76**

MERLOT NAPA VALLEY (★★★): Uneven early on but steadily improving. At its best it's rich, supple and complex.

1991: A delicate wine that's bright, supple and generous, offering ripe currant, blackberry and vanilla aromas and flavors. Finishes with polished tannins. **90**

1990: Tight, youthful and dense, with chewy currant, black cherry, herb and mineral flavors framed by toasty oak notes. **87**

1989: Ripe and balanced, with tight plum, oak, currant and spice flavors that stay with you. **84**

1988: Weedy, herbal aromas and flavors crowd out the modest streak of currant flavor in this lean, tannic wine. **82**

1987: Generous, supple and distinctive, with caramel, smoke, cherry and strawberry aromas and flavors. Firm without being harsh. **89**

1986: Unbearably woody and dry up front, overpowering the ripe currant and spice flavors. **72**

1985: Distinctively cedary and pungent on the nose, with firm, vivid flavors of black cherry, tobacco, tea and spice, finishing with firm tannins. **84**

HAWK CREST

This is a second label for Stag's Leap Wine Cellars (see listing).

HAYWOOD WINERY

Sonoma Valley
F: 1980. **O:** Racke USA. **W:** Dave Rosenthal, Peter Haywood. **S:** None.

OVERALL	$8-20	★★

WINE RATINGS

Cabernet Sauvignon	
California Vintner's Select	★★
Cabernet Sauvignon Sonoma Valley	
Los Chamizal Vineyard	★★
Chardonnay California Vintner's Select	★★
Zinfandel Sonoma Valley	★★★
Zinfandel Sonoma Valley	
Los Chamizal Vineyard	★★★
Zinfandel Sonoma Valley	
Rocky Terrace	★★★

WINERY DATA
C: 80,000. **V:** 90 acres in Sonoma Valley. **G:** Zinfandel (22 acres), Cabernet Sauvignon (20), Merlot (10), Chardonnay (33), Other (5). **P:** Chardonnay, Cabernet Sauvignon (California).

Former building contractor Peter Haywood planted a 90-acre vineyard in the hills above Sonoma in the late 1970s before starting his winery in 1980. Haywood's greatest success was with his mountain-grown Los Chamizal Vineyard Zinfandel, which proved among the best in Sonoma during the 1980s, with intense, spicy, peppery fruit flavors. Haywood's Riesling was also excellent early on. Cabernet, Chadonnay and Sauvignon Blanc were inconsistent, the former being intense yet highly tannic and the latter ranging from high in alcohol to austere and thin. By the late 1980s the winery was experiencing financial difficulties and Haywood sold the brand to Racke USA, owner of Buena Vista Winery, which shifted the brand's production to its Carneros winery; Haywood sold his winery facility to Ravenswood. Zinfandel from Los Chamizal remains the best wine, as the average-quality Cabernet and Chardonnay now carry a California appellation and Vintner's Select designations.

TASTING NOTES

CABERNET SAUVIGNON CALIFORNIA VINTNER'S SELECT (★★):
1991: Firm and intense, a compact, youthful wine with spice, currant and light oak shadings. **83**

CABERNET SAUVIGNON SONOMA VALLEY LOS CHAMIZAL VINEYARD (★★): Inconsistent and usually exceedingly tannic and austere.
1989: This crisp and narrow wine shows more earth and leather than fruit flavors at this stage, although a splash of currant sneaks through on the finish. **84**
1988: Tough and chewy, with hard-edged tannins, but it also has a tight core of herbal currant and black cherry flavors. **85**

1985: Good but simple for the vintage, with earthy currant flavors and dry tannins. **84**

1984: Lean, trim and tannic, with a tart beam of earthy currant flavors. Best after 1997, but will always be tannic. **83**

1983: Tannic to a fault; will never come around. **74**

1981: Mature, with complex, earthy currant, tar and spice flavors, but still very tannic. **85**

CHARDONNAY CALIFORNIA VINTNER'S SELECT (★★):
1993: Tastes off-dry, with a spicy, Riesling-like edge to the subtle pear and apple notes. **82**

1992: Serves up pleasant, spicy pear and cedary oak flavors that stay with you. **84**

ZINFANDEL SONOMA VALLEY (★★★):
1990: A crisp wine with earthy raspberry and cherry flavors and a peppery, spicy edge. **84**

1989: Tart and crisp, with earthy raspberry flavors that ring true for Zinfandel, but they finish without focus, turning murky. **85**

1988: Smooth, plush and velvety, this is a warm and generous wine with delicious ripe cherry and berry flavors and a nice dash of spice and pepper on the finish. **89**

1986: Offers early drinking allure like a cru Beaujolais. Has plenty of ripe, sweet raspberry flavor, firm acidity and modest tannins. Medium-bodied and smooth. **89**

1984: Rich and tasty, with high extract and layers of ripe raspberry, cassis and cherry flavors, a smooth, fleshy texture and firm but smooth tannins. Another terrific Zin from Haywood. They don't get much better than this. **92**

ZINFANDEL SONOMA VALLEY LOS CHAMIZAL VINEYARD (★★★): Impressive for its varietal integrity and its concentrated blackberry and pepper notes. Tannic, but ages well.

1991: Dry and tannic, with a tarry, smoky edge to the fruit flavors, which seem trapped in the austerity of the tannins. **85**

1990: Lean and spicy, with a narrow band of leathery flavors, but on the finish wild berry and cherry notes come through. **85**

1989: Spicy, earthy nuances add grace to the crisply focused, intense plum and berry flavors. **85**

1988: Lean in texture but concentrated in flavor, with firm raspberry and cherry flavors lasting well into the long finish. **86**

ZINFANDEL SONOMA VALLEY ROCKY TERRACE (★★★):
1992: An oaky wine that's woody and tannic, but spicy cherry, cedar and anise notes come through. **86**

HEITZ WINE CELLARS

St. Helena, Napa Valley
F: 1961. **O:** Heitz Wine Cellars. **W:** David Heitz. **S:** None.

OVERALL	$7-65	★★★

WINE RATINGS

Cabernet Sauvignon Napa Valley	★★★
Cabernet Sauvignon Napa Valley Bella Oaks Vineyard	★★★
Cabernet Sauvignon Napa Valley Martha's Vineyard	★★★★★
Cabernet Sauvignon Napa Valley Trailside Vineyard	★★★
Chardonnay Napa Valley	★★
Zinfandel Napa Valley Heitz Vineyard	★

WINERY DATA

C: 40,000. **V:** 292 acres in Napa Valley, Howell Mountain, Rutherford. **G:** Cabernet Sauvignon (196 acres), Chardonnay (34), Zinfandel (32), Grignolino (15), Merlot (12). **P:** Cabernet Sauvignon (Napa Valley).

Joe Heitz will be best remembered for his minty, currant-laced Martha's Vineyard Cabernet Sauvignons, which helped catapult Napa Valley wines to international fame. But that's just part of the story. Heitz moved to Napa Valley in the 1950s with his wife, Alice, after graduating from Fresno State College, and worked in the wine lab at Beaulieu Vineyard with André Tchelistcheff for several years. In 1961 he and Alice bought a small winery on Highway 29 (now the Heitz tasting room) and began buying bulk wines, blending them and selling them under the Heitz Wine Cellars label. Heitz had a hand in many of the wines being crafted in Napa in that era, including Stony Hill's; he had a close relationship with Fred and Eleanor McCrea, Stony Hill's owners. He was friends with wine connoisseur Barney Rhodes, one of the investors who helped finance Heitz Cellars early on by buying two vintages of Hanzell Chardonnay and Pinot Noir at auction, which Heitz bottled and sold under his label to wide critical acclaim. More significantly, Rhodes and his wife, Belle, planted the first 12 acres of what became the 34-acre Martha's Vineyard after Tom and Martha May bought it in 1964. In 1965 Heitz made his first Cabernet and a year later agreed to buy the Mays' Martha's Vineyard Cabernet. It proved so distinctive that Heitz decided to bottle it separately. The Mays too became partners in the Heitz business, along with wine writer/author Bob Thompson, author of *The Wine Atlas of California*.

Heitz has shown a deft hand with winemaking, making complex and ageworthy Chardonnays and Zinfandels and a rich, sweet dessert wine called Angelica, made from Mission grapes. He has also made a fine Grignolino Rosé and Johannisberg Riesling, along with a Pinot Noir that varied in quality. The Martha's Vineyard Cabernet emerged as the star, with its distinctive minty currant and blackberry flavors, dark color and great intensity and depth. From the first bottling in 1966 through the 1990 vintage, it has been among California's leading Cabernets, proving time and again that it's among the most ageworthy. Heitz's success with Cabernet led to other vineyard-designated wines, the main one being the Rhodes' Bella Oaks Vineyard in Rutherford. Heitz also made 1977 and 1978 bottlings from Fay Vineyard in the Stags Leap District, which is now owned by Stag's Leap Wine Cellars. More recently Heitz has produced a Cabernet from the 100-acre Trailside Vineyard (formerly Shown & Sons) near Conn Creek Winery on the Silverado Trail, which the Heitz family purchased in 1984, adding a portion of Wildwood Vineyard in 1986.

In the mid-1980s, Heitz's Cabernets came under fire from some critics who found a musty or bacterial flaw in the wines. I've tasted a mustiness in the Bella Oaks bottling, particularly the 1984 vintage, and have encountered bottle variation with the Napa Valley and Martha's Vineyard bottlings too, but not to the same degree as the Bella Oaks. It's unclear what may have caused the musty or bacterial edge, and critics are sharply divided on the topic. It may be a matter of faulty corks or bad barrels, or a combination of both. It may also be a matter of stylistic preference. Heitz's style is far from mainstream. The Heitz Cabernets are all 100 percent Cabernet, spend a long time in oak (42 months) and another full year in bottle before release. Most producers today sell their wines soon after they're bottled. Thus the Heitz Cabernets always taste more mature on release, as they should, especially when compared with the current Cabernet style of ripe, plush, rich and supple fruit flavors framed by toasty, buttery, spicy oak. Similarly, the Heitz Chardonnays are not lees aged, barrel fermented or put through malolactic fermentations. In that context, the full Heitz wine lineup—particularly the Chardonnay, Pinot Noir and Zinfandel—are well out of step with their Napa peers and often stand out for their rustic features. In any case, Cabernet remains the star, Heitz's favorite wine and the grape that grows best in Napa Valley. The winery, with Heitz's eldest son, David, as winemaker, produces some 40,000 cases of wine, nearly half of that Cabernet. Martha's Vineyard production is 4,000 cases, while Bella Oaks is about 3,000.

The Heitzes do understand the importance of controlling their grape sources. The family has steadily been adding vineyard property and now owns 292 acres of vineyard, 196 of that being Cabernet followed by Chardonnay (34), Zinfandel (32), Grignolino (15) and Merlot (12), which may find its way into the Heitz Cabernets of the future. The winery bought 576 acres on a parcel that straddles Pope Valley and Howell Mountain, with 160 acres in vines.

TASTING NOTES

CABERNET SAUVIGNON NAPA VALLEY (★★★): More rustic these days, but usually solid, marked by cedary currant and spice notes, often benefitting from small doses of Martha's, Bella's and Trailside grapes. Bottlings from the 1960s and 1970s were often superb.

1990: Strikes a nice balance between spicy, cedary oak and ripe cherry and currant flavors, turning smooth and supple on the finish. Has good intensity and depth. **90**

1989: Supple and elegant, with spicy cedar, mint and currant notes that are smooth and polished. **88**

1988: Ripe and smooth, with generous chocolate and spice overtones to the plum, prune and currant aromas and flavors. **88**

1987: Distinctive, earthy and generous, with a strong beam of mint, spice and currant aromas and flavors. Has subtlety and intensity, but also a streak of earthiness. **90**

1986: A bit funky on the nose, with pungent earth and cedar notes, but the cedary spice and fruit flavors make it better on the palate. **85**

1985: An herbal, earthy wine with a velvety texture and generous flavors. Broad and flavorful, with more cedar and brown sugar than fruit. **80**

1984: Earthy, tarry aromas and flavors intrude on the soft, supple texture and good concentration of cedar and ripe cherry flavors at the core. **86**

1983: Leans toward the minty spectrum of Cabernet, it's medium-bodied, with faint hints of cherry, cedar and spice. Turns woody on the finish. **80**

CABERNET SAUVIGNON NAPA VALLEY BELLA OAKS VINEYARD (★★★): Has never lived up to the Martha's, but is usually very good in a lighter and less distinctive style, with moderate fruit concentration but no real signature.

1990: Solid but unexciting, with a chewy core of currant, mint and spice, turning austere and tannic on the finish. **85**

1989: Displays elegant cedar, currant and cherry aromas and flavors, but it loses its intensity on the finish, where the flavors turn diffuse. **84**

1988: Firm in texture, with a decidedly earthy edge and hints of mustiness, but it offers focused, herb-scented prune and black cherry flavors. **81**

1987: Distinctive in its earthy style, with the fruit showing through the cedar, wet wood and tobacco flavors that dominate this medium-weight wine. **81**

1986: Big and assertive, with intense, concentrated herb, cherry, currant and plum flavors that are firmly tannic and long on the finish. **89**

1985: Complex, with bright, vivid black cherry, spice and mint notes, firm yet elegant, with a long, clean, crisp finish that echoes cherry and cedar. **88**

1984: Serious bottle variation, with many earthy, musty bottles. **74**

1983: A toasty wine with chocolate, currant and black cherry flavors that are rich and concentrated. **86**

1982: Subtle, with tight, mature cedar, plum and currant flavors. **85**

1981: Very elegant and refined, typical of the vintage, displaying ripe cherry, plum and cranberry flavors and a cedary richness. **85**

1980: Mature now, with earthy currant and oak flavors. **87**

1978: Ripe, with mature plum, cherry and spice flavors that are fleshy. **89**

1977: With beautiful aromas and complex flavors, the 1977 has been drinking well for several years and is fully mature now. The rich, ripe black cherry, cranberry and spicy cedar nuances are supple and elegant. **91**

1976: Past its prime but holding, with mature Cabernet flavors. **81**

CABERNET SAUVIGNON NAPA VALLEY MARTHA'S VINEYARD (★★★★★): From 1966 to 1980, the star of Napa Valley Cabernets, with its signature deep color and rich, minty chocolate, currant and blackberry flavors. The wines of the 1980s have been good but variable, as the style has gotten more rustic.

1990: Marked by mint and currant with a cedary oak edge, turning smooth and supple with good depth and intensity before finishing with firm tannins. **90**

1989: Dark, rich and intensely flavored, this is a youthful and tightly wound Martha's that's opening up, with spicy mint, cherry and currant flavors that turn supple and generous on the finish. **90**

1988: A successful 1988 that combines the classic Martha's cedar and mint notes with supple currant and spice flavors. Balanced and ready to drink now, but there are enough tannins to cellar. **87**

1987: Deep, dense and dark, a powerful wine, with distinctive currant, mint and eucalyptus flavors, turning gamy and chocolaty on the finish. **91**

1986: Dense and chewy, with firm tannins and an earthy core of currant, mint and cedar flavors. A bit funky; best after 1996. **90**

1985: Incredibly rich, elegant and complex, with tiers of currant, black cherry, spice and mint flavors that are deep and concentrated. **94**

1984: Beautifully defined and richly concentrated, with deep, complex, vibrant black cherry, currant, cedar and creamy vanilla flavors that are impeccably balanced. **92**

1983: Supple for the vintage, with chocolate, currant and plum flavors that pick up firm, hard tannins on the finish. **88**

1982: Powerful and concentrated, yet with rounded edges that display depth and finesse. A beautifully crafted wine with lots of mint and currant flavors. **90**

1981: Deep and intense, with a rich concentration of ripe currant, plum and cherry flavors with cedar and mint notes. Has great harmony, balance and finesse. **89**

1980: Very forward and flavorful, with ripe, generous, bright cherry, plum, anise and cedar nuances that are beautifully focused and very long on the finish. **91**

1979: A rich, bold, dramatic Martha's, intense yet elegant and supple, with round, smooth tannins and a long, gorgeous aftertaste that echoes the mint, fruit and floral notes. **93**

1978: Supple and elegant, with rich, intense, complex cedar, coffee, currant and plum flavors and fine tannins. **91**

1977: Mature, with generous ripe cherry, plum and currant flavors, a nice overlay of peppery, cedary oak and fine balance and length. **90**

1976: Mature, with ripe but drying plum and currant flavors and a good dose of tannin. **85**

1975: Mature but intense, with complex cedar, chocolate and cherry flavors that are softening. **92**

1974: Now at its best, this classic offers extraordinary richness, depth and complexity, with deep currant, mint, spice and cassis flavors. **97**

1973: Impressive for its rich core of cedar, chocolate and currant flavors and smooth, supple texture. Mature. **92**

1972: A weak vintage with modest, drying flavors. **75**

1970: Mature but aging magnificently, with tiers of complex currant, mint, anise and cedar flavors. Deep and complex, rich and concentrated. **97**

1969: Elegant, with great intensity and depth and the characteristic Martha's mintiness that complements the rich currant and cherry flavors. Great length on the finish. **95**

1968: A big, deep, extremely rich and concentrated wine, packed with complex, ripe currant, cedar and spice flavors that are fully mature, with great persistence and depth of flavor on the finish. A stunning wine. **99**

1967: Holding up; it's a bit earthy, with bright cherry, cedar and spice flavors that are lively on the finish. **86**

1966: Still a marvelous wine, with complex currant, earth, mint and cherry flavors and a delicate touch of cedar and cinnamon on the finish. Perfectly balanced. **92**

CABERNET SAUVIGNON NAPA VALLEY TRAILSIDE VINEYARD (★★★): This property, on rich soils near Caymus, should serve Heitz well. It's great Cabernet country.

1989: Intense and lively, rich and supple, with tiers of spicy currant, black cherry, vanilla and toasty oak flavors. A wonderful sense of harmony and finesse. **89**

CHARDONNAY NAPA VALLEY (★★): Well off the pace these days, often with tired, earthy, overly mature flavors.

1993: Lacks focus, with a modest range of earthy pear and oak notes. **78**

ZINFANDEL NAPA VALLEY HEITZ VINEYARD (★): Tired, earthy and lacking the bright, rich, vibrant flavors found in the best.

1989: A pungent, weedy, musty wine that turns earthy and sour on the finish. Another example of how poorly many 1989s fared. **67**

1988: Vanilla and maple flavors from oak aging give this earthy, almost musty Zinfandel a smooth, polished veneer. **78**

THE HESS COLLECTION WINERY
Mount Veeder, Napa Valley
F: 1986. **O:** The Hess Collection Winery. **W:** Randle Johnson. **S:** Hess Select.

OVERALL	$10-38	★★★★

WINE RATINGS

Cabernet Sauvignon Mount Veeder	★★★★★
Cabernet Sauvignon Mount Veeder Reserve	★★★★★
Chardonnay Mount Veeder	★★★
Chardonnay Napa Valley	★★★
Merlot Napa Valley	★★★
Hess Select Cabernet Sauvignon California	★★
Hess Select Chardonnay California	★★
Hess Select Pinot Noir California	★★
Hess Select Pinot Noir Santa Maria Valley Bien Nacido Vineyard	★★

WINERY DATA
C: 125,000. **V:** 695 acres in Mount Veeder, Napa Valley and Monterey County. **G:** Cabernet Sauvignon (166 acres), Chardonnay (61), Merlot (26), Cabernet Franc (6). **P:** None.

Swiss entrepreneur Donald Hess came to California in 1978 searching for new springs to expand Valser, his mineral water company. He immediately took a liking to Napa Valley wines and decided to start a winery. Being Swiss, he liked the mountains, and bought more than 500 acres of land on Mount Veeder, including several hundred already planted to vines by William Hill. Hess has since expanded his plantings to cover some 259 acres, although phylloxera has forced him to replant large sections of the vineyard. Cabernet (at 166 acres), Chardonnay (at 61 acres) and Merlot (with 26 acres) dominate.

When the Christian Brothers abandoned their Mont La Salle Winery on Mount Veeder, Hess signed a 50-year lease and began an extensive remodelling that resulted in not only a modernized, high-tech, tourist-friendly winery, but also a museum to house Hess's magnificent modern art collection (hence the winery's double-entendre name). While the initial focus was on Mount Veeder estate-grown Cabernet and Chardonnay, Merlot has since been added, along with a second line of California-appellation wines (Cabernet, Chardonnay and Pinot Noir), called Hess Select, from grapes grown primarily in Monterey on a 350-acre property owned by Hess. Total production by 1995 was approaching 125,000 cases, led by 50,000 cases of Hess Select Chardonnay and 25,000 cases of Hess Select Cabernet. The Mount Veeder wines comprise some 25,000 cases, with 12,000 cases of Cabernet and 14,000 of Chardonnay. Winemaker Randle Johnson has fine-tuned the style to capture the depth and intensity of Mount Veeder-grown grapes, balancing it well with oak and a sense of elegance.

TASTING NOTES

CABERNET SAUVIGNON MOUNT VEEDER (★★★★★), RESERVE (★★★★★): Dark, intense and concentrated, capable of uncommon depth and complexities while keeping the tannins under control. A reserve in 250-case lots appears in special years and is a shade bolder and oakier. So far they age very well.

1991: There's a wonderful sense of harmony and finesse, with ripe, concentrated currant, plum and black cherry flavors and spicy oak notes that add complexity. **92**

1990: Firm and compact, with a tight band of chunky currant, plum, spice and oak flavors that need short-term cellaring to soften and evolve. **90**

1989: Lean, green and herbal, with tough, chewy tannins that override the plum and cherry flavors. **82**

1988: Ripe and smooth, with complex currant and plum flavors that are broad and generous. Layers of prune and anise notes add complexity to the finish. **88**

1987: Strikes a pleasant balance between the opulent, ripe, rich currant and black cherry flavors and the herb and lavish oak notes. Deep, plush and concentrated. **94**

1986: Intense, rich, smooth and elegant, with layers of well defined black cherry, currant and toasty oak flavors that are beautifully integrated. **91**

1985: A terrific wine, lavishly oaked, rich, smooth, supple and concentrated, with great depth and intensity and delicious black cherry, cedar, vanilla and anise flavors. **92**

1983: Still lean and austere, offering ripe cherry, currant and cedar flavors of moderate depth and intensity. **84**

Reserve 1990: Bold, rich and intensely concentrated, with compact, tannic fruit flavors. On the finish the spicy black cherry, currant and mineral notes are focused and complex. **90**

Reserve 1989: An oaky wine, but the currant, wild berry and black cherry flavors are now coming to the front, giving it a greater sense of proportion and depth. Complex and concentrated. **89**

Reserve 1987: Massively flavorful, with chewy tannins and a rich core of currant, plum, blackberry and cedar aromas and flavors, echoing anise and spice on the finish. **96**

Reserve 1986: Remarkably rich, supple, deep and concentrated, with tiers of black cherry, currant and toasty French oak flavors. **93**

Reserve 1984: Still bold, ripe and complex, with currant, spice, anise and cherry flavors, straddling the line between youth and maturity, picking up cedar and coffee notes from age. **91**

Reserve 1983: Lean and austere, with tight tannins and sharply defined black cherry and currant flavors. **88**

CHARDONNAY VARIOUS BOTTLINGS (★★★): Starts out tight and lean but expands, revealing its intensity and depth of flavor. Worthy of short-term cellaring.

Mount Veeder 1991: Crisp, firm and elegant, tightly wound, with ripe, spicy pear, citrus and light oak shadings. **87**

Napa Valley 1993: Medium-bodied, with ripe pear and peach notes that pick up a light toasty oak shading. **84**

Napa Valley 1992: Starts out lean but the flavors build, with ripe pear, toast and spice notes. Gains richness and depth on the finish, where smoky oak comes into play. **89**

MERLOT NAPA VALLEY (★★★):
1989: Very attractive, with ripe plum and cherry flavors and a supple texture. **86**

Hess Select Cabernet Sauvignon California (★★): A good value. It can be bright and fruity with supple tannins, or a shade leaner and simpler.
1992: Ripe and fruity, with a pretty array of black cherry, plum, cedar and spice flavors, finishing with mild tannins, good length and a hint of mint. **87**
1991: Lean and crisp, with modest berry and tobacco aromas and flavors, but the finish is green and tight. **82**
1990: Soft and fragrant, with simple red cherry and plum aromas and flavors. **80**

Hess Select Chardonnay California (★★): Very well made in a ripe and fruity style.
1993: Firm and lively, with intense grapefruit, citrus and pear flavors that turn complex. **86**
1992: Simple and spicy, with a pretty core of pear, citrus and oak flavors, picking up a grapefruit edge on the finish. **84**

Hess Select Pinot Noir California (★★), Santa Maria Valley Bien Nacido Vineyard (★★): Pleasant, with appealing cherry, herb and spice notes. The Bien Nacido bottling is well made, capturing the style of the vineyard.
California 1993: Simple, with pleasant cherry, herb and spice notes. **83**
Bien Nacido Vineyard 1992: Intense and spicy, with a firm band of pepper, leather, cola and cherry flavors, finishing with crisp tannins. **85**

Hess Select
This is a second label of The Hess Collection Winery (see listing).

Hidden Cellars Winery
Mendocino County
F: 1981. **O:** Hidden Cellars Winery Inc. **W:** John Buechsenstein. **S:** None.

Overall	$8-20	★★★

Wine Ratings

Chardonnay Mendocino County	★★★
Chardonnay Mendocino County Organically Grown	★★
Chardonnay Mendocino County Reserve	★★★
Johannisberg Riesling Mendocino County	★★
Meritage White Mendocino County Alchemy	★★★
Sauvignon Blanc Mendocino County	★★★
Sauvignon Blanc Mendocino County Organically Grown	★★★
Zinfandel Mendocino County	★★★
Zinfandel Mendocino County McAdams Vineyard	★★★
Zinfandel Mendocino County Pacini Vineyard	★★★

WINERY DATA
C: 25,000. **V:** None. **G:** None. **P:** Chardonnay, Sauvignon Blanc, Sémillon, Zinfandel (Mendocino), Johannisberg Riesling (Potter Valley).

Dennis Patton founded Hidden Cellars in Talmage, east of Ukiah, and has built the brand up to 25,000 cases with a product mix that includes Chardonnay, a white Meritage called Alchemy, Johannisberg Riesling, Sauvignon Blanc and Zinfandel, all from purchased Mendocino County grapes. The lineup is solid, as Patton has zeroed in on many of the grapes that grow well in Mendocino County.

Tasting Notes

Chardonnay Mendocino County (★★★), Reserve (★★★): Medium-weight, with ripe, focused fruit flavors and light oak shadings. The Reserve is more intense.
1993: Pleasantly fruity, with ripe pear, apple and nectarine notes. **83**
1992: Ripe, smooth, elegant and polished, with spicy pear, butterscotch and melon flavors that are long and lingering on the finish. **88**
1991: Simple and sturdy, with a coarse texture robbing the apple and pear flavors of their charm. **78**
Reserve 1992: Impressive for its ripe, rich and complex flavors of concentrated pear, honey, spice and vanilla that linger on a long, full finish. **89**

Chardonnay Mendocino County Organically Grown (★★): Good but not as complex and refined as the standard bottling.
1992: Intense and lively, with tiers of citrus, pineapple and pear flavors that pick up a slightly tart edge on the finish. **84**

JOHANNISBERG RIESLING MENDOCINO COUNTY (★★):
Ripe and fruity, with floral apricot notes.
1993: Fragrant and distinctly floral, with a nice bead of apricot flavor carrying through the off-dry finish. **86**
1992: Very sweet but still fresh and lively. A Moscato style of Riesling, with modest spritz and nice, light peach and apple flavors. Drink with dessert. **83**

MERITAGE WHITE MENDOCINO COUNTY ALCHEMY (★★★): A blend of Sémillon and Sauvignon Blanc dominated by the former, it succeeds with an attractive array of flavors.
1992: Ripe and spicy, a generous wine with a woody edge to the honey, fig and citrus flavors. **87**

SAUVIGNON BLANC VARIOUS BOTTLINGS (★★★): Also well made, complex and flavorful, while taming Sauvignon Blanc's herbaceous nature.
Mendocino County 1993: Smooth, round and more complex than most Sauvignons, with an earthy, mineral edge to the honey and pear flavors. **85**
Mendocino County Organically Grown 1992: Strikes a nice balance between intense fig, melon and citrus notes, with a spicy edge on the finish. **85**

ZINFANDEL MENDOCINO COUNTY (★★★):
1992: A solid, rustic Zin with bright, ripe cherry, spice and earthy raspberry flavors, finishing with firm tannins. **85**
1991: Crisp and refreshing, with bright, rich cherry, raspberry, tar, pepper and anise flavors that are elegantly balanced, finishing with spicy, supple tannins. **89**
1990: Tart, lean and focused, with crisp cherry, raspberry and cranberry flavors that take on a peppery edge on the finish. **88**

ZINFANDEL MENDOCINO COUNTY McADAMS VINEYARD (★★★):
1993: Medium-weight, but balanced with appealing berry and cherry notes. **83**

ZINFANDEL MENDOCINO COUNTY PACINI VINEYARD (★★★): Serves up classic Zinfandel flavors, with pretty, ripe fruit and a peppery edge.
1989: Offers plenty of fresh berry flavor accented by spice notes, but has a tart, vinegary edge. **81**
1988: Brimming with appealing cherry and mixed berry aromas and flavors, but held in check by a firm structure and tannins. **85**

WILLIAM HILL WINERY
Napa Valley
F: 1976. **O:** The Wine Alliance. **W:** Jill Davis. **S:** None.

OVERALL	$10-24	★★★

WINE RATINGS

Cabernet Sauvignon Napa Valley Gold Label Reserve	★★★
Cabernet Sauvignon Napa Valley Silver Label	★★
Chardonnay Napa Valley	★★★
Merlot Napa Valley	★★
Sauvignon Blanc Napa Valley	★★

WINERY DATA
C: 125,000. **V:** 101 acres in Napa Valley. **G:** Chardonnay (66 acres), Cabernet Sauvignon (55). **P:** Sauvignon Blanc (Napa Valley), Chardonnay (Napa Valley), Merlot (Napa Valley), Cabernet Sauvignon (Napa Valley), Cabernet Franc (Napa Valley), Petite Verdot (Napa Valley).

William Hill has always been a believer in mountain-grown grapes, favoring intensity and concentration in his wines. In the early 1970s, after graduating from Stanford with a master's degree in business administration, Hill moved to Napa Valley and developed a vineyard on Diamond Mountain (now Sterling's Diamond Mountain Ranch) before moving south to Mount Veeder, where he planted his own vineyard and then started William Hill Winery in 1976. The first commercial wines were the 1978 Cabernet and 1980 Chardonnay, and they were well received. The Cabernets through 1983 were entirely Mount Veeder-grown, but by the mid-1980s Hill began blending grapes from his estate vineyard in Soda Canyon. He also continued investing in and developing vineyards, most notably the Atlas Peak Vineyards. He made his wines in various locations in the city of Napa.

In 1985 Hill sold the Atlas Peak Vineyards and three years later, needing cash to build a winery, entered into an agreement that led to his selling his name and winery to The Wine Alliance—a subsidiary of the British drinks firm Allied Domecq—which also owns Clos du Bois and Callaway. In 1993 Hill severed his ties with Wine Alliance and embarked on plans to develop Domain Hill & Mayes (see listing), a diversified wine company based on vineyard estates, with John Mayes, a longtime business associate. Although Hill sold his 70-

acre Mount Veeder vineyard to Kendall-Jackson in 1994, he still has widespread vineyard holdings throughout Napa, Sonoma and Mendocino Counties and has branched into Oregon with Van Duzer.

After an impressive start, by the late 1980s William Hill Winery had settled into producing a line of good but unexceptional wines. The winery has experienced tremendous growth, and production now exceeds 125,000 cases, with Cabernet and Chardonnay, both regular and Reserve bottlings, still the main focus. Merlot and Sauvignon Blanc have been added to the product mix. In 1994 Wine Alliance hired Jill Davis from Buena Vista Winery to oversee winemaking, but I suspect this winery would have been better off in the long run severing its ties with the Hill name entirely and giving itself a new name and a new image, as Wine World did when it took the old Estrella River Winery and renamed it Meridian.

TASTING NOTES

CABERNET SAUVIGNON NAPA VALLEY GOLD LABEL RESERVE (★★★): Deep, ripe and complex early on, with dark cherry and herb notes. It's on very solid ground through the 1987 vintage, but the style changed in the mid-1980s and the wines became leaner, tarter and more austere. Early vintages from 1978 to 1986 aged well.
1991: Lean and austere, with a narrow band of spice, cedar and currant flavors. **84**
1990: Green olive and herbal notes tend to obscure the modest currant and berry flavors in this smooth-textured, appealing wine. **87**
1989: Flavorful, with a narrow band of currant, black cherry and herb flavors, but it's also tannic and tightly wound, with a green edge. **85**
1988: Tart, with mint and currant flavors, firm tannins and an earthy edge. **84**
1987: A rich core of focused, concentrated currant, black cherry and plum flavors balances beautifully with finely integrated tannins. **88**
1986: Intense and concentrated, a rich but compact Cabernet with crisp acidity and firm tannins. The pretty cassis, toast and vanilla flavors are enticing. **90**
1985: Tight and concentrated, with dry tannins and cedary oak, but the ripe cherry flavors peek through the tight structure. **88**
1984: Tight and compact, with a thin beam of ripe black currant and cherry flavors that are just beginning to peek through. **88**

1983: Mature, but retaining its tight, hard and tannic profile. Drink while the fruit is still there. **82**
1982: Tight and compact, with a narrow beam of spicy black cherry, currant and cedar flavors. Nearing its peak. **88**
1981: Mature and ready to drink, with modest cherry and currant flavors that are losing their intensity. **84**
1980: Bold and compact, mature now, with black cherry, currant, herb and spicy cedar notes that turn earthy. **87**
1979: Smooth, supple and seductive, with attractive cedar and cigar box aromas and ripe black cherry, currant and spice notes. **90**
1978: Deeply colored and richly flavored, it gushes with fruit, with a tight core of currant, cherry and wild berry flavors that pick up pretty chocolate and buttery oak nuances on the finish. Still firmly tannic, but at its peak. **92**

CABERNET SAUVIGNON NAPA VALLEY SILVER LABEL (★★): Leaner and more austere, it's aimed at value.
1989: Firm, tannic and ultimately simple, with a modest level of olive, currant and smoke flavors. **82**
1987: Lavishly oaked, with dill and toasty oak nuances and tart raspberry and cherry flavors. **85**
1985: Complex, tart and dense, with ripe plum, cherry and cassis flavors and a perfumed nose. **85**

CHARDONNAY NAPA VALLEY (★★★): Followed a pattern similar to the Cabernet, shifting in style from ripe to more austere, with tart, thin flavors.
1993: Medium-weight with ripe pear and oaky flavors that are well balanced. **82**
1992: Tight and firm, still a bit green, but the tart pear and apple flavors are intense and focused, and the light oak shadings on the finish add complexity. **88**

MERLOT NAPA VALLEY (★★): Early efforts are unimpressive, marked by green, herbal, not-quite-ripe flavors.
1991: Earthy, with a chunky, herbal, weedy edge and chewy tannins. **82**

SAUVIGNON BLANC NAPA VALLEY (★★): Sturdy, with appealing herb, melon and pear notes.
1993: Smooth in texture, with citrusy pear and floral flavors that linger. **81**
1992: Sturdy and flavorful, with generous herb, melon and pear flavors plus a touch of vanilla on the finish. **85**

HITCHING POST WINERY
Santa Maria Valley
F: 1980. **O:** Frank Ostini. **W:** Frank Ostini. **S:** None.

OVERALL	$14-25	★★★

WINE RATINGS

Pinot Noir Santa Maria Valley	★★★
Pinot Noir Santa Ynez Valley	
Sanford & Benedict Vineyard	★★★

WINERY DATA
C: 300. **V:** None. **G:** None. **P:** Pinot Noir (Santa Maria Valley and Santa Ynez Valley).

Pinot Noir-lover Frank Ostini owns the Buellton-based Hitching Post restaurant and wine brand, which uses grapes purchased from Santa Maria Valley and the Sanford & Benedict Vineyard in Santa Ynez Valley. Through the years several winemakers have assisted Ostini, including Lane Tanner, his former wife, and currently Jim Clendenen of Au Bon Climat. I have tasted most of the Hitching Post Pinot Noirs, and there's no mistaking the high quality across the board, all the more impressive given Pinot's difficult personality. Both wines reflect their appellations, with ripe black cherry, herb and cola notes, striving for elegance and finesse. Production is usually a few hundred cases, although Ostini has recently expanded and is intent on building production to 2,000 cases. The Hitching Post restaurant is an excellent choice for older vintages and a fun place to eat.

TASTING NOTES

PINOT NOIR SANTA MARIA VALLEY (★★★): Often rustic, but improving and showing more consistency.
1991: Earth, sage and herb aromas give way to earthy cherry flavors, finishing with a spicy edge. **86**
1990: Ripe and fruity for a young Hitching Post Pinot, with intense, complex, concentrated plum, cherry, anise and oak flavors. **91**
1989: Lots of flavor, with cola, currant, plum and spice notes in a tight, compact, complex package, finishing with subtle oak shadings. **88**
1988: Remarkably complex, with ripe, intense, grapey flavors that take on an earthy, leathery edge, especially on the finish, where the tannins kick in. This is a tough, gutsy wine that needs further cellaring. **90**

1987: Classic Hitching Post Pinot Noir, intense and potent, with wonderful cola, plum, cherry and spice flavors and a texture that's developing silk and polish, but at the same time is very firm and intense. **92**
1986: A tight, firm and tannic wine that's hard and acidic, with hints of plum and currant coming through crisp, rugged tannins. **82**
1985: The weakest Hitching Post, picked underripe at 21.5 Brix, it displays an underripe character, with herb and rhubarb flavors that are lean and tannic. Holding, but not going anywhere. **79**
1984: Ripe, firm and tannic, but with a pretty core of currant, plum and cherry aromas and flavors. **87**
1983: Intense, complex and tannic, with a solid core of earth, spice, cola and cherry aromas and flavors. **88**
Early Pick 1982: One of two bottlings made this year, this wine is from the early pick. It's intense but more delicate than the late pick, with complex currant, plum and cedar aromas. **85**
Late Pick 1982: The second of two wines made this vintage, this is the late pick, which came after the rains. It's a curious wine, very ripe and raisiny, with hints of currant and earth. **82**
1981: The first Pinot Noir made by this Santa Ynez Valley cult producer. I found it mature and pickley, with a strong volatile character; it's complex in its own curious way. **80**

PINOT NOIR SANTA YNEZ VALLEY SANFORD & BENEDICT VINEYARD (★★★):
1991: Lean and earthy, with a leathery edge to the black cherry and spice flavors, finishing with firm, drying tannins. **86**
1989: From a great vintage in Santa Ynez Valley, this is a ripe, intense and fruity wine with a big spine and a distinctive Pinot Noir character. **88**
1988: Serves up lots of flavor and tannins, with rich, earthy cola, plum, currant, and spice flavors. **87**
1987: Though 1987 was a mixed vintage in this area for Pinot Noir, this is a tight, firm wine with a nice core of plum, currant and cherry flavors. **88**
1985: Lean and firm, with earthy currant and plum flavors that come across as simple, but this wine is better than the 1985 Santa Maria bottling. **84**

PAUL HOBBS CELLARS
Sonoma County
F: 1991. **O:** Paul Hobbs. **W:** Paul Hobbs. **S:** None.

OVERALL	$24-30	★★★

WINE RATINGS

Cabernet Sauvignon Carneros Hyde Vineyard	★★★
Chardonnay Sonoma Mountain Richard Dinner Vineyard	★★★★
Pinot Noir Carneros Hyde Vineyard	★★★

WINERY DATA
C: 3,500. **V:** None. **G:** None. **P:** Cabernet Sauvignon (Howell Mountain), Pinot Noir (Carneros), Chardonnay (Sonoma Mountain), Merlot (Napa Valley), Cabernet Sauvignon (Carneros).

Paul Hobbs worked with Opus One in the early 1980s and was winemaker at Simi from 1985 to 1991 before launching his own brand, using space at Kunde Estate Winery in Kenwood and purchased grapes from a number of excellent sources. Hobbs's 3,500-case lineup includes Cabernet and Pinot Noir from Hyde Vineyard in Carneros, Chardonnay from Richard Dinner Vineyard on Sonoma Mountain, a second Cabernet from Liparita Vineyard on Howell Mountain and Merlot from Michael Black Vineyard near Napa. All of the early wines have been impressive, except for a 1992 Pinot Noir that displayed a pungent, earthy character.

TASTING NOTES

CABERNET SAUVIGNON CARNEROS HYDE VINEYARD (★★★):
1991: Firm, ripe and intense, with a rich, focused core of currant, black cherry, mineral and herb notes. Turns supple and complex on the finish, where the tannins and buttery oak kick in. **91**

CHARDONNAY SONOMA MOUNTAIN RICHARD DINNER VINEYARD (★★★★): Impressive for its richness, concentration and complexity.
1993: Understated, with a ripe core of pear, honey and toasty oak flavors that are pleasant but missing the extra dimensions found in earlier vintages. **86**
1992: Rich and full-bodied, with an earthy streak to the ripe pear and spicy oak flavors. Packs in lots of bold, delicious Chardonnay flavors. **91**
1991: Wonderfully rich, smoky and complex, with tiers of butterscotch, pear, spice and honey notes. Turns smooth and silky on the finish, with extra depth and dimensions. A stunning debut. **93**

PINOT NOIR CARNEROS HYDE VINEYARD (★★★): Tight and firm in 1991, but earthy and funky in 1992.
1992: Earthy and barnyardy; it's hard to find the fruit. **74**
1991: Firm and tight, with an earthy edge that blends well with the raspberry and cherry aromas and flavors. It finishes with firm tannins and a sense of austerity. **87**

HOMEWOOD WINERY
Sonoma Valley
F: 1988. **O:** MNH Inc. **W:** David Homewood. **S:** None.

OVERALL	$12-15	★★

WINE RATINGS

Zinfandel Dry Creek Valley Quinn Vineyard	★★
Zinfandel Sonoma Valley 110-Year-Old Vines	★★

WINERY DATA
C: 2,250. **V:** 1 acre in Carneros. **G:** Chardonnay (1 acre). **P:** N/A.

David Homewood founded this 2,250-case winery in Sonoma in 1988 with a focus on Zinfandel from two sources, 110-year-old vines in Sonoma Valley and Quinn Vineyard in Dry Creek Valley. The Sonoma Valley 1992 is the showier of the two, with spicy cherry and raspberry flavors and less wood than the 1992 Quinn bottling, which is heavily oaked. Carneros Chardonnay and Alexander Valley Cabernet are also made.

TASTING NOTES

ZINFANDEL VARIOUS BOTTLINGS (★★):
Dry Creek Valley Quinn Vineyard 1992: Firm and tight, with oak flavors and drying tannins. Underneath all that is a compact core of raspberry and berry aromas and flavors. Could offer a little more fruit and a little less wood. **79**

Sonoma Valley 110-Year-Old Vines 1992: Shows more spicy cherry and raspberry flavors and less overt wood than the Quinn Vineyard bottling, yet shares its firmness and tannic structure. Could stand to lose some tannin, though. **83**

LOUIS HONIG CELLARS
Rutherford, Napa Valley
F: 1964. **O:** Bill & Nancy Honig, Daniel & Sue Weinstein. **W:** James Hall. **S:** None.

OVERALL	$10-15	★★

WINE RATINGS

Cabernet Sauvignon Napa Valley	★★
Sauvignon Blanc Napa Valley	★★

WINERY DATA
C: 24,500. **V:** 68 acres in Napa Valley. **G:** Sauvignon Blanc (35 acres), Cabernet Sauvignon (30), Merlot (3). **P:** None.

In 1966 Louis Honig bought a partially planted 67-acre property in Rutherford from Charlie Wagner of Caymus and began replanting the remaining acreage. In 1980 Honig's son Bill, better known then as California's former superintendent of schools, and Daniel Weinstein, his son-in-law, began making small lots of Sauvignon Blanc, which has steadily increased to about 22,500 cases. Along the way Cabernet Sauvignon (2,000 cases) became part of the product mix. James Hall, a partner in Patz & Hall, is winemaker, and several wineries (Rocking Horse and Patz & Hall) use Honig's facilities for custom-crushing and barrel aging.

TASTING NOTES

CABERNET SAUVIGNON NAPA VALLEY (★★): Medium-weight, with herb and plum flavors, but no match at all for Caymus, its neighbor to the east.
1988: A medium-bodied Cabernet with herb and plum flavors and a dominant layer of oak and tannins. **83**

SAUVIGNON BLANC NAPA VALLEY (★★): Better suited to be grown on this property, its quality varies, but it can be pungently herbaceous.
1993: Herbal, vegetal notes tip this into the odd category. **80**
1991: Stylish but not very fruity, with vague toast and butter aromas and flavors. A solid-feeling wine that fades a bit on the finish. **80**

HOP KILN WINERY
Russian River Valley
F: 1975. **O:** The Hop Kiln Winery Inc. **W:** L. Steven Strobl. **S:** None.

OVERALL	$8-18	★★★

WINE RATINGS

Cabernet Sauvignon Russian River Valley	★★
Chardonnay Russian River Valley	
M. Griffin Vineyards	★★★
Gewürztraminer Russian River Valley	
M. Griffin Vineyards	★★
Johannisberg Riesling Russian River	
Valley M. Griffin Vineyards	★★
Petite Sirah Russian River Valley	
M. Griffin Vineyards	★★
Petite Sirah Sonoma County	★★
Red Table Wine Russian River Valley	
M. Griffin Vineyards Valdiguie	★★
Red Table Wine Sonoma County	
Marty Griffin's Big Red	★★
Zinfandel Russian River Valley	★★★
Zinfandel Russian River Valley Primitivo	★★★

WINERY DATA
C: 9,000. **V:** 36 acres in Russian River Valley. **G:** Cabernet Sauvignon (3 acres), Gewürztraminer (4), Riesling (7), Zinfandel (13), Chardonnay (6), Rhône Type (3). **P:** Zinfandel (Dry Creek Valley).

Marty Griffin caught the wine bug in 1964 on a trip to Italy, where he studied winemaking. A year later he started making Zinfandel as a home winemaker, going commercial in 1975 in the Russian River Valley. A physician by profession, Griffin, now in his 70's, has had a long-running flair for Zinfandel. He holds the trademark for the name Primitivo, the southern Italian grape that may have genetic links to Zinfandel. For his Primitivo bottling, the grapevines must be at least 50 years old; they yield a very intriguing Zinfandel, with bold ripe fruit flavors and deep color. Roughly half his acres are planted to red grapes, including Zinfandel and Cabernet, and he also buys grapes from area vineyards. Chardonnay and Riesling are rooted in his vineyard as well, and he makes a sparkling wine from Gewürztraminer. Today 3,000 cases of Hop Kiln's 9,000-case production is devoted to Zinfandel. He makes 2,000 cases of Marty Griffin's Big Red, a blend of Zinfandel, Petite Sirah, Napa Gamay and Cabernet that is often a rich, hearty wine and an excellent value. One year a California wine competition awarded Big Red a gold medal over Opus One, favoring power and intensity over harmony and finesse. The winery is modeled after a hop kiln from 1905, and is worth a visit.

TASTING NOTES

CABERNET SAUVIGNON RUSSIAN RIVER VALLEY (★★): Highly variable, as Cabernet in Russian River can often be.
1991: Firm and intense, with racy black cherry and cider flavors. **83**
1990: Ripe and straightforward, this is a youthful, intense and firmly tannic wine with a narrow band of spice, raspberry and cherry notes. **84**
1989: Earthy, thin and uninteresting. **72**

CHARDONNAY RUSSIAN RIVER VALLEY M. GRIFFIN VINEYARDS (★★★): Improving of late, but variable in style and quality, ranging from simple to complex.
1993: Intense and spicy, with complex pear, vanilla, toast and butter notes that fan out, giving it added depth and richness. **89**
1992: Crisp in texture, but it packs a lot of fruit and spice into its elegant frame, offering pear and apple notes with a touch of nutmeg. **87**
1991: Lean, toasty and almost sappy, this narrow-gauge wine shows nice buttery, toasty oak, green apple and vanilla flavors. **85**

GEWÜRZTRAMINER RUSSIAN RIVER VALLEY M. GRIFFIN VINEYARDS (★★): This temperamental grape produces a wine that's highly variable, with rose petal and spice notes at its best.
1993: Dry and modest in scope, with rose petal and apple flavors that emerge gently on the finish. **82**

JOHANNISBERG RIESLING RUSSIAN RIVER VALLEY M. GRIFFIN VINEYARDS (★★): Sweet and floral, but pleasant when chilled.
1993: Frankly sweet but balanced, with a sort of austerity that keeps the peach, honey and floral flavors in check. **83**
1992: Simple and fruity, a sweet, soft-textured wine with appealing apple and peach flavors and a soft finish. **82**

PETITE SIRAH VARIOUS BOTTLINGS (★★): Can be classic, dark, ripe and peppery, with firm tannins, or simply too tannic for its own good.
Russian River Valley M. Griffin Vineyards 1989: Dark, ripe and peppery, this is a classic that is dry and firmly tannic, capable of aging through the decade. Last vintage from the Hop Kiln vineyard. **88**
Russian River Valley M. Griffin Vineyards 1987: Simple fruit and firm tannins manage to strike a balance that makes this wine drinkable, but it lacks extra qualities. **82**
Sonoma County 1991: A nice black pepper edge gives this sturdy, chunky wine some style, adding nuances to the plum and berry flavors. **84**

RED TABLE WINE RUSSIAN RIVER VALLEY M. GRIFFIN VINEYARDS VALDIGUIE (★★):
1991: Solidly built, fruity and spicy, slightly gamy, a distinctive wine that makes up in flavor for its rough-and-tumble structure. Valdiguie is the grape variety often identified as Gamay in California. **82**
1990: Tannic and ripe, with stewed plum and cherry flavors and hints of nutmeg and toast. **77**

ZINFANDEL RUSSIAN RIVER VALLEY (★★★): Varies from medium- to full-bodied, intense, with berry and spice flavors at its best.
1992: Rich, spicy and complex, with peppery cherry and wild berry flavors that pick up a tar and oak edge. **86**
1991: Bright and lively, with ripe, lush, spicy cherry and raspberry flavors that pick up an anise edge on the finish. **84**
1990: Firm and focused, with lean, grapey blackberry and slightly raisiny flavors that extend into a solid finish. **85**
1988: Ripe and rich, with generous plum, cherry and vanilla aromas and flavors held in check by a structure of firm tannins and alcohol. **88**
1986: Smooth and velvety, with ripe, wild berry flavors on a firm framework of acidity and moderate tannins. **85**

RED TABLE WINE SONOMA COUNTY MARTY GRIFFIN'S BIG RED (★★): This blend of grapes is usually intense and powerful, particularly appealing to those who like their wines big, ripe and tannic.
1992: Austere, with thin, earthy dried cherry flavors that turn metallic. **81**

1990: Almost like a late-harvest Zinfandel, full-bodied, with prune and raisin flavors, apparent sweetness. It's wild and woolly, accented by oak, and probably best with cheese or barbecue. **81**

1988: Deep in color and intense in aroma and flavor yet relatively gentle on the palate, offering appealing berry and plum flavors and a supple texture. **85**

1987: A powerful wine that lets its blueberry, raspberry and plum flavors shine through. **89**

1986: Firm, tannic, clean and concentrated, with fresh cherry and blackberry flavors, crisp acidity and nice oak accents. **85**

Reserve NV: Firm, tight and tannic, a tightly wound and compact Zin with sharply focused cherry and raspberry flavors that are rich and tannic. **87**

ZINFANDEL RUSSIAN RIVER VALLEY PRIMITIVO (★★★), RESERVE (★★★): Dark, ripe and intense, high in alcohol and extract. Ages well.

1992: Ripe and racy, with a gamy edge to the wild raspberry and cherry flavors. Tasty now but can age through 1997. **85**

1991: A peppery, blackberry-scented wine that's distinctive, full-bodied, deep in color and moderately tannic. **87**

1990: Smooth and ripe, with focused plum, cherry and rose petal aromas and flavors that meld nicely into the rich chocolate and vanilla finish. **85**

1988: Deep, dark, ripe, intense and powerful, with plenty of tannin to complement the muscular plum, raspberry and cherry flavors. There's nothing subtle about it, but the intensity of fruit is so enjoyable that it almost makes you forget the tannin. **89**

1985: A concentrated, very ripe Zinfandel that tastes like blackberry jam. **80**

Reserve 1985: Packs a wallop; deeply colored, with equally deep blackberry and black cherry flavors and plenty of soft tannins. **90**

HOPE FARMS WINERY
Paso Robles
F: 1990. O: The Hope Family. W: Stephen Rasmussen. S: None.

OVERALL	$9-12	★★

WINE RATINGS		
Cabernet Blend Paso Robles Claret		★★

WINERY DATA
C: 5,000. V: N/A. G: N/A. P: N/A.

The Hope family began as grape growers in the Paso Robles area, and with the 1989 vintage introduced a Cabernet and later a Claret-Cabernet blend. Also under consideration are plans for Chardonnay, Sauvignon Blanc, Merlot and Zinfandel, with the winery's production at the 5,000-case level. The Cabernet 1989 is intense, with cherry and currant flavors and a tarry edge, while the 1990 shows more oak. The 1991 Claret is light and spicy, with herb, cherry and currant notes.

TASTING NOTES

VARIOUS BOTTLINGS:

Cabernet Blend Paso Robles Claret 1991: Light, with spicy herb and cedar notes. Finishes with a hint of cherry and currant and mild tannins. **81**

Cabernet Sauvignon Paso Robles 1990: An oaky wine marked by toasty, buttery flavors, but enough anise and cherry notes emerge to make it interesting. **84**

Cabernet Sauvignon Paso Robles 1989: Intense and juicy, with lots of ripe plum, cherry and currant flavors, but the finish turns raisiny with a tarry, minty edge. **84**

HOUTZ VINEYARDS
Santa Ynez Valley
F: 1982. O: David & Margy Houtz. W: David Houtz. S: None.

OVERALL	$10-12	NR

WINE RATINGS		
Cabernet Sauvignon Santa Ynez Valley		NR
Chardonnay Santa Ynez Valley		NR
Chenin Blanc Santa Ynez Valley		NR

WINERY DATA
C: 4,000. V: 16 acres in Santa Ynez Valley. G: Sauvignon Blanc, Chardonnay, Cabernet Sauvignon. P: None.

David Houtz left real estate in Los Angeles for wine-growing in Los Olivos in the Santa Ynez Valley, planting a 16-acre vineyard and starting his 4,000-case winery in 1984. Houtz's offerings include Cabernet, Chardonnay and Chenin Blanc.

ROBERT HUNTER WINERY
Sonoma Valley
F: 1980. **O:** Robert Hunter. **W:** Robert Hunter. **S:** None.

| OVERALL | $25 | ★★ |

WINE RATINGS
Sparkling Wine Sonoma Valley
   Brut de Noirs ★★

WINERY DATA
C: N/A. **V:** 43 acres in Sonoma Valley. **G:** N/A. **P:** None.

Sonoma Valley grape grower Robert Hunter sold Chardonnay and Pinot Noir to Sonoma wineries before starting his *méthode champenoise* sparkling wine brand in 1980, eventually building production to 8,000 cases. By the late 1980s, however, the wines were discontinued, only to be restarted in 1994 with the release of a 1991 Brut de Noirs marked by lean, earthy flavors.

TASTING NOTES

SPARKLING WINE SONOMA VALLEY BRUT DE NOIRS (★★):
1991: Lean and earthy, with rough-hewn pear and spice notes; a tough wine to warm up to. **80**

HUSCH VINEYARDS
Anderson Valley
F: 1971. **O:** Husch Vineyards Inc. **W:** Fritz Meier. **S:** None.

| OVERALL | $8-18 | ★★★ |

WINE RATINGS
Cabernet Sauvignon Mendocino County La Ribera Ranch ★★★
Cabernet Sauvignon Mendocino County North Field Select ★★
Chardonnay Anderson Valley Special Reserve ★★★
Chardonnay Mendocino County ★★★
Chenin Blanc Mendocino County La Ribera Ranch ★★
Gewürztraminer Anderson Valley Late Harvest ★★★
Pinot Noir Anderson Valley ★★
Sauvignon Blanc Mendocino County ★★★
Sauvignon Blanc Mendocino County La Ribera Ranch ★★★

WINERY DATA
C: 30,000. **V:** 202 acres in Anderson Valley and Mendocino County. **G:** Chardonnay (90 acres), Sauvignon Blanc (44), Pinot Noir (20), Cabernet Sauvignon (20), Gewürztraminer (12), Chenin Blanc (4), Zinfandel (2), Carignane (10). **P:** None.

In 1971 Tony Husch established the first winery in Anderson Valley since Prohibition, but his business success was mixed and he sold it in 1979 to the Oswald family, longtime grape growers. The winery now has 202 acres in vines, 75 in Anderson Valley. Chardonnay (90 acres) dominates, followed by Sauvignon Blanc (44), Pinot Noir and Cabernet (20 each). The winery's 30,000-case output includes those varietal wines, along with Chenin Blanc and Gewürztraminer, all estate-grown. Three wines, the Cabernet, Chardonnay and Sauvignon Blanc, carry a La Ribera Ranch designation. Another Cabernet carries the North Field Select designation.

TASTING NOTES

CABERNET SAUVIGNON MENDOCINO COUNTY LA RIBERA RANCH (★★★): La Ribera is more complex and concentrated in warmer years, although less complex and flavorful of late.
1992: Tight and firm, with a narrow band of spicy currant flavors. **83**
1991: Lean and simple, with modest cherry and currant notes. **84**
1990: An elegant, complex, youthful wine that has finesse and grace. Layers of spice, cherry, toast and currant flavors fold together on the finish. **88**
1989: Light and cedary, with simple berry and cherry flavors. **79**
1988: Firm and lively, with lots of appealing, ripe currant and plum flavors and hints of black pepper and vanilla. **86**
1987: Rich, deep and concentrated, with generous black cherry, nutmeg and chocolate notes that persist into the long finish. **88**

CABERNET SAUVIGNON MENDOCINO COUNTY NORTH FIELD SELECT (★★): Clean and correct, marked by herb and dill notes and modest currant and cherry fruit. Mildly tannic. La Ribera is more complex and concentrated in warmer years, as the appellation dictates ripeness.

1991: Relies too heavily on strong dill and oak notes, which overshadow the narrow band of currant flavor. **81**

1990: Firm and intense, with ripe cherry, currant, anise and spice flavors that turn chunky and tannic on the finish. **87**

1989: Strives for complexity with its cedary, buttery oak flavors. It's crisp and firm on the palate, with a narrow beam of currant and black cherry notes. **84**

1988: Firm and tasty if not especially concentrated, showing appealing blackberry and black currant flavors with a hint of mint. **84**

1987: Firm, rich and concentrated, with ripe, supple currant, cedar, cherry, herb and chocolate flavors, finishing with firm tannins. **87**

Chardonnay Various Bottlings (★★★): Emphasizes ripe fruity flavors in a well executed style.

Anderson Valley Special Reserve 1992: Distinct for its ripe pear and spicy notes, but it loses its intensity and focus on the finish. **85**

Mendocino County 1993: Intense and lively, with a grassy edge to the pear and apple notes. **85**

Mendocino County 1992: Crisp and flinty, with tart pear, apricot and spice flavors. **84**

Chenin Blanc Mendocino County La Ribera Ranch (★★): Off-dry with good fruit flavors, but nothing special.

1994: Light, charming and generous with its green apple and sweet pear fruit. Not too sweet. **85**

1993: Lightly sweet and fruity, with a leafy-herbal streak running through the green apple flavor. **82**

Gewürztraminer Anderson Valley Late Harvest (★★★):

1993: Soft and sweet, with recognizable Gewürztraminer spice and a touch of bitterness to enliven the syrupy finish. Very tasty and the flavors persist nicely. **87**

Pinot Noir Anderson Valley (★★): Consistently good and a good value, with recent vintages showing more depth and intensity.

1992: Ripe and intense, with a pretty core of black cherry, plum and spice flavors. **87**

1991: Intense and spicy, with raspberry and black cherry flavors that turn elegant and racy. **84**

1990: Very light, with pleasant strawberry, rhubarb and spice flavors. **81**

1989: Packs lots of flavor into a light, easy-to-drink structure. A medium-bodied, delicate wine with fresh, spicy plum and cherry flavors. **87**

1988: Tough and tannic but not heavy-handed, with tea, herb and plum aromas and flavors. **84**

1987: Decent, with ripe berry, brown sugar and cherry flavors, but it's also rather simple and lacking complexity. **80**

1986: Tastes like a Bouzy Rouge—light, thin and delicate, but pleasing. **81**

1985: Meaty, smoky cherry flavors are rich and delicate, with crisp acidity and firm tannins. **84**

Sauvignon Blanc Mendocino County La Ribera Ranch (★★★): Offers good intensity and moderately rich flavors.

1994: Light and juicy, a nice mouthful of passion fruit, grapefruit and pineapple flavors that persists on the lively finish. **87**

1992: Crisp and lively, with bright green apple and lemon aromas and flavors, slightly herbal and honeyed on the finish. **86**

Indian Springs Vineyards
Penn Valley, Nevada County
F: 1981. **O:** Dennis & David Ball, Karen Swink. **W:** John Cleos, Jed Steele. **S:** None.

Overall	$8-17	★★

Wine Ratings	
Cabernet Franc Nevada County	★★
Cabernet Sauvignon Nevada County	★★
Merlot Nevada County	★★
Sangiovese Nevada County	★★
Syrah Nevada County	★★

Winery Data
C: 8,000. **V:** 111 acres in Nevada County. **G:** Chardonnay (51 acres), Sémillon (2), Merlot (21), Cabernet Sauvignon (17), Cabernet Franc (12), Sangiovese (2), Nebbiolo (0.5). **P:** None.

With the addition of Jed Steele (Steele Wines, Fess Parker, Villa Mt. Eden) as the consulting winemaker,

Indian Springs (of Penn Valley in the Sierra Foothills northeast of Sacramento) hopes to upgrade the overall quality of its all-red lineup. The 8,000-case production includes Cabernet Franc, Cabernet Sauvignon, Merlot, Sangiovese and Syrah, all from the winery's 111 acres of vines.

TASTING NOTES

CABERNET SAUVIGNON NEVADA COUNTY (★★): Solid if rustic, with compact fruit and firm tannins.
1991: Strikes a nice balance between cedary oak and ripe currant flavors; picks up a hint of coffee on the finish before the tannins kick in. **82**
1990: A rustic, youthful Cabernet with earthy, tannic currant flavors that turn spicy on the finish, but in the end the tannins hang tough. **80**

MERLOT NEVADA COUNTY (★★): Improving, as recent vintages show more supple, polished flavors.
1992: Smooth and supple, with a nice range of currant, herb and spice flavors. Has the intensity and tannins for short-term cellaring. **84**
1991: Supple and fruity, showing a nice core of cherry and berry flavors and light oak shadings. Finishes with a nice touch of fruit and firm tannins. **84**
1990: Ripe, spicy and not too tannic, with bright, lively black cherry, currant, tar and tobacco flavors. **84**
1989: A big, ripe, full-bodied Merlot with exuberant black cherry and raisin flavors, plenty of crisp acidity and moderate tannins. The black cherry nuances linger nicely on the finish. Distinctive and full of character. **85**

INGLENOOK-NAPA VALLEY
Ukiah, Mendocino County
F: 1879. O: Canandaigua Wine Co. W: John Richburg. S: None.

OVERALL	$10-38	★★

WINE RATINGS	
Cabernet Sauvignon Napa Valley	★★
Cabernet Sauvignon Napa Valley Reserve Cask	★★★
Cabernet Sauvignon Napa Valley Reunion	★★★
Merlot Napa Valley Reserve	★★

WINERY DATA
C: N/A. **V:** None. **G:** None. **P:** N/A.

The rise and fall of Inglenook is one of the sad chapters in California wine history. Founded in 1879 by Finnish fur trader Gustav Niebaum, Inglenook first rose to prominence in the late 1800s and early 1900s. Niebaum, an ambitious, energetic man, built his handsome stone winery in Rutherford west of Highway 29. He hoped to produce great wines at any cost and by many accounts he did. In 1989 I tasted the Inglenook 1897 Claret Medoc-Type, a wine that still had plenty of life in its aromas and flavors. Niebaum died in 1908, and Prohibition closed the winery until 1933, when it reopened under the direction of Carl Bundschu, a partner in Bacchus Wines of Sonoma. Amazingly, in the first vintage after repeal Inglenook produced a stunning 1933 Cabernet that aged gloriously, with a deep, dark color and rich, complex, concentrated flavors.

In 1939 John Daniel Jr., Niebaum's grandnephew, took over, marking the beginning of an era that would extend to 1964. Daniel, along with winemaker George Deuer, maintained exceptionally high standards, with severe evaluations of their wines. Daniel's motto was "pride, not profits," and he was known to declassify wines that didn't meet his rigid standards. Inglenook produced a succession of fabulous wines from the 1940s through the 1950s, notably the extraordinary 1941 Cabernet, but by the early 1960s things began to unravel at Inglenook. In 1964 Daniel sold the winery to Allied Grape Growers (which subsequently became a part of United Vintners and later of Heublein) and the Napanook Vineyard in Yountville to his daughters (see Dominus Estate).

In 1969 Heublein took over and began to expand production, introducing Inglenook Navalle, a line of California-appellation jug wines and vintage-dated varietals that once sold 4 million cases a year. By the 1980s the brands had become so commingled that "Napa Valley" was attached to the original Inglenook's name to avoid confusion. In the 1980s Dennis Fife and John Richburg attempted to revive the winery and succeeded in upgrading quality, reintroducing the Cask designation and later adding a Reunion Cabernet that brought together the three main vineyards that had gone into the great Cask Cabernets of the Daniel era.

Still the winery struggled, and eventually Heublein sold the winemaking faciltes and then the brand name to Canandaigua Wine Co., which moved production of Inglenook-Napa Valley to Ukiah in Mendocino County. Richburg has been retained as a winemaking consultant. In late 1994, the historic Inglenook Chateau, aging *chai* and surrounding vineyard were sold to Francis Ford Coppola, owner of neighboring Niebaum-Coppola Estate. The future of the Inglenook *brand*, however, appears more uncertain than ever.

TASTING NOTES

CABERNET SAUVIGNON NAPA VALLEY RESERVE CASK (★★★): Vintages from the 1940s and 1950s are still holding up quite well, but then you have to fast-forward to the 1980s to find any depth or complexity. The youngest vintages are tight and tannic.

1988: Lean and austere, with a tight, narrow range of flavors that turn watery. Hints of currant and berry don't last. **84**

1987: Firm, tight and concentrated, with rich, focused currant, cedar and cherry aromas and flavors that turn complex on the finish, with hints of tobacco and oak. **87**

1986: A rich, concentrated wine with smoky cedar, currant and black cherry flavors that are tightly focused, firmly tannic and well structured. **87**

1985: Smooth and polished, with intense cherry, currant, mint and herb aromas and flavors framed by hints of cedar. A bit tannic but balanced, and almost elegant right through the finish. **87**

1984: Ripe and exotic, with lots of coffee, cedar and spice overtones to the gentle, very ripe cherry and raspberry flavors. A stylish wine with plenty of tannin to support it. **90**

1983: Cedar and menthol notes tend to outshine the fruit at this stage, and there's lots of tannin. **88**

1982: A tight, austere 1982 that is quite tannic and will require long cellaring to come around, if it ever does. **85**

1981: Developing well, with rich, ripe, supple, generous cassis and black cherry flavors, turning a bit dry and tannic. **87**

1980: Mature and rich, concentrated and supple, with ripe currant, black cherry and spicy oak flavors. **88**

1978: Mature, with generous ripe plum and anise flavors that have shed most of their tannins. **83**

1966: Aging very well, fully mature, but it has held its fruit and elegant, claret-like personality. Rich and full-bodied, with currant, plum and anise flavors that are long and full on the finish. **89**

1959: Aging amazingly well, another delicious Inglenook Cabernet from a first-class vintage. Ripe, complex and firm, with layers of currant, black cherry and plum flavors that are long and persistent on the finish. **96**

1958: Ripe and forward, fully mature, a delicious wine from a great vintage, with mint, cherry and spice flavors, plenty of depth and finesse and a long, persistent finish. Youthful for its age, the last of the great Daniel Cabernets. **94**

1955: Great balance and depth from a fine vintage, ripe and mature, with rich cedar, herb, olive and plum flavors that are intense and lively and a long, full finish. **93**

1951: Warm, rich, supple and complex, a wonderfully engaging wine that spills forth pretty currant, anise and cherry flavors that linger gently on the palate. It's silky, complex and graceful, and can age for another decade or more. A fabulous wine. **96**

1949: With a wonderful bouquet of dried fruit and flowers, the 1949 wraps up the fabulous 1940s decade for Inglenook, with smooth, rich, supple, fully mature fruit that tastes like liquid anise, supplemented with plum, currant, smoke and cherry flavors. **92**

1946: Another extremely ripe, big, chewy, chunky Cabernet that is fully developed, with wonderful black cherry, anise, cedar and plum flavors that are complex. Beautiful dried fruit flavors echo on the finish, along with some volatile acidity. **87**

1943: Earthy, with a slight mustiness that clears up, the 1943 is another of the terrific vintages of the 1940s for Inglenook. The tart plum, anise and black cherry flavors are fully mature. **91**

1941: Absolutely sensational and undoubtedly one of the greatest California Cabernets ever produced, the 1941 is the kind of wine that comes around once in a lifetime. This wine is amazing for its youthful vitality, incredible depth, complexity of flavor and staying power. Few wines in the world ever achieve this height of intensity, and it appears to have the stamina to last another 20 to 30 years. From an extremely ripe vintage, the raisin, plum, currant, herb and tea flavors are very concentrated and sharply defined. **100**

1933: In fantastic condition, with a healthy, deep red-garnet color, wonderful spice, mint, rose petal and mature plum aromas, and complex, rich, elegant, faded plum, rose petal and spice flavors that turn to chocolate, cedar and coffee with aeration. **95**

1897: One of the oldest California Cabernets in existence, this treasure is still hanging on, providing a wealth of information and insight into how California Cabs age. A blend of Cabernet with a dollop of Zinfandel, it reflects the Bordeaux heritage in its name and still offers smoke, anise, orange and tea notes to complement the fading black cherry and ripe plum flavors. Very light in color, it gained in the glass for more than an hour. Short of perfection, yet brilliant in its own way. **87**

CABERNET SAUVIGNON NAPA VALLEY REUNION (★★★): Introduced with the 1983 vintage. Quality was sound early on, although the wines have turned leaner and more austere, with hard-edged tannins.

1986: Still tight and tannic, with a complex band of cedar, black cherry, currant and anise flavors. **88**

1985: Austere, with compact, concentrated, spicy black cherry, currant and cedary oak flavors. **89**

1984: Ripe, smooth and elegant, with supple, jammy cherry and raspberry flavors, finishing with smooth tannins and a light oak edge. **91**

1983: Big, intense and tannic, mature now but still rugged, with currant, cherry and spice notes. **88**

MERLOT NAPA VALLEY RESERVE (★★):
1988: Tight and tough, with lean currant and cherry notes that turn tannic on the finish. **83**

INNISFREE
Napa Valley
F: 1984. **O:** Joseph Phelps. **W:** Craig Williams. **S:** None.

OVERALL	$11-12	★★

WINE RATINGS

Cabernet Sauvignon Napa Valley	★★
Pinot Noir California	NR

WINERY DATA
C: 20,000. **V:** None. **G:** None. **P:** N/A.

Joseph Phelps started this winery in 1984 and it now produces some 20,000 cases of Cabernet, Chardonnay and Pinot Noir, but quality has rarely risen above average. The winery was considering phasing out this brand in 1995.

TASTING NOTES

VARIOUS BOTTLINGS:
Cabernet Sauvignon Napa Valley 1990: Intense, focused, rich and spicy, with incredibly fruity flavors. The cherry, currant and oak flavors fold together. **88**
Pinot Noir California 1990: Light and pleasant, with slightly herbal, smoky notes to complement the modest cherry flavor. **84**

IRON HORSE VINEYARDS
Russian River Valley
F: 1978. **O:** Audrey & Barry Sterling, Forrest Tancer and Joy Anne Sterling. **W:** Forrest Tancer. **S:** Tin Pony.

OVERALL	$12-28	★★★

WINE RATINGS

Cabernet Blend Alexander Valley	
T-T Vineyards Cabernets	★★★
Chardonnay Green Valley-Sonoma	★★★
Chardonnay Sonoma County Cuvée Joy	★★★
Fumé Blanc Alexander Valley	
T-T Vineyards	★★★
Pinot Noir Green Valley-Sonoma	★★★
Sparkling Wine Green Valley-Sonoma	
Blanc de Blancs	★★★★
Sparkling Wine Green Valley-Sonoma	
Brut Late Disgorged	★★★
Sparkling Wine Green Valley-Sonoma	
Brut Rosé	★★★
Sparkling Wine Green Valley-Sonoma	
Brut Vrais Amis	★★★
Sparkling Wine Green Valley-Sonoma	
Demi-Sec	★★★
Sparkling Wine Green Valley-Sonoma	
Wedding Cuvée	★★★

WINERY DATA
C: 40,000. V: 205 acres in Sonoma County Green Valley, Alexander Valley. G: Chardonnay (81 acres), Pinot Noir (61), Sauvignon Blanc (14), Viognier (9), Cabernet Sauvignon (16), Merlot (3), Cabernet Franc (3), Sangiovese (5). P: None.

Barry and Audrey Sterling founded this winery in 1976, naming it after a railroad stop called Iron Horse. Some 205 of their 300-plus acres are in vines, with Green Valley-grown Chardonnay (81 acres) and Pinot Noir (61 acres) dominating, a large portion of which goes into the winery's line of sparkling wines. Under the direction of winemaker and part-owner Forrest Tancer, the 40,000-case Iron Horse Vineyards' product mix ranges from Cabernet, Chardonnay and Pinot Noir to vintage-dated sparkling wines. Quality is solid across the board, although the sparkling wines seem to have inched ahead in recent years, perhaps due to a joint venture with Laurent-Perrier of Champagne, which helped develop a new vineyard. There are plans for a co-produced wine by decade's end.

TASTING NOTES

CABERNET BLEND ALEXANDER VALLEY T-T VINEYARDS CABERNETS (★★★): Consistent if at times on the lean side, it features ripe, bright flavors and is usually elegant and well mannered. It's called Cabernets because the blend includes Franc.

1990: Rustic and tannic, with currant and berry flavors that are ripe and chunky. **87**
1989: Supple, with bright, focused cherry and currant flavors that turn elegant and spicy. **86**
1988: A focused, polished wine with distinctive plum and currant flavors. **85**
1987: Firm and tight, with tannins dominating now, but it has generous plum, black cherry and currant flavors underneath. **86**
1986: Ripe and complex, with plum, floral, cedar and spice flavors. **88**
1985: Delicate, complex and beautifully balanced, with ripe black cherry, currant, cedar and spice flavors and firm tannins. **87**

CABERNET SAUVIGNON ALEXANDER VALLEY (★★★):
1984: A moderately rich wine offering ripe plum, currant, black cherry and cedary anise flavors. **86**

1983: Supple cherry, currant and cedary oak flavors that are pleasant enough. **82**
1982: Mature, with ripe black cherry, herb and currant flavors that are tight and closed now. **83**
1981: Lean, with a crisp band of plum and cedar flavors. **79**
1980: Ripe and generous, offering black cherry and currant flavors that are mildly tannic. **86**
1979: Rich and supple, with cherry, raspberry and chocolate flavors, firm structure, gentle intensity and understated elegance. Plenty of vitality in this wine. Gaining every step of the way. **91**
1978: Mature herb, cedar, plum and spice flavors that offer a modest amount of complexity and delicacy. **80**

CHARDONNAY GREEN VALLEY-SONOMA (★★★): Austere and flinty, with tart green apple and spice notes that reflect the coolness of this climate. Very consistent, though, and ages well.

1993: Marked by tight, compact green apple and pear notes, it's crisp and refreshing with a fruity aftertaste. **87**
1992: Crisp and lean, with spicy apple and pear flavors that turn elegant on the finish. **86**
1991: Lean and spicy, with a vibrant streak of green apple, ginger and nutmeg flavors and a solid echo of pear and vanilla on the finish. An understated wine that gains complexity. **91**

CHARDONNAY SONOMA COUNTY CUVÉE JOY (★★★):
1993: Intense, with a crisp, juicy core of grapefruit and citrus flavors that pick up a nice oaky edge on the finish. Tight and complex. **90**

FUMÉ BLANC ALEXANDER VALLEY T-T VINEYARDS (★★★): Strives for delicacy and usually succeeds, but is sometimes thin and light.

1994: Ripe and round, packed with floral and tropical fruit flavors that remain rich and focused through the soft finish. Twenty five percent Viognier makes it an unusual blend that fills out the palate without much wood. **87**
1993: Ripe and fruity, a soft-textured wine that pours out nectarine, herb and vanilla flavors. **87**

PINOT NOIR GREEN VALLEY-SONOMA (★★★): Varies in quality and style; it's often lean and tannic, while other times fuller and fruitier.

1992: Intense and tannic, a dense and oaky wine that packs in lots of chunky, ripe plum flavors that turn tannic on the finish. **87**
1988: Delicate and well proportioned, with herb, tea and spicy cherry flavors that are crisp and tannic. **85**
1987: A tight, hard-edged, unusually woody wine with just a hint of plum and cherry flavors. **72**
1986: Tart, crisp, and focused, with herb and tea aromas, raspberry flavors and firm tannins. **88**
1980: Aging very well, displaying a complex array of herb, dried cherry, anise and oak flavors, finishing with a chunky, tannic aftertaste. **87**

SPARKLING WINE GREEN VALLEY-SONOMA VARIOUS BOTTLINGS (★★★):
Blanc de Blancs 1988: Crisp, tart and lean, with lemon, spice, apple and grapefruit flavors that are rich, concentrated and intense. Well balanced and lively; may be even better with additional bottle time. **90**
Brut Late Disgorged 1988: Austere, with flinty, mineral and earth notes that add to the lemon flavors. **82**
Brut Rosé 1989: Simple and correct, with a hint of spicy black cherry flavor, but lacks complexity. **81**
Brut Vrais Amis 1989: Smooth and creamy, with crisp, tart apple, pear and spicy flavors that are clean and complex. **87**
Demi-Sec 1989: Not too sweet, offering simple fruit and spice aromas and flavors. **82**
Wedding Cuvée 1991: Bright and fruity, with a grapefruit edge to the delicate raspberry flavors. **87**

J

This is a second label for sparkling wine produced by Jordan Vineyard and Winery (see listing).

JACKSON VALLEY VINEYARDS
Amador County
F: 1985. **O:** Fred & Patricia Anderson. **W:** John L. Bree, Allen Kreitzer. **S:** None.

OVERALL	$5-15	★★

WINE RATINGS	
Zinfandel Amador County	★★

WINERY DATA
C: 20,000. **V:** 50 acres in Amador County. **G:** Chenin Blanc (22 acres), Chardonnay (23), Other (5). **P:** Zinfandel, Cabernet Sauvignon, Cabernet Franc, Nebbiolo, Sangiovese (Amador County).

Fred and Patricia Anderson own Jackson Valley Vineyards, which was founded in 1985 and produces 20,000 cases a year of Chardonnay, a Port-style dessert wine, white table wine and Zinfandel. The 1990 Zinfandel Amador County offers high-profile oak that dominates the spicy fruit flavors.

TASTING NOTES

ZINFANDEL AMADOR COUNTY (★★):
1990: High-profile oak aromas and flavors tend to overpower the modest fruit in this smooth-textured, slightly spicy, highly drinkable Zinfandel. **83**

JADE MOUNTAIN WINERY
Napa Valley
F: 1984. **O:** James C. Paras. **W:** Douglas Danielak. **S:** None.

OVERALL	$13-18	★★★

WINE RATINGS	
Mourvèdre California Unfiltered	★★
Rhône Blend California La Provençale	★★
Syrah Napa Valley	★★★★

WINERY DATA
C: 3,000. **V:** 22 acres in Mount Veeder. **G:** Syrah, Mourvèdre, Viognier, Grenache, Cabernet Sauvignon, Merlot. **P:** Mourvèdre (Contra Costa County), Syrah, Merlot (Napa Valley).

Owner James Paras and winemaker Douglas Danielak of Jade Mountain believe Syrah will be California's star grape in the future. This 3,000-case winery leases space from White Rock Vineyards in the hills east of Napa, using Mourvèdre grapes from the Antioch and Oakley areas in Contra Costa County, and Syrah from Carneros, its own Jade Mountain Ranch (part of the old Veedercrest vineyard) and the Cloverdale area in Northern Sonoma. The rich and concentrated Syrah is among the state's best, and the winery also makes Rhône-style blends called Les Jumeaux (made from Cabernet, Mourvèdre, Grenache and Syrah) and La Provençale (Grenache, Mourvèdre and Syrah). Viognier and Mourvèdre are also part of the changing lineup.

TASTING NOTES

MOURVÈDRE CALIFORNIA (★★):
1990: Crisp and fruity, with a gamy, peppery edge that hints at olive on the finish. **81**
Unfiltered 1990: A firm, sturdy wine, with pleasant blackberry, toast and vanilla flavors and firm tannins. **83**

RHÔNE BLEND CALIFORNIA LA PROVENÇALE (★★):
1992: Firm and tight, with an earthy band of cherry, wild berry, anise and mineral-edge, finishing with crisp tannins and good length. Can stand short-term cellaring. **88**
1990: Sturdy and simple, with appealing blackberry and pepper flavors. **80**

SYRAH NAPA VALLEY (★★★★): Dark and intense, with rich flavors and a supple texture.
1992: Well crafted, elegant in style and body, with an attractive core of currant and cherry fruit, although it loses its intensity on the finish. Mildly tannic. **87**

JAEGER FAMILY WINE CO.
St. Helena, Napa Valley
F: 1978. O: Jaeger Family. W: Joe Cafaro. S: None.

OVERALL	$19	★★

WINE RATINGS

Merlot Napa Valley Inglewood Vineyard	★★

WINERY DATA
C: 5,000. V: 25 acres in Napa Valley. G: Merlot (19.5 acres), Cabernet Sauvignon (2.5), Cabernet Franc (2.5). P: None.

Pomerol lovers Bill and Lila Jaeger, partners in both Freemark Abbey and Rutherford Hill Wineries, farm the 25-acre Inglewood Vineyard near St. Helena for their 5,000-case brand. Most of their vines are Merlot, with about 5 acres split between Cabernet Sauvignon and Cabernet Franc. The wines were more appealing in the early 1980s than at decade's end, when they became leaner and thinner.

TASTING NOTES

MERLOT NAPA VALLEY INGLEWOOD VINEYARD (★★):
There has been a steady erosion in quality since the complex wines offered in 1985 and 1986. They are now typically lean, with herb and earth notes.
1989: Crisp, lean and tannic, a hollow wine with shallow flavors. **77**
1988: Crisp, spicy and still moderately tannic, showing a lean beam of tobacco-scented berry, prune and chocolate flavors. **81**
1987: A rustic wine that's tough and unfocused, with ripe plum and berry flavors lurking behind a wall of tannin and a woody, metallic edge. **81**
1986: Firm, well balanced and modestly fruity, with black currant and herb flavors. **83**
1985: Complex and compact, with ripe black cherry flavors, full, firm tannins and good acidity. **89**

JARVIS
Napa Valley
F: 1985. O: William & Leticia Jarvis. W: Dimitri Tchelistcheff. S: None.

OVERALL	$34-48	★★★

WINE RATINGS

Cabernet Franc Napa Valley	★★
Cabernet Sauvignon Napa Valley	★★★
Chardonnay Napa Valley	★★★

WINERY DATA
C: 5,000. V: 37 acres in Napa Valley. G: Cabernet Sauvignon, Chardonnay, Merlot, Malbec, Petit Verdot. P: None.

In 1985, wine lovers William and Leticia Jarvis bought a 1,400-acre country estate in the hills east of Napa as a weekend retreat, but quickly decided to pursue grape growing, planting the first 25 acres of their 37-acre vineyard and selling the grapes to Clos Du Val and Grgich Hills Cellar. By the late 1980s, the Jarvises decided to enter the wine business, tunneling out a 45,000-square-foot subterranean winery at a cost of more than $20 million. As the owner of Wiltron, an international electronics firm, Jarvis traveled to France and Europe and added to his appreciation of fine wine. In 1992, the winery, under the direction of Dimitri Tchelistcheff, produced its first estate-grown wines, a

Cabernet Franc, Cabernet Sauvignon and Chardonnay, with a 1993 Merlot to follow. The vineyard is rooted in three different areas on the property, at an elevation of 1,000 feet above sea level. The debut wines were very impressive for their elegance and finesse. Worth watching.

TASTING NOTES

CABERNET FRANC NAPA VALLEY (★★):
1992: Marked by a stalky tobacco and green herb edge, enough currant and cedary oak flavors come into play to keep it in balance. **86**

CABERNET SAUVIGNON NAPA VALLEY (★★★):
1992: Supple and polished, a wine of finesse and grace, with ripe black cherry, currant, cedar and tobacco notes, finishing with mild, integrated tannins. **90**

CHARDONNAY NAPA VALLEY (★★★):
1992: Elegant and well balanced, with a smooth core of creamy pear, honey and butterscotch notes, finishing with a light, toasty oak edge. The finish lingers. **90**

JEKEL VINEYARDS
Monterey County
F: 1978. **O:** Brown-Forman Inc. **W:** Rick Boyer. **S:** None.

OVERALL	$10-25	★★

WINE RATINGS

Cabernet Franc Monterey County	★★
Cabernet Sauvignon Arroyo Seco	★★
Chardonnay Arroyo Seco	
Gravelstone Vineyard	★★
Malbec Arroyo Seco	
The Sanctuary Estate	NR
Meritage Red Arroyo Seco	
The Sanctuary Estate Symmetry	★★
Merlot Arroyo Seco The Sanctuary Estate	★★
Pinot Noir Arroyo Seco	★★
White Riesling Arroyo Seco	★★★

WINERY DATA
C: 65,000. **V:** 295 acres in Arroyo Seco. **G:** Chardonnay (170 acres), Johannisberg Riesling (19), Pinot Noir (22), Merlot (48), Cabernet Sauvignon (36). **P:** Pinot Noir (Arroyo Seco).

Bill and Gus Jekel, the founders twin of Jekel Vineyards, made a major commitment to Monterey County, planting vineyards there in the 1970s and launching their winery in 1978, focusing on Cabernet, Chardonnay and Riesling. At first the whites held a distinct edge in quality, as the Cabernet struggled to ripen beyond the herb, bell pepper and tobacco flavors that so often characterize Cabernets grown in a climate that is too cool. Despite that, Jekel enjoyed success with Cabernet, winning a following even if critics often panned the wines. By the late 1980s Monterey Cabernets suffered from such a poor reputation that it seriously damaged sales of wines across the board and the Jekels decided to sell the winery and vineyards. In 1990 Jekel became part of the ill-fated Vintech group, which failed financially, and the Jekels resumed ownership of the winery only to sell it to Brown-Forman, which also added Fetzer to its holdings.

Jekel owns 295 acres of vineyard, led by Chardonnay (170 acres), Merlot (48) and Cabernet (36), and the product mix is weighted toward whites, with Chardonnay at 30,000 cases and Riesling at 7,000 cases. Cabernet, Merlot and Symmetry, a Meritage red from Sanctuary Estate, account for 20,000 cases. Of all the wines, Riesling has been the steadiest and most appealing varietal, made in styles from off-dry to sweet to late-harvest.

TASTING NOTES

CABERNET FRANC MONTEREY COUNTY (★★):
1990: Marked by cedary oak flavors, a narrow band of cherry and currant emerges, but it turns stalky on the finish. **82**

CABERNET SAUVIGNON ARROYO SECO (★★): Tough, tanninc and chewy, marked by herb, bell pepper and green flavors. While out of the mainstream, this wine has its followers.
1990: Firm, intense and tannic, but with enough currant and berry flavors to keep your interest. **84**
1989: Tough and chewy, with a tight, hard-edged core of black cherry and currant flavors, but it's a little green around the edges and is quite tannic. **81**
1988: Tough and tannic, with some ripe fruit attempting to peek through, finishing herbal and smoky. **80**
1986: Very vegetal, with olive, bell pepper and onion flavors. **83**

**CHARDONNAY ARROYO SECO GRAVELSTONE VINEYARD
(★★):** Early efforts were very ripe, heavily oaked and
high in extract, but recently the wines have been simpler.
1993: Lean and spicy, simple and pleasant with its apple
and toast flavors. **82**
1992: Clean and fruity with a modest band of pear and
spice, turning toasty on the finish. **84**

MALBEC ARROYO SECO THE SANCTUARY ESTATE (NR):
1992: Big, ripe, intense and tannic, but at this stage the
fruit is overpowered by the tannins. Well focused, but it
needs time. **83**

**MERITAGE RED ARROYO SECO THE SANCTUARY
ESTATE SYMMETRY (★★):**
1989: Complete and well balanced for a 1989, with spicy
currant, anise and cedar notes, and the tannins are firm
and well mannered. Picks up blackberry nuances and
crisp, dry tannins on the finish. **85**

MERLOT ARROYO SECO THE SANCTUARY ESTATE (★★):
1992: Intense and tannic, with firm herb, spice, mineral
and currant flavors; turns dry and tannic on the finish. **83**

PINOT NOIR ARROYO SECO (★★):
1992: Tasty, with spicy, buttery oak notes and a nice core
of cherry and plum aromas and flavors. **84**

WHITE RIESLING ARROYO SECO (★★★): Appealing for
its forward fruitiness and floral notes.
1991: A fine imitation of Mosel Valley kabinett. Off-dry,
crisp and minerally, with lively peach and apple flavors. **85**

JEPSON VINEYARDS
Mendocino County
F: 1985. **O:** Jepson Ltd. **W:** Kurt Lurgnei. **S:** None.

OVERALL	$9-16	★★

WINE RATINGS

Chardonnay Mendocino County	★★
Sauvignon Blanc Mendocino County	★★
Sparkling Wine Mendocino County Brut	★★
Sparkling Wine Mendocino County Blanc de Blancs	★★

WINERY DATA
C: 10,000. **V:** 110 acres in Mendocino. **G:** Chardonnay
(80 acres), French Colombard (11), Sauvignon Blanc (18),
Viognier (1). **P:** None.

Banker Robert Jepson purchased the former Estate
William Baccala facility in 1985, in the process acquiring a modern winery, 110 acres of vineyard and an alam-
bic still. The winery's focus is on Sauvignon Blanc,
Chardonnay and sparkling wine, along with a brandy, all
made in lots of fewer than 3,000 cases. Quality varies.

TASTING NOTES

CHARDONNAY MENDOCINO COUNTY (★★): Lightly fruity.
1993: Smooth in texture, spicy in flavor, focusing its
pear and spice flavors through the lively structure. **85**
1992: Ripe and juicy, with a flinty edge to the pear and
apple notes, with spicy oak notes. **87**
1991: Decadent flavors go over the top, robbing this of
freshness and making it seem spoiled. **68**
1990: A ripe, spicy, generous wine, offering appealing
pineapple, pear and vanilla aromas and flavors. Finishes
creamy and rich without excess weight. A softer style of
Chardonnay. **90**

SAUVIGNON BLANC MENDOCINO COUNTY (★★):
1992: Soft and fruity, almost sweet on the palate, with a
candied edge to the finish. **77**

SPARKLING WINE VARIOUS BOTTLINGS (★★):
Blanc de Blancs 1988: Crisp, lean and elegant with citrus, grapefruit and lime flavors that turn to butter, spice
and toast on the finish. Complex and lively with a burst
of fruit on the finish. Drink through 1996. **88**
Brut 1989: Smooth and elegant, with spicy pear, vanilla
and crisp apple notes. Finishes with a soft aftertaste. **85**

JOHNSON'S ALEXANDER VALLEY WINES
Alexander Valley
F: 1968. **O:** Rancho Sotoyome Inc. **W:** Ellen M.
Johnson. **S:** None.

OVERALL	$6-25	NR

WINE RATINGS
Blush Alexander Valley White Zinfandel   NR

Cabernet Sauvignon Alexander Valley	NR
Chardonnay Alexander Valley	NR
Pinot Noir Alexander Valley	NR

WINERY DATA
C: 3,000. **V:** 38 acres in Alexander Valley. **G:** Pinot Noir (16 acres), Chardonnay (12), Zinfandel (4), Cabernet Sauvignon (3), Johannisberg Riesling (3). **P:** None.

This 3,000-case, family-owned winery produces estate-grown Alexander Valley Cabernet, Chardonnay, Pinot Noir and white Zinfandel from its 38 acres, selling most of its wines directly to the public.

JORDAN VINEYARD AND WINERY
Alexander Valley
F: 1972. **O:** Jordan Vineyard and Winery. **W:** Rob Davis. **S:** J.

OVERALL	$22-25	★★★

WINE RATINGS

Cabernet Sauvignon Alexander Valley	★★★
Chardonnay Alexander Valley	★★
J Sparkling Wine Sonoma County Brut	★★★

WINERY DATA
C: 75,000. **V:** 265 acres in Alexander Valley. **G:** Chardonnay, Cabernet Sauvignon, Cabernet Franc, Merlot. **P:** None.

Denver oil and gas executive Tom Jordan and his wife, Sally, spent a small fortune on vineyards and a lavish Bordeaux-style chateau in Alexander Valley that was completed in 1976, when Jordan made its first Cabernet from purchased grapes. By 1978 the estate vineyards were mature enough for the first estate-bottled Cabernet. In the mid-1980s Chardonnay joined the lineup, and in the '90's, so did J, a sparkling-wine brand and company. The Jordan Cabernet 1976 was a big hit from the moment it was introduced in 1980, memorable for its bright fruit flavors, spicy cinnamon and cedary oak nuances and smooth, polished texture. The Cabernets are wonderful to drink on release and in the first few years but not to cellar, making them perfect for restaurant sales. The Chardonnay has not enjoyed the same success.

The style has swung from ultraripe and oaky to earthy and unfocused. J, the sparkling wine, was introduced with the 1987 vintage as a business venture between Jordan and his daughter Judy, and operated separately from Jordan until 1994. It's a blend of Russian River-grown Chardonnay and Pinot Noir. The winery owns 265 acres of vineyard, with production about 75,000 cases.

TASTING NOTES

CABERNET SAUVIGNON ALEXANDER VALLEY (★★★): Supple, elegant and refined, with a polished texture, herb, cherry and currant flavors and soft tannins. Best early on.
1991: Supple and elegant, with smooth, polished, medium-weight cherry, currant, herb and anise notes and with mild tannins. **87**
1990: Supple and elegant, with spicy black cherry and plum notes and mild tannins. **87**
1989: Spicy herb and currant aromas and flavors turn earthy and leathery. **84**
1988: Crisp and lively, with nice herb, currant, spice and vanilla flavors. **85**
1987: Beginning to soften, with generous herb, olive, plum and cherry flavors that are quite inviting. **90**
1986: Ripe, smooth, rich, complex and wonderfully proportioned, with currant, plum, nutmeg and cedar flavors. **88**
1985: Ripe and floral, with touches of herb, bell pepper, currant and plum flavors that are enticingly supple and complex. **88**
1984: Supple and smooth, marked by the characteristic Alexander Valley herbal cherry and green olive flavors. **86**

CHARDONNAY ALEXANDER VALLEY (★★): Steadily improving, in a ripe, well oaked style, although it lacks the Cabernet's focus and elegance.
1992: Medium-weight, with crisp pear and apple shadings, finishing with a crisp snappy edge. Reflects a different style for Jordan, as it's less opulent and oaky. **86**
1991: A lean, crisp wine with fresh apple and pear notes and light oak, a stylistic change from the riper, oakier style of the past. **83**

J SPARKLING WINE SONOMA COUNTY BRUT (★★★): Ripe, fruity and complex, with rich flavors and good depth.
1990: Mature with spicy pear, vanilla and apple notes of moderate depth and complexity. Lacks the extra dimensions you might hope for, but it's pleasing nonetheless. **87**

1989: Intense, lively, crisp and focused, displaying a broad range of honey, pear, toast and spice flavors that are subtle and harmonious. Finishes with a burst of flavor. Tastes delicious now, but should drink well for the next few years. **89**

1987: Good, solid, crisp and clean, with tart apple and floral flavors rounded out by creamy, slightly nutty accents. The first sparkling wine from Jordan. **88**

JORY WINERY

GILROY, SANTA CLARA COUNTY
F: 1987. **O:** The Jory Group. **W:** Stillman B. Brown. **S:** None.

OVERALL	$10-13	★★★

WINE RATINGS

Chardonnay California White Zeppelin Blimp de Blanc	NR
Chardonnay Santa Clara County Selected Clone	★★
Pinot Noir California San Ysidro Vineyard	★★
Red Table Wine California Black Hand Mano Nero	★★
Zinfandel California Old Barrister Cuvée 91	★★

WINERY DATA
C: 3,500. **V:** None. **G:** None. **P:** Chardonnay (Santa Clara Valley, Monterey County), Zinfandel, Merlot (Santa Clara, San Benito), Cabernet Sauvignon, Merlot, Nebbiolo, Petite Sirah (Contra Costa, Paso Robles, San Luis Obispo).

Winemaker Stillman Brown founded this winery to make wines for local restaurants, moving first into the old Novitiate Winery near Los Gatos and then into the old Bertero Winery west of Gilroy. The 3,500-case winery's most serious endeavors are Chardonnay and Pinot Noir, but it has the most fun with a series of California-appellation, proprietary red blends: Black Hand Mano Nero, a blend of Pinot Nero, Sangiovese and Petite Sirah; Bon Jory Red, from 70- to 100-year-old vines, a blend of Pinot Nero, Primitivo, Mataro, Sangiovese, Carignane, Syrah, Cabernet Sauvignon, Merlot and Negrette, which features more different grapes than any other wine I know of; The Emperor's, a blend of similar grapes; White Zeppelin Chardonnay; and Old Barrister, a blend of Zinfandel, Primitivo and Syrah.

TASTING NOTES

VARIOUS BOTTLINGS:
Chardonnay California White Zeppelin Blimp de Blanc 1992: A fat, round wine but the flavors veer off into a sweet, candied earthiness before returning to the flight pattern with a core of pear and peach flavors. **83**

Chardonnay Santa Clara County Selected Clone 1992: Coarse and oaky, with more toasty, buttery wood than pear flavors showing. **82**

Pinot Noir California San Ysidro Vineyard 1989: Offers appealing ripe plum flavor, but it's one-dimensional. **80**

Red Table Wine California Black Hand Mano Nera 1993: Dark in color, with ripe, intense, spicy raspberry flavors. **85**

Red Table Wine California Red Zeppelin Bon Jory Red 1989: A tremendous value in a balanced, complex wine that's fresh and spicy, offering supple berry and cedar notes. **88**

Rhône Blend California Red Zeppelin II The Emperor's Reserve 1990: Smells spicy and fruity, with hints of leather and wood, and rich, lush plum, cherry and raspberry flavors come pouring through on the palate. This Rhône-style blend delivers a lot of flavor, but it's not too tannic. **86**

Zinfandel California Old Barrister Cuvée 91 1991: Earthy and tannic, with a medicinal edge to the raspberry and wild berry flavors. It's also very dry and tannic on the finish. **81**

JOULLIAN VINEYARDS

Carmel Valley
F: 1982. **O:** Joullian & Co. **W:** Raymond E. Watson III. **S:** Cépage.

OVERALL	$8-18	★★

WINE RATINGS

Cabernet Sauvignon Carmel Valley	NR
Chardonnay Monterey County	★★
Chardonnay Monterey County Family Reserve	★★
Sauvignon Blanc Carmel Valley	★★
Sauvignon Blanc Carmel Valley Family Reserve	★★

WINERY DATA
C: 10,000. **V:** 40 acres in Carmel Valley. **G:** Cabernet Sauvignon (15 acres), Merlot (2), Cabernet Franc (1), Sauvignon Blanc (8), Sémillon (2), Chardonnay (11), Zinfandel (1). **P:** Chardonnay (Santa Lucia Highlands), Chardonnay (Monterey).

Joullian Vineyards in Carmel Valley dates to 1982, when Ray Watson, brother of pro golfer Tom Watson, purchased a vineyard next to Durney, having taken a liking to Durney's Cabernets. Today the 40 acres of vines are planted to seven mainstream varietals, with Cabernet (15 acres) the leader. Chardonnay is purchased from Monterey County and Santa Lucia Highlands, and production is about 10,000 cases. The Cabernet so far has been lean and unimpressive, while the Chardonnay has varied in quality; it's overmanipulated one year, lean and thin the next. The Sauvignon Blanc has fared the best.

TASTING NOTES

CABERNET SAUVIGNON CARMEL VALLEY (NR):
1989: Firm and tannic, with a narrow band of earthy fruit flavors. Doubtful that this one's going anywhere. **80**

CHARDONNAY MONTEREY COUNTY (★★), FAMILY RESERVE (★★):
1993: Medium-bodied with enough ripe pear and citrus notes to hold your interest, even if the flavors are modest. **82**
1992: Woody flavors stand out and dominate. There are hints of pear and peach before the oak takes over. **81**
1991: Crisp and flavorful, with lively pear, lemon and nutmeg aromas and flavors that remain light and appealing through the finish. **84**
Family Reserve 1992: Bold, ripe and complex, with a rich and complex core of honey, pear, toast and spice, all folding together for a wonderful aftertaste echoing fruit and oak. **89**
Family Reserve 1991: Strives for complexity with its smoky, toasty oak overlay, but that can't quite overcome the charred, earthy notes. This is a solid wine, but perhaps a bit over-produced. **84**

SAUVIGNON BLANC CARMEL VALLEY (★★):
1992: Sturdy, spicy and round, maybe a little sweet, but balanced and drinkable. **84**

Family Reserve 1992: Spicy, toasty flavors dominate this soft-textured, buttery wine. **85**

JOYA WINERY
Napa Valley
F: 1993. **O:** Joya Wine Co. Inc. **W:** Russell G. Joy. **S:** None.

OVERALL	$8-12	★★

WINE RATINGS

Pinot Blanc Napa Valley	★★
Zinfandel Napa Valley	★★

WINERY DATA
C: 1,000. **V:** None. **G:** None. **P:** Pinot Blanc, Zinfandel (Napa Valley).

Russell and Deborah Joy founded Joya Wine Co. in Napa in 1993, releasing a 1991 Napa Pinot Blanc marked by a smooth, buttery texture, and a 1992 Napa Zinfandel made in a big, ripe, jammy style. Initial production was around 1,000 cases, with Napa Cabernet and Chardonnay just coming on line. All wines are made from purchased grapes.

TASTING NOTES

VARIOUS BOTTLINGS (★★):
Pinot Blanc Napa Valley 1991: Smooth and buttery, with a floral edge to the modest flavors, and the finish is soft and a little spicy. **83**
Zinfandel Napa Valley 1992: A big, ripe, jammy wine with tannins to match. A juniper berry note gives it an earthy edge, but there's enough wild berry flavor to admire. Finishes with crisp tannins. **86**

JUDD'S HILL
St. Helena, Napa Valley
F: 1985. **O:** Finkelstein Vineyards. **W:** Art Finkelstein. **S:** None.

OVERALL	$24-26	★★★

WINE RATINGS

Cabernet Sauvignon Napa Valley	★★★

WINERY DATA
C: 1,500. V: 11 acres in Napa Valley. G: Cabernet Sauvignon (7 acres), Merlot (2), Cabernet Franc (2). P: Cabernet Sauvignon, Cabernet Franc (Napa Valley), Merlot (Knights Valley).

Art and Bunnie Finkelstein, co-founders and former owners of Whitehall Lane Winery in St. Helena, shifted gears after selling that winery and started a 1,500-case Cabernet-only brand named after their son. The Finkelsteins own 11 acres, and their Cabernet includes a portion of Merlot from Knights Valley. Some of their wine is sold directly to consumers.

TASTING NOTES

CABERNET SAUVIGNON NAPA VALLEY (★★★): Off to a good start. Impressive for its richness, depth and purity of flavor. No track record for aging, but the wines drink well on release. Worth watching.
1991: Packs in lots of ripe, juicy plum and currant flavors, with an elegant, supple, polished texture, picking up subtle herb, tea, spice and tobacco notes. **93**
1990: Framed with buttery oak, it is lean, elegant and compact, with cherry and currant flavors that are tightly wrapped. **89**
1989: Offers a pretty dose of cherry and currant flavors, with coffee, vanilla and cola notes that turn intense and tannic. **89**

JULIANA VINEYARDS
Pope Valley, Napa County
F: 1992. O: Buttes Resource Co. W: Tucker Catlin. S: None.

OVERALL	$N/A	NR

WINERY DATA
C: N/A. V: 860 acres in Pope Valley. G: N/A. P: None.

This is a sprawling, 4,700-acre ranch in Pope Valley, northeast of Napa Valley, with 860 acres in vines. Just about every grape worth growing is being grown or studied here, although the emphasis is on red grapes. The intention is to sell most of the grapes and focus on small-case production of wines made from the best parts of the vineyard. Frog's Leap, Merryvale, St. Clement, Robert

Pepi, Rutherford Hill, The Hess Collection and William Hill were among its early customers. Tucker Catlin, a former vice president of vineyard operations for Sterling Vineyards, is president of the vineyard and is overseeing the project for the Houston-based owner.

JUSTIN VINEYARDS & WINERY
Paso Robles
F: 1981. O: Justin & Deborah Baldwin. W: Steve Glossner. S: Epoch.

OVERALL	$18-25	★★★

WINE RATINGS

Cabernet Blend San Luis Obispo County Isosceles Reserve	★★★
Cabernet Blend San Luis Obispo County Justification	★★★
Cabernet Franc San Luis Obispo County	★★★
Cabernet Sauvignon San Luis Obispo County	★★★
Cabernet Sauvignon San Luis Obispo County Society Reserve	★★★
Chardonnay Central Coast Barrel Fermented	★★★
Chardonnay San Luis Obispo County	★★★
Port San Luis Obispo County Obtuse	★★

WINERY DATA
C: 11,000. V: 74 acres in San Luis Obispo County. G: Chardonnay (25 acres), Cabernet Sauvignon (28), Merlot County, Cabernet Franc (10), Muscat (1), Italian Type (1). P: None.

Investment banker Justin Baldwin began planting his 74-acre vineyard 15 miles west of Paso Robles in the early 1980s, making his first wine with the 1987 vintage. Production is 11,000 cases and quality is high; the wines—Cabernet Sauvignon, Cabernet Franc, Isosceles Cabernet blend, Merlot and Chardonnay—all strive for deep, rich flavors, and so far have been on target more often than not. Given the successes, it's a winery worth watching.

TASTING NOTES

CABERNET BLEND SAN LUIS OBISPO COUNTY ISOSCELES RESERVE (★★★): A soulful wine that can be rich, supple and brilliant in some years and marked by strong leathery flavors in others. This bottling has carried both the Paso Robles and broader San Luis Obispo appellations.

1991: A big, ripe wine with bright black cherry and plum flavors. Picks up earthy tannins on the finish, along with a gamy edge. **84**

1990: Packed with ripe cherry and currant flavors yet firmly tannic, revealing a solid core of fruit. Picks up toasty, buttery oak and an earthy note on the finish. **88**

1989: Earthy and leathery, with plum and currant flavors and a leathery finish. **83**

1988: A tough, slightly bitter wine with tightly wrapped flavors that barely hint at currants and herbs. **75**

1987: Very rich and concentrated, with broad cherry, plum and chocolate aromas and flavors that spread across the palate, turning smooth and plush. **90**

CABERNET BLEND SAN LUIS OBISPO COUNTY JUSTIFICATION (★★★):
1992: Leans toward the vegetal side of Merlot, with a racy edge to the cherry and plum flavors, but the texture is smooth despite ample tannins. Doesn't shortchange you on flavor. **87**

CABERNET FRANC SAN LUIS OBISPO COUNTY (★★★): Shows more richness, depth and flavor than most from California.
1991: Deeply colored, with rich, chewy tannins to match and intriguing plum and black cherry flavors. **87**
1989: Charming and flavorful, with light tannins and plenty of violet, blueberry, cherry and berry flavors. **86**

CABERNET SAUVIGNON SAN LUIS OBISPO COUNTY (★★★): Broad, ripe, supple and complex when it's right, which is most of the time.
1991: Rich and supple, with a pretty core of vivid currant, plum and chocolate flavors that are complex and concentrated, focused and lively. **89**
1990: An earthy, leathery, oaky edge detracts from the ripe fruit. Perhaps with time these flavors will become more integrated, but at this stage it's a warning signal. Tasted twice, with consistent notes. Try in 1997. **80**
1989: Strikes a pleasant balance between ripe fruit flavors and a moderately rich texture, with currant, plum and cedar notes and a leathery aftertaste. **83**
1988: Tannic and tough on the palate, with very ripe, almost pruny flavors. **77**

Society Reserve 1991: Ripe and juicy, with plump, generous plum and cherry flavors and light oak shadings. **88**

CHARDONNAY VARIOUS BOTTLINGS (★★★): Packs in lots of bold, ripe and exotic flavors, but maintains its elegance.
Central Coast Barrel Fermented 1991: Elegant, smooth, ripe and creamy, with pretty honey, pear, butter and hazelnut flavors that are rich and focused. **89**
San Luis Obispo County 1992: An elegant wine with smoky, toasty, buttery oak and ripe pear and fig flavors. **87**

PORT SAN LUIS OBISPO COUNTY OBTUSE (★★):
1992: Sweet and spicy, a Port-style dessert wine with ripe cherry and currant flavors, finishing with chewy tannins and a seam of elegance, picking up a hint of chocolate on the finish. **84**

KALIN CELLARS
Novato, Marin County
F: 1976. **O:** Terrance & Frances Leighton. **W:** Terrance Leighton. **S:** None.

OVERALL	$26-30	★★★

WINE RATINGS

Cabernet Sauvignon Sonoma County Reserve	★★
Chardonnay Various Bottlings	★★★
Pinot Noir Sonoma County	★★

WINERY DATA
C: 6,000. **V:** None. **G:** None. **P:** Chardonnay, Pinot Noir, Cabernet Sauvignon (Sonoma County), Chardonnay, Sémillon (Livermore Valley), Sauvignon Blanc (Potter Valley).

Terry Leighton is a microbiologist at the University of California at Berkeley who indulges his fascination with extended wild yeast fermentations and wine in his spare time. From a rented warehouse in Novato in Marin County, Leighton makes wines from purchased grapes. I've had very mixed experiences with the wines, but can write off some poor showings to bottle variation and bad storage. Some of the reds, namely Cabernet and Pinot Noir, have been prematurely tired, with pale brown colors and fruit that lacks freshness. Chardonnay too has varied, but of late the wines have been sound, complex and flavorful. Even the 1988 Chardonnays I tried during research for this book had aged well. Production hovers around 6,000 cases, including sparkling wine.

TASTING NOTES

CABERNET SAUVIGNON SONOMA COUNTY RESERVE (★★): Looks older than the vintages should have, with mature flavors to match.
1988: Big and a bit rugged, with lots of black cherry and currant flavors shaded by a significant complement of toasty oak. **81**
1985: A mature wine with weedy, earthy aromas and black currant and olive flavors that turn tart on the finish. **83**

CHARDONNAY VARIOUS BOTTLINGS (★★★): Improving, with more richness and depth. Their extended cellaring prior to release is curious; the 1990s were being sold when most California wineries were about to release their 1993s.
Livermore Valley Cuvée W 1990: Mature with honey, apricot and pear flavors that pick up an earthy mineral flavor. **84**
Sonoma County Cuvée CH 1990: Bold, ripe, rich and supple, with a silky texture and tiers of honey, pear, spice and hazelnut flavors that gently unfold. Complex and concentrated. **91**
Sonoma County Cuvée LD 1990: Soft and showing mature spice, honey and hazelnut flavors that linger, turning complex. **87**
Sonoma County Cuvée LR 1989: A medium-weight, polished wine showing pleasant pear and apple flavors and a hint of oak. **80**
Sonoma County Cuvée LV 1989: Lean and earthy, with a metallic edge to the astringent green apple flavors. **70**
Potter Valley Cuvée BL 1988: Elegant and balanced, with ripe pear, pineapple and nutmeg flavors. **86**
Sonoma County Cuvée DD 1988: Deep and complex, with tiers of pear, honey, earth and butterscotch that are rich and concentrated. **87**
Sonoma County Cuvée LD 1988: Aging well, with complex honey, pear, herb and spice flavors and a smooth, silky texture. **87**

PINOT NOIR (★★): Usually light and simple, but can stray into earthier territory.

KARLY WINES
Amador County
F: 1980. **O:** Larry & Karly Cobb. **W:** Larry Cobb. **S:** None.

OVERALL	$8-15	★★

WINE RATINGS

Cabernet Sauvignon El Dorado County Stromberg Carpenter Vineyard	★★
Chardonnay Edna Valley MacGregor Vineyard	★★
Petite Sirah Amador County Not So Petite Sirah	★★
Sauvignon Blanc Amador County	★★
Syrah Amador County	★★
Zinfandel Amador County	★★
Zinfandel Amador County Pokerville	★★
Zinfandel Amador County Sadie Upton Vineyard	★★

WINERY DATA
C: 10,000. **V:** 20 acres in Amador County. **G:** Sauvignon Blanc (6 acres), Zinfandel (3), Petite Sirah (2), Syrah (3), Mourvèdre (2), Marsanne (2), Roussanne (1), Muscat (1). **P:** Zinfandel, Grenache (Amador County).

Larry "Buck" Cobb and his wife, Karly, founded this 10,000-case, Amador-based winery in 1980, using their 20-acre vineyard as an anchor and buying other grapes to augment their lineup. In 1995 the owners indicated they were making some switches, adding Marsanne and Syrah and dropping Chardonnay, which they had made from grapes purchased in Edna Valley. Zinfandel is their best and most reliable wine, although all the wines are well made, fairly priced and reflective of their appellations.

TASTING NOTES

CABERNET SAUVIGNON EL DORADO COUNTY STROMBERG CARPENTER VINEYARD (★★):
1991: An earthy, herbal wine with muddled currant and plum flavors. Can stand short-term cellaring to soften. Best after 1996. **82**

CHARDONNAY EDNA VALLEY MACGREGOR VINEYARD (★★): Ripe and flavorful, with a spicy honey edge.
1992: A sturdy, flavorful white wine with a spicy honey edge to the apple flavors. **81**

1991: Fresh and spicy, with a slight honey edge to the basic pear and apple flavors. **84**

Petite Sirah Amador County Not So Petite Sirah (★★): Smooth, with a wild berry edge to the flavors.
1991: Smooth and flavorful, with a wild edge to the berry character. The finish is slightly gamy. **83**

Sauvignon Blanc Amador County (★★):
1993: Smooth and fruity, a generous wine with definite leafy, herbal overtones to the pear and melon flavors. **83**

Syrah Amador County (★★):
1992: Ripe and chewy, a solid wine that beams its plum and berry flavors through chunky tannins. **85**

Zinfandel Various Bottlings (★★): Released in various bottlings, including Sadie Upton Vineyard. Quality varies, but at its best the earthy berry and tar flavors are right on target.
Amador County 1992: Intense and a bit raw, with just enough spicy cherry and raspberry flavors. **82**
Amador County 1990: Ripe and jammy, intense and tannic, with wild berry and earthy cherry notes. **86**
Amador County Pokerville 1990: Pleasantly earthy, with sweet plum and cherry flavors and an elegant texture. **88**
Amador County 1989: Thick in texture, tasting cooked, buttery, nutty and bitter on the finish. Reminds me more of Brazil nuts than fruit. Drinkable with hearty food. **74**
Amador County Sadie Upton Vineyard 1992: A ripe, jammy wine that gushes with fresh black cherry, raspberry and plum flavors before picking up an earthy tannic edge. **88**
Amador County Sadie Upton Vineyard 1991: Earthy and gamy, with coarse, leathery Zinfandel flavors. **77**
Amador County Sadie Upton Vineyard 1989: Earthy, but the raspberry and herb flavors come through. **81**

Keegan Cellars
Sonoma County
F: 1994. **O:** Eugenia Keegan. **W:** Eugenia Keegan. **S:** None.

Overall	$20	NR

Wine Ratings

Pinot Noir Russian River Valley	NR

Winery Data
C: N/A. **V:** None **G:** None. **P:** Pinot Noir (Russian River Valley).

Former Bouchaine Vineyards president Eugenia Keegan made her first Pinot Noir in 1994, with plans to market it beginning in 1996. She hopes to eventually plant her own vineyard on the Sonoma coast, build a small gravity flow winery and make an estate-bottled Pinot Noir. She is currently making her wine at the former Balverne Winery in Sonoma. Keegan began her winemaking career working with Joseph Swan and served as Bouchaine's president from 1986 through 1995. Also in the works is a small lot of Alexander Valley Zinfandel.

Robert Keenan Winery
Spring Mountain, Napa Valley
F: 1894. **O:** Robert Keenan Winery. **W:** Matthew K. Cookson. **S:** None.

Overall	$15-25	★★

Wine Ratings

Cabernet Sauvignon Napa Valley	★★
Chardonnay Napa Valley	★★
Merlot Napa Valley	★★

Winery Data
C: 10,000. **V:** 49 acres in Spring Mountain. **G:** Merlot (12 acres), Cabernet Sauvignon (13), Cabernet Franc (2), Chardonnay (21). **P:** Merlot (Carneros).

Robert Keenan purchased the old, defunct Conradi Winery at the 1,700-foot level on Spring Mountain in 1974, replanting some 49 acres to Cabernet, Cabernet Franc, Chardonnay and Merlot and introducing his first wines with the 1977 vintage. After a string of high-extract, overly tannic and excessively oaky wines in the late 1970s, Keenan redefined its style with an impressive series of opulent, polished Cabernets, but by decade's end the wines had turned leaner and more austere. Merlot, made partly from Carneros-grown grapes, also seemed to peak in quality in the mid-1980s, as recent vintages have been less interesting. The Chardonnays have been made in a lean, crisp style. Production is 10,000 cases. Nils Venge, owner/winemaker of Saddleback Cellars and formerly with Groth, is now a consultant.

TASTING NOTES

CABERNET SAUVIGNON NAPA VALLEY (★★): Increasingly lean and austere, with a tannic edge and insufficient fruit to keep it in balance. The vintages from the mid-1980s had more flesh and body.

1989: Tight and firm, with a narrow band of plum, currant, leather and earth flavors and crisp tannins. **83**

1988: Aromatic and flavorful, with more currant and berry flavors than most '88s. Turns a little tannic and tight on the finish, but is a generous wine from beginning to end. **85**

1987: Firm and tart, with sharp berry and toast aromas and flavors supported by crisp acidity and a minimum of tannin. **86**

1986: Rich and ripe, with firm tannins and toasty French oak nuances, loaded with ripe, fleshy, pretty black cherry flavors. **90**

1985: Lean and elegant, with a narrow band of ripe cherry, plum and cedar flavors. **86**

1984: Ripe and smoky, with pretty, well defined currant and cherry flavors that are firm and tannic. **91**

1983: Tight, lean and mature, with ripe currant and plum flavors and firm tannins. **87**

1982: Mature but still on the lean side, with tight plum, currant and cedar flavors that are complex. **88**

1981: Has ripe fruit flavors, but tastes dry, with oaky tannins. **83**

1980: Dry, tannic and oaky, but true to Keenan's style in this era. Just a hint of cherry and plum flavors come through. **80**

1979: Packs in lots of plum and berry flavors, but is dry and tannic to a fault. **74**

1978: Smells attractive, but is chunky and clumsy, with hard, oaky Cabernet flavors. **78**

1977: Hard, dry and tannic, with a barnyard edge that's unappealing. **69**

CHARDONNAY NAPA VALLEY (★★): Medium-weight, lean and lemony, with light oak shadings.

1992: Rich and smoky, with toasty oak flavors that add complexity and depth to the ripe pear and apple notes. **87**

1991: Solid, with ripe lemon and pear flavors that turn spicy from oak. **83**

MERLOT NAPA VALLEY (★★): Among the leaders in the early 1980s, but quality has dipped as the wines have become leaner and more tannic, following the pattern of the Cabernet.

1990: Tough, chewy and tannic, with an earthy, leathery edge to the currant and cherry notes. **83**

1989: A rough-hewn wine with hard oak and tannins overshadowing the currant and berry notes. **82**

1988: Firm and tight, with gritty tannins, but the ripe plum, blueberry and cherry flavors turn supple and smooth. **84**

1987: Lean, rich and concentrated, with pretty herb, raspberry, currant and spice flavors. **88**

1986: Complex, ripe, smooth and elegant, with a tight, rich core of currant, herb and cherry aromas and flavors. **87**

1985: Lots of weedy tobacco flavors, but also has enough plum and anise notes. **83**

1984: Big, ripe and tannic, with a tight core of cherry, tobacco and plum flavors. **90**

1983: Fully mature, supple and complex, with currant, herb, earth and cedar flavors. **86**

1982: Firm, dark and tannic, with nicely balanced, tart currant, chocolate and coffee flavors. **87**

Vintners Selection 1990: Smooth and polished, with a pretty vanilla and spice edge to the currant and blackberry flavors. **88**

KELTIE BROOK

This is a second label for MacRostie Winery (see listing).

KENDALL-JACKSON

Sonoma County

F: 1982. **O:** Jess Jackson. **W:** John Hawley. **S:** None.

OVERALL	$10-60	★★★

WINE RATINGS

Cabernet Franc California	
Vintner's Reserve	★★
Cabernet Sauvignon California	
Grand Reserve	★★★

Cabernet Sauvignon California
 Vintner's Reserve ★★
Chardonnay California Grand Reserve ★★★
Chardonnay California
 Late Harvest Select NR
Chardonnay California
 Vintner's Reserve ★★
Chardonnay Santa Maria Valley
 Camelot Vineyard ★★★
Chardonnay Sonoma Valley
 Durell Vineyard ★★★
Chenin Blanc California
 Vintner's Reserve ★★
Gewürztraminer California
 Vintner's Reserve ★★
Johannisberg Riesling California
 Vintner's Reserve ★★
Johannisberg Riesling California
 Late Harvest Select ★★★
Meritage Red California Cardinale ★★★★
Meritage White California Royale ★★★
Merlot Alexander Valley ★★★
Merlot California Grand Reserve ★★★
Pinot Noir California Grand Reserve ★★★
Pinot Noir California Vintner's Reserve ★★
Sauvignon Blanc California
 Grand Reserve ★★★
Sauvignon Blanc California
 Vintner's Reserve ★★
Syrah California Grand Reserve ★★★
Syrah California Vintner's Reserve ★★★
Syrah Sonoma Valley Durell Vineyard ★★★
Zinfandel Anderson Valley
 Ciapusci Vineyard ★★★
Zinfandel Anderson Valley
 DuPratt Vineyard ★★★
Zinfandel California Grand Reserve ★★★
Zinfandel California Vintner's Reserve ★★
Zinfandel Mendocino County
 Zeni Vineyard ★★★

WINERY DATA

C: 1,300,000. **V:** 5,000. **G:** Chardonnay, Pinot Blanc, Pinot Noir, Sangiovese, Syrah, Viognier (Santa Maria Bench), Chardonnay, Pinot Noir (Russian River Valley), Chardonnay, Merlot, Pinot Noir, Sémillon, Viognier, Riesling (Arroyo Seco), Chardonnay, Merlot, Pinot Noir, Sémillon, Viognier, Riesling (Santa Lucia Highlands), Chardonnay, Gewürztraminer, Zinfandel (Mendocino), Chardonnay (Anderson Valley), Chardonnay, Muscat, Sauvignon Blanc, Sémillon, Viognier, Riesling (Clear Lake), Merlot, Pinot Noir (Carneros), Merlot, Zinfandel (Dry Creek), Cabernet Sauvignon, Chardonnay, Zinfandel (Alexander Valley). **P:** N/A.

San Francisco attorney Jess Stonestreet Jackson started planting wine grapes at his Lake County retreat in 1974 before deciding to try his hand at winemaking in 1982. An arrested fermentation of his first wine led to a sweet Chardonnay with residual sugar, but Jackson sold the wine anyway and it proved enormously popular with consumers. Building on the straightforward fruitiness of its Vintner's Reserve Chardonnay, Kendall-Jackson grew quickly throughout the decade, reaching several hundred thousand cases by decade's end. It now produces an estimated 1.3 million cases, nearly half of that the ever-popular Vintner's Select Chardonnay and an increasingly high volume of Vintner's Select Cabernet (250,000 to 300,000 cases).

With savvy winemaker Jed Steele calling the shots, Kendall-Jackson focused on securing grape sources, choosing not to limit itself to Napa and Sonoma but looking farther south to the Central Coast, where it found excellent Chardonnay vineyards in Santa Maria Valley and Santa Barbara. One major coup came with the purchase of the 1,000-acre Tepusquet Vineyard in Santa Maria. Those grapes helped fuel K-J's growth and provided the foundation for Cambria Winery. Jackson then acquired Edmeades in 1988; Stephen Zellerbach, renaming it Stonestreet, in 1989; and in 1994 both Vinwood, a large modernized winemaking facility north of Healdsburg, and Robert Pepi Winery in Napa Valley. K-J keeps adding vineyards—it now has some 5,000 acres in vines—and new brands (La Crema, Gauer Estate).

While Chardonnay and Cabernet roll up big sales numbers, K-J also focuses on designer wines. Jackson gave Steele enough leeway to experiment with smaller lots of wines; when Steele found the right grapes, he kept the wine separate, leading to vineyard-designated Chardonnay, Zinfandel and Syrah, usually made in 200- to 500-case lots. K-J's finest wines are now bottled under the Grand Reserve designation, except for its proprietary red, the Cabernet-based Cardinale, which by the mid-1990s appeared headed toward a Napa Valley appellation as Jackson's staff focused on Napa for premium-quality Cabernet grapes. Underscoring K-J's commitment to reach the top in California wine, Jackson hired the talented winemaker

Charles Thomas from Robert Mondavi Winery in 1994, his assignment being to further fine-tune the top wines. Thomas joined a K-J staff already deep in experience, including Tom Selfridge, former president and winemaker at Beaulieu; John Hawley, former winemaker for Clos du Bois; and Pete Downs, former winemaker for Chateau St. Jean's sparkling wines. As the decade unfolds, K-J and its satellite wineries appear poised for continued growth as the individual wineries develop their specialties and K-J hones its best wines.

TASTING NOTES

CABERNET FRANC CALIFORNIA VINTNER'S RESERVE (★★):
1992: This wine has a green herbal and cedary oak edge to the spicy currant and berry notes. **82**

CABERNET SAUVIGNON CALIFORNIA GRAND RESERVE (★★★): Richer and more polished than the Vintner's Reserve, with currant and cherry flavors and more toasty oak. Shows steady improvement.
1991: Bright, ripe and rich, with layers of currant, black cherry and spice flavors that are focused and concentrated. **89**
1990: Ripe and generous, with a strong current of fruit flavors, firm tannins and an herbal edge. **90**
1988: Light and simple, with hints of raspberry, black cherry, spice and leather flavors. **83**
1987: Smooth and spicy, with supple currant, berry and vanilla flavors that linger on the finish. **87**
1986: Smooth and silky, with ripe plum and red cherry flavors, turning a bit herbal and vegetal on the finish. **85**
1985: Sleek and elegant, with an overlay of toasty French oak and layers of spice, currant, cassis and cherry flavors underneath. **91**

CABERNET SAUVIGNON CALIFORNIA VINTNER'S RESERVE (★★): Serves up ripe, forward fruit flavors with light oak shadings and mild tannins.
1992: Firm, with a tight core of currant, cedar and tobacco notes that pick up a minty note and chewy tannins. **82**
1991: Pleasantly fruity, with grape, herb, cherry and currant notes framed by light oak, finishing with firm tannins. **83**
1990: Light and fruity, with straight-on Cabernet flavors that offer hints of plum and cherry, but the finish turns dry and oaky and ends rather abruptly. **83**

CHARDONNAY CALIFORNIA GRAND RESERVE (★★★): Elegant, well oaked and refined. Improving.
1993: Effusively fruity, with pretty pear, spice, pineapple and creamy vanilla flavors that fold together nicely in a seamless, elegant package. **90**
1992: Smooth, ripe and creamy, with complex, elegant pear, toast and spice flavors. **90**
1991: Spicy and lively, with honey, pear and vanilla flavors that are focused and harmonious. **85**

CHARDONNAY CALIFORNIA LATE HARVEST SELECT (NR):
1993: Ripe and honeyed, centered around some pretty pear fruit that persists into a gentle finish. **85**

CHARDONNAY CALIFORNIA VINTNER'S RESERVE (★★):
1993: Ripe and fruity, with a pretty band of pear and spice flavors, finishing with honey and vanilla notes. **85**

CHARDONNAY SANTA MARIA VALLEY CAMELOT VINEYARD (★★★):
1993: Offers attractive ripe pear, apple, honey and citrus notes and holds its focus on the finish, where it turns elegant. **88**
1992: Firm and flinty, an intense and focused wine, with spicy pear, honey and light, toasty oak shadings. **88**
1991: Ripe, smooth and intense, with buttery pear and apple flavors complemented by toasty oak and spice notes. **89**

CHARDONNAY SONOMA VALLEY DURELL VINEYARD (★★★):
1991: Simple and unexciting, with ripe pear, apple and spice flavors that turn to custard and nutmeg. **80**

CHENIN BLANC CALIFORNIA VINTNER'S RESERVE (★★):
1992: Light and direct, off-dry, showing fresh apple and leafy flavors, polished on the finish. **84**

GEWÜRZTRAMINER CALIFORNIA VINTNER'S RESERVE (★★):
1993: Bright and refreshing, a simple wine with pleasant pear and spice flavors. **82**

JOHANNISBERG RIESLING CALIFORNIA LATE HARVEST SELECT (★★★):
1993: Ripe and very sweet, soft enough that it seems syrupy, more unctuous than rich. Echoes honey and floral notes on the finish. **86**

JOHANNISBERG RIESLING CALIFORNIA VINTNER'S RESERVE (★★):
1993: Soft, a little sweet, with modest apple and citrus flavors. **80**
1992: Soft and fragrant, with bright peach and apple flavors and a piney edge. **84**

MERITAGE RED CALIFORNIA CARDINALE (★★★★):
Ripe and tightly wound, usually well focused, with lots of flavor and depth, but at times it's a shade too tart and austere.
1990: Bold, ripe, smooth and polished, with layers of plum, currant, cherry and blueberry flavors that are focused and lively. **91**
1989: An earthy, rough-hewn wine with chunky currant, herb and oak flavors. **86**
1988: Light and spicy, with ripe cherry and prune notes that pick up a touch of anise on a smooth finish. **85**
1987: Rich, ripe and concentrated, with plum, blueberry and currant flavors laced with spicy oak. Vanilla and cinnamon notes emerge on the long finish. **92**
1986: Lean and tannic, with intense, ripe aromas and flavors of currant and cherry and firm, crisp tannins. **91**
1985: Delivers a lot of richness and complexity, with pretty currant, cherry and plum flavors, finishing with toasty, buttery oak. **94**
1984: Ripe, with supple cassis and plum flavors framed by smoky, spicy oak notes. **84**

MERITAGE WHITE CALIFORNIA ROYALE (★★★):
1994: Bright and intriguing, with passion fruit, citrus and pear flavors that just don't quit. If there is oak, it is well submerged. Delicious. **89**
1992: Soft and fragrant, offering pear, spice and herb character in a gentle package. **85**

MERLOT CALIFORNIA GRAND RESERVE (★★★): Has yet to achieve the depth and flavor of the Cabernet, but is consistently well made, with medium-bodied currant, cherry and spice notes.
1991: Serves up a pretty array of ripe, supple cherry, plum and strawberry flavors, with appealing spice notes and mild tannins. **86**

MERLOT CALIFORNIA VINTNER'S RESERVE (★★):
1992: Crisp and austere, with a narrow band of spicy currant and herb notes, picking up a cedary edge on the finish. **82**

1991: Serves up smooth currant, chocolate, herb and spicy, buttery oak flavors. **87**
1990: A solid wine with ripe currant, cherry and spicy oak flavors, but it also has a leathery, barnyardy edge. **83**
1989: Lean, earthy and vegetal, with tart plum and tobacco notes. Not quite ripe. **75**
1988: A lively wine with generous spice, plum and berry aromas and flavors that come together on the finish. **84**

PINOT NOIR CALIFORNIA GRAND RESERVE (★★★):
Supple and elegant, with appealing cherry, cola and spice flavors.
1993: Supple and elegant, marked by toasty oak, and the ripe cherry and spicy plum flavors slide through past the soft tannins. **88**
1992: Smooth and supple, an elegant Pinot Noir with herb, cola and spicy cherry flavors and light, buttery oak notes. **86**

PINOT NOIR CALIFORNIA VINTNER'S RESERVE (★★):
Light and simple but serviceable.
1993: Firm and spicy, with a narrow band of herb and black cherry fruit. **83**
1992: Tight and firm, showing a tough veil of tannin, but underneath the cherry and cedar flavors are appealing. **82**
1991: Light and simple, with herb and pepper notes that turn to tar and tea on the finish. **80**
1990: Crisp, light and lively, with a nice bead of raspberry, vanilla and gamey flavors. **82**

SAUVIGNON BLANC CALIFORNIA GRAND RESERVE (★★★): Tight and complex, taming the grape's herbal tendencies.
1993: Ripe and broad, a harmonious wine with a sweet layer of smoky oak, pear and honey flavors. **86**
1992: Crisp and bright, offering some nice herbal grace notes to the lemony melody. A stylish wine that remains lively through the long finish. **87**

SAUVIGNON BLANC CALIFORNIA VINTNER'S RESERVE (★★): The Vintner's is simpler, with lightly herbal flavors.
1993: Sturdy, simple and lightly herbal, softly fruity at the core. **82**

SYRAH CALIFORNIA GRAND RESERVE (★★★):
1991: Rich and mouthfilling, a beautifully balanced red with upfront blackberry, black cherry and black pepper flavors. **88**

1990: Bold, rich and spicy, with plush, jammy plum, raspberry and cherry flavors that are smooth and polished. **88**

SYRAH CALIFORNIA VINTNER'S RESERVE (★★★):
1990: Dense and peppery, with a tight core of plum and berry aromas and flavors. **83**

SYRAH SONOMA VALLEY DURELL VINEYARD (★★★):
Among the best: dark and well focused, with rich fruit flavors and lots of depth.
1990: Smooth and supple, with polished herb, currant and spice flavors, finishing with mild tannins. **85**
1988: Ripe and smooth, with supple berry and plum flavors and a nice touch of new oak. **89**
1987: Ripe and supple, with a burst of plum and berry flavors framed by vanilla, toast and black pepper. **90**
1986: Supple and rich, with loads of spicy cherry, beautiful sweet oak and cinnamon flavors, turning voluptuous and succulent on the finish. **92**

ZINFANDEL ANDERSON VALLEY CIAPUSCI VINEYARD (★★★):
1989: An oaky wine with spicy, buttery aromas that override the peppery plum flavors. **82**
1988: Tannic and oaky, with hard-edged, smoky, toasty wood notes dominating the subdued berry flavors. **77**
1987: A claret-style Zin with ripe pepper, raspberry and earth aromas and flavors, framed by toasty oak. **88**
1984: Delivers a nice core of spice, pepper and ripe raspberry flavors, with mild tannins. **86**

ZINFANDEL ANDERSON VALLEY DUPRATT VINEYARD (★★★):
1990: Ripe and spicy, with pepper, cherry and raspberry flavors and toasty, buttery oak notes. **88**
1987: Ripe and focused, rich and elegant, with layers of plum, raspberry, vanilla and toasty oak flavors. **90**
1986: Thick and intense, bold and assertive, with rich pepper and berry notes and ample oak. **85**

ZINFANDEL CALIFORNIA GRAND RESERVE (★★★): Tight and supple, with focused spice and raspberry notes.
1992: Lightly fruity, with simple berry notes and firm tannins. **84**
1991: Crisp, firm and very tannic, this wine has a lean core of spicy berry flavors that hang together. **86**

1990: Dark and inky, packing in lots of rich, spicy raspberry, cherry and wild berry flavors, turning spicy and elegant. **89**

ZINFANDEL CALIFORNIA VINTNER'S RESERVE (★★):
More variable with lighter, less focused flavors.
1992: Firm and tannic, with a gritty texture and hints of wild berry and spicy raspberry. **83**
1991: A light, refreshing wine with cherry and raspberry flavors that are crisp and tight. **84**
1990: Ripe and intense, with peppery Zinfandel flavors that turn to menthol. **78**
1989: Light and fruity, well focused, with raspberry and currant flavors. **84**

ZINFANDEL MENDOCINO COUNTY (★★★):
1987: Earthy and complex, with fresh, ripe cherry, plum and raspberry flavors that are rich and intense. **88**
1986: Fresh and packed with blackberry flavors, pure and clean, with overtones of black pepper and cedar. **86**

ZINFANDEL MENDOCINO COUNTY ZENI VINEYARD (★★★):
1990: Firm and peppery, with classic plummy Zin flavors underneath. **83**

KATHRYN KENNEDY WINERY
Santa Cruz Mountains
F: 1979. **O:** Kathryn Kennedy Winery Inc. **W:** Marty Mathis. **S:** Lateral.

OVERALL	$54	★★★

WINE RATINGS	
Cabernet Blend California Lateral	★★★
Cabernet Sauvignon	
Santa Cruz Mountains	★★★

WINERY DATA
C: 1,000. **V:** 9 acres in Santa Cruz Mountains. **G:** Cabernet Sauvignon (9 acres). **P:** Merlot (Santa Clara County), Merlot (Monterey County), Merlot, Cabernet Franc, Cabernet Sauvignon (Santa Cruz Mountains), Merlot, Cabernet Franc (Nevada County), Cabernet Franc (Napa County).

Owner Kathryn Kennedy established this 9-acre Cabernet vineyard to protect her from real estate developers who coveted this property. Kennedy took wine-growing seriously, attending viticultural and winemaking classes, and decided to focus on Cabernet while adding a second wine from purchased grapes, a Merlot-Cabernet Franc-Cabernet Sauvignon blend called Lateral, made from vineyard sources as diverse as Napa, Nevada County, Monterey and Santa Cruz. Combined production is 1,000 cases, divided between the two wines. Given the pressures to develop in this area, with prices running several hundred thousand dollars an acre, this is clearly a labor of love.

TASTING NOTES

CABERNET SAUVIGNON SANTA CRUZ MOUNTAINS (★★★): Aptly reflects the appellation, with its earthy currant and herb flavors and firm tannins, but it can be ripe and opulent too. Ages well.

1991: Walks a tightrope between its earthy juniper berry and peppery cherry notes. Firmly tannic. **87**

1990: Earthy and oaky, with a potent tannin level, but it has rich, earthy currant and spice flavors too. **89**

1989: Tight and firm, with intense black cherry, currant, herb and cedary oak flavors. **87**

1988: Smooth, lush and polished, with supple, complex anise, currant and plum aromas and flavors, mild tannins and herbal oak shadings. **88**

1987: Deep, rich and concentrated, a potent wine that packs in currant, plum and anise flavors supported by crisp, firm tannins. **90**

1986: Rich and polished, with a complex bouquet of black cherry and currant aromas and flavors and spicy, buttery oak shadings. **89**

1985: Broad, ripe and complex, with concentrated currant, herb, spice and cherry flavors that are intense and framed by spicy, toasty oak and firm tannins. **91**

1984: Opulent, with rich, ripe currant, plum and black cherry flavors framed by toasty, spicy oak. **88**

1983: Austere, with firm, tight, leathery tannins that submerge the ripe currant and berry notes. **84**

1982: Ripe and flavorful, with firm currant, berry and mineral flavors that pick up a tannic edge. **88**

1981: Supple and complex, with broad layers of rich, fleshy currant, anise and black cherry flavors that are plush and concentrated. **91**

1980: Smooth, ripe and generous, with spicy currant and anise flavors that turn lean and focused. **88**

CABERNET BLEND CALIFORNIA LATERAL (★★★): Well crafted, often showing off more of Merlot's herbal characteristics, backed by solid tannins.

1991: Austere, with a tannic edge and enough ripe currant, plum and tar flavors to keep in balance. **86**

1990: Firm, focused and spicy, with supple cherry, cinnamon and raspberry flavors blending together. **88**

1989: Oaky and spicy, with a smooth texture and modest berry and dill flavors. **84**

1988: Deliciously rich and fruity, with layers of ripe plum, cherry, currant and raspberry flavors that have a nice smoky edge. **87**

KENWOOD VINEYARDS
Sonoma Valley
F: 1970. **O:** Kenwood Vineyards. **W:** Michael Lee. **S:** None.

OVERALL	$9-40	★★★

WINE RATINGS	
Cabernet Sauvignon Sonoma Valley	★★★
Cabernet Sauvignon Sonoma Valley Artist Series	★★★★
Cabernet Sauvignon Sonoma Valley Jack London Vineyard	★★★
Chardonnay Sonoma Valley	★★
Chardonnay Sonoma Valley Beltane Ranch	★★★
Chardonnay Sonoma Valley Reserve	★★★
Chardonnay Sonoma Valley Yulupa Vineyard	★★★
Merlot Sonoma County	★★
Merlot Sonoma Valley Jack London Vineyard	★★★
Merlot Sonoma Valley Massara Vineyards	★★★
Pinot Noir Sonoma Valley Jack London Vineyard	★★
Sauvignon Blanc Sonoma County	★★★
Zinfandel Sonoma Valley	★★★
Zinfandel Sonoma Valley Barricia Estate Vineyard	★★★
Zinfandel Sonoma Valley Jack London Vineyard	★★★

Winery Data

C: 210,000. V: 125 acres in Sonoma Valley. G: Chardonnay (58 acres), Sauvignon Blanc (37), Cabernet Sauvignon (18), Merlot (12). P: Pinot Noir, Syrah, Sauvignon Blanc, Merlot, Zinfandel, Chardonnay, Cabernet Sauvignon, Cabernet Franc (Sonoma Valley), Chardonnay, Pinot Noir, Sauvignon Blanc (Russian River Valley), Sauvignon Blanc, Merlot, Cabernet Sauvignon (Dry Creek, Alexander Valley).

John Sheela's family farmed grapes in the Central Valley before he decided fine wine might have a future in California. When the old Pagani Winery in Kenwood came up for sale, Sheela put together a partnership to buy it in 1970, a group that included his college roommate and future brother-in-law, Marty Lee, and eventually more of the Lee family, including Marty's parents and his younger brother Mike, who became winemaker. Progress with all Kenwood's wines has been steady since its revival under the Sheela-Lee regime, with reds getting a slight nod over whites overall, despite the winery's huge success with Sauvignon Blanc and improvements with Chardonnay.

Today the winery owns 125 acres of vines, mostly Chardonnay and Sauvignon Blanc, and prefers hillside-grown grapes. It has contracts to buy from several key vineyards that it uses for vineyard-designated wines, among them Milo Shepard's Jack London Vineyard at the base of Sonoma Mountain for Cabernet, Merlot, Pinot Noir and Zinfandel; Beltane Ranch and Yulupa Vineyard in Sonoma Valley for Chardonnay; and Barricia in Sonoma Valley for Zinfandel. The flagship is the Artist Series Cabernet, which combines Marty and Mike's passion for art and fine wine. The winery commissions a leading artist (à la Mouton-Rothschild) to design or sell a piece of art for use on the label, then selects the best lots of Cabernet. Production is 210,000 cases, with nearly one-third devoted to Sauvignon Blanc.

Tasting Notes

Cabernet Sauvignon Sonoma Valley (★★★):

1991: Austere and tannic, with chunky herb and currant flavors, framed by oak. **82**

1990: Distinctively minty and mildly tannic, weaving cherry and currant flavors through the minty notes. **84**

1989: Firm, focused and flavorful, offering distinctive spicy and minty characteristics, with rich currant and plum flavors. **88**

1987: Dark, rich and intense, but also shows a tight, tannic edge. The chocolate, black cherry, currant and berry flavors shine through, picking up a nice touch of toasty oak. **90**

1986: Aromatic, with a minty, meaty nose, but lean, rich and tannic on the palate, with a pretty core of black cherry and currant flavors framed by oak. Turns tannic. **86**

1985: A big, robust wine packed with rich, ripe plum, currant and black cherry flavors and a good dose of tannin and oak. **88**

1984: Lots of plum, cherry and anise flavors in a fleshy wine that's now mature. **83**

Cabernet Sauvignon Sonoma Valley Artist Series

(★★★★): The Artist Series ranks among the state's best, its only shortcoming being that it can be exceedingly tough and tannic. It can also be unusually supple and charming in so-called off vintages.

1991: Firm and compact, with a tight, narrow band of spicy currant, cedar, oak and mineral notes. Picks up an earthy edge on the finish, but hangs together. **90**

1990: Hard-edged and tannic, with mint, herb and tart berry flavors framed by cedar notes. **86**

1989: Firm, rich and deeply flavored, packed with spicy currant, plum and cherry flavors framed by spicy, buttery oak notes. **91**

1988: Tight and tough, with a cedary tobacco edge to the currant and earth flavors. It's softening with time. **85**

1987: Ripe and supple, with plush currant, cherry, anise and buttery oak flavors that fold together nicely. **90**

1986: Rich, smooth and layered, with ripe, lush black cherry, currant, cedar, toast and spice flavors all in exquisite balance, finishing with delicacy and finesse. **92**

1985: Elegant and refined, typical of the vintage, offering plenty of currant, cassis, cedar and spice flavors, fine tannins and good length. **91**

1984: Big, ripe and deeply concentrated, with complex black cherry, spice and plum flavors to match firm tannins. **93**

1983: Mature, still lean and firm, with elegant fruit flavors, fine tannins and a pretty spice and cedar aftertaste. **87**

1982: Tight, lean and concentrated, with spice, cedar, earth and plum flavors now emerging from the tannins. **87**

1981: Aging well, with ripe plum, currant and cassis flavors and a fleshy texture. **89**

1980: A weedy, vegetal wine that lacks the appeal of most Artist Series bottlings. **80**

1979: Mature and drying, but holding its complex chocolate, plum, anise and spice flavors. **90**

1978: Mature and drinking well, with supple cedar, cinnamon, currant and plum flavors and a long, full finish. The grapes came from Laurel Glen and Steiner Vineyards, and were aged in French oak for the first time. **90**

1977: Mature and declining, with modest plum, anise and mint flavors. **82**

1976: Fading, with pungent earthy flavors. **75**

1975: Well past its prime but valuable as a collectible, so if you still have a bottle, don't open it. **73**

CABERNET SAUVIGNON SONOMA VALLEY JACK LONDON VINEYARD (★★★):

1991: Serves up ripe plum and cherry flavors before picking up a trace of bitterness from wood. **83**

1989: Deep, dark and plush, with supple currant, plum and anise flavors and smooth, earthy tannins. **87**

1987: Packs plenty of ripe cherry and currant flavors into the tannic structure, with hints of spice and vanilla. **91**

1986: Deep in color and fairly tannic, it's spicy and minty, with very intense Cabernet flavors. **88**

1985: Very dark, ripe and concentrated, but the tannins turn smooth, with mint and cherry flavors. **89**

1984: Concentrated and tannic, with supple chocolate, cherry and berry flavors that turn smooth. **89**

CHARDONNAY SONOMA VALLEY (★★), RESERVE (★★★):

1993: Ripe and pleasantly fruity, with pear, citrus and spicy notes that hang together. **84**

1992: Crisp and medium-bodied, with light pear and oak notes. **83**

1991: Fresh and lively, with apple, butter, vanilla and oak flavors. **85**

Reserve 1993: Compact with medium-weight pear, oak and spice notes, but not the extra dimensions of some vintages. **87**

Reserve 1992: Subtle and elegant, with medium-weight spice, pear and nutmeg flavors. **84**

Reserve 1991: Intense and lively, showing a ripe, rich, focused core of spicy pear, vanilla and hazelnut flavors. **91**

CHARDONNAY SONOMA VALLEY BELTANE RANCH (★★★):

1993: Medium-weight with spicy pear, apricot and spicy oak notes of modest proportion. **84**

CHARDONNAY SONOMA VALLEY YULUPA VINEYARD (★★★):

1993: Marked by minty edge that turns to a piney oak flavor that overrides pear and apple fruit. Disjointed at this stage. **83**

1992: Elegant, with ripe pear, spice and vanilla flavors, picking up a hint of nutmeg on the finish. **85**

1991: Young, ripe and intense, with spicy pineapple, pear, citrus and apple flavors. **87**

MERLOT SONOMA COUNTY (★★):

1992: Lean with a cedar and tobacco edge, but it thins out and the plum flavors lack depth. **83**

1991: Lean, oaky and simple, with modest herb and currant notes. **81**

1990: Smooth, soft and elegant, with rich, supple herb, currant and plum flavors and supple tannins. **87**

1989: Crisp and fruity, with light berry and currant flavors that toughen up on the finish. **83**

MERLOT SONOMA VALLEY JACK LONDON VINEYARD (★★★):

1991: Rugged tannins and a deep color, with spicy cedar, plum and currant notes. **87**

1990: Lean, with hints of berry and currant, picking up toast, smoke and tobacco flavors. **82**

MERLOT SONOMA VALLEY MASSARA VINEYARDS (★★★):

1992: Tight and cedary, with a lean band of cherry and currant; needs short-term cellaring to soften as the tannins are substantial. **84**

PINOT NOIR SONOMA VALLEY JACK LONDON VINEYARD (★★): The weakest red, it is usually on the herbal, weedy side of the flavor spectrum, but it gets ripe once in a while and can be more flavorful and full-bodied.

1992: Earthy and a bit funky, with candied cherry flavors that are one-dimensional. **80**

1991: Light and simple, with weedy plum and cherry notes. **79**

1990: Ripe, jammy fruit flavors mark this medium-bodied, nicely oaked Pinot. **85**

1989: Tart and light, with modest cherry and plum flavors. **80**

SAUVIGNON BLANC SONOMA COUNTY (★★★): Among the top five in the mid-1980s and still among the best, with clearly defined and very appealing herb, spice, grass and pear flavors. Remarkably consistent.

1993: Crisp, floral and lively, with smoothly integrated apple fruit character. **84**
1992: This wine shows Kenwood at the top of its Sauvignon Blanc game. The herb and citrus flavors pick up fig and spice notes on the finish. **86**

ZINFANDEL SONOMA VALLEY (★★★):
1992: Supple and spicy, with an elegant band of peppery berry flavors. Finishes with firm tannins. **84**
1991: Firm and compact, with a narrow band of spicy cherry flavors. **82**
1990: Firm, tight and oaky, with an elegant core of spicy berry and plum flavors. **86**
1988: Drinkable and pleasant, with appealing wild berry and toast flavors. **82**
1987: Rich and elegant, with supple raspberry, cherry and spicy plum flavors that are fresh and lively. **90**
1985: Juicy blackberry and cherry flavors are mature and a touch earthy. **89**
1984: Ripe, rich and tarry, complex and concentrated, with berry, tar and spice notes. **87**

ZINFANDEL SONOMA VALLEY BARRICIA ESTATE VINEYARD (★★★):
1991: A big, oaky and tannic wine packed with rich, briary, wild berry and cherry flavors and dry tannins. **84**
1990: Supple, with ripe, rich plum, cherry, vanilla and spice flavors that are sharply focused and opulent. **88**

ZINFANDEL SONOMA VALLEY JACK LONDON VINEYARD (★★★): Sound, packed with spicy, peppery berry flavors, framed by light oak and firm tannins.
1992: Light and fruity, with simple earthy berry flavors that turn elegant and simple. **82**
1991: Lean and tight, with a narrow beam of earthy berry and limestone flavors that turn tannic. **86**
1990: Broad, ripe and complex, with intense raspberry, cherry, spice and buttery oak shadings. **88**
1989: Crisply focused and tart, with lively plum and berry aromas and flavors that finish strong. **83**
1987: Attractive for its ripe raspberry, cherry and vanilla notes and elegant balance. Firmly tannic. **88**

JOHN KERR WINES
Santa Maria Valley
F: 1986. O: John Kerr. W: John Kerr. S: None.

OVERALL	$19-30	★★

WINE RATINGS
Chardonnay Santa Barbara County	★★
Pinot Noir Santa Barbara County	★★

WINERY DATA
C: 1,000. V: None. G: None. P: Chardonnay, Merlot, Syrah, Muscat, Pinot Noir (Santa Barbara).

John Kerr began his winemaking career at the historic Brookside Winery near Los Angeles in the early 1970s, and has worked for several wineries (notably Byron, Chalone and Jekel), but his own brand dates to 1986, when he began making small lots of Chardonnay and Pinot Noir. Production hovers around 1,000 cases, with the wines made from purchased grapes. So far quality has not risen to the level of Byron's. The 1991 Chardonnay Santa Barbara offered a narrow band of flavors, while the 1990 Pinot Noir had a funky, bitter edge. It was followed by a much better 1991, which served up a wide range of cherry, berry, earth and spice flavors.

TASTING NOTES

VARIOUS BOTTLINGS (★★):
Chardonnay Santa Barbara County 1991: Fresh and simple, with a narrow band of pear, nectarine and spice flavors. **80**
Pinot Noir Santa Barbara County 1991: Delivers a wide range of cherry, berry, earth and spice notes that unfold elegantly and subtly. **85**
Pinot Noir Santa Barbara County 1990: A funky wine with pungent earth, beet and cola flavors that have a bitter, oaky finish. **80**

KISTLER VINEYARDS
Sonoma County
F: 1978. O: Kistler Family. W: Stephen W. Kistler. S: None.

OVERALL	$22-50	★★★★★

WINE RATINGS
Cabernet Sauvignon Sonoma Valley Kistler Estate Vineyard	★★★
Chardonnay Russian River Valley Dutton Ranch	★★★★★

Chardonnay Russian River Valley
  Vine Hill Road Vineyard ★★★★★
Chardonnay Sonoma Coast ★★★★★
Chardonnay Sonoma County ★★★★★
Chardonnay Sonoma County
  Cuvée Cathleen ★★★★★
Chardonnay Sonoma Mountain
  McCrea Vineyard ★★★★★
Chardonnay Sonoma Valley
  Durell Vineyard ★★★★★
Chardonnay Sonoma Valley
  Kistler Estate Vineyard ★★★★★
Pinot Noir Russian River Valley
  Cuvée Catherine ★★★
Pinot Noir Russian River Valley
  Dutton Ranch ★★★
Pinot Noir Sonoma Mountain
  McCrea Vineyard ★★★

WINERY DATA

C: 18,000. **V:** 123 acres in Russian River Valley, Sonoma Valley, Sonoma Mountain. **G:** Chardonnay (96 acres), Pinot Noir (27). **P:** Chardonnay (Sonoma Valley), Chardonnay (Sonoma Coast), Chardonnay (Russian River Valley), Pinot Noir (Sonoma Coast).

Steve Kistler studied English at Stanford, hoping for a career as a writer, but found wine-making more to his liking. In the late 1970s he teamed up with Mark Bixler, a chemistry wiz, and with the backing of the Kistler family the duo founded Kistler Vineyards in 1978. Considering how consistently excellent Kistler's seven different Chardonnays are, you could make a strong case for crowning him king of Chardonnay. There are a few Chardonnays in the state that rival Kistler's, but no one is putting out seven to match these. It's mindboggling how complex and intricate these wines are every year, and while each of the bottlings has distinctive features, they are more alike than dissimilar.

The winery's 18,000 cases are dominated by Chardonnay, and it's vineyard holdings now measure 123 acres, including 96 in Chardonnay and 27 in Pinot Noir. The Chardonnays are all barrel-fermented, undergo full malolactic fermentation and are aged on their lees, and wild (or natural) yeast fermentations are often part of the formula. Kistler is a big fan of different yeast strains and uses them to achieve the broadest range of flavors possible. He prefers his wines to have a doughy, hazelnut flavor, a character sometimes found in great white Burgundies, and part of this is achieved through his vinification techniques. The wines typically display a bold, rich, creamy texture, tiers of fruit and spice flavors and remarkably long finishes.

The Cabernets and Pinot Noirs are not in the same league as the Chardonnays—at least not yet—although the Cabernet is made in a very deliberate and consistent style. The Pinot Noir is not new to the lineup, but it has not been a main focus until just recently. The Sonoma Coast and Cuvée Cathleen Chardonnays, as well as a Cuvée Catherine Pinot Noir, are new additions to the lineup.

TASTING NOTES

CABERNET SAUVIGNON SONOMA VALLEY KISTLER ESTATE VINEYARD (★★★): Dark, intense and usually quite compact and tannic. In cooler years it displays a strong herb, bell pepper and stemmy edge, while in warmer years those flavors are less evident and currant and cherry notes emerge.
1991: Marked by herb, coffee and black olive notes, it's smooth and supple with polished currant and plum flavors, finishing with a complex aftertaste and fine tannins. Ready now through 2000. Shows more restraint with tannins than past vintages. **90**
1990: Rich and velvety, with a coffee-tobacco streak running through the modest berry and beet flavors. **86**
1988: Firm and focused, with a strong beam of bell pepper, cherry and tobacco flavors. Firmly tannic. **86**
1987: A weedy wine with pretty black currant, plum and spice flavors, and also a good dose of herb and mint notes and firm tannins. **83**
1986: Ripe and distinctively peppery—black, bell and chili—turning soft, lush and generous on the palate. Still firmly tannic. **86**
1985: Remarkably complex and elegant, with well focused plum, spice and pepper notes that are very enticing. The tannins are firm but supple for Kistler. **92**

CHARDONNAY RUSSIAN RIVER VALLEY DUTTON RANCH (★★★★★):
1992: Intense and lively, with layers of tightly wound

pear, spice, vanilla and nutmeg flavors, held together by crisp acidity and finishing with a long, full aftertaste that lingers. **92**
1991: Ripe and refreshing, with rich, intense pear, spice, hazelnut and earth flavors that turn silky. **92**
1990: Ripe and creamy, with fresh pear, herb, smoke and butter notes that are neatly focused and well integrated. **88**
1989: Intense and complex, with pretty floral aromas and a solid core of pear, butter, toast and spice flavors. **89**

CHARDONNAY RUSSIAN RIVER VALLEY VINE HILL ROAD VINEYARD (★★★★★):
1992: Ripe, rich and exotic, with layers of pear, toast, hazelnut and smoky oak, all folding together into a complex and concentrated wine. **91**
1991: Rich and complex, combining a generous core of pear, pineapple, spice and earth notes with a smooth, supple texture, turning smoky and toasty. **92**
1990: Complex and deep, with rich, ripe pear, apple and spice flavors framed by toasty, buttery oak notes. **90**

CHARDONNAY SONOMA COAST (★★★★★):
1993: Well oaked, with smoky, toasty oak flavors, but a pretty core of elegant pear and spice, picking up the hazelnut notes, finishing with a complex aftertaste. **89**

CHARDONNAY SONOMA COUNTY (★★★★★):
1992: Packs in lots of ripe, fresh, lively pear, nectarine, spice and honey notes, turning smooth and elegant, with a fleshy texture. **93**

CHARDONNAY SONOMA COUNTY CUVÉE CATHLEEN (★★★★★):
1992: Remarkably complex with ripe, rich pear, fig and smoky oak flavors, turning complex and lingering on the finish. First Cuvée Catherine bottling, named after Steve Kistler's sister. **92**

CHARDONNAY SONOMA MOUNTAIN McCREA VINEYARD (★★★★★):
1992: Youthful and tight, with smoky, toasty pear and spice flavors slowly unfolding, revealing more depth and complexity. **92**
1991: Bold, ripe and complex, loaded with tiers of citrus, pear, fig and spicy wood nuances that turn smooth and creamy. **91**

1990: Exuberantly fruity and full-bodied, with tons of grapefruit, pear, cream, butter and vanilla flavors. **92**
1989: Broad pineapple and grapefruit flavors are generously layered with the new oak notes of vanilla and butter. **88**
1988: Remarkably rich, concentrated and elegant, with tiers of pear, lemon, melon and stony mineral flavors. **92**

CHARDONNAY SONOMA VALLEY DURELL VINEYARD (★★★★★):
1993: Smooth, ripe and harmonious, with a rich complex core of pear, hazelnut, honey and spice notes, finishing with a smoky oak aftertaste. **91**
Sand Hill 1992: Ripe and assertive, brimming with rich pear and apple flavors framed by toasty oak, spicy pear and honey notes. **91**
Sand Hill 1991: Tight and concentrated, with a toasty oak edge, this is rich and flavorful, showing pear, apple and spice flavors. **90**
Sand Hill 1990: Rich, dense and enormously concentrated, with toasty, buttery notes over tight peach and pear flavors that turn creamy. **93**
1989: Ripe, spicy and buttery in flavor, with rich pear, honey and vanilla notes that fill the mouth and really last on the finish. Complex and generous. **90**
1988: A wonderfully delicious wine, with pure, rich, elegant, subtle pear, melon, spice and citrus notes all contributing to the complexity and depth. **90**

CHARDONNAY SONOMA VALLEY KISTLER ESTATE VINEYARD (★★★★★):
1992: A rich, high-extract, enormously complex blend of ripe pear, apple and spice flavors and toasty, smoky, buttery oak nuances. **94**
1991: Bright and lively, with juicy pear, apple and pineapple flavors that are framed by pretty, toasty, buttery oak flavors, turning elegant and smoky. **90**
1990: Enormously complex and deep, with rich, concentrated pear, pineapple, citrus and hazelnut flavors that glide across the palate. Finishes with a long, smoky, toasty aftertaste. **92**
1989: Generous, ripe and buttery, packed with layers of pear, pineapple, nutmeg and vanilla flavors that turn complex. **91**
1988: Oozing with rich, opulent, delicious pear, honey, vanilla, lemon and spicy nutmeg flavors that explode on the palate, displaying uncommon finesse and a smooth, creamy texture. **94**

PINOT NOIR VARIOUS BOTTLINGS (★★★): Steadily improving, although it shares the Cabernet's hard, stemmy, tannic qualities and could offer more fruit.

Russian River Valley Cuvée Catherine 1991: Firm and tannic, with a coarse, stemmy, woody edge to the tight cherry and raspberry flavors. Try after 1996. **85**

Russian River Valley Dutton Ranch 1986: Loads of ripe raspberry, cherry and blackberry flavors and firm tannins that are softening. **86**

Russian River Valley Dutton Ranch 1984: Ripe and tannic, with broad tar, cherry and spice flavors and firm, gripping tannins. May always be tannic. **84**

Sonoma Mountain McCrea Vineyard 1992: Serves up a ripe, supple core of black cherry, anise and currant flavors that turn smooth and polished despite a firm tannic backbone. **88**

KLEIN
Santa Cruz Mountains
F: 1986. O: Arturo Klein. W: Arturo Klein. S: None.

OVERALL	$18-22	★★

WINE RATINGS
Cabernet Sauvignon
  Santa Cruz Mountains   ★★

WINERY DATA
C: 400. V: 3 acres in Santa Cruz Mountains. G: Cabernet Sauvignon. P: None.

Swiss banker Arturo Klein owns this 3-acre, 400-case, Cabernet-only winery in the Santa Cruz appellation. Quality varies, ranging from dense and concentrated to earthy and funky.

TASTING NOTES

CABERNET SAUVIGNON SANTA CRUZ MOUNTAINS (★★):
1990: Deep and dark, it turns earthy and mulchy on the palate. **81**
1989: A spicy, cedary wine with ample ripe berry and plum flavors. **85**
1988: Strong smoke and tobacco notes override the currant and berry flavors. **83**
1987: Big, intense and tannic, with bell pepper, olive and currant flavors, finishing with toasty oak. **87**

1986: Densely concentrated, with complex smoke and ripe plum flavors. **89**

KONRAD ESTATE
Mendocino County
F: 1982. O: Konrad Estate Winery Inc. W: Victor Simon John Buechsenstein. S: None.

OVERALL	$9-18	★★

WINE RATINGS
Barbera Amador County	★★★
Charbono Mendocino County	★★
Chardonnay Mendocino County	★★
Meritage Red Mendocino County	
Mélange a Trois	★★
Petite Sirah Mendocino County	★★
Port Mendocino County	
Petite Sirah Port Admiral's Quinta	NR
Zinfandel Mendocino County	★★
Zinfandel Mendocino County	
Ricetti Vineyard	★★

WINERY DATA
C: 5,000. V: 12 acres in Mendocino. G: Zinfandel (8 acres), Petite Sirah (4). P: Chardonnay (Mendocino), Cabernet Sauvignon (Mendocino), Merlot (Mendocino), Cabernet Franc (Mendocino), Charbono (Mendocino).

Konrad Estate is a 5,000-case winery based in Redwood Valley in Mendocino County, with 12 acres in vines and a roster that includes Barbera from Amador County, Charbono, Chardonnay, Petite Sirah Port, a red Meritage called Mélange a Trois, Petite Sirah and Zinfandel from Mendocino. The wines are sound, although quality varies. The 1992 Barbera from Amador is dark and well crafted, with a wild berry edge to it.

TASTING NOTES

BARBERA AMADOR COUNTY (★★★):
1992: Well crafted and dark, with an earthy currant and wild berry edge that turns to mineral and spice. **87**

CHARBONO MENDOCINO COUNTY (★★): Earthy, with a dry, leathery edge.
1992: Earthy, with a leathery edge to the plum flavors. **82**

CHARDONNAY MENDOCINO COUNTY (★★): Often simple, with modest fruit flavors, although the 1991 is rich and buttery.
1992: Simple, with modest, toasty apple flavors. **77**
1991: Ripe and buttery, with bold, spicy pineapple, fig and pear notes. **88**

MERITAGE RED MENDOCINO COUNTY MÉLANGE A TROIS (★★): Lean and crisp, with appealing fruit flavors.
1991: Crisp in texture, jammy and intense, showing currant and berry flavors and hints of vanilla and toast on the finish. **86**
1989: Tight and firm, with rich currant, cherry and anise flavors that offer fine depth and concentration. Turns tannic. **85**

PETITE SIRAH MENDOCINO COUNTY (★★): Bright, with chunky fruit flavors and dry tannins.
1991: Bright in flavor, chunky in texture, slipping some nice blackberry and spice flavors through the tannins. **82**

PORT MENDOCINO COUNTY PETITE SIRAH PORT ADMIRAL'S QUINTA (NR):
1990: An awkward, Port-style wine that's coarse and sweet, with decadent floral aromas and flavors. Extremely tannic. **74**

ZINFANDEL VARIOUS BOTTLINGS (★★): Variable, ranging from lean and crisp to fuller-bodied, with blackberry and plum flavors.
Mendocino County 1991: Crisp and austere, with more drying tannins than cherry and raspberry flavors. **80**
Mendocino County 1990: Chewy, concentrated and distinctive, offering blackberry, plum, black pepper and dill flavors. **87**
Mendocino County 1989: Packed with ripe berry flavors and accented by cinnamon notes, but also quite tannic. **84**
Mendocino County Ricetti Vineyard 1990: Classic peppery Zinfandel flavors, bright, spicy and complex, with hints of tar, cedar and anise adding to the pepper and berry notes. **88**

KORBEL CHAMPAGNE CELLARS
Russian River Valley
F: 1882. **O:** Gary B. & Richie C. Heck. **W:** Greg Gessner. **S:** Armstrong Ridge.

OVERALL	$10-15	★★

WINE RATINGS

Cabernet Sauvignon Alexander Valley	NR
Chardonnay Russian River Valley	★★
Sparkling Wine California Blanc de Noirs Cuvée Master's Reserve	★
Sparkling Wine California Blanc de Blancs	★
Sparkling Wine California Brut	★
Sparkling Wine California Natural	★★
Sparkling Wine California Rosé	★

WINERY DATA
C: 1,500,000. **V:** 400 acres in Russian River Valley. **G:** Chardonnay (170 acres), Pinot Noir (90), French Colombard (45). **P:** N/A.

Korbel Champagne Cellars in Russian River is a beautiful old winery with scenic landscaped gardens and brilliant flower arrangements. It is one of the largest wineries in California, producing between 1.5 million and 2 million cases of *méthode champenoise* sparkling wine. Even though quality has been uneven of late, these modest and modestly priced wines offer good value. A Brut, Brut Natural, Blanc de Blancs, Blanc de Noirs and Rosé lead the way, although the winery added Sonoma County Chardonnay and Alexander Valley Cabernet in the 1990s. A new, high-end sparkling cuvée was in the works in 1994.

TASTING NOTES

VARIOUS BOTTLINGS:
Cabernet Sauvignon Alexander Valley 1991: Earthy, leathery, dry and tannic. Just a hint of fruit sneaks through. Marginal. **73**
Chardonnay Russian River Valley 1993: Smooth and creamy, medium-bodied with ripe pear, fig and apricot flavors, finishing with a spicy edge. Well crafted. **85**
Chardonnay Sonoma County 1992: Strikes a nice balance between light pear and apple notes and spicy oak flavors. **82**
Chardonnay Sonoma County 1991: An odd earthy streak runs through the ripe pear and spice flavors. **70**
Sparkling Wine California Blanc de Noirs Cuvée Master's Reserve 1990: Tastes sweet, with crisp, tinny pear, cherry and citrus notes. **78**

Sparkling Wine California Natural NV: Tastes off-dry, with cherry and candied fruit flavors, but it's crisp and clean. **80**

CHARLES KRUG WINERY
St. Helena, Napa Valley
F: 1861. **O:** C. Mondavi & Sons. **W:** John Moynier. **S:** C.K. Mondavi.

OVERALL	$9-28	★★★

WINE RATINGS

Cabernet Sauvignon Napa Valley	★★
Cabernet Sauvignon Napa Valley Vintage Selection	★★★
Chardonnay Reserve	★★★
Chardonnay Napa Valley	★★
Merlot Napa Valley	★★
Pinot Noir Carneros	★★
Zinfandel Napa Valley	★★

WINERY DATA
C: 650,000. **V:** 1,000 acres in Napa Valley. **G:** Cabernet Sauvignon, Chardonnay, Chenin Blanc, Merlot, Pinot Noir, Zinfandel (Napa Valley). **P:** N/A.

Russian immigrant Charles Krug founded this winery in St. Helena in 1861, establishing a 540-acre estate and vineyard. Phylloxera (at the end of the 19th century) and Prohibition doomed the winery, and it closed until 1943, when another immigrant, Italian-born Cesare Mondavi, bought the winery at the urging of his son Robert, who had scouted out Napa Valley with an eye to moving his family's wine business there from Lodi. The Mondavi era featured Cesare and sons Robert and Peter overseeing winemaking, production and marketing. Charles Krug's flagship wine was the Vintage Selection Cabernet, which the winery started producing in 1946. Krug's quality and volume grew through the 1960s, and Krug became one of Napa's big four—along with Beaulieu, Inglenook and Louis Martini.

In the early 1960s family tensions over wine styles and future directions led to a bitter falling out between Robert and Peter, with Robert departing to start his own winery in 1966 and Peter remaining in charge of Charles Krug. Robert prevailed in a lawsuit against his family, which diverted both money and key vineyards

from the Krug winery, leading by the early 1970s to a period of decline. Only the Vintage Selection Cabernet held its own, as the vineyard source shifted to western Yountville. By the mid-1980s, Krug was back on solid footing following a major renovation and while its wines are improved, they are still more mainstream than cutting edge. Occasionally though, wines such as the 1990 and 1992 Carneros Reserve Chardonnays indicate the potential of the winery's considerable vineyard holdings throughout the valley, measuring some 1,000 acres spread out in nine vineyards. Moreover, the winery is experimenting with Bordeaux-style blends and new Reserve wines.

TASTING NOTES

CABERNET SAUVIGNON NAPA VALLEY (★★): Uneven; thin, light and herbal one year, full-bodied and flavorful the next.
1991: Ripe and fleshy, with spicy plum and currant flavors that finish with soft tannins and a touch of anise and light oak shadings. **88**
1990: Firm and tight, but with a nice core of black cherry, currant and plum flavors underneath. **88**
1989: Ripe and supple, with a narrow band of plum and currant-laced fruit that turns crisp on the finish with mild tannins. **83**
1988: A squeaky-clean wine that's tart and hollow. **73**
1987: Crisp and focused, with berry and spice aromas and orange peel and caramel flavors. **79**
1986: A big, sturdy, flavorful wine packed with herb, currant, cherry and chocolate flavors. **87**

CABERNET SAUVIGNON NAPA VALLEY VINTAGE SELECTION (★★★): Can be rich and plush, with deep, concentrated flavors. It was generally sound during the 1980s. Ages well.
1990: Marked by ripe plum and currant flavors that are direct and unevolved, with firm tannins, but lacking extra dimensions early on. **87**
1988: Deep, dark and complex, offering tart, intense, lively currant, mineral and black cherry flavors that pick up a slightly vegetal edge on the finish, where it's tannic. **87**
1986: Rich and lively, with ripe black cherry, pepper, currant and spice flavors that are complex and concentrated, almost opulent. **92**

1985: A ripe, supple wine with spicy, mature currant and cherry flavors that linger on the finish. **89**
1984: Beautifully balanced, with a solid backbone of acid and ripe, jammy flavors delivered in an elegant package, with berry, currant and mint notes. **88**
1983: Oaky and tannic, but with the Krug trademark of ripe, jammy berry, raspberry and cedar notes. **82**
1981: Complex and inviting, with mature anise, plum, tar and currant flavors, finishing with hints of cedar and spice. **87**
1980: Considerable bottle variation. At its best it offers tart black cherry and spice notes, but there are bottles that taste as if they're going through malolactic fermentation. **75**
1979: Mature and high in extract, with plum, prune, cherry and anise flavors. **82**
1977: The anise, plum and prune flavors are dry and fading. **74**
1974: Mature, with an earthy edge to the supple currant and plum flavors. Dries out on the finish. **81**
Lot F1 1974: From Fay Vineyard in Stags Leap. Mature, with rich, supple flavors that are drying out after a long run of excellence. **88**
1968: Past its prime but showing the signature ripe plum flavor that characterizes the Vintage Select. **80**
1961: Still displays pretty rose petal and plum flavors and great persistence on the finish. **89**
1959: Very pleasant the last time I tried it, with a complex, smoky cedar aroma and rich, mature plum flavor. **85**
1958: Past its prime, but it still shows rich, complex ripe plum and currant flavors. **85**
1956: Fading now, but for a long time a tremendous wine, supple, elegant and serving up ripe plum flavors. **90**
1952: Elegant and spicy, with rich, mature plum and prune flavors. Still in fine condition the last time I tried it. **90**
1951: The 1951 vintage in Napa was excellent, and the Krug displays very ripe, jammy, sweet fruit flavors of good depth and intensity. Better a decade ago, but still holding on. **85**
1950: The faint cherry and plum flavors are thin and drying. **79**
1946: Showing ripe cedar, cassis and plum flavors and a touch of tannin on the finish. At its peak, it was an excellent wine. **88**

CHARDONNAY CARNEROS RESERVE (★★★): This Reserve has shown signs of brilliance, depth and intensity.

1992: Despite a leesy edge, the ripe pear and honey flavors are accented with spicy oak and nutmeg notes. **89**
1991: Crisp, tart and leesy, with pear, pineapple and spicy nutmeg flavors. **87**

CHARDONNAY NAPA VALLEY (★★):
1993: Light and simple, with delicate pear and spice flavors. **81**
1992: Ripe pear, citrus and oak flavors pick up a toasty, buttery edge. **84**

MERLOT NAPA VALLEY (★★): Correct and balanced, but lacking the extra dimensions of the best.
1992: Lean and trim, with a narrow band of currant and spice flavors. **83**
1991: This wine has a green tobacco edge to the plum flavor. **81**
1990: Dark in color, smooth in texture, with ample plum, raspberry and tobacco notes. **85**
1989: Crisp and lean, with tart cherry and sage notes. **84**

PINOT NOIR CARNEROS (★★): Light and herbal, with tarry flavors and modest depth.
1992: Tart and earthy, with a spicy raspberry edge. **82**
1990: Marked by ripe cherry, cedar and herb flavors and hints of oak. **78**
1989: Light and silky, with hints of currant, cherry and spice flavors. **82**
1987: Well balanced and sharply focused, with a tight core of cherry and plum flavors. Firm tannins and toasty oak notes add complexity and echo on the finish. **87**
1985: Light, spicy and tealike, with austere strawberry and toast flavors that turn silky. **81**

ZINFANDEL NAPA VALLEY (★★): Simple, with crisp, modest flavors.
1992: Simple, with earthy Zin notes of modest proportion and distinction. **81**
1990: Tart and lean, with cedar and cherry aromas and flavors. **74**
1989: Lean, with raspberry and strawberry flavors that turn light and crisp. **83**

KUNDE ESTATE WINERY
Kenwood, Sonoma Valley
F: 1989. **O:** Kunde Family. **W:** David Noyes. **S:** None.

OVERALL	$10-19	★★★

WINE RATINGS

Cabernet Sauvignon Sonoma Valley	★★★
Chardonnay Sonoma Valley	★★★
Chardonnay Sonoma Valley	
Estate Reserve	★★★
Chardonnay Sonoma Valley	
Kinneybrook Vineyard	★★★
Chardonnay Sonoma Valley	
Wildwood Vineyard	★★★
Meritage Red Sonoma Valley	
Louis Kunde Founder's Reserve	★★★
Merlot Sonoma Valley	★
Sauvignon Blanc Sonoma Valley	
Magnolia Lane	NR
Viognier Sonoma Valley	★★★
Zinfandel Sonoma Valley	
The Shaw Vineyard Century Vines	★★

WINERY DATA

C: 50,000. V: 700 acres in Sonoma Valley. G: Chardonnay (150 acres), Cabernet Sauvignon (100), Merlot (71), Zinfandel (70), Sauvignon Blanc (30). P: None.

The Kundes started planting grapes in Sonoma Valley in 1904, and their hillside vineyards were long a source for Sebastiani Vineyards, which bought most of theirgrapes until 1990. Sebastiani used parts of Kunde's vineyard for its vineyard-designated wines, Bell, Kinneybrook and Wildwood. In 1989 Kunde Estate Winery got off to a good start with a series of wines including Chardonnay, Meritage red and Zinfandel, although quality varied in subsequent vintages, possibly due to rapid expansion: plans called for the winery to grow from 32,000 to 110,000 cases by decade's end. Kunde Estate spreads out over 2,000 acres, with 650 planted to grapes in seven different microclimates that rise up 1,200 feet above the valley floor.

TASTING NOTES

CABERNET SAUVIGNON SONOMA VALLEY (★★★):
1990: Ripe, supple and complex, with generous berry, currant and toast flavors, finishing with firm tannins. **87**

CHARDONNAY VARIOUS BOTTLINGS (★★★): Ripe and well focused, with rich, complex fruit flavors and light oak shadings.

Sonoma Valley 1992: Ripe and spicy, with a pretty core of buttery pear, hazelnut and fig flavors. **88**
Sonoma Valley 1991: Elegant and focused, with pretty pear, nectarine, honey and vanilla flavors and a nice oak edge. **89**
Sonoma Valley Estate Reserve 1992: Spicy and concentrated, with pretty pear, fig and anise notes that are firm and focused. **89**
Sonoma Valley Kinneybrook Vineyard 1992: Intense and chunky, with heavy-handed pear and butterscotch flavors that turn oaky. **82**
Sonoma Valley Wildwood Vineyard 1992: Firm and tight, a compact wine with ripe, spicy pear and oak flavors that turn coarse. **82**

MERITAGE RED SONOMA VALLEY LOUIS KUNDE FOUNDER'S RESERVE (★★★): Firm, tannic and chocolaty, with rich, intense fruit flavors.
1990: Firm and focused, a spicy, toasty, chocolate-scented wine with a modest core of currant and plum flavors. **88**
1989: Ripe, rich and spicy, with a Syrah-like edge, packing in lots of currant, anise, earth and tar flavors. The texture is thick and plush, with supple tannins. **89**

MERLOT SONOMA VALLEY (★):
1991: Surprisingly earthy and tarry, devoid of fruit. Off the pace for Kunde. **77**

SAUVIGNON BLANC SONOMA VALLEY MAGNOLIA LANE (NR):
1993: Smooth and distinctly herbal, a light wine with a resiny edge. **80**

VIOGNIER SONOMA VALLEY (★★★):
1993: Deliciously fresh, floral and spicy, a bright, fruity wine with exotic overtones. Focused and supple on the finish. **88**

ZINFANDEL SONOMA VALLEY THE SHAW VINEYARD CENTURY VINES (★★): Marked by a lean, narrow band of fruit flavors.
1992: Earthy and a bit funky, with drying fruit flavors. Misses the mark. **74**
1991: Tart and crisp, with pepper, black cherry and spice notes that turn elegant. **83**
1990: Intense and focused, with ripe plum and berry flavors that turn soft. **84**

LA CREMA
Sonoma County
F: 1979. **O:** Jess Jackson. **W:** Dan Goldfield. **S:** None.

OVERALL	$11-20	★★★

WINE RATINGS

Chardonnay California	★★★
Chardonnay California Reserve	★★★
Pinot Noir California	★★★
Pinot Noir California Reserve	★★★

WINERY DATA
C: 100,000. **V:** 38 acres in Green Valley. **G:** Chardonnay, Pinot Noir. **P:** Chardonnay, Pinot Noir (Sonoma Valley), Chardonnay, Pinot Noir (Santa Barbara), Chardonnay, Pinot Noir (Monterey), Chardonnay (Napa Valley), Chardonnay, Pinot Noir (Mendocino), Pinot Noir (Marin).

Burgundy-inspired La Crema changed hands twice before Jess Jackson of Kendall-Jackson bought it in 1993. La Crema was founded in 1979 as La Crema Vinera in a dreary warehouse in Petaluma, where it remained until 1983, when New Yorker Jason Korman and a group of investors bought the brand. The new owners expanded production and introduced a line of cash-flow wines before running into financial troubles which forced them sell the winery via bankruptcy to Jackson, the highest bidder. Through the years the Chardonnays have held a slight edge over the Pinot Noirs, although the former has had its share of quality swings.

Standard and Reserve bottlings of both La Crema wines carry the California appellation, the belief being that complex wines are best created through blending different vineyards. "In an average year, would a little Chambertin help a Richebourg?" asks winemaker Dan Goldfield. "Yes, it can." Both the Chardonnay and Pinot Noir are mixtures of grapes grown in Russian River, Santa Barbara, Mendocino, Marin, Anderson Valley and Potter Valley. Production is 100,000 cases, 70,000 of that being Chardonnay. Reserves are made in lots of a few thousand cases.

TASTING NOTES

CHARDONNAY CALIFORNIA (★★★), RESERVE (★★★): Well oaked, with rich, complex, creamy flavors. Usually very good, sometimes earthy, sometimes outstanding.
1992: Elegant and refined, with creamy pear, spice, hazelnut and toasty oak flavors. **87**

Reserve 1993: Hits the right notes, with clean, correct pear, light oak and spice notes, finishing with a crisp edge. **85**
Reserve 1992: Rich and bold, with complex, concentrated buttery pear and spice flavors. **90**

PINOT NOIR CALIFORNIA (★★★), RESERVE (★★★): Not as complex as the Chardonnay but flavorful, with cherry, earth, herb and leather notes.
1992: Tight, firm and tannic, with a core of plum, rhubarb and cola flavors. **84**
1991: Raw and tight, not showing much fruit. **78**
1986: Spicy and elegant, with pretty strawberry, black cherry and cinnamon flavors that are lean and concentrated. **89**
1985: Powerful and ripe, smooth and elegantly balanced, with complex cherry, plum, clove and smoke flavors. **90**
Reserve 1993: Tight and tannic, with a lean beam of earthy berry and mineral flavors. **85**
Reserve 1992: Intense and lively, complex and concentrated, with ripe cherry, earth and buttery oak flavors. **88**
Reserve 1991: Pungent, gamy and earthy in the extreme. **79**
Reserve 1990: Crisply focused, lean and lively, with appealing ripe raspberry, black cherry, tea and spice flavors. **85**
Reserve 1986: Extremely ripe, with plum and cherry jam flavors that are rich and powerful. **85**

LA CROSSE
This is a second label for Beaucanon Winery (see listing).

LA FAMIGLIA DE ROBERT MONDAVI
This is a second label for Robert Mondavi Winery (see listing).

LA JOTA VINEYARD CO.
Howell Mountain
F: 1982. **O:** Bill & Joan Smith. **W:** Bill Smith, Helen Turley. **S:** Little J.

OVERALL	$18-38	★★★

WINE RATINGS

Cabernet Franc Howell Mountain	★★★
Cabernet Sauvignon Howell Mountain	★★★

Petite Sirah Howell Mountain	NR
Viognier Howell Mountain	★★★
Viognier Howell Mountain Sweet	NR
Zinfandel Howell Mountain	NR

WINERY DATA

C: 5,000. **V:** 28 acres in Howell Mountain. **G:** Cabernet Sauvignon (18 acres), Cabernet Franc (4), Merlot (3), Viognier (3). **P:** None.

Oilman and home winemaker Bill Smith came to Napa Valley to find vineyard land for a development investment, and after accomplishing that goal decided along with his wife, Joan, that a combination weekend retreat and vineyard sounded even better. While scouting around Howell Mountain, Smith discovered a rustic stone winery built in 1895 by Frederick Hess. By 1982 the Smiths had found a winemaker, neighbor Randy Dunn, and their first La Jota Vineyard Co. Cabernet was released, followed by Zinfandel and later Cabernet Franc, Viognier, Marsanne and Roussanne.

There's no disputing that La Jota Cabernets are distinctive, intense, rustic, concentrated and tannic. But my many experiences with the wines show that they often dry out and turn ponderous and tannic before evolving into something more complex and intricate as they promise in their youth. Looking back at years of notes, I find that I've always liked the Cabernets far more out of barrel and on release than after they've been cellared. The Smiths are also concerned about their wines and in 1993 retained Helen Turley to help tame the tannins. Production hovers around 5,000 cases from the winery's 28 acres in vines, the majority planted to red Bordeaux varieties. In 1991 the winery split its Cabernet production, focusing on its estate Howell Mountain Anniversary Series bottling and a lower-priced Howell Mountain selection.

TASTING NOTES

CABERNET FRANC HOWELL MOUNTAIN (★★★): Lighter than the Cabernet Sauvignon, with appealing flavors, but lacking focus.
1992: Well oaked but not overdone, with buttery, spicy overtones and a pretty core of currant and cherry flavors that fan out. **89**
1991: Smooth, ripe and polished, with pretty, toasty oak, cherry and currant flavors. **86**

1990: Light and appealing, with herb, tobacco and cedar notes overriding the currant and spice. Mild tannins. **83**
1988: A fine Cabernet Franc with layers of currant, plum, vanilla and spice notes. **84**
1986: Mature, with earthy cedar, anise and currant flavors that pick up grainy tannins on the finish. **84**

CABERNET SAUVIGNON HOWELL MOUNTAIN (★★★): Solid, intense and austere. The compact fruit flavors struggle against significant tannins and oak. Early vintages have not evolved and are somewhat disappointing.
1992: Solid with a chunky core of earthy currant and tobacco, turning supple in texture but with ample tannins for short-term cellaring. **88**
10th Anniversary Release 1991: Big, rich, chewy and tannic, packed with cedar, currant, earth and oak flavors. Deeply colored and firmly structured, this brawny wine needs time to soften. **87**
1990: Firm and supple, with intense currant, anise and herb notes that turn smooth and fleshy on the finish despite ample tannins. **86**
1989: An appealing 1989 with earthy currant and cherry notes that turn oaky. **83**
1988: The spicy, peppery flavors turn tannic and gutsy, with modest cherry and plum notes. **85**
1987: Austere, dry and oaky, with a narrow band of cedary earth and currant notes that dry up on the finish. Unimpressive in my last tasting. **82**
1986: A solid wine with cedar, oak and currant notes, developing a supple, silky texture despite ample tannins and a good dose of oak. It's doubtful that it will live up to earlier expectations. **85**
1985: Still austere, with tightly wound tobacco and currant notes, and I wonder whether it will evolve into a more complex and compelling wine with further cellaring. **83**
1984: Heavy oak dominates, leaving a dry, tannic finish, but the cherry and currant flavors struggle to work through the oak and tannins. **83**
1983: Tight, thin and austere, with the cherry and currant flavors drying up. **79**
Napa Valley 1982: Dry and austere, with its fruit dropping out, turning oaky. **79**

PETITE SIRAH HOWELL MOUNTAIN (NR):
1992: Ripe and chewy, a nicely shaped wine that shows typical Petite Sirah tannins but offers appealing spice, oak and blackberry aromas and flavors. **87**

VIOGNIER HOWELL MOUNTAIN (★★★): Intense and spicy, true to the variety, but essentially one-dimensional. **1991:** Firm and supple, with ripe, rich pear, earth, honey and spice flavors that are complex. **89**
Sweet 1993: Very ripe, honeyed and unctuous, with hay-like overtones to the sweet pear and cereal flavors. Tasty if highly unusual. **85**

ZINFANDEL HOWELL MOUNTAIN (NR): Intense, peppery and spicy, sharing the appellation's firm tannins.
1987: Very tough and tannic, with intense cherry flavor that battles the tannins. **83**

LA PETITE VIGNE
This is a second label for Pine Ridge Winery (see listing).

LAKE SONOMA WINERY
Alexander Valley
F: 1977. O: Lake Sonoma Winery Co. W: Don Polson. S: None.

OVERALL	$10-16	★
WINE RATINGS		
Cinsault Dry Creek Valley		
Vintner's Reserve		NR
Merlot Dry Creek Valley		
Yoakim Bridge Ranch		★★
Zinfandel Dry Creek Valley		★

WINERY DATA
C: 3,000. V: 10 acres in Dry Creek Valley. G: Merlot (4 acres), Zinfandel (4), Cinsault (2). P: Zinfandel, Merlot, Cinsault (Dry Creek).

This winery was originally Diablo Vista Vineyards in Contra Costa County. In 1982 it was purchased by the Polson family, which already owned 10 acres of vineyard in Dry Creek Valley near the Lake Sonoma dam rooted to small portions of Cinsault, Merlot and Zinfandel. The 3,000-case winery augments its grape output with purchases. Quality varies, occasionally rising above average.

TASTING NOTES

CINSAULT DRY CREEK VALLEY VINTNER'S RESERVE (NR):
1991: An awkward, earthy, murky blend of cherry and plum flavors. **73**

MERLOT DRY CREEK VALLEY YOAKIM BRIDGE RANCH (★★): Solid, marked by earthy, leathery flavors in a medium-bodied style.
1991: Big and powerful, definitely leathery, showing bright currant and berry aromas and flavors before the barnyardy notes take over. **83**
1990: Lively and complex, with earthy aromas to the concentrated, fresh cherry flavors. **86**

ZINFANDEL DRY CREEK VALLEY (★): Earthy and funky flavors appear more often than not, which is unusual for this appellation.
1990: Another earthy, gamy Zinfandel from Lake Sonoma, which reflects a consistent style from this producer even if the flavors are a bit off-target. **72**
1989: Ripe and spicy, with a pleasant band of cedar, chocolate and wild berry flavors. **84**

LAKESPRING WINERY
Napa Valley
F: 1980. O: Canandaigua Wine Co. W: Randy Mason. S: None.

OVERALL	$9-15	★★
WINE RATINGS		
Cabernet Sauvignon Napa Valley		★★
Chardonnay Napa Valley		★★
Merlot Napa Valley Yount Mill Vineyard		★★
Sauvignon Blanc Napa Valley		
Yount Mill Vineyard		★★

WINERY DATA
C: N/A. V: N/A. G: None. P: N/A.

The Battat brothers—Frank, Harry and Ralph—founded Lakespring Winery near Yountville using mostly purchased grapes, with the huge Pelissa Vineyard being a major source for the winery's Cabernet and Merlot. These wines were big, ripe and often weedy, and they held an edge over the highly variable Chardonnay and Sauvignon Blanc. After years of slow sales and declining quality, production dropped from 25,000 cases to half that before the Battats decided to get out of the business, selling the brand to Canandaigua and the winery to Franus and Havens. Lakespring's future is unclear.

TASTING NOTES

CABERNET SAUVIGNON NAPA VALLEY (★★): In steady decline since the early 1980s, it's a big, ripe, intense and weedy wine marked by dry tannins.
1990: Firm and chewy, showing a solid beam of currant and berry flavors shining through the thick veil of tannin. **87**
Reserve Selection 1988: Shows stinky, swampy aromas and raisiny, vegetal flavors. **74**
1987: Firm, focused and decidedly minty, with solid currant and berry flavors that extend into a tannic finish. **84**
1986: Mature, with drying tannins and an earthy, weedy edge to the currant and cherry flavors. **88**
1985: Has turned austere and dry, with the greenish tannins now showing more presence. There are lots of currant and wild berry flavors, but it lacks focus and harmony. **84**
Reserve Selection 1984: This ultraripe wine is mature, with deep, weedy black currant, earth and spice flavors. **88**
Vintage Selection 1982: While showy early on, it has taken on a dry, tannic, earthy profile. **82**
1981: Lean and tight, with mint, anise and plum flavors that turn dry and tannic. **86**
1980: A big, rich, high-extract wine that's mature and turning earthy, with dry currant flavors. **82**

CHARDONNAY NAPA VALLEY (★★): Crisp and lightly fruity, although variable.
1992: Crisp and lightly fruity, turning astringent on the finish. **81**

MERLOT NAPA VALLEY YOUNT MILL VINEYARD (★★): Shares the Cabernet's weedy, tannic edge.
1990: Firm and focused, offering ripe plum, currant and black cherry flavors and nice smoky, spicy notes. **88**
1988: Tight and austere, with strong oak and menthol notes and tiers of currant, plum and cherry flavors. **85**

SAUVIGNON BLANC NAPA VALLEY YOUNT MILL VINEYARD (★★):
1993: Fresh and herbal, with a nice core of peach and melon flavors. **83**

LAKEWOOD
Clear Lake, Lake County
F: 1974. **O:** Jess Jackson. **W:** Dave Rosenthal. **S:** None.

OVERALL	$9-12	★★★

WINE RATINGS

Sauvignon Blanc Clear Lake	★★
Sauvignon Blend Clear Lake Chevriot	★★★
Sémillon Clear Lake	★★

WINERY DATA
C: 5,000. **V:** 71 acres in Clear Lake. **G:** Sémillon (29 acres), Sauvignon Blanc (12), Chardonnay (24), Muscat Canelli (3), Viognier (2), Sangiovese (1). **P:** None.

This is the original winery Jess Jackson used to launch Kendall-Jackson (see listing) back in 1974. He planted vineyards then but didn't make wine until 1982. Jackson decided to create a separate brand—Lakewood—with this location near Clear Lake as its base. The focus at Lakewood will be on Clear Lake-grown Sauvignon Blanc, Sémillon and a blend of the two grapes. The winery owns 71 acres, split among Chardonnay (24 acres), Sémillon (29), Sauvignon Blanc (12), Muscat Canelli (3), Viognier (2) and Sangiovese (1). Early indications were that the Sauvignon Blanc and Sémillon aptly reflected the appellation, which is well suited for these grape varieties.

TASTING NOTES

SAUVIGNON BLANC CLEAR LAKE (★★):
1993: Lean and crisp, with hints of herb, melon and grass notes. **84**

SAUVIGNON BLEND CLEAR LAKE CHEVRIOT (★★★):
1993: Crisp and focused, bright with toasty green apple and spice flavors. Livelier than most oak-apparent Sauvignons. **86**
1992: A 50-50 blend of Sémillon and Sauvignon Blanc, it strikes a fine balance between the two, with rich, smoky fig, sweet pea and pear flavors. **88**

SÉMILLON CLEAR LAKE (★★):
1993: A little rough around the edges, but the ripe fig, herb and pear flavors ring true. **85**

LAMBERT BRIDGE
Sonoma County
F: 1975. O: Lambert Bridge Winery Inc. W: Julia Baird Iantosca, Merry Edwards. S: None.

OVERALL	$7-15	★★

WINE RATINGS	
Cabernet Sauvignon Sonoma County	★★
Chardonnay Dry Creek Valley	★★
Fumé Blanc Sonoma County	★
Merlot Sonoma County	★★
Zinfandel Dry Creek Valley	★★

WINERY DATA
C: N/A. V: 2 acres in Dry Creek Valley. G: Cabernet Sauvignon (2 acres). P: Chardonnay, Cabernet Sauvignon, Merlot, Cabernet Franc (Dry Creek Valley), Chardonnay, Cabernet Sauvignon (Alexander Valley), Chardonnay (Russian River), Chardonnay (Sonoma Valley), Sauvignon Blanc, Sémillon, Zinfandel (Dry Creek Valley), Pinot Noir (Russian River, Carneros).

Jerry Lambert founded this Dry Creek winery in 1975, six years after buying a 120-acre site. The early product mix included Cabernet, Chardonnay and Merlot, growing to 25,000 cases by the end of the 1980s. A protracted legal dispute with its distributors, however, drained Lambert Bridge financially and it closed in 1992, reopening a year later under new ownership and with Merry Edwards as consultant.

TASTING NOTES

CABERNET SAUVIGNON SONOMA COUNTY (★★): Marked by green olive and herb notes, it's quite tannic but consistent.
1991: Dark, firm, tannic and tightly wound, with currant and spice flavors wrapped in tannins. 84
1989: Marked by a minty edge, with simple flavors that fade. 80
1984: Spicy herb and green olive aromas are followed by plum, black currant and herb flavors. 80

CHARDONNAY DRY CREEK VALLEY (★★): Good but unexciting, although the 1993 showed more depth and appeal.
1993: Nicely focused and flavorful, with ripe apple and pear flavors. 84
1992: Soft and fruity, a simple wine with a brash, sappy streak running through it. 80

FUMÉ BLANC SONOMA COUNTY (★):
1993: Light, fruity and appealing, with pear and smoky herbal flavors lingering on the delicate finish. 81
1992: Simple, herbal aromas and flavors characterize this sturdy, slightly sweet wine. 78

MERLOT SONOMA COUNTY (★★): The strongest of the red wines, erratic but at times smooth and polished, with complex flavors.
1992: Smooth and polished, with supple currant, berry and cherry flavors, finishing with a smoky, toasty oak edge and mild tannins. 87
1991: Austere, with firm tannins and a narrow band of herb and wild berry flavors. 79
1989: Lean, with herb, black cherry, currant and spice flavors and firm tannins. 85

ZINFANDEL DRY CREEK VALLEY (★★): Sturdy, hard-edged and tannic.
1992: Earthy and tannic, with a hard-edged core of tarry fruit flavors. 84

LAMBORN FAMILY VINEYARDS
Howell Mountain
F: 1987. O: Robert & Janet Lamborn. W: Robert Lamborn, Edward Lemon. S: None.

OVERALL	$15-18	★★

WINE RATINGS	
Zinfandel Howell Mountain	★★

WINERY DATA
C: 2,300. V: 9 acres in Howell Mountain. G: Zinfandel (9 acres). P: None.

Private investigator Bob Lamborn, who worked on the Patty Hearst kidnapping, bought his 9-acre vineyard on Howell Mountain in 1972, inspired by the Napa Valley wine renaissance and the desire for a weekend retreat. For years he commuted on weekends to Howell Mountain from Oakland, where he operated his P.I. business, and made home wine for several years. In 1979 he replanted his vineyard and in 1982 he started selling wine under the Lamborn Family Vineyards label. His neighbor, Randy Dunn, helped with the first few vintages. Winemaking is kept to the basics, with no razzle-dazzle. Production is around 2,300 cases. Despite stylistic swings, Lamborn's Zinfandel is typically Howell Mountain in its tightness and austerity. A small portion of his grape crop goes to Rocking Horse, which bottles a Zin with the Lamborn Family designation.

TASTING NOTES

ZINFANDEL HOWELL MOUNTAIN (★★): Austere and tightly wound, with a narrow band of wild berry and earth flavors.
The Phoenix Vintage 1991: A tough, tannic and chewy wine with tart cherry, plum and spice flavors. **82**
1990: Austere, with wild berry, spice and earth notes and firm tannins. **85**
1988: Big, tough and flavorful, with lots of ripe blackberry, cedar and toast flavors. **89**
1987: Intense and tannic, with dry raspberry and cherry flavors that are very tight and concentrated. **84**

LANDMARK VINEYARDS
Kenwood, Sonoma Valley
F: 1974. **O:** Damaris Deere W. Ethridge & Michael Colhoun. **W:** Eric Stern, Helen Turley. **S:** None.

OVERALL	$14-19	★★★

WINE RATINGS

Chardonnay Alexander Valley	
Damaris Vineyards Reserve	★★★
Chardonnay Sonoma County Overlook	★★
Chardonnay Sonoma Valley	
Two Williams Vineyard	★★★

WINERY DATA
C: 16,000. **V:** 20 acres in Sonoma Valley. **G:** Chardonnay. **P:** Chardonnay (Alexander Valley), Chardonnay (Russian River), Chardonnay (Sonoma Valley).

Bill Mabry and his family founded Landmark in Windsor in 1974, producing several popular varietals before moving the winery to a new home in Kenwood in Sonoma Valley in 1990 after urban encroachment forced the winery out. The move coincided with the winery's acquisition by Damaris Deere W. Ethridge, leaving Mabry to oversee operations. Mabry left soon after and Michael Colhoun has taken over day-to-day manage-

ment. The focus in the 1990s has been on Chardonnay, but Cabernet, Fumé Blanc, Merlot, Pinot Noir and Zinfandel were in production and headed toward the market. Helen Turley (of Marcassin) also signed on as a consultant, another sign the winery is intent on improving its wines. The winery owns 20 acres, with production about 16,000 cases.

TASTING NOTES

CHARDONNAY ALEXANDER VALLEY DAMARIS VINEYARD RESERVE (★★★): This is the star, as it should be—it's rich, ripe and complex. Worth watching.
1993: Ripe, smooth and creamy, with lush pear, vanilla and light toast shadings that turn smooth and silky on the finish. **90**
1992: Fresh and lively, with apple and pear flavors that are simple and one-dimensional. **82**
1991: Ripe, luscious and complex, with spicy honey, pineapple, pear, vanilla and fig aromas and flavors. **91**

CHARDONNAY SONOMA COUNTY OVERLOOK (★★): Lighter, with appealing fruit flavors.
1993: Firm and compact, with spicy pear, fig and citrus notes that pick up a light, toasty oak edge. **88**
1992: Serves up pretty pear, nectarine and apple flavors that zing across the palate, picking up toasty oak notes. **87**

CHARDONNAY SONOMA VALLEY TWO WILLIAMS VINEYARD (★★★): This wine is polished and complex.
1992: Packed with flavor, a polished, flinty wine that throws off sparks of apple, vanilla and spice along the way. **90**

LAS MONTAÑAS WINERY
Sonoma Valley
F: 1982. **O:** Aleta Apgar. **W:** Aleta Apgar. **S:** None.

OVERALL	$12-14	NR

WINE RATINGS

Cabernet Sauvignon Sonoma Valley	NR
Zinfandel Sonoma Valley	NR

WINERY DATA
C: 1,500. **V:** N/A. **G:** Cabernet Sauvignon, Zinfandel. **P:** None.

This is literally a one-woman show. Owner Aleta Apgar makes some 1,500 cases a year from her steep hillside vineyard in Sonoma Valley, with Cabernet and Zinfandel the focus. Quality has been marginal, occasionally good.

LAS VIÑAS WINERY
Lodi, Central Valley
F: 1986. **O:** The Cotta Family. **W:** John Cotta. **S:** None.

OVERALL	$6	★

WINE RATINGS

Cabernet Sauvignon California	
Private Reserve	NR

WINERY DATA
C: 12,000. **V:** 800 acres in Lodi. **G:** N/A. **P:** N/A.

The Cotta family owns some 800 acres in vines in Lodi. After decades of farming in the Central Valley, the family started producing wine in 1986 under the Las Viñas Winery name, selling Cabernet, Chardonnay and Zinfandel, with case volume at 12,000.

TASTING NOTES

CABERNET SAUVIGNON CALIFORNIA PRIVATE RESERVE (NR):
1988: An earthy wine with leathery aromas and slightly muddy fruit flavors. Still, it's a decent red. **78**

LATERAL
This is a second label for Kathryn Kennedy (see listing).

LAUREL GLEN VINEYARD
Sonoma Mountain
F: 1977. **O:** Patrick Campbell. **W:** Patrick Campbell. **S:** Counterpoint, Terra Rosa.

OVERALL	$10-30	★★★★

WINE RATINGS

Cabernet Sauvignon Sonoma Mountain	★★★★
Counterpoint Cabernet Sauvignon	
Sonoma Mountain	★★★
Terra Rosa Cabernet Sauvignon	
Napa Valley	★★★

WINERY DATA
C: 40,000. **V:** 40 acres in Sonoma Mountain. **G:** Cabernet Sauvignon (32 acres), Cabernet Franc (3), Merlot (4), Sangiovese (0.5), Syrah (0.5). **P:** None.

Patrick Campbell earned a degree in English and a master's degree in the philosophy of religion from Harvard's Divinity School before choosing grape growing as his calling. After selling his Sonoma Mountain Cabernet grapes to Chateau St. Jean, Kenwood and others, Campbell made experimental wines at home in 1978 and 1979, two of the best Cabernets from that era that I've ever tasted. Both wines are remarkably dark in color, rich in flavor and, as of 1995, still vibrant and alive. By 1981 Campbell began bottling his own wine from this gently sloping vineyard on Sonoma Mountain. With the exception of a poor 1983, the Laurel Glen Cabernets are among the most exciting wines made in California. Most of Laurel Glen's 40 acres are devoted to Cabernet, but small portions of the vineyard are planted to Cabernet Franc, Merlot, Sangiovese and Syrah, each of which might someday make it into the Laurel Glen brand. Two other Cabernets support the estate wine: Counterpoint, which carries a Sonoma Mountain appellation, and Terra Rosa, a brand that carries the Napa Valley appellation and has rapidly grown to 30,000 cases.

TASTING NOTES

CABERNET SAUVIGNON SONOMA MOUNTAIN (★★★★):
Can be brilliant, complex, supple, rich in fruit flavors and distinctively elegant, but it's also variable on occasion.
1991: Dense and concentrated, earthy and leathery, but it opens up to reveal spicy currant and black cherry flavors that turn elegant on the finish despite ample tannins. **89**
1990: Firm and flavorful, its spicy plum and berry aromas and flavors fan across the palate, hinting at bell pepper and herbs on the finish. **90**
Laurel Glen Reserve 1990: Firm in texture, with tightly wound berry, plum, cedar and tobacco flavors that wrestle with the tannins. **88**
1989: Deeply concentrated, with minty, cedary aromas and deep cherry and currant flavors accented by the spice and vanilla of oak. Chewy tannins. **88**
1988: A successful '88, brimming with bright, ripe grape, currant and black cherry flavors and pretty oak notes. Intense and deep. **89**
1987: Openly forward and fruity, with complex, toasty oak, currant, spice and cherry flavors that are smooth and

polished, finishing with a firm tannic grip that bodes well for the future. **92**

1986: Hard, tight and tannic, with firm plum and currant flavors finishing with a chewy, tannic aftertaste. **88**

1985: Ripe, smooth, supple and elegant, with vibrant black cherry, currant and plum flavors that finish with round, smooth tannins and toasty oak shadings. **91**

1984: Tart, with focused, complex cherry and plum flavors in an elegant style. It has medium intensity and depth of flavor, yet the flavors linger. **87**

1983: Lean and vinegary, with spicy plum and pruny notes. A difficult wine to warm up to, although it does not show the musty character that was so prevalent in earlier tastings. **75**

1982: Lean and tart, with an earthy, cedary quality on top of the ripe black cherry flavor. **79**

1981: This remains a magnificent wine with beautifully focused black cherry, currant, plum and cedar flavors that are smooth and supple, with fine, integrated tannins. **93**

COUNTERPOINT CABERNET SAUVIGNON SONOMA MOUNTAIN (★★★): Can rival the estate Cab in the best years, with well defined, complex fruit flavors.

1991: Dense, chewy and complex, with pretty black cherry, blackberry and currant flavors and a wide array of bay leaf, smoke and tar notes. Tannic too. **90**

1990: Firmly tannic, with tightly wound herb, currant and leather notes and a dry, tannic tobacco edge. **87**

1989: Ripe and plummy, with firm oak shadings, it is also firmly tannic. **85**

1988: Firm and oaky, with tight currant and berry flavors, but like most '88s it's short on depth and richness. **85**

1987: Rich, bold and complex, with dense currant, anise and plum flavors framed by toasty, buttery oak. Still firmly tannic, rivaling the '87 Laurel Glen. **90**

TERRA ROSA CABERNET SAUVIGNON NAPA VALLEY (★★★): Excellent value in ripe, complex Cabernet.

1992: Ripe with smooth, supple cherry, berry, spice and attractive buttery oak flavors, but it offers good depth intensity, finishing with firm tannins. **88**

1990: Expands on the palate, revealing currant, spice and toasty oak flavors, and the finish is firm and tannic. **89**

1989: Strikes a nice balance between ripe, supple currant and cherry flavors and buttery oak shadings. **86**

1988: Attractive, with ripe, cherry, currant and spicy floral notes that are showy up front. **85**

1987: Big and tough but harmonious, with a wealth of cherry, currant and berry aromas and flavors along with toasty coffee and oak notes and firm tannins. **86**

LAURIER
Sonoma County
F: 1978. **O:** Bronco Wine Co. **W:** Merry Edwards. **S:** None.

OVERALL	$15	★★★

WINE RATINGS

Chardonnay Sonoma County (V & G)	★★★

WINERY DATA
C: 13,000. **V:** None. **G:** None. **P:** Chardonnay (Sonoma), Pinot Noir (Sonoma).

Originally named Domaine Laurier under the founding Shilo family, this winery enjoyed moderate success through its first decade before being sold to Fred Franzia of Bronco Wine Co. in 1991. The focus is on barrel-fermented Chardonnay and small lots of Pinot Noir, with Merry Edwards (of Merry Vintners and others) overseeing winemaking.

TASTING NOTES

CHARDONNAY SONOMA COUNTY (★★★):
1992: Elegant and graceful, a wine of finesse and flavor, with toasty pear and buttery oak notes. **88**

LAVA CAP WINERY
El Dorado County
F: 1986. **O:** Lava Springs, Inc. **W:** Thomas Jones. **S:** None.

OVERALL	$10	★★

WINE RATINGS

Cabernet Sauvignon El Dorado County	★★
Merlot El Dorado County	★★
Zinfandel El Dorado County	★

WINERY DATA
C: 8,000. **V:** 30 acres in El Dorado County. **G:** N/A. **P:** N/A.

Lava Cap is a 30-acre vineyard owned by the Jones family from which they produce 8,000 cases of Cabernet, Chardonnay, Merlot, Sauvignon Blanc and Zinfandel, some of which is grown in their volcanic soils. The 1989 Cabernet El Dorado shows attractive currant and berry flavors with a buzz of tannin, and the Merlot 1990 is firm and chewy, with a band of plum, cherry and spice flavors. The Zinfandels from 1989 through 1991 are far less impressive, earthy and tired, often with off flavors.

TASTING NOTES

CABERNET SAUVIGNON EL DORADO COUNTY (★★):
1989: Lean and crisp, with ripe currant and berry flavors. Finishes with a buzz of tannin. **85**

MERLOT EL DORADO COUNTY (★★):
1990: Firm and chewy, with a nice band of plum, cherry and spice flavors. **84**

ZINFANDEL EL DORADO COUNTY (★):
1991: Tired, with earthy, gamy oak flavors and not much fruit. **73**
1990: Light in flavor, with leather, spice and other mature notes. **77**
1989: Light and simple, with modest cherry and cedar flavors. **77**

LAZY CREEK VINEYARDS
Anderson Valley
F: 1974. **O:** Lazy Creek Vineyards Inc. **W:** Johann Kobler. **S:** None.

OVERALL	$10-15	★★

WINE RATINGS	
Chardonnay Anderson Valley	★★
Pinot Noir Anderson Valley	★★★

WINERY DATA
C: 5,000. **V:** 20 acres in Anderson Valley. **G:** Gewürztraminer (4 acres), Chardonnay (8), Pinot Noir (8). **P:** None.

Former restaurateur Johann Kobler and his wife, Theresa, own this 20-acre vineyard estate in Anderson Valley from which they produce 5,000 cases of Chardonnay, Gewürztraminer and Pinot Noir. All three wines are well made, with Pinot Noir the most complex and Gewürztraminer the most distinctive.

TASTING NOTES

CHARDONNAY ANDERSON VALLEY (★★): Aims for a directly. fruity style, with the 1992 tasting as if a dollop of Gewürztraminer were added.
1993: A little earthy, with simple orange-scented apple flavors. **75**
1992: Has a curious Gewürztraminer edge, but enough spice and fruit to hold your interest. **82**
1991: Fruity and spicy, featuring green apple, vanilla and nutmeg flavors. **86**

PINOT NOIR ANDERSON VALLEY (★★★): Intense and fruity, marked by ripe, bright plum and black cherry flavors.
1991: Firm and tight, with a nice core of plum and currant aromas and flavors that turn tannic. **83**
Private Reserve 1988: Intense and concentrated, with ripe, rich plum, black cherry and currant aromas and flavors. **87**
1987: Ripe and fruity, with pretty black cherry and boysenberry aromas and flavors. **86**

LEEWARD WINERY
Ventura County
F: 1979. **O:** Leeward Winery Inc. **W:** Erick Cinnamon. **S:** None.

OVERALL	$11-16	★★

WINE RATINGS	
Cabernet Sauvignon Alexander Valley	★
Chardonnay Central Coast	★★
Chardonnay Edna Valley Reserve	★
Chardonnay Ventura County	NR
Merlot Napa Valley	★★
Pinot Noir Santa Barbara County	★

WINERY DATA
C: 12,000. **V:** None. **G:** None. **P:** Chardonnay (Edna Valley), Merlot (Napa Valley), Pinot Noir (Santa Barbara).

Home winemakers Chuck Gardner and Chuck Brigham went commercial in 1979, initially making wine in basements and garages before moving into a warehouse in Ventura. Chardonnay, carrying both an Edna Valley and Central Coast appellation, is the main focus of this 12,000-

case winery, with a few hundred cases each of Cabernet from Alexander Valley, Merlot from Napa Valley and Pinot Noir from Santa Barbara County also part of the roster. Quality varies; the wines are occasionally good but are often marked by odd aromas and flavors.

TASTING NOTES

CABERNET SAUVIGNON ALEXANDER VALLEY (★): Both the 1988 and 1991 vintages have shallow fruit flavors.
1991: Tough and chewy, a tannic wine with modest currant and berry flavors. **81**
1988: Herbal, smoky, earthy flavors dominate this tannic wine. **78**

CHARDONNAY VARIOUS BOTTLINGS:
Central Coast 1992: Stretches the range of flavors a bit too far, with strong leesy, ripe, almost sour pineapple flavors. **79**
Central Coast 1991: Smooth and flavorful, with lots of ripe apricot, pineapple and butter aromas and flavors. **85**
Edna Valley Reserve 1993: A fruity style with tart apple, pineapple and spice notes, solid and well made. **86**
Edna Valley Reserve 1992: Shows off ripe, exotic guava, pineapple and tropical fruit flavors, but it loses its focus on the finish, where it's woody. **85**
Edna Valley Paragon Vineyard Reserve 1991: A funky, bitter, earthy wine with orange and nectarine flavors that taste stripped. **74**
Monterey County 1991: Lean, with a citrus and grapefruit edge. **82**
Ventura County 1992: Earthy, with a sour pineapple edge to the flavors. **81**

MERLOT NAPA VALLEY (★★): Highly variable, lean and hollow one year, fruity the next.
1992: Lean and hollow, with a slim, bland band of simple herb and fruit flavors. **74**
1991: An oaky wine with chunky currant and cherry flavors that are one-dimensional. **81**
1989: Crisp and fruity, with well defined berry and currant flavors and hints of toast and vanilla on the finish. **83**

PINOT NOIR SANTA BARBARA COUNTY (★): Marked by funky, gamy flavors, well off the pace.
1990: Austere, with funky, earthy flavors that detract from the core of currant and berry notes. **76**

1989: Tight, firm and gamy, with strong charred-oak flavors that dominate the plum and currant notes underneath. Bitingly tannic. **79**

LEWIS CELLARS
Napa Valley
F: 1995. **O:** Randy & Debbie Lewis. **W:** Joe Cafaro. **S:** None.

OVERALL	$26-30	★★★

WINE RATINGS

Chardonnay Napa Valley	
Oakville Ranch Reserve	★★★

WINERY DATA
C: N/A. **V:** None. **G:** None. **P:** Chardonnay, Cabernet Sauvignon (Oakville).

Former Oakville Ranch partners Randy and Debbie Lewis formed their own winery in 1995, following the death of Bob Miner, who owned the vineyard for their Oakville Ranch wines. Oakville Ranch will continue, but early plans were for the Lewises to buy grapes from that vineyard with Joe Cafaro overseeing winemaking. Cabernet from 1992 was planned to join the 1993 Chardonnay.

TASTING NOTES

CHARDONNAY NAPA VALLEY OAKVILLE RANCH RESERVE (★★★):
1993: Ripe and spicy, with a pretty core of fig, pear, nectarine and toasty oak, all folding together, finishing with complex aftertaste that picks up fruit and oak. **90**

LIBERTY SCHOOL
This is a second label of Caymus Vineyards (see listing).

LIMERICK LANE
Russian River Valley
F: 1986. **O:** Michael F. Collins. **W:** Michael F. Collins. **S:** None.

OVERALL $7-14 ★★

WINE RATINGS

Sauvignon Blanc Russian River Valley
   Collins Vineyard ★
Zinfandel Russian River Valley ★★★

WINERY DATA

C: 3,500. V: 30 acres in Russian River Valley. G: Zinfandel.
P: None.

Limerick Lane specializes in Russian River-grown Zinfandel from Collins Vineyard, producing some 3,500 cases a year at its Limerick Lane address in Healdsburg. The wine has been highly variable in its past four vintages.

TASTING NOTES

SAUVIGNON BLANC RUSSIAN RIVER VALLEY COLLINS VINEYARD (★):
1992: Tastes vinegary and pickley, with little freshness or snap. **69**

ZINFANDEL RUSSIAN RIVER VALLEY (★★★): Quality is extremely variable, with very ripe and flavorful Zinfandels in 1990 and 1991, but a terribly flawed effort in 1989.
1991: Big and dramatic, loaded with rich plum, black cherry and black pepper flavors. **88**
1990: Ripe and rich, with a smoky edge to the ripe plum and blackberry flavors. **89**
1989: Earthy, mulchy and pickley. A bizarre wine that has multiple flaws. **61**

LIMUR WINERY

St. Helena, Napa Valley
F: 1985. O: Charles & Eleanor de Limur. W: Jeff Sowells. S: None.

OVERALL $16 ★★

WINE RATINGS

Chardonnay Napa Valley ★★

WINERY DATA

C: 400. V: 2 acres in Rutherford. G: Chardonnay (Napa Valley). P: None.

Charles de Limur farms 2 acres of Chardonnay in Rutherford for his 400-case-a-year endeavor, making this one of the valley's smallest producers.

TASTING NOTES

CHARDONNAY NAPA VALLEY (★★): Made in a crisp, lean style with modest fruit flavors.
1992: Tart and a bit green, with a narrow band of spicy apple and peach flavors. **83**
1991: Crisp and fruity, offering a nice burst of apple and lemon flavors. **83**

LIPARITA CELLARS

Howell Mountain
F: 1984. O: Liparita Wine Co. Inc. W: Merry Edwards. S: None.

OVERALL $24-28 ★★

WINE RATINGS

Cabernet Sauvignon Howell Mountain ★★★
Chardonnay Howell Mountain ★★
Merlot Howell Mountain NR

WINERY DATA

C: 4,000. V: 80 acres in Howell Mountain. G: Chardonnay (35 acres), Cabernet Sauvignon (25), Merlot (13), Sauvignon Blanc (7). P: None.

San Franciscan Robert Burrows has revived this 80-acre vineyard and old winery on Howell Mountain, selling part of his crop to Chateau Montelena, Peter Michael and others over the years. Beginning in 1987 he began making small lots of Chardonnay, followed a few years later by Cabernet and Merlot. Quality is on a steady rise, with production at 4,000 cases. Worth watching.

TASTING NOTES

CABERNET SAUVIGNON HOWELL MOUNTAIN (★★★): True-to-form Howell Mountain Cab, with its density and chewy tannins.
1991: Compact and a bit rustic, with an earthy, leathery edge to the tannic currant and mineral flavors. **86**
1990: Smooth and flavorful, a dense, chewy wine that's packed with currant, anise and black cherry flavors. **88**

CHARDONNAY HOWELL MOUNTAIN (★★): Improving; the 1992 served up bright, lively flavors.
1992: Bright and fruity, with layers of apricot, apple and grapefruit flavors. **88**
1991: Perfumed and spicy, with a Muscat edge, but also a woody, earthy streak. **82**

MERLOT HOWELL MOUNTAIN (NR): The 1991 was marked by an earthy, leathery edge.
1991: An earthy, leathery, oaky edge dominates the fruit flavors. **83**

LIVERMORE VALLEY CELLARS

Livermore Valley
F: 1978. **O:** Chris & Beverly Lagiss. **W:** Tim Sauer. **S:** None.

OVERALL	$5-15	NR

WINE RATINGS	
Cabernet Sauvignon Livermore Valley	NR
Chardonnay Livermore Valley	NR
French Colombard Livermore Valley	NR
Zinfandel Livermore Valley	NR

WINERY DATA
C: 1,000. **V:** 34 acres in Livermore Valley. **G:** Golden Chasselas (12 acres), Riesling (4), French Colombard (4), Chardonnay (4), Servant (1). **P:** Chardonnay (Livermore Valley), Cabernet Sauvignon (Livermore Valley), Zinfandel (Livermore Valley).

Since 1978 the Lagiss family has been making about 1,000 cases of wine yearly from its 34-acre vineyard between Livermore and Pleasanton. For years Wente Bros. bought all the grapes from this vineyard. Now, Livermore Valley's all-white lineup includes Chardonnay, Grey Riesling, French Colombard and even Golden Chasselas and Servant. Cabernet, Chardonnay and Zinfandel are purchased from the Toy and Graham vineyards, also in Livermore Valley.

LIVINGSTON WINES

St. Helena, Napa Valley
F: 1984. **O:** John L. & Diane F. Livingston. **W:** Greg Graham. **S:** H. W. Helms.

OVERALL	$18-30	★★★★

WINE RATINGS	
Cabernet Sauvignon Napa Valley Moffett Vineyard	★★★★
Cabernet Sauvignon Napa Valley Stanley's Selection	★★

WINERY DATA
C: 4,000. **V:** 10 acres in Rutherford. **G:** Cabernet Sauvignon (9 acres), Cabernet Franc (0.5), Merlot (0.5). **P:** Chardonnay (Carneros).

John and Diane Livingston own the 10-acre Moffett Vineyard in west Rutherford, from which they produce their Livingston Cabernet from vines planted in 1969. A second Cabernet called Stanley's Selection comes from grapes grown on Howell Mountain. Livingston wines are rich and concentrated and age well.

TASTING NOTES

CABERNET SAUVIGNON NAPA VALLEY MOFFETT VINEYARD (★★★★): Dark, ripe and intense, with loads of flavor and full-bodied tannins. Only the 1985 is off the pace. Ages well; the 1984 is still young and complex.
1991: Very ripe and decadent, with earthy black cherry and currant flavors. Finishes with gritty tannins and a mineral edge. **90**
1990: Ripe, supple and elegant, with layers of complex, concentrated cedar, black cherry, currant and plum flavors. Has a wonderful sense of harmony and finesse, finishing with chewy tannins and a mineral edge. **92**
1989: Despite an earthy edge it's elegant, with cedar, anise and spice notes adding complexity. Firmly tannic. **87**
1988: Supple, complex and harmonious, with ripe plum, currant, black cherry and anise flavors that pick up a touch of cedar on the finish. **87**
1987: Beautifully balanced, rich, complex and concentrated, with a beam of crisp, juicy black cherry, plum and cedary oak flavors. The tannins are supple and fleshy and the acidity is crisp. **93**
1986: Tight, firm and intense, lean and tannic, but the earthy currant and oak flavors are deftly balanced, with fine depth and an elegant aftertaste. **89**
1985: A good but not exceptional 1985, with subdued currant and black cherry notes that have a cedary edge, but it lacks focus. Perhaps it needs more time. **85**

1984: This remains a wonderfully ripe, fleshy and supple wine with bright, rich black cherry and currant flavors that are youthful and vibrant. The tannins are supple yet firm. **92**

CABERNET SAUVIGNON NAPA VALLEY STANLEY'S SELECTION (★★): Tannic and austere, with more herb and cedary oak notes than fruit flavors. Pricey for a second-line wine.
1992: Firm, tight and tannic, with a core of earthy currant and cedary oak and menthol underneath. Best after 1997. **87**
1991: Herbal and smoky, with a band of austere currant and spice notes. **83**
1990: Tight, firm and tannic, with ripe currant, black cherry and spice flavors and just the right touch of oak seasoning. **88**
1989: Tannic, but the fruit keeps pace, with pretty cherry, currant and oak flavors. **85**

LOCKWOOD VINEYARD
Monterey County
F: 1986. **O:** Paul Toppen, Butch Lindley & Phil Johnson.
W: Stephen Pessagno. **S:** None.

OVERALL	$9-18	★★

WINE RATINGS

Cabernet Sauvignon Monterey County	★★
Cabernet Sauvignon Monterey County Partners' Reserve	★★
Chardonnay Monterey County	★★
Chardonnay Monterey County Partners' Reserve	★★
Merlot Monterey County	★★
Sauvignon Blanc Monterey County	★★★

WINERY DATA
C: 75,000. **V:** 1,650 acres in Monterey County. **G:** Cabernet Sauvignon (500 acres), Chardonnay (900), Chenin Blanc, Merlot, Pinot Blanc, Pinot Noir, Riesling, Sauvignon Blanc. **P:** None.

Seizing on the popularity of Monterey grapes, Paul Toppen, Butch Lindley and Phil Johnson formed a partnership in 1981 and planted a large vineyard now covering 1,650 acres in vines, with more than 900 acres in Chardonnay and nearly 500 in Cabernet, plus smaller amounts of Chenin Blanc, Merlot, Riesling, Sauvignon Blanc, Pinot Blanc and Pinot Noir. In 1986 Lockwood began production and now bottles four main wines, Cabernet, Chardonnay, Merlot and Sauvignon Blanc, all well balanced and appealing wines that are well oaked. Production is near 75,000 cases, with an aggressive direct-marketing campaign.

TASTING NOTES

CABERNET SAUVIGNON MONTEREY COUNTY (★★), PARTNERS' RESERVE (★★): Improving, with well oaked and well focused flavors that avoid the vegetal notes that mar so many reds from this area.
1992: A well oaked style with vanilla and toasty flavors, but enough supple cherry and herb notes to balance and give it some dimension. **86**
1991: Complex and inviting, with a broad array of toasty, buttery oak, currant, herb and spice flavors. **88**
Partners' Reserve 1991: Firm and compact, with tightly wound currant, plum and cherry notes framed by cedary oak. Austere and tannic. **84**
Partners' Reserve 1990: Firm, ripe and intense, with spicy boysenberry, cherry and currant flavors that gain complexity. **87**

CHARDONNAY MONTEREY COUNTY (★★), PARTNERS' RESERVE (★★): Features bright and attractive fruit flavors framed by toasty, spicy oak.
1992: Strikes a nice balance between ripe pear, peach and spice flavors and light, toasty, smoky oak. **84**
1991: Crisp and spicy, displaying a nice thread of green apple flavor and a tart, spicy finish. **84**
Partners' Reserve 1992: Earthy with a citrus and grapefruit edge to the ripe pear and honeyed flavors. **83**
Partners' Reserve 1991: Firm, tight and concentrated, with a beam of grapefruit and apple flavors shaded by nutmeg, vanilla and butter overtones. **89**

MERLOT MONTEREY COUNTY (★★): Smooth and polished, medium-weight, well crafted.
1992: Smooth and polished, with spicy cherry, cedar and raspberry flavors. **84**
1991: Ripe and plush, with fleshy tar, cherry, prune and plum notes that hold their complexity. **87**

SAUVIGNON BLANC MONTEREY COUNTY (★★★): Tames the grape's herbal tendencies; it's a rich and complex wine with plenty of flavor.
1992: Smooth and spicy, with a nice core of fig, honey and spice overtones. **87**

LOGAN WINERY
This is a second label for Robert Talbott Vineyards (see listing).

J. LOHR WINERY
San Jose, Santa Clara County
F: 1974. **O:** J. Lohr Winery Inc. **W:** Jeff Runquist. **S:** None.

OVERALL	$6-22	★★★

WINE RATINGS

Cabernet Sauvignon California Cypress	★★
Cabernet Sauvignon	
Paso Robles Seven Oaks	★★★
Chardonnay California Cypress	★★★
Chardonnay Monterey County Riverstone	★★★
Fumé Blanc California Cypress	★★
Merlot California Cypress	★★

WINERY DATA
C: 250,000. **V:** 1,164 acres in Monterey, Paso Robles, Napa Valley, Clarksburg. **G:** Cabernet Sauvignon (380 acres), Chardonnay (500), Johannisberg Riesling (50), Gamay (13), Merlot (31), Cabernet Franc (15), Pinot Blanc (47), Syrah (12), Chenin Blanc (86), Sauvignon Blanc (30). **P:** Petite Sirah (Clarksburg), Chardonnay (Monterey), Cabernet Sauvignon (Paso Robles), Gamay (Monterey).

Jerry Lohr had a successful career in construction and development before turning to grape growing and winemaking in Monterey. After planting a 280-acre vineyard in the Greenfield area, he and his then-partner, Bernie Turgeon, purchased an old brewery in San Jose, which they converted for winemaking. After a spotty first decade, the winery has expanded its vineyard holdings to 1,164 acres, with more than 400 acres in Monterey and Paso Robles, 217 in Clarksburg and 32 in Napa Valley, and steadily upgraded its wines. Chardonnay, with 500 acres, dominates the plantings, followed by Cabernet (380), Chenin Blanc (86), Johannisberg Riesling (50)

and Pinot Blanc (47). The wine lineup ranges from Amador County White Zinfandel to Monterey Gamay to Napa Cabernet, which has appeared under the Carol's Vineyard designation.

TASTING NOTES

CABERNET SAUVIGNON CALIFORNIA CYPRESS (★★):
1991: Shows off its toasty, buttery oak and has enough fruit to match. A good value. **82**
1990: Despite a toasty, smoky wood overlay, there's a nice core of spicy fruit flavors underneath, and on the finish the fruit and wood hang together nicely. Lots of flavor and character, especially at this price. **86**

CABERNET SAUVIGNON PASO ROBLES SEVEN OAKS (★★★): Steadily improving, elegant and well oaked, but with enough fruit to keep it in balance.
1991: Relies on toasty, buttery oak for much of its flavor—as the label implies—and that's pleasing, but it also has enough ripe fruit flavors to keep it interesting. **84**
1990: A ripe and showy wine with buttery oak flavors, but underneath the spicy wood are pretty cherry and currant notes. **87**
1989: Lavishly oaked, with intense vanilla and spice notes, but also a core of lush, ripe plum and currant flavors. **89**
1988: A jammy wine with currant and raspberry flavors that are very ripe, but it's hollow at mid-palate. **83**
1987: Very stylish with its cedar, plum and cherry flavors. **86**

CHARDONNAY CALIFORNIA CYPRESS (★★★):
1992: A simple but pleasant Chardonnay with spicy apple, pear and light oak notes. **83**

CHARDONNAY MONTEREY COUNTY RIVERSTONE (★★★):
Combines ripe fruit with creamy oak flavors. Well balanced.
1992: Combines ripe peach and pear flavors with creamy, toasty, buttery oak. **85**
1991: Smooth, spicy and gentle, with a silky texture, vanilla aromas and pear and apricot flavors. **89**

FUMÉ BLANC CALIFORNIA CYPRESS (★★):
1993: Ripe, round and generous, smooth-textured, with nice honey and fig notes on the finish. A little sweet, but balanced. **86**
1992: Ripe and spicy, an oaky wine with modest fruit flavors, not especially varietal but pleasant. **81**

Merlot California Cypress (★★):
1992: Smooth and oaky, with supple plum and prune notes. **86**
1991: Simple and fruity, with a woody edge and fleshy cherry and herb notes. **82**

LOLONIS WINERY
Mendocino County
F: 1920. **O:** Lolonis Vineyards. **W:** Jed Steele. **S:** None.

OVERALL	$10-24	★★

WINE RATINGS

Cabernet Sauvignon Mendocino County Private Reserve	★★
Chardonnay Mendocino County Estate Reserve	★★
Zinfandel Mendocino County	★★
Zinfandel Mendocino County Private Reserve	★★

WINERY DATA
C: 16,000. **V:** 300 acres in Mendocino. **G:** Sauvignon Blanc (25 acres), Petite Sirah (15), Chardonnay (96), Pinot Noir (13), Zinfandel (65), Cabernet Sauvignon (50), Merlot (25), Gamay Beaujolais (11). **P:** None.

The Lolonis family has been growing grapes in Mendocino since 1920, selling to customers such as Fetzer, Parducci and now Steele Wines. With Jed Steele overseeing winemaking, Lolonis now produces 16,000 cases a year, using a fraction of its 300 acres in grapes. The main focus is on Cabernet, Chardonnay, Petite Sirah and Zinfandel. Quality has consistently been good, but with Steele on board, look for steady improvement.

TASTING NOTES

CABERNET SAUVIGNON MENDOCINO COUNTY PRIVATE RESERVE (★★): Firm and focused, if on the lean, compact side.
1989: Firm and focused, with a crisp texture and plum, berry and cherry flavors shaded by spicy oak. **84**

CHARDONNAY MENDOCINO COUNTY ESTATE RESERVE (★★): Lean, marked by tart green apple and spice flavors, in contrast to earlier efforts that were very ripe and bold.
1991: Lean, crisp and fruity, showing an appealing core of green apple and pineapple flavors that turn spicy. **83**

ZINFANDEL MENDOCINO COUNTY (★★), PRIVATE RESERVE (★★): Inconsistent, but can hit the mark with its pepper and raspberry flavors.
1991: Ripe, with a jammy berry character, finishing with crisp tannins. **83**
1990: Tight and rugged, with a core of tannic cherry, spice and oak flavors. **85**
Private Reserve 1991: Lean and firm, with spicy raspberry, leather and anise notes that turn tannic. **85**
Private Reserve 1990: Intense and focused, with bright pepper, plum and raspberry aromas and flavors that capture the essence of Zinfandel. **89**
Private Reserve 1989: Rich and flavorful, with plenty of ripe blackberry, cherry and spice flavors that have a slightly pickley edge, all of it rounded by oak. **83**
Private Reserve Lot 2 1989: Lean and tough, with strong herbal flavors obscuring the modest fruit notes. **76**

LONE OAK ESTATES
This is a second label for Smith and Hook (see listing).

LONG VINEYARDS
St. Helena, Napa Valley
F: 1977. **O:** Long Vineyards Inc. **W:** Sandi Belcher, Zelma Long. **S:** None.

OVERALL	$18-30	★★★

WINE RATINGS

Cabernet Sauvignon Napa Valley	★★★
Chardonnay Napa Valley	★★★★★
Johannisberg Riesling Napa Valley	★★★
Johannisberg Riesling Napa Valley Botrytis	★★★
Pinot Grigio Napa Valley	★★

WINERY DATA
C: 3,500. **V:** 18 acres in Napa Valley. **G:** Chardonnay (14 acres), Riesling (3), Cabernet Sauvignon (1). **P:** Pinot Grigio (Napa), Sauvignon Blanc (Carneros).

Bob and Zelma Long founded this winery in the hills east of Napa with Long's parents as financial backers. The two have since divorced, but they remain partners, producing 3,500 cases of wine each year, a mixture of Cabernet, Chardonnay, Johannisberg Riesling,

Sauvignon Blanc from Carneros and Pinot Grigio, also from purchased grapes. Long Vineyards is on Pritchard Hill near Chappellet, and their Cabernet grapes come from a tiny 30-year-old experimental vineyard in Oakville near Robert Mondavi and Martha's Vineyard.

TASTING NOTES

CABERNET SAUVIGNON NAPA VALLEY (★★★): Elegant and supple, very complex and fruity on release, with mild tannins. Early vintages have not aged that well.
1990: Thick, dense and tannic, with rich currant, chocolate, mint and berry flavors that spread out on the palate. A big, ripe, opulent wine. **89**
1986: Delicious for its pure black cherry, currant and spice flavors, supple tannins and a measure of delicacy and finesse. **86**
1985: Mature, with earthy plum, toasty oak and spicy black cherry flavors that are smooth and fleshy. **87**
1984: Elegant, supple and balanced, with pretty plum, currant and cranberry flavors that are mildly tannic. **86**
1983: Light and simple, from a lesser year. **78**
1980: Rich, ripe and complex, loaded with currant, cherry and spice flavors that are deep and mature. The tannins are softening. **88**
1979: Aging well, mature now, with ripe cherry, currant, cranberry and spice flavors that are elegant and smooth. The tannins are soft. **88**

CHARDONNAY NAPA VALLEY (★★★★★): Ripe, smooth, complex and elegant, with very good aging ability. Best a year or two after release.
1992: Firm and intense, with a tight core of spice, pear, apple and toasty oak shadings, giving it depth and a sense of elegance. **89**
1991: A spicy, rich, round and complex wine that's smooth and generous, offering layers of butter, toast, pear, apple and honey flavors. **91**
1990: Ripe, rich and creamy, with layers of honey, pear, toast and vanilla flavors that dance on the palate. **90**
1989: Rich, smooth and elegant, offering lots of nutmeg, almond, pear, peach and honey aromas and flavors. **91**
1988: Beautifully defined pear, apple, citrus and melon flavors and subtle vanilla and spicy oak seasoning, impeccable balance and a long, delicious aftertaste. **93**
1987: Displaying a wealth of complex pear, honey and vanilla flavors that are well defined and well focused. **90**

1986: Amazing complexity and flavor, with a pretty earthiness to complement the fresh, ripe pear, apple, vanilla and nutmeg flavors. **92**
1985: Shows a shade more richness and finesse than the 1984, offering pure apple, pear, spice, honey and vanilla flavors that are beautifully balanced, finishing with remarkable elegance and subtlety. Terrific now and should hold up through the decade. **91**

JOHANNISBERG RIESLING NAPA VALLEY BOTRYTIS (★★★):
1990: Sweet and fruity, with peach and lemon flavors that pick up honey notes on the finish. **86**
1983: Aging exceptionally well, with clean, ripe honey, pear and apricot flavors. Finishes with a crisp, dry aftertaste. With the zingy acidity, it should age for another decade. **89**

RICHARD LONGORIA WINES
Santa Ynez Valley
F: 1982. **O:** Richard & Diana Longoria. **W:** Richard Longoria. **S:** None.

OVERALL	$16-20	★★

WINE RATINGS

Cabernet Sauvignon Santa Ynez Valley	★★
Chardonnay Santa Barbara County	★★
Chardonnay Santa Ynez Valley Huber Vineyard	★★
Merlot Santa Ynez Valley	★★
Pinot Noir Santa Maria Valley Bien Nacido Vineyard	★★★

WINERY DATA
C: 1,500. **V:** None. **G:** None. **P:** Chardonnay (Santa Ynez), Pinot Noir, Merlot, Cabernet Franc (Santa Maria).

Richard Longoria has a long track record with Santa Barbara winegrowing, with stints at J. Carey and now Gainey Vineyard. On the side, he and his wife, Diana, make about 1,500 cases a year of Cabernet Sauvignon (and sometimes Cabernet Franc), Chardonnay, Merlot and Pinot Noir, all from purchased grapes and all from Santa Ynez Valley except the Pinot Noir, which comes from Bien Nacido and occasionally Sanford & Benedict.

TASTING NOTES

CABERNET SAUVIGNON SANTA YNEZ VALLEY (★★):
Lean and racy, marked by leather and herb notes.
1990: Lean and racy, showing more spicy oak than fruit aromas and flavors, although berry and herbal notes come through. **83**

CHARDONNAY VARIOUS BOTTLINGS (★★): Ripe, intense and well oaked.
Santa Barbara County 1992: Marked by a strong leesy and toasty oak edge, the ripe pear and pineapple flavors gain intensity on the finish. **87**
Santa Ynez Valley Huber Vineyard 1993: A cedary oak edge dominates at this stage, with ripe pear, spice and apple notes underneath. Well balanced, with flavors that stay focused. **86**

MERLOT SANTA YNEZ VALLEY (★★): Works better than the Cabernet, with appealing fruit flavors and a touch of herb.
1990: Supple and ripe, with currant, plum and spice notes that are mildly tannic. **85**

PINOT NOIR VARIOUS BOTTLINGS (★★★): Marked by cola and earth notes, but enough ripe cherry and spice flavors come through to make it attractive.
Santa Maria Valley Bien Nacido Vineyard 1993: Intense and well focused, with an earthy, herbal edge to the cherry and cola notes. Tight and tannic, it can stand short-term cellaring into 1996 to soften a bit. **86**
Santa Ynez Valley Benedict Vineyard 1989: A pretty blend of cola and cherry aromas and flavors that are firm, rich and spicy. Moderate tannins make it drinkable. **86**
Santa Ynez Valley Benedict Vineyard 1988: An earthy, leathery wine that's firm and tight, with cedar, anise and gamy currant flavors. **87**
Santa Ynez Valley Benedict Vineyard 1987: Ripe, smooth and generous, with spicy anise, cola and fruit flavors and mild tannins. **88**

THE LUCAS WINERY
Lodi, Central Valley
F: 1978. **O:** David Lucas. **W:** David Lucas. **S:** None.

OVERALL	$7	★★

WINE RATINGS

Zinfandel	★★

WINERY DATA
C: 1,000. **V:** 20 acres in Lodi. **G:** Zinfandel. **P:** None.

Dave Lucas manages vineyards for Robert Mondavi winery and knows the state's wine appellations well. He and his wife, Tamara, begain growing Zinfandel in the 1970s and now produce a thousand cases a year from their 20-acre Lodi Vineyard, a portion of which was planted in the 1930s.

LYETH
Alexander Valley
F: 1981. **O:** Boisset U.S.A. **W:** Bill Arbios. **S:** None.

OVERALL	$8-18	★★★

WINE RATINGS

Cabernet Blend Alexander Valley	★★★
Cabernet Sauvignon Alexander Valley	★★★
Chardonnay Sonoma County	★★

WINERY DATA
C: 32,000. **V:** None. **G:** None. **P:** Malvasia Bianca, Sémillon, Sauvignon Blanc (Sonoma County), Cabernet Sauvignon, Merlot, Cabernet Franc, Chardonnay (Alexander Valley), Chardonnay (Dry Creek Valley).

Founder Munro "Chip" Lyeth advocated Bordeaux blends for his red and white table wines and enjoyed a string of successful vintages before he died in a tragic plane crash. From there the winery struggled, first being acquired by Vintech, which failed financially. The vineyards in Alexander Valley were then sold to Gallo, the winery went to Silver Oak and the brand was sold to Jean-Claude Boisset, who is making Cabernet and Chardonnay under the Lyeth label at another location.

TASTING NOTES

CABERNET BLEND ALEXANDER VALLEY (★★★):
1992: Elegant with cedar, coffee, cherry and berry flavors that are supple and polished, finishing with firm tannins and good length. Best after 1996. **87**

1991: Firm and austere, with a tannic edge, but the ripe cherry, plum and wild berry flavors are complex and appealing. **87**

1988: Smooth, supple and approachable, with pleasant, pretty cherry, anise and rhubarb flavors. **84**

1987: Definitely herbal, bordering on vegetal, with a strong smoky edge to the currant and cedar flavors. **83**

1986: Aromatic but lean on the palate, this elegant wine features herb, toast and currant aromas and flavors that linger on the focused finish. **88**

1985: Rich and supple, with layers of lively plum, currant and cedar flavors that are thick and concentrated, bordered by ample tannins and a soft, smooth texture. **86**

CABERNET SAUVIGNON ALEXANDER VALLEY (★★★): Graceful if a shade tannic, but with a pleasant range of flavors; the vintages from 1981 to 1987 were made by the original Lyeth winery.

1990: Graceful and elegant, with a pleasant blend of currant, spice and plum aromas and flavors and soft, fine tannins. **88**

1985: Has aged well but not exceptionally, with an earthy cedar and herb edge to the currant and anise flavors. **87**

1984: Mature now, with an earthy edge to the ripe plum flavors. **85**

CHARDONNAY SONOMA COUNTY (★★): Variable quality so far, ranging from simple to complex.

1993: Young and unfocused, with coarse, spicy, typical Chardonnay flavors. **82**

1992: Smooth and creamy, with ripe apple, pineapple and spicy citrus flavors that are elegant and lively, finishing with a nutmeg edge. **88**

1991: Smooth and elegant, with spicy pear and vanilla flavors that are fresh and light. **83**

LYTTON SPRINGS WINERY
Sonoma County
F: 1959. **O:** Ridge Vineyards Inc. **W:** Paul Draper. **S:** None.

OVERALL	$16	★★★★

WINE RATINGS

Cabernet Sauvignon Mendocino		
County Private Reserve		★★
Zinfandel Sonoma County		★★★★★

WINERY DATA
C: 7,800. **V:** 45 acres in Dry Creek Valley. **G:** Zinfandel (35 acres), Petite Sirah (7), Carignane (1), Grenache (2). **P:** Zinfandel, Carignane, Alicante Bouschet (Sonoma), Petite Sirah (Alexander Valley).

Lytton Springs has been synonymous with great Zinfandels since the 1970s, when Ridge Vineyards began bottling a vineyard-designated wine from these turn-of-the-century Dry Creek Valley vines. Founding partners B.W. Walters and Richard Sherwin started making a Zin of their own as the Ridge bottling gained popularity. In 1991 Ridge purchased the 45-acre vineyard and winery building, and now makes 7,800 cases of Lytton Springs Zinfandel. The vineyard is on the eastern edge of Dry Creek Valley near where it meets Alexander Valley, a very warm part of the area. Full ripeness usually means alcohol levels at 14.5 percent or higher, yet the wines carry it well.

TASTING NOTES

CABERNET SAUVIGNON MENDOCINO COUNTY PRIVATE RESERVE (★★):
1988: The spicy raspberry and currant notes have a pickley edge. **80**

1987: A big, high-extract wine with raisin, currant, black cherry, plum and spicy oak flavors. **88**

ZINFANDEL SONOMA COUNTY (★★★★★): Ultraripe and deeply colored, with intense, often jammy plum and raspberry flavors that can have a spicy, tarry edge. Ages well, but hits its peak on release and is best in its youth.

1992: Deeply colored, thick and rich, a tight and compact wine that packs in black cherry, blueberry and raspberry flavors. With all its power, it manages to remain sleek and polished. **89**

1988: Ripe and jammy, with beautifully defined raspberry aromas and flavors and hints of plum, nutmeg, vanilla and toast, turning elegant. **90**

1987: Very ripe, powerful and toasty, with concentrated pepper, raspberry and plum flavors held in careful check by a firm structure and fine tannins. **88**

1986: Built like a claret, with a ripe boysenberry and plum edge to the toasty flavors, turning tannic. **87**

1985: An inky purple color, with intense plum and vanilla flavors that turn supple and elegant. **90**

MACROSTIE WINERY
Carneros
F: 1987. O: Steven & Thale MacRostie. W: Steven MacRostie. S: Keltie Brook.

OVERALL	$16-23	★★★

WINE RATINGS	
Chardonnay Carneros	★★★
Merlot Carneros	★★
Pinot Noir Carneros	★★
Keltie Brook Pinot Noir Carneros Unfiltered	★★

WINERY DATA
C: 9,000. V: None. G: None. P: Chardonnay, Merlot, Cabernet Franc, Pinot Noir (Carneros).

After serving as winemaker at Hacienda Winery from 1975 to 1987, Steve MacRostie started his own winery, focusing on Sangiacomo-grown Chardonnay and smaller lots of Merlot and Pinot Noir. All grapes are purchased and production has grown to 9,000 cases.

TASTING NOTES

CHARDONNAY CARNEROS (★★★): Well crafted in a highly manipulated style, with lots of flavor and finesse.
1993: This wine is straightforward and bright against a supple background, laying out its youthful pear and floral flavors. **85**
1992: Crisp and spicy, a toasty wine with relatively modest fruit intensity. **86**
1991: Smooth and harmonious, with a nice array of ripe pear, spice, citrus and pineapple flavors framed by toasty oak. **88**
Reserve 1992: A subtle wine that folds in some lovely spice and honey notes on the long, elegant finish, all of it wrapped around a nice core of apple and quince flavors. **91**

MERLOT CARNEROS (★★): Lean and earthy so far, in need of a little more ripeness.
1992: Lean and trim, with a cedary vanilla edge to a tight core of berry and currant flavors. **85**
1991: Lean, firm and earthy, with a barnyardy edge to the currant and cherry notes. **82**

PINOT NOIR CARNEROS (★★): Similar to the Merlot in its trim, austere style.
1992: Young and chewy, showing a firm, tannic edge, but it has enough ripe fruit flavors to merit watching. **84**

KELTIE BROOK PINOT NOIR CARNEROS UNFILTERED (★★):
1991: Soft and light in texture and flavor but very appealing, especially the plum and currant flavors that linger on the finish, hinting at spice and toast. **84**

MADRONA VINEYARDS
Camino, El Dorado County
F: 1973. O: Richard & Leslie Bush. W: Hugh Chappelle. S: None.

OVERALL	$7-11	★★

WINE RATINGS	
Cabernet Sauvignon El Dorado County	★★
Chardonnay El Dorado County	★★

WINERY DATA
C: 10,000. V: 32 acres in El Dorado County.
G: Gewürztraminer (0.5 acres), Chardonnay (6), Cabernet Sauvignon (7), Merlot (2), Cabernet Franc (2), Zinfandel (7), Johannisberg Riesling (5). P: None.

Madrona Vineyards lays claim to having California's highest grapevines, as its 32 acres of estate vineyards rise to an elevation of 3,000 feet. Cabernet, Chardonnay, Merlot, Cabernet Franc and Zinfandel are among the mix for its 10,000 case output. Chardonnay is the most appealing; the 1992 El Dorado serves up ripe apple, pear and cedary oak notes.

TASTING NOTES

VARIOUS BOTTLINGS (★★):
Cabernet Sauvignon El Dorado County 1991: Elegant with a floral and grapey currant edge that's pleasing to drink. **81**
Chardonnay El Dorado County 1993: Clean and appealing for its ripe pear and custard flavors that turn elegant and refined on the finish. **85**
Chardonnay El Dorado County 1992: Ripe and spicy, with pretty pear, apple and cedary oak flavors. **84**

MAHONEY ESTATE

This is a second label of Carneros Creek Winery (see listing).

MAISON DEUTZ WINERY

Arroyo Grande, San Luis Obispo County
F: 1981. O: Pressoir Deutz & Wine World Estates. W: Christian Roguenant. S: None.

OVERALL	$15-23	★★★

WINE RATINGS

Sparkling Wine San Luis Obispo County Blanc de Noirs	★★
Sparkling Wine San Luis Obispo County Brut Cuvée	★★
Sparkling Wine San Luis Obispo County Brut Reserve	★★★
Sparkling Wine San Luis Obispo County Brut Rosé	★★★

WINERY DATA
C: 30,000. V: 160 acres in San Luis Obispo County. G: Chardonnay (60 acres), Pinot Noir (60), Pinot Blanc (40). P: None.

This is a joint venture between Deutz Champagne of France and Wine World Estates, owner of Beringer, Chateau Souverain, Meridian and Napa Ridge. The project is part of the great French Champagne land rush to California in the 1970s and 1980s, led by Domaine Chandon, Roederer, Piper Heidsieck and Taittinger. The winery in Arroyo Grande has 160 acres in vines in the San Luis-Arroyo Grande area, 60 acres each of Chardonnay and Pinot Noir and 40 of Pinot Blanc. Volume is now 30,000 cases and quality ranges from very good to excellent.

TASTING NOTES

SPARKLING WINE SAN LUIS OBISPO COUNTY BLANC DE NOIRS (★★): Leans on Pinot Noir for its intense flavors, but lacks the complexity found in the other wines.
NV: Pale salmon in color with light strawberry and spice flavors, but not quite as rich and complex as the first attempt. **82**

SPARKLING WINE SAN LUIS OBISPO COUNTY BRUT RESERVE (★★★): The most complex, with concentrated toasty pear and spice flavors.
1990: Tart and spicy, with a narrow band of citrus, herb and pear flavors. Intense and concentrated, with a long, full finish, although the flavors are unusual. **85**

MANZANITA

Alexander Valley
F: 1980. O: Steve Koster. W: Steve Koster. S: None.

OVERALL	$15	★★

WINE RATINGS

Zinfandel Alexander Valley	★★

WINERY DATA
C: 1,500. V: N/A. G: N/A. P: Cabernet Sauvignon, Chardonnay (Napa Valley), Zinfandel (Alexander Valley).

Steve Koster owns this brand, using leased space and purchased grapes to produce Napa Valley Cabernet, Chardonnay and Alexander Valley Zinfandel. The 1988 Zin is an excellent wine, with bright, focused blackberry, cherry and anise notes. Production is 1,500 cases.

TASTING NOTES

ZINFANDEL ALEXANDER VALLEY (★★):
1988: Well crafted, bright and lively, with focused blackberry, black cherry and anise flavors. **89**

MARCASSIN WINERY

Oakville, Napa Valley
F: 1990. O: Helen Turley. W: Helen Turley, John Wetlaufer. S: None.

OVERALL	$36-50	★★★★★

WINE RATINGS

Chardonnay Alexander Valley Gauer Ranch Upper Barn	★★★★★
Chardonnay Carneros Hudson Vineyard	★★★★★
Chardonnay Sonoma County Lorenzo Vineyard	★★★★★

WINERY DATA

C: 1,200. V: 10 acres in Sonoma Coast. G: Chardonnay (Alexander Valley, Carneros). P: None.

After making excellent wines for B. R. Cohn and Peter Michael, Helen Turley founded her own brand, Marcassin (which means little wild boar). She and her husband, John Wetlaufer, have planted 5 acres each to Chardonnay and Pinot Noir on the Sonoma coast near Fort Ross. She is still a very busy consultant, and in 1995 counted her brother's new winery, Turley Wine Cellars, as a client, along with Bryant Family Vineyard, Canepa, Colgin, Green and Red, Harrison, La Jota, Landmark, Martinelli, Pahlmeyer and Swanson. Turley's formula for success is straightforward: she seeks vineyards that hold crop loads to 2 tons per acre, cool climates for Chardonnay and Pinot Noir, natural yeast fermentations, judicious use of oak and minimal handling, including avoiding filtration. Her early success with Chardonnay from Gauer's Upper Barn vineyard and Lorenzo Vineyard near Occidental puts her out in front of the pack. These wines are ultra rich, ripe and creamy, loaded with deep, complex flavors. Her work with Turley Wine Cellars Zinfandel and Petite Sirah is simply amazing. Marcassin's production will never amount to much, even when her dense-spacing vineyard comes into full production. But the quality is very high, and her wines and those of her clients are definitely worth watching. Production should level off around 1,200 cases.

TASTING NOTES

CHARDONNAY ALEXANDER VALLEY GAUER RANCH UPPER BARN (★★★★★):

1993: Ultra rich and toasty, with bold, complex pear, pineapple, spice, honey and hazelnut flavors that are intense and complex, gaining nuance on the finish. Succeeds with uncommon complexity and depth for the vintage. **92**

1992: Very rich, ripe and creamy, with complex toast, pear, spice and honey notes that are mouth-filling. A no-holds-barred wine that packs in lots of flavor, with a long, full finish. **94**

CHARDONNAY CARNEROS HUDSON VINEYARD (★★★★★):

1993: Smoky and perfumed, with polished honey, pear and butterscotch notes that gain complexity and depth on the finish. Has a sense of harmony and finesse. **92**

CHARDONNAY SONOMA COUNTY LORENZO VINEYARD (★★★★★):

1993: Well oaked, with bold, rich and concentrated tiers of honey, pear and toasty oak flavors that are ripe and well focused, finishing with a long complex aftertaste. **91**

1992: Extremely rich and creamy, with layers of complex pear, spice, honey and butterscotch flavors on a long, full finish. For all its richness, it's wonderfully elegant. **93**

MARIETTA CELLARS
Sonoma County
F: 1979. O: Chris Bilbro. W: Chris Bilbro. S: None.

OVERALL	$8-16	★★

WINE RATINGS

Port Alexander Valley	★★
Red Table Wine Sonoma County Old Vine Red Lot 14 NV	★★
Zinfandel Sonoma County	★★

WINERY DATA

C: 15,000. V: 22 acres in Alexander Valley. G: Zinfandel, Petite Sirah, Carignare. P: Cabernet Sauvignon, Merlot, Cabernet Franc, Zinfandel, Petite Sirah (Sonoma County).

Chris Bilbro, whose family once owned Bandiera, produces 15,000 cases a year using 15 acres of winery-owned Zinfandel and Petite Sirah and buying Cabernet from Sonoma County. The all-red lineup includes those varieties, made in a bold, ripe, high-extract style. Zinfandel is the leader, although it's been several vintages since I've seen new releases.

TASTING NOTES

VARIOUS BOTTLINGS (★★):

Port Alexander Valley 1989: Smells and tastes like a really good late harvest Zinfandel, smooth and berryish, not too sweet, with a solid mouthful of fruit and spice on the finish. **86**

Red Table Wine Sonoma County Old Vine Red Lot 14
NV: Ripe with sweet cherry and berry fruit that turns soft and supple. **83**
Zinfandel Sonoma County 1992: A ripe, jammy, effusively fruity style, with wild berry, black cherry and raspberry flavors. Has lots of tannin too, but it's appealing. **85**

MARK WEST VINEYARDS
Russian River Valley
F: 1976. **O:** Associated Vintners Group. **W:** Kerry Damskey. **S:** None.

OVERALL	$9-20	★★

WINE RATINGS

Chardonnay Russian River Valley	
Barrel Fermented	★★
Gewürztraminer Russian River Valley	★★
Pinot Noir Russian River Valley	★★
Sauvignon Blanc Russian River Valley	★★

WINERY DATA
C: 10,000. **V:** 66 acres in Russian River Valley. **G:** Chardonnay (34 acres), Gewürztraminer (15), Merlot (7), Pinot Noir (10). **P:** Sauvignon Blanc (Russian River Valley).

Bob and Joan Ellis founded this winery and vineyard in 1976 near Mark West Creek, focusing on Chardonnay, Gewürztraminer, Riesling and Pinot Noir with production peaking at 25,000 cases. Quality with both Chardonnay and Pinot Noir has ranged from fair to good, although the most recent Chardonnay is impressive. The winery has undergone several ownership changes, the most recent being in 1994 when it was acquired by the Associated Vintners Group (owners of McDowell Valley Vineyards). Plans call for the winery to focus on Chardonnay, Gewürztraminer, Pinot Noir and Sauvignon Blanc. The limited distribution Robert Rue Zinfandels, from vines planted in 1906, are bright and lively. Their future is undetermined.

TASTING NOTES

CHARDONNAY RUSSIAN RIVER VALLEY BARREL FERMENTED (★★): Improving after a series of simple wines, with 1992 impressive for its richness and depth.
1992: Best Mark West ever. Complex, with layers of smoky, toasty oak, spicy pear, peach and vanilla notes and a smooth texture. **89**

1991: Solid, with intense pear, spice, peach and vanilla flavors that pick up a honey edge. **85**
Estate Reserve 1991: A simple, refreshing Chardonnay that shows spicy apple flavors a light citrus touch. **81**

PINOT NOIR RUSSIAN RIVER VALLEY (★★): On the lighter side, with simple tea, cherry and strawberry notes.
1991: Tea, strawberry and herb flavors are accented by toasty, buttery oak notes in this lean wine. **84**
1990: Crisp and narrow, with spicy cola and cherry notes of moderate depth and intensity. **83**

MARKHAM VINEYARDS
St. Helena, Napa Valley
F: 1977. **O:** Merican Corp. **W:** Rob Hunter. **S:** Glass Mountain Quarry.

OVERALL	$8-25	★★★★

WINE RATINGS

Cabernet Sauvignon Napa Valley	★★★
Chardonnay Napa Valley	
Barrel Fermented	★★★★
Glass Mountain Quarry	
Cabernet Sauvignon California	★★
Glass Mountain Quarry	
Chardonnay California	★★
Laurent Cellars Cabernet Sauvignon	
Napa Valley Reserve	★★
Laurent Cellars Chardonnay Napa Valley	★★★
Merlot Napa Valley	★★★★
Sauvignon Blanc Napa Valley	★★★

WINERY DATA
C: 150,000. **V:** 253 acres in Napa Valley. **G:** Muscat (8 acres), Sauvignon Blanc (14), Chardonnay (49), Sémillon (2), Merlot (79), Cabernet Sauvignon (55), Cabernet Franc (10), Petite Verdot (3). **P:** Chardonnay, Sauvignon Blanc, Sémillon, Cabernet Sauvignon, Cabernet Franc, Merlot (Napa Valley).

Former advertising executive Bruce Markham founded this winery in 1977, hiring Bryan del Bondio, the young son of Al del Bondio, a longtime Inglenook employee, to run the winery. Markham's old stone winery north of St. Helena was built in 1876 and remodeled in time for the 1978 vintage. In 1988 Markham tired of the wine business and sold it to Sanraku, Japan's largest winemaker, which proceeded with an extensive remodelling of the facility.

Bruce Markham's legacy lies in the vineyards he acquired, including 55 acres of Cabernet in Yountville next to Napanook and Dominus Estate. Today Markham's vineyard holdings total 253 acres, spread out from Yountville to Calistoga, with the Napa Ranch, near Oak Knoll, devoted primarily to Chardonnay, and both the Calistoga and Yountville ranches planted to Bordeaux varieties. Each of the main wines is produced in significant lots: 20,000 cases of Cabernet, 14,000 of Chardonnay, 32,000 of Merlot and 16,000 of Sauvignon Blanc. Two second labels—the value-oriented Glass Mountain Quarry brand and the newly repositioned, reserve-status Laurent line—round out the roster. Quality across the board was solid into the 1990s, although case volume appears to be threatening quality control.

TASTING NOTES

CABERNET SAUVIGNON NAPA VALLEY (★★★): Bold, ripe and fruity, with supple currant and black cherry flavors and mild tannins. A few vintages have been sweet beyond ripeness. Ages well.

1991: Spicy, with pretty currant, plum and cherry notes that add complexity and depth. Firmly tannic. **88**

1990: Ripe in flavor and firmly tannic, an opulent wine with spicy, chocolaty plum, berry and currant flavors pushing through the tannins on the finish. **90**

1989: Delivers ripe currant and cherry flavors with subtle vanilla, herb and spice shadings, finishing with fine tannins. **87**

1988: Crisp and fruity, offering nice black cherry and spice flavors, but it thins out on the finish. **80**

1987: Offers a solid core of ripe, rich cherry, currant, plum and mint flavors and a slap of oak. Firmly tannic. **87**

1986: Well articulated currant and berry flavors run through this smoothly balanced, harmonious wine that turns elegant and supple on a long finish. **87**

1985: Lean in structure but brimming with generous blackberry and vanilla flavors that turn complex. **91**

1984: Elegantly balanced, with oaky nuances and fresh currant and black cherry flavors that are subtle and delicate. **87**

1983: Lean and tannic, but with more fruit concentration, plushness and elegance than most Markhams. Tight and austere on the finish. **88**

1982: A solid 1982, showcasing the sharply focused black cherry and currant flavors. Mature now. **88**

1981: Lean, tannic and more austere than previous vintages, but it has a rich concentration of ripe cherry and currant flavors. **86**

1980: Supple black cherry, anise and currant flavors, with tannins that are softening. **85**

1979: Lean, complex and tannic, with an elegant seam of black cherry and currant flavors. **88**

1978: Mature, with ripe, chewy currant and cherry flavors and firm tannins, making it long on flavor but short on finesse. **86**

CHARDONNAY NAPA VALLEY BARREL FERMENTED (★★★★): Ripe, smooth and creamy, with up-front fruity flavors, appealing oak and a sense of elegance.

1993: Pleasantly ripe and full bodied, with attractive pear, ginger, quince and spice notes, a distinctive wine with personality and finesse. **91**

1992: Ripe, smooth and complex, with layers of creamy vanilla, pear, spice, honey and hazelnut flavors. **90**

1991: Smooth and complex, with tiers of toasty oak, pear, spice and pineapple flavors that fold together nicely. **88**

MERLOT NAPA VALLEY (★★★★): Among the best, bold, ripe and complex, with supple tannins. Ages well.

1992: Ripe and chewy, with chunky black cherry, currant and mineral flavors, finishing with firm tannins and fine length. **88**

1991: Supple and refined, with complex and compact coffee, currant and cedar notes that turn smooth and fan out on the finish. **87**

1990: Bold, ripe and opulent, brimming with rich, complex currant and black cherry flavors that turn smooth and polished. **92**

1989: A solid 1989 that's rich and full-bodied, with layers of currant and black cherry flavors that are long and smooth on the finish. **88**

1988: Rich and flavorful, with intense yet supple currant, cherry, raspberry and anise flavors that are silky-smooth and a persistent finish that echoes fruit. **90**

1987: Complex and supple, a fine 1987, with minty currant notes that turn smooth and rich on the palate. **92**

1985: Rich and vibrant, with silky, complex currant, black cherry, spice and cedar notes that are focused and engaging, finishing with fine length and excellent balance. **93**

1984: Ripe, rich and full-bodied, with broad, complex black cherry, currant and spice notes framed by toasty, buttery oak. **92**

1983: Austere, like most 1983s, with lean, spicy currant flavors that are vibrant but not very generous. **81**

1982: A solid 1982 with mature black cherry and plum aromas and flavors. Oak sticks out on the finish. **84**

1981: Tight and one-dimensional, with an herbaceous edge to the currant flavor. Turns dry and oaky on the finish. **83**

1980: Entirely from Fay Vineyard in the Stags Leap District, this wine is fully mature, with spicy cedar and plum flavors. **85**

SAUVIGNON BLANC NAPA VALLEY (★★★): A touch sweet but very fine, with grassy pear and citrus notes and deft oak shadings.

1994: Bright and focused, showing lots of sweet tropical fruit, floral and herb flavors that swirl through the finish. **87**

1993: Floral, spicy and juicier than most 1993s, with a passion fruit character running through it and lingering on the finish. **89**

1992: There's a touch of sweetness but also a rich core of fig, herb, toast and spice flavors that turn smooth and fan out. **88**

GLASS MOUNTAIN QUARRY VARIOUS BOTTLINGS (★★):
1993: Well oaked, with toasty buttery aromas and just the right mix of ripe pear and spice notes to achieve balance. **84**

1991: Appealing, with honey, spice, peach and apple flavors. **82**

1990: Ripe and supple, offering generous currant, plum and herb flavors. **84**

LAURENT CELLARS CABERNET SAUVIGNON NAPA VALLEY RESERVE (★★): The initial offerings were good but incomplete. Expect this new line to feature Markham's best Cabernet.

1991: Supple and round, with light currant and black cherry notes that turn elegant and polished on the finish. **85**

1990: Supple and elegant, with spicy, cedary oak, black cherry and currant flavors that turn smooth and silky. **85**

1988: Supple, with well defined plum and currant aromas and flavors shaded by herb and toast notes. Finishes with a solid dose of tannin. **87**

LAURENT CELLARS CHARDONNAY NAPA VALLEY RESERVE (★★★): Like the Cabernet, it's not yet head and shoulders above the standard Chardonnay, but the aim is to take it there.

1991: Smooth and tangy, with an orange-blossom edge to the creamy pear and spice aromas and flavors. **88**

MARTIN BROTHERS WINERY
Paso Robles
F: 1981. **O:** Martin & MacFarlane Inc. **W:** Dominic Martin. **S:** None.

OVERALL	$10-25	★★

WINE RATINGS

Cabernet Blend Paso Robles Etrusco	★★
Sparkling Wine California	
Moscato Allegro	NR
Zinfandel Paso Robles Primitiva	★★

WINERY DATA
C: 16,000. **V:** 58 acres in Paso Robles. **G:** Chardonnay (30 acres), Nebbiolo (10), Zinfandel (5), Petite Verdot (2), Sangiovese (5), Pinot Grigio (3), Barbera (2), Dolcetto (1). **P:** Chardonnay, Nebbiolo, Zinfandel, Sangiovese (Paso Robles), Malvasia Bianca, Italian Type (Central Coast).

The Martin family purchased a run-down dairy with 80-plus acres of land and created their own wine estate, which now includes 58 acres of vineyards, mostly Chardonnay (30 acres), but also noteworthy for Nebbiolo (10 acres), Sangiovese (5 acres) and smaller parcels of Pinot Grigio, Barbera and Dolcetto. Increasingly the focus has shifted to Italian varietal wines, including a Cabernet-Sangiovese blend called Etrusco, a Zinfandel called Primitiva, a Sangiovese called Il Palio and a Nebbiolo called Vecchio. The winery also produces a series of dessert-style wines, again modeled after Italian wines of a similar style, including a vin santo (Malvasia Bianca) and Aleatico. Production is 16,000 cases, with Chardonnay the volume leader at 2,600. Overall quality has been uneven, with a few impressive wines and several that miss.

TASTING NOTES

CABERNET BLEND PASO ROBLES ETRUSCO (★★): A blend of 85 percent Cabernet Sauvignon with Sangiovese. The 1990 and 1991 show improvement, with complex flavors, but the 1992 is less concentrated.

1992: Ripe, round and fruity, a pleasant mouthful of currant and berry flavors. **82**

1991: The best from Martin Brothers. A Cabernet-Sangiovese blend that serves up pretty currant, black cherry, anise and berry flavors. **89**

1990: A light, fruity wine with ripe plum and currant flavors that have a hint of strawberry and raspberry. **85**

SPARKLING WINE CALIFORNIA MOSCATO ALLEGRO (NR): **1992:** Simple, fruity and soft, with a vaguely cucumber edge to the pear and vanilla flavors. **77**

ZINFANDEL PASO ROBLES PRIMITIVA (★★): Lean, with modest fruit flavors.

1992: Simple and fruity, with a light color and modest berry flavors. **83**

1991: Firm and intense, with an earthy, gamy edge to the wild berry flavors. **84**

1990: Light and lean, with a spicy, toasty edge to the raspberry flavors. **82**

MARTINELLI WINERY
Russian River Valley
F: 1987. O: Lee & Carolyn Martinelli. W: Steve Ryan, Helen Turley. S: None.

OVERALL	$10-20	★★

WINE RATINGS

Chardonnay Russian River Valley	★★
Sauvignon Blanc Russian River Valley	NR
Zinfandel Russian River Valley	
Jackass Vineyard	★★★

WINERY DATA
C: 3,000. V: 158 acres in Russian River Valley. G: Zinfandel (12 acres), Chardonnay (100), Sauvignon Blanc (12), Muscat (2), Gewürztraminer (12), Pinot Noir (20). P: None.

The Martinellis have been grape growers in Russian River since 1905 and preside over 158 acres of vines, mostly Chardonnay (100 acres), with smaller parcels of Pinot Noir (20), Gewürztraminer, Sauvignon Blanc and Zinfandel (12 acres each). It is best known for its Zinfandel, and Williams & Selyem Winery produced a hearty Zinfandel from the property for a decade. In 1987 the winery began making small lots of Zinfandel from the Jackass Vineyard (and now Jackass Hill as well), along with Chardonnay and Sauvignon Blanc. Helen Turley (of Marcassin and others) is consulting.

TASTING NOTES

CHARDONNAY RUSSIAN RIVER VALLEY (★★): Improving. The 1992 is rich and complex, brimming with elegant pear, spice and pineapple flavors.

1992: Smooth, polished and brimming with spicy, elegant pear and pineapple flavors. **88**

SAUVIGNON BLANC RUSSIAN RIVER VALLEY (NR): **1993:** Sweet and peppery, an off-putting wine. **71**

ZINFANDEL RUSSIAN RIVER VALLEY JACKASS VINEYARD (★★★): This vineyard is capable of producing ripe, intense, potent Zinfandel (see notes from Williams & Selyem), but so far the wines have been lean and trim. The 1993 vintage shows considerably more stuffing.

1992: Intense and lively, with earthy, tarry raspberry and cherry flavors that are ripe and focused. Firmly tannic. **88**

1991: Smooth-textured, fresh and lively, with distinctive grape, berry and earth flavors. **81**

1990: Bold, ripe and jammy, oozing with deep, concentrated plum, currant and black cherry flavors. Firmly tannic and rich on the finish. **91**

1989: Light and simple, with earthy mineral flavors obscuring modest fruit. **71**

1988: A peppery wine that's light and charming, with cherry, strawberry and spice accents. **85**

LOUIS M. MARTINI WINERY
St. Helena, Napa Valley
F: 1922. O: The Martini Family. W: Michael Martini. S: None.

OVERALL	$8-23	★★★

WINE RATINGS

Barbera California	★★
Cabernet Sauvignon	
Napa Valley Reserve	★★★
Cabernet Sauvignon North Coast	★★
Cabernet Sauvignon Sonoma Valley	
Monte Rosso Vineyard Selection	★★★
Chardonnay Napa Valley	★★★

Chardonnay Napa Valley Reserve ★★★
Gewürztraminer Russian River Valley ★★
Merlot North Coast ★★
Merlot Russian River Valley
 Los Vinedos del Rio Vineyard Selection ★★★
Pinot Noir Carneros ★★
Zinfandel Sonoma Valley NR

WINERY DATA
C: 200,000. **V:** 536 acres in Napa Valley, Sonoma County, Lake County. **G:** Barbera (5 acres), Cabernet Franc (9), Cabernet Sauvignon (175), Zinfandel (74), Chardonnay (26), Folle Blanche (6), Gamay Beaujolais (10), Gewürztraminer (23), Johannisberg Riesling (22), Merlot (115). **P:** Cabernet Sauvignon, Chardonnay, Merlot, Sauvignon Blanc (Napa Valley), Barbera (California).

Louis M. Martini is one of the great names in California wine. He moved this family-owned and operated winery from the Central Valley town of Kingsburg to St. Helena in 1934 and quickly established a reputation for savvy winemaking. From the outset, the Martini winery was a no-frills, low-key, quality-oriented operation that relied on keen winemaking and precision farming. Martini has its roots in a number of excellent vineyards, the most famous being the Monte Rosso Vineyard in the eastern hills of Sonoma Valley at the 1,000-foot elevation, acquired in 1938. It is planted primarily to Cabernet and Zinfandel, and the winery uses it for vineyard-designated wines. Martini bought the 200-acre La Loma Vineyard in Carneros, a source of the winery's Pinot Noir and Chardonnay, and in 1962 Las Amigas Vineyard (200 acres in Carneros), adding acreage in 1974. Also acquired in 1962 was Los Vinedos del Rio Vineyard in Russian River Valley, which is planted to several varieties, but is best known for the winery's vineyard-designated Merlot. Altogether the Martinis own 536 acres: 358 in Sonoma County, 117 in Napa Valley and 61 in Lake County. All the major grape varieties are grown, led by Cabernet at 175 acres, Merlot at 115 and Zinfandel at 74.

Longtime drinkers of old Martini wines— Barberas, Cabernets, Zinfandels, Pinot Noirs, even Rieslings and Gewürztraminers—know full well how excellent and well crafted these wines were. The best Cabernets from the 1940s, 1950s and 1960s have all aged exceptionally well. By the 1970s, the Martini wines began to undergo stylistic changes, one major change being the shift to small oak barrels, which the winery long resisted, having enjoyed success aging its wine in larger tanks. The winery was caught by surprise—as were many others—by the white wine boom of the 1970s, and lagged behind the leaders with Chardonnay. Since the 1970s, quality across the board has varied. There have been several excellent wines, particularly the Reserve Cabernet, Reserve Chardonnay and Merlot, but often the wines taste light and ordinary, less concentrated and less complex than the state's best.

TASTING NOTES

BARBERA CALIFORNIA (★★): Light, with pleasant berry and spice notes; older vintages from the 1960s and 1970s are still very fine.
1987: A crisp, zesty red with appealing berry aromas and flavors and smoke and dill overtones. **83**

CABERNET SAUVIGNON NORTH COAST (★★): Light, with herb and cherry notes, but sometimes diluted.
1990: Green, tannic and herbal, a simple, hard-edged wine. **79**

CABERNET SAUVIGNON NAPA VALLEY RESERVE (★★★): Inconsistent: ripe and full one year, lean and thin the next.
1989: Lean and earthy, with just enough currant flavor to make it appealing. **81**
1988: A light, simple Cabernet with herbal, grassy flavors. **78**
1987: Elegant, with pretty currant and black cherry flavors, a touch of herb and spice and fine, firm tannins. **87**

CABERNET SAUVIGNON SONOMA VALLEY MONTE ROSSO VINEYARD SELECTION (★★★): Inconsistent like the Reserve: at times complex and flavorful, other times simple and lacking focus. Older wines carry various designations.
1990: Firm and lean, with a core of tight, tannic currant, herb and mint notes, finishing with green tannins. **82**
1988: A crisp, austere, tannic wine with modest mint and currant flavors. Hollow in the middle. **81**
1986: Pleasant and attractive, with supple black cherry and currant notes. **84**
1984: Ripe, supple and understated for the vintage, with plum and currant flavors that turn simple. **85**

Special Selection 1978: Mature and complex, with supple cedar, olive, anise and black cherry flavors. **80**

Special Selection 1968: Mature and fading now after a long run of excellence, with earthy, tarry, dried fruit flavors, but worth a try if you can find it. **84**

Special Selection 1966: Past its prime, but it remains an elegant and complex wine. **87**

Special Selection 1964: Well past its prime but still complex, with cedar, black cherry and anise flavors. **83**

CHARDONNAY VARIOUS BOTTLINGS (★★★): Improving of late, showing richer, fuller flavors.

Carneros 1991: Delivers ripe, spicy pear and pineapple flavors, but the buttery oak note stands apart. **84**

Napa Valley 1992: Ripe and creamy, with pear, apple and spice flavors that are appealing. **86**

Napa Valley 1991: Simple, fruity and easygoing, with modest green apple and spice aromas and flavors that persist on the light finish. **82**

Napa Valley Reserve 1991: Intense and lively, with pretty pear, spice, hazelnut and nectarine flavors that are focused and concentrated. **88**

GEWÜRZTRAMINER RUSSIAN RIVER VALLEY (★★): Medium-weight, with modest varietal intensity.

1992: Fresh and lively, showing some nice floral and spice overtones to the basic pear and apple flavors, balanced and refreshingly dry. **85**

MERLOT NORTH COAST (★★): This bottling of Merlot is light and herbal.

1992: Light and crisp, simple berry flavors on a lively structure. **81**

1991: Simple and fruity, with a cranberry and cherry streak that turns tart and earthy. **82**

MERLOT RUSSIAN RIVER VALLEY LOS VINEDOS DEL RIO VINEYARD SELECTION (★★★): Can be complex, with supple flavors and excellent length.

1990: Ripe and supple, with a band of crisp, focused currant, bell pepper and herb notes and soft tannins. **87**

PINOT NOIR CARNEROS (★★): Often carrying La Loma designation, it is lightly fruity, with herb and mushroom notes.

1992: Smooth and ripe with appealing plum, cherry and anise notes and a delicate aftertase with mild tannins. **86**

La Loma Vineyard 1990: Light and balanced, with cherry and mushroom flavors and modest tannins. **83**

1988: Smooth and generous, with nicely focused currant flavors. **85**

ZINFANDEL SONOMA VALLEY (★★): Light and fruity, with modest pepper, berry and spice notes.

1992: Well oaked and a bit murky, with the focus on cedar and spice, but on the finish hints of cherry and berry come through, making it more appealing. **84**

MARTZ VINEYARDS
Yorkville, Mendocino County
F: 1989. **O:** Martz Vineyards Inc. **W:** Larry W. Martz.
S: None.

OVERALL	$8-10	NR

WINE RATINGS	
Cabernet Sauvignon	
Mendocino County	NR
Symphony Mendocino County	NR
Zinfandel Mendocino County	NR

WINERY DATA
C: 1,500. **V:** 8 acres in Mendocino. **G:** Merlot (3 acres), Symphony (2), Chardonnay (2), Flora (1). **P:** Zinfandel (Mendocino County).

This winery is producing Cabernet Sauvignon, Symphony and Zinfandel, all carrying a Mendocino appellation, a portion of the grapes coming from an 8-acre estate vineyard. Production is 1,500 cases.

MASTANTUONO
San Luis Obispo County
F: 1976. **O:** Mastantuono Inc. **W:** Pasquale Mastantuono.
S: Templeton Winery.

OVERALL	$6-13	★★

WINE RATINGS	
Red Table Wine California Carminello	NR

WINERY DATA

C: 11,000. **V:** None. **G:** None. **P:** Barbera (California), Chenin Blanc (Central Coast), Zinfandel (San Luis Obispo County).

Mastantuono Winery in Templeton dates to 1976 when Pasquale Mastantuono began producing wine. Today production is 11,000 cases, with a product mix that relies on purchased grapes from several appellations, including Barbera (California), Chenin Blanc (Central Coast), White Zinfandel (Paso Robles) and Zinfandel (Templeton). Distribution is limited, quality ordinary.

MATANZAS CREEK WINERY
Sonoma Valley

F: 1977. **O:** Matanzas Creek Winery. **W:** Bill Parker, Susan Reed. **S:** Journey.

OVERALL	$14-70	★★★★★

WINE RATINGS

Chardonnay Sonoma Valley	★★★★★
Chardonnay Sonoma Valley Journey	★★★★★
Merlot Sonoma Valley	★★★★★
Sauvignon Blanc Sonoma County	★★★★

WINERY DATA

C: 35,000. **V:** 42 acres in Sonoma Valley. **G:** Chardonnay (29 acres), Merlot (11), Cabernet Sauvignon (1). **P:** Chardonnay, Sauvignon Blanc, Sémillon, Merlot, Cabernet Franc (Sonoma County).

Matanzas Creek is one of those rare wineries that keeps on refining and improving its wines. Owners Sandra and Bill MacIver founded this Bennett Valley winery in 1978 with a product mix that included Cabernet, Chardonnay, Merlot, Pinot

Noir and Sauvignon Blanc. After only average results with Cabernet and disappointing results with Pinot Noir, the MacIvers narrowed the focus to the three wines they excel with—Chardonnay, including a luxury-priced bottling called Journey ($75), Merlot and Sauvignon Blanc.

While all these wines are among the best of their kind, the MacIvers' success with Merlot stands out because the varietal is relatively new to California and is difficult to grow. The winery owns 42 acres: 29 are planted to Chardonnay, 11 to Merlot and the rest to Cabernet. Sauvignon Blanc and Chardonnay are also purchased.

TASTING NOTES

CHARDONNAY SONOMA VALLEY (★★★★★): Starts out tight and flinty, but opens up to reveal a tight and concentrated core of complex flavors. Packs in lots of intensity with a deft hand, and the oak is well balanced. Best early on but can stand short-term cellaring.
1992: Austere and flinty, with bright green apple and spicy pear notes that are complex and vibrant. **89**
1991: Rich, ripe and generous, with honey, pear and vanilla aromas and flavors, remaining flavorful and concentrated through the solid finish. **90**
1990: Wonderfully rich and elegant fig, cream and spice flavors are sharply focused, with pretty, toasty oak shadings. **92**
1988: Attractive, with ripe tropical fruit, apple, pineapple, peach and pear flavors that are sharply focused, finishing with honey and vanilla notes. **91**

CHARDONNAY SONOMA VALLEY JOURNEY (★★★★★):
1990: Deeply concentrated, with tiers of pear, citrus, buttery oak and spice notes that are intense and lively, but what's most impressive is the remarkable complexity and length of the finish. **94**

MERLOT SONOMA VALLEY (★★★★★): Impeccably balanced, ripe, rich, lush, complex and well oaked. Has small portions of Cabernet Sauvignon and Cabernet Franc. Ages well but reaches a pleasant drinking peak early, too.
1992: Dark in color, with lots of rich currant, herb, tobacco and buttery oak, but given its weight and flavor it retains a sense of elegance. **91**
1991: A rich, tight and compact Merlot that displays lots of ripe currant, cherry, herb and vanilla notes from oak aging. Picks up a pretty coffee and cola edge on the finish. **89**
1990: Rich, young and concentrated, with tiers of currant, cherry and plum flavors that pick up coffee and cedar. Firm and tannic. **92**

1989: Ripe and generous, with tiers of complex, smoky currant, plum and cherry flavors and tannins that are fine and polished. **90**

1988: Effusively fruity, with ripe berry, cherry and currant flavors and hints of tar and spice. Firmly tannic. **88**

1987: Smooth, supple and generous, with buttery oak, ripe currant, cherry and plum flavors and very fine, integrated tannins. The finish is long, full, rich and complex. **93**

1986: Tight and tannic, with a seam of elegance and finesse and finely integrated currant, spice and plum flavors that gain on the finish. **88**

1984: Ripe and fleshy, elegant and balanced, with pretty plum and currant notes that gain a touch of anise on the finish. **87**

1983: Tart, green and tannic, with green plum and spicy tar notes. **77**

1982: Hard, green and uneven, with tannic, peppery flavors. **74**

1981: Austere, with green herb and plum notes that are coarse and tight. **78**

1980: Ultraripe and pruny, with raisiny plum flavors that are biting, tannic and drying. **80**

1979: Hard and tannic, with stemmy, green, underripe coffee and cedar flavors. **74**

1978: Still quite oaky, which is the dominant flavor, but underneath there are ripe currant and plum flavors that turn raisiny and tannic. **87**

SAUVIGNON BLANC SONOMA COUNTY (★★★★): Very refined and elegant, with just the right balance of herb, spice, citrus and pear flavors and subtle oak shadings.

1993: Crisp and bright, a lively wine with appealing pear and vanilla flavors shaded by a light touch of grapefruit and herb. **87**

MAYACAMAS VINEYARDS
Mount Veeder, Napa Valley
F: 1889. **O:** Mayacamas Vineyards. **W:** Robert B. Travers. **S:** None.

OVERALL	$10-25	★★★★

WINE RATINGS
Cabernet Sauvignon Napa Valley	★★★★
Chardonnay Napa Valley	★★★★
Pinot Noir Napa Valley	★
Sauvignon Blanc Napa Valley	★★★

WINERY DATA
C: 5,000. **V:** 50 acres in Mount Veeder. **G:** Chardonnay (32 acres), Cabernet Sauvignon (12), Sauvignon Blanc (3), Pinot Noir (2), Merlot (1). **P:** None.

Mayacamas Vineyards was one of California's original boutique wineries. The stone winery was built in 1889 in a remote location some 2,000 feet up on Mount Veeder and rejuvenated as a winery in 1941 by Jack and Mary Taylor. In 1968 former stockbroker Robert Travers and his wife, Noni, bought the winery and vineyard, and it was during their tenure that Mayacamas became famous for its intensely flavored and often firmly tannic mountain-grown Cabernets. The wines from the late 1960s to the mid-1980s are widely admired for their authenticity, rustic personalities, rich fruit concentration and ageworthiness. Vintages such as 1968, 1969, 1970, 1973, 1974, 1977, 1978 and 1979 rank among the best from California. In the 1980s quality dipped, as the wines became more herbaceous, lighter, less focused and less concentrated.

Mayacamas has an impressive track record with Chardonnay, too. It is one of the few Chardonnays still made in the traditional California style—no malolactic fermentation and minimal oak flavoring. It too ages well, starting out lean and trim but gaining depth, earthy nuances and complexity with age. For years Mayacamas produced a Zinfandel, often in a late-harvest style, but now the winery focuses on the two main varieties plus Pinot Noir and Sauvignon Blanc. All of its wines are from its 50 acres of estate vineyards.

TASTING NOTES

CABERNET SAUVIGNON NAPA VALLEY (★★★★): Older vintages are well worth the search for their sheer expression of the Mount Veeder appellation, but the most recent vintages are lighter and less compelling.

1987: Mature and cedary, with plum and cherry flavors and spice notes on the finish. **81**

1986: Strongly herbal and vegetal, with a green olive edge to the black cherry and currant notes. **82**

1985: Tough and tannic, with an earthy edge to the cherry, cassis and smoke aromas and flavors. **85**

1984: Tight, earthy and tannic, with a beam of gamy currant and tar flavors. Still rough and tumble; better after 1997. **87**

1983: Turning lean and thin, with a narrow band of cedary currant and spice notes. **86**

1982: A mediocre wine from a difficult vintage, with herbal, weedy flavors that detract. The structure is fine, but the flavors are off. **77**

1981: Mature, with a lean, smoky, cedary edge to the currant and cherry flavors. **88**

1980: Rich, smoky and gamy, loaded with currant, anise and earth flavors. Finishes with firm tannins; better after 1998. **89**

1979: Has peaked but remains complex and flavorful, with mature, earthy currant, spice and mineral flavors, finishing with mild tannins. Still one of the best 1979s. **90**

1978: Ripe and spicy, with black cherry, tar and smoke nuances that turn firm and tight on the finish. The tannins are softening, but there is still depth and substance to this vibrant wine. **93**

1977: Dark and inky, packed with plush black cherry, currant, mineral and cedary oak flavors. A big, dramatic, complex and deeply concentrated wine that still has a long life ahead of it. May be the best of the 1977s. **95**

1975: Dark and rich, with a rustic edge to the cedar, earth and currant flavors. This remains a classic 1970s Mayacamas Cabernet with its sheer power and intensity. **89**

1974: It's holding its deep color, but the aromas of earthy currant, berry and spice turn drier on the palate and the finish is short. The tannins have softened and it's still a tight and concentrated wine. **88**

1973: Mature, with a smooth texture, but the currant and herb flavors are taking on an earthier profile. May always have a deep color. **88**

1972: Mature, with a spicy currant and plum edge. Most of the tannins have faded. **82**

1971: Supple and fully mature, with complex plum, cedar, spice and mineral flavors, good depth and richness and moderate tannins. **85**

1970: Still inky dark and tightly wound, with layers of ripe currant, mineral, anise and spice flavors, picking up a cedary edge on the finish, where the tannins are still evident. This massive, concentrated wine shows little sign of age or of losing its wealth of flavor. **97**

1969: Mature, with an earthy, leathery streak to the dusty Cabernet flavors, picking up complex tar, spice and currant notes that linger on the finish. **89**

1968: This wine has wonderful perfumed aromas of ripe, mature Cabernet. On the palate it is smooth and supple, with pretty currant, dried black cherry and anise flavors that linger on the finish. **90**

CHARDONNAY NAPA VALLEY (★★★★): Starts out tight and flinty, but give it a year or two and it blossoms, turning earthy and complex. Ages very well.

1990: Ripe and fruity, with pear, nectarine and spice characteristics, but without the heavy hand of oak. Lets the fruit speak clearly. **89**

1989: Fresh and vibrant, with elegant nectarine, pear and apple notes that turn complex, gaining an earthy edge. **88**

1987: Has loads of pear, lemon and apple flavors, but it's bound by plenty of acidity and a spicy note on the finish. This wine is a good bet to improve in the cellar through 1999. **86**

1986: Shows the benefits of cellaring, with mature flavors of anise, pear and spice, but also shows signs of maturity, with almond and caramel notes. **86**

1985: Beautifully balanced and tightly wound, with complex apple, peach, honey and toast flavors that unfold. **90**

PINOT NOIR NAPA VALLEY (★): Light and thin, often overly tannic for the fruit, marked by tea and herb flavors. Good only occasionally.

1988: Thin and astringent, with lean, green, woody nuances and only a hint of plum flavor. **68**

1987: Firm and tannic, with very ripe, almost rustic aromas and flavors of plum, prune and pepper. **80**

1986: Light in color, meaty tasting and meager, with barnyardy aromas and cherry and spice notes. **67**

SAUVIGNON BLANC NAPA VALLEY (★★★): Intense and flinty, with tart citrus and spice notes.

1990: Crisp, lean and tangy, with mouth-cleansing acidity, attractive grapefruit and herbal flavors and added complexity from mineral and earth notes. **87**

MAZZOCCO VINEYARDS
Sonoma County

F: 1985. O: Mazzocco Vineyards Inc. W: Phyllis Zouzounis. S: None.

OVERALL	$14-28	★★

WINE RATINGS

Cabernet Blend Sonoma County Matrix	★★
Cabernet Sauvignon Sonoma County	★★
Chardonnay Alexander Valley	
River Lane Vineyard	★★

Merlot Dry Creek Valley	★
Zinfandel Sonoma County	★★★

WINERY DATA
C: 15,000. **V:** 42 acres in Alexander Valley, Dry Creek Valley. **G:** Chardonnay (28 acres), Cabernet Sauvignon (10), Cabernet Franc (1), Merlot (2.2), Malbec (0.5). **P:** Zinfandel (Dry Creek Valley), Zinfandel (Alexander Valley), Cabernet Sauvignon (Alexander Valley), Chardonnay (Dry Creek Valley), Petite Sirah (Dry Creek Valley).

Thomas Mazzocco is a famous eye surgeon who fell in love with winegrowing, establishing a 15,000-case winery in Alexander Valley that uses both estate-grown grapes from its 42 acres of vineyards and purchased grapes. Both the Cabernet Blend, called Matrix, and the Merlot carry the Dry Creek Valley appellation, while the Cabernet, Chardonnay and Zinfandel carry the broader Sonoma County appellation. By the late 1980s the winery's production was headed toward 30,000 cases, and Mazzocco sold the winery to Vintech, an investment group that went out of business a year later. Mazzocco then reacquired his winery.

TASTING NOTES

CABERNET BLEND SONOMA COUNTY MATRIX (★★): After an impressive 1987, the style has turned leaner.
1990: Lean and compact, with a narrow band of spice, currant and bell pepper notes. **82**
1989: Round and flavorful, with appealing blackberry and currant flavors livened up by a dose of spicy oak. **86**
1987: Big, ripe and complex, with supple black cherry and currant flavors, spiced up with plenty of oak. **91**

CABERNET SAUVIGNON ALEXANDER VALLEY CLARET STYLE (★★): Uneven in quality, but it has on occasion been ripe and complex, with appealing flavors.
1988: Hard and tight, with smoky, tarry plum, cherry and currant flavors. Firmly tannic. **85**
1987: Delicious layers of complex, concentrated, rich cassis, currant, vanilla and plum flavors. **90**
1986: Its tannic personality overrides the cherry and currant flavors. **78**

CABERNET SAUVIGNON SONOMA COUNTY (★★):
1991: Supple and spicy, with ripe, smooth black cherry, earth and currant flavors that fold together with soft tannins. **88**

1989: Crisp and tough, with a tannic texture and modest currant and plum flavors. **81**

CHARDONNAY ALEXANDER VALLEY RIVER LANE VINEYARD (★★): Well made in a crisp, tightly reined-in, medium-weight style.
1993: A touch earthy, with grapefruit, citrus and pear shadings, but turning tart and lean on the finish. **83**
1992: Fresh and crisp, with a focused band of citrus, pear and light oak flavors that turn elegant and refined on the finish. **86**
1991: Tart, firm and flinty, with crisp lemon, peach and spice flavors that are tightly reined in. **86**

MERLOT DRY CREEK VALLEY (★): An unfiltered 1989 estate wine that is supple and flavorful, but subsequent vintages are lean, tannic and gamy.
1991: Lean, tannic and hard-edged, devoid of fruit. **78**
1989: An earthy, gamy wine with herb and tobacco notes. **78**
Unfiltered 1989: Supple, flavorful and complex, with nicely modulated cherry, cedar, chocolate and earth flavors on a frame of moderate tannins. **88**

ZINFANDEL SONOMA COUNTY (★★★): The most consistent Mazzocco wine, ripe and fruity, with cherry and berry flavors framed by toasty oak. Has carried various appellations.
1992: Elegant and fruity, with ripe strawberry and raspberry flavors and firm tannins. **86**
1991: Complex, with toasty, buttery oak and spicy raspberry and cherry flavors that linger. **88**
1990: Toasty and heavily oaked, with dried cherry, plum and currant flavors battling their way through the wood. **87**
1988: Ripe and rich, with deep, concentrated cherry and berry flavors, finishing with spicy oak. **89**
1986: Lean and spicy, with smoky berry aromas and flavors and jammy intensity, turning elegant. **88**

PETER McCOY VINEYARDS
Calistoga, Napa Valley
F: 1980. **O:** Peter McCoy. **W:** Peter McCoy. **S:** None.

OVERALL	$19	★★

WINE RATINGS
Chardonnay Knights Valley	
Clos des Pierres	★★

WINERY DATA
C: 1,900. V: 20 acres in Knights Valley. G: Chardonnay (20 acres). P: None.

This is a 1,900-case winery that focuses on Knights Valley-grown Chardonnay from a 20-acre estate vineyard. Very limited distribution.

TASTING NOTES

CHARDONNAY KNIGHTS VALLEY CLOS DES PIERRES (★★):
1992: Medium-weight, with earthy citrus and pear notes that linger on the finish. **85**

McDOWELL VALLEY VINEYARDS
McDowell Valley, Mendocino County
F: 1979. O: Crawford & Keehn Family. W: William Crawford. S: None.

OVERALL	$9-25	★★

WINE RATINGS

Cabernet Sauvignon Mendocino County	★★
Chardonnay Mendocino County	★★
Rhône Blend McDowell Valley	
Les Vieux Cépages	★★
Syrah Mendocino County	★★
Viognier Mendocino County	★★
Zinfandel McDowell Valley	★★

WINERY DATA
C: 40,000. V: 312 acres in McDowell Valley, Mendocino. G: Grenache, Viognier, Syrah (141 acres), Chardonnay (75), Cabernet Sauvignon (60), Sauvignon Blanc (36). P: None.

In 1970 Richard and Karen Keehn purchased a large ranch east of Hopland with the intention of growing grapes and selling them, but as so often happens it made greater financial sense to make wine also, which they did beginning in 1979. Today the 40,000-case winery owns 312 acres and has its own American Viticultural Appellation. Some 141 acres are planted to Rhône varieites (Syrah, Grenache and Viognier), with which the winery has enjoyed better success than with the California standards of Cabernet and Chardonnay, which are ordinary.

TASTING NOTES

CABERNET SAUVIGNON MENDOCINO COUNTY (★★):
Lean and austere, with just enough fruit to keep it interesting.
1990: This firm, flavorful wine has a decadent edge to the basic black cherry flavors and finishes with a wisp of almond. **82**

CHARDONNAY MENDOCINO COUNTY (★★): Good but nothing more, with medium-weight fruit and oak flavors.
1992: A well turned wine, shading its solid pear flavors with hints of spice, toast and vanilla. **86**

RHÔNE BLEND McDOWELL VALLEY LES VIEUX CÉPAGES (★★): Solid, with appealing flavors, but not the extra dimensions the best Rhône-style reds offer.
1990: Complex, with spice, berry and toasty oak flavors that are well integrated. **86**

SYRAH MENDOCINO COUNTY (★★): Light and fruity, with early drinking allure.
1990: Ripe and chunky, a chewy wine with plum and pepper flavors sneaking in; not as generous as it could be. May be better from 1996. **82**

VIOGNIER MENDOCINO COUNTY (★★): Ripe, with strong spice and honey notes.
1992: Rich, intense and lively, with spicy pear, peach and nectarine flavors that are fresh and complex. **84**

ZINFANDEL McDOWELL VALLEY (★★): Lean and tannic, often leathery in flavor.
1990: Simple and tough in texture, with modest leather and plum aromas and flavors that soften a bit on the finish. **79**

McHENRY VINEYARD
Santa Cruz Mountains
F: 1980. O: Henry, Linda, Dean & Jane McHenry. W: Henry McHenry. S: None.

OVERALL	$13-18	★★

WINE RATINGS

Chardonnay Santa Cruz Mountains	★★
Pinot Noir Santa Cruz Mountains	★★

WINERY DATA

C: 400. V: 4 acres in Santa Cruz Mountains. G: Chardonnay, Pinot Noir. P: None.

This is a tiny winery that makes small amounts of Pinot Noir and even smaller amounts of Chardonnay from 4 acres of estate vineyard. Most of the 400 cases are sold at the winery on Bonny Doon Road and in limited outlets throughout the San Francisco Bay Area.

MEADOW GLEN

This is a second label for Rabbit Ridge Vineyards (see listing).

THE MEEKER VINEYARD

Dry Creek Valley

F: 1984. O: Charles R. Meeker. W: Michael J. Loykasek. S: None.

OVERALL	$8-16	★★

WINE RATINGS

Cabernet Sauvignon Dry Creek Valley	★★
Cabernet Sauvignon Dry Creek Valley Gold Leaf Cuvée	★★
Cabernet Sauvignon Dry Creek Valley Scharf Family Vineyard	★★
Chardonnay Dry Creek Valley Second Rack	★
Sauvignon Blanc Dry Creek Valley Gold Leaf Cuvée	★★
Zinfandel Dry Creek Valley	★★
Zinfandel Dry Creek Valley Gold Leaf Cuvée	★★★
Zinfandel Sonoma County Sonoma Cuvée	★★

WINERY DATA

C: 6,000. V: 40 acres in Dry Creek Valley. G: Zinfandel (14 acres), Cabernet Sauvignon (10), Chardonnay (12), Merlot (3), Cabernet Franc (1). P: Zinfandel, Cabernet Sauvignon, Sauvignon Blanc (Dry Creek Valley), Zinfandel (Russian River Valley).

Charles Meeker founded his 6,000-case winery in Dry Creek Valley in 1984, and he now uses 40 acres of estate vineyard and purchased grapes to produce four main wines: a Cabernet and a Gold Leaf Cuvée Cab, a white table wine dominated by Chardonnay, and two Zinfandels. Quality is average, except for the Zinfandel, which can be very good.

TASTING NOTES

CABERNET SAUVIGNON DRY CREEK VALLEY (★★), GOLD LEAF CUVÉE (★★): The Gold Leaf Cuvée has been lean, hard and tannic of late, with the standard bottling offering more fruit.
1988: Pleasantly rich and fruity, with polished currant, berry and plum flavors that turn tannic. **85**
1987: Delivers cassis and chocolate flavors that turn tight and firm. **87**
1986: Heavy-handed tannins override the cherry and currant flavors. **72**
1985: Tough and tannic, with rough-hewn wood aromas and astringent textures. **76**
1984: Hard and tannic, with light plum, anise and spice notes. **78**
Gold Leaf Cuvée 1991: Lean and firm, with a trim band of currant and cherry flavors. **78**
Gold Leaf Cuvée 1990: Tight and lean, with a narrow band of cedar and currant flavors. **82**
Scharf Family Vineyard 1990: Ripe and intense, with spicy, peppery aromas and a compact core of black cherry and currant flavors. **84**

CHARDONNAY DRY CREEK VALLEY SECOND RACK (★): Heavy-handed style that can stray from the main focus of fruitiness.
1992: Earthy, with a funky, woody edge. **76**

SAUVIGNON BLANC DRY CREEK VALLEY GOLD LEAF CUVÉE (★★):
1993: Light and distinctively herbal, with a little pear flavor at the core and sweet peas around the edges. **85**

ZINFANDEL DRY CREEK VALLEY (★★), GOLD LEAF CUVÉE (★★★): Features ripe, bright fruit flavors, with the Gold Leaf Cuvée richer and fuller, but both bottlings are variable in quality.
1991: Intense and floral, with ripe, spicy berry and cherry flavors that taste rugged. **82**

First Rack 1991: Smooth and supple, with pretty spice and cherry jam flavors and mild tannins. **86**

1989: Ripe and rugged, full of cherry, currant and plum flavors and considerable tannin. **80**

1988: Ripe and tart at the same time, with sharply focused blackberry, plum and toast flavors. **82**

1987: Elegantly balanced, with fresh, crisp, lively raspberry and cherry flavors and light oak notes. **85**

1986: Has bright, fresh raspberry and cherry flavors but is also quite tannic. **83**

1985: Impressive for its lively blackberry, raspberry and strawberry aromas and flavors, picking up hints of nutmeg, vanilla and butter. **88**

Gold Leaf Cuvée 1992: Lean and simple, with a narrow band of fruit that's barely ripe, and the finish is tannic. **80**

Gold Leaf Cuvée 1991: Tight, firm and tannic, with modest cherry and raspberry flavors on the finish. **84**

Gold Leaf Cuvée 1990: Crisp and lively, with a band of rich, focused raspberry, cherry and currant flavors flanked by firm, drying tannins. **90**

Gold Leaf Reserve 1989: Very dark, with jammy berry aromas, but it's woody, tannic and lean on the palate. **81**

ZINFANDEL SONOMA COUNTY SONOMA CUVÉE (★★):
1992: Smooth and polished, with elegant wild berry and cherry flavors. **84**

MELIM VINEYARD AND WINERY
Alexander Valley
F: 1971. **O:** Melim Ltd. **W:** Mario Derrieo, Kerry Damskey. **S:** None.

OVERALL $8-15 ★

WINE RATINGS
Cabernet Sauvignon Alexander
  Valley Reserve ★
Chardonnay Alexander
  Valley Reserve ★

WINERY DATA
C: 10,000. **V:** 63 acres in Alexander Valley. **G:** Cabernet Sauvignon (30 acres), Merlot (10), Cabernet Franc (5), Chardonnay (18). **P:** None.

This label was originally Maacama Creek, in Alexander Valley, used for a series of estate-grown

wines. Quality of the Cabernet Reserve Alexander Valley and Chardonnay ranged from fair to average.

TASTING NOTES

CABERNET SAUVIGNON ALEXANDER VALLEY RESERVE (★):
1992: It's lean, dry and tannic, which doesn't give the fruit much chance. **77**
1991: An oaky wine in which the wood overshadows the simple fruit flavors. **75**
1990: A light, fruity wine with plum, cherry and cedar notes. **81**
1989: A thick, chewy wine with ripe, vibrant fruit flavors and supple tannins. **86**

CHARDONNAY ALEXANDER VALLEY RESERVE (★):
1992: Crisp and lively, a simple, citrusy wine with a tart finish. **79**

MENDOCINO HILL
Mendocino County
F: 1989. **O:** Richard Sherwin. **W:** Darrell Holbrook. **S:** None.

OVERALL $15 ★★

WINE RATINGS
Cabernet Sauvignon Mendocino County ★★

WINERY DATA
C: 3,000. **V:** 85 acres in Mendocino County. **G:** Cabernet Sauvignon (60 acres), Merlot (15), Sangiovese (5), Syrah (5). **P:** None.

Former Lytton Springs owner Richard Sherwin owns this Mendocino Cabernet-only brand, which makes some 3,000 cases in a rugged, rustic style.

TASTING NOTES

CABERNET SAUVIGNON MENDOCINO COUNTY (★★):
1989: Tight and firm, with leathery tannins, but also pretty, juicy black cherry, currant, anise and vanilla flavors that are focused, intense and concentrated. Finishes with a hint of dill. Has lots of potential, but hands off until 1997. **88**

MER ET SOLEIL
Gonzales, Monterey County
F: 1992. **O:** Chuck Wagner. **W:** Chuck Wagner. **S:** None.

OVERALL	$25	★★★

WINE RATINGS

Chardonnay Monterey County	★★★

WINERY DATA

C: 2,500 **V:** 100 acres in Monterey County.
G: Chardonnay (65 acres), Viognier (12), Pinot Blanc, Marsanne, Roussanne, Pinot Gris, Sangiovese, Nebbiolo, Dolcetto (less than 5 acres each). **P:** None.

Caymus owner and winemaker Chuck Wagner branched out from Napa Valley in 1992 with the purchase of land in Monterey County, where he owns 100 acres in vines and a new winery called Mer et Soleil (Sea and Sun), focusing on barrel-fermented, Burgundian-style Chardonnay. Wagner toyed with Chardonnay at Caymus for years with mixed results before turning to Monterey, where it excels. "In my eyes, it's an area of California that's never been dealt with properly," he says. His interest is in matching soil and microclimate with the right grape varieties.

Mer et Soleil's vineyard is dominated by Chardonnay (65 acres), followed by Viognier (12 acres) and smaller lots of Pinot Blanc, Roussanne, Pinot Gris, Sangiovese, Nebbiolo and Dolcetto—all of which Wagner intends to vinify experimentally. But he indicated that it's unlikely he will make more than one or two wines commercially other than Chardonnay, focusing on the grapes he believes have the most potential and selling the remaining grape production to others. The initial production of 1,100 cases from the 1992 vintage was priced at $25 and sold entirely outside California. Production is expected to stay in the 2,500-case range.

MERIDIAN VINEYARDS
Paso Robles
F: 1988. **O:** Wine World Estates. **W:** Charles Ortman. **S:** None.

OVERALL	$9-16	★★★

WINE RATINGS

Cabernet Sauvignon Paso Robles	★★★
Chardonnay Edna Valley	★★★
Chardonnay Santa Barbara County	★★★
Chardonnay Santa Barbara County Reserve	★★★
Pinot Blanc Santa Barbara County	★★
Pinot Noir Edna Valley Reserve	★★
Pinot Noir Santa Barbara County	★★
Pinot Noir Santa Barbara County Reserve	★★
Sauvignon Blanc California	★★
Syrah Paso Robles	★★★
Zinfandel Paso Robles	★★

WINERY DATA

C: 100,000. **V:** 3,250 in Central Coast. **G:** Cabernet Sauvignon (350 acres), Chardonnay (2,400), Gewürztraminer (150), Pinot Noir (59), Riesling (68), Syrah (42). **P:** Pinot Noir (Santa Barbara County), Chardonnay (Edna Valley), Sauvignon Blanc (Napa Valley, Sonoma County), Zinfandel (Paso Robles).

Winemaker Chuck Ortman, who had a hand in making wines at Spring Mountain, Far Niente and others as a consultant, started this brand in 1984, making small lots of wine before selling the name to Wine World Estates (owner of Beringer, Chateau Souverain and Maison Deutz). Wine World bought the old Estrella River Winery and retooled it for the Meridian brand. Significantly, Meridian owns 3,250 acres in vines, making it one of the state's largest vineyard owners. The biggest planting is a staggering 2,400 acres of Chardonnay, most of that in Santa Barbara County; there are substantial amounts of Cabernet (350 acres), Gewürztraminer (150), Riesling (68), Pinot Noir (59) and Syrah (42) as well. Plantings in Paso Robles total 454 acres, mostly reds, and in Edna Valley, 100 acres. Production is about 100,000 cases, with room to grow. Meridian's vineyards are a prime grape source for Wine World's Napa Ridge brand and for many other wineries.

TASTING NOTES

CABERNET SAUVIGNON PASO ROBLES (★★★): Early maturing but well balanced, with ripe fruit and herb shadings. Not worth cellaring.
1990: Crisp and lean, with bright cherry and berry flavors of modest proportions. **83**
1989: Delivers ripe, supple black cherry, plum and currant aromas and flavors that finish with a tobacco and spice edge. **87**

1988: Showy on release but maturing fast, with an earthy edge to the cedar and currant notes. **86**

CHARDONNAY EDNA VALLEY (★★★):
1993: Simple with a modest band of earth, spice and light pear flavors. **85**
1992: Firm and compact, with an earthy edge to the ripe pear and spicy butterscotch flavors. **86**
1991: Tight and focused, with a core of rich, spicy pear, honey and earth flavors framed by toasty, buttery oak notes. **88**

CHARDONNAY SANTA BARBARA COUNTY (★★★) RESERVE (★★★): Consistently has a nice sense of proportion and a delicate balance between ripe, spicy fruit flavors and light oak shadings.
1993: Medium-weight, with ripe pear, apple and spice notes that are pleasing. **85**
1992: Earthy, with a solid core of pear and pineapple flavors that pick up wood and citrus notes. **85**
1991: Intense and concentrated, showing a wide spectrum of tropical fruit, toasty oak and earth flavors. **85**
Reserve 1993: A shade fuller and richer, well oaked, with creamy vanilla, pear, spice and hazelnut notes. **89**

PINOT BLANC SANTA BARBARA COUNTY (★★):
Appealing for its direct fruitiness and varietal character.
1993: Subtle, with ripe pear and spice flavors and a hint of orange blossom in the background. **86**

PINOT NOIR EDNA VALLEY RESERVE (★★):
1991: Serves up an intriguing array of herb, cola, spice and black cherry flavors that are tightly wound, with rich tannins. **86**

PINOT NOIR SANTA BARBARA COUNTY (★★), RESERVE (★★): On the lighter side so far, with a narrow band of herb flavors, but the winery is making a big push with this varietal, so better things may come.
1993: Light with simple cherry, herb and berry notes, picking up an earthy edge on the finish. **82**
1992: Lean and fruity, with simple spice, cherry, herb and tea notes. **83**
1991: Light and thin, showing herb, tea and light cherry flavors. **80**
1990: Shows a decent core of tart cherry and raspberry flavors, but lacks complexity. More like a Beaujolais. **80**

Reserve 1991: Lean and crisp, but the fleshy flavors build, with herb, cola, black cherry and spicy notes adding complexity. **85**

SAUVIGNON BLANC CALIFORNIA (★★): New to the line-up, it's light and fragrant, with spicy overtones to the pear and apple flavors.
1993: Bright and fragrant, lively with apple and pear flavors, shaded with a touch of herb, finishing smooth. **86**
1992: Light and fragrant, with lots of herbal, spicy overtones to the basic apple and nectarine flavors, finishing with a touch of lemon and celery. **83**

SYRAH PASO ROBLES (★★★): Quality varies, but the best vintages show fine depth and rich fruit flavors. Other years have been lighter.
1991: Soft, broad and spicy, with jammy berry and pepper notes and mild tannins. **83**
1990: Crisp and plummy, with pleasant currant, berry and spice notes. **86**
1988: Dark and spicy, with cedar, blackberry and wild raspberry flavors, turning complex on the finish. **88**

ZINFANDEL PASO ROBLES (★★): Good but unexceptional, with lean flavors and firm tannins.
1990: Tight, firm and oaky, with cedar, pepper, wild berry and cherry notes. Firmly tannic. **86**
1989: Chunky and tannic, with ripe blackberry, cherry and anise flavors. **85**

THE MERRY VINTNERS
Sonoma County
F: 1984. O: Merry Vintners. W: Merry Edwards. S: None.

OVERALL	$12-15	NR

Merry is Merry Edwards, the well known winemaker who had a hand in Mount Eden (from 1974 to 1976) and Matanzas Creek (1977 to 1983) before starting her own winery focusing on Chardonnay. Production was about 7,500 cases of several different bottlings, including a Reserve, which was ripe, complex and well oaked but inconsistent. The winery planned to close in 1995.

MERRYVALE VINEYARDS
St. Helena, Napa Valley

F: 1983. **O:** Jack Schlatter, William Harlan, Robin Lail & John Montgomery. **W:** Robert J. Levy, Michel Rolland. **S:** Sunny St. Helena.

OVERALL	$10-36	★★★

WINE RATINGS

Cabernet Sauvignon Napa Valley	★★★
Chardonnay Napa Valley Reserve	★★★★★
Chardonnay Napa Valley Starmont	★★★
Meritage Red Napa Valley Profile	★★★
Meritage White Napa Valley	★★★
Merlot Napa Valley	★★
Sauvignon Blanc Napa Valley	★★★

WINERY DATA

C: 30,000. **V:** 150 acres in Napa Valley. **G:** Sauvignon Blanc (25 acres), Cabernet Sauvignon (25), Merlot (45), Cabernet Franc (4), Petite Verdot (1), Chardonnay (50). **P:** Cabernet Sauvignon (Napa Valley), Merlot (Napa Valley), Cabernet Franc (Napa Valley), Sémillon (Napa Valley), Chardonnay (Napa Valley), Sauvignon Blanc (Napa Valley), Pinot Blanc (Napa Valley).

This partnership brought together real estate developers Bill Harlan of Harlan Estate, the late Peter Stocker, John Montgomery and Robin Lail, John Daniel's daughter and a former partner at Dominus Estate. With the 1983 vintage, Merryvale, named after the Merryvale building in San Francisco, introduced a Bordeaux-style red made from purchased grapes, following that with Chardonnay, Merlot and a white Meritage. Early on, Ric Forman oversaw winemaking, which is now under the supervision of Robert Levy, who gets consulting advice from Château Le Bon Pasteur's Michel Rolland. The partners also own the Sunny St. Helena winery in St. Helena, where they produce the Merryvale wines along with a value-oriented line of varietals under the Sunny St. Helena label. While the red table wine now called Profile held an early lead in quality, it has been surpassed by the Chardonnay—the Reserve is among the state's richest and most complex. Merryvale owns 150 acres planted to Chardonnay (50 acres), Merlot (45 acres), Cabernet (25) and Sauvigon Blanc (25), but the winery still buys grapes. Production is 30,000 cases.

TASTING NOTES

CABERNET SAUVIGNON NAPA VALLEY (★★★): Well made, but marked by hard tannins and a tight band of fruit flavors.

1991: Dense, chewy and tannic, but underneath is a core of rich mint, currant and mineral flavors. **87**

1990: Ripe and round, with a core of concentrated currant, plum and vanilla flavors. Firmly tannic. **88**

1989: Elegant and flavorful, with a brilliant beam of spicy currant, plum and blackberry flavors and smoothly integrated tannins. **90**

1988: Tough, tannic and oaky, with hard-edged currant, plum and black cherry flavors. **86**

CHARDONNAY NAPA VALLEY RESERVE (★★★★★): Has quickly moved to the top of the class in Napa. It's consistenly rich, smooth, creamy and complex, well oaked and capable of improving for several years. The 1990 was tremendous in 1995, but 1992 missed the mark.

1993: Medium-bodied, with smoky, toasty oak and ripe pear flavors, elegant and refined for the vintage. Finishes with an appealing aftertaste. **88**

1992: Awkward, with tart pear and pineapple flavors that lack finesse. **84**

1991: Tart, tight and firm, with a complex core of pear, pineapple and citrus flavors. Takes on a complex seductive, smoky, toasty note on the finish. **91**

CHARDONNAY NAPA VALLEY STARMONT (★★★): Can be rich and complex too, but they usually don't possess the depth and concentration of the Reserve.

1993: Appealing for its forward fruitiness, with ripe pear, peach and apple notes of modest depth, but not up to Merryvale's standards. **84**

1992: Balances ripe, spicy pear notes with toasty nutmeg and hazelnut flavors, turning complex. **88**

1991: Smoky, buttery and complex, with ripe, rich, concentrated pear, spice and apple flavors that are focused and lively. **90**

MERITAGE RED NAPA VALLEY PROFILE (★★★): Tends to be crisp and austere rather than rich and generous, with tightly reined-in fruit flavors and hard tannins.

1990: Crisp and lean, with pretty currant and black cherry fruit, but the acidity and crispness dominate on a brisk finish. **86**

1989: Tight, firm and crisp, with currant, spice and berry flavors that are hollow in the middle. **86**

1988: Crisp and lively, a tightly reined-in wine with modest Cabernet flavors and firm tannins. **85**

1987: Hard and oaky, with wood dominating the currant and plum flavors. Tannic. **83**

1986: Firm tannins dominate this austere wine, overshadowing the cherry and currant flavors underneath. **86**

1985: Mature, with pretty vanilla, mint, cherry and currant flavors that are starting to unfold from the tannin's grip. **91**

1984: Lean and austere, with distinct cedar, black cherry and herb flavors that are developing nicely. **86**

1983: Mature, with crisp currant, black cherry, mint and floral notes that are framed by firm tannins. **87**

MERITAGE WHITE NAPA VALLEY (★★★):

1993: Elegant with moderately rich pear, fig, melon and herb notes. **85**

1992: Complex and spicy, with vanilla, lemon, grapefruit and herb flavors. **87**

MERLOT NAPA VALLEY (★★): Tight and firm, although recent vintages are a little more generous.

1991: Tight and firm, with balanced oak, currant and bay leaf flavors, turning austere and tannic. **84**

1990: Ripe and racy, with intense, heady plum and currant flavors and spicy, peppery oak shadings. Firmly tannic. **85**

1989: Tough, lean and hard-edged, with firm, drying tannins and a tight core of currant and plum flavors. **84**

SAUVIGNON BLANC NAPA VALLEY (★★★): Strikes a nice balance between herb and pear flavors and light oak shadings.

1993: Simple and fruity, sturdy enough to carry through the spicy pineapple flavors on the finish. **83**

1992: Simple, crisp and spicy, displaying a nice beam of apple and herb flavors. The finish is fresh and stylish. **83**

MEV

This is a second label for Mount Eden Vineyards (see listing).

PETER MICHAEL WINERY
Knights Valley

F: 1982. **O:** Peter Michael Winery, Inc. **W:** Mark Aubert, Helen Turley. **S:** None.

OVERALL	$26-30	★★★★

WINE RATINGS

Cabernet Sauvignon Knights Valley	
Les Pavots	★★★
Chardonnay Napa County Clos du Ciel	★★★★★
Chardonnay Napa Valley Cuvée Indigene	★★★★★
Chardonnay Sonoma County Mon Plaisir	★★★★★

WINERY DATA

C: 6,000. **V:** 65 acres in Knights Valley. **G:** Cabernet Sauvignon, Merlot, Cabernet Franc (50 acres), Chardonnay (15). **P:** Chardonnay (Howell Mountain), Chardonnay (Alexander Valley).

Peter Michael Winery is based in Sonoma County's Knights Valley, and its beautiful winery building is situated at the foot of a steep grade that leads to the vineyards and a lovely view of Mount St. Helena. Owner Peter Michael is a London-born computer engineer who bought the 600-acre estate as a vacation retreat, and he spends about a month there each year. With the help of Helen Turley, Michael purchases Chardonnay grapes from Gauer Estate in Alexander Valley and Howell Mountain in Napa, but he hopes the wines will eventually be entirely estate-grown from his 65 acres of vines. The Cabernet, Les Pavots ("the poppies"), is a Bordeaux-style red from Michael's own vineyard. The Chardonnays are rich and distinctive; all three share a full-throttle Burgundian character, with rich, creamy textures, hazelnut and spice notes and deep, complex flavors. Les Pavots is not yet in that class, as it is often marked by green herb and bell pepper notes.

TASTING NOTES

CABERNET SAUVIGNON KNIGHTS VALLEY LES PAVOTS (★★★): Variable so far; ripe and full-bodied one year, lean and tannic the next. But the 1991 showed more focus, ripe fruit flavors and depth.

1991: Turns earthy and leathery, with a gamy streak, but there's enough currant and cherry fruit to maintain a delicate balance. **87**

1990: Smoky, earthy and gamy, with a meaty edge to the flavors, this is a tough, tannic, hard-edged wine whose future is questionable. Needs cellaring in hopes the tannins will soften, but don't bet on that. **80**

1989: Sharp and chewy, with a tealike, tannic bite to the spicy dill, currant and berry flavors. **79**

1988: Rich and full-bodied, showing layers of plum, currant, coffee and cedar flavors before the tannins clamp down on the finish. **88**

CHARDONNAY NAPA COUNTY CLOS DU CIEL (★★★★★):

1992: Smooth, elegant and polished, with pretty pear, honey, hazelnut and floral notes that are rich and focused, finishing with a pretty aftertaste. **91**

1991: Smooth and polished, with appealing honey, butterscotch and apple flavors. **88**

CHARDONNAY NAPA VALLEY CUVÉE INDIGENE (★★★★★):

1992: Bold, ripe and concentrated, a seamless wine with layers of honey, pear, toast and hazelnut flavors that turn rich and complex on a long full finish. **93**

1990: Absolutely delicious, ripe, smooth and creamy, with rich pear, nutmeg and fig flavors and subtle oak and earth shadings. Wonderful harmony and finesse, depth and length. **94**

CHARDONNAY SONOMA COUNTY MON PLAISIR (★★★★★):

1992: Firm and compact, with a trim band of spice, pear, hazelnut and vanilla-laced oak flavors, finishing with a rich, complex aftertaste. **92**

1989: Extremely rich and buttery, with lots of butterscotch, honey and brown sugar flavors that are full, oaky and assertive. **88**

MICHEL-SCHLUMBERGER

Dry Creek Valley

F: 1979. **O:** Jacques Schlumberger & Michel Vineyards Inc. **W:** Fred Payne. **S:** Domaine Michel.

OVERALL	$18-35	★★

WINE RATINGS

Cabernet Sauvignon Dry Creek Valley	★★
Cabernet Sauvignon Sonoma County	★★
Chardonnay Dry Creek Valley	★★
Merlot Dry Creek Valley	★★

WINERY DATA

C: 14,000. **V:** 50 acres in Dry Creek Valley. **G:** Chardonnay (27 acres), Cabernet Sauvignon (15), Merlot (5), Cabernet Franc (3). **P:** Cabernet Sauvignon (Dry Creek Valley).

Swiss investment banker Jean-Jacques Michel founded this Dry Creek Winery in 1987 after admiring the success of his close friend Tom Jordan of Jordan Vineyard and Winery. The winery is beautiful, but the wines have never really taken off. Both the Cabernet and Chardonnay are consistently underachievers, often with bland, dull flavors despite repeated efforts to upgrade quality. The winery owns 50 acres in Sonoma dominated by Chardonnay (27 acres), and production is 14,000 cases, with Merlot new to the lineup. In 1993 Jacques Schlumberger, whose family produces wine in Alsace, France, became majority owner and managing partner.

TASTING NOTES

CABERNET SAUVIGNON DRY CREEK VALLEY (★★): Tends toward lean, austere and often oaky flavors without sufficient richness or focus to achieve balance.

1991: Ripe and spicy, with a modest grapey Cabernet edge to the flavors and not much more. **81**

1990: Austere and tannic, with an oaky edge and modest currant and cherry flavors. **82**

Michel Vineyard 1988: Lean and hollow, with thin, spicy currant and herb notes that turn austere and tannic. **82**

CABERNET SAUVIGNON SONOMA COUNTY (★★):

1990: Crisp and lean, with a narrow band of currant, cedar and spice flavors. **82**

1989: Lean and herbal, with a thin band of currant and spice flavors that turn austere. **81**

1988: Sharp, lean and tannic, with very modest cherry and plum flavors to stand up to the rough texture. **80**

1987: A tight, tough wine that's tannic and hard-edged, with plum, tobacco, herb and oak flavors. **82**

1986: The rugged tannins overpower the thin plum and cherry flavors. **75**

1984: Solid but oaky and tannic, with jammy cherry, blackberry and vanilla flavors. **86**

CHARDONNAY DRY CREEK VALLEY (★★): Lean and simple, in the lower third of Sonoma producers in quality.
1992: Lean and smoky, with tight, thin spice and pear flavors that fade. **83**
1991: Lean and simple, with earth and oak flavors that dominate the fruit. **79**

MERLOT DRY CREEK VALLEY (★★):
1991: Lean and hard, with a tannic, narrow band of fruit that dries out on the finish. **80**

MIETZ CELLARS

Sonoma County
F: 1989. **O:** Keith & Nancy Mietz. **W:** Keith Mietz.
S: Single Tree Vineyards.

OVERALL	$17	★★

WINE RATINGS

Merlot Sonoma County	★★

WINERY DATA
C: 3,000. **V:** 13.5 acres in Russian River Valley, Dry Creek Valley. **G:** Merlot (11.5 acres), Cabernet Sauvignon (2).
P: Merlot (Dry Creek Valley).

Santa Rosa fireman Keith Meitz and his family specialize in Sonoma County Merlot, a portion of which is grown in their 13 acres of vines in Russian River and Dry Creek. Production is 3,000 cases. The 1989 is a solid debut wine, but the bottlings have been less impressive since. A Single Tree Vineyard-designated Merlot was added in 1993.

TASTING NOTES

MERLOT SONOMA COUNTY (★★): After a harmonious 1989, subsequent vintages have been ordinary.
1991: Crisp and lively, with fresh berry and currant flavors that turn supple. **85**
1990: Firm and chunky, with ripe currant and vanilla flavors. **81**
1989: A remarkably harmonious and supple wine with ripe cherry and plum flavors and spicy oak shadings. **88**

MILANO WINERY

Mendocino County
F: 1977. **O:** Milano Inc. **W:** Jim Milone. **S:** None.

OVERALL	$8-12	★★

WINE RATINGS

Cabernet Sauvignon Mendocino County Sanel Valley Vineyard	NR
Zinfandel Mendocino County Sanel Valley Vineyard	★★

WINERY DATA
C: 3,500. **V:** None. **G:** None. **P:** Chardonnay, Cabernet Sauvignon, Zinfandel, Merlot (Mendocino).

Jim Milone founded this 3,500-case winery in Hopland in a remodeled hop kiln, focusing on Mendocino-grown Cabernet, Chardonnay, Zinfandel and a Zinfandel-Cab blend, all from purchased grapes grown in Sanel Valley Vineyard. The Zinfandel has a slight edge on the Cabernet; production of the Chardonnay is only 100 cases.

TASTING NOTES

CABERNET SAUVIGNON MENDOCINO COUNTY SANEL VALLEY VINEYARD (NR):
1985: Delivers ripe plum and cherry flavors with ample oak shadings. **82**

ZINFANDEL MENDOCINO COUNTY SANEL VALLEY VINEYARD (★★): Appealing, with true varietal character.
1990: Mature, with ripe, supple wild berry, cherry, tar and spice flavors that turn soft and fleshy. **85**
1988: A pretty core of ripe, elegant raspberry and black cherry flavors, with firm tannins. **85**

MILAT VINEYARDS

St. Helena, Napa Valley
F: 1986. **O:** Milat Family. **W:** Bob & Mike Milat.
S: None.

OVERALL	$14	★★

WINE RATINGS

Cabernet Sauvignon Napa Valley	NR

Chardonnay Napa Valley	NR
Chenin Blanc Napa Valley	NR
Zinfandel Napa Valley	NR

WINERY DATA
C: 3,000. V: 22 acres in Napa Valley. G: Chenin Blanc (4 acres), Cabernet Sauvignon (8), Merlot (2), Zinfandel (2.5), Chardonnay (2). P: None.

Brothers Bob and Mike Milat produce 3,000 cases of wine that they sell primarily from their winery south of St. Helena on Highway 29. The family owns 22 acres in Napa Valley and the product mix includes Cabernet, Chardonnay, Chenin Blanc and Zinfandel.

MILL CREEK VINEYARDS
Dry Creek Valley
F: 1976. O: William & Yvonne Kreck, James & Elizabeth Kreck. W: Hank Skewis III, Dennis Hill. S: Felta Springs, Mill Creek Ranches.

OVERALL	$7-14	★★

WINE RATINGS
Cabernet Sauvignon Dry Creek Valley	★★
Chardonnay Dry Creek Valley	★★
Gewürztraminer Dry Creek Valley	★★
Merlot Dry Creek Valley	★★
Sauvignon Blanc Dry Creek Valley	★★

WINERY DATA
C: 12,000. V: 65 acres in Dry Creek Valley. G: Merlot, Sauvignon Blanc, Cabernet Sauvignon, Chardonnay, Gewürztraminer. P: None.

In 1965 the Kreck family started planting what is now a 65-acre vineyard in southern Dry Creek Valley, selling part of the crop but keeping enough to produce 12,000 cases a year of Cabernet, Cabernet Blush, Chardonnay, Gewürztraminer, Merlot and Sauvignon Blanc, with Merlot at 3,000 cases the volume leader. The wines range in quality from ordinary to good. For a period in the 1980s Mill Creek was among California's pioneers with Merlot, although quality has tapered off.

TASTING NOTES

CABERNET SAUVIGNON DRY CREEK VALLEY (★★):

1991: Firm and tight, with a narrow band of herb, currant and berry notes. 83

CHARDONNAY DRY CREEK VALLEY (★★):
1993: Up and front fruitness is appealing with apple, pear and spice flavors turning a touch coarse on the finish. 87

GEWÜRZTRAMINER DRY CREEK VALLEY (★★):
1993: Soft and lively, a brightly fruity wine with floral pear and spice aromas and flavors. 84
1992: Soft and fruity, with appealing melon and pear flavors mingling with a touch of spice on the fresh finish. 82

MERLOT DRY CREEK VALLEY (★★): The style lacks focus and quality varies, with the wines often showing weedy, herbaceous flavors.
1991: Oaky and leathery, with ripe currant and cherry flavors underneath. 83
1990: Light in texture, with plenty of currant and plum flavors and nice hints of toast and earth emerging. 84
1989: Smooth and soft, with bright, full raspberry and pepper flavors. 82
1988: Weedy, herbaceous and grassy, with a touch of floral plum flavors. 77
1987: Spicy, herbal overtones add interest to the cherry and plum flavors, echoing cedar and tobacco notes on the finish. 84

SAUVIGNON BLANC DRY CREEK VALLEY (★★):
1993: Smooth and spicy, balancing crisp grapefruit against spicy oak in a light to medium-weight wine. 86

MIRABELLE CELLARS
This is a second label for Schramsberg Vineyards (see listing).

MIRASSOU VINEYARDS
San Jose, Santa Clara County
F: 1854. O: Mirassou Brothers. W: Tom Stulz. S: None.

OVERALL	$6-14	★★

WINE RATINGS
Cabernet Sauvignon Monterey County Family Selection	★★

Cabernet Sauvignon Monterey County
   Harvest Reserve Limited Bottling   ★★
Chardonnay Monterey County
   Family Selection   ★★
Chardonnay Monterey County
   Harvest Reserve   ★★
Chardonnay Santa Clara County
   140th Anniversary Selection   ★★
Chenin Blanc Monterey County
   Family Selection Dry   ★★
Johannisberg Riesling Monterey County
   Select Late Harvest Reserve   ★★
Merlot Central Coast Family Selection   ★★
Petite Sirah Monterey County
   Family Selection   ★★
Pinot Blanc Monterey County
   Family Selection White Burgundy   ★★
Pinot Blanc Monterey County
   Harvest Reserve   ★★
Pinot Noir Monterey County
   Family Selection   ★
Pinot Noir Monterey County
   Harvest Reserve Limited Bottling   ★
Sauvignon Blanc California   ★★
Sparkling Wines Monterey County   ★★
Zinfandel Central Coast
   Family Selection   ★
Zinfandel Santa Clara Valley
   Harvest Reserve   ★

WINERY DATA

C: 250,000. **V:** 689 acres in Monterey County, Santa Clara County. **G:** Chardonnay (131 acres), Pinot Blanc (87), Pinot Noir (62), Merlot (27), Johannisberg Riesling (43), Other Red (51), Gamay (54), Other White (72), Sylvaner (44), Cabernet Sauvignon (52). **P:** Cabernet Franc (California), Merlot (Central Coast).

Mirassou Vineyards in Santa Clara, which traces its origins to 1854, is now run by the fifth generation of winemakers, making the Mirassous among the oldest winemaking families in California. The family played an important role in bringing vine cuttings to California, but it wasn't until the 1940s that the winery began to shift production from bulk wines to better wines with the Mirassou name attached. The wines of the 1970s and early 1980s were often marked by herbaceous flavors, but the family has persisted in its efforts to raise quality and the wines now on the market are better than any it has produced in the past 40 years. Production is 250,000 cases, most of it ordinary wine from the winery's nearly 700 acres in vines. The best wines appear under the Family Selection and Harvest Reserve designations, with Pinot Blanc and Chardonnay the quality leaders, along with the *méthode champenoise* sparking wines, which are steadily improving.

TASTING NOTES

CABERNET SAUVIGNON MONTEREY COUNTY FAMILY SELECTION (★★), HARVEST RESERVE LIMITED BOTTLING (★★): Carries both the Monterey and California appellations. Too often the wines are heavily herbaceous.

Family Selection 1991: Marked by earthy, gamy, vegetal flavors, with green tannins. **74**

Family Selection 1990: Solid and medium-bodied, with eucalyptus aromas, black cherry flavors and firm tannins. **81**

Family Selection 1986: Ripe and minty, with smooth cherry, tobacco and herb flavors. **83**

Harvest Reserve 1990: Austere for a 1990, with crisp herb and currant flavors. **79**

CHARDONNAY MONTEREY COUNTY FAMILY SELECTION (★★), HARVEST RESERVE (★★): Both bottlings are simple and correct, occasionally providing more depth and complexity.

Family Selection 1993: Bright and lively, with fresh, ripe pear, honey and apple notes that hold together. Excellent in a light, easy drinking style . **84**

Family Selection 1991: Crisp, spicy and more than a bit earthy, showing modest honey and pear notes. **81**

Harvest Reserve 1993: Well focused, with good intensity to the ripe pear, apple and honeyed notes and pretty oak shadings. Impressive for its fruit and balance. **87**

Harvest Reserve 1992: Strikes a pleasant balance between ripe pear, fig and smoky oak flavors, with a long, lingering aftertaste. Another impressive Mirassou Chardonnay. **87**

Harvest Reserve 1991: Smooth, ripe and generous, with spicy, toasty pear and hazelnut flavors that linger on the finish. **85**

CHENIN BLANC MONTEREY COUNTY FAMILY SELECTION DRY (★★):

1993: Lively, citrusy, a generous, dry wine with appealing orange and pear flavors that linger. **85**

JOHANNISBERG RIESLING MONTEREY COUNTY SELECT LATE HARVEST RESERVE (★★):
1992: Sweet, unctuous and generous, with honey and caramel aromas and flavors, and the finish is spicy and a little syrupy. **85**

MERLOT CENTRAL COAST FAMILY SELECTION (★★): Light and simple, with modest herb and cherry notes.
1992: Bright and floral, the currant flavors sneaking in on the slightly tannic finish. **84**
1991: Laced with pepper, cherry and currant flavors, but lacking polish and finesse. **80**
1990: A lightly flavored Merlot with modest herb and cherry notes. **80**

PETITE SIRAH MONTEREY COUNTY FAMILY SELECTION (★★):
1991: Coarse in texture, but the berry and pepper flavors ring true. **81**

PINOT BLANC MONTEREY COUNTY FAMILY SELECTION (★★), HARVEST RESERVE (★★): Can be the winery's most complex wine. The impressive 1991 is rich and buttery.
Family Selection White Burgundy 1993: Light but sturdy, with a tarry, spicy edge to the basic pear flavors. **81**
Harvest Reserve 1993: Medium-weight and a touch earthy with a juniper berry edge to the ripe pear notes. **82**
Harvest Reserve 1991: Smooth and ripe, with generous, buttery pear and melon aromas and flavors. The finish is round, echoing fruit and honey notes. **86**

PINOT NOIR MONTEREY COUNTY FAMILY SELECTION (★), HARVEST RESERVE LIMITED BOTTLING (★): Usually light and simple, marked by herb and pepper notes.
Family Selection 1990: Light and simple, with hints of cherry and strawberry flavors. **75**
Harvest Reserve 1991: Lean and trim, with a meaty, smoky edge to the berry flavors, but turning tannic on the finish. **83**

SAUVIGNON BLANC CALIFORNIA (★★):
1993: Soft and simple, showing nice grapefruit and floral flavors that linger on the finish. Appealing. **85**
1992: Simple and soft, an appealing white wine with a slightly herbal edge. **80**

ZINFANDEL CENTRAL COAST FAMILY SELECTION (★), SANTA CLARA COUNTY HARVEST RESERVE (★): Highly variable: earthy and gamy one year, fruity and appealing the next.
Family Selection 1992: On the lighter side both in color and body, but with appealing cherry and berry notes of modest proportions. **83**
Harvest Reserve 1991: Earthy and gamy, with a strong woody edge. **79**
Harvest Reserve 1990: Wild and fruity, with distinctive raspberry, spice and rhubarb flavors. **82**

MISSION VIEW VINEYARDS & WINERY
San Luis Obispo County
F: 1979. O: Mission View Inc. W: Tom Meyers. S: None.

OVERALL	$9-18	★★

WINE RATINGS
Cabernet Sauvignon Paso Robles	★★
Chardonnay San Luis Obispo County	★
Merlot Paso Robles Limited Release	★
Sauvignon Blanc San Luis Obispo County	★

WINERY DATA
C: 2,100. V: 40 acres in Paso Robles. G: Cabernet Sauvignon, Chardonnay, Pinot Noir, Zinfandel (San Luis Obispo County). P: None.

Mission View produces 2,100 cases a year from its 40 acres of vines, with a product mix that includes Cabernet, Chardonnay, Pinot Noir and Zinfandel, all of decent quality, with Cabernet the leader so far.

TASTING NOTES

CABERNET SAUVIGNON PASO ROBLES (★★): Clean and balanced, with straightforward flavors.
1990: A straightforward wine with ripe currant and cherry notes. **82**
1989: Correct and balanced, with a core of decent plum and currant flavors, oak shadings and herb and spice notes. **84**
1988: Smooth and round, with a core of pretty cherry and raspberry flavors and soft tannins. **86**

CHARDONNAY SAN LUIS OBISPO COUNTY (★):
1993: Dull and a bit earthy, but it's palatable. **77**

MERLOT PASO ROBLES LIMITED RELEASE (★):
1992: Light with an herbal edge to the modest cherry and berry fruit. **76**

SAUVIGNON BLANC SAN LUIS OBISPO COUNTY (★):
1993: Oddly vegetal, with a celery-like edge to the modest apple fruit. **78**

CHARLES B. MITCHELL VINEYARDS
El Dorado County
F: 1994. **O:** Charles B. Mitchell Vineyards. **W:** Charles B. Mitchell, Mark Foster. **S:** None.

OVERALL	$6-14	NR

WINE RATINGS

Cabernet Sauvignon El Dorado County	NR
Sauvignon Blanc El Dorado County	NR

WINERY DATA
C: 2,400. **V:** 10 acres in El Dorado County. **G:** Sémillon, Sauvignon Blanc, Cabernet Sauvignon, Cabernet Franc, Merlot, Petite Sirah. **P:** Cabernet Sauvignon, Zinfandel (El Dorado).

This is a new winery founded in 1994 by Charlie Mitchell, who produces 2,400 cases of El Dorado-grown Cabernet and Sauvignon Blanc, with standard and Reserve bottlings of both planned.

ROBERT MONDAVI WINERY
Oakville, Napa Valley
F: 1966. **O:** Robert Mondavi Inc. **W:** Timothy J. Mondavi. **S:** Robert Mondavi-Woodbridge, La Famiglia de Robert Mondavi.

OVERALL	$6-56	★★★★★

WINE RATINGS

Cabernet Sauvignon Napa Valley	★★★★
Cabernet Sauvignon Napa Valley Reserve	★★★★★
Chardonnay Carneros	★★★★★
Chardonnay Napa Valley	★★★
Chardonnay Napa Valley Reserve	★★★★★
Fumé Blanc Napa Valley	★★★
Fumé Blanc Napa Valley To-Kalon Vineyard Reserve	★★★
Johannisberg Riesling Napa Valley	★
Merlot Napa Valley	★★★
Muscat Napa Valley Moscato d'Oro	NR
Pinot Noir Carneros	★★★
Pinot Noir Napa Valley	★★★
Pinot Noir Napa Valley Reserve	★★★★★
Zinfandel Napa Valley	★★★★
La Famiglia di Robert Mondavi Barbera California	★★★
La Famiglia di Robert Mondavi Malvasia Bianca California	★★★
La Famiglia di Robert Mondavi Sangiovese California	★★★
La Famiglia di Robert Mondavi Tocai Fruliani California	★★★
Robert Mondavi-Woodbridge Cabernet Sauvignon California	★★
Robert Mondavi-Woodbridge Chardonnay California	★★
Robert Mondavi-Woodbridge Sauvignon Blanc California	★★
Robert Mondavi-Woodbridge Zinfandel California	★★

WINERY DATA
C: 450,000. **V:** 1,300 acres in Oakville, Stags Leap District, Carneros. **G & P:** Cabernet Sauvignon, Cabernet Franc, Merlot, Sangiovese, Pinot Noir, Zinfandel, Chardonnay, Sauvignon Blanc, Sémillon (Napa Valley), Cabernet Sauvignon, Cabernet Franc, Merlot (Stag's Leap), Cabernet Sauvignon, Cabernet Franc, Sauvignon Blanc, Sémillon (Rutherford), Cabernet Sauvignon, Cabernet Franc, Chardonnay, Merlot, Pinot Noir, Sauvignon Blanc, Sémillon (Carneros).

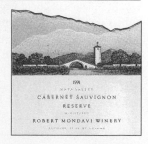

Robert Mondavi remains the single greatest influence on modern California wine. Through his energy, vision, innovation and determination, Mondavi set California wine on the path to greatness when the industry was struggling to regain its momentum after Prohibition, the Great Depression and World War II.

Robert convinced his parents, Cesare and Rosa Mondavi, that Napa Valley held the future for California wine, and the Mondavi family bought the old Charles Krug Winery in St. Helena in 1943. For the next two decades the Mondavis worked on fine-tuning their wines and, just as importantly, Robert worked on building a broader market for California wines. He traveled extensively in the United States and Europe, promoting California wines domestically while studying the great European wine estates first-hand. Mondavi recognized that California wines needed to compete with the great French wines to earn international acclaim, and saw as his models the great Bordeaux and red and white Burgundies.

After being ousted from Krug, Mondavi started his own winery in Oakville in 1966 with the help of his eldest son, Michael, and Rainier Brewing Co. There he resumed his efforts to refine and polish his wines through innovative techniques aimed at raising quality. The early Mondavi wines reflected the experimental state of California wine, with Gamay, Petite Sirah, Riesling and Zinfandel all part of the lineup. By the early 1970s the winery had narrowed its focus, emphasizing Cabernet and Chardonnay, and then by the 1980s adding Fumé Blanc and Pinot Noir.

One key to the winery's success is that Mondavi emerged from Krug with choice vineyard sites and continued to acquire the best vineyards and secure long-term contracts with growers willing to follow his directives. The most important vineyard among the winery's 1,300 acres is the To-Kalon Vineyard, with 500-plus acres in vines, mostly Cabernet, situated around the southern boundaries of the Oakville winery. The winery also has substantial plantings in the Stag's Leap District (398) and in Carneros (362), the latter devoted primaily to Chardonnay and Pinot Noir.

Mondavi's accomplishments are many, beginning with superb Cabernets, especially the Reserve line. He has also had great success with Chardonnay, Sauvignon Blanc—which he renamed Fumé Blanc when sales sagged—and Pinot Noir, as well as with dessert wines, *méthode champenoise* sparkling wine (since discontinued), Zinfandel and Merlot. In 1995 the winery introduced its first Italian-style wines, including Barbera, Malvasia Bianca, Sangiovese and Tocai. Robert's son Timothy has overseen winemaking since the late 1970s and deserves credit for many of the advancements. All things considered, this winery, which now makes more than 450,000 cases of Napa Valley and Carneros wines, offers an impressive lineup, including many cutting-edge wines.

TASTING NOTES

CABERNET SAUVIGNON NAPA VALLEY (★★★★): Typically supple and elegant, with ripe, sharply focused currant, black cherry, mint and spice flavors. Showy on release and should be enjoyed early on.
1992: Smooth and elegant, with a rich, supple core of currant, black cherry and cedary oak, all beautifully proportioned with mild tannins. **91**
1991: A racy wine with lots of ripe, juicy currant, plum and black cherry flavors, picking up toasty oak notes on the finish. **90**
1990: Dark, dense and tannic, but remarkably supple for such a big wine, offering lots of currant, cherry and bitter almond flavors and ample tannins. **90**
1989: Lean and astringent, with a mint and currant flavor emerging between the layers of tannins. **84**
1988: Has lots of dark cherry, chocolate, currant, herb and plum flavors, but it's also quite tannic and firm and is hollow in the middle. **83**
1987: Crisp in structure, with complex currant, cherry and plum flavors shaded with a nice touch of oak. **87**
1986: Classic Cabernet aromas and flavors, with a beam of bright currant, toast, vanilla and spice notes. **90**
1985: Distinct currant, cassis, cherry and vanilla flavors that are elegant and focused, with harmonious tannins and subtle oak flavors. **94**
1967: Lean and losing its fruit. Best to enjoy soon. **79**
1966: Classic Mondavi flavors and aromas. Once you identify the smoky plum, currant, mint and anise notes, you've found the thread that strings subsequent vintages together. **88**

CABERNET SAUVIGNON NAPA VALLEY RESERVE (★★★★★): Richer and fuller than the Napa bottling, but also early maturing, reaching a pleasant drinking plateau within a year or two of release. Ages well in some years, but even the 1984, 1985, 1986 and 1987 have peaked and should be consumed. The To-Kalon Vineyard in Oakville is the primary source for the Reserve, which some day will probably carry both Oakville and To-Kalon designations.

1992: Dense and compact, with a tight, rich core of earthy currant, cedar, spice and cherry, finishing with chewy tannins and good length. Can stand cellaring into 1998. **91**

1991: Dense, compact and firmly tannic, with a beam of mint, currant and chocolate flavors. This is a big, rough-and-tumble wine with high extract. **90**

1990: Deeply colored and richly flavored, with an intriguing array of spicy black cherry, currant, mineral and cedary oak flavors leading to a firm, tannic edge. **91**

1989: Ripe and firm, with intense, chewy currant and plum flavors, but also has a good dose of tannin and oak. **85**

1988: Firm and tight in its austerity, this wine offers mint, currant, earth, tobacco and bay leaf flavors. Turns dry and hollow on the finish. **85**

1987: Firm and concentrated in the style of the '85 and '86 Reserves. Packs in plenty of flavor, echoing currant, anise and plum on the finish. **94**

1986: Elegant and complex, with a gamy currant and mint edge to the earthy Cabernet flavors. Well crafted, but it loses its zest on the finish. **92**

1985: Mature, with cedar, currant and light oak shadings, it comes across as simple and lacking complexity. **86**

1984: Ripe and firm, with supple black cherry, currant, anise and oak flavors. Balanced and complex. **90**

1983: Austere like the '82, with more tannins than fruit. **82**

1982: A hard-edged, tannic wine with minty currant flavors that turn thin. **82**

1981: Austere and devoid of most its fruit. A weak Reserve that has peaked. **83**

1980: Tastes thin and stripped, with a hint of mint and currant. **80**

1979: Tight, firm and concentrated, showing more spine than the '78 but not the breadth of flavor. A different style, but very impressive. **91**

1978: Ripe, smooth and polished, with complex currant, anise and oak flavors that finish with fleshy tannins. **91**

1977: Still showing plenty of ripe currant, cedar and spice flavors that are elegant. **87**

1976: It has ripe currant and plum aromas, but it tastes dry and tannic. A drought-year wine that's fairly typical of the vintage. **84**

1975: The 1975 was always elegant and delicate, but its best years are past, leaving it with a leathery currant edge that's drying. **86**

1974: Mature and elegant, with ripe currant, coffee and cedar flavors and a smooth, plush texture. **87**

1973: Most impressive the last time I tried it, ripe and concentrated, with complex cassis, currant and anise notes flanked by firm tannins. **90**

1972: Never a vintage to get excited about, it's a pleasant, earthy wine. **78**

1971: Firm and concentrated, with high extract and currant and spice flavors. A muscular wine that's sturdy and complex. **91**

1970: Long one of my favorites, it's a great wine from a great vintage, packed with ripe currant, herb, olive, spice and cherry flavors that linger. **92**

1969: Elegant and stylish, with pretty currant and spice flavors. Still showing ample oak and tannin. **91**

1968: From a ripe, rich vintage, it's packed with complex flavors of currant, cedar, spice and mint. **88**

CHARDONNAY CARNEROS (★★★★★): The Carneros bottling rings true for that appellation, with its bright pineapple and citrus notes.

1992: Beautifully crafted, rich, complex and focused, with a pretty array of ripe pear, pineapple and citrus flavors, framed by toasty oak and nutmeg. **92**

1991: Light in texture, focused and flavorful, with generous pineapple, pear and apple flavors balanced by a nice touch of vanilla and spice. **90**

CHARDONNAY NAPA VALLEY (★★★): Starts out lean and crisp but turns complex and concentrated.

Unfiltered 1993: Lean and tart, with a narrow band of apple, pear and light oak, that folds together on the finish. **85**

1992: Tightly wound and sharply focused, with a complex band of pear, toasty oak and hazelnut flavors. **91**

1991: An austere wine with tight, flinty peach and apple flavors that are intense and concentrated. **90**

CHARDONNAY NAPA VALLEY RESERVE (★★★★★): Richer and more complex, with a core of tight, focused fruit flavors and deft oak shadings.

1993: Elegant and refined, with a pretty array of ripe pear, smoky, toasty oak and hints of vanilla and nutmeg; a seamless wine that's rich and complex. **91**

1992: Remarkably elegant and complex, with tiers of ripe, polished pear, peach, nectarine and honey flavors framed by toasty vanilla and oak. **92**

1991: Tight and complex, with a core of pretty, spicy honey, pear and vanilla flavors that are smooth and elegant, providing a nice blend of fruit and oak. **90**

1990: Bold, rich and striking for its complexity and depth, with lots of smoky oak, pear, fig and melon flavors, finishing with a creamy texture and fine length. Beautifully balanced, long and delicious. **92**
1988: Aging exceptionally well, with youthful, vibrant, complex Chardonnay flavors that echo peach, pear, spice and nutmeg. **91**
1986: Elegant and delicate, with subtle pear, melon, smoke and spicy citrus notes that are complex and long on the finish. A deliberately elegant and restrained wine that follows the 1985 in reshaping the Reserve style. **89**
1985: A distinctively elegant and subtle wine that offers attractive, ripe, well balanced pear, earth and lemon notes that are gentle and enticing, finishing with a touch of smokiness. **88**

FUMÉ BLANC NAPA VALLEY (★★★): An early leader of this varietal, but quality zigzagged through the 1980s. Recent vintages are more on the mark.
1993: Crisply flavorful, harmonizing its pear, citrus, toast and herb flavors, hinting at anise on the lively finish. **88**
1992: Ripe and quite herbal, with grapefruit and pear flavors at the core, a clear expression of full-fledged Sauvignon Blanc. **89**
1991: Lean and crisp, with tight fig, citrus and spice notes that are alive and vibrant; a step up from the lightweight 1990. **87**

FUMÉ BLANC NAPA VALLEY TO-KALON VINEYARD RESERVE (★★★): The Reserve carries the To-Kalon Vineyard designation and at its best is sharply focused and complex with herb, spice and oak notes that are well proportioned.
Unfiltered 1993: Lots of green, herbal notes weave through the brisk pear and apple fruit in this lively wine. **86**
1992: Complex and elegant, with tiers of smoke, fig and pear flavors. **89**

JOHANNISBERG RIESLING NAPA VALLEY (★): The weakest wine, often syrupy and dull. It's hard to figure why the winery bothers.
1991: Pine and earth flavors tend to obscure the delicate fruit in this soft example of an off-dry Riesling. Pleasant enough, but not distinctive. **76**

MERLOT NAPA VALLEY (★★★): Steadily improving since its introduction in 1989, marked by complex herb and currant flavors. Worth watching.
1991: Complex, vibrant and focused, with cherry, currant and spicy oak flavors that pick up chocolate and toasty oak notes on the finish. Firmly tannic. **89**
1990: Tight and firm, with a meaty, leathery edge to the plum and currant aromas and flavors. **86**
1989: Ripe and tannic, with plenty of plum and currant aromas and flavors, but they're buried under a layer of gritty tannins. **87**

MUSCAT NAPA VALLEY MOSCATO D'ORO (NR):
1991: Light, simple and flawed by a soapy flavor that obscures the modest fruit. **70**

PINOT NOIR CARNEROS (★★★): New but may evolve into something more complex and distinctive. Worth watching.
1992: Crisp and firm, with a delicate band of cherry, cola and spice notes, framed by light oak. **86**
1991: Elegant and spicy, with a beam of pretty black cherry and leather flavors. **88**

PINOT NOIR NAPA VALLEY (★★★):
1992: Simple, with a core of pleasant cherry and spice flavors. **84**
1991: Supple, ripe and fruity, displaying plum and spice flavors, light oak notes and firm tannins. **85**
1990: Light, fresh and fruity, with lively cherry and strawberry flavors accented by sweet oak notes. **86**
1989: Smells pretty, with currant, cherry and oak aromas, turning supple on the finish. **86**
1988: Deep in color and ripe in flavor, with a distinctive mintiness that adds complexity to the fresh, full, rich, broad black cherry and spice notes. **89**
1987: Delivers ripe black cherry and meaty flavors, turning earthy, but brimming with rich fruit and spice. **88**
1986: Fully mature, with dried cherry and plum flavors that are herbal and spicy. **85**
1985: Earth, spice, tea and cherry flavors turn earthy and decadent on the finish. **79**

PINOT NOIR NAPA VALLEY RESERVE (★★★★★): Among the leaders, it's very consistent, marked by herb and black cherry flavors, with judicious oak and attractive earthy nuances. Drinks well early.

Unfiltered 1992: Tight and firm, with a crisp band of tart black cherry and spice notes. Finishes with a short aftertaste; short-term cellaring may help. **87**

1991: Broad, ripe and supple, with complex cherry, strawberry and earth notes. **89**

1990: Splendid use of spicy, toasty oak to add complexity to the rich currant and raspberry flavors. **92**

1989: A successful '89, smooth, ripe and supple, with pleasing plum, black cherry and spice flavors. **90**

1988: A sleeper that has evolved into a rich and complex wine with tight, concentrated black cherry and spice flavors. **91**

1987: Has closed up, turning tight and tannic, with complex cherry, cola and spice flavors emerging on the finish. **87**

1986: Possessing classic Burgundian aromas, it's lavishly oaked, with true Pinot Noir flavors that are elegant and complex, echoing plum and cherry notes on a long, full aftertaste. **91**

1985: Remarkably complex, with toasty oak, fresh cherry, leather and spice flavors that are rich and elegant. Mature. **92**

ZINFANDEL NAPA VALLEY (★★★★): After more than a decade's hiatus, Zinfandel is back, impressive for its ripe, lush wild berry flavors and sense of elegance and refinement.

1993: Medium-weight, with strawberry, berry and cherry notes of modest proportions. **84**

1992: Ripe, rich and supple, with plush cherry, raspberry and plum flavors and supple tannins. **92**

LA FAMIGLIA DI ROBERT MONDAVI VARIOUS BOTTLINGS (★★★):

Barbera California 1993: Delicate with pretty cherry, berry and plum notes that finish with soft tannins and a sense of elegance. **87**

Malvasia Bianca California 1993: Smells ripe and exotic, with pungent spicy notes, but is better focused on the palate, where those flavors are well defined. **85**

Sangiovese California 1993: Supple with complex cherry, raspberry and plum flavors and mild tannins. **87**

Tocai Fruliani California 1993: Marked by citrus and grapefruit notes, a modest but crisp and well made wine. **86**

ROBERT MONDAVI-WOODBRIDGE VARIOUS BOTTLINGS (★★):

Cabernet Sauvignon California 1992: An herbal wine with spicy currant and berry notes. Simple but appealing. **82**

Chardonnay California 1993: Ripe with a fruity, earthy edge to the pear and cedary notes. **81**

Chardonnay California 1992: Crisp and simple, a light wine with bright citrus flavors. **80**

Sauvignon Blanc California 1993: Smooth and appealing, with generous pineapple, passion fruit and citrus flavors that persist on the lively finish. **85**

Sauvignon Blanc California 1992: Crisp and fruity, with grassy pear, herb and lemon notes that are complex and delicate. This is the best Mondavi Woodbridge bottling in several years and is a great value. **85**

Zinfandel California 1992: Light and diluted, with simple cherry and strawberry notes. **77**

C. K. MONDAVI WINES

This is a second label for Charles Krug Winery (see listing).

ROBERT MONDAVI-WOODBRIDGE

This is a second label for Robert Mondavi Winery (see listing).

MONT ST. JOHN CELLARS
Carneros
F: 1979. **O:** Bartolucci Family. **W:** Andrea Bartolucci. **S:** Poppy Hill.

OVERALL	$13-18	★★

WINE RATINGS	
Cabernet Sauvignon Napa Valley	★★
Chardonnay Carneros Madonna Vineyards	★★
Chardonnay Carneros Organically Grown Grapes	★★
Pinot Noir Carneros	★★
Poppy Hill Merlot Napa Valley Founder's Selection	★★

WINERY DATA
C: 18,000. **V:** 138 acres in Carneros. **G:** Pinot Noir, Chardonnay. **P:** Cabernet.

The Bartolucci family, which has winemaking ties in Napa dating to 1922, founded this winery in Carneros in 1979, focusing on Cabernet, Chardonnay and Pinot Noir from 138 acres in vines. Their holdings include the Madonna Vineyard, known for its Chardonnay and Pinot Noir, and they also use purchased grapes. The earlier Bartolucci winemaking ventures included the Madonna Winery, once one of the state's largest. The 18,000-case winery relies heavily on tourists, since its location on the Carneros Highway is ideal as one of the first stops in Napa. The quality of the wines has varied.

TASTING NOTES

CABERNET SAUVIGNON NAPA VALLEY (★★): Can be ripe and supple, but is usually made in a rustic style.
1987: Smells and tastes old and metallic, with astringent, green currant flavors that miss the mark. Marginal quality. **70**

CHARDONNAY CARNEROS MADONNA VINEYARDS (★★): Clean and correct, but missing the extra dimensions found in the best Carneros Chardonnays.
1993: Simple with a crisp band of earthy citrus and pear notes. Medium-weight. **82**
1992: Lean in texture but sharply focused, and there's a nice tension between fruit and oak, with the apple and pear flavors winning out in the end. **87**

CHARDONNAY CARNEROS ORGANICALLY GROWN GRAPES (★★):
1993: Intense and earthy, but it holds together, with a solid core of grapefruit and citrus notes and a hint of pear. **85**
1992: Smooth and polished, a lighter Chardonnay with pretty pear and floral flavors. **85**

PINOT NOIR CARNEROS (★★): Soft and fruity in an appealing, ready-to-drink style.
1989: Soft and fleshy, with ripe cherry, cola and oak flavors that are bright and lively. A light wine. **85**

POPPY HILL MERLOT NAPA VALLEY FOUNDER'S SELECTION (★★):
1991: Ripe and inviting, with a core of pretty, supple currant, cherry and herb flavors. Finishes with chewy tannins, so cellaring until 1996 should soften it. **84**

MONTE VERDE
This is a second label of Arciero Winery (see listing).

MONTE VOLPE
Mendocino County
F: 1990. **O:** Gregory Graziano & Lowell Stone. **W:** Gregory Graziano. **S:** None.

OVERALL	$8-25	★★
WINE RATINGS		
Barbera Mendocino County		★★★
Muscat Mendocino County		★★
Pinot Bianco Mendocino County		★★
Sangiovese Mendocino County		★★

WINERY DATA
C: 5,000. **V:** 90 acres in Mendocino County. **G:** Barbera, Muscat, Pinot Blanc, Sangiovese. **P:** N/A.

Greg Graziano, winemaker for Hidden Cellars in Mendocino, and vineyardist Lowell Stone, who owns Fox Hill Vineyard (Monte Volpe in Italian) are partners in this venture, which specializes in Italian-style wines, including Barbera, Pinot Bianco, Sangiovese and Muscat. The 1991 Barbera displays intense, exotic strawberry and cherry flavors, while the 1992 Sangiovese is supple, with currant and berry notes. The Pinot Bianco and Muscat are less impressive.

TASTING NOTES

VARIOUS BOTTLINGS :
Barbera Mendocino County 1991: Intense and exotic, with ripe, vibrant strawberry and cherry flavors and a crisp, lively finish. **87**
Muscat Mendocino County 1991: Frankly sweet, with generous peach and pear flavors scented by touches of resin and spice. More reminiscent of a late-harvest Riesling than a Muscat. Balanced and refreshing. **80**
Pinot Bianco Mendocino County 1993: Bright and fruity, a zingy wine with lively pear and resin flavors. **84**
Sangiovese Mendocino County 1992: Supple and fruity, gently unfolding its soft currant and berry flavors. **86**

MONTEREY PENINSULA WINERY
Monterey County
F: 1974. **O:** Rutherford Benchmarks, Inc. **W:** Tom Bates.
S: Monterey Cellars.

OVERALL	$7-18	★★

WINE RATINGS
Barbera California Vineyard
   View Pleasant Hill   NR
Cabernet Sauvignon Monterey County   ★★
Chardonnay Monterey County
   Sleepy Hollow Vineyard   NR
Pinot Noir Monterey County
   Sleepy Hollow Vineyard   ★★
White Riesling Monterey County
   Sleepy Hollow Vineyard Late Harvest   NR
Zinfandel Amador County Ferrero Ranch   ★★

WINERY DATA
C: 5,000. **V:** None. **G:** None. **P:** Cabernet Sauvignon,
Chardonnay, Merlot, Pinot Blanc, Pinot Noir (Montery County),
Pinot Blanc (Arroyo Seco), Zinfandel (Amador County),
Zinfandel (Lodi).

Two Monterey dentists founded this winery in 1974,
producing a broad array of wines, including multiple bottlings of Zinfandel (even late-harvest bottlings), Riesling,
Cabernet and Chardonnay. Quality from this 10,000-case
winery is highly variable. Perhaps the recent change in
ownership will even out this winery's performance.

TASTING NOTES

**BARBERA CALIFORNIA VINEYARD VIEW PLEASANT
HILL (NR):**
1989: Light and spicy, with a gamy edge to the modest
plum and herb flavors. **78**

CABERNET SAUVIGNON MONTEREY COUNTY (★★):
Variable, but usually marked by herbal flavors.
1986: Mature, with supple herb and currant notes that
pick up a chocolate edge. **84**
Doctor's Reserve 1986: Displays mature herb and spice
flavors and delivers a solid core of currant and plum
flavors. **86**

**CHARDONNAY MONTEREY COUNTY SLEEPY HOLLOW
VINEYARD (NR):**
1989: Rich and intense, with layers of ripe pear, pineapple and spice flavors, but it also has an odd earthy flavor
that doesn't quite come clean on the finish. **83**

**PINOT NOIR MONTEREY COUNTY SLEEPY HOLLOW
VINEYARD (★★):** Ranges from dark and chewy to downright funky.
1992: Supple and elegant, with pretty cherry, vanilla and
spice notes. **83**
1989: Funky and earthy, with vegetal onion and cherry
aromas and flavors. **76**
1987: Dark, ripe and tannic, with intense, deep plum,
herb, earth and cherry flavors. **86**

**WHITE RIESLING MONTEREY COUNTY SLEEPY HOLLOW
VINEYARD LATE HARVEST (NR):**
1989: Has a deep gold color, a soft, round texture and
caramel, honey and apricot aromas and flavors that extend
into a bright finish. Rich, sweet and fully mature. **89**

ZINFANDEL AMADOR COUNTY FERRERO RANCH (★★):
Variable, but usually rustic and austere.
1991: Intense and tannic, with earthy, tarry raspberry flavors. Can stand short-term cellaring to soften. **80**
1990: Austere and earthy, with bramble and berry flavors. **80**
Doctor's Reserve 1987: Ripe and full-bodied, a rustic
wine with berry and plum flavors. **83**

THE MONTEREY VINEYARD
Monterey County
F: 1973. **O:** Seagram Classics Wine Co. **W:** Phil
Franscioni. **S:** None.

OVERALL	$6-13	★★

WINE RATINGS
Cabernet Sauvignon Monterey County
   Limited Release   ★★
Chardonnay Monterey County Classic   ★
Chardonnay Monterey County
   Limited Release   ★
Pinot Noir Monterey County Classic   ★

WINERY DATA

C: 550,000. V: 1,162 acres in Monterey County. G: Merlot (150 acres), Chenin Blanc (180). P: None.

The Monterey Vineyard began as an ambitious venture aimed at capitalizing on the widespread vineyard plantings in Monterey and the belief that the right grapes were matched with the proper terroir. Hindsight shows that this optimism was premature, and the winery struggled, especially with red wines that couldn't shake the herbal, vegetal qualities that often dominate Monterey reds. Richard Peterson left Beaulieu Vineyard in Napa in 1973 to oversee production, joining wine writer Gerald Asher, then a wine importer affiliated with Seagram. In 1977 the winery was sold to Coca-Cola, which in turn sold it to Seagram in 1983. Volume today is around 550,000 cases of wines that are generally good quality and sound values. The product line is divided between Classic varietal wines and Limited Release wines of superior quality. Wines include everything from Merlot to Sauvignon Blanc to white Zinfandel.

TASTING NOTES

CABERNET SAUVIGNON MONTEREY COUNTY LIMITED RELEASE (★★): Well oaked for this price range, but drinks easily.
1990: Marked by spicy, toasty oak, it delivers enough cedar and fruit flavors to make it interesting. Well balanced and easy to drink. **84**

CHARDONNAY MONTEREY COUNTY CLASSIC (★), LIMITED RELEASE (★): Variable, but can stray into pungently earthy flavors.
Classic 1993: An earthy wine with a strong citrus and grapefruit edge to the typical Chardonnay flavors. **79**
Limited Release 1993: Smooth and polished, unfolding its generous pear, citrus and spicy oak flavors over a gentle structure; its flavors lingering nicely. **85**

PINOT NOIR MONTEREY COUNTY CLASSIC (★): Often lean and stemmy, with modest fruit flavors.
1992: Lean and earthy, with a smoky, meaty edge to the flavors. **77**

MONTEVINA WINES
Amador County
F: 1970. O: Sierra Sunrise Vineyards Inc. W: Jeffrey B. Meyers. S: None.

OVERALL	$7-12	★★
WINE RATINGS		
Aleatico Amador County		NR
Barbera Amador County Reserve		★★
Cabernet Sauvignon California		★
Red Table Wine Amador County Matrimonio		NR
Red Table Wine Amador County Montanaro		NR
Sangiovese Amador County		NR
Zinfandel Amador County		★★
Zinfandel Amador County Brioso		★
Zinfandel Amador County Reserve		★★

WINERY DATA

C: 65,000. V: 145 acres in Amador County. G: Zinfandel (50 acres), Barbera (61), Sauvignon Blanc (19), Aleatico (3), Nebbiolo (3), Refosco (9). P: Zinfandel, Barbera (Amador County).

In 1988 the Trinchero family, owners of Sutter Home, purchased Montevina Wines, which under founder Cary Gott, had played a leading role in developing Amador County wine styles in the 1970s. Since the Trinchero takeover, quality has risen and hopes are high for richer, more complex wines. The winery owns 145 acres in vines, dominated by Barbera (61 acres) and Zinfandel (50), with the focus on Barbera, Sangiovese and Zinfandel. The Zin is made in a traditional and a lighter style, the latter called Brioso.

TASTING NOTES

ALEATICO AMADOR COUNTY (NR):
1993: Very light red, very light aromas and flavors, moderately sweet and simple. **78**

BARBERA AMADOR COUNTY RESERVE (★★): Impressive for its ripe, bright fruit.
1990: Tart, lively and flavorful, with bright currant and raspberry flavors and toasty oak. **82**
1987: Ripe and fruity, with lean raspberry, plum and anise flavors that turn complex. **89**

CABERNET SAUVIGNON CALIFORNIA (★): Light and simple, with herbal overtones.
1990: A smooth, herbal wine that's fairly simple, showing decent plum and cherry flavors. **80**

1989: Lean and tight, with a strong herbal component to the aromas and flavors, hinting slightly at plum on the tight finish. **78**

RED TABLE WINE AMADOR COUNTY MATRIMONIO (NR):
1992: Crisp in texture with a nice thread of smooth black currant and berry flavors that bring some suppleness to the finish. **84**

RED TABLE WINE AMADOR COUNTY MONTANARO (NR):
1992: Light in texture, a little chewy with tannins but the plum and black cherry flavors hold their own on the finish. **85**

SANGIOVESE AMADOR COUNTY (NR):
1992: A dead ringer for a Zinfandel, full-bodied, spicy and rippling with plum and blackberry flavors that echo like stewed plums on the finish. **86**

ZINFANDEL AMADOR COUNTY (★★): Light, with pepper and berry notes.
1990: Elegant, with distinctive pepper and raspberry flavors. **82**

ZINFANDEL AMADOR COUNTY BRIOSO (★): Light, with simple grape flavors.
1993: A lighter style marked by ripe strawberry and cherry jam notes, it's supple and appealing. **83**
1991: A light, Beaujolais-style Zinfandel that would be best served chilled. The strawberry flavor is appealing and the tannins are light. **77**

ZINFANDEL AMADOR COUNTY RESERVE (★★): Rustic, with earthy berry flavors.
1991: Ripe, with jammy wild berry and cherry flavors. **82**
1989: This tasty, old-style Zin packs in lots of rich berry, pepper, chocolate and sage notes. **87**

MONTICELLO CELLARS
Napa Valley
F: 1980. **O:** Jay Corley. **W:** John McKay. **S:** None.

OVERALL $15-30 ★★★

WINE RATINGS

Cabernet Sauvignon Napa Valley Corley Reserve	★★★
Cabernet Sauvignon Napa Valley Jefferson Cuvée	★★★
Chardonnay Napa Valley	★★
Chardonnay Napa Valley Corley Reserve	★★★★
Merlot Napa Valley	★★★
Pinot Noir Napa Valley	★★★
Pinot Noir Napa Valley Corley Family Vineyards	★★★

WINERY DATA
C: 18,000. **V:** 95 acres in Napa Valley. **G:** Chardonnay (65 acres), Pinot Noir (17), Sémillon (1), Merlot (12). **P:** None.

Monticello Cellars and its hospitality center are a replica of Thomas Jefferson's Virginia home, Monticello. Jay Corley began as a grape grower, but founded this winery in 1980, producing Cabernet and Chardonnay and smaller lots of Merlot and Pinot Noir. Monticello makes 18,000 cases of wine a year, dominated by a Jefferson Cuvée Cabernet (5,000 cases) and Corley Family Chardonnay (5,000); the winery has been on steady ground with both wines from the outset. The Cabernet is purchased from a number of vineyards upvalley, where it's warmer, but the winery's 65 acres of Chardonnay prove that this cool area doesn't bake the flavors out of this varietal. Pinot Noir on occasion has been complex, while Merlot, the newcomer, is without a track record. Gewürztraminer and Sauvignon Blanc have also been made. Early in the 1980s Corley put together a business group that started Domaine Montreaux, a *méthode champenoise* sparkling-wine producer near Monticello. But when its style failed to catch on due to wild stylistic swings, the winery was sold and the Domaine Montreaux brand moved to Monticello. John McKay, late of Vichon and Merlion, signed on as winemaker in 1994.

TASTING NOTES

CABERNET SAUVIGNON NAPA VALLEY CORLEY RESERVE (★★★): Solid and consistent, with strong oak notes and bold, rich fruit flavors to match. Ages well.
1991: Firm and austere, with good intensity and ripe chewy cherry and earthy currant flavors that are big and rambunctious. Will need time in the bottle to soften. Try after 2001. **85**

1989: Bright and full-bodied, with lively cherry and plum flavors that are deep and intense. **85**
1987: Mature and tannic, but the concentrated currant, cedar and cherry flavors push through. **87**
1986: Alluring, with pretty black cherry and currant flavors, a lush texture and fine, supple tannins. **88**
1985: Supple and elegant, with ripe plum, cherry and spicy currant flavors in a sleek, lean style. **88**
1984: Dense and concentrated, with rich, thick black currant, plum and cherry flavors and supple tannins. Mature. **89**
1983: Firm, concentrated and mature, with earthy currant, spice and cedar flavors. **86**
1982: Mature, with smooth, concentrated black currant, cherry, earth and anise flavors. **88**

CABERNET SAUVIGNON NAPA VALLEY JEFFERSON CUVÉE (★★★): Similar in quality to the Reserve, usually deep and complex, with rich, oaky flavors.
1989: Ripe and mature, a lean-textured wine with appealing cedar, coffee and berry flavors. **86**
1988: Austere and tight, with bright, firm currant, black cherry and plum flavors. **85**
1987: Intense, sharply focused and richly concentrated, with bright black cherry, currant, herb and spice notes turning complex. **90**
1986: Deep and complex, with focused herb, cherry, spice and currant flavors and fine tannins. **89**
1985: Ripe and supple, with currant, cherry and vanilla flavors. **87**
1984: Pretty currant, tar and black cherry flavors that turn vivid and elegant. **88**

CHARDONNAY NAPA VALLEY (★★):
1991: Bright and fruity, showing a smooth range of apple, cream and spice flavors. **83**

CHARDONNAY NAPA VALLEY CORLEY RESERVE (★★★★): Ripe, bold, intense and complex. The 1992 is extraordinary with tiers of flavor.
1992: Bold, rich and concentrated, with a pretty core of pear, honey, spice and apple flavors that turn smooth and creamy with toasty oak notes. **94**
1991: Tight, lean and oaky, with hints of pear, spice and nutmeg flavors. **86**

MERLOT NAPA VALLEY (★★★):
1990: Deeply colored, with floral aromas and ripe plum and berry flavors accented by spicy oak notes. **86**

PINOT NOIR NAPA VALLEY CORLEY FAMILY VINEYARDS (★★★): Complex and distinctive early on, but less impressive of late.
1992: Elegant and well focused, with deft balance between ripe cherry, spice, wild berry and pretty vanilla notes. A classy wine with well defined fruit and a long aftertaste. **88**
1991: Lean and raw, featuring chewy, tannic plum and cherry flavors. **81**
1990: Ripe and fruity, with rich cherry, plum and berry flavors that are intense and complex. **86**
1988: Complex and richly flavored, with a range of black cherry, currant, spice and oak notes. **89**
1987: Laced with herb and cherry flavors that broaden into tea, rose petal, and toasty oak. **85**
1986: Silky and elegant, delicate and graceful, this wine has turned into a wonderful Pinot Noir, with sweet plum, cherry and raspberry flavors that turn to spicy anise on the finish. **91**
1984: Ripe, smooth, smoky and complex, with a broad array of black cherry, anise, orange peel and spice notes that are rich and delicate. **91**

MONTPELLIER
Ceres
F: 1989. **O:** Classic Wines of California. **W:** Richard Peterson. **S:** None.

OVERALL	$7-8	★

WINE RATINGS	
Chardonnay California	★
Merlot California	★
Sauvignon Blanc California	★★

WINERY DATA
C: N/A. **V:** None. **G:** None. **P:** Chardonnay, Merlot, Cabernet Sauvignon, Pinot Noir, Zinfandel, Sauvignon Blanc (California).

This joint venture brought together Michael Mondavi, Robert Mondavi's wife, Margrit Biever, and the Franzia brothers (of Bronco Wine Co.). Montpellier makes California-appellation Cabernet, Chardonnay, Sauvignon Blanc, Zinfandel, white Zinfandel and Merlot aimed at the fighting-varietal market. When the Robert Mondavi Winery went public, Michael Mondavi and Margrit Biever sold their interests to Bronco's Classic Wines of California.

TASTING NOTES

VARIOUS BOTTLINGS:
Chardonnay California 1992 (★): Earthy, gamy and bitter, a disappointingly sour and awkward wine. Misses the mark. **70**
Merlot California 1992 (★): Offers spicy strawberry and raspberry flavors in a light and simple style. **80**
Sauvignon Blanc California 1992 (★★): Herbal and peppery, but it's smooth and graceful enough to remain in balance. **82**

MOONDANCE CELLARS
Sonoma Valley
F: 1992. **O:** David Cohen. **W:** Charlie Tolbert. **S:** None.

OVERALL	$10-16	★★★

WINE RATINGS

Cabernet Sauvignon Napa Valley	★★
Merlot Napa Valley	★★★
Zinfandel Sonoma Valley	★★★

WINERY DATA
C: 3,500. **V:** None. **G:** None. **P:** N/A.

David Cohen founded this 3,500-case brand in Sonoma in 1992, focusing on Napa Valley Cabernet, Merlot and Petite Sirah and Sonoma Valley Zinfandel, all from purchased grapes. Both the Merlot and Zinfandel were well made in the early vintages.

TASTING NOTES

CABERNET SAUVIGNON NAPA VALLEY (★★):
1992: Marked by cedary tobacco and earthy nuances, just enough herb and currant flavors come through to keep it in balance. Best after 1996, but it may always be tannic. **82**

MERLOT NAPA VALLEY (★★★): Well crafted, smooth and elegant, with solid fruit flavors and supple tannins.
1992: Smooth, open and generous, with chewy currant, blackberry and toast flavors that are focused. **87**
1990: Elegant and delicately balanced, with crisp black cherry and currant flavors, finishing with supple tannins. **86**

ZINFANDEL SONOMA VALLEY (★★★): Impressive in the first vintage.

1992: Smooth, ripe and polished, offering ripe cherry, currant and wild berry notes that turn complex. **88**

Z MOORE WINERY
Russian River Valley
F: 1985. **O:** Daniel Moore & Natalie Zuccarelli Moore. **W:** Daniel Moore. **S:** Quaff.

OVERALL	$10-14	★★★

WINE RATINGS

Cabernet Sauvignon Sonoma County	★★★
Gewürztraminer Russian River Valley Barrel Fermented	★★★
Gewürztraminer Russian River Valley McIlroy/Martinelli Barrel Fermented Puncheon Select	★★★
Petite Sirah Mendocino County	★★★
Red Table Wine Mendocino County Donato	★★★
Riesling Monterey County	★★★
Zinfandel Sonoma County	★★★

WINERY DATA
C: 5,000. **V:** None. **G:** None. **P:** Gewürztraminer (Russian River Valley), Riesling (Monterey County), Petite Sirah (Mendocino County), Zinfandel, Cabernet Sauvignon (Sonoma County).

Z Moore takes its name from Daniel Moore and Natalie Zuccarelli-Moore, who founded this Russian River Valley winery in 1987, earning a following for Gewürztraminer, most of which comes from the highly regarded Martinelli Vineyard. The 5,000-case winery makes several styles of Gewürztraminer: barrel fermented dry (1,200 cases), Puncheon select (400 cases separated from the main line of Gewürz) and new barrel select (164 cases). Small amounts of White Riesling (Monterey), Petite Sirah (Mendocino), Cabernet (Sonoma) and Zinfandel (Sonoma) are also produced. Donato is a Zinfandel blend that includes Petite Sirah (40 percent) and Cabernet (10 percent).

TASTING NOTES

GEWÜRZTRAMINER RUSSIAN RIVER VALLEY BARREL FERMENTED (★★★): Captures the essence of

Gewürztraminer with its exotic spiciness; floral and fruity at its best.

1991: Focused and flavorful, a firm, full-bodied, dry Gewürztraminer that displays classic rose petal, grapefruit and spice notes that carry onto the long finish. **89**

McIlroy/Martinelli Puncheon Select 1991: Modest and restrained in both aroma and flavor, this lightly floral wine comes off as dry and refreshing, but curiously lacking in Gewürztraminer character. **82**

RED TABLE WINE MENDOCINO COUNTY DONATO (★★★): A fine example of a Zinfandel blend, with Petite Sirah and Cabernet adding flavor and backbone.

1990: Lends credibility to Zinfandel blends, with its spicy berry, pepper and currant notes. It's 50 percent Zinfandel, 40 percent Petite Sirah and 10 percent Cabernet Sauvignon. **87**

MORAGA
Bel Air, Los Angeles County
F: 1982. **O:** Tom & Ruth Jones. **W:** Tony Soter. **S:** None.

OVERALL	$50	★★★

WINE RATINGS

Cabernet Sauvignon Bel Air	★★★

WINERY DATA
C: 650. **V:** 6 acres in Bel Air. **G:** Cabernet Sauvignon (4 acres), Cabernet Franc (1), Merlot (1). **P:** None.

Aeronautical engineer Tom Jones headed Northrop Aviation and helped develop the B2 Stealth Bomber while creating a unique vineyard in the fashionable Los Angeles suburb of Bel Air. Jones began planting what is undoubtedly one of the state's most expensive vineyards in 1978 in shale and calcareous soils that were once part of the ocean bottom. By 1982 the vineyard was expanded, only to be attacked by Pierce's disease, requiring total replanting. The vineyard now measures 6 acres and is devoted to red Bordeaux varieties, planted in extremely dense spacing of 1,600 vines per acre. Tony Soter (of Étude, Spottswoode, Niebaum-Coppola and Araujo Estate) is winemaker, with Soter's Winery in Napa the crush pad and barrel-aging facility. Production began with a few hundred cases, with plans to grow to 1,000 cases.

TASTING NOTES

CABERNET SAUVIGNON BEL AIR (★★★): Shows a steady style, with earth and mineral flavors adding dimension to the supple currant and cherry notes.

1991: Well crafted and flavorful, with a supple texture and broad, complex currant and black cherry fruit and mild tannins. **89**

1990: Has worked its way out of its youthful oaky edge, showing more currant and anise-laced fruit. **84**

1989: Deep and ripe, with generous black cherry, plum and anise flavors, finishing with an earthy, tannic edge. **87**

MORGAN WINERY
Monterey County
F: 1982. **O:** Morgan Winery Inc. **W:** Joseph M. Davis. **S:** None.

OVERALL	$11-27	★★★

WINE RATINGS

Cabernet Sauvignon Carmel Valley	★★★
Chardonnay Monterey County	★★
Chardonnay Monterey County Reserve	★★★
Pinot Noir California	★★
Pinot Noir Carneros Reserve	★★★
Pinot Noir Monterey County	★★
Pinot Noir Monterey County Reserve	★★★
Sauvignon Blanc Sonoma County	★★★
Zinfandel Sonoma County	★★

WINERY DATA
C: 30,000. **V:** None. **G:** None. **P:** Chardonnay, Pinot Noir (Monterey), Sauvignon Blanc (Sonoma County), Pinot Noir (Carneros), Cabernet Sauvignon (Carmel Valley).

Dan Lee made wine for Jekel Vineyard and Durney Vineyard before he and his family founded Morgan in 1982. Lee's experience with Monterey vineyards led to early successes with a Chardonnay and a Reserve, and he has since shown a deft hand with Carmel Valley Cabernet, Monterey and Carneros-grown Pinot Noir, Dry Creek Valley Viognier and Zinfandel, and Sauvignon Blanc. Production has steadily risen to 30,000 cases, with all the grapes purchased.

TASTING NOTES

CABERNET SAUVIGNON CARMEL VALLEY (★★★):
Uneven, although the 1986, 1987 and 1991 are excellent, well oaked and complex. In cooler years the tannins can be hard and astringent.

1991: Lavishly oaked and firmly tannic, complex and chewy, with currant and cherry flavors. **88**

1990: Harsh, burnt-tobacco flavors rob it of its charm. **77**

1989: Tough and unyielding, with a layer of ripe plum and currant flavors trying to get through the heavy-duty tannins. **83**

1988: Has plenty of currant, herb and cherry aromas, but turns tight and tart on the palate, with hard tannins. **81**

1987: Big, dense and rich, packed with complex ripe currant, cherry and plum flavors flanked by firm tannins. **92**

1986: Elegant and refined, with polished mint, herb, currant and plum flavors that turn rich and supple. **89**

CHARDONNAY MONTEREY COUNTY (★★), RESERVE (★★★): Usually well crafted, balancing fruit flavors with oak. The Reserve is fuller, oakier and more complex.

1993: Lightly fruity, with pear, apple, earth and melon notes, finishing with a mild spicy edge. **83**

1992: Gamy, with a slightly sour note that overrides the spice, pear and vanilla notes, finishing with a toasty edge. **85**

1991: A heavy-handed wine that is smooth in texture, but has an earthy, toasty, almost mossy edge to the apple and vanilla flavors. **77**

Reserve 1992: Intense and sharply focused, with a rich band of honey, pear, spice and nutmeg flavors that fold together nicely, turning complex. **88**

Reserve 1991: Ripe, smooth and polished, with elegant pear, toast and honey notes. **86**

PINOT NOIR CALIFORNIA (★★):

1993: Light and medium-bodied, with modest herb and cherry notes. **83**

1992: A blend of Carneros and Monterey grapes, this is a well oaked wine that's intense and spicy, with hints of herb and black cherry. **85**

1991: Lean and sharply focused, with a solid beam of black cherry and currant aromas and flavors enhanced by thyme and coffee notes. **81**

1990: Pleasantly fruity, with currant, berry, vanilla and spice flavors in an elegant, smooth, polished package. **89**

1989: Light in color, but it has a rich texture and pretty berry, cherry and vanilla aromas. **85**

1988: Mint, menthol and camphor aromas dominate the bright cherry flavor. **75**

1987: Smooth and spicy, a lighter wine with rhubarb flavors and a cinnamon-clove edge to the plum and cherry notes. **81**

1986: Ripe and fleshy, with supple raspberry flavors. **84**

PINOT NOIR CARNEROS RESERVE (★★★):

1992: Firm and intense, a shade on the tannic side, but the core of black cherry, spice and herb notes are focused and concentrated. Ample tannins on the finish. **87**

1991: Distinctively minty and spicy in aroma and flavor; pleasing if one-dimensional. **84**

1990: A big, oaky wine with rich tannins well integrated with the cherry and strawberry flavors. **89**

PINOT NOIR MONTEREY COUNTY (★★):

1991: Ripe and straightforward, offering nice cherry and plum notes, but finishes with a bitter edge. **81**

PINOT NOIR MONTEREY COUNTY RESERVE (★★★):

1992: Supple and elegant, with a pretty array of herb, tea and black cherry flavors that are ripe and focused. **87**

1990: Complex and elegant, with attractive toast and spice aromas followed by tasty cherry, cola and plum flavors that linger. **90**

SAUVIGNON BLANC SONOMA COUNTY (★★★): Strikes a nice balance between herbal fruit flavors and oak shadings.

1994: Crisp and juicy, fairly glowing with vanilla-scented pear and tropical fruit flavors, just a touch of herb on the finish. **86**

1992: Frankly varietal, reminiscent of Sancerre with its lively apple and melon flavors and distinctive leafy berry overtones. **89**

ZINFANDEL SONOMA COUNTY (★★):

1993: Tart, lean and a touch earthy with a thin band of raspberry fruit. **82**

MOSBY WINERY
Santa Barbara County
F: 1979. **O:** Bill & Jeri Mosby. **W:** Bill Mosby. **S:** None.

OVERALL	$11-16	NR

WINE RATINGS
Nebbiolo Santa Barbara County
   Rosso di Nebbiolo   NR
Sangiovese Santa Barbara County
   Vigna Della Casa Vecchia   NR

WINERY DATA
C: 7,500. V: 37 acres in Santa Ynez Valley. G: Chardonnay, Gewürztraminer, Pinot Noir, Riesling. P: N/A.

A home winemaker since age 17, Bill Mosby began this winery in 1979 as Vega Vineyards near Buellton. He owns 37 acres of vineyards planted to Chardonnay, Gewürztraminer, Pinot Noir and Riesling. Recently Nebbiolo, Sangiovese, Pinot Grigio and Zinfandel have been part of the product mix. Production is about 7,500 cases.

TASTING NOTES

VARIOUS BOTTLINGS (NR):
Nebbiolo Santa Barbara County Rosso di Nebbiolo 1991: Soft and slightly chewy, but with a distinctive profile, offering currant, raspberry and anise flavors that linger on the slightly tannic finish. **83**
Sangiovese Santa Barbara County Vigna Della Casa Vecchia 1993: Chewy, simple, modest in flavor but tannic enough to want until 1997-98. **79**

MOSHIN VINEYARDS
Russian River Valley
F: 1989. O: The Moshin Vineyards. W: Richard Moshin, Gary Farrell. S: None.

OVERALL	$9-25	★★

WINE RATINGS
Pinot Noir Russian River Valley   ★★
White Table Wine Russian
   River Valley Blanc de Noir   NR

WINERY DATA
C: 1,000. V: 10 acres in Russian River Valley. G: Pinot Noir (10 acres). P: None.

Santa Cruz teacher Richard Moshin sold Pinot Noir to Davis Bynum for years before starting his own 1,000-case winery using his 10-acre Russian River vineyard. The focus is on Pinot Noir, with two styles, a standard and a Reserve bottling. Gary Farrell is consulting winemaker.

TASTING NOTES

PINOT NOIR RUSSIAN RIVER VALLEY (★★): A lighter style with delicate flavors.
1992: A shade more depth and flavor than the 1991 but still on the modest side, with herb, cherry and spice notes. **83**
1991: Light, with subtle herb, tea and cranberry flavors of modest proportions. **81**

WHITE TABLE WINE RUSSIAN RIVER VALLEY BLANC DE NOIR (NR):
1993: Broad and lightly fruity, a touch of berry on the palate and a touch of color giving it a fleshy look. Finishes dry. **86**

MOUNT EDEN VINEYARDS
Santa Cruz Mountains
F: 1972. O: Mount Eden Vineyards Inc. W: F. Jeffrey Patterson. S: MEV.

OVERALL	$15-35	★★★★

WINE RATINGS
Cabernet Sauvignon
   Santa Cruz Mountains   ★★★
Cabernet Sauvignon
   Santa Cruz Mountains
   Lathweisen Ridge   ★★★
Cabernet Sauvignon
   Santa Cruz Mountains
   Old Vine Reserve   ★★★
Chardonnay Edna Valley
   MacGregor Vineyard   ★★★
Chardonnay Santa Barbara County   ★★★
Chardonnay Santa Cruz Mountains   ★★★★
Pinot Noir Edna Valley   ★★★
Pinot Noir Santa Cruz Mountains   ★★★

WINERY DATA

C: 8,500. V: 50 acres in Santa Cruz Mountains. G: Pinot Noir (7 acres), Chardonnay (20), Cabernet Sauvignon (23). P: Chardonnay (Edna Valley).

Mount Eden Vineyards is the former Martin Ray Winery, which Ray founded in the Santa Cruz Mountains in the early 1940s. After protracted legal battles among investors, the property was split. Martin Ray and his family took the lower half of the property and maintained the name. The remaining investors took over the winery facility and renamed it. The winery produces some 8,500 cases a year from its estate vineyards, which are divided among Cabernet (23 acres), Chardonnay (20) and Pinot Noir (7), each yielding wines that are intense and complex. In 1985 the winery began making a MacGregor Vineyard Edna Valley Chardonnay, at 5,000 cases the winery's largest volume wine, added to improve cash flow. In 1990 an Old Vine Reserve Cabernet was added. Each of the wines can be outstanding, but vintage variations are significant, as the cool climate can affect the Cabernet and Pinot Noir adversely. A Lathweisen Ridge Cabernet has been made since the 1980s.

TASTING NOTES

CABERNET SAUVIGNON SANTA CRUZ MOUNTAINS (★★★):
1992: Lean, tannic and leathery, with the currant and berry fruit buried underneath. Turns dry and austere on the finish. **83**
1989: Firm and focused, with a tight core of chunky currant, anise, cherry and oak flavors that are neatly wound together. **86**
1988: Distinctively herbal, smooth, round and mildly tannic, and the currant, herb and cherry flavors persist on the finish. **86**
1987: Tough, hard-edged, and tannic, with a charred, smoky green bean and ash flavor. **65**
Young Vine Cuvée 1987: Smoky, racy aromas and flavors characterize this hard-edged, somewhat woody wine. **85**
1986: A lean, firm wine with pretty floral and bright cherry flavors. **85**
1985: This producer's best effort since 1978, it's mature, with a lean core of currant and earthy berry flavors. **86**
1984: Lean and trim, with ripe black cherry and currant flavors and crisp acidity. **84**

1983: Lean and tannic, with just a hint of fruit. **77**
1982: Thin and tannic, mediocre as Mt. Edens go, but 1982 was a difficult vintage in this area. **70**
1981: Tight, lean and firm, with pretty currant and cherry flavors and firm tannins. **85**
1980: Mature, with earthy currant flavors that turn tannic. **85**
1979: Earthy, with unripe flavors. **69**
1978: An oaky wine with ripe plum and currant flavors and hints of pepper and mint. **86**
1977: Best of this era, a big, thick wine loaded with intense black currant, spice, chocolate and cherry flavors. **91**
1976: Very ripe, with a raisiny edge to the fruit flavors. Turns dry and earthy. **83**
1975: Mature, with an earthy edge to the black cherry, currant, toast and cedar flavors. Still impressive. **92**
1974: Mature, with a deep, dark color and flavors to match, ripe, rich and complex, with currant, cherry, tar and spice notes that turn earthy, dry and tannic on the finish. **88**
1973: Remains a big, chewy, high-extract wine with thick tannins and ripe currant, black cherry and cedar flavors. **91**
1972: Mature and fading, with earthy currant and berry flavors. **82**

CABERNET SAUVIGNON SANTA CRUZ MOUNTAINS LATHWEISEN RIDGE (★★★):
1990: Ripe, generous and muscular, with thick-textured herb, earth, currant and black cherry aromas and flavors. The tannins are fine in texture and well integrated. Should be at its best after 1998. **88**
1989: Has hard-edged tannins, with a modest core of currant and plum flavors underneath. **84**
1988: Has a firm, stiff structure, with ripe blackberry, black cherry and cedar flavors that are full and concentrated. **87**

CABERNET SAUVIGNON SANTA CRUZ MOUNTAINS OLD VINE RESERVE (★★★):
1991: Lean and firm, with a tight core of herb, black cherry and cedary flavors that turn supple on the finish, although the tannins are tight on the finish. Best after 1997. **88**
1990: Dark and dense, a sturdy wine with solid currant, black cherry, smoke and caramel flavors. **85**

Chardonnay Edna Valley MacGregor Vineyard
(★★★): The MacGregor packs in lots of intensity
and flavor.
1993: A decadent style that's earthy and funky, but the
rich, complex pear, honey, toast and spicy flavors build to
a full, complex aftertaste. **90**
1992: Firm and focused, with delicate layers of honey,
pear and hazelnut flavors that turn elegant and spicy. **89**
1991: Broad and rich, with spicy pear, honey and oaky
flavors that are full blown. **85**

Chardonnay Santa Barbara County (★★★):
1990: Earthy, ripe and concentrated, with pretty citrus,
honey, pineapple and cedary oak flavors that are sharply
focused and lively through the finish. **89**

Chardonnay Santa Cruz Mountains (★★★★): The
estate Chardonnay can be awesome, enormously rich
and complex.
1988: Firm and slightly tannic, but the smoky pear and
nutmeg aromas and flavors are beautifully focused and
linger enticingly on the finish. A sturdy wine. **88**
1987: Lavishly oak aged, with butterscotch, pear and
spicy flavors that are woody, but it has a smooth texture
and good length on the finish. The smoky aftertaste is
pretty. **88**
1986: A shade richer and more complex than the 1985, it
is also very elegant and subtle, with pear, lemon, honey
and spicy oak adding delicate flavor notes that linger on
the palate. **88**
1985: Elegant and refined, impeccably balanced, with
pretty pear, lemon, honey and subtle toast notes, a youthful wine that while drinking well now can still age.
Finish is elegant and delicate. **87**

Pinot Noir Edna Valley (★★★):
1991: A complex wine that matches ripe cherry and
plum flavors with herb and spice notes. **84**

Pinot Noir Santa Cruz Mountains (★★★): Ranges
from stunning, rich and complex when ripe to tannic and
green in cold years.
1990: Dark and plummy in color and flavor, turning crisp
and tannic. **86**
1989: Meaty, smoky flavors surround a solid core of
black cherry and spice. **85**

1987: Tart and tannic, with a green edge to the raspberry
flavors. **79**
1985: A beautifully elegant wine with soft, silky cherry,
spice and vanilla flavors, firm tannins and toasty oak. **90**
1984: Mature and still tannic, with an earthy edge to the
cherry, strawberry and cinnamon flavors. **86**

Mount Konocti Winery
Clear Lake, Lake County
F: 1974. **O:** Lake County Vintners, J & GP Inc. & Wines
Not Inc. **W:** John Clews, Jed Steele. **S:** None.

Overall	$7-13	★★

Wine Ratings

Cabernet Franc Lake County Kelsey	★★★
Cabernet Sauvignon Lake County Kelsey	★★
Chardonnay California Grand Reserve	★★★
Chardonnay California Kelsey	★★
Fumé Blanc Lake County	★★
Fumé Blanc Lake County Grand Reserve	★★
Meritage Red Clear Lake	★★
Merlot Lake County	★★
White Table Wine Lake County Sémillon-Chardonnay	NR

Winery Data
C: 45,000. **V:** 300 acres in Lake County. **G:** Cabernet
Sauvignon (120 acres), Merlot (20), Cabernet Franc (10), Syrah
(10), Sauvignon Blanc (70), Sémillon (10), Chardonnay (10),
Riesling (10), Zinfandel (20), Chenin Blanc (20).
P: Chardonnay (Mendocino County).

This winery began as a cooperative venture owned and
operated by more than a dozen Lake County grape growers. In 1979 a winery was built to consolidate and
expand production and as the wines improved the need
arose for a sales and marketing arm. In 1983 the
Parducci family in Mendocino became a 50 percent partner and the wines continued to improve, with Sauvignon
Blanc, Chardonnay and Cabernet leading the way. In
1992 Jed Steele (of Steele Wines), a longtime advocate
of Lake County grapes, joined the winemaking team as a
consultant. Clearly these are well-made wines across the
board. Both the reds and whites are a shade lighter than
those grown in Napa or Sonoma, but that's not necessarily
bad. The reds, with softer tannins, have an immediate

allure and the whites are delicate and refreshing. Production is 45,000 cases, drawing from some 300 acres of vineyards.

TASTING NOTES

CABERNET FRANC LAKE COUNTY KELSEY (★★★): Light but flavorful in an easy-drinking style.
1992: Light but flavorful, with spicy currant, cedar and toast notes and light tannins. **85**
1988: Grapey and supple, with easy-drinking plum and raspberry notes. **83**

CABERNET SAUVIGNON LAKE COUNTY KELSEY (★★): Medium-weight, with ripe fruit flavors and mild tannins.
1992: Youthful and still a bit grapey, not to mention tannic. **84**
1990: Light and simple, with a bit of an herb and beet edge to the currant flavors, finishing with a touch of tar. **82**
1989: Crisp in texture, with tightly reined-in raspberry and cola flavors, turning tannic. **81**
1986: Elegant and stylish, with supple plum and currant flavors and a touch of bell pepper and herb that adds complexity. **83**
1985: Firm and concentrated, with cherry and blackberry flavors that turn tannic and complex. **88**

CHARDONNAY CALIFORNIA GRAND RESERVE (★★★), KELSEY (★★): The Grand Reserve 1992 shows uncommon richness and depth for this winery.
Grand Reserve 1992: The best Konocti Chardonnay, it's rich, smooth and complex, with creamy pear, vanilla, honey and smoke flavors. **88**
Kelsey 1992: Simple and fruity, with an anise edge to the basic apple flavors. **76**

FUMÉ BLANC LAKE COUNTY (★★), GRAND RESERVE (★★): Delicate, with herb, spice and pear notes.
1994: Bright and tasty, generous with its pear, papaya and spice flavors, hinting at honey on the finish. **85**
1993: Lean and citrusy, with a distinct grapefruit character running through the finish. **85**
1992: A crisp, juicy Sauvignon Blanc with bright grapefruit flavors and good balance. Enjoy well chilled. **84**
Grand Reserve 1992: Bright and spicy, marked by smooth, sweet oak flavors, echoing pear and vanilla on the finish. **86**

MERITAGE RED CLEAR LAKE (★★): Smooth, polished and medium-weight.
1987: Smooth and generous, with hints of dill and celery around a core of sweet cherry, currant, cedar and tobacco flavors. **84**

MERLOT LAKE COUNTY (★★): Light and fruity, one of the best in this style.
1992: Light and fruity, with fresh, ripe cherry, berry and vanilla flavors. **85**
1989: Offers attractive black cherry and blackberry flavors and a hint of plum. **83**
1988: Tannic, with supple currant and berry aromas. **82**
1987: Lean and citrusy, with vaguely defined olive and toast flavors. **73**
1985: Supple and elegant, with spicy cherry, herb and plum flavors and just the right dose of tannin. **83**

WHITE TABLE WINE LAKE COUNTY SÉMILLON-CHARDONNAY (NR):
1993: Simple and a little herbal, with a sappy edge to the basic apple flavors. **82**

MOUNT PALOMAR WINERY
Temecula
F: 1975. **O:** Poole Properties. **W:** Etienne Cowper. **S:** Castelleto.

OVERALL	$7-20	★★

WINE RATINGS

Cabernet Sauvignon Temecula	★
Chardonnay Temecula	★
Chardonnay Temecula Reserve	★★
Sauvignon Blanc Temecula	★
Sauvignon Blanc Temecula Reserve	★★
Castelletto Cortese Temecula	★★
Castelletto Sangiovese Temecula	★

WINERY DATA
C: 16,000. **V:** 92 acres in Temecula. **G:** Chardonnay (47 acres), Johannisberg Riesling (14), Sauvignon Blanc (8), Cabernet Sauvignon (8), Sangiovese (5), Merlot (4), Cortese (2), Palomino (1), Syrah (1), Other Red (2). **P:** None.

John Poole owned and operated KBIG radio on Catalina Island through 1969 before turning to winemaking in Temecula. The winery makes 16,000 cases from its 92 acres in vineyards, with a product mix that includes Temecula-grown Cabernet, Chardonnay, Cortese, Sauvignon Blanc and Sangiovese. The wines have been ordinary, although the Cortese (the grape that makes Gavi in Italy) and Sangiovese, both bottled under the new Castelletto label, are significant improvements over earlier efforts.

TASTING NOTES

VARIOUS BOTTLINGS:
Cabernet Sauvignon Temecula 1991: Earthy and funky, with weedy bell pepper flavors that turn leathery on the finish. **74**

Chardonnay Temecula 1992: The gluey canned pineapple flavors don't quite make it. Marginal quality. **72**

Chardonnay Temecula Reserve 1993: Clean and correct, with a spicy, grassy edge to the pear-laced flavors. **83**

Chardonnay Temecula Reserve 1992: An elegant, reserved wine with light pear, oak and spice flavors, finishing with a citrus and grapefruit edge. **84**

Sauvignon Blanc Temecula 1993: Light and refreshing, a delicately herbal wine with a slightly sweet finish. **79**

Sauvignon Blanc Temecula Reserve 1993: Light and varietally true, a smooth-textured wine with tamed Sauvignon Blanc flavors that lean toward grapefruit and spice. **82**

Castelletto Cortese Temecula 1993: Cortese is the grape that makes Gavi in the Piedmont region of Italy. This version is a fresh, enticing, lively wine with pear and floral flavors that linger nicely on the finish. **87**

Castelletto Sangiovese Temecula 1992: Light, earthy, with unwelcome barnyard notes. **73**

Castelletto Sangiovese Temecula 1991: A modestly ripe and smoky Sangiovese with herb, olive and spicy cherry notes and light tannins. **82**

MOUNT VEEDER WINERY
Mount Veeder, Napa Valley
F: 1972. **O:** Eckes Family & Augustin Huneeus.
W: Darice Spinelli. **S:** None.

OVERALL	$18-40	★★★

WINE RATINGS
Cabernet Sauvignon Napa Valley	★★★
Chardonnay Napa Valley	★★★
Meritage Red Napa Valley Reserve	★★★

WINERY DATA
C: 8,800. **V:** 33 acres in Mount Veeder. **G:** Cabernet Sauvignon (11 acres), Cabernet Franc (7), Merlot (8), Malbec (1), Petite Verdot (1), Chardonnay (5). **P:** None.

Michael and Arlene Bernstein founded this winery in 1972, making a series of good but often tannic and rustic mountain-grown Cabernets and Zinfandels. In 1982 they sold the winery to Henry and Lisele Matheson, who expanded operations to nearly 5,000 cases, but they too found the wine business a financial drain and in 1989 sold it to the owners of Franciscan Vineyards. The thread of consistency through most of the past decade was winemaker Peter Franus (of Franus), who finally departed in 1993 after starting his own small brand focusing on Zinfandel. The modern Mount Veeder produces 8,800 cases, mostly Cabernet-based reds, including a Mount Veeder-appellation Meritage and a Napa Valley-appellation Cabernet. The Napa Valley appellation reflects the winery's acknowledgement that some supple, valley-floor grapes help tame the often austere and chewy tannins of Mount Veeder. Chardonnay is also part of the mix. Quality has been on the upswing.

TASTING NOTES

CABERNET SAUVIGNON MOUNT VEEDER (NR):
1986: Complex, with modest vanilla, cherry, cedar and herb flavors supported by smooth yet supple tannins. **87**

1985: Firm and tight, with ripe black cherry, blueberry, earth and mineral flavors that turn tannic. **85**

1984: Ripe, firm and flavorful, with layers of berry, black cherry and plum flavors and a touch of jam from the ripe fruit. **86**

1983: Firm and tannic, yet there's a core of ripe, mature plum and black cherry flavors underneath. **83**

1982: Weedy, thin and vegetal, an apparent victim of harvest rain. **68**

1981: An earthy wine with a mushroom edge to the typical Cabernet flavors. **75**

1980: Ripe, smooth and supple, with ripe black cherry and currant flavors and spice and mineral nuances. **87**

1979: A stylish wine with complex cedar, earth, currant, plum and spice flavors, turning earthy and mature on the finish. **92**
1978: Very ripe, with complex plum, currant, spice and anise flavors that finish with earthy tannins. **86**
1977: Ripe, supple and oaky, with spicy mint and cherry flavors and a gamy edge. **85**
1976: Earthy, with a juniper berry and metallic edge. **74**
1975: High in extract, firm and tannic, with ripe cherry and plum flavors and a touch of gamy earthiness. **80**
1974: Dry and tannic, fading, with an earthy edge to the flavors. **80**

CABERNET SAUVIGNON NAPA VALLEY (★★★): Showing more harmony and finesse recently, especially the brilliant 1990.
1991: Serves up ripe currant and black cherry flavors, picking up a cedar and spice edge on the finish, but it's tough and chewy. **86**
1990: Opulent and chewy, with rich, pretty black cherry, currant and plum flavors, finishing with a delicious encore of fruit and oak. Wonderful depth. **94**
1989: Firm and tight, with ripe plum and currant flavors and a crisp texture. **82**
1987: Spicy and focused, showing elegant plum, currant and herb notes before the firm, drying tannins kick in. **85**
1986: A big, blunt wine with very ripe flavors of raisin and currant, finishing with strong tannins. **83**
1984: Rich and supple tar, tobacco, plum, currant and spicy flavors finish with firm tannins. **83**
1974: Still sturdy, with strong, dry oak flavors. There are ripe, lean, earthy currant and cedar notes, but it's drying on the finish. **85**

CHARDONNAY NAPA VALLEY (★★★): Tight and flinty, striking a nice balance between ripe fruit and toasty oak.
1992: Pleasantly balanced, with ripe, spicy pear and toast flavors, picking up peach and smoky oak notes. **88**
1991: Tight and intense, with an earthy, almost dirty edge to the pear and spice flavors. **76**

MERITAGE RED NAPA VALLEY RESERVE (★★★): Variable, lighter than the Cabernet, but the 1990 Reserve is superb.
1991: Elegant in style, with attractive earth, anise and currant flavors, but on the palate it turns crisp and lean, with a beet and cedar edge. **84**

1990: Elegant and supple, with a blend of rich, spicy currant, berry and buttery oak flavors. **92**
1989: Elegant, with toasty oak shadings adding complexity to the cherry and currant flavors. **86**
1988: Firm in texture, with crisp plum and berry flavors emerging through the strong tannins. **83**

ROBERT MUELLER CELLARS
Russian River Valley
F: 1991. **O:** Robert Mueller. **W:** Robert Mueller. **S:** Foss Creek Cellars.

OVERALL	$13-30	★★

WINE RATINGS

Chardonnay Russian River Valley LB Barrel Fermented	★★★
Foss Creek Cabernet Sauvignon Sonoma County	★★
Foss Creek Chardonnay Central Coast Barrel Fermented	★★
Foss Creek Chardonnay Sonoma County 85% Barrel Fermented	★★

WINERY DATA
C: 1,000. **V:** None. **G:** None. **P:** Chardonnay, Pinot Noir (Sonoma County).

Robert Mueller started his 1,000-case Chardonnay and Pinot Noir winery in 1991 using purchased grapes from the Russian River appellation. So far the quality of the Chardonnay has been high.

TASTING NOTES

CHARDONNAY RUSSIAN RIVER VALLEY LB BARREL FERMENTED (★★★): Big, ripe and generous, well oaked and complex.
1992: Intense and spicy, with rich apricot, pear, honey and oak flavors that fold together nicely, with a rich smoky aftertaste. **90**
1991: Smooth, rich and creamy, with spicy honey, pear, butter and toast flavors, picking up nutmeg and butterscotch on the finish. **91**

FOSS CREEK VARIOUS BOTTLINGS (★★);
Cabernet Sauvignon Sonoma County 1991: Simple

but pleasing, with cedar, coffee, herb and currant flavors that finish with a tannic edge; fairly priced. **82**
Chardonnay Central Coast Barrel Fermented 1992: Smooth and fruity, its apple, earth and honey flavors last nicely through the lingering finish. **86**
Chardonnay Sonoma County 85% Barrel Fermented 1992: Lean, lively and zingy, with citrus, apple and pear flavors. **81**

MUMM NAPA VALLEY
Rutherford, Napa Valley
F: 1986. **O:** Seagram Classics Wine Co. **W:** Greg Fowler. **S:** None.

OVERALL	$14-30	★★★

WINE RATINGS

Sparkling Wine Carneros Winery Lake Vineyard Brut	★★★
Sparkling Wine Napa Valley Blanc de Blancs	★★★
Sparkling Wine Napa Valley Blanc de Noirs	★★★
Sparkling Wine Napa Valley Cuvée Napa Brut	★★★
Sparkling Wine Napa Valley Cuvée Napa Brut Reserve	★★★
Sparkling Wine Napa Valley DVX	★★★★
Sparkling Wine Napa Valley Prestige Cuvée Brut	★★★

WINERY DATA
C: 210,000. **V:** 112 acres in Carneros. **G:** Pinot Gris (6 acres), Pinot Meunier (10), Pinot Noir (65), Chardonnay (31). **P:** Pinot Gris, Pinot Meunier, Pinot Noir, Chardonnay (Napa Valley), Pinot Noir (Santa Barbara), Pinot Noir, Chardonnay (Carneros).

A joint venture between Mumm of Champagne, France, and Seagram Classics Wine Co., the California wine branch of spirits giant Seagram. Plans began in 1983, with the first *méthode champenoise* sparkling wine appearing in 1986, made at the foot of Sterling Vineyards. A winery on Silverado Trail was completed in 1988, in time to meet growing expansion that now has the winery producing 210,000 cases of uniformly high-quality sparkling wines. The winery owns 112 acres spread throughout Napa Valley, which gives winemaker Greg Fowler a lot of flexibility and contributes to the wines' complexity. The product mix ranges from Blanc de Blancs (Chardonnay and Pinot Gris), Blanc de Noirs (mostly Pinot Noir), Brut Prestige (mostly Pinot Noir), DVX (a *tête de cuvée* named after Guy Devaux, the founding winemaker and former chairman, which is 50% Chardonnay and 50% Pinot Noir), Vintage Reserve (when appropriate), and a vineyard-designated Winery Lake bottling from a Seagram-owned vineyard in Carneros. DVX and the Winery Lake bottling rank among the state's best.

TASTING NOTES

SPARKLING WINE CARNEROS WINERY LAKE BRUT (★★★): Tight and sharply focused, a fine example of Carneros-grown fruit with its spice, pear, pineapple and cherry notes.
1989: Tight and tart, with spicy lemon and citrus notes that are focused and creamy on the finish. Clean and well balanced. **87**

SPARKLING WINE NAPA VALLEY BLANC DE BLANCS (★★★): Crisp and intense, marked by ripe pear and vanilla notes.
NV: Spicy and refreshing, a creamy wine with vanilla and toast overtones to the pear and lemon aromas and flavors. **87**

SPARKLING WINE NAPA VALLEY BLANC DE NOIRS (★★★): Pink, with cherry and strawberry notes, reflective of Pinot Noir.
NV: Frankly pink in color, with watermelon and strawberry aromas and flavors in a pastel level of intensity, and the finish is light, slightly sweet and pleasant. **84**

SPARKLING WINE NAPA VALLEY PRESTIGE CUVÉE BRUT (★★★): Complex cherry and vanilla flavors are focused and lively.
NV: This wine grows on you, with its subtle cherry, vanilla and spice flavors that start out simple but gain complexity on the finish. **88**

SPARKLING WINE NAPA VALLEY CUVÉE NAPA BRUT (★★★), RESERVE (★★★):
NV: Attractive for its ripe, earthy black cherry and spice flavors. Holds together nicely, finishing with richness and depth. **87**

Reserve 1989: Solid, with modest spice, pear and hazelnut flavors that build on the finish, where they turn elegant. 87

Reserve 1987: Elegant and lively, with fresh, ripe pear, spice, vanilla and toast notes offering complexity and finesse. Well balanced, with a long, clean finish. 87

SPARKLING WINE NAPA VALLEY DVX (★ ★ ★ ★): Uncommon depth, richness and complexity.

1990: Crisp and clean, with a band of toast, ginger, pear and spice. Gains depth and complexity on the finish, where the flavors fan out. Mumm's new prestige cuvée. 90

MURPHY-GOODE ESTATE WINERY
Alexander Valley
F: 1985. O: MTGR Inc. W: Christina Benz. S: Goode & Ready.

OVERALL	$10-24	★ ★ ★

WINE RATINGS

Cabernet Sauvignon Alexander Valley	★ ★ ★
Cabernet Sauvignon Alexander Valley Murphy Ranch	★ ★ ★
Chardonnay Alexander Valley	★ ★ ★
Chardonnay Alexander Valley Reserve	★ ★ ★
Chardonnay Russian River Valley J & K Murphy Vineyard	★ ★ ★
Chardonnay Russian River Valley J & K Murphy Vineyard Reserve	★ ★ ★
Fumé Blanc Alexander Valley	★ ★ ★
Fumé Blanc Alexander Valley Reserve	★ ★ ★
Merlot Alexander Valley Murphy Ranch	★ ★
Pinot Blanc Alexander Valley	★ ★
Sauvignon Blanc Alexander Valley Dry	★ ★ ★
Goode & Ready Cabernet Sauvignon Alexander Valley The Second Cabernet	NR

WINERY DATA
C: 65,000. V: 345 acres in Alexander Valley. G: Chardonnay (100 acres), Sauvignon Blanc (120), Pinot Blanc (25), Gewürztraminer (15), Muscat Canelli (5), Merlot (40), Cabernet Sauvignon (30), Pinot Noir (10). P: Chardonnay (Russian River), Zinfandel (Dry Creek Valley).

This is a partnership that includes Dale Goode, Tim Murphy and Dave Ready. Goode and Murphy were grape growers in Alexander Valley before founding the winery in 1985. This winery has substantial vineyard holdings, with 345 acres in vines, led by 100 acres of Chardonnay and 120 acres of Sauvignon Blanc. With Christina Benz as winemaker, the style has evolved into what is now a very attractive line of well oaked and flavorful wines, including Cabernet, Chardonnay, Merlot, Pinot Blanc and Sauvignon Blanc, with Reserve bottlings of Chardonnay and Sauvignon Blanc. All the wines carry the Alexander Valley appellation, although a Dry Creek Valley Zinfandel is planned. Production is 65,000 cases.

TASTING NOTES

CABERNET SAUVIGNON ALEXANDER VALLEY (★ ★ ★):
1992: Ripe, supple and loaded with plum, black cherry and currant flavors, finishing with a toasty oak edge. 89
1987: Effusively fruity, brimming with currant and raspberry flavors and fine tannins. 89

CABERNET SAUVIGNON ALEXANDER VALLEY MURPHY RANCH (★ ★ ★): Features ripe fruit flavors, supple texture and mild tannins, increasingly marked by toasty oak. Best on release.
1992: Firm and crisp, with a narrow band of dried cherry, chocolate and plum flavors that finish with a good dose of tannin and toasty oak. 87
1991: A heavy-handed wine marked by strong, smoky oak notes that override the spicy currant flavors. 83
1990: Ripe, with moderately rich plum, chocolate and currant flavors that turn supple and spicy. 85
1989: Dense and chewy, with hard oak notes and tannins that dominate the currant and cherry aromas and flavors. 82
1988: Offers pretty, intense berry, jam, currant and black cherry flavors and ample tannins. 87
1986: Intense and lively, with layers of cedar, spice, ripe cherry and plum flavors. 90

CHARDONNAY VARIOUS BOTTLINGS (★ ★ ★): Also showing more oak and better focus, with ripe, intense fruit flavors.
Alexander Valley 1993: Tastes a little disjointed, with the acidity standing apart, but the ripe pear and apple-laced flavors hold together. 86
Alexander Valley 1992: Clean, elegant and lively, with crisp pear, citrus and hazelnut flavors that fan out on the finish. 86
Alexander Valley Reserve 1992: Rich, creamy and

utterly delicious, serving up layers of ripe apple, pear and honey notes and a pretty overlay of spicy, toasty oak. **92**
Alexander Valley Murphy Ranch 1991: Young and tart, with green apple flavors that don't taste quite ripe. **80**
Russian River Valley J & K Murphy Vineyard 1993: Bold with smoky, toasty oak and a tight, concentrated core of pear, spice, honey and butterscotch flavors that are complex and compelling. **92**
Russian River Valley J & K Murphy Vineyard Reserve 1993: A lot of oaky flavors, but it wears it well, with floral and spicy aromas with a tangerine edge to the pear and oak flavors, but it folds together nicely on the finish where it turns smoky. **90**

FUMÉ BLANC ALEXANDER VALLEY (★★★), RESERVE (★★★): Oaky with toast and fig notes.
1994: Light and smooth, its vibrant nectarine and spice flavors humming nicely on the finish. Not much that says Sauvignon, but tasty and long. **87**
Reserve 1993: Smooth and elegant, with a buttery, creamy texture and flavors that weave in pear and citrus. **89**
Reserve 1992: Smooth, ripe and creamy, with soft fig, melon and buttery oak flavors. Complex and harmonious on the finish. **88**

MERLOT ALEXANDER VALLEY MURPHY RANCH (★★): Not in the same league as the other wines, but appealing in a supple, medium-weight style.
1992: Deeply colored, well oaked and firmly tannic, with chewy currant and cherry flavors. **83**
1991: Delivers ripe black cherry and oak aromas with flavors to match, finishing with firm tannins and more oak. **83**
1990: Tightly packed with ripe currant and blackberry flavors, with a strong tannic edge. **83**
1989: Fruity, with cola and sassafras accents to the cherry flavors. Moderate tannins. **82**
1986 Alexander Valley Premier Vineyard: The spicy, floral berry flavors are complemented by smooth, tasty vanilla notes and soft, fleshy tannins. **90**

PINOT BLANC VARIOUS BOTTLINGS (★★): Lots of oak here, too. It's more variable in quality, but the fruit flavors are attractive.
Alexander Valley 1992: An oaky wine, rather like a rich, round Chardonnay, it's buttery and spicy, showing enough pear and apple flavor to keep it in balance. **83**

Alexander Valley Melon de Bourgogne Barrel Fermented 1993: Soft and fruity, a delicate wine with a spicy edge to the pretty pear and citrus flavors, finishing with a light touch of oak. **88**
Alexander Valley Melon de Bourgogne Barrel Fermented 1991: Young and oaky, with tart green apple and pear flavors that turn to citrus on the finish. **83**

SAUVIGNON BLANC ALEXANDER VALLEY DRY (★★★): **1993:** Light and slightly herbal, a crisp wine with bright grapefruit and sage flavors. **86**

GOODE & READY CABERNET SAUVIGNON ALEXANDER VALLEY THE SECOND CABERNET (NR): **1989:** Soft and generous, with nice, oak-framed plum and currant flavors that turn spicy. **80**

MURRIETA'S WELL
Livermore Valley
F: 1990. O: Philip R. Wente & Sergio Traverso. W: Sergio Traverso. S: None.

OVERALL	$16-28	★★★

WINE RATINGS

Cabernet Blend Livermore Valley Vendimia	★★★
Sauvignon Blend Livermore Valley Vendimia	★★
Zinfandel Livermore Valley	★★★

WINERY DATA
C: 5,000. V: None. G: None. P: Cabernet Sauvignon, Sauvignon Blanc, Zinfandel, Sémillon, Merlot (Livermore Valley).

This is a partnership between veteran California winemakers Sergio Traverso (formerly of Sterling and Concannon) and Philip Wente (of Wente Bros.) focusing on Livermore Valley wines, with 5,000 cases of two upscale blends (a Bordeaux red and white) and a Zinfandel. The grapes come from the historic Louis Mel Vineyard, a 90-acre vineyard that dates to the 1880s.

TASTING NOTES

CABERNET BLEND LIVERMORE VALLEY VENDIMIA (★★★): A claret-style wine that aims for finesse and elegance rather than sheer varietal strength.

1991: Earthy with a tarry, smoky edge to the currant and berry flavors. **84**

1990: A claret-style blend with cedar, plum and green olive flavors and firm tannins. It's 60 percent Cabernet, 11 percent Merlot, 2 percent Cabernet Franc and 4 percent Zinfandel. **85**

SAUVIGNON BLEND LIVERMORE VALLEY VENDIMIA (★★): A blend of Sauvignon Blanc, Sémillon and Muscat Canelli, it's moderately rich and avoids the racy character of pungent Sauvignon Blanc.

1992: Smooth and polished, round in texture, an elegant wine that shows citrus-tinged pear and spicy vanilla flavors. **88**

ZINFANDEL LIVERMORE VALLEY (★★★): Intense and marked by spicy pepper and wild berry flavors; a bit on the rustic side.

1991: An exotic wine brimming with fresh, ripe, juicy, rich wild berry, cherry and raspberry jam flavors. **88**

1989: Ripe, lean and oaky, with classic raspberry and pepper aromas and a tarry edge that turns funky and earthy on the long finish. **83**

NALLE WINERY
Dry Creek Valley
F: 1984. **O:** Nalle Winery Inc. **W:** Doug Nalle. **S:** None.

OVERALL	$16-18	★★★★

WINE RATINGS

Cabernet Sauvignon Dry Creek Valley	★★★
Zinfandel Dry Creek Valley	★★★★

WINERY DATA
C: 2,500. **V:** None. **G:** None. **P:** Zinfandel, Petite Sirah (Dry Creek Valley).

After working at Jordan, Souverain, Balverne and Quivira, Doug Nalle zeroed in on Dry Creek Valley Zinfandel as his speciality, beginning with the 1984 vintage. All the grapes are purchased from old vines and the wine includes a dash of Petite Sirah. Production has hovered around 2,500 cases and quality has been very high. A small amount of Cabernet is also made occasionally, also from Dry Creek Valley grapes, but it's a shade lighter and less intriguing than the Zinfandel, which is usually the case with these two grapes in Dry Creek.

TASTING NOTES

CABERNET SAUVIGNON DRY CREEK VALLEY (★★★): Appealing for its forward cherry and currant flavors and mild tannins.

1990: Firm and focused, with bright blackberry and currant aromas and flavors, chunky tannins and an austere finish. **85**

1987: Tight and firm, with currant, red cherry and raspberry flavors and firm tannins. **89**

ZINFANDEL DRY CREEK VALLEY (★★★★): Combines ripe, intense, well focused fruit flavors with a sense of polish and finesse. Drinks best early on.

1992: Supple and fruity, with hints of floral and wild berry notes. Tannins are mild but firm. **85**

1991: Lean and supple, with pretty raspberry and cherry flavors and a touch of buttery oak. **86**

1990: Smooth and generous, with plenty of blackberry, blueberry and vanilla aromas and flavors that keep pouring through. **89**

1989: Fresh and fruity, with solid blackberry and black cherry flavors that hint at vanilla on the finish. **85**

1988: Offers beautiful wild berry, cherry and raspberry flavors, picking up toast and black pepper on the finish. **89**

1987: Beautifully crafted, ripe and brimming with complex, focused raspberry, vanilla and floral flavors. **92**

1986: Very stylish and richly fruity, with buttery oak notes adding to pretty wild berry and raspberry flavors. **90**

1985: Bright, vivid black cherry, raspberry and vanilla flavors turn smooth and supple. Mature. **88**

NAPA CREEK WINERY
Rutherford
F: 1980. **O:** Bronco Wine Co. **W:** None. **S:** None.

The late Jack Schultz founded this winery on the Silverado Trail, building volume to about 15,000 cases, with occasionally good wines but more often rather ordinary ones. In the late 1980s the winery faced financial hardships and was sold to the Bronco Wine Co. Its future in 1995 was unclear.

NAPA RIDGE

St. Helena, Napa Valley
F: 1986. **O:** Wine World Estates. **W:** David Schlottman.
S: None.

OVERALL	$4-13	★★★

WINE RATINGS

Cabernet Sauvignon Central Coast	
Oak Barrel	★★
Cabernet Sauvignon North Coast Coastal	
Oak Barrel	★★
Chardonnay Central Coast	★★★
Chardonnay Central Coast Coastal Vines	★★★
Chardonnay Central Coast Special Select	★★★
Chardonnay Napa Valley Coastal Reserve	★★★
Chardonnay Napa Valley	
Frisinger Vineyard	★★★
Chardonnay North Coast	★★★
Chardonnay North	
Coast Coastal Reserve	★★★
Merlot North Coast Coastal	★★
Pinot Noir North Coast Coastal	★★
Sauvignon Blanc North Coast Coastal	★★
Zinfandel Central Coast Coastal	NR

WINERY DATA
C: 1,000,000. **V:** N/A. **G:** N/A. **P:** N/A.

There is no actual Napa Ridge or Napa Ridge Winery; the name is a brand started by Wine World Estates, owner of Beringer, Souverain and Meridian, to compete in the fighting-varietal category of wines. Napa Ridge has become an enormous success, both as a business venture and for its high-quality, affordably priced wines. Winemaker David Schottman has a wealth of Wine World vineyards to choose from, from Santa Barbara to Sonoma, and that diversity is reflected in the broad Central Coast and North Coast appellations. Case volume is 1,000,000, with a lineup that stretches from Cabernet to Chardonnay to white Zinfandel, made at Beringer.

TASTING NOTES

CABERNET SAUVIGNON VARIOUS BOTTLINGS (★★): Made in a lightly fruity, ready-to-drink style. The Reserve shows more depth and finesse.

Central Coast 1992: Ripe and fruity, with a core of black cherry and wild berry jam flavors that has a tannic edge. **87**

Central Coast Oak Barrel 1991: Supple and generous, with pretty wild berry and cherry flavors. **84**

Napa Valley Coastal Reserve 1989: A wine that's lean, smooth and silky, with tightly knit tannins and focused blackberry and currant aromas and flavors. Needs to lose some tannin; best after 1996 or '97. **85**

North Coast Coastal Oak Barrel 1992: Austere, with crisp currant and cherry notes of modest depth and proportion. **79**

North Coast Coastal Oak Barrel 1991: Light and fruity, a simple Cabernet with berry and cherry overtones and soft tannins. **77**

North Coast Reserve 1990: A good but ultimately simple Cabernet with ripe, coarse fruit notes and firm tannins. **82**

North Coast Coastal 1989: Solidly fruity and firm in texture, with appealing black cherry and currant flavors shaded by herbs. **79**

North Coast Coastal Reserve 1989: Good balance of flavor and oak, with ripe, spicy cherry and currant notes that pick up a toasty, cedary edge on the finish. **87**

CHARDONNAY VARIOUS BOTTLINGS (★★★): Steadily improving, complex, polished and well oaked, with plenty of ripe, juicy fruit flavors.

Central Coast Coastal Vines 1993: Lightly fruity, with spicy pear and grapefruit notes; easy to drink. **83**

Central Coast Special Select 1993: Ripe and rich, with spicy pear, honey and light oak shadings. **86**

Napa Valley Coastal Reserve 1993: Appealing for its complex fruit flavors, with tiers of citrus, pear and spice that stay focused, gaining complexity and length. **86**

Napa Valley Frisinger Vineyard 1993: Elegant with a deft balance between the bright pear and lemony flavors and light spicy oak shadings. **88**

North Coast 1992: Crisp and lean, with a thin band of citrus and apple flavors. **78**

North Coast Coastal Reserve 1992: A spicy wine with pretty pear, oak and honey notes that are elegant and lively. **86**

MERLOT NORTH COAST COASTAL (★★): Light and pleasant.

1992: Chewy with a pretty core of herb, currant and vanilla flavors that fold together nicely, finishing with a pretty cherry and spice edge. **87**
1991: A lighter style of Merlot with spicy fruit flavors that echo currant and cherry. **84**

PINOT NOIR NORTH COAST COASTAL (★★): Appealing for its direct fruit flavors.
1993: Leans toward the herb and tea side of Pinot Noir, but finishes with a nice touch of toasty oak and black cherry. **84**
1991: A nice, simple red offering appealing strawberry and raspberry flavors. **83**

SAUVIGNON BLANC NORTH COAST COASTAL (★★): Simple but balanced.
1993: Simple and appealing, offering peach and pear flavors with an earthy, herbal edge. **81**
1992: Crisp and simple, a nice white wine with little to identify it as Sauvignon Blanc. **79**

ZINFANDEL CENTRAL COAST COASTAL (NR): Early efforts were disappointing, not of the same caliber as the Chardonnay or Cabernet.
1990: Simple, earthy and gamy, showing a sour edge to the cherry and raspberry flavors. Drinkable, but not up to par for Napa Ridge. **76**

NAVARRO VINEYARDS
Anderson Valley
F: 1974. **O:** Ted Bennett & Deborah Cahn. **W:** Ted Bennett. **S:** Indian Creek.

OVERALL	$7-17	★★★★

WINE RATINGS

Blush Anderson Valley Pinot Gris	★★
Cabernet Sauvignon Mendocino County	★★★
Chardonnay Anderson Valley	★★★
Chardonnay Anderson Valley Premiere Reserve	★★★★
Gewürztraminer Anderson Valley Dry	★★★
Gewürztraminer North Coast Late Harvest Sweet	★★★★
Pinot Noir Anderson Valley	★★
Pinot Noir Anderson Valley Méthode l'Ancienne	★★★
Red Table Wine Mendocino County Petits Villages	NR
Sauvignon Blanc Mendocino County Cuvée 128	★★★
Sparkling Wine Anderson Valley Brut	★★
White Riesling Anderson Valley	★★
White Table Wine Mendocino County Edelzwicker	NR
Zinfandel Mendocino County	★★★

WINERY DATA
C: 20,000. **V:** 75 acres in Anderson Valley. **G:** Gewürztraminer (29 acres), Pinot Noir (23), Chardonnay (16), Johannisberg Riesling (4), Muscat (3). **P:** Pinot Noir (Anderson Valley), Johannisberg Riesling (Anderson Valley), Pinot Gris (Anderson Valley), Zinfandel (Mendocino), Cabernet Sauvignon (Mendocino).

Ted Bennett and Deborah Cahn built their beautiful winery in picturesque Anderson Valley in 1974, moving from the Bay Area, where Bennett had owned Pacific Stereo, a chain of music stores. They initially focused on Gewürztraminer but have since added a full lineup that includes Cabernet, Riesling (made in three styles, from dry to late harvest) and Pinot Noir. All Navarro's wines are superbly crafted and very consistent from year to year. Bennett and Cahn have high standards and resist selling inferior wines—a trap too many wineries fall into. Production is 20,000 cases from 75 acres of winery-owned vineyards. Wines such as Cabernet and Zinfandel are made from purchased grapes grown in warmer inland vineyards. Anderson Valley is one of California's coolest climates, ideal for many of the wines Navarro excels at. As good as these wines are, quality keeps improving. The dessert wines are among the state's best.

TASTING NOTES

BLUSH ANDERSON VALLEY PINOT GRIS (★★): New to the lineup, it's clean, correct and varietally true.
1993: Clean and spicy, with bright, fresh pear, apple and honey notes. **85**

CABERNET SAUVIGNON MENDOCINO COUNTY (★★★): Never flashy or dramatic, but well crafted and consistent, with deft balance and a sense of harmony.
1989: Delivers enough currant and spice notes to balance the herb and earth flavors. **82**

1988: A slim but complex wine that shows off its buttery oak and ripe, spicy currant flavors. **86**

1987: Classy, ripe, smooth and balanced, with a core of rich, plush currant, cherry and plum flavors and subtle, buttery oak notes. **88**

1986: Complex, weaving plum, cherry and spice flavors through a medium-weight structure. **87**

1985: A good '85 with ripe currant and black cherry flavors that lead to firm tannins. **87**

Chardonnay Anderson Valley (★★★): Solid, with intense fruit and spice notes.

1993: Solid, with ripe, appealing pear, apple and spice notes, finishing with light oak. **83**

1992: Smooth and creamy, with a spicy wood and nutmeg edge to the ripe pear and apple flavors. **86**

Chardonnay Anderson Valley Premiere Reserve (★★★★): Very consistent, with a fine balance between ripe pear and fig notes and vanilla-tinged oak. Ages well.

1992: Supple and fruity, with ripe, complex pear and apple flavors and light oak shadings. **87**

1991: Bold, ripe, rich and creamy, with pretty spice and vanilla flavors, but also a load of pear, apple, citrus and toast notes on a long, full finish. **91**

Gewürztraminer Anderson Valley Dry (★★★): Floral and spicy, hitting the right flavor notes.

1993: Light and floral, with a touch of grapefruit and pear sneaking in behind the floral, spicy notes. The finish is a little flat. **84**

1992: Floral and spice notes surround a core of lively grapefruit and litchi flavors. It's dry, gentle and appealing, with a beautiful balance of fruit and spice. **88**

Gewürztraminer North Coast Late Harvest Sweet (★★★★): May be California's first in this style; utterly delicious.

1991: Smooth, sweet and lively, with dazzling spice, apricot, honey and rose petal notes. **90**

Pinot Noir Anderson Valley Méthode l'Ancienne (★★★): Elegant, with delicate berry and cherry flavors and light oak in the background.

1991: Elegant, with delicate cherry and blackberry flavors that are bright and vivid and a finish that echoes those flavors. **86**

1990: Fresh and lively, with bright berry, tar, anise and raspberry flavors, picking up an earthy edge on the finish. **86**

1989: An elegant wine with crisp cherry, raspberry and spice flavors that take on a nice oaky edge on the finish. **87**

1988: Ripe and supple, with delicate cherry, raspberry, vanilla and spice flavors that are focused and elegant. **89**

1987: Earthy, gamy aromas and flavors tend to shoulder past the cherry and spice notes. **85**

1986: Mature, with earthy plum and black cherry aromas and flavors that take on a pleasant mushroom note on the finish. **85**

1985: Aging well, with spicy cherry and plum flavors and a bright red color. **86**

Pinot Noir Various Bottlings (★★): Lighter than the Methode l'Ancienne but tasty, with appealing Pinot Noir character.

Anderson Valley Clone 54 1992: Like a Beaujolais with its fresh, snappy grape, black cherry and wild berry flavors. **87**

Anderson Valley Deep End Blend 1989: Intense, deep and flavorful, with ripe plum, raspberry and cherry notes that are focused and long. **87**

Red Table Wine Mendocino County Petits Villages (NR):

1993: Very light and fruity, a Beaujolais-style wine with an appealing berry and watermelon character. A blend of several varieties, including Grenache, Pinot Noir and Gamay. **83**

Sauvignon Blanc Mendocino County Cuvée 128 (★★★): Superb and intense, with rich fruit flavors and fine balance.

1993: Light and smooth in texture and vibrant in flavor, with melon, pear, citrus and floral notes. **88**

1992: Supple and flavorful, with generous pear, spice, vanilla and fig flavors that turn complex. **88**

Sparkling Wine Anderson Valley Brut (★★): A solid if rustic sparkling wine with generous pear, spice and vanilla flavors.

NV: Tastes off-dry, with ripe, spicy pear, hazelnut and vanilla notes. Simple but appealing. **83**

WHITE RIESLING ANDERSON VALLEY (★★):
1992: Light and slightly sweet, with apricot and floral flavors that extend into a solid finish. Could be a little more delicate. **83**

WHITE TABLE WINE MENDOCINO COUNTY EDEL-ZWICKER (NR):
1990: Fresh, smooth and off-dry, with appealing pear, apricot and spice aromas and flavors and a nice balance of sweetness and crispness on the finish. Perfect for a picnic. **84**

ZINFANDEL MENDOCINO COUNTY (★★★):
1992: Ripe, with a wild, gamy, jammy edge to the cherry and plum flavors. **85**
1991: Well crafted, with ripe cherry and raspberry flavors framed by light, toasty oak and just the right dose of tannin. **86**

NELSON ESTATE
Sonoma County
F: 1986. **O:** David Nelson. **W:** Kerry Damskey. **S:** None.

OVERALL	$15	★★

WINE RATINGS

Cabernet Franc Sonoma County	★★

WINERY DATA
C: 3,000. **V:** 85 acres in Sonoma County. **G:** Cabernet Franc, Merlot, Chardonnay, Pinot Noir. **P:** Sauvignon Blanc (Rutherford), Chardonnay (Carneros, Oakville), Merlot (Oakville), Zinfandel (Alexander Valley).

Commercial airline pilot David Nelson owns a 20-acre vineyard in Bennett Valley, where he produces Cabernet Franc and small amounts of Cabernet Sauvignon and Merlot. So far the quality is ordinary, and the wines are marked by stalky flavors, a tradmark of Cabernet Franc.

TASTING NOTES

CABERNET FRANC SONOMA COUNTY(★★): Unimpressive, with a green, unripe edge.
1990: Tastes green as in not quite ripe, with a cedary edge to the tart fruit flavors. **78**
1987: Delivers modest herb, olive and plum flavors, and the wood is attractive. **82**

NEVADA CITY WINERY
Nevada County
F: 1980. **O:** N.C.W.G. Inc. **W:** Mark Foster. **S:** None.

OVERALL	$9-15	★★

WINE RATINGS

Cabernet Sauvignon Sierra Foothills	★★
Chardonnay Nevada County Barrel Fermented	★★
Meritage Red Nevada County Claret The Director's Reserve	★★
Zinfandel Sierra Foothills	★★

WINERY DATA
C: 8,500. **V:** None. **G:** None. **P:** Cabernet Sauvignon, Cabernet Franc, Zinfandel, Gewürztraminer, Chardonnay, Charbono (Nevada County), Gewürztraminer (Sonoma County).

Former lawyer Alan Hayley founded this winery in 1980, with a marketing strategy that targeted the tourist trade that visits this city on the way to the Sierra Nevada. Some 8,500 cases are produced, including Cabernet and Chardonnay, and also Douce Noir, a Rhône-style blend of Charbono, Mourvèdre and Grenache. All the wines are made from purchased grapes.

TASTING NOTES

VARIOUS BOTTLINGS (★★):
Cabernet Sauvignon Sierra Foothills 1989: Firm, ripe and chunky, with generous black cherry and currant flavors wrapped tightly in tannin. **81**
Chardonnay Nevada County Barrel Fermented 1993: Refreshingly fruity with appealing pear, apple and light citrus notes, holding its flavor through the finish. **86**
Chardonnay Nevada County Barrel Fermented 1992: Light and fruity, with an earthy mineral edge on the finish. Balanced and pleasing. **83**
Meritage Red Nevada County Claret The Director's Reserve 1989: Dark in color and deeply flavored, with firm tannins, tight acidity and straightforward fruit. Doesn't have a lot of complexity but is very solidly put together. It's 49 percent Cabernet Sauvignon. **83**
Zinfandel Sierra Foothills 1991: A well proportioned Zin with spicy berry and pepper notes that take on a meaty edge on the finish. The flavors have staying power and the price is right. **85**

NEWLAN VINEYARDS AND WINERY
Napa Valley
F: 1980. **O:** Newlan Vineyards and Winery. **W:** Glen Newlan. **S:** Napa Villages.

OVERALL	$10-28	★★★

WINE RATINGS
Cabernet Sauvignon Napa Valley	★★★
Chardonnay Napa Valley Reserve	★★
Johannisberg Riesling Napa Valley Late Harvest	★★★
Pinot Noir Napa Valley	★★
Zinfandel Napa Valley	★★★

WINERY DATA
C: 10,000. **V:** 27 acres in Napa Valley. **G:** Pinot Noir (16 acres), Cabernet Sauvignon (11). **P:** Zinfandel (Napa Valley), Chardonnay (Napa Valley), Johannisberg Riesling (Napa Valley).

Former Lockheed engineer Bruce Newlan opted for a winemaking career, first as a partner in Alatera Vineyards before starting his own winery in 1981 north of Napa. Today Newlan is a family-run operation, using 27 acres of estate vineyard, including 16 acres of Pinot Noir and 11 acres of Cabernet. Chardonnay, Riesling and Zinfandel are purchased, along with a small amount of School House Pinot Noir grown on Spring Mountain. That wine is bottled under the Vieilles Vignes label.

TASTING NOTES

CABERNET SAUVIGNON NAPA VALLEY (★★★): Solid but unspectacular, with a spicy edge to the currant and spice notes.
1990: Broad and ripe, with black cherry, currant and wild berry flavors that are tightly wound, finishing with dry, gritty tannins. **86**
1988: Tight and peppery, with a lean core of currant and earthy berry flavors. **84**
1987: Ripe, smooth and generous, with complex currant, plum and spicy mint notes. **88**
1986: A remarkably elegant and flavorful '86 with a pretty core of black cherry, currant, raspberry and anise flavors and cedary oak notes. **88**
1985: Combines ripe, supple plum and cherry flavors framed by just the right touch of oak. **87**

CHARDONNAY NAPA VALLEY RESERVE (★★): Clean and well made, but lacks extra dimensions.
1991: Soft, round and spicy, a moderately flavorful wine with pear and grapefruit notes. **83**

JOHANNISBERG RIESLING NAPA VALLEY LATE HARVEST (★★★): Sweet, with appealing honey, spice and apricot flavors.
1992: Sweet and syrupy, a mouthful of spice, honey, apricot and floral flavors that become unctuous and round on the silky finish. **88**
1991: Sweet, soft and pillowy, a wine you can sink into like a soft sofa, with generous honey, spice and apricot aromas and flavors. The finish is sweet enough to warrant waiting until 1996 or 1997 to lose some of the sugar. **89**

PINOT NOIR VARIOUS BOTTLINGS (★★): Medium-weight and solid, occasionally very good, with spicy cherry and berry notes, but often lean and minty. Vieilles Vignes is inconsistent too, as the School House vineyard is old and struggles each year to ripen.
Napa Valley 1992: Lean and crisp, with a minty edge and modest fruit flavors. **83**
Napa Valley 1991: Distinctively minty and plummy, with a good dose of chewy oak. **80**
Napa Valley 1989: Solid, generous and spicy, with focused black cherry, strawberry and spicy toast flavors. **87**
Napa Valley 1988: Firm, tart and focused, with spice, blackberry and vanilla notes that are hard-edged. **81**
Napa Valley 1987: Ripe and broad, with minty aromas, full flavors of cherry and strawberry and a velvety texture. **81**
Napa Valley 1985: Rich, velvety, round and full, a beautifully polished, graceful wine. **88**
Napa Valley 1980: Aging well but in decline, with spicy, minty cherry and tobacco flavors. **83**
Napa Valley Napa-Villages 1991: A light but pleasant wine with strawberry and cranberry notes, picking up an earthy edge. **81**
Napa Valley Reserve 1991: A pleasant mouthful of plum and spice flavors, turning dry. **84**
Napa Valley School House Vieilles Vignes 1991: Tart, with a green tea edge to the cherry flavor, which barely tastes ripe. **79**
Napa Valley Vieilles Vignes 1990: Richer and riper than the 1991 but similar in weight and flavor profile, with intense, smoky, spicy herb and cherry flavors. **87**

Napa Valley Vieilles Vignes 1989: Mature, with elegant, spicy, smoky Pinot Noir flavors that pick up an herb and cola accent on the finish. **85**

ZINFANDEL NAPA VALLEY (★★★): Consistent, with spicy, peppery qualities.
1992: Spicy and peppery, it's a lean and compact wine with firm, drying tannins. **86**
1991: Features bright, ripe, spicy berry and cherry flavors and soft, fleshy tannins. **89**

NEWTON VINEYARD
St. Helena, Napa Valley
F: 1978. **O:** Peter & Su Hua Newton. **W:** John Kongsgaard, Michel Rolland. **S:** Newtonian.

OVERALL	$13-20	★★★

WINE RATINGS

Cabernet Sauvignon Napa Valley	★★★
Chardonnay Napa Valley	★★★
Meritage Red Napa Valley Claret	★★★
Merlot Napa Valley	★★★

WINERY DATA
C: 30,000. **V:** 170 acres in Napa Valley. **G:** Chardonnay (40 acres), Merlot (50), Petite Verdot (15), Cabernet Franc (15), Chardonnay (50). **P:** Chardonnay.

Peter Newton headed a group of investors that founded Sterling Vineyards in 1967 and hired Ric Forman as winemaker. While Sterling experienced its share of hits and misses, by the time Newton sold it to the Coca-Cola Bottling Co. in 1977 it ranked among the leaders in Cabernet, Merlot and Sauvignon Blanc. After selling Sterling, Newton and Forman started a new winery on Spring Mountain, to be called Forman. But at the last minute the two partners had a falling out and Forman departed to start his own winery (Forman) after making the first few vintages of Newton Cabernet. The winery focuses on estate-grown Cabernet and Merlot, while the Chardonnay includes some purchased grapes from Carneros. Production is about 30,000 cases and quality is high and consistent across the board under the winemaking direction of John Kongsgaard.

TASTING NOTES

CABERNET SAUVIGNON NAPA VALLEY (★★★): Complex and supple, with well focused flavors and mild, polished tannins. Ages well.
1989: Rough and chewy, with ripe currant and cherry flavors and firm tannins. **84**
1988: Firm and focused, with ripe currant, plum and raspberry flavors shaded by cedar and tobacco notes. **87**
1987: Offers attractive spice, herb, anise and dill notes, but there's a tight core of currant and cherry flavors behind them. Firmly tannic. **87**
1986: Elegant and refined, with focused chocolate, toast, currant and plum flavors, hinting at olives on the finish. **90**
1985: Firm and slightly tannic, but supple enough to carry off the ripe berry and currant flavors. **89**
1984: Big and round, with ripe, complex cherry, plum and chocolate flavors. **88**
1983: Complex, with mature, drying currant, anise and earth flavors. **85**

CHARDONNAY NAPA VALLEY (★★★): Well oaked; the Reserve-style unfiltered wine spends close to two years in barrel, but has fruit and finesse to match the oak.
1992: Ripe fruit gives a sweet impression, with spicy pear, apricot and nectarine flavors that are focused and lively. **87**
1991: Lean, firm and focused, with a beam of concentrated, spicy lemon, apple and pear flavors. **89**

MERITAGE RED NAPA VALLEY CLARET (★★★): Shares the suppleness and finesse of the Cabernet.
1992: Spicy, with ripe plum and cherry flavors that are moderately rich and well focused. **88**
1991: Rich and supple, with ripe cherry and currant flavors and a hint of toast and spice. The tannins are supple. **87**
1990: Appealing for its ripe currant, chocolate and plum flavors. Modest tannins. **85**
1988: Subtle and complex, with ripe currant, black cherry and cedar flavors, supple tannins and fine balance. Picks up toasty tobacco, herb and mint notes on the finish. **87**

MERLOT NAPA VALLEY (★★★): Typical Merlot in its variability, but can be among the best when it's fully ripe and concentrated.

1989: Plush and concentrated, with rich currant, earth and toasty, buttery oak flavors. **88**

1987: Austere, with lean herb, cherry, currant and bell pepper flavors. **84**

1986: Complex, with herb, cherry, tobacco and toasty oak notes. **83**

1985: Combines beautiful fruit and oak flavors in a lush but firmly structured wine, echoing sweet plum, cherry, cedar and butter notes. **91**

NEYERS
Napa Valley
F: 1980. **O:** Bruce Neyers. **W:** Bruce Neyers. **S:** None.

OVERALL	$15-20	★★
WINE RATINGS		
Cabernet Sauvignon Napa Valley		★★
Chardonnay Carneros		★★
Merlot Napa Valley		★★

WINERY DATA
C: 5,000. **V:** None. **G:** None. **P:** Chardonnay (Carneros), Merlot (Napa Valley).

Bruce Neyers worked at Mayacamas and Joseph Phelps Vineyards before starting his brand on the side, producing some 5,000 cases of Cabernet, Chardonnay and Merlot, all from purchased grapes. Quality was ordinary, as the wines were typically on the lean, austere side, lacking richness and generosity. Neyers left Phelps in 1992 to head a wine import firm, but the brand has continued.

TASTING NOTES

VARIOUS BOTTLINGS (★★):
Chardonnay Carneros 1993: Serves up ripe pear, apple and pineapple flavors and adds light oak shadings. **86**
Merlot Napa Valley 1992: Firm and compact, with a tight core of cedar, currant and black cherry flavors, finishing with firm tannins. **84**

NICHELINI WINERY
St. Helena, Napa Valley
F: 1890. **O:** Nichelini Winery, Inc. **W:** Greg Boeger. **S:** None.

OVERALL	$9-12	★★
WINE RATINGS		
Cabernet Sauvignon Napa Valley		★
Cabernet Sauvignon Napa Valley		
Joseph A. Nichelini Vineyards		★★
Sauvignon Blanc Napa Valley		
Joseph A. Nichelini Vineyards		NR

WINERY DATA
C: 2,500. **V:** 100 acres in Napa Valley. **G:** Zinfandel old vines (7 acres), Zinfandel (60), Merlot (10), Cabernet Sauvignon (10), Chenin Blanc (10), Sauvignon Vert (3). **P:** None.

Nichelini Winery in Chiles Valley east of Napa Valley dates to 1890. The old winery is worth a visit if you want a glimpse of history, but the wines have only been fair. In the 1990s Greg Boeger, owner of Boeger Winery, revived the Nichelini brand and began producing Zinfandel from the winery's 100 acres of vines, many of them a century old. The 1988 Zinfandel is crisp and pleasant, with modest berry and cherry notes.

TASTING NOTES

VARIOUS BOTTLINGS:
Cabernet Sauvignon Napa Valley 1988: Crisp and clean, with modest cherry and plum flavors. **81**
Cabernet Sauvignon Napa Valley Joseph A. Nichelini Vineyards 1989: Earthy with a lean cedary edge that's drying and tannic. **77**
Sauvignon Blanc Napa Valley Joseph A. Nichelini Vineyards 1993: Ripe and floral, a creamy, supple wine with a modest level of pear and vanilla flavors, echoing floral notes. **82**

GUSTAVE NIEBAUM
This is a second label for Niebaum-Coppola Estate Winery (see listing).

NIEBAUM-COPPOLA ESTATE WINERY
Rutherford, Napa Valley
F: 1975. **O:** Francis Ford & Eleanor Coppola. **W:** Scott McLeod, Tony Soter. **S:** Gustave Niebaum, Edizione Pennino.

OVERALL $14-60   ★★★★

WINE RATINGS

Cabernet Franc Napa Valley
    Francis Coppola Family Wines   ★★
Meritage Red Napa Valley Rubicon   ★★★★
Merlot Napa Valley Francis Coppola
    Family Wines   ★★
Zinfandel Napa Valley Edizione Pennino   ★★★
Gustave Niebaum Cabernet Sauvignon
    Napa Valley Reference   NR
Gustave Niebaum Cabernet Sauvignon
    Napa Valley Mast Vineyard   NR
Gustave Niebaum Cabernet Sauvignon
    Napa Valley Tench Vineyard   NR
Gustave Niebaum Chardonnay
    Napa Valley Reference   NR
Gustave Niebaum Merlot
    Napa Valley Reference   NR

WINERY DATA

C: 5,000. V: 125 acres in Rutherford. G: Cabernet Sauvignon (55 acres), Cabernet Franc (19), Merlot (14), Zinfandel (12), Chardonnay (3), Viognier (2). P: None.

Filmmaker Francis Ford Coppola and his wife, Eleanor, purchased the old home of Inglenook founder Gustave Niebaum in 1975 and began making wine from the old Inglenook vineyard shortly thereafter. The goal was to create long-lived wines in the mold of the great Inglenook Cask Cabernets of the Niebaum and later John Daniel era. Having enjoyed Inglenook wines that dated to the turn of the century, Coppola focused on a style of wine that would age well over the long term, and that remains the goal today.

The winery's production is 5,000 cases, led by the proprietary red table wine called Rubicon (2,000 cases), with another 2,000 cases of Cabernet Franc and 1,000 cases of Zinfandel; the latter is bottled under the Edizione Pennino label, named after Coppola's maternal grandfather. Merlot joined the lineup in 1991. Scott McLeod is the winemaker, while Tony Soter (of Étude Wines) consults as the winery aims to polish Rubicon's chewy tannins and give it more finesse. In 1995 Coppola bought the old Inglenook chateau and 80 acres of vineyard, effectively reuniting most of Gustave Niebaum's old estate. Plans are to keep the old chateau open for visitors and revive the Gustave Niebaum label that Inglenook's former owners, Heublein Inc., once used. The Coppolas own 125 acres in vines, selling a portion of their grape crop to various wineries.

TASTING NOTES

CABERNET FRANC NAPA VALLEY FRANCIS COPPOLA FAMILY WINES (★★):
1991: Earthy, leathery flavors dominate the currant notes, and it has a bitter edge. **81**
1990: Tight, dense and gamy, with oak showing more than the currant and violet notes. **84**

MERITAGE RED NAPA VALLEY RUBICON (★★★★): A remarkably steady performer since its 1978 debut, it's a dense, tannic, chewy, even rustic wine that ages very slowly. Recognizing the hardness of many vintages, the winery now uses nearly 95 percent Cabernet, and the 1990 and 1991 vintages appear to be the best in the winery's history, with more richness, brighter flavors and more depth.
1991: Best Niebuam-Coppola ever, it's dense, chewy, complex and loaded with currant, anise, spice and cedar notes. Has a wonderful sense of harmony and finesse. **93**
1990: Bold, ripe and fleshy, with deep, concentrated plum, currant, anise and tar notes framed by light oak shadings. **90**
1989: Tough and chewy, with hard-core tannins that override the smoky herb and currant flavors. **87**
1988: Herb and mint aromas give way to a core of taut, chewy currant and cherry flavors, and the finish is austere and tannic. **86**
1987: Smooth, mature and chewy, with robust cherry, anise and leather flavors that meld nicely. **88**
1986: Mature, with a complex, earthy currant edge to the flavors that adds to the menthol and mint notes. Tannic and oaky. **89**
1985: Tannic and concentrated, with earthy, spicy aromas and ripe plum and anise flavors that pick up a mineral edge. **88**
1984: Gaining richness and depth with age, with layers of chewy currant, black cherry and earthy, tarry notes. **89**
1982: Earthy and tannic, with ripe, mature currant and cherry flavors that are still tightly wound. **87**
1981: Ripe, forward and supple, with plum, cherry and currant flavors that are mature, turning dry and earthy. **87**

1980: Big, intense and tannic, with drying cedar, plum and black cherry flavors. **87**

1979: Deeply colored, with rustic, potent herb and currant flavors that turn earthy and gamy. **84**

1978: Mature, with complex currant, earth and cedar flavors that turn supple on the finish. **87**

MERLOT NAPA VALLEY FRANCIS COPPOLA FAMILY WINES (★★):

1991: Firm and flavorful, with ripe currant and blackberry flavors at the core and a strong gamy, oaky streak. **86**

ZINFANDEL NAPA VALLEY EDIZIONE PENNINO (★★★): Impressive for its intensity and earthy raspberry flavors. Tilts toward the tannic side.

1992: Ripe and lush, with pretty tar, earth and berry flavors framed by toasty oak. **88**

1991: Ripe, intense, tannic and spicy, with a band of rich, chunky pepper and plum flavors. **88**

1990: Supple and elegant, with tar, anise, raspberry and smoke notes that turn smooth and spicy. **88**

1989: Pleasantly ripe and fruity, with classic pepper and wild berry flavors that turn floral on the finish. **87**

GUSTAVE NIEBAUM VARIOUS BOTTLINGS (NR): These were made at Inglenook-Napa Valley before Coppola bought the brand in 1995.

Cabernet Sauvignon Napa Valley Reference 1989: Firm and focused, with pleasant currant and plum aromas and flavors, turning tannic. **85**

Cabernet Sauvignon Napa Valley Reference 1985: Ripe and lively, with spice, anise and fresh berry and currant flavors that are intense and complex. **87**

Cabernet Sauvignon Napa Valley Mast Vineyard 1987: Firm and tannic, with tight plum, currant and chocolate flavors that pick up spice and tobacco. **87**

Cabernet Sauvignon Napa Valley Tench Vineyard 1988: Hard and tight, with earthy tannins that override the currant flavors. **80**

Cabernet Sauvignon Napa Valley Tench Vineyard 1986: Intense and tannic, with ripe plum, vanilla, spice and cherry flavors that work to the surface. **88**

Chardonnay Napa Valley Reference 1991: Simple and correct, displaying a core of spicy pear and apple aromas and flavors. **81**

Merlot Napa Valley Reference 1989: Lean, overly tart and woody. **72**

NORMAN VINEYARDS
Paso Robles
F: 1992. **O:** Norman Vineyards. **W:** Robert Nadeau. **S:** None.

OVERALL	$9-15	★★★

WINE RATINGS		
Cabernet Sauvignon Paso Robles		★★★
Cabernet Sauvignon Paso Robles No Nonsense Red		NR
Zinfandel Paso Robles		★★★

WINERY DATA
C: 2,500. **V:** 37 acres in Paso Robles. **G:** Cabernet Sauvignon (16 acres), Chardonnay (11), Merlot (2), Zinfandel (7), Barbera (1). **P:** Cabernet Franc, Pinot Noir (Paso Robles).

This new winery uses Paso Robles-grown grapes for its Cabernet and Zinfandel. Two versions of the 1992 Cabernet were offered: a standard bottling that's supple and elegant, with herb, cherry and currant flavors, and a No Nonsense Red bottling, a tightly wound wine laced with herb and cedar notes. The 1992 Zinfandel shows impressive ripe, spicy cherry and herb notes.

TASTING NOTES

CABERNET SAUVIGNON PASO ROBLES (★★★):

1992: Supple and elegant, with pretty herb, cherry and currant flavors. **87**

No Nonsense Red 1992: The herb, cedar, currant and berry flavors are tight and compact, finishing with firm tannins. **82**

ZINFANDEL PASO ROBLES (★★★):

1993: Ripe and plush, with rich, supple black cherry, raspberry and wild berry flavors that are bright and lively. Finishes with a firm tannic edge that's smooth, not biting. **90**

1992: Ripe and spicy, with a pretty band of herb and cherry flavors that turn rich and supple. **88**

OAKFORD VINEYARDS
Oakville, Napa Valley
F: 1986. **O:** Charles & Catherine Ball. **W:** Larry Ball, Bob Levy. **S:** None.

OVERALL	$30	★★★

WINE RATINGS

Cabernet Sauvignon Napa Valley	★★★

WINERY DATA
C: 1,000. **V:** 8 acres in Oakville. **G:** Cabernet Sauvignon. **P:** None.

Charles and Catherine Ball established this 8-acre, 1,000-case winery in the hills above Oakville in 1986, where they focus on Cabernet Sauvignon. The name Oakford combines Oakville and Rutherford. The wines are custom-crushed at Sunny St. Helena Winery.

TASTING NOTES

CABERNET NAPA VALLEY (★★★): Supple and well balanced, leaning toward elegant, with spicy currant flavors and mild tannins. No track record for aging.
1990: Solid and chunky, with pretty currant, spice and mineral flavors and light oak shadings. Firmly tannic. **88**
1989: Elegant, with spice, mint, earth and currant flavors, finishing with firm tannins. **84**
1988: Crisp and compact, with a band of pleasant cherry and currant flavors framed by light oak shadings. **87**
1987: Supple, complex and firm, with very ripe plum and cherry notes and firm tannins. **88**

OAKVILLE RANCH VINEYARDS
Oakville, Napa Valley
F: 1989. **O:** Mary Miner. **W:** Joe Cafaro. **S:** None.

OVERALL	$18-32	★★★★

WINE RATINGS

Cabernet Sauvignon Napa Valley	★★★★
Cabernet Sauvignon Napa Valley Lewis Select	★★★★
Cabernet Sauvignon Napa Valley Reserve	★★★★
Chardonnay Napa Valley ORV	★★★
Chardonnay Napa Valley Vista Vineyard	★★★

WINERY DATA
C: 4,000. **V:** 56 acres in Napa Valley. **G:** Cabernet Sauvignon (35 acres), Chardonnay (15), Merlot (4), Cabernet Franc (2). **P:** None.

This winery merges high tech with high speed. With his wife Mary, the late Bob Miner (founder of Oracle Systems Corp., the computer software giant) established the winery's 56 acres of Cabernet and Chardonnay in the hills east of Oakville, where they owned a 334-acre ranch. They started the winery with partners Debbie and Randy Lewis, the latter a former race car driver who once finished 14th in the Indianapolis 500. Quality, especially with Cabernet, has been exceptional under the direction of winemaker Joe Cafaro. Production is in the 4,000-case range, but is expected to grow as the vineyard matures. In 1994, Miner's death led to a breakup of the partnership with the Lewises, who formed their own wine brand, Lewis Cellars (see listing), retaining Cafaro as winemaker. Oakville Ranch, however is still worth watching.

TASTING NOTES

CABERNET SAUVIGNON NAPA VALLEY (★★★★): Dark, rich, plush and concentrated. Strong start; should age well.
1991: Serves up rich, supple, complex, ripe currant, cherry, plum and chocolate flavors, finishing with a good dose of oak. **90**
Reserve 1991: Packs in lots of black cherry, currant, mineral and spice flavors, turning smooth and supple on the palate, finishing with a long, rich, concentrated aftertaste. Mild tannins make it approachable, but it's best to cellar short-term into 1997. **92**
1990: Smooth, complex and stylish, with a strong, spicy streak of cedar, currant and plum aromas and flavors, and the finish is silky and elegant. **93**
1989: Dark, rich and potent, with intense, deeply concentrated currant, plum and berry flavors, spicy vanilla and oak shadings and fine tannins. **88**

CABERNET SAUVIGNON NAPA VALLEY LEWIS SELECT (★★★★): Impressive for its broad, rich, complex fruit flavors and mellow tannins. Appears well suited for mid-term aging.

1991: Ripe and plush, with rich currant, cherry and chocolate notes framed by toasty, buttery oak. Deep, complex and concentrated. **91**

CHARDONNAY NAPA VALLEY ORV (★★★): Consistently well made, intense and concentrated, with plenty of flavor and the right amount of oak.
1992: Ripe, smooth and creamy, with pretty pear and toasty oak flavors that turn smoky on the finish. **88**
1991: Intense and oaky, with concentrated pear, spice and citrus flavors that turn smooth and creamy. **88**

CHARDONNAY NAPA VALLEY VISTA VINEYARD (★★★):
1993: Elegant and understated with ripe pear and melon notes that turn smooth and polished on the finish. **90**
1992: A big, ripe, buttery wine with spicy pear, nectarine and vanilla flavors, picking up smoky notes on the finish. **87**
1991: Tight and firm, offering lemon, pear and grapefruit flavors that are lean and crisp. **88**

OBESTER WINERY
Mendocino County
F: 1977. **O:** Obester Winery Inc. **W:** Bruce Regalia.
S: Gemello Winery.

OVERALL	$8-15	★★

WINE RATINGS

Chardonnay Mendocino County	★★
Chardonnay Mendocino County Barrel Fermented	★
Gewürztraminer Anderson Valley	★★
Pinot Noir Anderson Valley	NR
Sangiovese Mendocino County	★★
Sauvignon Blanc Mendocino County	★★
Zinfandel Mendocino County	NR

WINERY DATA
C: 10,000. **V:** 10 acres in Anderson Valley, Mendocino County. **G:** Chardonnay (5 acres), Pinot Noir (3), Gewürztraminer (2). **P:** Zinfandel, Sauvignon Blanc, Sangiovese, Chardonnay, Pinot Noir (Mendocino County), Sémillon, Gewürztraminer (Anderson Valley), Johannisberg Riesling (Monterey County).

After a decade in Half Moon Bay south of San Francisco, Obester moved in 1989 to Anderson Valley in Mendocino County, where it produces 10,000 cases a year of Chardonnay, Gewürztraminer, Johannisberg Riesling, Pinot Noir, Sangiovese, Sauvignon Blanc, Sémillon and Zinfandel, primarily from purchased grapes. Quality has ranged from ordinary to good.

TASTING NOTES

CHARDONNAY MENDOCINO COUNTY (★★), BARREL FERMENTED (★): Variable; well oaked one year and austere the next. The Barrel Fermented bottling strays into earthier flavors and is less appealing.
1991: Austere and flinty but well focused, with a band of pear and apple flavors. Lively acidity on the finish keeps the flavors alive. **85**
1988: Offers lots of toasty, buttery oak, but has a core of nice pear and lemon flavors, too. Balanced, elegant and perfectly enjoyable. **83**
Barrel Fermented 1990: Sturdy and spicy, with earthy, buttery flavors that hint at pear somewhere in the middle. Drinkable, but not for everyone. **78**
Barrel Fermented 1989: Intense oak and vegetal flavors are difficult to warm up to, and the fruit is simple and turns watery. Barely decent. **71**

GEWÜRZTRAMINER ANDERSON VALLEY (★★): Off-dry, with just the right measure of spicy fruit flavors.
1992: Just barely off-dry, spicy and varietally correct, a good candidate for an apéritif. **84**

PINOT NOIR ANDERSON VALLEY (NR): The 1992 has a volatile edge that dominates the cherry notes.
1992: A wine with a vinegary, volatile edge that overshadows the raspberry and cherry flavors. Finishes with firm tannins. Perhaps cellaring a year will make it more appealing. **78**

SANGIOVESE MENDOCINO COUNTY (★★):
1993: Soft in texture, bright in flavor, with modest strawberry and mildly grapey character. **83**
1992: Intense but a little green, with spicy, assertive raspberry and earth flavors. Could use a little polish and finesse. **79**

SAUVIGNON BLANC MENDOCINO COUNTY (★★): Intense and well focused, with ripe flavors. Best of the lineup.
1993: Slightly raisiny, earthy edge to the modest fruit keeps this a little off balance. **80**

1992: Intense and focused on spicy grapefruit and pear flavors. Finishes with good length. **85**

1991: Smooth, round and ripe, offering solid pear and spice aromas and flavors shaded by an appropriate hint of herbs. All the right flavors linger on the finish. **85**

ZINFANDEL MENDOCINO COUNTY (NR): The 1991 is packed with intense cherry and raspberry flavors and high in alcohol.

1991: Intense and spicy, with bright cherry and raspberry flavors that take on a hot and jammy edge on the finish. Despite firm tannins, it's developing a supple texture. The label claims it's 16 percent alcohol. **84**

OCTOPUS MOUNTAIN
Anderson Valley
F: 1989. **O:** Pete and Will Dennison. **W:** Pete and Will Dennison. **S:** None.

OVERALL	$9-14	★★

WINE RATINGS	
Cabernet Sauvignon Anderson Valley	
Dennison Vineyard	★★
Chardonnay Anderson Valley	
Dennison Vineyard	★★
Pinot Noir Anderson Valley	
Dennison Vineyard	★★

WINERY DATA
C: 5,000. **V:** N/A. **G:** Cabernet Sauvignon, Chardonnay, Pinot Noir, Riesling. **P:** N/A.

This winery uses Anderson Valley grapes from Dennison Vineyard for its Cabernet, Chardonnay and Pinot Noir, each of which deserves decent marks. A portion of the Dennison family's grapes are sold to wineries including Edmeades, Steele and Briceland.

TASTING NOTES

CABERNET SAUVIGNON ANDERSON VALLEY DENNISON VINEYARD (★★): Solid if unexciting; Cabernet often struggles to ripen in Anderson Valley.

1991: Ripe and intense, with a grapey currant and cherry edge to the flavors, finishing with firm tannins. **82**

1989: Pretty plum, currant and cherry flavors are ripe and rich but also tight and hard, with firm tannins that are a bit green. Has good intensity but could use a bit more depth. **83**

CHARDONNAY ANDERSON VALLEY DENNISON VINEYARD (★★):
1990: Light and lively, with definite butterscotch overtones to the crisp green apple and spice aromas and flavors, finishing with a smack of lemon. A pleasant drink with real character. **84**

PINOT NOIR ANDERSON VALLEY DENNISON VINEYARD (★★): Light in style, but the flavors are appealing.
1991: Light and elegant, with fine plum and blackberry flavors that shine through the soft, plush texture. **85**
1989: Pretty, light and smooth, with appealing plum, cherry and spice aromas and flavors, crisp balance and polished, soft tannins to round it out. **86**

THE OJAI VINEYARD
Santa Barbara County
F: 1983. **O:** Adam Tolmach & Helen Hardenbergh. **W:** Adam Tolmach. **S:** None.

OVERALL	$15-25	★★★

WINE RATINGS	
Chardonnay Arroyo Grande Valley	★★★
Chardonnay Arroyo Grande Valley	
Reserve	★★★
Chardonnay Santa Barbara County	★★★
Chardonnay Santa Barbara County	
Reserve	★★★
Pinot Noir Santa Barbara County	★★
Syrah California	★★★

WINERY DATA
C: 4,500. **V:** 5.5 acres in California. **G:** Syrah (2.5 acres), Sauvignon Blanc (2), Sémillon (1). **P:** Pinot Noir, Chardonnay, Sauvignon Blanc, Sémillon, Syrah (Santa Barbara County), Chardonnay (Arroyo Grande).

Adam and Helen Tolmach were partners at Au Bon Climat before branching out and developing their own 5.5-acre vineyard in Ventura's Ojai Valley. This 4,500-case winery offers a wide array of wines made in small case lots, including two vineyard-designated Chardonnays (Bien Nacido and Talley, with a Reserve bottling of each), Pinot Noir (Bien Nacido), Sauvignon Blanc (California and Buttonwood Farms) and Syrah (California), the latter being the wine most connoisseurs associate with Ojai. Quality is very good, but short of outstanding.

TASTING NOTES

CHARDONNAY ARROYO GRANDE VALLEY (★★★), RESERVE (★★★): Variable in style, ranging from well oaked to more directly fruity, but usually well balanced and appealing. The Reserve bottlings show more oak.
1993: A medium-bodied style with a modest range of spice, pear and light oak shadings. Holds together through the finish. **86**
Reserve 1992: An oaky wine with rich honey, apricot, pear and smoky oak flavors. **88**
Reserve 1991: Heavy oak flavors are present throughout, but there's also a nice core of spicy pear flavors that give it added complexity. **87**

CHARDONNAY SANTA BARBARA COUNTY (★★★), RESERVE (★★★):
1992: Clean and correct, with spicy pear, honey, pine and oak shadings. **88**
1991: An oaky wine that serves up spicy pear and tropical fruit flavors. **84**
Reserve 1993: Ripe and appealing, with spicy pear, pineapple and melon notes that are moderately complex, folding together on the finish. **87**
Reserve 1992: Compact and flavorful, with pear, toast and spice flavors that hang with you. **86**

PINOT NOIR SANTA BARBARA COUNTY (★★):
1993: Well balanced, with ripe plum, black cherry and vanilla shadings, focused and flavorful. Finishes with tight tannins. **86**

SYRAH CALIFORNIA (★★★★): Consistently well made, with distinctive peppery notes.
1992: Distinctively spicy and peppery, it serves up complex black cherry, plum and cedar flavors. **84**
1991: Broad in texture and bright in flavor, with distinctive black pepper, cherry and raspberry flavors. **87**

OPTIMA
Sonoma County
F: 1984. **O:** Greg Smith. **W:** Michael Duffy. **S:** None.

OVERALL	$25-30	★★★

WINE RATINGS
Cabernet Sauvignon Alexander Valley	★★★
Chardonnay Sonoma County	★★★

WINERY DATA
C: 2,300. **V:** None. **G:** None. **P:** Cabernet Sauvignon, Cabernet Franc, Merlot, Petite Sirah, Zinfandel (Sonoma County), Chardonnay (Carneros).

This is a partnership between Mike Duffy, winemaker at Field Stone, and Greg Smith, who now owns Fitch Mountain Winery. Optima, which began as a Cabernet-only venture, relies on purchased grapes from Field Stone's vineyards in Alexander Valley, even though the label has shown both Sonoma County and Alexander Valley appellations. Chardonnay from Carneros joined the lineup in 1989. Quality has been high, as the Cabernets in particular are ripe and well oaked. A tasting of all the wines in 1994, however, showed they had not aged well at all.

TASTING NOTES

CABERNET SAUVIGNON ALEXANDER VALLEY (★★★): The early wines were very showy on release, with opulent fruit and buttery oak flavors, but age has not been kind. Best to drink early on.
1991: Young and tight, but it opens to reveal pretty, ripe black cherry and currant flavors that stay rich and focused. **88**
1990: Tannic and oaky, with spicy currant, chocolate and berry flavors, but it lacks focus and harmony. **82**
1989: Earthy and metallic, with dry, raisiny flavors. **79**
1988: Oaky, with berry and currant flavors that turn simple. **84**
1987: The lavish, buttery oak dominates the currant and berry flavors. **83**
1986: Coarse and oaky, with firm tannins and hints of currant. Tough, dry and chewy. **79**
1985: Mature, with earthy flavors and hints of currant and cedar. **81**

1984: Aging well, with fresh, ripe currant, plum and mint notes and drying tannins. **87**

CHARDONNAY SONOMA COUNTY (★★★): Shares the Cabernet's ripe intensity and heavy oak.

1992: Toasty, cedary oak dominates, but there are hints of pear and spice flavors. **85**

1991: Ripe, smooth, rich and concentrated, with layers of pear, spice, honey and vanilla flavors. Shows a good measure of finesse and grace. **89**

OPUS ONE

Oakville, Napa Valley

F: 1979. **O:** Baroness Philippine de Rothschild & Robert Mondavi. **W:** Genevieve Janssens. **S:** None.

OVERALL	$75	★★★★★

WINE RATINGS

Cabernet Blend Napa Valley Opus One	★★★★★

WINERY DATA

C: 23,000. **V:** 108 acres in Oakville, Napa Valley. **G:** Cabernet Sauvignon, Cabernet Franc (Napa Valley). **P:** None.

Opus One is the celebrated joint venture between Robert Mondavi Winery in Napa Valley and the late Baron Philippe de Rothschild of Château Mouton-Rothschild in Pauillac, France, who died in 1988. It is the marriage of two great winemaking families as well as two fortunes: the winery cost roughly $20 million and the families own 108 acres of expensive vineyard land in the Oakville area. With the first vintage in 1979, Opus One set out to downplay Cabernet's aggressive flavors, aiming more for elegance and finesse. The style that has evolved since features more classic Napa Valley Cabernet flavors and expensive oak shadings, but also a core of rich, complex fruit flavors. Production has risen to 23,000 cases and at $65 a bottle, it remains one of California's most expensive wines. Opus One's grapes now come entirely from winery-owned vineyards in Oakville. Quality is uniformly sensational. Genevieve Janssens oversees winemaking production.

TASTING NOTES

CABERNET BLEND NAPA VALLEY OPUS ONE (★★★★★): Increasingly reliant on estate-grown Cabernet (now 95 percent of the blend), it features bold, ripe, rich and complex flavors and generally supple tannins, although with the 1991 vintage it appeared the winery was aiming to build more longevity into the wine. Early vintages have aged only moderately well; the wine reaches an early drinking pleateau. Best within the first few years of its life.

1991: Rich and tannic, a potent wine that shows dense currant, anise and black cherry flavors before picking up a chalky chocolate edge on the finish. **93**

1990: A chunky, chewy, sturdy wine that shows perfumed currant and berry flavors, all wrapped in several layers of fine tannins. Complex and concentrated. **94**

1989: Firm and flavorful, with generous, ripe currant, blackberry and cherry flavors shaded by spicy oak and a touch of earth. Firmly tannic. **89**

1988: Ripe, rich and focused, with solid vanilla, spice, currant, plum and blackberry flavors that reverberate on the long finish. Well integrated tannins. **90**

1987: A great marriage of fruit and oak, with amazingly deep, rich, concentrated currant, black cherry, anise and plum flavors that keep on developing. Supple tannins. **98**

1986: Amazingly rich and concentrated, with beautiful currant, plum, black cherry, herb and spice flavors that are elegant and sharply defined. The tannins are softening. **96**

1985: The best of the early Opus Ones, it's fully mature and complex, with rich, ripe supple currant, anise and black cherry flavors, finishing with soft tannins. **94**

1984: Mature, with the rich, complex currant, black cherry, cedar and anise flavors turning a touch earthy. Tannins are smooth and polished. **92**

1983: Fully mature and declining, this is still a fine bottle of wine, but drink soon because the ripe fruit is fading. **88**

1982: Mature and taking on an earthy currant and anise edge. Drinking well now, but the tannins are drying. **88**

1981: Has peaked, with dry, earthy, complex currant and berry flavors, but it has shed its youthful charm and should be consumed soon. **88**

1980: Still big and ripe but softening, allowing the currant, anise, cedar and spice flavors to flow. Mature. **89**

1979: Showing its age, with the earthy side of the currant and cherry flavors showing. Mature and a shade past its prime. **88**

ORGANIC WINE WORKS

This is a second label of Hallcrest Vineyards (see listing).

PACHECO RANCH WINERY

Novato, Marin County
F: 1979. **O:** Rowland, Meves & Schultes Partners. **W:** John S. O'Neill, T. J. Meves. **S:** None.

OVERALL	$10	★
WINE RATINGS		
Cabernet Sauvignon Marin County		★

WINERY DATA
C: 1,000. **V:** 7 acres in Marin County. **G:** Cabernet Sauvignon (7 acres). **P:** None.

This winery is located on a 100-acre ranch in Ignacio in northern Marin County, where Cabernet Sauvignon is planted. My last note is for the 1985 vintage (76), which is marked by strong menthol flavors and an odd smoky, medicinal edge. Production is around 1,000 cases.

PAGE MILL WINERY

Los Altos Hills, Santa Clara County
F: 1976. **O:** Richard, Alison & Diane Stark. **W:** Richard Stark, Diane Stark. **S:** None.

OVERALL	$12-18	★★
WINE RATINGS		
Cabernet Sauvignon Napa Valley V. & L. Eisele Vineyard		★★
Chardonnay California Cuvée Select		★★
Chardonnay Santa Barbara County Bien Nacido Vineyard		★★
Chardonnay Santa Clara County Elizabeth Garbett Vineyard		★★
Pinot Noir Santa Barbara County Bien Nacido Vineyard		★★

WINERY DATA
C: 3,000. **V:** None. **G:** None. **P:** Sauvignon Blanc (San Luis Obispo), Pinot Noir (Santa Maria Valley), Chardonnay (Santa Clara County), Cabernet Sauvignon (Napa Valley).

Owner-winemaker Richard Stark buys grapes from throughout California for this 3,000-case winery, which he founded in 1976. Quality has varied significantly; most of the time the wines are average to good. Cabernet comes from Volker Eisele Vineyard in Chiles Valley, Chardonnay is from Santa Clara, Pinot Noir is from Bien Nacido in Santa Maria and Sauvignon Blanc comes from San Luis Obispo.

TASTING NOTES

CABERNET SAUVIGNON NAPA VALLEY V. & L. EISELE VINEYARD (★★): Good in 1988, but heavily oaked in 1989.
1989: Strong woody aromas turn to dry, woody flavors on the palate. Doesn't quite have the fruit concentration to match the oak. **74**
1988: Ripe and spicy, with currant and plum flavors that are well balanced for a 1988. Finishes with a firm, tannic edge, but there's a fruity aftertaste. **84**

CHARDONNAY VARIOUS BOTTLINGS (★★): Variable; the 1991 Bien Nacido is appealing, while the 1992 California misses the mark.
California Cuvée Select 1992: Light and spicy, with generous, focused, slightly sweet, nutty pear flavors. The finish is soft, with a touch of honey. **79**
Santa Barbara County Bien Nacido Vineyard 1991: Intense and sharply focused, with rich, lively lemon, pear, butter and nutmeg flavors, all of which adds up to a complex and engaging wine. **88**
Santa Clara County Elizabeth Garbett Vineyard 1992: Simple, fruity and spicy, showing focused pear, peach and honey aromas and flavors that glide smoothly to a satisfying finish, echoing fruit and honey. **86**

PINOT NOIR SANTA BARBARA COUNTY BIEN NACIDO VINEYARD (★★): Reflects the vineyard's cola, herb, earth and cherry flavors in a medium-bodied style.
1991: Firm, ripe, broad, complex and well balanced, with a spicy aftertaste and mild tannins. Approachable now, but worthy of cellaring through 2000. **86**
1990: Spicy, with herb and cola aromas and earthy, leathery cherry flavors. A supple wine that does not appear to have the depth, richness or concentration for extended cellaring. **84**

PAHLMEYER
Napa Valley
F: 1985. **O:** Jayson Pahlmeyer. **W:** Jayson Pahlmeyer, Helen Turley. **S:** None.

OVERALL	$24-34	★★★

WINE RATINGS

Cabernet Blend Napa Valley	★★★★
Chardonnay Napa Valley	★★★
Merlot Napa Valley Caldwell Vineyard	★★

WINERY DATA
C: 4,000. **V:** None. **G:** None. **P:** Cabernet Sauvignon, Malbec (Napa Valley), Chardonnay (Napa Valley), Cabernet Franc (Napa Valley), Merlot (Napa Valley), Petite Verdot (Napa Valley), Malbec (Napa Valley).

Lawyer Jayson Pahlmeyer found he was reading more wine journals than law journals, so he changed careers in 1985, teaming up first with vineyard owner John Caldwell (Caldwell Vineyard) and then Randy Dunn, who oversaw winemaking through the 1992 vintage. Most of Caldwell Vineyard is planted to Cabernet, with smaller portions of Merlot, Cabernet Franc and other Bordeaux varieties. The vineyard is located in the Coombsville area east of the city of Napa, which yields a distinctively austere and firmly tannic wine. After 1993, Pahlmeyer stopped buying Caldwell Vineyard Cabernet and signed on with several new vineyards, so it's likely the wine style will change—perhaps considerably, since Helen Turley became winemaker in 1993. Worth watching.

TASTING NOTES

CABERNET BLEND NAPA VALLEY (★★★★): Uniformly high quality, intense, complex and concentrated, with firm tannins and an austere edge to the flavors. Ages well, but the track record is limited. Has carried several designations over the years.
1992: Dense and chewy, with complex currant, herb and tobacco notes that turn supple despite youthful tannins. **88**
1991: Dense and compact, firmly tannic and hard-edged, with just a glimpse of currant and cherry pushing through on the finish. Needs time, but may always be dry and tannic. **84**
1990: Ripe and intense, with pretty herb, mint, spice and currant flavors, picking up tobacco and cherry notes on a tannic finish. **90**

Minty Cuvée 1990: Potently minty, a flavor that overrides all else, with just a hint of currant and cedar emerging on the finish. For fans of mint-dominated Cabernet. **82**
1989: Deeply colored, austere and complex, with rich currant, spice, mineral and oak shadings that are intense. **88**
1988: Deeply concentrated, intense and flavorful, with lively currant, mint, cherry and oak flavors that combine to give it complexity and richness. Firmly tannic. **90**
1987: Elegant, rich and complex, with wonderful aromas and spicy currant, black cherry and cedar flavors, finishing with a long, lean aftertaste. **91**
1986: Tight and firm, with spicy currant, anise and cedar flavors that are sharply focused, lean and disciplined. Still youthful and compact. **89**

CHARDONNAY NAPA VALLEY (★★★): The 1991 was sensational on release, but it quickly faded to a rather good—not extraordinary Chardonnay. Subsequent vintages are more ordinary.
1993: Strikes a nice balance between spicy oak and ripe pear, peach and pineapple-laced flavors, finishing with good depth and richness. **89**
1992: Mature in color and flavor, with slightly oxidized pear, honey and toast flavors that turn rich and smoky on the finish. **86**
1991: A sensational wine that defines Burgundian complexity, with spicy pear, hazelnut and butterscotch flavors, a creamy texture and a long, full finish. **90**

MERLOT NAPA VALLEY CALDWELL VINEYARD (★★): Austere and tight, with modest flavors and ample tannins. Not in the same class as the red table wine.
1991: Tight and firm, an austere and youthful wine with an earthy, cedary edge to the herb and currant flavors. **83**
1990: Austere and tight, showing a narrow band of cedar, currant, herb and tobacco flavors. Pleasant and well balanced, with firm tannins, but the flavors taper off on the finish. The first Merlot from Pahlmeyer. **85**

PARADIGM
Oakville, Napa Valley
F: 1975. **O:** Ren & Marilyn Harris. **W:** Heidi Peterson Barrett. **S:** None.

OVERALL	$28	★★★

WINE RATINGS

Cabernet Sauvignon Napa Valley   ★★★

WINERY DATA

C: 2,500. V: 50 acres in Oakville. G: Cabernet Sauvignon (28 acres), Merlot (18), Cabernet Franc (2), Zinfandel (2). P: None.

This vineyard was established in 1975, but in 1991 Ren and Marilyn Harris bought the property and established the Paradigm label for limited-production Cabernet Sauvignon. The vineyard, located in Oakville, has 50 acres in vines and is planted to Cabernet (28), Merlot (18), Cabernet Franc (2) and Zinfandel (2), most of which are sold to other wineries. Heidi Peterson Barrett (Dalla Valle) is winemaker, and Cabernet production is in the 2,500-case range. Zinfandel (150 cases) is also in the works. Worth watching.

TASTING NOTES

CABERNET SAUVIGNON NAPA VALLEY (★★★): Solid effort in 1991 as it is well focused, with complex flavors. **1991:** Firm, supple and complex, with pretty anise, currant and cherry flavors framed by toasty, smoky oak. Impressive for its richness and depth. **90**

PARAISO SPRINGS VINEYARDS
Monterey County

F: 1987. O: Richard & Claudia Smith. W: Philip Zorn. S: None.

OVERALL   **$7-20**   ★★

WINE RATINGS

Chardonnay Santa Lucia Highlands Barrel Fermented	★★
Gewürztraminer Santa Lucia Highlands	★★
Johannisberg Riesling Santa Lucia Highlands Late Harvest Hand Selected	★★
Pinot Blanc Monterey County	★★
Pinot Noir Carneros	★

WINERY DATA

C: 4,500. V: 200 acres in Santa Lucia Highlands. G: Chardonnay (63 acres), Pinot Blanc (9), Pinot Noir (52), Gewürztraminer (25), Johannisberg Riesling (51). P: None.

In 1987, Richard and Claudia Smith founded Paraiso Springs after developing a 200-acre vineyard planted primarily to white wine varieties, led by Chardonnay (63 acres) and Johannisberg Riesling (51) but also containing 52 acres of Pinot Noir. Quality has ranged from ordinary to good, with production at 4,500 cases.

TASTING NOTES

VARIOUS BOTTLINGS:

Chardonnay Monterey County Barrel Fermented 1991: Earthy and buttery notes override the spicy pear and fig flavors, but the flavors grow on you after a couple of sips. Especially appealing if you like your Chardonnays with buttery oak. **84**

Chardonnay Santa Lucia Highlands Barrel Fermented 1993: Well oaked, with a grapey perfumed aroma, turning more complex and focused on the finish where the citrus, pear and toasty oak flavors turn elegant. **86**

Gewürztraminer Santa Lucia Highlands 1993: With its rose petal and pear aromas and flavors, this fairly dry wine performs lightly and appealingly through the fine finish. **84**

Johannisberg Riesling Santa Lucia Highlands Late Harvest Hand Selected 1993: Light, sweet and very smooth, a little sugary but the floral apricot flavors sneak in on the finish. Best from 1997. **85**

Pinot Blanc Monterey County 1991: Crisp and spicy around a light core of pear and apple flavors. **82**

Pinot Noir Carneros 1991: Tough and tannic, with an earthy bite and not much fruit. Simple at best. **77**

PARDUCCI WINE CELLARS
Mendocino County

F: 1933. O: TMI Inc. W: Tom Monostori. S: None.

OVERALL   **$5-15**   ★★

WINE RATINGS

Cabernet Franc Mendocino County	★★
Cabernet Sauvignon Mendocino County	★★
Chardonnay Mendocino County	★★
Merlot North Coast	★★
Petite Sirah Mendocino County	★★
Pinot Noir Mendocino County	★★

Red Table Wine Mendocino County
   Bono-Sirah   ★★
Sauvignon Blanc North Coast   ★★
Zinfandel Mendocino County   ★★

WINERY DATA

C: 400,000. **V:** 262 acres in Mendocino County. **G:** Chardonnay (81 acres), Sauvignon Blanc (34), Chenin Blanc (7), Cabernet Sauvignon (24), Merlot (35), Sémillon (11), Flora (12), Zinfandel (13), French Colombard (15), Other Red (30). **P:** None.

The Parducci family settled in wooded Mendocino County at the turn of the century, pioneering grapegrowing and winemaking in most of the appellations that are now associated with Mendocino wines. In 1933 the Parduccis started their winery, buying and growing grapes for a wide variety of wines. By the 1960s and 1970s, John Parducci had tested, proved and disproved many theories about winegrowing in Mendocino, laying the foundation for modern-day thinking about what grows best where. He was also a leader in using new techniques such as barrel fermentation, *sur lie* aging and blending Merlot with Cabernet. The winery excelled with red wines, finding Petite Sirah, Cabernet Sauvignon and Zinfandel ideally suited for many areas in Mendocino, but found itself out of style in the 1970s as the white wine boom hit. By 1972, the Parducci family needed cash and sold the winery to Teachers Management & Investment (TMI Inc.), which retained the Parduccis to run the winery; but a long-running management dispute led to John Parducci's departure in 1994 and subsequent battle for control of the winery, which Parducci lost in 1995. The winery owns 262 acres of vines and produces some 400,000 cases of wine, excelling at Sauvignon Blanc; most of the lineup is clean, correct and balanced, with modest varietal character. The Cellarmaster Selection wines are richer and oakier. Always good values.

TASTING NOTES

CABERNET FRANC MENDOCINO COUNTY (★★):
1989: Firm and fruity, with a velvety texture and generous currant and vanilla aromas and flavors that persist on the finish. **85**

CABERNET SAUVIGNON MENDOCINO COUNTY (★★): Light and herbal with spicy Cabernet flavors and mild tannins.

1991: Smooth and polished, with more depth and character than this wine's had in previous vintages, showing off ripe plum and smoky oak flavors. **84**
1989: Soft and fruity, a sturdy wine that offers a mouthful of berry and anise flavors. The finish is simple and straightforward. **84**

CHARDONNAY MENDOCINO COUNTY (★★): A fruity style that doesn't emphasize oak.
1993: Tart and green, with crisp pear and apple notes. For fans of Chardonnay without oak. **81**
1991: Simple, fruity and lively, offering nice lemon and apple flavors and a touch of vanilla. **81**

MERLOT NORTH COAST (★★): Supple and well balanced, with light herb and currant notes.
1992: Bright and fruity and a little chewy, but generous with its currant and blackberry flavors. **85**
1990: Firm in texture and a bit tannic, with nice currant and cedar flavors struggling to emerge. **82**

PETITE SIRAH MENDOCINO COUNTY (★★): Medium-weight, but with the right pepper and berry notes.
1991: A little chewy, with vanilla-scented strawberry and plum flavors that linger sweetly on the finish. **84**
1989: Has a firm texture, with a solid core of blackberry flavor poking through the layer of tannins. **80**

PINOT NOIR MENDOCINO COUNTY (★★): Light and elegant, but pleasant enough.
1992: Snappy and grapey, like a Beaujolais with its cherry notes, but enjoyable on those terms. **83**
1990: Light and elegant, with pretty berry, cherry and spice flavors that are well focused, crisp acidity and soft tannins. **85**
1988: Light and delicate, with fresh, lively cherry and berry aromas and flavors and overtones of vanilla and spice. **85**
Cellarmaster Selection 1987: Gentle and fragrant, offering lovely spice, berry and currant aromas and flavors shaded by a touch of tea on the finish. **84**

RED TABLE WINE MENDOCINO COUNTY BONO-SIRAH (★★):
1990: Soft and fruity, with exuberant plum, blackberry and currant aromas and flavors, hinting at vanilla and spice on the finish. An appealing blend of 70 percent Charbono with Carignane and Petite Sirah. **82**

SAUVIGNON BLANC NORTH COAST (★★): Serves up pure varietal character, but avoids excesses.

1993: Simple, floral flavors on a lean frame. **79**

1990: Tart and fresh, with peach, herb and fig notes that are tasty and lingering. **82**

ZINFANDEL MENDOCINO COUNTY (★★): Elegant with wild berry and spicy notes.

1992: Crisp and a bit woody, with the oak overshadowing the light berry flavors. **82**

1991: Despite an earthy, gamy edge, this is a solid glass of Zinfandel with rustic spice and berry flavors. **82**

1990: Lean and crisp, with a narrow band of cherry and spice notes that turn tannic. **83**

FESS PARKER WINERY
Santa Barbara County
F: 1987. **O:** Fess & Eli Parker. **W:** Eli Parker, Jed Steele. **S:** None.

OVERALL	$9-18	★★★

WINE RATINGS

Chardonnay Santa Barbara County	★★★
Chardonnay Santa Barbara County American Tradition Reserve	★★★
Johannisberg Riesling Santa Barbara County	★★
Pinot Noir Santa Barbara County	★★
Syrah Santa Barbara County	★★

WINERY DATA
C: 25,000. **V:** 19 acres in Santa Barbara County. **G:** Chardonnay (13.5 acres), Riesling, Merlot, Syrah, Viognier, Marsanne. **P:** None.

Retired actor Fess Parker, famous for his roles as Davey Crockett and Daniel Boone, produces, with his family, 25,000 cases of wine from a mixture of estate-grown and purchased grapes from the Central Coast and Santa Barbara County appellations. Parker's son, Eli, is the winemaker, coached by consultant Jed Steele (Steele Wines). The product mix includes Chardonnay, a Muscat Canelli dessert wine, Merlot, Pinot Noir, Riesling and Syrah, with reserve-style wines carrying the American Tradition designation. All the wines were on solid ground as of 1994, with Chardonnay holding an edge in quality, and a new Syrah impressive out of barrel.

TASTING NOTES

CHARDONNAY SANTA BARBARA COUNTY (★★★), AMERICAN TRADITION RESERVE (★★★): Made in a ripe, round and generous style, emphasizing the fruit.

1993: Forward, ripe and generous, with pretty pear, peach and spice flavors that are broad and complex. **87**

1992: Ripe peach and pear flavors turn creamy and spicy. **85**

American Tradition Reserve 1993: Smooth and polished, with ripe pear, honey and spice notes, framed by light toasty oak shadings. **88**

American Tradition Reserve 1992: Ripe and round, a generous wine with a smooth texture and plenty of pear and spice flavors at the core. **88**

JOHANNISBERG RIESLING SANTA BARBARA COUNTY (★★):

1993: Light, refreshing and a little sweet, with appealing peach and apple flavors. **84**

PINOT NOIR SANTA BARBARA COUNTY (★★): The 1993 was supple, with exotic berry, cherry and plum flavors.

1993: Supple and fruity, with exotic wild berry, cherry and plum flavors. **86**

SYRAH SANTA BARBARA COUNTY (★★): Based on the first vintages and barrel samples, this could be a wine to watch from Parker, as it serves up lots of flavor.

1992: Ripe and succulent, a sturdy wine with plum, berry and spice flavors that turn silky. **85**

PATZ & HALL WINE CO.
Napa Valley
F: 1988. **O:** Patz & Hall Wine Co. **W:** James Hall. **S:** None.

OVERALL	$25-30	★★★★★

WINE RATINGS

Chardonnay Napa Valley	★★★★★

WINERY DATA
C: 1,200. **V:** None. **G:** None. **P:** Chardonnay (Napa Valley, Carneros, Mt. Veeder), Pinot Noir (Russian River Valley).

Donald Patz, marketing director for Girard, and James Hall, winemaker at Honig and for Rocking Horse, met while working at Flora Springs Winery. In 1988, they pooled $5,000 each in capital and started their own brand, aiming for a distinctive Burgundian

style of Chardonnay. Despite that shoestring budget, they found two solid grape sources: Caldwell Vineyard in Coombsville, east of Napa, and Hyde Vineyard in Carneros. As the 1988 harvest ended, John Caldwell had extra grapes and offered them to Patz & Hall on a pay-when-you-can basis. That gave them more fruit than they anticipated and they needed more barrel space, so they borrowed $20,000 from Hall's father. Production has increased to 1,200 cases for the 1992 vintage, up from 1,000 in 1991. Patz and Hall are considering adding a second Chardonnay that may carry a vineyard designation, as well as a red wine, with Pinot Noir a candidate.

TASTING NOTES

CHARDONNAY NAPA VALLEY (★★★★★): Full-blown Burgundian techniques and toasty, buttery oak add texture and flavor dimension to the ripe and succulent fruit. Serves up lots of up front flavor right on release.
1993: Delivers a mouthful of ripe pear, peach, honey and hazelnut flavors, turning rich and elegant on the finish where the flavors persist. Beautifully crafted. **91**
1992: Spicy, rich and generous, with complex and distinctive nectarine, vanilla and spice aromas and flavors. **91**
1991: Wonderfully complex, with bold, ripe, concentrated pear, fig, citrus and vanilla flavors that are deep and intense. A real mouthful. **92**

PEACHY CANYON WINERY
Paso Robles
F: 1987. **O:** Douglas & Nancy Beckett. **W:** Douglas Beckett, Robert Nadeau. **S:** None.

OVERALL	$12-22	★★★

WINE RATINGS
Cabernet Sauvignon Central Coast	★★★
Cabernet Sauvignon Paso Robles	★★★
Merlot Paso Robles	★★★
Zinfandel Paso Robles	★★★
Zinfandel Paso Robles Dusi Ranch	★★★
Zinfandel Paso Robles Especial	★★★
Zinfandel Paso Robles Westside	★★★

WINERY DATA
C: 5,000. **V:** 8 acres in Paso Robles. **G:** Zinfandel.
P: Zinfandel (Paso Robles), Zinfandel (El Dorado), Merlot (Paso Robles), Cabernet Sauvignon (Central Coast).

Doug Beckett owned a chain of liquor stores before turning to winemaking, first buying land in Paso Robles and a then taking a stab at home winemaking. In 1987, Peachy Canyon released its first wines, with Beckett focusing on old-vine Cabernet Sauvignon and Zinfandel, including a vineyard-designated Dusi Ranch bottling, long a source of excellent Zinfandel for Ridge Vineyards. Merlot was added in 1992, but Zinfandel is still the specialty, with four bottlings: Dusi Ranch, Especial, Old Vine and Westside. Quality is high, with wines that consistently feature bold, bright and ripe, juicy flavors. Worth watching.

TASTING NOTES

CABERNET SAUVIGNON CENTRAL COAST (★★★): Has carried both the Central Coast and Paso Robles appellations, with wines that are ripe and juicy, with bright, lush flavors.
1992: A very ripe wine with intense black cherry and berry flavors. Finishes with firm tannins. **87**
1991: Bold, ripe, intense and fleshy, with gorgeous cherry, currant and plum flavors, picking up an earthy, herbal edge on the finish. Mildly tannic. **90**
1990: Tough, tannic and chewy, with tight plum and raspberry flavors and spicy oak seasoning. **85**

MERLOT PASO ROBLES (★★★):
1992: Well oaked, but the ripe plum and cherry-laced fruit stands up to it, turning complex and elegant on the finish, where the flavors marry well. **91**

ZINFANDEL PASO ROBLES (★★★):
1989: A racy wine with wild berry and beet flavors that are a little off the mark. **80**

ZINFANDEL PASO ROBLES DUSI RANCH (★★★):
1992: Lean, with a narrow band of earthy, spicy flavors. Not as rich and supple as the regular bottling, but the flavors build on the finish. **85**

ZINFANDEL PASO ROBLES ESPECIAL (★★★):
Consistently bright and lively, with lush cherry and wild berry flavors framed by spicy new oak.
1991: Bright and lively, with ripe, tart, jammy cherry and raspberry flavors that linger. **85**
1990: The stamp of spicy new oak gives style to this full-bodied, firmly tannic, very fruity Zinfandel with berry and cherry flavors. **90**
1989: Ripe, supple and generous, with layers of plum, black cherry and spice flavors. **89**

ZINFANDEL PASO ROBLES WESTSIDE (★★★):
1992: Supple and generous, with pretty, ripe cherry and blackberry flavors that are complex and concentrated. **88**
1991: Ripe, almost sweet-tasting, packed with berry and cherry flavors, finishing with gnarly tannins. **84**
1990: Ripe and bold, with bright, vivid blackberry, plum, prune and spice flavors. **91**

ROBERT PECOTA WINERY
Calistoga, Napa Valley
F: 1978. **O:** Robert Pecota. **W:** Robert Pecota. **S:** None.

OVERALL	$7-20	★★★

WINE RATINGS

Cabernet Sauvignon Napa Valley	
Kara's Vineyard	★★★
Merlot Napa Valley	
Steven Andre Vineyard	★★★
Muscat Napa Valley Muscato di Andrea	★★★
Muscat Napa Valley Sweet Andrea Select	★★★
Sauvignon Blanc Napa Valley	★★★

WINERY DATA
C: 20,000. **V:** 50 acres in Napa Valley. **G:** Sauvignon Blanc (17 acres), Cabernet Sauvignon (13), Merlot (20). **P:** Muscat, Cabernet Franc, Gamay Beaujolais (Napa Valley).

Robert Pecota worked for Beringer Vineyards in the 1970s, developing vineyards and buying grapes before starting his winery in 1978. He focused initially on Chardonnay, Muscat Canelli, and Cabernet Sauvignon, including the 10-acre vineyard-designated Kara's Vineyard, named after his daughter. Pecota added a Steven Andre Merlot in 1989, named after his son. A Canepa Vineyard Chardonnay from Alexander Valley, produced for a decade, has been dropped. Pecota owns 50 acres of vineyard, dominated by Merlot (20 acres), Cabernet (13 acres) and Sauvignon Blanc (17 acres). Production is 20,000 cases, and includes well crafted Cabernet, Merlot and Muscat Canelli. Sauvignon Blanc has been more variable.

TASTING NOTES

CABERNET SAUVIGNON NAPA VALLEY KARA'S VINEYARD (★★★): Made in a supple, polished, moderately tannic style, it can hit highs, as in 1987 and 1991, and even the 1988 was superior to the vintage.
1991: Fresh and lively, with ripe currant, berry and spice flavors and fine but firm tannins, turning complex and elegant. **90**
1990: A lighter 1990 with supple herb, cherry and currant notes that turn smooth and moderately oaky on the finish. **85**
1989: Firm and tight, with smoky cedar and currant flavors that turn hard, tannic and astringent. **78**
1988: Smooth and generous, with well proportioned black cherry, currant and plum flavors shaded by herb, bay leaf and chocolate notes. Supple tannins. **89**
1987: Serves up pretty, ripe black cherry, toast and spice notes, but the tannins really clamp down on the finish, where it turns austere. **90**
1986: Mature, with supple black cherry, currant and spice nuances that linger. **87**
1985: Lean and crisp, with a narrow band of black cherry and currant flavors in a modest, not-too-tannic style. **85**
1984: Brimming with fresh, ripe, supple black cherry and berry flavors. Mature. **85**
1982: Mature, with an earthy edge to the berry, cherry and spicy oak flavors. **83**

MERLOT NAPA VALLEY STEVEN ANDRE VINEYARD (★★★): Shows the same polish and finesse as the Cabernet, featuring ripe flavors and ample oak shadings.
1992: Ripe and oaky but well proportioned, with pretty cherry and currant notes that blend in well with the wood and tannins. **87**

1991: Smooth, supple and complex, with pretty, toasty, buttery oak aromas, ripe cherry and plum flavors and soft tannins. **89**

1990: Ripe and plush, with rich currant, plum and herb flavors and pretty toasty, vanilla oak nuances. **88**

1989: Has appealing blackberry and currant flavors, but tastes hard and a bit woody. **86**

MUSCAT NAPA VALLEY MUSCATO DI ANDREA (★★★): Light and sweet, drinks well early.

1992: Light and delicately sweet, with appealing orange, lemon and pear aromas and flavors. The finish is bright and fruity without being cloying. **84**

1991: Fruity and focused, a lightly sweet dessert wine with charming pear and peach aromas and flavors. The finish is balanced and refreshing. **83**

1987: Fresh, sweet and lively, with zesty orange and tangerine flavors and a smooth texture. Intense and interesting. Could stand a year or two in the cellar to develop complexity. **85**

MUSCAT NAPA VALLEY SWEET ANDREA SELECT (★★★):
1990: Soft and sweet, with a perfumed character that never quite blossoms into richness. Simple and drinkable, finishing with a hint of toffee. **81**

SAUVIGNON BLANC NAPA VALLEY (★★★): Ripe with refreshing herb, fruit and spice notes.

1994: Light and flavorful, showing herb and peach flavors that linger nicely on the bright finish. **85**

1993: Ripe and refreshing, with complex pear, spice and grapefruit flavors. **87**

J. PEDRONCELLI WINERY
Alexander Valley
F: 1904. **O:** Jim & John Pedroncelli. **W:** John Pedroncelli. **S:** None.

OVERALL	$6-14	★★

WINE RATINGS

Cabernet Sauvignon Dry Creek Valley	★★
Cabernet Sauvignon Dry Creek Valley Reserve	★★
Chardonnay Dry Creek Valley	★★
Fumé Blanc Dry Creek Valley	★★
Merlot Dry Creek Valley	★
Pinot Noir Dry Creek Valley	★
Red Table Wine Sonoma County Primitivo Misto	NR
Zinfandel Dry Creek Valley	★★

WINERY DATA
C: 90,000. **V:** 110 acres in Dry Creek Valley. **G:** Zinfandel (40 acres), Sangiovese (6), Cabernet Sauvignon (27), Merlot (16), Gamay (8), Chardonnay (8), Petite Sirah (5). **P:** Chardonnay, Gamay, Cabernet Sauvignon, Pinot Noir, Zinfandel, Sauvignon Blanc, Merlot (Dry Creek Valley), Cabernet Sauvignon, Chenin Blanc (Alexander Valley).

Family-owned J. Pedroncelli Winery dates to 1904 and throughout its history the philosophy has been to make affordable, well balanced, easy-to-drink wines. Brothers John and Jim Pedroncelli have overseen operations for the past three decades, with John as winemaker and Jim in charge of sales and marketing. The winery owns 110 acres of vineyard in Dry Creek Valley from which, along with purchased grapes, it makes a wide range of wines including Cabernet, Chardonnay, Chenin Blanc, Gamay, Merlot, Pinot Noir, Sauvignon Blanc, white Zinfandel and Zinfandel. The house style through the lineup features simple but pleasant varietal flavors and minimal oak influence. Perhaps it's just me, but quality seems to have dipped with the past few vintages. With most of the grapes grown in Dry Creek, it's no surprise that reds such as Cabernet and Zinfandel usually fare better than Pinot Noir or Chardonnay.

TASTING NOTES

CABERNET SAUVIGNON DRY CREEK VALLEY (★★), RESERVE (★★): Rustic with mature cedar, herb and modest fruit flavors.

1991: Lean and earthy, with a bitter, oaky edge. Dries out. **75**

1990: Very light and herbal for a 1990, and lacking the character you usually find in Pedroncelli reds. **73**

Reserve 1988: Simple, fruity and crisp, with straightforward currant and tobacco aromas and flavors. **78**

Reserve 1986: Dark, rich and tannic, packed with currant, herb and tobacco flavors that turn a bit funky and tarry on the finish. **78**

CHARDONNAY DRY CREEK VALLEY (★★): Ripe and openly fruity at its best, but variable of late.

1993: Simple, straightforward and spicy, with a touch of a tannic bite on the finish. **80**

1992: Lean and a bit earthy, with simple pear and grapefruit notes. **79**

FUMÉ BLANC DRY CREEK VALLEY (★★): Light with crisp, earthy flavors.

1992: Crisp and light, with an earthy component to the modest fruit flavors. **77**

MERLOT DRY CREEK VALLEY (★): Variable, simple and fruity one year, lean and bitter the next.

1990: Simple and fruity, with nice plum and cherry flavors that turn lean. **83**

1989: Bitter and murky, with green, stemmy menthol flavors. **74**

PINOT NOIR DRY CREEK VALLEY (★):

1992: Earthy, with a tarry edge to the cranberry flavors. Tannic finish. **79**

1991: Reminiscent of Gamay, but the fresh, snappy, grapey flavors are appealing. **82**

RED TABLE WINE SONOMA COUNTY PRIMITIVO MISTO (NR):

1991: Earthy and gamy, it comes up short on fruit. **75**

ZINFANDEL DRY CREEK VALLEY (★★): Highly variable of late—disappointing, given the high quality of Dry Creek Zinfandel this past decade.

1990: Has well balanced crushed pepper, violet and raspberry flavors. **85**

1989: Light and gamy, with tarry berry and earth notes that dry out and turn simple. **77**

1988: Smooth, supple and flavorful, with bright raspberry, strawberry and cherry flavors. Not particularly intense, but pleasant and lively. **84**

1987: Extremely dry and almost sour on the finish. **65**

PEJU PROVINCE WINERY
Rutherford, Napa Valley
F: 1983. **O:** Anthony & Herta Peju. **W:** Anthony Peju, Lisa Van de Water. **S:** Carnival.

OVERALL	$16-35	★★★

WINE RATINGS

Cabernet Sauvignon Napa Valley	★★★
Cabernet Sauvignon Napa Valley HB Vineyard	★★★
Chardonnay Napa Valley	★★
Chardonnay Napa Valley HB Vineyard	★★
Meritage Red Napa Valley	NR
Sauvignon Blanc Napa Valley Late Harvest Special Select	★★

WINERY DATA
C: 8,000. **V:** 22 acres in Napa Valley. **G:** Cabernet Sauvignon (10 acres), Chardonnay (6), Cabernet Franc (2.75), Merlot (3), Petite Verdot (0.25). **P:** Cabernet Sauvignon, Chardonnay, Sauvignon Blanc, Cabernet Franc, French Colombard (Napa Valley), French Colombard (Sonoma County).

Tony Peju ran a nursery in Los Angeles before deciding to start a winery in Napa Valley, purchasing a vineyard in Rutherford that now measures 22 acres. After a long battle with the county regarding the winery design, Peju Province was completed in 1989. The winery's strength is Cabernet from its HB Vineyard (named for Herta Behensky Peju), but it was uprooted for replanting in 1995, a victim of phylloxera. Chardonnay, including an HB Vineyard bottling, Late Harvest Sauvignon Blanc and a red Meritage are also produced, with total production 8,000 cases.

TASTING NOTES

CABERNET SAUVIGNON NAPA VALLEY (★★★), HB VINEYARD (★★★): Variable of late, but often well crafted, with ripe, rich fruit that's characteristic of the Rutherford appellation.

1991: A touch earthy and vinegary, but the cherry and plum flavors come through on the finish, even if they lack focus and turn chewy and tannic. A rustic style that grows on you. **85**

1989: Ripe and tannic, with fresh, firm plum and currant flavors and hints of coffee and currant **85**

HB Vineyard 1991: Dark and well focused, with spicy plum, cherry and currant flavors that are tight and a bit austere now. Short-term cellaring into 1997 should help. **86**

HB Vineyard 1990: Smooth and plush, with a rich core of smoky currant, spice and mineral flavors. **88**

HB Vineyard 1989: There's an earthy, minty edge to the currant, herb and oak flavors, and it thins out on the finish. **83**

HB Vineyard 1988: Barely enough currant and berry flavors to sneak past the smoky charcoal flavors. **80**

HB Vineyard Special Selection 1988: Crisp and lively, with plum and currant flavors that carry through to the finish. **87**

HB Vineyard 1987: Tannic and potent, with gamy, pepper and currant flavors, turning tannic on the finish. **87**

HB Vineyard 1986: Rich and plush, with layers of cherry, currant, cinnamon and cedar flavors and fine tannins. **89**

CHARDONNAY NAPA VALLEY (★★), HB VINEYARD (★★): Less inspiring than the Cabernet, often lean and simple for Napa, but the 1993 Barrel Fermented showed marked improvement.

1993: A touch earthy, with a smoky toasty oak edge, but just enough ripe pear and apple-laced fruit to keep it in balance. **86**

1992: Serves up a range of spicy grapefruit, pear and apple flavors. **84**

1991: A funky, woody note detracts from the ripe pear and apple flavors. **75**

HB Vineyard 1993: Complex, with ripe, rich pear and smoky, toasty oak flavors. **88**

HB Vineyard 1992: Relies a little too much on toasty oak, which dominates the pear and apple flavors. **83**

HB Vineyard 1991: Spicy, with earthy pear flavors that lack focus. **82**

MERITAGE RED NAPA VALLEY (NR):
1992: Very ripe and juicy, with bright black cherry and plum flavors. Mild tannins. **87**

SAUVIGNON BLANC NAPA VALLEY LATE HARVEST SPECIAL SELECT (★★): Sweet, with a marked spicy edge.
1992: Very sweet, silky and supple, and a rose petal Gewürztraminer-like character sneaks in on the finish. Very fine, if a bit syrupy. **87**

PELLEGRINI WINERY
Russian River Valley

F: 1933. **O:** Pellegrini Family Vineyards. **W:** Merry Edwards. **S:** Cloverdale Ranch, Côtes de Sonoma, Olivet Lane Estate.

OVERALL	$7-13	★★

WINE RATINGS	
Barbera Sonoma Valley Old Vines	★★
Zinfandel Sonoma County Old Vines	★★
Cloverdale Ranch Cabernet Sauvignon Alexander Valley Estate Cuvée	★★
Côtes de Sonoma Cabernet Sauvignon Sonoma County	★★
Côtes de Sonoma Chardonnay Sonoma County	★★
Côtes de Sonoma Red Table Wine Sonoma County Deux Cépages	★★
Côtes de Sonoma Sauvignon Blanc Sonoma County	★★
Olivet Lane Estate Chardonnay Russian River Valley	★★
Olivet Lane Estate Pinot Noir Russian River Valley	★★

WINERY DATA
C: 20,000. **V:** 65 acres in Russian River Valley. **G:** Chardonnay, Pinot Noir (Russian River Valley). **P:** None.

The Pellegrini family owns this winery, which has 65 acres of Chardonnay and Pinot Noir in Russian River Valley. The Pinot, from the Pellegrinis' Olivet Lane Vineyard, was made famous by the Williams & Selyem Winery, which bottles a vineyard-designated Pinot Noir from this property. Merry Edwards' arrival as winemaker is giving the wines a little more polish and finesse. Production has risen to 20,000 cases.

TASTING NOTES

BARBERA SONOMA VALLEY OLD VINES (★★):
1993: Lighter, with watery berry, earth and spice notes. **81**

ZINFANDEL SONOMA COUNTY OLD VINES (★★):
1993: Crisp and compact, with a narrow band of simple berry flavors. **81**

CLOVERDALE RANCH CABERNET SAUVIGNON ALEXANDER VALLEY ESTATE CUVÉE (★★):
1991: Medium-bodied, with cedary currant and spice notes. **83**

1989: Nicely balanced and broad in flavor, with plum, spice and herb notes. **84**

1988: Light in texture, but has a firm backbone to support the modest red cherry and nutmeg flavors. **82**

CÔTES DE SONOMA VARIOUS BOTTLINGS (★★):

Cabernet Sauvignon Sonoma County 1990: A toasty, oaky characteristic gives a nice spicy accent to the smooth cherry and plum flavors. **83**

Cabernet Sauvignon Sonoma County 1989: Supple and generous, with ripe strawberry, cherry, plum and spice flavors. **83**

Chardonnay Sonoma County 1993: Fresh and flavorful, simple but brimming with pear and nectarine character that lingers on the finish. **84**

Chardonnay Sonoma County 1992: Fresh and spicy, with bright pear and nutmeg aromas and flavors and a smooth, elegant finish. **86**

Red Table Wine Sonoma County Deux Cépages 1990: Light in color, with a stalky edge. **73**

Sauvignon Blanc Sonoma County 1994: Crisp and lively, with a touch of floral character to spice up the green apple and green berry flavors. **83**

Sauvignon Blanc Sonoma County 1993: A gentle wine showing plenty of pear flavor with a touch of herbs, echoing a bit of anise on the finish. **85**

OLIVET LANE ESTATE CHARDONNAY RUSSIAN RIVER VALLEY (★★): Light and simple, with modest fruit flavors.

1992: Light and simple, with modest, spicy pear and wood flavors that gain intensity. **84**

OLIVET LANE ESTATE PINOT NOIR RUSSIAN RIVER VALLEY (★★): A lighter style that lacks the opulence of Williams & Selyem's bottling.

1992: Oaky and drying, with spicy cherry and currant aromas, but the oak dominates. **84**

1991: Ripe, rich and fruity, displaying crisp, well defined plum and cherry flavors that are well focused and lively. Firmly tannic. **84**

1988: Light in color but smooth and flavorful, with abundant black cherry, pepper and spice notes. **85**

ROBERT PEPI WINERY
Oakville, Napa Valley
F: 1981. **O:** Jess Jackson. **W:** Jon Engelskirger. **S:** None.

OVERALL	$11-25	★★★

WINE RATINGS

Cabernet Sauvignon Napa Valley Vine Hill Ranch	★★★
Chardonnay Napa Valley Puncheon Fermented	★★
Sangiovese Napa Valley Colline di Sassi	★★
Sauvignon Blanc Napa Valley Reserve Selection	★★★
Sauvignon Blanc Napa Valley Two-Heart Canopy	★★★

WINERY DATA

C: 25,000. **V:** 60 acres in Oakville. **G:** Sauvignon Blanc (24 acres), Chardonnay (3), Sangiovese (12), Merlot (11), Sémillon (4), Cabernet Sauvignon (4), Viognier (1), Other (1). **P:** Sangiovese (Napa Valley, Amador, Santa Barbara).

San Francisco fur dresser Robert Pepi bought a partially planted 70-acre property north of Yountville in 1966 as a country retirement home, replanting the property to Sauvignon Blanc and Chardonnay and eventually building a winery there in 1981. He was joined by his son Robert Jr., who oversaw production of Cabernet (from Vine Hill Ranch west of the winery), Chardonnay, Sauvignon Blanc and later a Sangiovese blend, among the first produced in California, bottled under the Colline di Sassi designation. Quality across the board has been good to very good. By the early 1990s, however, the winery experienced financial strains. Robert Jr. departed to Conn Creek Winery, and in 1994 Robert Sr. sold the winery to Jess Jackson, head of the Kendall-Jackson family of wineries. At the time of purchase, indications were the Robert Pepi name would be retained and the winery would focus on high-end Cabernet, using grapes from the former William Hill Winery Mount Veeder property Jackson had acquired earlier. Worth watching.

TASTING NOTES

CABERNET SAUVIGNON NAPA VALLEY VINE HILL RANCH (★★★): Consistently austere, with firm tannins and a narrow band of fruit, but true to the character of the vineyard.

1989: Serves up moderately rich currant and cherry flavors, finishing with firm tannins. **85**

1988: Ripe and fleshy, with moderately rich, complex cherry, plum and currant flavors that turn smooth on the finish. **87**

1987: A minty, herbal, camphor-laced wine with a solid concentration of rich black cherry, currant, cedar and chocolate flavors. Firmly tannic. **88**

1986: A tough, hard-edged, tannic wine, but the currant, earth, mineral and cherry flavors are compact. **88**

1985: Spicy and exotic, with dense berry and currant flavors and overtones of mint, eucalyptus and clove. **86**

1984: Lean and firm, with enough black cherry and cedary oak flavors to keep in balance. **87**

CHARDONNAY NAPA VALLEY PUNCHEON FERMENTED (★★): Variable, ranging from good to very good on occasion, but usually a bit on the lean side.

1992: Medium-weight, with ripe pear and apricot notes of modest proportions, but lacks the extra dimensions. Finishes with an earthy, oaky edge. **85**

1991: Ripe and spicy, with layers of pear, peach, pineapple and vanilla flavors in a crisp, delicate style. **88**

SANGIOVESE NAPA VALLEY COLLINE DI SASSI (★★): Shares a leanness that runs through all the Pepi wines, variable in quality but not quite meeting expectations. Includes 10 percent Cabernet.

1991: Lean but nicely focused, with ripe berry and tobacco flavors. **83**

1990: A gamy, weedy wine that's light and simple, with hints of berry flavor. Lacks focus and definition. **75**

1989: Firm and smooth, with an oaky edge, but also attractive cherry, plum and raspberry flavors. **83**

SAUVIGNON BLANC NAPA VALLEY RESERVE SELECTION (★★★), TWO-HEART CANOPY (★★★): Lean too, but the crispness works better with this variety than other Pepi wines.

Reserve Selection 1993: Round and generous, filling the mouth with citrusy pear, peach and vanilla flavors that remain lively through the richly balanced finish. **88**

Reserve Selection 1992: Crisp and delicately fruity, but the flavors never quite come into focus. **84**

Two-Heart Canopy 1994: Distinctly herbal and toasty, a lean wine with modest fruit to balance. **84**

Two-Heart Canopy 1993: Bright and fruity, with generous pear and vanilla flavors and a slight onion edge. **86**

PEPPERWOOD GROVE

This is a second label of Cecchetti Sebastiani Cellars (see listing).

PEPPERWOOD SPRINGS VINEYARDS
Anderson Valley
F: 1981. **O:** Gary & Phyllis Kaliher. **W:** Gary Kaliher. **S:** None.

OVERALL	$10-15	★

WINE RATINGS

Pinot Noir Anderson Valley	★
Pinot Noir Mendocino County Vidmar Vineyard	★

WINERY DATA
C: 1,000. **V:** 7 acres in Anderson Valley. **G:** Pinot Noir (Anderson Valley). **P:** None.

Larry Parsons, who was blind from birth and so printed his labels in Braille, founded this small Anderson Valley winery in 1981. He scored some early successes with Pinot Noir, but then died in a tragic auto accident. Gary and Phyllis Kaliher bought the property and have continued to focus on Pinot Noir with only fair results. Both the 1991 bottlings, one from Anderson Valley and a second from Vidmar Vineyard in Mendocino, were mediocre in quality.

TASTING NOTES

PINOT NOIR VARIOUS BOTTLINGS (★):
Anderson Valley 1991: Ripe, firm and minty, with chewy plum and spice notes that come through on a tannic finish. It's never going to be more than a simple wine. **79**

Mendocino County Vidmar Vineyard 1991: Light and gamy, with juniper berry and spice flavors that aren't very interesting. **74**

MARIO PERELLI-MINETTI WINERY

St. Helena, Napa Valley
F: 1977. **O:** Mario Perelli-Minetti. **W:** Bruce Bradley, Kellie Carlin. **S:** None.

OVERALL	$13-15	★★

WINE RATINGS	
Cabernet Sauvignon Napa Valley	★★

WINERY DATA
C: 5,000. **V:** 8 acres in Napa Valley. **G:** Cabernet Sauvignon, Chardonnay. **P:** None.

Mario Perelli-Minetti managed his family's once giant winery in the Central Valley before setting up a small winery in Napa Valley in 1977, focusing on small lots of Cabernet and Chardonnay. In 1988 a winery in Rutherford on the Silverado Trail was built. After a modest start, Cabernet quality is on the upswing.

TASTING NOTES

CABERNET SAUVIGNON NAPA VALLEY (★★): Variable quality as no consistent style is evident, although the well crafted 1990 is the best offering.
1990: Firm and compact, with a tight band of rich, supple plum, currant, spice and cedary oak flavors. **88**
1988: Distinctly minty and spicy, with ripe currant and berry flavors that offer moderate depth and richness. **86**
1987: Lean in texture but focused, with pleasant currant and berry flavors that turn spicy and chunky. **83**

PETERSON WINERY

Dry Creek Valley
F: 1983. **O:** Fred Peterson & Bill Hambrecht. **W:** Fred Peterson. **S:** None.

OVERALL	$13-16	★★

WINE RATINGS	
Cabernet Sauvignon Dry Creek Valley	★★
Chardonnay Anderson Valley	★★
Zinfandel Dry Creek Valley	★★

WINERY DATA
C: 3,500. **V:** None. **G:** None. **P:** Zinfandel, Merlot, Cabernet Sauvignon (Dry Creek Valley), Chardonnay (Anderson Valley).

Peterson Winery is the former Belvedere Winery. It is still owned by Fred Peterson and Bill Hambrecht, but under the new setup Hambrecht Vineyards sells grapes from its 531 acres in vines to Peterson Winery, which produces 3,500 cases of Cabernet (Bradford Mountain), Chardonnay, Merlot and Zinfandel (Dry Creek Valley and Bradford Mountain). Hambrecht's vineyards are spread out among Alexander Valley (240 acres), Dry Creek Valley (235) and Anderson Valley (56), with Chardonnay (140 acres) and Zinfandel in Dry Creek (75) the largest plantings, followed by Cabernet (60) and Merlot (30). The Bradford Mountain vineyard is also owned by Hambrecht. The name change from Belvedere to Peterson took place in 1995.

TASTING NOTES

VARIOUS BOTTLINGS (★★):
Cabernet Sauvignon Dry Creek Valley 1992: Medium-bodied, with a leathery edge to the cedar and berry flavors, finishing with a dry tannic edge. Short-term cellaring may help soften it. **83**
Chardonnay Anderson Valley 1993: Firm and compact, with a medium-weight beam of pear and citrus flavors that fold together on the finish. **84**
Zinfandel Dry Creek Valley 1993: Tart, tight and tannic, with a crisp earthy edge to the cherry and wild berry flavors. Needs short-term cellaring. **84**

JOSEPH PHELPS VINEYARDS

St. Helena, Napa Valley
F: 1973. **O:** Stone Bridge Cellars. **W:** Craig Williams. **S:** Vin du Mistral.

OVERALL	$10-50	★★★★

WINE RATINGS	
Cabernet Blend Napa Valley Insignia	★★★★★
Cabernet Sauvignon Napa Valley	★★★
Cabernet Sauvignon Napa Valley Backus Vineyard	★★★★
Cabernet Sauvignon Napa Valley Eisele Vineyard	★★★★
Chardonnay Carneros	★★★
Gewürztraminer California	★★★
Grenache California Vin du Mistral Rosé	★★★

Johannisberg Riesling Napa Valley ★★
Merlot Napa Valley ★★★
Rhône Blend California Vin du Mistral
Le Mistral ★★★
Sauvignon Blanc Napa Valley ★★
Scheurebe Napa Valley Special Select ★★★★
Sémillon Napa Valley Délice du Sémillon ★★★
Syrah Napa Valley Vin du Mistral ★★★
Viognier Napa Valley Vin du Mistral ★★★★
Zinfandel Alexander Valley ★★★

WINERY DATA

C: 85,000. V: 337 acres in Napa Valley, Stags Leap District, Rutherford, Carneros. G: Chardonnay (69 acres), Cabernet Sauvignon (76), Merlot (24), Viognier (36), Syrah (12), Sauvignon Blanc, Sémillon (36), Grenache, Mourvèdre (15), Other (69). P: Chardonnay (Carneros, Napa Valley), Cabernet Sauvignon (Napa Valley), Merlot (Napa Valley).

Building contractor Joseph Phelps came to California from Colorado in the early 1970s and built Souverain (now Rutherford Hill Winery) in Napa, followed by a Souverain in Sonoma County (now Chateau Souverain) before deciding wine was right for him. By 1973 he had built his winery in a narrow fold of hills east of Napa Valley off Taplin Road. With 337 acres in vines, Phelps is among the largest vineyard owners in Napa. The vineyards are well dispersed throughout the valley, and are dominated by Cabernet (76 acres) and Chardonnay (69), with plan-ting in Stags Leap, Rutherford and Carneros. Phelps has also been a low-key but influential leader, pioneering vineyard-designated wines (Eisele and Backus Cabernets and Sangiacomo Chardonnay), a Bordeaux-inspired red blend (Insignia), richly flavored dessert wines (Riesling, Scheurebe and Gewürztraminer) and a line of Rhône-inspired wines bottled under the Vin du Mistral label. Craig Williams has been winemaker since 1983, having replaced Walter Schug, who helped get Phelps off to a great start. Production is 85,000 cases.

TASTING NOTES

CABERNET BLEND NAPA VALLEY INSIGNIA (★★★★★):

Has often rivaled the Eisele bottling for depth, concentration and complexity, but of late this blend of Cabernet, Merlot and Cabernet Franc has been less opulent and it's often marked by strong minty qualities, which the winery is hoping to minimize if not erase with future efforts. Still, many memorable classics that age exceptionally well.

1991: Dark and intense, with pretty aromas and tight, dense currant, mineral, tar and cedary oak that's a touch astringent. Needs cellaring until 1998 to soften. **90**

1990: Firm and compact, with herb and currant flavors that turn lean and tannic on the finish. **88**

1989: Smooth and polished, with a beam of bright raspberry, cherry and currant flavors shining through the firm texture, hinting at leather and mint on the finish. **87**

1988: There's a wealth of rich currant, cedar and coffee flavors, with hints of mint, bay leaf and menthol. Firmly tannic. **86**

1986: Enormously deep, rich, supple and complex, with enticing black cherry, currant, mineral, toast and anise flavors that are seductive and long. Mature now but still ageworthy. **95**

1985: Amazingly complex and concentrated, with layers of ripe black cherry, currant and mint flavors that are sharply focused, beautifully proportioned and supple. Distinctive for its elegance and complexity. **96**

1984: Firm, tight and compact, with a tough edge to the black currant and mint flavors, finishing with crisp, lean tannins. **89**

1983: Intense and concentrated, packed with rich berry, mint, currant and cedar notes that are now mature. Still firmly tannic. **89**

1982: Developing nicely, with a smooth texture, rounded tannins and a woody, earthy edge to the currant and berry flavors. **85**

1981: Sleek and elegant, brimming with fresh, ripe currant, cherry and plum flavors that are bright and lively. Supple and mature. **92**

1980: Lean but very concentrated, with ripe plum, currant, spice and mineral flavors that are tight and tannic. **90**

1979: A sleek, seductive, beautifully focused wine that's fully mature now, with rich, ripe, supple black cherry, currant, anise and mint flavors, turning smooth and supple. **90**

1978: Complex and oaky, with intense, spicy currant, anise and herb flavors. Impeccably balanced, deep and long. **92**

1977: Smooth and elegant, with mature earth, herb and cedar complexities that add to the ripe black cherry and plum flavors. **91**

1976: Bold, supple and very ripe, smooth and satiny, with black cherry, currant, anise, mint and oak flavors that are concentrated and powerful. **93**

1975: A Merlot-dominated Insignia that is decidedly herbal and minty, yet elegant and concentrated. **85**

1974: Aging well, with a tight, compact core of spice, mineral and racy fruit flavors, finishing with rich, chewy tannins and a coffee and cedar aftertaste. **88**

Cabernet Sauvignon Napa Valley (★★★): The 1991 hails Phelps' move to 100 percent Cabernet and it's a rich, chewy, deeply complex wine, clearly the best effort in many years. Fine value given its quality.

1992: Dark and intense, with a compact core of black cherry, currant and anise flavors, turning earthy and leathery on the finish. **87**

1991: Young and concentrated, with firm black cherry and currant flavors that are pure and ripe, finishing with a light oak and spice edge. Impressive for its focus and elegance. **90**

1990: Firm and flavorful, with ripe currant and cherry flavors that are firmly tannic. **85**

1989: Tight, tannic and leathery, with a thin base of currant and cherry aromas and flavors. **78**

1988: Distinctive for its mint and dill aromas, and it has a core of rich, tasty currant, plum and berry notes. Firmly tannic. **85**

1987: Herbal, vegetal, gamy aromas and flavors turn murky and unpleasant on the finish. **75**

1985: A wine with pronounced herb and mint notes that complement the ripe currant and cherry flavors. **84**

1984: Distinctly minty and chocolaty, with rich, elegant cherry and berry flavors, smooth, supple tannins and a woody finish. **89**

Cabernet Sauvignon Napa Valley Backus Vineyard (★★★★): Steadily improving with a wonderful 1990 bottling, dark, intense and well focused, increasingly reliant on Cabernet for the entire blend. Ages well.

1991: Hard-edged, dark and inky, packed with chewy, tannic plum and cherry flavors, this is a big, powerful wine. **90**

1989: Rich and minty, with currant and spice flavors that are concentrated and vibrant, finishing with tight tannins and pretty oak shadings. **88**

1987: An elegant wine with ripe, supple plum, mint, herb and currant flavors that are framed by toasty oak and dry, rounded tannins. **88**

1986: Deep, concentrated and intense, with thick currant, plum and spicy mint flavors that are firm and elegant, wrapped in thick tannins. **89**

1985: A rich, sleek, distinctive wine with spice, mint and chocolate flavors and bright cherry and plum notes that stand up to the firm tannins. **90**

1984: Ripe and mature, with spicy cherry, plum and mineral flavors that are lean and crisp. **86**

1983: Tight, lean and crisp, with ripe, mature cherry, chocolate and mint flavors. **85**

1981: Mature but appealing, with lush, ripe cherry, currant, plum and spicy mineral flavors that are very seductive. The tannins are soft and smooth but still potent. **91**

1978: Ripe and concentrated, with currant, earth, mineral and toasty oak flavors. **89**

1977: Fully mature now, with smooth, rich, supple chocolate, plum, spice and toast flavors. **86**

Cabernet Sauvignon Napa Valley Eisele Vineyard (★★★★): Some of Napa's most dramatic, rich, plush and deeply concentrated wines have appeared under this designation. Uncommonly thick and complex, with grand aging potential. Capable of lasting 25 to 30 years. Last bottling was 1991, as Eisele Vineyard is now owned by Araujo Estate.

1991: Shows spicy black cherry and currant flavors before the chewy tannins creep in, turning intense and tannic on the finish. **89**

1989: Lean and crisp, with a leathery edge to the classic currant, mineral and earth flavors that are characteristic of this vineyard. Firmly tannic. **87**

1987: Rich and focused, with a leathery edge to the complex currant and mineral flavors. Focused and balanced, with fine but ample tannins. **88**

1986: A pungently earthy wine with barnyard and leather notes overriding the ripe currant and cherry flavors. **77**

1985: Bold and rich, with concentrated currant, plum, toast, cinnamon and anise flavors that are deep, intense and lively, finishing with firm yet integrated tannins. **94**

1984: A firmly structured wine with a tight core of rich currant and spicy mineral flavors. Mature but still tannic. **87**

1983: Still quite tannic, with tightly knit cedar, currant and plum flavors masked by rough-hewn tannins that are chewy on the finish. **86**

1982: Mature but still taut, with modest earthy mineral and currant flavors. **84**

1981: Wonderfully rich and complex, loaded with currant, herb, anise and mineral flavors that turn deep and concentrated. **93**

1979: Rich and concentrated, with currant, plum, cedar, earth and mineral flavors that are thick and deeply concentrated. **92**

1978: An amazing wine that's intense and powerful, packed with deep, persistent, concentrated currant, anise, herb and oak flavors, finishing with thick, round tannins. Marvelous. **97**

1977: Ripe and mature, with plum and black cherry flavors that are thick, lean and rich. **85**

1975: Deep, rich and enticingly complex, with dense cedar, cigar box, black currant and chocolate notes that unfold on the palate, turning thick, rich and unctuous on the finish. **97**

CHARDONNAY VARIOUS BOTTLINGS (★★★): Variable, but well oaked, elegant and complex at its best.

Chardonnay Carneros 1992: Rich, complex and elegant, with toasty oak and spicy pear notes. **89**

Chardonnay Napa Valley 1991: Tight, lean and crisp, with a nice range of pear, vanilla and spice flavors and a creamy, supple texture. **86**

GEWÜRZTRAMINER CALIFORNIA (★★★):
1992: Soft and smooth, with an earthy edge to the modest pear and floral aromas and flavors. **82**

GRENACHE CALIFORNIA VIN DU MISTRAL ROSÉ (★★★): Made in a rosé style, with ripe, snappy fruit that's versatile on the table.

1993: A pretty rosé, bright with strawberry and raspberry flavors that extend into a lively finish. Drink it fresh. **87**

1992: A serious, dry rosé that's crisp and snappy, with berry, strawberry and plum notes and hints of pepper and spice. **87**

1990: Very fruity and fresh, with a brilliant color and lovely pepper-scented blackberry and cherry flavors. **87**

JOHANNISBERG RIESLING NAPA VALLEY (★★):
1990: Mature and slightly off-dry, with earth and pineapple flavors and a touch of honey. The finish is slightly bitter as well. **77**

MERLOT NAPA VALLEY (★★★): Leaner and more austere than the other Phelps reds, but pleasant enough.

1991: Crisp and austere, a tough-textured wine with a modest beam of currant flavor. **83**

1990: Spicy and medium-bodied, with blackberry and plum flavors and a tannic finish. **83**

1989: Firm and tight, with concentrated raspberry and cherry aromas and flavors and oak notes lingering on the finish. **88**

1987: The herb, bay leaf and vegetal aromas and flavors overwhelm the currant notes. **80**

RHÔNE BLEND CALIFORNIA VIN DU MISTRAL LE MISTRAL (★★★): A red Rhône blend that relies heavily on Grenache, it's spicy, complex and elegant.

1992: An earthy wine with ripe, peppery Syrah and Grenache flavors. **85**

1991: Bright and spicy, like a Chateauneuf-du-Pape, offering intense berry flavor and a touch of black pepper. **84**

1990: Solid, with currant, plum and berry notes that finish with firm tannins. **85**

1989: Fruity and lively, with a strain of tannin to match the plum and berry flavors and a distinctive salt-and-pepper edge. **85**

SAUVIGNON BLANC NAPA VALLEY (★★):
1992: Crisp and flinty, with an austere edge of grapefruit, fig and spice. Taut and compact. **85**

SCHEUREBE NAPA VALLEY SPECIAL SELECT (★★★★): Bold, ripe and delicious dessert-style wine marked by ripe apricot, honey, pear and buttery flavors. This is the only one of this variety in California that I know of.

1989: Sweet but not cloying, with focused peach, berry and tropical fruit aromas and flavors. Has elegance and plenty of flavor on the finish. **88**

SÉMILLON NAPA VALLEY DÉLICE DU SÉMILLON (★★★): This dessert wine flirts with greatness, at its best ripe and complex, but often less concentrated.

1990: Nice peach and floral flavors fill up this sweet, straightforward dessert wine. The flavors lack concentration and depth, but are appealing. **81**

SYRAH NAPA VALLEY VIN DU MISTRAL (★★★): Variable, but ripe and complex with plum and mineral notes at its best.

1991: Firm and chewy, loaded with bright blackberry and black pepper flavors that poke through the tannic finish. **88**

1990: Elegant and polished, with spicy berry flavors that are pure and appealing. **84**

1989: Smooth and plush, with simple ripe cherry and currant flavors and a touch of spice. **84**
1988: A complex, flavorful Syrah that balances gamy, earthy aromas with ample grape and berry flavors. **87**
1987: Earthy pepper, herb and dill aromas and flavors tend to dominate this sturdy, rustic wine. **81**
1986: Smooth, focused and harmonious, with gentle black cherry, leather and nutmeg flavors and velvety tannins. **88**

VIOGNIER NAPA VALLEY VIN DU MISTRAL (★★★★): Among the elite, as it achieves richness and complexity without relying on a one-dimensional spicy quality.
1992: Floral, creamy and spicy, with pretty pear, apple, honey and vanilla flavors that turn rich and complex. **90**

ZINFANDEL ALEXANDER VALLEY (★★★): Like the Merlot, not in the class of Phelps' best reds, but well balanced and improving.
1990: Lean and focused, with plenty of ripe plum and cherry flavors scented with more than a hint of vanilla and spice from oak. **88**
1989: Full of wild berry and raspberry flavors, with a gamy, peppery edge on the finish. **82**

R. H. PHILLIPS VINEYARD
Esparto, Central Valley
F: 1983. **O:** R. H. Phillips Inc. **W:** Barry Bergman. **S:** Diamond G, Chateau St. Nicholas.

OVERALL	$6-10	★★

WINE RATINGS

Cabernet Sauvignon California	★★
Chardonnay Dunnigan Hills Barrel Cuvée	★★
Mourvèdre California EXP	★★
Rhône Blend California Alliance	★★★
Sauvignon Blanc California	
Night Harvest	★★
Syrah California EXP	★★★
Viognier Dunnigan Hills EXP	★★

WINERY DATA
C: 350,000. **V:** 698 acres in California. **G:** Rhône Type (10 acres), Grenache (8), Merlot (15), Sauvignon Blanc (184), Sémillon (44), Chardonnay (251), Syrah (112), Other White (7), Viognier (14), Cabernet Sauvignon (46). **P:** Chardonnay (California).

Esparto-based R.H. Phillips, which owns 698 acres in vines and produces 350,000 cases a year, makes a strong case for the high quality of winegrowing in Yolo County, due east of Napa Valley and northwest of Sacramento. All the wines are well crafted and carry the California or Dunnigan Hills appellations. The Syrah EXP stands out for its opulence and pure varietal character; the Mourvèdre is also worth seeking out.

TASTING NOTES

CABERNET SAUVIGNON CALIFORNIA (★★): Crisp and straightforward, with modest flavors and intensity.
1991: Crisp and straightforward, a light, simple wine with an herbal edge. **82**

CHARDONNAY DUNNIGAN HILLS BARREL CUVÉE (★★): Crisp and simple, with medium-weight pear and spice notes.
1994: Simple and fruity, centering around peach and apple flavors. **83**
1993: Well balanced, with pretty pear, spice and light oak shadings, all focused with a lingering aftertaste. **85**
1992: Crisp and simple, with a spicy edge to the modest pear and apple flavors and a solid finish. **83**

MOURVÈDRE CALIFORNIA EXP (★★):
1990: Lean and earthy, with spicy plum and cherry flavors that turn stemmy on the finish. Balanced and moderately tannic. **83**

RHÔNE BLEND CALIFORNIA ALLIANCE (★★★):
1989: Firm and flavorful, with a nice range of cherry, raspberry and plum flavors shaded by black pepper and spice notes. **88**

SAUVIGNON BLANC CALIFORNIA NIGHT HARVEST (★★★): Well made, with ripe, intense flavors, while avoiding the grape's excesses.
1992: Smooth, appealing and soft in texture, with polished edges. Offers apple, pear and slightly herbal aromas and flavors. **84**

SYRAH CALIFORNIA EXP (★★★): Can be excellent as the 1988 demonstrated with its lush concentration of fruit.
1989: Well balanced raspberry and black cherry flavors

are flanked by hints of sweet vanilla and pepper and tight, crisp tannins. **86**

1988: Ripe and opulent, with a luscious concentration of black cherry, plum and strawberry flavors and hints of pepper and smoke. **91**

1987: Modest in flavor and firm in structure, but not much to excite the senses. **80**

VIOGNIER DUNNIGAN HILLS EXP (★★): Variable, but usually solid with good varietal character.

1993: Ripe, round and bubbling over with fruit, mixing its nectarine, pear and almond flavors artfully, finishing supple and smooth. **86**

1992: Tart, lean and austere, with tightly reined-in citrus and earth flavors. Could use a little more flavor and flesh. **79**

PINE RIDGE WINERY
Napa Valley
F: 1978. **O:** R. Gary Andrus & Leucadia International. **W:** R. Gary Andrus, Stacy Clark. **S:** Silverwood, La Petite Vigne.

OVERALL	$8-65	★★★

WINE RATINGS
Cabernet Sauvignon Diamond Mountain	★★
Cabernet Sauvignon Napa Valley Andrus Reserve	★★★
Cabernet Sauvignon Napa Valley Rutherford Cuvée	★★
Cabernet Sauvignon Stags Leap District	★★★
Chardonnay Napa Valley Knollside Cuvée	★★★
Chardonnay Stags Leap District	★★★
Chardonnay Stags Leap District Vieille Vigne	★★★
Merlot Carneros	★★
Merlot Napa Valley Selected Cuvée	★★
La Petite Vigne Chenin Blanc Napa Valley	★★

WINERY DATA
C: 80,000. **V:** 203 acres in Stags Leap District, Oakville, Rutherford, Carneros. **G:** Cabernet Sauvignon (54 acres), Cabernet Franc (9), Merlot (78), Petite Verdot (7), Malbec (5). **P:** Chenin Blanc (Napa Valley), Cabernet Sauvignon (Howell Mountain).

Gary and Nancy Andrus founded Pine Ridge in the Stags Leap District in 1978 with a focus on vineyard and/or appellation-oriented wines (Rutherford and Stags Leap), using grapes from their vineyards and buying grapes from Diamond Mountain and Howell Mountain as well. Quality across the board is very good, occasionally outstanding with both Chardonnay and Cabernet. During the late 1980s, quality dipped in two difficult vintages, 1988 and 1989; however, the winery appears to have regained its focus and recent vintages have shown more depth and better balance. To Andrus' credit, he declassified wines in lesser years, owning up to the wines' shortcomings. Leucadia International became a majority shareholder in the early 1990s, providing a needed cash infusion to expand operations and production, which now tops 80,000 cases.

TASTING NOTES

CABERNET SAUVIGNON DIAMOND MOUNTAIN (★★): The Diamond Mountain bottling is austere and dominated by a minty earthiness that comes across as one-dimensional.

1988: Tight and perfumed, with a cedar and mint edge that overshadows the modest berry and currant notes. **82**

1987: Crisp and austere, with a thin beam of tart black cherry and plum flavors, finishing with crisp, watery tannins. **80**

1986: Attractive for its ripe currant, cherry and plum flavors, framed by firm tannins and ample oak. **84**

CABERNET SAUVIGNON NAPA VALLEY ANDRUS RESERVE (★★★): The Andrus Reserve, which comes from the owner's home vineyard in Rutherford, can be richer and more complex, but it can also be of medium-weight intensity and not as complex as the $60 price would suggest.

1991: Crisp and straightforward, with a tobacco edge to the modest fruit flavors. **85**

1988: Tough and tannic, with a medicinal edge to the solid core of currant, black cherry and plum flavors. **82**

1986: An extremely oaky wine with camphor and mint notes that come across as dry and woody on the palate. **79**

Cuvée Duet 1985: Firm, with simple currant and berry flavors. **83**

1984: Has not evolved, with crisp blackberry and spice flavors that turn lean. **82**

1983: Mature, with crisp tannins and appealing currant and anise flavors that turn lean. **88**

1980: Past its peak but holding, with ripe, supple cherry and currant flavors that turn thin on the finish. **85**

CABERNET SAUVIGNON NAPA VALLEY RUTHERFORD CUVÉE (★★): Smooth and supple, with well focused cherry and currant fruit.

1991: Supple, with forward cherry and berry flavors that firm up on the finish. **84**

1990: The currant and cherry flavors are supple and pleasing, but the oak has a smoky green edge to it that detracts from the quality. **82**

1987: An earthy, herbal wine marked by dill aromas, turning tight and tart on the finish. **77**

1986: Lean and focused, with mint and menthol running through the tart cherry and currant flavors. **84**

1985: Has not gained in the bottle. It remains a simple, correct wine with modest currant and berry notes. **87**

CABERNET SAUVIGNON STAGS LEAP DISTRICT (★★★): Supple and shows a sense of elegant and understated fruit.

1992: Strives for complexity with its intensity and oak shadings, but this tightly wound Cabernet is firmly tannic and just showing a hint of currant, herb and plum flavors. **87**

1991: Combines ripe, intense currant, cherry and spice flavors with cedary oak, finishing with elegant, firm tannins. **89**

1990: A drying, charred, green oak edge takes away from the crisp black cherry and currant flavors. **78**

1987: Tight and minty, with more herb than currant and cherry flavors. Dry tannins. **83**

CHARDONNAY VARIOUS BOTTLINGS (★★★): Serves up ripe and well focused fruit from Oak Knoll and Stags Leap, but the oak often carries a cedary sawdust edge that I find less appealing.

Napa Valley Knollside Cuvée 1992: Good intensity and range of flavor, with spice, pear and dried apricot flavors that hang with you. **86**

Stags Leap District 1993: Shows more depth and flavor than most from this vintage, as the ripe pear, apple and honey notes pick up a pretty toasty oak edge on the finish. **89**

Stags Leap District Vieille Vigne 1992: Intense and smoky, with a core of rich, complex spice, pear, honey and vanilla flavors. **89**

MERLOT VARIOUS BOTTLINGS (★★): Simple, with modest herb and currant fruit, again marked by dusty oak flavors.

Carneros 1992: Crisp and firm, with a cedary edge to the currant and cherry flavors, finishing with tight tannins. **85**

Napa Valley Selected Cuvée 1991: Enough currant and spice flavors come through to offset the earthy, herbal notes. **83**

Napa Valley Selected Cuvée 1989: Overwhelming wood suffocates the fruit underneath. **73**

Napa Valley Selected Cuvée 1988: The oak is strong, with menthol and dill notes that turn dry and mask the ripe plum and cherry flavors. **80**

Napa Valley Selected Cuvée 1987: Has plenty of oak and herb notes and lean, elegant currant and plum aromas and flavors. **88**

Napa Valley Selected Cuvée 1986: Lean and tart, with firm tannins and good concentration of plum and currant flavors. **80**

LA PETITE VIGNE CHENIN BLANC NAPA VALLEY (★★): Off-dry, with ripe, juicy fruit.

1993: Barrel fermented, with toasty oak flavors that match up well with the rich and spicy apple, pear, honey and melon notes. Includes 8 percent Chardonnay. **87**

PINNACLES

This is a second label for Estancia (see listing).

PIPER SONOMA CELLARS

Sonoma County
F: 1980. **O:** Piper Heidsieck Inc. **W:** Rob McNeill. **S:** Bearboat.

OVERALL	$14-28	★★★

WINE RATINGS

Sparkling Wine Sonoma County	
Blanc de Noirs	★★★
Sparkling Wine Sonoma County Brut	★★★
Sparkling Wine Sonoma County	
Tête de Cuvée	★★★
Bearboat Pinot Noir Russian River Valley	★

WINERY DATA
C: 100,000. **V:** 84 acres in Russian River Valley. **G:** Pinot Noir (62.5 acres), Chardonnay (17.5), Cabernet Sauvignon (4).

P: Pinot Noir (Alexander Valley, Dry Creek Valley, Russian River Valley), Chardonnay (Russian River Valley), Rhône Type (Russian River, Dry Creek Valley), Pinot Blanc (Alexander Valley).

I n 1980, Piper Heidsieck, the French Champagne house, and Renfield Imports formed a joint venture to build Piper Sonoma, but since 1988 Heidsieck has been the sole proprietor. All four of the *méthode champenoise* sparkling wines are consistently well crafted, with a house style that emphasizes crisp, intense, tightly wound fruit flavors. Bearboat Pinot Noir is a new non-sparkling entry. Production is 100,000 cases.

TASTING NOTES

SPARKLING WINE SONOMA COUNTY BLANC DE NOIRS (★★★): Dominated by Pinot Noir (95 percent), it features tightly wound spice and cherry notes that turn rich and creamy. Ages well.
NV: Tight and firm, offering spicy cherry and cream flavors that are focused and lively. **87**

SPARKLING WINE SONOMA COUNTY BRUT SELECT CUVÉE (★★★): Also reliant on Pinot Noir (75 percent); spice, earth and black cherry flavors are evident.
1989: No mistaking the fruit here, with ripe, spicy black cherry and subtle plum notes. Keeps its flavors on the finish. **88**
NV: Despite an earthy streak, the pear, black cherry and spice flavors prevail, making it complex. **87**

SPARKLING WINE SONOMA COUNTY TÊTE DE CUVÉE (★★★): Produced in superior vintages and vintage-dated, it is structured for long-term aging, aged on the yeast for six years.
1985: Lean and trim, with earthy citrus flavors that are tightly wound, gaining modest depth on the finish. Doesn't deliver the complexity you expect from a Tête de Cuvée. **86**

BEARBOAT PINOT NOIR RUSSIAN RIVER VALLEY (★):
1992: Light and thin, with a shallow band of spicy cherry flavors. Marginal quality, but the label's cute. **77**

PLAM VINEYARDS & WINERY
Yountville, Napa Valley
F: 1984. **O:** Plam Vineyards & Winery. **W:** Kenneth H. Plam, Tom Eddy. **S:** None.

OVERALL	$6-30	★★

WINE RATINGS	
Cabernet Sauvignon California	★★
Cabernet Sauvignon Napa Valley	★★
Chardonnay Napa Valley	★★
Merlot Napa Valley	★★

WINERY DATA
C: 1,700. **V:** 6 acres in Napa Valley. **G:** Chardonnay (3 acres), Merlot (3). **P:** Cabernet Sauvignon (Napa Valley).

B ay Area engineer Ken Plam purchased the old Hopper Creek Vineyard north of Yountville in 1984, where he and his family own six acres of vines, split between Chardonnay and Merlot. The 1,700-case winery focuses on Cabernet, Chardonnay and Merlot, and since 1992 has retained Tom Eddy as the winemaking consultant. The main focus and best wine has been Cabernet, albeit with radical quality swings. Chardonnay often rises to good, but can also be way off the mark. The winery has skipped several vintages while reorganizing.

TASTING NOTES

CABERNET SAUVIGNON VARIOUS BOTTLINGS (★★): Solid with 1985 and 1986, but funky in 1988. No consistent house style.
California 1992: Smooth and polished, with earthy herb, cherry and a spicy pickley edge, finishing with fine tannins. **82**
Napa Valley 1992: Intense and concentrated, with tiers of spice, currant, cedar and smoky oak flavors. **88**
Napa Valley 1988: A strong barnyard note dominates the currant, anise and berry flavors. **79**
Napa Valley 1986: Elegant, with appealing currant, plum and black cherry flavors that pick up coffee and cedar notes. **87**
Napa Valley 1985: Mature, with simple herb, anise and cedar flavors, picking up a trace of cherry and currant on the finish. **86**

Poppy Hill

This is a second label for Mont St. John Cellars (see listing).

Porter Creek Vineyards

Russian River Valley
F: 1982. **O:** George R. Davis. **W:** George R. Davis. **S:** None.

Overall	$14-23	NR

WINE RATINGS	
Chardonnay Russian River Valley	NR
Pinot Noir Russian River Valley	NR

WINERY DATA
C: 1,500. **V:** 20 acres in Russian River Valley. **G:** Pinot Noir (11 acres), Chardonnay (9). **P:** None.

Porter Creek Vineyards is a 1,500-case winery in Healdsburg founded in 1982 by George Davis, who owns 11 acres of Chardonnay and 9 acres of Pinot Noir in the Russian River Valley appellation. The focus is on those two Burgundian varieties, with two bottlings of the Pinot Noir: Creekside and Hillside. Chardonnay at 800 cases is the volume leader. Very limited distribution, although plans are to expand case production.

Bernard Pradel Cellars

Napa Valley
F: 1983. **O:** Chateaulin Inc. **W:** Bernard Pradel. **S:** None.

Overall	$14-24	★★★

WINE RATINGS	
Cabernet Sauvignon Napa Valley Limited Barrel Selection	★★
Cabernet Sauvignon Napa Valley Howell Mountain Ranch	★★

WINERY DATA
C: 2,500. **V:** 19 acres in Howell Mountain, Yountville. **G:** Cabernet Sauvignon (17 acres), Merlot (1), Cabernet Franc (0.5). **P:** None.

French-born Bernard Pradel, whose family has winemaking roots in Chablis, worked as a chef in Oregon and Napa before turning to wine. In 1983 he started his 2,500-case winery, using his 19 acres of Cabernet, Merlot and Cabernet Franc for a Bordeaux-style red he labels Cabernet. Quality has been variable and distribution limited. A Howell Mountain Cabernet joined the lineup in 1991. Within the wine trade, Pradel is known for having devised and patented a combined stainless steel and wooden barrel. It's essentially a stainless steel barrel with the ends removed; in their place are oak ends that can be shaved, reversed and replaced, minimizing the cost for new oak barrels.

TASTING NOTES

CABERNET SAUVIGNON NAPA VALLEY LIMITED BARREL SELECTION (★★): The 1984 and 1985 vintages showed a measure of harmony and finesse, but other vintages have been unfocused, marked by lean flavors.
1990: Smooth and supple, with a mineral and cedar edge to the cherry and plum notes. Finishes with smooth tannins and a mature edge. **85**
1989: Lean and crisp, with trim blackberry and currant flavors shaded by herb and toast notes. **81**
1988: Harsh in texture and strongly herbal in flavor, with more vegetal notes than fruit. **80**
1987: Simple but pleasant, with very intense, ripe currant, dill and cherry notes. **84**
1986: Big and full-bodied, with currant and chocolate flavors that turn simple and oaky. **82**
1985: Firm and harmonious, with ripe cherry and berry flavors. **86**
1984: Deep, dark and ripe, silky and appealing on the palate, with plum and black cherry flavors. **86**

CABERNET SAUVIGNON NAPA VALLEY HOWELL MOUNTAIN RANCH (★★):
1992: A touch earthy, with a cedary oak edge, but some pleasant fruit flavors too, with hints of herb and cherry. Finishes with firm but not overwhelming tannins. **85**
1991: Offers a hint of cherry and berry jam before the dense earthy tannins clamp down. Packs a wallop but needs considerable cellar time to soften. **87**

PRAGER WINERY & PORT WORKS
St. Helena, Napa Valley
F: 1980. O: Jim & Imogene Prager. W: Jim Prager, John Prager. S: La Croix.

OVERALL	$30-35	★★

WINE RATINGS

Cabernet Sauvignon Napa Valley Port	★★
Petite Sirah Napa Valley Port	★★
Pinot Noir Napa Valley Port	★★

WINERY DATA
C: 3,600. V: 0.5 acres in Napa Valley. G: Port Type. P: Cabernet Sauvignon, Petite Sirah, Zinfandel, Riesling (Napa Valley), Chardonnay (Carneros).

Since 1980, Jim Prager has run a low-key, small-scale winery using purchased Napa Valley grapes for his line of ports. Production is 3,600 cases and distribution is limited, as much of the wine is sold from the winery, which is located behind Sutter Home near St. Helena. Port-style Cabernet, Petite Sirah and Pinot Noir are among the offerings.

PRESTON VINEYARDS
Dry Creek Valley
F: 1973. O: Lou & Susan Preston. W: Kevin Hamel. S: None.

OVERALL	$9-18	★★★

WINE RATINGS

Barbera Dry Creek Valley	★★★
Cabernet Sauvignon Dry Creek Valley	★★★
Chenin Blanc Dry Creek Valley	
Barrel Aged	★★★
Gamay Beaujolais Dry Creek Valley	★★★
Marsanne Dry Creek Valley	
Organically Grown Grapes	★★★
Rhône Blend Dry Creek Valley Faux	★★★
Rhône Blend Dry Creek Valley	
Sirah-Syrah	★★★
Sauvignon Blanc Dry Creek Valley	
Cuvée de Fumé	★★
Syrah Dry Creek Valley	★★★
Viognier Dry Creek Valley	★★★
Zinfandel Dry Creek Valley	★★★

WINERY DATA
C: 20,000. V: 120 acres in Dry Creek Valley. G: Sauvignon Blanc, Barbera, Carignane, Grenache, Syrah, Sangiovese and Viognier (Dry Creek Valley). P: None.

Preston Vineyards in Dry Creek Valley is a family-run operation that switched from grape growing to winemaking. With 120 acres in vines, the Prestons have a wide variety of grapes to choose from, with Sauvignon Blanc the acreage leader (25 acres) and Barbera, Carignane, Grenache, Syrah, Sangiovese and Viognier also part of the mix. The uniformly high and consistent quality of their wines is testimony to the Prestons' viticultural and enological capabilities. While all the wines are well made, the winery has taken a fancy to Rhône-style varieties, including Marsanne and Viognier. Chardonnay is conspicuous by its absence. Interestingly, none of the wines undergo malolactic fermentation and all of the reds are styled for immediate consumption.

TASTING NOTES

BARBERA DRY CREEK VALLEY (★★★): Steadily improving with a ripe, tart beam of fruit.
1992: Brimming with fresh, ripe raspberry, cherry and wild berry flavors that turn complex. **88**
1990: Lean, lively and fruity, a crisp red wine with pleasant raspberry and plum flavors. **82**
1989: Tart, crisp and fruity, with intense, moderately rich berry, plum and raspberry flavors. **86**

CABERNET SAUVIGNON DRY CREEK VALLEY (★★★): Medium-weight, with modest fruit concentration but overall well crafted and balanced.
1990: Firm, compact and tightly wound, with currant, black cherry and spice flavors that linger on. Firmly tannic. **87**
1989: Lean and crisp, with a core of modest blackberry and earthy herbal flavors. **81**
1988: A charming, fruity wine with an oaky edge. **80**
1987: Firm and tannic but with a solid core of rich, ripe currant and black cherry flavors that turn rugged. **88**
1986: Firm and concentrated, brimming with ripe cherry and currant flavors, picking up a trace of spicy oak. **87**

1985: A supple, elegant wine with ripe black cherry and currant flavors that are complex. **87**

1984: Ripe, with well defined currant, cedar, cassis and raspberry flavors that are smooth and supple. **86**

Chenin Blanc Dry Creek Valley Barrel Aged (★★★): Barrel aged, with good varietal character.

1992: Soft and fruity but dry, with a lemony edge to liven up the spicy melon and almond flavors, finishing with welcome generosity. **86**

Gamay Beaujolais Dry Creek Valley (★★★):

1994: Dark in color, effusively fruity, with bright berry flavors and smooth texture. Drink it while it's fresh and zingy. **87**

Marsanne Dry Creek Valley Organically Grown Grapes (★★★): Medium-bodied, but the varietal character is true with honey, pear and spice notes.

1994: Soft, ripe and silky, with a vanilla note running through the fruit bowl flavors. Finishes bright and appealing. **87**

1993: Medium-bodied, with a spicy honeysuckle edge. **83**

1992: Fresh and lively, with pretty spice, pear, floral and grapefruit flavors that turn smooth and polished. **88**

1991: Fresh and lively, with bright honey, pear and citrus flavors that are rich and focused, finishing with a smooth, creamy texture. **88**

Rhône Blend Dry Creek Valley Faux (★★★): Began as Faux-Castel—a play on Beaucastel, the great Rhône estate—it is now just called Faux, a blend of Rhône varieties made in a supple, medium-intensity style.

1993: Smooth and generous, and a spicy edge adds character to the black cherry and berry flavors that linger on the solid finish. **85**

1992: Dark in color, bright in flavor, a mildly chewy wine with berry and cherry flavors echoing on the finish. **83**

1991: Dark in color, with peppery plum and currant flavors that are ripe and lively, like a Beaujolais-Villages. **85**

1990: Tough and tannic, with raspberry and blackberry flavors pressing against the veil of astringency. **82**

Rhône Blend Dry Creek Valley Sirah-Syrah (★★★): A unique blend of these two grapes, as apparently the Prestons know what they planted. Vibrant and intense, with pepper and firm tannins.

1989: The crisp, lean texture lacks generosity, showing plum and cherry flavors. **78**

1986: Vibrant and floral, with oak-tinged blackberry and blueberry flavors. **90**

Sauvignon Blanc Dry Creek Valley Cuvée de Fumé (★★): Lightly fruity, with 20 percent Chenin Blanc added.

1993: Lean and crisp, a racy wine that has a green edge to the tobacco-scented pear. **86**

Organically Grown Grapes 1993: Round in texture but citrusy at the core, dressed up with a touch of ripe pear and toast. **83**

1992: Lightly fruity, with balanced herb, citrus and perfumed sweet pea flavors. **84**

Syrah Dry Creek Valley (★★★):

1992: Dark in color, with an alluring core of earthy currant, cedar and spice flavors that are tightly wound, finishing with rich tannins. **88**

1991: Dark in color, with a core of rich, earthy, concentrated currant, spice and mineral flavors. **87**

1990: Ripe, grapey and dark in color, with lots of raspberry, wild berry and cherry notes. **85**

Viognier Dry Creek Valley (★★★): Steadily improving, with pretty honey and spice-tinged fruit.

1994: Spicy, soft and fresh, a peppery edge to the simple pear flavors that last on the finish. **85**

1993: Light, with spice and honey notes. **82**

Zinfandel Dry Creek Valley (★★★): Medium weight and intensity, but attractive fruit flavors and mild tannins.

Old Vines Old Clones 1993: Rich and oaky, with a solid core of cedary oak and berry flavors, a complete package that turns spicy, complex and tannic. **88**

1992: Ripe, chunky and rustic, with rich, complex raspberry, cherry and blackberry flavors. **89**

1991: Ripe and fruity, with pretty black cherry, wild berry and anise notes. Finishes with soft tannins. **86**

1990: Soft and lush, with ripe, supple raspberry and cherry flavors that are fresh and lively. Supple tannins. **87**

1989: Nice proportions for an '89, with fresh berry and currant notes and smooth tannins. **84**

1988: Lighter in style, with charming strawberry and blackberry flavors that are immediately likable. **86**

1987: Intense, with ripe raspberry and cherry flavors framed by toasty oak notes. **83**

PRIDE MOUNTAIN VINEYARDS
St. Helena, Napa Valley
F: 1990. **O:** Jim & Carolyn Pride. **W:** Bob Foley.
S: None.

OVERALL	$18-20	★★★

WINE RATINGS

Cabernet Franc Napa Valley	★★
Cabernet Sauvignon Napa Valley	★★★
Chardonnay Napa Valley	
Mountain Vineyards	★★★
Merlot Napa Valley	★★★

WINERY DATA
C: 5,000. **V:** 70 acres in Napa Valley. **G:** Cabernet Sauvignon (25 acres), Merlot (30), Cabernet Franc (4), Petite Verdot (2), Chardonnay (6). **P:** Chardonnay, Merlot (Napa Valley).

Jim and Carolyn Pride bought 170 acres of volcanic earth on Spring Mountain in 1989, 2,000 feet above the valley floor and sitting on the Napa-Sonoma county line. Starting slowly with Cabernet, Cabernet Franc, Chardonnay and Merlot, production from their 70 acres in vines (and some purchased grapes) is at around 5,000 cases and headed toward 9,000 cases, with Bob Foley, the former winemaker at Markham, making the wines. Pride Mountain Vineyards was once known as Summit Winery. The first vines were planted in 1869. In 1995, the wines were made at Chappellet, but plans are to build a winery on the property.

TASTING NOTES

CABERNET FRANC NAPA VALLEY (★★):
1992: Dense, chewy and firmly tannic, with an intriguing tobacco edge to the currant and leather flavors. **83**

CABERNET SAUVIGNON NAPA VALLEY (★★★):
Impressive start, with ripe, rich, lush and complex flavors, supported by smooth but firm tannins and the right dose of oak.
1991: Ripe, smooth and polished, with plush cherry, currant and toasty oak flavors, finishing with richness, depth and concentration and supple tannins. **92**

CHARDONNAY NAPA VALLEY MOUNTAIN VINEYARDS (★★★): An understated style that reminds me of a young Stony Hill for its flinty, crisp mineral and tart fruit flavors. Well balanced, with the accent on fruit, not oak.
1993: Ripe with spicy, creamy pear and apple-laced fruit, turning elegant and delicate on the finish. **87**
1992: Tight and firm, with sleek apricot, pear and vanilla flavors that turn to hazelnut and honey on the finish. **88**
1991: Crisp and lively, with a bright core of apple, spice and vanilla flavors. **85**

MERLOT NAPA VALLEY (★★★): Early vintages are well made, with ripe flavors and good balance.
1992: An herbal wine, but the black cherry and cedar flavors come through the supple tannins. **85**
1991: Supple, smooth and spicy, with cedary plum, anise and currant aromas and flavors. Supple tannins. **88**

Q. C. FLY
This is a second label of Bouchaine Vineyards (see listing).

QUADY WINERY
Madera, Central Valley
F: 1977. **O:** Quady Winery Inc. **W:** Michael Blaylock.
S: None.

OVERALL	$9-13	★★★

WINE RATINGS

Black Muscat California Elysium	★★★
Orange Muscat California Electra	★★★
Orange Muscat California Essensia	★★★
Port Amador County Starboard	★★
Port California LBV	★★

WINERY DATA
C: 15,000. **V:** 1 acre in Madera. **G:** N/A. **P:** Orange and Black Muscat (California), Other (Amador).

After working for a now defunct Lodi winery, Andrew Quady decided to focus on port-style wines, beginning with Amador County Zinfandel followed by a string of uniquely styled dessert wines made from Muscat varieties. Elysium is made from Black Muscat, Essensia is made from Orange Muscat, Electra is a low-alcohol

Orange Muscat, and all are exceptionally well done. The Port is called Starboard, a play on the nautical opposite of Port; the grapes come from Frank's Vineyard, planted to traditional port varieties, including Tinta Cao, Tinta Amerela, Valdepenas and Bastardo. Total production is 15,000 cases.

TASTING NOTES

BLACK MUSCAT CALIFORNIA ELYSIUM (★★★): Dark and amazingly fruity, with a unique range of flavors.
1993: Smooth and lightly sweet, with plum and litchi flavors that dance delicately. Appealing for its unique fruit flavors. **87**
1992: Incredibly fruity and almost effervescent, with wild, jammy aromas and flavors. Sweet though not rich, with grape, raspberry and plum flavors. **82**
1990: Firm in texture and ebulliently fruity, with terrific blackberry, Muscat and nutmeg flavors. **86**

ORANGE MUSCAT CALIFORNIA ELECTRA (★★★): Sweet, with an appealing range of flavors.
1993: Light and sweet, with orange and peach flavors that glide smoothly across the palate. Drink while it's fresh. **83**
1992: Sweet and amazingly fresh, with appealing orange, pear and litchi aromas and flavors. Disarmingly fresh and juicy on the palate, and low enough in alcohol that it almost tastes like juice. **86**

ORANGE MUSCAT CALIFORNIA ESSENSIA (★★★): Shows off all the aromatic spiciness of Orange Muscat, but variable of late.
1993: Sweet and appealing, with a definite citrusy edge to the honey and pear flavors. **84**
1985: A harsh, bitter edge takes away from the sweet plum flavors. **73**

PORT VARIOUS BOTTLINGS (★★):
Amador County Starboard Batch 88 Rich Ruby 1988: Very rich and spicy, a well crafted, Port-like wine with concentration and character. **87**
Amador County Starboard 1987: Ripe and sweet, with cherry and plum notes, showing more alcoholic harshness than is desirable. **81**
Amador County Frank's Vineyard Starboard 1989: Ripe and rich, with layers of plum, prune, chocolate and pepper flavors, hinting at coffee and spice on the finish. **87**

California LBV 1991: Light in color, lightly plummy and spicy in flavor, a smooth wine. **81**

QUAFF
This is a second label for Z Moore Winery (see listing).

QUAIL RIDGE CELLARS
Napa Valley
F: 1978. **O:** Rutherford Benchmarks Inc. **W:** Elaine Wellesley. **S:** None.

OVERALL	$10-30	★★

WINE RATINGS	
Cabernet Sauvignon Napa Valley	★★
Chardonnay Napa Valley	★★
Merlot Napa Valley	★★
Sauvignon Blanc Napa Valley	★★

WINERY DATA
C: 30,000. **V:** None. **G:** None. **P:** Cabernet Sauvignon, Chardonnay, Merlot, Sauvignon Blanc (Napa Valley).

In the late 1970s, Elaine Wellesley and her late husband, Jesse Corallo, developed a small vineyard on Mount Veeder. The wines were made in an old stone building on Atlas Peak Road near the Silverado Country Club. In 1988, needing cash and a stronger market presence, the winery was sold to Heublein, with Wellesley retained as winemaker. When Heublein decided to divest itself of Inglenook, it also sold Quail Ridge to Rutherford Benchmarks, a group of investors headed by former Beaulieu general manager Anthony Bell. Once again, Wellesley survived. As of 1994, production had risen to 30,000 cases, all from purchased grapes, with a lineup that included Cabernet, Chardonnay, Merlot and Sauvignon Blanc. Despite all the changes, quality has remained good, and occasionally exceptional.

TASTING NOTES

CABERNET SAUVIGNON NAPA VALLEY (★★): A dip in quality after the brilliant 1987, as recent efforts have lacked fruit and depth.
1990: Modestly fruity and medium-weight, with hints of anise and currant. **85**
1989: Tough in texture, with tannic currant and berry flavors. **82**

1988: Simple, light and fruity, with plum and cherry notes and a hint of oak. **80**

1987: A big, ripe, chewy wine packed with concentrated cherry, plum, chocolate, cedar and smoke flavors that are tight and complex. **90**

Reserve 1987: Ripe and fruity, with a nice core of plum, cherry, cedar and spice flavors, but not up to the quality of the regular bottling. **87**

1986: A rich, smooth, seductive wine with pretty, toasty, oaky, ripe currant, cherry, tobacco and anise flavors that are broad and complex. Firm tannins. **89**

1985: Tough and tannic, with tobacco, herb and cherry flavors masked by a wall of tannin, closed and bitter. **80**

1984: Ripe and rich, with mature currant, plum and spicy oak flavors that are very intense and lively. **88**

CHARDONNAY NAPA VALLEY (★★): Usually well oaked, but with just enough fruit concentration to measure up.

1991: Oaky, with vanilla and toasty notes, finishing with pear and fig flavors. **84**

MERLOT NAPA VALLEY (★★): Uneven quality, light and smooth one year, ripe and jammy the next.

1990: Tastes green, with herb, tobacco and currant notes, but needs more fruit. **81**

1989: Light and fruity, with a distinctive herbal cast to the modest toast flavors. **79**

1988: Light, and smooth, with herb-scented plum and cherry flavors and a vanilla edge. **82**

1987: Ripe, with jammy berry and plum flavors, turning tight and tart on the finish. **86**

1985: Thick, rich, soft and luscious, with black cherry, herb and chocolate flavors, fine tannins and a plum aftertaste. **88**

SAUVIGNON BLANC NAPA VALLEY (★★): Clean and refreshing, with a nice core of fruit.

1992: Soft and refreshing, with ripe fig, vanilla and citrus notes, picking up light toasty oak on the finish. A delicate and pleasantly balanced wine. **85**

QUARTET

This is a second label for Roederer Estate (see listing).

QUINTESSA

Rutherford, Napa Valley

F: 1990. **O:** Huneeus Family. **W:** Alan Tenscher. **S:** None.

WINERY DATA

C: 1,000. **V:** 180 acres in Rutherford, Napa Valley. **G:** Cabernet Sauvignon, Cabernet Franc, Merlot. **P:** None.

In 1990, Agustin Huneeus headed a group of investors, including his partners at Franciscan, in purchasing a huge property in Rutherford, north of Conn Creek Winery, where 180 acres are now planted: 108 in Cabernet, 54 in Merlot and 18 Cabernet Franc. Plans are to build production to 20,000 cases, focusing on a Meritage red, Cabernet, Cabernet Franc and Merlot, each from the best single block on the property. Wines were planned for late 1996 or 1997.

QUIVIRA VINEYARDS

Dry Creek Valley

F: 1981. **O:** Holly & Henry Wendt. **W:** Grady Wann, Mary Ann Graf. **S:** Atlantis.

OVERALL	$10-15	★★★

WINE RATINGS

Cabernet Blend Dry Creek Valley	
Cabernet Cuvée	★★★
Rhône Blend Dry Creek Valley	
Dry Creek Cuvée	★★
Sauvignon Blanc Dry Creek Valley	★★★
Sauvignon Blanc Dry Creek Valley	
Reserve	★★★
Zinfandel Dry Creek Valley	★★★★

WINERY DATA

C: 20,000. **V:** 72.5 acres in Dry Creek Valley. **G:** Petite Sirah, Mourvèdre, Syrah, Cabernet Franc, Merlot, Sauvignon Blanc, Zinfandel, Grenache, Cabernet Sauvignon, Sémillon. **P:** None.

Holly and Henry Wendt founded Quivira in Dry Creek Valley in 1981 as a country retreat where they could ease into retirement. The Wendts spend time at their estate as time permits, as Henry is chairman of SmithKline Beecham, a $7-billion pharmaceutical giant. The Wendts hired Doug Nalle (Nalle Winery) to oversee winemaking at the outset, with an initial focus on Sauvignon Blanc and Zinfandel, later adding Cabernet and a red table wine blending Grenache, Syrah and Zinfandel. Production is now 20,000 cases, all estate bottled.

TASTING NOTES

CABERNET BLEND DRY CREEK VALLEY CABERNET CUVÉE (★★★): Steadily improving, classic Dry Creek weight and proportion, with appealing currant, cherry and cedary oak flavors, and mild tannins.

1991: Lean and earthy, with a narrow band of cherry and cedar, but it needs a little more flesh and flavor. **82**

1990: Tight and firm, with appealing currant, cherry and cedary oak flavors combined with firm, drying tannins. **87**

1989: Crisp, elegant and stylish, with bright cherry and raspberry flavors that have a pleasant, earthy, tarry edge, finishing with firm tannins. **86**

1988: Subtle, shaped by cedary oak but showing a core of elegant cherry and currant flavors. **84**

1987: Ripe, rich and rough-hewn, with chunky cherry, currant and earth flavors that are a bit coarse. **87**

RHÔNE BLEND DRY CREEK VALLEY DRY CREEK CUVÉE (★★): Good, but not in the class of Quivira's other reds—yet.

1993: A ripe and fruity style, with a ripe, grapey and cherry edge. Can be served chilled. A blend of Grenache, Mourvèdre, Syrah and Zinfandel. **84**

1992: A chunky, Rhône-style blend with raspberry and spice flavors. **85**

SAUVIGNON BLANC DRY CREEK VALLEY (★★★), RESERVE (★★★): Can be among the state's best, lean and delicate, with a tight core of citrus and pear-laced fruit.

1993: Light and fragrant, floral more than herbal, with citrusy flavors on the finish. **85**

1992: Beautifully balanced, lean and delicate, with spicy, herbal peach and honey flavors, and the finish is silky and smooth. **89**

Reserve 1993: Light and snappy, a bit of resiny flavor adding some interest to the bright pear fruit. **84**

Reserve 1992: Bright and buttery, medium-weight, smooth in texture, with a touch of fig to balance the butterscotch flavors. **84**

ZINFANDEL DRY CREEK VALLEY (★★★★): Remarkably consistent, with impeccible balance and just the right mix of berry and pepper. Mild tannins. Drinks best on release.

1992: Smooth, rich and complex, with ripe, concentrated wild berry, raspberry and spice notes that finish with toasty oak shadings. **89**

1991: Complex, full-bodied and stylish, with toasty, earthy, spicy notes accenting the solid berry and cherry flavors. **90**

1990: Smooth, ripe and generous, offering brilliant raspberry and plum aromas and flavors, turning more toward plum and spice on the long, round finish. **90**

1989: Lively and focused, with wild berry and plum flavors and a hint of earthiness. **84**

1988: The appealing ripe plum, black pepper and wild berry flavors are seductive, finishing with firm tannins. **88**

1987: Effusively fruity, teeming with pepper, raspberry, spice and jam notes framed by tannins and a touch of wood. **88**

1986: Effusively fruity, with supple strawberry notes, but reined in and firmly wrapped in just enough tannin. **88**

1984: Mature now, but still offering earthy raspberry flavors. **88**

QUPE CELLARS
Santa Maria Valley
F: 1982. **O:** Robert N. Lindquist. **W:** Robert N. Lindquist, Jim Adelman. **S:** None.

OVERALL	$11-25	★★★★

WINE RATINGS

Chardonnay Santa Barbara County	
Sierra Madre Vineyard	★★★
Marsanne Santa Barbara County	
Los Olivos Vineyard	★★★★
Rhône Blend Santa Barbara County	
Los Olivos Cuvée	★★★
Syrah Central Coast	★★★★
Syrah Santa Barbara County	
Bien Nacido Vineyard	★★★★
Viognier Santa Barbara County	★★★★

WINERY DATA
C: 10,000. **V:** 10 acres in Santa Barbara County. **G:** Syrah (3.25 acres), Merlot (4), Viognier (2), Mourvèdre (1). **P:** Syrah, Chardonnay, Viognier (Santa Barbara County), Syrah (Monterey), Syrah (Paso Robles).

After leaving Zaca Mesa Winery, where he worked with Ken Brown (Byron) and Jim Clendenen (Au Bon Climat), Bob Lindquist shifted his focus from traditional California wines (i.e. Cabernet, Pinot Noir and Sauvignon) to Rhône-style reds, taking an early interest in Syrah and adding Marsanne and Viognier. But also kept a hand in Chardonnay, which is made in a rich and dramatic style. Lindquist owns 10 acres in vines, which are planted to Rhône varieties. He also purchases grapes from Bien Nacido (Syrah) and Sierra Madre (Chardonnay). The Syrah is often blended with grapes purchased in Monterey, Paso Robles and Santa Barbara; hence it carries a Central Coast appellation of late, and is the winery's volume leader at 4,000 cases. A Bien Nacido Vineyard Syrah and Sierra Madre Chardonnay Reserve are two specialty wines.

TASTING NOTES

CHARDONNAY SANTA BARBARA COUNTY SIERRA MADRE VINEYARD (★★★), RESERVE (★★★): Bold and ripe, well oaked and concentrated.
1993: Beautifully crafted, bold, ripe and creamy, with a pretty array of complex pear, honey, toast and spicy flavors that are concentrated. **90**
Reserve 1993: Marked by a slight botrytis edge, with honey and fig notes that straighten out on the finish, where the flavors linger. **88**

MARSANNE SANTA BARBARA COUNTY LOS OLIVOS VINEYARDS (★★★★): Shows what is possible with this grape in California, as early efforts are ripe and well focused, with delicious flavors.
1991: Has delicious honey, vanilla and pear flavors, lively acidity and fine balance. It's rich, complex and appealing. **91**

RHÔNE BLEND SANTA BARBARA COUNTY LOS OLIVOS CUVÉE (★★★):
1989: Hearty and full-bodied, with a smooth texture and an earthy edge to the generous plum, cherry and spice flavors, turning murky with a vegetal edge. **85**

SYRAH CENTRAL COAST (★★★★): A leader with this grape, uniformly ripe, complex and deep in fruit concentration. Ages well.
1991: Ripe and fleshy, brimming with generous, complex black cherry, raspberry and currant flavors and earthy oak shadings. **90**

1989: Smooth and focused, with generous berry and spice flavors that edge toward cedary, earthy complexity. **87**
1988: Serves up ripe, rich, attractive spice, pepper, plum and earth flavors. Complex. **90**
1987: Firm and flavorful, with nicely focused raspberry, floral, toast and vanilla flavors and supple tannins. **88**

SYRAH SANTA BARBARA COUNTY BIEN NACIDO VINEYARD (★★★★):
1990: Wonderful depth, richness and complexity, with spicy cherry, pepper and currant flavors that are intense and concentrated. **92**
1989: Powerful and spicy, with a cedar, toast and pepper edge to the central core of plum and cherry flavors. **89**
1987: Distinctive, robust and ripe. Extremely dark in color, peppery and gamy in flavor, with smoke, anise and black cherry notes. **83**

RABBIT RIDGE VINEYARDS
Russian River Valley
F: 1985. **O:** Erich Russell & Darryl Simmons. **W:** Erich Russell. **S:** Meadow Glen.

OVERALL	$7-20	★★

WINE RATINGS

Cabernet Sauvignon Sonoma County Rabbit Ridge Ranch	★★
Chardonnay Russian River Valley Rabbit Ridge Ranch	★★★
Chardonnay Sonoma County	★★
Merlot Carneros Sangiacomo Vineyard	★★
Petite Sirah Sonoma County	★★
Red Table Wine California Oddux Reserve Red	★★
Rhône Blend California Allure	★★
Sangiovese Dry Creek Valley Coniglio Selezione	★★
White Table Wine North Coast Mystique	★★
Zinfandel Dry Creek Valley	★★
Zinfandel Sonoma County San Lorenzo Vineyard Reserve	★★★★

WINERY DATA
C: 30,000. **V:** 40 acres in Russian River Valley. **G:** Chardonnay (15 acres), Viognier (4), Sauvignon Blanc (5), Cabernet Sauvignon (8), Cabernet Franc (8). **P:** Chardonnay (Sonoma Valley), Zinfandel (Dry Creek Valley).

Erich Russell and his wife, Catherine, began developing their 40-acre Russian River vineyard in 1985. Today the winery is producing 30,000 cases, using both estate-grown and purchased grapes, and Russell is devoting himself full-time to the winery after a stint as winemaker at Belvedere. The lineup includes Cabernet (Sonoma County), Chardonnay (Russian River and Sonoma County bottlings), Petite Sirah, a Rhône blend called Allure (California) and Zinfandel, which has carried the Dry Creek, Sonoma County, Russian River Rabbit Ridge Ranch and San Lorenzo Vineyard Reserve designations.

TASTING NOTES

CABERNET SAUVIGNON SONOMA COUNTY RABBIT RIDGE RANCH (★★): Variable, with a successful 1988 and 1990, but less inspiring 1989.
1990: Firm, compact and tannic, this tightly wound Cabernet opens up with currant, anise and spicy wood flavors before turning dry and finishing with chewy tannins. Needs cellaring but may not outgrow its tannins. **86**
1989: A heavy-handed, oaky and tannic wine with little to offer. **77**
1988: Has pretty currant, black cherry, plum and spice flavors neatly framed by heavy oak. Despite the tannins and wood, the fruit pours through on the aftertaste. Try after 1996. **89**

CHARDONNAY VARIOUS BOTTLINGS (★★★): Variable too, impressive with its 1991 and 1993 Rabbit Ridge Ranch, but other bottlings are less fulfilling.
Russian River Valley Rabbit Ridge Reserve 1993: Intensely spicy with lichee nut, pear and honeyed notes, a bold and full-bodied Chardonnay with good depth. **88**
Russian River Valley Rabbit Ridge 1991: Smooth, broad, rich, complex and creamy, with layers of pear, spice, vanilla and honey flavors. **89**
Sonoma County 1992: Tastes sweet beyond ripeness, with a slightly sour pineapple edge. **80**
Sonoma County 1991: Despite an earthy edge, there are spicy nutmeg, peach and pear flavors that turn gamy. **84**

MERLOT CARNEROS SANGIACOMO VINEYARD (★★):
1992: Smooth and polished, spice-scented berry and black cherry flavors folding neatly between the delicate sparks of toasty oak. Nicely balanced all the way around, best from 1996. **86**

PETITE SIRAH SONOMA COUNTY (★★):
1990: Rich in flavor and dense with soft tannins, with grapey plum flavors. Slightly stale in aroma, but makes up for it on the chocolaty finish. **80**

RED TABLE WINE CALIFORNIA ODDUX RESERVE RED (NR):
1990: Half of a very good wine, with great spice and vanilla from new oak barrels, but it has harsh tannins and little fruit to back it all up. Stylish on the nose, but out of balance on the palate. **78**

RHÔNE BLEND CALIFORNIA ALLURE (★★): Nothing special so far, as the flavors are modest.
1991: A touch herbaceous, but it serves up enough pleasant fruit flavors to keep it in balance. **82**
1990: Lean and a bit oaky, with a narrow band of cherry and spice flavors that remain tight and tannic through the finish. **83**
1989: A straightforward, Rhône-style red wine offering ripe cherry and spice flavors. Definitely mature, showing earthy aromas and a finish that turns a little harsh, with muddled tomato notes. **81**

SANGIOVESE DRY CREEK VALLEY CONIGLIO SELEZIONE (★★):
1992: Supple and polished, with cedary oak and ripe cherry and berry notes. **84**

WHITE TABLE WINE NORTH COAST MYSTIQUE (★★):
1993: Light and bright, simple and straightforward, showing off its buttery pear fruit with freshness. **85**

ZINFANDEL SONOMA COUNTY SAN LORENZO VINEYARD RESERVE (★★★★): From low yield, old vines grown in Alexander Valley and Russian River Valley, this is a dark, rich and dramatic style, packed with juicy berry and mineral flavors. The 1993 is in the same class as the fine 1991.
1991: Dark, ripe and jammy, with rich wild berry and plum aromas and flavors, turning chewy with firm tannins. **90**

ZINFANDEL VARIOUS BOTTLINGS (★★): The 1991 vintage offers hope this is where the winery is headed with Zinfandel, as two bottlings, the Dry Creek and San Lorenzo Vineyard Reserve were both excellent.

Dry Creek Valley 1993: Mild-mannered, with spicy berry and cherry fruit of modest proportions. **85**

Dry Creek Valley 1992: An oaky wine with gritty tannins and a coarse core of tarry fruit flavors. **80**

Dry Creek Valley 1991: Sturdily built, with firm tannins and pepper and wild berry flavors. **87**

Dry Creek Valley 1990: Tough and tannic, with a strong gamy edge to the blackberry and toast flavors. **73**

Russian River Valley Rabbit Ridge Ranch 1988: A firm, focused, claret-style wine that offers attractive blackberry and cherry flavors. **86**

Sonoma County 1989: Firm and concentrated, with a strong dose of blackberry and plum flavors shaded by leafy cedar overtones. **86**

RADANOVICH VINEYARDS & WINERY
Mariposa, Sierra Foothills
F: 1986. O: Radanovich Family. W: George P. Radanovich. S: None.

OVERALL	$11-18	★

WINE RATINGS

Cabernet Sauvignon Sierra Foothills Mariposa County	★
Merlot Sierra Foothills	★
Zinfandel Sierra Foothills Mariposa County	★

WINERY DATA
C: 2,000. V: 20 acres in Mariposa County. G: Sauvignon Blanc, Zinfandel. P: None.

This 2,000-case family-owned winery in Mariposa owns some 20 acres of Sauvignon Blanc and Zinfandel, with both being made into wines, the latter in both a red and white version. Cabernet and Merlot have also been added. Quality is ordinary. In 1994, founder-winemaker George Radanovich was elected to the U.S. House of Representatives.

TASTING NOTES

VARIOUS BOTTLINGS (★):
Cabernet Sauvignon Sierra Foothills Mariposa County 1989: A rustic wine with leathery Zinfandel-like flavors that range from pruny to briary. Needs hearty fare to soften the rough, chewy tannins. **77**

Merlot Sierra Foothills 1991: Simple, fruity and a little earthy, a medium-weight wine with modest but appealing flavors and moderate tannins. **82**

Zinfandel Sierra Foothills Mariposa County 1989: Thin and diluted, with earthy, leathery flavors that barely pass as Zinfandel. Flat and dull on the finish. Drinkable, but barely. **72**

A. RAFANELLI WINERY
Dry Creek Valley
F: 1974. O: Patricia Lee & David A. Rafanelli. W: David A. Rafanelli. S: None.

OVERALL	$13-17	★★★★

WINE RATINGS

Cabernet Sauvignon Dry Creek Valley	★★★★
Zinfandel Dry Creek Valley	★★★★

WINERY DATA
C: 8,000. V: 53 acres in Dry Creek Valley. G: Cabernet Sauvignon (19 acres), Zinfandel (24), Merlot (8), Petite Sirah (2). P: None.

If one were accepting nominations for California's most underrated winery, A. Rafanelli would have to be given serious consideration. The family has been growing grapes in Dry Creek Valley since the 1950s, when Americo and Alberto Rafanelli purchased a large property in Dry Creek planted to various varieties, which they sold to Sonoma wineries. In 1974, the family began making small lots of wine, and even today production is on a small scale, with 8,000 cases, roughly two-thirds Zinfandel and one-third Cabernet. Both the Cabernet and Zinfandel come from old vines and they share a pure if not rustic quality that emphasizes the ripeness, depth and concentration of the fruit. They are formidable wines and very consistent from year to year; they drink exceptionally well and represent excellent value. Under winemaker David Rafanelli, quality continues to improve.

TASTING NOTES

CABERNET SAUVIGNON DRY CREEK VALLEY (★★★★):
Uniformly rich, intense and flavorful, jam-packed with complex and concentrated flavors and firm, but plush

tannins. Oak is in the background. Contains 5 percent Merlot, ages well.

1991: Firm and intense, with ripe, juicy currant, black cherry and spicy oak flavors that turn rustic and chunky, but the flavors run deep and rich. **91**

1990: Intense, spicy and elegant, a lavish wine that delivers a broad array of berry, currant and nutmeg flavors, hinting at vanilla and coffee on the finish. **90**

1988: Firm, concentrated and deep, with ripe, chunky cherry and plum flavors and vanilla, chocolate and oak notes. Supple tannins. **90**

1987: Pretty cherry, currant, herb and smoky, seasoned oak flavors are well proportioned, turning complex and intriguing. **91**

1986: Marvelously concentrated, with cassis and cherry flavors framed by toasty vanilla overtones that make it harmonious. **91**

1985: Dense and concentrated, a rustic style with some odd flavors and hard, tannic fruit notes. **78**

ZINFANDEL DRY CREEK VALLEY (★★★★): Shares the Cabernet's intensity, with bold, ripe, direct fruit flavors and a sense of harmony and finesse. Contains 5 percent Petite Sirah. Ages well too.

1992: Intense and tannic, with pretty, toasty oak, concentrated blackberry and cherry flavors that linger on the finish. **89**

1991: Ripe and generous, with bright raspberry, blackberry and plum flavors wrapped neatly in spicy oak, echoing berry and vanilla on the finish. **89**

1990: Solid and chunky, with rich, intense berry, cherry and raspberry flavors that are deep and concentrated, finishing with a dry, oaky, slightly earthy edge. **90**

1989: Aromatic, with a firm, crisp texture and plenty of plum and blackberry flavors to ride a solid stream of fine tannins. **85**

1988: Massively proportioned, with elegant, ripe raspberry, plum and cherry flavors that turn complex and concentrated, seasoned by spicy dill and oak notes. **90**

1987: Offers juicy raspberry and berry flavors that pick up a touch of gaminess on the finish. **84**

1986: Firm and concentrated, layered with blackberry, cassis and plum flavors, cedary overtones from spicy oak and a bracing touch of acidity and tannin to wrap it up. **91**

RAMSEY

This is a second label for Kent Rasmussen Winery (see listing).

RANCHO SISQUOC WINERY
Santa Maria Valley
F: 1972. **O:** Flood Ranch Co. **W:** Stephan Bedford. **S:** None.

OVERALL	$9-27	★★

WINE RATINGS

Cabernet Blend Santa Maria Valley Red Cellar Select	★★
Cabernet Sauvignon Santa Maria Valley	★★
Chardonnay Santa Maria Valley	★★
Merlot Santa Maria Valley	★★
Sauvignon Blanc Santa Maria Valley	★★

WINERY DATA

C: 8,000. **V:** 210 acres in Santa Maria Valley. **G:** Sauvignon Blanc (25 acres), Chardonnay (40), Sylvaner (10), Merlot (10), Cabernet Franc (5), Johannisberg Riesling (40), Cabernet Sauvignon (70), Malbec (3), Mourvèdre (3), Syrah (3). **P:** None.

Rancho Sisquoc Winery is part of the sprawling 38,000-acre Flood Ranch, a diversified agricultural concern that grows a variety of crops. The oldest part of this 210-acre Santa Maria Valley vineyard was planted in 1968, making it one of the oldest in Santa Barbara County. As such, it has sold grapes to many area wineries. The acreage leader is, perhaps surprisingly, Cabernet (70 acres), with which the winery excells. Chardonnay and Johannisberg Riesling both have 40 acres in vines. Farming is still the main endeavor, as the winery makes but 8,000 cases.

TASTING NOTES

CABERNET BLEND SANTA MARIA VALLEY RED CELLAR SELECT (★★): Features ripe, bright, complex fruit flavors.

1990: Ripe and fleshy, with bright, complex, concentrated cherry, currant and spice flavors that show a delicate balance. **88**

1989: Velvety in texture, with a gamy edge to the fairly rich currant, chocolate and cedar aromas and flavors. **87**

CABERNET SAUVIGNON SANTA MARIA VALLEY (★★): One of the best Cabernets in an area where Cabernet often struggles and is marked by pronounced vegetal notes. Quality is variable.

1991: A herbaceous wine that's moderately rich and spicy, picking up cherry and plum flavors on the finish, where a little bell pepper sneaks in. **84**

1990: Light and simple, with a sour green edge to the modest plum and currant flavors. **76**

1989: Firm and focused, showing tight, elegant currant, cedar and spice flavors. **85**

1986: Pronounced vegetal and herbal flavors dominate in a wine that has limited appeal. **73**

CHARDONNAY SANTA MARIA VALLEY (★★): Less exciting than many from this area, but it can be rich and earthy with deep flavors.

1992: Clean and correct, with ripe, spicy pear and citrus notes of modest depth. **81**

1991: Ripe and round, with a decidedly earthy edge to the Burgundian apple and pear flavors, finishing with butter and oak. **85**

MERLOT SANTA MARIA VALLEY (★★): Lean and simple, with modest fruit flavors.

1991: Lean and slightly astringent, but it has modest flavors of chocolate and berry that echo lightly the finish. **80**

SAUVIGNON BLANC SANTA MARIA VALLEY (★★): Offers pure, ripe varietal character, but lacks finesse.

1992: Ripe and broad, with flavors that lean more toward pineapple and grapefruit than herbs, finishing a little chunky. **81**

KENT RASMUSSEN WINERY
Carneros

F: 1986. **O:** Kent Rasmussen & Celia Ramsey. **W:** Kent Rasmussen. **S:** Ramsey.

OVERALL	$19-21	★★★

WINE RATINGS

Cabernet Sauvignon Napa Valley	★★
Chardonnay Napa Valley	★★★
Pinot Noir Carneros	★★★
Ramsey Merlot Napa Valley	★★★
Ramsey Pinot Noir Carneros	★★
Ramsey Sangiovese California	★★

WINERY DATA

C: 5,000. **V:** 14 acres in Carneros. **G:** Pinot Noir. **P:** Chardonnay (Napa Valley), Pinot Noir (Carneros), Dolcetto (Napa Valley), Syrah (California).

Kent Rasmussen's winemaking credentials include stints in South Africa and Australia, but most of his experience is with Napa Valley and Carneros-grown grapes. In 1986 he purchased a small vineyard that now measures 14 acres in vines, all devoted to Pinot Noir, but his wine portfolio of 5,000 cases includes Chardonnay, Dolcetto, Sangiovese, Syrah and Alicante Bouschet made from purchased grapes. Sangiovese, Merlot and Pinot Noir have appeared under the Ramsey label.

TASTING NOTES

CABERNET SAUVIGNON NAPA VALLEY (★★):
1988: Firm, flavorful and definitely earthy, with a strong core of blackberry and currant flavors shaded by hints of leather. **83**

CHARDONNAY NAPA VALLEY (★★★): Can be intense and lively, well oaked and complex.

1992: Firm and supple, with spicy pear, toasty oak and light earthy flavors, finishing with a burst of fruit. **87**

1991: Intense and lively, with complex, concentrated flavors of toasty oak, spicy pear and creamy vanilla. **90**

PINOT NOIR CARNEROS (★★★): Solid and well made but shy of outstanding, marked by complex fruit flavors in the best years.

1992: Tight and firm, softening a bit in texture, with herb, cherry and cedar notes. **87**

1991: Tight, firm and intense, with a nice core of currant, herb and spice flavors that turn dry and tannic. **88**

1990: Solid, with generous, smoothly integrated black cherry, black currant, toast and spice flavors. **86**

1988: An earthy, juniper berry flavor overrides the spicy cherry and plum notes, picking up a woody, tannic edge. **84**

RAMSEY MERLOT NAPA VALLEY (★★★): Well made, with complex flavors, but not the extra dimensions of the best.

1992: Features bright plum, wild berry and cherry notes, but turns lean and austere on the finish. **87**
1991: Smooth, spicy and generous, brimming with elegant blackberry, vanilla and nutmeg flavors. **88**
1989: A decadent wine that has plenty of lively fruit flavors to back up the earthy, barnyardy aromas and finish. Firmly tannic. **86**

RAMSEY PINOT NOIR CARNEROS (★★): Simple with decent flavors, but a step down from the Rasmussen.
1992: Firm, tight and tannic, with compact flavors of dried cherry and tobacco. **82**
1991: Spicy, herbal and firm, hinting at cherry and earth on the finish. The finish is tannic. **81**

RAMSEY SANGIOVESE CALIFORNIA (★★):
1992: Lean and a little leathery, with earthy berry flavors shooting through the finish. **82**

RAVENSWOOD
Sonoma Valley
F: 1976. **O:** Reed Foster & Joel Peterson. **W:** Joel Peterson. **S:** None.

OVERALL	$8-40	★★★★

WINE RATINGS

Cabernet Blend Sonoma County Mountain Claret	★★
Cabernet Blend Sonoma Mountain Pickberry Vineyard	★★★
Cabernet Sauvignon Sonoma County	★★
Cabernet Sauvignon Sonoma Valley Gregory Vineyard	★★
Chardonnay North Coast Vintners Blend	★★
Chardonnay Sonoma Valley	★★
Merlot Carneros Sangiacomo Vineyard	★★★
Merlot North Coast Vintners Blend	★★
Merlot Sonoma County	★★
Zinfandel Napa Valley Dickerson Vineyard	★★★★★
Zinfandel North Coast Vintners Blend	★★
Zinfandel Sonoma County	★★★★
Zinfandel Sonoma Valley Belloni	★★★★
Zinfandel Sonoma Valley Cooke	★★★★
Zinfandel Sonoma Valley Old Hill Vineyard	★★★★

WINERY DATA
C: 90,000. **V:** 14 acres in Carneros Valley. **G:** Pinot Noir. **P:** Cabernet Sauvignon (Sonoma County), Chardonnay (North Coast, Sonoma Valley), Merlot (Carneros, North Coast, Sonoma County), Zinfandel (Sonoma County).

Joel Peterson, winemaker and co-founder of Ravenswood, grew up with fine wine-loving parents, and developed a keen palate at a young age. His fascination with wine led to his working for Joseph Swan in the early 1970s before he started Ravenswood in 1976; he was joined in 1981 by Reed Foster, who provided financial backing to expand operations. Most of Ravenswood's wines are made from purchased grapes. The winery's strength is ripe, full-throttle Zinfandel from a series of mostly old-vine, dry-farmed vineyards, mostly in Sonoma Valley, which makes a strong case for Sonoma Valley Zinfandel. When it comes to understanding how and where Zinfandel grows best, and recognizing the wine's strengths and limitations, Peterson has few peers. He is so in tune with his Zinfandel vineyards and the resultant wines that they routinely overshadow his other fine wines, none of which rises to the heights of the Belloni (Sonoma Valley), Cooke (Sonoma Valley), Dickerson (Napa Valley) or Old Hill Vineyards (Sonoma Valley) Zinfandel.

Having achieved such success with Zinfandel, at times it appears that Peterson tries to cull as much character from Cabernet Chardonnay and Merlot, but somehow comes up just short. Ravenswood's finest Cabernet-style wine is a proprietary blend that includes Merlot and Cabernet Franc from Pickberry Vineyard on Sonoma Mountain. Chardonnay comes from several sources, but the Sangiacomo bottling is often excellent. In 1991, Ravenswood moved into the old Haywood winery, and production is now 90,000 cases.

TASTING NOTES

CABERNET BLEND SONOMA COUNTY MOUNTAIN CLARET (★★):
1992: Marked by herb and cedary notes, the narrow band of currant and cherry emerge on the finish, giving it more depth and shape. Best after 1996. **84**

CABERNET BLEND SONOMA MOUNTAIN PICKBERRY VINEYARD (★★★): Shares the same intensity and range of flavors as Ravenswood's Zinfandels, but often to its detriment, as it comes across as a Zinfandel-style Cabernet with wild flavors and brambly tannins.

1992: Dense, dark and chewy, with a tight core of tannins submerging the earthy currant and berry flavors. **86**

1991: The pretty berry, spice, currant and tobacco flavors are soft, rich and fleshy, with modest tannins. **83**

1990: Ripe, smooth and polished, a supple wine with prune, chocolate and cola aromas and flavors, echoing a hint of cherry on the finish. **86**

1989: Complex and inviting, with pretty spice, cedar, black cherry and currant flavors that have just the right touch of tannin. **89**

1988: Soft and ripe, with jammy plum and cherry flavors of modest depth. **82**

1986: Tannic and drying, with appealing anise, plum and currant flavors that are concentrated and focused. **87**

CABERNET SAUVIGNON SONOMA COUNTY (★★):

1992: Smoky, with toasty oak that gives the currant and plum flavors a slight bitter edge. **86**

1991: Tight and chewy, with a narrow, compact band of currant and tar flavors. **84**

1989: Lean and firm, with a supple core of cherry and currant flavors. **84**

1988: Elegant and complex, with intense, concentrated currant, spice, cedar and herb flavors that are well integrated and well defined. **89**

1987: Herbal green olive aromas and flavors push to the front of this supple, velvety wine, joining black cherry and currant flavors on the finish. **84**

1986: Mature, still showing its oak and tannin, but the currant and cherry flavors are appealing. **86**

1985: A big, muscular, tannic and concentrated wine with mature mint and cherry flavors. **85**

CABERNET SAUVIGNON SONOMA VALLEY GREGORY VINEYARD (★★): Tight and lean, marked by herbal notes.

1990: Definitely herbal, with strong mint, sage and tarragon aromas and flavors, and the finish is soft and minty more than fruity. **84**

1989: Aromatically pleasing, with minty currant notes, but leaner and shyer on the palate. **85**

1988: Tough and oaky, with decent cherry and plum flavors accented by cedar and vanilla notes. **80**

CHARDONNAY VARIOUS BOTTLINGS (★★):

North Coast Vintners Blend 1993: Tart and flinty, with a green edge to the pear and apple flavors. **84**

Sonoma Valley 1991: An earthy, mossy wine that misses the mark. **71**

MERLOT CARNEROS SANGIACOMO VINEYARD (★★★): This Sangiacomo bottling packs in lots of flavors and is nearing the class of Ravenswood's Zinfandels. Worth watching.

1992: Dense, chewy and tannic, but there's enough currant, herb and cedary oak flavors to hold your interest, picking up a nice tobacco edge on the finish. **86**

1990: Ripe, firm and generous, with tasty plum and cherry flavors that have a spicy anise and oak edge. **88**

1989: Chunky and lively, with supple currant, cherry and blackberry flavors shaded by anise and cedar notes. **90**

MERLOT VARIOUS BOTTLINGS (★★): Ranges from good to very good, with soft, sharply focused flavors at its best.

North Coast Vintners Blend 1992: Well proportioned, with supple, earthy berry and cherry flavors that pick up a spicy edge. **84**

Sonoma County 1992: Tight and tannic, with a band of minty currant that peeks through; best to cellar into 1996 to soften, but it may always be on the tannic side. **85**

Sonoma County 1990: Firm in texture, with appealing raspberry, blackberry, spice and vanilla flavors. **85**

Sonoma County 1989: Dense and tannic, with austere plum and currant flavors framed by hard-edged oak. **86**

Sonoma County 1987: Soft and generous at first, with sharply focused cherry and plum flavors that linger. **87**

Sonoma County 1986: Tough, tannic wood overrides the fragile plum and cherry flavors. **80**

ZINFANDEL NAPA VALLEY DICKERSON VINEYARD (★★★★★): This Napa vineyard consistently yields a rich, supple minty currant core of Zinfandel fruit. Ages well.

1992: Firm, tight, crisp and tannic, with spicy raspberry, wild berry and black cherry flavors that are intense and sharply focused, gaining a minty edge on the finish. **91**

1991: Distinctively minty and spicy, showing ripe raspberry and cherry flavors, but the mint flavors dominate. The tannins are polished. **87**

1990: A delicious Zin, ripe, rich and tannic, with tiers of berry, raspberry and cherry flavors that zoom across the palate. **92**

1989: Spicy, oaky notes lead to ripe, intense raspberry flavors and firm tannins. **87**

1988: Marked by strong eucalyptus and menthol flavors, with chunky red cherry and raspberry flavors that persist on the finish. **84**

1987: Tart, intense and tannic, with ripe, powerful plum, blueberry and cherry flavors that are sharply focused. **86**

1986: Tight and tannic, with ripe raspberry and cherry flavors and a touch of vanilla on the finish. **88**

1983: Tight and sharply focused, with ripe plum and spice notes and a smoky, cedary edge. **87**

1981: Mature but holding, with intense plum, raisin and spice flavors that turn tannic. **85**

ZINFANDEL NORTH COAST VINTNERS BLEND (★★):
1992: Simple and fruity, with plum and cherry flavors that turn spicy and earthy on the finish. **83**

ZINFANDEL SONOMA COUNTY (★★★★): In the years it's made, this Zinfandel blended from all the Sonoma Vineyards can be excellent, supple and complex.

1992: Bright and lively, with spicy cherry, raspberry, plum and currant flavors, turning elegant, with a supple texture and light, toasty oak shadings. **91**

1990: A mouthful of fruit and tannin, offering rich, intense plum and blackberry flavors framed by toasty, buttery oak notes. **89**

1989: Solid and chewy, with a firm texture and ample plum and berry flavors. **82**

1988: Firm and tannic, with tart, well defined plum and berry flavors that linger. **86**

1987: Despite the tannins, this has attractive raspberry flavors that are spicy, peppery and well balanced. **88**

1986: Massive and fruity, deep and rich, with raspberry and plum flavors and a tannic, powerful finish. **88**

1985: Mature with earthy, anise and berry notes, fading on the finish. **80**

ZINFANDEL SONOMA VALLEY BELLONI (★★★★): Very ripe and dense, packed with rich fruit flavors that fan out.

1992: Big, rich, intense and tannic, packing in loads of black cherry, wild berry, spice and floral flavors. **89**

1991: Tight and firm, with rich, tannic cherry and raspberry flavors that are youthful, concentrated and sharply focused. **89**

ZINFANDEL SONOMA VALLEY COOKE (★★★★): Big, ripe, deep and concentrated, loaded with fruit and character.

1992: Tight and compact, with a firm tannic edge to the ripe cherry, raspberry and spice flavors that are rich and focused. **91**

1991: Big, deep, rich and concentrated, with ripe, intense tar, cherry, raspberry and spice flavors wrapped firmly in tannins. **88**

1990: Bold, ripe, intense and chewy, with layers of powerful, tannic currant, raspberry, cherry and plum flavors surrounded by spicy oak notes that linger. **90**

1987: An intense, lively wine that's dense, deep, rich and concentrated, with pretty raspberry and pepper notes on the finish. **88**

ZINFANDEL SONOMA VALLEY OLD HILL VINEYARD (★★★★): Serves up lots of bold, ripe, aromatic flavors, with great intensity. Usually quite tannic.

1992: Perfumed and floral, with bright, ripe cherry and raspberry jam flavors that border on the exotic. Finishes with crisp tannins. **92**

1991: Tight and firm, with plenty of raspberry and cherry flavors peeking through the cedary, spicy oak and chewy tannins. **87**

1990: A ripe, potent Zinfandel loaded with ripe blackberry, black cherry, spice, floral and earth flavors. **89**

1987: Intensely tannic and packed with ripe raspberry, cherry, plum and spice flavors that are powerful and enduring. **87**

1986: Very rich and concentrated, blanketed by soft tannins, and the blueberry and raspberry flavors are complemented by black pepper and toasty oak shadings. **92**

MARTIN RAY WINERY
F: 1937. **O:** Codera Wine Group Inc. **W:** Greg Graziano. **S:** None.

OVERALL	$24-28	★★★

WINE RATINGS

Cabernet Sauvignon Napa Valley	★★★

Chardonnay California Mariage ★★★

WINERY DATA
C: 6,000. V: None. G: None. P: Cabernet Sauvignon (Napa Valley), Chardonnay (California), Pinot Noir (Sonoma, Monterey, Mendocino).

After owning Paul Masson Winery from 1936 to 1943, Martin Ray established a winery and vineyard in the Santa Cruz Mountains, where he produced a number of important (indeed legendary in some quarters) Cabernets, Chardonnays and Pinot Noirs, both from his property and purchased grapes. In 1972, a dispute among investors led to the property being divided, with the former Martin Ray Winery facility being renamed Mount Eden, and Ray moving to a separate facility at a lower elevation. He died in 1976, and without him the brand withered. In 1991, Courtney Benham received permission from Ray's estate to use the name and the brand was revived, with two excellent wines. The 1991 Cabernet, made from Howell Mountain grapes, showed tremendous depth and concentration; a 1992 Chardonnay, California appellation, with grapes from Santa Cruz, Monterey, Anderson Valley and Sonoma, was intense and lively. Initial production was 3,000 cases of each, with Pinot Noir planned for the future. The first wines were made at Mendocino's Domaine Saint Gregory winery, but Benham hopes to locate a site in Santa Clara and relocate the winery there.

TASTING NOTES

CABERNET SAUVIGNON NAPA VALLEY (★★★):
1991: Rich, ripe, supple and intense, with tiers of currant, black cherry, plum and spice notes, gaining depth from the toasty, buttery oak nuances. **91**

CHARDONNAY CALIFORNIA MARIAGE (★★★):
1992: Intense and lively, with supple, complex layers of spicy pear, honey, toast and smoky oak flavors. **91**

RAYMOND VINEYARD AND CELLAR
St. Helena, Napa Valley
F: 1971. O: Kirin Brewery. W: Walter Raymond, Kenn Vigoda. S: None.

OVERALL	$10-40	★★★

WINE RATINGS
Cabernet Sauvignon California Amberhill	★★
Cabernet Sauvignon Napa Valley	★★★
Cabernet Sauvignon Napa Valley Private Reserve	★★★
Chardonnay California Amberhill	★★
Chardonnay California Selection	★★
Chardonnay Napa Valley	★★★
Chardonnay Napa Valley Private Reserve	★★★
Meritage Red Napa Valley Private Reserve	★★★
Pinot Noir Napa Valley	★★
Sauvignon Blanc Napa Valley	★★

WINERY DATA
C: 165,000. V: 450 acres in Napa Valley, Monterey. G: Chardonnay (362 acres), Cabernet Sauvignon (31), Merlot (44), Pinot Noir (12). P: Chardonnay (Napa, Sonoma County), Cabernet Sauvignon (Napa Valley), Merlot (Napa Valley), Cabernet Franc (Napa Valley), Sauvignon Blanc (Napa Valley), Sémillon (Napa Valley).

The Raymonds are one of the oldest winemaking families in Napa Valley. The family owned Beringer Vineyards until 1971, when they sold it to Nestlé and the Labruyere family of France. With money from the winery sale, Roy Raymond Sr. bought a 90-acre parcel on Zinfandel Lane, where he and his sons Roy Jr. and Walt founded this winery. In 1988 part-interest in the winery was sold to Kirin Brewing Co. of Japan. The Raymonds remained in control of management and production, and since then production has risen substantially to 165,000 cases. The winery owns 450 acres of vineyard, including 300 acres in Monterey which fuel the Raymonds' California-appellation Chardonnay and Amberhill line. The Napa Valley wines, both the Napa Valley and Reserve bottlings, are very well crafted, although in recent vintages there has been less distance between the two lines than was evident in the mid-1980s.

TASTING NOTES

CABERNET SAUVIGNON CALIFORNIA AMBERHILL (★★):
1991: Pleasantly balanced, with spicy, toasty oak and supple currant and cherry flavors. **84**

CABERNET SAUVIGNON NAPA VALLEY (★★★): Marked by fine balance, fine tannins and a range of flavors that runs from spicy black cherry, to earth, tar and cedary oak.

1991: Supple, but with an earthy, leathery edge to the currant and plum-laced fruit, leaving a dry tannic edge. **85**

1990: Firm, chunky and pleasantly fruity, with buttery oak, cedar, currant and plum flavors. **88**

1989: Firm and focused, with a nice range of spice, currant, cherry, chocolate and vanilla flavors. **87**

1988: Firm and tight for an '88, with plum, cedar and currant flavors of moderate richness and concentration. Not too tannic. **85**

1987: Delivers ripe cherry and currant flavors, but is distinctive for its mint and bay leaf notes. **83**

1986: Firm and tight, with rich plum and berry flavors that are beautifully focused straight through to the finish, where the buttery oak adds complexity. **90**

1985: Green bell pepper, olive and tobacco aromas and flavors tend to nudge past the vague currant flavors. **84**

1978: Ripe and intense, with lively currant and herb aromas and flavors, finishing with a spicy anise aftertaste. **86**

CABERNET SAUVIGNON NAPA VALLEY PRIVATE RESERVE (★★★): The Reserve bottling is usually a shade more intense and concentrated, but not always.

1990: Supple, with well integrated herb, currant and spicy, buttery oak flavors and fleshy tannins. **88**

1988: Supple and complex, with spicy currant, herb, anise and cedary oak flavors. **88**

1986: Elegant and polished, with spicy oak notes and juicy currant, herb, dill and plum flavors that are complex. **88**

1985: Smooth and elegant, with well defined currant, plum, herb, cedar and smoky oak flavors that finish with plush tannins. **88**

1984: Ripe and supple, with generous cherry, plum, cedar, anise and olive flavors. **88**

1983: Mature and retaining its tannic edge, with herb, currant and plum flavors emerging on the finish. **84**

1982: Mature, with smoky, herbal berry flavors that finish with smooth tannins. **86**

1981: At its peak, serving up fresh herb, currant and anise flavors. **87**

1980: A herbaceous wine laced with herb, tea, spice and cherry flavors that are elegant and graceful. **85**

CHARDONNAY CALIFORNIA AMBERHILL (★★):

1993: Pleasantly fruity, with ripe pear, apple and citrus notes. **83**

1992: Plenty of bold, ripe and creamy apple, pear and spice flavors. **84**

1991: Lean and fruity, with a nice apple and lemon zing to the flavors that persists into a lively finish. **83**

CHARDONNAY NAPA VALLEY (★★★), PRIVATE RESERVE (★★★): Features bold, ripe, juicy Chardonnay flavors that are well oaked, displaying vanilla and buttery notes. Recent vintages have been a shade less opulent and less concentrated.

1992: Lean and crisp, with a narrow band of tart apple and pear flavors that are well focused. **85**

1991: A subtle wine that's correct and balanced, with a narrow band of spicy pear and vanilla flavors. **85**

Private Reserve 1992: Ripe, smooth and polished, with an elegant core of spicy pear, apple and light vanilla oak shadings, but not the usual gusto found in Raymond Reserve Chardonnay. **87**

Private Reserve 1991: Ripe, rich and intense, with spicy pear, fig and toasty oak flavors that are just beginning to unfold into a complex and creamy wine. **89**

MERITAGE RED NAPA VALLEY PRIVATE RESERVE (★★★): Shares the weight, flavor and tannin profile of the Cabernet. The 1990 was finely crafted.

1989: Smooth and elegant, with aromatic spicy and leathery overtones to the currant, mineral and cedar flavors. **89**

1990: Delivers bright, lively black cherry, currant and plum flavors that are rich, focused and elegant, finishing with a long, fruity aftertaste and smooth tannins. **90**

PINOT NOIR NAPA VALLEY (★★):

1992: Tight, with an earthy, stemmy edge, but enough fruit comes through to make it appealing, with hints of dried cherry. **83**

SAUVIGNON BLANC NAPA VALLEY (★★): A new addition, the initial offerings were mixed, with the 1992 marked by strong weedy flavors.

1993: Spicy, floral flavors run through this straightforward, slightly vegetal wine. **81**

1992: Shows weedy, woody flavors on a sturdy frame, but has little charm. **77**

RENAISSANCE VINEYARD & WINERY
North Yuba, Sierra Foothills
F: 1978. **O:** Fellowship of Friends. **W:** Gideon Beinstock, Paul Flitcroft. **S:** Da Vinci.

OVERALL	$8-35	★★

WINE RATINGS

Cabernet Sauvignon North Yuba	NR
Riesling North Yuba Dry	NR
Sauvignon Blanc North Yuba	★★
Sauvignon Blanc North Yuba	
Select Late Harvest	★★

WINERY DATA
C: 30,000. **V:** 365 acres in North Yuba. **G:** Cabernet Sauvignon (168 acres), Sauvignon Blanc (78), Riesling (38), Chardonnay (36), Merlot (25), Zinfandel (15), Cabernet Franc (2), Pinot Noir (2). **P:** None.

Renaissance Vineyard and Winery, owned by the Fellowship of Friends, a philosophical group based in the San Francisco Bay Area, farms 365 acres of grapes in the North Yuba foothills. It's a unique setup situated in a unique locale, as this is the lone vineyard in this remote northern California county. The fellowship has invested some $16 million in planting these vines and building a winery, which produces 30,000 cases of wine, including Cabernet (15,000 cases), Chardonnay (2,000), Riesling and Sauvignon Blanc (10,000 cases), along with dessert-style Riesling and Sauvignon Blanc. Optimism is high about the potential and the wines have impressed some critics. My own notes indicate the wines have been bizarre to ordinary to good, but clearly this is a serious endeavor and given time it may yield more compelling wines. Worth watching.

TASTING NOTES

VARIOUS BOTTLINGS:
Cabernet Sauvignon North Yuba 1990: Ripe, with a slight raisiny edge, turning coarse and finishing with gritty tannins. **81**

Riesling North Yuba Dry 1992: Light and refreshing, flavors centered around grapefruit, finishing a tad sweet. **85**
Sauvignon Blanc North Yuba 1992: Aggressively floral aromas and flavors mark this as an unusual wine, but there are some nice pear and apple notes as well. **83**
Sauvignon Blanc North Yuba Select Late Harvest 1991: Sweet and fresh, with nice pear and apricot fruit that lingers on the solid finish. Tasty now, maybe best from 1997. **85**

RENWOOD WINERY
Amador County
F: 1979. **O:** Renwood Wineries Inc. **W:** Scott Harvey. **S:** Santino Wines.

OVERALL	$6-30	★★★

WINE RATINGS

Barbera Amador County	★★★
Port Shenandoah Valley Late	
Bottled Vintage	★★
Zinfandel Amador County	★★★
Zinfandel Shenandoah Valley	
Grandpère Vineyard	★★★

WINERY DATA
C: 40,000. **V:** 34 acres in Amador County. **G:** Zinfandel (16 acres), Barbera (6), Viognier (6), Syrah (6). **P:** Zinfandel, Muscat Canelli, Barbera, Nebbiolo, Syrah, Sauvignon Blanc, Sémillon, Sangiovese (Amador County).

Renwood is the former Santino Winery. Scott Harvey started his brand there in 1991 while working for Santino, but when the owners decided to sell the winery, he was able to put together a deal to buy it in 1994. Renwood produces 40,000 cases, including wines still made under the Santino brand. The wide-ranging lineup includes Barbera, Fumé Blanc, Nebbiolo, Sangiovese, Sémillon, Syrah, Viognier and Zinfandel (5 different bottlings, including white Zinfandel and a Grandpère Vineyard bottling). So far the Barbera and Zinfandels are most impressive and most widely distributed, but clearly there are some fine wines in this stable, which makes it worth watching. Sangiovese dates only to 1992, Syrah 1991 and Viognier 1992.

Tasting Notes

Barbera Amador County (★★★): Two bottlings are made, an Amador County and Linsteadt (500 cases). The standard features ripe, tight, sharply focused flavors.
1992: Firm and fruity, but strays toward an undertone of horsy flavor. Finishes with firm black cherry flavors. **82**
1991: Ripe and intense, with tart raspberry and blackberry flavors that are bright and vivid. Impressive. **86**

Port Shenandoah Valley Late Bottled Vintage (★★):
1989: A lighter style of Port, with nicely focused black cherry and blackberry flavors, slightly smoky and with a delicate grip on the finish. Solid to drink now, best from 1997-1998. **85**

Zinfandel Amador County (★★★):
1991: Tight and tannic, with a core of hard-edged wild berry and cherry flavors, finishing with drying tannins and an earthy, tarry edge. **83**

Zinfandel Shenandoah Valley Grandpère Vineyard (★★★): The Grandpère Vineyard (125-year-old vines), is the one to watch, as it is intense and complex.
1992: Dark in color, with very ripe jam, raisin, plum and black cherry flavors that are intense and concentrated, finishing with firm tannins. **88**
1991: Intense and firmly tannic, with briary chocolate and wild berry flavors that turn complex if a bit biting on the finish. **86**

RETZLAFF VINEYARDS
Livermore Valley
F: 1986. O: Bob & Gloria Taylor. W: Bob Taylor. S: None.

Overall	$14-18	★

Wine Ratings	
Cabernet Sauvignon Livermore Valley	NR

Winery Data
C: 3,000. V: 14 acres in Livermore. G: Cabernet Sauvignon (4 acres), Merlot (2), Chardonnay (4), Sauvignon Blanc (2), Riesling (2). P: None.

Bob and Gloria Taylor own this 3,000-case winery. Using 14 acres of winery-owned vineyards in Livermore Valley, they produce Cabernet, Chardonnay (Alameda County), Merlot and Sauvignon Blanc (Amador County). Quality is ordinary.

RICHARDSON VINEYARDS
Sonoma Valley
F: 1980. O: Dennis, Carolyn & Evelyn Richardson & Al Wighton Jr. W: Dennis Richardson. S: None.

Overall	$12-15	★★★

Wine Ratings	
Cabernet Sauvignon Sonoma Valley	
Horne Vineyard	★★
Merlot Carneros	★★★
Pinot Noir Carneros	
Sangiacomo Vineyard	★★★
Zinfandel Sonoma Valley	
Nora's Vineyard	★★★

Winery Data
C: 2,500. V: None. G: None. P: Pinot Noir, Merlot (Carneros), Zinfandel, Cabernet Sauvignon, Cabernet Franc (Sonoma Valley).

This partnership operates a 2,500-case winery on the Sonoma side of Carneros, using purchased grapes for Cabernet (Horne Vineyard), Merlot, Pinot Noir (Sangiacomo) and Zinfandel (Nora's Vineyard, Sonoma Valley), with Merlot, Pinot Noir and Zinfandel the quality leaders.

Tasting Notes

Cabernet Sauvignon Sonoma Valley Horne Vineyard (★★): Variable quality, although the 1991 Horne Vineyard was impressive for its complex flavors.
1992: An earthy, minty wine that turns rustic and tannic, devoid of charm. **79**
1991: Ripe, intense and jammy, with lush, complex blackberry and currant flavors that turn spicy and chewy on a tannic finish. **89**
1990: Firm, focused and decidedly earthy, showing a barnyard streak that dominates. **73**

1989: Decidedly minty, with strong menthol flavors that dominate the cherry and berry notes. **78**

MERLOT CARNEROS (★★★): Consistently well made, with both Gregory Vineyard and Sangiocomo Vineyards used as vineyard-designations on occasion.

1992: Gains complexity and finesse, with tiers of ripe cherry, plum and spice flavors that linger. **87**

1991: Hard, tart and tannic, with a tight core of currant, spice and anise flavors. **86**

1990: Deep and full-bodied, full of cassis, earth and smoke aromas that are backed up by complex fruit flavors. **89**

1989: Firmly tannic, with a strong streak of currant flavor shaded by chocolate and cedar notes and an herbal overlay. **83**

Sangiacomo & Gregory Vineyards 1991: Clumsy, with cedar, spice and oak flavors showing more prominently than the fruit. **82**

Sangiacomo Vineyard 1990: Thick and flavorful, with layers of herb, plum and currant flavors backed by full but soft tannins. **87**

PINOT NOIR CARNEROS SANGIACOMO VINEYARD (★★★): Solid and reliable through most of the 1980s, but less inspiring of late.

1991: Simple, sturdy and flavorful, with currant and spice flavors that turn smoky. **80**

1990: Soft and fleshy, with cola, berry, earth and oak flavors, thinning on the finish. **83**

1989: Deep in color, with plenty of ripe raspberry, spice, loganberry and currant flavors. **86**

1987: Distinctive, rich and enticing, with layers of smoky bacon, plum and black cherry flavors. **88**

1986: Firm, focused and fruity, with berry flavors that are nicely integrated with oak. **85**

ZINFANDEL SONOMA VALLEY NORA'S VINEYARD (★★★): Made in a bold, assertive style.

1992: Bold, ripe and intense, with layers of spicy raspberry, tar and cedary oak flavors. **89**

RIDGE VINEYARDS
Santa Cruz Mountains
F: 1959. **O:** Otsuka America. **W:** Paul Draper. **S:** None.

OVERALL $14-75   ★★★★★

WINE RATINGS

Cabernet Sauvignon Napa County York Creek	★★
Cabernet Sauvignon Santa Cruz Mountains	★★★
Cabernet Sauvignon Santa Cruz Mountains Monte Bello	★★★★★
Chardonnay Santa Cruz Mountains	★★★★
Merlot Napa County York Creek	★★
Merlot Sonoma County Bradford Mountain Vineyard	★★
Petite Sirah Napa County York Creek	★★
Rhône Blend California Evangelo Vineyards Mataro-Mourvèdre	NR
Zinfandel Dry Creek Valley Lytton Springs	★★★★★
Zinfandel Howell Mountain	★★
Zinfandel Napa County York Creek	NR
Zinfandel Paso Robles	★★★★
Zinfandel Paso Robles Dusi Ranch	★★★★
Zinfandel Sonoma County	★★★
Zinfandel Sonoma County Geyserville	★★★★
Zinfandel Sonoma Valley Pagani Ranch	★★★★

WINERY DATA
C: 50,000. **V:** 150 acres in Santa Cruz Mountains and Dry Creek Valley. **G:** Cabernet Sauvignon (98 acres), Merlot (6), Petite Verdot (3), Cabernet Franc (2), Zinfandel (34). **P:** Cabernet Sauvignon, Chardonnay, Merlot (Santa Cruz Mountains), Carignane, Zinfandel, Petite Sirah, Mataro (Sonoma County, Contra Costa County).

The amazing thing about Ridge Vineyards is that its wines just keep getting better. This winery not only excels with its Monte Bello Cabernet and various vineyard-designated Zinfandels, but each of the wines keeps improving, with small refinements here and there. To top things off, in the 1990s Ridge is producing superb Chardonnays.

Ridge began in 1959, when a trio of Stanford Research Institute engineers, headed by Dave Bennion, bought an abandoned winery and the Monte Bello vineyard high atop the steep Santa Cruz Mountains above

Cupertino. Bennion and his colleagues began tending the vines on weekends and started making small lots of wine from the Monte Bello vineyard, while also seeking out old Zinfandel, Petite Sirah and other Italian field blend varietals from Amador County, Dry Creek Valley (Lytton Springs), Alexander Valley (Geyserville), Mendocino, Napa Valley (York Creek), Paso Robles (Dusi Ranch), and later Howell Mountain (Beatty Ranch) and just about anywhere else they could find grapes that suited their style. Employing basic, if not rustic, winemaking techniques, Ridge developed its own style of big, ripe and often tannic wines which quickly won a devout following. By the mid-1960s, the winery was producing a Monte Bello Cabernet along with as many as six or seven other red wines, most Zinfandels. The wines were so good—and popular—that the owners began to convert the winery from a hobby to a business. It soon became apparent that running the winery required more than weekend management, and in 1969, Ridge hired the talented Paul Draper as winemaker, putting him in charge of shaping the styles, which he has done admirably.

With its rich soils and cool climate, Monte Bello's 2,600-foot elevation is considered an ideal location for Cabernet Sauvignon. Its proximity to the Pacific Ocean, less than 20 miles away, provides for many damp, foggy mornings and brisk, breezy afternoons, which allow the grapes to ripen slowly and evenly. (The only drawback is that in some years it is a shade too cool and the grapes struggle to ripen.) Draper credits the wine's quality to provide the vineyard's maturity (most of the vines are 40 years old or older), the wild, natural yeasts which provide natural fermentation, and the fact that Ridge does little in the way of filtration to manipulate its wines.

Through the years, Ridge has stayed its course, gradually adding Cabernet and Petite Sirah from York Creek (Spring Mountain, Napa Valley), Merlot from Bradford Mountain (Sonoma), Chardonnay (Howell Mountain and Santa Cruz Mountains), Mataro (Bridgehead, Contra Costa County) and another Zinfandel (Pagani Ranch, Sonoma). In 1986, Ridge's partners decided to sell the winery, with the buyer being Otsuka, a large diversified firm based in Japan.

The winery owns 150 acres in vines, 59 in the Santa Cruz Mountains, including Monte Bello. It also bought the Lytton Springs Winery and vineyard (45 acres) in 1991, maintaining its long, successful asso-

ciation with that winery by keeping the vineyard and brand name alive. Production is 50,000 cases, but some things don't change. The lineup is still heavily weighted toward reds, most of which are at the top of their classes.

TASTING NOTES

CABERNET SAUVIGNON NAPA COUNTY YORK CREEK (★★): Disappointing in recent vintages, after a run of good to very good wines dating to the 1970s. Has lacked the richness of fruit and complexity to measure up to the wood and hard tannins. Both the 1988 and the 1989 were mediocre.

1991: Youthful and tight, with smoke and currant flavors that are plush but tannic. **84**

1990: Solid and chunky in texture, with a green, herbal edge to the prune and berry flavors. **88**

1987: Firm and chunky, with smoky, woody notes to the ripe plum and currant flavors. **85**

1986: Has a pleasing if rustic core of black currant, cedar and spicy cherry flavors. **88**

1985: Mature and losing its fruit, turning earthy and dry. Drink it before the cherry and currant flavors dry out. **86**

1984: Ripe and fruity, with layers of ripe, supple black cherry, currant, floral and spice flavors. **85**

1983: Lean and crisp, overly tannic. **73**

1982: Lean, hard, tannic and oaky. **73**

1981: Lean and oaky, with dry tannins. **74**

1980: Ripe and jammy, packed with earthy currant, black cherry and plum flavors, supported by firm tannins. Mature. **85**

1979: Extremely ripe and mature, almost raisiny, with drying tannins. **86**

1978: Elegant, with cedary tobacco and currant flavors, but it turns blunt and tannic. **87**

1977: A very pleasant 1977 with ripe plum, cherry and spicy currant flavors. **88**

1976: Extremely ripe, with pruny, earthy flavors. **68**

1975: Extremely ripe, with earthy plum, currant and black cherry flavors. **87**

1974: Smooth and mature, with supple currant, cherry and spicy oak flavors. **85**

CABERNET SAUVIGNON SANTA CRUZ MOUNTAINS (★★★): The Santa Cruz bottling, which includes Jimsomare Vineyard (once a vineyard-designated wine) has been green, tannic and funky on occasions, but is now steadily improving. Recent bottlings feature ripe, focused fruit flavors and supple tannins.

1992: Intense and focused, with supple, elegant currant, earth and black cherry flavors framed by toasty, cedary oak. **89**

1991: A tough, chewy, earthy wine that packs in lots of flavor, with layers of currant, chocolate, mineral and tar. **89**

1990: Dense and earthy, with a nice layer of focused currant and blackberry flavors to go with the toasty, gamy overtones. **85**

1989: Medium-weight, with chocolate, earth, cedar and bay leaf flavors and firm tannins. **82**

1986: Funky, with intense oak and barnyard flavors. **68**

1985: The exaggerated oak and vegetal flavors are austere and tannic. **64**

1983: This declassified Monte Bello has decent black currant and cherry flavors, but give Ridge credit for putting it under a second label. **84**

CABERNET SAUVIGNON SANTA CRUZ MOUNTAINS MONTE BELLO (★★★★★): Among California's elite, very consistently dark, concentrated and flavorful, with complex current, earth and mushroom flavors that develop nicely over time. Moderately tannic, it ages exceptionally well, reaching a peak at about six to seven years after vintage date, and is capable of aging 20 to 25 years. Contains about 15 percent Merlot.

1991: Complex and inviting, with a pleasant range of currant, vanilla and herb flavors that fold together nicely, finishing with depth, richness and concentration. Best to cellar into 1997, but then it should last another decade. **93**

1990: Earthy, cedary flavors dominate this dark, chunky, solidly built wine. It's tannic on the palate, finishing with black cherry and spice notes. **92**

1989: Ripe, rich, smooth and complex, with currant, plum and black cherry flavors and chocolate, vanilla and spice notes, finishing with fine tannins. **90**

1988: Marked by meaty, vegetal and smoky flavors wrapped tightly around a modest core of raspberry and currant, turning raw and tough. **82**

1987: Powerful and complex but marked by earth, mushroom and leather overtones to the deep, concentrated currant flavor. **88**

1986: The oak has folded into the black cherry and currant flavors, giving it a greater sense of balance and elegance. **85**

1985: Beautifully defined and rich, with layers of cedar, plum, black cherry and vanilla flavors supported by firm, lean tannins and a great aftertaste of fruit and minerals. **95**

1984: Mature now, with a supple earthiness joining the ripe currant, black cherry, vanilla and spice flavors. **88**

1982: Tough and tannic, a victim of harvest rains. **75**

1981: Elegant and complex, with firm, compact black currant, plum and cherry aromas and flavors that are well proportioned. **89**

1980: Still lacks focus, and the oak and moderately ripe fruit flavors lack harmony. **80**

1978: Elegant and mature, with ripe, concentrated plum, currant and spice flavors that turn earthy and complex. The tannins are supple. **92**

1977: A shade past its peek, it is very deep and concentrated, with cedar, black currant and cherry flavors that are complex and firmly tannic. **92**

1976: Ripe and raisiny, with drying tannins; past its peak. **83**

1975: Supple and lively, with ripe, complex fruit flavors that are mature and complex. **88**

1974: Deep ruby, with ripe, spicy currant and anise flavors that are fresh, rich and focused, turning smooth and elegant on the finish. There's a wonderful sense of harmony and proportion and the tannins are mild. **94**

1973: Lively, elegant and complex, with mint, cedar, sweet black cherry and anise flavors. **87**

1972: Past its prime, with earthy mushroom aromas, but there are pretty fruit flavors and a touch of bell pepper on the finish. **82**

1971: Fully mature and at its peak, offering prune, plum, cedar and tobacco flavors. **85**

1970: The Monte Bello of the decade, a supple, complex, harmonious wine with layers of currant, anise, cedary oak and earthy mineral flavors. **96**

1969: Amazingly elegant and youthful, with bright, complex spice, plum, black cherry and floral flavors that echo on the finish. **92**

1968: Mature and drying, but there's still a pleasant core of chocolate, cedar and oak flavors. **87**

1965: Complex and elegant, past its prime but holding, with classic cigar box aromas and mature cherry and bell pepper flavors. **86**

1964: Beautifully crafted, smooth and mellow, with complex, well focused Cabernet flavors, cigar box aromas and fine length. **90**

C*hardonnay* S*anta* C*ruz* M*ountains* (★★★★):
Increasingly impressive for its bold, ripe, complex fruit
flavors and deft oak shadings. Poised to join the top
echelon.

1992: Ripe and complex, with a pretty assortment of spice,
pear, honey and toasty, buttery oak, with a persistence on
the finish that builds. Another beauty from Ridge. **92**

1991: Bold, ripe, rich and complex, with tiers of concentrated pear, honey, toast and vanilla flavors. **92**

M*erlot* N*apa* C*ounty* Y*ork* C*reek* (★★):

1991: Light and spicy, with an austere, woody edge to
the modest blackberry flavors. **80**

1990: There are smoky, toasty, charred oak shadings to
the herb and currant aromas and flavors. **82**

M*erlot* S*onoma* C*ounty* B*radford* M*ountain*
V*ineyard* (★★): Highly variable, excellent in 1990, but
marginal in several vintages prior.

1990: Bright and flavorful, a charming wine with a nice
range of berry, plum, mint and spice aromas and flavors. **89**

1989: Medium-bodied, with mild tannins and modest
cherry and plum flavors. **82**

1987: Despite ripe plum aromas, this is tight and tannic,
with a green edge and a little stemminess. **75**

1986: Extremely woody and vegetal, with thin, uninspired red wine flavors. **72**

P*etite* S*irah* N*apa* C*ounty* Y*ork* C*reek* (★★): Can
be ruggedly tannic, with the peppery fruit struggling
to compete.

1991: Dark and tannic, with intense ripe plum, pepper
and spice notes that linger. **87**

1987: The inky black color foreshadows the licorice and
leather flavors that dominate this rich, intense wine. **76**

1985: Ripe and pretty, with crushed pepper and floral
notes to complement the fresh berry flavors. **87**

R*hône* B*lend* C*alifornia* E*vangelo* V*ineyards*
M*ataro*-M*ourvèdre* (NR):

1990: Gamy, smoky, toasty aromas and flavors shoulder
past the modest fruit in this medium-weight, closed-
in red. **73**

Z*infandel* D*ry* C*reek* V*alley* L*ytton* S*prings*
(★★★★★): A great vineyard and wine capable of
achieving uncommon depth, richness and complexity.

Big, ripe and flavorful, it showcases what Zinfandel can
achieve and does it often. Includes up to 20 percent Petite
Sirah and Carignane.

1993: Ripe, rich and supple, with complex jammy cherry, plum, tar and spice flavors, all complex and concentrated, with a long plush aftertaste that keeps pumping
out the flavor. **91**

1992: Bright, lush and rich, brimming with ripe, juicy
wild berry, jam and pepper flavors, this wine hangs
together extremely well. **91**

1991: Full-blown and fully oaked, displaying a fine, deep
color, rich fruit flavors and polished tannins. Lush and
plush in texture and sweet with vanilla and spice. **91**

1990: A sturdy, solid, old-style Zin that's bursting with
jammy, peppery raspberry and plum flavors. Weaves in a
nice touch of oak on the finish. **89**

1989: Firm and tannic, with a delicate balance between
the distinctive oak and barnyard flavors. **82**

1988: Tart and fruity, with berry and plum flavors that
turn a bit sour on the finish. **82**

1987: Ultraripe and complex, teeming with jammy, spicy,
peppery flavors and finishing with richness and finesse. **91**

1986: Firm and ripe, with enough supple smoothness to
let the raspberry and plum flavors show through, and
there's a touch of buttery toast on the finish. **88**

1985: Big, rich and tasty, with ripe berry flavors and
spicy, oaky nuances that are well integrated in a thick,
full-bodied style. **83**

1974: Mature but holding, with spicy, leathery, smoky
fruit flavors. **83**

Z*infandel* H*owell* M*ountain* (★★):

1990: Lean and leathery, with barnyard aromas and flavors and a tough texture. **80**

1989: Dense and deeply flavored, with pepper and blackberry notes on top of firm, chewy tannins. **87**

1988: Ripe and earthy, with burnt coffee overtones to the
dark plum and cherry flavors. **82**

1987: Ripe and earthy, with supple, moderately rich, typical Zinfandel flavors. **83**

Z*infandel* N*apa* C*ounty* Y*ork* C*reek* (NR):

1991: Ripe, spicy and opulent, a juicy wine with cherry
and raspberry flavors and a good dose of tannins. **88**

Z*infandel* P*aso* R*obles* (★★★★), D*usi* R*anch*
(★★★★): Can be variable, as Zinfandel is, but at its best
brilliant, with bright, ripe, lush and complex fruit.

1991: Deep in color, with ripe, spicy, jammy berry, cherry, raspberry and plum flavors that turn earthy and complex on the finish. **90**

1990: Smooth and gentle, with pleasant cherry and spice flavors. **84**

1989: There are spicy oak and modest barnyard overtones to the ripe raspberry and plum flavors. **84**

1987: Earthy and gamy, with attractive wild berry and spice notes that give it complexity. **85**

1986: An old-fashioned wine with jammy raspberry flavors and a woody, tannic edge. **81**

Dusi Ranch 1992: Bold, ripe and jammy, a super-ripe wine with lush black cherry and plum flavors. **90**

ZINFANDEL SONOMA COUNTY (★★★):

1990: Ripe and fleshy, with a pretty core of spicy raspberry aromas and flavors framed by toasty oak, earth and dill notes. **86**

1989: An earthy wine with dill and mineral notes backed by straightforward berry flavor. **80**

1988: Earthy, leathery and firmly tannic, with firm berry and cherry flavors that turn supple and generous. **88**

ZINFANDEL SONOMA COUNTY GEYSERVILLE (★★★★):
Steady, ranging from very good to excellent, with rich, complex fruit flavors. Blend is 20 percent Carignane and 15 percent Petite Sirah.

1992: A controversial style with its lush, ripe fruit and earthy, leathery flavors, finishing with a horsey barnyard edge that detracts. **86**

1991: Bold, ripe, rich and concentrated, offering a core of elegant currant, spice, herb and meat flavors. The color is dark and the texture is smooth and supple. **90**

1990: Firm and focused, with hearty wild berry and oak flavors that fold together nicely. **87**

1989: Full-bodied, flavorful and velvety in texture, with straightforward blueberry and blackberry flavors. **84**

1988: Spicy vanilla nuances add grace and complexity to this distinctive wine that's oozing with blackberry and boysenberry flavors. **90**

1987: Intense and well focused, mature now with a complex array of wild berry, spice, cedar and tarry notes, and a long finish. **88**

1986: Lean and firm, with plenty of berry aromas and flavors and plenty of oak too. **79**

1985: A rich, intense, tannic Zin that's loaded with berry and pepper flavors. **83**

ZINFANDEL SONOMA VALLEY PAGANI RANCH (★★★★):
A new star, bold, ripe and jammy, it's typically very ripe and carried a Late Picked designation in 1992.

1992: Packs in lots of ripe, jammy flavors yet maintains its elegance and finesse. The black cherry, wild berry and currant notes are intense and concentrated. **93**

1991: Beautiful, dark, ripe, spicy plum, cherry and raspberry flavors turn dense and chewy, picking up a tarry edge, with smooth but substantial tannins. **89**

RITCHIE CREEK VINEYARDS
St. Helena, Napa Valley
F: 1967. **O:** R. Pete Minor. **W:** R. Pete Minor. **S:** Richard Minor.

OVERALL	$18	★★★

WINE RATINGS

Cabernet Sauvignon Napa Valley	★★★

WINERY DATA
C: 1,200. **V:** 8 acres in Spring Mountain. **G:** Chardonnay (3 acres), Cabernet Sauvignon, Merlot (4). **P:** None.

In the mid-1960s, Santa Rosa dentist Pete Minor caught wine fever and bought a large parcel of land at the 2,000-foot elevation on Spring Mountain. He began planting his eight-acre Cabernet and Chardonnay vineyard an acre a year, commencing commercial winemaking in 1974. Without grape purchases, production is limited to 1,200 cases a year, which has held steady for more than a decade. The tree-shrouded vineyard makes for a cool climate, but the Cabernet does especially well here, rendering very consistent wines from year to year.

TASTING NOTES

CABERNET SAUVIGNON NAPA VALLEY (★★★): Elegant with an earthy, mushroom edge to the currant and cherry flavors. Rustic but well crafted. Includes 8 percent Merlot.

1991: Firm, with herb, olive and tar overtones to the ripe currant and black cherry flavors. Rich and balanced, with an earthy mushroom and tar edge. **91**

1990: Spicy, with pepper, currant and earthy tobacco flavors that turn smooth and soft. **89**

1985: Mature and rustic, with supple currant, coffee and herb notes that turn complex. **87**

1978: Hard and tannic, an austere wine in which the tannins dominate. **78**

RIVER ROAD VINEYARD
Russian River Valley
F: 1977. **O:** Gary Mills. **W:** Gary Mills. **S:** None.

OVERALL	$5-10	NR

WINE RATINGS		
Cabernet Sauvignon Sonoma County		NR
Chardonnay Sonoma County		NR

WINERY DATA
C: 14,000. **V:** 78 acres in Russian River Valley. **G:** Chardonnay. **P:** Chardonnay, Cabernet Sauvignon (Sonoma County).

Founder-winemaker Gary Mills farms 78 acres of Chardonnay in Russian River Valley and augments that by buying Sonoma-grown Cabernet and Chardonnay for his 14,000-case winery in Forestville. Chardonnay at 8,000 cases dominates. Cabernet is in the 2,000-case range. Distribution is limited. No recent notes.

RIVER RUN VINTNERS
Watsonville
F: 1978. **O:** Kris Arneson & J. P. Pauloski. **W:** J. P. Pauloski. **S:** None.

OVERALL	$7-18	NR

WINE RATINGS		
Cabernet Sauvignon Mendocino County		NR
Merlot San Benito County		NR
Syrah California		NR
Zinfandel California		NR

WINERY DATA
C: 3,000. **V:** None. **G:** None. **P:** Merlot, Cabernet Sauvignon (Redwood Valley), Syrah (Monterey), Zinfandel, Merlot (San Benito County), Zinfandel, Syrah (Paso Robles), Mourvèdre (Contra Costa).

This 3,000-case winery in Watsonville buys all the grapes for its lineup, which includes Cabernet, Chardonnay, Merlot, Syrah and Zinfandel. Vineyard sources include Contra Costa (Mourvèdre), Monterey (Syrah), Redwood Valley (Cabernet and Merlot), and San Benito County (Merlot and Zinfandel). No recent notes.

RIVERSIDE FARMS
This is a second label for Foppiano Vineyards (see listing).

ROCHE WINERY
Carneros
F: 1989. **O:** Joseph & Genevieve Roche. **W:** Steve MacRostie. **S:** None.

OVERALL	$9-30	★★

WINE RATINGS		
Chardonnay Carneros		★★
Pinot Noir Carneros		★★

WINERY DATA
C: 6,000. **V:** 26 acres in Carneros. **G:** Chardonnay (14 acres), Pinot Noir (9), Merlot (3). **P:** None.

Joseph and Genevieve Roche purchased 2,500 acres in Carneros in 1977 with an eye to retirement. They eased into grape growing and then winemaking, constructing a winery in 1989 on the Carneros Highway in Sonoma. Today they farm 26 acres of Pinot Noir, Chardonnay and Merlot, and after a good start with Pinot Noir, the winery has settled into a line of good but unspectacular wines, a bit surprising given winemaker Steve MacRostie's success with Chardonnay at Hacienda and Macrostie. Production is about 6,000 cases.

TASTING NOTES

CHARDONNAY CARNEROS (★★): Tight and firm, on the crisp side with medium-bodied flavors.
Barrel Select Reserve 1992: Strikes a nice balance between spicy, toasty oak and ripe pear and apple flavors, giving it an elegant finish. **85**
1991: Firm, crisp and spicy, with subtle pear and apple flavors that could be a little brighter. **85**

PINOT NOIR CARNEROS (★★): Simple, light and fruity, a wine that neither inspires nor offends.
1990: Offers ripe berry flavors with raspberry and cherry notes, but it turns thin, firm and tight on the finish, with gritty tannins. **83**

1989: Light, tart and flavorful, with lively, slightly candied sour cherry and raspberry flavors. **81**

1988: Crisp, clean and narrow, with light, spicy cherry and berry notes. **80**

Reserve 1990: Simple, ripe and fleshy, with a band of intriguing spice, cherry, currant, oak and nutmeg flavors. **83**

Unfiltered 1991: Shows a core of pretty, spicy currant and black cherry flavors, mild tannins and a fruity finish. **84**

Unfiltered 1989: Woody, varnishlike flavors dominate. **78**

J. ROCHIOLI VINEYARD & WINERY
Russian River Valley

F: 1982. **O:** Tom & Joe Rochioli. **W:** Tom Rochioli. **S:** None.

OVERALL	$11-38	★★★★★

WINE RATINGS

Cabernet Sauvignon Russian River Valley	
Neoma's Vineyard Private Reserve	★★
Chardonnay Russian River Valley	★★★★
Chardonnay Russian	
River Valley Reserve	★★★★★
Pinot Noir Russian River Valley	★★★★
Pinot Noir Russian River Valley Reserve	★★★★★
Sauvignon Blanc Russian River Valley	★★★
Sauvignon Blanc Russian River	
Valley Reserve	★★★★
Zinfandel Russian River Valley	
Sodini Vineyard	★★★★

WINERY DATA
C: 8,000. **V:** 110 acres in Russian River Valley. **G:** Chardonnay (35 acres), Pinot Noir (38), Sauvignon Blanc (13), Gamay (10), Other (14). **P:** None.

After years of supplying area wineries with wonderful grapes, J. Rochioli Vineyards is about to receive the recognition it richly deserves. The wines from this Russian River Valley estate have steadily gained in quality, so much so that the current offerings, from Chardonnay to Pinot Noir to Sauvignon Blanc to Zinfandel, are now among California's pacesetters.

The Rochioli family—like the Wagners at Caymus, or the Rafanellis—are first and foremost farmers with excellent land. Add to this precision farming, where the right grapes, clones and rootstock are rooted in the proper soils, and you have a recipe for superb grapes.

Joe Rochioli began planting vineyards in 1959 on family-owned property dating to 1938. Early on he became convinced that this was the place for Pinot Noir, Chardonnay and Sauvignon Blanc—and was well ahead of his time with these varieties. Today the Rochiolis—father Joe who oversees the vineyards and son Tom the winemaker—farm 110 acres, led by Pinot Noir (38 acres) and Chardonnay (35 acres), the top two wines. Cabernet and Zinfandel are planted on the higher slopes of the vineyard. Two versions of the Chardonnay, Pinot Noir and Sauvignon Blanc are offered, a regular and a Reserve. Both lines are superb.

Since the Rochiolis sell much of their crop, production is in the 8,000-case range, but that could easily double. One wonders whether they will expand the Pinot Noir plantings, given the uniquely high quality of the grapes. Williams & Selyem buy and bottle a Rochioli Vineyard Pinot Noir and Gary Farrell and Davis Bynum also buy Rochioli grapes.

TASTING NOTES

CABERNET SAUVIGNON RUSSIAN RIVER VALLEY NEOMA'S VINEYARD PRIVATE RESERVE (★★): Improving, with earlier vintages being hard, tight and austere. Recent offerings are riper as the winery pays more attention to this wine.

1991: Smooth and ripe, with generous currant and blackberry aromas and flavors and hints of vanilla and spice on the long finish. **86**

1990: Shows a complexity and finesse missing in earlier vintages, with spicy, buttery, ripe cherry, currant and plum flavors. **87**

1989: Elegant, with spicy currant and plum flavors. **84**

1988: Simple, with spicy plum and currant flavors, but like most 1988s it's hollow after mid-palate and it turns tannic. **81**

1987: Tightly knit, with compact currant, berry, oak and spice flavors. **84**

1986: Lean and austere, with firm tannins and meaty, spicy, hard-edged currant and berry flavors. **83**

1985: Tight and firm, with currant and cedar flavors that turn hard on the finish. **83**

1983: Mature, with dried prune and plum aromas, but it's one-dimensional and firmly tannic. **82**

1982: Mature and past its prime, with earthy cedar and tar flavors that turn dry and tannic. **80**

CHARDONNAY RUSSIAN RIVER VALLEY (★★★★): This bottling is ripe, bold and juicy, with loads of rich fruit and ample oak.

1993: Combines ripe pear and apricot flavor with deft oak shadings, in a clean and well balanced wine. **85**

1992: Creamy and spicy, with supple pear, honey and apple notes that are ripe, rich and focused. **90**

1991: Intense and spicy, with pretty orange, pear, vanilla and toast flavors that are bright, with a toasty oak edge. **90**

CHARDONNAY RUSSIAN RIVER VALLEY RESERVE (★★★★★): The Reserve is sleek, intense, and tightly wound, showing depth, complexity and sophistication. Ages well.

1993: Serves up plenty of elegant flavors, with apple, pear, caramel and honey notes that are medium-weight but persistent, turning complex. **90**

1992: Sleek, elegant and concentrated, beautifully crafted, loaded with rich, complex honey, pear, nutmeg and spice flavors. **93**

1991: Intense and lively, with ripe, spicy, buttery notes adding to the rich core of pear, fig and honey flavors. Bright and vibrant. **91**

PINOT NOIR RUSSIAN RIVER VALLEY (★★★★): The regular is riper, fuller and fruitier than the Reserve, while still complex and concentrated.

1991: Bright, ripe and spicy, with pretty floral, cherry, raspberry and anise flavors that are rich and concentrated. Picks up hints of cola and vanilla on the finish. **90**

1990: Broad, ripe and complex, with spicy plum, cherry and raspberry flavors that turn tight and firm. Picks up tea and herb notes on the finish. **88**

1989: A lighter vintage with spicy herb, tea and cedar flavors and a cherry note that comes through on the finish. Well balanced and tasty. **84**

1988: Ripe and openly fruity on the nose, but not as rich or opulent on the palate. Finishes with cherry, raspberry and anise flavors. **86**

1987: An austere vintage with a gamy edge, but on the finish the cherry and raspberry flavors show. **85**

1986: Ripe and spicy, with complex black cherry and raspberry aromas and flavors, finishing with a firmly tannic edge. **90**

1985: A meaty, smoky edge adds complexity to the ripe, spicy cherry and raspberry flavors. **88**

1984: Sweet and rich, almost silky on the palate, with ripe plum, cherry and clove flavors. It's fairly complex on the nose as well. **84**

1982: Aging well, with firm plum and cherry aromas and flavors. Dry tannins and oak show on the finish. **85**

PINOT NOIR RUSSIAN RIVER VALLEY RESERVE (★★★★★): This bottling is rich, plush and concentrated, with uncommon depth and finesse. Smaller lots carry designations from within the vineyard, such as Western and Eastern Block.

Western Block 1992: Deep in color, with a core of rich, ripe black cherry, currant, anise and spicy oak shadings that run deep and long on the finish. **92**

1991: Amazingly complex and concentrated, packed with cherry, spice, raspberry and currant aromas and flavors framed by toasty, smoky, buttery oak notes that add an extra dimension. **93**

1990: A tremendously rich, complex and concentrated wine with tiers of black cherry, vanilla, bacon and smoke flavors that are intense and focused. **92**

Lot 9 1990: Inspired by DRC techniques using whole berry clusters and stem contact, this is a big, rich and tannic wine, with a massive concentration of cherry and raspberry flavors that have the requisite hard tannins and stemmy edge. **85**

1989: Shows depth and concentration, with ripe cherry, raspberry, nutmeg and toasty, spicy oak flavors, finishing with a long, crisp aftertaste. **88**

1988: Broad, ripe, rich and complex, with deep cherry, plum and currant notes, finishing with meaty, smoky, toasty oak flavors. **90**

1986: Tightly wound, firm and intense, with concentrated spice, cherry and raspberry flavors. Tannins and oak clamp down on the finish. **85**

SAUVIGNON BLANC RUSSIAN RIVER VALLEY (★★★): Fruitier and more forward than the Reserve.

1994: Lean and lively, showing distinctly herbal, floral overtones to the basic green apple flavors. Finishes a little simple. **84**

1993: Spicy and flavorful, a flowery wine with a crisp apple character and lingering finish. **87**
1990: Has rich fig and citrus notes, with a finish that's crisp and lingering, picking up honey and vanilla. **89**

SAUVIGNON BLANC RUSSIAN RIVER VALLEY RESERVE (★★★★): Crisp, flinty and tightly wound, ranking among the best.
1993: Ripe, broad and toasty, a spicy, aromatic wine that leans strongly toward oaky flavors. **88**
1992: Understated, with spicy fig, grapefruit and citrus flavors that are long and elegant. **88**

ZINFANDEL RUSSIAN RIVER VALLEY SODINI VINEYARD (★★★★): New at Rochioli, but shows the winery's fine winemaking craftsmanship; a beautifully balanced, rich and fruity wine.
1992: Smooth, ripe and polished, with bright, lively cherry, raspberry and currant flavors that turn elegant and refined on the finish. **91**

ROCKING HORSE
Napa Valley
F: 1989. **O:** Rocking Horse Winery Inc. **W:** James Hall. **S:** None.

OVERALL	$14-24	★★★

WINE RATINGS
Cabernet Sauvignon Napa Valley Garvey Family Vineyard	★★★
Cabernet Sauvignon Napa Valley Hillside Cuvée	★★★
Cabernet Sauvignon Stags Leap District Robinson Vineyard	★★★
Zinfandel Howell Mountain Lamborn Family Vineyard	★★★

WINERY DATA
C: 2,000. **V:** None. **G:** None. **P:** Zinfandel (Howell Mountain), Cabernet Sauvignon (Stags Leap District), Cabernet Sauvignon (Rutherford).

Furniture store owner Jeff Doran and his partner Brian Zealear were home winemakers for years before turning commercial in 1989, with small lots of vineyard-designated wines from Lamborn Family Vineyard (Howell Mountain Zinfandel), Garvey Family (Rutherford Cabernet) and Robinson Vineyard (Stags Leap Cabernet). With James Hall (Honig, Patz & Hall) making the wines, the quality has been very good, with wines that well reflect their varietal characters as well as the areas in which they're grown. Production is 2,000 cases, with all grapes purchased.

TASTING NOTES

CABERNET SAUVIGNON NAPA VALLEY GARVEY FAMILY VINEYARD (★★★):
1992: Firm and focused, with a band of oaky currant and plum flavors. **86**

CABERNET SAUVIGNON NAPA VALLEY HILLSIDE CUVÉE (★★★):
1991: Chewy, chunky, tannic and sturdy, with earthy currant, blackberry and tar notes on the finish. **84**
1989: Tight, rich and focused, with lavishly oaked currant and berry flavors. Firmly tannic. **87**

CABERNET SAUVIGNON STAGS LEAP DISTRICT ROBINSON VINEYARD (★★★): Shows off the elegance and finesse of the vineyard.
1992: Tight and firm, with a narrow band of focused currant, black cherry and mineral flavors, finishing with crisp tannins. **85**
1991: Smooth and stylish, offering generous plum, berry, chocolate, vanilla and spice aromas and flavors, and the finish is silky and seductive. **90**
1990: Firm, tight, youthful and flavorful, with focused plum and currant flavors that are fleshy and balanced, finishing with fine tannins. **91**
1986: Straightforward, with pleasant currant and berry flavors and mild tannins. **84**

ZINFANDEL HOWELL MOUNTAIN LAMBORN FAMILY VINEYARD (★★★): Reflects the vineyard's earthy, peppery qualities, with the 1991 showing the winery's steady improvement with this variety.
1991: Complex and inviting, with ripe, spicy, buttery oak notes adding richness to the cherry and berry flavors. **88**
1990: A rich, earthy, mulchy and peppery wine that's distinctive, finishing with soft tannins. **84**
1989: A racy wine with blueberry and spice flavors that hit the mark for Zin. **84**

ROEDERER ESTATE
Anderson Valley
F: 1986. **O:** Roederer Estate Inc. **W:** Michel Salgues.
S: Quartet.

OVERALL	$16-35	★★★★

WINE RATINGS	
Sparkling Wine Anderson Valley Brut	★★★
Sparkling Wine Anderson Valley Brut	
L'Ermitage Prestige Cuvée	★★★★

WINERY DATA
C: 60,000. **V:** 350 acres in Anderson Valley. **G:** Chardonnay
(200 acres), Pinot Noir (150). **P:** None.

Roederer, the French Champagne producer, zeroed in on the cool Anderson Valley climate for its sparkling wines and that decision has already proven fortuitous, as these estate-grown wines show remarkable depth, richness and complexity. In fact, Roederer is the lone French Champagne house in California to grow all its grapes, which are rooted in diverse soils covering some 350 acres in vines, with Chardonnay at 200 acres and Pinot Noir comprising the rest. The winemaker is Michel Salgues, a Ph.D in enology from Montpellier, France. The combination of a cool climate, intensely flavored grapes and deft winemaking (along with the use of oak barrels for aging young cuvées) has moved Roederer to the head of the class in California. The non-vintage Brut (56,000 cases) is rich and toasty, with complex flavors, excellent depth and rich flavors. The L'Ermitage Prestige Cuvée (4,600) is vintage dated and raises the ante with richness, depth and finesse. For my taste, it's the finest sparkling wine in California. Given its rapid ascent, it's worth watching to see how much better this wine can become as the vineyards mature and winemakers become more familiar with their grapes. A third non-vintage cuvée was in the works as of the 1992 vintage, a 50-50 blend of Chardonnay and Pinot Noir.

TASTING NOTES

SPARKLING WINE ANDERSON VALLEY BRUT NV (★★★):
Intense and concentrated, with tiers of honey, pear and hazelnut flavors, the result of a blend that is 70 percent Chardonnay. A remarkable value that shows complexity and finesse.

NV: Spicy, with ripe pear, hazelnut, honey and butter notes, it serves up a wide range of complex flavors and finishes with an elegant touch. **90**

SPARKLING WINE ANDERSON VALLEY BRUT L'ERMITAGE PRESTIGE CUVÉE (★★★★): Rich and creamy, with toasty pear, spice, hazelnut and honeyed notes, amazingly long and complex on the finish. Setting the pace in California. Fifty-six percent Chardonnay.
1989: A wonderful example of just how good California bubbly can be. Creamy and rich, a toasty wine with pear and hazelnut notes that keep singing on the finish. Graceful, with style and plenty of flavor, a lot like a fine Champagne. **92**

ROLLING HILLS VINEYARDS
Santa Maria Valley
F: 1981. **O:** Edward A. Pagor Jr. **W:** Edward A. Pagor Jr.
S: None.

OVERALL	$6-7	★★

WINE RATINGS	
Cabernet Sauvignon California	NR
Pinot Noir Santa Maria Valley	NR

WINERY DATA
C: 1,000. **V:** 5 acres in Temecula. **G:** Cabernet Sauvignon.
P: None.

This winery in Camarillo, north of Los Angeles, produces about 1,000 cases a year, using grapes from its 5-acre vineyard in Temecula. The 1987 Cabernet California leaned toward oaky flavors, but had enough concentration and black cherry flavors to make it interesting. It proved more appealing than the 1985 Pinot Noir Santa Maria Valley, which tasted overly mature with earthy flavors.

TASTING NOTES

VARIOUS BOTTLINGS (NR):
Cabernet Sauvignon California 1987: Woody at this young age but has a great concentration of black cherry and currant flavors plus strong tannins. A deliciously fruity, long finish indicates it may improve nicely if cellared. **86**
Pinot Noir Santa Maria Valley 1985: Mature color and aromas, with spicy orange and earth flavors. **77**

ROMBAUER VINEYARDS
St. Helena, Napa Valley
F: 1980. **O:** Koerner & Joan Rombauer. **W:** Greg Graham. **S:** None.

OVERALL	$18-35	★★★

WINE RATINGS
Cabernet Franc Napa Valley	NR
Cabernet Sauvignon Napa Valley	★★
Cabernet Sauvignon Napa Valley Le Meilleur du Chai	★★★
Chardonnay Carneros	★★★
Merlot Napa Valley	★★
Zinfandel Napa Valley	★★

WINERY DATA
C: 18,000. **V:** 18 acres in Napa Valley. **G:** Zinfandel **P:** Chardonnay (Carneros), Cabernet Sauvignon, Merlot, Petite Verdot, Cabernet Franc (Napa Valley).

Former commercial airline pilot Koerner Rombauer and his wife Joan were investors in Conn Creek Winery before building their own facility on Silverado Trail north of St. Helena, where they produce 18,000 cases under the Rombauer label, along with running a diversified custom-crush and barrel aging facility. The focus is on Carneros-grown Chardonnay (6,000), which is steadily improving, along with Cabernet, Merlot and a reserve-style red called Le Meilleur du Chai (best of the cellar).

TASTING NOTES

CABERNET FRANC NAPA VALLEY (NR):
1990: Smooth, supple and generous, offering ripe, spicy, toasty currant and plum aromas and flavors that turn elegant and lively on the finish. **85**

CABERNET SAUVIGNON NAPA VALLEY (★★): Less complex and complete now than during the mid-1980s, as the wines are crisper and leaner, with narrow flavors.
1990: Has moderately ripe cherry and currant flavors, finishing with firm tannins and a touch of oak. **86**
1989: Tough and chewy, with an earthy, leathery edge to the currant and berry flavors, turning dry and horsey. **78**
1987: Supple, with herb, currant and black cherry flavors, chewy tannins and a touch of anise. **85**

1986: Firm and tannic, but the underlying texture is smooth and silky, with flavors that are subtle and concentrated. Plum, currant and chocolate flavors slide smoothly into a long and tasty finish. **88**
1985: Lean and crisp, but it lacks drama and richness, with modest black cherry, currant and mint flavors. **85**
1984: Fruity and elegant, lacking richness and depth, with modest currant and plum flavors. **84**

CABERNET SAUVIGNON NAPA VALLEY LE MEILLEUR DU CHAI (★★★):
1987: Starts out nicely, with ripe plum and currant flavors, but it turns austere on the finish and the tannins dominate. **83**
1986: Ripe, tight and lean, with well defined currant, cherry and spicy oak flavors that are elegant and complex. **89**
1985: Lean and austere, with a distinctive minty component along with cedar and black cherry flavors that turn crisp. **89**
1984: Distinctive for its richness and elegance, with supple cedar, black cherry, spice and anise flavors. **88**
1983: A big, thick, muscular and tannic wine with layers of cedar, currant, mint and chocolate flavors. **85**

CHARDONNAY CARNEROS (★★★): Vastly improved, as recent vintages are ripe, smooth, rich and complex, with a bright beam of flavors.
1993: Serves up lots of ripe, juicy pear, fig and pineapple flavors framed by toasty, buttery oak, all folding together into a delicious wine. **92**
1992: Packs in lots of ripe pear, honey, smoke and vanilla flavors that turn rich and complex on the finish. **88**
1991: Ripe and rich, packed with smooth, complex honey, pear and butterscotch flavors. **91**

MERLOT NAPA VALLEY (★★): Tight and lean, with a crisp band of flavors.
1991: Tight and intense, with a narrow range of herb, tobacco and currant notes. **82**
1990: Tough and tight, with berry and red cherry flavors that work through the tannins. **84**
1989: The spicy oak is heavy-handed, making it difficult to tell whether there are sufficient currant and cherry flavors. **84**
1987: Attractive for its suppleness and ripe plum, tobacco and herb notes. Mild tannins. **87**

1986: Excessively woody, with firm tannins and ripe cherry and currant flavors. **78**

ZINFANDEL NAPA VALLEY (★★):
1993: Combines toasty buttery oak with zesty Zinfandel flavors, picking up lots of spice, earth and raspberry notes. Strikes a nice balance of fruit and oak. **88**

ROSENBLUM CELLARS
Alameda, Alameda County
F: 1978. **O:** Rosenblum Cellars. **W:** Kent Rosenblum.
S: None.

OVERALL	$8-30	★★★

WINE RATINGS

Cabernet Blend Napa Valley	
Holbrook Mitchell Vineyard Trio	★★
Cabernet Sauvignon Napa Valley	
George Hendry Vineyard	★★★
Merlot Napa Valley Holbrook	
Mitchell Vineyard	★★
Merlot Russian River Valley	★★
Merlot Russian River Valley	
Lone Oak Vineyard	★★
Pinot Noir Napa Valley	
George Hendry Vineyard	★★
Pinot Noir Russian River Valley	
Ellis Ranch	★★
Zinfandel Contra Costa County	★★★
Zinfandel Mount Veeder Brandlin Ranch	★★★
Zinfandel Napa Valley	
George Hendry Vineyard	★★★
Zinfandel Paso Robles	
Richard Sauret Vineyard	★★★
Zinfandel Sonoma County	★★★
Zinfandel Sonoma Valley Samsel	
Vineyard Maggie's Reserve	★★★★

WINERY DATA
C: 25,000. **V:** 32 acres in Russian River Valley. **G:** Chardonnay (18 acres), Merlot (14). **P:** Zinfandel, Cabernet Sauvignon, Carignane, Petite Sirah, Cabernet Franc, Merlot (Napa Valley), Zinfandel (Paso Robles), Carignane, Zinfandel, Merlot (Sonoma), Zinfandel, Mourvèdre (Contra Costa).

Veterinarian Kent Rosenblum has built his winery to 25,000 cases with an impressive lineup of wines, led by a series of vineyard-designated and appellation-oriented Zinfandels. One year he produced some eight different bottlings, with Contra Costa, Mount Veeder, Napa, Paso Robles and Sonoma Valley represented, and an Alexander Valley bottling beginning with the 1993 vintage. Black Muscat (California), Cabernet (Napa Valley), Carignane (Napa), Merlot (Russian River), Petite Sirah (Napa Valley), Pinot Noir (Russian River), Sémillon (Sonoma County) and sparkling wine (Sonoma County) have joined the lineup. Each of the wines is well balanced, with the reds notable for their supple textures and polished tannins. The standout Zin: Samsel Vineyard Maggie's Reserve, which offers uncommon finesse and flavor.

TASTING NOTES

CABERNET BLEND NAPA VALLEY HOLBROOK MITCHELL VINEYARD TRIO (★★): Effusively fruity, often marked by strong herbal flavors.
1992: Very ripe, brimming with stewed plum and black cherry flavors that turn soft and fleshy. **85**
1991: Strongly herbal, with powerful mint, oregano and vanilla aromas and flavors running through the solid currant and earth notes. **86**
1990: The complex currant, cherry and mint flavors are still a bit rough and tannic. **87**

CABERNET SAUVIGNON NAPA VALLEY GEORGE HENDRY VINEYARD (★★★): Ripe and intense too, with a shade more depth than the Mitchell bottling.
Reserve 1991: Ripe and intense, with a firm band of raspberry, cherry and currant flavors, turning tannic. **88**
1990: Distinctive for its minty herbal notes, and the currant flavor takes on a dill and oak edge on the way to a dense, chewy, tannic finish. **84**

MERLOT VARIOUS BOTTLINGS (★★): Has carried both the Napa Valley and Russian River Valley appellations, ranging from good to very good depending on the year.
Napa Valley Holbrook Mitchell Vineyard 1989: Offers attractive plum and cherry flavors up front, but then the tannins dominate with a vicelike grip. **80**
Russian River Valley 1989: Dark, tight and concentrated, with ripe cherry, currant and mint flavors that finish with firm tannins. **85**

Russian River Valley Lone Oak Vineyard 1990: Tight, tart and lean, with modest berry flavors and an earthy, toasty finish. **81**

Pinot Noir Various Bottlings (★★): Has carried both the Napa Valley and Russian River Valley appellations, with variable quality.
Napa Valley George Hendry Vineyard 1990: Earthy and dull, with a hard edge of tannin and modest flavors. **73**
Russian River Valley Ellis Ranch 1991: Earthy, vegetal notes clash with the modest blackberry and pickle flavors. **80**

Zinfandel Contra Costa County (★★★):
1992: Lean, earthy and gamy, with hints of fruit coming through on the finish. **83**
1991: Effusively fruity, with pretty jam, black cherry, plum, pepper and floral flavors that turn rich and firm on the finish. **90**
1990: Bright and concentrated, with focused, jammy raspberry and blackberry aromas and flavors and hints of toast and tobacco. **87**

Zinfandel Mount Veeder Brandlin Ranch (★★★):
1992: Tight and firm, with a core of chewy plum and wild berry flavors, turning austere and tannic. **86**
1991: A big, ripe Zin packed with firm tannins and supple currant and berry flavors. **88**

Zinfandel Napa Valley George Hendry Vineyard (★★★):
1990: Ripe and spicy, with intense plum, cherry and raspberry flavors that are smooth and polished. **86**
1989: Ripe, crisp and fruity, with a chewy, tannic texture, finishing with hints of cedar and chocolate. **84**
1987: Earthy, herbal notes overshadow the raspberry flavors. **77**
Reserve 1992: Ripe and fruity up front, with spicy, supple cherry, raspberry and buttery oak flavors. **86**
Reserve 1990: Smooth, rich and complex, with deep raspberry, loganberry and currant notes, framed by spicy, cedary oak and a tarry edge. **89**
Reserve 1988: Firm and tannic, with spicy, earthy blackberry and cherry aromas and flavors and a tannic edge. **84**

Zinfandel Paso Robles Richard Sauret Vineyard (★★★):
1992: Lays out ripe, supple, focused black cherry and raspberry flavors that are fresh and lively, finishing with firm tannins. **87**
1991: Bright raspberry flavors and a touch of oak give this wine complexity and finesse. **88**
1990: Firm and ripe, with generous black cherry and plum flavors and well integrated tannins. **87**

Zinfandel Sonoma County (★★★):
1992: Firm and compact, with a narrow band of currant and earth flavors that turn tannic. **84**
1991: Rich, fruity, fresh and almost jammy, with raspberry, cherry and plum flavors. **86**
1990: Ripe and fleshy, with rich raspberry and wild berry flavors that are complex and concentrated. **88**

Zinfandel Sonoma Valley Samsel Vineyard Maggie's Reserve (★★★★): One of the state's best.
1992: A sumptuous Zin with layers of ripe cherry, berry, raspberry and plum flavors that turn spicy on the finish. **89**
1991: Great, bright, vibrant fruit flavors fill out this exuberant Zinfandel. It shows concentrated cherry, plum and raspberry flavors that are simply delicious, fine balance and lots of body. **91**
1990: Ripe, rich and fruity, with intense raspberry, tar, anise, pepper and spice flavors that are concentrated and lively, finishing with polished tannins. **90**

ROSENTHAL - THE MALIBU ESTATE
Malibu, Los Angeles County
F: 1987. O: George Rosenthal. W: George Rosenthal. S: None.

OVERALL	$20	★★★

WINE RATINGS		
Cabernet Sauvignon California		★★★

WINERY DATA
C: 5,000. V: 15 acres in South Coast. G: Cabernet Sauvignon, Chardonnay, Merlot. P: None.

Rosenthal - The Malibu Estate and Moraga in Bel Air are Southern California's two leading fine wine estates. Real estate investor George Rosenthal founded this 15-

acre estate in 1987, initially focusing on Cabernet (beginning with the 1991 vintage), and adding Chardonnay (1994) and Merlot (1995), all from his Malibu Canyon property, which rises to an elevation of 1,510 feet. The Cabernet impressed in 1991, under the winemaking direction of Bruno D'Alfonso of Sanford. An application for a Malibu Hills appellation was pending in 1995.

TASTING NOTES

CABERNET SAUVIGNON CALIFORNIA (★★★): Off to a good start, with a wine that's well focused and flavorful. Worth watching.
1991: Elegant and concentrated, combining tart, ripe, spicy fruit flavors with toasty, buttery oak. Finishes with lots of flavor and finesse and a good dose of tannins. **91**

ROUDON-SMITH WINERY
Santa Cruz Mountains
F: 1972. **O:** Roudon-Smith Vineyard Inc. **W:** Bob Roudon. **S:** None.

OVERALL	$10-15	★★

WINE RATINGS	
Cabernet Sauvignon California	NR
Chardonnay Central Coast	NR
Chardonnay Santa Cruz Mountains	NR
Petite Sirah San Luis Obispo County	NR
Pinot Noir Santa Cruz Mountains	★★
Pinot Noir Santa Cruz Mountains Cox Vineyard	★★
Zinfandel San Luis Obispo County	NR

WINERY DATA
C: 10,000. **V:** 5 acres in Santa Cruz Mountains. **G:** Chardonnay (5 acres). **P:** Zinfandel, Petite Sirah (San Luis Obispo), Cabernet Sauvignon, Chardonnay (Santa Cruz Mountains), Cabernet Sauvignon (California), Merlot (Paso Robles), Chardonnay (Monterey).

Amdahl Inc. electrical engineers Bob Roudon and Jim Smith, along with their wives, Anna Maria and June, wanted a country lifestyle, so they started this winery in Santa Cruz. They make 10,000 cases a year, focusing on Cabernet, Chardonnay (from Central Coast and an estate vineyard in Santa Cruz), and smaller lots of Petite Sirah and Zinfandel. The lineup varies each year; generally the quality is fair if rustic.

TASTING NOTES

VARIOUS BOTTLINGS:
Cabernet Sauvignon California 1991: A safe and correct Cabernet that's fairly priced, but has no real distinctive features. The light Cabernet and oak flavors are pleasant. **77**
Pinot Noir Santa Cruz Mountains 1989: Tough, lean and chewy, with gritty tannins and stemmy tea flavors. Needs more fruit to achieve balance. Drinkable, but there are plenty of better wines. **70**
Pinot Noir Santa Cruz Mountains Cox Vineyard 1989: Lean and earthy, showing herb, spice and cherry flavors that are focused and balanced. **82**
Pinot Noir Santa Cruz Mountains Cox Vineyard 1987: Elegant and well defined, with pretty cherry, plum, spice and toast notes framed by firm but fine tannins and finishing with good length. **84**

ROUND HILL WINERY
St. Helena, Napa Valley
F: 1977. **O:** Round Hill Winery Inc. **W:** Mark Swain. **S:** Rutherford Ranch.

OVERALL	$7-12	★★

WINE RATINGS	
Cabernet Sauvignon California	★★
Cabernet Sauvignon Napa Valley Reserve	★★★
Chardonnay California	★★
Chardonnay Napa Valley Reserve	★★
Chardonnay Napa Valley Van Asperen Reserve	★★
Fumé Blanc Napa Valley	NR
Merlot California	★★
Merlot Napa Valley Reserve	★★
Zinfandel Napa Valley	★★★
Rutherford Ranch Chardonnay Napa Valley	★★
Rutherford Ranch Merlot Napa Valley	★★
Rutherford Ranch Sauvignon Blanc Napa Valley	★★
Rutherford Ranch Zinfandel Napa Valley	★★★

WINERY DATA
C: 375,000. **V:** 28 acres in Napa Valley. **G:** Cabernet Sauvignon (24 acres), Gamay (4). **P:** Chardonnay, Cabernet Sauvignon, Merlot, Zinfandel, Sauvignon Blanc (Napa), Chardonnay (Central Coast), Cabernet Sauvignon, Merlot (Sierra Foothills), Cabernet Sauvignon (Lodi), Merlot (South Coast).

Round Hill evolved out of Ernie and Virginia Van Asperen's chain of Ernie's wine and spirits stores, where they bought bulk wines and bottled them under the Ernie's label. The Ernie's chain proved so successful that they sold it and expanded Round Hill, and even built a winery on Silverado Trail. The key to operating a successful negociant brand is the ability to tap into high quality bulk wines that either aren't wanted by other wineries or that don't fit into their main blends. Round Hill did that better than most, providing a consistent line of popular varietals (Cabernets and Chardonnays), but also such wines as Gewürztraminer and Petite Sirah.

By the mid-1980s many less renowned wineries zeroed in on what became known as fighting (i.e. inexpensive) varietals, which involved not only the purchase of bulk wines but also some in-house crushing and vinification of purchased grapes. Round Hill today is diversified, crushing and vinifying its own grapes, buying bulk wines and offering a custom label business that services restaurants, hotels and resorts. The winery focuses on Cabernet, Chardonnay, Merlot, Sauvignon Blanc and Zinfandel, with the best wines appearing under the Reserve designation. Rutherford Ranch is an affiliated brand, originally intended to represent Round Hill's reserve-style wines, but later separated and developed into an independent line.

TASTING NOTES

CABERNET SAUVIGNON CALIFORNIA (★★):
1991: Simple but correct, with mature Cabernet and oak flavors. Firmly tannic. **80**

CABERNET SAUVIGNON NAPA VALLEY RESERVE (★★★):
Variable but usually in sync with the vintage, with moderate fruit concentration and mild tannins.
1990: Firm and chunky, with a narrow band of earthy currant and mineral flavors, finishing with firm tannins. **84**
1989: Austere as 1989s go, with crisp, firm, chunky currant and black cherry aromas and flavors on a narrow framework. Cellaring should soften this wine, but it's not going to outgrow the vintage personality. **83**

CHARDONNAY VARIOUS BOTTLINGS (★★): Light, with simple fruit flavors and light oak shadings. Good value.
California 1993: Young and tart, with a green edge to the pear and apple flavors, but it fans out on the finish, holds its fruit and gains complexity. **86**

California 1992: Light and simple, showing some nice peach and vanilla aromas and flavors. **81**
Napa Valley Reserve 1993: Hard and woody, with toasty oak flavors dominating the pear and grapefruit flavors, finishing with a touch of bitterness from wood. **82**
Napa Valley Reserve 1991: Firm and simple, with a modest level of pear and spice aromas and flavors. **81**
Napa Valley Van Asperen Reserve 1993: Bright and fruity, with a cidery apple flavor at the core and spicy oak on the finish. Ready now. **83**
Napa Valley Van Asperen Reserve 1992: Crisp and lean, with simple earthy, grassy pear flavors. **81**

FUMÉ BLANC NAPA VALLEY (NR):
1993: Bright and fruity, an exuberant wine with immediately appealing peach and vanilla flavors that linger. **85**

MERLOT VARIOUS BOTTLINGS (★★): Variable in quality, but rises to good in the best years.
California 1992: Earthy, oaky flavors override the simple Merlot notes. **77**
Napa Valley Reserve 1991: Sleek and elegant, with mint, herb and currant flavors. **83**

ZINFANDEL NAPA VALLEY (★★★): The best of the reds, with spicy wild berry flavors.
1990: Ripe and rich, with a solid dose of oak that lingers on the palate, and the plum, cherry and spice flavors are attractive. **85**
1988: Very well made in the claret style, with oak-tinged blackberry, cherry and nutmeg flavors. **89**

RUTHERFORD RANCH VARIOUS BOTTLINGS (★★):
Chardonnay Napa Valley 1993: Up-front ripe and fruity in a very direct and appealing style, graced by pear, apple and spice notes. **87**
Chardonnay Napa Valley 1992: Fresh, lively and focused, bright with apple and pear fruit that keeps bouncing through the finish. **86**
Merlot Napa Valley 1992: Lean and a little chewy, showing a bead of blackberry and tar flavor that extends into the finish. Best from 1997. **82**
Merlot Napa Valley 1990: Spicy, with modest cherry notes that have a stylish, spicy oak accent. **82**
Sauvignon Blanc Napa Valley 1993: Crisp and juicy, a flavorful wine with generous apple, lemon and sweet pea flavors. **85**

ROYCE VINEYARDS
Sonoma County
F: 1987. **O:** John Duarte. **W:** John Duarte. **S:** None.

OVERALL	$10-16	★★

WINE RATINGS	
Cabernet Sauvignon Napa Valley	NR
Cabernet Sauvignon Sonoma County	NR
Chardonnay California	NR
Merlot Napa Valley Reserve	★★
Merlot Sonoma County	★★

WINERY DATA
C: 13,000. **V:** None. **G:** None. **P:** N/A.

Jack Duarte, who works in the wine trade in Louisiana, owns this brand, which operates out of Healdsburg. He offers Cabernet, Chardonnay and Merlot, all blended from bulk wines and carrying differing appellations. Quality is ordinary to good, with production estimated at 13,000 cases. In 1994, Duarte was among a group of investors who bought Quail Ridge Winery in Napa Valley and several other properties.

TASTING NOTES

VARIOUS BOTTLINGS:
Cabernet Sauvignon Napa Valley 1989: Lean and crisp, with herbal, cedary aromas and flavors. It's thin on fruit, but the finish is spicy and chocolaty. **77**
Cabernet Sauvignon Sonoma County 1987: Ripe and chunky, with leather notes running through the ripe cherry and currant flavors. **80**
Chardonnay California 1991: Simple, tart and straightforward, with appealing nectarine, spice and apple notes. **78**
Merlot Napa Valley Reserve 1990: This ripe, generous wine offers raisiny plum flavors and definite leathery, gamy characteristics as well. **81**
Merlot Sonoma County 1991: Wild and flavorful, offering herb, chocolate, plum and blackberry aromas and flavors and a firm, tasty finish. **85**

RUBISSOW-SARGENT
Berkeley, Alameda County
F: 1987. **O:** Rubissow Sargent Wine Co. **W:** Tony Sargent. **S:** None.

OVERALL	$15-18	★★

WINE RATINGS	
Cabernet Blend Mount Veeder Les Trompettes	★★
Cabernet Sauvignon Mount Veeder	★★
Merlot Mount Veeder	★★

WINERY DATA
C: 2,500. **V:** 18 acres in Mount Veeder. **G:** Cabernet Sauvignon (7 acres), Merlot (9), Cabernet Franc (2). **P:** None.

George Rubissow and Tony Sargent own 18 acres on Mount Veeder planted to Bordeaux varieties, from which they produce some 2,500 cases, including a Cabernet blend called Les Trompettes, Cabernet and Merlot. Quality has ranged from average to good. Early vintages were made at The Hess Collection.

TASTING NOTES

CABERNET BLEND MOUNT VEEDER LES TROMPETTES (★★): Variable in first efforts, but the 1990 was a marked improvement.
1990: Firm and compact, with earthy Cabernet flavors that finish with crisp tannins. Needs short-term cellaring to soften; better after 1997. **85**
1989: Lean, tannic and earthy, typical of the 1989 vintage with its hollow, murky flavors. **79**

CABERNET SAUVIGNON MOUNT VEEDER (★★): Lean and on the green, austere side.
1990: Lean and a bit green, with austere cedar, currant and spice notes, but it could use a little more richness and depth. Best after 1997. **84**
1988: Tough and tannic, with a modest concentration of cedar, currant and berry flavors. **85**

MERLOT MOUNT VEEDER (★★): The best of the wines so far, but no track record.
1990: Rich and lavishly oaked, but the complex fruit flavors stand up to the wood. **86**

RUSTRIDGE VINEYARDS & WINERY
St. Helena, Napa Valley
F: 1985. **O:** Susan, Stan, Grant & Angela Meyer.
W: Merry Edwards. **S:** None.

OVERALL   **$15-30**   ★★

WINE RATINGS

Cabernet Sauvignon Napa Valley	NR
Chardonnay Napa Valley	NR
Zinfandel Napa Valley	NR
Zinfandel Blend Napa Valley	
Cabernet Zinfandel	NR

WINERY DATA

C: 10,000. **V:** 54 acres in Chiles Valley. **G:** Cabernet Sauvignon, Chardonnay, Zinfandel. **P:** None.

The Meyer family owns this small winery and 54-acre vineyard in Chiles Valley and focuses on Cabernet, Chardonnay, Zinfandel and a Cab-Zin blend, with production in the 10,000-case range. Quality is fair to good.

RUTHERFORD HILL WINERY
Rutherford, Napa Valley
F: 1976. **O:** Rutherford Hill Winery Partners. **W:** Kevin Robinson. **S:** None.

OVERALL   **$10-21**   ★★

WINE RATINGS

Cabernet Sauvignon Napa Valley	★★
Cabernet Sauvignon Napa Valley XVS	★★
Chardonnay Napa Valley XVS Reserve	★★
Chardonnay Napa Valley	
Jaeger Vineyards	★★
Merlot Napa Valley XVS Reserve	★★
Zinfandel Napa Valley	NR
Zinfandel Port Napa Valley	NR

WINERY DATA

C: 80,000. **V:** 46 acres in Napa Valley. **G:** Chardonnay. **P:** Chardonnay, Merlot, Cabernet Sauvignon, Cabernet Franc, Zinfandel (Napa Valley).

Rutherford Hill is owned by a partnership headed by Bill Jaeger and Chuck Carpy and has close ties to Freemark Abbey. It operates out of the original Souverain Winery in the hills east of Napa near Round Hill. In the early 1980s, the winery decided to focus on Merlot—Bill Jaeger's favorite wine—and has expanded production of that wine to 45,000 cases; although quality has declined in recent vintages. Cabernet, Chardonnay, Zinfandel and a Zinfandel Port are also produced. They too are of ordinary to good quality. The winery seems to value volume over quality.

TASTING NOTES

CABERNET SAUVIGNON NAPA VALLEY (★★): Better in the early 1980s than of late, as most recent wines have been austere with modest flavors.
1991: Austere and tannic, with drying Cabernet flavors of modest depth. **81**
1987: Showing signs of maturity, with cedary herbal notes and a hint of coffee, but also pretty currant and spice flavors that linger. **82**
XVS 1987: Stemmy tea aromas and flavors pervade this lean-textured wine that shows modest herb notes. **86**
1986: Musty, muddy aromas and flavors override the fruit. **68**
1985: Extremely herbal, with layers of chocolate, currant, berry and oak flavors. **82**
1984: Deep and concentrated, smoothly textured, with ripe black cherry and currant flavors. **84**

CHARDONNAY VARIOUS BOTTLINGS: (★★): Ordinary to good, with modest fruit flavors, but well off the pace of Napa's best.
NAPA VALLEY JAEGER VINEYARDS 1992: Medium-weight, with a grassy edge to the pear and spice notes. **82**
NAPA VALLEY XVS RESERVE 1992: Marked by ripe, spicy pear and light oak shadings, but ultimately simple. **83**
NAPA VALLEY XVS RESERVE 1991: Crisp and spicy, a toasty wine with grapefruit and pineapple flavors sneaking in on the finish. **83**
MERLOT NAPA VALLEY XVS RESERVE (★★): Increasingly lean and tannic, with herb and currant notes of medium depth.
1992: Tight and intense, with a woody, cedary edge to the rich currant and black cherry flavors. Finishes with a firm tannic edge. **85**
1991: Lean and trim, with simple berry and cherry flavors. **82**

RUTHERFORD RANCH
This is a second label for Round Hill Winery (see listing).

Saddleback Cellars
Oakville, Napa Valley
F: 1981. **O:** Nils & Dianna L. Venge. **W:** Nils Venge. **S:** Vine Haven.

OVERALL	$13-25	★★

WINE RATINGS

Cabernet Sauvignon Napa Valley	★★
Chardonnay Napa Valley	★
Pinot Blanc Napa Valley	★★

WINERY DATA
C: 2,800. **V:** 15 acres in Oakville. **G:** Chardonnay (4.5 acres), Pinot Blanc (2.8), Cabernet Sauvignon (7.5), Pinot Grigio (0.2). **P:** Zinfandel (St. Helena), Sangiovese (Oakville), Sauvignon Blanc (Pope Valley).

Nils Venge, who excelled as winemaker at Villa Mt. Eden (1974-1982) and Groth Vineyards (1982-1994), started Saddleback as a sideline, with production at 2,800 cases until 1994, when he departed Groth, started a consulting business and planned to expand this winery to 10,000 cases. Quality has been mediocre given Venge's success with Cabernet at Groth, but the 1991 Cabernet showed considerable improvement. Worth watching.

TASTING NOTES

CABERNET SAUVIGNON NAPA VALLEY (★★): Simple and ordinary until the 1991, which showed richness and flair.
1991: Rich and oaky, with pretty currant, black cherry and buttery oak flavors that fold together, creating a complex and flavorful wine. **90**
1988: Gamy, leathery, tarry aromas and flavors wind up flabby and soft, with little fruit. **73**
Family Reserve 1989: A weedy, herbal Cabernet, but it's true to the vintage, finishing with a hint of Cabernet fruit. **83**
Family Reserve 1988: Lean and simple, with an herbal edge to the woody flavors. **78**

CHARDONNAY NAPA VALLEY (★):
1993: Modest pear and apple flavors are ripe and floral, but there's a coarseness to the texture. **81**
1992: Simple and coarse, grassy in flavor, like biting into an unripe apple. **73**
1991: Tart and simple, with green apple and unripe pineapple flavors. **78**

PINOT BLANC NAPA VALLEY (★★):
1990: Vibrant and concentrated, showing apple and melon flavors overlaid with buttery accents. **82**

St. Amant Winery
Sierra Foothills
F: 1990. **O:** Richard S. & Barbara Spencer. **W:** Richard Spencer, Paul Wofford. **S:** None.

OVERALL	$9-18	NR

WINE RATINGS

Port Amador County Vintage Port	NR
Port Amador County Zinfandel Port	NR
Red Table Wine Amador County	NR

WINERY DATA
C: 3,000. **V:** 34 acres in Amador County. **G:** Zinfandel (16 acres), Other (18). **P:** None.

Founded in 1990, this Stockton-based winery produces 3,000 cases of red wine, focusing on its estate-grown Amador County grapes. A Vintage Port using traditional Port varieties, a Zinfandel Port and a red table wine round out the lineup. The winery owns 34 acres, 16 of them planted to Zinfandel.

St. Andrew's Winery
Napa Valley
F: 1979. **O:** Mike Moone, Richard Lemon & David Freed. **S:** None.

OVERALL	$12-20	★★

WINE RATINGS

Cabernet Sauvignon Napa Valley	★★
Chardonnay Napa Valley	★★

WINERY DATA
C: 4,100. **V:** 32 acres in Napa Valley. **G:** Chardonnay (32 acres). **P:** Cabernet Sauvignon.

Swiss-born Irme Vizkelety founded this 32-acre winery estate on Silverado Trail in 1979, focusing on ripe, supple Chardonnays in the 2,000-case range. It had grown to nearly 15,000 cases by the time it was sold to

Clos Du Val's owner, John Goelet, in 1989. After expanding production, Goelet sold the winery facility (but not the brand) in 1995 to a partnership: Mike Moone, a former Beringer executive, Napa attorney Richard Lemon, and David Freed of UCC Vineyards, who renamed it Luna Vineyards. The new emphasis will be on Sangiovese and Pinot Grigio, with plans to grow to 30,000 cases. Both the Cabernet and Chardonnay were made in smooth, ripe and easy-drinking style. The status and future of the St. Andrews brand is uncertain.

TASTING NOTES

CABERNET SAUVIGNON NAPA VALLEY (★★):
1986: Impressive for its elegance and balance, this wine manages to provide attractive cherry, currant, herb and spicy oak flavors. **85**

CHARDONNAY NAPA VALLEY (★★): Capable of achieving outstanding complexity in the mid-1980s, but increasingly simple and fruity as production expanded.
1993: Simple, with floral and pear notes that finish with a cloying edge. **82**
1992: Simple and appealing, with spicy pear and apple flavors. **83**

ST. CLEMENT VINEYARDS
St. Helena, Napa Valley
F: 1975. **O:** Sapporo USA. **W:** Dennis Johns. **S:** None.

OVERALL	$11-30	★★★★

WINE RATINGS

Cabernet Blend Napa Valley Oroppas	★★★★★
Cabernet Sauvignon Napa Valley	★★★★
Chardonnay Carneros Abbott's Vineyard	★★★★
Merlot Napa Valley	★★★
Sauvignon Blanc Napa Valley	★★★

WINERY DATA
C: 12,000. **V:** 38 acres in Carneros, Napa Valley. **G:** Cabernet Sauvignon (2 acres), Merlot (5), Chardonnay (31). **P:** Sauvignon Blanc (Napa Valley), Cabernet Sauvignon (Napa Valley), Merlot (Napa Valley), Cabernet Franc (Napa Valley).

Eye surgeon William Casey founded St. Clement in 1975 and developed this small winery around Cabernet, Chardonnay and Merlot. Casey owned the winery until 1987 when Japanese brewer Sapporo USA purchased it, later adding vineyards (Abbott's Vineyard in Carneros) along with Merlot and a Cabernet blend called Oroppas (Sapporo spelled backward). Quality across the board has been consistently high with all varietals, a tribute to the winemaking skills of Dennis Johns, who has been in that position since 1979. Each of the wines shares a house style that features intense, tightly wound fruit flavors, deft balance and light oak shadings. The Cabernet, for instance, owes much of its excellence to the fact that the grapes come from two superb sources: Spottswoode and Staglin. Cabernet (4,600 cases) is the volume leader, but only slightly ahead of Chardonnay (4,000). Total production is 12,000 cases.

TASTING NOTES

CABERNET BLEND NAPA VALLEY OROPPAS (★★★★): Absolutely delicious in first two tries, offering bold, ripe, deep and complex fruit flavors.
1992: A terrific wine with a rich core of ripe plum, black cherry, currant and new oak flavors, all of which are bright and well focused, finishing with a long, full, rich aftertaste. **95**
1991: Bold, ripe, rich and generous, with tiers of supple black cherry, currant, spice and anise flavors, all sharply focused and picking up pretty toasty oak and coffee notes on a long finish. **94**

CABERNET SAUVIGNON NAPA VALLEY (★★★★): With Spottswoode and Staglin grapes to draw upon, quality is very high, with well focused wines that feature rich, complex flavors. Reducing the tannin level makes current offerings even more supple and appealing. Older vintages have aged well.
1991: Tight and compact but well focused, with intense, spicy currant, black cherry and anise notes that turn elegant and supple. **90**
1990: Firm and chunky, with a full complement of currant, berry and spice aromas and flavors, picking up hints of herb and toast on the finish. **90**
1989: Crisp and tannic, but with enough currant and spicy fruit to enjoy. **84**
1988: Delivers modest plum, currant, cherry and spicy oak flavors. Firmly tannic too. **86**
1987: Offers a pretty display of ripe, rich currant, plum

and blackberry flavors, with subtle oak shadings in the background. **90**

1986: Delivers ripe currant and berry flavors touched by herbs and toast on the finish; intense and concentrated. **90**

1985: Firm, round and elegant, with complex, polished cherry and currant flavors balanced against smoky, toasty oak. **90**

1984: Mature but still delivering ripe cherry and currant flavors that turn spicy. **87**

1983: Has turned dry and tannic, with mature, earthy currant and spice notes. **85**

1982: Mature, with tight, tannic, earthy currant and berry flavors. **87**

1981: Austere and tannic, with earthy, spicy plum and currant notes. **85**

1980: A thin, lean wine with modest currant and plum flavors. **82**

1979: Mature and drying, with a firm core of earthy, spicy currant and cherry notes. **87**

1978: Earthy and mature, with ripe but drying cherry, currant, mineral and plum flavors. **88**

1977: Past its peak, turning dry and oaky, with most of the fruit turning earthy. **85**

NV: A blend of two vintages, 1975 and 1976, it leans toward the 1976 in character with its drying Cabernet flavors. **84**

CHARDONNAY CARNEROS ABBOTT'S VINEYARD (★★★★): Bright, complex and well focused, with the emphasis on ripe fruit flavors and just the right touch of toasty, smoky oak. Ages well.

1993: Simple and uncomplicated, with spicy pear and honey notes. **84**

1992: Elegant and classy, with tart pear, pineapple and spicy oak flavors that are tight and concentrated. **91**

1991: Builds from simple honey and pear notes to a more complex and broad-shouldered wine, with toast, earth and complex spicy flavors. **90**

CHARDONNAY NAPA VALLEY (★★★★):
1991: Lean, with focused lemon and green apple flavors that turn crisp and lively. **86**

MERLOT NAPA VALLEY (★★★): Improving and can be excellent as in 1987, but it is variable, as Merlot is prone to be. Usually well balanced and focused. Drinks well early.

1992: Ripe and chunky, with plush cherry, earth, currant and light oak shadings that turn spicy and fruity on the finish. **89**

1991: Tough and tannic, making it hard for the currant and black cherry flavors to emerge from the tannins. **83**

1990: Dense, firm and focused, with ripe blackberry and toast flavors and hints of ash on the finish. **87**

1989: Ripe, with generous, buttery cedar aromas and currant and spice flavors. **86**

1987: Tight and complex, with tart, sharply focused currant, anise and buttery oak flavors that turn earthy. **90**

1986: Hard and tannic, with a backward core of currant and cedar flavors. **79**

1985: Smooth and cedary, with ripe currant and black cherry flavors that are broad and supple, turning complex. **88**

1983: Smoky and tannic, with a thin band of fruit flavors. **81**

SAUVIGNON BLANC NAPA VALLEY (★★★): Distinct with its complex blend of spicy oak and herb, pear, spice and flinty notes.

1994: Lean and focused, with definite cigar box, cedary overtones to the pear and fig flavors. **87**

1993: Floral pear flavors and a soft texture linger nicely on the delicate finish. **84**

ST. FRANCIS WINERY
Sonoma Valley
F: 1979. **O:** Kobrand Corp., Joseph Martin & Lloyd Canton. **W:** Tom Mackey. **S:** None.

OVERALL	$11-26	★★★★

WINE RATINGS	
Cabernet Franc Sonoma Valley	NR
Cabernet Sauvignon Sonoma County	★★★
Cabernet Sauvignon Sonoma Valley Reserve	★★★
Chardonnay Sonoma County	★★
Chardonnay Sonoma Valley Reserve	★★★★
Gewürztraminer Sonoma County	★★
Merlot Sonoma Valley	★★★
Merlot Sonoma Valley Reserve	★★★★
Zinfandel Sonoma Valley Old Vines	★★★

WINERY DATA

C: 100,000. **V:** 90 acres in Sonoma Valley. **G:** Cabernet Franc, Cabernet Sauvignon, Merlot. **P:** Cabernet Sauvignon, Chardonnay, Gewürztraminer (Sonoma County).

Joe Martin set up St. Francis Winery across the highway from Chateau St. Jean. He has steadily built production to 100,000 cases, using some 90 acres of winery-owned vineyard and purchased grapes. Cabernet and Chardonnay with a Sonoma County appellation both top 25,000 cases and Merlot is at 14,000. Reserve-style wines are made for each variety. Old vine Zinfandel (2,000) is new to the lineup. Each of the wines made by Tom Mackey is marked by smoky, toasty, buttery American oak, but they're all well balanced, with rich fruit to stand up to the oak. Only the Chardonnay Reserve is aged in French wood.

TASTING NOTES

CABERNET FRANC SONOMA VALLEY (NR):

1989: A heavy hand of oak dominates this earthy, rough-hewn wine, with cherry and plum emerging on the finish. **83**

CABERNET SAUVIGNON SONOMA COUNTY (★★★):

Usually ripe and flavorful, but it can have a strong herb and bell pepper edge. Well oaked, drinks well early.
1992: Serves up a nice array of bright, ripe Cabernet flavors, but it's still tannic. **85**
1991: Intense and earthy, with bell pepper notes and chocolate, herb and currant flavors. Modest tannins. **84**
1990: Smooth and ripe, with a generous beam of plum and currant flavors and a nice touch of toasty oak. **89**
1989: Light and lively, a silky-textured wine with appealing currant, berry and herb flavors. **84**
1988: Loaded with ripe, rich currant, cherry and plum flavors and an array of herbal scents, it is also lavishly oaked. **89**
1986: Firm, fruity and generous, full-bodied and robust, with focused cassis and cherry flavors and solid tannins. **89**

CABERNET SAUVIGNON SONOMA COUNTY RESERVE

(★★★): A shade fuller than the regular bottling, but often more elegant and polished too. Made in a similar style that balances ripe fruit with spicy oak.

1991: Complex and enticing, with exotic cedar, coffee and vanilla aromas and supple currant, cherry and chocolate flavors. **88**

CABERNET SAUVIGNON SONOMA VALLEY (★★★):

1990: Broad, rich and supple, a beautifully balanced wine with complex currant, anise, spice and cherry aromas and flavors and toasty, buttery oak. **92**
1989: Supple and elegant, with a fine balance between ripe, spicy currant and berry flavors and cedary oak notes. Has firm tannins. **89**
1987: Ripe, intense and concentrated, with tiers of herb, currant, tobacco and spice notes and fine tannins. **89**
1986: Crisp and intense, with concentrated herb, currant and spice flavors that are persistent and lingering on the finish. **86**

CABERNET SAUVIGNON SONOMA VALLEY RESERVE (★★★):

1989: Shows depth, intensity and complexity, with pretty currant, cherry, earth and tar notes and pretty oak shadings. **89**
1988: Combines ripe currant, herb and cedar notes with a fleshy texture and firm tannins. **87**
1986: Opulent currant and cedar flavors permeate this harmonious, seamless wine that's smooth and supple. **94**

CHARDONNAY SONOMA VALLEY (★★): Shows the strains

of growth, with 28,000 cases, but features ripe pear, apple and cedary oak flavors.
1993: A little heavy-handed with buttery oak flavors, which override the pear and spice notes. **82**
1992: Compact, with tight pear, hazelnut, spice and oak flavors that finish with a blunt edge. **84**
1991: Spicy, light and lively, with pleasant apple, melon and nutmeg notes. **84**

CHARDONNAY SONOMA VALLEY RESERVE (★★★★):

Bold and complex, with lots of rich fruit and oak flavors.
1993: Distinctive for its smoky, toasty oak flavors which blend together nicely with the ripe, spicy pear and fig flavors. **90**
1992: Complex and concentrated, beautifully crafted, with smoky, toasty oak that leads to ripe, smooth spice, pear, apple and pineapple flavors. **91**
1991: Smooth and spicy, with a nice hazelnut edge to the pear and pineapple flavors, and the finish is firm and toasty. **85**

GEWÜRZTRAMINER SONOMA COUNTY (★★): Less interesting of late, as it is soft and simple with modest flavor.
1992: Soft, almost watery, with bitter almond and sweet, grapey flavors trying to achieve varietal intensity and falling short. **73**

MERLOT SONOMA VALLEY (★★★): Well oaked and regaining its stature after a rough patch in the late 1980s.
1991: Meaty and spicy aromas turn to supple herb, oak and currant flavors. **86**
1990: Smooth and elegant, offering distinctive blackberry, anise and spice aromas and flavors and a strong, clear finish. **88**
1989: Has offbeat smoke and bacon aromas, rhubarb and plum flavors and a smoky finish. **79**
1988: Lavishly oaked, with layers of herb, tea, currant and spice notes. **82**
1987: Extremely herbal, tobaccolike and smoky, turning vegetal. **80**
1986: Fruity and herbal, with sweet currant and plum flavors, lean, firm tannins, medium body and moderate depth. **85**

MERLOT SONOMA VALLEY RESERVE (★★★★): Remarkably complex, accentuating the herbal, spice and chocolate flavors of Merlot. It too is well oaked, with mild tannins.
1992: Rich, smooth and polished, with a supple core of currant, herb, oak and black cherry flavors; a wonderfully complex and focused wine. **93**
1991: An herbal wine that turns richly fruity, showing currant and cherry notes, lavish oak and a smooth texture. **89**
1990: Ripe, round and spicy, with generous plum, chocolate, currant and vanilla flavors and a plush, velvety finish. **91**
1989: Exotic, with plenty of expensive oak accents over an exuberant base of blueberry and herb flavor, turning supple. **90**
1988: Weedy herb and black cherry flavors turn medicinal on the aftertaste. **82**
1986: Marked by rich, opulent plum, cherry, herb and vanilla flavors, magnificent depth and concentration. **91**

ZINFANDEL SONOMA VALLEY OLD VINES (★★★): Also made from old vines, including the Pagani Vineyard (used by Ridge), it is gaining in quality, striking a fine

balance between ripe, complex fruit and St. Francis's signature of toasty oak.
1992: Spicy and aromatic, with bay leaf and dill notes, but a gamy, ripe berry edge emerges. **87**
1990: Complex and well integrated, with ripe, rich blueberry, plum and cherry aromas and flavors and pretty, toasty, buttery oak. **88**
1989: Elegant and spicy, with focused, generous black cherry, blackberry, vanilla and nutmeg flavors. **85**

ST. SUPÉRY VINEYARD & WINERY
Rutherford, Napa Valley
F: 1982. **O:** Skalli Family. **W:** Robert Broman.
S: Bonverre, Mount Madrona.

OVERALL	$9-15	★★★

WINE RATINGS

Cabernet Sauvignon Napa Valley	
Dollarhide Ranch	★★★
Chardonnay Napa Valley	
Dollarhide Ranch	★★
Merlot Napa Valley Dollarhide Ranch	★★★
Muscat California	NR
Sauvignon Blanc Napa Valley	
Dollarhide Ranch	★★
Bonverre Cabernet Sauvignon California	
Lot Number 9	NR
Bonverre Chardonnay California	
Lot Number 14	NR
Bonverre Merlot California	
Lot Number 11	NR
Bonverre Sauvignon Blanc	
Napa Valley Lot Number 10	NR

WINERY DATA
C: 100,000. **V:** 488 acres in Napa Valley. **G:** Cabernet Sauvignon (174 acres), Cabernet Franc (86), Zinfandel (4), Chardonnay (122), Sauvignon Blanc (74), Muscat (5), Sémillon (11). **P:** None.

The Skalli family of France, owners of a giant, diversified food and wine company, began this winery with the purchase of a vineyard property in Pope Valley, northeast of Napa Valley. The vineyard, named Dollarhide Ranch, covers nearly 400 acres and is planted to a wide variety of grapes. St. Supéry takes its name from French winemaker Edward St. Supéry who in 1899 made wine on the property in Rutherford on Highway 29, where the modern winery sits today. The winery's quick ascent to 100,000 cases is impressive, given that the quality of its wines is good across the board. The goal here is not to make Napa's greatest wines—merely good ones that sell for reasonable prices. The lineup is targeted toward the most popular varietals: Cabernet, Chardonnay, Merlot and Sauvignon Blanc. All of the wines carry the broader Napa Valley appellation, but also indicate the more specific designation: Dollarhide Ranch. Bonverre and Mount Madrona are second labels.

TASTING NOTES

CABERNET SAUVIGNON NAPA VALLEY DOLLARHIDE RANCH (★★★): Consistent, with supple, well balanced cherry, herb and currant flavors with mild tannins. Ready on release. The Limited Edition reserve-style wine debuted in 1989 and was better than most from that vintage.
1990: Ripe, flavorful and complex, with moderately intense cherry, currant and anise flavors and a nice, cedary vanilla overlay of oak. **86**
1989: Ripe and chewy, packed with blueberry, currant and plum flavors and finishing with smooth tannins. **85**
Limited Edition 1989: Intense, with wild berry, cherry and currant notes and austere tannins, gaining complexity. **88**
1988: Features ripe plum, jam and spice flavors that are lively and intense up front before the tannins kick in. **85**
1987: Crisp and elegant, with a pretty core of currant, plum, anise and oak flavors that finish with soft tannins. **86**

CHARDONNAY NAPA VALLEY DOLLARHIDE RANCH (★★): Emphasizes the fruit, with ripe, uncomplicated flavors, but good balance and minimal oak influence.
1993: Lean and simple, with coarse pear and citrus notes, but it lacks focus and harmony. **81**
1992: Chunky, straightforward and flavorful, offering decent pear and citrus notes, but it flattens out a little on the finish. **83**
1991: Well balanced, with ripe, creamy pear and apple flavors and subtle oak and spice notes. **86**

MERLOT NAPA VALLEY DOLLARHIDE RANCH (★★★): Well balanced, with pleasantly ripe fruit flavors and a supple texture.
1992: Lightly fruity, with modest fruit concentration of berry and cherry, leaving the tannins to stand out. **80**
1991: Young and firm, with crisp herb, cherry and currant flavors of modest depth and richness. **85**
1990: Pleasantly fruity, with ripe, intense, spicy currant and cherry flavors that pick up cedar and tobacco notes on the finish. **86**
1989: Firm and fresh, with generous currant, plum and raspberry flavors that turn complex and supple. **87**

MUSCAT CALIFORNIA (NR):
1992: Light in texture and off-dry, with appealing apple and pear flavors, but there's an earthy edge that takes away from the pleasant fruit. **76**

SAUVIGNON BLANC NAPA VALLEY DOLLARHIDE RANCH (★★): Crisp, with a flinty pear and mineral edge.
1992: Simple and direct, with a core of ripe pear, herb and grapefruit flavors. **84**

BONVERRE VARIOUS BOTTLINGS (NR):
Cabernet Sauvignon California Lot Number 9 1991: A good value in affordable Cabernet, with bright, fresh currant, herb and oak shadings. Balanced and pleasing to drink. **83**
Chardonnay California Lot Number 14 1992: Light and simple, easy to drink, echoing a touch of apple. **78**
Merlot California Lot Number 11 1992: Light and fruity, with simple wild berry flavors. Average quality. **76**
Sauvignon Blanc Napa Valley Lot Number 10 1992: Minty, herbal flavors overwhelm the modest pear flavors in this soft-textured wine. It seems almost sweet. **77**

SAINTSBURY
Carneros
F: 1981. **O:** Richard A. Ward & David W. Graves. **W:** William P. Knuttel. **S:** None.

OVERALL	$11-30	★★★★

WINE RATINGS

Chardonnay Carneros	★★★
Chardonnay Carneros Reserve	★★★★
Pinot Noir Carneros	★★★

Pinot Noir Carneros Garnet ★★★
Pinot Noir Carneros Reserve ★★★★

WINERY DATA
C: 45,000. V: 54 acres in Carneros. G: Pinot Noir (44 acres), Chardonnay (10). P: Pinot Noir, Chardonnay (Carneros).

Inspired by a love of Burgundy, longtime friends David Graves and Richard Ward formed a partnership in 1981 focusing on Burgundian-style wines, naming their Carneros-based winery after British wine writer George Saintsbury ("Notes On A Cellarbook"). With its beautifully crafted Chardonnays and Pinot Noirs, Saintsbury has been a model of intelligent winemaking on several counts. The winery's style emphasizes ripe fruit flavors and supple textures and the ratio between quality and price is high. Because of that, Saintsbury has been able to both increase volume and steadily improve quality. Saintsbury's success is tied to a trio of Pinot Noirs, ranging from its supple, delicate, easy-drinking Garnet, to its standard Carneros bottling to its Reserve wine, which features richer fruit and more oak seasoning. Chardonnay, too, is remarkably well crafted, split into two styles, a Carneros and a Reserve bottling. Saintsbury purchases most of its grapes, which gives it a diverse mix of clones, soil and climatic differences. With that diversity, the wines are very consistent from year to year, even given vintage vagaries. Production is 45,000 cases, led by 15,000 cases each of Carneros Chardonnay and Pinot Noir.

TASTING NOTES

CHARDONNAY CARNEROS (★★★): Rich and complex, well oaked with lots of tropical fruit flavors.
1993: Appealing for its direct pear, spice and creamy vanilla notes. Medium weight. **85**
1992: Youthful and spicy, it shows off ripe pear, apple and oak flavors that turn elegant and stylish. **85**
1991: Complex and lively, with elegant vanilla, pear, honey and spice flavors that fold together nicely. **87**

CHARDONNAY CARNEROS RESERVE (★★★★): Fuller and richer, intense and concentrated, with bold oak and fruit flavors.
1993: Intense and spicy, with ripe pear, apple and butterscotch flavors that turn complex and smoky on the finish. **89**

1992: Tight and focused, with a rich core of pear, pineapple and citrus notes that turn spicy and complex, with light oak shadings. **91**
1991: Complex and classy, with layers of ripe pear, honey, spice and subtle earth notes framed by pretty, toasty, smoky oak. **92**

PINOT NOIR CARNEROS (★★★): A shade less complex and concentrated with recent vintages, but through most of the 1980s it bordered on outstanding. Ages well, turning earthy and complex.
1992: Delicate, with fresh, crisp cherry, strawberry and spice flavors, picking up a pleasant earthy edge on the finish. **85**
1991: Tight and firm, with intense earth, spice and cherry notes and a tannic edge that gives it a tougher profile. **87**
1990: Ripe, rich and complex, with sharply focused cherry, earth, cola and rhubarb flavors that are tightly knit, finishing with firm tannins. **90**
1989: Crisp and focused, with ripe black cherry, plum and toast flavors that linger. **85**
1988: Elegant, with spicy raspberry and cherry flavors that turn supple and earthy, and a complex aftertaste. **91**
1987: Firm, with pretty cherry, earth, strawberry and toasty oak flavors. **87**
1986: Mature, rich and tasty, with a decadent edge to the ripe strawberry, cherry, spice and oak flavors. **92**
1985: At its peak, it has taken on a decadent, earthy, tarry edge that adds flavor and complexity to the spicy cherry and wild berry flavors. **87**

PINOT NOIR CARNEROS GARNET (★★★): Very appealing for early drinking, light in color but flavorful with spicy strawberry and cherry notes.
1993: Spicy and lively, with pretty cherry and subtle earth notes. **86**
1992: Light, fruity and pleasant, displaying floral overtones to the berry flavors. **84**
1991: Light and fruity, with generous currant, strawberry and spice aromas and flavors. **88**

PINOT NOIR CARNEROS RESERVE (★★★★): Deep rich and concentrated, with an earthy streak to the ripe cherry and plum fruit. Well oaked with toasty, spicy flavors. Ages well so far.
1992: Complex and flavorful, with ripe, spicy black cherry, herb, cedar and earth nuances. **89**

1991: Rich, intense and concentrated, with an earthy, decadent edge to the ripe cherry and spice flavors. **89**
1990: Complex, with ripe, rich and concentrated plum, spice and buttery oak flavors that fan out, adding depth. **92**

SALAMANDRE WINE CELLARS
Santa Cruz Mountains
F: 1985. **O:** Wells Shoemaker. **W:** Wells Shoemaker. **S:** None.

OVERALL	$5-18	NR

WINE RATINGS	
Chardonnay Arroyo Seco	NR
Chardonnay Santa Cruz Mountains	
Matteson Vineyard	NR
Merlot Arroyo Seco	NR
Pinot Noir Santa Cruz	
Mountains Vineyard	NR

WINERY DATA
C: 2,000. **V:** None. **G:** None. **P:** Chardonnay, Pinot Noir (Santa Cruz Mountains), Chardonnay, Merlot, Sauvignon Blanc, Zinfandel (Arroyo Seco).

Founder-winemaker Dr. Wells Shoemaker owns this 2,000-case brand based in Aptos, which makes small lots of Chardonnay (Arroyo Seco and Santa Cruz, Matteson Vineyard), Merlot (Arroyo Seco) and Pinot Noir (Santa Cruz, Matteson Vineyard). No recent notes.

SALMON CREEK
F: 1990. **O:** Bronco Wine Co. **W:** N/A. **S:** None.

OVERALL	$12-18	★★

WINE RATINGS	
Chardonnay Carneros	★★

WINERY DATA
C: 2,000. **V:** None. **G:** None. **P:** Chardonnay.

This 1,000-case Chardonnay-only wine brand was founded by Daniel Baron, former general manager of Dominus Estate, who sold the brand to Bronco Wine Co.

in 1994 after joining Silver Oak. Expect production to grow significantly.

TASTING NOTES

CHARDONNAY CARNEROS (★★):
1993: Relies heavily on oak at this stage, but enough ripe pear and pineapple fruit comes through on the finish to hold your interest. **85**

SAN SABA VINEYARD
Monterey County
F: 1975. **O:** San Saba Vineyard Inc. **W:** Joel Burnstein. **S:** Bocage.

OVERALL	$10-15	★★

WINE RATINGS	
Cabernet Sauvignon Monterey County	★★
Bocage Cabernet Sauvignon	
Monterey County Proprietor's Cuvée	★★
Bocage Merlot Monterey County	
Proprietor's Cuvée	★

WINERY DATA
C: 6,000. **V:** 68 acres in Monterey County. **G:** Cabernet Sauvignon (30 acres), Merlot (15), Chardonnay (23). **P:** None.

San Saba Vineyard dates to 1975 and has 68 acres in vines in the western hills of Salinas Valley, where it focuses on Cabernet, Chardonnay and Merlot under the San Saba and Bocage labels. The 1990 Cabernet (Monterey) was impressive for its balance and finesse. Distribution is limited.

TASTING NOTES

CABERNET SAUVIGNON MONTEREY COUNTY (★★): Only one recent note, but the 1990 showed well, with well focused flavors.
1990: A nice, tasty blend of spicy, toasty oak and supple currant and herb flavors, finishing with a caramel edge and fine, polished tannins. **88**

BOCAGE VARIOUS BOTTLINGS:
Cabernet Sauvignon Monterey County Proprietor's Cuvée 1990: Pungently weedy and vegetal. **70**

Merlot Monterey County Proprietor's Cuvée 1990:
Leans toward the weedy, herbal, bell pepper end of the
Merlot spectrum, but it's balanced and appealing
nonetheless. **84**

Merlot Monterey County Proprietor's Cuvée 1989:
Nice herbal aromas, but the flavors turn heavily vegetal,
spoiling the experience for me. Rather than fruit, the flavors run toward beets and tomatoes. **74**

SANFORD WINERY
Santa Barbara County
F: 1981. **O:** J. Richard & Thekla B. Sanford. **W:** Bruno
D'Alfonso. **S:** None.

OVERALL	$10-30	★★★★★

WINE RATINGS

Blush Santa Barbara County Vin Gris	★★
Chardonnay Santa Barbara County	★★★★
Chardonnay Santa Barbara County	
Barrel Select	★★★★★
Chardonnay Santa Ynez Valley	★★★★
Pinot Noir Santa Barbara County	★★★★
Pinot Noir Santa Barbara	
County Sanford & Benedict Vineyard	
Barrel Select	★★★★★
Sauvignon Blanc Santa Barbara County	★★★

WINERY DATA
C: 30,000. **V:** 20 acres in Santa Barbara County. **G:** Pinot Noir
(8 acres), Chardonnay (8). **P:** Chardonnay, Pinot Noir,
Sauvignon Blanc (Santa Barbara County).

Sanford Winery began
in the early 1970s, when
Richard Sanford and
Michael Benedict par-
layed their wine interests
into the establishment of
the 112-acre Sanford & Benedict Vineyard in Santa Ynez
Valley, where they believed the soil and climate would be
ideal for their passion, Pinot Noir. At the time it looked
like a long shot, but after the first few wines from their
property it became apparent that they were right on the
money with their vineyard site. In 1980, the partnership
dissolved over differences in style and the winery's direction, and Sanford formed his own winery, eventually set-

tling in a warehouse in Buellton. Benedict managed the
vineyard for several years before selling it to Robert and
Janice Atkins of London, who in turn hired Sanford to
manage it, thereby reuniting him with his original vineyard in time for the 1990 vintage.

Using mostly purchased grapes from the best vineyards in the area (Bien Nacido, Sierra Madre,
Cottonwood Canyon), winemaker Bruno D'Alfonso has
developed a remarkably distinctive (and consistent) house
style. Each of the winery's specialties—Chardonnay
(three wines), Pinot Noir (two wines) and Sauvignon
Blanc—features a bold and exotic range of flavors,
intensely varietal and marked by rich, smooth textures.
Even the Pinot Noir Blanc is fresh and snappy. Production
is in the 30,000-case range, nearly two-thirds white.
Sanford plans to build a winery and add vineyard acreage
near his original vineyard site.

The Sanford & Benedict Vineyard is the source for
the Signature Series, which gives six wineries (Au Bon
Climat, Babcock, Foxen, Gainey, Lane Tanner and
Sanford) enough grapes for six barrels of wine, with each
winery bottling its own signature Pinot Noir and a barrel
from each blended together for a vineyard house wine.
The Barrel Select bottlings of Chardonnay and Pinot Noir
rank among California's finest.

TASTING NOTES

BLUSH SANTA BARBARA COUNTY VIN GRIS (★★): Fresh
and snappy, ideal for warm weather drinking.
1991: Crisp and snappy, with a burnt orange and spice
edge. Drinks cleanly and easily, with more flavor than
most blush wines deliver. **84**

CHARDONNAY SANTA BARBARA COUNTY (★★★★):
Consistently delivers rich, creamy, complex tropical
fruit flavors.
1993: Complex and full-bodied, well oaked and flavorful, with ripe pear, honey and earthy notes that turn rich
and complex on the finish. **90**
1992: Firm and focused, with tight pear, spice and honey
notes that turn elegant and spicy on the finish. **88**
1991: Bold, ripe, rich and tasty, with concentrated pear,
pineapple, honey and toast flavors that turn complex,
earthy and creamy on the finish. **91**

CHARDONNAY SANTA BARBARA COUNTY BARREL SELECT (★★★★★): The Barrel Select raises the ante, displaying even more fruit and oak with uncommon depth and finesse. Ages well.

1992: Well crafted, with a nice marriage of honey, pear, citrus and spicy, toasty oak, all folding together neatly on the finish, where the flavors echo. **90**

1991: Complex, with spice, pear, pineapple and honey notes that gain a toasty, buttery edge from oak, turning smooth and elegant. **91**

CHARDONNAY SANTA YNEZ VALLEY (★★★★):

1993: Lean and crisp, with spicy pear, citrus and pineapple notes, turning complex and well focused. **86**

1992: Ripe and fruity, with creamy pear, honey and apple flavors that gain depth and complexity on the finish. A new wine and style from Sanford, as it did not undergo malolactic fermentation. **88**

PINOT NOIR SANTA BARBARA COUNTY (★★★★): While early vintages were often variable, the most recent efforts have yielded ripe, well focused wines marked by herb, black cherry, earth and cola flavors.

1992: Strikes a fine balance between spicy herb and ripe black cherry flavors, picking up an earthy anise note on the supple finish. **88**

1991: Ripe and elegant, with a distinctive earthy, woody edge to the herb, cherry and spice notes. **87**

1990: Bold, ripe, rich and lush, with tiers of pretty black cherry, raspberry, spice and toast flavors that are sharply focused, firm tannins and great complexity. **89**

1989: Has wonderful depth and complexity, with sharply focused plum, spice, currant, smoke and earth notes that are finely woven together. The finish is broad and complex. **93**

1988: Intense, elegant, complex and concentrated, with layers of cherry, plum, earth, spice and cola flavors. **91**

1987: An earthy wine with decadent mushroom, tar and cedar flavors. **80**

1986: Fully mature, with spicy herb and tea aromas that turn to black cherry flavors, finishing with crisp acidity and fine length. **87**

1985: More youthful than the Barrel Select, with spicy cherry, herb and earth notes that turn elegant. **83**

1982: Light and acidic, with barely a trace of drying fruit. Marginal. **73**

1979: Bottled under the Sanford & Benedict label, it offers strong tar and rhubarb notes blended nicely with the cherry and plum flavors. Still firmly tannic. **89**

PINOT NOIR SANTA BARBARA COUNTY SANFORD & BENEDICT VINEYARD BARREL SELECT (★★★★★): The Barrel Select can be absolutely stunning, well dressed in toasty, smoky oak, but usually with sufficient fruit to measure up to it. Ages exceptionally well, although the Barrel Select, curiously, does not always turn out to be the better of the two wines over time.

1992: Firm and tight, with a narrow beam of herb, spice and dried cherry flavors, finishing with crisp tannins. **88**

1991: Supple and elegant, with focused cherry, herb, cola and berry flavors that are rich and polished. Part of the Signature Series, it's a blend of six different wines. **88**

1990: Wonderfully rich and decadent, concentrated and enormously complex, with ripe cherry, cola, earth and spice flavors that are uncommonly deep and persistent. **94**

1989: Simply wonderful, ripe, smooth and creamy, it's a classic Sanford Pinot, with broad, rich, complex raspberry, plum, cherry, earth and spice notes. Soft tannins give it a supple texture. **95**

1986: Bold, ripe, rich and intense, packed with spicy black cherry, herb, tea and mint flavors, a wonderfully complex and elegant wine with a long, lingering finish and soft tannins. **92**

1985: Starts out elegant and spicy, with earthy black cherry flavors, but it dries out. **79**

1984: Mature but firm and intense, with pretty smoky, meaty, orange rind, cherry and earth notes. A complex wine with polish and finesse. **92**

PINOT NOIR VARIOUS BOTTLINGS:

Central Coast 1984: Rich, sweet and flavorful, with a sour note that detracts. **85**

Central Coast 1983: Fully mature, with herb, black cherry, tea and spice notes that are smooth, soft and elegant. **86**

Santa Ynez Valley 1984: Mature but firm and intense, with pretty, smoky, meaty orange rind and earth notes. Wonderful complexity and finesse. Tasted from a magnum. **92**

Santa Ynez Valley 1980: Pungent and vegetal; past its prime. **70**

Santa Ynez Valley 1977: Bottled under the Sanford & Benedict label. An odd wine that's deep in color, with a strong earthy rhubarb and rubber edge. **76**

Santa Ynez Valley 1976: Bottled under the Sanford & Benedict label. Ripe and complex, with mature cola, rhubarb and beet flavors. A decadent but intriguing wine. **89**
Santa Ynez Valley 1975: Bottled under the Sanford & Benedict label. Amazingly ripe, smooth and complex, with spicy black cherry, earth and anise flavors that are rich and silky, finishing with great length and finesse. **94**

Sauvignon Blanc Santa Barbara County (★★★): Intensely varietal, with pungent herb, citrus and grassy flavors, but serves up so much flavor it's delicious.
1993: Smooth and supple, with modest fruit flavors popping through on the finish. **82**
1991: Has unique flavors of rich honey, grapefruit and asparagus, with a grassy, vegetal edge. **85**

Santa Barbara Winery
Santa Barbara County
F: 1962. **O:** Pierre Lafond. **W:** Bruce McGuire. **S:** Mission Canyon.

Overall	$8-30	★★★

Wine Ratings

Cabernet Sauvignon Santa Ynez Valley	★★
Cabernet Sauvignon Santa Ynez Valley Reserve	★★
Chardonnay Santa Ynez Valley	★★
Chardonnay Santa Ynez Valley Lafond Vineyard	★★★
Chardonnay Santa Ynez Valley Reserve	★★★
Johannisberg Riesling Santa Barbara County	★★
Pinot Noir Santa Barbara County	★★
Pinot Noir Santa Barbara County Reserve	★★★
Sauvignon Blanc Santa Ynez Valley	★
Sauvignon Blanc Santa Ynez Valley Reserve	★
Zinfandel San Luis Obispo County Saucelito Canyon Vineyard	★★
Zinfandel Santa Ynez Valley Beaujour	★★
Zinfandel Santa Ynez Valley Late Harvest Essence	NR
Zinfandel Santa Ynez Valley Lafond Vineyard	★★

Winery Data

C: 26,000. **V:** 63 acres in Santa Ynez Valley. **G:** Chardonnay (23 acres), Riesling (12), Pinot Noir (5), Zinfandel (9), Cabernet Sauvignon (6), Sauvignon Blanc (8). **P:** Pinot Noir (Santa Maria Valley).

Santa Barbara Winery dates to 1962, when architect Pierre Lafond decided to build a winery, marking the first winemaking in the county since Prohibition. Santa Barbara began making dessert wines which were sold locally, but by 1972 it had expanded operations and now it produces 26,000 cases. Much of its fruit is grown in its 63-acre vineyard in Santa Ynez Valley, which is dominated by Chardonnay (23 acres). Despite the volume, most of the winery's dozen offerings are made in batches of less than 1,000 cases, with many wines made in two styles, including a reserve. All the wines carry either the Santa Ynez or broader Santa Barbara County appellations. The Reserve Chardonnay and Reserve Pinot Noir are the quality leaders, although the entire lineup is well crafted.

Tasting Notes

Cabernet Sauvignon Santa Ynez Valley (★★), Reserve (★★): Variable—it can feature bright cherry and strawberry notes and also veer into stronger herbal flavors that are more characteristic of the region.
1991: Strong herb, bell pepper and earth flavors are hard to look past in this one. **75**
1990: Intense and herbaceous, with spice, onion, cherry and currant notes. **83**
1989: Dense, weedy and vegetal, a classic Santa Ynez Cabernet with hints of currant and berry flavors. **79**
1988: A simple, brightly fruity wine with concentrated strawberry and raspberry aromas and flavors, shading toward tea on the finish. **83**
Reserve 1991: Intense and spicy, with a racy bell pepper and herb edge to the currant and cherry flavors. **84**
Reserve 1990: Smells like a sauté of onions and bell peppers, but it picks up hints of cherry and spice. **83**
Reserve 1989: A deeply colored, nicely pumped up Cabernet with dominant herbal and olive flavors accented by oak notes. **82**
Reserve 1988: A crisp, herbal wine with a nice berry component that balances the flavors. **83**

CHARDONNAY SANTA YNEZ VALLEY (★★):
1992: An elegant wine that's showing a bit too much wood at this stage. The oak dominates the ripe, spicy pear and peach flavors. **84**

CHARDONNAY SANTA YNEZ VALLEY RESERVE (★★★):
Openly fruity and well oaked in an appealing style.
1993: Rich and buttery, with an attractive butterscotch flavor that adds complexity to the ripe pear and honey notes that linger on the finish. Well made. **89**
1992: Firm and focused, brimming with fresh, ripe pear and pineapple flavors that are framed by light, toasty, smoky oak. **89**
1991: An uncomplicated wine that's smooth and buttery, with spicy pear and citrus notes that turn soft and fleshy. **86**

CHARDONNAY SANTA YNEZ VALLEY LAFOND VINEYARD (★★★):
1992: Strives for complexity with its array of toasty oak and ripe pear and butterscotch, turning supple and elegant. **89**
1991: Broad, generous and silky, offering plenty of apple, pear and spice flavors and a strong finish. Delicious. **88**

JOHANNISBERG RIESLING SANTA BARBARA COUNTY (★★): Can be sweet and sugary, or better focused with peach and pineapple flavors.
1992: A clean, fresh, California-style Riesling that's light-bodied and fruity, with good peach and apple flavors. Has crisp acidity and no finish. Drink with a mild cheese and good French bread on a warm summer day. **82**
1990: Sugary and simple, with a sour edge to the finish. The flavors run toward pear and apple. Drinkable, if odd. **71**
1988: Good and simple. A pleasant, slightly sweet, fruity wine that's soft in structure. **76**
1987: Very flavorful and focused, with full peach and pineapple flavors, a sense of depth and a lingering, fruity finish. Off-dry and well balanced. **84**

PINOT NOIR SANTA BARBARA COUNTY (★★): Variable in quality and style, at its best it is complex and well oaked, with pretty ripe fruit flavors.
1991: Tight, firm and austere, with a narrow band of herb, cola and cherry flavors. **82**

1990: Light, aromatic and deftly balanced, offering herb-scented cherry, berry, spice and cola flavors. **87**
1989: Light and velvety, with spicy, tea-scented cherry and plum flavors. **84**
1986: Walks on the wild side with its cooked beet flavors, but it's palatable. **80**

PINOT NOIR SANTA BARBARA COUNTY RESERVE (★★★): Well oaked, with ripe fruit flavors. Offers more depth and complexity than the non-Reserve.
1991: Lean, crisp and herbal, with cola and berry notes that turn austere on the finish. **79**
1990: Earthy and leathery, with cola and berry notes that turn simple. **83**
1989: Ripe and smoky, silky and polished, with exotic plum, blackberry, bacon and earth flavors. **87**
1987: Elegant and beautifully balanced, with toasty, complex cherry and strawberry flavors and a hint of vanilla. **89**

SAUVIGNON BLANC VARIOUS BOTTLINGS (★): A weak link, as it strays into pungent earthy and vegetal flavors.
Santa Ynez Valley 1993: Laced with rose petal and herb flavors, this one keeps a solid core of pear and ginger floating through the finish. **83**
Santa Ynez Valley Reserve 1993: Lean and spicy, more oak than fruit, sneaking in a touch of herb on the finish. **80**
Santa Ynez Valley Reserve 1992: Herbal, almost vegetal on the nose, but the pineapple and citrus flavors come up nicely on the palate. Perhaps a little sweet, but an enjoyable drink. **85**
Santa Ynez Valley Reserve 1987: Oaky, earthy aromas and flavors dominate this heavy-handed wine. **68**
Santa Ynez Valley Valley View Vineyards 1987: Very oaky. A buttery character dominates the aromas and flavors, but there's just enough fruit underneath to keep it in line. **72**

ZINFANDEL SANTA YNEZ VALLEY BEAUJOUR (★★):
A Beaujolais style as the name implies, with a grapey appeal.
1994: Ripe and grapey like a Beaujolais, it's best served chilled. **82**
1993: Deep color, but the flavors don't quite match. It's pleasant enough, with grapey Zin notes. Can be served chilled. **84**

1992: Youthful and lively, a nouveau-style Zinfandel that's effusively fruity. **80**

1991: A Beaujolais-style Zin, fresh and lively, loaded with plum, berry and tropical fruit aromas and flavors, yet remaining lean and crisp. **84**

1987: Fresh, jammy strawberry and raspberry flavors. **82**

ZINFANDEL SANTA YNEZ VALLEY LAFOND VINEYARD (★★): Good when the cherry and spice flavors dominate. Medium-bodied.

1992: Ripe and spicy, with rustic, tarry fruit flavors that turn dry and tannic on the finish. **85**

1991: A firm, tight young Zin that's tart and lean, with flavors that range from herb and olive to black cherry and oak. **83**

ZINFANDEL VARIOUS BOTTLINGS:

San Luis Obispo County Saucelito Canyon Vineyard 1990: Firm and focused, with pleasant red cherry and spice aromas and flavors that are smooth and appealing. Has a compact grace. **84**

San Luis Obispo County Saucelito Canyon Vineyard 1989: Smooth and ripe, with gentle plum and berry flavors. **82**

Santa Ynez Valley Late Harvest Essence 1993: A sweet Zinfandel with syrupy grape juice, and nice plum and black cherry fruit. **87**

SANTA CRUZ MOUNTAIN VINEYARD
Santa Cruz Mountains
F: 1974. O: Ken D. Burnap. W: Jeff L. Emery. S: None.

OVERALL	$12-20	★★★

WINE RATINGS

Cabernet Sauvignon Santa Cruz Mountains Bates Ranch	★★★
Chardonnay Santa Cruz Mountains	NR
Merlot California	★★
Petite Sirah Santa Cruz Mountains	NR
Pinot Noir Santa Cruz Mountains	★★★★
Pinot Noir Santa Cruz Mountains Matteson Vineyard	★★★

WINERY DATA
C: 4,000. V: 14 acres in Santa Cruz Mountains. G: Pinot Noir . P: Pinot Noir, Cabernet Sauvignon, Chardonnay, Duriff (Santa Cruz Mountains), Merlot.

Ken Burnap's quest for the perfect vineyard led him to the rugged Santa Cruz Mountains, where the former restaurateur (The Hobbit in Orange County) owns 14 acres of Pinot Noir (his passion) and a 4,000-case winery. He makes Cabernet, Chardonnay (two barrels), Merlot, Petite Sirah and two bottlings of Pinot Noir. Each of Burnap's wines shows a rustic, even rugged, personality, which renders reds earthy and ultraripe, intensely tannic and in need of cellaring—if only for a few years. Few California Cabernets can match the sheer concentration and tannic intensity of Burnap's Bates Ranch bottling. The Pinot Noirs, while well out of the mainstream, age and gain better than most, although they are difficult to warm up to in their youth.

TASTING NOTES

CABERNET SAUVIGNON SANTA CRUZ MOUNTAINS BATES RANCH (★★★): Typically dark, intense, earthy and packed with fruit and tannins, almost always in need of short-term cellaring. Ages well, while retaining its rustic qualities.

1989: Tough and hard-edged, firmly tannic, displaying earthy, mulchy, leafy, barely ripe Cabernet flavors. A miss. **71**

1988: Appealing for its ripe, jammy cherry and currant flavors and intensity, finishing with herb notes and firm tannins. **87**

1987: Deep, dark and ripe, with brooding mineral, herb and spice aromas, currant, black cherry and prune flavors and gripping tannins. **91**

1986: Thick and rich, with a marvelous density of currant, plum and cedar flavors and hints of herbs on the finish. Firmly tannic. **89**

1985: Firm, tight and austere, with layers of rich, ripe, lean black cherry, herb, spice and cedar flavors and firm tannins. **92**

1984: Ripe, lean and focused, with attractive black cherry, currant, spice and cedar notes and crisp, firm tannins. **87**

1983: Crisp, lean and austere, with a tight core of tannic, earthy currant flavors. **84**

1982: From a rainy vintage, it is earthy and woody, with barely ripe fruit. **75**

1981: Heavily oaked, with a dry, woody flavor that dominates the fruit. **80**

1980: Extremely ripe, with heady black cherry and currant flavors that are supple and concentrated, supported by firm tannins. **86**

1979: Tough, dry and earthy, with hints of cedar and black currant. **81**

1978: Very ripe and intense, with stewed plum and cherry flavors that are concentrated and oaky, finishing with tight, firm tannins. **88**

MERLOT CALIFORNIA (★★): Maintains the winery's style of intense character despite the California appellation.

1991: Deeply colored and richly fruity, with an abundance of ripe, grapey currant flavors joined by firm tannins. **89**

1989: Dark, dense and decidedly herbal, with tarry black cherry flavors that struggle with a layer of tannin. **83**

PINOT NOIR SANTA CRUZ MOUNTAINS (★★★★): Intense and potent, very ripe and concentrated, often earthy, occasionally funky, but usually consistent and capable of aging 10 to 15 years.

1990: Earthy and decadent, with black cherry and spicy oak flavors struggling to work through the funkiness. **81**

1989: Intense, ripe and powerful, with lively raspberry, black cherry, spice and toast aromas and flavors. **90**

1988: Rich, ripe and opulent, with intense cherry, currant and gamy Pinot Noir flavors framed by spicy, toasty oak. Firmly tannic. **92**

1987: This is a tight, firm, focused and concentrated wine with rich, spicy currant, herb, oak and earth notes. **90**

1985: Deep and dark, with a rich concentration of deeply scented black cherry, plum and spice flavors and a thick dose of tannin. **89**

PINOT NOIR SANTA CRUZ MOUNTAINS MATTESON VINEYARD (★★★):

1990: Ripe and generous, with a juniper berry, smoke and toffee edge that overrides the black cherry and currant flavors. **87**

1989: Rich, smooth and complex, with spicy currant, herb, anise and nutmeg flavors and a velvety texture. **87**

SANTA YNEZ WINERY
Santa Ynez Valley
F: 1975. **O:** Doug Scott. **W:** Bill Spencer. **S:** None.

OVERALL	$8-25	★★

WINE RATINGS

Cabernet Blend Santa Barbara County	
Cabernet Merlot	NR
Pinot Noir Santa Maria Valley	NR
Zinfandel Paso Robles	NR

WINERY DATA
C: 18,000. **V:** None. **G:** None. **P:** N/A.

Begun as Santa Ynez Valley Winer, (the name has since been shortened). Doug Scott purchased the winery in 1988 and now produces 18,000 cases, including Cabernet, Chardonnay, Pinot Noir, Zinfandel and white Zinfandel, with quality ranging from fair to good.

TASTING NOTES

VARIOUS BOTTLINGS (NR):
Cabernet Blend Santa Barbara County Cabernet Merlot 1987: Light, fruity and very herbal, with limited appeal. **72**
Pinot Noir Santa Maria Valley 1987: Tart and sour, with earthy, gamy Pinot Noir flavors. Avoid. **62**
Zinfandel Paso Robles 1987: Effusively fruity and jammy, showing plum, berry, oak and spice flavors. **84**

SANTINO WINES
This is a second label for Renwood Winery (see listing).

SARAH'S VINEYARD
Santa Clara County
F: 1978. **O:** Marilyn Clark, Debra & Craig McManigal, Donna & Steve Hicks. **W:** Marilyn Clark. **S:** None.

OVERALL	$24-50	★★★

WINE RATINGS

Chardonnay Santa Clara County	★★★
Chardonnay Santa Clara County Lot II	★★★
Merlot Santa Clara County	NR

WINERY DATA

C: 2,000. V: 9 acres in Santa Clara Valley. G: Chardonnay (8 acres), Pinot Noir (1). P: Merlot (San Luis Obispo).

The winery's focus is on Chardonnay, Merlot and Pinot Noir. It produces 2,000 cases, with plans for an Italian-variety blend with the 1991 vintage. After early successes with the Sarah's Vineyard Chardonnay in the mid-1980s, quality dipped, although the most recent offerings have been much better balanced.

TASTING NOTES

CHARDONNAY SANTA CLARA COUNTY (★★★):

1993: Combines intense citrus and grapefruit flavors with touches of honey, pear and peach, adding up to a complex and elegant wine with fine length and an earthy note. **89**

1992: Ripe and intense, with spicy peach, pear, honey and light toasty oak shadings. Combines richness with finesse and polish. **89**

Lot II 1992: Ripe with apricot, honey and toasty buttery oak, a full-bodied and well oaked wine that holds together. **88**

V. SATTUI WINERY

St. Helena, Napa Valley
F: 1885. O: Daryl Sattui. W: Rick Rosenbrand. S: None.

OVERALL	$10-35	★★★

WINE RATINGS

Cabernet Sauvignon Napa Valley Preston Vineyard	★★★
Cabernet Sauvignon Napa Valley Preston Vineyard Reserve Stock	★★★
Cabernet Sauvignon Napa Valley Suzanne's Vineyard	★★★
Chardonnay Napa Valley	★★★
Chardonnay Napa Valley Carsi Vineyard Barrel Fermented	★★★
Merlot Napa Valley	★★
Sauvignon Blanc Napa Valley	★★
Zinfandel Howell Mountain	★★★
Zinfandel Napa Valley Suzanne's Vineyard	★★★

WINERY DATA

C: 40,000. V: 59 acres in Napa Valley. G: Chardonnay (24 acres), Zinfandel (7), Cabernet Sauvignon (17), Sauvignon Blanc (7), Johannisberg Riesling (4). P: Zinfandel (Howell Mountain), Cabernet Sauvignon (Rutherford), Johannisberg Riesling (Napa Valley).

V. Sattui Winery is undoubtedly among Napa Valley's most profitable enterprises. Tourists know it as a one-stop winery-deli-picnic destination on Highway 29 south of St. Helena, where Darryl Sattui plays host to tens of thousands of visitors each year. Those who've visited the winery and tasted the wines can attest to the quality (which is very good) and diversity of his products. The winery owns 59 acres of vineyard and produces 40,000 cases, most of which is sold directly to tourists at the highest profit margins. The lineup ranges from Cabernet (three bottlings) and Chardonnay to Madeira, Johannisberg Riesling, Muscat, Sauvignon Blanc and Zinfandel (two bottlings). Quality across the board is high, with Cabernet holding an edge. Because of the clientele, the wines are styled for immediate consumption.

TASTING NOTES

CABERNET SAUVIGNON NAPA VALLEY PRESTON VINEYARD (★★★):

1991: Strikes a nice balance between spicy oak and sweet, ripe fruit. Mild tannins. **87**

1988: Smooth and concentrated, with a solid core of cherry, currant and plum flavors, finishing with a leathery edge. **86**

1986: Sharply focused, with spicy oak, but the elegant, delicate cherry and currant flavors echo on the finish. **88**

1985: Elegant and refined, with pretty black cherry and currant flavors, a subtle dose of toasty oak and fine, light tannins. **87**

1984: Impressive for its delicate and elegant structure and currant, plum and cherry flavors. Mature. **86**

CABERNET SAUVIGNON NAPA VALLEY PRESTON VINEYARD RESERVE STOCK (★★★): Shows a sense of elegance and fine proportion, with a complex core of currant and cedary oak flavors and fine tannins.

1991: Serves up ripe spice, plum and black cherry flavors, turning smooth and supple on the finish. **90**

1988: Marked by ripe currant, toast and spice flavors, firm tannins and a supple texture. **87**
1987: Delivers currant, mineral and vanilla flavors that are firmly tannic but true to the vintage. **86**

CABERNET SAUVIGNON NAPA VALLEY SUZANNE'S VINEYARD (★★★):
1991: Firm and compact, with ample tannins to shed and a core of crisp cherry and currant flavors. **86**
1989: Firm and crisp, with hard plum and currant flavors that pick up a spicy oak edge, but in the end the austerity wins out. **81**

CHARDONNAY NAPA VALLEY (★★★):
1992: Simple and direct, a fruity wine with a spicy edge. **82**

CHARDONNAY NAPA VALLEY CARSI VINEYARD BARREL FERMENTED (★★★):
1993: Has extremely spicy, almost peppery pear and vanilla flavors against a silky background. **88**
1992: Serves up ripe pineapple, citrus and pear flavors that turn spicy on the finish. **87**
1991: Crisp and lively, a spicy wine with bright apple and peach flavors shining through. **86**

MERLOT NAPA VALLEY (★★):
1989: Light and grapey, appealing to drink now. **80**

SAUVIGNON BLANC NAPA VALLEY (★★):
1993: Brightly focused, a flavorful wine that veers off toward earthy and herbal notes, with a touch of grapefruit. **82**

ZINFANDEL HOWELL MOUNTAIN (★★★): The Howell Mountain bottling reflects the winery's efforts to achieve balance and early drinking allure.
1991: A rustic wine with cedar, pepper, raspberry and exotic spice flavors, turning smooth and tarry on the finish. **86**

SAUCELITO CANYON VINEYARD
Arroyo Grande, San Luis Obispo County
F: 1974. **O:** William & Nancy Greenough. **W:** William Greenough. **S:** None.

OVERALL $12-14   ★★★

WINE RATINGS
Zinfandel Arroyo Grande Valley   ★★★

WINERY DATA
C: 2,500. **V:** 12 acres in Arroyo Grande. **G:** Zinfandel (10 acres), Cabernet Sauvignon (2). **P:** None.

Upon buying a remote 100-acre ranch in Arroyo Grande Valley in 1974, Bill Greenough discovered the remnants of an old winery and an even older and much neglected Zinfandel vineyard, which dated back to 1880. Greenough revived the Zinfandel vines and planted more, including one acre of Cabernet. The winery's focus is on Zinfandel, with production at 2,500 cases. The style is shaped by picking the grapes at varying degrees of ripeness, ranging from tart young berries (harvested at around 21.5 Brix), which gives the wine firm acidity and bright fruit notes, to riper berries (24 Brix), which provide a jammy, tarry edge. Quality has been uniformly high.

TASTING NOTES

ZINFANDEL ARROYO GRANDE VALLEY (★★★): Elegant and flavorful, ripe and polished, with supple cherry and berry flavors and smooth tannins.
1992: Ripe and jammy, with wild berry, black cherry and plum flavors that are fleshy and focused. **87**
1991: Elegant and flavorful, brimming with fresh, ripe, lively raspberry and cherry aromas and flavors that gain complexity. **88**
1990: A rich-textured, polished wine that's ripe and round, with appealing blackberry and plum flavors layered with a touch of anise, toast and vanilla. **85**
1989: Ripe, with jammy plum and raspberry flavors that are smooth and supple, turning complex on the finish. **89**
1986: Ripe and seductive, like a full-bodied Burgundy, with slightly earthy, exotic aromas and polished fruit and black pepper flavors. **87**

SAUSAL WINERY
Alexander Valley
F: 1973. **O:** Sausal Winery Inc. **W:** Dave Demostene. **S:** None.

OVERALL $9-14   ★★★

WINE RATINGS

Cabernet Sauvignon Alexander Valley ★★

Zinfandel Alexander Valley ★★★

Zinfandel Alexander Valley
Private Reserve ★★★

WINERY DATA

C: 10,000. V: 64 acres in Alexander Valley. G: Zinfandel (41 acres), Cabernet Sauvignon (7), Chardonnay (8), Sangiovese (4), Malbec (2), French Colombard (2). P: None.

In 1953, Leo Demostene purchased the Sausal Ranch in Alexander Valley, expanding a vineyard that dated to the mid-1920s. The winery started commercial winemaking in 1974, a year after Demostene died. Grgich Hills and Joseph Phelps purchased the Zinfandel grapes for several years, but production has gradually expanded to 10,000 cases, with Cabernet and three bottlings of Zinfandel—the winery's strength, with 41 acres in vines.

TASTING NOTES

CABERNET SAUVIGNON ALEXANDER VALLEY (★★): Medium-weight with modest flavors. Ordinary, especially when compared with the Zinfandels.

1988: Tart and crisp, a simple but pleasing medium-bodied Cabernet with currant and plum flavors. **84**

ZINFANDEL ALEXANDER VALLEY (★★★), PRIVATE RESERVE (★★★): Very consistent, with ripe, supple flavors and fine balance.

1993: Firm and intense, with a well focused core of earthy plum, cherry and raspberry fruit that's rich and concentrated. Packs in lots of intensity and flavor. Best after 1996. **88**

1992: Big, ripe and smooth, with pretty plum and blackberry flavors and a satiny texture. **89**

1990: Ripe, fruity and elegant, with spicy, peppery raspberry and cherry aromas and flavors. Mild tannins. **85**

1989: The salt and pepper aromas and earthy berry flavors are modest and unfocused. **79**

1988: Ripe and full-bodied, with firm tannins and plum, cherry and spice flavors **82**

1987: Lean and tight, with green, leafy overtones to the raspberry flavors. **83**

Private Reserve 1992: Ripe and round, packed with vanilla-scented plum and berry flavors. **87**

Private Reserve 1991: Spicy and peppery, with elegant cherry and raspberry flavors and fine tannins. **87**

Private Reserve 1988: Ripe and focused, showing a nice balance of berry, currant and vanilla flavors and hints of smoke on the smooth finish. **88**

SCHARFFENBERGER CELLARS
Anderson Valley

F: 1981. O: Scharffenberger Cellars Inc. W: Tex Sawyer. S: None.

OVERALL $17-23 ★★★

WINE RATINGS

Sparkling Wine Mendocino County
Blanc de Blancs ★★★

Sparkling Wine Mendocino County
Brut Sparkling Wine ★★★

Mendocino County Brut Rosé ★★★
Sparkling Wine

Mendocino County Cremant Extra Dry ★★★

WINERY DATA

C: 30,000. V: 58 acres in Anderson Valley. G: Chardonnay (27 acres), Pinot Noir (28), Pinot Meunier (3). P: Pinot Noir, Chardonnay (Anderson Valley).

As a college student, John Scharffenberger studied biogeography and land use management, an ideal background for a career in winemaking, which he launched in 1981 with financial backing from his family. His early efforts with sparkling wines followed a pattern in California—where winemakers harvested the grapes early at low sugar levels, believing that the wines needed bracing acidity to survive a secondary fermentation and still maintain backbone. By the mid-1980s production was 25,000 cases and in 1989 Scharffenberger persuaded Pommery, the French Champagne house, to buy his operation and join other French producers (Chandon, Piper, Deutz and Taittinger) who believe that California sparkling wine has a future. All of Scharffenberger's grapes are grown in the cool, coastal Anderson Valley, including 58 acres' worth that are winery-owned. The focus is on four cuvées—the excellent Blanc de Blancs (all Chardonnay), Brut, Brut Rosé and a Cremant (extra dry, which really means slightly sweet). Quality is high and improving.

TASTING NOTES

SPARKLING WINE MENDOCINO COUNTY BLANC DE BLANCS (★★★): The leader so far, vintage dated, with a rich, creamy, complex core of fruit accented by toasty oak and hazelnut flavors. 100 percent Chardonnay.
1989: Smooth and lively, with a lemony edge to the vanilla, pear and toast aromas and flavors, nicely balanced and appealing through the crisp finish. **89**

SPARKLING WINE MENDOCINO COUNTY BRUT (★★★): A blend of Chardonnay and Pinot Noir, it too is rich, smooth and polished, with more black cherry and spice flavors.
1989: Smooth and elegant, with spice, black cherry and raspberry flavors that fold together nicely and a long finish that echoes fruit. **87**
NV: Supple and balanced, with ripe, spicy pear, toast and honey notes that linger. **86**

SPARKLING WINE MENDOCINO COUNTY BRUT ROSÉ (★★★): Includes a small portion of Chardonnay, but it's the Pinot Noir flavors that dominate.
NV: A winy sort of sparkling wine with distinctive Pinot Noir aromas and flavors, touching on earth, berry and cherry notes. **88**

SPARKLING WINE MENDOCINO COUNTY CREMANT EXTRA DRY (★★★): Off-dry, with ripe fruity flavors.
NV: Tastes off-dry, with a hint of sweetness, but the toast, pear and vanilla flavors are focused. **87**

F. SCHERRER WINES
Sonoma County
F: 1991. **O:** Fred Scherrer. **W:** Fred Scherrer. **S:** None.

OVERALL	$16	★★★

WINE RATINGS

Zinfandel Alexander Valley Old Vines	★★★

WINERY DATA
C: 1,000. **V:** 28 acres in Alexander Valley. **G:** Zinfandel (17 acres), Chardonnay (4), Cabernet Sauvignon (7). **P:** None.

This new winery is focused on old-vines Zinfandel grown in Alexander Valley, with its most recent vintages (1991 and 1992) right on target, with supple fruit flavors.

TASTING NOTES

ZINFANDEL ALEXANDER VALLEY OLD VINES (★★★): Early efforts show a deft hand with this variety, as the wines are well focused, bright and lively, with supple tannins.
1993: Tight and compact, with a coarse edge to the dense black cherry, raspberry and earthy notes, finishing with chewy tannins. **87**
1992: Firm and fleshy, with a core of ripe, supple black cherry, plum and spice flavors. **90**
Unfiltered 1991: Smooth and polished, with bright raspberry and blackberry flavors that pick up hints of vanilla and black pepper on the finish. **87**

SCHOOL HOUSE
Spring Mountain, Napa Valley
F: 1956. **O:** John Gantner Jr. **W:** Bruce Scotland. **S:** None.

OVERALL	$35	★★

WINE RATINGS

Pinot Noir Napa Valley	★★

WINERY DATA
C: 1,500. **V:** 13 acres in Spring Mountain. **G:** Chardonnay (4 acres), Pinot Noir (6), Other (3). **P:** None.

School House vineyard on Spring Mountain represents an early attempt in Napa Valley at replicating Burgundian excellence. Its three founders—author Frank Schoonmaker, Inglenook's John Daniel Jr. and John Gantner—were among the great wine connoisseurs and thinkers of the era. After a long look throughout the valley for an ideal Pinot Noir setting, the site on Spring Mountain was chosen, and planting began in the 1940s, with the early wines made by another famous Napa vintner—Fred McCrea of Stony Hill. No winery was ever built at the School House site; through the years the estate's wines were made at several Napa and Sonoma wineries. In their time, the Pinot Noirs were considered excellent, complex and ageworthy, and they served as an inspiration for a number of winemakers. Today, John Gantner Jr. is working to revive the struggling vineyard and his father's dream.

TASTING NOTES

PINOT NOIR NAPA VALLEY (★★): After a long period of ordinary wines, the 1992 and 1993 vintages appeared to be significant improvements, with both wines offering attractive fruit, sage and earthy notes. Earlier vintages, including 1958, 1959 and 1976 have aged well, but the 1974, 1978 and 1980 vintages had not.
1992: Elegant with spice, sage, herb, tea and black cherry, characteristic of this vineyard's past performances. **85**
1976: Ripe and complex with intense raspberry, currant and anise flavors that turn earthy and tannic on the finish. **84**

SCHRAMSBERG VINEYARDS
Calistoga, Napa Valley
F: 1862. **O:** Jack & Jamie Davies. **W:** Mike Reynolds. **S:** J. Schram, Mirabelle Cellars.

OVERALL	$22-50	★★★

WINE RATINGS

Sparkling Wine Napa Valley Blanc de Blancs	★★★
Sparkling Wine Napa Valley Blanc de Noirs	★★★
Sparkling Wine Napa Valley Brut	★★★
Sparkling Wine Napa Valley Brut Rosé Cuvée de Pinot	★★★
Sparkling Wine Napa Valley Cremant Demi-Sec	★★★
Sparkling Wine Napa Valley J. Schram	★★★★

WINERY DATA
C: 40,000. **V:** 54 acres in Napa Valley. **G:** Chardonnay 30 acres), Pinot Noir (24). **P:** Pinot Noir, Chardonnay, Pinot Blanc, Pinot Meunier, Flora (Napa Valley).

Jack and Jamie Davies revived the historic Jacob Schram property mid-way between St. Helena and Calistoga in 1965, naming their winery after the pioneer who first made wine there in 1862 and whose wines were praised by Robert Louis Stevenson. The Davies came to Napa knowing little about winemaking, but with a desire to succeed and a sense of style and commitment. The early Schramsberg Champagnes (as they're called) set new quality standards in California. Production is now 40,000 cases, part of it from 54 acres of estate-grown grapes. Quality is high across the board, with the new prestige cuvée, J. Schram, introduced with the 1987 vintage.

TASTING NOTES

SPARKLING WINE NAPA VALLEY BRUT (★★★):
1989: Tastes mature, with a slightly oxidized pear note, but on the finish it turns smooth and spicy with a vanilla edge. **87**

SPARKLING WINE NAPA VALLEY BRUT ROSÉ CUVÉE DE PINOT (★★★): Variable, often showing mature flavors, but it can be complex and flavorful.
1990: Offers a pretty array of ripe cherry and strawberry flavors that are firm and lively, finishing with a clean, fruity aftertaste. **87**

SPARKLING WINE NAPA VALLEY CREMANT DEMI-SEC (★★★): Off-dry, with spicy fig and honey notes.
1989: Off-dry, with honey, pear and spice notes that finish with a rich aftertaste. **87**

SPARKLING WINE NAPA VALLEY J. SCHRAM (★★★★): Easily the best, offering uncommon richness, depth and concentration; complex and well focused. A blend of Chardonnay and Pinot Noir.
1989: Bold, ripe and spicy, with a pretty array of honey, pear, nut and vanilla, turning rich and creamy on the finish. Impressive for its finesse and concentration. **90**
1988: Rich, intense and concentrated, with sharply focused pear, spice, vanilla and smoke notes that fold together in a complex and inviting way. **90**

SCHUETZ-OLES
Napa Valley
F: 1993. **O:** Rick Schuetz & Russ Oles. **W:** Rick Schuetz. **S:** None.

OVERALL	$14-15	★★★

WINE RATINGS

Chardonnay Napa Valley Chappell Vineyard	★★
Zinfandel Napa Valley Korte Ranch	★★★

WINERY DATA
C: 3,200. V: None. G: None. P: Chardonnay, Zinfandel, Petite Sirah (Napa Valley).

Rick Schuetz and Russ Oles formed a partnership in 1993 to produce a small line of vineyard-designated, Napa Valley wines. Oles, a farmer, owns 20 acres of Chardonnay near St. Helena which is called the Chappell Vineyard, while Schuetz, a vineyard manager and winemaker, manages the other two vineyards used by the winery. Zinfandel comes from 75-year-old vines grown at the Korte Ranch (owned by Hal Pagendarm), while Petite Sirah comes from the Rattlesnake Acres vineyard in Calistoga. Zinfandel at 2,000 cases is the volume leader, followed by Chardonnay at 1,000 cases. Some 200 cases of Petite Sirah are produced.

TASTING NOTES

CHARDONNAY NAPA VALLEY CHAPPELL VINEYARD (★★):
1993: Medium-weight and crisp, with an earthy, leesy edge to the pear and citrus flavors. **82**

ZINFANDEL NAPA VALLEY KORTE RANCH (★★★):
Impressive for its flavor, complexity and finesse.
1992: Firm and compact, well proportioned, striking a nice balance between currant, black cherry and toasty oak flavors. Has a measure of finesse. **89**

SCHUG CARNEROS ESTATE
Carneros
F: 1980. O: Walter & Gertrud Schug. W: Walter Schug. S: L'Étage.

OVERALL	$15-25	★★

WINE RATINGS
Cabernet Sauvignon Sonoma Valley Heritage Reserve	NR
Chardonnay Carneros	★★
Chardonnay Sonoma Valley	★★
Pinot Noir Carneros	★★
Pinot Noir Carneros Heritage Reserve	★★
Sauvignon Blanc Sonoma Valley	NR

WINERY DATA
C: 10,000. V: 3.5 acres in Carneros. G: Pinot Noir (3.5 acres). P: Chardonnay, Pinot Noir, Sauvignon Blanc, Gamay (Carneros), Chardonnay, Sauvignon Blanc, Cabernet Sauvignon, Merlot, Cabernet Franc (Sonoma Valley).

After a remarkable decade as winemaker for Joseph Phelps, where he produced a number of quintessential California wines (Eisele Vineyard Cabernet, Insignia and amazingly complex dessert-style wines), Walter Schug stepped out on his own with the 1980 vintage, aiming for a different style of wines. Indeed the focus—primarily on Carneros-grown Chardonnay and Pinot Noir—and style—much leaner, earthier and with a narrower range of flavors—reflect that desire, although to my taste Schug's wines are far less interesting than those he crafted at Phelps. Production is 10,000 cases, with a Sonoma Valley Cabernet blend (Heritage Reserve) recently added, and with recent vintages quality has edged up, if ever so slightly.

TASTING NOTES

CABERNET SAUVIGNON SONOMA VALLEY HERITAGE RESERVE (NR): The debut from the 1992 vintage was rich and grapey.
1992: Young and a bit grapey, with the rough edges you'd expect from a barrel sample, but the currant, black cherry, mineral and spicy oak flavors are appealing. **86**

CHARDONNAY VARIOUS BOTTLINGS (★★): Quality is highly variable, with wines that are often short on fruit and frankly bland. Recent vintages are still variable.
Chardonnay Carneros 1993: Marked by an earthy edge to the ripe pear and apple flavors, finishing with a funky leesy edge. **78**
Chardonnay Carneros Barrel Fermented 1992: Firm and one-dimensional, with light fruit aromas and flavors that fail to excite. The oak tastes hard and disjointed. **80**
Chardonnay Sonoma Valley 1993: On the simple side, with ripe pear, toast and vanilla notes. **83**
Chardonnay Sonoma Valley 1992: Lean, with shallow fruit flavors that echo pear and apple notes. **82**

PINOT NOIR VARIOUS BOTTLINGS (★★): Lean, earthy and ultimately simple, lacking the richness and depth found in so many Carneros Pinot Noirs.

Carneros 1993: Tight and firm, with a band of earthy cherry, spice and cedary oak, but it fills out on the finish, where the flavors come to life. Shows Schug is making progress. **86**

Carneros 1992: Tough and leathery, with drying tannins and just a trace of fruit. Turns bitter, with a tealike edge. **78**

Carneros 1991: Dark in color, rich and earthy, with cherry and spice notes. **83**

Carneros Heritage Reserve 1991: Intense and spicy, with elegant herb, black cherry and earthy raspberry flavors. **84**

Carneros 1990: Mature, with earthy, leafy flavors, but short on ripe fruit. **78**

Carneros Beckstoffer Vineyard 1990: Simple, with mature plum, tea, earth and wood flavors. Prematurely tired. **80**

Carneros Beckstoffer Vineyard 1989: Lean and green, with leafy herb and tea notes but minimal fruit. **74**

Carneros Beckstoffer Vineyard 1988: Light and simple, with cherry, earth and strawberry flavors, turning bitter. **79**

Carneros Beckstoffer Vineyard 1987: Has a tough leather and mushroom quality that obscures the black cherry notes. **81**

Carneros Beckstoffer Vineyard 1986: Aromatically pleasing, with complex spice, tea and cherry flavors. **85**

Napa Valley Heinemann Vineyard Reserve 1989: A simple, earthy, bland Pinot that doesn't merit Reserve status. **78**

Napa Valley Heinemann Vineyard Reserve 1985: Crisp and tight-textured, with lean, mature tea, spice and plum aromas. **83**

SAUVIGNON BLANC SONOMA VALLEY (NR):
1993: A coarse-textured wine with strange vegetal and pine flavors. **73**

SEA RIDGE WINERY
Sonoma Coast
F: 1980. **O:** Dan & Dee Wickham. **W:** Dan Wickham.
S: None.

OVERALL	$12-20	★★

WINE RATINGS

Merlot Sonoma Coast Occidental Vineyard	NR
Pinot Noir Sonoma Coast Hirsch Vineyard	★★
Zinfandel Sonoma Coast Occidental Vineyard	★★

WINERY DATA
C: 1,500. **V:** None. **G:** None. **P:** Pinot Noir, Zinfandel, Merlot (Sonoma Coast).

Sea Ridge buys grapes grown three miles from the Pacific Ocean—about as close to the ocean as they can get and still ripen. Owners Dan and Dee Wickham chose this cool locale, near the Sonoma County town of Cazadero, because of its proximity to the ocean. All the grapes for their 1,500-case winery are purchased. As of 1995, the focus was on production of Merlot, Pinot Noir and Zinfandel. Chardonnay has been discontinued.

TASTING NOTES

MERLOT SONOMA COAST OCCIDENTAL VINEYARD (NR): This wine debuted in 1989.
1989: Deeply flavored, with intense, almost chocolaty flavors of black cherry and black pepper. Firm tannins. **84**

PINOT NOIR SONOMA COAST HIRSCH VINEYARD (★★): The winery is best known for this variety; quality is good, but on the lean side.
1990: Tastes and smells like a peppery Beaujolais, but it's pleasant enough. **82**
1989: Crisp plum and cherry flavors lead to a stemmy, greenish edge that turns peppery and slightly bitter. **81**

ZINFANDEL SONOMA COAST OCCIDENTAL VINEYARD (★★): Like the Pinot Noir, the 1990 and 1991 were on the austere side.
1991: Ultraripe and jammy, with a raw edge to the wild blackberry and raspberry flavors. **82**
1990: Austere and earthy, showing a lean band of cherry and cranberry flavors, but the earthiness dominates. **80**

SEAVEY VINEYARD
St. Helena, Napa Valley
F: 1990. **O:** William & Mary Seavey. **W:** Gary Galleron.
S: None.

OVERALL	$16-26	★★★

WINE RATINGS

Cabernet Sauvignon Napa Valley	★★★
Chardonnay Napa Valley	★★

WINERY DATA

C: 1,500. **V:** 33 acres in Napa Valley. **G:** Cabernet Sauvignon (20 acres), Chardonnay (13). **P:** None.

San Francisco attorney Bill Seavey bought an old 143-acre ranch in Conn Valley in 1979 that was once the Franco-Swiss Cellar, built around 1881. Seavey restored the old stone cellar and planted a 33-acre vineyard beginning in 1981, dividing it nearly equally between Cabernet and Chardonnay. The first commercial release was the 1990 vintage, with Gary Galleron (formerly of Grace Family Vineyard now at Whitehall Lane) overseeing winemaking. The Cabernet (1,200 cases) has been impressive for its rich, complex core of fruit and mineral flavors. Production is expected to grow to 4,000 cases, with Seavey still selling a portion of his grapes. Chardonnay (300 cases) is sold primarily through a winery mailing list. Worth watching.

TASTING NOTES

CABERNET SAUVIGNON NAPA VALLEY (★★★): Dark, rich and complex, with well focused cherry, currant, mineral and spice notes. Has the power and finesse to age.

1991: Impressive for its focus on ripe, rich, red currant, mineral and cherry flavors, finishing with mild tannins and an oak and mineral edge. **90**

1990: Dark, rich, chewy and supple, with layers of currant, anise, cherry and cedary oak flavors, finishing with supple tannins. **89**

CHARDONNAY NAPA VALLEY (★★): The debut in 1992 showed elegant fruit and light oak shadings.

1992: Rich and smoky, with intense, complex pear and spice notes. **87**

SEBASTIANI VINEYARDS

Sonoma Valley

F: 1904. **O:** Sebastiani Family. **W:** Mary Sullivan, Mark Lyon. **S:** Vendange, Richard Cuneo.

OVERALL	$6-24	★★★

WINE RATINGS

Barbera Sonoma County Sonoma Series	★★
Cabernet Franc Sonoma Valley Sonoma Series	★★
Cabernet Sauvignon Sonoma Valley Sonoma Series	★★★
Cabernet Sauvignon Sonoma Valley Cherryblock Old Vines	★★★
Chardonnay Russian River Valley Dutton Ranch	★★★
Chardonnay Sonoma Valley Reserve	★★★
Chardonnay Sonoma Valley Sonoma Series	★★
Merlot Sonoma Valley Sonoma Series	★★
Mourvèdre Sonoma County Sonoma Series	NR
Syrah Sonoma County Sonoma Series	NR
Zinfandel Sonoma County Sonoma Series	★★
Richard Cuneo Sparkling Wine Sonoma County Brut Cuvée de Chardonnay	★★★

WINERY DATA

C: 6,000,000. **V:** 291 acres in Carneros, Sonoma Valley. **G:** Chardonnay (136 acres), Gewürztraminer (7), Cabernet Sauvignon (33), Merlot (5), Cabernet Franc (4), Pinot Noir (106). **P:** Chardonnay, Cabernet Sauvignon, Cabernet Franc, Merlot, Zinfandel, Mourvèdre (Sonoma Valley), Cabernet Sauvignon, Chardonnay, Cabernet Franc, Merlot, Zinfandel, Pinot Noir (Russian River Valley), Chardonnay (Green Valley), Chardonnay, Cabernet Sauvignon, Cabernet Franc, Merlot, Zinfandel, Barbera, Syrah (Dry Creek Valley), Chardonnay, Cabernet Sauvignon, Cabernet Franc, Zinfandel, Merlot, Sauvignon Blanc, Chenin Blanc, Barbera (Alexander Valley), Pinot Noir (Carneros).

Sebastiani Vineyards dates to 1904, when Italian immigrant Samuele Sebastiani purchased a small winery in Sonoma, where he produced wines by buying both grapes and bulk wines; he sold the wines in San Francisco. In 1944, his son, August, took charge and began slowly building volume, so that by the 1960s and 1970s, Sebastiani Vineyards was one of the largest wine producers in the state. A shrewd businessman, August Sebastiani succeeded with mass marketing programs for his bulk wines. As the market began to shift in the 1970s—moving away from sweet wines and red wines to dry wines and eventually dry white wines—Sebastiani found itself out of style and behind the times. Technology and innovation were replacing traditional techniques—with wineries moving away from redwood tanks and rustic red wines (blends of Zinfandel, Petite Sirah, Gamay and others) to temperature-controlled stainless steel fermenters, small French oak barrels and varietals such as Cabernet and Chardonnay. Sebastiani continued to sell large volumes of wine but struggled to keep pace as consumers began drinking less wine overall, instead focusing on better quality wines at higher prices.

At the time of August's death in 1980, Sebastiani Vineyards was in need of a major overhaul. His son, Sam, gradually reduced the winery's volume from 2.4 million cases and slowly raised quality, with vineyard-designated Cabernets (Eagle Vineyard), and a greater emphasis on quality varietals (Chardonnay, Sauvignon Blanc). Shrinking case volume and strong disagreements from within the family led to Sam's ouster in 1986. He departed with his wife Vicki to found Viansa (on the Carneros Highway in Southern Sonoma) and August's youngest son, Don, took over.

Under Don's direction, the winery has pursued the best of both worlds. Quality has continued to improve and the winery has also grown in volume, reaching nearly 6 million cases by 1995. The winery buys most of its grapes, and owns a winemaking facility in Lodi where the Vendange and August Sebastiani lines are produced under a California appellation. The winery owns 291 acres in vines, dominated by Chardonnay (136 acres) and Pinot Noir (106). The best wines are bottled under the Sebastiani Vineyards Sonoma Series label and carry either the Sonoma Valley or Sonoma County appellations. Wines include Barbera, Cabernet, Chardonnay, Merlot, Syrah and Zinfandel, including Reserve bottlings of several. Richard Cuneo Sparkling Wine appeared in the mid-1980s as Sebastiani bought finished cuvées from Sonoma-Cutrer, when that winery decided not to pursue sparkling wine.

TASTING NOTES

BARBERA (★★): Steadily improving, as it usually has a well focused core of tart berry and cherry fruit.
1992: Crisp and juicy, lively with blackberry, black cherry and spice flavors that jump lightly through the finish. **86**
1989: Tart and crisp, with earthy cherry flavors that are focused and lively. **82**

1988: Elegant and refined, with bright, moderately rich berry, anise and boysenberry flavors that are well focused. **85**
1987: Ripe and fruity, with generous blackberry and raspberry flavors. **86**

CABERNET FRANC SONOMA COUNTY (★★): Improving too, with a smoky, leathery edge to the currant flavors.
1989: Appealing for its ripe, supple, complex spice, currant and plum flavors. **86**

CABERNET SAUVIGNON VARIOUS BOTTLINGS (★★★): Elegant and medium-bodied, with cedary currant, spice and light oak shadings. The Estates Group series of vineyard-designated wines proved too complicated to market successfully and has been dropped in favor of standard and Reserve bottings.
1991: Distinct for its spicy, minty notes, it serves up pretty currant and berry flavors, finishing with spice and firm tannins. **85**
1990: Lean, with a narrow band of oak and currant flavors. **80**
1989: Layers of oak, plum and black cherry flavors are nicely accented by cedar and spice notes. **82**
1988: Soft and gentle, with modest cranberry and currant flavors, turning simple. **77**
Reserve 1988: Juicy, fruity and accessible, with ripe plum and cherry flavors and moderate tannins. **83**
Reserve 1987: Dark, supple and complex, with ripe plum, cherry and currant notes, finishing with soft, firm tannins and subtle oak shadings. **87**
Reserve 1986: Ripe and complex, with plum, currant and black cherry flavors that turn supple despite firm tannins. **85**
Reserve 1985: Ripe and flavorful, with pleasant currant, plum and herb flavors that are developing a smooth, supple texture. **85**
Reserve 1978: Smooth and mature, with coffee, currant and chocolate notes. **83**
Cherryblock Old Vines 1991: Firm and intense, with moderately rich and concentrated cherry, spice and currant flavors and chunky tannins. **88**
Cherryblock Old Vines 1989: Tough, with coarse tannins and modest currant and plum flavors that turn a bit raisiny. **82**
Cherryblock 1987: Firmly tannic, with coffee, cedar, currant and olive flavors that are distinctive and focused. **84**

CHARDONNAY RUSSIAN RIVER VALLEY DUTTON RANCH (★★★): New in 1993, an important quality statement.
1993: Complex, with bold, ripe, creamy pear, hazelnut and spicy nuances, turning elegant and rich on the finish. Sebastiani's finest Chardonnay. **90**

CHARDONNAY SONOMA VALLEY RESERVE (★★★), SONOMA SERIES (★★): Clean and well balanced, emphasizing pure ripe fruit. The Reserve shows more buttery oak flavors.
1993: Smooth and creamy, with appealing apple, pear and vanilla shadings that unfold and hang together on the finish, where it picks up a toasty edge. **87**
1992: The pleasant, spicy pear and nutmeg flavors are simple, with light oak shadings. **83**
1991: Oaky notes of butter and spice dominate the modest, tart orange and grapefruit notes. **84**
Reserve 1991: Lean and silky, with vibrant green apple, vanilla and peach flavors and a smooth texture. **86**

MERLOT SONOMA VALLEY SONOMA SERIES (★★): Medium-bodied, with modest fruit complexity, but well balanced.
1992: Lean and chewy tannins dominate the cedar and currant flavors. **82**
1991: Light, fruity and spicy, with simple plum and blackberry flavors shaded by vanilla and clove notes. **84**
1990: Tight and tannic, offering black cherry and tobacco flavors, ending with firm tannins. **82**
1989: Spicy and elegant, with pretty cherry and raspberry flavors sustained by crisp, lively acidity. **84**

SYRAH SONOMA COUNTY SONOMA SERIES (NR):
1992: Ripe, rich and smoky, with a supple core of currant and spice flavors that are complex and focused, finishing with a tannic edge. **86**

ZINFANDEL SONOMA COUNTY SONOMA SERIES (★★): Shares the winery style with clean, medium-weight cherry, spice and wild berry notes.
1991: A thin band of spice picks up hints of cherry and raspberry on the finish. **83**
1989: Ripe, flavorful and full-bodied, with attractive plum and cherry flavors. **85**
1988: Crisp and elegant, with pepper, berry and plum flavors, finishing with fine tannins. **84**

Family Selection 1985: A claret-style Zin with appealing cherry, berry, cedar and spice flavors, turning smooth and concentrated. **88**

RICHARD CUNEO SPARKLING WINE SONOMA COUNTY BRUT CUVÉE DE CHARDONNAY (★★★): Intense and concentrated, well oaked and complex.
1991: Intense and lively, with pretty honey, butter and pear flavors that fold together nicely, gaining depth and length on the finish. **88**

SEGHESIO WINERY
Sonoma County
F: 1985. **O:** Seghesio Family. **W:** Ted Seghesio. **S:** None.

OVERALL	$8-14	★★

WINE RATINGS

Cabernet Sauvignon Sonoma County	★★
Carignane Alexander Valley Old Vines	★★
Chardonnay Sonoma County	★★
Pinot Noir Russian River Valley	★★
Pinot Noir Sonoma County	★★
Sangiovese Alexander Valley Chianti Station Old Vine	★★
Sangiovese Alexander Valley Vitigno Toscano	★★
Sauvignon Blanc Sonoma County	★★
Zinfandel Alexander Valley Old Vine Reserve	★★
Zinfandel Sonoma County	★★

WINERY DATA
C: 120,000. **V:** 245 acres in Dry Creek Valley, Russian River Valley, Alexander Valley. **G:** Zinfandel (100 acres), Cabernet Sauvignon (60), Chardonnay (60), Sauvignon Blanc (25). **P:** None.

This is another old-time Sonoma winery, which dates to 1902. For most of that history it was a bulk winery, selling finished wines to others for bottling or blending. In 1985, the family turned to commercial winemaking using its own name, and quality has steadily risen, thanks to extensive vineyard holdings in Alexander, Dry Creek and Russian River Valleys. The 245 acres under vine are still dominated by reds, with Zinfandel (100 acres) the leader, followed by Cabernet and Chardonnay (60 acres each). A

Sangiovese field blend called Chianti Station, Sauvignon Blanc and white Zinfandel are also part of the 120,000-case mix. Given the vineyard resources, a little fine-tuning of the winemaking could work wonders. Currently these wines reflect simple styles and honest prices.

TASTING NOTES

CABERNET SAUVIGNON SONOMA COUNTY (★★): Well balanced, with medium-weight currant and cherry flavors. **1992:** Firm and intense, with a pretty core of grapey fruit flavors, finishing with hints of currant and cherry. **84** **1991:** Tart and lean, with crisp cherry and raspberry flavors. **83**

CARIGNANE ALEXANDER VALLEY OLD VINES (★★): **1992:** Bright and fruity, with medium-weight strawberry and guava flavors and a jammy edge on the finish. **84**

CHARDONNAY SONOMA COUNTY (★★): Appealing for its bright, fresh, fruity style. **1993:** Crisp and fruity, generous with its spiced apple and vanilla flavors that lose a little focus on the finish. **82** **1992:** Smooth and generous, a mouthful of fresh peach and apple flavor, and the finish is bright and lively. **85** **1991:** A crisply focused, lean, simple wine with nice green apple and spice notes. **83**

PINOT NOIR VARIOUS BOTTLINGS (★★): Light and often on the green side with tart cherry and strawberry notes, but it drinks easy. **Russian River Valley 1991:** Simple and straightforward, with spicy berry notes of modest depth. **81** **Russian River Valley 1990:** Tough and a bit green around the edges, appealing on the finish, where the cherry and tea flavors take shape. **78** **Russian River Valley 1988:** Crisp, tart and juicy, with bracing acidity to support the slightly jammy plum and wild berry flavors. **83** **Russian River Valley 1987:** Light and smooth, with pretty strawberry and peach aromas and flavors that are very pleasant and appealing. **84** **Russian River Valley Reserve 1987:** Firm and concentrated, offering strawberry and cherry flavors and firm tannins. **83** **Sonoma County 1993:** Light with spicy herb and cherry notes, turning earthy. **83**

SANGIOVESE ALEXANDER VALLEY CHIANTI STATION OLD VINE (★★), VITIGNO TOSCANO (★★): The former includes a dose of Cabernet Sauvignon, while the latter is 100 percent Sangiovese from old vines. Medium-bodied and well proportioned. **Chianti Station Old Vine 1990:** Spicy, fruity, vanilla-scented red cherry flavors run through this tart, medium-weight wine . **86** **Vitigno Toscano 1991:** Exciting and vibrant, with ripe, rich cherry, currant and spice flavors and smooth tannins. **87**

SAUVIGNON BLANC SONOMA COUNTY (★★): Intense with earthy pear and grassy notes. **1993:** Intense, with spicy citrus, pear and grapefruit notes. **85**

ZINFANDEL VARIOUS BOTTLINGS (★★): Improving, but mostly a medium-bodied style with a pleasant thread of cherry and raspberry flavors. **Alexander Valley Old Vine Reserve 1990:** Despite attractive berry and cherry aromas, this is harsh and severe on the palate, with sharp, hard-edged tannins. **83** **Alexander Valley Reserve 1988:** Rich, fruity and almost opulent, with generous berry, cherry and plum flavors on a smooth-textured background. **88** **Alexander Valley Reserve 1986:** Heavily oaked, with toast and cedar flavors that dominate. **80** **Northern Sonoma 1987:** Full-bodied, with firm tannins and nice blueberry and cherry flavors. **85** **Northern Sonoma 1986:** Crisp, lively and elegant, with simple berry and oak flavors of moderate depth and intensity. **80** **Sonoma County 1992:** Clean and flavorful, with bright, fresh black cherry, wild berry and raspberry flavors that are crisp and focused. **88** **Sonoma County 1991:** Crisp and tart, with pepper, cherry and spice flavors, turning firm. **84** **Sonoma County 1990:** Firm and focused, with lively raspberry, spice and vanilla flavors. **85** **Sonoma County 1989:** Firm and focused, with spicy vanilla aromas and plum and berry flavors, turning spicy on the finish. **84** **Sonoma County 1988:** Crisp, fruity and smooth in texture, with lively raspberry, blackberry and cinnamon flavors. **86**

SELENE WINES
Napa Valley
F: 1991. **O:** Mia Klein. **W:** Mia Klein, Tony Soter. **S:** None.

OVERALL	$18-25	★★★

WINE RATINGS

Merlot Napa Valley	★★★
Sauvignon Blanc Carneros	
Hyde Vineyard	★★★

WINERY DATA
C: 1,200. **V:** None. **G:** None. **P:** Merlot (Napa Valley), Sauvignon Blanc (Carneros).

Mia Klein worked briefly at Spottswoode before starting her brand, which specializes in Merlot and Sauvignon Blanc from purchased grapes. Production has reached 1,200 cases, led by Sauvignon Blanc at 800 cases. The Sauvignon Blanc came from Hyde Vineyard in Carneros, while the Merlot comes from Madrona Ranch in St. Helena from 1991 through 1993, shifting to Caldwell Vineyard in Coombsville for the 1994 vintage. Quality has been high. She continues to work with Tony Soter of Étude Wines, who consults at Araujo, Niebaum-Coppola Estate, Moraga and Spottswoode.

TASTING NOTES

MERLOT NAPA VALLEY (★★★): Off to a very good start with the first vintage, a wine that shows pretty fruit flavors, harmony and finesse.
1991: An intriguing wine with pretty fruit flavors, echoing wild berry, cherry, spice and tobacco notes, picking up an earthy, chocolate edge on a firmly tannic finish. **88**

SAUVIGNON BLANC CARNEROS HYDE VINEYARD (★★★): From Hyde Vineyard, the first wine showed excellent depth, richness and complexity.
1993: Balanced toward fruity, appealing for its pear and ever-so-slightly herbal flavors that last on the smooth finish. **86**
1992: Ripe, smooth and complex, with delicious, creamy fig, citrus, pear and spice flavors. **90**

SEQUOIA GROVE VINEYARDS
Rutherford, Napa Valley
F: 1978. **O:** James Allen, Angelo Brutico & Kobrand Corp. **W:** James Allen. **S:** Allen Family.

OVERALL	$14-30	★★★

WINE RATINGS

Cabernet Sauvignon Napa Valley	★★★
Cabernet Sauvignon Napa Valley	
Estate Reserve	★★★★
Chardonnay Carneros	★★
Chardonnay Napa Valley	
Estate Reserve	★★★

WINERY DATA
C: 25,000. **V:** 22 acres in Rutherford. **G:** Cabernet Sauvignon (10 acres), Cabernet Franc (1), Merlot and Petite Verdot (1), Chardonnay (10). **P:** Chardonnay (Carneros), Cabernet Sauvignon, Chardonnay (Napa Valley).

Brothers Jim and Steve Allen toyed with home winemaking for years before buying a property in Rutherford where they established Sequoia Grove, named after a cluster of towering Sequoias on the property. The focus from the start has been on Cabernet and Chardonnay, with early vintages carrying different appellations (Napa Valley and Alexander Valley for Cabernet) along with different lot numbers. In 1985 the focus narrowed to two Cabernets (Estate Reserve and Napa Valley) and two Chardonnays (Napa Valley and Carneros), the latter from a vineyard the Allens purchased in conjunction with a partnership that evolved into the Taittinger Domaine Carneros sparkling wine venture. Production is 25,000 cases, evenly divided between the two grapes.

TASTING NOTES

CABERNET SAUVIGNON NAPA VALLEY (★★★): Ripe, rich, well oaked and well crafted.
1992: Deep, intense and lively, with a rich core of earthy currant, chocolate, cedar and vanilla, finishing with a long, tannic and complex aftertaste. Has harmony and finesse. **90**
1991: Firm, ripe and focused, with a beam of currant, black cherry and plum flavors. **88**
1990: Firm and compact, with a rich, chewy core of currant, tobacco, earth and mineral notes that are complex and concentrated. **90**
1989: Crisp and firm, with simple flavors that echo currant and plum, but it turns herbal and tannic. **80**
1988: Very firm and focused, with ripe currant and black cherry flavors at the core and layers of smoke and herbal oak nuances. **87**

1987: A solid wine with generous, meaty, smoky notes and currant and plum flavors emerging on the finish. **87**

1986: Mature, ripe currant, spice and berry flavors, turning supple. **86**

1985: Mature and losing its intensity, but still worth drinking for its supple currant and earth notes. **86**

1984: Sturdy, with mature, earthy plum, anise, cherry and olive flavors. **85**

1983: Lean and thin, with ripe cherry and mint flavors of modest depth. **75**

1982: Lean and tannic, with its earthy currant flavors drying up. **82**

1981: Dry and mature, still oaky and tannic. **78**

Cabernet Sauvignon Napa Valley Estate Reserve (★★★★): Capable of achieving uncommon suppleness and complexity. Early Sequoia Grove Cabernets have not aged well, so drinking them early is best advised.

1992: Serves up a complex range of flavors, with tiers of currant, coffee, cedar and toasty oak, all well focused, finishing with firm tannins and a leathery edge. **89**

1991: Ripe, firm and focused, with a core of intense currant, cherry, plum and spice flavors, turning supple and smoky. **91**

1990: Smooth and supple, a very soft-textured wine with a nice array of spice, chocolate, currant and prune flavors that turn supple and complex. **91**

1989: Seductive, ripe, round and generous, with a nice tension between the supple plum, black cherry and currant flavors and the spicy oak finish. **90**

Chardonnay Carneros (★★), Napa Valley Estate Reserve (★★★): The former is lean and crisp, missing the rich, full-bodied flavors found in the early Sequoia Grove Chardonnays. The Estate Reserve is riper and oakier, but still a shade leaner than it used to be.

1993: Earthy, with a marked grapefruit and citrus edge, turning lean and simple on the finish. **83**

1992: Crisp, with juicy peach, citrus and nectarine flavors that are tightly wound but well proportioned. **86**

1991: Tart, lean and green, with crisp apple and pear notes that border on ripeness. **82**

Estate Reserve 1993: Leans toward the earthy citrus and grapefruit side of Chardonnay, which isn't very pretty without more fruit. **82**

Estate Reserve 1992: Lean and intense, with ripe pear and apple flavors that turn rich and spicy on the finish, where it picks up a smoky edge. **88**

Estate Reserve 1991: Tight and compact, with a thin strip of buttery pear flavors, but the finish comes up short. **82**

Shafer Vineyards
Napa Valley
F: 1979. **O:** Shafer Family. **W:** Elias Fernandez. **S:** None.

Overall	$16-45	★★★★

Wine Ratings

Cabernet Sauvignon Stags Leap District	★★★★
Cabernet Sauvignon Stags Leap District Hillside Select	★★★★★
Chardonnay Napa Valley	★★★
Chardonnay Napa Valley Barrel Select	★★★
Merlot Stags Leap District	★★★★
Sangiovese Stags Leap District Firebreak	★★

Winery Data
C: 24,000. **V:** 140 acres in Napa Valley, Stags Leap District, Carneros. **G:** Chardonnay (53 acres), Merlot (37), Cabernet Franc (5), Cabernet Sauvignon (39), Sangiovese (6). **P:** Chardonnay, Merlot (Carneros), Merlot, Cabernet Sauvignon, Cabernet Franc (Stags Leap District).

John Shafer left a 23-year career in book publishing in Chicago for a career change and a back-to-the-land lifestyle, buying vineyard land in the Stags Leap District. Concentrating his plantings on Cabernet Sauvignon and Merlot, Shafer released his first Cabernet with the 1978 vintage and in a 1994 tasting, this wine had just reached an amazingly complex peak. The early lineup also included Zinfandel, but by the mid-1980s the winery had narrowed its focus to estate-grown Cabernet (Hillside Select and Stags Leap District bottlings), Merlot, Chardonnay and a Sangiovese blend called Firebreak. Production is at 24,000 cases, drawing from the winery's 140 acres of vineyard, including 53 acres of Carneros Chardonnay. Quality across the board is very high and continues to improve. Even Chardonnay, which lagged early on, is increasingly on target. Firebreak was new with the 1991 vintage.

TASTING NOTES

CABERNET SAUVIGNON STAGS LEAP DISTRICT (★★★★):
More forward and polished than the Hillside Select, but
it's just as complex and satisfying. Matures earlier, as it
is very drinkable on release and in its first few years.
1991: Rich and supple, with focused earth, tobacco and
currant flavors that pick up a cedary oak edge and mineral notes. **90**
1990: Ripe and generous, with plum, blackberry, prune
and chocolate flavors that turn supple and delicate. **90**
1989: Polished cherry and currant flavors turn elegant and
full-bodied, accented by vanilla and cedar from oak. **86**
1988: Crisp and lively, with pleasant plum, berry and coffee aromas and flavors, hinting at cedar on the finish. **88**
1987: Supple and complex, with ripe currant and cherry
flavors framed by toasty, spicy oak that turns chocolaty.
Hints of vanilla and berry come through on the finish. **92**
1986: Elegant and polished, with plenty of tannin to
carry the cedar, tobacco, currant and plum flavors
through to a long finish. **93**
1985: Delivers sharply defined ripe cherry, cassis, currant
and spice flavors that have a gentle underlying intensity. **91**
1984: Offers harmony and finesse, with beautifully integrated, smooth, ripe, fleshy cherry, currant, vanilla and
spice flavors and supple tannins. **91**
1983: Lean, concentrated, elegant and well focused, with
rich, ripe black cherry, currant, herb and mint flavors. **87**
1982: Tight and concentrated, with a firm structure and
plenty of herb, cherry and cassis flavors. **88**
1980: A herbaceous wine in which the bell pepper and
herbs override the cherry and currant flavors. **82**
1979: Ripe, opulent and flavorful, with cherry and currant flavors that are drying out. **88**
1978: Wonderful complexity and depth, with ripe, complex, focused currant and spice flavors and tannins that
have just recently turned supple without losing fruit. **94**

**CABERNET SAUVIGNON STAGS LEAP DISTRICT HILLSIDE
SELECT (★★★★★):** Ripe, intense, complex and well
focused, brimming with rich fruit and just the right touch
of oak. Grapes come from the sloping hillside vineyard
that surrounds the winery. Ages well, peaking at 5 to 7
years of age, but capable of lasting 15 years or more.
Started with the 1983 vintage, it is among the best in
Stags Leap and Napa Valley.
1991: Rich, thick and plush, with a tight core of currant,
mineral, cedar and black cherry fruit that's complex and

deeply concentrated. **93**
1990: A wine with harmony, finesse, excellent depth and
richness, and the supple, complex, toasty oak, currant,
herb, spice and mineral flavors finish with firm, plush
tannins. **94**
1989: Solid and well crafted, with ripe, pretty currant,
mineral, spice, tar and earth notes, turning firmly tannic
on the finish. **88**
1988: Supple and forward, with coffee and currant flavors that are pleasing. **85**
1987: Ripe and plush, with polished herb, currant and
spice notes that offer a wonderful sense of harmony and
finesse, earning high marks for its supple, polished texture and breadth of flavor. **92**
1986: Rambunctious, with austere tannins and ripe fruit
dominating. There's a Port-like quality to the currant and
herb notes. **89**
1985: A seamless wine that displays tremendous harmony and finesse, with supple, bright, complex and opulent
currant, anise, spice and cedary oak flavors. **94**
1984: Complex and concentrated, with plush black cherry and currant flavors that are silky and polished, finishing with spicy anise notes. **90**
1983: Austere, with firm tannins holding an edge over
the currant, cherry and herb notes. **86**

**CHARDONNAY NAPA VALLEY (★★★), BARREL SELECT
(★★★):** Steadily improving, with the emphasis on ripe,
forward fruit and ample oak shadings.
1992: Fresh, bright and lively, with tight fig, oak and
nutmeg shadings that linger. **88**
Barrel Select 1993: Elegant and refined, ripe and fruity,
with snappy pear and apple-laced fruit and light oak
shadings. **88**
Barrel Select 1992: Has clean, fresh pear and vanilla flavors that are nicely balanced. **85**
Barrel Select 1991: Tight and focused, with spicy pear,
nutmeg and melon flavors and pretty oak shadings.
Impeccable balance. **91**

MERLOT STAGS LEAP DISTRICT (★★★★): Forward, supple and polished, very appealing to drink on release as it
serves up lots of ripe, juicy fruit and is not weighted down
with tannins. Ages well, but is best to drink early on.
1992: A smooth and elegant wine with cedary oak and
currant flavors that are well integrated, finishing with a
pretty berry aftertaste. **88**

1991: Supple, ripe and generous, with rich, fleshy currant, anise, herb and cherry aromas and flavors that are focused and lively. **89**

1990: Full, rich and generous, with complex currant, chocolate and herb aromas and flavors shaded by sweet oak. **91**

1989: Offers pretty ripe black cherry, currant, spice and cedar flavors that are elegant and polished. **87**

1988: Elegant, with pretty plum, currant and olive notes and a coarse finish. **83**

1987: Lavishly oaked, with rich, supple, concentrated currant, spice and plum flavors that linger on the finish. **92**

1986: Fine concentration and depth, with ripe plum and raspberry notes adding to the toasty, chocolaty flavors. **91**

SANGIOVESE STAGS LEAP DISTRICT FIREBREAK (★★): An evolving style that showed improvement in its first two vintages, showcasing the spice and anise notes of Sangiovese. Includes 20 percent Cabernet for color and backbone.

1992: Rich in flavor, sinewy and chewy, lacing its ripe black cherry and berry flavors with anise and gamy notes that linger. **87**

1991: Firm and flavorful, a soft-textured wine with solid currant and violet flavors. **84**

SHENANDOAH VINEYARDS
Amador County
F: 1977. **O:** Leon & Shirley Sobon. **W:** Leon Sobon. **S:** None.

OVERALL	$8-10	★★

WINE RATINGS

Black Muscat Amador County	NR
Cabernet Sauvignon Amador County	★★
Orange Muscat Amador County	NR
Sauvignon Blanc Amador County	NR
Zinfandel Amador County	★★
Zinfandel Amador County Special Reserve	★★
Zinfandel Blend Amador County Zingiovese	★★
Zinfandel Blend Sierra Foothills Zinfandel-Sirah	NR

WINERY DATA
C: 20,000. **V:** 42 acres in California Shenandoah Valley. **G:** Muscat Canelli (2 acres), Zinfandel (35), Sauvignon Blanc (3.5), Cabernet Sauvignon (4), Viognier (7). **P:** Zinfandel (Fiddletown), Zinfandel (California Shenandoah Valley).

Silicon Valley research scientist Leon Sobon shifted gears, going commercial after a career as a home winemaker. The focus (and strength) of Shenandoah has always been Amador-grown Zinfandel (although the Cabernet of late has been superior). The lineup also includes Cabernet, two dessert wines (Black Muscat and Orange Muscat) and Sauvignon Blanc, all carrying the Amador appellation. Quality is only fair across the board. In 1989, the Sobons purchased the old D'Agostini Winery and renamed it Sobon Estate (see listing).

TASTING NOTES

CABERNET FRANC AMADOR COUNTY VARIETAL ADVENTURE SERIES (NR):
1989: Pleasantly fruity, with soft, rich plum, currant and cherry flavors that are mildly tannic. **85**

CABERNET SAUVIGNON AMADOR COUNTY (★★): Variable, but impressive in 1992, which lends hope for the future.
1992: Delivers bright, juicy black cherry, plum and currant flavors, picking up spice and toasty oak on the finish. **88**
1991: An earthy wine that needs food to tame the flavors. **79**

ORANGE MUSCAT AMADOR COUNTY (NR):
1992: Aromatic, with orange, spice and pear aromas and flavors, a solid dessert wine that's balanced and refreshing. **84**

SAUVIGNON BLANC AMADOR COUNTY (NR):
1993: Smooth and polished, a silky wine with citrusy pear and mineral flavors. **82**

ZINFANDEL AMADOR COUNTY SPECIAL RESERVE (★★): Variable, but somewhat disappointing of late.
1992: Smells floral and fruity but tastes a bit earthy, with anise and wild berry notes. **83**
1991: Faint strawberry and tea flavors make this a light, thin wine. Think of it as a dry rosé and it's not bad, but it's not much of a Zinfandel. **76**

ZINFANDEL BLEND AMADOR COUNTY ZINGIOVESE (★★):
1993: Dry and tannic, with just enough fruit to hold your interest, but it doesn't do justice to either grape. **77**

ZINFANDEL BLEND SIERRA FOOTHILLS ZINFANDEL-SIRAH (NR):
1991: Bold, ripe and Port-like, with dense, dry and chewy tannins. It's hard for the ripe plum flavor to fight through. Better after 1998, but it will probably still be tannic. **81**

SHOOTING STAR
This is a second label for Steele Wines (see listing).

SIERRA VISTA
El Dorado County
F: 1974. O: John M. & Barbara A. MacCready. W: John MacCready. S: None.

OVERALL	$13-22	★★

WINE RATINGS
Cabernet Blend El Dorado County	
Lynelle	NR
Cabernet Sauvignon El Dorado County	★★
Cabernet Sauvignon El Dorado	
County Five Star Reserve	★★
Chardonnay El Dorado County	NR
Fumé Blanc El Dorado County	NR
Rhône Blend El Dorado County	
Fleur de Montagne	NR
Syrah El Dorado County	NR
Viognier El Dorado County	NR
Zinfandel El Dorado County	NR

WINERY DATA
C: 7,500. **V:** 20 acres in El Dorado. **G:** Chardonnay (4 acres), Viognier (2.5), Cabernet Sauvignon (9), Syrah (4.5). **P:** Grenache (El Dorado), Cinsault (El Dorado), Mourvèdre (El Dorado), Zinfandel (El Dorado).

Beginning in 1972, John and Barbara MacCready began planting their 20-acre vineyard in El Dorado County; commercial winemaking commenced in 1974, using both estate-grown and purchased grapes. Production is 7,500 cases, with a product mix that includes Cabernet, a Cabernet blend (Lynelle), Chardonnay, Fumé Blanc, Rhône-style red (Fleur de Montagne), Syrah, Viognier and Zinfandel. Cabernet holds the edge in quality and distribution.

TASTING NOTES

CABERNET SAUVIGNON EL DORADO COUNTY (★★):
Variable, ranging from chewy to crisp and simple.
1989: Crisp and simple, with a bit more tannin than the modest raspberry and spice flavors need. **76**
1988: Chewy, concentrated and focused, with rough-hewn black cherry and currant flavors. **84**
Five Star Reserve 1991: Pleasantly earthy, with supple spice and currant notes, a flavorful wine that's tannic and just a bit short on finesse, finishing with gritty tannins. Worth short-term cellaring. **84**

SIGNORELLO VINEYARDS
Napa Valley
F: 1985. O: Raymond Signorello Sr. & Raymond Signorello Jr. W: Raymond Signorello Jr. S: None.

OVERALL	$18-32	★★★★

WINE RATINGS
Cabernet Sauvignon Napa Valley	★★★
Cabernet Sauvignon Napa Valley	
Founder's Reserve	★★★★
Chardonnay Napa Valley	★★★
Chardonnay Napa Valley	
Founder's Reserve	★★★★
Merlot Napa Valley	★★★
Petite Sirah Napa Valley	★★★
Pinot Noir North Coast	
Founder's Reserve	★★★
Red Table Wine Napa Valley Il Taglio	★★★
Sauvignon Blanc Napa Valley	★★★
Sémillon Napa Valley Barrel Fermented	★★★
White Table Wine Napa Valley Il Taglio	NR
Zinfandel Napa Valley	
Unfined Unfiltered	★★

WINERY DATA
C: 4,000. **V:** 39 acres in Napa Valley. **G:** Cabernet Sauvignon (10.5 acres), Merlot (5.5), Cabernet Franc (3), Sémillon (3), Chardonnay (15), Viognier (0.5), Syrah (2). **P:** Pinot Noir (Carneros), Pinot Noir (Russian River).

Ray Signorello Sr., who runs a successful natural resources company in Canada, bought a 100-acre property in the Oak Knoll area of Napa south of the Stags Leap District, where he farmed grapes for nearly a decade before starting a winery with his son, Ray Jr. The Signorellos still sell grapes, but since 1985 the winery has been producing wines from both its own and purchased grapes. Production has slowly grown to 4,000 cases with a diversified mix that includes two Cabernets (including a Founder's Reserve), two Chardonnays (another Founder's Reserve), Merlot, Petite Sirah, Pinot Noir (Carneros and Russian River), Sauvignon Blanc, Sémillon and Zinfandel. A small amount of Il Taglio, an Italian-inspired blend, is also offered. Quality is uniformly high across the board, as recent vintages have shown more depth and richness. Only Zinfandel missed the mark. Worth watching.

TASTING NOTES

CABERNET SAUVIGNON NAPA VALLEY (★★★):
1991: Supple, with ripe plum, currant and spicy oak flavors that finish with mild tannins and an earthy note. **87**
1990: Beautifully crafted, with a core of rich, elegant, spicy cherry, currant, anise and buttery oak flavors, turning supple and silky. **90**

CABERNET SAUVIGNON NAPA VALLEY FOUNDER'S RESERVE (★★★★):
Shows a deft house style with bold, ripe, seductive fruit flavors that are well oaked, keeping the tannins in check. Impressive, but no track record for aging.
1992: Smooth and polished for such a young wine, with an appealing array of black cherry, currant, plum and spice, finishing with light oak and firm tannins. Best after 1997. **90**
1991: Rich and chewy, packed with currant, mineral, herb and tobacco flavors that open up, leading to a firm tannic edge and pretty oak shadings. **90**
1990: Ripe, round and chewy, a complex wine with brilliantly focused currant, chocolate and buttery oak flavors that linger. **92**
1989: Ripe and chewy, with powerful currant, plum and cherry aromas and flavors framed by spicy vanilla and oak. **85**
1988: Ripe and complex, with deep, tannic, peppery berry flavors, smoky chocolate nuances and a deep plush texture. Superb for the vintage. **90**

CHARDONNAY NAPA VALLEY (★★★):
1993: Lavishly oaked, with a smoky, charred edge, but the creamy pear and vanilla flavors come through. **88**
1992: Bold, ripe and buttery, with spicy pear, fig, honey and vanilla flavors that turn complex. **91**
1991: Delicate and complex, with layers of honey, pear, vanilla and nutmeg flavors, a smooth, supple texture and spicy honey notes. **91**

CHARDONNAY NAPA VALLEY FOUNDER'S RESERVE (★★★★):
Also well oaked, with prominent vanilla and toasty, buttery notes, but also a rich, high extract core of fruit.
1993: Intense and concentrated, with ripe pear, pineapple and nectarine notes that turn complex, with a long aftertaste, picking up citrus. **90**
1992: Firm and compact, complex and concentrated, with a tight, narrow band of flinty citrus, nutmeg and pineapple flavors. **88**

MERLOT NAPA VALLEY (★★★):
Spicy and elegant, with a pretty core of currant and cherry fruit, framed by oak.
1990: Spicy and elegant, with a core of supple cherry and plum flavors and light oak shadings. **86**

PETITE SIRAH NAPA VALLEY (★★★):
The 1990 was stunning, packed with rich, supple fruit in a style that's most appealing. Hopefully it is a wine that will be continued.
1990: Supple, warm and rich, with plum and floral aromas and a solid core of peppery, spicy currant flavors, finishing with chewy tannins. **91**

PINOT NOIR NORTH COAST FOUNDER'S RESERVE (★★★):
Carries the North Coast appellation because it combines Carneros grapes with a small portion purchased in Russian River Valley. Not as dramatic as the other reds, but very well made, delicate on occasion but rustic other times.
1991: Has pungent, spicy aromas and delivers ripe fruit flavors that pick up vanilla from oak, turning complex. **87**
1990: Pungent minty flavors dominate the light, spicy plum notes. **82**
1989: Mint, dill and pickle flavors overshadow the plum and cherry notes. Has lots of oak and tannin, too, making for a heavy-handed, rustic wine. **78**
1988: A ripe, stylish wine that emphasizes spicy vanilla flavors from aging in new oak barrels. **85**

RED TABLE WINE NAPA VALLEY IL TAGLIO (★★★):
1991: Light and lean, with distinctive herb and tobacco aromas and berry and black cherry flavors. **86**

SAUVIGNON BLANC NAPA VALLEY (★★★): Oak again plays a prominent role, giving a buttery edge to the herb and grassy varietal notes.
1993: Bold, ripe and buttery, with rich pear, vanilla, cream and spice notes that are full and deep. **91**
1992: Intensely varietal, with pungent Sauvignon Blanc aromas and flavors and tiers of citrus, fig, pear and spice notes. **87**

SÉMILLON NAPA VALLEY BARREL FERMENTED (★★★):
1993: Ripe and spicy, generous with its oaky pear and lanolin flavors, finishing strong. **86**
1992: An excellent Sémillon, rich with fig, melon and butter notes. **89**

WHITE TABLE WINE NAPA VALLEY IL TAGLIO (NR):
1991: Crisp and earthy, with a strong mineral component to go along with the creamy orange and pear flavors. **81**

ZINFANDEL NAPA VALLEY UNFINED UNFILTERED (★★):
The 1990 was lean and austere, lacking the supple character of the other reds.
1993: Marked by lots of toasty, smoky oak, so much so the fruit struggles to peek through. Just a hint of earthy berry and spice so far, so short-term cellaring is advised. May always be tannic. **86**
1990: Hard, lean and austere, with spiky tannins and harsh acidity covering the ripe plum and cherry flavors. **75**

SILVER MOUNTAIN VINEYARDS
Monterey County
F: 1979. **O:** Jerold O'Brien. **W:** Jerold O'Brien. **S:** Skyland Ridge.

OVERALL	$10-14	★★

WINE RATINGS

Chardonnay Monterey County	★★

WINERY DATA
C: 2,000. **V:** 12 acres in Santa Cruz Mountains. **G:** Chardonnay (7 acres). **P:** Chardonnay (Monterey), Zinfandel (Santa Clara), Cabernet Sauvignon (Monterey).

In 1979, former Air Force pilot Jerold O'Brien purchased 17 acres in the Los Gatos Mountains, where he farms 12 acres of vines, using both estate-grown and purchased grapes for his 2,000-case winery. Monterey Chardonnay from Ventana Vineyard is the main focus (1,000 cases), with smaller lots of estate Chardonnay, Monterey Cabernet and Zinfandel.

TASTING NOTES

CHARDONNAY MONTEREY COUNTY (★★): Made in an elegant, understated style.
1991: Elegant and stylish, with ripe, spicy pear, peach and light toasty oak flavors. **84**

SILVER OAK CELLARS
Oakville, Napa Valley
F: 1972. **O:** Justin Meyer & Raymond T. Duncan. **W:** Justin R. Meyer. **S:** None.

OVERALL	$32-50	★★★★

WINE RATINGS

Cabernet Sauvignon Alexander Valley	★★★★
Cabernet Sauvignon Napa Valley	★★★★
Cabernet Sauvignon Napa Valley Bonny's Vineyard	★★★★

WINERY DATA
C: 38,000. **V:** 250 acres in Alexander Valley, Napa Valley. **G:** Cabernet Sauvignon. **P:** None.

When Justin Meyer and Raymond Duncan founded Silver Oak Cellars in 1972, few would have predicted it would become one of California's most successful, and probably profitable, wineries. Meyer, a former member of the Christian Brothers order, and Duncan, a Colorado oilman, focused on Cabernet Sauvignon only (100 percent) with Silver Oak, and initially used only Alexander Valley grapes despite being based in Napa Valley (Oakville since 1982). By 1979, Silver Oak added two more Cabernets, one a Napa Valley bottling, primarily from Calistoga-area grapes, and a second from Meyer's own vineyard, Bonny's in Oakville, which is named after his wife. Total production is 38,000 cases from 250 winery-owned acres, and despite the winery's holding the wines for five years, they sell out almost instantly at high prices: $32 for the Napa and Alexander Valley and $50 for the Bonny's, although after 1991 the Bonny's was dropped, with the grapes headed for the Napa Valley bottling.

Meyer's philosophy is simple: his wines should be ready to drink and enjoy on release, so he polishes the tannins with extended barrel aging (mostly American oak at $175 a barrel compared to $450 a barrel for French) and ages them in bottle as well. The Alexander Valley Cabernet (30,000 cases) is laced with herb and cedary oak flavors and showcases that appellation's smooth tannins. The Napa Valley (7,700 cases), too, is round and harmonious, often a shade richer and more structured. The Bonny's Vineyard (1,000 cases) often is marked by strong herbaceous and pickle barrel notes, but I've found the wine can change dramatically in the bottle, and those flavors often subside, leaving the fruit more prominent. Because of their distinctive features, Silver Oak wines have their critics, but consumers speak loud and clear that this is a wine style they love. What's surprising is that for all Silver Oak's success, few wineries have tried to mirror the style.

TASTING NOTES

CABERNET SAUVIGNON ALEXANDER VALLEY (★★★★): Supple, complex and well oaked, with a strong cedar, vanilla and herbal streak, but also a wealth of rich, polished currant-laced fruit and supple tannins. Drinks well on release and ages well up to 10 years and beyond. Best and most consistent Alexander Valley Cabernet.

1990: An herbal wine with a peppery dill edge, turning smooth and supple and finishing with plum and cherry notes and soft tannins. **89**

1989: Soft and fleshy, with herb, currant, plum and earth notes on the finish. **82**

1988: Stylish, rich and complex, with classy, smoky oak notes adding to the dense, chewy core of currant and herb flavors. **90**

1987: Despite a heavy toast flavor, there are plenty of currant, black cherry, plum and herb flavors neatly wound together, with supple tannins. **89**

1986: Smooth, harmonious and distinctive, with well integrated currant, smoke, herb and meat aromas and flavors marked by lavish oak. **93**

1985: Enormously rich, complex and concentrated, with layers of ripe, fleshy, intense plum, currant, cedar and anise flavors that are lively and elegant. **95**

1984: Complex and supple, with cedar, vanilla, cherry and plum flavors that are fresh and lively. **89**

1983: Rich, supple and tannic, with earthy currant and cedar flavors. **85**

1982: Still tight, lean and tannic, with a cedary edge to the plum and currant notes. **88**

1981: A ripe, supple, complex 1981 with distinctive green olive and ripe plum flavors, turning mature. **86**

1980: Very ripe, almost jammy and Port-like in aroma, this is a deeply concentrated wine packed with mature, earthy plum, currant and spicy jam notes that are full-bodied. **88**

1979: Elegant and complex, with tart black cherry, currant and cedar flavors that are backed by fine, firm tannins. **85**

1978: Bold, ripe and complex, with smoky herb, currant and chocolate flavors. A seductive wine that's smooth and polished, with depth and richness. **91**

1977: Ripe, rich and supple, with complex plum, currant and cedary oak flavors that are bright and lively. **88**

1976: Has peaked, with deep, rich and drying cherry, chocolate and earth notes. **84**

1975: Mature but still elegant and refined, with spicy cherry and plum flavors that turn supple and a touch earthy. **88**

1974: Fully mature and light in color, with smoky currant and stewed plum flavors that turn smooth and soft on the finish. **84**

1973: Still quite oaky, with the mature Cabernet flavors fading. **80**

1972: Still impressive, with earthy, mature cherry, cedar and smoky anise flavors. **83**

CABERNET SAUVIGNON NAPA VALLEY (★★★★): Similar in style to the Alexander Valley bottling, but shows Napa's structure and deeper tannic strength. Complex and ageworthy too.

1990: Lavishly oaked, with pretty, complex spice, herb, currant and black cherry flavors that pick up a smoky edge on the finish. **91**

1989: Complex and supple, with ripe prune and chocolate flavors that turn to herb and spice. **86**

1988: Round in texture, with tightly wrapped cherry, tobacco and anise flavors extending into a long finish, hinting at toast and spice. **88**

1987: Offers currant, bay leaf, herb and plum flavors that are austere and compact now, but have good depth and concentration. **89**

1986: Beautifully crafted, firm and rich, with complex currant and dill flavors that are rich, powerful and long on the finish. **92**

1985: Remarkably intense and tannic, with tight currant, cherry and plum flavors that are strong and persistent. **88**

1984: Rich, with a core of black cherry, herb, dill and spice flavors that turn supple and complex. **87**

1983: Lean and light, with a vegetal edge to the currant flavors, turning tannic. **74**

1982: Mature now but still impressive for its cherry and currant flavors accented by spicy oak notes. **86**

1981: Lavishly oaked, perhaps to a fault. The fruit struggles to compete. **79**

1980: Marked by tar and vegetal flavors of modest appeal. **73**

1979: Still hard and drying, with the plum and herb flavors turning earthy. **81**

CABERNET SAUVIGNON NAPA VALLEY BONNY'S VINEYARD (★★★★): Steadily improving with recent vintages showing less of a herbaceous edge and more fruit. Dropped after the 1991 vintage.

1987: Lavishly oaked, with a pungent, weedy, herbaceous edge to the broad, complex black cherry and currant flavors and bell pepper, anise and olive notes. **88**

1986: A powerful, aromatic wine that's developed a level of maturity and complexity that suits its nicely focused currant, black cherry and pepper flavors. **88**

1985: Showing tremendous improvement, having evolved into a richer, fuller, fruitier wine with plush, racy black cherry, currant and anise flavors. **90**

1984: Marked by supple, complex green olive, plum and spicy tobacco notes along with bell pepper flavors that are deep and long. **84**

1983: A lighter wine that's mature, with the signature herb, dill and currant notes. **82**

1981: Mature and fading, with a decadent edge to the cherry and spice flavors. **77**

1980: Marked by pungent vegetal, pickle and green chili pepper flavors. **73**

1979: Potent pickle, chili pepper and vegetable flavors fail to make it into the fruit zone. **72**

SILVERADO HILL CELLARS
Napa Valley
F: 1979. **O:** Minami Kyushu Co. **W:** John D. Nemeth. **S:** None.

OVERALL	$10	★★

WINE RATINGS

Chardonnay Napa Valley	★★

WINERY DATA
C: 20,000. **V:** 36 acres in Napa Valley. **G:** Chardonnay (27 acres). **P:** Merlot (Napa Valley).

This winery has survived despite changes in ownership. In 1979, John D. Nemeth headed a group of investors who founded Pannonia winery, which in 1982 became Louis K. Mihaly Vineyards before it was sold in 1987 to Minami Kyushu Co. of Japan. The 30,000-case winery owns 36 acres on the Silverado Trail north of Napa, planted primarily to Chardonnay, which is the main focus. Nemeth has stayed on as winemaker.

TASTING NOTES

CHARDONNAY NAPA VALLEY (★★): Improving with appealing pear and citrus notes.

1993: Marked by an herbal grassy edge, almost like a Sauvignon Blanc, with pear and citrus notes. **82**

1992: Smooth and polished on the surface, it's a crisp-textured wine underneath that offers plenty of pear and grapefruit flavors. **87**

Winemaker's Traditional Methode 1993: Crisp and simple, with a lean band of pear and citrus notes that pick up a light floral edge. **83**

SILVERADO VINEYARDS
Stags Leap District, Napa Valley
F: 1981. **O:** The Silverado Vineyards Inc. **W:** John Stuart. **S:** None.

OVERALL	$10-45	★★★★

WINE RATINGS

Cabernet Sauvignon Stags Leap District	★★★★
Cabernet Sauvignon Stags Leap District Limited Reserve	★★★★★
Chardonnay Napa Valley	★★★
Chardonnay Napa Valley Limited Reserve	★★★★★
Dessert Napa Valley	NR
Merlot Stags Leap District	★★★

Sangiovese Napa Valley	NR
Sauvignon Blanc Napa Valley	★★★

WINERY DATA

C: 85,000. **V:** 340 acres in Napa Valley. **G:** Cabernet Sauvignon (115 acres), Merlot (61), Cabernet Franc (9), Chardonnay (93), Sangiovese (18), Sauvignon Blanc (40), Zinfandel (4). **P:** Chardonnay, Sauvignon Blanc (Napa Valley).

Silverado Vineyards is owned by the family of the late Walt Disney. After purchasing this large property on Silverado Trail in the Stags Leap District in 1976, Lillian Disney and her family planted grapes and began winemaking in 1981, producing excellent wines ever since. The winery owns 340 acres, dominated by Cabernet (115 acres) and Chardonnay (93), from which it produces 85,000 cases, with Chardonnay at 40,000 cases the volume leader, followed by Sauvignon Blanc (20,000 cases), Cabernet (15,000) and Merlot (10,000), all modestly priced given their quality. Jack Stuart has been winemaker since the start and has steadily improved the wines' quality, as well as achieving new heights with the Limited Reserve Cabernet and Chardonnay, both of which are extraordinary. While all the wines are well made, the reds hold a slight edge in quality. A Sangiovese bottling was slated to begin with the 1992 vintage and a Zinfandel is in the works once new plantings mature.

TASTING NOTES

CABERNET SAUVIGNON STAGS LEAP DISTRICT (★★★★): Bright and lively, well focused with complex cherry, currant and olive notes with supple tannins. Well balanced for early consumption.

1992: Firm and rich, with complex cherry, anise, currant and cedary oak flavors. Young, intense and tannic, but in need of short-term cellaring. Best after 1998. **90**

1991: Bright and lively, ripe and richly concentrated, with focused cherry, berry and currant flavors, finishing with firm tannins. **93**

1990: Smooth, polished and elegant, offering complex plum, currant, spice and vanilla aromas and flavors that are smoothly blended, ending with supple tannins. **90**

1989: Soft and simple, with a stalky edge to the modest currant and chocolate flavors. **81**

1988: Marked by grapey cherry and currant flavors, finishing with moderate tannins. **86**

1987: Ripe, round and lively, brimming with spicy straw-berry and currant flavors, turning smooth, elegant and complex. **92**

1986: Mature, with a tight band of spicy black cherry, cassis, currant, raspberry and toasty French oak flavors. **90**

1985: Beautifully styled, elegant and supple, with rich currant, black cherry, raspberry and vanilla flavors and buttery nuances on the finish. **92**

1984: Mature, with an earthy, decadent edge to the currant, plum and cherry flavors, but it delivers a lot of flavor. **91**

1983: This wine has peaked. It remains tannic, but still delivers lots of flavor, with a core of chunky cassis, currant and black cherry flavors. **88**

1982: Fully mature and a shade past its prime, with earthy cherry, oak, chocolate and mint flavors that turn decadent on the finish. **88**

1981: Past its peak now but still pleasing, with a complex array of mature Cabernet flavors. **90**

CABERNET SAUVIGNON STAGS LEAP DISTRICT LIMITED RESERVE (★★★★★): Uncommon richness, depth and concentration, lavishly oaked but beautifully proportioned. No track record for aging, but it drinks well early and has a sense of harmony. No 1992 produced.

1991: Another stunner; dark, ripe, rich and complex with a wide range of black cherry, plum and currant flavors, framed by toasty, buttery oak and a long complex finish. **95**

1990: Beautifully crafted, ripe, rich and complex, with currant, black cherry, cedar, vanilla and spice flavors that unfold to reveal wonderful depth and uncommon complexities. **97**

1987: Dense, concentrated and brimming with plum and currant flavors, with gentle bay leaf and anise overtones and layers of spice and cedar on the long finish. A remarkably delicious wine. **95**

1986: Plush and generous, with rich, sharply focused, delicious cherry, plum, currant, oak and spice flavors that are tight and concentrated. **96**

CHARDONNAY NAPA VALLEY (★★★): Features lots of ripe fruit flavors and pretty oak shadings.

1993: Tart with crisp apple, peach and citrus flavors. What's there is pretty but it fails to develop on the finish. **87**

1992: Well proportioned, with creamy pear, hazelnut and spice notes that turn delicate on the finish. **87**

1991: Intense, spicy and lively, a vibrant wine with focused pineapple, lemon and nutmeg flavors. The finish is tight and concentrated. **89**

CHARDONNAY NAPA VALLEY LIMITED RESERVE (★★★★★): Enormously complex and concentrated, with lots of rich fruit and oak in a dramatic style.
1992: Bold, ripe and complex, with rich, compact pear, toasty smoke and butter flavors. **92**

DESSERT NAPA VALLEY (NR):
NV: Deliciously rich and concentrated, with tiers of fig, honey, pear, apricot and toast flavors that turn smooth and lush, picking up a smoky aftertaste. The label doesn't indicate grapes, vintage or appellation beyond Napa. **93**

MERLOT STAGS LEAP DISTRICT (★★★): Typically firm and well focused, with attractive fruit flavors, mild tannins and early drinking appeal.
1992: Firm and focused, with a nice core of cherry and mint flavors poking through the chewy tannins. **85**
1991: Firm and focused, with a tight, compact band of currant, cherry, anise and cedary oak flavors that hang together **88**
1990: A spicy, toasty Merlot that's lean in profile, supple in texture and focused on plum and blackberry flavors. **87**
1989: Intense, focused blueberry and cherry flavors mark this supple, medium-bodied wine. **85**
1988: Ripe, crisp and juicy, with elegant black cherry, plum and currant flavors and modest tannins. **85**
1987: Big and firm, with plenty of raspberry and plum aromas and flavors before the tannins firm up on the finish. **90**
1986: Sharply defined, with tiers of currant, plum, and black cherry flavors that are wrapped in thick, firm, drying tannins. **89**

SAUVIGNON BLANC NAPA VALLEY (★★★): Strikes a fine balance between herb, fruit and light oak shadings.
1993: There are crisp grapefruit flavors up front in this refreshing wine that fades on the finish. **84**
1992: Rich and complex, packed with herb, citrus, fig and spice flavors. Hints of Sémillon, wonderful balance and uncommon depth. **90**

SILVERWOOD
This is a second label for Pine Ridge Winery (see listing).

SIMI WINERY
Alexander Valley
F: 1876. **O:** Moët-Hennessy/Louis Vuitton. **W:** Nick Goldschmidt. **S:** None.

OVERALL	$9-35	★★★★

WINE RATINGS

Cabernet Sauvignon Alexander Valley	★★★
Cabernet Sauvignon Alexander Valley Reserve	★★★★
Chardonnay Sonoma County	★★★
Chardonnay Sonoma County Reserve	★★★★★
Meritage White Sonoma County Sendal	★★★
Red Table Wine North Coast Altaire	NR
Sauvignon Blanc Sonoma County	★★★

WINERY DATA
C: 150,000. **V:** 273 acres in Alexander Valley, Russian River Valley. **G:** Cabernet Sauvignon (100 acres), Chardonnay (122), Sauvignon Blanc (19), Cabernet Franc (16), Merlot (13), Petite Verdot (3). **P:** Chardonnay (Carneros, Sonoma Coast Mendocino), Cabernet Sauvignon (Alexander Valley), Sauvignon Blanc (Sonoma County, Carneros), Sémillon (Sonoma County).

Dating back to 1876, Simi was founded by the Simi family and family-owned until 1969, when they were forced to sell. A series of ownership changes followed—each improving the winery—with the current owner, Moët-Hennessy/Louis Vuitton, taking over in 1981. Two years earlier, Simi had hired the talented Zelma Long as winemaker, luring her from Robert Mondavi Winery, and her arrival led to yet another round of refinements and improvements from the vineyard to the barrel room.

Simi draws on its 273 acres of estate vineyards, including Chardonnay (122 acres in Russian River) and Cabernet (100 acres in Alexander Valley) but it also relies on purchased grapes. Cabernet (30,000 cases) and Chardonnay (80,000 cases) are the volume leaders, with smaller lots of Reserve wines for both. Quality has been high—as have expectations, many of which have been realized—especially with the Reserve Chardonnay, which is remarkably complex and ageworthy. The Cabernets have been less inspiring. However, the winery's newly planted vineyard is now in production and noted Bordeaux enologist Michel Rolland (Château Le Bon-Pasteur) is consulting and helping to shape the style, so hopes are high that quality will rise. Production is 150,000 cases.

TASTING NOTES

CABERNET SAUVIGNON ALEXANDER VALLEY (★★★): Variable, usually good to very good, as it can be elegant and complex, but it takes a long time to come around. Has carried both the Alexander Valley and Sonoma County appellations.

1989: Tough and tannic, with earthy barnyard and leather flavors that override the modest berry notes. **77**

1988: Firm and focused, with a nice core of currant and berry flavors. **84**

1987: Rich, complex and enticing, with intense, well integrated cherry, toast, currant, plum and chocolate flavors. **89**

1986: This compact and concentrated wine delivers ripe currant and black cherry flavors. **85**

1985: Elegantly crafted, with sharply focused currant, cherry, herb and oak flavors folding together. **91**

1984: Smooth and supple, with bright cherry, cranberry and raspberry flavors in an elegant style. **86**

CABERNET SAUVIGNON ALEXANDER VALLEY RESERVE (★★★★): Consistently very good, occasionally outstanding, but often ponderous with hard tannins and a hard edge that doesn't soften. Mid-1980s bottlings have not gained.

1991: Supple and harmonious, bold and rich, with bright black cherry, currant, mineral and spice notes, finishing with firm tannins. **92**

Centennial Edition 1990: An earthy wine with just enough supple plum and cherry flavors to fight off the earthiness. **84**

1988: Deftly balanced, rich and focused, combining depth and concentration with chewy currant, anise, earth and cedar notes. **87**

1987: Tough and tannic, with solidly concentrated cherry and currant flavors and plenty of gamy, earthy notes and firm tannins. **88**

1986: Balanced and flavorful, with an elegant feel and plenty of currant, berry and tobacco flavors that echo plum and chocolate. Firm tannins. **89**

1985: Dense, rich and complex, offering coffee, cherry, nutmeg, plum, herb and currant flavors, finishing with plush tannins. **90**

1984: Brimming with ripe currant, plum and spice flavors that turn supple, with modest tannins. **88**

1982: Lean and concentrated, with a tannic edge to the anise and plum flavors. **85**

1981: Smells and tastes mature, turning smoky and spicy on the finish. Drying up. **86**

1980: Oaky and tannic, very tight and backward, in danger of drying up. **80**

1979: Firm, oaky and still tannic, with mature, earthy berry, plum and spice components. **84**

Special Reserve 1974: Distinctive for its weedy, herbal edge, it is well past its peak, finishing on a spicy, tarry note. **82**

CHARDONNAY SONOMA COUNTY (★★★): Elegant and fruity, with complex oak adding dimension, but the fruit is the focus.

1991: Pretty and elegant, with floral, spicy pear and nutmeg notes that turn smooth, silky and pleasing on the aftertaste. **85**

CHARDONNAY SONOMA COUNTY RESERVE (★★★★★): Among the state's elite, combining deep, ripe, rich and complex fruit flavors with pretty oak shadings. Ages exceptionally well. The winery holds the wine for two years for additional bottle age. Increasingly reliant on Russian River grapes.

1989: Intense and earthy, offering ripe, spicy pineapple flavors, but it is also a little funky, with hints of honey and botrytis that make it taste even earthier on the finish. A good 1989. **82**

1988: A fully mature, buttery, honeyed Chardonnay that's soft and elegant. Nutty pear and vanilla flavors linger on the finish. **89**

1987: Smooth and fruity, with a real sense of elegance to the melon, pear and honey aromas and flavors, turning spicy and honeyed on the finish. Medium-weight. 1,800 cases made. **92**

1986: Ultrarich, complex and toasty, with layers of ripe pear, apple, lemon and nutmeg flavors that unfold on the palate in this very elegant and enticing wine. Beautifully proportioned, it picks up a pretty butterscotch note on the long and pleasing finish. **92**

1985: Wonderfully complex, subtle and elegant, with fresh, ripe, rich pear, lemon and buttery toast flavors that are impeccably balanced, long and full on the finish. Not quite the concentration of some of the earlier Reserves. **91**

MERITAGE WHITE SONOMA COUNTY SENDAL (★★★): Combines Sauvignon Blanc with a smaller dose of Sémillon, rendering a complex and well crafted wine.
1992: Broad and toasty, a bit of onion intruding around the edges of the light, herbal, smoky pear flavors. **84**
1991: Ripe and generous, with a fig edge to the buttery pineapple flavors. A smooth wine that shows some extra dimensions. **88**

RED TABLE WINE NORTH COAST ALTAIRE (NR):
1992: Light and herbal, showing citrus and strawberry flavors at the center. An usual red wine with some white-wine flavors. **78**

SAUVIGNON BLANC SONOMA COUNTY (★★★): Strikes a nice balance between herb, citrus and pear-laced fruit and light oak notes.
1993: Soft and fruity, with a floral edge to the slightly honeyed pear flavors. **84**

ROBERT SINSKEY VINEYARDS
Stags Leap District, Napa Valley
F: 1986. **O:** Sinskey Vineyards Inc. **W:** Jeff Virnig.
S: Aries.

OVERALL	$10-28	★★★

WINE RATINGS
Cabernet Sauvignon Stags Leap District	NR
Chardonnay Carneros	★★★
Meritage Red Carneros RSV	
Claret Reserve	★★★
Meritage Red Stags Leap District	
RSV Claret Reserve	★★★
Merlot Carneros	★★★
Pinot Noir Carneros	★★★
Aries Cabernet Sauvignon Napa Valley	★★
Aries Merlot Carneros	★★
Aries Pinot Noir Carneros	★★
Aries Pinot Noir Carneros Cuvée Vivace	★★

WINERY DATA
C: 10,000. **V:** 100 acres in Carneros, Stags Leap District.
G: Merlot (30 acres), Cabernet Franc (7), Cabernet Sauvignon (15), Pinot Noir (36), Chardonnay (11), Zinfandel (1). **P:** None.

Robert Sinskey, an eye surgeon, was a founding partner at Acacia and acquired a 35-acre Carneros vineyard before Acacia was sold to the Chalone Wine Group. After the sale, Sinksey purchased the property on the Silverado Trail where the current Sinskey winery stands. Having planted Chardonnay, Merlot and Pinot Noir, Sinskey hired Joe Cafaro, who had had a brief stint with Acacia when it toyed with Bordeaux-style wines. The winery produces 10,000 cases, with Merlot and Pinot Noir the volume leaders at 3,000 cases each, and there are two Claret Reserve bottlings, one from Carneros and the other from Stags Leap District. Chardonnay production is declining, at 1,000 cases. The winery owns 95 acres in Carneros, dominated by Pinot Noir (36 acres) and Merlot (30 acres), along with 5 acres in Stags Leap. The goal is to be all estate-bottled. Aries, the winery's second label, offers good value in Merlot and Pinot Noir.

TASTING NOTES

CABERNET SAUVIGNON STAGS LEAP DISTRICT (NR):
1989: Tight and intense, with deep, focused currant and spice flavors held in check by firm tannins and crisp acidity. **88**

CHARDONNAY CARNEROS (★★★): Made in a tart, tight style, with crisp, intense fruit that's typical of Carneros.
1993: Tart with a green apple and pear edge, this is a young wine with a definite lemony streak. Can stand short-term cellaring. **87**
1992: Tart, tight and intense, with crisp citrus, pear and pineapple flavors that pick up a pretty toasty oak edge. **87**
1991: Tart, tight and concentrated, showing lemon, spice and toast aromas and flavors and hints of peach and honey on the long finish. **88**

MERITAGE RED CARNEROS RSV CLARET RESERVE (★★★):
1990: Tight, firm and focused, with cedar, ripe cherry, plum and wild berry flavors that turn supple on the finish. **87**
1989: Austere, with tightly wound currant, cherry and plum flavors framed by toasty oak. It's 55 percent Cabernet Franc, 25 percent Merlot and 20 percent Cabernet Sauvignon. **85**
1988: Tight and firm, with hard-edged currant and oak flavors. It's 59 percent Cabernet Sauvignon, 22 percent Merlot and 19 percent Cabernet Franc. **83**

MERITAGE RED STAGS LEAP DISTRICT RSV CLARET RESERVE (★★★):
1991: Dark, intense and firmly tannic, but attractive currant, spice, mineral and cherry flavors emerge on the finish. **88**

MERLOT CARNEROS (★★★): More variable than the Claret, as it can be elegant and harmonious or harder edged.
1990: Soft and supple, a generous wine with chocolate and toast overtones to the ripe plum and currant flavors. **86**
1989: Earthy and chewy, with firm currant, herb and oak flavors that are coarse and blunt. **82**
1987: Elegant and harmonious, with ripe currant, plum, black cherry and oak flavors that are well integrated, finishing with firm tannins. **88**
1986: Deeply colored, with a leathery, woody edge to the herb, spice and currant flavors. **83**

PINOT NOIR CARNEROS (★★★): Variable too, but improving, as the 1990 is broad, ripe and voluptuous.
1992: Heavily oaked, with a meaty, smoky, gamy edge that dominates the ripe plum and cherry flavors. **83**
1991: Lean, firm and tannic, with ripe cherry and plum flavors, turning firm on the finish. **82**
1990: Broad, ripe and spicy, with intense, concentrated black cherry, plum, earth and tar notes and fine tannins. **89**
1988: Ripe and generous, with leathery, earthy plum flavors and a tannic finish. **81**
1987: Elegant, with ripe plum, spice and cherry flavors that are appealing. **86**
RSV Reserve 1990: Straight and simple, with woody flavors and faint echoes of cherry and spice. **80**

ARIES VARIOUS BOTTLINGS (★★):
Cabernet Sauvignon Napa Valley 1990: Intense and vibrant, with chewy plum and currant flavors that are ripe and complex, picking up anise and spice notes on a tannic finish. **87**
Merlot Carneros 1989: Crisp and lively, with generous raspberry and leather flavors that focus nicely on the finish, where there's a hint of citrus. **86**
Pinot Noir Carneros 1992: Bright and fruity like a Beaujolais, offering ripe cherry and plum flavors. **85**
Pinot Noir Carneros 1991: Firm and flavorful, with generous currant, blackberry and spice flavors. **84**
Pinot Noir Carneros Cuvée Vivace 1989: A strong, horsey, leathery flavor detracts from the wine. **70**

SKY VINEYARDS
Napa Valley
F: 1979. **O:** Lore Olds & Linn Briner. **W:** Lore Olds. **S:** None.

OVERALL	$16	★★★★

WINE RATINGS		
Zinfandel Mount Veeder		★★★★

WINERY DATA
C: 2,000. **V:** 12 acres. **G:** Zinfandel. **P:** None.

On the Mount Veeder ridge that separates Napa and Sonoma Valleys, owner-winemaker Lore Olds farms 12 acres of Zinfandel, producing 2,000 cases made in a bold, ripe, juicy style that's distinctive and very consistent as well as ageworthy.

TASTING NOTES

ZINFANDEL MOUNT VEEDER (★★★★): Intense and ultraripe, with bold, ripe, complex flavors that are often exotic. Can be tannic and high in alcohol, but ages rather well.
1990: Ripe and exotic, with peppery aromas, stewed plum and prune notes and high-octane alcohol. **88**
1989: Intense and spicy, with peppery cherry, raspberry and anise flavors that are fresh and lively. **87**
1988: The herb and raspberry aromas promise more than this lean, tart wine delivers on the palate. Ruggedly tannic. **78**
1987: Bold, rich and thick, brimming with fresh, ripe blackberry, cherry and jam flavors that are smooth and supple. **90**
1985: Peppery, fruity and concentrated, with raspberry notes that turn supple and tannic. **88**

SMITH AND HOOK
Monterey County
F: 1979. **O:** Smith and Hook Winery. **W:** Art Nathan. **S:** Hahn Estates, Lone Oak Estates.

OVERALL	$18-30	★★

WINE RATINGS		
Cabernet Sauvignon Santa Lucia Highlands		★★
Merlot Santa Lucia Highlands		★★

Lone Oak Cabernet Sauvignon
  Monterey County   ★★

WINERY DATA
C: 50,000. **V:** 921 acres in Arroyo Seco, Santa Lucia Highlands.
G: Chardonnay (308 acres), Merlot (248), Cabernet Sauvignon
(182), Cabernet Franc (75), Viognier (14), Nebbiolo (5),
Sauvignon Blanc (21), Gewürztraminer (41), Chenin Blanc (27).
P: None.

Smith and Hook, the marriage of two large vineyards,
owns 921 acres of grapevines, including a beautifully terraced 250-acre parcel west of Highway 101 near
Soledad. The winery's focus is on Bordeaux-style reds,
based on Cabernet and Merlot, and it makes 50,000
cases, occasionally buying Napa County grapes for both
Cabernet and Merlot. The winery makes two other labels,
Hahn Estates (see listing) and Lone Oak Estates, from its
considerable holdings. There are plans to build separate
wineries for the individual brands.

TASTING NOTES

CABERNET SAUVIGNON SANTA LUCIA HIGHLANDS (★★):
Improving but variable, often well oaked and marked by
herbal flavors.
1991: A big, ripe, herbal wine with layers of cedar, currant, coffee and spice notes. **86**
1990: An oaky wine that's complex and concentrated,
with herb, currant, tobacco and spice flavors framed by
toasty, buttery wood. **87**
1988: Strong, almost overbearing herb and bay leaf flavors dominate the currant and berry notes. It's also quite
tannic and oaky. **80**

MERLOT SANTA LUCIA HIGHLANDS (★★): Usually
marked by strong herb and bell pepper flavors, disappointing in 1991.
1992: Well oaked with herb and currant flavors that pick
up a spicy wood flavor on the finish. **85**
1991: Earthy, rubbery flavors dominate this one. **74**
1990: Lean and tart, with an austere vegetal and bell
pepper edge to the light cherry notes. **81**
1989: An extreme, off-putting wine with vegetal and rubbery flavors. **70**
1988: Simple plum and herb flavors give it modest
appeal. **80**
1987: Marked by strong bell pepper and herbal flavors,
finishing with ripe currant and pepper flavors. **83**

1986: Lush and appealing, with herb, bell pepper, chocolate and plum flavors. **86**

**LONE OAK CABERNET SAUVIGNON MONTEREY
COUNTY (★★):**
1992: An herbal wine with spice and bell pepper notes. **79**

SMITH-MADRONE VINEYARD
Spring Mountain, Napa Valley
F: 1971. **O:** Smith-Madrone Vineyard and Winery.
W: Charles Smith. **S:** None.

OVERALL   **$9-15**   ★★

WINE RATINGS
Cabernet Sauvignon Napa Valley   ★★
Chardonnay Napa Valley   ★★★
Johannisberg Riesling Napa Valley   ★★★

WINERY DATA
C: 5,000. **V:** 32 acres in Napa Valley. **G:** Cabernet Sauvignon
(13 acres), Chardonnay (13), Riesling (6). **P:** None.

Brothers Stuart and Charles Smith led a group of
investors headed by family members which bought 200
acres on Spring Mountain in 1971; they planted vines in
1973, and initially focused their winemaking efforts on
Riesling and Chardonnay. They were inspired by Stony
Hill's success with those varietals on property below
theirs on Spring Mountain. The winery added Cabernet
in 1978 and has been plagued by erratic stylistic and
quality swings. Production is 5,000 cases. In 1994 the
Smith brothers decided to take the winery public with a
stock offering, a plan that was subsequently dropped.

TASTING NOTES

CABERNET SAUVIGNON NAPA VALLEY (★★): Highly variable, usually less inspiring than either the Chardonnay or
Riesling. Quality ranges from fair to good. No recent vintage notes as the winery has an irregular release pattern.
1985: Tired and mature on release, with earthy cedar,
coffee and herb notes. **80**
1984: Best of the early wines, ripe, complex and mature
now, with currant, earth and cedary notes. **85**
1983: Like most 1983s, tannic and drying. **79**

SMOTHERS BROTHERS WINES
Sonoma Valley
F: 1977. **O:** Smothers Inc. **W:** Richard Arrowood.
S: None.

OVERALL	$16-18	★★

WINE RATINGS

Cabernet Sauvignon Sonoma Valley	
Remick Ridge Ranch	★★

WINERY DATA
C: 4,000. **V:** 28 acres in Sonoma Valley. **G:** Chardonnay
(16 acres), Cabernet Sauvignon (10), Merlot (2). **P:** None.

Comedians Tom and Dick Smothers first bought a vineyard in the Santa Cruz Mountains (Vine Hill) before moving to Sonoma Valley, where they farm 28 acres of vines—Chardonnay (16 acres), Cabernet (10) and Merlot (2)—at the Remick Ridge Ranch. Production is 4,000 cases, with quality ranging from ordinary to good. Richard Arrowood is the winemaker, so quality should continue to improve.

TASTING NOTES

CABERNET SAUVIGNON SONOMA VALLEY REMICK RIDGE RANCH (★★): Simple and uninspired so far.
1990: Medium-bodied, with moderately rich currant, cherry and oak flavors. **84**
1989: Light and simple, with herb, currant and spice notes. **82**

SOBON ESTATE
Shenandoah Valley
F: 1856. **O:** Leon & Shirley Sobon. **W:** Leon Sobon.
S: None.

OVERALL	$6-17	★★

WINE RATINGS

Cabernet Franc Shenandoah Valley	NR
Rhône Blend Shenandoah Valley	
Rhône Rouge	NR
Rhône Blend Shenandoah Valley Rosé	NR
Syrah Shenandoah Valley	★★
Viognier Shenandoah Valley	NR
Zinfandel Fiddletown Lubenko	★★
Zinfandel Shenandoah Valley	★★
Zinfandel Sierra Foothills	★★

WINERY DATA
C: 6,000. **V:** 85 acres in Shenandoah Valley, Fiddletown.
G: Muscat Canelli (2 acres), Zinfandel (35), Sauvignon Blanc
(3.5), Cabernet Sauvignon (4), Viognier (7), Cabernet Franc
(3.5), Rhône Red (11), Sangiovese (1), Orange Muscat (1).
P: Zinfandel (Fiddletown), Zinfandel (Shenandoah Valley).

In 1989, Leon and Shirley Sobon bought the old and run-down D'Agostini Winery (founded in 1856) in the Shenandoah Valley and began replanting the vineyards and restoring the winery, which they renamed Sobon Estate. The 6,000-case winery focuses on Cabernet Franc, Syrah, Viognier and Zinfandel, the former three from Shenandoah Valley, and the Zinfandel carrying both the Shenandoah Valley and Sierra Foothills designations. Syrah and Zin are the quality leaders. The winery's 85 acres of vineyards are the major source, dominated by Zinfandel (35 acres).

TASTING NOTES

CABERNET FRANC SHENANDOAH VALLEY (NR): Crisp and fruity in 1990, but with a stalky edge to the plum and cherry notes.
1990: Crisp and fruity, with a hint of stalkiness on the finish after the cherry and plum flavors have their say. A pleasant wine. **81**

RHÔNE BLEND SHENANDOAH VALLEY RHÔNE ROUGE (NR):
1992: Intensely spicy, with an earthy, tarry, bell pepper edge to the currant and cherry notes underneath. **86**

RHÔNE BLEND SHENANDOAH VALLEY ROSÉ (NR):
1994: Dry, fresh and lively, gently unfolding its watermelon and spice flavors. **82**

SYRAH SHENANDOAH VALLEY (★★): Improving and may be the best wine for the future.
1991: Intense and deeply colored, with tight, compact, concentrated Syrah flavors that turn meaty and spicy. **82**
1990: Crisp and fruity, with ripe currant, pepper and cherry aromas and flavors. **86**

VIOGNIER SHENANDOAH VALLEY (NR): Ripe and supple in 1993, with tropical fruit, spice and earthy notes.

1993: Ripe and supple, with tropical fruit, spice and slightly earthy overtones. **84**

ZINFANDEL VARIOUS BOTTLINGS (★★): Variable but can be intense and powerful.

Zinfandel Fiddletown Lubenko 1992: Very ripe and tannic, with a pruney edge that's dry and tannic. **82**

Zinfandel Shenandoah Valley 1992: Rustic, with jammy cherry and berry flavors and a tarry edge, turning tannic and earthy on the finish. **81**

Zinfandel Shenandoah Valley 1988: Full-bodied, ripe and powerful, with generous plum, toast, chocolate and vanilla flavors supported by firm tannins. **88**

Zinfandel Shenandoah Valley Old Vines Sobon Estate 1990: Austere, tannic and earthy, a tough and chewy wine with just a hint of berry and cherry flavors showing. **78**

Zinfandel Shenandoah Valley Rocky Top 1992: Ripe, almost jammy, with wild berry and cherry flavors that turn exotic, finishing with chewy tannins. **82**

Zinfandel Sierra Foothills 1990: Tough and chewy, with lean, earthy berry and plum flavors buried beneath the tannins. **81**

Zinfandel Sierra Foothills 1989: Firm, roasted and tannic, a classic, old-style Zin that offers plenty of berry aromas and flavors. **86**

SODA CANYON VINEYARDS
Napa Valley
F: 1979. **O:** John Furtado. **W:** John Furtado. **S:** None.

OVERALL	$10	★★

WINE RATINGS	
Chardonnay Napa Valley	★★

WINERY DATA
C: 2,800. **V:** 12 acres in Napa Valley. **G:** Chardonnay. **P:** None.

John Furtado owns and operates this 2,800-case Chardonnay winery, which uses grapes from its 12-acre estate vineyard in Soda Canyon, an area east of the Silverado Trail near the Silverado Country Club. Quality is ordinary to good.

TASTING NOTES

CHARDONNAY NAPA VALLEY (★★): Quality varies in this rustic-styled Chardonnay, which often relies heavily on oaky flavors.

14th Leaf 1992: Simple, with spicy pear and light cedary notes that fan out on the finish. **83**

13th Leaf 1991: Relies heavily on smoky, oaky flavors, but delivers enough spicy fig and pear flavors to keep in balance. **85**

SOLIS WINERY
Santa Clara County
F: 1989. **O:** Rancho De Solis. **W:** David Vanni, Corey Wilson. **S:** None.

OVERALL	$8-12	★★

WINE RATINGS	
Chardonnay Santa Clara County	
Barrel Fermented	★★
Merlot Santa Clara County	★★
Pinot Noir Santa Clara County	★
Zinfandel Blend Santa Clara	
County Old Vines Seducente	★

WINERY DATA
C: 8,000. **V:** 12 acres in Santa Clara County. **G:** Chardonnay, Merlot, Pinot Noir, Zinfandel. **P:** None.

David Vanni bought this historic winery in 1989, renaming it Solis, after it had been known for decades as the Bertero Winery (1917) and for a briefer period as Summerhill Vineyards. Using grapes from a 12-acre vineyard, along with purchased grapes, Solis produces 8,000 cases of wine, mainly Chardonnay and Merlot; Pinot Noir and Zinfandel are also produced on occasion. Quality is ordinary.

TASTING NOTES

VARIOUS BOTTLINGS:
Chardonnay Santa Clara County Barrel Fermented 1991: Has a definite French character, with earthy, toasty oak aromas and nicely integrated pear and apple flavors that join in through the finish. **85**

Merlot Santa Clara County 1991: A smooth, soft, herbal Merlot with cherry, anise and olive flavors. Straightforward and slightly tannic. **81**

Pinot Noir Santa Clara County 1988: A modest wine with simple plum and cherry flavors, a trace of Pinot Noir character and mild tannins. **78**

Zinfandel Blend Santa Clara County Old Vines Seducente 1991: Lean and chewy, a little soft around the middle, with plum flavor and a citrus bite on the finish. Unbalanced. **79**

SOLITUDE WINES
Sonoma County
F: 1986. O: Richard Litsch. W: Richard Litsch. S: None.

OVERALL	$17-21	★★

WINE RATINGS

Chardonnay Carneros Sangiacomo Vineyard	★★★
Pinot Noir Sonoma County	★★

WINERY DATA
C: 2,000. V: None. G: None. P: Chardonnay, Pinot Noir (Carneros), Pinot Noir (Carneros), Pinot Noir (Russian River Valley).

Now using Sangiacomo-grown Chardonnay and Pinot Noir, so far the former has the quality lead, as the 1991 was elegant, spicy, smooth and polished, with creamy pear, vanilla, honey and nutmeg shadings. The 1991 Pinot Noir offered gamy, rubbery red-wine flavors, but not much varietal character.

TASTING NOTES

CHARDONNAY CARNEROS SANGIACOMO VINEYARD (★★★):
1993: Openly fruity, with ripe pear, apple and pretty spice flavors that are elegant and appealing, picking up spicy smoky oak flavors. **90**
1991: Elegant, spicy, smooth and polished, with creamy pear, vanilla, honey and nutmeg shadings. **89**

PINOT NOIR SONOMA COUNTY (★★):
1992: Ripe and supple, laced with herb, black cherry and spice notes that turn simple on the finish. Ready. **84**
1991: Marginal, with gamy, rubbery, nondescript red-wine flavors. **75**

SONOMA CREEK WINERY
Sonoma Valley
F: 1987. O: Robert F. Thomas C. & Suzanne Larson. W: David Dobson. S: None.

OVERALL	$10-25	★★

WINE RATINGS

Cabernet Sauvignon Sonoma Valley Reserve	★
Chardonnay Carneros	★★
Merlot Sonoma Valley Sangiacomo Vineyard	NR
Pinot Noir Carneros	NR
Zinfandel Sonoma County	★

WINERY DATA
C: 20,000. V: 45 acres in Carneros. G: Chardonnay. P: Zinfandel (Sonoma County), Cabernet Sauvignon (Sonoma County), Cabernet Sauvignon (Sonoma Valley), Pinot Noir (Carneros), Merlot (Sonoma Valley).

The Larson family farmed these 45 acres in Carneros before turning commercial in 1987. Using their Chardonnay-only vineyard and buying grapes, they've built production to 20,000 cases of Cabernet, Chardonnay, Merlot, Pinot Noir and Zinfandel. Chardonnay and Merlot are the early quality leaders, with the other wines ranging from thin and ordinary to good.

TASTING NOTES

CABERNET SAUVIGNON SONOMA VALLEY RESERVE (★): Unusually tannic and hard-edged, with grapes from Sonoma Valley.
1991: Ripe, with a racy wild berry and herbal edge and a tannic finish. **84**
1988: Tight, tough tannins run roughshod over the modest cherry and plum flavors, making it a risk to buy. **74**

CHARDONNAY CARNEROS (★★): Highly variable with two 1992 bottlings, the oxidized Barrel Fermented bottling and the attractively fruity Estate Bottled offering.
1993: Light and gently spicy, a smooth-textured wine that displays some warm spice and honey-scented pear flavors that taper a bit on the finish. **84**
Barrel Fermented 1992: Crisp and thin, with a candied, earthy, oxidized edge to the flavors. Marginal quality. **70**

Organically Grown Estate Bottled 1992: Elegant and refined, with pretty pear, spice and hazelnut flavors framed by light, toasty oak shadings. **87**

Merlot Sonoma Valley Sangiacomo Vineyard (NR): **1992:** Deep, dark, dense and tannic, with herb, cedar and currant flavors. **85**

Pinot Noir Carneros (NR): Light and simple. **1992:** Light and simple, with a hollow strip of spicy cherry and oak flavors. **77**

Zinfandel Sonoma County (★): Has failed to impress in two vintages. **1992:** Earthy and gamy, with a dry, leathery edge to the Zin flavors. **78** **1990:** Crisp, with modest raspberry, tobacco and spice flavors. **78**

SONOMA-CUTRER VINEYARDS
Sonoma Coast
F: 1973. O: Sonoma-Cutrer Vineyards. W: Terry Adams, Bill Bonetti. S: None.

OVERALL	$14-21	★★★

WINE RATINGS

Chardonnay Sonoma Coast Cutrer Vineyard	★★★
Chardonnay Sonoma Coast Les Pierres	★★★
Chardonnay Sonoma Coast Russian River Ranches	★★★

WINERY DATA
C: 80,000. V: 500 acres in Sonoma Coast. G: Chardonnay
P: Chardonnay (Sonoma Coast).

Sonoma-Cutrer Vineyards began in 1973 as a grape-growing business, but by the early 1980s shifted to wine-making, with the highly regarded Bill Bonetti (Charles Krug) overseeing production of three different Chardonnay bottlings designed for long aging. The winery has stuck with Chardonnay and owns some 500 acres in vines, ranging from Russian River Valley to Carneros (Les Pierres). Plans to introduce a sparkling wine were dropped in the mid-1980s but there has been talk of producing small amounts of Pinot Noir in the future.

Sonoma-Cutrer is known for its ultramodern, state-of-the-art winemaking facility. To call Sonoma-Cutrer a specialist winery is an understatement, and not quite accurate. "Perfectionist" is more appropriate. No winery goes to such lengths to preserve the quality of its grapes from the vineyard to the bottle, yet despite that and early successes in the mid-1980s, quality has tapered off in recent vintages as production has risen to 80,000 cases. Given all that is done to achieve perfection, complexity and ageworthiness, Sonoma-Cutrer's Chardonnays age only moderately well. By the early 1990s, the winery was rethinking its entire philosophy from vineyard to barrel. Having taken a much closer look at what's done in Burgundy, and why, they've concluded that the winery's style—with no malolactic fermentation—needed an overhaul, or at the least, a retooling.

TASTING NOTES

Chardonnay Sonoma Coast Cutrer Vineyard (★★★): The steadiest performer of late, it is ripe and intense, with crisp pear and peach-laced fruit. **1992:** Well focused, with a pretty core of pear, spice, oak and honey, finishing with a spicy oak edge. **88** **1991:** Smooth and complex, intense and lively, with pear and spice notes. **88** **1990:** Tart, tight and flinty, with crisp citrus, grapefruit and tangy pear flavors and subtle oak shadings. **87**

Chardonnay Sonoma Coast Les Pierres (★★★): A star in the 1980s, but a victim of phylloxera and variable quality since 1988. Les Pierres, "the stones" in French, is a single vineyard wine that takes its name from the stony, rocky soil that usually shows up in the wines as a stony, flinty, mineral character. Can age well, but vintages from the 1980s have peaked. The vineyard was replanted in the early 1990s. **1991:** A subtle, flinty style with mature pear, spice, honey and light toast shadings that pick up a citrus edge. **88** **1990:** Crisp and flinty, with spicy pear, apple and nutmeg flavors that offer a hint of maturity. Stays lean and focused through the finish. **87** **1989:** Complex and lively, with creamy pear, peach, vanilla and butterscotch flavors and a solid dose of oak. It's balanced and creamy, with good depth and a pretty follow-through. **86** **1988:** The finest Les Pierres since 1981, it's tart, crisp,

lean and elegant, with lively, flinty pear, mineral, lemon and spice notes enlivened by bracing acidity and subtle, smoky oak shadings. Showing complexity and grace. **93**
1987: Tight, tart and flinty like a barrel-aged Chablis, with complex, concentrated pear, citrus, spice and honey notes that are well structured. **90**

CHARDONNAY SONOMA COAST RUSSIAN RIVER RANCHES (★★★): This wine comes from a trio of winery-owned vineyards and it's usually ripe and fruity with light oak shadings.
1993: Young and crisp, with a citrus and grapefruit flavor that has a bitter edge, but it may come around with short-term cellaring. **84**
1992: Tight and flinty, with earthy pear and spice flavors that turn perfumed on the finish. **83**
1991: A tart, slightly green Chardonnay offering crisp pear, green apple and spice notes, but it shows an earthy edge. **84**
1990: Tart, intense and lively, with subtle pear, peach and spice notes that are well focused. **86**
1989: Fruity and generous, with ripe pear and spice flavors that are accented by butter and vanilla notes. A slightly rough texture holds it back. **82**
1988: Intense and elegant, with sharply defined, crisp pear and pineapple flavors that zip across the palate, held in check by zingy acidity and gaining complexity and subtlety on the finish. **88**

SONOMA-LOEB
Sonoma County
F: 1990. **O:** John L. Loeb Jr. **W:** Phillip Titus. **S:** Sonoma-Loeb Cellars.

OVERALL	$16-26	★★★

WINE RATINGS

Chardonnay Sonoma County Ambassador John L. Loeb Jr.'s Private Reserve	★★★

WINERY DATA
C: 1,750. **V:** 50 acres in Alexander Valley. **G:** Chardonnay (30 acres), Cabernet Sauvignon (20). **P:** Chardonnay (Sonoma County, Carneros).

John Loeb Jr., former U.S. ambassador to Denmark, bought land in Sonoma County as a tax shelter in the 1970s, but he picked good Chardonnay turf, settling next to Robert Young Vineyards in Alexander Valley, with another vineyard in the Russian River Valley near Davis Bynum Winery. Loeb sold his grapes to Fetzer, Clos du Bois and Piper-Sonoma before turning to winemaking, encouraged by Seagram Classics' Sam Bronfman II. The goal is to make Burgundian-style Chardonnays and early results are encouraging. A Cabernet is also in the works for this winery, which plans to grow beyond its current 1,750-case output.

TASTING NOTES

CHARDONNAY SONOMA COUNTY AMBASSADOR JOHN L. LOEB JR.'S PRIVATE RESERVE (★★★): Carries the broader Sonoma County appellation with vineyards in Alexander Valley and Russian River. The early wines are well oaked and richly fruity, with polished textures. Not much distinction with the Private Reserve bottling.
1993: A touch woody at first, but it opens up with ripe pear, peach and vanilla flavors that turn smooth and elegant. **89**
1992: Smooth and creamy, with a leesy, earthy edge and soft, fleshy, spicy pear, honey and vanilla flavors. **89**
1991: Smooth, ripe and lively, with a rich, focused core of creamy pear, honey and nutmeg flavors that are complex. **90**
Private Reserve 1991: Tight and firm, framed by toasty oak shadings, with nice, ripe melon and pear flavors and a hint of smoke. **89**

SONORA WINERY & PORT WORKS
Amador County
F: 1986. **O:** Richard Matranga & Michael Brogan. **W:** Richard Matranga. **S:** None.

OVERALL	$14-16	NR

WINE RATINGS

Port Amador County	NR
Zinfandel Sonoma County	NR

WINERY DATA
C: 2,500. **V:** 1 acre in Sierra Foothills. **G:** Potr Type (1 acre). **P:** Zinfandel (Amador County), Zinfandel (Sonoma County).

Richard Matranga heads this limited partnership which specializes in dessert-style wines, including a

Vintage Port, using the classic Portuguese grapes Souzao, Tinta Cao, Touriga Nacional and Alveralhao, all from Amador County. Zinfandel comes from 90-year-old vines in Sonoma County. Production is 2,500 cases, with limited distribution. No recent notes.

SOQUEL VINEYARDS
Santa Cruz Mountains
F: 1987. **O:** Peter Bargetto, Paul Bargetto & Jon Morgan. **W:** Paul Bargetto, Peter Bargetto. **S:** None.

OVERALL	$18-25	★★

WINE RATINGS

Cabernet Sauvignon	
Santa Cruz Mountains	★★
Cabernet Sauvignon Stags Leap District	★★
Chardonnay Santa Cruz Mountains	★
Pinot Noir Santa Cruz Mountains	★★
Zinfandel Alexander Valley	NR

WINERY DATA
C: 2,000. **V:** None. **G:** None. **P:** Cabernet Sauvignon, Pinot Noir, Chardonnay (Santa Cruz Mountains), Cabernet Sauvignon (Stags Leap District).

Paul and Peter Bargetto, of the Bargetto Winery family, are reviving the former Grover Gulch Winery in Santa Cruz, with a lineup that includes Cabernet from the Santa Cruz Mountains and Stags Leap District, Chardonnay (Santa Cruz Mountains), Pinot Noir (Santa Cruz Mountains) and Zinfandel (Alexander Valley). Production is around 2,000 cases, with wines of fair to above-average quality.

TASTING NOTES

CABERNET SAUVIGNON SANTA CRUZ MOUNTAINS (★★): Firm and intense, with spicy flavors and tight tannins. A Special Reserve appeared in 1989.
1991: Firm, tannic and intense, with a distinctive meaty, peppery edge to the currant flavors. **86**
1990: Supple and fruity, with spicy plum and black currant flavors that turn spicy, firm and tannic. **88**
Special Reserve 1989: Bright and lively, with generous blackberry, raspberry and currant flavors shaded by herb and toast notes. Tannic. **84**

CABERNET SAUVIGNON STAGS LEAP DISTRICT (★★): On the lean side for Stags Leap grapes. Less impressive than the Santa Cruz bottlings.
1991: Tart and lean, with a green edge to the cherry and plum flavors. **83**
1990: Firm and fruity, with black cherry and plum notes that are a little rough around the edges. **85**
1989: This lean, focused wine is tightly tannic and woody, but nice raspberry, strawberry and cherry flavors peek through on the finish. **83**

CHARDONNAY SANTA CRUZ MOUNTAINS (★): Uninspired so far, with an odd 1991.
1991: Marked by tart, oaky, brackish pear flavors that don't blend together. **75**

PINOT NOIR SANTA CRUZ MOUNTAINS (★★): Variable in the past two vintages.
1991: Lean and tough, with a hint of tea and plum flavors peeking through. **80**
1990: A tight, tart Pinot with modest raspberry and cherry flavors. **86**

ZINFANDEL ALEXANDER VALLEY (NR):
1991: Simple and fruity, with crisp raspberry flavors and an ample layer of toasty, buttery oak. **79**

SPOTTSWOODE WINERY
St. Helena, Napa Valley
F: 1982. **O:** Mary Novak. **W:** Pam Starr, Tony Soter. **S:** None.

OVERALL	$12-40	★★★★★

WINE RATINGS

Cabernet Sauvignon Napa Valley	★★★★★
Sauvignon Blanc Napa Valley	★★★

WINERY DATA
C: 8,000. **V:** 40 acres in Napa Valley. **G:** Cabernet Sauvignon (32 acres), Cabernet Franc (3), Sauvignon Blanc (5). **P:** Sauvignon Blanc, Sémillon (Napa Valley).

In its first decade, Spottswoode produced a succession of beautifully crafted Cabernets and the winery now stands as one of California's premiere Cabernet estates. The key, of course, is in the soils and climate of its vineyard, which is situated in an area capable of yielding consistently excellent, rich and deeply concentrated wines with suitably thick but polished tannins. Owner-founder Mary Novak and her late husband Jack moved to Napa

Valley in the early 1970s to ease into a country lifestyle, and ended up purchasing one of the valley's great vineyards. Mary Novak still oversees operations, having had the wisdom (and good fortune) to hire Tony Soter early on as winemaker (he still consults); he had a hand in shaping and refining the style. Most of the 40-acre vineyard on the western outskirts of St. Helena is planted to Cabernet (32 acres) and Cabernet Franc (3) with the remaining five acres rooted in Sauvignon Blanc. Winery production is 8,000 cases, led by Cabernet (5,000 cases). The Sauvignon Blanc is a blend of estate and purchased grapes.

TASTING NOTES

CABERNET SAUVIGNON NAPA VALLEY (★★★★★): Uniformly rich and well focused, with deep, complex and concentrated currant, black cherry, and spicy flavors. Well oaked but not overdone. Tannins are thick but polished and well integrated. Ages well up to 10 years, as the wines from the early and mid-1980s are holding up.
1991: Ripe, smooth and polished, packing in pretty currant, black cherry and anise flavors that are rich and focused, complex and concentrated, finishing with plush tannins. **93**
1990: Ripe, opulent, rich and intense, with pretty plum, berry, currant, spice and cedary, buttery oak flavors, finishing with supple tannins. **91**
1989: Smooth and polished, a pretty wine with black cherry and spice flavors and integrated tannins that turn supple. **89**
1988: Well focused, with supple, well defined currant, berry and plum aromas and flavors that carry through into a finish that features fine tannins. **90**
1987: Rich, potent and aristocratic, with supple, plush blackberry, currant and cherry flavors, picking up vanilla, herb and nutmeg in the aromas and on the long finish. **96**
1986: Beautifully defined currant, black cherry, cassis, anise and toasty oak flavors unfold gracefully, turning supple and complex, with firm tannins. **96**

1985: Elegantly styled, with a massive concentration of rich, ripe currant, cherry and cassis flavors, floral and herb aromas and black cherry on the finish. **95**
1984: Ripe, supple and harmonious, with pretty toasty oak, ripe plum, cassis and currant flavors that are rich and generous. Mature. **90**
1983: Impressive for its structure and firm tannins, which allow the cassis, currant, plum and mint flavors to emerge. Complex and mature. **88**
1982: Firm and deeply concentrated, with tight, thick tannins wrapped around an abundance of ripe plum, cherry and cassis flavors. **88**

SAUVIGNON BLANC NAPA VALLEY (★★★): Crisp and well focused, too, with citrus, herb and mineral notes.
1994: Smooth and supple, a harmonious wine with tropical fruit and spice flavors and just a hint of anise on the finish. **87**
1993: Fresh, floral and concentrated, with focused grapefruit, pear and earthy mineral flavors. **85**

SPRING MOUNTAIN VINEYARDS
Spring Mountain, Napa Valley
F: 1968. **O:** Good Wine Co. **W:** Thomas Ferrell. **S:** None.

OVERALL	$20	NR

WINE RATINGS		
Cabernet Sauvignon Napa Valley		NR

WINERY DATA
C: N/A. **V:** 100 acres in Napa Valley. **G:** Cabernet Sauvignon, Merlot. **P:** None.

Mike Robbins turned from real estate to winegrowing in the 1960s, buying property and building a winery at the base of Spring Mountain. By the end of the 1960s, the winery had established a solid reputation for Chardonnay and Cabernet, under the winemaking direction of Chuck Ortman (Meridian), relying on both estate-grown and purchased grapes. But the wine business did not prove as lucrative as real estate, and when finances tightened and profits narrowed, Robbins first agreed to let his winery be the backdrop for the "Falcon Crest" TV series, then bottled a wine under the same name. He then let quality slip by failing to reinvest in his business. When Robbins sold the Wildwood Vineyard in Rutherford (near Caymus), the winery was robbed of its best vineyard for Cabernet and slowly the brand faded from the market.

Robbins put the winery up for sale in the late 1980s and kept dropping the price until a group of investors, headed by Jacob Safra, hired Tom Ferrell (ex-Inglenook winemaker and Sterling Vineyards' president) to buy the property out of bankruptcy in 1990. Shortly thereafter, the group acquired two other out-of-business wineries nearby, Chateau Chevalier and Streblow. By 1994, the Good Wine Co. had acquired nearly 400 acres on Spring Mountain, 100 of them in vines, and plans to focus on Cabernet, Chardonnay and Sauvignon Blanc at Spring Mountain, and Rhône-style wines at Chateau Chevalier. In 1995, after years of trying to keep the group's identity secret in order to secure more vineyards, Safra was exposed as the money behind Good Wine, and he paid $4 million to buy half of the 385-acre Draper Vineyard, also on Spring Mountain. The first of the new Spring Mountain wines were planned for release in 1995, and production is expected to expand to the 15,000-case range.

TASTING NOTES

CABERNET SAUVIGNON NAPA VALLEY (NR): It's been a long time since this wine was produced, but older vintages, dating to 1968, are worth the try. The best Spring Mountain ever made is the Lot H 68-69, half of which came from Heitz Martha's Vineyard.

1986: The best in a long time, with ripe black cherry and currant flavors that are sharply defined, finishing with toasty oak. **86**

1985: Correct but unexciting, with simple berry, cherry and currant flavors. **83**

1984: Pleasing with its supple black cherry, currant, anise and plum flavors. **85**

1983: Plenty of tannin, overriding the plum and currant flavors. **78**

Lot H 68-69 NV: A blend of wines from the '68 and '69 vintages that includes Heitz Martha's '69; it's mature and cedary now. **83**

STAGLIN FAMILY VINEYARD
Rutherford, Napa Valley
F: 1985. **O:** Garen & Shari Staglin. **W:** Celia Masyczek. **S:** None.

OVERALL	$20-28	★★★

WINE RATINGS

Cabernet Sauvignon Napa Valley	★★★
Chardonnay Napa Valley	NR
Sangiovese Napa Valley Stagliano	NR

WINERY DATA
C: 2,000. **V:** 50 acres in Rutherford. **G:** Cabernet Sauvignon (37 acres), Chardonnay (10), Cabernet Franc (2), Sangiovese (1). **P:** None.

Staglin Family Vineyard in Rutherford dates to 1985, and this 50-acre estate is dominated by Cabernet (37 acres), with smaller parcels of Chardonnay (10), Cabernet Franc and Sangiovese (called Stagliano). Cathy Corison had a hand in the early wines, which were made in very small case numbers. The Cabernets have shown steady improvement, and are reflective of the Rutherford appellation with their plush fruit flavors and fine tannins. A portion of the Cabernet crop is sold to Corison and St. Clement. Worth watching.

TASTING NOTES

CABERNET NAPA VALLEY (★★★): Keeps improving, with well focused and complex fruit flavors and mild, supple tannins.

1991: Intense, lively and tightly wound, with lovely, supple plum and currant flavors that pick up a spicy, cedary edge. **88**

1990: Tight, firm and oaky, with vanilla and chocolate notes showing through and black cherry and currant flavors underneath. **88**

1989: Smooth and supple, with artful oak and spice shadings to the ripe plum and blackberry flavors. **87**

SANGIOVESE NAPA VALLEY STAGLIANO (NR): Only 75 cases with the first vintage, but it was well oaked and complex.

1993: Framed by supple, toasty oak, the cherry, currant and wild berry flavors stay focused, turning spicy. **88**

STAG'S LEAP WINE CELLARS
Stags Leap District, Napa Valley
F: 1972. **O:** Warren & Barbara Winiarski. **W:** Warren Winiarski. **S:** Hawk Crest.

OVERALL	$17-88	★★★★

WINE RATINGS

Cabernet Blend Napa Valley Cask 23	★★★★★
Cabernet Sauvignon Napa Valley	★★★
Cabernet Sauvignon Napa Valley Fay Vineyard	★★★★
Cabernet Sauvignon Stags Leap District SLV	★★★★
Chardonnay Napa Valley	★★★
Chardonnay Napa Valley Reserve	★★★★
Merlot Napa Valley	★★★
Petite Sirah Napa Valley	★★★
Sauvignon Blanc Napa Valley Rancho Chimiles	★★
White Riesling Napa Valley	★★
Hawk Crest Sauvignon Blanc California	★★

WINERY DATA

C: 140,000. **V:** 113 acres in Stags Leap District. **G:** Cabernet Sauvignon (Stags Leap District). **P:** Cabernet Sauvignon, Chardonnay, Merlot, Sauvignon Blanc, Johannisberg Riesling, Petite Sirah.

With its second vintage, Stag's Leap Wine Cellars vaulted to international fame, when its 1973 Cabernet placed first in the famous Paris Tasting of 1976. That blind tasting featured French critics as judges, pairing first-growth Bordeaux (Mouton Rothschild, Haut-Brion, Montrosé and Leoville-Las Cases), with prominent California Cabernets (Clos Du Val, Mayacamas and Ridge Monte Bello). Stag's Leap's first-place finish the "tasting heard round the world," generated enormous publicity for the winery.

Stag's Leap founders Warren and Barbara Winiarski left Chicago in the 1960s, with Warren, a former lecturer in Greek classics at the University of Chicago, abandoning his academic career for winemaking. Once in Napa, he worked for Lee Stewart at the old Souverain Winery and later joined Robert Mondavi Winery before putting together a group of investors to start his own winery. The initial focus was on Cabernet from a 45-acre vineyard near the winery. Later the winery made headlines during a protracted legal battle with Stags' Leap Winery over who owned the Stag's Leap name (irrespective of spelling). Eventually both wineries were allowed to use it, having started at about the same time.

Currently production is 140,000 cases, with a series of Cabernets (Cask 23, SLV, and Fay Vineyard bottlings) still the stars, but also Chardonnay, Merlot, Petite Sirah, Riesling and Sauvignon Blanc, a large portion of which is bottled under the Hawk Crest label. Even though the winery remains best known for its rich and distinctive Cabernets, the Chardonnay Reserve since the mid-1980s has been remarkably well crafted. The winery owns 113 acres, including the famous Fay Vineyard, which the winery acquired in 1986 and replanted, releasing a Fay Vineyard bottling with the 1989 vintage.

TASTING NOTES

CABERNET BLEND NAPA VALLEY CASK 23 (★★★★★): A blend of Fay Vineyard and SLV (Stag's Leap Vineyard), it is variable. At its best it is among the most complex and distinctive of California Cabernets, capable of rendering amazingly complex, intricate and ageworthy wines marked by plush herb, olive, currant, coffee and spicy flavors with smooth polished tannins. It can also be pungently earthy, with a mulchy, weedy, tobacco edge. Ages exceptionally well. Produced only in exceptional years, with 1,000 cases. The 1991 sold for $75 a bottle, making it among the most expensive.
1991: Tightly wound and tannic, but loaded with currant, coffee, herb and anise flavors that run rich, deep and long. Complex and concentrated. **92**
1990: Remarkably rich, supple, concentrated and complex, with spicy cherry, currant, plum, olive and herb notes. **94**
1987: Has become progressively more earthy and mulchy, not very appealing. **80**
1986: Has turned funky, with an earthy, mulchy edge. **82**
1985: Amazingly complex and concentrated, an elegant, polished and refined wine that serves up ripe, sharply focused black cherry, currant and cedar flavors. A magnificent wine of great distinction. **98**
1984: Mature, with lush, expansive herb, currant, anise and herb flavors that turn supple. **89**
1983: Remarkably well balanced and concentrated, with intense, spicy cherry flavors that stand up to the firm tannins. **86**
1979: Soft, supple and harmonious, with black cherry and herb flavors that are rich, complex and persistent. **88**
1978: Tastes effusively fruity, with fleshy currant, spice and oak flavors that are complex. **92**
1977: Fully mature, with complex cedar, herb, cherry and spice notes that turn supple. **89**

1974: Rich and supple, vibrant and complex, with currant, tar, tobacco and spice notes that turn smooth and polished, silky and elegant. **94**

CABERNET SAUVIGNON NAPA VALLEY (★★★): A mixture of purchased grapes from hillside and valley floor grapes in Rutherford, Soda Canyon and Wooden Valley, it features supple, complex fruit flavors and light oak shadings. Not as deep and concentrated as the winery's best. Drinks best early.

1991: Firm, focused and supple, with herb and leather aromas and berry and currant flavors, finishing with a bite of tannin and a hint of vanilla. **87**

1990: Sleek and flavorful, with pretty mint and currant aromas, a smooth texture and supple tannins. **89**

1989: Crisp and distinctive, with mint and bay leaf flavors and firm tannins. **83**

1988: Ripe and generous, with berry and currant aromas and flavors that turn complex. **87**

CABERNET SAUVIGNON NAPA VALLEY FAY VINEYARD (★★★★): Capable too of uncommon richness, harmony and finesse, but it often strays into earthier, mulchier flavors. Ages well, peaking at 10 years.

1991: Rich and intense, with an earthy edge to the currant and cherry flavors, picking up tobacco and herb notes. **88**

1990: A firm, weighty wine with rich, spicy currant and sandalwood notes, finishing with firm, complex tannins. **90**

1989: Marked by an oaky, herbaceous edge to the currant and plum aromas and flavors, finishing with light tannins. **84**

SLV/Fay Vineyard Blend 1989: A crisp, thin wine with tight currant, earth and cedar flavors of modest depth. **80**

CABERNET SAUVIGNON STAGS LEAP DISTRICT SLV (★★★★): Rivals Cask 23 in best years, with distinctive flavors, complexity and finesse.

1990: Smooth, supple and complex, with rich, intense herb, currant, olive, coffee and cedar flavors that fan out, finishing with fine tannins and excellent depth. **90**

1988: Smooth and supple, with a core of currant, herb and cherry flavors that are lively and firmly tannic. **87**

1987: Decidedly herbal, earthy and ripe, with rich plum, cherry, dill and pickle flavors that turn dry and bitter. **77**

1986: Distinctively rich and elegant, with firm acidity and delicate tannins and layers of cedar, currant and black cherry flavors. **89**

1985: Ripe and concentrated, brimming with currant, cherry, spice and cedar flavors that turn supple, with well integrated tannins. **94**

1984: Very ripe and flavorful, loaded with supple cherry, cedar, currant and anise flavors that are broad and lush, with smooth, supple tannins. **89**

1981: Attractive, with ripe currant, cedar and cherry flavors and a nice touch of toasty vanilla oak. **88**

1978: Rich, smooth and concentrated, delicately balanced, with spice, cedar and cherry flavors. **89**

Lot 2 1978: Minty herbal notes add complexity to the fleshy, forward Cabernet flavors. **88**

1977: Ripe and earthy yet elegant and harmonious, with mature, complex cherry, cedar and currant flavors. **85**

Lot 2 1977: Similar to Lot 1, with cedar and chocolate flavors that are rich and satisfying on the finish. **88**

1974: Plenty of fruit, harmony, elegance and grace. At its peak now, it should be consumed while the fruit is still fresh, concentrated and lively on the palate. **87**

1973: The famous Paris Tasting winner showed very well the last time I tried it, with complex aromas and spicy cherry, cedar, toast and chocolate flavors. **86**

1972: The first vintage from Stag's Leap Wine Cellars is old and fading. **70**

CHARDONNAY NAPA VALLEY (★★★): Steadily improving, with ripe fruit flavors and a smooth silky texture. Best on release.

1993: Ripe and spicy, with pretty pear, light oak, hazelnut and buttery flavors, turning elegant and refined. **88**

1992: Tight and flinty, with lemony pear and light oak shadings. Complex. **88**

CHARDONNAY NAPA VALLEY RESERVE (★★★★): Increasingly among the best, with bold, ripe and complex flavors, pretty spicy, toasty oak shadings and an elegant polished texture. Best on release.

1993: Ripe with buttery pear, tropical fruit and spicy notes that are focused and elegant through the finish. **89**

1992: Ripe, smooth and polished, with pear, fig, citrus and spicy oak flavors, elegant and refined. **90**

1991: Complex and harmonious, with layers of ripe, rich pear, spice, honey and vanilla flavors, picking up toasty, smoky oak notes that linger. **91**

MERLOT NAPA VALLEY (★★★): Offers a broad range of flavors, with herb, tobacco, black cherry and coffee notes, and smooth tannins.

1991: True to form, with a broad range of decadent herb, earth, tobacco, plum and currant flavors. **87**

1990: Tight, firm and intense, with focused, ripe flavors of currant, plum and black cherry framed by toasty, spicy oak notes. **87**

1985: Rich and concentrated, with intense plum and chocolate flavors and a touch of earthiness. **86**

PETITE SIRAH NAPA VALLEY (★★★): Dark in color, with firm tannins and rich fruit. A solid wine.

1991: Dark in color and tannic but relatively light in flavor, with appealing plum and berry flavors. **85**

1987: Intense in color, with spicy cassis and blackberry flavors that turn tannic and earthy. **87**

1985: Well balanced, ripe and supple, with ripe plum, earth and berry flavors that combine depth and elegance. **85**

SAUVIGNON BLANC NAPA VALLEY RANCHO CHIMILES (★★): Usually good, in a medium-bodied style with herb, pear and spice notes.

1993: Extremely floral and a little candied, not as fresh and appealing as it could be. **77**

1992: An austere, flinty wine with ripe grapefruit and herb flavors that turn coarse and biting on the finish, where it tastes like bitter grapefruit skin. **82**

WHITE RIESLING NAPA VALLEY (★★):

1992: Fruity, sappy and bright, with peach, apple and pine aromas and flavors, finishing on the dry side with plenty of fruit and life. **86**

HAWK CREST SAUVIGNON BLANC CALIFORNIA (★★): Good value, with simple fruit flavors.

1993: Light, simple and slightly earthy around a light core of pear flavor. **79**

STAGS' LEAP WINERY
Stags Leap District, Napa Valley
F: 1893. **O:** The Doumani Family. **W:** Robert Brittan. **S:** None.

OVERALL	$17-20	★★★

WINE RATINGS

Cabernet Sauvignon Napa Valley	★★
Merlot Napa Valley	★★
Petite Sirah Napa Valley	★★★★

WINERY DATA

C: 36,000. **V:** 121 acres in Stags Leap District. **G:** Cabernet Sauvignon (58 acres), Merlot (42), Petite Sirah (19). **P:** Chardonnay (Napa Valley).

Stags' Leap Winery is the lesser known of the two Stags Leap wineries, but its history dates to 1893 when it was named Stags' Leap Manor. When Carl Doumani bought it in 1972 he decided to focus on his favorite (and best) wine, Petite Sirah, and his version is among the finest in the state. The winery owns 121 acres at the base of the Stags Leap rock outcropping, dominated by Cabernet (58 acres) and Merlot (42), with 19 acres of old vine Petite Sirah. The 36,000-case output is led by Merlot (12,000 cases), Cabernet (10,000) and Chardonnay (6,000), with Chenin Blanc, another winery favorite, discontinued after 1992.

TASTING NOTES

CABERNET SAUVIGNON NAPA VALLEY (★★): Steadily improving as the winery builds more depth and richness into the wines, which have been medium-bodied and somewhat simple.

1991: Austere, with a peppery edge to the Cabernet flavors and lots of chewy tannins to shed. **85**

1989: Firm and spicy, with a band of pleasant currant, plum and black cherry flavors. **86**

1987: A strong herbal note dominates the ripe plum and currant flavors and it's quite oaky, but the flavors are concentrated and persistent. **88**

1986: Leans toward the herbal side of Cabernet, with plenty of currant and plum flavors. **88**

1985: Restrained, with pepper and berry flavors, lacking the richness and opulence of the best 1985s. **85**

1984: Big, chunky and massive, with concentrated tannins and hints of cassis, plum and spicy anise flavors. **87**

MERLOT NAPA VALLEY (★★): Variable as Merlot goes, ranging from light and simple to ripe and plush as in 1989.

1990: Light, with modest black cherry flavors marred by an earthy, leathery note. **78**

1989: Plush, spicy and generous, with opulent currant, plum and chocolate flavors. **87**

1987: Firm and fruity, with a nice oaky edge to the ripe plum and currant flavors. **85**

1986: Distinctively Merlot, with ripe cherry and spice notes, an herbal edge, a supple oak texture and firm but soft tannins. **84**

PETITE SIRAH NAPA VALLEY (★★★★): Can be enormously bold, rich, dense and peppery with firm tannins. Capable of aging for 10 to 15 years in the best vintages.

1990: Bold, ripe and richly fruity, with layers of fresh, spicy cherry, plum, anise and tar notes. It has wonderful balance and a sense of harmony and finesse. **91**

1989: A light (for Stags' Leap) vintage with moderate depth and intensity to the cherry and plum flavors. **84**

1988: Ripe, supple and fruity, with toasty plum and cherry flavors that are elegant. **86**

Reserve 1988: Firm and austere, with ample tannins, yet the texture at mid-palate is smooth, with floral, plum and cherry notes. **86**

1987: Extremely oaky, with charred, buttery oak flavors that overpower the cherry and plum notes. **83**

Petite Syrah 1987: Firm, tannic and flavorful, with generous blackberry, black cherry and smoke flavors. **82**

1986: Supple and elegant, with ripe black cherry, earth, tar and spice notes. **87**

1985: Simple and lightly fruity, with cherry and plum flavors that are pleasant and of modest concentration. **84**

1984: Marked by a wild, earthy, leathery edge, with spicy cherry and plum flavors and a slightly horsey edge. **85**

1983: Austere, dry and tannic, with fruit that's dropping out. **82**

1982: Earthy and austere, with a tight, tannic core of cherry, pepper and spice flavors. **86**

1981: Its modest flavors taste stripped. **80**

1980: An earthy, tarry wine with fruit that's dropping out. **80**

1979: Lean, austere and unripe, with earthy cherry notes. **79**

1978: Big, ripe and chewy, with rich, dark currant and black cherry flavors that pick up a nice, earthy mineral edge on the finish. **89**

1977: Dry and lean, with tannic cherry and plum aromas that turn dry on the palate. **83**

1976: Rich, ripe, intense and tannic, with ripe plum and raisin flavors that have a coarse texture. **89**

1975: Austere and tight, with a narrow band of spice and fruit flavors. **84**

1974: A big, ripe, slightly alcoholic wine, almost a caricature of Petite Sirah with its intense, rich pepper and plum flavors. Lacks finesse and finishes with an earthy mineral edge. **87**

1973: Smooth in texture, it is not quite as complex as the 1972 but offers ripe, spicy plum and cherry flavors. **88**

1972: Deep in color, with delicious, ripe black cherry and plum flavors and peppery, spicy mineral aromas that turn to anise and cedar on the palate. **91**

P. AND M. STAIGER
Santa Cruz Mountains
F: 1973. **O:** Paul & Marjorie Staiger. **W:** Paul Staiger. **S:** None.

OVERALL	$12-14	★★

WINE RATINGS

Cabernet Sauvignon	
Santa Cruz Mountains	★★
Chardonnay Santa Cruz Mountains	★★

WINERY DATA
C: 400. **V:** 5 acres in Santa Cruz Mountains. **G:** Chardonnay (2 acres), Cabernet Sauvignon (2), Merlot (1). **P:** None.

Paul and Marjorie Staiger own this small hillside vineyard and winery, producing 400 cases of Cabernet and Chardonnay from their 5-acre property. Distribution is very limited, and the 1992 Chardonnay Santa Cruz Mountains showed a strong green apple and oak edge with an astringent texture.

TASTING NOTES

CHARDONNAY SANTA CRUZ MOUNTAINS (★★):

1993: Marked by citrus and grapefruit notes, with just enough pear and spice to keep in balance. Good value. **83**

1992: This wine displays a strong green apple and oak edge, complete with an astringent mouthfeel on the finish. Lacks the extra complexity you might expect from this vintage. **80**

STAR HILL WINES
Napa Valley
F: 1986. **O:** Jacob & Sally Goldenberg. **W:** Jacob Goldenberg. **S:** Pacific Star Winery.

OVERALL	$19-24	★★

WINE RATINGS

Cabernet Sauvignon Napa Valley Bartolucci Vineyard Doc's Reserve	★★
Chardonnay Napa Valley	★★
Pinot Noir Napa Valley Doc's Reserve	★★

WINERY DATA
C: 2,900. **V:** 10 acres in Napa Valley. **G:** Pinot Noir. **P:** Mataro (Oakley), Merlot (Stags Leap), Cabernet Sauvignon (Napa Valley).

Dentist Jacob Goldenberg and his wife, Sally, were home winemakers before starting their winery in 1986, focusing initially on Burgundian varieties, and later adding Cabernet Sauvignon and a Cabernet blend. Production is 2,900 cases, with both the Cabernet and Pinot Noir earning good ratings.

TASTING NOTES

CABERNET SAUVIGNON NAPA VALLEY BARTOLUCCI VINEYARD DOC'S RESERVE (★★): Ordinary for Napa Cabernet, quality varies.
1990: Firm, with a tobacco and juniper berry edge to the basic black currant flavor. **82**
1987: Ripe and lavishly oaked, offering black cherry and currant flavors that persist on the finish. **87**

PINOT NOIR NAPA VALLEY DOC'S RESERVE (★★): Better balanced than the Cabernet, but still rather simple.
1988: Ripe and oaky, with black cherry and currant flavors lavishly accented with a toasty, minty oak character. **82**
1987: Offers intriguing flavors of vanilla, chocolate, cherry and spice, finishing with crisp acidity. **87**

STEELE WINES
Lake County
F: 1991. **O:** Jed & Marie Steele. **W:** Jed Steele. **S:** Shooting Star.

OVERALL	$13-26	★★★

WINE RATINGS

Chardonnay California	★★★
Chardonnay Carneros Sangiacomo Vineyard	★★★★
Chardonnay Mendocino County Dennison Vineyard	★★★
Chardonnay Mendocino County DuPratt Vineyard	★★★★
Chardonnay Mendocino County Lolonis Vineyard	★★★★
Chardonnay Santa Barbara County Bien Nacido Vineyard	★★★★
Chardonnay Sonoma Valley Durell Vineyard	★★★★
Pinot Blanc Santa Barbara County Bien Nacido Vineyard	★★★★
Pinot Noir Carneros	★★★★
Pinot Noir Carneros Sangiacomo Vineyard	★★★★
Pinot Noir Mendocino County DuPratt Vineyard	★★★
Pinot Noir Santa Barbara County Bien Nacido Vineyard	★★★
Pinot Noir Sonoma Valley Durell Vineyard	★★★
Zinfandel Clear Lake Catfish Vineyard	★★★★
Zinfandel Mendocino County Pacini Vineyard	★★★
Shooting Star Blush Mendocino County Pacini Vineyard Zin Gris	NR
Shooting Star Cabernet Franc Clear Lake	★★★
Shooting Star Chardonnay Mendocino County	★★
Shooting Star Merlot Clear Lake	★★★
Shooting Star Pinot Noir Mendocino County	★★★
Shooting Star Zinfandel Clear Lake	★★★
Shooting Star Zinfandel Lake County	★★★

WINERY DATA
C: 8,000. **V:** None. **G:** None. **P:** Chardonnay, Zinfandel (Mendocino), Chardonnay, Pinot Noir (Carneros), Chardonnay (Santa Barbara).

Jed Steele's been around long enough to know you can make great wine without owning vineyards. (The secret is to buy grapes from great vineyards). His career has included, among other things, a stint at the old Edmeades Winery (Anderson Valley) before joining Kendall-Jackson as chief winemaker from 1982-89, when production topped 1 million cases. Among Steele's talents is an ability to tap into superb vineyards (Bien Nacido in Santa Barbara, Dennison in Mendocino, DuPratt in Mendocino, Durell in Sonoma Valley, Lolonis in Mendocino and Sangiacomo in Carneros) and to make harmonious wines that are complex and easy to drink. While the Steele label (and second label Shooting Star) is now at 8,000 cases, he still consults on and shapes the style of wines from Wildhurst, Konocti, Villa Mt. Eden, Conn Creek and Fess Parker. Steele Wines focuses on Chardonnay, Pinot Blanc, Pinot Noir and Zinfandel, with smaller lots of Shooting Star Cabernet Franc, Chardonnay and Merlot.

TASTING NOTES

CHARDONNAY CALIFORNIA (★★★):
1993: Spicy, with modest ripe pear and light oak shadings. Elegant and well balanced, but not especially complex. **86**
1992: Spicy and a bit earthy, but it serves up lots of pretty pear, spice, vanilla and oak flavors that turn elegant. **90**
1991: Ripe, smooth and complex, with tiers of vanilla, pear, spice and honey flavors framed by toasty oak shadings. **87**

CHARDONNAY CARNEROS SANGIACOMO VINEYARD (★★★★):
1992: Smooth and silky, with layers of complex honey, pear, toast and spice flavors that are rich and focused, elegant and refined. **90**
1991: Broad, rich, bright and complex, with layers of spicy pear, buttery oak, pineapple and honey notes that are focused. **90**

CHARDONNAY MENDOCINO COUNTY DENNISON VINEYARD (★★★):
1992: Tight and firm, with compact citrus, pear and cedary oak flavors that turn smoky on the finish. **89**

CHARDONNAY MENDOCINO COUNTY DuPRATT VINEYARD (★★★★):
1993: Bright and fruity, with a focused beam of pear,

spice, apple and buttery notes, turning supple and complex. **91**
1992: An elegant wine with ripe, spicy pear and honey notes that hang together nicely. **86**
1991: Delicious, rich and creamy, with toasty pear, spice, honey and butter notes that are complex and intriguing. **92**

CHARDONNAY MENDOCINO COUNTY LOLONIS VINEYARD (★★★★):
1993: Ripe and spicy, with a smooth texture and pretty pear, toasty oak and buttery notes, turning complex on the finish. **90**
1992: Crisp and focused, with pretty peach, spice, apple and fig flavors that fan out on the palate, giving it added richness. **92**
1991: Broad, ripe and creamy, with a rich, complex band of pear, vanilla, honey and spice flavors that turn smooth and smoky. **91**

CHARDONNAY SANTA BARBARA COUNTY BIEN NACIDO VINEYARD (★★★★):
1993: Marked by bright, ripe pear and honeyed notes, well oaked, turning spicy and earthy on the finish. **89**
1992: Firm and tightly wound, and the spicy pear and hazelnut flavors open to reveal more richness and depth. **90**

CHARDONNAY SONOMA VALLEY DURELL VINEYARD (★★★★):
1992: Firm, intense and lively, complex and compelling, with layers of fig, vanilla, honey and hazelnut flavors that are sharply focused. **92**

PINOT BLANC SANTA BARBARA COUNTY BIEN NACIDO VINEYARD (★★★★):
1993: Smooth and spicy, showing a lot of nutmeg and almond character to liven up the melon and apple flavors, and some real depth. **89**
1992: Rich and complex, with tiers of honey, pear, pineapple and spice flavors and a long, full finish that picks up the buttery oak nuances. **91**

PINOT NOIR CARNEROS (★★★★):
1993: Smooth and elegant, with a pretty core of toasty vanilla-tinged oak and ripe black cherry fruit. Folds together nicely, turning complex on the finish. **90**
1992: Smooth and polished, with spicy black cherry and plum flavors framed by toasty, buttery oak. **88**
1991: Complex and intriguing, combining cherry and currant flavors with toasty, buttery oak notes. **90**

PINOT NOIR CARNEROS SANGIACOMO VINEYARD (★★★★):
1993: Well oaked with smoky toasty aromas, but with enough ripe cherry, and wild berry flavors to match, coming together on the finish. **88**
1991: Wonderful complexity of flavor, with toasty, buttery oak and elegant, rich, spicy raspberry and cherry notes. **90**

PINOT NOIR MENDOCINO COUNTY DUPRATT VINE-YARD (★★★):
1992: Young, tight and intense, featuring spicy cherry and plum flavors and toasty, buttery oak. **86**

PINOT NOIR SANTA BARBARA COUNTY BIEN NACIDO VINEYARD (★★★):
1993: Marked by a spicy, peppery edge, almost with a Syrah-like edge, but the cherry and earthy nuances come through. **86**

PINOT NOIR SONOMA VALLEY DURELL VINEYARD (★★★):
1993: Lush and complex, with tiers of toasty, buttery oak, black cherry and currant flavors that fold together in a ripe, supple manner. **88**
1992: Smooth, supple and polished, with subtle plum and spice aromas and flavors that echo on the finish. **87**

ZINFANDEL CLEAR LAKE CATFISH VINEYARD (★★★★):
Well oaked, but has the rich fruit to stand up to it.
1993: Complex, with a nice balance between the spicy, toasty oak and the ripe cherry and raspberry fruit. Turns supple on a long fruity finish. **89**
1992: Shows off smoky, buttery oak and pretty currant and blackberry flavors in a smooth, polished, claret-style wine that may even remind you of a Pinot Noir. **90**
1991: Offers pretty, spicy, toasty oak and a solid core of peppery currant and berry aromas and flavors. **90**

ZINFANDEL MENDOCINO COUNTY PACINI VINEYARD (★★★): Tart and lean, but the flavors fan out, gaining depth.
1993: Tight and firm, well oaked with toasty, buttery flavors, but also a good core of wild berry and cherry-laced fruit. Finishes with firm tannins. **87**
1992: Lean and earthy, with wild berry and cherry flavors coming through. **84**
1991: Both tart and rich, with intense earth, cherry and raspberry notes around a sharp, tannic core of classic Zinfandel flavors. Tight and tannic, with crisp acidity. **87**

SHOOTING STAR VARIOUS BOTTLINGS:
Blush Mendocino County Pacini Vineyard Zin Gris 1994: Dry and a little funky, an earthy wine with only modest charms. **78**
Cabernet Franc Clear Lake 1992: Light, smooth and fleshy, with an herbal edge to the currant and berry notes. **83**
Cabernet Franc Lake County 1991: Impressive for its richness and polish, this is a complex and supple wine with tiers of currant and plum flavors framed by toasty, smoky, buttery oak. **88**
Chardonnay Mendocino County 1993: Has an earthy edge to the pear and spice flavors. **82**
Merlot Clear Lake 1992: Light in color, with pretty, toasty oak, spicy cherry and currant flavors. **87**
Merlot Lake County 1991: Marked by toasty, buttery oak and full of flavor, with spicy currant and herb notes that are rich and concentrated. **88**
Pinot Noir Mendocino County 1993: Well oaked, with vanilla and toasty oak flavors that complement the black cherry and spice flavors. **86**
Zinfandel Clear Lake 1993: Well oaked, but that only adds flavor to the elegant wild berry and cherry flavors. **87**
Zinfandel Lake County 1993: Supple and polished, with pretty wild berry, raspberry and blueberry flavors that are ripe and appealing. **87**

STELTZNER VINEYARDS
Stags Leap District, Napa Valley
F: 1983. **O:** Richard & Christine Steltzner. **W:** Richard Steltzner. **S:** None.

OVERALL	$11-45	★★★

WINE RATINGS

Cabernet Blend Stags Leap District Claret	★★
Cabernet Sauvignon Stags Leap District	★★★
Merlot Stags Leap District	★★
Sauvignon Blanc Napa Valley Oak Knoll Ranch	★★

WINERY DATA
C: 12,000. **V:** 96 acres in Stags Leap District, Napa Valley.
G: Pinot Chardonnay (10 acres), Sauvignon Blanc (8), Cabernet Sauvignon (40), Merlot (5), Cabernet Franc (3), Sangiovese (1).
P: None.

Richard Steltzner grew grapes, and planted and managed other people's vineyards (Diamond Creek and Spring Mountain) for more than a decade before easing into winemaking. The 1973 Conn Creek Cabernet is a memorable bottling from his vineyard's grapes. In 1977, using his 96-acre Stags Leap District Vineyard, he started producing Cabernet; since then he's added Claret, Merlot and Sauvignon Blanc. Quality across the board is very good. The reds share a chunky, rustic edge, especially compared with other Stags Leap District offerings, but they hold up well. Production is 12,000 cases and headed upward, as a new winery and caves were completed in 1995.

TASTING NOTES

CABERNET BLEND STAGS LEAP DISTRICT CLARET (★★): Lean and earthy, with decent flavor, but less interesting of late.
1992: Tight, with hard currant, cedary oak and earth notes. **84**
1991: A lean and earthy wine with some pretty, ripe, juicy cherry and berry flavors. **84**
1990: Ripe and juicy, with intense plum and black cherry flavors that are lively and supple. **87**

CABERNET SAUVIGNON STAGS LEAP DISTRICT (★★★): Variable, but ripe, intense, openly fruity and firmly tannic at its best. Makes no pretense at finesse, but packs in lots of chewy flavors. Ages well up to 10 years.
1991: Chunky, with ripe cherry and currant flavors that turn earthy and tannic. **85**
Commemorative 1991: Earthy and tannic, with a leathery edge to the currant and cherry flavors. It opens up with aeration. **85**
1990: Firm and compact, with focused currant, cherry and spice flavors that finish with crisp tannins. **87**
1988: Light and simple, with currant aromas and flavors tinged with a touch of earthiness and gaminess. **82**
1987: Offers herb, currant, cherry and spice flavors that hang together nicely, but it's tight. **85**
1986: Full-bodied, with ripe currant, cassis, black cherry and cedary oak flavors. **88**
1985: Firm and tight, with a gamy edge to the black cherry, raspberry, currant and plum flavors. **88**
1984: Turning tannic and austere, with cherry, berry and anise flavors that finish with gripping tannins. **87**
1983: Crisp and austere, with firm tannins now overshadowing the earthy fruit flavors. **83**

1981: Mature, with an earthy, dry edge to the plum and currant flavors. **84**
1980: Tart, compact and mature, with an earthy edge to the currant flavors. **85**
1978: Ripe and plush, with complex currant, plum and cherry aromas and flavors and smooth tannins on the finish. **88**
1977: Pleasant but past its prime, with drying Cabernet flavors. **82**

MERLOT STAGS LEAP DISTRICT (★★): Lacks the depth and intensity of the Cabernet, but is pleasant enough with its herb and cherry notes.
1992: Lean and trim, with a narrow band of cedar and berry flavors. **82**
1991: Modest plum and currant flavors finish with a tannic edge. **83**
1990: Intense and herbal, with bright cherry and spice flavors that turn to sour cherry on the finish, where gritty tannins emerge. **84**
1989: Firm, spicy and marked by oak, with a solid cherry flavor shaded by toffee and walnut notes. **84**

SAUVIGNON BLANC NAPA VALLEY OAK KNOLL RANCH (★★): Fruity, with herb and pear notes, but it can lack focus and intensity.
1991: Solid, drinkable and pleasantly flavorful, showing slightly floral nectarine and herb aromas and flavors and a smooth finish. **81**

ROBERT STEMMLER WINERY
Sonoma County
F: 1977. **O:** Racke USA. **W:** Robert Stemmler. **S:** None.

OVERALL	$20	★

WINE RATINGS

Pinot Noir Sonoma County	★

WINERY DATA
C: 8,000. **V:** None. **G:** None. **P:** Pinot Noir (Sonoma County).

Robert Stemmler has had a hand in many California wines, having worked for Charles Krug, Inglenook, Simi, and Caymus (for the 1974 vintage) before starting his winery in 1977. Through the years, Stemmler has made several varieties, but recently the focus has been on

Sonoma County-grown Pinot Noir, with quality on a steady decline since the early 1980s. The most recent offerings have been light, thin and uninteresting, at the same time that Sonoma County Pinot Noir generally has been on a steady rise.

TASTING NOTES

PINOT NOIR SONOMA COUNTY (★): Light, thin and hollow, without much fruit.
1991: Light, with modest herb, tea and spicy cherry notes. **78**
1990: Light and thin, with herbal cola flavors overshadowing the modest plum note. **80**
1989: A crisp, hollow wine that's devoid of fruit. **71**
1988: Lean and funky, with vinegary tea and herb flavors. **71**
1987: Austere, firm and tannic, with modest coffee, cedar, cherry and toast notes. **82**

STERLING VINEYARDS
Calistoga, Napa Valley
F: 1964. O: Seagram Classics Wine Co. W: Bill Dyer. S: None.

OVERALL	$9-40	★★★

WINE RATINGS	
Cabernet Blend Napa Valley Reserve	★★★★
Cabernet Blend Napa Valley	
Three Palms Vineyard	★★★
Cabernet Sauvignon Napa Valley	★★
Cabernet Sauvignon Napa Valley	
Diamond Mountain Ranch	★★
Chardonnay Carneros	
Winery Lake Vineyard	★★
Chardonnay Napa Valley	★★
Chardonnay Napa Valley	
Diamond Mountain Ranch	★★
Merlot Napa Valley	★★
Pinot Noir Carneros	
Winery Lake Vineyard	★
Sauvignon Blanc Napa Valley	★★

WINERY DATA
C: 230,000. V: 824 acres in Napa Valley, Carneros, Rutherford.
G: Chardonnay (161 acres), Sauvignon Blanc (105), Sémillon (30), Cabernet Sauvignon (235), Cabernet Franc (50), Merlot (142), Malbec (1), Petite Verdot (17), Pinot Noir (83). P: Petite Verdot, Zinfandel, Sangiovese, Chardonnay, Sauvignon Blanc, Sémillon, Cabernet Sauvignon, Cabernet Franc, Merlot (Napa Valley), Chardonnay, Cabernet Sauvignon, Merlot (Rutherford), Merlot (Knights Valley), Sémillon, Merlot (Oakville), Merlot, Chardonnay (Carneros), Mourvèdre (Contra Costa County).

In the early 1960s, a group of Sterling International Paper Co. executives headed by Peter Newton founded Sterling Vineyards, building the white, monastic-looking winery on a hill south of Calistoga with the goal of creating a tourist destination, complete with a tram ride to the top of the hill. Sterling hired Ric Forman as winemaker for the 1969 vintage, focusing on Bordeaux-style wines (red and white), plus Chardonnay. By 1977, Sterling's owners decided to sell. Newton and Forman left to start a winery together, then went their separate ways, each emerging with his own winery. The Coca-Cola Bottling Co. of Atlanta became Sterling's new owner until 1983, when the winery was sold to Seagram.

Quality through the early years was usually very good, especially with Cabernet, Sauvignon Blanc and Merlot. In the early 1980s, Sterling's Diamond Mountain Ranch vineyard began producing grapes for two lines of vineyard-designated wines (Cabernet and Chardonnay). Sterling acquired Winery Lake Vineyard in Carneros in 1986 and began producing vineyard-designated Chardonnay and Pinot Noir. As volume has risen to 230,000 cases, though, quality has slipped across the board, as the Cabernet, Chardonnay, Merlot and Sauvignon Blanc have become lighter and simpler. Moreover, the vineyard-designated wines, while at times distinctive, have also at times been disappointing.

Sterling has considerable vineyard holdings to draw upon, with 824 acres in vines, led by Cabernet (235 acres), Chardonnay (161), Merlot (142) and Sauvignon Blanc (105). The four standard bottlings of Cabernet, Chardonnay, Merlot and Sauvignon Blanc are each made in the 50,000-case range, and the winery plans to further increase production. Bill Dyer, an employee since 1977, has been winemaker since 1985, enjoying his greatest success with the often brilliant Sterling Reserve, a Cabernet-based red that is often among the state's best.

TASTING NOTES

CABERNET BLEND NAPA VALLEY RESERVE (★★★★): Sterling's best wine by a wide margin, typically dark, ripe, rich, complex and well oaked, with smooth, polished tannins. Ages well, peaking at about five to eight years.

1991: Firm, dark and intense, with complex currant, black cherry, cedar and spice flavors, showing the most depth and finesse of any Sterling Cabernet since 1986. **91**

1990: Elegant, with spicy oak and vanilla notes and supple currant and black cherry flavors. **87**

1989: Delivers ripe currant, black cherry, anise and spice flavors, then frames them with toasty, buttery, smoky oak notes. **88**

1988: Modestly flavorful, with drying, tough tannins dominating the tart cherry and herb flavors. **85**

1987: Deep and concentrated, with black cherry, currant, chocolate, coffee and herb flavors that are sharply focused. **90**

1986: Firm and compact, packed with complex currant, anise and plum flavors that turn elegant, with a polished texture and a complex aftertaste. **93**

1985: A supple, elegant and complex wine packed into a firm package, it's powerful, smooth, supple and finely focused, glowing with plum, cherry and cassis flavors that are deep and concentrated. **96**

1984: Beautifully defined, rich, supple and concentrated, with layers of ripe plum, currant, mint and spice flavors that are intense yet fine. **90**

1983: Extremely dry and tannic, very austere and concentrated, with lean mint, currant and berry flavors. **82**

1982: Marked by weedy, mulchy and herbal flavors. **75**

1981: Austere and tannic, with a drying edge to the modest currant, cherry and oak flavors. **83**

1980: Mature, with rich, earthy plum, black cherry and smoky oak flavors. It has peaked. **88**

1979: A dry, dusty oakiness overrides the currant and spice flavors. **77**

1978: Smooth, polished, fully mature and showing well, with intense currant, herb and olive flavors that are complex and lingering. **90**

1974: Along with an earthy tannic streak, this wine offers complex spice, tart black cherry and mature currant flavors that turn dry on the finish. **83**

1973: Mature, with a core of hearty, earthy currant and spicy wood flavors. **85**

CABERNET BLEND NAPA VALLEY THREE PALMS VINEYARD (★★★): More tannic and austere than the Reserve, as the vineyard south of the winery yields more austere wines, as evidenced by Duckhorn's bottling which is similar in texture and weight to Sterling's.

1991: Tight, youthful and chewy, packing in ripe berry and currant flavors and ample tannins. **86**

1988: Tight and firm, with attractive plum, currant, spice and tobacco flavors. **85**

1987: Big and tannic, with a core of currant and black cherry flavors, but the tannins really box it in. **87**

1986: Rich, supple, tannic and flavorful, with decent depth and ripe currant and plum notes. **85**

1985: Graced with ripe currant, black cherry and plum flavors along with buttery oak, offering depth and complexity. **89**

CABERNET SAUVIGNON NAPA VALLEY (★★): Has declined in quality, often lean and herbal with earthy flavors.

1991: An earthy, gamy flavor dominates the fruit in this one, turning dry and leathery on the finish. **82**

1990: Tightly wound, a firm-textured wine with a compact array of berry, currant and leather flavors. **83**

1989: Austere, with modest currant, anise and cherry flavors, it shows woody oak shadings and firm tannins. **83**

1988: Lean and simple, with narrow herb and currant notes. **80**

1987: Offers blueberry, raspberry and plum flavors, with firm tannins lurking just beneath the surface. **85**

1986: Under the hard, tight tannins there's a tight, concentrated, elegant wine with layers of cassis, plum and black cherry flavors. **87**

1985: Firm and elegantly balanced, with focused red cherry, plum and currant flavors and the right touch of wood. **89**

CABERNET SAUVIGNON NAPA VALLEY DIAMOND MOUNTAIN RANCH (★★): Less complex and focused of late, as it comes across as simple, earthy and tannic.

1991: Earthy, dry, leathery and tannic, with hints of herb, currant and mineral emerging on the finish. **83**

1990: Hard and tannic, with a green edge to the Cabernet flavors. **81**

1989: Tough, tannic, hard and woody, with a decidedly gamy edge to the ripe Cabernet flavors. **79**

1987: Intense, with chewy black cherry, plum and currant flavors that pick up herb and earth notes. **86**

1986: Austere, with firm, dry tannins and aromatic plum and cherry notes, deeply concentrated and built for cellaring. Has the potential for greatness, but patience is required. **87**

1985: Firm and hard, with cedary, oaky aromas and ripe plum and berry flavors that are clamped down by the tannins. **85**

1984: Very ripe, with complex berry, cherry, plum and chocolate flavors along with a touch of anise, turning dry and tannic. **84**

CHARDONNAY CARNEROS WINERY LAKE VINEYARD (★★): Has sharply declined in quality, hitting bottom in 1992 with an earthy, metallic wine.

1993: Lean and earthy, with a coarse edge to the grapefruit and citrus notes. **78**

1992: Earthy and bitter, devoid of ripe fruit, with a papery, musty edge. **67**

1991: Marked by a strong, earthy, leesy edge, but it picks up spicy apple and pear flavors. **81**

CHARDONNAY NAPA VALLEY (★★): Lean and simple, with modest fruit flavors and often an earthy edge.

1993: Earthy and a touch bitter, but it straightens out on the finish where the pear and spice flavors are more appealing. **82**

Sterling Collections Z Lot 1993: Ripe, smooth and creamy, with a slight bitter edge from oak, but the fruit rises to the occasion, with enough pear and spice to keep balance. **85**

1992: Spicy, sappy flavors tend to overshadow the modest fruit. **81**

1991: Crisp, earthy and spicy, with a mineral edge to the slightly bitter apple and almond flavors. **78**

CHARDONNAY NAPA VALLEY DIAMOND MOUNTAIN RANCH (★★): While successful in the mid-1980s, it too is increasingly lean and hard-edged, probably growing in an area too warm for Chardonnay. At its best, the flinty pear and mineral flavors are well focused.

1992: A tightly reined-in style, with a flinty edge to the spicy pear, apple, nutmeg and toasty oak shadings. **84**

1991: Austere and oaky, with wood dominating, nearly devoid of fruit. **81**

MERLOT VARIOUS BOTTLINGS (★★): Has also declined in quality, with modest fruit flavors.

1991: The green, cedary wood dominates this wine on both the nose and the palate. **79**

1990: A crisp-textured, herb-scented Merlot that offers tart plum flavors. **82**

Three Palms Vineyard 1990: Lean and strongly herbal, but it finishes with a nice turn toward sweet plum and spice flavors. **82**

1989: Modest plum and raspberry flavors are shaded by a smooth touch of oak. **82**

1988: Tight and compact, with layers of herb, raspberry, spice and plum flavors that turn firm and tannic on the finish. **83**

1987: Firm and tannic, with modest currant and cherry flavors. **83**

1986: An herbal wine with oak overshadowing the plum and black cherry flavors. **84**

1985: Lean and well crafted, with subtle cherry, currant and spice flavors and a hard edge of tannin. **83**

PINOT NOIR CARNEROS WINERY LAKE VINEYARD (★): After an impressive debut wine in 1986, these wines have become increasingly light and simple, with a thin band of fruit, and they are often marred by mulchy, earthy flavors.

1992: A bit clumsy, with sharp tannins and wild berry flavors that turn earthy and bitter. **73**

1991: Firm and tannic, but whatever fruit it has seems submerged under a wash of horsey cola, smoke and leather flavors. **78**

1990: Meaty and spicy, with soy, cola and earth flavors that turn woody on the finish. **73**

1989: Fragrant and delicate, with spicy cherry flavors that are crisp and lean. **83**

1988: Light in texture but fragrant, spicy and oaky, with very nice raspberry, caramel and nutmeg flavors. **83**

1987: Light and simple, showing less fruit now than on release. **81**

1986: Aging well, with earthy black cherry, cedar and currant notes that are rich and fleshy. **87**

SAUVIGNON BLANC NAPA VALLEY (★★): Once a leader, the most recent bottlings have been light and thin, marked by herb and onion flavors.

1993: Clean and bright, with just a narrow streak of

tobacco and herb running through the modest pear and peach flavors. **80**

1992: Strongly herbal, oniony and bitter, picking up a little fruit in the middle. **72**

STEVENOT WINERY
Sierra Foothills

F: 1974. **O:** Barden D. Stevenot. **W:** Chuck Hovey. **S:** None.

OVERALL	$7-11	★★

WINE RATINGS

Blush Calaveras County White Zinfandel	NR
Cabernet Sauvignon	
Calaveras County Reserve	★★
Cabernet Sauvignon California	★★
Chardonnay Calaveras County Reserve	★
Chardonnay Sierra Foothills	★
Merlot North Coast Reserve	NR
Zinfandel Calaveras County	NR

WINERY DATA

C: 40,000. **V:** 28 acres in Calaveras County. **G:** Chardonnay (18 acres), Cabernet Sauvignon (4), Merlot (1), Zinfandel (5). **P:** Merlot, Cabernet Sauvignon, Chardonnay, Zinfandel (El Dorado), Merlot, Cabernet Sauvignon, Chardonnay, Zinfandel (Calaveras), Merlot (Mariposa).

Barden Stevenot bought an old cattle ranch in 1969 before developing a 28-acre vineyard and opening a winery in 1978, building a brand that now produces 40,000 cases, with the focus on Cabernet, Chardonnay, Merlot and Zinfandel. Quality ranges from fair to good, with the Reserve Cabernets the leaders. White Zinfandel, at 30,000 cases, is the production leader.

TASTING NOTES

CABERNET SAUVIGNON VARIOUS BOTTLINGS (★★): Carries varying appellations, with medium-weight, solidly fruity but unexceptional wines.

Amador County Grand Reserve 1988: Offers modest ripe cherry, currant and anise notes that are crisp and moderately tannic. **83**

Calaveras County Grand Reserve 1987: Full-bodied, sturdy and tannic, with earthy currant notes. **82**

Calaveras County Reserve 1992: Manages to balance its ripe berry and cherry fruit with an earthy, slightly rubbery edge. **82**

Calaveras County Reserve 1991: Rich, intense and spicy, with floral, plum and cedary oak flavors. **84**

Calaveras County Reserve 1990: A stylish, solidly fruity wine with a deep color and plum flavor, firm but fine tannins and a lingering finish. **84**

California 1991: A light, fruity Cabernet that's smooth and supple, with a strong layer of oak. **83**

CHARDONNAY VARIOUS BOTTLINGS (★):

Calaveras County Barrel Fermented 1992: Earthy, with tart grapefruit and citrus notes. A good white table wine, but lacks true varietal character. **74**

Calaveras County Reserve 1993: Crisp and flinty with a grapefruit edge to the flavors. **82**

California 1992: Crisp, lean and simple, with tart pear and apple flavors. **79**

Sierra Foothills 1993: Crisp, with a flinty, earthy edge to the pear and apple notes. **82**

MERLOT NORTH COAST (NR):

1991: Herbal aromas, cranberry flavors and a green, vegetal note throughout make this a tart Merlot. A simple wine that turns astringent on the finish. **75**

STONEGATE WINERY
Calistoga, Napa Valley

F: 1973. **O:** Stonegate Inc. **W:** David Spaulding. **S:** None.

OVERALL	$10-24	★★

WINE RATINGS

Cabernet Franc Napa Valley	NR
Cabernet Sauvignon Napa Valley	★★
Chardonnay Sonoma County	
Bella Vista Vineyard	★★
Meritage Red Napa Valley Reserve	★★
Merlot Napa Valley	★★

WINERY DATA

C: 12,500. **V:** 32 acres in Napa Valley. **G:** Cabernet Sauvignon (11 acres), Merlot (7), Chardonnay (3), Sauvignon Blanc (11). **P:** Cabernet Sauvignon, Merlot, Chardonnay, Sauvignon Blanc (Napa Valley), Chardonnay (Sonoma County).

In 1969, Jim Spaulding, a journalism professor, moved his family to Napa Valley, purchased mountain property for vineyards and established Stonegate off Highway 29 south of Calistoga near Sterling Vineyards. His son David Spaulding is winemaker, presiding over the 12,500-case winery which focuses on a Cabernet Blend (Meritage), Cabernet Franc (Pershing Hills Vineyard), Chardonnay (Bella Vista Vineyard, Sonoma) and Sauvignon Blanc. A portion of the grapes come from family-owned vineyards which total 32 acres and include Cabernet, Merlot, Chardonnay and Sauvignon Blanc. Quality is highly variable, good at best.

TASTING NOTES

CABERNET FRANC NAPA VALLEY (NR):
1990: Heavy-handed oak dominates the aromas and flavors, overpowering the fruit underneath. Turns green and leafy on the finish. Time in the bottle may have helped. **81**

CABERNET SAUVIGNON NAPA VALLEY (★★): Has become increasingly lean, hard and tannic, with a modest level of fruit and a high level of tannin.
1990: An earthy wine with a gamy streak that runs through the Cabernet flavors. **81**
1989: Lean and austere, with currant and berry flavors that turn tannic and astringent. **80**
1988: Firm and tannic, with a modest level of plum, currant and spice flavors fighting green astringency. **84**
1987: Lean, with cedary black currant aromas and flavors that turn green and tart. **82**
1986: Earthy, ultraripe and coffeelike, a soft but tannic wine that's awkward. **86**
1978: Ripe and oaky, packing in lots of plum, currant and spicy wood flavors and rugged tannins. Shows good depth and richness. **87**

CHARDONNAY SONOMA COUNTY BELLA VISTA VINEYARD (★★): Variable, but often lean and earthy, without the bright fruit and pretty oak flavors so many Chardonnays offer.
1991: Lean and earthy, with some funky notes. **83**

MERITAGE RED NAPA VALLEY RESERVE (★★):
1988: Crisp, tight and lean, with spicy currant, herb and cedar notes. **83**
1987: Firm in texture, with tart acidity running under the complex anise-scented currant and blackberry flavors. **83**

MERLOT NAPA VALLEY (★★): Variable too, with hard tannins and wood dominating. Has carried both the Pershing Vineyard and Spaulding Vineyard designations.
1989: A chunky wine with a band of rough currant, berry, cedar and coffee flavors. **86**
1988: Hard and oaky, with a strong woody component that shoulders past the modest berry flavor. **81**
Pershing Vineyard 1987: Offers toast, herb and spice aromas, but woody, oaky notes override the ripe plum and currant flavors. **83**
Spaulding Vineyard 1987: Elegant, ripe and supple, with plenty of herb, menthol, currant and plum flavors that ride soft tannins. **85**
1986: Oaky and woody, but the currant and plum flavors stand up to it. **82**

STONESTREET
Chalk Hill, Sonoma County
F: 1988. **O:** Jess Jackson. **W:** Stephen Test. **S:** None.

OVERALL	$20-35	★★★

WINE RATINGS

Cabernet Blend Alexander Valley Legacy	★★★
Cabernet Sauvignon Alexander Valley	★★★
Chardonnay Sonoma County	★★★★
Gewürztraminer Anderson Valley	★★★
Merlot Alexander Valley	★★★
Pinot Noir Sonoma County	★★★

WINERY DATA
C: 19,000. **V:** 95 acres in Chalk Hill. **G:** Cabernet Sauvignon, Merlot. **P:** Chardonnay, Pinot Noir (Sonoma County), Gewürztraminer (Anderson Valley).

Stonestreet, yet another of Jess Jackson's (Kendall-Jackson) properties, was acquired in 1988 and has 95 acres in the Chalk Hill appellation and production at 19,000 cases, but headed upward. The original home of Stephen Zellerbach (1973), later the home of William Baccala, it is now Jackson's home too; he named the estate after his grandfather. Under the direction of Stephen Test, the quality of the wines has been very good and steadily improving, with a Meritage red (Legacy), Chardonnay, Gewürztraminer, Merlot and Pinot Noir that are all impressive.

TASTING NOTES

CABERNET BLEND ALEXANDER VALLEY LEGACY (★★★): Reached new heights with the dazzling 1991, rich and complex, well oaked with tannins in check.
1991: Smooth, plush and elegant, with a core of rich, focused plum and currant flavors, turning mildly tannic. **91**
1990: Crisp and spicy, with a spicy chocolate edge to the core of modest berry and currant flavors. **86**

CABERNET SAUVIGNON ALEXANDER VALLEY (★★★): Good but nothing more in 1988 and 1989 as the best grapes were headed toward the Legacy bottling in subsequent vintages.
1991: Smooth and elegant, with appealing cherry, currant and cedary notes, finishing with good length and crisp tannins. **87**
1989: Has ripe currant and spicy oak flavors with a strong herbal, floral edge and a note of green bean and bell pepper. **82**
1988: Crisp and fruity, with modestly intense currant, plum and smoke aromas and flavors laced with an herbal, woody overtone. **82**

CHARDONNAY SONOMA COUNTY (★★★★): Rich and creamy, well oaked but packs in lots of complex flavors. Improving.
1993: Another remarkable Chardonnay from Stonestreet, this is a rich, toasty, complex wine with tiers of pear, spice, toast and smoky oak, altogether a real mouthful. **92**
1992: Ripe, rich and oaky, with a pleasant range of toasty, buttery pear and spicy flavors that fan out and turn complex. **90**
1991: Smooth and elegant, with a band of pretty, ripe pear, honey, spice and apple flavors. **88**

GEWÜRZTRAMINER ANDERSON VALLEY (★★★): Captures the essence of the varietal with its spicy flavors.
1993: Soft and very spicy, with strong nutmeg, allspice and rose petal notes and light fruit echoing on the finish. **85**
1991: On the dry side, this soft-textured wine offers modest apple and pine aromas and flavors. **78**

MERLOT ALEXANDER VALLEY (★★★): Rich and complex, with a nice balance between ripe fruit and spicy oak seasonings.
1992: Smooth and supple, with rich chocolate and cherry

fruit and plush, supple tannins. First from the Alexander Valley estate vineyard. **89**
1991: Rich, complex and polished, with deep, concentrated, firmly structured plum, currant and anise flavors that pick up earth and coffee notes with the tannins. **87**
1990: Shows off herb, cola and currant flavors, but ultimately it's a simple wine that's dry and tannic. **82**
1989: Ripe, intense and concentrated, with pretty spice, currant and anise flavors framed by toasty, smoky oak notes. **88**

PINOT NOIR SONOMA COUNTY (★★★): Improving too, with herb and cherry-laced fruit.
1992: Laced with herb, cherry and tobacco flavors, turning chunky and tannic on the finish. **85**
1991: Smooth, velvety and elegant, showing nice plum, currant, toast, cola and spice flavors. **89**
1990: Smells great but is tight and astringent. A lean wine with a thread of berry flavor struggling to get past the tough tannins. **83**

STONY HILL VINEYARD
St. Helena, Napa Valley
F: 1948. O: McCrea Family. W: Michael Chelini. S: None.

OVERALL	$23-30	★★★★

WINE RATINGS

Chardonnay Napa Valley	★★★★★
Chardonnay Napa Valley SHV	★★★
Gewürztraminer Napa Valley	★★★
Johannisberg Riesling Napa Valley	★★★

WINERY DATA
C: 5,000. V: 40 acres in Napa Valley. G: Chardonnay (25 acres), Riesling (9), Gewürztraminer (4), Sémillon (2). P: Chardonnay, Riesling (Napa Valley).

When Fred and Eleanor McCrea founded Stony Hill Vineyard as a weekend retreat in 1943, no one imagined this tiny winery would come to symbolize the ultimate quest for quality. North of St. Helena in the western hills near Napa Valley-Bothe State Park, Stony Hill took its name from the rugged terrain. Once in Napa, the McCreas became fascinated with a winemaking lifestyle and even had a hand in others' wines, such as School

House. In 1946 they began planting their vineyard at 1 to 2 acres a year. The McCreas focused on Pinot Chardonnay, then a relatively scarce grape variety in California, on a hunch that it would grow well in their soil. Later they added smaller plots of Riesling and Pinot Blanc, still later Gewürztraminer, Sémillon and a few dozen Pinot Noir vines. Their first Chardonnay grapes were harvested in 1950, and their first commercial release followed in 1952, but production was very small, with only a few barrels and often fewer than 100 cases. Winemaking was primitive by current standards: The McCreas picked grapes when they tasted ripe and used old brandy barrels for aging in a tiny stone winery.

Although the winery had the size and appearance of a hobby, the McCreas took winemaking seriously and slowly built production to the 3,000-case range, always paying the greatest attention to quality and detail. The Stony Hill Chardonnay style emphasized tight, tart, flinty green apple and pear notes early on, but what really set these wines apart from others was their ability to age and develop for years. There are many great Chardonnays in this winery's history, as wines from the 1960s still seem suspended in time, light yellow-straw in color, with wonderful balance, flavor, richness and depth, with little indication of decline. The McCreas held crop loads to 1 ton per acre, which maximized concentration and ensured their ability to manage and harvest grapes under ideal circumstances. The wine was aged in old oak barrels, which minimized oxidation and premature aging.

Only in the late 1980s and early 1990s have the wines taken a dip in quality. Much of the 40-acre vineyard has been replanted, a victim of Pierce's disease, and grapes have been bought from Howell Mountain, both for a SHV bottling and now part of the main Stony Hill line. While the most recent vintages have seemed simpler and fruitier that those of yesteryear, it remains to be seen how wines from the new plantings evolve. By the late 1990s, the vineyard should be fully replanted and the grapes mature enough to indicate future quality. Most of the Chardonnay, Riesling (800 cases) and Gewürztraminer (200 cases) are sold via a mailing list. Still worth watching.

TASTING NOTES

CHARDONNAY NAPA VALLEY (★★★★★): Even though the most recent vintages have lacked the depth and focus of the glory years, this remains a great estate based on its amazing track record for superb wines, dating back to the 1950s. These wines do not undergo malolactic fermentation, are not *sur lie* aged, nor do they see the insides of toasty French oak barrels. As such, they are often lean, floral, tart and subtle wines that need time in the bottle.

1992: Austere and earthy, with a metallic edge to the pineapple and citrus flavors. **83**

1991: Elegant and vibrant, with pretty peach, nectarine and spice nuances. **88**

1990: Firm, tight and spicy, with compact pear, apple and light citrus notes that come through on the finish. **88**

1988: Wonderfully complex and elegant, with tiers of pure pear, honey and melon flavors and a charming touch of spicy nutmeg and oak seasoning. **90**

1986: Ripe, rich and full of fresh pear, honey, nutmeg and oak flavors, this is a very youthful wine that needs time to fill out. The flavors are focused and well balanced, with all the ingredients to move up a notch or two. **87**

1985: Ripe and rich, with intense, sharply focused pear, honey, toast, melon and nutmeg flavors that are remarkably elegant and smooth. **92**

1984: Very ripe and forward, with generous pear, melon, spice flavors and subtle pine and oak shadings. **90**

1982: Quite successful for this troubled vintage, it has with age become more pleasing, with elegant, delicate, creamy pear and melon flavors and fine balance, finishing with good length. At its peak. **85**

1981: Typical of the vintage, very ripe, rich and forward, big and full, with spice, honey, pear, vanilla and nutmeg flavors that glide across the palate with a creamy, smooth texture. At its peak. **86**

1980: Aging gracefully; rich, full-bodied and ripe, with intense honey, pear, spice and vanilla flavors all neatly knit and balanced. This wine is ready to drink, although it has the depth and richness to gain for a few more years. **86**

1979: Deep, mature color, with toasty hazelnut, spice and fig flavors, but in decline and beginning to lose its fruit. Drink soon. **81**

1978: Fully mature, yellow-gold, a bit alcoholic but holding up well, with rich, ripe pear, lemon, honey, spice and cocoa flavors and a soft, smooth texture. Not likely to improve; drink soon. **85**

1977: Almost opposite in style from the 1976, high in acidity and austere in character, with fresh, vibrant pear, citrus and melon notes that are clean and refreshing.

Delicate, with excellent balance, it still has years of life ahead. **91**

1976: Very rich, bold and ripe, with layers of honey, pear, toast and butter flavors that offer excellent depth. With aeration it develops further complexities and subtleties. One of the few successes of the 1976 vintage. **88**

1975: A sulfur quality is evident in this wine; a strong flavor and aroma and a coarseness on the palate. It has a charm of its own, but some may not be able to look past the sulfur. **75**

1974: Appears to have more oak and sulfur than fruit, giving it a slight rubbery flavor. It's pleasant, but those especially sensitive to sulfur may find that quality distracting. **73**

1973: Fading now, but early on it was quite lovely. Delicate, with pretty pear and melon flavors. **79**

1972: Elegant and delicate, with pear, anise and spice notes that are a bit blunt, it's a very good wine from a difficult vintage. **83**

1971: Fresh and open when first poured, but not quite as full in the glass, where the ginger, pear and vanilla flavors are delicate and light. Past its prime but still enjoyable. **80**

1970: Ripe, rich, smooth and complex, in peak condition, with distinctive vanilla flavors, a creamy texture and hints of pear, spice and honey. **92**

1968: A wine of great concentration and depth that may still be a few years from peaking. It offers intense honey, pear, spice and vanilla flavors that are rich, elegant and very sharply focused. **93**

1965: Forward and fruity, with a silky smooth texture and honey, pear, melon and spice nuances that are amazingly persistent, elegant and impeccably balanced. Acidity carries the flavors on and on. **90**

1964: The greatest Stony Hill ever produced and the finest California Chardonnay I've ever tasted, the 1964 opens up to reveal rich, intense, deeply concentrated fruit flavors that echo earth, mushroom, honey, toast and pear notes before developing a creamy butterscotch aftertaste. **98**

1962: Absolutely wonderful, complex and elegant, with subtlety and finesse and sharply focused pear, honey, butterscotch and nutmeg flavors that fan out on the palate. **96**

1960: Remarkably youthful and lively for a 30-something Chardonnay, still quite rich, with delicate pear, pineapple and spice flavors, deftly balanced, with a creamy vanilla texture and a long, lingering finish. **88**

CHARDONNAY NAPA VALLEY SHV (★★★):
1993: Despite floral aromas, it's tight and trim to drink, with a narrow band of pear and spice that fans out on the finish. **86**

STONY RIDGE WINERY
Livermore Valley
F: 1975. **O:** Monica Scotto. **W:** Dominic Scotto. **S:** None.

OVERALL	$6-14	★

WINE RATINGS

Cabernet Sauvignon California	★
Cabernet Sauvignon Napa Valley	
Limited Release	★
Merlot North Coast Limited Release	★★

WINERY DATA
C: 20,000. **V:** None. **G:** None. **P:** Cabernet Sauvignon (Napa Valley), Chardonnay (California), Merlot (North Coast).

Development having squeezed the original Stony Ridge winery out of business, the Scotto family intends to revive the brand, using a new facility and focusing on some 20,000 cases of Cabernet (California and Napa Valley), Merlot (North Coast) and white Zinfandel.

TASTING NOTES

VARIOUS BOTTLINGS:

Cabernet Sauvignon California 1989: Lean and a little bit leathery, with a vegetal edge to the modest plum and berry flavors. **78**

Cabernet Sauvignon Napa Valley Limited Release 1989: A robust, rustic red wine with a solid shot of tannin. Not very distinctive, but appealing as a basic, full-bodied wine for everyday occasions. **78**

Merlot North Coast Limited Release 1991: Pleasantly ripe and fruity, with pure, supple berry, cherry and spice flavors, finishing with complexity, length and lots of fruity notes. Easy to drink, and at a fair price. **85**

Merlot North Coast Limited Release 1990: A well balanced, medium-bodied, moderately tannic Merlot that blends fresh cherry and herb flavors. Good and hearty. **82**

STORRS WINERY

Santa Cruz Mountains

F: 1988. O: Stephen J. Storrs & Pamela Bianchini-Storrs. W: Stephen J. Storrs. S: None.

OVERALL	$15-19	★★

WINE RATINGS	
Chardonnay Santa Cruz Mountains Christie Vineyard	★★
Chardonnay Santa Cruz Mountains Vanumanutagi Vineyards	★★
Gewürztraminer Monterey County	★★
Merlot Santa Clara County San Ysidro Vineyard	★★
Zinfandel California Beauregard Ranch Ben Lomond Mountain	★★

WINERY DATA
C: 4,000. V: None. G: None. P: Chardonnay, Zinfandel (Santa Cruz Mountains), Merlot (San Ysidro), Gewürztraminer (Monterey).

In 1988, Stephen and Pamela Storrs, two enologists, founded this small winery in Santa Cruz, focusing on four bottlings of Santa Cruz Mountain-grown Chardonnay (Beauregard Ranch, Christie Vineyard, Dirk Vineyard and a blend of all three), Monterey Gewürztraminer, San Ysidro Vineyard Merlot and Beauregard Ranch Zinfandel. Total production by 1994 was in the 4,000-case range, with limited distribution.

TASTING NOTES

VARIOUS BOTTLINGS:
Chardonnay Santa Cruz Mountains Christie Vineyard Mountain Vineyard Collection 1993: More complete than most 1993s, with supple pear, honey and light oak notes. **85**
Chardonnay Santa Cruz Mountains Vanumanutagi Vineyards 1993: Young and fruity, with attractive peach, pear and vanilla notes that are clean and well proportioned. **86**
Zinfandel California Beauregard Ranch Ben Lomond Mountain 1990: Firm, with spicy raspberry and vanilla flavors and a twang of pickle on the finish. **82**

STORY WINERY

Shenandoah Valley

F: 1973. O: Bruce & Jan Tichenor. W: Bruce Tichenor. S: None.

OVERALL	$10-16	★★

WINE RATINGS	
Zinfandel Shenandoah Valley	★★

WINERY DATA
C: 2,500. V: 42 acres in Shenandoah Valley. G: Zinfandel (38 acres), Chenin Blanc (2), Barbera (1), Mission (1). P: None.

Bruce and Jan Tichenor own 42 of the oldest vineyard acres in Amador County, from which they produce some 2,500 cases a year. Their specialty is Zinfandel, which carries the Shenandoah appellation.

TASTING NOTES

ZINFANDEL SHENANDOAH VALLEY (★★): Usually earthy, with ripe cherry and berry fruit.
1991: Earthy and complex, with ripe, supple raspberry and cherry aromas and flavors, ending with buttery oak. **86**
1990: Gamy and a bit earthy, but it hangs together, picking up ripe berry and cherry notes. **83**

STORYBOOK MOUNTAIN VINEYARDS

Calistoga, Napa Valley

F: 1976. O: Jerry B. & Sigrid M. Seps. W: Jerry B. Seps. S: None.

OVERALL	$15-25	★★★

WINE RATINGS	
Zinfandel Howell Mountain	★★★
Zinfandel Napa Valley Reserve	★★★

WINERY DATA
C: 9,000. V: 40 acres in Napa. G: Zinfandel. P: Zinfandel (Howell Mountain).

Jerry Seps taught history at Stanford University before turning to wine, first as an apprentice for Joseph Swan in Sonoma. He started his winery in 1976 with the purchase of the old Grimm Brothers Winery (founded 1882) north of Calistoga, which was planted to Zinfandel. This quickly became Storybook Mountain's specialty. Seps' goals: to craft long-lived and ageworthy Zinfandel (which he does) and to raise its image among wine lovers (he's done that too, having helped found ZAP, Zinfandel Advocates and Producers). His 40-acre vineyard yields wines of distinctive character; the Reserve wines in particular are big, ripe, intense and earthy, traits many feel make Storybook's the quintessential mountain-grown Zinfandel, even though heavy-handed. Production is 9,000 cases, including a new bottling from purchased Howell Mountain grapes.

TASTING NOTES

ZINFANDEL HOWELL MOUNTAIN (★★★): Can be brilliant, with classic pepper and berry flavors, but it can also be ruggedly earthy, tannic and disjointed, depending on the year.
1991: Austere, with a core of tight, firm and focused black cherry, raspberry and spice notes, turning tannic. **87**
1990: Crisp and lively, with peppery strawberry and raspberry aromas and flavors, and the finish is lean and a little leafy. **83**
1989: Very peppery, tannic and woody smelling, with lean fruit flavors and an earthy, tannic finish. **80**
1988: Ripe, with a solid, tannic core of pepper and berry flavors. **79**
1987: A mouthful of fruit cloaked with tannin, this rich wine has bright raspberry, berry and spice flavors. **88**
1986: Ripe and redolent of black pepper and plum flavors like a Syrah, a big, inky, tannic, gentle giant of a wine. **88**

ZINFANDEL NAPA VALLEY RESERVE (★★★): Similar to the regular bottling in its inconsistency and earthy tannins, but the early 1980s vintages have aged well, surrendering their fresh raspberry fruit to earthy, anise and tarry notes, but softening nonetheless. Recent vintages appear more variable and may show better with short-term cellaring.
1991: Ripe, intense and spicy, but it turns hollow in the middle, showing a pruny edge that turns earthy and gamy, with gritty tannins. **84**
1989: Dense, oaky and earthy, this is a tough and chewy 1989 with its fruit submerged beneath the oak and earth. **71**
1988: Powerful, full-bodied and tannic, with peppery aromas and ample blackberry, tart cherry and spice flavors. **86**

1987: Amazingly ripe and powerful, with deep, rich, complex berry, cherry, pepper and spice flavors, turning very tannic. **89**
1986: Spicy, firm in texture and fragrant, with black pepper and raspberry aromas and flavors. **82**
1985: Extremely concentrated and tannic, with ripe, jammy plum and berry flavors, finishing with pepper and spice. **88**
1984: Ripe, concentrated and tannic, brimming with ripe cherry, raspberry and plum flavors with a touch of mint. **88**

STRATFORD WINERY
Oakville, Napa Valley
F: 1982. **O:** Hoxsey Winery Investors & Yount Mill Vineyards. **W:** Kerry Signoracci. **S:** Canterbury.

OVERALL	$9	★★

WINE RATINGS	
Cabernet Sauvignon California	★★
Chardonnay California	★★
Merlot California	★★
Sauvignon Blanc	
California Partners' Reserve	★★
Zinfandel California	★★

WINERY DATA
C: 20,000. **V:** 370 acres in Napa Valley. **G:** Cabernet Sauvignon (150 acres), Chardonnay (70), Sauvignon Blanc (100), Merlot (80). **P:** None.

This upscale negociant brand focuses on popular varietals, namely Chardonnay, Cabernet, Merlot, Sauvignon Blanc and Zinfandel. In 1994, a group of investors, headed by Andrew Hoxsey, owner of Napa Wine Co. in Oakville (where brands such as Marcassin, Fife, Bay View, Colgin, Pahlmeyer and Staglin are produced), purchased the brand and will now use Hoxsey's family's considerable vineyard holding (Yount Mill Vineyard) in and around the Yountville area to produce a new line of estate-bottled wines. Production is expected to remain in the 20,000-case range. Canterbury is a second label.

TASTING NOTES

VARIOUS BOTTLINGS (★★):
Cabernet Sauvignon California 1990: Light and fruity,

with a floral edge to the basic currant flavors, finishing with modest tannins. **81**

Chardonnay California 1991: Fresh, fruity and simple, showing crisp green apple and spice aromas and flavors. The finish is a bit austere. **82**

Merlot California 1991: Youthful, tight and vibrant, with herb, black cherry and currant flavors that ring true for Merlot. Picks up a spicy edge on the finish, but tastes closed and tannic now. **84**

Sauvignon Blanc California Partners' Reserve 1991: Crisp and flavorful, offering a bright beam of citrus, pear and grassy herb flavors. The finish is focused and lively, with a distinct echo of grapefruit. **85**

Zinfandel California 1991: Light, fruity, spicy and velvety, a well tempered example of fresh berry and vanilla characteristics. The finish is lively. **83**

STRAUS VINEYARDS
Napa Valley
F: 1986. **O:** Straus Vineyards Inc. **W:** Alan Philips. **S:** None.

OVERALL	$17	★★★

WINE RATINGS

Merlot Napa Valley	★★★

WINERY DATA
C: 1,500. **V:** None. **G:** None. **P:** Merlot (Napa Valley).

Beginning in 1986, Lisa and Phillip Toohey started this 1,500-case brand in St. Helena named after Toohey's grandfather. The winery makes only Merlot, all from purchased grapes in Napa Valley. The first five vintages have shown that the Tooheys have a fine hand for Merlot, as the wines are well crafted, balancing ripe fruit and oak.

TASTING NOTES

MERLOT NAPA VALLEY (★★★): Quality runs with the vintages, as the 1986, 1987 and 1990 all show ripe, lively fruit, while the 1988 and 1989 are leaner and less harmonious.

1991: Smooth and elegant, with a smoky oak edge to the currant, black cherry and mineral flavors. **85**

1990: Fresh and lively, with spicy plum, cherry and raspberry flavors that are crisp and firm. **85**

1989: Hard-edged and woody, with a chunky fruit component but lacking finesse. **81**

1988: A weedy, herbal wine with more herbs and spice than fruit, turning vegetal. **82**

1987: Deliciously focused and concentrated, with appealing plum and cherry flavors, a firm texture and mild tannins. **87**

1986: Smells wonderful, but it needs time to soften the tannins and let the currant, vanilla and toast flavors emerge. **89**

RODNEY STRONG VINEYARDS
Russian River Valley
F: 1959. **O:** Klein Family Vintners Inc. **W:** Richard B. Sayre. **S:** None.

OVERALL	$9-30	★★★

WINE RATINGS

Cabernet Sauvignon Northern Sonoma Alexander's Crown	★★★
Cabernet Sauvignon Northern Sonoma Reserve	★★★
Cabernet Sauvignon Sonoma Coast	★★
Chardonnay Chalk Hill Chalk Hill Vineyard	★★
Chardonnay Sonoma County	★★
Merlot Sonoma County	★★
Pinot Noir Russian River Valley River East Vineyard	★★
Sauvignon Blanc Northern Sonoma Charlotte's Home Vineyard	★★★
Zinfandel Russian River Valley River West Vineyard Old Vines	★★★

WINERY DATA
C: 180,000. **V:** 460 acres in Sonoma County. **G:** Cabernet Sauvignon (100 acres), Chardonnay (275), Merlot, Pinot Noir, Sauvignon Blanc, Zinfandel. **P:** None.

Rodney Strong Vineyards has gone through more changes than most. It began in 1959 as Tiburon Vintners, then became Windsor Vineyards, a wine mail-order business. In 1970 it was renamed Sonoma Vineyards before shifting gears again, becoming Rodney Strong Vineyards. Through it all, Rodney Strong oversaw winemaking and management before easing into semi-retirement in 1995. The winery has generally produced good to very good wines, its star being the Alexander's Crown Cabernet Vineyard in Alexander Valley, which dates to 1974. Production is 180,000 cases under the Strong label, drawing from 460 acres of vineyard, led by Chardonnay (275 acres) and Cabernet (100). Along with the Crown bottling, Chalk Hill Chardonnay, River East Vineyard Pinot Noir, Charlotte's Home Vineyard Sauvignon Blanc and River West Old Vines Zinfandel are featured wines. In 1989, Klein Foods purchased the winery and vineyards, with plans to scale back production slightly, while upgrading quality. Sonoma County Chardonnay and Cabernet at 50,000 cases each are the volume leaders.

Tasting Notes

Cabernet Sauvignon Northern Sonoma Alexander's Crown (★★★): Can be rich and complex, but more variable of late, with more medium-bodied flavors than rich, concentrated fruit. Older bottlings carried the Sonoma Vineyards label.

1990: Firm and tasty, a soft-textured wine with a green bean edge to the plum and currant flavors. Firmly tannic. **86**

1988: Smooth and generous, with layers of ripe currant, blackberry and buttery oak flavors. Finishes with a sense of polish and elegance. **91**

1987: Elegant and lively, with a ripe currant edge to the plum and cherry flavors and tannins that are firm and rounded. **89**

1985: An elegant but oaky bottling with light currant and cherry notes that turn earthy and simple on the finish. **83**

1984: A good 1984 with supple black cherry, herb and anise notes, finishing with soft tannins and a leafy edge. **82**

1979: Firm, intense and tannic but holding on, with mature, cedary Cabernet flavors. **84**

1978: On its last legs, with fading cedary, earthy notes that dry out. **77**

1977: Old and faded, with an earthy, cedary edge but no fruit. **73**

1976: Ripe, rich, intense and youthful, with spicy, jammy fruit flavors. **87**

1975: Old but pleasing, with spicy, cedary currant flavors that fade on the finish. **83**

1974: Past its prime but still enjoyable, with spicy anise and cedar notes. **83**

Cabernet Sauvignon Northern Sonoma Reserve (★★★): Carries the Northern Sonoma appellation lately, and is steadily improving, well oaked, with well focused fruit that's complex and elegant.

1990: Dark, ripe and rich, with currant, chocolate and toasty oak flavors that turn supple and elegant, with polished tannins. **90**

1988: Ripe and flavorful, with firm tannins underpinning the straightforward Cabernet flavors. **84**

1987: Intensely flavored and chewy, with lots of rich currant, mint and chocolate nuances and toasty oak notes, turning supple. **90**

Cabernet Sauvignon Sonoma Coast (★★): Lean and crisp, with a narrow band of fruit.

1992: A rustic style marked by cedary oak, currant and berry flavors, with firm tannins. Best after 1996. **83**

1991: Firm, intense and tannic, with a narrow band of spicy fruit flavors. **82**

1990: Lean and a bit on the green side, with herb, bell pepper and green bean notes. **81**

Chardonnay Chalk Hill Chalk Hill Vineyard (★★): Variable quality in 1991 and 1992, but it lacks the extra dimensions the best Sonoma Chardonnays display.

1993: Well balanced in a medium-bodied style, with ripe pear, apple, honey and spice notes. **85**

1992: Ripe and fruity, with spicy pear and honey notes. **87**

1991: Marked by a funky, clumsy, woody edge to the ripe citrus and pear notes. **74**

Chardonnay Sonoma County (★★): Medium-weight, with ripe fruit and light oak shadings.

1993: Simple and straightforward, with ripe pear and apple-laced fruit. **83**

1992: A ripe, spicy, floral wine with hints of peach and honey. **82**

Merlot Sonoma County (★★): New to the lineup, light- and medium-bodied.

1992: Lean and crisp, with herb, plum and spice notes that turn elegant. **84**

Pinot Noir Russian River Valley River East Vineyard (★★): Light in color, body and texture, but with attractive tea, herb and cherry notes. Best to drink early on.

1992: Marked by an earthy, herbal edge to the modest tea and cherry notes. **83**
1991: Delicate and spicy, offering pretty floral, strawberry and cherry flavors that are elegant. **87**
1990: Tannic, with oaky cola, vanilla and anise flavors. **82**
1985: Elegant and balanced, with mature cherry, toast, herb and plum flavors. **83**

SAUVIGNON BLANC NORTHERN SONOMA CHARLOTTE'S HOME VINEYARD (★★★): Offers good intensity and lots of ripe fruit flavors.
1994: Smooth and fruity in a tropical-fruit sort of way, with a wave of leafy, herbal flavors washing over the finish. **84**
1993: Fruity and spicy, echoing nectarine and vanilla flavors. **85**

ZINFANDEL RUSSIAN RIVER VALLEY RIVER WEST VINEYARD OLD VINES (★★★): From old vines, it's an elegant wine, well oaked with peppery berry notes.
1992: Well oaked but with a bright core of cherry and raspberry fruit to match it. Drinks well now, with a long, fruity aftertaste. **86**
1991: Light in color and weight, offering pepper and spicy cherry flavors framed by light oak. **82**
1990: Elegant and stylish, with spicy oak notes adding complexity to the ripe cherry and raspberry flavors. **86**
1988: Polished, with pretty vanilla, raspberry and spice flavors that finish with smooth tannins. **89**
1987: Light in color, with more vanilla and spicy oak characteristics than cherry and strawberry flavors. **82**

SULLIVAN VINEYARDS WINERY
Rutherford, Napa Valley
F: 1979. **O:** Sullivan Vineyards Inc. **W:** Jim Sullivan.
S: None.

OVERALL	$23-30	★★★

WINE RATINGS

Cabernet Sauvignon Napa Valley	★★★
Cabernet Sauvignon Napa Valley Private Reserve	★★★
Merlot Napa Valley	★★★

WINERY DATA
C: 3,000. **V:** 26 acres in Rutherford. **G:** Cabernet Sauvignon (6 acres), Merlot (6), Chardonnay (8), Chenin Blanc (6). **P:** Cabernet Sauvignon (Rutherford).

Graphic designer Jim Sullivan converted from home to commercial winemaking in 1979, buying the first four acres of what is now a 26-acre vineyard in Rutherford, east of Franciscan, where he specializes in Cabernet, Cabernet Reserve (made from older vines, planted in 1972) and Merlot, with production totaling 3,000 cases. While both wines are made in a dense, rustic, often tannic style, needing several years of aging to soften, they are very consistent.

TASTING NOTES

CABERNET NAPA VALLEY (★★★), PRIVATE RESERVE (★★★): Intense, tannic and often earthy, but with a solid core of chunky fruit and ample oak shadings. Needs three to five years after the vintage to calm down.
1992: Chunky and grapey, with chocolate, currant and oak flavors that finish with firm tannins. **88**
1991: Smoky and toasty, severe and harsh, with a green edge to the flavors. **78**
1990: Austere, with a tight, compact band of concentrated currant, spice and cedary oak flavors, finishing with a firm tannic grip. **87**
1989: Youthful and raw, with generous black currant and blackberry flavors, chewy tannins and gamy overtones. **84**
1984: Mature, with an earthy currant edge to the cedary oak flavors that are softening and turning complex. **87**
Private Reserve 1991: Young and tight, with a green edge to the currant and cherry flavors. **84**
Private Reserve 1990: Big, ripe, firm and rich, with cherry, currant and spice flavors that turn supple, finishing with firm tannins. **88**
Private Reserve 1989: An oaky wine that has enough currant and cherry flavors to give it balance. **86**
Private Reserve 1988: Dark in color, bold, deep and concentrated, with firm, hard-edged tannins and currant, plum and cedar flavors. **83**

MERLOT NAPA VALLEY (★★★): Shares the Cabernet's intensity and high tannin level, but can surprise in years such as 1989 when it's better balanced. Needs time too.

1992: Dense, with a chocolaty edge to the currant and cherry flavors, but it's very tannic and oaky and in need of cellaring. **88**

1991: Austere and tight, with a firm, tannic edge to the spicy currant flavors that are struggling to emerge. **84**

1990: Lean and austere, with a narrow band of cedar, currant and spice flavors, firmly tannic. **84**

1989: Austere and tight, with a firm, tannic edge to the spicy currant flavors. **86**

1987: Firm and focused, with complex currant and cedar flavors, finishing with firm tannins. **88**

SUMMIT LAKE VINEYARDS & WINERY
Howell Mountain

F: 1985. **O:** Robert J. & Susan M. Brakesman. **W:** Robert J. Brakesman. **S:** None.

OVERALL	$12	★★

WINE RATINGS

Zinfandel Howell Mountain	★★

WINERY DATA

C: 1,500. **V:** 14 acres on Howell Mountain. **G:** Zinfandel (10 acres). **P:** None.

Howell Mountain Zinfandel lovers Robert and Susan Brakesman founded this 1,500-case Zinfandel-only winery in 1985, using their 14 acres of vines (10 in Zin) at the 2,200-foot level. Quality has been consistently good, with 1987 the best of recent offerings.

TASTING NOTES

ZINFANDEL HOWELL MOUNTAIN (★★): Intense, lean and peppery in 1988 and 1989, but somewhat fruitier in 1987.

1989: The peppery, spicy aromas turn austere, earthy and firm on the palate. **84**

1988: Firm, ripe and peppery, with minty berry flavors that turn tannic. **82**

1987: Intense, ripe and jammy, with lively black pepper and berry flavors . **87**

1986: Tart, with fresh berry, raspberry and spice notes. **84**

1985: Very firm and tart, with ripe raspberry flavors and a touch of oak and earthiness. **86**

SUNRISE WINERY
Santa Cruz Mountains

F: 1976. **O:** Ronald & Rolayne Stortz. **W:** Rolayne Stortz. **S:** None.

OVERALL	$7-22	NR

WINE RATINGS

Cabernet Sauvignon Santa Cruz Mountains Arata Vineyard	NR
Chardonnay Livermore Valley Beyers Ranch	NR
Pinot Blanc Santa Cruz Mountains St. Charles Vineyard	NR
Zinfandel Santa Cruz Mountains Picchetti Ranch	NR

WINERY DATA

C: 2,500. **V:** 3 acres in Santa Cruz Mountains. **G:** Zinfandel (3 acres). **P:** Cabernet Sauvignon, Chardonnay, Pinot Blanc (Santa Cruz Mountains), Chardonnay (Livermore Valley).

Ronald and Rolayne Stortz own this 2,500-case winery on Montebello Road in Cupertino, where they farm three acres of Zinfandel and buy Cabernet (from Arata Vineyard, Santa Cruz), Chardonnay (Beyers Ranch, Livermore Valley), Pinot Blanc (St. Charles Vineyard, Santa Cruz) and Zinfandel (Picchetti Ranch, Santa Cruz) to round out production. Distribution is very limited.

SUTTER HOME WINERY
St. Helena, Napa Valley

F: 1874. **O:** Louis Trinchero, Roger Trinchero & Vera Trinchero-Torres. **W:** Gary Branham. **S:** None.

OVERALL	$4-12	★★

WINE RATINGS

Cabernet Sauvignon Napa Valley Reserve	★★
Chardonnay California	★★
Chenin Blanc California	NR
Merlot California	★★
Sauvignon Blanc California	★★
Zinfandel California	★★

WINERY DATA

C: 5,500,000. **V:** 2,654 acres in Napa County, Amador County, Lake County, Glenn County, Colusa County, Sacramento County. **G:** Zinfandel (1,560 acres), Chardonnay (510), Cabernet Sauvignon (210), Barbera (170), Gewürztraminer (90), Merlot (80), Other (33.5). **P:** Chardonnay (Central Coast, North Coast), Sauvignon Blanc (Central Coast, North Coast), Chenin Blanc (Central Coast, North Coast), Gewürztraminer (Central Coast, North Coast), Cabernet Sauvignon (North Coast), Zinfandel (North Coast, Amador County), Merlot (North Coast), Gamay (North Coast), Pinot Noir (North Coast).

The original Sutter Home Winery dates to 1874. The Trinchero family bought the winery in 1947, bottling a wide assortment of wines, and in 1968, Louis "Bob" Trinchero launched Amador County Zinfandel, which the winery produced through the 1970s. In 1972, Sutter Home experimented with a blanc de noirs, pressing Zinfandel grapes and leaving just a pink tinge and hint of sweetness, labeling it white Zinfandel. That and other so-called "blush" wines triggered an explosion of similarly styled wines, but Sutter Home's proved the most successful, and its name became synonymous with white Zin.

The success of white Zin propelled Sutter Home to great financial heights, and the winery has added other varietals, including Cabernet, Chardonnay, Merlot, Sauvignon Blanc and Zinfandel, all made in a light- to medium-bodied, easy-to-drink style. Production now tops 5 million cases and the winery has vast vineyard resources, measuring 2,654 acres in vines (mostly in the Sacramento Valley), led by 1,560 acres of Zinfandel. Amador Zin is still part of the product mix, albeit a small part, and the winery has extended its holdings in Amador, buying the Montevina Winery. It has also resumed producing Napa Valley appellation wines, led by a Cabernet.

TASTING NOTES

CABERNET SAUVIGNON VARIOUS BOTTLINGS (★★): Good but unexceptional with the early tries.
Napa Valley Reserve 1991: Spicy, with focused currant and cherry flavors that turn smooth, with mild tannins. **84**
Napa Valley Centennial Selection Reserve 1990: Crisp and flavorful, with a beam of generous wild berry flavor. **87**

CHARDONNAY CALIFORNIA (★★): Simple and lightly fruity, but a decent value.

1993: Marred by a tinny, canned grapefruit edge, it's drinkable but below average. **74**
1992: Crisp and simple, offering a glint of apple in the background. **79**

CHENIN BLANC CALIFORNIA (NR):
1993: An attempt to make a more complex style of Chenin Blanc, but it veers off toward earthiness rather than centering around pretty fruit. **79**

MERLOT CALIFORNIA (★★): Light and simple too, with modest herbal flavors.
1992: Firm in texture and a little weak on intensity, but what's there is pleasant. Softens on the finish and gets a wee bit sweet. **79**

SAUVIGNON BLANC CALIFORNIA (★★): Simple with a citrus edge to the flavors.
1992: Crisp, simple and citrusy, a lively wine with tartness to balance the sweet edge. **79**

ZINFANDEL VARIOUS BOTTLINGS (★★): Well balanced, with tarry berry and earthy notes.
California 1992: Light and simple, with hints of raspberry and strawberry flavors. **75**
Amador County Centennial Selection 1990: Fresh, ripe and supple, with pretty raspberry, tar and spice notes. **84**

JOSEPH SWAN VINEYARDS
Sonoma County
F: 1969. **O:** June Swan. **W:** Rod Berglund. **S:** Trenton Cellars.

OVERALL	$14-22	★★★

WINE RATINGS

Cabernet Sauvignon Sonoma Mountain Steiner Vineyard	NR
Pinot Noir Russian River Valley	★★
Pinot Noir Sonoma Mountain Steiner Vineyard	★★
Red Table Wine Russian River Valley Côtes du Rosa	NR
Zinfandel Russian River Valley Frati Ranch	★★★

Zinfandel Russian River Valley
  V.H.S.R. Vineyard ★★★
Zinfandel Sonoma Valley
  Stellwagen Vineyard ★★

WINERY DATA

C: 3,800. **V:** 10 acres in Russian River Valley. **G:** Pinot Noir (5 acres), Chardonnay (5). **P:** Zinfandel (Russian River Valley), Zinfandel (Sonoma Valley), Pinot Noir (Sonoma Mountain), Pinot Noir (Russian River Valley), Carignane (Russian River Valley).

Over the years, Joseph Swan, a former airline pilot, has become a Zinfandel legend. Among his many admirers and pupils were Joel Peterson (Ravenswood) and Jerry Seps (Storybook Mountain), both of whom credit Swan's passion and success with Zinfandel for their pursuit of that wine. For many, Swan Zinfandels typified the big, bold, ripe, high-extract style of the 1970s—many of them aged well, further encouraging the style, however exaggerated. In the 1980s, Swan lost some of his key vineyards and quality dipped, with Pinot Noir emerging as his best wine. Following Swan's death in 1988, son-in-law Rod Berglund became winemaker. The most recent Zinfandels are very well crafted, with vineyard-designated wines part of the mix. Production hovers around 3,800 cases, with 10 acres owned by the winery, divided between Chardonnay and Pinot Noir.

TASTING NOTES

CABERNET SAUVIGNON SONOMA MOUNTAIN STEINER VINEYARD (NR): The first wine proved a curiosity, but better things may be in store.
1990: An odd mixture of ripe plum and blueberry flavors with dill and pickle notes, resulting in a stylish wine that has its pluses and minuses. **84**

PINOT NOIR VARIOUS BOTTLINGS (★★): Steadily improving, but still marked by variable quality, ripe and fruity one year, lean and less ripe the next.
Russian River Valley 1991: Tight and chewy, with an earthy streak to the wild berry flavors. Turns gamy and tannic on the finish. **83**
Russian River Valley 1990: Crisp and rustic, with spicy raspberry, black cherry and anise notes that take on a pleasing earthy berry edge. **88**
Sonoma Coast 1988: Smells attractive, with pepper and cherry notes, but it tastes woody, tannic and dry. **79**

Sonoma Coast 1985: Mature, with earthy plum, cherry, cedar and spice flavors. **87**
Sonoma Mountain Steiner Vineyard 1993: Youthful and earthy, with a green edge to the wild berry and cherry notes. **84**
Sonoma Mountain Steiner Vineyard 1992: Appealing for its bright black cherry, berry and tar notes, but showing enough tannin for short-term cellaring. **88**
Sonoma Mountain Wolfspierre Vineyard 1992: Tart and crisp, with an earthy edge to the wild berry and raspberry flavors. **86**

RED TABLE WINE RUSSIAN RIVER VALLEY CÔTES DU ROSA (NR):
1991: Rich, ripe and plummy, with a floral edge to the raspberry, grape and spice flavors. **88**

ZINFANDEL RUSSIAN RIVER VALLEY FRATI RANCH (★★★): Worth watching after the lush and complex 1992 bottling.
1992: Very dark and jammy, with layers of ripe wild berry, black cherry and plum flavors. **92**

ZINFANDEL RUSSIAN RIVER VALLEY V.H.S.R. VINEYARD (★★★): Rivaled the Frati Ranch for richness and complexity in 1992. Worth watching.
1992: Dark, rich and chocolaty, with intense, focused wild berry and black cherry flavors that are ripe and lively. **92**

ZINFANDEL SONOMA COUNTY (★★): Steadily improving, but has stylistic and quality swings.
1989: Tart, green and simple, with a thin band of berry notes. **80**
1988: Exotic pepper and spice aromas are appealing, and the blackberry flavors are built on a firm foundation of well integrated tannins **82**
1987: Light and bright, with jammy berry and toast flavors that finish with firm tannins. **86**
1986: Attractive for its pure, ripe, spicy flavors and peppery notes that play off the delicious cherry and jam nuances. **89**

ZINFANDEL SONOMA VALLEY STELLWAGEN VINEYARD (★★): Quality and stylistic swings make this one hard to peg. Has been the weakest of the Zinfandel bottlings.
1992: Dill, oregano and bay leaf aromas and flavors render it one-dimensional. **77**

1989: An offbeat wine with tart cranberry and menthol flavors that miss the mark. **80**

1987: Firm and tannic, with pepper, cherry, raspberry and jam flavors seasoned by nutmeg and spice. **86**

Zinfandel Sonoma County Ziegler Vineyard (NR): Ripe with pretty cherry, spice and pepper notes.

1987: Very ripe, with cherry and raspberry notes and pepper seasoning. **86**

Swanson Vineyards
Rutherford, Napa Valley

F: 1985. **O:** W. Clarke Swanson, Jr. **W:** Marco S. Cappelli, Helen Turley. **S:** Cygnet.

Overall	$16-25	★★★

Wine Ratings
Cabernet Sauvignon Napa Valley	★★★
Chardonnay Carneros	★★★
Chardonnay Napa Valley Reserve	★★★★
Merlot Napa Valley	★★★
Sangiovese Napa Valley	★★★
Sémillon Napa Valley Late Harvest	★★
Syrah Napa Valley	★★★
Zinfandel Napa Valley	NR

Winery Data
C: 10,000. **V:** 120 acres in Oakville, Rutherford.
G: Merlot (56 acres), Sauvignon Blanc (10), Syrah (13), Cabernet Sauvignon (11), Cabernet Franc (3), Petite Sirah (3), Chardonnay (24). **P:** Chardonnay (Carneros), Cabernet Sauvignon, Sauvignon Blanc (Oakville), Sémillon (Napa Valley), Cabernet Sauvignon (Rutherford), Cabernet Sauvignon (Mount Veeder).

Swanson Foods heir W. Clarke Swanson Jr. purchased a large vineyard in Oakville in 1985. He then bought the former Cassayre-Forni winery in Rutherford, where his 10,000-case winery operates today. Expanding vineyards, Swanson now owns 120 acres in vines, led by Merlot (56), Chardonnay (24) and a prized Syrah vineyard in Yountville (13) that for years was the source of grapes for Sean Thackrey's Orion Syrah bottlings. Under the winemaking direction of Marco Capelli and Helen Turley, quality across the board has been high.

Tasting Notes

Cabernet Sauvignon Napa Valley (★★★): Poised for greatness, the 1987 to 1990 vintages have been right on the mark for each vintage, with bold, ripe, supple and complex wines in the best years. Worth watching.

1991: Supple and complex, rich and flavorful, laced with buttery oak and full of ripe cherry, currant and spice flavors, turning tannic. **90**

1990: Deep, dense and elegant, its ripe berry, cherry and currant flavors wrapped in a tight blanket of fine tannin, echoing toast and spice on the finish. **89**

1988: Hard and chewy, but the ripe currant, earth and oak flavors are appealing if a bit hollow. **82**

1987: Firm and tight, with chewy tannins, but delivering a solid core of currant and black cherry flavor, turning spicy. **90**

Chardonnay Carneros (★★★): Firm and well focused, with a nice balance between ripe fruit and oak.

1993: Shows good intensity and breadth of flavor, with ripe pear, peach, spice and honey notes, with a nice touch of oak. **88**

1992: Serves up a bright, ripe beam of peach, pear and melon-laced fruit, turning supple and elegant on the finish. **89**

1991: Firm and intense, with a solid core of ripe pineapple and citrus flavors framed by toasty oak. **87**

Chardonnay Napa Valley Reserve (★★★★): A shade richer, fuller and more complex than the regular bottling.

1990: Brimming with fresh, ripe flavors, offering tiers of pear, citrus, honey and spice notes that are intense and lively, finishing with subtle toast and nutmeg notes. **90**

Merlot Napa Valley (★★★): Improving as the style shows more focus and finesse.

1992: Marked by cedary oak and a leathery edge, the wild berry and cherry battles the tannins right up to the finish. Needs time. **86**

1991: Ripe and supple, with smooth, rich plum, herb and spicy pepper notes that are intense and concentrated. **89**

1990: Hard and tannic, a medium-weight wine with modest fruit flavors and a strong leafy, woody component. **82**

SANGIOVESE NAPA VALLEY (★★★): Another wine that's poised for greatness, as young vines mature and the style becomes more refined. Combines ripe, complex fruit with a sense of elegance and finesse.

1992: Ripe and complex, pouring out its pure plum, berry and spicy vanilla character in a supple package. **91**
1991: Smooth and elegant, with smoky cherry, plum and anise notes framed by toasty, buttery oak flavors. **88**

SÉMILLON NAPA VALLEY LATE HARVEST (★★):
1991: Sweet and silky, unfolding its delicious fig, tobacco and honey flavors nicely. Gets a little sugary on the finish, but should be at its best from 1997-1998. **88**
1988: Distinctive almond, toast, fig and honey aromas and flavors come off sweet and a little sticky, but it would be pleasant to drink with or after dessert. **80**

SYRAH NAPA VALLEY (★★★): Should be great as the replanted vineyard matures, but given Thackrey's success with these grapes they should yield wonderful wines.
1992: Dark and inky, with a tight band of spice, prune, currant and meaty Syrah flavors. The tannins coat the mouth and win hands down. **89**

ZINFANDEL NAPA VALLEY (NR): The last bottling was with the 1988 vintage.
1988: Heavily oaked, with a core of currant and plum aromas and flavors that turn peppery. **85**

SYCAMORE CREEK VINEYARDS
Morgan Hill, Santa Clara County
F: 1975. **O:** Koshu Budoshu Honpo Co. Ltd. **W:** Hideki Yamaki, Corey Wilson. **S:** None.

OVERALL	$8-13	NR

WINE RATINGS

Cabernet Sauvignon Santa Clara County	NR
Chardonnay Santa Clara County	NR
Johannisberg Riesling	
Santa Clara County	NR

WINERY DATA
C: 10,000. **V:** 14 acres in Santa Clara County. **G:** Chardonnay (7 acres), Cabernet Sauvignon (7). **P:** None.

This 10,000-case winery in the Uvas Valley west of Morgan Hill was founded by Terry Parks, but since 1989 has been owned by Japanese interests, Koshu Budoshu Honpo Co. Ltd. It now focuses on estate-grown Cabernet and Chardonnay, with smaller lots of Johannisberg Riesling. Distribution is very limited.

TAFT STREET WINERY
Sonoma County
F: 1982. **O:** Taft Street Inc. **W:** John Tierney. **S:** None.

OVERALL	$7-13	★★

WINE RATINGS

Chardonnay Sonoma County	★★
Sauvignon Blanc Sonoma County	★★

WINERY DATA
C: 39,000. **V:** None. **G:** None. **P:** Chardonnay (Russian River, Alexander Valley), Merlot (Russian River, Dry Creek, Alexander Valley), Sauvignon Blanc (Sonoma County).

Taft Street is a 39,000-case operation producing Sonoma County Chardonnay, Merlot and Sauvignon Blanc, with Chardonnay (18,500) the volume leader. Known for good values; quality falls in the fair to good range.

TASTING NOTES

VARIOUS BOTTLINGS (★★):
Chardonnay Sonoma County 1993: Smooth and creamy, with ripe pear, apple and spice notes that turn elegant and soft on the finish. Ready. **86**
Sauvignon Blanc Sonoma County 1993: Soft and simple, a gently fruity wine to drink soon. **77**

ROBERT TALBOTT VINEYARDS
Monterey County
F: 1982. **O:** Robert Talbott Inc. **W:** Sam Balderas. **S:** Logan Winery.

OVERALL	$25-34	★★★★

WINE RATINGS

Chardonnay Monterey County	★★★★
Chardonnay Monterey County	
Diamond T Estate	★★★★

Logan Winery Chardonnay
  Monterey County ★★

WINERY DATA
C: 14,000. **V:** 134 acres in Monterey. **G:** Chardonnay.
P: Chardonnay (Monterey).

The Talbott family (of necktie fame) founded this Carmel Valley winery in 1983, focusing on Chardonnay, from both purchased grapes and its own 134-acre property, Diamond T Estate vineyard. Since the late 1980s, quality has been very high, with a series of rich, complex and well oaked wines that serve up lots of flavor and finesse. The two main wines, Diamond T and Monterey, are made in similar Burgundian styles. Logan, a second label, has offered good values.

TASTING NOTES

CHARDONNAY MONTEREY COUNTY (★★★★), DIAMOND T (★★★★): Combines bold, ripe, juicy fruit with toasty, smoky oak, rendering rich and complex wines with deep, full-bodied flavors.
1992: Ripe and complex, with earthy pear and pineapple flavors that pick up a nice touch of toasty oak on the finish. Finish goes on and on. **91**
Diamond T Estate 1991: Rich, complex and lively, with pretty spice, pear, apple and melon notes that are bright and elegant. **90**

LOGAN WINERY CHARDONNAY MONTEREY COUNTY (★★): Simple with elegant pear and citrus notes.
1993: Earthy with a pungent, grassy edge to the pear and apple notes, but it has appealing flavors and is elegant. **84**
1992: Elegant, with simple, pleasant pear, peach and spice notes. **84**
1991: Fruity, with a focused, spicy edge to the apple and pear aromas and flavors. **84**

TALLEY VINEYARDS
Arroyo Grande, San Luis Obispo County
F: 1986. **O:** Talley Family. **W:** Steve Rasmussen.
S: None.

OVERALL $18-30 ★★

WINE RATINGS
Chardonnay Arroyo Grande Valley ★★
Pinot Noir Arroyo Grande Valley ★★

WINERY DATA
C: 6,000. **V:** 102 acres in Arroyo Grande Valley, Edna Valley. **G:** Chardonnay (80 acres), Pinot Noir (12), Sauvignon Blanc (5), Riesling (1), Other (4). **P:** None.

Longtime farmers in Arroyo Grande Valley, the Talley family turned to planting vineyards in 1982 and to winemaking in 1986, while still selling a portion of their 102 acres in grapes to customers such as Au Bon Climat. They've slowly built production to 6,000 cases, with Chardonnay and Pinot Noir the main wines. So far Au Bon Climat has a quality edge with Talley grapes, but this winery is worth watching.

TASTING NOTES

CHARDONNAY ARROYO GRANDE VALLEY (★★): Lean and crisp, but expectations are high for this wine and vineyard, as the 1993 was a marked improvement.
1993: Pleasantly fruity, with light pear, honey and spice notes that are well focused in a medium-bodied style. Shows more depth and finesse than most 1993s. **88**
1991: Lean and crisp, with simple apple and vanilla flavors. **81**

PINOT NOIR ARROYO GRANDE VALLEY (★★): Marked by quality and stylistic swings, impressive in 1990, so better things may come.
1992: Tight and compact, with a tannic edge to the herb, cola and fruit flavors. **82**
1990: Dark in color, with firm, tight black cherry and currant flavors that are closed now, but it finishes with a pretty array of fruit. **87**
1989: Tannic, with modest cherry, blackberry and spice notes. **75**

IVAN TAMAS WINERY
Livermore Valley
F: 1984. **O:** Ivan Tamas Fuezy. **W:** Ivan Tamas. **S:** None.

OVERALL $7-9 ★★

WINE RATINGS
Cabernet Sauvignon Livermore Valley
    Le Clan des Quatre Vineyards   ★
Chardonnay Livermore Valley
    Hayes Ranch   ★★
Sauvignon Blanc Livermore Valley
    Figoni Ranch   ★★

WINERY DATA
C: 45,000. V: None. G: None. P: Cabernet Sauvignon (Livermore Valley), Chardonnay (Livermore Valley), Sauvignon Blanc, Sémillon (Livermore Valley), Other (Livermore Valley).

This negociant brand owned by Ivan Tamas Fuezy with Steve Mirassou as a partner has grown to 45,000 cases of Cabernet, Chardonnay, Trebbiano and Sauvignon Blanc, all from purchased grapes. Chardonnay at 20,000 cases is the volume leader. All the wines carry the Livermore Valley appellation, with Hayes Ranch (Chardonnay) and Figoni Ranch (Sauvignon Blanc) as vineyard-designated wines. Quality is usually fair, but occasionally good.

TASTING NOTES

VARIOUS BOTTLINGS:
Cabernet Sauvignon Livermore Valley Le Clan des Quatre Vineyards 1991: Smells fruity and floral, but it turns earthy and herbal on the palate, drying out on the finish. Decent but nothing more. **77**
Chardonnay Livermore Valley Hayes Ranch 1993: Light and pleasantly fruity, generous with its fresh pear and apple fruit that lingers on the finish. Ready now. **84**
Chardonnay Livermore Valley Hayes Ranch 1992: Lean and a bit earthy, with citrus and pear notes of modest depth. **82**
Sauvignon Blanc Livermore Valley Figoni Ranch 1992: Light and crisp, with simple green apple and lemon flavors. **82**

LANE TANNER
Santa Maria Valley
F: 1989. O: Lane Tanner. W: Lane Tanner. S: None.

OVERALL $20-30 ★★

WINE RATINGS
Pinot Noir Santa Barbara County   ★★
Pinot Noir Santa Ynez Valley
    Sanford & Benedict Vineyard   ★★

WINERY DATA
C: 1,500. V: None. G: None. P: Pinot Noir (Santa Maria Valley), Pinot Noir (Santa Ynez Valley).

Chemist Lane Tanner worked for Mount Konocti, Zaca Mesa, Firestone and Hitching Post wineries before starting her own 1,500-case Pinot Noir-only brand using grapes bought from Sierra Madre, Bien Nacido and Sanford & Benedict vineyards. The Sanford & Benedict wine is part of the Signature Series, for which six local producers are each sold 3 tons of Pinot Noir, to make wines that reflect their own individual styles. Tanner's wine carries the Santa Barbara appellation.

TASTING NOTES

PINOT NOIR VARIOUS BOTTLINGS (★★): The style avoids overripe grapes, aiming for a racy, delicate style of Pinot Noir that's lighter and more elegant than many from this area. Worth watching.
Santa Barbara County 1992: A spicy, peppery wine with racy fruit flavors that echo cherry and vegetal notes. **84**
Santa Barbara County 1991: Gamy and earthy, with leathery, herbal flavors that overshadow the spicy cherry and currant notes. **79**
Santa Barbara County Sierra Madre Vineyard 1990: A firm yet delicate wine with earthy, spicy black cherry and cedar notes that are intense. **85**
Santa Barbara County Sierra Madre Vineyard Hitching Post 1987: Simple and pleasant, with ripe raspberry, spice, vanilla and nutmeg flavors that linger. **81**
Santa Ynez Valley Sanford & Benedict Vineyard 1992: Thin and tart, with a lean core of earthy berry flavors. **82**
Santa Ynez Valley Sanford & Benedict Vineyard 1991: Dark, rich and tightly wound, serving up full-bodied herb, cherry and spice flavors that are compact, firm and tannic. **88**
Santa Ynez Valley Sanford & Benedict Vineyard 1989: Ripe and compact, with generous cherry, raspberry and tobacco flavors. **85**

TEAL LAKE CELLARS

This is a second label for Cache Cellars (see listing).

TEMPLETON WINERY

This is a second label for Mastantuono (see listing).

TERRA ROSA

This is a second label for Laurel Glen Vineyard (see listing).

THE TERRACES

Napa Valley
F: 1985. **O:** W. Hogue Vineyards Family Corp. **W:** Wayne Hogue, Chuck Wagner. **S:** None.

OVERALL	$16-40	★★★

WINE RATINGS

Cabernet Sauvignon Napa Valley		★★★
Zinfandel Napa Valley		★★★

WINERY DATA
C: 700. **V:** 7 acres in Rutherford. **G:** Cabernet Sauvignon (4 acres), Zinfandel (3). **P:** None.

Personal investment counselor Wayne Hogue was born and raised on a farm in Riverside, in Southern California, and in 1977 he bought his Napa Valley vineyard off Silverado Trail. It's a 7-acre vineyard planted to Cabernet Sauvignon and Zinfandel, with winemaking handled by Chuck Wagner of Caymus Vineyards. Both the Zinfandel and Cabernet reflect Wagner's effort to stretch the band of flavors and frame them with toasty oak. The Cabernet spends 36 months in oak, almost a year longer than most Napa Valley Cabernets. Production and distribution are limited. Best to write the winery in Rutherford to obtain the wines.

TASTING NOTES

CABERNET SAUVIGNON NAPA VALLEY (★★★): Despite a few brilliant vintages, quality has dipped slightly; whether it's just the vintages or a stylistic change is unclear. Certainly the wines from 1986 and 1987 were exciting, with complex flavors and fine tannins.
1990: The extremely leathery and tannic notes override the cedar, black currant and plum flavors that lurk beneath. **86**

1989: Dark, rich and supple, it offers rich currant, herb and anise flavors that are polished and fleshy, with shades of light vanilla oak. **88**
1988: Firm and lean, with a tight range of currant, cedar and anise flavors and oaky vanilla nuances. **88**
1987: Dark and complex, with layers of herb, currant and cherry flavors, packed with firm tannins and fine depth. **92**
1986: Rich, deep, complex and concentrated, with toasty currant, spice and herb aromas and flavors, a ripe, profound, powerful wine. **91**

ZINFANDEL NAPA VALLEY (★★★): Shares the Cabernet's intensity and range of flavors, with fine balance and pretty oak shadings.
1991: A claret-style Zin with rich, ripe cherry, anise and spice notes that turn smooth and supple. **87**
1990: Ripe and fleshy, with pretty oak, toast and spice flavors that add complexity to the raspberry and earthy cherry notes. **88**
1989: Lavishly oaked, with strong, toasty dill flavors, but underneath is a solid core of ripe berry and cherry notes that turn to raspberry on the finish. **88**
1988: Combines smoky, spicy aromas with blueberry and ripe cherry flavors for a stylish, complex wine. **86**
1987: Concentrated, intense raspberry and plum flavors are framed by lavish spice and mint nuances from oak. **89**
1985: Shows rich, ripe plum and raspberry flavors and a hint of chocolate. **87**

SEAN H. THACKREY & CO.

Bolinas, Marin County
F: 1980. **O:** Sean H. Thackrey. **W:** Sean H. Thackrey. **S:** None.

OVERALL	$15-30	★★★

WINE RATINGS

Syrah Napa Valley Orion		★★★

WINERY DATA
C: 2,000. **V:** None. **G:** None. **P:** Petite Sirah, Syrah (Napa Valley), Mourvèdre, Syrah, Grenache, Nebbiolo (California).

Professional art dealer Sean Thackrey thought winemaking might be a creative outlet for himself. In 1980 he started making small lots of wine, gradually focusing on what he calls "native American varietals," mostly old-vine Mourvèdre, Petite Sirah and Syrah, all from purchased grapes. For years, his key Syrah vineyard was in Yountville, but it has since been purchased by Swanson. A second key vineyard source, Marston Vineyard on Spring Mountain, provided Petite Sirah, but it has since been leased to Beringer, and is currently being replanted. Thackrey is now focusing on Rossi Vineyard near Spottswoode in St. Helena for his Syrah. The vines, planted in 1905, yield a half-ton per acre. Pleiades is a blend of lesser wines, aimed for immediate consumption.

TASTING NOTES

SYRAH NAPA VALLEY ORION (★★★): Despite changing vineyard sources, the style remains ripe and high extract, well oaked with big, but polished tannins. Ages well.
1990: Big, rich, dark and chewy, with potent plum, cherry and leather flavors that pick up an earthy, peppery edge. **83**
1989: Intense, ripe, deep and rich, with tiers of plum, cherry and chocolate flavors, finishing with lavish oak and firm tannins. **90**
1988: Ripe, rich and generous, glowing with meaty berry and pepper flavors that are smooth, polished and tannic. **89**
1987: Dark, dense and remarkably supple, with layers of plum and cherry flavors graced with hints of mint and spice, rounded out with delicious oak. **92**
1986: Deep, dense and dark, with mint and pepper overtones to the plum and cherry flavors. **89**

THOMAS-HSI
Napa Valley
F: 1988. **O:** Charles Thomas & Lili Hsi Thomas. **W:** Charles Thomas. **S:** None.

OVERALL	$18	★★★

WINE RATINGS	
Chardonnay Napa Valley	★★★

WINERY DATA
C: 180. **V:** None. **G:** None. **P:** Chardonnay (Napa Valley).

One of California's smallest commercial brands, Thomas-Hsi is a 180-case Chardonnay-only venture with the husband-wife team of Charles Thomas and Lili Hsi. Thomas is the talented former winemaker for Robert Mondavi who in 1994 moved to Kendall-Jackson, and Hsi is a wine marketer also employed by Kendall-Jackson. Your best chance to buy the wines is to contact the winery.

TASTING NOTES

CHARDONNAY NAPA VALLEY (★★★): Well crafted, with a complex array of flavors, medium oak shadings and good intensity.
1991: Firm and concentrated, with a spicy, earthy citrus and grapefruit edge to the ripe pear flavors and light oak shadings. **87**

TIFFANY HILL
Arroyo Grande, San Luis Obispo County
F: 1986. **O:** Paragon Vineyard Co. Inc. **W:** Gary Mosby. **S:** None.

OVERALL	$20	NR

WINE RATINGS	
Chardonnay Edna Valley	NR

WINERY DATA
C: 3,000. **V:** N/A. **G:** N/A. **P:** N/A.

Ed Nivens, owner of Paragon Vineyards in Edna Valley, the major supplier of Chardonnay to Edna Valley Vineyards, owns this brand, which bottles some 3,000 cases of Chardonnay each year. Distribution is very limited.

TIN PONY
This is a second label of Iron Horse Vineyards (see listing).

TOBIN JAMES
Paso Robles
F: 1987. **O:** Tobin James Shumrick. **W:** Tobin James Shumrick. **S:** None.

OVERALL	$11-20	★★★

WINE RATINGS	
Cabernet Sauvignon Paso Robles	
Private Stash	★★

Cabernet Sauvignon San Luis Obispo
County Twilight ★★
Chardonnay Paso Robles ★★★
Merlot Paso Robles Full Moon ★★
Merlot San Luis Obispo County
Made in the Shade ★★
Pinot Noir Santa Barbara
County Black Tie ★★
Pinot Noir Santa Barbara
County Sunshine ★★
Zinfandel Paso Robles Big Shot ★★
Zinfandel Paso Robles Big Time ★★
Zinfandel Paso Robles
Blue Moon Reserve ★★
Zinfandel Paso Robles Solar Flair ★★★
Zinfandel Paso Robles Sure Fire ★★★

WINERY DATA
C: 6,000. **V:** None. **G:** None. **P:** Cabernet Sauvignon, Chardonnay, Merlot, Zinfandel (San Luis Obispo County), Pinot Noir (Santa Barbara County).

Tobin James "Toby" Shumrick worked for Eberle Winery in the early 1980s before moving on to Peachy Canyon Winery in 1984, where he started his own brand. He has focused on Paso Robles-grown Cabernet, Chardonnay and Zinfandel (including standard, Reserve and late-harvest bottlings), along with Pinot Noir purchased from Monterey and Santa Barbara Counties. Most of the wines carry exotic nicknames, such as Big Shot and Blue Moon Reserve Zinfandels, Made in the Shade Merlot, Private Stash Cabernet and Solar Flair, a dessert-style Zinfandel.

TASTING NOTES

CABERNET SAUVIGNON VARIOUS BOTTLINGS (★★): Features ripe, bright and juicy fruit flavors of moderate depth and concentration, typical of the area.
Paso Robles Private Stash 1990: Ripe and smooth, with rich currant, plum and black cherry flavors and firm tannins. **84**
Paso Robles Private Stash 1989: Offers layers of intense plum, currant and cherry flavors. **88**
San Luis Obispo County Twilight 1991: Fresh and fruity, displaying jammy cherry, berry and raspberry flavors that ooze across the palate. **86**

CHARDONNAY PASO ROBLES (★★★): Ripe, rich and complex.

1991: Ripe and rich, with bold pear and pineapple flavors and subtle, buttery oak shadings. **89**

MERLOT VARIOUS BOTTLINGS (★★): Shares the Cabernet's bright fruit and weight, with a touch of herbs.
Paso Robles Full Moon 1991: Brimming with ripe, juicy raspberry and cranberry aromas and flavors, this is an unusual if not distinctive style of Merlot. **86**
San Luis Obispo County Made in the Shade 1992: Bright and fruity, with spicy herb and currant flavors that are quite appealing. **84**

PINOT NOIR VARIOUS BOTTLINGS (★★): Distinctive for its earthy cola and cherry notes.
Santa Barbara County Black Tie 1992: Intense and spicy, with a narrow beam of cherry and herb notes. Best after 1995. **84**
Santa Barbara County Sunshine 1990: Supple, elegant and delicate, brimming with fresh, ripe, spicy plum, cherry and anise notes that are firm and concentrated. **88**

ZINFANDEL VARIOUS BOTTLINGS: Offers lots of ripe, almost jammy berry and raspberry flavors, ample alcohol and smooth tannins; the dessert-style bottling is good, but shows why so many wineries stopped making this intense and high-octane wine.
Paso Robles Big Shot 1990: A bold, ripe, seductive wine that packs in lots of flavor. The cherry, raspberry, plum and spice flavors are smooth and potent. **88**
Paso Robles Big Time 1991: Smooth and fruity, with generous blackberry and plum aromas and flavors that remain on the velvety finish. **82**
Paso Robles Blue Moon Reserve 1991: Firm and flavorful, with a nice shot of wild berry, plum and spice aromas and flavors, finishing with a touch of toast. **84**
Paso Robles Blue Moon Reserve 1990: Tart and earthy, with a gamy, tannic edge, this chewy wine is for fans of hearty, spicy, peppery Zinfandel. **84**
Paso Robles Solar Flair 1992: Sweet and ripe, with cherry, berry and spice flavors. Tobin James is making a very appealing late-harvest Zin that succeeds with ripe fruit but doesn't overpower you with tannins. **84**
Paso Robles Solar Flair 1991: A sweet, dessert-style Zinfandel that packs in a pretty band of ripe cherry and raspberry flavors that are supple and lively. Would work nicely after dinner with a wedge of cheese. Masks its 15.4 percent alcohol quite well. **87**

Paso Robles Sure Fire 1991: An unusual wine, halfway between late harvest and Port, showing very smooth, ripe black cherry and plum flavors and a touch of raisin and a modest Portlike grip on the finish. Not terribly sweet. Ready now. **86**

PHILIP TOGNI VINEYARD
Spring Mountain, Napa Valley
F: 1983. O: Brigitta & Philip Togni. W: Philip Togni.
S: Tanbark Hill.

OVERALL	$14-32	★★★★

WINE RATINGS	
Black Muscat Napa Valley	★★★★
Cabernet Sauvignon Napa Valley	★★★★
Sauvignon Blanc Napa Valley	★★★

WINERY DATA
C: 2,500. V: 10.5 acres on Spring Mountain. G: Cabernet Sauvignon, Sauvignon Blanc, Black Muscat (Napa Valley). P: None.

Philip Togni's wine resumé goes like this: A graduate of the University of Bordeaux, where he studied under Emile Peynaud, he began making wine in 1954 at Château Lascombes in Margaux. In 1958 he worked at Mayacamas, followed by a stint at Chalone (where he was the first winemaker), then E. & J. Gallo, Chappellet and Cuvaison. In 1983 he and his wife Brigitta founded their estate winery on a steep slope on Spring Mountain. Production remains small at 2,500 cases, with Cabernet the volume leader at 1,750 cases, followed by smaller amounts of Sauvignon Blanc and Black Muscat. Quality is high across the board, with wines of enormous varietal intensity.

TASTING NOTES

CABERNET SAUVIGNON NAPA VALLEY (★★★★): Ultraripe, high extract, dense and chewy, packed with flavor and substantial tannins, but it comes off as well balanced and the early wines are aging well. Peaks at five years after vintage.
1992: Deep, dark and tannic, this one packs a wallop of fruit and tannin but there's a solid core of earthy currant, tar and spice flavors. **91**

1991: Rich and complex, with lovely herb and mineral notes adding complexity to the mouth-filling currant and berry flavors. **90**
1990: Plush and flavorful, with deep, concentrated plum, currant, blackberry, pepper and anise flavors that extend onto a smooth, supple finish. **92**
1989: Tough and tannic, with herbal, tarry, gamy notes around a core of ripe, jammy currant and berry flavors. **84**
1988: Deliciously rich and concentrated, with intense, ripe plum, black cherry, vanilla, sage and spice notes that are long and full on the palate. Firmly tannic. **90**
1987: Plush and generous, with lots of ripe currant, cassis, mint and plum flavors that are rich, deep, supple, wonderfully thick and complex, finishing with firm tannins. **94**
1986: A big, rich, concentrated wine, firmly tannic, with sharply defined black currant flavors that are thick and powerful. **90**
1985: Lavishly oaked, with a spicy cedar note that overrides the thick, austere, concentrated black currant, plum and cherry flavors. Firmly tannic. **89**
1984: Cedary oak notes overshadow the ripe, earthy plum and currant flavors. **85**
1983: Still hard, tight and tannic, with a core of weedy black currant flavors framed by spicy, cedary oak. **84**

SAUVIGNON BLANC NAPA VALLEY (★★★): Stretches the range of flavors on this varietal, often to extremes with intense, pungent, grassy flavors.
1992: Shows exaggerated Sauvignon Blanc flavors that range from wildly herbaceous to fig and citrus. **87**

TOPAZ
Napa Valley
F: 1988. O: Jeff Sowells. W: Jeff Sowells. S: None.

OVERALL	$16-25	★★

WINE RATINGS	
Cabernet Blend Napa Valley	
Rouge de Trois	NR

WINERY DATA
C: 300. V: None. G: None. P: N/A.

Jeff Sowells works as a consultant in addition to making a few hundred cases of two wines: a dessert-style wine using Sauvignon Blanc and Sémillon and a Cabernet blend called Rouge de Trois (mostly Cabernet, with 25 percent Merlot and 15 percent Cabernet Franc).

TASTING NOTES

CABERNET BLEND NAPA VALLEY ROUGE DE TROIS (NR):
1990: A vegetal wine with green bean and herb notes and hints of currant and berry flavors that add complexity. Balanced and not too tannic. It's 60 percent Cabernet Sauvignon, 25 percent Merlot and 15 percent Cabernet Franc. **82**

TOPOLOS
Sonoma County
F: 1963. O: Michael, Jerry & Christine Topolos. W: Jac Jacobs. S: None.

OVERALL	$9-20	★★

WINE RATINGS

Cabernet Blend Sonoma County Riserva	★
Cabernet Sauvignon Sonoma County	★
Chardonnay Sonoma County	
Dry Farmed Old Vines	
Barrel Fermented	★
Pinot Noir Sonoma Mountain	
Dry Farmed	★
Zinfandel Sonoma County	★★
Zinfandel Sonoma County Ultimo	★★
Zinfandel Sonoma County Rossi Ranch	★★

WINERY DATA
C: 18,000. V: 50 acres in Sonoma Mountain, Russian River, Sonoma County. G: Cabernet Sauvignon, Chardonnay, Pinot Noir, Zinfandel. P: None.

Red wine specialist Topolos has shortened its name (from Topolos at Russian River) and added Chardonnay, but Alicante Bouschet, Petite Sirah and Zinfandel (Rossi Ranch) are the wines it is best known for (although Cabernet and Pinot Noir are also part of the product mix). The Topolos family, owners since 1978, have 50 acres in vines, and quality is generally in the fair to good range. Production is 18,000 cases.

TASTING NOTES

CABERNET BLEND SONOMA COUNTY RISERVA (★):
1991: Intense and peppery, with more beet and herb notes than classic currant or cherry flavors. **79**

CABERNET SAUVIGNON SONOMA COUNTY (★): Recent vintages have been lean and lacking in ripe fruit flavors.
1992: Lean and tannic, with a narrow band of herb, cranberry and raspberry flavors. **83**

CHARDONNAY SONOMA COUNTY DRY FARMED OLD VINES BARREL FERMENTED (★): Crisp and lean, with a lemony edge and not much ripe fruit.
1992: Tart and oaky, a mouth-puckering wine that finishes with a touch of lemon. **79**

PINOT NOIR SONOMA MOUNTAIN DRY FARMED (★): The Sonoma Mountain 1992 was simple in a great year.
1992: Doesn't have the richness or complexity that its appearance suggests. Simple, with light flavors. **79**

ZINFANDEL SONOMA COUNTY (★★):
1992: Firm, tight, compact and earthy, but spicy raspberry flavors sneak through. **84**
1991: Tart and lean, with a narrow band of cherry and cranberry flavors. **81**

ZINFANDEL SONOMA COUNTY ULTIMO OLD VINES (★★):
1992: Austere, with a green, unripe edge to the flavors, but on the finish the peppery raspberry and blackberry flavors stay with you; needs food to take off the tannic edge. **83**
1991: Strives for complexity with its intensity and tannins, showing minty currant and raspberry flavors. **84**
1988: Earthy, tannic and rustic, with hard-edged berry and cherry flavors buried under the tannins. **77**

ZINFANDEL SONOMA COUNTY ROSSI RANCH (★★): The best of the reds, but only good, as it too is made in a crisp, lean style.
1992: Austere, with a leathery, pickley edge to the raspberry flavors. **78**
1991: Crisp and lean, with spicy, earthy, berry notes. **85**
1990: Dark, thick and extremely youthful, full of extract and color, loaded with weedy currant and blackberry flavors. **84**

1989: The tart, puckering texture lets only a portion of the ripe blackberry and spice flavors through. **84**

MARIMAR TORRES ESTATE
Green Valley-Sonoma
F: 1978. **O:** Torres Family. **W:** Barbara Lindblom. **S:** None.

OVERALL	$20-25	★★★★

WINE RATINGS

Chardonnay Green Valley-Sonoma Don Miguel Vineyard	★★★★
Pinot Noir Green Valley-Sonoma Don Miguel Vineyard	★★★

WINERY DATA
C: 10,000. **V:** 45 acres in Green Valley-Sonoma. **G:** Chardonnay (30 acres), Pinot Noir (15), Parellada (0.5). **P:** None.

Marimar Torres is a member of the well-known Torres wine family of Spain. In 1983, Torres, along with her father Miguel, ended a search for prime California vineyard property in Sonoma's Green Valley. She now presides over the 45-acre Don Miguel Vineyard, which is planted to Chardonnay (30 acres) and Pinot Noir (15 acres). Production is 10,000 cases, with Chardonnay holding an edge in quality.

TASTING NOTES

CHARDONNAY GREEN VALLEY-SONOMA DON MIGUEL VINEYARD (★★★★): Beautifully crafted, ripe, rich, smooth and polished, with intense fruit flavors and lots of oak.
1992: Rich, smooth and polished, with a creamy texture and ripe, broad pear, apple and spice notes, turning elegant and refined. **91**
1991: Rich, smooth and complex, with layers of honey, pear, toast and hazelnut flavors. **90**

PINOT NOIR GREEN VALLEY-SONOMA DON MIGUEL VINEYARD (★★★): Improving, with herb and cherry-laced fruit and deft oak shadings.
1992: Ripe and supple, with a trim band of plum, herb and cherry flavors. **86**

TREFETHEN VINEYARDS
Napa Valley
F: 1973. **O:** Trefethen Family. **W:** Peter Luthi. **S:** Eshcol.

OVERALL	$9-19	★★★

WINE RATINGS

Cabernet Sauvignon Napa Valley	★★
Cabernet Sauvignon Napa Valley Reserve	★★★
Chardonnay Napa Valley	★★★
Pinot Noir Napa Valley	★
White Riesling Napa Valley	★★

WINERY DATA
C: 95,000. **V:** 573 acres in Napa Valley. **G:** Chardonnay (226 acres), Cabernet Sauvignon (108), Merlot (32), Riesling (40), Cabernet Franc (4), Pinot Noir (163). **P:** Chardonnay, Cabernet Sauvignon (Napa Valley).

In 1968, former Kaiser Industries executive Gene Trefethen and his wife Katie purchased the old Eschol estate north of Napa, where in 1973 their son, John, and his wife, Janet, founded Trefethen Vineyards. The family has a large vineyard (573 acres) dominated by Chardonnay (226 acres), Pinot Noir (163) and Cabernet (108). The winery's (and vineyard's) strength is Chardonnay, although the Cabernet is well balanced and best in warmest years. A new Estate Reserve Cabernet, using hillside grapes, shows more intensity.

TASTING NOTES

CABERNET SAUVIGNON NAPA VALLEY (★★): Medium-bodied, well balanced with herb and cherry notes and mild tannins.
1989: Lean and compact, with spicy dried cherry and plum flavors, it picks up herbal, leathery notes and light oak shadings. **84**
1988: Lean and crisp, with modest berry and currant flavors that smooth out. **82**
1987: Marked by ripe cherry, strawberry and tobacco flavors that turn cedary. **86**
1986: Firmly tannic, but the ripe currant, plum and cherry flavors are attractive. **84**

CABERNET SAUVIGNON NAPA VALLEY RESERVE (★★★): Shows more depth, intensity and complexity. Aged in bottle at the winery for a later release.

1989: Marked by pleasant cedary oak, herb and currant flavors and mild tannins. **86**

1986: Very firm and astringent, with mature spice, herb and toast flavors complementing the cherry and currant notes. **82**

Chardonnay Napa Valley (★★★): Once among Napa's best it is now more ordinary. The style remains the same, but the resulting wines come across as simple and fruity. No malolactic, barrel fermentation or *sur lie* aging. Little new oak either. Can age well, but often older vintages that are held back for longer aging are tired on release.

1993: Crisp and flinty, with a citrus and spice edge to the pear and melon notes. Oak stays in the background. **86**

1992: Crisp and simple, on the austere side, with modest leafy, floral apple flavors. **83**

Trentadue Winery
Alexander Valley
F: 1969. **O:** Leo & Evelyn Trentadue. **W:** Chris Gebhardt. **S:** None.

Overall	$10-11	★★

Wine Ratings

Cabernet Sauvignon Dry Creek Valley	★
Chardonnay Alexander Valley	★
Sangiovese Alexander Valley	★★
Zinfandel Sonoma County	★★

Winery Data
C: 28,000. **V:** 187 acres in Alexander Valley, Dry Creek. **G:** Sangiovese (5 acres), Carignane (13), Merlot (44), Petite Sirah (11), Cabernet Sauvignon (25), Zinfandel (55), Chardonnay (10), Sémillon (3), Aleatico (1), Gamay (3). **P:** Petite Sirah, Zinfandel (Russian River Valley), Carignane, Petite Sirah, Zinfandel (Alexander Valley).

Rustic reds are still the main focus at Trentadue Winery off of Highway 101 east of Chateau Souverain near Geyserville. The family owns 187 acres in vines, the majority in red varieties. Case production is 28,000 with quality in the fair to good range.

Tasting Notes

Cabernet Sauvignon Dry Creek Valley (★): The 1989 showcases the rustic, chunky, tannic house style.

1989: A ripe, chunky, tannic Cabernet made in a hearty style. **77**

Chardonnay Alexander Valley (★): The 1992 strayed into smoky, meaty flavors, well off the mark for this variety.

1992: Smoky, meaty flavors dominate, so much so that the spicy pear flavors struggle to fight through. **78**

Sangiovese Alexander Valley (★★): Impressive, with the 1991 marked by bright floral, berry and cherry notes.

1991: Admirable for its fresh, bright floral, berry and cherry notes. **85**

Zinfandel Sonoma County (★★): The best of the wines, it can be ripe and flavorful, with good balance.

1992: Firm, ripe and intense, with solid, spicy mint and cherry flavors that pick up earthy, gamy notes. **88**

Truchard Vineyards
Carneros
F: 1989. **O:** Tony & Jo Ann Truchard. **W:** Ken Bernards. **S:** None.

Overall	$17-22	★★★

Wine Ratings

Cabernet Sauvignon Carneros	★★★
Chardonnay Carneros	★★★★
Merlot Carneros	★★
Pinot Noir Carneros	★★★
Syrah Carneros	★★★★

Winery Data
C: 7,000. **V:** 169 acres in Carneros. **G:** Syrah (4 acres), Chardonnay, Merlot, Pinot Noir. **P:** None.

When Tony and Jo Ann Truchard decided to buy land and plant grapes in 1973, they chose Carneros, where land was far less expensive than in Napa and the potential for winegrowing largely unknown. It proved a wise move, as the Truchards have assembed 169 acres in vineyards on a sloping grade that extends to the northern boundary of Carneros west of the city of Napa. The winery's (and the vineyard's) focus is on Chardonnay, Merlot, Pinot Noir and Syrah, the latter showing tremendous potential on the steep rocky soils at the top of the Truchard hillside. The Truchards' Chardonnay, Merlot and Pinot Noir grapes are popular among area wineries; Acacia and Duckhorn are among the dozens who've purchased them and been pleased with their quality. Now retired from his medical practice, Tony Truchard oversees the vineyard, and the goal is to isolate the best sections of the vineyard for his own wines, yet still sell grapes. Production is 7,000 cases but headed upward, with quality high across the board. Worth watching.

TASTING NOTES

CABERNET SAUVIGNON CARNEROS (★★★): Typically smooth and polished, with supple currant, spice and chocolate notes.
1991: Supple and compact, a well proportioned Cabernet with currant and cherry flavors that turn tannic. **87**
1990: Ripe and spicy, with pepper and currant notes that pick up pretty toast and buttery oak flavors. **86**
1989: Smooth and buttery, with a chocolaty, spicy vanilla streak running through the prune and black cherry flavors. **85**

CHARDONNAY CARNEROS (★★★★): Ripe with deft balance between rich, tropical fruit and pretty oak shadings.
1993: Elegant, with well defined pear, spice and smoky oak shadings, turning moderately rich on the finish. **89**
1992: Intense and lively, with a band of elegant, spicy pear, pineapple, vanilla and nutmeg flavors. **90**
1991: Packs in a lot of flavor, with spice, pear, apple and pineapple notes, finishing with complexity, depth and a hint of smoky oak. **90**
1990: Firm and focused, with straight-ahead apricot and pear aromas and flavors that are crisp and appealing. **82**

MERLOT CARNEROS (★★): Solid in a medium-bodied style, with attractive herb, currant and anise notes.
1991: Firm and spicy, with herb, currant, black cherry and anise notes. **85**
1990: Strong herb and chocolate notes run through to the crisp, spicy finish. A lean wine with attractive flavors. **85**
1989: Sturdy, with simple raspberry and plum flavors, turning lean and tannic. **81**

PINOT NOIR CARNEROS (★★★): On the lighter, delicate style of late after a very ripe 1989, but the style emphasizes fleshy fruit and light oak.

1992: Smooth, delicate and soft in texture, with appealing black cherry and spice flavors. **84**
1991: Light and simple, with appealing raspberry and blackberry flavors. **82**
1990: Firm and fragrant, with a pleasant loganberry edge to the cola, cherry and oak notes. **86**
1989: Rich, ripe cherry, plum and currant flavors lead to hints of anise and spicy oak. **88**

SYRAH CARNEROS (★★★★): May well be the star, as the 1992 and 1993 show tremendous richness, depth and character, and intensity without weight. Shows classic Syrah flavors with finesse.
1993: Rich and exotic, with ripe plum jam, cherry, spice and mineral flavors, turning complex and elegant with plush tannins. **93**
1992: Delivers classic pepper, tobacco and spicy cherry flavors, with firm, crisp tannins and a pretty anise aftertaste. **89**

TUDAL WINERY
St. Helena, Napa Valley
F: 1979. **O:** Tudal Family. **W:** Arnold Tudal. **S:** None.

OVERALL	$18	★★★

WINE RATINGS

Cabernet Sauvignon Napa Valley	★★★

WINERY DATA
C: 1,800. **V:** 7 acres in Napa Valley. **G:** Cabernet Sauvignon (7 acres). **P:** None.

Replacing an old walnut grove with vines, Arnold Tudal founded this small vineyard and winery north of St. Helena in 1979. The 7-acre Cabernet vineyard produces 1,800 cases a year, with wines that are consistently good but short of outstanding.

TASTING NOTES

CABERNET SAUVIGNON NAPA VALLEY (★★★): Quality runs with the vintages, and in very good, ripe years the fruit is ripe and polished with mild tannins and modest oak shadings. Drinks well early.
1990: Smooth, supple and stylish, a spicy wine with ripe currant and chocolate flavors extending onto a generous finish. **88**

1989: Lean, oaky and sour, simple and diluted, with hints of oak and plum. **74**

1988: Simple, tart and crisp, with earthy currant and berry flavors that turn tannic. **80**

1986: Impressive for its elegance and sharply focused, fresh, ripe, rich black cherry and currant flavors. **87**

1985: Elegant and well proportioned, with layers of ripe cherry, currant and cedar flavors, turning supple. **87**

1984: Combines richness with elegance, offering ripe black cherry and currant flavors and a touch of spicy oak. **89**

TULOCAY WINERY
Napa Valley
F: 1975. **O:** William Cadman. **W:** William Cadman. **S:** None.

OVERALL	$12-14	★★

WINE RATINGS

Cabernet Sauvignon Napa Valley Cliff Vineyard	★★
Cabernet Sauvignon Napa Valley DeCelles Vineyard	★★
Cabernet Sauvignon Napa Valley Egan Vineyard	★
Chardonnay Napa Valley DeCelles Vineyard	★★
Pinot Noir Napa Valley Haynes Vineyard	★
Zinfandel Napa Valley Casanova Vineyards	★★

WINERY DATA
C: 2,000. **V:** None. **G:** None. **P:** Pinot Noir, Cabernet Sauvignon, Zinfandel, Chardonnay (Napa Valley).

Former stockbroker William Cadman has worked at several Napa wineries, and on the side makes 2,000 cases of Cabernet, Chardonnay, Pinot Noir and Zinfandel, all from purchased grapes. The wines are often lean and earthy, simple by Napa standards, but occasionally they receive good marks. Each of the wines carries a vineyard designation.

TASTING NOTES

CABERNET SAUVIGNON NAPA VALLEY CLIFF VINEYARD (★★): Good on occasion, but variable as the 1990 demonstrated.

1991: A touch earthy, with a barnyard edge, but there's a modest level of plum and cherry flavors. **85**

1990: Earthy, with a metallic edge to the flavors. **74**

CABERNET SAUVIGNON NAPA VALLEY DECELLES VINEYARD (★★):

1991: Laced with herb and black olive flavors that add complexity to the spicy cherry and currant notes. **87**

CABERNET SAUVIGNON NAPA VALLEY EGAN VINEYARD (★):

1988: Extremely tannic, firm and tight, holding its ample currant and plum flavors in check. **84**

1987: Intensely weedy and herbal, with more vegetables than fruit pouring through. **74**

CHARDONNAY NAPA VALLEY DECELLES VINEYARD (★★): Improving lately with riper fruit flavors and fewer earthy notes.

1993: Has a hint of earthiness on the nose, but it's more palatable to drink, with ripe pear and oak shadings of modest depth. **83**

1991: Ripe, smooth and polished, with spicy pear, pineapple and buttery oak flavors that are complex. **87**

PINOT NOIR NAPA VALLEY HAYNES VINEYARD (★): Light, simple and earthy, with modest fruit notes.

1989: Sweet oak flavors of vanilla and spice dominate the modest cherry and cola notes. **76**

1988: Leathery, with a swampy edge. **75**

TURLEY WINE CELLARS
St. Helena, Napa Valley
F: 1993. **O:** Larry & Suzanne Turley. **W:** Helen Turley. **S:** None.

OVERALL	$20-25	★★★★

WINE RATINGS

Zinfandel Napa Valley Aida Vineyard	★★★★
Zinfandel Napa Valley Hayne Vineyard	★★★★
Zinfandel Napa Valley Moore Vineyard	★★★★

WINERY DATA
C: 3,500. **V:** None. **G:** None. **P:** Zinfandel (Napa Valley).

Frog's Leap co-founder Larry Turley and his wife Suzanne were partners in Frog's Leap Winery, but as that winery grew to 40,000-plus cases the Turleys decided to sell their interest and focus on small-case production of vineyard-designated Zinfandels from their property, the original Frog Farm north of St. Helena (after which Frog's Leap was named). Other vineyards include: Aida near St. Helena; Hayne, an 88-year-old vineyard near St. Helena; Moore, off Silverado Trail in northeast Napa Valley; Whitney, north of Calistoga; and Sears on Howell Mountain. Petite Sirah and Sauvignon Blanc are also produced. Turley's sister, Helen, is winemaker and focuses on reduced crop load, high-extract, richly concentrated wines. Early results are most impressive, with wines due to be released in 1995. Worth watching.

TASTING NOTES

ZINFANDEL VARIOUS BOTTLINGS (★★★★): Tasted from barrel and bottle before release, each shared a rich core of intense fruit flavors and fine balance.
Napa Valley Aida Vineyard 1993: Dark, rich and intense, with potent wild berry, chocolate, cherry and buttery oak with full-blown but polished tannins. **93**
Napa Valley Hayne Vineyard 1993: Enormously complex and concentrated, with well focused wild berry, black cherry and currant flavors, finishing with buttery oak and supple tannins. **95**
Napa Valley Moore Vineyard 1993: Tight, tart and compact, with spice, pepper and berry notes and crisp tannins. **88**

TURNBULL WINE CELLARS
Oakville, Napa Valley
F: 1979. **O:** Patrick S. O'Dell. **W:** Kristin Belair.
S: None.

OVERALL	$20	★★★

WINE RATINGS

Cabernet Sauvignon Napa Valley	★★★

WINERY DATA
C: 5,000. **V:** 64 acres in Oakville. **G:** Cabernet Sauvignon (30 acres), Merlot (14), Cabernet Franc (6), Sangiovese (6), Syrah (3), Zinfandel (1), Sémillon (2), Sauvignon Musque (2). **P:** None.

Lawyer Reverdy Johnson and architect William Turnbull founded Johnson Turnbull and produced their first Cabernet in 1979, having decided that their vineyard produced exceptional grapes and that owning a weekend retreat vineyard involved more work than they imagined. With some 20 acres of Cabernet and Cabernet Franc in Oakville, Johnson Turnbull built production to 5,000 cases by the mid-1980s. The style of wine was characterized by a strong mint, bay leaf and oregano character, so pronounced that the partners began producing two Cabernets in 1986: Vineyard Selection 67 emphasizing the oregano quality and Vineyard Selection 82 showcasing brilliant currant and cherry notes. By the late 1980s, their vineyard fell victim to phylloxera and needed to be replanted. In 1993, the winery was sold to Patrick O'Dell, who changed the name to Turnbull Wine Cellars, retained winemaker Kristin Belair and added property, expanding the winery's vineyard holdings to 64 acres. A Merlot bottling is a planned addition to the lineup.

TASTING NOTES

CABERNET SAUVIGNON NAPA VALLEY (★★★): Quality varies depending on the strengh of the minty-oregano character, but when that character's downplayed the wine displays a pretty core of currant and cherry.
1991: Shows the classic mint and bay leaf aromas of this vineyard, and it also delivers juicy currant and cherry flavors. **88**
1990: A decidedly minty wine on a lean, austere frame. **80**
1989: Distinctive for its minty edge, it turns lean, with cherry, strawberry and spice notes that finish with gritty tannins. **85**
1988: A minty, herbal wine with a nice burst of berry and currant flavors. **84**
1985: Spicy and minty, with subtle earth and currant flavors. **86**
1984: Supple, but marked by potent, spicy herb, plum, currant and cherry flavors that linger. **85**
1983: Lean and drying, picking up an earthy edge to the currant and mint notes. **85**

1982: Simple and mature, with an earthy, tannic edge to the currant and spice flavors. **81**

1981: Mature, with earthy currant and plum flavors that complement the spicy notes. **87**

1980: Spicy and full-bodied, with mint, oregano and complex herb flavors. **84**

1979: Lean and minty, with spicy bay leaf, herb and cassis flavors. Mature. **83**

Vineyard Selection 67 1990: Potently minty, but with a nice currant and plum edge underneath, turning supple. **87**

Vineyard Selection 67 1989: Spicy and minty yet crisp and austere, with hints of cherry and currant flavors. Firmly tannic. **85**

Vineyard Selection 67 1988: Marked by a spicy oregano aroma, but there's a nice core of currant, mint and eucalyptus flavors. **86**

Vineyard Selection 67 1987: Minty menthol aromas give way to ripe, rich black cherry, plum and currant flavors. **88**

Vineyard Selection 67 1986: Dense, with potent herb, bay leaf and spice notes. **86**

Vineyard Selection 82 1986: Intense and concentrated, with tart black cherry, currant, spice and cedar flavors that are sharply focused and framed by firm tannins and toasty oak. **89**

T VINE
Napa Valley
F: 1992. **O:** Greg Brown. **W:** Greg Brown. **S:** None.

OVERALL	$10	★★

WINE RATINGS	
Zinfandel Napa Valley	★★

WINERY DATA
C: 2,000. **V:** None. **G:** None. **P:** N/A.

Greg Brown produces 2,000 cases of mostly Zinfandel but also makes small quantities of Cabernet Sauvignon, Chardonnay and Sauvignon Blanc, with even smaller portions of Grenache and a Port from Petite Sirah and Alicante Bouschet.

TASTING NOTES

ZINFANDEL NAPA VALLEY (★★):
1992: Attractive for its ripe wild berry and cherry flavors made in a light and simple style. **83**

TWIN HILLS WINERY
Paso Robles
F: 1982. **O:** Caroline Scott & Glenn Reid. **W:** Caroline Scott. **S:** James J's.

OVERALL	$7-10	NR

WINE RATINGS	
Cabernet Sauvignon Paso Robles	NR
Chardonnay Paso Robles Reserve	NR
Zinfandel Paso Robles	NR

WINERY DATA
C: 5,000. **V:** 43 acres in Paso Robles. **G:** Chardonnay (20 acres), Zinfandel (15), Cabernet Sauvignon (3), Other (5). **P:** None.

James Lockshaw founded this winery in San Luis Obispo, after buying a ranch that included a vineyard. He expanded it to more than 40 acres, growing (and often producing) Cabernet, Chardonnay and Zinfandel, with production in the 10,000 case range. Since 1991, the winery has been owned by Caroline Scott and Glenn Reid, who have cut production in half to 5,000 cases and are offering a wide variety of small case lot wines, ranging from the standards such as Cabernet and Chardonnay to a blush wine, Zinfandel, Sherry and Port. Distribution is limited.

TASTING NOTES

VARIOUS BOTTLINGS (NR):
Cabernet Sauvignon Paso Robles 1991: Earthy and tanky, with a sour edge. **72**
Chardonnay Paso Robles Reserve 1992: Simple and a bit coarse, but the pineapple and spice flavors have appeal. **80**
Zinfandel Paso Robles 1991: Firm, lean and tannic, with a tight core of earthy raspberry and plum flavors. Turns tannic and gritty on the finish. **80**

M. G. VALLEJO
This is a second label of Glen Ellen Winery (see listing).

VALLEY OF THE MOON WINERY
Sonoma Valley
F: 1857. **O:** Harry Parducci. **W:** Harry Parducci Jr. **S:** None.

OVERALL	$5-25	NR

WINE RATINGS

Cabernet Sauvignon Sonoma Valley	NR
Zinfandel Sonoma Valley Reserve	NR

WINERY DATA
C: 25,000. V: 65 acres in Sonoma Valley. G: N/A. P: None.

Generic table wines are the main business of this 25,000-case winery in Glen Ellen. Its finer wines are sold from the tasting room and receive limited distribution. Quality is ordinary.

VAN DER HEYDEN VINEYARD
Napa Valley
F: 1977. O: Andre & Sande Van Der Heyden. W: Andre Van Der Heyden. S: None.

OVERALL	$10-18	★★

WINE RATINGS

Cabernet Sauvignon Alexander Valley	★★
Chardonnay Napa Valley	★
Chardonnay Napa Valley Private Reserve	★

WINERY DATA
C: 2,000. V: 14 acres in Napa Valley. G: Chardonnay (10 acres), Cabernet Sauvignon (4). P: None.

Andre and Sande Van Der Heyden own this 2,000-case winery, which uses grapes both from its own 14 acres of vineyard in Napa Valley and from Alexander Valley. Chardonnay at 1,200 cases is the volume leader, with smaller lots of Cabernet (Alexander Valley and Napa, each 300 cases) and three dessert-style wines: Riesling, Sémillon and a Cabernet. Recent bottlings have failed to impress.

TASTING NOTES

VARIOUS BOTTLINGS:
Cabernet Sauvignon Alexander Valley 1987: Tough and tannic, with a modest level of plum and spice flavors. **80**
Chardonnay Napa Valley 1991: A curious wine that's earthy and gamy, with perfumed fruit aromas, but overall it's funky. **75**

Chardonnay Napa Valley Private Reserve 1989: Lean and crisp, with modest peach and nectarine flavors and an austere, slightly astringent texture. Hints at honey on the finish. **78**

VENDANGE
This is a second label for Sebastiani Vineyards (see listing).

VENTANA VINEYARDS
Monterey County
F: 1978. O: Ventana Vineyards Winery Inc. W: Douglas Meador. S: La Tournelle.

OVERALL	$6-14	★★

WINE RATINGS

Chardonnay Monterey County	
Gold Stripe Selection	★★★
Chenin Blanc Monterey County	★★
Johannisberg Riesling Monterey County	★★
Merlot Monterey County	NR
Pinot Blanc Monterey County	NR
Sauvignon Blanc Monterey County	★★
Syrah Monterey County	NR

WINERY DATA
C: 40,000. V: 271 acres in Monterey County. G: Chardonnay (130 acres), Riesling (38), Sauvignon Blanc (26), Gewürztraminer (16), Chenin Blanc (14). P: Merlot, Pinot Blanc, Syrah (Monterey County).

Douglas Meador's Ventana Vineyard has experienced a checkered financial past, but Meador persists with a wide range of vineyard research; the 271-acre vineyard is a source of grapes to many wineries. Production has grown to 40,000 cases, led by the Gold Stripe Chardonnay (10,000 cases), which continues to improve after a serious dip in the mid-1980s when the winery and vineyard underwent a costly financial reorganization. Chenin Blanc, Johannisberg Riesling, Merlot, Pinot Blanc, Sauvignon Blanc and Syrah are also produced in smaller case quantities.

TASTING NOTES

CHARDONNAY MONTEREY COUNTY GOLD STRIPE SELECTION (★★★): Emphasizes bold, ripe and fleshy

Chardonnay flavors, with pretty oak shadings. Elegant and well proportioned. Worth watching.

1992: Appealing for its ripe pear, honey, spice and light oak shadings, all folding together nicely, with a butter and vanilla edge. **88**

1991: Smooth, ripe and creamy, with spice, pear, fig and vanilla notes that turn silky and elegant. **88**

Crystal 1990: Earthy, complex and sweet, a nicely put together wine that shows shadings of pear, honey and toast. **86**

1989: Pleasant peach, pear, earth and apple flavors are ripe, tart and clean, with good depth and intensity. Picks up interesting honey and spicy oak notes on the aftertaste. **87**

CHENIN BLANC MONTEREY COUNTY (★★):
1993: Soft and fragrant, a leafy, minty character carrying through stronger than the fruit. Ready now. **81**

JOHANNISBERG RIESLING MONTEREY COUNTY (★★):
1993: Smooth and appealing, a soft wine with modest apple and pear flavors that linger on the finish. **84**

1992: Soft and fruity, with a mineral edge to the pineapple and pear fruit. Finishes on the dry side. **82**

SAUVIGNON BLANC MONTEREY COUNTY (★★):
1993: Ripe and refreshing, a round, harmonious example of fruit-centered Sauvignon that lavishes spice and tobacco nuances on the pear, fig and honey character. **89**

1991: Smells like celery, but the soft, figgy flavors remain in balance. Seems a bit sweet, however. **77**

VIADER VINEYARDS
Howell Mountain
F: 1987. **O:** Viader Vineyards Inc. **W:** Tony Soter. **S:** None.

OVERALL	$28	★★★★

WINE RATINGS
Cabernet Blend Napa Valley	★★★★

WINERY DATA
C: 1,843. **V:** 18 acres in Napa Valley. **G:** Cabernet Sauvignon (10 acres), Cabernet Franc (8). **P:** None.

Argentine-born Delia Viader owns a densely planted 18-acre Cabernet and Cabernet Franc vineyard on Howell Mountain, where she produces just over 1,800 cases of wine, with a St. Emilion-style blend in mind. With Tony Soter (Étude, Spottswoode and others) as winemaking consultant, quality is very high. Worth watching.

TASTING NOTES

CABERNET BLEND NAPA VALLEY (★★★★): Very impressive in the first vintages, as the wines uniformly offer ripe, complex and fleshy currant, earth, anise and smoky oak flavors, with supple tannins. A blend of 60 percent Cabernet Sauvignon and 40 percent Cabernet Franc. No track record for aging, but the wines have the depth and balance to improve.

1992: Well oaked, with strong vanilla and chocolate notes, but a rich, complex core of currant and cherry fruit to match. Makes for an intriguing range of flavors. Has the tannic strength to cellar into 1997. **88**

1991: Supple and generous, with layers of ripe plum, currant, anise and smoke flavors, finishing with rich, plush tannins. **91**

1990: Ripe, complex and concentrated, with a core of rich currant, earth and berry flavors, finishing with toasty oak and supple tannins. **91**

1989: Smooth and polished, with complex cedar, spice, chocolate and cherry flavors that turn supple on the finish. **89**

VIANO VINEYARDS
Contra Costa County
F: 1946. **O:** Clement A. Viano. **W:** Clement Viano. **S:** None.

OVERALL	$8-10	★★

WINE RATINGS
Cabernet Sauvignon Contra Costa County	★★
Chardonnay Contra Costa County	★★
Dessert Contra Costa County	★★
Zinfandel Contra Costa County	★★

WINERY DATA

C: 2,000. V: 60 acres in Contra Costa County. G: Cabernet Sauvignon, Chardonnay, Zinfandel. P: None.

The Viano family founded this winery in Martinez in 1946, and owns 60 acres of vineyards from which come about 2,000 cases of Cabernet, Chardonnay, dessert wine and Zinfandel. Zinfandel at 800 cases is the volume leader. All the wines carry a Contra Costa County appellation. Distribution is very limited.

TASTING NOTES

VARIOUS BOTTLINGS (★★):

Cabernet Sauvignon California Reserve Selection 1988: Mature, with a cedary aroma and austere currant and spice notes that turn tannic on the finish. Can stand another year or so of cellaring. **81**

Dessert Contra Costa County Reserve Selection 1988: Dense, dark and chewy, a solid late-harvest Zin that shows off complex tarry and smoky, toasty oak flavors. **86**

Zinfandel Contra Costa County Sand Rock Hill Vineyard Reserve 1991: A very ripe and oaky style that somehow hangs together. The cherry and raspberry fruit borders on jammy and it's tannic and hot on the finish, but food should take off some of the rough edges. **80**

Zinfandel Contra Costa County Sand Rock Hill Vineyard Reserve 1989: Sweet and spicy, this offering from a new winery has a soft texture and brown sugar flavor running through it; highly unusual but not altogether unlikable. **81**

VIANSA WINERY
Sonoma Valley
F: 1988. O: Sam & Vicki Sebastiani. W: Sam Sebastiani. S: None.

OVERALL	$11-70	★★

WINE RATINGS

Cabernet Sauvignon	
Napa-Sonoma Counties	★★
Cabernet Sauvignon	
Napa-Sonoma Counties Reserve	★★
Chardonnay Sonoma Valley	★★
Nebbiolo California Nebbiolo	★★
Red Table Wine Napa County Thalia	★★
Zinfandel Blend Sonoma Valley Prindelo	★★

WINERY DATA

C: 12,000. V: 2 acres in Carneros. G: Sangiovese (1.5 acres), Malvasia Bianca (0.25), Vernaccia (0.3). P: Brunello (Amador), Nebbiolo (Sonoma, Amador), Trebbiano (California).

After working for and leading Sebastiani Vineyards for most of his life, Sam Sebastiani was ousted as president of the historic Sonoma winery in 1986 after a bitter family dispute about the winery's future. He and his wife, Vicki, promptly started Sam J. Sebastiani Vineyards, but due to market confusions with Sebastiani Vineyards, changed the name to Viansa (short for Vicki and Sam). They later built an attractive Italian villa-style winery on Highway 121 in Carneros, where they cater to tourists, selling some 12,000 cases of wine, mostly from purchased grapes. The long-term plan is to focus on native Italian varietals such as Sangiovese and Nebbiolo. Quality ranges from fair to good, but the real test will come with the introduction of the new wines due after 1995.

TASTING NOTES

VARIOUS BOTTLINGS:

Cabernet Blend Napa-Sonoma Counties Obsidian 1987: Austere, with crisp raspberry, cherry, herb and spice notes, but it has a supple texture before the tannins develop. **85**

Cabernet Blend Napa-Sonoma Counties Riserva Anatra Rosso 1989: An earthy, barnyardy wine that's tannic and austere. **80**

Cabernet Sauvignon Napa-Sonoma Counties 1988: Ripe and fruity, but rife with gamy, leathery flavors. **76**

Cabernet Sauvignon Napa-Sonoma Counties Reserve 1988: Simple and austere, with a narrow band of currant and earth notes and cedary tannins. **78**

Nebbiolo California Nebbiolo 1990: Light and spicy, with herb, tea and cherry flavors. **81**

Red Table Wine Napa County Thalia 1990: Ripe and plummy, with an earthy, oaky edge, but pleasantly balanced and drinkable. **83**

Zinfandel Blend Sonoma Valley Prindelo 1991: Ripe and gamy in almost equal proportions, it tastes unbalanced. **80**

Vichon Winery
Oakville, Napa Valley
F: 1980. **O:** Robert Mondavi Inc. **W:** Karen Culler.
S: None.

OVERALL	$9-28	★★★

Wine Ratings

Cabernet Sauvignon California Coastal Selection	★★
Cabernet Sauvignon Napa Valley	★★
Cabernet Sauvignon Stags Leap District	★★★
Chardonnay California Coastal Selection	★★
Chardonnay Napa Valley	★★★
Merlot California Coastal Selection	★★
Merlot Napa Valley	★★★
Sauvignon Blend Napa Valley Chevrignon	★★

Winery Data

C: 110,000. **V:** 4.5 acres in Napa Valley. **G:** Cabernet Sauvignon, Malbec. **P:** Cabernet Sauvignon, Merlot, Chardonnay, Sémillon, Sauvignon Blanc (Napa Valley), Cabernet Sauvignon, Merlot, Chardonnay (Sonoma, Santa Maria, San Luis Obispo, Monterey).

Vichon Winery was founded in 1980 by a limited partnership that included leading restaurateurs and hoteliers. "Vichon" came from the three limited partners—George Vierra, Peter Brucher and Doug Watson. Vierra oversaw winemaking with John McKay, focusing on Cabernet, Chardonnay and a Sauvignon Blanc blend called Chevrignon. In 1984 the partnership built a winery on the Oakville Grade, but investors were disappointed in the financial forecast and sold the operation to Robert Mondavi Winery in 1985. Merlot, an SLD (for Stags Leap District) Cabernet bottling, and a new line of value-oriented Coastal Selection wines have been added, boosting production to 110,000 cases, much of that from grapes grown in the south and central coast.

Tasting Notes

Cabernet Sauvignon Califorma Coastal Selection (★★): Well balanced, with supple cherry and herb notes, made for immediate consumption.
1992: Complex and elegant, with tiers of black cherry, spice and cedary oak flavors. **84**

1991: A good but simple wine with grapey Cabernet flavors that pick up herb and oak notes. **82**

Cabernet Sauvignon Napa Valley (★★): Medium-bodied, with good fruit flavors and light oak shadings, but fairly typical of Napa Cabernet.
1991: Light and herbal, with spicy currant, plum and cedary oak flavors. **84**
1990: Intense and spicy, with pretty cherry, currant, anise and cedar notes that turn rich, supple, smooth and concentrated. **88**
1989: Ripe, rich and concentrated, wrapped in a solid layer of tannin, offering a wide band of plum, blackberry and currant flavors. **89**
1988: A modest Cabernet with a seductive overlay of toast, spice and oak flavors. **84**

Cabernet Sauvignon Stags Leap District (★★★): Stags Leap District Cabernet is the star, often very rich and flavorful, with supple tannins and fine balance.
1990: Firm, chewy and flavorful, showing a nice glow of plum, currant and anise flavors, finishing with overtones of cedar, tobacco and herb. **91**
1989: Smooth, ripe and polished, with a pretty core of currant, berry, vanilla, spice and cedar flavors and a supple texture. **88**
1988: Well proportioned, with an elegant balance of currant, plum and vanilla aromas and flavors, offering subtle hints of spice, tar and chocolate. **88**
1987: A graceful, elegant, harmonious wine with subtle but rich currant, cherry and vanilla flavors that build on the finish. **87**
1986: Elegant and sophisticated, offering ripe herb, cherry, currant and anise flavors that are supported by supple tannins. **88**
1985: Rich, ripe and supple, mature now, with layers of black cherry, currant and spice flavors. **90**

Chardonnay California Coastal Selection (★★): Clean, ripe and fruity, a good value.
1993: Clean and fruity, with a citrus edge that holds the pear and spice flavors together. **82**

Chardonnay Napa Valley (★★★): Steady, with a tight core of spicy pear and light oak shadings. Well balanced.
1993: Light with modest pear and spice notes that hang with you, but ultimately it's simple. **83**

1992: Smooth, ripe and creamy, with spicy pear, apple, nutmeg and vanilla flavors that are focused and elegant. **88**
1991: Spicy and elegant, with a silky texture and appealing pear, apple and vanilla flavors in a smooth and polished package. **89**

MERLOT CALIFORNIA COASTAL SELECTION (★★): Crisp and fruity, with herb and cherry notes.
1992: Crisp and fruity, with simple cherry and currant flavors and mild tannins. **83**

MERLOT NAPA VALLEY (★★★): Lacks the consistency of the SLD Cabernet, but can be very good with dense, complex flavors.
1991: Solid and chunky, with grapey currant flavors that lack finesse. **82**
1990: Densely flavored, full of tannins, with supple currant, plum and spice flavors. **89**
1989: Ripe, spicy and rounded, with supple currant, tobacco and vanilla flavors. **87**
1988: Marked by modest currant, cherry and plum flavors. **81**
1987: Intense, with layers of ripe, supple plum and currant flavors that are well oaked and elegantly balanced. **89**
1986: Offers pretty spice, herb and currant flavors that are persistent from start to finish. **86**

SAUVIGNON BLEND NAPA VALLEY CHEVRIGNON (★★):
1993: Smooth, harmonious and delicately herbal atop a layer of pretty apple and pear fruit. **85**

VILLA HELENA WINERY
St. Helena, Napa Valley
F: 1984. **O:** Donald W. & Lydia H. McGrath. **W:** Don McGrath. **S:** None.

OVERALL	$8-20	★

WINE RATINGS
Cabernet Sauvignon	
Napa Valley Baron von Kees Vineyard	★
Chardonnay Napa Valley	NR
Viognier Napa Valley	★★

WINERY DATA
C: 2,000. **V:** 4 acres in Napa Valley. **G:** Viognier. **P:** Cabernet Sauvignon, Chardonnay (Napa Valley).

Donald and Lydia McGrath own this 2,000-case winery that focuses on Napa Valley-grown Cabernet, Chardonnay and Viognier, the latter grown in a family-owned four-acre vineyard near St. Helena. Distribution is limited and quality has been variable.

TASTING NOTES

CABERNET SAUVIGNON NAPA VALLEY BARON VON KEES VINEYARD (★): The 1990 was marked by dense, weedy, unripe fruit.
1990: Dense, weedy and vegetal, this Cabernet is difficult to like. Tastes like underripe grapes from young, overcropped vines. Marginal quality. **71**

VIOGNIER NAPA VALLEY (★★):
1992: Spicy and elegant, showing pretty, crisp pear, honey and hazelnut flavors that are fresh and lively. Finishes with a mouthwatering burst of acidity. **87**

VILLA MT. EDEN
St. Helena, Napa Valley
F: 1970. **O:** Stimson Lane Vineyards & Estates. **W:** Mike McGrath, Jed Steele. **S:** None.

OVERALL	$8-45	★★★

WINE RATINGS
Cabernet Sauvignon	
California Cellar Select	★★
Cabernet Sauvignon Mendocino County	
Signature Series	★★★★
Cabernet Sauvignon Napa Valley	★★
Cabernet Sauvignon Napa Valley	
Grand Reserve	★★
Chardonnay California Cellar Select	★★
Chardonnay Carneros Grand Reserve	★★★
Chardonnay Santa Barbara County	
Signature Series	★★★★
Merlot Napa Valley Grand Reserve	★★★
Pinot Blanc Santa Maria Valley	
Bien Nacido Vineyard Grand Reserve	★★★
Pinot Noir California Cellar Select	★★
Pinot Noir Carneros Grand Reserve	★★
Pinot Noir Santa Maria Valley	
Bien Nacido Vineyard Grand Reserve	★★
Zinfandel California Cellar Select	★★

WINERY DATA

C: 107,300. V: None. G: None. P: Cabernet Sauvignon (Napa Valley, Sonoma Valley), Pinot Noir (Mendocino, Carneros, Santa Barbara County), Zinfandel (Napa Valley, Mendocino), Merlot (Napa Valley), Chardonnay (Sonoma Valley, Carneros, Napa Valley, Monterey, Santa Barbara County).

This Oakville winery dates to 1881 and was rejuvenated in 1970 by James and Anne McWilliams, the latter the granddaughter of A.P. Giannini, founder of Bank of America. After early success, including fine 1974 and 1978 Cabernets made by Nils Venge, quality declined, and in 1982 Venge departed to Groth Vineyards. In 1986 the McWilliamses sold the winery to Stimson Lane, the owner of Chateau Ste. Michelle in Washington. Since the takeover, the focus has been on building the volume of Cabernet, Chardonnay, Merlot, Pinot Noir and Zinfandel, with appellations ranging from California to Carneros to Napa Valley. The winery owns no vineyards.

The Cellar Select Chardonnay (64,000) is the volume leader in the winery's 107,300-case output. Cabernet, Chardonnay, Merlot and Pinot Noir are made in Cellar Select and Grand Reserve styles. The new Signature Series Cabernet, with grapes from Anderson Valley, was a blockbuster in 1992.

TASTING NOTES

CABERNET SAUVIGNON CALIFORNIA CELLAR SELECT (★★): Clean and fruity, a good value in supple Cabernet.
1991: A good, simple, correct Cabernet without any extra dimensions. **82**

CABERNET SAUVIGNON MENDOCINO COUNTY SIGNATURE SERIES (★★★★): From Anderson Valley, the 1992 packed in lots of rich, complex flavors and loads of toasty buttery oak. Worth watching.
1992: Firm and chunky, with a tight, concentrated beam of cherry and currant fruit, finishing with firm tannins and a long toasty aftertaste. **92**

CABERNET SAUVIGNON NAPA VALLEY (★★), GRAND RESERVE (★★): Shows more richness, depth and concentration than the Cellar Select, but is still more mainstream Napa Cabernet than exceptional.
1990: Ripe and spicy, with currant flavors and cedary oak notes. **86**

1987: Smooth and plush, with ripe currant and cherry flavors that turn smooth and supple. **88**
1986: Pleasant, with ripe, well defined cherry and currant flavors and toasty oak. **84**
1978: Showing better than it usually does, this wine is ripe and opulent, with currant and plum flavors that turn smoky and decadent on the finish. **85**
1974: Remains a healthy ruby-garnet, with a pretty perfumed, floral aroma and rich, focused cherry and currant flavors. **90**
Grand Reserve 1991: Tight and a touch green, with firm tannins and just enough ripe currant and berry flavors. **83**
Grand Reserve 1990: The best Villa Mt. Eden Cabernet in years, it is an elegant and flavorful wine with currant and cherry notes framed by light, toasty oak. Drink it now or cellar it through the decade. **87**
Grand Reserve 1989: Simple, with currant and black cherry flavors and fine tannins. **84**
Grand Reserve 1988: Ripe and generous, with a soft, creamy texture and lively currant, plum and berry flavors. **86**

CHARDONNAY CALIFORNIA CELLAR SELECT (★★): Clean and fruity, with simple flavors.
1993: Ripe and fruity, with good depth and intensity to the pear and apple notes, turning elegant on the finish. **85**
1992: Elegant and fruity, with light pear, apple, spice and oak shadings. **83**

CHARDONNAY CARNEROS GRAND RESERVE (★★★): Bright, lively, intense and well focused, with pretty oak shadings.
1993: Showy with its smoky, toasty, buttery oak and spicy pear and apple flavors, turning smooth and complex, with finesse and grace. **91**
1992: A lovely blend of ripe, spicy pear and fig flavors and toasty buttery oak. **88**
1991: Lean and crisp, with elegant pear, pineapple and spice flavors that turn to honey and toast. **87**

CHARDONNAY SANTA BARBARA COUNTY SIGNATURE SERIES (★★★★):
1993: Makes quite a statement about where Villa Mt. Eden is headed. Bold, ripe and creamy, with ultrarich

tropical fruit, pear, honey, toast and spice flavors that fold together, finishing with excellent length, depth and concentration. Alas only 235 cases. **93**

MERLOT NAPA VALLEY GRAND RESERVE (★★★): Strikes a nice balance between herb and cherry-laced fruit with light oak notes.
1991: Smooth and supple, with currant and berry flavors and a nice touch of spice. **85**
1990: Elegant and complex, with spice, herb and mineral notes adding to the supple plum and currant flavors. The texture is smooth and fleshy, and the finish is long and lingering. Enjoyable now, but has sufficient tannins to age through 1997. **88**

PINOT BLANC SANTA MARIA VALLEY BIEN NACIDO VINEYARD GRAND RESERVE (★★★): Impressive for its bright, rich, complex flavors and deft oak shadings.
1993: Bold, ripe and creamy, with spice, pear and apple flavors that fold together nicely. **88**

PINOT NOIR VARIOUS BOTTLINGS (★★): Smooth and polished, with simple fruit flavors.
California Cellar Select 1993: Simple and correct, with a nice band of herb, cola, cherry and spice notes. **83**
Carneros Grand Reserve 1991: Supple and flavorful, with soft cherry, raspberry and plum notes. **84**
Napa Valley 1988: Lean and woody, with pleasant strawberry, herb and plum flavors. **82**
Santa Maria Valley Bien Nacido Vineyard Grand Reserve 1993: Smooth and polished, with appealing cherry, vanilla and light spice notes. **84**

ZINFANDEL CALIFORNIA CELLAR SELECT (★★): Medium-bodied, with simple but pleasant Zinfandel flavors.
1992: Firm and compact, with a tight band of earthy, tarry fruit flavors and light oak shadings. **84**
1991: Supple and fruity, with a core of nice raspberry, cherry and spice flavors. **86**
1990: Firm and focused, with spicy toast, berry and plum flavors. **84**
1989: Lean and lively, with appealing raspberry and wild berry flavors. **86**

VINE CLIFF CELLARS
Napa Valley
F: 1990. **O:** Vine Cliff Cellars. **W:** John R. Gibson. **S:** None.

OVERALL	$25-35	★★★

WINE RATINGS

Cabernet Sauvignon Napa Valley	★★★
Chardonnay Napa Valley	
Proprietress Reserve	★★★

WINERY DATA
C: 3,500. **V:** 22 acres in Napa Valley. **G:** Cabernet Sauvignon (20 acres), Cabernet Franc (0.5), Merlot (2). **P:** Chardonnay, Merlot (Napa Valley).

Crown Sterling Suites president Charles Sweeney and his wife Nell revived an old winery built on their property back in 1871 and planted 22 acres of terraced vineyard to Bordeaux varieties for their Vine Cliff Cellars winery on Silverado Trail in Oakville. Production is 3,500 cases, including a Proprietress Reserve Chardonnay made from Liparita Vineyard on Howell Mountain. Quality is very high. Worth watching.

TASTING NOTES

CABERNET SAUVIGNON NAPA VALLEY (★★★): Continues to improve, with elegant, well focused, deftly balanced wines that are balanced for aging.
1991: Elegant, with cedar, tobacco and currant flavors that fold together nicely. **88**
1990: Tight and firm, with chewy cherry and herb flavors that finish with mild tannins. **87**

CHARDONNAY NAPA VALLEY PROPRIETRESS RESERVE (★★★): Packs in lots of rich, complex flavors and is well oaked but balanced.
1993: Well oaked, but the rich core of pear, pineapple and spice come through in an elegant way. **89**

VINE HAVEN
This is a second label for Saddleback Cellars (see listing).

VITA NOVA
Santa Barbara County
F: 1987. O: Jim Clendenen & Bob Lindquist. W: Jim Clendenen, Bob Lindquist. S: None.

OVERALL	$18-25	★★★

WINE RATINGS

Cabernet Blend Santa Barbara County Reservatum	★★
Chardonnay Santa Barbara County	★★★
Sauvignon Blend Santa Barbara County Reservatum	★★★

WINERY DATA
C: 3,000. V: None. G: None. P: N/A.

Vita Nova is headed by two well-known winemakers, Jim Clendenen (Au Bon Climat) and Bob Lindquist (Qupe), who in 1987 began making Bordeaux-style wines. One is made from Cabernet and Merlot, the other from Sauvignon Blanc and Sémillon; both appear under the Reservatum name. Chardonnay has since been added to the winery's 3,000-case output. Distribution is very limited.

TASTING NOTES

CABERNET BLEND SANTA BARBARA COUNTY RESERVATUM (★★): Struggles to avoid the herb and vegetal flavors that plague Santa Barbara Cabernets, but it can offer appealing cherry and currant notes.
1986: Attractive, with ripe currant, chocolate and spicy oak flavors that fold together. **87**

VON STRASSER VINEYARDS
Calistoga, Napa Valley
F: 1990. O: Teale Creek Associates. W: Rudy von Strasser. S: Freestone.

OVERALL	$28	★★★

WINE RATINGS

Cabernet Sauvignon Diamond Mountain	★★★

WINERY DATA
C: 1,500. V: 10 acres in Napa Valley. G: Cabernet Sauvignon (8.5 acres), Merlot (0.5), Petite Verdot (1). P: Chardonnay (Napa Valley).

Rudy and Rita von Strasser bought the former Roddis Vineyard on Diamond Mountain in 1990, using the Cabernet Sauvignon estate vineyard for their wine. The vineyard, while close to the dusty Volcanic Hill Vineyard at Diamond Creek, has yet to produce wines of Volcanic Hill's caliber. The von Strassers hope to change that. Roddis Cabernets (1978 to 1984) were an odd mix of ruggedly tannic and technically flawed wines. Pine Ridge purchased grapes from the vineyard for its Diamond Mountain bottling (1986 and 1987), but it too failed to impress, as it was often marked by a potent minty character. Rudy von Strasser, who worked nearby at Newton, intends to make a richer, fleshier style of Cabernet and so far that style is evident in the early wines. Chardonnay comes from purchased grapes. Production is 1,500 cases.

TASTING NOTES

CABERNET SAUVIGNON DIAMOND MOUNTAIN (★★★): Consistently well made and focused, with appealing currant, herb and pretty oak shadings. Time will tell how the wines age, but they're well balanced and reflective of the appellation.
1992: Tough, chewy and tannic, with a core of muscular, earthy currant and cherry flavors submerged beneath the tannins. **88**
1991: Ripe and chewy, youthful and tannic, with ripe currant, plum and mint flavors emerging on the finish. **88**
1990: Tight and firm, with herb, anise and currant flavors that turn supple and elegant on the finish. Tannins are fine and soft at this stage. **89**

VOSS VINEYARDS
Napa Valley
F: 1991. O: S. Smith & Son and Negociants U.S.A. W: Simon Adams. S: None.

OVERALL	$9-16	★★

WINE RATINGS

Cabernet Sauvignon	NR
Chardonnay Napa Valley	★★
Merlot Napa Valley	★★
Sauvignon Blanc Napa Valley	★★★
Zinfandel Alexander Valley	★

WINERY DATA

C: 7,000. **V:** None. **G:** None. **P:** Cabernet Sauvignon, Chardonnay, Merlot, Sauvignon Blanc, Zinfandel (Napa Valley, Alexander Valley).

Australian Robert Hill Smith, whose family owns several wineries including Yalumba, owns this negociant brand; its 7,000 cases of Cabernet, Chardonnay, Merlot, Sauvignon Blanc and Zinfandel are made from purchased grapes grown in Napa and Alexander Valleys. Quality has been good.

TASTING NOTES

CHARDONNAY NAPA VALLEY (★★): Variable in early vintages, but at its best it offers clean, ripe apple and pear-laced fruit.
1992: Earthy, green and lean, with a minty edge to the apple flavors. **83**
1991: Firm and focused, with toasty, spicy, mineral-scented pear and pineapple flavors. **85**

MERLOT NAPA VALLEY (★★): Variable too, the 1992 is a clear improvement over the green, stalky 1991.
1992: Tight and firm, with a compact band of currant, cedar, oak and herb notes. **83**
1991: Lean and green, this is a hard-edged wine with more tobacco and cedar flavors than fruit. Perhaps with cellaring it will reveal more fruit flavors. Tasted twice with consistent notes. **75**

SAUVIGNON BLANC NAPA VALLEY (★★★):
1993: Fresh and lively, with a fruity center and nice anise and herb overtones, distinctly varietal and nicely balanced. **88**

ZINFANDEL ALEXANDER VALLEY (★):
1992: Soft and a little raisiny, with a bitter edge to the tannic finish. Bites back on the finish. **77**

WEIBEL VINEYARDS
Mendocino County
F: 1939. **O:** Weibel Vineyards. **W:** Richard T. Casquerio. **S:** None.

OVERALL	$5-10	★★

WINE RATINGS

Cabernet Sauvignon Mendocino County	★★
Chardonnay Mendocino County	★★
Chenin Blanc Mendocino County	★★
Pinot Noir Mendocino County	★

WINERY DATA
C: 900,000. **V:** 1,100 acres in Mendocino County. **G:** Cabernet Sauvignon, Chardonnay, Chenin Blanc, Pinot Noir. **P:** None.

Weibel Vineyards dates back to 1939 and for years was best known for its Green Hungarian, a light and fruity white wine. This family-owned winery was founded by Swiss immigrant Rudolph Weibel and his son, Fred, who built a prosperous business in Fremont, near San Jose, bottling wine under different brand names for various customers. As urban sprawl surrounded the winery, increasing land prices, the Weibels sold their Fremont property and moved to Mendocino, where they now own 1,100 acres and produce 900,000 cases, with the best wines being simple, easy-drinking varieties such as Cabernet, Chardonnay, Chenin Blanc and Pinot Noir. At this writing, the Weibel Winery has just been purchased by Mendocino County growers Bill Pauli and Charles Barra.

WEINSTOCK CELLARS
Sonoma County
F: 1984. **O:** Weinstock Cellars. **W:** Robert Weinstock. **S:** None.

OVERALL	$9	NR

WINE RATINGS

Blush Sonoma County White Zinfandel	NR
Chardonnay Sonoma County	NR
Gamay Sonoma County	NR
Pinot Noir Sonoma County	NR

WINERY DATA
C: 25,000. **V:** None. **G:** None. **P:** Chardonnay, Gamay, Pinot Noir, Zinfandel (Sonoma County).

Family-owned Weinstock Cellars produces 25,000 cases of Chardonnay, Gamay, Pinot Noir and white Zinfandel, all from purchased grapes in Sonoma County and Alexander Valley. Quality ranges from fair to good, with several Kosher wines also part of the lineup.

WELLINGTON VINEYARDS

Sonoma Valley
F: 1986. **O:** Wellington Vineyards. **W:** Peter Wellington.
S: None.

OVERALL	$8-16	★★

WINE RATINGS

Cabernet Sauvignon Mount Veeder Random Ridge Vineyard	★★
Cabernet Sauvignon Sonoma County Mohrhardt Ridge Vineyard	★★
Chardonnay Sonoma Valley Barrel Fermented	★★
Merlot Sonoma County	NR
Red Table Wine Sonoma Valley Criolla Old Vines	★★
Zinfandel Sonoma Valley 100-Year-Old Vines	★★
Zinfandel Sonoma Valley Casa Santinamaria	★★

WINERY DATA
C: 4,000. **V:** 24 acres in Sonoma Valley. **G:** Merlot (6 acres), Chardonnay (3), Zinfandel (2), Cabernet Sauvignon (1), Rhône Type (11). **P:** Cabernet Sauvignon (Sonoma County, Mount Veeder), Cabernet Franc (Mount Veeder), Zinfandel (Sonoma Valley), Syrah (Russian River Valley), Chardonnay (Sonoma Valley).

The Wellington family founded this 4,000-case winery in Glen Ellen in Sonoma Valley. It includes an old vineyard which has been expanded to 24 acres, and is now used as a part of the winery's diverse mix of Cabernet, Chardonnay, Merlot, red table wine and Zinfandel. Most are made in small lots, sometimes only 100 to 300 cases.

TASTING NOTES

CABERNET SAUVIGNON MOUNT VEEDER RANDOM RIDGE VINEYARD (★★): This bottling is a shade more tannic and intense than the Mohrhardt Ridge bottling.
1991: An earthy wine with racy currant and plum flavors to offset the earthiness. **83**
1990: Ripe and earthy, a mouthful of plum, spice and oak flavors. **86**
1989: Ripe, intense and tannic, with crisp currant and cherry aromas and flavors that are concentrated. **86**

CABERNET SAUVIGNON SONOMA COUNTY MOHRHARDT RIDGE VINEYARD (★★): This bottling offers ripe, earthy flavors, not as tannic as the Random Ridge.
1991: Spicy, with ripe plum, cherry and currant flavors that are focused and lively. **85**
1990: Robust and full-bodied, with plenty of currant and black cherry flavors and lots of tannins. **83**
1989: Offers nice, spicy berry aromas and flavors framed by toasty, buttery oak notes. **85**

CHARDONNAY SONOMA VALLEY BARREL FERMENTED (★★): Variable. The 1992 was well off the mark. The 1991 was more appealing.
1993: Potently floral and perfumed, with a strong wood and honeysuckle edge that dominates. Gains more fruit on the finish. **84**
Lot 2 1993: Floral and perfumed, with a narrow band of spicy pear and apricot flavors, finishing with chewy oak notes. **81**
1992: Marked by odd candied flavors that turn grapey, crisp and perfumed. **70**
1991: Ripe and round, with spicy, earthy notes that add complexity to the pear and pineapple flavors. **88**

MERLOT SONOMA COUNTY (NR):
1991: Chewy, with a minty currant edge that's built around solid tannins. **84**

RED TABLE WINE SONOMA VALLEY CRIOLLA OLD VINES (★★): A field blend that's dominated by Alicante Bouschet, with appealing cherry and wild berry flavors.
1991: A ripe, fruity red offering jammy raspberry, plum and anise flavors, finishing with a touch of cedar. **85**
1990: Smooth and generous, with well defined raspberry and blackberry flavors and a supple, velvety finish. **85**

ZINFANDEL VARIOUS BOTTLINGS (★★): Well crafted wines in 1992, with ripe fruity flavors. The Casa Santinamaria is a shade earthier.
Sonoma Valley 100-Year-Old Vines 1992: Ripe, with bright, jammy black cherry, wild berry and plum flavors, turning supple. **87**
Sonoma Valley Casa Santinamaria 1992: Dark, ripe and intense, with jammy cherry and wild berry flavors that turn supple and earthy. **84**

WENTE BROS.
Livermore Valley
F: 1883. **O:** Wente Family. **W:** Willy Joslin. **S:** None.

OVERALL	$7-16	★★★

WINE RATINGS
Cabernet Sauvignon
   Livermore Valley Charles Wetmore
      Vineyard Estate Reserve   ★★
Chardonnay Arroyo Seco Riva Ranch   ★★★
Chardonnay Central Coast
   Wente Family Estate Selection   ★★★
Chardonnay Livermore Valley
   Herman Wente Vineyard Reserve   ★★★
Merlot Livermore Valley Crane Ridge   ★★
Sauvignon Blanc Livermore Valley
   Wente Family Estate Selection   ★★

WINERY DATA
C: 350,000. **V:** 1,977 acres in Livermore Valley, Arroyo Seco.
G: Cabernet Franc (15 acres), Cabernet Sauvignon (188), Chardonnay (974), Chenin Blanc (48), French Colombard (35).
P: None.

O ne of California's true wine dynasties, Wente Bros. dates to 1883 and is now run by the family's fourth generation of winemakers. From its base in Livermore Valley, Wente has enjoyed success with white wines both before and after Prohibition, planting many of the old world varieties (which it sold as bulk wines) during its early years and refining many varietals after Repeal, including Sémillon, Sauvignon Blanc, Grey Riesling, Pinot Blanc and Chardonnay. In 1981, Wente purchased the old Cresta Blanca winery site and replanted the vineyard, calling it the Charles Wetmore Vineyard. In 1992 Philip Wente joined forces with Sergio Traverso, forming Murrieta's Well (see listing), and in 1992 the winery bought Concannon Vineyards (see listing). Today the winery makes 350,000 cases, owns 1,977 acres in vines (974 of that Chardonnay, with nearly 600 acres in Arroyo Seco, Monterey). Central Coast Chardonnay at 100,000 cases is the volume leader, followed by California Cabernet (50,000 cases), Chenin Blanc (Le Blanc de Blancs, 30,000 cases), and blush (30,000 cases). The Herman Wente Reserve from Livermore Valley and the Riva Ranch (Arroyo Seco) Chardonnays lead in quality.

TASTING NOTES

CABERNET SAUVIGNON LIVERMORE VALLEY CHARLES WETMORE VINEYARD ESTATE RESERVE (★★): Solid with ripe Cabernet flavors, but not the depth and richness found in Napa or Sonoma bottlings.
1991: Leans toward the earthy, leathery end of the Cabernet spectrum, turning dry on the finish. **82**
1990: Leans toward the herbal end of the Cabernet spectrum, but picks up supple currant and spice flavors. **86**
1989: A weedy, herbal wine with a core of currant and earth flavors that fold together. **84**
1987: Ripe, supple and graceful, with appealing blackberry and currant flavors shaded by herb and mint overtones. **86**
1986: Smooth and mature, with tobacco, herb, leather, plum and chocolate flavors. Modest tannins. **82**

CHARDONNAY ARROYO SECO RIVA RANCH (★★★):
1992: Smooth and silky, with elegant pear, spice and honey notes, medium-bodied and well crafted. **85**
1991: Fresh and fruity, with nicely defined apple, grapefruit, lemon and pear flavors that turn spicy. **87**

CHARDONNAY CENTRAL COAST WENTE FAMILY ESTATE SELECTION (★★★): Good value in bright, ripe, fruity Chardonnay.
1993: Crisp, with a slightly coarse texture, but appealing pear and apple flavors. **85**
1992: Fresh and spicy, with pleasant apple, pear and nutmeg flavors. **84**

CHARDONNAY LIVERMORE VALLEY HERMAN WENTE VINEYARD RESERVE (★★★): Shows more depth, intensity and complexity than the other bottlings.
1991: Well balanced, with intense pear, apple and vanilla flavors, turning smooth and elegant. **88**

MERLOT LIVERMORE VALLEY CRANE RIDGE (★★): Good, well balanced, but lacks extra dimensions.
1991: An oaky, earthy wine that slowly picks up ripe cherry and plum flavors. **84**
1990: Smooth and supple, with tarry currant, herb and tobacco notes. **84**

SAUVIGNON BLANC LIVERMORE VALLEY WENTE FAMILY ESTATE SELECTION (★★): Clean and fruity, if simple, with grassy pear notes.

1993: Smooth and spicy, with pineapple and herb flavors that extend into a generous finish. **85**
1992: Simple and soft, with a hint of apple and a pleasant grassy edge. **83**

WERMUTH WINERY
Calistoga, Napa Valley
F: 1981. O: Ralph & Smitty Wermuth. W: Ralph Wermuth. S: None.

OVERALL	$8-10	★

WINE RATINGS

French Colombard Napa Valley	NR
Gamay Napa Valley	NR
Zinfandel Napa Valley	NR

WINERY DATA
C: 4,000. V: 2 acres in Napa Valley. G: Colombard (1 acre), Gamay (1). P: Zinfandel (Napa Valley).

The Wermuths own this 4,000-case winery, which produces Napa Valley Colombard, Gamay and Zinfandel, all of ordinary quality.

WESTWOOD WINERY
El Dorado County
F: 1984. O: Umbert A. Urch & Elizabeth A. Stoltz. W: Umbert A. Urch. S: None.

OVERALL	$10-20	NR

WINE RATINGS

Barbera El Dorado County Ritchie Vineyard	NR

WINERY DATA
C: 4,000. V: None. G: None. P: Pinot Noir (Napa, Carneros, El Dorado), Barbera, Charbono, Chardonnay, Johannisberg Riesling, Merlot, Syrah (El Dorado).

Bert Urch buys all his grapes for this brand, from Napa Valley and on occasion El Dorado County. All of the wines are made in small case lots (usually fewer than 500 cases) with very limited distribution. Among the wines offered from El Dorado Barbera, Charbono (and Rosé), Chardonnay, Merlot, Pinot Noir, Johannisberg Riesling and Syrah. Those from Napa: Pinot Noir Haynes Vineyard and Roders Vineyard.

WHALER VINEYARD
Mendocino County
F: 1981. O: Russ & Ann Nyborg. W: Russ Nyborg, Jed Steele. S: None.

OVERALL	$10-14	★★

WINE RATINGS

Zinfandel Mendocino County	★★
Zinfandel Mendocino County Flagship	★★★

WINERY DATA
C: 1,800. V: 24 acres in Mendocino. G: Zinfandel (23 acres), Syrah (1). P: None.

Whaler Vineyard produces 1,800 cases of its specialty, Zinfandel, with two bottlings, both from its 24-acre vineyard. Owners Russ and Ann Nyborg hired Jed Steele as a consultant in 1991.

TASTING NOTES

ZINFANDEL MENDOCINO COUNTY (★★): Good, with ripe wild berry flavors and firm tannins.
1992: Firmly tannic, with supple wild berry and blueberry flavors. **84**
1991: Displays intriguing wild raspberry and blueberry flavors that are firm and tight. **84**
1990: Tannic in texture but light in flavor, with slightly earthy overtones to the modest berry flavors. **81**
1989: Crisp and modest, with a thread of mature spice and berry flavors. **83**

ZINFANDEL MENDOCINO COUNTY FLAGSHIP (★★★): Intense and lively, with juicy, complex fruit flavors.
1992: Ripe, with juicy plum and black cherry flavors that are focused and lively, finishing with firm tannins. **87**
1991: Sleek and elegant, displaying pretty spice, earth, oak and raspberry flavors that are complex and concentrated. **87**
1990: Light and appealing, with raspberry and wild berry aromas and flavors that persist on the lively finish. **85**

WHEELER WINERY
Sonoma County
F: 1970. **O:** Boisset USA. **W:** Bill Arbios. **S:** None.

OVERALL	$8-12	★★

WINE RATINGS

Cabernet Sauvignon Dry Creek Valley	
Norse Vineyard Private Reserve	★★
Chardonnay Sonoma County	★★★
Merlot Dry Creek Valley	NR
Red Table Wine California Quintet	NR
Sauvignon Blanc Sonoma County	★★
Zinfandel Dry Creek Valley	★★

WINERY DATA
C: 18,000. **V:** None. **G:** None. **P:** Cabernet Sauvignon, Chardonnay, Sauvignon Blanc, Zinfandel.

William and Ingrid Wheeler purchased a 175-acre property in Dry Creek Valley in 1970, planting 30 hillside acres to Cabernet and Zinfandel, with the former designated Norse Vineyard. Chardonnay, Sauvignon Blanc and a red Rhône blend (Mourvèdre and Syrah), all from purchased grapes, were also part of the wine mix, which reached 20,000 cases. But financial constraints forced the Wheelers to take on a partner, the French investment firm Paribas Domaines, in 1989; in 1992 they sold the winery to Jean-Claude Boisset. The Wheelers' greatest success was with Chardonnay, as the Norse Vineyard Cabernet was typically hard, tannic and laced with herbal flavors. It's unclear what the new direction will be, as the vineyard may be used to support Boisset's other emerging brands, including Christophe and Lyeth.

TASTING NOTES

CABERNET SAUVIGNON DRY CREEK VALLEY NORSE VINEYARD PRIVATE RESERVE (★★): Early 1980s vintages were dense and tannic, with earthy herbal flavors. More recently the wines are middle-of-the-road.
1991: Firm and compact, with medium-weight spice, vanilla and black cherry flavors. **84**
1989: Light and fairly fruity, with berry aromas and modest tannins. **81**
1988: A tart, firm, medium-weight Cabernet with good raspberry and cherry flavors. **83**
1987: Despite hard-edged tannins, modest plum, chocolate and currant flavors emerge. **84**

1986: Marked by heavy oak flavors that dominate the cherry and currant notes. **83**

CHARDONNAY SONOMA COUNTY (★★★): Well balanced, smooth and flavorful, with complex flavors.
1993: Good intensity and depth for the vintage, with a complex core of honey, pear, vanilla and spice, turning elegant on the finish. **84**
1992: Complex and flavorful, with toasty, buttery oak overshadowing the spicy pear flavors. **87**
1991: Ripe, lush and spicy, with a core of rich pear, peach and nectarine flavors. **91**

MERLOT DRY CREEK VALLEY (NR):
1992: Tries to be ripe and broad, but comes a little off balance, citrusy at the center and chewy at the edges. **79**

RED TABLE WINE CALIFORNIA QUINTET (NR):
1990: Medium-bodied, peppery in aroma, light in flavor and mature now, this red wine has simple carrot and berry flavors. **76**

SAUVIGNON BLANC SONOMA COUNTY (★★): Strikes a nice balance between herbs and fruit.
1992: Smooth and distinctively herbal, with a minty note that carries through the finish against a citrusy pear background. **86**

ZINFANDEL DRY CREEK VALLEY (★★): Good, but below par for Dry Creek, as it offers only modest fruit flavors.
1992: Well oaked and polished, with pretty cherry, wild berry and plum flavors, gaining complexity and finesse through the finish. Ready now, even with the tannins. **87**
1991: Simple and correct, with modest berry flavors. **80**

WHITCRAFT WINERY
Santa Maria Valley
F: 1985. **O:** Christopher Whitcraft. **W:** Christopher Whitcraft. **S:** None.

OVERALL	$22-35	★★★

WINE RATINGS

Chardonnay Santa Maria Valley	
Bien Nacido Vineyard	★★★
Pinot Noir Russian River Valley	
Olivet Lane Vineyard	★★★

Pinot Noir Santa Maria Valley
  Bien Nacido Vineyard   ★★★

Winery Data
C: 1,500. V: None. G: None. P: Chardonnay, Pinot Noir (Santa Maria Valley and Olivet Lane).

Former wine retailer and wholesaler Chris Whitcraft and his wife, Kathleen, own this 1,500-case brand which uses purchased grapes from Bien Nacido in Santa Maria Valley (Chardonnay and Pinot Noir) and Olivet Lane in Russian River Valley (just Pinot Noir) for its two Burgundian-inspired wines. Early indications are Whitcraft is on target with both varieties. Worth watching.

Tasting Notes

Chardonnay Santa Maria Valley Bien Nacido Vineyard (★★★): Rich and Burgundian, well focused and flavorful.
1993: Intense, with bright, tart citrus, pineapple and pear notes that are sharply focused, finishing with a pretty nectarine edge. **89**
1992: Bold, rich and buttery, with high-extract pear, apple and toast notes. **88**

Pinot Noir Russian River Valley Olivet Lane Vineyard (★★★): Impressive too for its focus on rich, supple fruit flavors and smooth tannins.
1992: Bright, distinctive and spicy, with ripe berry and currant underpinnings. **90**
1991: Supple, rich and complex, with silky smooth currant, raspberry and spicy cherry notes that take on an earthy, tarry edge. **88**

Pinot Noir Santa Maria Valley Bien Nacido Vineyard (★★★): Packs in lots of rich, complex flavors, with the vineyard's classic earthy herb, cola and cherry flavors.
1993: Bright and lively, with fresh, ripe, elegant cherry, strawberry and plummy notes, picking up a leathery edge on the finish when the tannins kick in. **88**
Q Block 1993: A shade denser and more compact than the other bottling from this vineyard, it delivers ripe plum and currant flavors that last into the finish. **90**
1992: Gutsy and flavorful, with mouth-filling plum and currant flavors that extend into a solid, slightly tannic finish. **88**

1991: Tight and tannic, with a leathery edge to the cola, cherry, spice and rhubarb flavors. **87**
1990: Ripe and focused, with lively cola, rhubarb and black cherry flavors framed by tight tannins and oak shadings. **88**

White Oak Vineyards & Winery
Sonoma County
F: 1978. O: Bill Myers. W: Paul Brasset. S: None.

Overall	$7-18	★★★

Wine Ratings

Cabernet Franc Alexander Valley	★★
Cabernet Sauvignon Alexander Valley	★★
Chardonnay Russian River Valley	
Poplar Ranch Private Reserve	★★★
Chardonnay Sonoma County	★★★
Chardonnay Sonoma County	
Myers Limited Reserve	★★★
Chenin Blanc California	★★
Sauvignon Blanc Sonoma County	★★
Zinfandel Alexander Valley	
Church Vineyard	★★★
Zinfandel Dry Creek Valley	
Saunders Vineyard	★★★
Zinfandel Sonoma County	★★★
Zinfandel Sonoma County	
Limited Reserve	★★★

Winery Data
C: 14,000. V: 10 acres in Alexander Valley. G: Zinfandel (4 acres), Chardonnay (2), Merlot (4). P: Zinfandel, Sauvignon Blanc (Dry Creek Valley), Zinfandel, Chardonnay, Cabernet Sauvignon, Cabernet Franc (Alexander Valley), Chardonnay, Sauvignon Blanc (Russian River Valley).

Bill Myers founded this 14,000-case winery in 1978, offering a complete lineup of popular varietals, from Cabernet to Zinfandel, in key Sonoma appellations. Chardonnay, at more than 5,000 cases, is the volume leader and one of the best two wines, Zinfandel being the other quality leader.

Tasting Notes

Cabernet Franc Alexander Valley (★★): Not made every year, but efforts so far have yielded consistent results, with well balanced and fruity wines that avoid the grape variety's stalky tendencies.

1992: Firm and compact, with chewy tannins and modest black cherry and berry flavors. **84**

1989: Fresh and fruity, with crisp acidity and cherry and plum flavors that turn soft and supple. **84**

CABERNET SAUVIGNON VARIOUS BOTTLINGS (★★): Appealing for its suppleness and mild tannins, it is consistently good to very good, but short of outstanding.

Alexander Valley 1991: Offers ripe, spicy and exotic wild berry and cherry flavors, but turns simple. **82**

Alexander Valley 1990: Smooth and pleasant, with a grapey edge, but ultimately simple. **84**

Alexander Valley 1988: Forward and pleasing, with cedary currant, spice and oak flavors. **85**

Alexander Valley Myers Limited Reserve 1985: Very tight and tannic in structure, but the ripe cherry flavors underneath are appealing. **84**

Sonoma County 1987: Very ripe, generous, chunky and a bit awkward now, but it offers plenty of currant and plum aromas and flavors. Has a vegetal edge that adds complexity. **85**

CHARDONNAY RUSSIAN RIVER VALLEY POPLAR RANCH PRIVATE RESERVE (★★★):

1993: A touch earthy and astringent, with just a hint of light pear and oak coming through. **82**

CHARDONNAY SONOMA COUNTY (★★★), MYERS LIMITED RESERVE (★★★): Less interesting and simpler of late, but mid- to late-1980s vintages of both wines showed more richness and depth.

1993: Marked by lean, earthy grapefruit and citrus flavors, but not much in the way of ripe fruit. **83**

1991: A spicy wine with simple pear and apple flavors. **80**

Myers Limited Reserve 1991: Marked by toasty oak that overrides the spice and pear flavors. **87**

CHENIN BLANC CALIFORNIA (★★):

1993: Bright, fruity and utterly charming, unfolding its melon, mint and pear flavors with grace and style. **87**

SAUVIGNON BLANC SONOMA COUNTY (★★): Good, with simple but correct flavors.

1993: Light and spicy, a lean wine with pear and herb flavors that soften on the finish. **83**

ZINFANDEL ALEXANDER VALLEY CHURCH VINEYARD (★★★):

1992: Rustic, with a green, wild berry streak to it. **80**

1990: Hard and oaky, with thin flavors that miss the mark. **73**

ZINFANDEL DRY CREEK VALLEY SAUNDERS VINEYARD (★★★): Captures the essence of Zinfandel with its spice and wild berry flavors.

1992: An earthy, spicy Zin with tar, pepper and wild berry flavors. **84**

1990: Ripe, inviting and firm, creamy-textured and oak-scented, offering rich raspberry, cherry, vanilla and spice flavors. **90**

ZINFANDEL SONOMA COUNTY (★★★), LIMITED RESERVE (★★★):

1992: Firm, tight and gamy, with wild berry, cherry and plum flavors and gritty tannins. **85**

1991: Solid, with ripe, intense cherry and raspberry aromas and flavors, finishing with a peppery, oaky edge. **87**

1989: Packed with ripe blackberry and raspberry flavors that linger on the finish. Firmly tannic. **85**

Limited Reserve 1992: Lean and tarry, showing a narrow band of cedar and spice notes before the cherry and wild berry flavors kick in. **86**

Limited Reserve 1991: Intense and lively, with a core of ripe, spicy cherry, raspberry and plum flavors, finishing with firm tannins. **88**

WHITE ROCK VINEYARDS
Napa Valley
F: 1986. **O:** Claire & Henri Vandendriessche. **W:** Douglas Danielak. **S:** None.

OVERALL	$19-22	★★★

WINE RATINGS

Chardonnay Napa Valley	★★★
Meritage Red Napa Valley Claret	★★★

WINERY DATA
C: 3,000. **V:** 36 acres in Napa Valley. **G:** Chardonnay (13 acres), Cabernet Sauvignon (18), Cabernet Franc (3), Merlot (1), Petite Verdot (1). **P:** None.

Henry and Claire Vandendriessche were looking for a home in the country in 1977 when they came across the Pettingill estate, a winery and vineyard that is tucked in a narrow fold of hills behind the Stags Leap rock outcropping and that dates to 1970. In 1979 the Vandendriessches bought the property and began planting 36 acres in vines, producing their first wines in 1986. They call their Bordeaux-style red "claret," as it is a blend of the classic varieties and made in a tight, austere style. The Chardonnay is crisp and flinty. Douglas Danielak, winemaker for Jade Mountain, is also White Rock's winemaker, and the Jade Mountain wines are aged in White Rock's caves.

TASTING NOTES

CHARDONNAY NAPA VALLEY (★★★): Consistently well made in a delicate, understated style, but with plenty of flavor and finesse.
1992: Crisp and compact, with a core of elegant, spicy pear and peach flavors. **87**
1991: Fresh, ripe and creamy, offering spicy vanilla, pear, honey and toast flavors that are elegant and refreshing. **88**

MERITAGE RED NAPA VALLEY CLARET (★★★): Austere, with a tight, narrow but focused band of currant, cedar and currant flavors. Improving.
1990: Tight and firm, with a narrow band of spice, cedary oak and plum flavors, turning tannic. **88**
1989: Tough and hard in texture, with an austere feel to it, offering a modest helping of earthy coffee and blackberry flavors. **83**
1988: Lean but flavorful, with a cedary edge to the basic Cabernet flavors. **84**
1986: Heavy-handed oak overrides the currant and cedar flavors. **80**

WHITEHALL LANE WINERY

St. Helena, Napa Valley
F: 1979. **O:** Thomas A. Leonardini. **W:** Gary Galleron. **S:** None.

OVERALL	$10-36	★★★

WINE RATINGS

Cabernet Sauvignon Napa Valley	★★★
Cabernet Sauvignon Napa Valley Reserve	★★★
Cabernet Sauvignon Napa Valley Morisoli Vineyard	★★★
Chardonnay Napa Valley	★★★
Meritage Red Napa Valley	NR
Merlot Knights Valley	★★
Pinot Noir Alexander Valley	★★
Sauvignon Blanc Napa Valley Barrel Fermented	★★

WINERY DATA

C: 13,000. **V:** 36 acres in Rutherford, St. Helena. **G:** Sauvignon Blanc (4 acres), Chardonnay (6), Merlot (14), Cabernet Sauvignon (10), Zinfandel (2). **P:** Merlot (Knights Valley), Chardonnay (Napa Valley), Sauvignon Blanc, Cabernet Sauvignon (Rutherford).

Brothers Art Finkelstein and Alan Steen founded this winery in Rutherford in 1979, one year after buying a vineyard which they replanted. In the interim, most of the grapes for their wines were purchased in Napa and Knights Valleys, with production in the 10,000-case range. In 1988, the winery was sold to Hideaki Ando of Japan, who owned it until financial constraints forced him to sell to entrepreneur Tom Leonardini, owner of the Napa Valley Winery Exchange, a wine shop in San Francisco. In 1994, the winery began upgrading its wines, hiring Gary Galleron (formerly of Grace Family Vineyard) as winemaker. Production is at 13,000 cases now and is projected to climb to 50,000 cases, including wines to be sold to be under a second label. The winery owns 36 acres, 22 in Rutherford and 14 in St. Helena, and buys grapes from Morisoli Vineyard in Rutherford for a vineyard-designated Cabernet. Knights Valley Merlot (3,200 cases) was the volume leader in 1995. Worth watching.

TASTING NOTES

CABERNET FRANC NAPA VALLEY (NR):
1990: Tight and firm, with smoky cherry, anise and berry flavors that turn complex. **86**
1989: Light and gentle, with mature cherry flavors and hints of sage and mint. **79**
1988: Complex and supple, with an array of pretty spice, vanilla, currant and chocolate flavors wrapped tightly in oak and tannins. **86**

CABERNET SAUVIGNON NAPA VALLEY (★★★): Good and improving, as the wines show better focus, smoother textures and more currant and cherry fruit. Early vintages have aged fairly well.

1991: Offers spicy currant, cherry and anise notes, finishing with modest tannins. **87**

1990: Smooth and polished, with appealing grape, currant and violet flavors that turn supple. **87**

1988: A distinctive minty edge dominates the bay leaf, currant and plum flavors. **85**

1987: Minty and herbal, with a narrow band of fruit flavor that's dominated by sage notes. **83**

1986: Mature but still firm, with minty currant and black cherry flavors that are fresh and vibrant, finishing with firm tannins. **87**

1985: Has peaked, showing mature mint, currant and cedary oak flavors. **88**

CABERNET SAUVIGNON NAPA VALLEY RESERVE (★★★): Solid the past few vintages, and a wine to watch, as the focus will be to raise the quality level with Napa's best. Ages well.

1991: Provides a nice core of currant, cherry and berry fruit that's framed by toast and supported by firm tannins. Best to cellar this one into 1997 or 1998 for it to soften. **89**

1990: Firm, intense and spicy, with a tight band of currant, cherry, anise and cedary oak flavors. **89**

1989: Distinctive for its minty, herbal edge, it's also complex and concentrated, with layers of currant and berry underneath. **87**

1988: Lean and focused, with distinctive mint, currant and cedary oak flavors that turn complex. **86**

1987: Tight and focused, with spice, mint and oak nuances, but there are also ripe, concentrated cherry, currant and raspberry flavors that turn silky. **90**

CABERNET SAUVIGNON NAPA VALLEY MORISOLI VINEYARD (★★★): The other wine to watch, as this vineyard yields excellent grapes for several Napa wines.

1991: Well constructed, with ripe plum, currant and cherry fruit and a sense of elegance and finesse. **88**

1990: Tight and intense, with a green edge to the currant and cherry notes, finishing with firm tannins. **87**

CHARDONNAY NAPA VALLEY (★★★): Improving, although the 1993 was light. The 1992 is a better model for what the winery hopes to achieve.

1993: Light and spicy, with ripe pear and cedary oak notes. **82**

1992: Ripe and toasty, with pretty, buttery oak notes adding richness and complexity to the spicy pear and fig flavors. **89**

MERITAGE RED NAPA VALLEY (NR): New in 1991; the challenge is to create a wine that will stand out in an already crowded Cabernet and Merlot lineup.

1991: Firm and tannic, with a tightly wound core of earthy currant and mineral flavors. **85**

MERLOT KNIGHTS VALLEY (★★): Typical of Knights Valley in its medium-bodied intensity and depth of flavors. Good but nothing more.

1992: Well focused, with pretty cherry and plum-laced flavors that turn spicy and tannic on the finish, where toasty oak comes into play. **88**

1991: Smooth and supple, with modest berry, spice and tobacco flavors, finishing with a touch of vanilla. **86**

1990: Spicy, supple and elegant, with layers of currant, toast and berry flavors that are tightly wound. **86**

1989: A wrapping of stylish, sweet oak surrounds the lush cherry and raspberry flavors. **84**

1988: Supple and fruity, with nice cherry, herb and plum flavors. **82**

1987: Pungent, with pickle and raspberry flavors, hinting at tarragon on the finish. **77**

PINOT NOIR VARIOUS BOTTLINGS (★★): Usually light and simple, with modest flavors, 1987 being the exception when it showed more depth.

Alexander Valley 1990: Light and simple, showing crisp tea, herb and plum notes but lacking depth and complexity. **82**

Alexander Valley 1988: Lavishly oaked, with wood dominating the cherry and spice flavors. **82**

Napa Valley 1987: Shows pretty red cherry, blueberry, oak and spice aromas, with flavors to match. **87**

Napa Valley 1985: An earthy, decadent wine that's lean and silky, with sweet spice on the finish. **82**

SAUVIGNON BLANC NAPA VALLEY BARREL FERMENTED (★★): Variable of late, but usually good and reliable.

1993: Herbal, foxy aromas and flavors are distinctive and funky. **81**

WILD HOG HILL VINEYARD
Sonoma County
F: 1990. **O:** Daniel & Marion Schoenfeld. **W:** Daniel Schoenfeld. **S:** None.

OVERALL $12-18   ★★

WINE RATINGS

Cabernet Sauvignon	NR
Pinot Noir Sonoma County	NR
Zinfandel	NR

WINERY DATA

C: 1,000. V: 5 acres in Sonoma Coast. G: Zinfandel (1 acre), Pinot Noir (3). P: Zinfandel, Pinot Noir (Russian River), Zinfandel (Sonoma Coast), Cabernet (Dry Creek Valley).

Michele Andrian and Joanne Wirth founded this 1,500-case winery, producing small lots of Chardonnay, Pinot Noir and Zinfandel from purchased grapes in Sonoma. Distribution was limited, with quality in the average to good range. In 1990, Daniel and Marion Schoenfield purchased the winery and reduced production to 1,000 cases, using a portion of their five acres in vines, four of which are Pinot Noir. Vineyard-designated wines were planned for Zinfandel (Porter Bass in Russian River Valley and Wild Hog Hill) and Pinot Noir (Wild Hog Hill). Cabernet is purchased from Dry Creek Valley.

WILD HORSE WINERY
San Luis Obispo County
F: 1983. O: Ken Volk. W: Ken Volk. S: None.

OVERALL $12-16   ★★★

WINE RATINGS

Cabernet Sauvignon	
Paso Robles Cheval Sauvage	★★★
Cabernet Sauvignon	
San Luis Obispo County	★★★
Chardonnay Central Coast	★★★
Malvasia Bianca Monterey County	NR
Merlot San Luis Obispo County	★★★
Pinot Blanc Monterey County	★★★
Pinot Blanc Santa Barbara County	
Bien Nacido Vineyard	★★★
Pinot Noir Central Coast	★★★
Red Table Wine Cienega Valley Negrette	NR
Zinfandel Paso Robles Unbridled	★★★

WINERY DATA

C: 40,000. V: 32 acres in San Luis Obispo County. G: Chardonnay, Pinot Noir, Cabernet Sauvignon. P: Cabernet Sauvignon, Chardonnay, Pinot Noir (Santa Barbara County).

Owner and winemaker Ken Volk founded Wild Horse Winery in 1983 with the idea of planting a vineyard and then reselling it, but changing directions, he soon decided to and turn to winemaking. The lineup of wines is solid across the board, including Cabernet, Chardonnay, Merlot, Pinot Blanc, Pinot Noir and a white table wine made from Malvasia. A reserve style line is bottled under the Cheval Sauvage label when the wine quality merits. The winery owns 32 acres in vines but also buys from key vineyards in the Central and South Coast. Cabernet comes from Paso Robles, Chardonnay and Merlot from the Central Coast, Pinot Blanc from Monterey, Pinot Noir from the Central Coast and Santa Barbara and Zinfandel from Paso Robles. Worth watching.

TASTING NOTES

CABERNET SAUVIGNON VARIOUS BOTTLINGS (★★★): Consistently well balanced and well focused, balancing ripe cherry and currant with herb and spice notes.
Paso Robles 1987: Ripe and full-bodied, with currant, plum and herb notes, but not too tannic. **88**
Paso Robles 1986: Balanced, with ripe currant, herb and spice notes, turning tannic. **86**
Paso Robles Cheval Sauvage 1987: Firm and tannic, with a good dose of oak, but it's also complex and concentrated, with tight currant and anise flavors. **85**
Paso Robles Wild Horse Vineyards 1985: Very jammy, with ripe cherry and spice flavors and tarry, vegetal nuances. **70**
San Luis Obispo County 1992: Smooth and generous, with supple plum, cherry, anise and berry notes, finishing with soft tannins. **87**

CHARDONNAY CENTRAL COAST (★★★): At its best, bright, ripe and lively, with intense fruit flavors.
1993: Lean, with a firm band of spice, pineapple and vegetal notes. **84**
1992: Ripe and spicy, with intense, creamy pear, fig and vanilla flavors that turn delicate and elegant. **87**

MALVASIA BIANCA MONTEREY COUNTY (NR): New with the 1993.

1993: Racy, with earthy pear and grapefruit flavors that are ripe and concentrated, finishing with a nutty edge. **86**

MERLOT VARIOUS BOTTLINGS (★★★): Steadily improving, as recent vintages show more richness and depth. Can be weedy and earthy, though, too.

Central Coast Cheval Sauvage 1990: Bold, rich and fruity, with complex, plush currant, raspberry and wild berry flavors that are intense and tannic. **89**

Central Coast 1989: Austere, with firm currant, anise and cherry aromas and flavors. Firmly tannic. **84**

Central Coast 1988: Firm and tannic, with ripe, weedy currant and cherry aromas and flavors. **85**

Central Coast 1987: Tart and crisp, with currant and cherry flavors. **80**

Central Coast 1986: Smells like a Pomerol, with earthy currant flavors that turn tannic and dry on the finish. **87**

San Luis Obispo County 1991: Firm and compact, with a tight band of cherry, herb and currant flavors, finishing with ample tannins; best after 1996. **85**

PINOT BLANC VARIOUS BOTTLINGS (★★★): Firm and well focused, with ripe, intense, well proportioned flavors.

Monterey County 1993: Broad, spicy and scented with vanilla, with pear flavor sneaking in on the finish. **83**

Santa Barbara County Bien Nacido Vineyard 1993: Ripe, complex, almost opulent, with a rich texture and marvelous pear, spice and honey flavors. **90**

PINOT NOIR VARIOUS BOTTLINGS (★★★): Can be enormously rich and complex, but usually strikes a fine balance between spicy cherry, herb, cola and earthy nuances. Ages well.

Central Coast 1993: Tight and firm, with a compact band of cherry, herb and currant notes. Drinks well now, but should age well short-term. **85**

Central Coast 1992: Firm, with a narrow band of leathery Pinot Noir flavors, but on the finish a hint of cherry and spice emerges. **82**

Central Coast 1991: Smooth, inviting and polished, with plush plum and black cherry aromas and flavors that persist through the finish. **87**

Paso Robles Cheval Sauvage 1990: Rich, deep, chewy and complex, with broad, wonderful cherry, raspberry, currant and plum flavors and plenty of intensity and concentration. Firmly tannic. **91**

Santa Barbara County 1990: Compact and focused, with earthy black cherry, nutmeg and spice flavors supported by crisp acidity and tannins. Balanced and drinkable now, but with time it should be smoother. **86**

Santa Barbara County 1989: Tight and firm, with strong oak flavors and a pretty core of rich raspberry and Pinot Noir aromas and flavors. **87**

Santa Barbara County 1988: Complex, with tart cherry, anise, oak and earth flavors and firm tannins. **87**

Santa Barbara County 1987: Dry, oaky notes dominate the ripe cherry, cola and herb aromas and flavors. Firmly tannic. **86**

Santa Barbara County 1986: Rich, full-bodied and firmly tannic, with ripe cherry, plum, spice and oak notes. **85**

Santa Barbara County 1985: Dry and oaky, with tart, ripe cherry flavor underneath. **82**

Santa Barbara County Cheval Sauvage 1989: Broad, rich and spicy, with solid cherry, cola, rhubarb and spice flavors that turn smooth until the earthy tannins emerge. **85**

Santa Maria Valley 1984: Broad and complex, with intense oak, earth, currant and gamy flavors that are complex and decadent. **88**

Santa Maria Valley Sierra Madre Vineyard 1986: Mature, earthy and leathery, with drying tannins. There are hints of cherry, cola and rhubarb flavors, but the tart acidity pushes the tannins. **84**

Santa Maria Valley Sierra Madre Vineyard 1983: Complex and delicate on the nose, with equally complex cherry, rhubarb, earth and cola flavors. **90**

RED TABLE WINE CIENEGA VALLEY NEGRETTE (NR): **1992:** Deeply colored, with ripe, supple berry, currant and spice flavors that are complex and hearty. Ready. **85**

ZINFANDEL VARIOUS BOTTLINGS (★★★): Improving, with the 1990 Unbridled offering ripe juicy fruit flavors and fine balance.

Paso Robles Unbridled 1990: Ripe and spicy, with a core of pretty, juicy, supple blackberry, raspberry and cherry flavors. **88**

1989: A pleasant claret-style Zin that features ripe cherry, pepper, spice and cedary oak flavors. **85**

WILDCAT
Sonoma Valley
F: 1985. **O:** Charles Ilgen. **W:** Charles Ilgen. **S:** None.

OVERALL	$20	★

WINE RATINGS

Merlot Sonoma Valley	★

WINERY DATA
C: 3,000. **V:** None. **G:** None. **P:** Merlot (Sonoma Valley).

Sonoma Valley grower Charles Ilgen produces 3,000 cases under the Wildcat label from purchased grapes. Distribution is very limited. Merlot quality has been unimpressive.

TASTING NOTES

MERLOT SONOMA VALLEY (★): Odd wines that lack focus and harmony.
1989: Tastes harsh, green and tannic, with little fruit underneath. Dominated by oak. **74**
1988: Awkward, with ripe raisin and rhubarb flavors and plenty of oak. **78**

WILDHURST VINEYARDS
Lake County
F: 1991. **O:** Myron Holdenried & Collin Brothers. **W:** Kathy Redman, Jed Steele. **S:** None.

OVERALL	$9-15	★★

WINE RATINGS

Cabernet Sauvignon Clear Lake	NR
Chardonnay California	★★
Fumé Blanc Clear Lake Reserve	NR
Johannisberg Riesling Clear Lake Dry	NR
Merlot Clear Lake	★★
Pinot Noir Mendocino County	NR
Zinfandel Clear Lake	★★

WINERY DATA
C: 12,000. **V:** 149 acres in Clear Lake. **G:** Sauvignon Blanc (20 acres), Zinfandel (40), Merlot (25), Cabernet Sauvignon (36), Chardonnay (18), Johannisberg Riesling (10). **P:** Chardonnay (Sonoma County).

A new winery in Lake County, founded in 1991, Wildhurst owns 149 acres in vines near Clear Lake, led by Zinfandel (40 acres) and Cabernet (36 acres). Wildhurst uses these, along with purchased grapes, to produce 12,000 cases a year, with Jed Steele (Steele Wines) consulting. Quality in early vintages has risen to good but is variable.

TASTING NOTES

CABERNET SAUVIGNON CLEAR LAKE (NR):
1991: Simple and oaky, with the wood masking the raspberry aromas and Cabernet flavors. Soft tannins. **76**

CHARDONNAY VARIOUS BOTTLINGS (★★): Inconsistent with the 1991 bottlings, although the Reserve was impressive.
California 1993: Crisp and spicy, with ripe apple, pear, honey and vanilla notes, turning complex and elegant on the finish, where the oak folds in nicely. Very well made. **85**
Sonoma County 1991: Floral and spicy, almost like a Riesling, a soft-textured wine with a polished feel, sweet on the finish. **80**
Sonoma County Reserve 1993: Smooth, round and spicy, a silky wine that spins out its oak-scented pear and apple fruit through a gentle finish. **85**
Sonoma County Reserve 1991: Ripe, smooth and creamy, with a sense of elegance and finesse to the toasty pear, spice and nutmeg flavors. **89**

FUMÉ BLANC CLEAR LAKE RESERVE (NR):
1993: Smooth and polished, spicy and fresh like a Chardonnay. Tasty now. **84**

MERLOT VARIOUS BOTTLINGS (★★): Well oaked, with modest fruit flavors, but so far no discernable style.
Clear Lake 1991: A tight, crisp, fruity Merlot that features ripe raspberry flavors and modest tannins. **84**
Lake County Reserve 1992: An oaky wine with toasty, buttery notes dominating, but cherry, currant and spice flavors emerge. **84**
Lake County Reserve 1991: Lean and spicy, with a strong, toasty oak component to the berry and currant notes. **87**

PINOT NOIR MENDOCINO COUNTY (NR): Made from Mendocino-grown grapes.
1992: Woody and cedary, lacking sufficient fruit to be interesting. **74**

RIESLING CLEAR LAKE DRY (NR):
1991: Light and crisp, with pleasant peach and pine aromas and flavors. Simple and refreshing; tastes just off-dry. **82**

ZINFANDEL CLEAR LAKE (★★): Offers appealing fruit flavors in a medium-bodied, balanced style.
1992: Intense and tannic, with a dry, earthy, briary edge. **80**
1991: Shows plum and prune flavors, toasty oak accents and an almost sweet finish. **86**
1990: Bright and fruity, with a firm texture and focused blackberry and black cherry aromas and flavors. **85**

WILLIAMS & SELYEM WINERY
Russian River Valley
F: 1981. **O:** Ed Selyem & Burt Williams. **W:** Burt Williams. **S:** None.

OVERALL	$20-60	★★★★★

WINE RATINGS

Chardonnay Russian River Valley Allen Vineyard	★★★★★
Pinot Noir Anderson Valley Ferrington Vineyard	★★★★
Pinot Noir Russian River Valley	★★★★
Pinot Noir Russian River Valley Allen Vineyard	★★★★★
Pinot Noir Russian River Valley Cohn Vineyard	★★★★
Pinot Noir Russian River Valley Olivet Lane Vineyard	★★★★
Pinot Noir Russian River Valley Rochioli Vineyard	★★★★★
Pinot Noir Sonoma Coast	★★★★
Pinot Noir Sonoma Coast Summa Vineyard	★★★★
Zinfandel Russian River Valley Leno·Martinelli Vineyard	★★★★★

WINERY DATA
C: 5,000. **V:** None. **G:** None. **P:** Pinot Noir (Russian River Valley), Pinot Noir (Sonoma Coast), Pinot Noir (Anderson Valley), Chardonnay (Russian River Valley), Zinfandel (Russian River Valley).

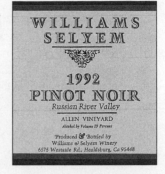

The emergence of Williams & Selyem as California's Pinot Noir leader is an improbable success story. In the early 1980s founders Burt Williams and Ed Selyem started making wine at Hacienda del Rio Winery in a garage in Fulton. Their first wine was a 1981 Zinfandel, but by 1982 they began their quest for great Pinot Noir, changing the winery's name when Hacienda Winery in Sonoma threatened a legal challenge. By the late 1980s, Williams retired as a typesetter and Selyem left his job as a wine retailer, devoting themselves full-time to winemaking.

With no vineyards of its own, Williams & Selyem is fortunate to have secured long-term contracts to buy some of Sonoma's best Pinot Noir from Rochioli and Allen Vineyards, along with Olivet Lane and Summa Vineyards. Ferrington Vineyard in Anderson Valley (Mendocino) impressed in its 1992 debut, and Cohn Vineyard, another Russian River vineyard, appeared with the 1993 vintage. A small portion of Zinfandel (Sonoma County) and a barrel or two of Allen Vineyard Chardonnay comprise the rest of the winery's 5,000-case production.

Quality across the board is exceptionally high, with a first decade that included many exciting wines, most notably the Pinot Noirs. There are no secrets to Williams & Selyem's success: they seek low-yield, fully ripened grapes from superb vineyard sources. The wines are well oaked, achieving extra flavor dimensions yet preserving the integrity of the fruit. In 1990, Williams & Selyem moved into a small facility near their key vineyard sources. The wines are sold mainly through a mailing list that is increasingly difficult to get on.

TASTING NOTES

CHARDONNAY RUSSIAN RIVER VALLEY ALLEN VINEYARD
(★★★★★): Very hard to get, as production in some
years is but 25 cases, (200 is the maximum), but this is
an ultraripe, high-alcohol (14.5%), intensely flavored and
well oaked style of wine. Ages well.
1993: Elegant and refined, with a subtle mix of pear,
spice, toast and apple flavors that fold together nicely,
turning smooth and complex. **91**
1992: Big, intense and flavorful, with lots of spicy pear
and honey notes that pick up the rich, toasty oak flavors
on the finish. **90**

PINOT NOIR ANDERSON VALLEY FERRINGTON VINEYARD
(★★★★): First appeared in 1992, with a tremendously
rich and complex wine. Worth watching.
1992: Combines ripe black cherry, spice and currant
notes with cedary oak flavors, all folded together nicely,
finishing with a complex aftertaste and firm tannins. **92**

PINOT NOIR RUSSIAN RIVER VALLEY (★★★★),
SONOMA COAST (★★★★): These bottlings are blends of
special lots of wines that aren't used in the vineyard-designated wines. The Sonoma Coast, from the coolest,
most westerly vineyards, is not produced every year, but
when it is made it shares the winery's house style of
ultraripe and complex flavors. The Russian River bottling
can claim similar attributes, even though the appellation
extends farther east. A Sonoma County bottling appeared
occasionally in the 1980s, but is rare. Ages well.
Russian River Valley 1993: Light but balanced, with
herb, black cherry and subtle spice and oak shadings. **85**
Russian River Valley 1992: Ripe, intense and fruity,
with elegant black cherry, plum and currant notes that
turn smooth and silky on the finish. **90**
Russian River Valley 1991: Smooth, ripe and exotic, an
opulent wine laced with blackberry, black cherry, currant
and plum flavors that all come together in a silky, supple
package. **93**
Russian River Valley 1990: Simply delicious, with its
lovely layering of currant, berry, vanilla and cocoa-butter
flavors, all resting on a silky texture that spins out the
flavors on a long finish. **93**
Sonoma Coast 1993: Light, with simple herb and cherry
notes of modest proportions. **83**

Sonoma Coast 1989: The nose is complex and aromatic,
and the cherry and rhubarb flavors are elegant and spicy. **87**
Sonoma Coast 1988: Remarkable for its rich, deep,
complex chocolate, cherry, toast and vanilla flavors that
are smooth and concentrated, backed with toasty oak and
firm, supple tannins. **92**
Sonoma County 1986: Lots of pretty aromas of fruit,
toast and cherries, followed by rich, ripe, spicy coffee,
strawberry and black cherry flavors. **91**
Sonoma County 1985: Light in color, turning pale garnet, with earthy, tarry herb and dried cherry flavors. An
elegant wine that's fully mature. **84**
Sonoma County 1982: Bottled under the Hacienda del
Rio label. Mature and aging very well, with tea, herb and
dried cherry flavors that turn delicate and floral notes on
the finish. **89**

PINOT NOIR RUSSIAN RIVER VALLEY ALLEN VINEYARD
(★★★★★): The Allen Vineyard borders the Rochioli
Vineyard and rivals it in quality, as it is capable of rendering enormously complex, rich and concentrated
wines, loaded with flavor and finesse. Ages well.
1992: Supple and flavorful, with currant, plum, smoke
and vanilla flavors that turn smooth and delicate on the
finish. **91**
1991: Complex and compelling, spicy and perfumed,
with rich, concentrated, sharply focused plum, black
cherry and raspberry flavors and an anise and tar edge on
the finish. **93**
1990: Ripe, rich and remarkably focused, with deeply
concentrated plum, cherry and spice aromas and flavors
that turn supple and complex. **93**
1989: Elegant and delicate, with complex plum and
black cherry aromas and flavors. **88**
1988: Amazing richness and depth, packed with complex
plum, cherry, raspberry and spice flavors that fill out on
the palate with a sumptuous, silky texture. **94**
1987: A remarkably rich and complex wine with layers
of black cherry, raspberry, chocolate and vanilla flavors
that are very harmonious and elegant, finishing with subtlety and delicacy. **92**

PINOT NOIR RUSSIAN RIVER VALLEY COHN VINEYARD
(★★★★): New in 1993, a lighter vintage, so it will take
a few more years before its quality and character can be
assessed.
1993: Medium-bodied, light in color, with an earthy cherry and herb streak, but it still lacks extra dimensions. **85**

PINOT NOIR RUSSIAN RIVER VALLEY OLIVET LANE VINEYARD (★★★★): Impressive, with bold, ripe, juicy Pinot Noir flavors that are complex and silky.

1993: Smooth and supple, with light cherry, earth and spicy notes, finishing with a firm, green tannic edge. **85**

1992: Has softened from a tannic beginning, now showing mature, black cherry, plum and wild berry notes, with a soft, fleshy aftertaste. **89**

1991: Rich, ripe and loaded with black cherry, plum, spice, raspberry and pretty oak flavors, all wrapped in a smooth, silky texture. **92**

1990: Ripe, smooth and velvety, more than a little tannic, with layers of plum, cherry, spice and oak aromas and flavors. **84**

1989: Ripe, round and fruity, with plush plum and black cherry flavors accented by toast and spice notes. **90**

PINOT NOIR RUSSIAN RIVER VALLEY ROCHIOLI VINEYARD (★★★★★): Among the finest, if not *the* finest Pinot Noir vineyard in California, consistently yielding wines of amazing depth, richness, concentration and flavor, with tiers of ripe cherry, plum, currant and wild berry. Ages well for up to a decade.

1992: Toasty, buttery oak gives way to ripe plum, strawberry and black cherry flavors before finishing with pretty vanilla, smoke and fruit flavors. Wonderful sense of harmony and finesse. **95**

1991: Rich, ripe and plummy, generous from start to finish, with plush, supple vanilla-scented fruit and spice flavors that are smooth and polished. **95**

1990: Ripe, supple and complex, with layers of rich cherry, raspberry, plum and anise flavors, finishing with mild tannins. Not as rich as the best bottlings from this winery. **91**

1989: Smooth and complex, with rich and supple cherry, herb and spicy wood flavors. **88**

1988: Beautifully proportioned, aromatic and elegant, with tiers of raspberry, plum, currant and cherry flavors to balance the vanilla and spice of oak, all of which keep growing on the finish. **94**

1987: Mature but holding, still displaying a ripe, supple core of elegant black cherry, spice and currant notes, finishing with a sense of harmony and finesse. **92**

1986: Deep in color and flavor, with richly perfumed aromas and concentrated plum and black cherry flavors that take on a spicy, minty edge. **93**

1985: Combines bold, ripe fruit with elegance and finesse, showing plum, currant and spicy herb flavors that are soft and fleshy, finishing with complex tar and earth notes. **89**

PINOT NOIR SONOMA COAST SUMMA VINEYARD (★★★★): This is a rare bottling, produced in extremely small quantities. The 1991 sold for $100 a bottle.

1991: Incredibly intense yet lithe and elegant, showing layer after layer of plum, berry, mineral and toast flavors that remain sharply focused through the long, slightly raw finish. **95**

1988: Mature and ready to drink, with spicy herb, tea and black cherry notes that are crisp and lighter than usual. **84**

ZINFANDEL RUSSIAN RIVER VALLEY LENO MARTINELLI VINEYARD (★★★★★): For a decade, 1981 to 1992, this Russian River vineyard was the source for a string of excellent Zins, made in a very ripe, high-extract, intense style with firm tannins, marked by wild berry, raspberry, anise and tarry flavors. Since 1992, Martinelli Winery has been bottling its own wine from this vineyard. Ages well.

1992: Packs in lots of juicy, ripe Zin flavors, with rich plum, cherry and raspberry notes that are firm and concentrated. **91**

1991: A beautifully crafted Zin with layers of bright, ripe, spicy raspberry, cherry and vanilla flavors. Intense and lively, with a long, full, lingering aftertaste. **92**

1990: Combines all the ripe, rich, intense flavors of this old vineyard with a sense of balance and finesse, showing tiers of spicy, peppery black cherry and raspberry flavors. **92**

1989: Crisp, elegant, supple and balanced, with black cherry, raspberry and anise flavors that linger long on the palate. **89**

1988: Stretches the ripeness to the edge of late harvest. This is a ripe, intense, jammy wine with elegant raspberry, black cherry and plum flavors that turn spicy on the finish. **89**

1987: Broad, ripe, rich and lush, with jammy, concentrated raspberry, plum and currant flavors that are polished and seductive, finishing with firm tannins. **90**

1986: Austere, tight, firm and focused, packing in lots of compact raspberry, anise and plum flavors that are bright and lively, finishing with a good dose of tannin. **88**

1985: Tight and lean but focused, with anise, black cherry, spice and raspberry flavors that are still firmly wound. **87**

1984: Intense and jammy, with raisin and Port-like flavors, but the richness, concentration, depth and alcohol stay in balance. Raspberry, anise and tar notes linger on a long, hot finish. **88**
1983: Tight, crisp and tannic, with plum and raspberry aromas and flavors that are still tightly tannic. **86**
Sonoma County 1982: Very ripe and jammy, with a funky, earthy edge, but it's big and concentrated. **84**
Sonoma County 1981: Bottled under the Hacienda del Rio label. Still youthful and vibrant, with tart, earthy plum and raspberry flavors that pick up a touch of anise and spice on the finish. **88**

WILSON-COLE CELLARS
This is a second label of Hafner (see listing).

WINDEMERE
Napa Valley
F: 1985. **O:** Kathy MacGregor-Bryan. **W:** Kathy MacGregor-Bryan. **S:** None.

OVERALL	$11-18	★★
WINE RATINGS		
Cabernet Sauvignon Napa Valley		★★
Chardonnay Edna Valley		
MacGregor Vineyard		★★
Zinfandel Paso Robles		NR

WINERY DATA
C: 2,000. **V:** None. **G:** None. **P:** Cabernet Sauvignon (Napa Valley), Chardonnay (Edna Valley), Zinfandel (Paso Robles).

Kathy MacGregor-Bryan produces 2,000 cases a year of Cabernet (Napa Valley), Chardonnay (Edna Valley) and Zinfandel (Paso Robles). She is the daughter of Andy MacGregor, owner of MacGregor Vineyard in Edna Valley, and produces a Chardonnay from that vineyard along with a Cabernet from Napa Valley grapes. At the time of this writing, she and her husband were planning to build a winery and expand production to 10,000 cases. Quality has been variable, ranging from fair to good.

TASTING NOTES

CABERNET SAUVIGNON NAPA VALLEY (★★): The 1990 was an improvement over the ordinary 1989.

1990: Firm and youthful, offering lots of complex, earthy currant flavors, with all of the parts in balance. **88**
1989: Tart and sharply focused, showing a narrow beam of ripe cherry, spice and tobacco characteristics shining through a veil of fine tannins. **83**

CHARDONNAY EDNA VALLEY MACGREGOR VINEYARD (★★): Variable, with 1992 a step up from the odd 1991.
1992: An intense, youthful wine with tart, ripe pear and pineapple flavors that finish with crisp, lemony acidity. **84**
1991: Tastes mature and excessively manipulated, with a sour edge to the pineapple and pear flavors. Some honey richness emerges on the finish. **77**

WING CANYON
Napa Valley
F: 1982. **O:** Palmer Williams Jenkins & Martha Jenkins. **W:** Bill Jenkins. **S:** None.

OVERALL	$18-20	NR
WINE RATINGS		
Cabernet Franc Mount Veeder		NR
Cabernet Sauvignon Mount Veeder		NR
Chardonnay Mount Veeder		NR
Merlot Mount Veeder		NR

WINERY DATA
C: 400. **V:** 10 acres in Mt. Veeder. **G:** Chardonnay (0.5 acres), Merlot (0.5), Cabernet Franc (0.5), Cabernet Sauvignon (8). **P:** None.

Wing Canyon on Mount Veeder is among the smallest California wineries, producing 400 cases, all from a 10-acre estate. At eight acres, Cabernet is the largest planted variety, yielding 200 cases. The three other types produce 48 cases each. The first wines were produced in 1991. Distribution is very limited.

CHRISTINE WOODS WINERY
Anderson Valley
F: 1982. **O:** Christine Woods Vineyards Inc. **W:** Vernon J. Rose. **S:** None.

OVERALL	$10-16	★

WINE RATINGS
Chardonnay Anderson Valley   ★
Pinot Noir Anderson Valley
   Estate Reserve   ★

WINERY DATA
C: 1,500. V: 15 acres in Anderson Valley. G: Pinot Noir
(8 acres), Chardonnay (6). P: None.

From its 15-acre Anderson Valley vineyard near
Roederer Estate, Christine Woods produces estate-grown
Chardonnay and Pinot Noir from a vineyard planted in
1982. Quality varies from fair to ordinary at best, as the
wines often display an earthy, murky edge. Production is
1,500 cases.

WOODSIDE VINEYARDS
Woodside, San Mateo County
F: 1960. O: Robert L. & Polly Mullen. W: Brian
Caselden. S: None.

OVERALL	$14-24	NR

WINE RATINGS
Cabernet Sauvignon
   Santa Cruz Mountains   NR
Chardonnay Santa Cruz Mountains   NR
French Colombard Santa Cruz Mountains NR
Zinfandel Santa Cruz Mountains   NR

WINERY DATA
C: 1,800. V: 40 acres in Santa Cruz Mountains. G: Chardonnay,
Cabernet Sauvignon, Zinfandel, French Colombard. P: None.

Woodside Vineyards is located in the wooded hills
between San Francisco and San Jose and produces 1,800
cases of wine a year, much of which comes from its 40
acres of Cabernet and Chardonnay grown in the Santa
Cruz appellation. Distribution is very limited.

YORK MOUNTAIN WINERY
San Luis Obispo County
F: 1970. O: Max Goldman. W: Steve Goldman. S: None.

OVERALL	$9-16	★

WINE RATINGS
Cabernet Sauvignon
   San Luis Obispo County   ★
Chardonnay San Luis Obispo County   ★★
Merlot San Luis Obispo County   ★
Pinot Noir San Luis Obispo County   ★
Zinfandel San Luis Obispo County   ★★

WINERY DATA
C: 5,000. V: 80 acres in York Mountain. G: Chardonnay
(8 acres), Cabernet Sauvignon (9), Pinot Noir (3), Merlot (2),
Grenache (7). P: Merlot, Zinfandel, Pinot Noir (Paso Robles).

York Mountain Winery dates to 1882, when the York
family built the old stone winery still used today. It was
revived in 1970 by Max Goldman, with his son and winemaker Steve overseeing the wines. Production is 5,000
cases, using both estate-grown and purchased grapes—
Cabernet, Chardonay, Merlot, Pinot Noir and Zinfandel—
all from the San Luis Obispo area. The estate vineyards
are in a very cool climate, which accounts for the green,
marginally ripe flavors often found in the wines. The
wines are largely unimpressive, ranging in quality from
poor to fair, occasionally hitting good marks. Fortified
wines are also produced. Most of the wine is sold to
tourists travelling from Highway 101 to the coast and on
to Cambria and Hearst's Castle.

TASTING NOTES

CABERNET SAUVIGNON SAN LUIS OBISPO COUNTY
(★★): Often overly tannic and austere, without sufficient
fruit to balance.
1989: Tannic, with an earthy menthol edge. **71**

CHARDONNAY SAN LUIS OBISPO COUNTY (★): Variable
quality, as it is often overmade with more oak and off flavors than pure fruit.
1993: Strikes a nice balance between ripe, earthy pear
and citrus notes and toasty buttery oak, finishing with a
lingering aftertaste. **84**
1992: Surprisingly dark and spicy for a '92, weaving a
harsh, toasty note into the otherwise smooth, earthy pear
flavors. **80**

MERLOT SAN LUIS OBISPO COUNTY (★): Simple and on
the borderline for acceptable quality.

1991: Simple, with a narrow strip of currant, herb and tobacco flavors. Marginal quality, but short-term cellaring should soften it. Tasted twice, with consistent results. **79**

PINOT NOIR SAN LUIS OBISPO COUNTY (★): The 1990 showed better than other recent York Mountain offerings. **1990:** Tart, lean and a bit green, with tea, herb and tobacco flavors dominating the fruit. Turns earthy and tannic on the finish, where it picks up a cola and cherry edge. **82**

ZINFANDEL SAN LUIS OBISPO COUNTY (★★): Rustic but showing more fruit and better balance than the other wines. **1990:** Ripe and spicy, with tart, crisp black cherry and raspberry flavors that linger. Not too tannic. **82**

YOUNG'S VINEYARD

Amador County
F: 1980. **O:** Steven & Annette Young. **W:** Stell Young, William Easton. **S:** None.

OVERALL	$10-13	NR

WINE RATINGS	
Cabernet Sauvignon Amador County	NR
Zinfandel Amador County	NR

WINERY DATA
C: 1,400. **V:** 10 acres in Amador County. **G:** Zinfandel (5 acres), Cabernet Sauvignon (2), Muscat (1), Syrah (2). **P:** None.

This 1,400-case winery in Plymouth produces small quantities of Cabernet and Zinfandel, both carrying the Amador County appellation, from its 10-acre estate vineyard. Very limited distribution.

ZACA MESA WINERY

Santa Barbara County
F: 1972. **O:** Cushman Winery Corp. **W:** Daniel R. Gehrs. **S:** None.

OVERALL	$12-19	★★★

WINE RATINGS	
Chardonnay Santa Barbara County	★★★
Chardonnay Santa Barbara County Chapel Vineyard	★★★
Chardonnay Santa Barbara County Zaca Vineyards	★★★
Pinot Noir Santa Barbara County Sierra Madre Vineyard	★★
Rhône Blend Santa Barbara County Cuvée Z	★★
Syrah Santa Barbara County	★★
Syrah Santa Barbara County Chapel Vineyard	★★

WINERY DATA
C: 25,000. **V:** 402 acres in Santa Barbara County. **G:** Rhône-type varieties Chardonnay, Pinot Noir. **P:** None.

In the early 1970s, oil executive Louis Ream mapped out a plan for Zaca Mesa Winery, built around some 340 acres in vines; production at one time reached 100,000 cases. Early on, Ken Brown (now at Byron) oversaw winemaking and a succession of now well-known winemakers—among them Jim Clendenen (Au Bon Climat, Vita Nova), Adam Tolmach (Ojai) and Bob Lindquist (Qupe)—assisted. Zaca Mesa experimented with a range of wines, including Cabernet, but found that Cabernet struggled to avoid being overly herbaceous.

The focus now is on the winery's 402 acres in vines, including a one-third ownership of the Sierra Madre Vineyard. Chardonnay (135 acres) is the acreage leader, with Pinot Noir and Rhône varieties also in the mix. Case volume has shrunk to 25,000 as the winery moves to improve quality. The hiring in 1993 of Daniel Gehrs (formerly of Congress Springs) should give the winery a boost. Quality is on the upswing, as the Chardonnays and Syrah are increasingly impressive. A line of Winemaker Alumni Series wines, made by former winemakers, shows where the winery wants to go in the future.

TASTING NOTES

CHARDONNAY VARIOUS BOTTLINGS (★★★): Steadily improving, with the Alumni Winemaker Series Chardonnay most impressive. The wines emphasize bright, ripe, juicy flavors with pretty oak shadings.
Santa Barbara County 1991: Tight and lemony, with reined-in citrus, pear and apple notes. **86**
Santa Barbara County Alumni Winemaker Series James A. Clendenen 1992: Ripe and creamy, offering a nice core of apricot, pear and vanilla flavors that turn complex. **90**

Santa Barbara County Chapel Vineyard 1992: Spicy and intense, very Burgundian, a rich, round wine that turns soft. **85**

Santa Barbara County Zaca Vineyards 1993: Lean and a little leafy in flavor, an attractive, floral wine that shows some nice apple flavor on the lively finish. **85**

PINOT NOIR VARIOUS BOTTLINGS (★★): Variable quality, as it often strays into earthy, vegetal flavors. Can be elegant and spicy, as in 1988. Has room to improve and indications are it will.

Santa Barbara County 1989: Carries the hallmark herb, cherry and vegetal notes of Santa Barbara Pinot Noir. **85**

Santa Barbara County Reserve 1990: Tough, tannic, gamy and earthy, with plum and cherry flavors lurking in the background. **74**

Santa Barbara County Reserve 1989: Earthy and vegetal, a distinctive style, but here the earthiness wins out over the plum notes. **73**

Santa Barbara County Reserve 1988: Elegant and spicy, with currant, cherry and rhubarb flavors that are intense and concentrated, but the finish lacks focus and turns tannic. **85**

Santa Barbara County Reserve 1987: Smooth, supple and flavorful, marked by oak and herb flavors. **82**

Santa Barbara County Sierra Madre Vineyard 1990: A solid wine with earthy cola and beet notes dominating the flavors. **82**

RHÔNE BLEND SANTA BARBARA COUNTY CUVÉE Z (★★): New to the lineup, but not overly impressive. The initial effort was light but the 1993 was better.

1993: Lean and flavorful, showing impressive complexity of berry, cherry and tar flavors. A hint of barnyard on the finish lends a touch of authenticity. **85**

1992: Light and smooth, a modest wine with gentle berry and earth flavors. **78**

SYRAH VARIOUS BOTTLINGS (★★): Medium-weight, with pleasant spicy cherry and peppery notes, but could use a little more richness. The Alumni Winemaker Series bottling is closer to the model, with its added richness.

Santa Barbara County 1990: Ripe, with classic black pepper, black cherry and currant aromas and flavors. **82**

Santa Barbara County 1989: Serves up a modest range of berry and cherry flavors and black pepper, tea and leather notes. **83**

Santa Barbara County Alumni Winemaker Series Bob Lindquist 1992: Ripe, round and generous, a complex wine that bursts with powerful blackberry, black cherry, black pepper and anise flavors. **89**

Santa Barbara County Chapel Vineyard 1992: Sturdy, with fresh plum, berry and spice flavors up front, turning chewy and tannic. **85**

ZAYANTE VINEYARDS
Santa Cruz Mountains
F: 1984. **O:** W. F. Nolten, Gregory Nolten & Kathleen Starkey. **W:** Gregory Nolten. **S:** None.

OVERALL	$14	NR

WINE RATINGS	
Chardonnay Santa Cruz Mountains	NR
Zinfandel Santa Cruz Mountains	NR

WINERY DATA
C: 1,000. **V:** 10 acres in Santa Cruz Mountains. **G:** Chardonnay (5 acres), Zinfandel (2), Syrah (2), Merlot (1). **P:** None.

This 10-acre Santa Cruz Mountain vineyard dates to 1984, but the first wines, Chardonnay and Zinfandel, were made in 1991. Production is around 1,000 cases.

ZD WINES
Napa Valley
F: 1969. **O:** de Leuze family. **W:** Julie de Leuze. **S:** None.

OVERALL	$14-25	★★★

WINE RATINGS	
Cabernet Sauvignon Napa Valley	★★★
Chardonnay California	★★★
Pinot Noir Carneros	★★

WINERY DATA
C: 20,000. **V:** 3 acres in Napa Valley. **G:** Cabernet Sauvignon. **P:** Chardonnay (Napa Valley, Sonoma, Monterey), Cabernet Sauvignon (Napa Valley), Pinot Noir (Carneros).

Aerospace engineers Gino Zepponi and Norman de Leuze founded ZD, starting first in Sonoma but later relocating to a site on Silverado Trail in Rutherford. The winery was expanded in 1990 to its current 20,000-case production. California-appellation Chardonnay (16,600 cases), with grapes coming from Carneros, Napa, Monterey, Santa Barbara and Santa Maria, remains the focal point, and the wines have a rich, earthy, distinctly Burgundian touch to them. Cabernet (from Napa Valley, including an occasional Reserve) and Pinot Noir (Carneros) are also part of the mix, each produced in the 1,500-case range. Quality across the board is very good to outstanding, with each of the wines showing an exotic edge. The winery is now owned entirely by the de Leuze family.

TASTING NOTES

CABERNET SAUVIGNON NAPA VALLEY (★★★): Typically firm and high in extract, with dense earthy tannins, but usually with enough ripe cherry and currant flavors to keep in balance. The winery's 3.5 acres of Cabernet are used for the reserve in exceptional years.

1990: A tight, austere wine that's showing more oak and tannin than fruit at this stage, but it has an appealing core of weedy black currant and spice flavors. **88**

1989: Walks a tightrope between earthy, barnyardy notes and modest fruit flavors. **78**

1988: Supple, with spicy oak notes, moderate cherry and plum flavors and firm tannins. **86**

1987: Smooth, rich and complex, packing in deep currant, plum, anise and oak flavors. **88**

Reserve 1987: Tough and earthy, with a powerful structure and broad, juicy black cherry and tobacco flavors. **89**

1986: Tight, firm and tannic, a backward wine that needs time for the spicy currant flavors to emerge. **85**

1985: Ripe, supple and complex, with nicely integrated currant, spice, anise and buttery oak flavors. **87**

1984: Tough, oaky and tannic, a blockbuster that's just beginning to reveal its ripe currant flavor. Turns dry and tannic. **85**

1983: Ripe, crisp and tannic, but with decent currant, plum and tar flavors that are persistent. **84**

1982: A strong weedy, almost vegetal streak runs through the fruit flavor. **83**

1981: Marked by herb, tar and currant flavors and oak shadings. **82**

1980: Bold, ripe and fleshy, with rich currant and plum flavors that border on raisiny. **84**

CHARDONNAY CALIFORNIA (★★★): A shade tighter of late, but the signature is bold, ripe, juicy and complex fruit that's well oaked in an opulent and distinctive style. Ages well.

25th Anniversary Vintage 1993: An exotic style with grapefruit, mango and guava flavors that stretch the band of flavors, but it turns simple and loses its intensity on the finish. **85**

1991: Tight, lean and a bit oaky, but it still packs in lots of ripe, spicy pear and lemon flavors and it's crisp and mouthwatering. **87**

PINOT NOIR CARNEROS (★★): The most variable wine, naturally, and ZD's least consistent, as it can be ripe and opulent at times, or hard-edged and tannic, with more wood than it needs.

1991: Hard, lean and dry, with more oak than fruit, which is unusual for ZD. **78**

1990: Ripe, smooth and plush, with tarry, earthy currant and plum flavors. **86**

1989: A tart, tight wine that's tannic and tough in texture, with raspberry and red cherry flavors and a drying finish. **82**

1988: An earthy wine with tiers of spice, pepper, plum and leather notes. **82**

1985: Hard-edged and woody, with an undercurrent of concentrated black cherry flavor plus hints of cassis and cinnamon. **79**

STEPHEN ZELLERBACH

This is a second label of Estate William Baccala (see listing).

ALL WINES TASTED BY WINERY

❖

ACACIA WINERY

84   1993 Chardonnay Carneros
87   1992 Chardonnay Carneros
83   1991 Chardonnay Carneros
89   1992 Chardonnay Carneros Reserve
89   1991 Chardonnay Carneros Marina Vineyard
85   1991 Chardonnay Napa Valley
83   1993 Pinot Noir Carneros
83   1991 Pinot Noir Carneros
86   1990 Pinot Noir Carneros
75   1989 Pinot Noir Carneros
85   1988 Pinot Noir Carneros
86   1987 Pinot Noir Carneros
86   1986 Pinot Noir Carneros
80   1985 Pinot Noir Carneros
80   1984 Pinot Noir Carneros
87   1992 Pinot Noir Carneros St. Clair Vineyard Reserve
83   1991 Pinot Noir Carneros St. Clair Vineyard
88   1990 Pinot Noir Carneros St. Clair Vineyard
85   1989 Pinot Noir Carneros St. Clair Vineyard
87   1988 Pinot Noir Carneros St. Clair Vineyard
84   1987 Pinot Noir Carneros St. Clair Vineyard
91   1986 Pinot Noir Carneros St. Clair Vineyard
86   1985 Pinot Noir Carneros St. Clair Vineyard
87   1984 Pinot Noir Carneros St. Clair Vineyard
85   1983 Pinot Noir Carneros St. Clair Vineyard
84   1982 Pinot Noir Carneros St. Clair Vineyard
79   1980 Pinot Noir Carneros St. Clair Vineyard
86   1979 Pinot Noir Carneros St. Clair Vineyard
82   1991 Pinot Noir Carneros Iund Vineyard
91   1986 Pinot Noir Carneros Iund Vineyard
87   1985 Pinot Noir Carneros Iund Vineyard
88   1984 Pinot Noir Carneros Iund Vineyard
83   1983 Pinot Noir Carneros Iund Vineyard
79   1981 Pinot Noir Carneros Iund Vineyard
70   1980 Pinot Noir Carneros Iund Vineyard
88   1982 Pinot Noir Carneros Lee Vineyard
79   1981 Pinot Noir Carneros Lee Vineyard
85   1979 Pinot Noir Carneros Lee Vineyard

87   1986 Pinot Noir Carneros Madonna Vineyard
87   1985 Pinot Noir Carneros Madonna Vineyard
82   1984 Pinot Noir Carneros Madonna Vineyard
79   1982 Pinot Noir Carneros Madonna Vineyard
87   1980 Pinot Noir Carneros Madonna Vineyard
85   1982 Pinot Noir Carneros Winery Lake Vineyard
78   1981 Pinot Noir Carneros Winery Lake Vineyard
85   1992 Caviste Zinfandel Napa Valley
86   1991 Caviste Zinfandel Napa Valley
86   1990 Caviste Zinfandel Napa Valley

ADELAIDA CELLARS

87   1988 Cabernet Sauvignon Paso Robles
89   1987 Cabernet Sauvignon Paso Robles
88   1991 Chardonnay San Luis Obispo County
87   1990 Chardonnay Paso Robles
87   1991 Chardonnay San Luis Obispo County Reserve
87   1991 Zinfandel San Luis Obispo County
82   1990 Zinfandel San Luis Obispo County
83   1989 Zinfandel Paso Robles
88   1988 Zinfandel Paso Robles

ADLER FELS

84   1992 Chardonnay Sonoma County
81   1992 Chardonnay Sonoma County Coleman Reserve
86   1991 Chardonnay Sonoma County Coleman Reserve
84   1992 Gewürztraminer Sonoma County
83   1992 Sauvignon Blanc Sonoma County

AHLGREN VINEYARD

76   1988 Cabernet Sauvignon Santa Cruz Mountains Bates Ranch
79   1991 Chardonnay Santa Cruz Mountains Buerge Vineyard
73   1991 Chardonnay Santa Cruz Mountains Mayers Vineyard

ALBAN VINEYARDS

84   1992 Roussanne San Luis Obispo County
86   1991 Roussanne San Luis Obispo County

84   1992 Viognier San Luis Obispo County
82   1991 Viognier San Luis Obispo County

ALDERBROOK WINERY

83   1993 Chardonnay Dry Creek Valley
85   1992 Chardonnay Dry Creek Valley
82   1990 Chardonnay Dry Creek Valley
87   1992 Meritage White Dry Creek Valley Duet
81   1990 Meritage White Dry Creek Valley Duet
85   1994 Sauvignon Blanc Dry Creek Valley
82   1993 Sauvignon Blanc Dry Creek Valley
80   1990 Sauvignon Blanc Dry Creek Valley
83   1993 Sémillon Dry Creek Valley
78   1992 Sémillon Dry Creek Valley
85   1990 Sémillon Dry Creek Valley
85   1993 Zinfandel Dry Creek Valley

ALEXANDER VALLEY FRUIT & TRADING CO.

82   1990 Dessert Wine Alexander Valley
81   1992 Zinfandel Dry Creek Valley

ALEXANDER VALLEY VINEYARDS

80   1993 Cabernet Sauvignon Alexander Valley
87   1992 Cabernet Sauvignon Alexander Valley
85   1991 Cabernet Sauvignon Alexander Valley
86   1989 Cabernet Sauvignon Alexander Valley
88   1988 Cabernet Sauvignon Alexander Valley
87   1987 Cabernet Sauvignon Alexander Valley
86   1986 Cabernet Sauvignon Alexander Valley
87   1985 Cabernet Sauvignon Alexander Valley
93   1984 Cabernet Sauvignon Alexander Valley
88   1983 Cabernet Sauvignon Alexander Valley
87   1982 Cabernet Sauvignon Alexander Valley
85   1981 Cabernet Sauvignon Alexander Valley
82   1980 Cabernet Sauvignon Alexander Valley
84   1979 Cabernet Sauvignon Alexander Valley
78   1978 Cabernet Sauvignon Alexander Valley
60   1976 Cabernet Sauvignon Alexander Valley
75   1975 Cabernet Sauvignon Alexander Valley
86   1992 Cabernet Sauvignon Alexander Valley Wetzel Family Estate

84   1991 Cabernet Sauvignon Alexander Valley Wetzel Family Estate

88   1990 Cabernet Sauvignon Alexander Valley Wetzel Family Estate

83   1990 Chardonnay Alexander Valley

84   1992 Chardonnay Alexander Valley Wetzel Family Estate

88   1991 Chardonnay Alexander Valley Wetzel Family Estate

80   1992 Gewürztraminer Alexander Valley

87   1992 Merlot Alexander Valley

86   1991 Merlot Alexander Valley

87   1990 Merlot Alexander Valley

84   1989 Merlot Alexander Valley

86   1992 Merlot Alexander Valley Wetzel Family Estate

77   1991 Merlot Alexander Valley Wetzel Family Estate

65   1989 Pinot Noir Alexander Valley

74   1987 Pinot Noir Alexander Valley

83   1990 Pinot Noir Alexander Valley Wetzel Family Estate

86   1991 Riesling Alexander Valley

76   1989 Zinfandel Alexander Valley Sin Zin

ALTAMURA WINERY AND VINEYARDS

88   1990 Cabernet Sauvignon Napa Valley

83   1989 Cabernet Sauvignon Napa Valley

85   1988 Cabernet Sauvignon Napa Valley

88   1990 Chardonnay Napa Valley

AMADOR FOOTHILL WINERY

82   1992 Sauvignon Blanc Shenandoah Valley Amador Fumé

78   1991 Zinfandel Fiddletown Eschen Vineyard

82   1990 Zinfandel Fiddletown Eschen Vineyard

82   1990 Zinfandel Shenandoah Valley Ferrero Vineyard

83   1990 Zinfandel Shenandoah Valley Grandpére Vineyard

S. ANDERSON VINEYARD

91   1991 Cabernet Sauvignon Stags Leap District Richard Chambers Vineyard

91   1990 Cabernet Sauvignon Stags Leap District Richard Chambers Vineyard

90   1989 Cabernet Sauvignon Stags Leap District Richard Chambers Vineyard

86   1993 Chardonnay Carneros

85   1992 Chardonnay Stags Leap District

85   1991 Chardonnay Stags Leap District

82   1990 Chardonnay Stags Leap District

89   1991 Chardonnay Stags Leap District Proprietor's Reserve

ANDERSON'S CONN VALLEY VINEYARDS

88   1991 Cabernet Sauvignon Napa Valley Estate Reserve

90   1990 Cabernet Sauvignon Napa Valley Estate Reserve

88   1989 Cabernet Sauvignon Napa Valley Estate Reserve

90   1988 Cabernet Sauvignon Napa Valley Estate Reserve

85   1992 Pinot Noir Napa Valley

84   1989 Pinot Noir Napa Valley Valhalla Vineyards

ARAUJO ESTATE WINES

93   1991 Cabernet Sauvignon Napa Valley Eisele Vineyard

ARCIERO WINERY

78   1990 Cabernet Sauvignon Paso Robles

79   1992 Chardonnay Paso Robles

86   1991 Chardonnay Paso Robles

84   1990 Chardonnay Paso Robles

79   1991 Nebbiolo Paso Robles

83   1992 Zinfandel Paso Robles

77   1988 Zinfandel Paso Robles

79   1988 Monte Verde Cabernet Sauvignon California Proprietor's Reserve

80   1987 Monte Verde Cabernet Sauvignon California Proprietor's Reserve

78   1990 Monte Verde Chardonnay Central Coast Proprietor's Reserve

ARMIDA WINERY

82   1992 Chardonnay Russian River Valley

88   1991 Chardonnay Russian River Valley

81   1990 Chardonnay Russian River Valley

86   1990 Merlot Russian River Valley

72   1992 Pinot Noir Russian River Valley

84   1991 Pinot Noir Russian River Valley

ARROWOOD VINEYARDS & WINERY

91   1991 Cabernet Sauvignon Sonoma County

91   1990 Cabernet Sauvignon Sonoma County

88   1989 Cabernet Sauvignon Sonoma County

87   1988 Cabernet Sauvignon Sonoma County

89   1987 Cabernet Sauvignon Sonoma County

90   1986 Cabernet Sauvignon Sonoma County

90   1985 Cabernet Sauvignon Sonoma County

88   1989 Cabernet Sauvignon Sonoma County Réserve Spéciale

87   1993 Chardonnay Sonoma County

91   1992 Chardonnay Sonoma County

88   1991 Chardonnay Sonoma County

88   1990 Chardonnay Sonoma County

92   1993 Chardonnay Sonoma County Cuvée Michel Berthoud

85   1992 Chardonnay Sonoma County Cuvée Michel Berthoud

90   1991 Chardonnay Sonoma County Réserve Spéciale

93   1990 Chardonnay Sonoma County Réserve Spéciale

91   1991 Merlot Sonoma County

91   1990 Merlot Sonoma County

88   1988 Merlot Sonoma County

85   1993 Viognier Russian River Valley Saralee's Vineyard

83   1992 Viognier Russian River Valley Saralee's Vineyard

96   1993 White Riesling Russian River Valley Oak Meadow Vineyard

87   1991 White Riesling Russian River Valley Oak Meadow Vineyard Select Late Harvest

87   1992 Domaine du Grand Archer Cabernet Sauvignon Sonoma County

89   1991 Domaine du Grand Archer Cabernet Sauvignon Sonoma County

82   1991 Domaine du Grand Archer Merlot Sonoma County

VINCENT ARROYO WINERY

88   1990 Cabernet Sauvignon Napa Valley

81   1989 Cabernet Sauvignon Napa Valley

85   1988 Cabernet Sauvignon Napa Valley

88   1987 Cabernet Sauvignon Napa Valley

ATLAS PEAK VINEYARDS

87   1991 Cabernet Sauvignon Napa Valley

85   1993 Chardonnay Atlas Peak

83   1990 Consenso Atlas Peak

83   1989 Consenso Atlas Peak

84   1992 Sangiovese Atlas Peak

82   1991 Sangiovese Atlas Peak

80   1990 Sangiovese Atlas Peak

82   1989 Sangiovese Atlas Peak

85   1992 Sangiovese Atlas Peak Reserve

AU BON CLIMAT

90   1993 Chardonnay Arroyo Grande Valley Talley Reserve

91   1992 Chardonnay Arroyo Grande Valley Talley Reserve

87   1990 Chardonnay Arroyo Grande Valley Talley Reserve

87   1993 Chardonnay Santa Barbara County

84   1990 Chardonnay Santa Barbara County

87   1993 Chardonnay Santa Barbara County Le Bouge D'à Côté

92 1992 Chardonnay Santa Barbara County Le Bouge D'à Côté
95 1990 Chardonnay Santa Barbara County Reserve
91 1989 Chardonnay Santa Barbara County Reserve
91 1988 Chardonnay Santa Barbara County Reserve
96 1987 Chardonnay Santa Barbara County Reserve
82 1987 Chardonnay Santa Barbara County Los Alamos Vineyard Reserve
92 1986 Chardonnay Santa Barbara County Reserve
93 1991 Chardonnay Santa Barbara County Bien Nacido Vineyard
91 1990 Chardonnay Santa Barbara County Bien Nacido Vineyard Reserve
89 1993 Chardonnay Santa Maria Valley Gold Coast Vineyard
83 1990 Pinot Blanc Santa Barbara County
87 1993 Pinot Noir Arroyo Grande Valley Talley and Paragon Vineyards
85 1993 Pinot Noir Santa Barbara County Bien Nacido Vineyard La Bauge Au-Dessus
92 1991 Pinot Noir Santa Barbara County Bien Nacido Vineyard La Bauge Au-Dessus
91 1990 Pinot Noir Santa Barbara County Bien Nacido Vineyard La Bauge Au-Dessus
87 1989 Pinot Noir Santa Barbara County Bien Nacido Vineyard La Bauge Au-Dessus
80 1988 Pinot Noir Santa Barbara County Bien Nacido Vineyard La Bauge Au-Dessus
84 1987 Pinot Noir Santa Barbara County Bien Nacido Vineyard La Bauge Au-Dessus
73 1985 Pinot Noir Santa Barbara County Bien Nacido Vineyard La Bauge Au-Dessus
86 1993 Pinot Noir Santa Maria Valley Rancho Vinedo Vineyard
86 1992 Pinot Noir Santa Maria Valley Rancho Vinedo Vineyard
86 1990 Pinot Noir Santa Maria Valley Rancho Vinedo Vineyard
83 1988 Pinot Noir Santa Maria Valley Rancho Vinedo Vineyard
91 1991 Pinot Noir Santa Ynez Valley Sanford & Benedict Vineyard
87 1989 Pinot Noir Santa Ynez Valley Benedict Vineyard
88 1987 Pinot Noir Santa Ynez Valley Benedict Vineyard

AUSTIN CELLARS

84 1991 Cabernet Sauvignon Santa Barbara County Mille Délices
80 1991 Cabernet Sauvignon Santa Barbara County Perry's Reserve
79 1991 Pinot Noir Santa Barbara County Reserve
72 1991 Sauvignon Blanc Santa Barbara County Reserve
70 1991 Sauvignon Blanc Santa Barbara County Lucas Vineyard

AZALEA SPRINGS

88 1991 Merlot Napa Valley

BABCOCK VINEYARDS

85 1993 Chardonnay Santa Barbara County
82 1990 Chardonnay Santa Barbara County
83 1990 Chardonnay Santa Barbara County Grand Cuvée
78 1991 Chardonnay Santa Ynez Valley
83 1993 Chardonnay Santa Ynez Valley Mt. Carmel Vineyard
85 1992 Pinot Noir Santa Ynez Valley
79 1991 Pinot Noir Santa Ynez Valley
70 1989 Pinot Noir Santa Ynez Valley Selected Barrels Reserve
85 1992 Pinot Noir Santa Ynez Valley Sanford & Benedict Vineyard
87 1991 Pinot Noir Santa Ynez Valley Benedict Vineyard
89 1992 Sauvignon Blanc Santa Ynez Valley 11 Oaks Ranch
83 1991 Sauvignon Blanc Santa Ynez Valley 11 Oaks Ranch

BAILEYANA

88 1993 Chardonnay Edna Valley Paragon Vineyard
88 1992 Chardonnay Edna Valley Paragon Vineyard
76 1991 Chardonnay Edna Valley Paragon Vineyard

BANCROFT VINEYARDS

86 1992 Chardonnay Howell Mountain
84 1990 Chardonnay Howell Mountain
89 1989 Chardonnay Howell Mountain

BANDIERA WINERY

83 1992 Cabernet Sauvignon Napa Valley
85 1991 Cabernet Sauvignon Napa Valley
87 1990 Cabernet Sauvignon Napa Valley
84 1993 Chardonnay Napa Valley
85 1992 Chardonnay Napa Valley
85 1991 Chardonnay Napa Valley
86 1993 Fumé Blanc Napa Valley

BANNISTER WINERY

89 1993 Chardonnay Russian River Valley Allen Vineyard
86 1992 Chardonnay Russian River Valley Allen Vineyard
88 1990 Chardonnay Russian River Valley Allen Vineyard
84 1992 Zinfandel Dry Creek Valley
83 1991 Zinfandel Dry Creek Valley

BARGETTO WINERY

84 1988 Cabernet Sauvignon Napa Valley Komes Ranch
83 1987 Cabernet Sauvignon Santa Cruz Mountains Bates Ranch
80 1993 Chardonnay Central Coast Cypress
82 1992 Chardonnay Central Coast Cypress
85 1991 Chardonnay Central Coast Cypress
82 1990 Chardonnay Central Coast Cypress
84 1993 Chardonnay Santa Cruz Mountains
83 1992 Chardonnay Santa Cruz Mountains
85 1990 Chardonnay Santa Cruz Mountains
83 1992 Gewürztraminer Monterey County
80 1989 Merlot Central Coast
78 1989 Pinot Noir Santa Cruz Mountains
79 1991 Sparkling Wine Santa Maria Valley Blanc de Noir 60th Anniversary 1933-1993

BARNETT VINEYARDS

87 1992 Cabernet Sauvignon Spring Mountain
90 1991 Cabernet Sauvignon Spring Mountain Rattlesnake Hill
83 1990 Cabernet Sauvignon Spring Mountain
86 1989 Cabernet Sauvignon Spring Mountain

BAYVIEW CELLARS

83 1991 Cabernet Sauvignon Napa Valley
88 1992 Chardonnay Carneros
77 1993 Gewürztraminer Napa Valley

BEAUCANON WINERY

86 1990 Cabernet Sauvignon Napa Valley
85 1992 Chardonnay Napa Valley
83 1991 Chardonnay Napa Valley
76 1991 Chardonnay Napa Valley Envie
83 1990 Chardonnay Napa Valley
77 1991 Merlot Napa Valley
81 1990 Merlot Napa Valley
73 1989 Merlot Napa Valley
84 1988 Merlot Napa Valley
77 1991 La Crosse Cabernet Sauvignon Napa Valley
77 1989 La Crosse Cabernet Sauvignon Napa Valley
83 1993 La Crosse Chardonnay Napa Valley
84 1992 La Crosse Chardonnay Napa Valley
85 1991 La Crosse Chardonnay Napa Valley
85 1993 La Crosse Merlot Napa Valley

BEAULIEU VINEYARD

82 1991 Cabernet Sauvignon Napa Valley Beau Tour
79 1990 Cabernet Sauvignon Napa Valley Claret Special Release
89 1990 Cabernet Sauvignon Napa Valley Georges de Latour Private Reserve

83 1989 Cabernet Sauvignon Napa Valley Georges de Latour Private Reserve

81 1988 Cabernet Sauvignon Napa Valley Georges de Latour Private Reserve

92 1987 Cabernet Sauvignon Napa Valley Georges de Latour Private Reserve

92 1986 Cabernet Sauvignon Napa Valley Georges de Latour Private Reserve

95 1985 Cabernet Sauvignon Napa Valley Georges de Latour Private Reserve

92 1984 Cabernet Sauvignon Napa Valley Georges de Latour Private Reserve

82 1983 Cabernet Sauvignon Napa Valley Georges de Latour Private Reserve

93 1982 Cabernet Sauvignon Napa Valley Georges de Latour Private Reserve

84 1981 Cabernet Sauvignon Napa Valley Georges de Latour Private Reserve

94 1980 Cabernet Sauvignon Napa Valley Georges de Latour Private Reserve

92 1979 Cabernet Sauvignon Napa Valley Georges de Latour Private Reserve

89 1978 Cabernet Sauvignon Napa Valley Georges de Latour Private Reserve

77 1977 Cabernet Sauvignon Napa Valley Georges de Latour Private Reserve

89 1976 Cabernet Sauvignon Napa Valley Georges de Latour Private Reserve

84 1975 Cabernet Sauvignon Napa Valley Georges de Latour Private Reserve

86 1974 Cabernet Sauvignon Napa Valley Georges de Latour Private Reserve

85 1973 Cabernet Sauvignon Napa Valley Georges de Latour Private Reserve

72 1972 Cabernet Sauvignon Napa Valley Georges de Latour Private Reserve

78 1971 Cabernet Sauvignon Napa Valley Georges de Latour Private Reserve

96 1970 Cabernet Sauvignon Napa Valley Georges de Latour Private Reserve

94 1969 Cabernet Sauvignon Napa Valley Georges de Latour Private Reserve

96 1968 Cabernet Sauvignon Napa Valley Georges de Latour Private Reserve

83 1967 Cabernet Sauvignon Napa Valley Georges de Latour Private Reserve

92 1966 Cabernet Sauvignon Napa Valley Georges de Latour Private Reserve

78 1965 Cabernet Sauvignon Napa Valley Georges de Latour Private Reserve

70 1964 Cabernet Sauvignon Napa Valley Georges de Latour Private Reserve

70 1963 Cabernet Sauvignon Napa Valley Georges de Latour Private Reserve

73 1962 Cabernet Sauvignon Napa Valley Georges de Latour Private Reserve

76 1961 Cabernet Sauvignon Napa Valley Georges de Latour Private Reserve

84 1960 Cabernet Sauvignon Napa Valley Georges de Latour Private Reserve

93 1959 Cabernet Sauvignon Napa Valley Georges de Latour Private Reserve

98 1958 Cabernet Sauvignon Napa Valley Georges de Latour Private Reserve

70 1957 Cabernet Sauvignon Napa Valley Georges de Latour Private Reserve

87 1956 Cabernet Sauvignon Napa Valley Georges de Latour Private Reserve

84 1955 Cabernet Sauvignon Napa Valley Georges de Latour Private Reserve

86 1954 Cabernet Sauvignon Napa Valley Georges de Latour Private Reserve

92 1953 Cabernet Sauvignon Napa Valley Georges de Latour Private Reserve

93 1952 Cabernet Sauvignon Napa Valley Georges de Latour Private Reserve

95 1951 Cabernet Sauvignon Napa Valley Georges de Latour Private Reserve

89 1950 Cabernet Sauvignon Napa Valley Georges de Latour Private Reserve

88 1949 Cabernet Sauvignon Napa Valley Georges de Latour Private Reserve

73 1948 Cabernet Sauvignon Napa Valley Georges de Latour Private Reserve

93 1947 Cabernet Sauvignon Napa Valley Georges de Latour Private Reserve

87 1946 Cabernet Sauvignon Napa Valley Georges de Latour Private Reserve

70 1945 Cabernet Sauvignon Napa Valley Georges de Latour Private Reserve

75 1944 Cabernet Sauvignon Napa Valley

87 1943 Cabernet Sauvignon Napa Valley Georges de Latour Private Reserve

85 1942 Cabernet Sauvignon Napa Valley Georges de Latour Private Reserve

89 1941 Cabernet Sauvignon Napa Valley Georges de Latour Private Reserve

89 1940 Cabernet Sauvignon Napa Valley Georges de Latour Private Reserve

91 1939 Cabernet Sauvignon Napa Valley Georges de Latour Private Reserve

86 1936 Cabernet Sauvignon Napa Valley Georges de Latour Private Reserve

85 1991 Cabernet Sauvignon Napa Valley Rutherford

85 1990 Cabernet Sauvignon Napa Valley Rutherford

86 1992 Chardonnay Carneros

88 1992 Chardonnay Carneros Carneros Reserve

88 1991 Chardonnay Carneros Carneros Reserve

83 1990 Chardonnay Carneros Carneros Reserve

86 1993 Chardonnay Napa Valley Beau Tour

83 1992 Chardonnay Napa Valley Beau Tour

82 1991 Chardonnay Napa Valley Beaufort

85 1990 Meritage Red Napa Valley

82 1991 Merlot Napa Valley Beau Tour

78 1992 Pinot Noir Carneros

86 1992 Pinot Noir Carneros Reserve

85 1991 Pinot Noir Carneros Reserve

84 1990 Pinot Noir Carneros Reserve

85 1989 Pinot Noir Carneros Reserve

87 1987 Pinot Noir Carneros Reserve

87 1986 Pinot Noir Carneros Reserve

95 1947 Pinot Noir Napa Valley

97 1946 Pinot Noir Napa Valley

79 1992 Pinot Noir Napa Valley Beau Tour

83 1994 Sauvignon Blanc California Beau Tour

83 1992 Sauvignon Blanc Napa Valley Dry

BELLEROSE VINEYARD

83 1986 Cabernet Blend Sonoma County Cuvée Bellerose

82 1985 Cabernet Blend Sonoma County Cuvée Bellerose

77 1984 Cabernet Blend Sonoma County Cuvée Bellerose

84 1988 Merlot Dry Creek Valley Reserve

69 1986 Merlot Sonoma County

73 1985 Merlot Sonoma County

77 1990 Sauvignon Blanc Dry Creek Valley Barrel Fermented Reserve

BELVEDERE WINERY

81 1985 Cabernet Sauvignon Alexander Valley Robert Young Vineyard Gifts of the Land

82 1991 Cabernet Sauvignon Sonoma County

84 1988 Cabernet Sauvignon Sonoma County Preferred Stock

84 1993 Chardonnay Sonoma County Preferred Stock

90 1992 Chardonnay Sonoma County Preferred Stock

89 1991 Chardonnay Sonoma County Preferred Stock

88 1990 Chardonnay Sonoma County Preferred Stock

87 1993 Chardonnay Alexander Valley

87 1992 Chardonnay Alexander Valley

86 1991 Chardonnay Alexander Valley

80 1990 Chardonnay Alexander Valley

88 1991 Chardonnay Russian River Valley

85 1990 Chardonnay Russian River Valley

86 1991 Zinfandel Dry Creek Valley

74 1990 Zinfandel Dry Creek Valley

85 1989 Zinfandel Dry Creek Valley

82 1991 Merlot Sonoma County

80 1990 Muscat Canelli Alexander Valley Late Harvest

BENZIGER FAMILY WINERY

84 1990 Cabernet Blend Sonoma Mountain A Tribute

86	1989 Cabernet Blend Sonoma Mountain A Tribute
86	1988 Cabernet Blend Sonoma Mountain A Tribute
85	1987 Cabernet Blend Sonoma Mountain A Tribute
83	1992 Cabernet Franc Alexander Valley Blue Rock Vineyard Imagery Series
85	1989 Cabernet Franc Alexander Valley Blue Rock Vineyard Imagery Series
87	1992 Cabernet Sauvignon Sonoma County
88	1991 Cabernet Sauvignon Sonoma County
84	1990 Cabernet Sauvignon Sonoma County
81	1989 Cabernet Sauvignon Sonoma County
84	1988 Cabernet Sauvignon Sonoma County
90	1987 Cabernet Sauvignon Sonoma County
82	1986 Cabernet Sauvignon Sonoma County
87	1992 Cabernet Sauvignon Knights Valley
84	1989 Cabernet Sauvignon Sonoma Mountain
85	1988 Cabernet Sauvignon Sonoma Mountain
85	1987 Cabernet Sauvignon Sonoma Valley
78	1986 Cabernet Sauvignon Sonoma Valley
83	1985 Cabernet Sauvignon Sonoma Valley
85	1993 Chardonnay Carneros Premiere Vineyard
88	1992 Chardonnay Carneros Premiere Vineyard
89	1991 Chardonnay Carneros Premiere Vineyard
87	1990 Chardonnay Carneros Premiere Vineyard
85	1992 Chardonnay Sonoma County
84	1994 Fumé Blanc Sonoma County
80	1993 Fumé Blanc Sonoma County
87	1992 Fumé Blanc Sonoma County
87	1992 Merlot Sonoma County
80	1991 Merlot Sonoma County
84	1990 Merlot Sonoma County
81	1989 Merlot Sonoma County
87	1988 Merlot Sonoma County
85	1992 Pinot Blanc Sonoma County
82	1991 Pinot Blanc Sonoma County
84	1993 Pinot Blanc Sonoma Mountain Skinner Vineyard Imagery Series
84	1991 Pinot Noir Sonoma County
84	1990 Pinot Noir Sonoma County
85	1989 Pinot Noir Sonoma County
86	1992 Sauvignon Blend Sonoma Mountain A Tribute White
83	1990 Sauvignon Blend Sonoma Mountain A Tribute White
83	1991 Sémillon Sonoma Mountain
83	1991 California Lagomarsino Vineyard Aleatico Blanc de Noirs Imagery Series
87	1990 Carneros Brut Imagery Series
84	1990 Syrah Paso Robles
86	1992 Zinfandel Sonoma County
87	1991 Zinfandel Sonoma County
84	1990 Zinfandel Sonoma County

83	1989 Zinfandel Sonoma County
87	1990 Zinfandel Port Dry Creek Valley Mayo Family & Carreras Vineyard Imagery Series

BERGFELD WINERY

83	1988 Cabernet Sauvignon Napa Valley
78	1990 Chardonnay Napa Valley
87	1989 Merlot Napa Valley

BERINGER VINEYARDS

87	1992 Cabernet Sauvignon Knights Valley
87	1991 Cabernet Sauvignon Knights Valley
88	1990 Cabernet Sauvignon Knights Valley
85	1989 Cabernet Sauvignon Knights Valley
86	1988 Cabernet Sauvignon Knights Valley
90	1987 Cabernet Sauvignon Knights Valley
87	1985 Cabernet Sauvignon Knights Valley
95	1991 Cabernet Sauvignon Napa Valley Private Reserve
95	1990 Cabernet Sauvignon Napa Valley Private Reserve
90	1989 Cabernet Sauvignon Napa Valley Private Reserve
88	1988 Cabernet Sauvignon Napa Valley Private Reserve
94	1987 Cabernet Sauvignon Napa Valley Private Reserve
97	1986 Cabernet Sauvignon Napa Valley Private Reserve
97	1985 Cabernet Sauvignon Napa Valley Private Reserve
94	1984 Cabernet Sauvignon Napa Valley Private Reserve
89	1983 Cabernet Sauvignon Napa Valley Private Reserve
91	1982 Cabernet Sauvignon Napa Valley Private Reserve
91	1981 Cabernet Sauvignon Napa Valley Private Reserve
89	1980 Cabernet Sauvignon Napa Valley Private Reserve
95	1978 Cabernet Sauvignon Napa Valley Private Reserve
88	1977 Cabernet Sauvignon Napa Valley Private Reserve
93	1991 Cabernet Sauvignon Napa Valley Chabot Vineyard
92	1990 Cabernet Sauvignon Napa Valley Chabot Vineyard
90	1989 Cabernet Sauvignon Napa Valley Chabot Vineyard
84	1988 Cabernet Sauvignon Napa Valley Chabot Vineyard
94	1987 Cabernet Sauvignon Napa Valley Chabot Vineyard

95	1986 Cabernet Sauvignon Napa Valley Chabot Vineyard
86	1985 Cabernet Sauvignon Napa Valley Chabot Vineyard
87	1984 Cabernet Sauvignon Napa Valley Chabot Vineyard
85	1983 Cabernet Sauvignon Napa Valley Chabot Vineyard
89	1982 Cabernet Sauvignon Napa Valley Chabot Vineyard
87	1981 Cabernet Sauvignon Napa Valley Chabot Vineyard
85	1980 Cabernet Sauvignon Napa Valley State Lane Vineyard Reserve
89	1979 Cabernet Sauvignon Napa Valley State Lane Vineyard Reserve
84	1993 Chardonnay Napa Valley
87	1992 Chardonnay Napa Valley
84	1991 Chardonnay Napa Valley
87	1992 Chardonnay Napa Valley Proprietor Grown
92	1993 Chardonnay Napa Valley Private Reserve
92	1992 Chardonnay Napa Valley Private Reserve
90	1991 Chardonnay Napa Valley Private Reserve
90	1990 Chardonnay Napa Valley Private Reserve
93	1992 Chardonnay Napa Valley Sbragia Limited Release
92	1991 Chardonnay Napa Valley Sbragia Limited Release
84	1991 Fumé Blanc Napa Valley
82	1994 Gamay Beaujolais Nouveau North Coast
88	1991 Meritage Red Knights Valley
84	1992 Meritage White Knights Valley
90	1991 Merlot Howell Mountain Bancroft Ranch
90	1990 Merlot Howell Mountain Bancroft Ranch
91	1989 Merlot Howell Mountain Bancroft Ranch
90	1988 Merlot Howell Mountain Bancroft Ranch
91	1987 Merlot Howell Mountain Bancroft Ranch
90	1990 Sauvignon Blanc Napa Valley Nightingale
95	1990 Sauvignon Blend Napa Valley Nightingale
91	1990 Sémillon Napa Valley Nightingale
93	1989 Sauvignon Blend Napa Valley Nightingale
91	1988 Sauvignon Blend Napa Valley Nightingale
92	1987 Sauvignon Blend Napa Valley Nightingale
93	1987 Sémillon Napa Valley Nightingale
88	1986 Sauvignon Blend Napa Valley Nightingale
89	1985 Sauvignon Blanc Napa Valley Nightingale
88	1985 Sauvignon Blend Napa Valley Nightingale
89	1985 Sémillon Napa Valley Nightingale
87	1983 Sauvignon Blanc Napa Valley Nightingale
84	1983 Sémillon Napa Valley Nightingale
87	1982 Sauvignon Blend Napa Valley Nightingale
91	1981 Sauvignon Blanc Napa Valley Nightingale

92   1981 Sémillon Napa Valley Nightingale

99   1980 Sauvignon Blend Napa Valley Nightingale

89   1993 Viognier Napa Valley Hudson Vineyard

87   1992 Viognier Napa Valley Hudson Vineyard

86   1991 Zinfandel Napa Valley

83   1990 Zinfandel Napa Valley

BERNARDUS VINEYARDS & WINERY

87   1993 Chardonnay

91   1992 Chardonnay

89   1991 Chardonnay California

86   1992 Pinot Noir Santa Barbara County Bien Nacido Vineyard

87   1993 Sauvignon Blanc Monterey County

87   1992 Sauvignon Blanc Monterey County

ROBERT BIALE VINEYARDS

84   1992 Zinfandel Napa Valley Aldo's Vineyard

91   1991 Zinfandel Napa Valley Aldo's Vineyard

BLACK MOUNTAIN

80   1990 Cabernet Sauvignon Alexander Valley Fat Cat

85   1988 Cabernet Sauvignon Alexander Valley Fat Cat

86   1986 Cabernet Sauvignon Alexander Valley Fat Cat

87   1985 Cabernet Sauvignon Alexander Valley Fat Cat

87   1991 Chardonnay Alexander Valley Douglass Hill

86   1990 Chardonnay Alexander Valley Gravel Bar

77   1990 Petite Sirah Alexander Valley Bosun Crest

87   1987 Petite Sirah Alexander Valley Bosun Crest

78   1990 Zinfandel Alexander Valley Cramer Ridge

77   1987 Zinfandel Alexander Valley Cramer Ridge

BLACK SHEEP VINTNERS

84   1991 Zinfandel Sierra Foothills

BLOCKHEADIA RINGNOSII

85   1993 Zinfandel Rutherford

88   1992 Zinfandel Rutherford

BLUE HERON LAKE WINERY

87   1992 Chardonnay Wild Horse Valley

BOEGER WINERY

84   1992 Barbera El Dorado County

84   1991 Barbera El Dorado County

81   1990 Barbera El Dorado County

85   1989 Barbera El Dorado County

83   1990 Cabernet Sauvignon El Dorado County

83   1989 Cabernet Sauvignon El Dorado County

85   1987 Cabernet Sauvignon El Dorado County

77   1985 Cabernet Sauvignon El Dorado County

81   1984 Cabernet Sauvignon El Dorado County

77   1989 Cabernet Sauvignon Napa Valley Joseph A. Nichelini Vineyards

87   1991 Chardonnay El Dorado County

85   1990 Chardonnay El Dorado County

84   1992 Johannisberg Riesling El Dorado County

83   1989 Meritage Red El Dorado County

86   1992 Merlot El Dorado County

86   1991 Merlot El Dorado County

78   1990 Merlot El Dorado County

86   1989 Merlot El Dorado County

83   1993 Sauvignon Blanc El Dorado County

84   1992 Sauvignon Blanc El Dorado County

84   1992 Zinfandel El Dorado County

87   1992 Zinfandel El Dorado County Walker Vineyard

87   1991 Zinfandel El Dorado County Walker Vineyard

90   1990 Zinfandel El Dorado County Walker Vineyard

84   1989 Zinfandel El Dorado County Walker Vineyard

85   1988 Zinfandel El Dorado County Walker Vineyard

86   1987 Zinfandel El Dorado County Walker Vineyard

81   1990 Zinfandel Napa Valley Joseph A. Nichelini Vineyards

80   1989 Zinfandel Napa Valley Joseph A. Nichelini Vineyards

85   1988 Zinfandel Napa Valley Joseph A. Nichelini Vineyards

BOGLE VINEYARDS

81   1992 Cabernet Sauvignon California

83   1990 Cabernet Sauvignon California

82   1993 Chardonnay California

81   1992 Chardonnay California

86   1992 Chardonnay California Reserve

83   1993 Fumé Blanc Lake County Dry

85   1992 Fumé Blanc Lake County Dry

83   1992 Merlot California

85   1991 Merlot California

82   1990 Merlot California

85   1992 Petite Sirah California

88   1991 Petite Sirah California

84   1992 Zinfandel California

BONNY DOON VINEYARD

82   1992 Blush California Vin Gris de Cigare

78   1990 Chardonnay Monterey County La Reina Vineyard

83   1990 Chardonnay Santa Cruz Mountains

78   1993 Chenin Blanc California Pacific Rim

87   1993 Grenache California Clos de Gilroy

84   1992 Grenache California Clos de Gilroy

84   1991 Grenache California Clos de Gilroy

87   1990 Grenache California Clos de Gilroy

88   1989 Grenache California Clos de Gilroy

87   1991 Mourvèdre California Old Telegram

84   1990 Mourvèdre California Old Telegram

85   1988 Mourvèdre California Old Telegram

90   1986 Mourvèdre California Old Telegram

88   1991 Rhône Blend California Le Cigare Volant

87   1990 Rhône Blend California Le Cigare Volant

80   1989 Rhône Blend California Le Cigare Volant

86   1988 Rhône Blend California Le Cigare Volant

85   1987 Rhône Blend California Le Cigare Volant

90   1986 Rhône Blend California Le Cigare Volant

88   1985 Rhône Blend California Le Cigare Volant

89   1992 Rhône Blend Santa Cruz Mountains Le Sophiste

88   1991 Rhône Blend Santa Cruz Mountains Le Sophiste

86   1989 Rhône Blend Santa Cruz Mountains Le Sophiste

92   1992 Muscat Canelli Monterey County Vin de Glaciere

85   1991 Malvasia Bianca Monterey County Vin de Glaciere

91   1990 Muscat Canelli California Vin de Glaciere

90   NV Framboise Santa Cruz Mountains

82   1992 Red Table Wine California Le Gaucher

87   1991 Red Table Wine California Pinot Meunier

83   1993 Sparkling Wine California Le Canard Froid Pinot Meunier

87   1992 White Riesling California Pacific Rim

88   1991 White Riesling California Pacific Rim

76   1990 White Table Wine California Grahm Crew Vin Blanc

85   1992 Ca' del Solo Muscat Monterey County Moscato del Solo

83   1991 Ca' del Solo Muscat Monterey County Moscato del Solo

86   NV Ca' del Solo Rhône Blend American Il Pescatore

84   1992 Ca' del Solo Rhône Blend California Big House Red

84   1991 Ca' del Solo Rhône Blend California Big House Red

85   1990 Ca' del Solo Rhône Blend California Big House Red

85   1993 Ca' del Solo White Table Wine California Il Pescatore

85   1992 Ca' del Solo White Table Wine Monterey County Malvasia Bianca

84   1990 Ca' del Solo White Table Wine Monterey County Malvasia Bianca

BOUCHAINE VINEYARDS

79   1991 Cabernet Franc Sonoma Valley Limited Release

83   1990 Cabernet Franc Sonoma Valley Limited Release

86   1992 Chardonnay Carneros

87   1991 Chardonnay Carneros

88   1991 Chardonnay Carneros Estate Reserve

84   1990 Chardonnay Carneros Estate Reserve

86   1991 Chardonnay Carneros Limited Release

87   1990 Chardonnay Carneros Sangiacomo Vineyard Limited Release

85   1990 Chardonnay Napa Valley

85   1993 Gewürztraminer Russian River Valley Dry

86   1992 Pinot Noir Carneros

82   1991 Pinot Noir Carneros

86   1990 Pinot Noir Carneros

82   1989 Pinot Noir Carneros

88   1991 Pinot Noir Carneros Reserve

82   1990 Pinot Noir Carneros Reserve

82   1991 Pinot Noir Russian River Valley Limited Release

84   1992 Q.C. Fly Chardonnay California

81   1992 Q.C. Fly Pinot Noir California

BRANDBORG CELLARS

84   1991 Pinot Noir Mendocino County

73   1990 Pinot Noir Mendocino County

86   1992 Pinot Noir Santa Maria Valley Bien Nacido Vineyard

84   1991 Pinot Noir Santa Maria Valley Bien Nacido Vineyard

78   1990 Pinot Noir Santa Maria Valley Bien Nacido Vineyard

87   1989 Pinot Noir Santa Barbara County

84   1989 Zinfandel Napa Valley

THE BRANDER VINEYARD

79   1990 Cabernet Blend Santa Ynez Valley Bouchet Tête de Cuvée

84   1989 Cabernet Blend Santa Ynez Valley Bouchet Tête de Cuvée

84   1993 Chardonnay Santa Ynez Valley Tête de Cuvée

78   1992 Chardonnay Santa Ynez Valley Tête de Cuvée

64   1990 Chardonnay Santa Ynez Valley Tête de Cuvée

82   1989 Merlot Santa Ynez Valley Three Flags

84   1994 Sauvignon Blanc Santa Ynez Valley

86   1993 Sauvignon Blanc Santa Ynez Valley

87   1992 Sauvignon Blanc Santa Ynez Valley

89   1993 Sauvignon Blanc Santa Ynez Valley Cuvée Nicolas

87   1992 Sauvignon Blanc Santa Ynez Valley Cuvée Nicolas

89   1994 Sauvignon Blend Santa Ynez Valley Cuvée Natalie

86   1993 Sauvignon Blend Santa Ynez Valley Cuvée Natalie

BRAREN PAULI WINERY

89   1990 Cabernet Sauvignon Dry Creek Valley

78   1989 Cabernet Sauvignon Dry Creek Valley Mauritson Vineyard

84   1987 Cabernet Sauvignon Mendocino County

85   1991 Merlot Alexander Valley

BRICELAND VINEYARDS

81   1992 Pinot Noir Humboldt County

83   1991 Pinot Noir Humboldt County

86   1992 Sauvignon Blanc Humboldt County

BRINDIAMO

76   1991 Cabernet Sauvignon California Limited Bottling

81   1992 Chardonnay California

77   1990 Pinot Noir Santa Barbara County Santa Maria Hills Vineyard Limited Bottling

86   1993 Red Table Wine South Coast Gioveto Limited Bottling

86   1993 Rhône Blend South Coast Rosso Vecchio Limited Bottling

80   1992 Rhône Blend South Coast Rosso Vecchio Limited Bottling

DAVID BRUCE WINERY

74   1991 Chardonnay San Ysidro

85   1990 Chardonnay Santa Cruz Mountains

84   1990 Chardonnay Santa Cruz Mountains Estate Reserve

74   1990 Chardonnay Santa Cruz Mountains Vineyard Selection

82   1991 Chardonnay Santa Cruz Mountains Meyley Vineyard

69   1990 Chardonnay Santa Cruz Mountains Meyley Vineyard

89   1991 Chardonnay Santa Cruz Mountains Split Rail Vineyard

85   1990 Pinot Noir Mendocino County Vintner's Select

88   1992 Pinot Noir Santa Cruz Mountains

87   1991 Pinot Noir Santa Cruz Mountains

91   1990 Pinot Noir Santa Cruz Mountains

75   1989 Pinot Noir Santa Cruz Mountains

91   1992 Pinot Noir Santa Cruz Mountains Estate Reserve

90   1991 Pinot Noir Santa Cruz Mountains Estate Reserve

91   1990 Pinot Noir Santa Cruz Mountains Estate Reserve

80   1990 Rhône Blend California Mr. Baggins

90   1990 Zinfandel San Luis Obispo County

BRUTOCAO CELLARS

82   1990 Cabernet Sauvignon Mendocino County

83   1988 Cabernet Sauvignon Mendocino County

82   1986 Cabernet Sauvignon Mendocino County

83   1991 Cabernet Sauvignon Mendocino County Proprietor's Special Reserve

82   1992 Cabernet Sauvignon Mendocino County Albert Vineyard

88   1991 Chardonnay Mendocino County

81   1988 Chardonnay Mendocino County

83   1993 Chardonnay Mendocino County Bliss Vineyard

84   1992 Chardonnay Mendocino County Bliss Vineyard

78   1992 Merlot Mendocino County

87   1991 Merlot Mendocino County

84   1988 Merlot Mendocino County

83   1992 Sauvignon Blanc Mendocino County

90   1991 Sauvignon Blanc Mendocino County

84   1992 Zinfandel Mendocino County

85   1991 Zinfandel Mendocino County Proprietor's Reserve

84   1993 Zinfandel Mendocino County Hopland Ranch

BUEHLER VINEYARDS

86   1991 Cabernet Sauvignon Napa Valley

86   1990 Cabernet Sauvignon Napa Valley

82   1989 Cabernet Sauvignon Napa Valley

85   1987 Cabernet Sauvignon Napa Valley

91   1991 Cabernet Sauvignon Napa Valley Reserve

85   1993 Chardonnay Russian River Valley

79   1993 Pinot Noir Central Coast

81   1993 Zinfandel Napa Valley

86   1992 Zinfandel Napa Valley

77   1990 Zinfandel Napa Valley

83   1989 Zinfandel Napa Valley

89   1987 Zinfandel Napa Valley

82   1992 Bon Marche Cabernet Sauvignon Napa Valley

84   1991 Bon Marche Cabernet Sauvignon Sonoma County

79   1992 Bon Marche Chardonnay Sonoma County

79   1990 Bon Marche Pinot Noir Napa Valley

86   1991 Bon Marche Pinot Noir Sonoma County

BUENA VISTA WINERY

87   1991 Cabernet Sauvignon Carneros

82   1990 Cabernet Sauvignon Carneros

83   1990 Cabernet Sauvignon Carneros Grand Reserve

86   1988 Cabernet Sauvignon Carneros Grand Reserve

88   1986 Cabernet Sauvignon Carneros Private Reserve

87   1985 Cabernet Sauvignon Carneros Private Reserve

87   1984 Cabernet Sauvignon Carneros Private Reserve

87   1983 Cabernet Sauvignon Carneros Private Reserve

85   1982 Cabernet Sauvignon Carneros Private Reserve

84   1979 Cabernet Sauvignon Sonoma Valley Special Selection

85   1978 Cabernet Sauvignon Sonoma Valley Special Selection

83   1992 Chardonnay Carneros

84   1991 Chardonnay Carneros

86   1991 Chardonnay Carneros Grand Reserve

80   1993 Gewürztraminer Carneros

82   1992 Merlot Carneros

82   1991 Merlot Carneros

86   1990 Merlot Carneros

82   1989 Merlot Carneros Grand Reserve

77   1992 Pinot Noir Carneros

80   1991 Pinot Noir Carneros

81   1990 Pinot Noir Carneros

83   1991 Pinot Noir Carneros Grand Reserve

86   1990 Pinot Noir Carneros Grand Reserve

79   1993 Sauvignon Blanc Lake County

BURGESS CELLARS

88   1990 Cabernet Sauvignon Napa Valley Vintage Selection

86   1989 Cabernet Sauvignon Napa Valley Vintage Selection

85   1988 Cabernet Sauvignon Napa Valley Vintage Selection

85   1987 Cabernet Sauvignon Napa Valley Vintage Selection

88   1986 Cabernet Sauvignon Napa Valley Vintage Selection

89   1985 Cabernet Sauvignon Napa Valley Vintage Selection

90   1984 Cabernet Sauvignon Napa Valley Vintage Selection

87   1983 Cabernet Sauvignon Napa Valley Vintage Selection

74   1974 Cabernet Sauvignon Napa Valley Vintage Selection

86   1993 Chardonnay Napa Valley Debourbage Barrel Fermented

83   1992 Chardonnay Napa Valley Triere Vineyard

86   1991 Chardonnay Napa Valley Triere Vineyard

81   1991 Zinfandel Napa Valley

84   1990 Zinfandel Napa Valley

80   1989 Zinfandel Napa Valley

BYINGTON WINERY & VINEYARDS

86   1987 Cabernet Sauvignon Napa Valley

83   1993 Chardonnay Mount Veeder

78   1990 Chardonnay Napa Valley

84   1993 Chardonnay Santa Cruz Mountains

84   1993 Chardonnay Santa Cruz Mountains Redwood Hill Vineyard

89   1991 Chardonnay Santa Cruz Mountains Redwood Hill Vineyard

83   1991 Merlot Sonoma County Bradford Mountain Vineyard

78   1991 Pinot Noir Santa Barbara County Bien Nacido Vineyard

80   1992 Sauvignon Blanc San Luis Obispo County French Camp Vineyard Dry

82   1992 Zinfandel Santa Clara County Calle Cielo Vineyard

DAVIS BYNUM WINERY

81   1989 Cabernet Sauvignon Sonoma County

79   1987 Cabernet Sauvignon Sonoma County

84   1992 Chardonnay Russian River Valley Allen-Griffin Vineyards Limited Release

81   1991 Chardonnay Russian River Valley Allen-Griffin Vineyards Limited Release

69   1991 Chardonnay Sonoma County

82   1994 Fumé Blanc Russian River Valley Shone Farm

85   1992 Fumé Blanc Russian River Valley Shone Farm

74   1992 Gewürztraminer Russian River Valley

81   1991 Merlot Russian River Valley Laureles Vineyard

84   1991 Pinot Noir Russian River Valley

72   1990 Pinot Noir Russian River Valley

88   1991 Pinot Noir Russian River Valley Limited Release

85   1990 Pinot Noir Russian River Valley Limited Release

87   1991 Zinfandel Russian River Valley

84   1990 Zinfandel Russian River Valley

BYRON VINEYARDS & WINERY

85   1990 Cabernet Sauvignon Santa Barbara County

82   1989 Cabernet Sauvignon Santa Barbara County

90   1993 Chardonnay Santa Barbara County

88   1992 Chardonnay Santa Barbara County

92   1991 Chardonnay Santa Barbara County

91   1993 Chardonnay Santa Barbara County Reserve

92   1992 Chardonnay Santa Barbara County Reserve

88   1991 Chardonnay Santa Barbara County Reserve

92   1990 Chardonnay Santa Barbara County Reserve

91   1992 Chardonnay Santa Maria Valley

91   1991 Chardonnay Santa Maria Valley

88   1991 Pinot Blanc Santa Barbara County

83   1992 Pinot Noir Santa Barbara County

87   1990 Pinot Noir Santa Barbara County

86   1992 Pinot Noir Santa Barbara County Reserve

88   1991 Pinot Noir Santa Barbara County Reserve

87   1990 Pinot Noir Santa Barbara County Reserve

87   1989 Pinot Noir Santa Barbara County Reserve

88   1988 Pinot Noir Santa Barbara County Reserve

82   1993 Sauvignon Blanc Santa Barbara County

90   1992 Sauvignon Blanc Santa Barbara County

CAFARO CELLARS

88   1991 Cabernet Sauvignon Napa Valley

84   1990 Cabernet Sauvignon Napa Valley

85   1989 Cabernet Sauvignon Napa Valley

81   1988 Cabernet Sauvignon Napa Valley

90   1987 Cabernet Sauvignon Napa Valley

93   1986 Cabernet Sauvignon Napa Valley

87   1990 Merlot Napa Valley

89   1988 Merlot Napa Valley

85   1987 Merlot Napa Valley

84   1986 Merlot Napa Valley

CAIN CELLARS

88   1992 Cabernet Blend Napa Valley Cuvée

81   1991 Cabernet Blend Napa Valley Cuvée

84   1989 Cabernet Blend Napa Valley Cuvée

85   1988 Cabernet Blend Napa Valley Cuvée

88   1987 Cabernet Sauvignon Napa Valley

89   1991 Meritage Red Napa Valley Cain Five

91   1990 Meritage Red Napa Valley Cain Five

87   1989 Meritage Red Napa Valley Cain Five

92   1987 Meritage Red Napa Valley Cain Five

90   1986 Meritage Red Napa Valley Cain Five

87   1985 Meritage Red Napa Valley Cain Five

85   1993 Sauvignon Blanc Monterey County Musqué

87   1992 Sauvignon Blanc Monterey County Musqué

CAKEBREAD CELLARS

88   1991 Cabernet Sauvignon Napa Valley

83   1990 Cabernet Sauvignon Napa Valley

87   1989 Cabernet Sauvignon Napa Valley

86   1988 Cabernet Sauvignon Napa Valley

89   1987 Cabernet Sauvignon Napa Valley

88   1986 Cabernet Sauvignon Napa Valley

84   1985 Cabernet Sauvignon Napa Valley

87   1984 Cabernet Sauvignon Napa Valley

77   1983 Cabernet Sauvignon Napa Valley

91   1974 Cabernet Sauvignon Napa Valley Lot 2

81   1988 Cabernet Sauvignon Napa Valley Rutherford Reserve

88   1987 Cabernet Sauvignon Napa Valley Rutherford Reserve

80   1986 Cabernet Sauvignon Napa Valley Rutherford Reserve

85   1985 Cabernet Sauvignon Napa Valley Rutherford Reserve

85   1984 Cabernet Sauvignon Napa Valley Rutherford Reserve

88   1983 Cabernet Sauvignon Napa Valley Rutherford Reserve

84   1993 Chardonnay Napa Valley

87   1992 Chardonnay Napa Valley

81 1991 Chardonnay Napa Valley
87 1992 Chardonnay Napa Valley Reserve
87 1992 Sauvignon Blanc Napa Valley
90 1992 Zinfandel Howell Mountain

CALE CELLARS

88 1993 Chardonnay Carneros Sangiacomo Vineyard
90 1992 Chardonnay Carneros Sangiacomo Vineyard

CALERA WINE CO.

88 1993 Chardonnay Central Coast
89 1992 Chardonnay Central Coast
89 1991 Chardonnay Central Coast
88 1990 Chardonnay Central Coast
89 1992 Chardonnay Mount Harlan
89 1990 Chardonnay Mount Harlan
73 1992 Pinot Noir Central Coast
84 1991 Pinot Noir Central Coast
87 1990 Pinot Noir Central Coast
85 1989 Pinot Noir Central Coast
82 1987 Pinot Noir Central Coast
88 1991 Pinot Noir Mount Harlan Jensen
87 1990 Pinot Noir Mount Harlan Jensen
89 1989 Pinot Noir Mount Harlan Jensen
92 1988 Pinot Noir Mount Harlan Jensen
93 1987 Pinot Noir Mount Harlan Jensen
91 1986 Pinot Noir Mount Harlan Jensen
92 1985 Pinot Noir Mount Harlan Jensen
93 1989 Pinot Noir Mount Harlan Mills
89 1988 Pinot Noir Mount Harlan Mills
91 1992 Pinot Noir Mount Harlan Reed
88 1989 Pinot Noir Mount Harlan Reed
85 1988 Pinot Noir Mount Harlan Reed
80 1987 Pinot Noir Mount Harlan Reed
89 1988 Pinot Noir Mount Harlan Selleck
92 1987 Pinot Noir Mount Harlan Selleck
85 1986 Pinot Noir Mount Harlan Selleck

CALLAWAY VINEYARD AND WINERY

79 1990 Cabernet Sauvignon California
79 1991 Cabernet Sauvignon California Hawk Watch
84 1993 Chardonnay Temecula Hawk Watch Calla-Lees
83 1992 Chardonnay Temecula Hawk Watch Calla-Lees
88 1990 Chardonnay Temecula Hawk Watch Calla-Lees
79 1991 Chenin Blanc Temecula Sweet Nancy Late Harvest
80 1993 Sauvignon Blanc Temecula
81 1993 Viognier Temecula
77 1991 White Riesling Temecula

CAMBRIA WINERY & VINEYARD

87 1993 Chardonnay Santa Maria Valley Katherine's Vineyard
85 1991 Chardonnay Santa Maria Valley Katherine's Vineyard
90 1990 Chardonnay Santa Maria Valley Katherine's Vineyard
91 1991 Chardonnay Santa Maria Valley Katherine's Vineyard Reserve
91 1993 Chardonnay Santa Maria Valley Reserve
91 1992 Chardonnay Santa Maria Valley Reserve
85 1991 Chardonnay Santa Maria Valley Reserve
90 1990 Chardonnay Santa Maria Valley Reserve
89 1989 Chardonnay Santa Maria Valley Reserve
85 1988 Chardonnay Santa Maria Valley Reserve
87 1993 Pinot Noir Santa Maria Valley Julia's Vineyard
87 1992 Pinot Noir Santa Maria Valley Julia's Vineyard
87 1991 Pinot Noir Santa Maria Valley Julia's Vineyard
80 1989 Pinot Noir Santa Maria Valley Julia's Vineyard
88 1988 Pinot Noir Santa Maria Valley Julia's Vineyard
86 1992 Pinot Noir Santa Maria Valley Reserve
86 1993 Sangiovese Santa Maria Valley Tepusquet Vineyard
88 1992 Syrah Santa Maria Valley Tepusquet Vineyard

CAMELOT

83 1992 Cabernet Sauvignon Central Coast
90 1993 Chardonnay Santa Barbara County
85 1993 Pinot Noir Central Coast

CANEPA CELLARS

88 1991 Chardonnay Alexander Valley

CARMENET VINEYARD

87 1992 Cabernet Sauvignon Sonoma County Dynamite Cabernet
85 1991 Cabernet Sauvignon Sonoma Valley Dynamite Cabernet
84 1990 Cabernet Sauvignon Sonoma Valley Moon Mountain Estate Vineyard
86 1989 Cabernet Sauvignon Sonoma Valley Moon Mountain Estate Vineyard
83 1989 Cabernet Sauvignon Sonoma Valley Moon Mountain Estate Vineyard Reserve
82 1992 Chardonnay Carneros Sangiacomo Vineyard
90 1991 Chardonnay Carneros Sangiacomo Vineyard
88 1989 Meritage Red Sonoma Valley
87 1988 Meritage Red Sonoma Valley
89 1987 Meritage Red Sonoma Valley

90 1986 Meritage Red Sonoma Valley
88 1985 Meritage Red Sonoma Valley
88 1984 Meritage Red Sonoma Valley
83 1983 Meritage Red Sonoma Valley
84 1982 Meritage Red Sonoma Valley
83 1993 Meritage White Edna Valley Paragon Vineyard
85 1992 Meritage White Edna Valley Paragon Vineyard

CARNEROS CREEK WINERY

82 1992 Chardonnay California Fleur de Carneros
84 1992 Chardonnay Carneros
84 1991 Chardonnay Carneros
88 1991 Pinot Noir Carneros
86 1990 Pinot Noir Carneros
85 1989 Pinot Noir Carneros
85 1988 Pinot Noir Carneros
85 1987 Pinot Noir Carneros
91 1986 Pinot Noir Carneros
85 1985 Pinot Noir Carneros
88 1984 Pinot Noir Carneros
90 1983 Pinot Noir Carneros
89 1978 Pinot Noir Carneros
87 1977 Pinot Noir Carneros
85 1976 Pinot Noir Carneros
81 1991 Pinot Noir Carneros Signature Reserve
80 1989 Pinot Noir Carneros Signature Reserve
89 1988 Pinot Noir Carneros Signature Reserve
87 1987 Pinot Noir Carneros Signature Reserve First Release
82 1993 Pinot Noir Carneros Fleur de Carneros
79 1992 Pinot Noir Carneros Fleur de Carneros
77 1991 Pinot Noir Carneros Fleur de Carneros
80 1990 Pinot Noir Carneros Fleur de Carneros
87 1992 Mahoney Estate Pinot Noir Carneros Las Piedras Vineyard

MAURICE CARRIE VINEYARDS AND WINERY

77 1991 Chardonnay Temecula
77 1991 Chardonnay Temecula Private Reserve
67 1990 Pinot Noir Santa Barbara County

CASTLE ROCK

84 1993 Chardonnay Napa Valley Barrel Fermented

CASTORO CELLARS

79 1991 Cabernet Blend Paso Robles Dieci Anni
84 1989 Cabernet Sauvignon Paso Robles
82 1991 Cabernet Sauvignon Paso Robles Reserve
82 1990 Cabernet Sauvignon Paso Robles Reserve
78 1991 Cabernet Sauvignon Paso Robles The Wine

80 1992 Chardonnay Paso Robles Reserve

84 1992 Chardonnay San Luis Obispo County

84 1991 Chardonnay San Luis Obispo County

78 1992 Chardonnay San Luis Obispo County
The Wine

77 1991 Pinot Noir Santa Barbara County

73 1990 Pinot Noir Santa Barbara County

82 1990 Zinfandel Paso Robles

84 1991 Zinfandel Paso Robles The Wine

CAYMUS VINEYARDS

91 1991 Cabernet Sauvignon Napa Valley

90 1990 Cabernet Sauvignon Napa Valley

88 1989 Cabernet Sauvignon Napa Valley

87 1988 Cabernet Sauvignon Napa Valley

92 1987 Cabernet Sauvignon Napa Valley

94 1986 Cabernet Sauvignon Napa Valley

92 1985 Cabernet Sauvignon Napa Valley

91 1984 Cabernet Sauvignon Napa Valley

84 1983 Cabernet Sauvignon Napa Valley

87 1982 Cabernet Sauvignon Napa Valley

88 1981 Cabernet Sauvignon Napa Valley

90 1980 Cabernet Sauvignon Napa Valley

91 1979 Cabernet Sauvignon Napa Valley

87 1978 Cabernet Sauvignon Napa Valley

77 1977 Cabernet Sauvignon Napa Valley

85 1976 Cabernet Sauvignon Napa Valley

89 1975 Cabernet Sauvignon Napa Valley

84 1974 Cabernet Sauvignon Napa Valley

93 1973 Cabernet Sauvignon Napa Valley

83 1972 Cabernet Sauvignon Napa Valley

99 1991 Cabernet Sauvignon Napa Valley Special
Selection

98 1990 Cabernet Sauvignon Napa Valley Special
Selection

93 1989 Cabernet Sauvignon Napa Valley Special
Selection

94 1988 Cabernet Sauvignon Napa Valley Special
Selection

98 1987 Cabernet Sauvignon Napa Valley Special
Selection

98 1986 Cabernet Sauvignon Napa Valley Special
Selection

99 1985 Cabernet Sauvignon Napa Valley Special
Selection

98 1984 Cabernet Sauvignon Napa Valley Special
Selection

91 1983 Cabernet Sauvignon Napa Valley Special
Selection

92 1982 Cabernet Sauvignon Napa Valley Special
Selection

93 1981 Cabernet Sauvignon Napa Valley Special
Selection

92 1980 Cabernet Sauvignon Napa Valley Special
Selection

94 1979 Cabernet Sauvignon Napa Valley Special
Selection

93 1978 Cabernet Sauvignon Napa Valley Special
Selection

90 1976 Cabernet Sauvignon Napa Valley Special
Selection

92 1975 Cabernet Sauvignon Napa Valley Special
Selection

88 1992 Conundrum California

92 1991 Conundrum California

84 1990 Pinot Noir Napa Valley Special Selection

78 1989 Pinot Noir Napa Valley Special Selection

82 1988 Pinot Noir Napa Valley Special Selection

86 1987 Pinot Noir Napa Valley Special Selection

82 1986 Pinot Noir Napa Valley Special Selection

88 1985 Pinot Noir Napa Valley Special Selection

85 1993 Sauvignon Blanc Napa Valley Barrel
Fermented

91 1992 Sauvignon Blanc Napa Valley Barrel
Fermented

89 1992 Zinfandel Napa Valley

82 1990 Zinfandel Napa Valley

83 1989 Zinfandel Napa Valley

80 1988 Zinfandel Napa Valley

85 1987 Zinfandel Napa Valley

89 1986 Zinfandel Napa Valley

83 1990 Liberty School Cabernet Sauvignon
California Vintner Select Series Three

85 1991 Liberty School White Table Wine California
Three Valley Select

CECCHETTI SEBASTIANI CELLARS

74 1989 Cabernet Sauvignon Alexander Valley

74 1990 Pepperwood Grove Cabernet Sauvignon
California

76 1992 Pepperwood Grove Chardonnay California

74 1994 Pepperwood Grove Gamay Beaujolais
California Nouveau

83 1993 Pepperwood Grove Pinot Noir California

78 1992 Pepperwood Grove Pinot Noir California
Cask Lot 1

86 1992 Pepperwood Grove Pinot Noir California
Cask Lot 2

84 1992 Pepperwood Grove Pinot Noir California
Cask Lot 3

CEDAR MOUNTAIN WINERY

86 1991 Cabernet Sauvignon Livermore Valley
Blanches Vineyard

89 1990 Cabernet Sauvignon Livermore Valley
Blanches Vineyard

84 1992 Chardonnay Livermore Valley Blanches
Vineyard

86 1991 Chardonnay Livermore Valley Blanches
Vineyard

79 1990 Chardonnay Livermore Valley Blanches
Vineyard

CHALK HILL WINERY

89 1991 Cabernet Sauvignon Chalk Hill

89 1990 Cabernet Sauvignon Chalk Hill

75 1989 Cabernet Sauvignon Chalk Hill

87 1988 Cabernet Sauvignon Chalk Hill

70 1987 Cabernet Sauvignon Chalk Hill

91 1993 Chardonnay Chalk Hill

84 1992 Chardonnay Chalk Hill

83 1991 Chardonnay Chalk Hill

91 1990 Chardonnay Chalk Hill

88 1993 Sauvignon Blanc Chalk Hill

87 1992 Sauvignon Blanc Chalk Hill

91 1986 Sémillon Chalk Hill

CHALONE VINEYARD

87 1993 Chardonnay Chalone

91 1992 Chardonnay Chalone

91 1991 Chardonnay Chalone

89 1990 Chardonnay Chalone

88 1989 Chardonnay Chalone

90 1988 Chardonnay Chalone

90 1987 Chardonnay Chalone

94 1986 Chardonnay Chalone

93 1992 Chardonnay Chalone Reserve

91 1991 Chardonnay Chalone Reserve

89 1990 Chardonnay Chalone Reserve

82 1989 Chardonnay Chalone Reserve

89 1988 Chardonnay Chalone Reserve

94 1985 Chardonnay Chalone Reserve

86 1992 Chenin Blanc Chalone

86 1992 Pinot Blanc Chalone

92 1991 Pinot Blanc Chalone

80 1990 Pinot Blanc Chalone

88 1989 Pinot Blanc Chalone

88 1991 Pinot Noir Chalone

90 1990 Pinot Noir Chalone

77 1989 Pinot Noir Chalone

83 1988 Pinot Noir Chalone

85 1987 Pinot Noir Chalone

84 1986 Pinot Noir Chalone

84 1985 Pinot Noir Chalone

85 1984 Pinot Noir Chalone

86 1983 Pinot Noir Chalone

84 1982 Pinot Noir Chalone

83 1981 Pinot Noir Chalone

88 1980 Pinot Noir Chalone

88 1979 Pinot Noir Chalone

92	1977 Pinot Noir Chalone
85	1990 Pinot Noir Chalone Reserve
83	1989 Pinot Noir Chalone Reserve
84	1988 Pinot Noir Chalone Reserve
86	1987 Pinot Noir Chalone Reserve
79	1986 Pinot Noir Chalone Reserve
75	1985 Pinot Noir Chalone Reserve
82	1984 Pinot Noir Chalone Reserve
80	1983 Pinot Noir Chalone Reserve
70	1982 Pinot Noir Chalone Reserve
88	1981 Pinot Noir Chalone Reserve
82	1980 Pinot Noir Chalone Reserve
85	1989 Gavilan Vineyards Chardonnay California
84	1993 Gavilan Vineyards Chardonnay Chalone
86	1992 Gavilan Vineyards Chardonnay Chalone
81	1992 Gavilan Vineyards Pinot Blanc Chalone
82	1992 Gavilan Vineyards Pinot Noir Chalone
78	1991 Gavilan Vineyards Pinot Noir Chalone

CHAMISAL VINEYARD

86	1991 Chardonnay Edna Valley
91	1989 Chardonnay Edna Valley Special Reserve

CHANSA CELLARS

77	1989 Chardonnay Santa Barbara County

CHAPPELLET VINEYARD

86	1992 Cabernet Sauvignon Napa Valley Pritchard Hill Estates
89	1991 Cabernet Sauvignon Napa Valley
80	1990 Cabernet Sauvignon Napa Valley
82	1989 Cabernet Sauvignon Napa Valley Signature
85	1988 Cabernet Sauvignon Napa Valley Reserve
89	1987 Cabernet Sauvignon Napa Valley Reserve
89	1986 Cabernet Sauvignon Napa Valley Reserve
88	1985 Cabernet Sauvignon Napa Valley Reserve
84	1984 Cabernet Sauvignon Napa Valley Reserve
77	1983 Cabernet Sauvignon Napa Valley
80	1982 Cabernet Sauvignon Napa Valley
85	1981 Cabernet Sauvignon Napa Valley
88	1980 Cabernet Sauvignon Napa Valley
79	1979 Cabernet Sauvignon Napa Valley
80	1977 Cabernet Sauvignon Napa Valley
76	1976 Cabernet Sauvignon Napa Valley
77	1975 Cabernet Sauvignon Napa Valley
68	1974 Cabernet Sauvignon Napa Valley
69	1973 Cabernet Sauvignon Napa Valley
67	1972 Cabernet Sauvignon Napa Valley
78	1971 Cabernet Sauvignon Napa Valley
84	1970 Cabernet Sauvignon Napa Valley
85	1969 Cabernet Sauvignon Napa Valley
82	1968 Cabernet Sauvignon Napa Valley

85	1992 Chardonnay Napa Valley
85	1992 Chenin Blanc Napa Valley Dry
85	1991 Chenin Blanc Napa Valley Dry
84	1992 Merlot Napa Valley
68	1989 Merlot Napa Valley
85	1988 Merlot Napa Valley
85	1987 Merlot Napa Valley
83	1986 Merlot Napa Valley
78	1985 Merlot Napa Valley

CHATEAU CHEVRE WINERY

83	1992 Chardonnay Napa Valley

CHATEAU DE BAUN

87	1993 Chardonnay Russian River Valley
85	1992 Chardonnay Russian River Valley
86	1991 Chardonnay Russian River Valley
82	1991 Pinot Noir Sonoma County
77	NV Sparkling Wine Sonoma County Brut
88	1993 Symphony Russian River Valley Finale Late Harvest
87	1989 Symphony Sonoma County Finale Late Harvest

CHATEAU DE LEU WINERY

78	1992 Chardonnay Green Valley-Solano
83	1991 Pinot Noir Napa Valley

CHATEAU JULIEN WINERY

79	1991 Chardonnay Monterey County Barrel Fermented
81	1990 Chardonnay Monterey County Barrel Fermented
80	1991 Chardonnay Monterey County Private Reserve
82	1991 Merlot Monterey County
86	1989 Merlot Monterey County
72	1988 Merlot Monterey County
85	1991 Merlot Monterey County Private Reserve
72	1991 Garland Ranch Chardonnay California

CHATEAU MONTELENA WINERY

90	1992 Cabernet Sauvignon Napa Valley Calistoga Cuvée
92	1991 Cabernet Sauvignon Napa Valley The Montelena Estate
90	1990 Cabernet Sauvignon Napa Valley The Montelena Estate
85	1989 Cabernet Sauvignon Napa Valley
87	1988 Cabernet Sauvignon Napa Valley
95	1987 Cabernet Sauvignon Napa Valley
93	1986 Cabernet Sauvignon Napa Valley
95	1985 Cabernet Sauvignon Napa Valley
94	1984 Cabernet Sauvignon Napa Valley

86	1983 Cabernet Sauvignon Napa Valley
89	1982 Cabernet Sauvignon Napa Valley
80	1981 Cabernet Sauvignon Napa Valley
86	1980 Cabernet Sauvignon Napa Valley
87	1979 Cabernet Sauvignon Napa Valley
96	1978 Cabernet Sauvignon Napa Valley
90	1977 Cabernet Sauvignon Napa Valley
90	1974 Cabernet Sauvignon Napa Valley
88	1976 Cabernet Sauvignon North Coast
86	1975 Cabernet Sauvignon North Coast
88	1979 Cabernet Sauvignon Sonoma County
87	1978 Cabernet Sauvignon Sonoma County
91	1977 Cabernet Sauvignon Sonoma County
88	1974 Cabernet Sauvignon Sonoma County
87	1973 Cabernet Sauvignon Sonoma County
90	1987 Chardonnay Alexander Valley
89	1986 Chardonnay Alexander Valley
91	1985 Chardonnay Alexander Valley
84	1993 Chardonnay Napa Valley
88	1992 Chardonnay Napa Valley 1972-1992 Anniversary
83	1991 Chardonnay Napa Valley
81	1990 Chardonnay Napa Valley
83	1989 Chardonnay Napa Valley
72	1987 Chardonnay Napa Valley
90	1986 Chardonnay Napa Valley
90	1985 Chardonnay Napa Valley
87	1992 Zinfandel Napa Valley
84	1991 Zinfandel Napa Valley
80	1989 Zinfandel Napa Valley
70	1987 Zinfandel Napa Valley

CHATEAU POTELLE

92	1992 Cabernet Sauvignon Mount Veeder V.G.S.
91	1990 Cabernet Sauvignon Mount Veeder V.G.S.
86	1990 Cabernet Sauvignon Napa Valley Cuvée 95
91	1991 Chardonnay Mount Veeder V.G.S.
88	1991 Chardonnay Napa Valley
80	1990 Chardonnay Napa Valley
87	1989 Chardonnay Napa Valley
86	1993 Sauvignon Blanc Napa Valley
92	1992 Zinfandel Mount Veeder V.G.S.
90	1990 Zinfandel Mount Veeder V.G.S.

CHATEAU SOUVERAIN

85	1992 Cabernet Sauvignon Alexander Valley
85	1991 Cabernet Sauvignon Alexander Valley
90	1990 Cabernet Sauvignon Alexander Valley
85	1989 Cabernet Sauvignon Alexander Valley
85	1988 Cabernet Sauvignon Alexander Valley
87	1987 Cabernet Sauvignon Alexander Valley

91   1991 Cabernet Sauvignon Alexander Valley Winemaker's Reserve

87   1990 Cabernet Sauvignon Alexander Valley Winemaker's Reserve

83   1988 Cabernet Sauvignon Alexander Valley Winemaker's Reserve

90   1990 Chardonnay Carneros Sangiacomo Vineyard

91   1992 Chardonnay Russian River Valley Allen Vineyard

88   1990 Chardonnay Russian River Valley Allen Vineyard

90   1992 Chardonnay Russian River Valley Allen Vineyard Reserve

90   1991 Chardonnay Russian River Valley Allen Vineyard Reserve

89   1993 Chardonnay Russian River Valley Rochioli Vineyard Reserve

84   1992 Chardonnay Sonoma County Barrel Fermented

85   1991 Chardonnay Sonoma County Barrel Fermented

88   1991 Chardonnay Sonoma Valley Durell Vineyard Reserve

85   1992 Merlot Alexander Valley

87   1991 Merlot Alexander Valley

86   1990 Merlot Alexander Valley

89   1989 Merlot Alexander Valley

87   1990 Merlot Sonoma County

84   1993 Pinot Noir Carneros Winemaker's Reserve

85   1992 Pinot Noir Carneros Winemaker's Reserve

84   1991 Pinot Noir Carneros Winemaker's Reserve

85   1994 Sauvignon Blanc Alexander Valley Barrel Fermented

87   1993 Sauvignon Blanc Alexander Valley Barrel Fermented

86   1992 Sauvignon Blanc Alexander Valley Barrel Fermented

87   1992 Zinfandel Dry Creek Valley Bradford Mountain Vineyard

87   1991 Zinfandel Dry Creek Valley Bradford Mountain Vineyard

84   1990 Zinfandel Dry Creek Valley Bradford Mountain Vineyard

82   1989 Zinfandel Dry Creek Valley Bradford Mountain Vineyard

85   1987 Zinfandel Dry Creek Valley Bradford Mountain Vineyard

CHATEAU ST. JEAN

83   1989 Cabernet Franc Sonoma Valley Jeanette Vineyards

86   1990 Cabernet Sauvignon Sonoma County

84   1989 Cabernet Sauvignon Sonoma County

83   1988 Cabernet Sauvignon Sonoma County

88   1987 Cabernet Sauvignon Sonoma Valley

90   1986 Cabernet Sauvignon Sonoma Valley

86   1985 Cabernet Sauvignon Sonoma Valley

87   1990 Cabernet Sauvignon Sonoma County Cinq Cépages

93   1990 Cabernet Sauvignon Sonoma County Reserve

85   1989 Cabernet Sauvignon Sonoma County Reserve

84   1988 Cabernet Sauvignon Sonoma County Reserve

93   1987 Cabernet Sauvignon Alexander Valley Reserve

86   1993 Chardonnay Alexander Valley Belle Terre Vineyard

90   1992 Chardonnay Alexander Valley Belle Terre Vineyard

88   1991 Chardonnay Alexander Valley Belle Terre Vineyard

87   1990 Chardonnay Alexander Valley Belle Terre Vineyard

88   1991 Chardonnay Alexander Valley Belle Terre Vineyard Reserve

91   1992 Chardonnay Alexander Valley Robert Young Vineyard

89   1991 Chardonnay Alexander Valley Robert Young Vineyard

90   1990 Chardonnay Alexander Valley Robert Young Vineyard

91   1991 Chardonnay Alexander Valley Robert Young Vineyard Reserve

92   1990 Chardonnay Alexander Valley Robert Young Vineyard Reserve

84   1992 Chardonnay Sonoma County

85   1991 Chardonnay Sonoma County

84   1993 Fumé Blanc Russian River Valley La Petite Étoile

80   1991 Fumé Blanc Russian River Valley La Petite Étoile

82   1993 Fumé Blanc Sonoma County Dry

85   1992 Fumé Blanc Sonoma County Dry

82   1992 Gewürztraminer Sonoma County

88   1988 Johannisberg Riesling Alexander Valley Hoot Owl Creek Vineyards Late Harvest Select

95   1989 Johannisberg Riesling Alexander Valley Hoot Owl Creek Vineyards Late Harvest Special Select

86   1992 Merlot Sonoma County

84   1991 Merlot Sonoma County

88   1990 Merlot Sonoma County

80   1989 Merlot Sonoma County

83   1990 Mourvèdre Sonoma Valley

86   1991 Pinot Noir Sonoma County

80   1990 Pinot Noir Sonoma County

CHATEAU WOLTNER

86   1993 Chardonnay Howell Mountain

84   1992 Chardonnay Howell Mountain

84   1991 Chardonnay Howell Mountain

82   1989 Chardonnay Howell Mountain

84   1993 Chardonnay Howell Mountain Estate Reserve

90   1992 Chardonnay Howell Mountain Estate Reserve

87   1991 Chardonnay Howell Mountain Estate Reserve

82   1993 Chardonnay Howell Mountain Frederique Vineyard

90   1992 Chardonnay Howell Mountain Frederique Vineyard

85   1991 Chardonnay Howell Mountain Frederique Vineyard

83   1993 Chardonnay Howell Mountain St. Thomas Vineyard

88   1992 Chardonnay Howell Mountain St. Thomas Vineyard

90   1990 Chardonnay Howell Mountain St. Thomas Vineyard

82   1993 Chardonnay Howell Mountain Titus Vineyard

88   1992 Chardonnay Howell Mountain Titus Vineyard

90   1991 Chardonnay Howell Mountain Titus Vineyard

CHATOM VINEYARDS

84   1992 Cabernet Sauvignon Calaveras County

83   1991 Cabernet Sauvignon Calaveras County

82   1993 Chardonnay Calaveras County

83   1991 Chardonnay Calaveras County

74   1992 Merlot Calaveras County

85   1991 Merlot Calaveras County

70   1992 Sangiovese Calaveras County

90   1993 Sauvignon Blanc Calaveras County

86   1991 Sauvignon Blanc Calaveras County Select

80   1991 Sauvignon Blanc Calaveras County Calaveras Fumé

87   1993 Sémillon Calaveras County

84   1992 Zinfandel Calaveras County

81   1991 Zinfandel Calaveras County

CHAUFFE-EAU CELLARS

85   1987 Cabernet Sauvignon Alexander Valley

87   1993 Chardonnay Carneros Sangiacomo Vineyard Sans Filtrage

89   1992 Chardonnay Carneros Sangiacomo Vineyard Sans Filtrage

86   1990 Chardonnay Carneros Sangiacomo Vineyard Sans Filtrage

86   1993 Chardonnay Russian River Valley Dutton Ranch Sans Filtrage

CHIMÉRE WINERY

83   1989 Chardonnay Edna Valley

83   1992 Merlot Santa Barbara County

76   1993 Pinot Blanc Santa Barbara County

CHIMNEY ROCK WINERY

84   1991 Cabernet Sauvignon Stags Leap District

85 1990 Cabernet Sauvignon Stags Leap District

82 1993 Chardonnay Carneros

82 1992 Chardonnay Stags Leap District

79 1991 Chardonnay Stags Leap District

77 1992 Fumé Blanc Napa Valley

88 1991 Meritage Red Stags Leap District Elevage

88 1990 Meritage Red Stags Leap District Elevage

82 1993 Sauvignon Blanc Napa Valley

CHRISTOPHER CREEK

84 1992 Syrah Russian River Valley

86 1990 Syrah Russian River Valley

CINNABAR VINEYARD & WINERY

85 1990 Cabernet Sauvignon Santa Cruz Mountains

82 1989 Cabernet Sauvignon Santa Cruz Mountains

82 1988 Cabernet Sauvignon Santa Cruz Mountains

87 1986 Cabernet Sauvignon Santa Cruz Mountains

85 1993 Chardonnay Santa Cruz Mountains

86 1992 Chardonnay Santa Cruz Mountains

91 1991 Chardonnay Santa Cruz Mountains Saratoga Estate

CLAIBORNE & CHURCHILL

87 1993 Chardonnay Edna Valley MacGregor Vineyard

80 1991 Chardonnay Edna Valley MacGregor Vineyard

85 1993 Gewürztraminer Central Coast Dry Alsatian Style

82 1991 Gewürztraminer Central Coast Dry Alsatian Style

88 1992 Pinot Noir Edna Valley MacGregor Vineyard

82 1991 Pinot Noir Edna Valley MacGregor Vineyard

78 1990 Pinot Noir Edna Valley MacGregor Vineyard

82 1993 Riesling Central Coast Dry Alsatian Style

85 1991 Riesling Central Coast Dry Alsatian Style

CLAUDIA SPRINGS WINERY

83 1993 Chardonnay Anderson Valley

86 1991 Pinot Noir Anderson Valley

81 1992 Zinfandel Mendocino County

CLINE CELLARS

83 1991 Carignane Contra Costa County

86 1990 Carignane Contra Costa County

75 1989 Merlot California

85 1989 Mourvèdre Contra Costa County

78 1989 Mourvèdre Contra Costa County Reserve

72 1990 Muscat Contra Costa County

82 1991 Rhône Blend Contra Costa County Cotes d'Oakley

89 1990 Rhône Blend Contra Costa County Oakley Cuvée

88 1989 Rhône Blend Contra Costa County Oakley Cuvée

90 1988 Rhône Blend Contra Costa County Oakley Cuvée

86 1990 Sémillon California Barrel Fermented

84 1991 Syrah Contra Costa County

84 1990 Syrah Contra Costa County

85 1993 Zinfandel Contra Costa County

84 1992 Zinfandel Contra Costa County

84 1991 Zinfandel Contra Costa County

86 1990 Zinfandel Contra Costa County

86 1989 Zinfandel Contra Costa County

89 1987 Zinfandel Contra Costa County

87 1993 Zinfandel Contra Costa County Big Break

87 1993 Zinfandel Contra Costa County Bridgehead

88 1993 Zinfandel Contra Costa County Reserve

89 1992 Zinfandel Contra Costa County Reserve

86 1991 Zinfandel Contra Costa County Reserve

82 1990 Zinfandel Contra Costa County Reserve

84 1989 Zinfandel Contra Costa County Reserve

87 1987 Zinfandel Contra Costa County Reserve

CLONINGER CELLARS

82 1990 Cabernet Sauvignon Monterey County

79 1991 Chardonnay Monterey County

CLOS DU BOIS

85 1991 Cabernet Franc Alexander Valley Reserve L'Etranger

86 1991 Cabernet Sauvignon Alexander Valley

87 1990 Cabernet Sauvignon Alexander Valley

92 1991 Cabernet Sauvignon Alexander Valley Winemaker's Reserve

87 1991 Cabernet Sauvignon Alexander Valley Briarcrest Vineyard

88 1990 Cabernet Sauvignon Alexander Valley Briarcrest Vineyard

80 1989 Cabernet Sauvignon Alexander Valley Briarcrest Vineyard

88 1987 Cabernet Sauvignon Alexander Valley Briarcrest Vineyard

87 1986 Cabernet Sauvignon Alexander Valley Briarcrest Vineyard

82 1985 Cabernet Sauvignon Alexander Valley Briarcrest Vineyard

87 1984 Cabernet Sauvignon Alexander Valley Briarcrest Vineyard

88 1991 Cabernet Sauvignon Alexander Valley Marlstone Vineyard

88 1990 Cabernet Sauvignon Alexander Valley Marlstone Vineyard

84 1989 Cabernet Sauvignon Alexander Valley Marlstone Vineyard

90 1987 Cabernet Sauvignon Alexander Valley Marlstone Vineyard

85 1986 Cabernet Sauvignon Alexander Valley Marlstone Vineyard

88 1985 Cabernet Sauvignon Alexander Valley Marlstone Vineyard

89 1984 Cabernet Sauvignon Alexander Valley Marlstone Vineyard

84 1993 Chardonnay Alexander Valley Barrel Fermented

84 1992 Chardonnay Alexander Valley Barrel Fermented

88 1993 Chardonnay Dry Creek Valley Calcaire Vineyard

89 1992 Chardonnay Dry Creek Valley Calcaire Vineyard

88 1991 Chardonnay Dry Creek Valley Calcaire Vineyard

83 1990 Chardonnay Dry Creek Valley Calcaire Vineyard

86 1993 Chardonnay Dry Creek Valley Flintwood Vineyard

87 1991 Chardonnay Dry Creek Valley Flintwood Vineyard

81 1990 Chardonnay Dry Creek Valley Flintwood Vineyard

79 1993 Gewürztraminer Alexander Valley Early Harvest

82 1991 Malbec Alexander Valley L'Etranger Reserve

87 1987 Malbec Alexander Valley L'Etranger Reserve

88 1992 Merlot Sonoma County

87 1991 Merlot Sonoma County

87 1990 Merlot Sonoma County

82 1989 Merlot Sonoma County

81 1988 Merlot Sonoma County

89 1987 Merlot Sonoma County

82 1990 Pinot Noir Sonoma County

80 1993 Sauvignon Blanc Alexander Valley Barrel Fermented

84 1994 Sauvignon Blanc Sonoma County

87 1992 Zinfandel Sonoma County

87 1991 Zinfandel Sonoma County

CLOS DU VAL

87 1990 Cabernet Sauvignon Napa Valley

82 1989 Cabernet Sauvignon Napa Valley

84 1990 Cabernet Sauvignon Stags Leap District

83 1989 Cabernet Sauvignon Stags Leap District

86 1988 Cabernet Sauvignon Stags Leap District

90 1987 Cabernet Sauvignon Stags Leap District

91 1986 Cabernet Sauvignon Stags Leap District

91 1985 Cabernet Sauvignon Stags Leap District

92 1984 Cabernet Sauvignon Stags Leap District

88 1990 Cabernet Sauvignon Stags Leap District Reserve

87 1988 Cabernet Sauvignon Stags Leap District Reserve

92 1987 Cabernet Sauvignon Stags Leap District Reserve

94 1985 Cabernet Sauvignon Stags Leap District Reserve

88 1982 Cabernet Sauvignon Stags Leap District Reserve

90 1979 Cabernet Sauvignon Stags Leap District Reserve

91 1978 Cabernet Sauvignon Stags Leap District Reserve

86 1993 Chardonnay Carneros Napa Valley Carneros Estate Special Select

85 1992 Chardonnay Carneros Napa Valley Carneros Estate

87 1991 Chardonnay Carneros Napa Valley Carneros Estate

84 1992 Merlot Stags Leap District

89 1991 Merlot Stags Leap District

86 1990 Merlot Stags Leap District

86 1989 Merlot Stags Leap District

90 1988 Merlot Stags Leap District

85 1987 Merlot Stags Leap District

86 1986 Merlot Stags Leap District

89 1985 Merlot Stags Leap District

87 1984 Merlot Stags Leap District

78 1990 Pinot Noir Carneros

81 1989 Pinot Noir Carneros

73 1991 Sémillon Stags Leap District

84 1991 Zinfandel Stags Leap District

74 1990 Zinfandel Stags Leap District

87 1989 Zinfandel Stags Leap District

85 1988 Zinfandel Stags Leap District

83 1987 Zinfandel Stags Leap District

87 1986 Zinfandel Stags Leap District

90 1985 Zinfandel Stags Leap District

CLOS LA CHANCE

88 1992 Cabernet Sauvignon Santa Cruz Mountains

89 1993 Chardonnay Santa Cruz Mountains

87 1992 Chardonnay Santa Cruz Mountains

CLOS PEGASE

85 1991 Cabernet Blend Napa Valley Hommage

86 1990 Cabernet Blend Napa Valley Hommage

87 1991 Cabernet Sauvignon Napa Valley

91 1990 Cabernet Sauvignon Napa Valley

82 1987 Cabernet Sauvignon Napa Valley

88 1986 Cabernet Sauvignon Napa Valley

86 1985 Cabernet Sauvignon Napa Valley

87 1993 Chardonnay Carneros Pegase Circle Reserve

83 1992 Chardonnay Carneros

87 1991 Chardonnay Carneros

80 1991 Merlot Napa Valley

86 1990 Merlot Napa Valley

79 1992 Sauvignon Blanc Napa Valley

CODORNIU NAPA

87 NV Sparkling Wine Napa Valley Brut Cuvée

B. R. COHN WINERY

82 1989 Cabernet Sauvignon Napa County Silver Label

87 1988 Cabernet Sauvignon Napa County Silver Label

90 1991 Cabernet Sauvignon Sonoma Valley Olive Hill Vineyard

90 1990 Cabernet Sauvignon Sonoma Valley Olive Hill Vineyard

84 1989 Cabernet Sauvignon Sonoma Valley Olive Hill Vineyard

86 1988 Cabernet Sauvignon Sonoma Valley Olive Hill Vineyard

92 1987 Cabernet Sauvignon Sonoma Valley Olive Hill Vineyard

92 1986 Cabernet Sauvignon Sonoma Valley Olive Hill Vineyard

94 1985 Cabernet Sauvignon Sonoma Valley Olive Hill Vineyard

85 1984 Cabernet Sauvignon Sonoma Valley Olive Hill Vineyard

84 1993 Chardonnay Carneros

87 1992 Chardonnay Carneros

82 1993 Chardonnay Carneros Joseph Herman Vineyard Reserve

88 1991 Chardonnay Napa Valley Silver Label

82 1989 Merlot Napa Valley Silver Label

80 1992 Merlot Napa-Sonoma Counties

84 1990 Merlot Napa-Sonoma Counties

COLGIN

92 1992 Cabernet Sauvignon Napa Valley Herb Lamb Vineyard

CONCANNON VINEYARD

78 1991 Cabernet Blend Livermore Valley Assemblage

84 1992 Cabernet Sauvignon Central Coast Selected Vineyards

79 1991 Cabernet Sauvignon Livermore Valley Concannon Estate Vineyard

84 1993 Chardonnay Central Coast Selected Vineyards

86 1992 Chardonnay Central Coast Selected Vineyards

82 1991 Chardonnay Central Coast Selected Vineyards

87 1993 Chardonnay Livermore Valley Reserve

89 1991 Chardonnay Livermore Valley Reserve

83 1991 Petite Sirah Central Coast

81 1991 Petite Sirah Livermore Valley Selected Vineyards

81 1992 Sauvignon Blanc Livermore Valley

80 1993 Sauvignon Blend Livermore Valley Assemblage

CONN CREEK WINERY

93 1991 Cabernet Blend Napa Valley Anthology

85 1991 Cabernet Sauvignon Napa Valley Barrel Select

88 1991 Cabernet Sauvignon Napa Valley Limited Release

84 1988 Cabernet Sauvignon Napa Valley Barrel Select

87 1987 Cabernet Sauvignon Napa Valley Barrel Select

87 1987 Cabernet Sauvignon Napa Valley Reserve

84 1985 Cabernet Sauvignon Napa Valley Barrel Select

87 1990 Merlot Napa Valley Barrel Select

80 1989 Merlot Napa Valley Barrel Select

86 1988 Merlot Napa Valley Barrel Select

87 1987 Merlot Napa Valley Barrel Select

R. & J. COOK

82 1989 Merlot Clarksburg

82 1991 Chestnut Hill Winery Cabernet Sauvignon California Coastal Cuvée

84 1990 Chestnut Hill Winery Cabernet Sauvignon California Coastal Cuvée

74 1991 Chestnut Hill Winery Chardonnay California

78 1992 Chestnut Hill Winery Merlot North Coast Coastal Cuvée

78 1991 Chestnut Hill Winery Merlot North Coast Coastal Cuvée

CORBETT CANYON VINEYARDS

80 1991 Cabernet Sauvignon California Coastal Classic

82 1991 Cabernet Sauvignon Napa Valley Reserve

84 1990 Cabernet Sauvignon Napa Valley Reserve

85 1989 Cabernet Sauvignon Napa Valley Reserve

80 1993 Chardonnay Central Coast Coastal Classic

75 1992 Chardonnay Central Coast Coastal Classic

81 1993 Chardonnay Santa Barbara County Reserve

82 1992 Chardonnay Santa Barbara County Reserve

82 1992 Merlot California Coastal Classic

82 1992 Pinot Noir Santa Barbara County Reserve

82 1992 Sauvignon Blanc Central Coast Coastal Classic

CORISON

89 1991 Cabernet Sauvignon Napa Valley

90 1990 Cabernet Sauvignon Napa Valley

86 1989 Cabernet Sauvignon Napa Valley

87 1988 Cabernet Sauvignon Napa Valley

90 1987 Cabernet Sauvignon Napa Valley

CORNERSTONE CELLARS

93 1991 Cabernet Sauvignon Howell Mountain

COSENTINO WINERY

83 1990 Cabernet Franc North Coast

78 1989 Cabernet Franc North Coast

80 1988 Cabernet Franc North Coast

81 1990 Cabernet Sauvignon Napa County

86 1989 Cabernet Sauvignon Napa County

87 1992 Cabernet Sauvignon Napa Valley

86 1991 Cabernet Sauvignon Napa Valley

84 1990 Cabernet Sauvignon Napa Valley

88 1992 Cabernet Sauvignon Napa Valley Punched Cap Fermented Unfined

86 1988 Cabernet Sauvignon North Coast

80 1987 Cabernet Sauvignon North Coast

84 1985 Cabernet Sauvignon North Coast

87 1990 Cabernet Sauvignon Napa Valley Reserve

80 1989 Cabernet Sauvignon Napa Valley The Winemaster

81 1988 Cabernet Sauvignon North Coast Reserve

86 1987 Cabernet Sauvignon North Coast Reserve

88 1986 Cabernet Sauvignon North Coast Reserve

81 1985 Cabernet Sauvignon North Coast Reserve

83 1993 Chardonnay Napa Valley

86 1992 Chardonnay Napa County

87 1991 Chardonnay Napa Valley

86 1993 Chardonnay Napa Valley The Sculptor

81 1992 Chardonnay Napa Valley The Sculptor

85 1991 Chardonnay Napa Valley The Sculptor

86 1990 Meritage Red California The Poet

81 1989 Meritage Red California The Poet

85 1988 Meritage Red California The Poet

85 1987 Meritage Red California The Poet

89 1991 Meritage Red Napa Valley M. Coz

92 1990 Meritage Red Napa Valley M. Coz

88 1989 Meritage Red Napa Valley M. Coz

87 1988 Meritage Red Napa Valley M. Coz

89 1992 Merlot Napa Valley

77 1991 Merlot Napa Valley

84 1990 Merlot Napa Valley

83 1989 Merlot Napa Valley

84 1993 Pinot Noir Carneros

86 1993 Pinot Noir Carneros Punched Cap Fermented

89 1992 Pinot Noir Carneros

82 1991 Pinot Noir Carneros

83 1990 Pinot Noir Napa Valley

83 1990 Pinot Noir Sonoma County

82 1989 Pinot Noir Sonoma County

85 1992 Sauvignon Blend Napa Valley The Novelist

87 1993 Zinfandel Sonoma County The Zin

88 1992 Zinfandel Sonoma County The Zin

89 1991 Zinfandel Sonoma County The Zin

88 1990 Zinfandel Sonoma County The Zin

80 1989 Crystal Valley Cellars Cabernet Sauvignon Napa Valley Unfined

77 1991 Crystal Valley Cellars Pinot Blanc Napa Valley

82 1992 Crystal Valley Cellars Sauvignon Blanc Napa Valley

COTTONWOOD CANYON

70 1991 Chardonnay Santa Barbara County

80 1990 Chardonnay Santa Barbara County

79 1990 Chardonnay Santa Barbara County Barrel Select

90 1989 Chardonnay Santa Barbara County Barrel Select

79 1990 Pinot Noir Santa Barbara County

86 1989 Pinot Noir Santa Barbara County

82 1989 Pinot Noir Santa Barbara County Barrel Select

THOMAS COYNE WINERY

84 1990 Merlot El Dorado County Quartz Hill Vineyard

84 1990 Merlot Sonoma County

CRESTON VINEYARDS & WINERY

85 1989 Cabernet Sauvignon Paso Robles

83 1989 Cabernet Sauvignon Paso Robles Winemaker's Selection

80 1988 Cabernet Sauvignon Paso Robles Winemaker's Selection

81 1990 Cabernet Sauvignon San Luis Obispo County

77 1992 Chardonnay Paso Robles

83 1991 Chardonnay Paso Robles

84 1991 Merlot Paso Robles

83 1992 Pinot Noir Paso Robles

74 1991 Pinot Noir Paso Robles

86 1994 White Table Wine Paso Robles Chevrier Blanc

78 1991 Zinfandel Paso Robles

87 1990 Zinfandel Paso Robles

CRICHTON HALL

84 1990 Chardonnay Napa Valley

CRONIN VINEYARDS

86 1990 Cabernet Blend California Joe's Cuvée

84 1990 Cabernet Sauvignon Santa Cruz Mountains

88 1989 Cabernet Sauvignon Santa Cruz Mountains

83 1988 Cabernet Sauvignon Santa Cruz Mountains

84 1987 Cabernet Sauvignon Santa Cruz Mountains

82 1990 Cabernet Sauvignon Stags Leap District Robinson Vineyard

85 1989 Cabernet Sauvignon Stags Leap District Robinson Vineyard

86 1988 Cabernet Sauvignon Stags Leap District Robinson Vineyard

89 1987 Cabernet Sauvignon Stags Leap District Robinson Vineyard

88 1986 Cabernet Sauvignon Stags Leap District Robinson Vineyard

85 1993 Chardonnay Alexander Valley Stuhlmuller Vineyard

88 1992 Chardonnay Alexander Valley Stuhlmuller Vineyard

88 1990 Chardonnay Alexander Valley Stuhlmuller Vineyard

82 1991 Chardonnay California Nancy's Cuvée

86 1992 Chardonnay Monterey County Ventana Vineyard

83 1991 Chardonnay Monterey County Ventana Vineyard

88 1990 Chardonnay Monterey County Ventana Vineyard

85 1993 Chardonnay Napa Valley

88 1992 Chardonnay Napa Valley

87 1991 Chardonnay Napa Valley

90 1990 Chardonnay Napa Valley

84 1993 Chardonnay Santa Cruz Mountains

89 1992 Chardonnay Santa Cruz Mountains

91 1991 Chardonnay Santa Cruz Mountains

91 1990 Chardonnay Santa Cruz Mountains

87 1991 Meritage Red Stags Leap District Robinson Vineyard Concerto

81 1991 Pinot Noir Santa Cruz Moutains Peter Martin Ray Vineyard

83 1990 Pinot Noir Santa Cruz Mountains Peter Martin Ray Vineyard

81 1988 Pinot Noir Santa Cruz Mountains Peter Martin Ray Vineyard

88 1992 Sauvignon Blend Napa Valley

84 1991 Sauvignon Blend Napa Valley

CULBERTSON WINERY

78 1994 Artist Series Cuvée de Frontignan

84 1994 Artist Series Cuvée Rouge

CUTLER CELLARS

88 1990 Cabernet Sauvignon Sonoma Valley Batto Ranch

88 1987 Cabernet Sauvignon Sonoma Valley Batto Ranch

86 1986 Cabernet Sauvignon Sonoma Valley Batto Ranch

91 1985 Cabernet Sauvignon Sonoma Valley Batto Ranch

89 1987 Meritage Red Sonoma Valley Satyre

85 1986 Meritage Red Sonoma Valley Satyre

CUVAISON WINERY

88 1991 Cabernet Sauvignon Napa Valley

88 1990 Cabernet Sauvignon Napa Valley

82 1989 Cabernet Sauvignon Napa Valley

82 1988 Cabernet Sauvignon Napa Valley

89 1987 Cabernet Sauvignon Napa Valley

90 1986 Cabernet Sauvignon Napa Valley

88 1985 Cabernet Sauvignon Napa Valley

88 1984 Cabernet Sauvignon Napa Valley

86 1993 Chardonnay Carneros

89 1992 Chardonnay Carneros

89 1991 Chardonnay Carneros

88 1990 Chardonnay Carneros

88 1993 Chardonnay Carneros Reserve

88 1992 Chardonnay Carneros Reserve

88 1990 Chardonnay Carneros Reserve

85 1991 Merlot Carneros

88 1990 Merlot Carneros

84 1989 Merlot Carneros

87 1988 Merlot Carneros

86 1987 Merlot Carneros

86 1986 Merlot Carneros

85 1985 Merlot Carneros

92 1984 Merlot Carneros

85 1992 Pinot Noir Carneros

87 1991 Pinot Noir Carneros

82 1992 Calistoga Vineyards Chardonnay Napa Valley

DALLA VALLE VINEYARDS

94 1992 Cabernet Blend Napa Valley Maya

90 1991 Cabernet Blend Napa Valley Maya

90 1990 Cabernet Blend Napa Valley Maya

91 1989 Cabernet Blend Napa Valley Maya

86 1988 Cabernet Blend Napa Valley Maya

92 1992 Cabernet Sauvignon Napa Valley

91 1991 Cabernet Sauvignon Napa Valley

93 1990 Cabernet Sauvignon Napa Valley

84 1989 Cabernet Sauvignon Napa Valley

88 1988 Cabernet Sauvignon Napa Valley

89 1987 Cabernet Sauvignon Napa Valley

84 1986 Cabernet Sauvignon Napa Valley

DE LOACH VINEYARDS

78 1991 Cabernet Sauvignon Russian River Valley

84 1990 Cabernet Sauvignon Russian River Valley

88 1992 Chardonnay Russian River Valley

88 1991 Chardonnay Russian River Valley

91 1992 Chardonnay Russian River Valley O.F.S.

91 1991 Chardonnay Russian River Valley O.F.S.

90 1990 Chardonnay Russian River Valley O.F.S.

85 1992 Chardonnay Sonoma County Sonoma Cuvée

88 1992 Gewürztraminer Russian River Valley Early Harvest

86 1991 Gewürztraminer Russian River Valley Late Harvest

89 1992 Merlot Russian River Valley

78 1991 Merlot Russian River Valley

82 1992 Pinot Noir Russian River Valley

74 1991 Pinot Noir Russian River Valley

82 1990 Pinot Noir Russian River Valley O.F.S.

81 1993 Fumé Blanc Russian River Valley

84 1993 Sauvignon Blanc Russian River Valley Dry

89 1992 Zinfandel Russian River Valley

83 1991 Zinfandel Russian River Valley

89 1990 Zinfandel Russian River Valley

82 1989 Zinfandel Russian River Valley

78 1988 Zinfandel Russian River Valley

90 1987 Zinfandel Russian River Valley

88 1986 Zinfandel Russian River Valley

82 1991 Zinfandel Russian River Valley Barbieri Ranch

82 1990 Zinfandel Russian River Valley Barbieri Ranch

85 1991 Zinfandel Russian River Valley Papera Ranch

81 1990 Zinfandel Russian River Valley Papera Ranch

86 1991 Zinfandel Russian River Valley Pelletti Ranch

87 1990 Zinfandel Russian River Valley Pelletti Ranch

DE LORIMIER WINERY

87 1992 Chardonnay Alexander Valley Clonal Select

84 1991 Chardonnay Alexander Valley Prism

80 1990 Chardonnay Alexander Valley Prism

85 1991 Meritage Red Alexander Valley Mosaic

77 1990 Meritage Red Alexander Valley Mosaic

81 1988 Meritage Red Alexander Valley Mosaic

89 1992 Meritage White Alexander Valley Spectrum

82 1991 Meritage White Alexander Valley Spectrum

DEER PARK WINERY

88 1990 Cabernet Sauvignon Howell Mountain Beatty Ranch Reserve

87 1988 Cabernet Sauvignon Howell Mountain Beatty Ranch Reserve

82 1987 Petite Sirah Howell Mountain

81 1990 Zinfandel Howell Mountain Beatty Ranch

83 1988 Zinfandel Howell Mountain Beatty Ranch

85 1987 Zinfandel Howell Mountain Beatty Ranch Reserve

DEHLINGER WINERY

75 1989 Cabernet Franc Russian River Valley

88 1991 Cabernet Sauvignon Russian River Valley

80 1990 Cabernet Sauvignon Russian River Valley

79 1989 Cabernet Sauvignon Russian River Valley

83 1988 Cabernet Sauvignon Russian River Valley

88 1987 Cabernet Sauvignon Russian River Valley

90 1986 Cabernet Sauvignon Russian River Valley

88 1993 Chardonnay Russian River Valley

84 1992 Chardonnay Russian River Valley

89 1991 Chardonnay Russian River Valley

92 1992 Chardonnay Russian River Valley Montrachet Cuvée

89 1990 Chardonnay Russian River Valley Montrachet Cuvée

88 1992 Pinot Noir Russian River Valley

87 1991 Pinot Noir Russian River Valley

85 1990 Pinot Noir Russian River Valley

80 1989 Pinot Noir Russian River Valley

89 1987 Pinot Noir Russian River Valley

88 1986 Pinot Noir Russian River Valley

88 1985 Pinot Noir Russian River Valley

87 1984 Pinot Noir Russian River Valley

91 1992 Pinot Noir Russian River Valley Reserve

91 1991 Pinot Noir Russian River Valley Reserve

81 1990 Pinot Noir Russian River Valley Reserve

93 1992 Syrah Russian River Valley

DEMOOR WINERY

78 1990 Cabernet Sauvignon Napa Valley

86 1989 Cabernet Sauvignon Napa Valley

80 1993 Chardonnay Napa Valley

83 1992 Chardonnay Napa Valley

82 1991 Chardonnay Napa Valley

76 1992 Sauvignon Blanc Napa Valley

87 1991 Zinfandel Napa Valley

DIAMOND CREEK VINEYARDS

93 1992 Cabernet Sauvignon Napa Valley Gravelly Meadow

92 1991 Cabernet Sauvignon Napa Valley Gravelly Meadow

92 1991 Cabernet Sauvignon Napa Valley Gravelly Meadow Lake Blend

90 1990 Cabernet Sauvignon Napa Valley Gravelly Meadow

83 1989 Cabernet Sauvignon Napa Valley Gravelly Meadow

87 1988 Cabernet Sauvignon Napa Valley Gravelly Meadow

90 1987 Cabernet Sauvignon Napa Valley Gravelly Meadow

94 1986 Cabernet Sauvignon Napa Valley Gravelly Meadow

92 1985 Cabernet Sauvignon Napa Valley Gravelly Meadow

94 1984 Cabernet Sauvignon Napa Valley Gravelly Meadow

88 1983 Cabernet Sauvignon Napa Valley Gravelly Meadow

89 1982 Cabernet Sauvignon Napa Valley Gravelly Meadow

89 1981 Cabernet Sauvignon Napa Valley Gravelly Meadow

92 1980 Cabernet Sauvignon Napa Valley Gravelly Meadow

92 1979 Cabernet Sauvignon Napa Valley Gravelly Meadow

95 1978 Cabernet Sauvignon Napa Valley Gravelly Meadow

89 1977 Cabernet Sauvignon Napa Valley Gravelly Meadow

85 1976 Cabernet Sauvignon Napa Valley Gravelly Meadow

85 1975 Cabernet Sauvignon Napa Valley Gravelly Meadow

94 1974 Cabernet Sauvignon Napa Valley Gravelly Meadow

94 1992 Cabernet Sauvignon Napa Valley Lake Vineyard

91 1990 Cabernet Sauvignon Napa Valley Lake Vineyard

92 1987 Cabernet Sauvignon Napa Valley Lake Vineyard

90 1984 Cabernet Sauvignon Napa Valley Lake Vineyard

98 1978 Cabernet Sauvignon Napa Valley Lake Vineyard

91 1992 Cabernet Sauvignon Napa Valley Red Rock Terrace

91 1991 Cabernet Sauvignon Napa Valley Red Rock Terrace

94 1991 Cabernet Sauvignon Napa Valley Red Rock Terrace Microclimate 3

89 1990 Cabernet Sauvignon Napa Valley Red Rock Terrace

88 1989 Cabernet Sauvignon Napa Valley Red Rock Terrace

88 1988 Cabernet Sauvignon Napa Valley Red Rock Terrace

94 1987 Cabernet Sauvignon Napa Valley Red Rock Terrace

95 1986 Cabernet Sauvignon Napa Valley Red Rock Terrace

93 1985 Cabernet Sauvignon Napa Valley Red Rock Terrace

96 1984 Cabernet Sauvignon Napa Valley Red Rock Terrace

88 1983 Cabernet Sauvignon Napa Valley Red Rock Terrace

87 1982 Cabernet Sauvignon Napa Valley Red Rock Terrace

91 1981 Cabernet Sauvignon Napa Valley Red Rock Terrace

86 1980 Cabernet Sauvignon Napa Valley Red Rock Terrace

92 1979 Cabernet Sauvignon Napa Valley Red Rock Terrace

95 1978 Cabernet Sauvignon Napa Valley Red Rock Terrace

88 1977 Cabernet Sauvignon Napa Valley Red Rock Terrace First Pick

94 1976 Cabernet Sauvignon Napa Valley Red Rock Terrace

88 1975 Cabernet Sauvignon Napa Valley Red Rock Terrace

92 1974 Cabernet Sauvignon Napa Valley Red Rock Terrace

74 1972 Cabernet Sauvignon Napa Valley Red Rock Terrace

87 1992 Cabernet Sauvignon Napa Valley Three Vineyard Blend

87 1990 Cabernet Sauvignon Napa Valley Three Vineyard Blend

81 1989 Cabernet Sauvignon Napa Valley Three Vineyard Blend

89 1985 Cabernet Sauvignon Napa Valley Three Vineyard Blend

89 1984 Cabernet Sauvignon Napa Valley Three Vineyard Blend

90 1981 Cabernet Sauvignon Napa Valley Three Vineyard Blend

91 1992 Cabernet Sauvignon Napa Valley Volcanic Hill

91 1991 Cabernet Sauvignon Napa Valley Volcanic Hill

93 1991 Cabernet Sauvignon Napa Valley Volcanic Hill Microclimate 4

90 1990 Cabernet Sauvignon Napa Valley Volcanic Hill

86 1989 Cabernet Sauvignon Napa Valley Volcanic Hill

88 1988 Cabernet Sauvignon Napa Valley Volcanic Hill

95 1987 Cabernet Sauvignon Napa Valley Volcanic Hill

96 1986 Cabernet Sauvignon Napa Valley Volcanic Hill

93 1985 Cabernet Sauvignon Napa Valley Volcanic Hill

94 1984 Cabernet Sauvignon Napa Valley Volcanic Hill

89 1983 Cabernet Sauvignon Napa Valley Volcanic Hill

89 1982 Cabernet Sauvignon Napa Valley Volcanic Hill

92 1981 Cabernet Sauvignon Napa Valley Volcanic Hill

90 1980 Cabernet Sauvignon Napa Valley Volcanic Hill

95 1979 Cabernet Sauvignon Napa Valley Volcanic Hill First Pick

94 1978 Cabernet Sauvignon Napa Valley Volcanic Hill

85 1977 Cabernet Sauvignon Napa Valley Volcanic Hill

87 1976 Cabernet Sauvignon Napa Valley Volcanic Hill

92 1975 Cabernet Sauvignon Napa Valley Volcanic Hill

89 1974 Cabernet Sauvignon Napa Valley Volcanic Hill

80 1973 Cabernet Sauvignon Napa Valley Volcanic Hill

83 1972 Cabernet Sauvignon Napa Valley Volcanic Hill

DICKERSON VINEYARD

85 1992 Cabernet Blend Napa Valley Ruby Cabernet Limited Reserve

87 1991 Cabernet Blend Napa Valley Ruby Cabernet Limited Reserve

90 1992 Merlot Napa Valley Limited Reserve

92 1991 Zinfandel Napa Valley Limited Reserve

DOMAIN HILL & MAYES

85 1991 Cabernet Sauvignon Napa Valley Clos Fontaine du Mont Reserve

87 1992 Chardonnay Napa Valley Clos Fontaine du Mont

DOMAINE CARNEROS

80 NV Sparkling Wine Carneros Brut

88 1988 Sparkling Wine Carneros Brut Blanc de Blancs

88 1989 Sparkling Wine Carneros Cuvée Taittinger

87 NV Sparkling Wine Carneros Cuvée Taittinger

DOMAINE CHANDON

80 NV Blanc de Noirs Carneros

85 NV Brut Cuvée Napa County

87 NV Brut Reserve Napa-Sonoma Counties

DOMAINE NAPA WINERY

82 1991 Chardonnay Napa Valley

84 1990 Merlot Napa Valley

81 1992 Sauvignon Blanc Napa Valley Michel A. Perret

DOMAINE SAINT GREGORY

85 1992 Chardonnay Mendocino County

86 1991 Chardonnay Mendocino County

81 1992 Pinot Noir Mendocino County

84 1991 Pinot Noir Mendocino County

86 1990 Pinot Noir Mendocino County

DOMAINE ST. GEORGE WINERY

85 1992 Cabernet Sauvignon California Vintage Reserve

83 1989 Cabernet Sauvignon Sonoma County Premier Cuvée Reserve

77 1988 Cabernet Sauvignon Sonoma County Premier Cuvée Reserve

80 1993 Chardonnay California Vintage Reserve

DOMINUS ESTATE

95 1991 Cabernet Sauvignon Napa Valley

93 1990 Cabernet Sauvignon Napa Valley

92	1989 Cabernet Sauvignon Napa Valley
88	1988 Cabernet Sauvignon Napa Valley
92	1987 Cabernet Sauvignon Napa Valley
88	1986 Cabernet Sauvignon Napa Valley
92	1985 Cabernet Sauvignon Napa Valley
85	1984 Cabernet Sauvignon Napa Valley
85	1983 Cabernet Sauvignon Napa Valley

DRY CREEK VINEYARD

83	1990 Cabernet Franc Dry Creek Valley
87	1991 Cabernet Sauvignon Dry Creek Valley
88	1990 Cabernet Sauvignon Dry Creek Valley
86	1989 Cabernet Sauvignon Dry Creek Valley
81	1988 Cabernet Sauvignon Dry Creek Valley
84	1987 Cabernet Sauvignon Dry Creek Valley
88	1986 Cabernet Sauvignon Dry Creek Valley
89	1985 Cabernet Sauvignon Dry Creek Valley
89	1991 Cabernet Sauvignon Dry Creek Valley Reserve
84	1993 Chardonnay Sonoma County
80	1992 Chardonnay Sonoma County
85	1991 Chardonnay Sonoma County
82	1990 Chardonnay Sonoma County
86	1992 Chardonnay Sonoma County Reserve
87	1991 Chardonnay Sonoma County 20th Anniversary Reserve
82	1993 Chenin Blanc California Dry
84	1993 Fumé Blanc Sonoma County
82	1992 Fumé Blanc Sonoma County
82	1992 Fumé Blanc Sonoma County Reserve
85	1991 Fumé Blanc Sonoma County Reserve
89	1990 Meritage Red Dry Creek Valley
86	1988 Meritage Red Dry Creek Valley
87	1987 Meritage Red Dry Creek Valley
80	1986 Meritage Red Dry Creek Valley
88	1985 Meritage Red Dry Creek Valley
88	1984 Meritage Red Sonoma County David S. Stare Vintner's Reserve
84	1992 Merlot Dry Creek Valley
84	1991 Merlot Dry Creek Valley
87	1990 Merlot Dry Creek Valley
86	1989 Merlot Dry Creek Valley
83	1988 Merlot Dry Creek Valley
87	1991 Merlot Dry Creek Valley Reserve
83	1991 Merlot Dry Creek Valley Bullock House Vineyard
83	1992 Zinfandel Dry Creek Valley Old Vines
87	1991 Zinfandel Dry Creek Valley Old Vines
85	1990 Zinfandel Dry Creek Valley Old Vines
85	1989 Zinfandel Dry Creek Valley Old Vines
86	1988 Zinfandel Dry Creek Valley Old Vines
85	1986 Zinfandel Dry Creek Valley Old Vines
88	1991 Zinfandel Dry Creek Valley Old Vines Reserve

DUCKHORN VINEYARDS

88	1991 Cabernet Blend Howell Mountain
88	1990 Cabernet Blend Howell Mountain
87	1989 Cabernet Blend Howell Mountain
93	1990 Cabernet Sauvignon Napa Valley
83	1989 Cabernet Sauvignon Napa Valley
85	1988 Cabernet Sauvignon Napa Valley
95	1987 Cabernet Sauvignon Napa Valley
94	1986 Cabernet Sauvignon Napa Valley
92	1985 Cabernet Sauvignon Napa Valley
91	1984 Cabernet Sauvignon Napa Valley
86	1983 Cabernet Sauvignon Napa Valley
88	1982 Cabernet Sauvignon Napa Valley
86	1981 Cabernet Sauvignon Napa Valley
91	1980 Cabernet Sauvignon Napa Valley
92	1978 Cabernet Sauvignon Napa Valley
88	1992 Merlot Napa Valley
89	1990 Merlot Napa Valley
86	1989 Merlot Napa Valley
86	1988 Merlot Napa Valley
93	1987 Merlot Napa Valley
85	1986 Merlot Napa Valley
95	1985 Merlot Napa Valley
92	1984 Merlot Napa Valley
90	1983 Merlot Napa Valley
92	1982 Merlot Napa Valley
87	1981 Merlot Napa Valley
91	1980 Merlot Napa Valley
91	1979 Merlot Napa Valley
84	1991 Merlot Napa Valley Three Palms Vineyard
83	1990 Merlot Napa Valley Three Palms Vineyard
87	1989 Merlot Napa Valley Three Palms Vineyard
87	1988 Merlot Napa Valley Three Palms Vineyard
90	1987 Merlot Napa Valley Three Palms Vineyard
84	1986 Merlot Napa Valley Three Palms Vineyard
91	1985 Merlot Napa Valley Three Palms Vineyard
87	1984 Merlot Napa Valley Three Palms Vineyard
92	1983 Merlot Napa Valley Three Palms Vineyard
87	1981 Merlot Napa Valley Three Palms Vineyard
88	1978 Merlot Napa Valley Three Palms Vineyard
88	1987 Merlot Napa Valley Vine Hill Ranch
83	1986 Merlot Napa Valley Vine Hill Ranch
86	1985 Merlot Napa Valley Vine Hill Ranch
85	1993 Sauvignon Blanc Napa Valley
89	1992 Sauvignon Blanc Napa Valley

DUNCAN PEAK VINEYARDS

85	1992 Cabernet Sauvignon Mendocino County
88	1991 Cabernet Sauvignon Mendocino County

DUNN VINEYARDS

92	1990 Cabernet Sauvignon Howell Mountain
89	1989 Cabernet Sauvignon Howell Mountain
90	1988 Cabernet Sauvignon Howell Mountain
95	1987 Cabernet Sauvignon Howell Mountain
96	1986 Cabernet Sauvignon Howell Mountain
88	1985 Cabernet Sauvignon Howell Mountain
96	1984 Cabernet Sauvignon Howell Mountain
91	1983 Cabernet Sauvignon Howell Mountain
94	1982 Cabernet Sauvignon Howell Mountain
93	1981 Cabernet Sauvignon Howell Mountain
95	1980 Cabernet Sauvignon Howell Mountain
94	1979 Cabernet Sauvignon Howell Mountain
90	1991 Cabernet Sauvignon Napa Valley
92	1990 Cabernet Sauvignon Napa Valley
89	1989 Cabernet Sauvignon Napa Valley
90	1988 Cabernet Sauvignon Napa Valley
94	1987 Cabernet Sauvignon Napa Valley
93	1986 Cabernet Sauvignon Napa Valley
93	1985 Cabernet Sauvignon Napa Valley
97	1984 Cabernet Sauvignon Napa Valley
91	1983 Cabernet Sauvignon Napa Valley
91	1982 Cabernet Sauvignon Napa Valley

DUNNEWOOD VINEYARDS

84	1991 Cabernet Sauvignon North Coast Barrel Select
83	1993 Chardonnay Carneros Gold Label Select
88	1992 Chardonnay Carneros Gold Label Select
80	1993 Chardonnay North Coast Barrel Select
83	1992 Chardonnay North Coast Barrel Select
82	1992 Merlot North Coast Barrel Select
78	1992 Sauvignon Blanc North Coast Barrel Select
80	1992 Zinfandel Sonoma Valley Barrel Select

DURNEY VINEYARD

86	1990 Cabernet Sauvignon Carmel Valley
83	1989 Cabernet Sauvignon Carmel Valley Reserve
84	1988 Cabernet Sauvignon Carmel Valley Reserve
84	1985 Cabernet Sauvignon Carmel Valley Reserve
86	1983 Cabernet Sauvignon Carmel Valley Reserve
76	1982 Cabernet Sauvignon Carmel Valley Reserve
74	1978 Cabernet Sauvignon Carmel Valley Reserve
84	1990 Chardonnay Carmel Valley
85	1993 Chenin Blanc Carmel Valley
80	1990 Pinot Noir Carmel Valley
80	1989 Pinot Noir Carmel Valley
80	1988 Pinot Noir Carmel Valley

DUXOUP

88	1987 Charbono Napa Valley
85	NV Gamay Dry Creek Valley 1990-1991

76 1988 Gamay Dry Creek Valley
86 1987 Gamay Dry Creek Valley
87 1987 Syrah Dry Creek Valley
85 1986 Syrah Dry Creek Valley

EBERLE WINERY

88 1991 Cabernet Sauvignon Paso Robles
84 1990 Cabernet Sauvignon Paso Robles
83 1989 Cabernet Sauvignon Paso Robles
86 1988 Cabernet Sauvignon Paso Robles
76 1987 Cabernet Sauvignon Paso Robles
85 1986 Cabernet Sauvignon Paso Robles
78 1987 Cabernet Sauvignon Paso Robles Reserve
78 1993 Chardonnay Paso Robles
83 1992 Chardonnay Paso Robles
82 1994 Muscat Canelli Paso Robles
81 1993 Muscat Canelli Paso Robles
86 1992 Syrah Paso Robles Fralich Vineyard
85 1991 Syrah Paso Robles Fralich Vineyard
78 1993 Viognier Paso Robles Fralich Vineyard
86 1993 Zinfandel Paso Robles Sauret Vineyard
82 1992 Zinfandel Paso Robles Sauret Vineyard
88 1990 Zinfandel Paso Robles Sauret Vineyard

TOM EDDY

91 1991 Cabernet Sauvignon Napa Valley

EDMEADES WINERY

88 1993 Chardonnay Anderson Valley Dennison Vineyard
82 1993 Chardonnay Mendocino County
86 1993 Pinot Noir Anderson Valley Dennison Vineyard
86 1990 Zinfandel Mendocino County Ciapusci Vineyard
88 1993 Zinfandel Mendocino County Zeni Vineyard
86 1992 Zinfandel North Coast

EDMUNDS ST. JOHN

88 1992 Rhône Blend California Les Cotes Sauvages
89 1991 Rhône Blend California Les Cotes Sauvages
88 1989 Rhône Blend California Les Cotes Sauvages
83 1988 Rhône Blend California Les Cotes Sauvages
83 1987 Rhône Blend California Les Cotes Sauvages
87 1986 Rhône Blend California Les Cotes Sauvages
85 1987 Rhône Blend California Les Cotes Sauvages Reserve
85 1988 Syrah Sonoma Valley
81 1987 Syrah California
91 1986 Syrah Sonoma County
91 1991 Syrah Sonoma Valley Durell Vineyard
90 1990 Syrah Sonoma Valley Durell Vineyard
89 1989 Syrah Sonoma Valley Durell Vineyard

87 1988 Syrah Sonoma Valley Durell Vineyard
89 1987 Syrah Sonoma Valley Durell Vineyard
85 1986 Syrah Sonoma Valley Durell Vineyard
88 1992 Viognier Knights Valley
88 1991 Zinfandel California
88 1990 Zinfandel Mount Veeder
90 1987 Cabernet Blend Napa Valley Les Fleurs du Chaparral
83 1991 Grenache El Dorado County Marchini Bianco
88 1986 Mourvèdre California
86 1991 Pinot Grigio El Dorado County
84 1992 Rhône Blend California El Nino
84 1989 Rhône Blend California Port O'Call New World Red Table Wine
87 1990 Rhône Blend Napa Valley Cuvée Wahluke

EDNA VALLEY VINEYARD

88 1993 Chardonnay Edna Valley
84 1992 Chardonnay Edna Valley
88 1991 Chardonnay Edna Valley
85 1991 Chardonnay Edna Valley Paragon Vineyard Reserve
83 1992 Pinot Noir Edna Valley
84 1990 Pinot Noir Edna Valley
86 1992 Pinot Noir Edna Valley Pagagon Vineyard Reserve

EL MOLINO

88 1993 Chardonnay Napa Valley
91 1992 Chardonnay Napa Valley
92 1991 Chardonnay Napa Valley
95 1990 Chardonnay Napa Valley
91 1992 Pinot Noir Napa Valley
89 1991 Pinot Noir Napa Valley
92 1990 Pinot Noir Napa County
86 1989 Pinot Noir Napa County
83 1988 Pinot Noir Napa County
85 1987 Pinot Noir Napa County
86 1986 Pinot Noir Carneros Abbott's Vineyard
88 1985 Pinot Noir Carneros Abbott's Vineyard
83 1984 Pinot Noir Carneros Abbott's Vineyard

ELIZABETH VINEYARDS

86 1992 Zinfandel Mendocino County
85 1990 Zinfandel Mendocino County

ELKHORN PEAK CELLARS

85 1993 Chardonnay Napa Valley Fagan Creek Vineyards
87 1992 Chardonnay Napa Valley Fagan Creek Vineyards
79 1992 Pinot Noir Napa Valley Fagan Creek Vineyards

ELLISTON VINEYARDS

84 1992 Cabernet Blend Napa Valley Captain's Claret
85 1991 Chardonnay Central Coast Sunol Valley Vineyard
82 1991 Pinot Blanc Central Coast Sunol Valley Vineyard

ELYSE VINEYARDS

84 1992 Red Table Wine Napa Valley Nero Misto
86 1991 Red Table Wine Napa Valley Nero Misto
86 1990 Red Table Wine Napa Valley Nero Misto
87 1992 Zinfandel Howell Mountain
85 1991 Zinfandel Howell Mountain
85 1992 Zinfandel Napa Valley Coeur du Val
88 1992 Zinfandel Napa Valley Morisoli Vineyard
87 1991 Zinfandel Napa Valley Morisoli Vineyard
88 1990 Zinfandel Napa Valley Morisoli Vineyard
85 1989 Zinfandel Napa Valley Morisoli Vineyard

ESTANCIA

82 1992 Cabernet Sauvignon Alexander Valley
85 1991 Cabernet Sauvignon Alexander Valley
86 1990 Cabernet Sauvignon Alexander Valley
85 1989 Cabernet Sauvignon Alexander Valley
81 1988 Cabernet Sauvignon Alexander Valley
87 1993 Chardonnay Monterey County
88 1992 Chardonnay Monterey County
86 1991 Chardonnay Monterey County
87 1993 Chardonnay Monterey County Reserve
85 1991 Meritage Red Alexander Valley
89 1990 Meritage Red Alexander Valley
85 1989 Meritage Red Alexander Valley
83 1988 Meritage Red Alexander Valley
88 1987 Meritage Red Alexander Valley
87 1993 Meritage White Monterey County
84 1992 Meritage White Monterey County
88 1992 Merlot Alexander Valley
84 1993 Pinot Noir Monterey County
83 1991 Sangiovese Alexander Valley
82 1994 Sauvignon Blanc Monterey County
82 1993 Sauvignon Blanc Monterey County
89 1992 Pinnacles Vineyard Chardonnay Monterey County
84 1991 Pinnacles Vineyard Chardonnay Monterey County
89 1991 Pinnacles Vineyard Pinot Noir Monterey County
79 1990 Pinnacles Vineyard Pinot Noir Monterey County
74 1988 Pinnacles Vineyard Pinot Noir Monterey County

ESTATE WILLIAM BACCALA

82 1992 Chardonnay Sonoma County

86 1991 Chardonnay Sonoma County

86 1991 Merlot Napa Valley

88 1990 Merlot Napa Valley

78 1991 Stephen Zellerbach Cabernet Sauvignon California

83 1993 Stephen Zellerbach Chardonnay California

78 1992 Stephen Zellerbach Sauvignon Blanc California

ESTRELLA RIVER WINERY

82 1992 Chardonnay California Proprietor's Reserve

80 1993 Sauvignon Blanc California Proprietor's Reserve

ÉTUDE WINES

90 1991 Cabernet Sauvignon Napa Valley

91 1990 Cabernet Sauvignon Napa Valley

87 1989 Cabernet Sauvignon Napa Valley

88 1987 Cabernet Sauvignon Napa Valley

92 1986 Cabernet Sauvignon Napa Valley

90 1985 Cabernet Sauvignon Napa Valley

89 1992 Pinot Noir Carneros

89 1991 Pinot Noir Carneros

87 1990 Pinot Noir Carneros

87 1989 Pinot Noir Carneros

87 1988 Pinot Noir Carneros

79 1987 Pinot Noir Carneros

84 1986 Pinot Noir Carneros

80 1985 Pinot Noir Carneros

77 1984 Pinot Noir Carneros

FALLENLEAF VINEYARD

77 1991 Chardonnay Carneros

80 1991 Sauvignon Blanc Sonoma Valley

FAR NIENTE WINERY

93 1992 Cabernet Sauvignon Napa Valley

88 1991 Cabernet Sauvignon Napa Valley

89 1990 Cabernet Sauvignon Napa Valley

86 1989 Cabernet Sauvignon Napa Valley

86 1988 Cabernet Sauvignon Napa Valley

88 1987 Cabernet Sauvignon Napa Valley

91 1986 Cabernet Sauvignon Napa Valley

90 1985 Cabernet Sauvignon Napa Valley

92 1984 Cabernet Sauvignon Napa Valley

84 1983 Cabernet Sauvignon Napa Valley

81 1982 Cabernet Sauvignon Napa Valley

87 1993 Chardonnay Napa Valley

89 1992 Chardonnay Napa Valley

89 1991 Chardonnay Napa Valley

90 1990 Chardonnay Napa Valley

89 1992 Dolce Sémillon Napa Valley

91 1991 Dolce Sémillon Napa Valley

95 1990 Dolce Sémillon Napa Valley

93 1989 Dolce Sémillon Napa Valley

FARELLA-PARK VINEYARDS

85 1991 Cabernet Sauvignon Napa Valley

83 1992 Chardonnay Napa Valley Barrel Fermented

84 1990 Merlot Napa Valley

84 1988 Merlot Napa Valley

75 1991 Sauvignon Blanc Napa Valley

GARY FARRELL WINES

89 1992 Cabernet Sauvignon Sonoma County Ladi's Vineyard

87 1991 Cabernet Sauvignon Sonoma County Ladi's Vineyard

89 1990 Cabernet Sauvignon Sonoma County Ladi's Vineyard

85 1989 Cabernet Sauvignon Sonoma County Ladi's Vineyard

85 1988 Cabernet Sauvignon Sonoma County Ladi's Vineyard

92 1991 Chardonnay Russian River Valley

92 1993 Chardonnay Russian River Valley Allen Vineyard

88 1992 Chardonnay Russian River Valley Allen Vineyard

92 1991 Chardonnay Russian River Valley Allen Vineyard

89 1993 Chardonnay Russian River Valley Westside Farms

83 1992 Merlot Sonoma County Ladi's Vineyard

88 1991 Merlot Sonoma County Ladi's Vineyard

89 1990 Merlot Sonoma County Ladi's Vineyard

88 1991 Pinot Noir Russian River Valley

89 1990 Pinot Noir Russian River Valley

87 1989 Pinot Noir Russian River Valley

90 1988 Pinot Noir Russian River Valley

85 1987 Pinot Noir Russian River Valley

90 1986 Pinot Noir Russian River Valley

88 1992 Pinot Noir Russian River Valley Allen Vineyard

87 1991 Pinot Noir Russian River Valley Allen Vineyard

95 1990 Pinot Noir Russian River Valley Allen Vineyard

91 1988 Pinot Noir Russian River Valley Allen Vineyard

84 1987 Pinot Noir Russian River Valley Allen Vineyard

84 1986 Pinot Noir Russian River Valley Allen Vineyard

85 1985 Pinot Noir Russian River Valley Allen Vineyard

86 1984 Pinot Noir Russian River Valley Allen Vineyard

87 1982 Pinot Noir Russian River Valley Allen Vineyard

85 1992 Pinot Noir Santa Barbara County Bien Nacido Vineyard

91 1990 Pinot Noir Santa Barbara County Bien Nacido Vineyard

93 1992 Sauvignon Blanc Russian River Valley Rochioli Vineyard

89 1993 Zinfandel Russian River Valley Collins Vineyard

92 1992 Zinfandel Russian River Valley

88 1991 Zinfandel Russian River Valley

88 1990 Zinfandel Russian River Valley Collins Vineyard

FENESTRA WINERY

78 1990 Cabernet Blend Livermore Valley

79 1991 Cabernet Sauvignon Livermore Valley

82 1990 Cabernet Sauvignon Livermore Valley

79 1989 Cabernet Sauvignon Monterey County Smith and Hook Vineyard

82 1993 Chardonnay Livermore Valley Toy Vineyard

75 1992 Chardonnay Livermore Valley Toy Vineyard

83 1991 Merlot Livermore Valley

89 1989 Merlot Livermore Valley Special Reserve

86 1992 Sémillon Livermore Valley

85 1992 White Table Wine Livermore Valley Semonnay

78 1991 Zinfandel Livermore Valley Special Reserve

80 1990 Zinfandel Livermore Valley

87 1989 Zinfandel Livermore Valley

FERRARI-CARANO WINERY

86 1991 Cabernet Sauvignon Sonoma County

89 1990 Cabernet Sauvignon Sonoma County

84 1988 Cabernet Sauvignon Sonoma County

84 1987 Cabernet Sauvignon Sonoma County

80 1986 Cabernet Sauvignon Sonoma County

85 1989 Cabernet Sauvignon Sonoma County Reserve

86 1988 Cabernet Sauvignon Sonoma County Reserve

83 1987 Cabernet Sauvignon Sonoma County Reserve

91 1993 Chardonnay Alexander Valley

93 1992 Chardonnay Alexander Valley

91 1991 Chardonnay Alexander Valley

91 1992 Chardonnay California Reserve

92 1991 Chardonnay California Reserve

92 1990 Chardonnay California Reserve

88 1993 Fumé Blanc Sonoma County

87 1993 Fumé Blanc Sonoma County Reserve

89 1991 Merlot Alexander Valley

87 1990 Merlot Alexander Valley

85 1989 Merlot Alexander Valley

85 1988 Merlot Alexander Valley

84 1987 Merlot Alexander Valley

87 1986 Merlot Alexander Valley

82 1990 Pinot Noir Napa-Sonoma Counties Rhonda's Reserve

85 1991 Sangiovese Alexander Valley

83 1991 Sauvignon Blanc Sonoma County Eldorado Gold

88 1989 Sauvignon Blanc Eldorado Gold

89 1992 Siena Sonoma County

90 1991 Siena Sonoma County

89 1992 Zinfandel Dry Creek Valley

90 1991 Zinfandel Dry Creek Valley

90 1990 Zinfandel Dry Creek Valley

GLORIA FERRER CHAMPAGNE CAVES

91 1993 Chardonnay Carneros

91 1992 Chardonnay Carneros

90 1991 Chardonnay Carneros

85 1991 Pinot Noir Carneros

86 1987 Carneros Late Disgorged Cuvée

86 NV Sonoma County

FETZER VINEYARDS

83 1990 Cabernet Sauvignon California Valley Oaks

83 1991 Cabernet Sauvignon North Coast Barrel Select

86 1990 Cabernet Sauvignon North Coast Barrel Select

83 1988 Cabernet Sauvignon Sonoma County Reserve

85 1987 Cabernet Sauvignon Sonoma County Reserve

88 1986 Cabernet Sauvignon Sonoma County Reserve

86 1985 Cabernet Sauvignon Sonoma County Reserve

81 1993 Chardonnay California Sundial

83 1992 Chardonnay California Sundial

87 1993 Chardonnay Mendocino County Barrel Select

85 1992 Chardonnay Mendocino County Barrel Select

84 1993 Chardonnay Mendocino County Bonterra Organically Grown

84 1992 Chardonnay Mendocino County Bonterra Organically Grown

88 1991 Chardonnay Mendocino County Bonterra Organically Grown

88 1993 Chardonnay Mendocino County Reserve

87 1991 Chardonnay Mendocino County Reserve

87 1993 Fumé Blanc Mendocino County

83 1992 Fumé Blanc Mendocino County

81 1992 Gewürztraminer California

86 1992 Johannisberg Rielsing California

91 1988 Johannisberg Rielsing Sonoma County Late Harvest

81 1992 Merlot California Eagle Peak

85 1990 Petite Sirah Mendocino County Reserve

84 1991 Pinot Noir California

88 1991 Pinot Noir California Barrel Select

84 1990 Pinot Noir California Reserve

87 1986 Pinot Noir Mendocino County Reserve

80 1992 Pinot Noir North Coast Barrel Select

86 1992 Pinot Noir Santa Barbara County Bien Nacido Vineyards

87 1992 Pinot Noir Sonoma County Olivet Lane Vineyard

83 1991 Red Table Wine Mendocino County Bonterra Organically Grown

83 1990 Red Table Wine Mendocino County Bonterra Organically Grown

79 1993 Sauvignon Blanc Mendocino County Barrel Select

85 1992 Sauvignon Blanc Mendocino County Barrel Select

85 1991 Sauvignon Blanc Mendocino County Barrel Select

86 1992 Zinfandel Mendocino County Barrel Select

84 1989 Zinfandel Mendocino County Barrel Select

87 1991 Zinfandel Mendocino County Reserve

88 1986 Zinfandel Mendocino County Reserve

80 1992 Bel Arbors Chardonnay California Founder's Selection

FICKLIN VINEYARD

84 1980 Port California Special Bottling No. 5

87 1983 Port California Special Bottling No. 6

78 NV Tinta Port California

FIDDLEHEAD CELLARS

88 1992 Pinot Noir Santa Maria Valley

82 1990 Pinot Noir Santa Maria Valley

FIELD STONE WINERY

84 1991 Cabernet Sauvignon

85 1989 Cabernet Sauvignon

85 1987 Cabernet Sauvignon

80 1990 Cabernet Sauvignon Hoot Owl Creek Vineyards

85 1986 Cabernet Sauvignon Hoot Owl Creek Vineyards

87 1985 Cabernet Sauvignon Hoot Owl Creek Vineyards

84 1990 Cabernet Sauvignon Staten Family Reserve

82 1989 Cabernet Sauvignon Staten Family Reserve

72 1987 Cabernet Sauvignon Staten Family Reserve

84 1985 Cabernet Sauvignon Turkey Hill Vineyard

88 1984 Cabernet Sauvignon Turkey Hill Vineyard

84 1990 Cabernet Sauvignon Vineyard Blend

82 1993 Chardonnay Sonoma County

80 1992 Chardonnay Sonoma County

89 1991 Chardonnay Sonoma County

81 1992 Gewürztraminer Sonoma County

83 1990 Petite Sirah Alexander Valley Old Vines

85 1988 Petite Sirah Alexander Valley

84 1987 Petite Sirah Alexander Valley

89 1992 Sauvignon Blanc Mendocino County Quillen Vineyard

FIELDBROOK VALLEY WINERY

81 1992 Chardonnay Mendocino County Redwood Valley Vineyard

84 1991 Merlot Napa Valley Frediani Vineyard

87 1992 Pinot Noir Napa Valley Beard Vineyard

83 1992 Sauvignon Blanc California Meredith Vineyard

83 1994 Sauvignon Blanc Mendocino County Webb Vineyard

87 1993 Sauvignon Blanc Mendocino County Webb Vineyard

87 1993 Zinfandel Mendocino County Pacini Vineyard

86 1992 Zinfandel Mendocino County Pacini Vineyard

84 1991 Zinfandel Mendocino County Pacini Vineyard

FIFE VINEYARDS

81 1991 Petite Sirah Napa Valley

87 1991 Petite Sirah Napa Valley Les Vieilles Vignes

88 1991 Zinfandel Napa Valley Fife Vineyard

85 1991 Zinfandel Napa Valley Les Vieilles Vignes

FIRESTONE VINEYARD

84 1991 Cabernet Sauvignon Santa Ynez Valley

83 1990 Cabernet Sauvignon Santa Ynez Valley

78 1989 Cabernet Sauvignon Santa Ynez Valley

84 1990 Cabernet Sauvignon Santa Ynez Valley Vintage Reserve

87 1993 Chardonnay Santa Ynez Valley Barrel Fermented

86 1992 Chardonnay Santa Ynez Valley Barrel Fermented

89 1991 Chardonnay Santa Ynez Valley Barrel Fermented

84 1992 Gewürztraminer California

84 1991 Johannisberg Riesling Santa Barbara County Selected Harvest

81 1992 Merlot Santa Ynez Valley

83 1991 Merlot Santa Ynez Valley

78 1990 Merlot Santa Ynez Valley

81 1992 Sauvignon Blanc Santa Ynez Valley

FISHER VINEYARDS

84 1991 Cabernet Sauvignon Napa Valley Coach Insignia

88 1991 Cabernet Sauvignon Sonoma County Wedding Vineyard

90 1990 Cabernet Sauvignon Napa-Sonoma Counties Coach Insignia

82 1989 Cabernet Sauvignon Napa-Sonoma Counties Coach Insignia

85 1987 Cabernet Sauvignon Napa-Sonoma Counties Coach Insignia

88 1986 Cabernet Sauvignon Sonoma County Coach Insignia

90 1985 Cabernet Sauvignon Sonoma County Coach Insignia

89 1984 Cabernet Sauvignon Sonoma County Coach Insignia

88 1993 Chardonnay Sonoma County Coach Insignia

86 1992 Chardonnay Sonoma County Coach Insignia

91 1991 Chardonnay Sonoma County Coach Insignia

85 1993 Chardonnay Sonoma County Whitney's Vineyard

88 1992 Chardonnay Sonoma County Whitney's Vineyard

90 1991 Chardonnay Sonoma County Whitney's Vineyard

87 1991 Merlot Napa Valley

FLORA SPRINGS WINE CO.

89 1987 Cabernet Sauvignon Napa Valley

85 1986 Cabernet Sauvignon Napa Valley

88 1985 Cabernet Sauvignon Napa Valley

96 1992 Cabernet Sauvignon Napa Valley Reserve

97 1991 Cabernet Sauvignon Napa Valley Reserve

88 1990 Cabernet Sauvignon Napa Valley Reserve

85 1989 Cabernet Sauvignon Napa Valley Reserve

84 1993 Chardonnay Napa Valley Barrel Fermented

90 1992 Chardonnay Napa Valley Barrel Fermented

91 1991 Chardonnay Napa Valley Barrel Fermented

92 1990 Chardonnay Napa Valley Barrel Fermented

91 1989 Chardonnay Napa Valley Barrel Fermented

91 1988 Chardonnay Napa Valley Barrel Fermented

93 1987 Chardonnay Napa Valley Barrel Fermented

87 1986 Chardonnay Napa Valley Barrel Fermented

85 1985 Chardonnay Napa Valley Barrel Fermented

89 1991 Meritage Red Napa Valley Trilogy

85 1990 Meritage Red Napa Valley Trilogy

85 1989 Meritage Red Napa Valley Trilogy

85 1988 Meritage Red Napa Valley Trilogy

90 1987 Meritage Red Napa Valley Trilogy

88 1986 Meritage Red Napa Valley Trilogy

88 1985 Meritage Red Napa Valley Trilogy

84 1984 Meritage Red Napa Valley Trilogy

86 1993 Sangiovese Napa Valley

89 1992 Sangiovese Napa Valley

85 1993 Sauvignon Blanc Napa Valley

77 1993 Sauvignon Blanc Napa Valley Soliloquy

82 1991 Sauvignon Blend Napa Valley Soliloquy

88 1990 Sauvignon Blend Napa Valley Soliloquy

88 1989 Sauvignon Blend Napa Valley Soliloquy

THOMAS FOGARTY WINERY

82 1992 Chardonnay Santa Cruz Mountains

86 1988 Pinot Noir Napa Valley

74 1989 Pinot Noir Santa Cruz Mountains

83 1988 Pinot Noir Santa Cruz Mountains

FOPPIANO VINEYARDS

80 1990 Cabernet Sauvignon Russian River Valley

83 1992 Merlot Russian River Valley

82 1991 Petite Sirah Sonoma County

87 1990 Petite Sirah Sonoma County

86 1988 Petite Sirah Russian River Valley

83 1986 Petite Sirah Russian River Valley

80 1991 Petite Sirah Napa Valley La Grande Petite

79 1987 Petite Sirah Reserve Le Grande Petite

81 1992 Sauvignon Blanc Dry Creek Valley

81 1993 Zinfandel Dry Creek Valley

87 1991 Zinfandel Dry Creek Valley

79 1987 Fox Mountain Cabernet Sauvignon Sonoma County Reserve

87 1986 Fox Mountain Cabernet Sauvignon Russian River Valley Reserve

75 1985 Fox Mountain Cabernet Sauvignon Russian River Valley Reserve

85 1984 Fox Mountain Cabernet Sauvignon Russian River Valley Reserve

FOREST GLEN

83 1992 Cabernet Sauvignon Sonoma County Barrel Select

85 1991 Cabernet Sauvignon Sonoma County Barrel Select

83 1990 Cabernet Sauvignon Sonoma County Barrel Select

83 1993 Chardonnay Sonoma County Barrel Fermented

90 1992 Chardonnay Sonoma County Barrel Fermented

FOREST HILL VINEYARD

85 1993 Chardonnay Napa Valley Private Reserve

90 1992 Chardonnay Napa Valley Private Reserve

90 1991 Chardonnay Napa Valley Private Reserve

FORMAN VINEYARD

92 1992 Cabernet Sauvignon Napa Valley

89 1991 Cabernet Sauvignon Napa Valley

90 1990 Cabernet Sauvignon Napa Valley

88 1989 Cabernet Sauvignon Napa Valley

88 1988 Cabernet Sauvignon Napa Valley

93 1987 Cabernet Sauvignon Napa Valley

93 1986 Cabernet Sauvignon Napa Valley

93 1985 Cabernet Sauvignon Napa Valley

92 1984 Cabernet Sauvignon Napa Valley

90 1983 Cabernet Sauvignon Napa Valley

89 1992 Chardonnay Napa Valley

89 1991 Chardonnay Napa Valley

90 1990 Chardonnay Napa Valley

88 1989 Chardonnay Napa Valley

92 1988 Chardonnay Napa Valley

89 1987 Chardonnay Napa Valley

92 1986 Chardonnay Napa Valley

93 1985 Chardonnay Napa Valley

85 1991 Chateau La Grande Roche Pinot Noir Napa Valley

FOXEN VINEYARD

87 1992 Cabernet Sauvignon Santa Barbara County

89 1991 Cabernet Sauvignon Santa Barbara County

84 1990 Cabernet Sauvignon Santa Barbara County

91 1989 Cabernet Sauvignon Santa Barbara County

89 1988 Cabernet Sauvignon Santa Barbara County

83 1990 Cabernet Sauvignon Santa Maria Valley

86 1989 Cabernet Sauvignon Santa Maria Valley

75 1988 Cabernet Sauvignon Santa Maria Valley

74 1987 Cabernet Sauvignon Santa Maria Valley

90 1993 Chardonnay Santa Maria Valley

84 1992 Chardonnay Santa Maria Valley

79 1991 Chardonnay Santa Maria Valley

85 1993 Chardonnay Santa Maria Valley Tinaquaic Vineyard

92 1992 Chardonnay Santa Maria Valley Tinaquaic Vineyard

83 1993 Chenin Blanc Santa Barbara County

87 1992 Chenin Blanc Santa Barbara County

88 1991 Merlot Santa Barbara County

87 1992 Pinot Noir Santa Maria Valley

88 1991 Pinot Noir Santa Maria Valley

89 1990 Pinot Noir Santa Maria Valley

84 1989 Pinot Noir Santa Maria Valley

85 1988 Pinot Noir Santa Maria Valley

86 1987 Pinot Noir Santa Maria Valley

86 1992 Pinot Noir Santa Ynez Valley Sanford & Benedict Vineyard

89 1991 Pinot Noir Santa Ynez Valley Sanford & Benedict Vineyard

FRANCISCAN VINEYARDS

82	1991 Cabernet Sauvignon Napa Valley Oakville Estate
88	1990 Cabernet Sauvignon Napa Valley Oakville Estate
87	1989 Cabernet Sauvignon Napa Valley Oakville Estate
81	1988 Cabernet Sauvignon Napa Valley Oakville Estate
87	1987 Cabernet Sauvignon Napa Valley Oakville Estate
84	1986 Cabernet Sauvignon Napa Valley Oakville Estate
81	1988 Cabernet Sauvignon Napa Valley Oakville Estate Reserve
84	1985 Cabernet Sauvignon Napa Valley Oakville Estate Reserve
90	1993 Chardonnay Napa Valley Oakville Estate Barrel Fermented
91	1992 Chardonnay Napa Valley Oakville Estate Barrel Fermented
89	1993 Chardonnay Napa Valley Oakville Estate Cuvée Sauvage
90	1992 Chardonnay Napa Valley Oakville Estate Cuvée Sauvage
91	1991 Chardonnay Napa Valley Oakville Estate Cuvée Sauvage
87	1990 Meritage Red Napa Valley Magnificat
86	1989 Meritage Red Napa Valley Magnificat
87	1988 Meritage Red Napa Valley Magnificat
88	1987 Meritage Red Napa Valley Magnificat
79	1986 Meritage Red Napa Valley Magnificat
90	1985 Meritage Red Napa Valley Magnificat
85	1991 Merlot Napa Valley Oakville Estate
87	1990 Merlot Napa Valley Oakville Estate
89	1991 Merlot Napa Valley Oakville Estate Reserve
86	1993 Zinfandel Napa Valley Oakville Estate
80	1992 Zinfandel Napa Valley Oakville Estate
85	1991 Zinfandel Napa Valley Oakville Estate
87	1990 Zinfandel Napa Valley Oakville Estate
88	1989 Zinfandel Napa Valley Oakville Estate
87	1988 Zinfandel Napa Valley Oakville Estate

FRANUS

88	1992 Zinfandel Mount Veeder Brandlin Vineyard
86	1991 Zinfandel Mount Veeder Brandlin Vineyard
89	1991 Zinfandel Napa Valley Late Picked
89	1992 Zinfandel Napa Valley Hendry Vineyard
90	1991 Zinfandel Napa Valley Hendry Vineyard
89	1990 Zinfandel Napa Valley Hendry Vineyard
86	1989 Zinfandel Napa Valley Hendry Vineyard
88	1988 Zinfandel Napa Valley Hendry Vineyard
88	1987 Zinfandel Napa Valley Hendry Vineyard

FREEMARK ABBEY WINERY

85	1991 Cabernet Sauvignon Napa Valley
83	1990 Cabernet Sauvignon Napa Valley
81	1989 Cabernet Sauvignon Napa Valley
90	1991 Cabernet Sauvignon Napa Valley Bosche
90	1990 Cabernet Sauvignon Napa Valley Bosche
87	1989 Cabernet Sauvignon Napa Valley Bosche
87	1987 Cabernet Sauvignon Napa Valley Bosche
86	1986 Cabernet Sauvignon Napa Valley Bosche
90	1985 Cabernet Sauvignon Napa Valley Bosche
87	1984 Cabernet Sauvignon Napa Valley Bosche
80	1983 Cabernet Sauvignon Napa Valley Bosche
88	1982 Cabernet Sauvignon Napa Valley Bosche
86	1981 Cabernet Sauvignon Napa Valley Bosche
88	1980 Cabernet Sauvignon Napa Valley Bosche
88	1979 Cabernet Sauvignon Napa Valley Bosche
87	1978 Cabernet Sauvignon Napa Valley Bosche
84	1976 Cabernet Sauvignon Napa Valley Bosche
85	1975 Cabernet Sauvignon Napa Valley Bosche
85	1974 Cabernet Sauvignon Napa Valley Bosche
89	1973 Cabernet Sauvignon Napa Valley Bosche
86	1971 Cabernet Sauvignon Napa Valley Bosche
91	1970 Cabernet Sauvignon Napa Valley Bosche
89	1990 Cabernet Sauvignon Napa Valley Sycamore Vineyard
86	1989 Cabernet Sauvignon Napa Valley Sycamore Vineyard
84	1988 Cabernet Sauvignon Napa Valley Sycamore Vineyard
90	1987 Cabernet Sauvignon Napa Valley Sycamore Vineyard
88	1986 Cabernet Sauvignon Napa Valley Sycamore Vineyard
85	1985 Cabernet Sauvignon Napa Valley Sycamore Vineyard
83	1992 Chardonnay Napa Valley
81	1991 Chardonnay Napa Valley
88	1991 Chardonnay Napa Valley Carpy Ranch
85	1990 Johannisberg Riesling Napa Valley
92	1991 Johannisberg Riesling Napa Valley Edelwein Gold
92	1989 Johannisberg Riesling Napa Valley Edelwein Gold
83	1992 Merlot Napa Valley
84	1991 Merlot Napa Valley
80	1989 Merlot Napa Valley

FREY WINERY

84	1992 Zinfandel Mendocino County
84	1990 Zinfandel Mendocino County

FRICK WINERY

79	1991 Zinfandel Dry Creek Valley

J. FRITZ CELLARS

85	1992 Chardonnay Russian River Valley Barrel Select
83	1992 Chardonnay Sonoma County
83	1994 Sauvignon Blanc Dry Creek Valley
86	1993 Sauvignon Blanc Dry Creek Valley
83	1992 Zinfandel Dry Creek Valley 80-Year-Old Vines
82	1991 Zinfandel Dry Creek Valley 80-Year-Old Vines
82	1990 Zinfandel Dry Creek Valley 80-Year-Old Vines

FROG'S LEAP WINERY

86	1991 Cabernet Sauvignon Napa Valley
88	1990 Cabernet Sauvignon Napa Valley
79	1989 Cabernet Sauvignon Napa Valley
86	1988 Cabernet Sauvignon Napa Valley
91	1987 Cabernet Sauvignon Napa Valley
91	1986 Cabernet Sauvignon Napa Valley
85	1985 Cabernet Sauvignon Napa Valley
92	1984 Cabernet Sauvignon Napa Valley
87	1992 Chardonnay Carneros
89	1991 Chardonnay Carneros
86	1991 Merlot Napa Valley
84	1990 Merlot Napa Valley
85	1992 Sauvignon Blanc Napa Valley
74	1992 Zinfandel Napa Valley
85	1991 Zinfandel Napa Valley
80	1990 Zinfandel Napa Valley
83	1989 Zinfandel Napa Valley
88	1988 Zinfandel Napa Valley

GABRIELLI WINERY

80	1992 Chardonnay Mendocino County
87	1991 Chardonnay Mendocino County
83	1992 Chardonnay Mendocino County Reserve
78	1991 Chardonnay Mendocino County Reserve
84	1991 White Table Wine Mendocino County Ascenza
86	1993 Zinfandel Mendocino County
85	1992 Zinfandel Mendocino County
85	1991 Zinfandel Mendocino County
85	1990 Zinfandel Mendocino County
84	1992 Zinfandel Mendocino County Reserve
84	1991 Zinfandel Mendocino County Reserve
82	1990 Zinfandel Mendocino County Reserve

THE GAINEY VINEYARD

88   1990 Cabernet Franc Santa Ynez Valley Limited Selection

77   1988 Cabernet Sauvignon Santa Maria Valley

77   1989 Cabernet Sauvignon Santa Ynez Valley

83   1989 Cabernet Sauvignon Santa Barbara County Limited Selection

75   1986 Cabernet Sauvignon Santa Barbara County Limited Selection

75   1988 Cabernet Sauvignon Santa Ynez Valley Limited Selection

86   1993 Chardonnay Santa Barbara County

84   1991 Chardonnay Santa Barbara County

91   1993 Chardonnay Santa Ynez Valley Limited Selection

91   1992 Chardonnay Santa Ynez Valley Limited Selection

83   1990 Merlot Santa Ynez Valley Limited Selection

89   1988 Merlot Santa Ynez Valley Limited Selection

81   1987 Merlot Santa Ynez Valley Limited Selection

87   1990 Pinot Noir Santa Barbara County

88   1986 Pinot Noir Santa Barbara County

74   1989 Pinot Noir Santa Maria Valley

88   1991 Pinot Noir Santa Ynez Valley Limited Selection

85   1990 Pinot Noir Santa Ynez Valley Limited Selection

83   1989 Pinot Noir Santa Ynez Valley Limited Selection

86   1988 Pinot Noir Santa Ynez Valley Limited Selection

85   1992 Riesling Santa Ynez Valley

82   1992 Sauvignon Blanc Santa Ynez Valley

83   1993 Sauvignon Blanc Santa Ynez Valley Limited Selection

E. & J. GALLO WINERY

91   1991 Cabernet Sauvignon Northern Sonoma

93   1990 Cabernet Sauvignon Northern Sonoma

90   1991 Cabernet Sauvignon Sonoma County Gallo Sonoma

86   1990 Cabernet Sauvignon Sonoma County Gallo Sonoma

88   1993 Chardonnay Northern Sonoma

91   1992 Chardonnay Northern Sonoma

92   1991 Chardonnay Northern Sonoma

87   1993 Chardonnay Sonoma County Gallo Sonoma

89   1992 Chardonnay Sonoma County Gallo Sonoma

89   1991 Chardonnay Sonoma County Gallo Sonoma

82   1992 Merlot Dry Creek Valley Frei Ranch Vineyard

87   1991 Merlot Dry Creek Valley Frei Ranch Vineyard

86   1992 Zinfandel Dry Creek Valley Frei Ranch Vineyard

91   1991 Zinfandel Dry Creek Valley Frei Ranch Vineyard

90   1990 Zinfandel Dry Creek Valley Frei Ranch Vineyard

GAN EDEN

80   1993 Black Muscat San Joaquin County

83   1989 Cabernet Sauvignon Alexander Valley

77   1988 Cabernet Sauvignon Alexander Valley

88   1993 Chardonnay Sonoma County

81   1993 Gewürztraminer Monterey County Late Harvest

83   1993 Sauvignon Blanc Sonoma County

83   1993 Sémillon Sonoma County

DANIEL GEHRS

84   1991 Chardonnay Monterey County

84   1993 Chenin Blanc Monterey County Le Chenay

83   1993 Chenin Blanc Santa Barbara County Le Cheniere

81   1993 Pinot Blanc Monterey County

83   1993 Sauvignon Blanc Monterey County Fumé En Vogue

84   1993 White Table Wine Monterey County Muscadet

GEORIS WINERY

87   1989 Merlot Carmel Valley

89   1987 Merlot Carmel Valley

77   1986 Merlot Carmel Valley

83   1985 Merlot Carmel Valley

GEYSER PEAK WINERY

77   1984 Cabernet Sauvignon Alexander Valley

85   1983 Cabernet Sauvignon Alexander Valley

90   1991 Cabernet Sauvignon Alexander Valley Estate Reserve

90   1990 Cabernet Sauvignon Alexander Valley Estate Reserve

87   1989 Cabernet Sauvignon Alexander Valley Estate Reserve

89   1987 Cabernet Sauvignon Alexander Valley Estate Reserve

82   1986 Cabernet Sauvignon Alexander Valley Estate Reserve

83   1985 Cabernet Sauvignon Alexander Valley Estate Reserve

84   1991 Cabernet Sauvignon Sonoma County

81   1990 Cabernet Sauvignon Sonoma County

80   1989 Cabernet Sauvignon Sonoma County

88   1987 Cabernet Sauvignon Sonoma County

90   1993 Chardonnay Alexander Valley Reserve

87   1992 Chardonnay Alexander Valley Reserve

85   1993 Chardonnay Sonoma County

80   1992 Gewürztraminer Sonoma County

93   1990 Johannisberg Riesling Mendocino County Late Harvest Selected Dried Berry

85   1991 Malbec Alexander Valley

91   1991 Meritage Red Alexander Valley Reserve Alexandre

90   1990 Meritage Red Alexander Valley Reserve Alexandre

88   1987 Meritage Red Alexander Valley Reserve Alexandre

89   1986 Meritage Red Alexander Valley Reserve Alexandre

87   1985 Meritage Red Alexander Valley Reserve Alexandre

84   1984 Meritage Red Alexander Valley Reserve Alexandre

83   1983 Meritage Red Alexander Valley Reserve Alexandre

85   1992 Merlot Alexander Valley

87   1991 Merlot Alexander Valley

79   1989 Petite Sirah Alexander Valley

82   1991 Petite Verdot Alexander Valley

87   1992 Port Alexander Valley Henry's Reserve Vintage Port

87   1993 Riesling Sonoma County Trione Vineyards Late Harvest Reserve

85   1994 Sauvignon Blanc Sonoma County

85   1993 Sauvignon Blanc Sonoma County

90   1991 Syrah Alexander Valley

91   1991 Syrah Alexander Valley Reserve

81   1993 White Table Wine California Semchard

78   1993 Canyon Road Chardonnay California

84   1992 Canyon Road Chardonnay California

85   1993 Canyon Road Sauvignon Blanc California

GIRARD WINERY

86   1991 Cabernet Sauvignon Napa Valley

87   1990 Cabernet Sauvignon Napa Valley

82   1989 Cabernet Sauvignon Napa Valley

85   1988 Cabernet Sauvignon Napa Valley

86   1987 Cabernet Sauvignon Napa Valley

88   1986 Cabernet Sauvignon Napa Valley

85   1985 Cabernet Sauvignon Napa Valley

87   1982 Cabernet Sauvignon Napa Valley

87   1991 Cabernet Sauvignon Napa Valley Reserve

86   1990 Cabernet Sauvignon Napa Valley Reserve

82   1989 Cabernet Sauvignon Napa Valley Reserve

88   1987 Cabernet Sauvignon Napa Valley Reserve

91   1986 Cabernet Sauvignon Napa Valley Reserve

89   1985 Cabernet Sauvignon Napa Valley Reserve

89   1984 Cabernet Sauvignon Napa Valley Reserve

88   1992 Chardonnay Napa Valley

90   1991 Chardonnay Napa Valley

89 1992 Chardonnay Napa Valley Reserve

83 1992 Chenin Blanc Napa Valley Dry

GLEN ELLEN WINERY

85 1993 Chardonnay California Proprietor's Reserve

84 1992 M. G. Vallejo Chardonnay California Harvest Select

83 1992 M. G. Vallejo Sauvignon Blanc California

GOLDEN CREEK VINEYARD

83 1991 Cabernet Blend Sonoma County Caberlot Reserve

80 1990 Cabernet Sauvignon Sonoma County

84 1991 Merlot Sonoma County Reserve

82 1990 Merlot Sonoma County Reserve

GRACE FAMILY VINEYARDS

88 1991 Cabernet Sauvignon Napa Valley

92 1990 Cabernet Sauvignon Napa Valley

90 1989 Cabernet Sauvignon Napa Valley

90 1988 Cabernet Sauvignon Napa Valley

97 1987 Cabernet Sauvignon Napa Valley

93 1986 Cabernet Sauvignon Napa Valley

95 1985 Cabernet Sauvignon Napa Valley

92 1984 Cabernet Sauvignon Napa Valley

93 1983 Cabernet Sauvignon Napa Valley

89 1982 Cabernet Sauvignon Napa Valley

88 1981 Cabernet Sauvignon Napa Valley

92 1980 Cabernet Sauvignon Napa Valley

92 1979 Cabernet Sauvignon Napa Valley

86 1978 Cabernet Sauvignon Napa Valley

GRAESER WINERY

79 1991 Cabernet Sauvignon Napa Valley

78 1992 Chardonnay Napa Valley Silverado Summers Vineyard

GRANITE SPRINGS WINERY

82 1990 Zinfandel El Dorado County

GREEN AND RED VINEYARD

84 1993 Chardonnay Napa Valley Catacula Vineyard

80 1992 Chardonnay Napa Valley Catacula Vineyard

88 1991 Chardonnay Napa Valley Catacula Vineyard

88 1992 Zinfandel Napa Valley Chiles Mill Vineyard

85 1991 Zinfandel Napa Valley Chiles Mill Vineyard

90 1990 Zinfandel Napa Valley Chiles Mill Vineyard

GREENSTONE WINERY

84 1990 Zinfandel Amador County

84 1987 Zinfandel Amador County

GREENWOOD RIDGE VINEYARDS

89 1992 Cabernet Sauvignon Anderson Valley

82 1991 Cabernet Sauvignon Anderson Valley

74 1989 Cabernet Sauvignon Anderson Valley

83 1988 Cabernet Sauvignon Anderson Valley

81 1990 Cabernet Sauvignon Anderson Valley Estate Reserve

87 1989 Cabernet Sauvignon Anderson Valley Estate Reserve

90 1992 Chardonnay Anderson Valley Du Pratt Vineyard

85 1993 Chardonnay Anderson Valley Late Harvest

83 1991 Chardonnay Mendocino County

86 1992 Merlot Anderson Valley

78 1991 Merlot Anderson Valley

85 1989 Merlot Anderson Valley

87 1990 Pinot Noir Anderson Valley

87 1989 Pinot Noir Anderson Valley

89 1993 Pinot Noir Anderson Valley Roederer Estate Vineyards

90 1992 Pinot Noir Anderson Valley Roederer Estate Vineyards

87 1991 Pinot Noir Mendocino County

80 1993 Sauvignon Blanc Anderson Valley

84 1992 Sauvignon Blanc Anderson Valley

85 1993 White Riesling Anderson Valley

89 1989 White Riesling Mendocino County Late Harvest

85 1991 Zinfandel Sonoma County

86 1990 Zinfandel Sonoma County

81 1989 Zinfandel Sonoma County

86 1988 Zinfandel Sonoma County

87 1993 Zinfandel Sonoma County Scherrer Vineyards

88 1992 Zinfandel Sonoma County Scherrer Vineyards

GRGICH HILLS CELLAR

87 1990 Cabernet Sauvignon Napa Valley

81 1989 Cabernet Sauvignon Napa Valley

84 1988 Cabernet Sauvignon Napa Valley

86 1987 Cabernet Sauvignon Napa Valley

88 1986 Cabernet Sauvignon Napa Valley

90 1985 Cabernet Sauvignon Napa Valley

89 1984 Cabernet Sauvignon Napa Valley

88 1983 Cabernet Sauvignon Napa Valley

87 1982 Cabernet Sauvignon Napa Valley

86 1981 Cabernet Sauvignon Napa Valley

90 1980 Cabernet Sauvignon Napa Valley

90 1992 Chardonnay Carneros Carneros Selection

88 1992 Chardonnay Napa Valley

88 1991 Chardonnay Napa Valley

89 1990 Chardonnay Napa Valley

88 1989 Chardonnay Napa Valley

90 1987 Chardonnay Napa Valley

92 1986 Chardonnay Napa Valley

92 1985 Chardonnay Napa Valley

85 1993 Fumé Blanc Napa Valley

84 1992 Fumé Blanc Napa Valley Dry

88 1993 Johannisberg Riesling Napa Valley Late Harvest

84 1992 Zinfandel Sonoma County

84 1991 Zinfandel Sonoma County

84 1990 Zinfandel Sonoma County

83 1989 Zinfandel Sonoma County

85 1988 Zinfandel Sonoma County

78 1987 Zinfandel Sonoma County

85 1986 Zinfandel Alexander Valley

GROTH VINEYARDS & WINERY

90 1991 Cabernet Sauvignon Napa Valley

90 1990 Cabernet Sauvignon Napa Valley

82 1989 Cabernet Sauvignon Napa Valley

79 1988 Cabernet Sauvignon Napa Valley

88 1987 Cabernet Sauvignon Napa Valley

90 1986 Cabernet Sauvignon Napa Valley

94 1985 Cabernet Sauvignon Napa Valley

88 1984 Cabernet Sauvignon Napa Valley

85 1983 Cabernet Sauvignon Napa Valley

88 1982 Cabernet Sauvignon Napa Valley

95 1991 Cabernet Sauvignon Napa Valley Reserve

94 1990 Cabernet Sauvignon Napa Valley Reserve

87 1989 Cabernet Sauvignon Napa Valley Reserve

87 1988 Cabernet Sauvignon Napa Valley Reserve

93 1987 Cabernet Sauvignon Napa Valley Reserve

89 1986 Cabernet Sauvignon Napa Valley Reserve

97 1985 Cabernet Sauvignon Napa Valley Reserve

92 1984 Cabernet Sauvignon Napa Valley Reserve

88 1983 Cabernet Sauvignon Napa Valley Reserve

84 1993 Chardonnay Napa Valley

83 1992 Chardonnay Napa Valley

86 1991 Chardonnay Napa Valley

82 1991 Merlot Napa Valley

85 1990 Merlot Napa Valley

83 1994 Sauvignon Blanc Napa Valley

83 1992 Sauvignon Blanc Napa Valley

GROVE STREET WINERY

75 1992 Cabernet Sauvignon California Vineyard Select

75 1992 Chardonnay Sonoma County

84 1992 Chardonnay Sonoma County Vintage Select

77 1993 Chardonnay Sonoma County Healdsburg Vineyard Select

GUENOC WINERY

70 1985 Cabernet Franc Lake County

88 1990 Cabernet Franc Napa Valley

87 1991 Cabernet Sauvignon Lake County

84 1990 Cabernet Sauvignon Lake County

77 1989 Cabernet Sauvignon Lake County

89 1987 Cabernet Sauvignon Lake County

78 1986 Cabernet Sauvignon Lake County

94 1991 Cabernet Sauvignon Napa Valley Beckstoffer Vineyard Reserve

92 1990 Cabernet Sauvignon Napa Valley Beckstoffer Vineyard Reserve

90 1989 Cabernet Sauvignon Napa Valley Beckstoffer Vineyard Reserve

92 1987 Cabernet Sauvignon Napa Valley Beckstoffer Vineyard Reserve

82 1991 Cabernet Sauvignon North Coast

85 1993 Chardonnay Guenoc Valley

89 1992 Chardonnay Guenoc Valley

85 1991 Chardonnay Guenoc Valley

90 1993 Chardonnay Guenoc Valley Genevieve Magoon Vineyard Reserve

89 1992 Chardonnay Guenoc Valley Genevieve Magoon Vineyard Reserve

88 1991 Chardonnay Guenoc Valley Genevieve Magoon Vineyard Reserve

90 1991 Meritage Red Lake County Langtry Estate

89 1990 Meritage Red Lake County Langtry Estate

87 1989 Meritage Red Lake County Langtry Estate

86 1988 Meritage Red Lake County Langtry Estate

89 1987 Meritage Red Lake County Langtry Estate

88 1993 Meritage White Guenoc Valley Langtry Estate

90 1992 Meritage White Guenoc Valley Langtry Estate

86 1987 Merlot Napa Lake Counties

87 1990 Petite Sirah North Coast

83 1989 Petite Sirah North Coast

86 1988 Petite Sirah North Coast

89 1992 Port California

87 1994 Sauvignon Blanc Guenoc Valley

82 1993 Sauvignon Blanc Guenoc Valley

86 1992 Sauvignon Blanc Guenoc Valley

83 1991 Zinfandel California

84 1990 Zinfandel California

85 1989 Zinfandel California

EMILIO GUGLIELMO WINERY

82 1992 Chardonnay Monterey County

78 1990 Merlot Napa Valley

75 1990 Pinot Noir Santa Clara Valley Private Reserve

70 1989 Red Table Wine Santa Clara County Claret 13th Limited Bottling

79 1989 Zinfandel Santa Clara Valley Private Reserve

GUILLIAMS VINEYARDS

86 1990 Cabernet Sauvignon Spring Mountain

80 1988 La Vieille Montagne Cabernet Sauvignon Napa Valley

81 1987 La Vieille Montagne Cabernet Sauvignon Napa Valley

84 1986 La Vieille Montagne Cabernet Sauvignon Napa Valley

GUNDLACH BUNDSCHU WINERY

87 1989 Cabernet Franc Sonoma Valley Rhinefarm Vineyards

89 1987 Cabernet Franc Sonoma Valley Rhinefarm Vineyards

87 1992 Cabernet Sauvignon Sonoma Valley Rhinefarm Vineyards

88 1991 Cabernet Sauvignon Sonoma Valley Rhinefarm Vineyards

83 1990 Cabernet Sauvignon Sonoma Valley Rhinefarm Vineyards

80 1989 Cabernet Sauvignon Sonoma Valley Rhinefarm Vineyards

85 1987 Cabernet Sauvignon Sonoma Valley Rhinefarm Vineyards

89 1986 Cabernet Sauvignon Sonoma Valley Rhinefarm Vineyards

91 1985 Cabernet Sauvignon Sonoma Valley Rhinefarm Vineyards

85 1984 Cabernet Sauvignon Sonoma Valley Rhinefarm Vineyards

84 1989 Cabernet Sauvignon Sonoma Valley Rhinefarm Vineyards Vintage Reserve

89 1987 Cabernet Sauvignon Sonoma Valley Rhinefarm Vineyards Vintage Reserve

83 1986 Cabernet Sauvignon Sonoma Valley Rhinefarm Vineyards Vintage Reserve

85 1991 Chardonnay Carneros Vineyard Special Selection

83 1991 Chardonnay Sonoma Valley

77 1992 Gewürztraminer Sonoma Valley Rhinefarm Vineyards

81 1990 Meritage Red Sonoma Valley Bearitage

84 1988 Merlot Sonoma Valley

87 1986 Merlot Sonoma Valley

88 1985 Merlot Sonoma Valley

82 1984 Merlot Sonoma Valley

80 1983 Merlot Sonoma Valley

83 1982 Merlot Sonoma Valley

84 1981 Merlot Sonoma Valley

88 1992 Merlot Sonoma Valley Rhinefarm Vineyards

85 1990 Merlot Sonoma Valley Rhinefarm Vineyards

80 1989 Merlot Sonoma Valley Rhinefarm Vineyards

81 1988 Merlot Sonoma Valley Rhinefarm Vineyards

87 1987 Merlot Sonoma Valley Rhinefarm Vineyards

91 1986 Merlot Sonoma Valley Rhinefarm Vineyards

92 1985 Merlot Sonoma Valley Rhinefarm Vineyards

82 1992 Pinot Noir Sonoma Valley Rhinefarm Vineyards

78 1991 Pinot Noir Sonoma Valley Rhinefarm Vineyards

83 1989 Pinot Noir Sonoma Valley Rhinefarm Vineyards

88 1988 Pinot Noir Sonoma Valley Rhinefarm Vineyards

87 1986 Pinot Noir Sonoma Valley Rhinefarm Vineyards

83 1993 White Riesling Sonoma Valley Dresel's Sonoma Riesling

82 1992 White Riesling Sonoma Valley Dresel's Sonoma Riesling

92 1992 Zinfandel Sonoma Valley

85 1991 Zinfandel Sonoma Valley

84 1989 Zinfandel Sonoma Valley

88 1988 Zinfandel Sonoma Valley

87 1987 Zinfandel Sonoma Valley

87 1990 Zinfandel Sonoma Valley Rhinefarm Vineyards

87 1989 Zinfandel Sonoma Valley Rhinefarm Vineyards

88 1988 Zinfandel Sonoma Valley Rhinefarm Vineyards

71 1987 Zinfandel Sonoma Valley Rhinefarm Vineyards

90 1986 Zinfandel Sonoma Valley Rhinefarm Vineyards

84 1985 Zinfandel Sonoma Valley Rhinefarm Vineyards

HAGAFEN CELLARS

77 1990 Cabernet Sauvignon Napa Valley

68 1989 Cabernet Sauvignon Napa Valley

88 1987 Cabernet Sauvignon Napa Valley

83 1988 Cabernet Sauvignon Napa Valley Reserve

85 1992 Chardonnay Napa Valley

86 1991 Chardonnay Napa Valley

82 1991 Chardonnay Napa Valley Reserve

86 1994 Johannisberg Riesling Napa Valley

84 1991 Johannisberg Riesling Napa Valley

77 1991 Pinot Noir Napa Valley

HAHN ESTATES

83 1992 Cabernet Sauvignon Santa Lucia Highlands

80 1991 Cabernet Sauvignon Santa Lucia Highlands

73 1989 Cabernet Sauvignon Santa Lucia Highlands

80 1988 Cabernet Sauvignon Santa Lucia Highlands

80 1990 Cabernet Sauvignon Santa Lucia Highlands

85 1993 Chardonnay Monterey County

89 1992 Chardonnay Monterey County

81 1992 Merlot Monterey County

84 1991 Merlot Monterey County

83 1990 Merlot Monterey County

86 1989 Merlot Monterey County

HALLCREST VINEYARDS

80 1990 Barbera El Dorado County
86 1990 Cabernet Sauvignon El Dorado County Covington Vineyard
85 1990 Cabernet Sauvignon El Dorado County De Cascabel Vineyard Proprietors Reserve
84 1990 Cabernet Sauvignon Santa Cruz Mountains Beauregard Ranch Proprietors Reserve
72 1991 Chardonnay California Fortuyn Cuvée
77 1991 Chardonnay Santa Cruz Mountains Meyley Vineyard
83 1991 Merlot El Dorado County De Cascabel Vineyard
87 1991 Merlot El Dorado County De Cascabel Vineyards Proprietors Reserve
83 1990 Zinfandel California Doe Mill Vineyard
77 1992 Organic Wine Works Chardonnay Mendocino County Redwood Valley Vineyards
71 1992 Organic Wine Works Fumé Blanc Napa Valley
80 1992 Organic Wine Works Merlot Butte County
73 1992 Organic Wine Works Pinot Noir Mendocino County
79 1992 Organic Wine Works Red Table Wine California A Notre Terre
83 1991 Organic Wine Works Red Table Wine California A Notre Terre
67 1992 Organic Wine Works Sémillon Napa Valley
86 1991 Organic Wine Works Zinfandel California
80 1992 Organic Wine Works Zinfandel Napa County

HANDLEY CELLARS

83 1992 Chardonnay Anderson Valley
80 1991 Chardonnay Anderson Valley
84 1992 Chardonnay Dry Creek Valley
84 1992 Pinot Noir Anderson Valley
84 1991 Pinot Noir Anderson Valley
87 1993 Sauvignon Blanc Dry Creek Valley
85 1992 Sauvignon Blanc Dry Creek Valley

HANNA WINERY

85 1991 Cabernet Sauvignon Alexander Valley
87 1990 Cabernet Sauvignon Alexander Valley
86 1988 Cabernet Sauvignon Alexander Valley
80 1987 Cabernet Sauvignon Alexander Valley
87 1986 Cabernet Sauvignon Alexander Valley
86 1985 Cabernet Sauvignon Alexander Valley
85 1992 Chardonnay Russian River Valley Reserve
86 1991 Chardonnay Sonoma County
82 1991 Merlot Alexander Valley
85 1990 Merlot Alexander Valley
85 1992 Pinot Noir Russian River Valley
85 1993 Sauvignon Blanc Sonoma County

HANZELL VINEYARDS

83 1990 Cabernet Sauvignon Sonoma Valley
82 1989 Cabernet Sauvignon Sonoma Valley
82 1988 Cabernet Sauvignon Sonoma Valley
84 1987 Cabernet Sauvignon Sonoma Valley
88 1986 Cabernet Sauvignon Sonoma Valley
91 1991 Chardonnay Sonoma Valley
89 1990 Chardonnay Sonoma Valley
90 1988 Chardonnay Sonoma Valley
89 1987 Chardonnay Sonoma Valley
87 1986 Chardonnay Sonoma Valley
90 1985 Chardonnay Sonoma Valley
84 1984 Chardonnay Sonoma Valley
84 1983 Chardonnay Sonoma Valley
89 1982 Chardonnay Sonoma Valley
86 1981 Chardonnay Sonoma Valley
90 1980 Chardonnay Sonoma Valley
85 1979 Chardonnay Sonoma Valley
95 1978 Chardonnay Sonoma Valley
86 1991 Pinot Noir Sonoma Valley
85 1990 Pinot Noir Sonoma Valley
88 1989 Pinot Noir Sonoma Valley
88 1988 Pinot Noir Sonoma Valley
87 1987 Pinot Noir Sonoma Valley
79 1986 Pinot Noir Sonoma Valley
85 1985 Pinot Noir Sonoma Valley
80 1984 Pinot Noir Sonoma Valley
83 1983 Pinot Noir Sonoma Valley
77 1982 Pinot Noir Sonoma Valley
83 1981 Pinot Noir Sonoma Valley
84 1980 Pinot Noir Sonoma Valley
95 1979 Pinot Noir Sonoma Valley
87 1978 Pinot Noir Sonoma Valley
87 1977 Pinot Noir Sonoma Valley
91 1976 Pinot Noir Sonoma Valley
92 1975 Pinot Noir Sonoma Valley
91 1974 Pinot Noir Sonoma Valley
89 1973 Pinot Noir Sonoma Valley
93 1972 Pinot Noir Sonoma Valley
92 1971 Pinot Noir Sonoma Valley
90 1970 Pinot Noir Sonoma Valley
87 1969 Pinot Noir Sonoma Valley
89 1968 Pinot Noir Sonoma Valley
86 1967 Pinot Noir Sonoma Valley
87 1966 Pinot Noir Sonoma Valley
93 1965 Pinot Noir Sonoma Valley
78 1962 Pinot Noir Sonoma Valley Heitz Bottling
97 1961 Pinot Noir Sonoma Valley Heitz Bottling

HARBOR WINERY

78 1991 Merlot Napa Valley Narsai David Vineyard

HARLAN ESTATE

93 1992 Cabernet Sauvignon Napa Valley
92 1991 Cabernet Sauvignon Napa Valley
93 1990 Cabernet Sauvignon Napa Valley

HARMONY CELLARS

77 1990 Cabernet Sauvignon Paso Robles
85 1989 Cabernet Sauvignon Paso Robles
82 1992 Chardonnay Paso Robles
88 1990 Pinot Noir Paso Robles

HARRISON VINEYARDS

88 1992 Cabernet Sauvignon Napa Valley
86 1991 Cabernet Sauvignon Napa Valley
87 1990 Cabernet Sauvignon Napa Valley
91 1989 Cabernet Sauvignon Napa Valley
91 1990 Cabernet Sauvignon Napa Valley Reserve
90 1993 Chardonnay Napa Valley
89 1992 Chardonnay Napa Valley
88 1991 Chardonnay Napa Valley

HART WINERY

82 1989 Cabernet Sauvignon Temecula Hansen Vineyard
80 1989 Merlot Temecula

HARTWELL VINEYARDS

92 1991 Cabernet Sauvignon Stags Leap District

HAVENS WINE CELLARS

88 1990 Merlot Carneros Truchard Vineyard Reserve
82 1989 Merlot Carneros Truchard Vineyard Reserve
76 1988 Merlot Carneros Truchard Vineyard Reserve
90 1991 Merlot Napa Valley
87 1990 Merlot Napa Valley
84 1989 Merlot Napa Valley
82 1988 Merlot Napa Valley
89 1987 Merlot Napa Valley
72 1986 Merlot Napa Valley
84 1985 Merlot Napa Valley

HAYWOOD WINERY

83 1991 Cabernet Sauvignon California Vintner's Select
84 1989 Cabernet Sauvignon Sonoma Valley Los Chamizal Vineyard
85 1988 Cabernet Sauvignon Sonoma Valley Los Chamizal Vineyard
84 1985 Cabernet Sauvignon Sonoma Valley Los Chamizal Vineyard
83 1984 Cabernet Sauvignon Sonoma Valley Los Chamizal Vineyard
74 1983 Cabernet Sauvignon Sonoma Valley Los Chamizal Vineyard

85 1981 Cabernet Sauvignon Sonoma Valley Los Chamizal Vineyard

82 1993 Chardonnay California Vintner's Select

84 1992 Chardonnay California Vintner's Select

84 1990 Zinfandel Sonoma Valley

85 1989 Zinfandel Sonoma Valley

89 1988 Zinfandel Sonoma Valley

89 1986 Zinfandel Sonoma Valley

92 1984 Zinfandel Sonoma Valley

85 1991 Zinfandel Sonoma Valley Los Chamizal Vineyard

85 1990 Zinfandel Sonoma Valley Los Chamizal Vineyard

85 1989 Zinfandel Sonoma Valley Los Chamizal Vineyard

86 1988 Zinfandel Sonoma Valley Los Chamizal Vineyard

86 1992 Zinfandel Sonoma Valley Rocky Terrace

HEITZ WINE CELLARS

90 1990 Cabernet Sauvignon Napa Valley

88 1989 Cabernet Sauvignon Napa Valley

88 1988 Cabernet Sauvignon Napa Valley

90 1987 Cabernet Sauvignon Napa Valley

85 1986 Cabernet Sauvignon Napa Valley

80 1985 Cabernet Sauvignon Napa Valley

86 1984 Cabernet Sauvignon Napa Valley

80 1983 Cabernet Sauvignon Napa Valley

85 1990 Cabernet Sauvignon Napa Valley Bella Oaks Vineyard

84 1989 Cabernet Sauvignon Napa Valley Bella Oaks Vineyard

81 1988 Cabernet Sauvignon Napa Valley Bella Oaks Vineyard

81 1987 Cabernet Sauvignon Napa Valley Bella Oaks Vineyard

89 1986 Cabernet Sauvignon Napa Valley Bella Oaks Vineyard

88 1985 Cabernet Sauvignon Napa Valley Bella Oaks Vineyard

74 1984 Cabernet Sauvignon Napa Valley Bella Oaks Vineyard

86 1983 Cabernet Sauvignon Napa Valley Bella Oaks Vineyard

85 1982 Cabernet Sauvignon Napa Valley Bella Oaks Vineyard

85 1981 Cabernet Sauvignon Napa Valley Bella Oaks Vineyard

87 1980 Cabernet Sauvignon Napa Valley Bella Oaks Vineyard

89 1978 Cabernet Sauvignon Napa Valley Bella Oaks Vineyard

91 1977 Cabernet Sauvignon Napa Valley Bella Oaks Vineyard

81 1976 Cabernet Sauvignon Napa Valley Bella Oaks Vineyard

90 1990 Cabernet Sauvignon Napa Valley Martha's Vineyard

90 1989 Cabernet Sauvignon Napa Valley Martha's Vineyard

87 1988 Cabernet Sauvignon Napa Valley Martha's Vineyard

91 1987 Cabernet Sauvignon Napa Valley Martha's Vineyard

90 1986 Cabernet Sauvignon Napa Valley Martha's Vineyard

98 1985 Cabernet Sauvignon Napa Valley Martha's Vineyard

92 1984 Cabernet Sauvignon Napa Valley Martha's Vineyard

88 1983 Cabernet Sauvignon Napa Valley Martha's Vineyard

90 1982 Cabernet Sauvignon Napa Valley Martha's Vineyard

89 1981 Cabernet Sauvignon Napa Valley Martha's Vineyard

91 1980 Cabernet Sauvignon Napa Valley Martha's Vineyard

93 1979 Cabernet Sauvignon Napa Valley Martha's Vineyard

91 1978 Cabernet Sauvignon Napa Valley Martha's Vineyard

90 1977 Cabernet Sauvignon Napa Valley Martha's Vineyard

85 1976 Cabernet Sauvignon Napa Valley Martha's Vineyard

92 1975 Cabernet Sauvignon Napa Valley Martha's Vineyard

97 1974 Cabernet Sauvignon Napa Valley Martha's Vineyard

92 1973 Cabernet Sauvignon Napa Valley Martha's Vineyard

75 1972 Cabernet Sauvignon Napa Valley Martha's Vineyard

97 1970 Cabernet Sauvignon Napa Valley Martha's Vineyard

95 1969 Cabernet Sauvignon Napa Valley Martha's Vineyard

99 1968 Cabernet Sauvignon Napa Valley Martha's Vineyard

86 1967 Cabernet Sauvignon Napa Valley Martha's Vineyard

92 1966 Cabernet Sauvignon Napa Valley Martha's Vineyard

89 1989 Cabernet Sauvignon Napa Valley Trailside Vineyard

70 1993 Chardonnay Napa Valley

67 1989 Zinfandel Napa Valley Heitz Vineyard

78 1988 Zinfandel Napa Valley Heitz Vineyard

THE HESS COLLECTION WINERY

92 1991 Cabernet Sauvignon Mount Veeder

90 1990 Cabernet Sauvignon Mount Veeder

82 1989 Cabernet Sauvignon Mount Veeder

88 1988 Cabernet Sauvignon Mount Veeder

94 1987 Cabernet Sauvignon Mount Veeder

91 1986 Cabernet Sauvignon Mount Veeder

96 1985 Cabernet Sauvignon Mount Veeder

84 1983 Cabernet Sauvignon Mount Veeder

90 1990 Cabernet Sauvignon Mount Veeder Reserve

89 1989 Cabernet Sauvignon Mount Veeder Reserve

96 1987 Cabernet Sauvignon Mount Veeder Reserve

93 1986 Cabernet Sauvignon Mount Veeder Reserve

91 1984 Cabernet Sauvignon Mount Veeder Reserve

88 1983 Cabernet Sauvignon Mount Veeder Reserve

84 1993 Chardonnay Napa Valley

89 1992 Chardonnay Napa Valley

87 1991 Chardonnay Mount Veeder

86 1989 Merlot Napa Valley

87 1992 Hess Select Cabernet Sauvignon California

82 1991 Hess Select Cabernet Sauvignon California

80 1990 Hess Select Cabernet Sauvignon California

86 1993 Hess Select Chardonnay California

84 1992 Hess Select Chardonnay California

83 1993 Hess Select Pinot Noir California

85 1993 Hess Select Pinot Noir Santa Maria Valley Bien Nacido Vineyard

HIDDEN CELLARS WINERY

83 1993 Chardonnay Mendocino County

88 1992 Chardonnay Mendocino County

78 1991 Chardonnay Mendocino County

89 1992 Chardonnay Mendocino County Reserve

84 1992 Chardonnay Mendocino County Organically Grown Grapes

86 1993 Johannisberg Riesling Mendocino County

83 1992 Johannisberg Riesling Mendocino County

87 1992 Meritage White Mendocino County Alchemy

85 1993 Sauvignon Blanc Mendocino County

85 1992 Sauvignon Blanc Mendocino County Organically Grown

85 1992 Zinfandel Mendocino County

89 1991 Zinfandel Mendocino County

88 1990 Zinfandel Mendocino County

83 1993 Zinfandel Mendocino County McAdams Vineyard

81 1989 Zinfandel Mendocino County Pacini Vineyard

85 1988 Zinfandel Mendocino County Pacini Vineyard

WILLIAM HILL WINERY

84 1991 Cabernet Sauvignon Napa Valley Gold Label Reserve

87   1990 Cabernet Sauvignon Napa Valley Gold Label Reserve

85   1989 Cabernet Sauvignon Napa Valley Gold Label Reserve

84   1988 Cabernet Sauvignon Napa Valley Gold Label Reserve

88   1987 Cabernet Sauvignon Napa Valley Gold Label Reserve

90   1986 Cabernet Sauvignon Napa Valley Gold Label Reserve

88   1985 Cabernet Sauvignon Napa Valley Gold Label Reserve

88   1984 Cabernet Sauvignon Napa Valley Gold Label Reserve

82   1983 Cabernet Sauvignon Napa Valley Gold Label Reserve

88   1982 Cabernet Sauvignon Napa Valley Gold Label Reserve

84   1981 Cabernet Sauvignon Napa Valley Gold Label Reserve

87   1980 Cabernet Sauvignon Napa Valley Gold Label Reserve

90   1979 Cabernet Sauvignon Napa Valley Gold Label Reserve

92   1978 Cabernet Sauvignon Napa Valley Gold Label Reserve

82   1989 Cabernet Sauvignon Napa Valley Silver Label

85   1987 Cabernet Sauvignon Napa Valley Silver Label

85   1985 Cabernet Sauvignon Napa Valley Silver Label

82   1993 Chardonnay Napa Valley

88   1992 Chardonnay Napa Valley

82   1991 Merlot Napa Valley

81   1993 Sauvignon Blanc Napa Valley

85   1992 Sauvignon Blanc Napa Valley

HITCHING POST WINERY

86   1991 Pinot Noir Santa Maria Valley

91   1990 Pinot Noir Santa Maria Valley

88   1989 Pinot Noir Santa Maria Valley

90   1988 Pinot Noir Santa Maria Valley

92   1987 Pinot Noir Santa Maria Valley

82   1986 Pinot Noir Santa Maria Valley

79   1985 Pinot Noir Santa Maria Valley

87   1984 Pinot Noir Santa Maria Valley

88   1983 Pinot Noir Santa Maria Valley

85   1982 Pinot Noir Santa Maria Valley Early Pick

82   1982 Pinot Noir Santa Maria Valley Late Pick

80   1981 Pinot Noir Santa Maria Valley

86   1991 Pinot Noir Santa Ynez Valley Sanford & Benedict Vineyard

88   1989 Pinot Noir Santa Ynez Valley Sanford & Benedict Vineyard

87   1988 Pinot Noir Santa Ynez Valley Sanford & Benedict Vineyard

88   1987 Pinot Noir Santa Ynez Valley Sanford & Benedict Vineyard

84   1985 Pinot Noir Santa Ynez Valley Sanford & Benedict Vineyard

PAUL HOBBS CELLARS

91   1991 Cabernet Sauvignon Carneros Hyde Vineyard

86   1993 Chardonnay Sonoma Mountain Richard Dinner Vineyard

91   1992 Chardonnay Sonoma Mountain Richard Dinner Vineyard

93   1991 Chardonnay Sonoma Mountain Richard Dinner Vineyard

74   1992 Pinot Noir Carneros Hyde Vineyard

87   1991 Pinot Noir Carneros Hyde Vineyard

HOMEWOOD WINERY

79   1992 Zinfandel Dry Creek Valley Quinn Vineyard

83   1992 Zinfandel Sonoma Valley 110-Year-Old Vines

LOUIS HONIG CELLARS

83   1988 Cabernet Sauvignon Napa Valley

80   1993 Sauvignon Blanc Napa Valley

80   1991 Sauvignon Blanc Napa Valley

HOP KILN WINERY

83   1991 Cabernet Sauvignon Russian River Valley

84   1990 Cabernet Sauvignon Russian River Valley

72   1989 Cabernet Sauvignon Russian River Valley

89   1993 Chardonnay Russian River Valley M. Griffin Vineyards

87   1992 Chardonnay Russian River Valley M. Griffin Vineyards

85   1991 Chardonnay Russian River Valley M. Griffin Vineyards

82   1993 Gewürztraminer Russian River Valley M. Griffin Vineyards

83   1993 Johannisberg Riesling Russian River Valley M. Griffin Vineyards

82   1992 Johannisberg Riesling Russian River Valley M. Griffin Vineyards

88   1989 Petite Sirah Russian River Valley M. Griffin Vineyards

82   1987 Petite Sirah Russian River Valley M. Griffin Vineyards

84   1991 Petite Sirah Sonoma County

82   1991 Red Table Wine Russian River Valley M. Griffin Vineyards Valdiguie

77   1990 Red Table Wine Russian River Valley M. Griffin Vineyards Valdiguie

81   1992 Red Table Wine Sonoma County Marty Griffin's Big Red

81   1990 Red Table Wine Sonoma County Marty Griffin's Big Red

85   1988 Red Table Wine Sonoma County Marty Griffin's Big Red

89   1987 Red Table Wine Sonoma County Marty Griffin's Big Red

85   1986 Red Table Wine Sonoma County Marty Griffin's Big Red

87   NV Red Table Wine Sonoma County Marty Griffin's Big Red Reserve

86   1992 Zinfandel Russian River Valley

84   1991 Zinfandel Russian River Valley

85   1990 Zinfandel Russian River Valley

88   1988 Zinfandel Russian River Valley

85   1986 Zinfandel Russian River Valley

85   1992 Zinfandel Russian River Valley Primitivo

87   1991 Zinfandel Russian River Valley Primitivo

85   1990 Zinfandel Russian River Valley Primitivo

89   1988 Zinfandel Russian River Valley Primitivo

80   1985 Zinfandel Russian River Valley Primitivo

90   NV Zinfandel Russian River Valley Primitivo Reserve

HOPE FARMS

81   1991 Cabernet Blend Paso Robles Claret

84   1990 Cabernet Sauvignon Paso Robles

84   1989 Cabernet Sauvignon Paso Robles

ROBERT HUNTER

80   1991 Sparkling Wine Sonoma Valley Brut de Noirs

HUSCH VINEYARDS

83   1992 Cabernet Sauvignon Mendocino County La Ribera Ranch

84   1991 Cabernet Sauvignon Mendocino County La Ribera Ranch

88   1990 Cabernet Sauvignon Mendocino County La Ribera Ranch

79   1989 Cabernet Sauvignon Mendocino County La Ribera Ranch

86   1988 Cabernet Sauvignon Mendocino County La Ribera Ranch

88   1987 Cabernet Sauvignon Mendocino County La Ribera Ranch

81   1991 Cabernet Sauvignon Mendocino County North Field Select

87   1990 Cabernet Sauvignon Mendocino County North Field Select

84   1989 Cabernet Sauvignon Mendocino County North Field Select

84   1988 Cabernet Sauvignon Mendocino County North Field Select

87   1987 Cabernet Sauvignon Mendocino County North Field Select

85   1992 Chardonnay Anderson Valley Special Reserve

85   1993 Chardonnay Mendocino County

84   1992 Chardonnay Mendocino County

85   1994 Chenin Blanc Mendocino County La Ribera Ranch

82 1993 Chenin Blanc Mendocino County La Ribera Ranch

87 1993 Gewürztraminer Anderson Valley Late Harvest

87 1992 Pinot Noir Anderson Valley

84 1991 Pinot Noir Anderson Valley

81 1990 Pinot Noir Anderson Valley

87 1989 Pinot Noir Anderson Valley

84 1988 Pinot Noir Anderson Valley

80 1987 Pinot Noir Anderson Valley

81 1986 Pinot Noir Anderson Valley

84 1985 Pinot Noir Anderson Valley

87 1994 Sauvignon Blanc Mendocino County La Ribera Ranch

86 1992 Sauvignon Blanc Mendocino County La Ribera Ranch

INDIAN SPRINGS VINEYARDS

82 1991 Cabernet Sauvignon Nevada County

80 1990 Cabernet Sauvignon Nevada County

84 1992 Merlot Nevada County

84 1991 Merlot Nevada County

84 1990 Merlot Sierra Foothills

85 1989 Merlot Sierra Foothills

INGLENOOK-NAPA VALLEY

84 1988 Cabernet Sauvignon Napa Valley Reserve Cask

87 1987 Cabernet Sauvignon Napa Valley Reserve Cask

87 1986 Cabernet Sauvignon Napa Valley Reserve Cask

87 1985 Cabernet Sauvignon Napa Valley Reserve Cask

90 1984 Cabernet Sauvignon Napa Valley Reserve Cask

88 1983 Cabernet Sauvignon Napa Valley Reserve Cask

85 1982 Cabernet Sauvignon Napa Valley Reserve Cask

87 1981 Cabernet Sauvignon Napa Valley Reserve Cask

88 1980 Cabernet Sauvignon Napa Valley Reserve Cask

83 1978 Cabernet Sauvignon Napa Valley Cask

89 1966 Cabernet Sauvignon Napa Valley Cask F-29

96 1959 Cabernet Sauvignon Napa Valley Cask J-6

94 1958 Cabernet Sauvignon Napa Valley Cask

93 1955 Cabernet Sauvignon Napa Valley Cask

96 1951 Cabernet Sauvignon Napa Valley

92 1949 Cabernet Sauvignon Napa Valley Cask

87 1946 Cabernet Sauvignon Napa Valley

91 1943 Cabernet Sauvignon Napa Valley

100 1941 Cabernet Sauvignon Napa Valley

95 1933 Cabernet Sauvignon Napa Valley

87 1897 Cabernet Sauvignon California Claret-Medoc Type

88 1986 Cabernet Sauvignon Napa Valley Reunion

89 1985 Cabernet Sauvignon Napa Valley Reunion

91 1984 Cabernet Sauvignon Napa Valley Reunion

88 1983 Cabernet Sauvignon Napa Valley Reunion

83 1988 Merlot Napa Valley Reserve

INNISFREE

88 1990 Cabernet Sauvignon Napa Valley

84 1990 Pinot Noir California

IRON HORSE VINEYARDS

87 1990 Cabernet Blend Alexander Valley T-T Vineyards Cabernets

86 1989 Cabernet Blend Alexander Valley T-T Vineyards Cabernets

85 1988 Cabernet Blend Alexander Valley T-T Vineyards Cabernets

86 1987 Cabernet Blend Alexander Valley T-T Vineyards Cabernets

88 1986 Cabernet Blend Alexander Valley T-T Vineyards Cabernets

87 1985 Cabernet Blend Alexander Valley T-T Vineyards Cabernets

86 1984 Cabernet Sauvignon Alexander Valley

82 1983 Cabernet Sauvignon Alexander Valley

83 1982 Cabernet Sauvignon Alexander Valley

79 1981 Cabernet Sauvignon Alexander Valley

86 1980 Cabernet Sauvignon Alexander Valley

91 1979 Cabernet Sauvignon Alexander Valley

80 1978 Cabernet Sauvignon Alexander Valley

87 1993 Chardonnay Green Valley-Sonoma

86 1992 Chardonnay Green Valley-Sonoma

91 1991 Chardonnay Green Valley-Sonoma

90 1993 Chardonnay Sonoma County Cuvée Joy

87 1994 Fumé Blanc Alexander Valley T-T Vineyards

87 1993 Fumé Blanc Alexander Valley T-T Vineyards

87 1992 Pinot Noir Green Valley-Sonoma

85 1988 Pinot Noir Green Valley-Sonoma

72 1987 Pinot Noir Green Valley-Sonoma

88 1986 Pinot Noir Green Valley-Sonoma

87 1980 Pinot Noir Sonoma County

90 1988 Sparkling Wine Green Valley-Sonoma Blanc de Blancs

82 1988 Sparkling Wine Green Valley-Sonoma Brut Late Disgorged

81 1989 Sparkling Wine Green Valley-Sonoma Brut Rosé

87 1989 Sparkling Wine Green Valley-Sonoma Brut Vrais Amis

82 1989 Sparkling Wine Green Valley-Sonoma Demi-Sec

87 1991 Sparkling Wine Green Valley-Sonoma Wedding Cuvée

JACKSON VALLEY VINEYARDS

83 1990 Zinfandel Amador County

JADE MOUNTAIN WINERY

81 1990 Mourvèdre California

83 1990 Mourvèdre California Unfiltered

88 1992 Rhône Blend California La Provencale

80 1990 Rhône Blend California La Provencale

87 1992 Syrah Napa Valley

JAEGER FAMILY WINE CO.

77 1989 Merlot Napa Valley Inglewood Vineyard

81 1988 Merlot Napa Valley Inglewood Vineyard

81 1987 Merlot Napa Valley Inglewood Vineyard

88 1986 Merlot Napa Valley Inglewood Vineyard

89 1985 Merlot Napa Valley Inglewood Vineyard

JARVIS

86 1992 Cabernet Franc Napa Valley

90 1992 Cabernet Sauvignon Napa Valley

90 1992 Chardonnay Napa Valley

JEKEL VINEYARDS

82 1990 Cabernet Franc Monterey County

84 1990 Cabernet Sauvignon Arroyo Seco

81 1989 Cabernet Sauvignon Arroyo Seco

80 1988 Cabernet Sauvignon Arroyo Seco

83 1986 Cabernet Sauvignon Arroyo Seco

82 1993 Chardonnay Arroyo Seco Gravelstone Vineyard

84 1992 Chardonnay Arroyo Seco Gravelstone Vineyard

83 1992 Malbec Arroyo Seco The Sanctuary Estate

85 1989 Meritage Red Arroyo Seco The Sanctuary Estate Symmetry

83 1992 Merlot Arroyo Seco The Sanctuary Estate

84 1992 Pinot Noir Arroyo Seco

85 1991 White Riesling Arroyo Seco

JEPSON VINEYARDS

85 1993 Chardonnay Mendocino County

87 1992 Chardonnay Mendocino County

68 1991 Chardonnay Mendocino County

90 1990 Chardonnay Mendocino County

77 1992 Sauvignon Blanc Mendocino County

85 1989 Brut Sparkling Wine

88 1988 Sparkling Wine Blanc de Blancs

JORDAN VINEYARD AND WINERY

87 1991 Cabernet Sauvignon Alexander Valley

87 1991 Cabernet Sauvignon Alexander Valley

87 1990 Cabernet Sauvignon Alexander Valley

84 1989 Cabernet Sauvignon Alexander Valley

85 1988 Cabernet Sauvignon Alexander Valley

90 1987 Cabernet Sauvignon Alexander Valley

88 1986 Cabernet Sauvignon Alexander Valley

88 1985 Cabernet Sauvignon Alexander Valley

86 1984 Cabernet Sauvignon Alexander Valley

86 1992 Chardonnay Alexander Valley

83 1991 Chardonnay Alexander Valley

87 1990 J Sparkling Wine Sonoma County Brut

89 1989 J Sparkling Wine Sonoma County Brut

88 1987 J Sparkling Wine Sonoma County Brut

JORY WINERY

83 1992 Chardonnay California White Zeppelin Blimp de Blanc

82 1992 Chardonnay Santa Clara County Selected Clone

80 1989 Pinot Noir California San Ysidro Vineyard

85 1993 Red Table Wine California Black Hand Mano Nera

88 1989 Red Table Wine California Red Zeppelin Bon Jory Red

86 1990 Rhône Blend California Red Zeppelin II The Emperor's Reserve

81 1991 Zinfandel California Old Barrister Cuvée 91

JOULLIAN VINEYARDS

80 1989 Cabernet Sauvignon Carmel Valley

82 1993 Chardonnay Monterey County

81 1992 Chardonnay Monterey County

84 1991 Chardonnay Monterey County

89 1992 Chardonnay Monterey County Family Reserve

84 1991 Chardonnay Monterey County Family Reserve

84 1992 Sauvignon Blanc Carmel Valley

85 1992 Sauvignon Blanc Carmel Valley Family Reserve

JOYA WINERY

83 1991 Pinot Blanc Napa Valley

86 1992 Zinfandel Napa Valley

JUDD'S HILL

93 1991 Cabernet Sauvignon Napa Valley

89 1990 Cabernet Sauvignon Napa Valley

89 1989 Cabernet Sauvignon Napa Valley

JUSTIN VINEYARDS & WINERY

84 1991 Cabernet Blend San Luis Obispo County Isosceles Reserve

88 1990 Cabernet Blend San Luis Obispo County Isosceles Reserve

83 1989 Cabernet Blend San Luis Obispo County Isosceles Reserve

75 1988 Cabernet Blend San Luis Obispo County Isosceles Reserve

90 1987 Cabernet Blend San Luis Obispo County Isosceles Reserve

87 1992 Cabernet Blend San Luis Obispo County Justification

87 1991 Cabernet Franc San Luis Obispo County

86 1989 Cabernet Franc San Luis Obispo County

89 1991 Cabernet Sauvignon San Luis Obispo County

80 1990 Cabernet Sauvignon San Luis Obispo County

83 1989 Cabernet Sauvignon San Luis Obispo County

77 1988 Cabernet Sauvignon San Luis Obispo County

88 1991 Cabernet Sauvignon San Luis Obispo County Society Reserve

89 1991 Chardonnay Central Coast Barrel Fermented

87 1992 Chardonnay San Luis Obispo County

84 1992 Port San Luis Obispo County Obtuse

KALIN CELLARS

81 1988 Cabernet Sauvignon Sonoma County Reserve

83 1985 Cabernet Sauvignon Sonoma County Reserve

84 1990 Chardonnay Livermore Valley Cuvée W

91 1990 Chardonnay Sonoma County Cuvée CH

87 1990 Chardonnay Sonoma County Cuvée LD

80 1989 Chardonnay Sonoma County Cuvée LR

70 1989 Chardonnay Sonoma County Cuvée LV

86 1988 Chardonnay Potter Valley Cuvée BL

87 1988 Chardonnay Sonoma County Cuvée DD

87 1988 Chardonnay Sonoma County Cuvée LD

KARLY WINES

82 1991 Cabernet Sauvignon El Dorado County Stromberg Carpenter Vineyard

81 1992 Chardonnay Edna Valley MacGregor Vineyard

84 1991 Chardonnay Edna Valley MacGregor Vineyard

83 1991 Petite Sirah Amador County Not So

83 1993 Sauvignon Blanc Amador County

85 1992 Syrah Amador County

82 1992 Zinfandel Amador County

86 1990 Zinfandel Amador County

74 1989 Zinfandel Amador County

88 1990 Zinfandel Amador County Pokerville

88 1992 Zinfandel Amador County Sadie Upton Vineyard

77 1991 Zinfandel Amador County Sadie Upton Vineyard

81 1989 Zinfandel Amador County Sadie Upton Vineyard

ROBERT KEENAN WINERY

83 1989 Cabernet Sauvignon Napa Valley

85 1988 Cabernet Sauvignon Napa Valley

86 1987 Cabernet Sauvignon Napa Valley

90 1986 Cabernet Sauvignon Napa Valley

86 1985 Cabernet Sauvignon Napa Valley

91 1984 Cabernet Sauvignon Napa Valley

87 1983 Cabernet Sauvignon Napa Valley

88 1982 Cabernet Sauvignon Napa Valley

83 1981 Cabernet Sauvignon Napa Valley

80 1980 Cabernet Sauvignon Napa Valley

74 1979 Cabernet Sauvignon Napa Valley

78 1978 Cabernet Sauvignon Napa Valley

69 1977 Cabernet Sauvignon Napa Valley

87 1992 Chardonnay Napa Valley

83 1991 Chardonnay Napa Valley

83 1990 Merlot Napa Valley

82 1989 Merlot Napa Valley

84 1988 Merlot Napa Valley

88 1987 Merlot Napa Valley

87 1986 Merlot Napa Valley

83 1985 Merlot Napa Valley

90 1984 Merlot Napa Valley

86 1983 Merlot Napa Valley

87 1982 Merlot Napa Valley

88 1990 Merlot Napa Valley Vintners Selection

KENDALL-JACKSON

82 1992 Cabernet Franc California Vintner's Reserve

89 1991 Cabernet Sauvignon California Grand Reserve

90 1990 Cabernet Sauvignon California Grand Reserve

83 1988 Cabernet Sauvignon California Grand Reserve

87 1987 Cabernet Sauvignon California Grand Reserve

85 1986 Cabernet Sauvignon California Grand Reserve

91 1985 Cabernet Sauvignon California Grand Reserve

82 1992 Cabernet Sauvignon California Vintner's Reserve

83 1991 Cabernet Sauvignon California Vintner's Reserve

83 1990 Cabernet Sauvignon California Vintner's Reserve

90 1993 Chardonnay California Grand Reserve

90 1992 Chardonnay California Grand Reserve

85 1991 Chardonnay California Grand Reserve

85 1993 Chardonnay California Late Harvest Select

85 1993 Chardonnay California Vintner's Reserve

88 1993 Chardonnay Santa Maria Valley Camelot Vineyard

88 1992 Chardonnay Santa Maria Valley Camelot Vineyard

89 1991 Chardonnay Santa Maria Valley Camelot Vineyard

80 1991 Chardonnay Sonoma Valley Durell Vineyard

84 1992 Chenin Blanc California Vintner's Reserve

82 1993 Gewürztraminer California Vintner's Reserve

86 1993 Johannisberg Riesling California Late Harvest Select

80 1993 Johannisberg Riesling California Vintner's Reserve

84 1992 Johannisberg Riesling California Vintner's Reserve

91 1990 Meritage Red California Cardinale

86 1989 Meritage Red California Cardinale

85 1988 Meritage Red California Cardinale

92 1987 Meritage Red California Cardinale

91 1986 Meritage Red California Cardinale

94 1985 Meritage Red California Cardinale

84 1984 Meritage Red California Cardinale

89 1994 Meritage White California Royale

85 1992 Meritage White California Royale

86 1991 Merlot California Grand Reserve

82 1992 Merlot California Vintner's Reserve

87 1991 Merlot California Vintner's Reserve

83 1990 Merlot California Vintner's Reserve

75 1989 Merlot California Vintner's Reserve

84 1988 Merlot California Vintner's Reserve

88 1993 Pinot Noir California Grand Reserve

86 1992 Pinot Noir California Grand Reserve

83 1993 Pinot Noir California Vintner's Reserve

82 1992 Pinot Noir California Vintner's Reserve

80 1991 Pinot Noir California Vintner's Reserve

82 1990 Pinot Noir California Vintner's Reserve

86 1993 Sauvignon Blanc California Grand Reserve

87 1992 Sauvignon Blanc California Grand Reserve

82 1993 Sauvignon Blanc California Vintner's Reserve

88 1991 Syrah California Grand Reserve

88 1990 Syrah California Grand Reserve

83 1990 Syrah California Vintner's Reserve

85 1990 Syrah Sonoma Valley Durell Vineyard

89 1988 Syrah Sonoma Valley Durell Vineyard

90 1987 Syrah Sonoma Valley Durell Vineyard

92 1986 Syrah Sonoma Valley Durell Vineyard

82 1989 Zinfandel Anderson Valley Ciapusci Vineyard

77 1988 Zinfandel Anderson Valley Ciapusci Vineyard

88 1987 Zinfandel Anderson Valley Ciapusci Vineyard

86 1984 Zinfandel Anderson Valley Ciapusci Vineyard

88 1990 Zinfandel Anderson Valley DuPratt Vineyard

90 1987 Zinfandel Anderson Valley DuPratt Vineyard

85 1986 Zinfandel Anderson Valley DuPratt Vineyard

84 1992 Zinfandel California Grand Reserve

86 1991 Zinfandel California Grand Reserve

89 1990 Zinfandel California Grand Reserve

83 1992 Zinfandel California Vintner's Reserve

84 1991 Zinfandel California Vintner's Reserve

78 1990 Zinfandel California Vintner's Reserve

84 1989 Zinfandel California Vintner's Reserve

88 1987 Zinfandel Mendocino County

86 1986 Zinfandel Mendocino County

83 1990 Zinfandel Mendocino County Zeni Vineyard

KATHRYN KENNEDY WINERY

87 1991 Cabernet Sauvignon Santa Cruz Mountains

89 1990 Cabernet Sauvignon Santa Cruz Mountains

87 1989 Cabernet Sauvignon Santa Cruz Mountains

88 1988 Cabernet Sauvignon Santa Cruz Mountains

90 1987 Cabernet Sauvignon Santa Cruz Mountains

89 1986 Cabernet Sauvignon Santa Cruz Mountains

91 1985 Cabernet Sauvignon Santa Cruz Mountains

88 1984 Cabernet Sauvignon Santa Cruz Mountains

84 1983 Cabernet Sauvignon Santa Cruz Mountains

88 1982 Cabernet Sauvignon Santa Cruz Mountains

91 1981 Cabernet Sauvignon Santa Cruz Mountains

88 1980 Cabernet Sauvignon Santa Cruz Mountains

86 1991 Cabernet Blend California Lateral

88 1990 Cabernet Blend California Lateral

84 1989 Cabernet Blend California Lateral

87 1988 Cabernet Blend California Lateral

KENWOOD VINEYARDS

82 1991 Cabernet Sauvignon Sonoma Valley

84 1990 Cabernet Sauvignon Sonoma Valley

88 1989 Cabernet Sauvignon Sonoma Valley

90 1987 Cabernet Sauvignon Sonoma Valley

86 1986 Cabernet Sauvignon Sonoma Valley

88 1985 Cabernet Sauvignon Sonoma Valley

83 1984 Cabernet Sauvignon Sonoma Valley

90 1991 Cabernet Sauvignon Sonoma Valley Artist Series

86 1990 Cabernet Sauvignon Sonoma Valley Artist Series

91 1989 Cabernet Sauvignon Sonoma Valley Artist Series

85 1988 Cabernet Sauvignon Sonoma Valley Artist Series

90 1987 Cabernet Sauvignon Sonoma Valley Artist Series

92 1986 Cabernet Sauvignon Sonoma Valley Artist Series

91 1985 Cabernet Sauvignon Sonoma Valley Artist Series

93 1984 Cabernet Sauvignon Sonoma Valley Artist Series

87 1983 Cabernet Sauvignon Sonoma Valley Artist Series

87 1982 Cabernet Sauvignon Sonoma Valley Artist Series

89 1981 Cabernet Sauvignon Sonoma Valley Artist Series

80 1980 Cabernet Sauvignon Sonoma Valley Artist Series

90 1979 Cabernet Sauvignon Sonoma Valley Artist Series

90 1978 Cabernet Sauvignon Sonoma Valley Artist Series

82 1977 Cabernet Sauvignon Sonoma Valley Artist Series

75 1976 Cabernet Sauvignon Sonoma Valley Artist Series

73 1975 Cabernet Sauvignon Sonoma Valley Artist Series

83 1991 Cabernet Sauvignon Sonoma Valley Jack London Vineyard

87 1989 Cabernet Sauvignon Sonoma Valley Jack London Vineyard

91 1987 Cabernet Sauvignon Sonoma Valley Jack London Vineyard

88 1986 Cabernet Sauvignon Sonoma Valley Jack London Vineyard

89 1985 Cabernet Sauvignon Sonoma Valley Jack London Vineyard

89 1984 Cabernet Sauvignon Sonoma Valley Jack London Vineyard

84 1993 Chardonnay Sonoma Valley

83 1992 Chardonnay Sonoma Valley

85 1991 Chardonnay Sonoma Valley

87 1993 Chardonnay Sonoma Valley Reserve

84 1992 Chardonnay Sonoma Valley Reserve

91 1991 Chardonnay Sonoma Valley Reserve

84 1993 Chardonnay Sonoma Valley Beltane Ranch

83 1993 Chardonnay Sonoma Valley Yulupa Vineyard

85 1992 Chardonnay Sonoma Valley Yulupa Vineyard

87 1991 Chardonnay Sonoma Valley Yulupa Vineyard

83 1992 Merlot Sonoma County

81 1991 Merlot Sonoma County

87 1990 Merlot Sonoma County

83 1989 Merlot Sonoma County

87 1991 Merlot Sonoma Valley Jack London Vineyard

82 1990 Merlot Sonoma Valley Jack London Vineyard

84 1992 Merlot Sonoma Valley Massara Vineyards

80 1992 Pinot Noir Sonoma Valley Jack London Vineyard

79 1991 Pinot Noir Sonoma Valley Jack London Vineyard

85 1990 Pinot Noir Sonoma Valley Jack London Vineyard

80 1989 Pinot Noir Sonoma Valley Jack London Vineyard

84 1993 Sauvignon Blanc Sonoma County

86 1992 Sauvignon Blanc Sonoma County

84 1992 Zinfandel Sonoma Valley

82 1991 Zinfandel Sonoma Valley

86 1990 Zinfandel Sonoma Valley

82 1988 Zinfandel Sonoma Valley

90 1987 Zinfandel Sonoma Valley

89 1985 Zinfandel Sonoma Valley

87 1984 Zinfandel Sonoma Valley

84 1991 Zinfandel Sonoma Valley Barricia Estate Vineyard

88 1990 Zinfandel Sonoma Valley Barricia Estate Vineyard

82 1992 Zinfandel Sonoma Valley Jack London Vineyard

86 1991 Zinfandel Sonoma Valley Jack London Vineyard

88 1990 Zinfandel Sonoma Valley Jack London Vineyard

83 1989 Zinfandel Sonoma Valley Jack London Vineyard

88 1987 Zinfandel Sonoma Valley Jack London Vineyard

J. KERR WINES

80 1991 Chardonnay Santa Barbara County

85 1991 Pinot Noir Santa Barbara County

80 1990 Pinot Noir Santa Barbara County

KISTLER VINEYARDS

90 1991 Cabernet Sauvignon Sonoma Valley Kistler Estate Vineyard

86 1990 Cabernet Sauvignon Sonoma Valley Kistler Estate Vineyard

86 1988 Cabernet Sauvignon Sonoma Valley Kistler Estate Vineyard

83 1987 Cabernet Sauvignon Sonoma Valley Kistler Estate Vineyard

86 1986 Cabernet Sauvignon Sonoma Valley Kistler Estate Vineyard

92 1985 Cabernet Sauvignon Sonoma Valley Kistler Estate Vineyard

92 1992 Chardonnay Russian River Valley Dutton Ranch

92 1991 Chardonnay Russian River Valley Dutton Ranch

88 1990 Chardonnay Russian River Valley Dutton Ranch

89 1989 Chardonnay Russian River Valley Dutton Ranch

91 1992 Chardonnay Russian River Valley Vine Hill Road Vineyard

92 1991 Chardonnay Russian River Valley Vine Hill Road Vineyard

90 1990 Chardonnay Russian River Valley Vine Hill Road Vineyard

89 1993 Chardonnay Sonoma Coast

93 1992 Chardonnay Sonoma County

92 1992 Chardonnay Sonoma County Cuvée Cathleen

92 1992 Chardonnay Sonoma Mountain McCrea Vineyard

91 1991 Chardonnay Sonoma Mountain McCrea Vineyard

92 1990 Chardonnay Sonoma Mountain McCrea Vineyard

88 1989 Chardonnay Sonoma Mountain McCrea Vineyard

92 1988 Chardonnay Sonoma Mountain McCrea Vineyard

91 1993 Chardonnay Sonoma Valley Durell Vineyard

91 1992 Chardonnay Sonoma Valley Durell Vineyard Sand Hill

90 1991 Chardonnay Sonoma Valley Durell Vineyard Sand Hill

93 1990 Chardonnay Sonoma Valley Durell Vineyard Sand Hill

90 1989 Chardonnay Sonoma Valley Durell Vineyard

90 1988 Chardonnay Sonoma Valley Durell Vineyard

94 1992 Chardonnay Sonoma Valley Kistler Estate Vineyard

90 1991 Chardonnay Sonoma Valley Kistler Estate Vineyard

92 1990 Chardonnay Sonoma Valley Kistler Estate Vineyard

91 1989 Chardonnay Sonoma Valley Kistler Estate Vineyard

94 1988 Chardonnay Sonoma Valley Kistler Estate Vineyard

85 1991 Pinot Noir Russian River Valley Cuvée Catherine

86 1986 Pinot Noir Russian River Valley Dutton Ranch

84 1984 Pinot Noir Russian River Valley Dutton Ranch

88 1992 Pinot Noir Sonoma Mountain McCrea Vineyard

KLEIN

81 1990 Cabernet Sauvignon Santa Cruz Mountains

85 1989 Cabernet Sauvignon Santa Cruz Mountains

83 1988 Cabernet Sauvignon Santa Cruz Mountains

87 1987 Cabernet Sauvignon Santa Cruz Mountains

89 1986 Cabernet Sauvignon Santa Cruz Mountains

KONRAD ESTATE

87 1992 Barbera Amador County

82 1992 Charbono Mendocino County

77 1992 Chardonnay Mendocino County

88 1991 Chardonnay Mendocino County

86 1991 Meritage Red Mendocino County Mélange a Trois

85 1989 Meritage Red Mendocino County Mélange a Trois

82 1991 Petite Sirah Mendocino County

74 1990 Port Mendocino County Petite Sirah Port Admiral's Quinta

80 1991 Zinfandel Mendocino County

87 1990 Zinfandel Mendocino County

84 1989 Zinfandel Mendocino County

88 1990 Zinfandel Mendocino County Ricetti Vineyard

KORBEL CHAMPAGNE CELLARS

73 1991 Cabernet Sauvignon Alexander Valley

85 1993 Chardonnay Russian River Valley

82 1992 Chardonnay Sonoma County

70 1991 Chardonnay Sonoma County

78 1990 Sparkling Wine California Blanc de Noirs Cuvée Master's Reserve

80 NV Sparkling Wine California Natural

CHARLES KRUG WINERY

88 1991 Cabernet Sauvignon Napa Valley

88 1990 Cabernet Sauvignon Napa Valley

83 1989 Cabernet Sauvignon Napa Valley

73 1988 Cabernet Sauvignon Napa Valley

79 1987 Cabernet Sauvignon Napa Valley

87 1986 Cabernet Sauvignon Napa Valley

87 1990 Cabernet Sauvignon Napa Valley Vintage Selection

87 1988 Cabernet Sauvignon Napa Valley Vintage Selection

92 1986 Cabernet Sauvignon Napa Valley Vintage Selection

89 1985 Cabernet Sauvignon Napa Valley Vintage Selection

88 1984 Cabernet Sauvignon Napa Valley Vintage Selection

82 1983 Cabernet Sauvignon Napa Valley Vintage Selection

87 1981 Cabernet Sauvignon Napa Valley Vintage Selection

75 1980 Cabernet Sauvignon Napa Valley Vintage Selection

82 1979 Cabernet Sauvignon Napa Valley Vintage Selection

78 1978 Cabernet Sauvignon Napa Valley Vintage Selection

74 1977 Cabernet Sauvignon Napa Valley Vintage Selection

81 1974 Cabernet Sauvignon Napa Valley Vintage Selection

88 1974 Cabernet Sauvignon Napa Valley Vintage Selection Lot F1

80 1968 Cabernet Sauvignon Napa Valley Vintage Selection

89 1961 Cabernet Sauvignon Napa Valley Vintage Selection

85 1959 Cabernet Sauvignon Napa Valley Vintage Selection

85 1958 Cabernet Sauvignon Napa Valley Vintage Selection

90 1956 Cabernet Sauvignon Napa Valley Vintage Selection

90 1952 Cabernet Sauvignon Napa Valley Vintage Selection

85 1951 Cabernet Sauvignon Napa Valley Vintage Selection

79 1950 Cabernet Sauvignon Napa Valley Vintage Selection

88 1946 Cabernet Sauvignon Napa Valley Vintage Selection

89 1992 Chardonnay Carneros Reserve

87 1991 Chardonnay Carneros Reserve

81 1993 Chardonnay Napa Valley

84 1992 Chardonnay Napa Valley

83 1992 Merlot Napa Valley

81 1991 Merlot Napa Valley

85 1990 Merlot Napa Valley

84 1989 Merlot Napa Valley

82   1992 Pinot Noir Carneros
78   1990 Pinot Noir Carneros
82   1989 Pinot Noir Carneros
87   1987 Pinot Noir Carneros
81   1985 Pinot Noir Carneros
81   1992 Zinfandel Napa Valley
74   1990 Zinfandel Napa Valley
83   1989 Zinfandel Napa Valley

KUNDE ESTATE WINERY

87   1990 Cabernet Sauvignon Sonoma Valley
88   1992 Chardonnay Sonoma Valley
89   1991 Chardonnay Sonoma Valley
89   1992 Chardonnay Sonoma Valley Estate Reserve
82   1992 Chardonnay Sonoma Valley Kinneybrook Vineyard
82   1992 Chardonnay Sonoma Valley Wildwood Vineyard
88   1990 Meritage Red Sonoma Valley Louis Kunde Founder's Reserve
89   1989 Meritage Red Sonoma Valley Louis Kunde Founder's Reserve
77   1991 Merlot Sonoma Valley
80   1993 Sauvignon Blanc Sonoma Valley Magnolia Lane
88   1993 Viognier Sonoma Valley
74   1992 Zinfandel Sonoma Valley The Shaw Vineyard Century Vines
83   1991 Zinfandel Sonoma Valley The Shaw Vineyard Century Vines
84   1990 Zinfandel Sonoma Valley The Shaw Vineyard Century Vines

LA CREMA

87   1992 Chardonnay California
85   1993 Chardonnay California Reserve
90   1992 Chardonnay California Reserve
84   1992 Pinot Noir California
78   1991 Pinot Noir California
89   1986 Pinot Noir California
90   1985 Pinot Noir California
85   1993 Pinot Noir California Reserve
88   1992 Pinot Noir California Reserve
79   1991 Pinot Noir California Reserve
85   1990 Pinot Noir California Reserve
85   1986 Pinot Noir California Reserve

LA JOTA VINEYARD CO.

89   1992 Cabernet Franc Howell Mountain
86   1991 Cabernet Franc Howell Mountain
83   1990 Cabernet Franc Howell Mountain
84   1988 Cabernet Franc Howell Mountain
84   1986 Cabernet Franc Howell Mountain

88   1992 Cabernet Sauvignon Howell Mountain
87   1991 Cabernet Sauvignon Howell Mountain 10th Anniversary Release
86   1990 Cabernet Sauvignon Howell Mountain
83   1989 Cabernet Sauvignon Howell Mountain
85   1988 Cabernet Sauvignon Howell Mountain
82   1987 Cabernet Sauvignon Howell Mountain
85   1986 Cabernet Sauvignon Howell Mountain
83   1985 Cabernet Sauvignon Howell Mountain
83   1984 Cabernet Sauvignon Howell Mountain
79   1983 Cabernet Sauvignon Howell Mountain
79   1982 Cabernet Sauvignon Howell Mountain Napa Valley
87   1992 Petite Sirah Howell Mountain
89   1991 Viognier Howell Mountain
85   1993 Viognier Howell Mountain Sweet
83   1987 Zinfandel Howell Mountain

LAKE SONOMA WINERY

73   1991 Cinsault Dry Creek Valley Vintner's Reserve
83   1991 Merlot Dry Creek Valley Yoakim Bridge Ranch
86   1990 Merlot Dry Creek Valley Yoakim Bridge Ranch
72   1990 Zinfandel Dry Creek Valley
84   1989 Zinfandel Dry Creek Valley

LAKESPRING WINERY

87   1990 Cabernet Sauvignon Napa Valley
74   1988 Cabernet Sauvignon Napa Valley Reserve Selection
84   1987 Cabernet Sauvignon Napa Valley
88   1986 Cabernet Sauvignon Napa Valley
84   1985 Cabernet Sauvignon Napa Valley
88   1984 Cabernet Sauvignon Napa Valley Reserve Selection
82   1982 Cabernet Sauvignon Napa Valley Vintage Selection
86   1981 Cabernet Sauvignon Napa Valley
82   1980 Cabernet Sauvignon Napa Valley
81   1992 Chardonnay Napa Valley
88   1990 Merlot Napa Valley Yount Mill Vineyard
85   1988 Merlot Napa Valley Yount Mill Vineyard
83   1993 Sauvignon Blanc Napa Valley Yount Mill Vineyard

LAKEWOOD

84   1993 Sauvignon Blanc Clear Lake
86   1993 Sauvignon Blend Clear Lake Chevriot
88   1992 Sauvignon Blend Clear Lake Chevriot
85   1993 Sémillon Clear Lake

LAMBERT BRIDGE

84   1991 Cabernet Sauvignon Sonoma County

80   1989 Cabernet Sauvignon Sonoma County
80   1984 Cabernet Sauvignon Sonoma County
84   1993 Chardonnay Dry Creek Valley
80   1992 Chardonnay Dry Creek Valley
81   1993 Fumé Blanc Sonoma County
78   1992 Fumé Blanc Sonoma County
87   1992 Merlot Sonoma County
79   1991 Merlot Sonoma County
85   1989 Merlot Sonoma County
84   1992 Zinfandel Dry Creek Valley

LAMBORN FAMILY VINEYARDS

82   1991 Zinfandel Howell Mountain The Phoenix Vintage
85   1990 Zinfandel Howell Mountain
89   1988 Zinfandel Howell Mountain
84   1987 Zinfandel Howell Mountain

LANDMARK VINEYARDS

90   1993 Chardonnay Alexander Valley Damaris Vineyard Reserve
82   1992 Chardonnay Alexander Valley Damaris Vineyard Reserve
91   1991 Chardonnay Alexander Valley Damaris Vineyard Reserve
88   1993 Chardonnay Sonoma County Overlook
87   1992 Chardonnay Sonoma County Overlook
90   1992 Chardonnay Sonoma Valley Two Williams Vineyard

LAS VIÑAS WINERY

78   1988 Cabernet Sauvignon California Private Reserve

LAUREL GLEN VINEYARD

89   1991 Cabernet Sauvignon Sonoma Mountain
90   1990 Cabernet Sauvignon Sonoma Mountain
88   1990 Laurel Glen Cabernet Sauvignon Sonoma Mountain Reserve
88   1989 Cabernet Sauvignon Sonoma Mountain
89   1988 Cabernet Sauvignon Sonoma Mountain
92   1987 Cabernet Sauvignon Sonoma Mountain
88   1986 Cabernet Sauvignon Sonoma Mountain
91   1985 Cabernet Sauvignon Sonoma Mountain
87   1984 Cabernet Sauvignon Sonoma Mountain
75   1983 Cabernet Sauvignon Sonoma Mountain
79   1982 Cabernet Sauvignon Sonoma Mountain
93   1981 Cabernet Sauvignon Sonoma Mountain
90   1991 Counterpoint Cabernet Sauvignon Sonoma Mountain
87   1990 Counterpoint Cabernet Sauvignon Sonoma Mountain
85   1989 Counterpoint Cabernet Sauvignon Sonoma Mountain

85 1988 Counterpoint Cabernet Sauvignon Sonoma Mountain

90 1987 Counterpoint Cabernet Sauvignon Sonoma Mountain

88 1992 Terra Rosa Cabernet Sauvignon Napa Valley

89 1990 Terra Rosa Cabernet Sauvignon Napa Valley

86 1989 Terra Rosa Cabernet Sauvignon Napa Valley

85 1988 Terra Rosa Cabernet Sauvignon Napa Valley

86 1987 Terra Rosa Cabernet Sauvignon Napa Valley

LAURIER

88 1992 Chardonnay Sonoma County

LAVA CAP WINERY

85 1989 Cabernet Sauvignon El Dorado County

84 1990 Merlot El Dorado County

73 1991 Zinfandel El Dorado County

77 1990 Zinfandel El Dorado County

77 1989 Zinfandel El Dorado County

LAZY CREEK VINEYARDS

75 1993 Chardonnay Anderson Valley

82 1992 Chardonnay Anderson Valley

86 1991 Chardonnay Anderson Valley

83 1991 Pinot Noir Anderson Valley

87 1988 Pinot Noir Anderson Valley Private Reserve

86 1987 Pinot Noir Anderson Valley

LEEWARD WINERY

81 1991 Cabernet Sauvignon Alexander Valley

78 1988 Cabernet Sauvignon Alexander Valley

79 1992 Chardonnay Central Coast

85 1991 Chardonnay Central Coast

86 1993 Chardonnay Edna Valley Reserve

85 1992 Chardonnay Edna Valley Reserve

74 1991 Chardonnay Edna Valley Paragon Vineyard Reserve

82 1991 Chardonnay Monterey County

81 1992 Chardonnay Ventura County

74 1992 Merlot Napa Valley

81 1991 Merlot Napa Valley

83 1989 Merlot Napa Valley

76 1990 Pinot Noir Santa Barbara County

79 1989 Pinot Noir Santa Barbara County

LEWIS CELLARS

90 1993 Chardonnay Napa Valley Oakville Ranch Reserve

LIMERICK LANE

69 1992 Sauvignon Blanc Russian River Valley Collins Vineyard

88 1991 Zinfandel Russian River Valley

89 1990 Zinfandel Russian River Valley

61 1989 Zinfandel Russian River Valley

LIMUR WINERY

83 1992 Chardonnay Napa Valley

83 1991 Chardonnay Napa Valley

LIPARITA CELLARS

86 1991 Cabernet Sauvignon Howell Mountain

88 1990 Cabernet Sauvignon Howell Mountain

88 1992 Chardonnay Howell Mountain

82 1991 Chardonnay Howell Mountain

83 1991 Merlot Howell Mountain

LIVINGSTON WINES

90 1991 Cabernet Sauvignon Napa Valley Moffett Vineyard

92 1990 Cabernet Sauvignon Napa Valley Moffett Vineyard

87 1989 Cabernet Sauvignon Napa Valley Moffett Vineyard

87 1988 Cabernet Sauvignon Napa Valley Moffett Vineyard

93 1987 Cabernet Sauvignon Napa Valley Moffett Vineyard

89 1986 Cabernet Sauvignon Napa Valley Moffett Vineyard

85 1985 Cabernet Sauvignon Napa Valley Moffett Vineyard

92 1984 Cabernet Sauvignon Napa Valley Moffett Vineyard

87 1992 Cabernet Sauvignon Napa Valley Stanley's Selection

83 1991 Cabernet Sauvignon Napa Valley Stanley's Selection

88 1990 Cabernet Sauvignon Napa Valley Stanley's Selection

85 1989 Cabernet Sauvignon Napa Valley Stanley's Selection

LOCKWOOD

86 1992 Cabernet Sauvignon Monterey County

88 1991 Cabernet Sauvignon Monterey County

84 1991 Cabernet Sauvignon Monterey County Partners' Reserve

87 1990 Cabernet Sauvignon Monterey County Partners' Reserve

84 1992 Chardonnay Monterey County

84 1991 Chardonnay Monterey County

83 1992 Chardonnay Monterey County Partners' Reserve

89 1991 Chardonnay Monterey County Partners' Reserve

84 1992 Merlot Monterey County

87 1991 Merlot Monterey County

87 1992 Sauvignon Blanc Monterey County

J. LOHR WINERY

82 1991 Cabernet Sauvignon California Cypress

86 1990 Cabernet Sauvignon California Cypress

84 1991 Cabernet Sauvignon Paso Robles Seven Oaks

87 1990 Cabernet Sauvignon Paso Robles Seven Oaks

89 1989 Cabernet Sauvignon Paso Robles Seven Oaks

83 1988 Cabernet Sauvignon Paso Robles Seven Oaks

86 1987 Cabernet Sauvignon Paso Robles Seven Oaks

83 1992 Chardonnay California Cypress

85 1992 Chardonnay Monterey County Riverstone

89 1991 Chardonnay Monterey County Riverstone

86 1993 Fumé Blanc California Cypress

81 1992 Fumé Blanc California Cypress

86 1992 Merlot California Cypress

82 1991 Merlot California Cypress

LOLONIS WINERY

84 1989 Cabernet Sauvignon Mendocino County Private Reserve

83 1991 Chardonnay Mendocino County Estate Reserve

83 1991 Zinfandel Mendocino County

85 1990 Zinfandel Mendocino County

85 1991 Zinfandel Mendocino County Private Reserve

89 1990 Zinfandel Mendocino County Private Reserve

83 1989 Zinfandel Mendocino County Private Reserve

76 1989 Zinfandel Mendocino County Private Reserve Lot 2

LONG VINEYARDS

89 1990 Cabernet Sauvignon Napa Valley

86 1986 Cabernet Sauvignon Napa Valley

87 1985 Cabernet Sauvignon Napa Valley

86 1984 Cabernet Sauvignon Napa Valley

78 1983 Cabernet Sauvignon Napa Valley

88 1980 Cabernet Sauvignon Napa Valley

88 1979 Cabernet Sauvignon Napa Valley

89 1992 Chardonnay Napa Valley

91 1991 Chardonnay Napa Valley

90 1990 Chardonnay Napa Valley

91 1989 Chardonnay Napa Valley

93 1988 Chardonnay Napa Valley

90 1987 Chardonnay Napa Valley

92 1986 Chardonnay Napa Valley

91 1985 Chardonnay Napa Valley

86 1990 Johannisberg Riesling Napa Valley Botrytis

89 1983 Johannisberg Riesling Napa Valley Botrytis

RICHARD LONGORIA WINES

83 1990 Cabernet Sauvignon Santa Ynez Valley

87 1992 Chardonnay Santa Barbara County

86 1993 Chardonnay Santa Ynez Valley Huber Vineyard

85 1990 Merlot Santa Ynez Valley

86 1993 Pinot Noir Santa Maria Valley Bien Nacido Vineyard

86 1989 Pinot Noir Santa Ynez Valley Benedict Vineyard

87 1988 Pinot Noir Santa Ynez Valley Benedict Vineyard

88 1987 Pinot Noir Santa Ynez Valley Benedict Vineyard

LYETH WINERY

87 1992 Cabernet Blend Alexander Valley

87 1991 Cabernet Blend Alexander Valley

84 1988 Cabernet Blend Alexander Valley

83 1987 Cabernet Blend Alexander Valley

88 1986 Cabernet Blend Alexander Valley

86 1985 Cabernet Blend Alexander Valley

88 1990 Cabernet Sauvignon Alexander Valley

87 1985 Cabernet Sauvignon Alexander Valley

85 1984 Cabernet Sauvignon Alexander Valley

82 1993 Chardonnay Sonoma County

88 1992 Chardonnay Sonoma County

83 1991 Chardonnay Sonoma County

LYTTON SPRINGS WINERY

80 1988 Cabernet Sauvignon Mendocino County Private Reserve

88 1987 Cabernet Sauvignon Mendocino County Private Reserve

89 1992 Zinfandel Sonoma County

90 1988 Zinfandel Sonoma County

88 1987 Zinfandel Sonoma County

87 1986 Zinfandel Sonoma County

90 1985 Zinfandel Sonoma County

MACROSTIE WINERY

85 1993 Chardonnay Carneros

86 1992 Chardonnay Carneros

88 1991 Chardonnay Carneros

91 1992 Chardonnay Carneros Reserve

85 1992 Merlot Carneros

82 1991 Merlot Carneros

84 1992 Pinot Noir Carneros

84 1991 Keltie Brook Pinot Noir Carneros Unfiltered

MADRONA VINEYARDS

81 1991 Cabernet Sauvignon El Dorado County

85 1993 Chardonnay El Dorado County

84 1992 Chardonnay El Dorado County

MAISON DEUTZ WINERY

82 NV Sparkling Wine San Luis Obispo County Blanc de Noirs

85 1990 Sparkling Wine San Luis Obispo County Brut Reserve

MANZANITA

89 1988 Zinfandel Alexander Valley

MARCASSIN WINERY

92 1993 Chardonnay Alexander Valley Gauer Ranch Upper Barn

94 1992 Chardonnay Alexander Valley Gauer Ranch Upper Barn

92 1993 Chardonnay Carneros Hudson Vineyard

91 1993 Chardonnay Sonoma County Lorenzo Vineyard

93 1992 Chardonnay Sonoma County Lorenzo Vineyard

MARIETTA CELLARS

86 1989 Port Alexander Valley

83 NV Red Table Wine Sonoma County Old Vine Red Lot 14

85 1992 Zinfandel Sonoma County

MARK WEST VINEYARDS

89 1992 Chardonnay Russian River Valley Barrel Fermented

85 1991 Chardonnay Russian River Valley Barrel Fermented

81 1991 Chardonnay Russian River Valley Estate Reserve

84 1991 Pinot Noir Russian River Valley

83 1990 Pinot Noir Russian River Valley

MARKHAM VINEYARDS

88 1991 Cabernet Sauvignon Napa Valley

90 1990 Cabernet Sauvignon Napa Valley

87 1989 Cabernet Sauvignon Napa Valley

80 1988 Cabernet Sauvignon Napa Valley

87 1987 Cabernet Sauvignon Napa Valley

87 1986 Cabernet Sauvignon Napa Valley

91 1985 Cabernet Sauvignon Napa Valley

87 1984 Cabernet Sauvignon Napa Valley

88 1983 Cabernet Sauvignon Napa Valley

88 1982 Cabernet Sauvignon Napa Valley

86 1981 Cabernet Sauvignon Napa Valley

85 1980 Cabernet Sauvignon Napa Valley

88 1979 Cabernet Sauvignon Napa Valley

86 1978 Cabernet Sauvignon Napa Valley

91 1993 Chardonnay Napa Valley Barrel Fermented

90 1992 Chardonnay Napa Valley Barrel Fermented

88 1991 Chardonnay Napa Valley Barrel Fermented

88 1992 Merlot Napa Valley

87 1991 Merlot Napa Valley

92 1990 Merlot Napa Valley

88 1989 Merlot Napa Valley

90 1988 Merlot Napa Valley

92 1987 Merlot Napa Valley

93 1985 Merlot Napa Valley

92 1984 Merlot Napa Valley

81 1983 Merlot Napa Valley

84 1982 Merlot Napa Valley

83 1981 Merlot Napa Valley

85 1980 Merlot Napa Valley

87 1994 Sauvignon Blanc Napa Valley

89 1993 Sauvignon Blanc Napa Valley

88 1992 Sauvignon Blanc Napa Valley

84 1990 Glass Mountain Quarry Cabernet Sauvignon California

84 1993 Glass Mountain Quarry Chardonnay California

82 1991 Glass Mountain Quarry Chardonnay California

87 1988 Laurent Cellars Cabernet Sauvignon Napa Valley

85 1991 Laurent Cellars Cabernet Sauvignon Napa Valley Reserve

85 1990 Laurent Cellars Cabernet Sauvignon Napa Valley Reserve

88 1991 Laurent Cellars Chardonnay Napa Valley

MARTIN BROTHERS WINERY

82 1992 Cabernet Blend Paso Robles Etrusco

89 1991 Cabernet Blend Paso Robles Etrusco

85 1990 Cabernet Blend Paso Robles Etrusco

77 1992 Sparkling Wine California Moscato Allegro

83 1992 Zinfandel Paso Robles Primitiva

84 1991 Zinfandel Paso Robles Primitiva

82 1990 Zinfandel Paso Robles Primitiva

MARTINELLI WINERY

88 1992 Chardonnay Russian River Valley

71 1993 Sauvignon Blanc Russian River Valley

88 1992 Zinfandel Russian River Valley Jackass Vineyard

81 1991 Zinfandel Russian River Valley Jackass Vineyard

91 1990 Zinfandel Russian River Valley Jackass Vineyard

71 1989 Zinfandel Russian River Valley

85 1988 Zinfandel Russian River Valley

LOUIS M. MARTINI WINERY

83 1987 Barbera California

79 1990 Cabernet Sauvignon North Coast

81 1989 Cabernet Sauvignon Napa Valley Reserve

78	1988 Cabernet Sauvignon Napa Valley Reserve
87	1987 Cabernet Sauvignon Napa Valley Reserve
82	1990 Cabernet Sauvignon Sonoma Valley Monte Rosso Vineyard Selection
81	1988 Cabernet Sauvignon Sonoma Valley Monte Rosso Vineyard Selection
84	1986 Cabernet Sauvignon Sonoma Valley Monte Rosso Vineyard Selection
85	1984 Cabernet Sauvignon Sonoma Valley Monte Rosso Vineyard Selection
80	1978 Cabernet Sauvignon Sonoma Valley Monte Rosso Special Selection
84	1968 Cabernet Sauvignon Sonoma Valley Monte Rosso Special Selection
87	1966 Cabernet Sauvignon Sonoma Valley Monte Rosso Special Selection
83	1964 Cabernet Sauvignon Sonoma Valley Monte Rosso Special Selection
84	1991 Chardonnay Carneros
86	1992 Chardonnay Napa Valley
82	1991 Chardonnay Napa Valley
88	1991 Chardonnay Napa Valley Reserve
85	1992 Gewürztraminer Russian River Valley
81	1992 Merlot North Coast
82	1991 Merlot North Coast
87	1990 Merlot Russian River Valley Los Vinedos del Rio Vineyard Selection
86	1992 Pinot Noir Carneros
83	1990 Pinot Noir Carneros La Loma Vineyard
85	1988 Pinot Noir Carneros
84	1992 Zinfandel Sonoma Valley

MATANZAS CREEK WINERY

89	1992 Chardonnay Sonoma Valley
90	1991 Chardonnay Sonoma Valley
92	1990 Chardonnay Sonoma Valley
91	1988 Chardonnay Sonoma County
94	1990 Chardonnay Sonoma Valley Journey
91	1992 Merlot Sonoma Valley
89	1991 Merlot Sonoma Valley
92	1990 Merlot Sonoma Valley
90	1989 Merlot Sonoma Valley
88	1988 Merlot Sonoma Valley
93	1987 Merlot Sonoma Valley
88	1986 Merlot Sonoma Valley
87	1984 Merlot Sonoma Valley
77	1983 Merlot Sonoma Valley
74	1982 Merlot Sonoma Valley
78	1981 Merlot Sonoma Valley
80	1980 Merlot Sonoma Valley
74	1979 Merlot Sonoma Valley
87	1978 Merlot Sonoma Valley
87	1993 Sauvignon Blanc Sonoma County

MAYACAMAS VINEYARDS

81	1987 Cabernet Sauvignon Napa Valley
82	1986 Cabernet Sauvignon Napa Valley
85	1985 Cabernet Sauvignon Napa Valley
87	1984 Cabernet Sauvignon Napa Valley
86	1983 Cabernet Sauvignon Napa Valley
77	1982 Cabernet Sauvignon Napa Valley
88	1981 Cabernet Sauvignon Napa Valley
89	1980 Cabernet Sauvignon Napa Valley
90	1979 Cabernet Sauvignon Napa Valley
93	1978 Cabernet Sauvignon Napa Valley
95	1977 Cabernet Sauvignon Napa Valley
89	1975 Cabernet Sauvignon Napa Valley
88	1974 Cabernet Sauvignon Napa Valley
88	1973 Cabernet Sauvignon Napa Valley
82	1972 Cabernet Sauvignon Napa Valley
85	1971 Cabernet Sauvignon Napa Valley
97	1970 Cabernet Sauvignon Napa Valley
89	1969 Cabernet Sauvignon Napa Valley
90	1968 Cabernet Sauvignon Napa Valley
89	1990 Chardonnay Napa Valley
88	1989 Chardonnay Napa Valley
86	1987 Chardonnay Napa Valley
86	1986 Chardonnay Napa Valley
90	1985 Chardonnay Napa Valley
68	1988 Pinot Noir Napa Valley
80	1987 Pinot Noir Napa Valley
67	1986 Pinot Noir Napa Valley
87	1990 Sauvignon Blanc Napa Valley

MAZZOCCO VINEYARDS

82	1990 Cabernet Blend Sonoma County Matrix
86	1989 Cabernet Blend Sonoma County Matrix
91	1987 Cabernet Blend Sonoma County Matrix
85	1988 Cabernet Sauvignon Alexander Valley Claret Style
90	1987 Cabernet Sauvignon Alexander Valley Claret Style
78	1986 Cabernet Sauvignon Alexander Valley Claret Style
88	1991 Cabernet Sauvignon Sonoma County
81	1989 Cabernet Sauvignon Sonoma County
83	1993 Chardonnay Alexander Valley River Lane Vineyard
86	1992 Chardonnay Alexander Valley River Lane Vineyard
86	1991 Chardonnay Alexander Valley River Lane Vineyard
78	1991 Merlot Dry Creek Valley
78	1989 Merlot Dry Creek Valley
88	1989 Merlot Dry Creek Valley Unfiltered
86	1992 Zinfandel Sonoma County

88	1991 Zinfandel Sonoma County
87	1990 Zinfandel Sonoma Valley
89	1988 Zinfandel Sonoma County
88	1986 Zinfandel Sonoma County

PETER McCOY VINEYARDS

85	1992 Chardonnay Knights Valley Clos des Pierres

McDOWELL VALLEY VINEYARDS

82	1990 Cabernet Sauvignon Mendocino County
86	1992 Chardonnay Mendocino County
86	1990 Rhône Blend McDowell Valley Les Vieux Cépages
82	1990 Syrah Mendocino County
84	1992 Viognier Mendocino County
79	1990 Zinfandel McDowell Valley

THE MEEKER VINEYARD

85	1988 Cabernet Sauvignon Dry Creek Valley
87	1987 Cabernet Sauvignon Dry Creek Valley
72	1986 Cabernet Sauvignon Dry Creek Valley
76	1985 Cabernet Sauvignon Dry Creek Valley
78	1984 Cabernet Sauvignon Dry Creek Valley
78	1991 Cabernet Sauvignon Dry Creek Valley Gold Leaf Cuvée
82	1990 Cabernet Sauvignon Dry Creek Valley Gold Leaf Cuvée
84	1990 Cabernet Sauvignon Dry Creek Valley Scharf Family Vineyard
76	1992 Chardonnay Dry Creek Valley Second Rack
85	1993 Sauvignon Blanc Dry Creek Valley Gold Leaf Cuvée
82	1991 Zinfandel Dry Creek Valley
86	1991 Zinfandel Dry Creek Valley First Rack
80	1989 Zinfandel Dry Creek Valley
82	1988 Zinfandel Dry Creek Valley
85	1987 Zinfandel Dry Creek Valley
83	1986 Zinfandel Dry Creek Valley
88	1985 Zinfandel Dry Creek Valley
80	1992 Zinfandel Dry Creek Valley Gold Leaf Cuvée
84	1991 Zinfandel Dry Creek Valley Gold Leaf Cuvée
90	1990 Zinfandel Dry Creek Valley Gold Leaf Cuvée
81	1989 Zinfandel Dry Creek Valley Gold Leaf Reserve
84	1992 Zinfandel Sonoma County Sonoma Cuvée

MELIM VINEYARD AND WINERY

77	1992 Maacama Creek Cabernet Sauvignon Alexander Valley Reserve
81	1990 Maacama Creek Cabernet Sauvignon Alexander Valley Reserve
86	1989 Maacama Creek Cabernet Sauvignon Alexander Valley Melim Vineyard

75 1991 Maacama Creek Cabernet Sauvignon Alexander Valley Melim Vineyard Reserve

79 1992 Maacama Creek Chardonnay Alexander Valley Melim Vineyard Reserve

MENDOCINO HILL

88 1989 Cabernet Sauvignon Mendocino County

MERIDIAN VINEYARDS

83 1990 Cabernet Sauvignon Paso Robles

87 1989 Cabernet Sauvignon Paso Robles

86 1988 Cabernet Sauvignon Paso Robles

85 1993 Chardonnay Edna Valley

86 1992 Chardonnay Edna Valley

88 1991 Chardonnay Edna Valley

85 1993 Chardonnay Santa Barbara County

85 1992 Chardonnay Santa Barbara County

85 1991 Chardonnay Santa Barbara County

89 1993 Chardonnay Santa Barbara County Reserve

86 1993 Pinot Blanc Santa Barbara County

86 1991 Pinot Noir Edna Valley Reserve

82 1993 Pinot Noir Santa Barbara County

83 1992 Pinot Noir Santa Barbara County

80 1991 Pinot Noir Santa Barbara County

80 1990 Pinot Noir Santa Barbara County

85 1991 Pinot Noir Santa Barbara County Reserve

86 1993 Sauvignon Blanc California

83 1992 Sauvignon Blanc California

83 1991 Syrah Paso Robles

86 1990 Syrah Paso Robles

88 1988 Syrah Paso Robles

86 1990 Zinfandel Paso Robles

85 1989 Zinfandel Paso Robles

MERRYVALE VINEYARDS

87 1991 Cabernet Sauvignon Napa Valley

88 1990 Cabernet Sauvignon Napa Valley

90 1989 Cabernet Sauvignon Napa Valley

86 1988 Cabernet Sauvignon Napa Valley

88 1993 Chardonnay Napa Valley Reserve

84 1992 Chardonnay Napa Valley Reserve

91 1991 Chardonnay Napa Valley Reserve

84 1993 Chardonnay Napa Valley Starmont

88 1992 Chardonnay Napa Valley Starmont

90 1991 Chardonnay Napa Valley Starmont

86 1990 Meritage Red Napa Valley Profile

86 1989 Meritage Red Napa Valley Profile

85 1988 Meritage Red Napa Valley Profile

83 1987 Meritage Red Napa Valley Profile

86 1986 Meritage Red Napa Valley Profile

91 1985 Meritage Red Napa Valley Profile

86 1984 Meritage Red Napa Valley Profile

87 1983 Meritage Red Napa Valley Profile

85 1993 Meritage White Napa Valley

87 1992 Meritage White Napa Valley

84 1991 Merlot Napa Valley

85 1990 Merlot Napa Valley

84 1989 Merlot Napa Valley

83 1993 Sauvignon Blanc Napa Valley

83 1992 Sauvignon Blanc Napa Valley

PETER MICHAEL WINERY

87 1991 Cabernet Sauvignon Knights Valley Les Pavots

80 1990 Cabernet Sauvignon Knights Valley Les Pavots

79 1989 Cabernet Sauvignon Knights Valley Les Pavots

88 1988 Cabernet Sauvignon Knights Valley Les Pavots

91 1992 Chardonnay Napa County Clos du Ciel

88 1991 Chardonnay Napa County Clos du Ciel

94 1990 Chardonnay Napa Valley Cuvée Indigene

93 1992 Chardonnay Napa Valley Cuvée Indigene

92 1992 Chardonnay Sonoma County Mon Plaisir

88 1989 Chardonnay Sonoma County Mon Plaisir

MICHEL-SCHLUMBERGER

81 1991 Cabernet Sauvignon Dry Creek Valley

82 1990 Cabernet Sauvignon Dry Creek Valley Reserve

82 1988 Cabernet Sauvignon Dry Creek Valley Michel Vineyard

82 1990 Cabernet Sauvignon Sonoma County

81 1989 Cabernet Sauvignon Sonoma County

80 1988 Cabernet Sauvignon Sonoma County

82 1987 Cabernet Sauvignon Sonoma County

75 1986 Cabernet Sauvignon Sonoma County

86 1984 Cabernet Sauvignon Sonoma County

83 1992 Chardonnay Dry Creek Valley

79 1991 Chardonnay Dry Creek Valley

80 1991 Merlot Dry Creek Valley

MIETZ CELLARS

85 1991 Merlot Sonoma County

81 1990 Merlot Sonoma County

88 1989 Merlot Sonoma County

MILANO WINERY

82 1985 Cabernet Sauvignon Mendocino County Sanel Valley Vineyard

85 1990 Zinfandel Mendocino County Sanel Valley Vineyard

85 1988 Zinfandel Mendocino County Sanel Valley Vineyard

MILL CREEK VINEYARDS

83 1991 Cabernet Sauvignon Dry Creek Valley

87 1993 Chardonnay Dry Creek Valley

84 1993 Gewürztraminer Dry Creek Valley

82 1992 Gewürztraminer Dry Creek Valley

83 1991 Merlot Dry Creek Valley

84 1990 Merlot Dry Creek Valley

82 1989 Merlot Dry Creek Valley

77 1988 Merlot Dry Creek Valley

84 1987 Merlot Dry Creek Valley

86 1993 Sauvignon Blanc Dry Creek Valley

MIRASSOU VINEYARDS

74 1991 Cabernet Sauvignon Monterey County Family Selection

81 1990 Cabernet Sauvignon Monterey County Family Selection

83 1986 Cabernet Sauvignon California Family Selection

79 1990 Cabernet Sauvignon Monterey County Harvest Reserve Limited Bottling

84 1993 Chardonnay Monterey County Family Selection

81 1991 Chardonnay Monterey County Family Selection

87 1993 Chardonnay Monterey County Harvest Reserve

87 1992 Chardonnay Monterey County Harvest Reserve

85 1991 Chardonnay Monterey County Harvest Reserve

85 1993 Chenin Blanc Monterey County Family Selection Dry

85 1992 Johannisberg Riesling Monterey County Select Late Harvest Reserve

84 1992 Merlot Central Coast Family Selection

80 1991 Merlot Central Coast Family Selection

80 1990 Merlot Monterey County Family Selection

81 1991 Petite Sirah Monterey County Family Selection

81 1993 Pinot Blanc Monterey County Family Selection White Burgundy

82 1993 Pinot Blanc Monterey County Harvest Reserve

86 1991 Pinot Blanc Monterey County Harvest Reserve

75 1990 Pinot Noir Monterey County Family Selection

83 1991 Pinot Noir Monterey County Harvest Selection Limited Bottling

85 1993 Sauvignon Blanc California

80 1992 Sauvignon Blanc California

83 1992 Zinfandel Central Coast Family Selection

79 1991 Zinfandel Santa Clara Valley Harvest Reserve

82 1990 Zinfandel Santa Clara Valley Harvest Reserve

MISSION VIEW VINEYARDS & WINERY

82 1990 Cabernet Sauvignon Paso Robles

84 1989 Cabernet Sauvignon Paso Robles

86 1988 Cabernet Sauvignon Paso Robles

77 1993 Chardonnay San Luis Obispo County

76 1992 Merlot Paso Robles

78 1993 Sauvignon Blanc San Luis Obispo County

ROBERT MONDAVI WINERY

91 1992 Cabernet Sauvignon Napa Valley

90 1991 Cabernet Sauvignon Napa Valley

90 1990 Cabernet Sauvignon Napa Valley

84 1989 Cabernet Sauvignon Napa Valley

83 1988 Cabernet Sauvignon Napa Valley

87 1987 Cabernet Sauvignon Napa Valley

90 1986 Cabernet Sauvignon Napa Valley

94 1985 Cabernet Sauvignon Napa Valley

79 1967 Cabernet Sauvignon Napa Valley

88 1966 Cabernet Sauvignon Napa Valley

91 1992 Cabernet Sauvignon Napa Valley Reserve

90 1991 Cabernet Sauvignon Napa Valley Reserve

91 1990 Cabernet Sauvignon Napa Valley Reserve

85 1989 Cabernet Sauvignon Napa Valley Reserve

85 1988 Cabernet Sauvignon Napa Valley Reserve

94 1987 Cabernet Sauvignon Napa Valley Reserve

92 1986 Cabernet Sauvignon Napa Valley Reserve

86 1985 Cabernet Sauvignon Napa Valley Reserve

90 1984 Cabernet Sauvignon Napa Valley Reserve

82 1983 Cabernet Sauvignon Napa Valley Reserve

82 1982 Cabernet Sauvignon Napa Valley Reserve

83 1981 Cabernet Sauvignon Napa Valley Reserve

80 1980 Cabernet Sauvignon Napa Valley Reserve

91 1979 Cabernet Sauvignon Napa Valley Reserve

91 1978 Cabernet Sauvignon Napa Valley Reserve

87 1977 Cabernet Sauvignon Napa Valley Reserve

84 1976 Cabernet Sauvignon Napa Valley Reserve

86 1975 Cabernet Sauvignon Napa Valley Reserve

87 1974 Cabernet Sauvignon Napa Valley Reserve

90 1973 Cabernet Sauvignon Napa Valley Reserve

78 1972 Cabernet Sauvignon Napa Valley Reserve

91 1971 Cabernet Sauvignon Napa Valley Reserve

92 1970 Cabernet Sauvignon Napa Valley Reserve

91 1969 Cabernet Sauvignon Napa Valley Reserve

88 1968 Cabernet Sauvignon Napa Valley Reserve

92 1992 Chardonnay Carneros

90 1991 Chardonnay Carneros

85 1993 Chardonnay Napa Valley Unfiltered

91 1992 Chardonnay Napa Valley

90 1991 Chardonnay Napa Valley

91 1993 Chardonnay Napa Valley Reserve

92 1992 Chardonnay Napa Valley Reserve

90 1991 Chardonnay Napa Valley Reserve

92 1990 Chardonnay Napa Valley Reserve

91 1988 Chardonnay Napa Valley Reserve

89 1986 Chardonnay Napa Valley Reserve

88 1985 Chardonnay Napa Valley Reserve

88 1993 Fumé Blanc Napa Valley

89 1992 Fumé Blanc Napa Valley

87 1991 Fumé Blanc Napa Valley

86 1993 Fumé Blanc Napa Valley To-Kalon Vineyard Reserve Unfiltered

89 1992 Fumé Blanc Napa Valley To-Kalon Vineyard Reserve

76 1991 Johannisberg Riesling Napa Valley

89 1991 Merlot Napa Valley

86 1990 Merlot Napa Valley

87 1989 Merlot Napa Valley

70 1991 Muscat Napa Valley Moscato d'Oro

86 1992 Pinot Noir Carneros

88 1991 Pinot Noir Carneros

84 1992 Pinot Noir Napa Valley

85 1991 Pinot Noir Napa Valley

86 1990 Pinot Noir Napa Valley

86 1989 Pinot Noir Napa Valley

89 1988 Pinot Noir Napa Valley

88 1987 Pinot Noir Napa Valley

85 1986 Pinot Noir Napa Valley

79 1985 Pinot Noir Napa Valley

87 1992 Pinot Noir Napa Valley Reserve Unfiltered

89 1991 Pinot Noir Napa Valley Reserve

92 1990 Pinot Noir Napa Valley Reserve

90 1989 Pinot Noir Napa Valley Reserve

91 1988 Pinot Noir Napa Valley Reserve

87 1987 Pinot Noir Napa Valley Reserve

91 1986 Pinot Noir Napa Valley Reserve

92 1985 Pinot Noir Napa Valley Reserve

84 1993 Zinfandel Napa Valley

86 1993 Zinfandel Napa Valley

92 1992 Zinfandel Napa Valley

87 1993 La Famiglia di Robert Mondavi Barbera California

85 1993 La Famiglia di Robert Mondavi Malvasia Bianca California

87 1993 La Famiglia di Robert Mondavi Sangiovese California

86 1993 La Famiglia di Robert Mondavi Tocai Fruliani California

82 1992 Robert Mondavi-Woodbridge Cabernet Sauvignon California

81 1993 Robert Mondavi-Woodbridge Chardonnay California

80 1992 Robert Mondavi-Woodbridge Chardonnay California

85 1993 Robert Mondavi-Woodbridge Sauvignon Blanc California

85 1992 Robert Mondavi-Woodbridge Sauvignon Blanc California

77 1992 Robert Mondavi-Woodbridge Zinfandel California

MONT ST. JOHN CELLARS

70 1987 Cabernet Sauvignon Napa Valley

82 1993 Chardonnay Carneros Madonna Vineyards

87 1992 Chardonnay Carneros Madonna Vineyards

85 1993 Chardonnay Carneros Organically Grown Grapes

85 1992 Chardonnay Carneros Organically Grown Grapes

85 1989 Pinot Noir Carneros

84 1991 Poppy Hill Merlot Napa Valley Founder's Selection

MONTE VOLPE

87 1991 Barbera Mendocino County

80 1991 Muscat Mendocino County

84 1993 Pinot Bianco Mendocino County

86 1992 Sangiovese Mendocino County

MONTEREY PENINSULA WINERY

78 1989 Barbera California Vineyard View Pleasant Hill

84 1986 Cabernet Sauvignon Monterey County

86 1986 Cabernet Sauvignon Monterey County Doctor's Reserve

83 1989 Chardonnay Monterey County Sleepy Hollow Vineyard

83 1992 Pinot Noir Monterey County Sleepy Hollow Vineyard

76 1989 Pinot Noir Monterey County Sleepy Hollow Vineyard

86 1987 Pinot Noir Monterey County Sleepy Hollow Vineyard

89 1989 White Riesling Monterey County Sleepy Hollow Vineyard Late Harvest

80 1991 Zinfandel Amador County Ferrero Ranch

80 1990 Zinfandel Amador County Ferrero Ranch

83 1987 Zinfandel Amador County Ferrero Ranch Doctor's Reserve

THE MONTEREY VINEYARD

84 1990 Cabernet Sauvignon Monterey County Limited Release

79 1993 Chardonnay Monterey County Classic

85 1993 Chardonnay Monterey County Limited Release

77 1992 Pinot Noir Monterey County Classic

MONTEVINA WINES

78 1993 Aleatico Amador County

82 1990 Barbera Amador County Reserve

89 1987 Barbera Amador County Reserve

80 1990 Cabernet Sauvignon California

78 1989 Cabernet Sauvignon California

84 1992 Red Table Wine Amador County Matrimonio

85 1992 Red Table Wine Amador County Montanaro

86 1992 Sangiovese Amador County

82 1990 Zinfandel Amador County

83 1993 Zinfandel Amador County Brioso

77 1991 Zinfandel Amador County Brioso

82 1991 Zinfandel Amador County Reserve

87 1989 Zinfandel Amador County Reserve

MONTICELLO CELLARS

85 1991 Cabernet Sauvignon Napa Valley Corley Reserve

85 1989 Cabernet Sauvignon Napa Valley Corley Reserve

87 1987 Cabernet Sauvignon Napa Valley Corley Reserve

88 1986 Cabernet Sauvignon Napa Valley Corley Reserve

88 1985 Cabernet Sauvignon Napa Valley Corley Reserve

89 1984 Cabernet Sauvignon Napa Valley Corley Reserve

86 1983 Cabernet Sauvignon Napa Valley Corley Reserve

88 1982 Cabernet Sauvignon Napa Valley Corley Reserve

86 1989 Cabernet Sauvignon Napa Valley Jefferson Cuvée

85 1988 Cabernet Sauvignon Napa Valley Jefferson Cuvée

90 1987 Cabernet Sauvignon Napa Valley Jefferson Cuvée

89 1986 Cabernet Sauvignon Napa Valley Jefferson Cuvée

87 1985 Cabernet Sauvignon Napa Valley Jefferson Cuvée

88 1984 Cabernet Sauvignon Napa Valley Jefferson Cuvée

83 1991 Chardonnay Napa Valley

94 1992 Chardonnay Napa Valley Corley Reserve

86 1991 Chardonnay Napa Valley Corley Reserve

86 1990 Merlot Napa Valley

88 1992 Pinot Noir Napa Valley Corley Family Vineyards

81 1991 Pinot Noir Napa Valley Corley Family Vineyards

86 1990 Pinot Noir Napa Valley Corley Family Vineyards

89 1988 Pinot Noir Napa Valley Corley Family Vineyards

85 1987 Pinot Noir Napa Valley Corley Family Vineyards

91 1986 Pinot Noir Napa Valley Corley Family Vineyards

91 1984 Pinot Noir Napa Valley Corley Family Vineyards

MONTPELLIER

70 1992 Chardonnay California

80 1992 Merlot California

82 1992 Sauvignon Blanc California

MOONDANCE CELLARS

82 1992 Cabernet Sauvignon Napa Valley

87 1992 Merlot Napa Valley

86 1990 Merlot Napa Valley

88 1992 Zinfandel Sonoma Valley

Z. MOORE WINERY

89 1991 Gewürztraminer Russian River Valley Barrel Fermented

82 1991 Gewürztraminer Russian River Valley McIlroy/Martinelli Barrel Fermented Puncheon Select

87 1990 Red Table Wine Mendocino County Danato

MORAGA

89 1991 Cabernet Sauvignon Bel Air

84 1990 Cabernet Sauvignon Bel Air

87 1989 Cabernet Sauvignon Bel Air

MORGAN WINERY

88 1991 Cabernet Sauvignon Carmel Valley

77 1990 Cabernet Sauvignon Carmel Valley

83 1989 Cabernet Sauvignon Carmel Valley

81 1988 Cabernet Sauvignon Carmel Valley

92 1987 Cabernet Sauvignon Carmel Valley

89 1986 Cabernet Sauvignon Carmel Valley

83 1993 Chardonnay Monterey County

85 1992 Chardonnay Monterey County

77 1991 Chardonnay Monterey County

88 1992 Chardonnay Monterey County Reserve

86 1991 Chardonnay Monterey County Reserve

83 1993 Pinot Noir California

85 1992 Pinot Noir California

81 1991 Pinot Noir California

89 1990 Pinot Noir California

85 1989 Pinot Noir California

75 1988 Pinot Noir California

81 1987 Pinot Noir California

84 1986 Pinot Noir California

87 1992 Pinot Noir Carneros Reserve

84 1991 Pinot Noir Carneros Reserve

89 1990 Pinot Noir Carneros Reserve

81 1991 Pinot Noir Monterey County

87 1992 Pinot Noir Monterey County Reserve

90 1990 Pinot Noir Monterey County Reserve

86 1994 Sauvignon Blanc Sonoma County

89 1992 Sauvignon Blanc Sonoma County

82 1993 Zinfandel Sonoma County

MOSBY WINERY

83 1991 Nebbiolo Santa Barbara County Rosso di Nebbiolo

79 1993 Sangiovese Santa Barbara County Vigna Della Casa Vecchia

MOSHIN VINEYARDS

83 1992 Pinot Noir Russian River Valley

81 1991 Pinot Noir Russian River Valley

86 1993 White Table Wine Russian River Valley Blanc de Noir Barrel Fermented

MOUNT EDEN VINEYARDS

83 1992 Cabernet Sauvignon Santa Cruz Mountains

86 1989 Cabernet Sauvignon Santa Cruz Mountains

86 1988 Cabernet Sauvignon Santa Cruz Mountains

65 1987 Cabernet Sauvignon Santa Cruz Mountains

85 1987 Cabernet Sauvignon Santa Cruz Mountains Young Vine Cuvée

85 1986 Cabernet Sauvignon Santa Cruz Mountains

86 1985 Cabernet Sauvignon Santa Cruz Mountains

84 1984 Cabernet Sauvignon Santa Cruz Mountains

77 1983 Cabernet Sauvignon Santa Cruz Mountains

70 1982 Cabernet Sauvignon Santa Cruz Mountains

85 1981 Cabernet Sauvignon Santa Cruz Mountains

85 1980 Cabernet Sauvignon Santa Cruz Mountains

69 1979 Cabernet Sauvignon Santa Cruz Mountains

86 1978 Cabernet Sauvignon Santa Cruz Mountains

91 1977 Cabernet Sauvignon Santa Cruz Mountains

83 1976 Cabernet Sauvignon Santa Cruz Mountains

92 1975 Cabernet Sauvignon Santa Cruz Mountains

88 1974 Cabernet Sauvignon Santa Cruz Mountains

91 1973 Cabernet Sauvignon Santa Cruz Mountains

82 1972 Cabernet Sauvignon Santa Cruz Mountains

88 1990 Cabernet Sauvignon Santa Cruz Mountains Lathweisen Ridge

84 1989 Cabernet Sauvignon Santa Cruz Mountains Lathweisen Ridge

87 1988 Cabernet Sauvignon Santa Cruz Mountains Lathweisen Ridge

88 1991 Cabernet Sauvignon Santa Cruz Mountains Old Vine Reserve

85 1990 Cabernet Sauvignon Santa Cruz Mountains Old Vine Reserve

90 1993 Chardonnay Edna Valley MacGregor Vineyard

89 1992 Chardonnay Edna Valley MacGregor Vineyard

85 1991 Chardonnay Edna Valley MacGregor Vineyard

89 1990 Chardonnay Santa Barbara County

88 1988 Chardonnay Santa Cruz Mountains
88 1987 Chardonnay Santa Cruz Mountains
88 1986 Chardonnay Santa Cruz Mountains
87 1985 Chardonnay Santa Cruz Mountains
84 1991 Pinot Noir Edna Valley
86 1990 Pinot Noir Santa Cruz Mountains
85 1989 Pinot Noir Santa Cruz Mountains
79 1987 Pinot Noir Santa Cruz Mountains
90 1985 Pinot Noir Santa Cruz Mountains
86 1984 Pinot Noir Santa Cruz Mountains

MOUNT KONOCTI WINERY

85 1992 Cabernet Franc Lake County Kelsey
83 1988 Cabernet Franc Lake County Kelsey
84 1992 Cabernet Sauvignon Lake County Kelsey
82 1990 Cabernet Sauvignon Lake County Kelsey
81 1989 Cabernet Sauvignon Lake County Kelsey
83 1986 Cabernet Sauvignon Lake County Kelsey
88 1985 Cabernet Sauvignon Lake County Kelsey
88 1992 Chardonnay California Grand Reserve
76 1992 Chardonnay California Kelsey
85 1994 Fumé Blanc Lake County
85 1993 Fumé Blanc Lake County
84 1992 Fumé Blanc Lake County
86 1992 Fumé Blanc Lake County Grand Reserve
84 1987 Meritage Red Clear Lake
85 1992 Merlot Lake County
83 1989 Merlot Lake County
82 1988 Merlot Lake County
73 1987 Merlot Lake County
83 1985 Merlot Lake County
82 1993 White Table Wine Lake County Sémillon-Chardonnay

MOUNT PALOMAR WINERY

74 1991 Cabernet Sauvignon Temecula
72 1992 Chardonnay Temecula
83 1993 Chardonnay Temecula Reserve
84 1992 Chardonnay Temecula Reserve
79 1993 Sauvignon Blanc Temecula
82 1993 Sauvignon Blanc Temecula Reserve
87 1993 Castelletto Cortese Temecula
73 1992 Castelletto Sangiovese Temecula
82 1991 Castelletto Sangiovese Temecula

MOUNT VEEDER WINERY

87 1986 Cabernet Sauvignon Mount Veeder Mount Veeder
85 1985 Cabernet Sauvignon Mount Veeder Mount Veeder
86 1984 Cabernet Sauvignon Mount Veeder Mount Veeder

83 1983 Cabernet Sauvignon Mount Veeder Mount Veeder
68 1982 Cabernet Sauvignon Mount Veeder Mount Veeder
75 1981 Cabernet Sauvignon Mount Veeder Mount Veeder
87 1980 Cabernet Sauvignon Mount Veeder Bernstein Vineyards
92 1979 Cabernet Sauvignon Mount Veeder Bernstein Vineyards
86 1978 Cabernet Sauvignon Mount Veeder Bernstein Vineyards
85 1977 Cabernet Sauvignon Mount Veeder Bernstein Vineyards
74 1976 Cabernet Sauvignon Mount Veeder Bernstein Vineyards
80 1975 Cabernet Sauvignon Mount Veeder Bernstein Vineyards
80 1974 Cabernet Sauvignon Mount Veeder Bernstein Vineyards
86 1991 Cabernet Sauvignon Napa Valley
94 1990 Cabernet Sauvignon Napa Valley
82 1989 Cabernet Sauvignon Napa Valley
85 1987 Cabernet Sauvignon Napa Valley
83 1986 Cabernet Sauvignon Napa Valley
83 1984 Cabernet Sauvignon Napa Valley
85 1974 Cabernet Sauvignon Napa Valley
88 1992 Chardonnay Napa Valley
76 1991 Chardonnay Napa Valley
84 1991 Meritage Red Napa Valley Reserve
92 1990 Meritage Red Napa Valley Reserve
86 1989 Meritage Red Napa Valley Reserve
83 1988 Meritage Red Napa Valley Reserve

ROBERT MUELLER CELLARS

90 1992 Chardonnay Russian River Valley LB Barrel Fermented
91 1991 Chardonnay Russian River Valley LB Barrel Fermented
82 1991 Foss Creek Cabernet Sauvignon Sonoma County
86 1992 Foss Creek Chardonnay Central Coast Barrel Fermented
81 1992 Foss Creek Chardonnay Sonoma County 85% Barrel Fermented

MUMM NAPA VALLEY

87 1989 Sparkling Wine Carneros Winery Lake Brut
87 NV Sparkling Wine Napa Valley Blanc de Blancs
84 NV Sparkling Wine Napa Valley Blanc de Noirs
88 NV Sparkling Wine Napa Valley Brut Prestige
87 NV Sparkling Wine Napa Valley Cuvée Napa Brut
87 1989 Sparkling Wine Napa Valley Cuvée Napa Brut Reserve

87 1987 Sparkling Wine Napa Valley Cuvée Napa Brut Reserve
90 1990 Sparkling Wine Napa Valley DVX

MURPHY-GOODE ESTATE WINERY

89 1992 Cabernet Sauvignon Alexander Valley
89 1987 Cabernet Sauvignon Alexander Valley
87 1992 Cabernet Sauvignon Alexander Valley Murphy Ranch
83 1991 Cabernet Sauvignon Alexander Valley Murphy Ranch
85 1990 Cabernet Sauvignon Alexander Valley Murphy Ranch
82 1989 Cabernet Sauvignon Alexander Valley Murphy Ranch
87 1988 Cabernet Sauvignon Alexander Valley Murphy Ranch
90 1986 Cabernet Sauvignon Alexander Valley Murphy Vineyard
86 1993 Chardonnay Alexander Valley
86 1992 Chardonnay Alexander Valley
92 1992 Chardonnay Alexander Valley Reserve
80 1991 Chardonnay Alexander Valley Murphy Ranch
92 1993 Chardonnay Russian River Valley J & K Murphy Vineyard
90 1993 Chardonnay Russian River Valley J & K Murphy Vineyard Reserve
87 1994 Fumé Blanc Alexander Valley
89 1993 Fumé Blanc Alexander Valley Reserve
88 1992 Fumé Blanc Alexander Valley Reserve
83 1992 Merlot Alexander Valley Murphy Ranch
83 1991 Merlot Alexander Valley Murphy Ranch
83 1990 Merlot Alexander Valley Murphy Ranch
82 1989 Merlot Alexander Valley Murphy Ranch
90 1986 Merlot Alexander Valley Premier Vineyard
88 1993 Pinot Blanc Alexander Valley Melon de Bourgogne Barrel Fermented
83 1992 Pinot Blanc Alexander Valley
83 1991 Pinot Blanc Alexander Melon de Bourgogne Barrel Fermented
86 1993 Sauvignon Blanc Alexander Valley Dry
80 1989 Goode-Ready Cabernet Sauvignon Alexander Valley The Second Cabernet

MURRIETA'S WELL

84 1991 Cabernet Blend Livermore Valley Vendimia
85 1990 Cabernet Blend Livermore Valley Vendimia
88 1992 Sauvignon Blend Livermore Valley Vendimia
88 1991 Zinfandel Livermore Valley
83 1989 Zinfandel Livermore Valley

NALLE WINERY

85 1990 Cabernet Sauvignon Dry Creek Valley
89 1987 Cabernet Sauvignon Dry Creek Valley

85	1992 Zinfandel Dry Creek Valley
86	1991 Zinfandel Dry Creek Valley
89	1990 Zinfandel Dry Creek Valley
85	1989 Zinfandel Dry Creek Valley
89	1988 Zinfandel Dry Creek Valley
92	1987 Zinfandel Dry Creek Valley
90	1986 Zinfandel Dry Creek Valley
88	1985 Zinfandel Dry Creek Valley

NAPA RIDGE

87	1992 Cabernet Sauvignon Central Coast
84	1991 Cabernet Sauvignon Central Coast Oak Barrel
85	1989 Cabernet Sauvignon Napa Valley Coastal Reserve
79	1992 Cabernet Sauvignon North Coast Coastal Oak Barrel
77	1991 Cabernet Sauvignon North Coast Coastal Oak Barrel
82	1990 Cabernet Sauvignon North Coast Reserve
79	1989 Cabernet Sauvignon North Coast Coastal
87	1989 Cabernet Sauvignon North Coast Coastal Reserve
83	1993 Chardonnay Central Coast Coastal Vines
86	1993 Chardonnay Central Coast Special Select
86	1993 Chardonnay Napa Valley Coastal Reserve
88	1993 Chardonnay Napa Valley Frilsinger Vineyard
78	1992 Chardonnay North Coast
86	1992 Chardonnay North Coast Coastal Reserve
87	1992 Merlot North Coast Coastal
84	1991 Merlot North Coast Coastal
84	1993 Pinot Noir North Coast Coastal
83	1991 Pinot Noir North Coast Coastal
81	1993 Sauvignon Blanc North Coast Coastal
79	1992 Sauvignon Blanc North Coast Coastal
76	1990 Zinfandel Central Coast Coastal

NAVARRO VINEYARDS

85	1993 Blush Anderson Valley Pinot Gris
82	1989 Cabernet Sauvignon Mendocino County
86	1988 Cabernet Sauvignon Mendocino County
88	1987 Cabernet Sauvignon Mendocino County
87	1986 Cabernet Sauvignon Mendocino County
87	1985 Cabernet Sauvignon Mendocino County
87	1992 Chardonnay Anderson Valley Premiere Reserve
91	1991 Chardonnay Anderson Valley Premiere Reserve
83	1993 Chardonnay Anderson Valley
86	1992 Chardonnay Anderson Valley
84	1993 Gewürztraminer Anderson Valley Dry
88	1992 Gewürztraminer Anderson Valley Dry
90	1991 Gewürztraminer North Coast Late Harvest Sweet

86	1991 Pinot Noir Anderson Valley Méthode l'Ancienne
86	1990 Pinot Noir Anderson Valley Méthode l'Ancienne
87	1989 Pinot Noir Anderson Valley Méthode l'Ancienne
89	1988 Pinot Noir Anderson Valley Méthode l'Ancienne
85	1987 Pinot Noir Anderson Valley Méthode l'Ancienne
85	1986 Pinot Noir Anderson Valley Méthode l'Ancienne
86	1985 Pinot Noir Anderson Valley Méthode l'Ancienne
87	1992 Pinot Noir Anderson Valley Clone 54
87	1989 Pinot Noir Anderson Valley Deep End Blend
83	1993 Red Table Wine Mendocino County Petits Villages
88	1993 Sauvignon Blanc Mendocino County Cuvée 128
88	1992 Sauvignon Blanc Mendocino County Cuvée 128
83	NV Sparkling Wine Anderson Valley Brut
83	1992 White Riesling Anderson Valley
84	1990 White Table Wine Mendocino County Edelzwicker
85	1992 Zinfandel Mendocino County
86	1991 Zinfandel Mendocino County

NELSON ESTATE

78	1990 Cabernet Franc Sonoma County
82	1987 Cabernet Franc Sonoma County

NEVADA CITY WINERY

81	1989 Cabernet Sauvignon Sierra Foothills
86	1993 Chardonnay Nevada County Barrel Fermented
83	1992 Chardonnay Nevada County Barrel Fermented
83	1989 Meritage Red Nevada County Claret The Director's Reserve
85	1991 Zinfandel Sierra Foothills

NEWLAN VINEYARDS AND WINERY

86	1990 Cabernet Sauvignon Napa Valley
84	1988 Cabernet Sauvignon Napa Valley
88	1987 Cabernet Sauvignon Napa Valley
88	1986 Cabernet Sauvignon Napa Valley
87	1985 Cabernet Sauvignon Napa Valley
83	1991 Chardonnay Napa Valley Reserve
88	1992 Johannisberg Riesling Napa Valley Late Harvest
89	1991 Johannisberg Riesling Napa Valley Late Harvest
83	1992 Pinot Noir Napa Valley
80	1991 Pinot Noir Napa Valley

87	1989 Pinot Noir Napa Valley
81	1988 Pinot Noir Napa Valley
81	1987 Pinot Noir Napa Valley
88	1985 Pinot Noir Napa Valley
83	1980 Pinot Noir Napa Valley
81	1991 Pinot Noir Napa Valley Napa-Villages
84	1991 Pinot Noir Napa Valley Reserve
79	1991 Pinot Noir Napa Valley School House Vieilles Vignes
87	1990 Pinot Noir Napa Valley Vieilles Vignes
85	1989 Pinot Noir Napa Valley Vieilles Vignes
86	1992 Zinfandel Napa Valley
89	1991 Zinfandel Napa Valley

NEWTON VINEYARD

84	1989 Cabernet Sauvignon Napa Valley
87	1988 Cabernet Sauvignon Napa Valley
87	1987 Cabernet Sauvignon Napa Valley
90	1986 Cabernet Sauvignon Napa Valley
89	1985 Cabernet Sauvignon Napa Valley
88	1984 Cabernet Sauvignon Napa Valley
85	1983 Cabernet Sauvignon Napa Valley
87	1992 Chardonnay Napa Valley
89	1991 Chardonnay Napa Valley
88	1992 Meritage Red Napa Valley Claret
87	1991 Meritage Red Napa Valley Claret
85	1990 Meritage Red Napa Valley Claret
87	1988 Meritage Red Napa Valley Claret
88	1989 Merlot Napa Valley
84	1987 Merlot Napa Valley
83	1986 Merlot Napa Valley
91	1985 Merlot Napa Valley

NEYERS

86	1993 Chardonnay Carneros
84	1992 Merlot Napa Valley

NICHELINI WINERY

81	1988 Cabernet Sauvignon Napa Valley
77	1989 Cabernet Sauvignon Napa Valley Joseph A. Nichelini Vineyards
82	1993 Sauvignon Blanc Napa Valley Joseph A. Nichelini Vineyards

NIEBAUM-COPPOLA ESTATE WINERY

81	1991 Cabernet Franc Napa Valley Francis Coppola Family Wines
84	1990 Cabernet Franc Napa Valley Francis Coppola Family Wines
93	1991 Meritage Red Napa Valley Rubicon
90	1990 Meritage Red Napa Valley Rubicon
87	1989 Meritage Red Napa Valley Rubicon
86	1988 Meritage Red Napa Valley Rubicon

88 1987 Meritage Red Napa Valley Rubicon
89 1986 Meritage Red Napa Valley Rubicon
88 1985 Meritage Red Napa Valley Rubicon
89 1984 Meritage Red Napa Valley Rubicon
87 1982 Meritage Red Napa Valley Rubicon
87 1981 Meritage Red Napa Valley Rubicon
87 1980 Meritage Red Napa Valley Rubicon
84 1979 Meritage Red Napa Valley Rubicon
87 1978 Meritage Red Napa Valley Rubicon
86 1991 Merlot Napa Valley Francis Coppola Family Wines
88 1992 Zinfandel Napa Valley Edizione Pennino
88 1991 Zinfandel Napa Valley Edizione Pennino
88 1990 Zinfandel Napa Valley Edizione Pennino
87 1989 Zinfandel Napa Valley Edizione Pennino
85 1989 Gustave Niebaum Cabernet Sauvignon Napa Valley Reference
87 1985 Gustave Niebaum Cabernet Sauvignon Napa Valley Reference
87 1987 Gustave Niebaum Cabernet Sauvignon Napa Valley Mast Vineyard
80 1988 Gustave Niebaum Cabernet Sauvignon Napa Valley Tench Vineyard
88 1986 Gustave Niebaum Cabernet Sauvignon Napa Valley Tench Vineyard
81 1991 Gustave Niebaum Chardonnay Napa Valley Reference
72 1989 Gustave Niebaum Merlot Napa Valley Reference

Norman Vineyard

87 1992 Cabernet Sauvignon Paso Robles
82 1992 Cabernet Sauvignon Paso Robles No Nonsense Red
90 1993 Zinfandel Paso Robles
88 1992 Zinfandel Paso Robles

Oakford Vineyards

88 1990 Cabernet Sauvignon Napa Valley
84 1989 Cabernet Sauvignon Napa Valley
87 1988 Cabernet Sauvignon Napa Valley
88 1987 Cabernet Sauvignon Napa Valley

Oakville Ranch Vineyards

90 1991 Cabernet Sauvignon Napa Valley
92 1991 Cabernet Sauvignon Napa Valley Reserve
93 1990 Cabernet Sauvignon Napa Valley
88 1989 Cabernet Sauvignon Napa Valley
91 1991 Cabernet Sauvignon Napa Valley Lewis Select
88 1992 Chardonnay Napa Valley ORV
88 1991 Chardonnay Napa Valley ORV
90 1993 Chardonnay Napa Valley Vista Vineyard
87 1992 Chardonnay Napa Valley Vista Vineyard
88 1991 Chardonnay Napa Valley Vista Vineyard

Obester Winery

85 1991 Chardonnay Mendocino County
83 1988 Chardonnay Mendocino County
78 1990 Chardonnay Mendocino County Barrel Fermented
71 1989 Chardonnay Mendocino County Barrel Fermented
84 1992 Gewürztraminer Anderson Valley
78 1992 Pinot Noir Anderson Valley
83 1993 Sangiovese Mendocino County
79 1992 Sangiovese Mendocino County
80 1993 Sauvignon Blanc Mendocino County
85 1992 Sauvignon Blanc Mendocino County
85 1991 Sauvignon Blanc Mendocino County
84 1991 Zinfandel Mendocino County

Octopus Mountain

82 1991 Cabernet Sauvignon Anderson Valley Dennison Vineyard
83 1989 Cabernet Sauvignon Anderson Valley Dennison Vineyard
84 1990 Chardonnay Anderson Valley Dennison Vineyard
85 1991 Pinot Noir Anderson Valley Dennison Vineyard
86 1989 Pinot Noir Anderson Valley Dennison Vineyard

The Ojai Vineyard

86 1993 Chardonnay Arroyo Grande Valley
88 1992 Chardonnay Arroyo Grande Valley Reserve
87 1991 Chardonnay Arroyo Grande Valley Reserve
88 1992 Chardonnay Santa Barbara County
84 1991 Chardonnay Santa Barbara County
87 1993 Chardonnay Santa Barbara County Reserve
86 1992 Chardonnay Santa Barbara County Reserve
86 1993 Pinot Noir Santa Barbara County
84 1992 Syrah California
87 1991 Syrah California

Optima

88 1991 Cabernet Sauvignon Alexander Valley
82 1990 Cabernet Sauvignon Alexander Valley
79 1989 Cabernet Sauvignon Alexander Valley
84 1988 Cabernet Sauvignon Alexander Valley
83 1987 Cabernet Sauvignon Alexander Valley
79 1986 Cabernet Sauvignon Alexander Valley
81 1985 Cabernet Sauvignon Alexander Valley
87 1984 Cabernet Sauvignon Alexander Valley
85 1992 Chardonnay Sonoma County
89 1991 Chardonnay Sonoma County

Opus One

93 1991 Cabernet Blend Napa Valley Opus One
94 1990 Cabernet Blend Napa Valley Opus One
89 1989 Cabernet Blend Napa Valley Opus One
90 1988 Cabernet Blend Napa Valley Opus One
98 1987 Cabernet Blend Napa Valley Opus One
96 1986 Cabernet Blend Napa Valley Opus One
94 1985 Cabernet Blend Napa Valley Opus One
92 1984 Cabernet Blend Napa Valley Opus One
88 1983 Cabernet Blend Napa Valley Opus One
88 1982 Cabernet Blend Napa Valley Opus One
88 1981 Cabernet Blend Napa Valley Opus One
89 1980 Cabernet Blend Napa Valley Opus One
88 1979 Cabernet Blend Napa Valley Opus One

Page Mill Winery

74 1989 Cabernet Sauvignon Napa Valley V. & L. Eisele Vineyard
84 1988 Cabernet Sauvignon Napa Valley V. & L. Eisele Vineyard
79 1992 Chardonnay California Cuvée Select
88 1991 Chardonnay Santa Barbara County Bien Nacido Vineyard
86 1992 Chardonnay Santa Clara County Elizabeth Garbett Vineyard
86 1991 Pinot Noir Santa Barbara County Bien Nacido Vineyard
84 1990 Pinot Noir Santa Barbara County Bien Nacido Vineyard

Pahlmeyer

88 1992 Cabernet Blend Napa Valley
84 1991 Cabernet Blend Napa Valley
90 1990 Cabernet Blend Napa Valley
82 1990 Cabernet Blend Napa Valley Minty Cuvée
88 1989 Cabernet Blend Napa Valley
90 1988 Cabernet Blend Napa Valley
91 1987 Cabernet Blend Napa Valley
89 1986 Cabernet Blend Napa Valley
89 1993 Chardonnay Napa Valley
86 1992 Chardonnay Napa Valley
90 1991 Chardonnay Napa Valley
83 1991 Merlot Napa Valley Caldwell Vineyard
85 1990 Merlot Napa Valley Caldwell Vineyard

Paradigm

90 1991 Cabernet Sauvignon Napa Valley

Paraiso Springs Vineyards

84 1991 Chardonnay Monterey County Barrel Fermented
86 1993 Chardonnay Santa Lucia Highlands Barrel Fermented

84   1993 Gewürztraminer Santa Lucia Highlands

85   1993 Johannisberg Riesling Santa Lucia Highlands Late Harvest Hand Selected

82   1991 Pinot Blanc Monterey County

77   1991 Pinot Noir Carneros

Parducci Wine Cellars

85   1989 Cabernet Franc Mendocino County

84   1991 Cabernet Sauvignon Mendocino County

84   1989 Cabernet Sauvignon Mendocino County

81   1993 Chardonnay Mendocino County

81   1991 Chardonnay Mendocino County

85   1992 Merlot North Coast

82   1990 Merlot North Coast

84   1991 Petite Sirah Mendocino County

80   1989 Petite Sirah Mendocino County

83   1992 Pinot Noir Mendocino County

85   1990 Pinot Noir Mendocino County

85   1988 Pinot Noir Mendocino County

84   1987 Pinot Noir Mendocino County Cellarmaster Selection

82   1990 Red Table Wine Mendocino County Bono-Sirah

79   1993 Sauvignon Blanc North Coast

82   1990 Sauvignon Blanc North Coast

82   1992 Zinfandel Mendocino County

82   1991 Zinfandel Mendocino County

83   1990 Zinfandel Mendocino County

Fess Parker Winery

87   1993 Chardonnay Santa Barbara County

85   1992 Chardonnay Santa Barbara County

88   1993 Chardonnay Santa Barbara County American Tradition Reserve

88   1992 Chardonnay Santa Barbara County American Tradition Reserve

84   1993 Johannisberg Riesling Santa Barbara County

86   1993 Pinot Noir Santa Barbara County

85   1992 Syrah Santa Barbara County

Patz & Hall Wine Co.

91   1993 Chardonnay Napa Valley

91   1992 Chardonnay Napa Valley

92   1991 Chardonnay Napa Valley

Peachy Canyon Winery

87   1992 Cabernet Sauvignon Central Coast

90   1991 Cabernet Sauvignon Central Coast

85   1990 Cabernet Sauvignon Central Coast

91   1992 Merlot Paso Robles

80   1989 Zinfandel Paso Robles

85   1992 Zinfandel Paso Robles Dusi Ranch

85   1991 Zinfandel Paso Robles Especial

90   1990 Zinfandel Paso Robles Especial

89   1989 Zinfandel Paso Robles Especial Reserve

88   1992 Zinfandel Paso Robles Westside

84   1991 Zinfandel Paso Robles Westside

91   1990 Zinfandel Paso Robles Westside

Robert Pecota Winery

83   1982 Cabernet Sauvignon Napa Valley

90   1991 Cabernet Sauvignon Napa Valley Kara's Vineyard

85   1990 Cabernet Sauvignon Napa Valley Kara's Vineyard

78   1989 Cabernet Sauvignon Napa Valley Kara's Vineyard

89   1988 Cabernet Sauvignon Napa Valley Kara's Vineyard

90   1987 Cabernet Sauvignon Napa Valley Kara's Vineyard

87   1986 Cabernet Sauvignon Napa Valley Kara's Vineyard

85   1985 Cabernet Sauvignon Napa Valley Kara's Vineyard

85   1984 Cabernet Sauvignon Napa Valley Kara's Vineyard

87   1992 Merlot Napa Valley Steven Andre Vineyard

89   1991 Merlot Napa Valley Steven Andre Vineyard

88   1990 Merlot Napa Valley Steven Andre Vineyard

86   1989 Merlot Napa Valley Steven Andre Vineyard

84   1992 Muscat Napa Valley Muscato di Andrea

83   1991 Muscat Napa Valley Muscato di Andrea

85   1987 Muscat Napa Valley Muscato di Andrea

81   1990 Muscat Napa Valley Sweet Andrea Select

85   1994 Sauvignon Blanc Napa Valley

87   1993 Sauvignon Blanc Napa Valley

J. Pedroncelli Winery

75   1991 Cabernet Sauvignon Dry Creek Valley

73   1990 Cabernet Sauvignon Dry Creek Valley

78   1988 Cabernet Sauvignon Dry Creek Valley Reserve

78   1986 Cabernet Sauvignon Dry Creek Valley Reserve

80   1993 Chardonnay Dry Creek Valley

79   1992 Chardonnay Dry Creek Valley

77   1992 Fumé Blanc Dry Creek Valley

83   1990 Merlot Dry Creek Valley

74   1989 Merlot Dry Creek Valley

79   1992 Pinot Noir Dry Creek Valley

82   1991 Pinot Noir Dry Creek Valley

75   1991 Red Table Wine Sonoma County Primitivo Misto

85   1990 Zinfandel Dry Creek Valley

77   1989 Zinfandel Dry Creek Valley

84   1988 Zinfandel Dry Creek Valley

65   1987 Zinfandel Dry Creek Valley

Peju Province Winery

85   1991 Cabernet Sauvignon Napa Valley

85   1989 Cabernet Sauvignon Napa Valley

86   1991 Cabernet Sauvignon Napa Valley HB Vineyard

88   1990 Cabernet Sauvignon Napa Valley HB Vineyard

83   1989 Cabernet Sauvignon Napa Valley HB Vineyard

80   1988 Cabernet Sauvignon Napa Valley HB Vineyard

87   1988 Cabernet Sauvignon Napa Valley HB Vineyard Special Selection

87   1987 Cabernet Sauvignon Napa Valley HB Vineyard

89   1986 Cabernet Sauvignon Napa Valley HB Vineyard

86   1993 Chardonnay Napa Valley

84   1992 Chardonnay Napa Valley

75   1991 Chardonnay Napa Valley

88   1993 Chardonnay Napa Valley HB Vineyard

83   1992 Chardonnay Napa Valley HB Vineyard

82   1991 Chardonnay Napa Valley HB Vineyard

87   1992 Meritage Red Napa Valley

87   1992 Sauvignon Blanc Napa Valley Late Harvest Special Select

Pellegrini Family Winery

81   1993 Barbera Sonoma Valley Old Vines

81   1993 Zinfandel Sonoma County Old Vines

83   1991 Cloverdale Ranch Cabernet Sauvignon Alexander Valley Estate Cuvée

84   1989 Cloverdale Ranch Cabernet Sauvignon Alexander Valley Estate Cuvée

82   1988 Cloverdale Ranch Cabernet Sauvignon Alexander Valley Estate Cuvée

83   1990 Cotes de Sonoma Cabernet Sauvignon Sonoma County

83   1989 Cotes de Sonoma Cabernet Sauvignon Sonoma County

84   1993 Cotes de Sonoma Chardonnay Sonoma County

86   1992 Cotes de Sonoma Chardonnay Sonoma County

73   1990 Cotes de Sonoma Red Table Wine Sonoma County Deux Cépages

83   1994 Cotes de Sonoma Sauvignon Blanc Sonoma County

85   1993 Cotes de Sonoma Sauvignon Blanc Sonoma County

84   1992 Olivet Lane Estate Chardonnay Russian River Valley

84   1992 Olivet Lane Estate Pinot Noir Russian River Valley

84   1991 Olivet Lane Estate Pinot Noir Russian River Valley

85 1988 Olivet Lane Estate Pinot Noir Russian River Valley

ROBERT PEPI WINERY

85 1989 Cabernet Sauvignon Napa Valley Vine Hill Ranch

87 1988 Cabernet Sauvignon Napa Valley Vine Hill Ranch

88 1987 Cabernet Sauvignon Napa Valley Vine Hill Ranch

88 1986 Cabernet Sauvignon Napa Valley Vine Hill Ranch

86 1985 Cabernet Sauvignon Napa Valley Vine Hill Ranch

87 1984 Cabernet Sauvignon Napa Valley Vine Hill Ranch

85 1992 Chardonnay Napa Valley Puncheon Fermented

88 1991 Chardonnay Napa Valley Puncheon Fermented

83 1991 Sangiovese Napa Valley Colline di Sassi

75 1990 Sangiovese Napa Valley Colline di Sassi

83 1989 Sangiovese Napa Valley Colline di Sassi

88 1993 Sauvignon Blanc Napa Valley Reserve Selection

84 1992 Sauvignon Blanc Napa Valley Reserve Selection

84 1994 Sauvignon Blanc Napa Valley Two-Heart Canopy

86 1993 Sauvignon Blanc Napa Valley Two-Heart Canopy

PEPPERWOOD SPRINGS VINEYARDS

79 1991 Pinot Noir Anderson Valley

74 1991 Pinot Noir Mendocino County Vidmar Vineyard

MARIO PERELLI-MINETTI WINERY

88 1990 Cabernet Sauvignon Napa Valley

86 1988 Cabernet Sauvignon Napa Valley

83 1987 Cabernet Sauvignon Napa Valley

PETERSON WINERY

83 1992 Cabernet Sauvignon Dry Creek Valley

84 1993 Chardonnay Anderson Valley

84 1993 Zinfandel Dry Creek Valley

JOSEPH PHELPS VINEYARDS

90 1991 Cabernet Blend Napa Valley Insignia

88 1990 Cabernet Blend Napa Valley Insignia

87 1989 Cabernet Blend Napa Valley Insignia

86 1988 Cabernet Blend Napa Valley Insignia

95 1986 Cabernet Blend Napa Valley Insignia

96 1985 Cabernet Blend Napa Valley Insignia

89 1984 Cabernet Blend Napa Valley Insignia

89 1983 Cabernet Blend Napa Valley Insignia

85 1982 Cabernet Blend Napa Valley Insignia

92 1981 Cabernet Blend Napa Valley Insignia

90 1980 Cabernet Blend Napa Valley Insignia

90 1979 Cabernet Blend Napa Valley Insignia

92 1978 Cabernet Blend Napa Valley Insignia

91 1977 Cabernet Blend Napa Valley Insignia

93 1976 Cabernet Blend Napa Valley Insignia

85 1975 Cabernet Blend Napa Valley Insignia

88 1974 Cabernet Blend Napa Valley Insignia

87 1992 Cabernet Sauvignon Napa Valley

90 1991 Cabernet Sauvignon Napa Valley

85 1990 Cabernet Sauvignon Napa Valley

78 1989 Cabernet Sauvignon Napa Valley

85 1988 Cabernet Sauvignon Napa Valley

75 1987 Cabernet Sauvignon Napa Valley

84 1985 Cabernet Sauvignon Napa Valley

89 1984 Cabernet Sauvignon Napa Valley

90 1991 Cabernet Sauvignon Napa Valley Backus Vineyard

88 1989 Cabernet Sauvignon Napa Valley Backus Vineyard

88 1987 Cabernet Sauvignon Napa Valley Backus Vineyard

89 1986 Cabernet Sauvignon Napa Valley Backus Vineyard

90 1985 Cabernet Sauvignon Napa Valley Backus Vineyard

86 1984 Cabernet Sauvignon Napa Valley Backus Vineyard

85 1983 Cabernet Sauvignon Napa Valley Backus Vineyard

91 1981 Cabernet Sauvignon Napa Valley Backus Vineyard

89 1978 Cabernet Sauvignon Napa Valley Backus Vineyard

86 1977 Cabernet Sauvignon Napa Valley Backus Vineyard

89 1991 Cabernet Sauvignon Napa Valley Eisele Vineyard

87 1989 Cabernet Sauvignon Napa Valley Eisele Vineyard

88 1987 Cabernet Sauvignon Napa Valley Eisele Vineyard

77 1986 Cabernet Sauvignon Napa Valley Eisele Vineyard

94 1985 Cabernet Sauvignon Napa Valley Eisele Vineyard

87 1984 Cabernet Sauvignon Napa Valley Eisele Vineyard

86 1983 Cabernet Sauvignon Napa Valley Eisele Vineyard

84 1982 Cabernet Sauvignon Napa Valley Eisele Vineyard

93 1981 Cabernet Sauvignon Napa Valley Eisele Vineyard

92 1979 Cabernet Sauvignon Napa Valley Eisele Vineyard

97 1978 Cabernet Sauvignon Napa Valley Eisele Vineyard

85 1977 Cabernet Sauvignon Napa Valley Eisele Vineyard

97 1975 Cabernet Sauvignon Napa Valley Eisele Vineyard

89 1992 Chardonnay Carneros

86 1991 Chardonnay Napa Valley

82 1992 Gewürztraminer California

87 1993 Grenache California Vin du Mistral Rosé

87 1992 Grenache California Vin du Mistral Rosé

87 1990 Grenache California Vin du Mistral Rosé

77 1990 Johannisberg Riesling Napa Valley

83 1991 Merlot Napa Valley

83 1990 Merlot Napa Valley

88 1989 Merlot Napa Valley

80 1987 Merlot Napa Valley

85 1992 Rhône Blend California Vin du Mistral Le Mistral

84 1991 Rhône Blend California Vin du Mistral Le Mistral

85 1990 Rhône Blend California Vin du Mistral Le Mistral

85 1989 Rhône Blend California Vin du Mistral Le Mistral

85 1992 Sauvignon Blanc Napa Valley

88 1989 Scheurebe Napa Valley Special Select

81 1990 Sémillon Napa Valley Delice du Sémillon

88 1991 Syrah Napa Valley Vin du Mistral

84 1990 Syrah Napa Valley Vin du Mistral

84 1989 Syrah Napa Valley Vin du Mistral

87 1988 Syrah Napa Valley Vin du Mistral

81 1987 Syrah Napa Valley Vin du Mistral

88 1986 Syrah Napa Valley Vin du Mistral

90 1992 Viognier Napa Valley Vin du Mistral

88 1990 Zinfandel Alexander Valley

82 1989 Zinfandel Alexander Valley

R. H. PHILLIPS VINEYARD

82 1991 Cabernet Sauvignon California

83 1994 Chardonnay Dunnigan Hills Barrel Cuvée

85 1993 Chardonnay California Barrel Cuvée

83 1992 Chardonnay California Barrel Cuvée

83 1990 Mourvèdre California EXP

88 1989 Rhône Blend California Alliance

84 1992 Sauvignon Blanc California Night Harvest

86 1989 Syrah California EXP

91 1988 Syrah California EXP

80 1987 Syrah California Reserve

86 1993 Viognier Dunnigan Hills EXP
79 1992 Viognier California EXP

PINE RIDGE WINERY

82 1988 Cabernet Sauvignon Diamond Mountain
80 1987 Cabernet Sauvignon Diamond Mountain
84 1986 Cabernet Sauvignon Diamond Mountain
85 1991 Cabernet Sauvignon Napa Valley Andrus Reserve
82 1988 Cabernet Sauvignon Napa Valley Andrus Reserve
79 1986 Cabernet Sauvignon Napa Valley Andrus Reserve
83 1985 Cabernet Sauvignon Napa Valley Andrus Reserve Cuvée Duet
82 1984 Cabernet Sauvignon Napa Valley Andrus Reserve
88 1983 Cabernet Sauvignon Napa Valley Andrus Reserve
85 1980 Cabernet Sauvignon Napa Valley Andrus Reserve
84 1991 Cabernet Sauvignon Napa Valley Rutherford Cuvée
82 1990 Cabernet Sauvignon Napa Valley Rutherford Cuvée
77 1987 Cabernet Sauvignon Napa Valley Rutherford Cuvée
84 1986 Cabernet Sauvignon Napa Valley Rutherford Cuvée
87 1985 Cabernet Sauvignon Napa Valley Rutherford Cuvée
87 1992 Cabernet Sauvignon Stags Leap District
89 1991 Cabernet Sauvignon Stags Leap District
78 1990 Cabernet Sauvignon Stags Leap District
83 1987 Cabernet Sauvignon Stags Leap District
86 1992 Chardonnay Napa Valley Knollside Cuvée
89 1993 Chardonnay Stags Leap District
89 1992 Chardonnay Stags Leap District Vieille Vigne
85 1992 Merlot Carneros
83 1991 Merlot Napa Valley Selected Cuvée
73 1989 Merlot Napa Valley Selected Cuvée
80 1988 Merlot Napa Valley Selected Cuvée
88 1987 Merlot Napa Valley Selected Cuvée
80 1986 Merlot Napa Valley Selected Cuvée
87 1993 La Petite Vigne Chenin Blanc Napa Valley

PIPER SONOMA CELLARS

87 NV Sparkling Wine Sonoma County Blanc de Noirs
88 1989 Sparkling Wine Sonoma County Brut Select Cuvée
87 NV Sparkling Wine Sonoma County Brut Select Cuvée

86 1985 Sparkling Wine Sonoma County Tête de Cuvée
77 1992 Bearboat Pinot Noir Russian River Valley

PLAM VINEYARDS & WINERY

82 1992 Cabernet Sauvignon California
88 1992 Cabernet Sauvignon Napa Valley
79 1988 Cabernet Sauvignon Napa Valley
87 1986 Cabernet Sauvignon Napa Valley
86 1985 Cabernet Sauvignon Napa Valley

BERNARD PRADEL CELLARS

85 1990 Cabernet Sauvignon Napa Valley Limited Barrel Selection
81 1989 Cabernet Sauvignon Napa Valley Limited Barrel Selection
80 1988 Cabernet Sauvignon Napa Valley Limited Barrel Selection
84 1987 Cabernet Sauvignon Napa Valley Limited Barrel Selection
82 1986 Cabernet Sauvignon Napa Valley Limited Barrel Selection
86 1985 Cabernet Sauvignon Napa Valley Limited Barrel Selection
86 1984 Cabernet Sauvignon Napa Valley Limited Barrel Selection
85 1992 Cabernet Sauvignon Napa Valley Howell Mountain Ranch
87 1991 Cabernet Sauvignon Napa Valley Howell Mountain Ranch

PRESTON VINEYARDS

88 1992 Barbera Dry Creek Valley
82 1990 Barbera Dry Creek Valley
86 1989 Barbera Dry Creek Valley
87 1990 Cabernet Sauvignon Dry Creek Valley
81 1989 Cabernet Sauvignon Dry Creek Valley
80 1988 Cabernet Sauvignon Dry Creek Valley
88 1987 Cabernet Sauvignon Dry Creek Valley
87 1986 Cabernet Sauvignon Dry Creek Valley
87 1985 Cabernet Sauvignon Dry Creek Valley
86 1984 Cabernet Sauvignon Dry Creek Valley
86 1992 Chenin Blanc Dry Creek Valley Barrel Aged
87 1994 Gamay Beaujolais Dry Creek Valley
87 1994 Marsanne Dry Creek Valley Organically Grown Grapes
83 1993 Marsanne Dry Creek Valley Organically Grown Grapes
88 1992 Marsanne Dry Creek Valley Organically Grown Grapes
88 1991 Marsanne Dry Creek Valley Organically Grown Grapes
85 1993 Rhône Blend Dry Creek Valley Faux
83 1992 Rhône Blend Dry Creek Valley Faux

85 1991 Rhône Blend Dry Creek Valley Faux
82 1990 Rhône Blend Dry Creek Valley Faux
78 1989 Rhône Blend Dry Creek Valley Sirah-Syrah
90 1986 Rhône Blend Dry Creek Valley Sirah-Syrah
86 1993 Sauvignon Blanc Dry Creek Valley Cuvée de Fumé
83 1993 Sauvignon Blanc Dry Creek Valley Organically Grown Grapes
84 1992 Sauvignon Blanc Dry Creek Valley Cuvée de Fumé
88 1992 Syrah Dry Creek Valley
87 1991 Syrah Dry Creek Valley
85 1990 Syrah Dry Creek Valley
85 1994 Viognier Dry Creek Valley
82 1993 Viognier Dry Creek Valley
88 1993 Zinfandel Dry Creek Valley Old Vines Old Clones
89 1992 Zinfandel Dry Creek Valley
86 1991 Zinfandel Dry Creek Valley
87 1990 Zinfandel Dry Creek Valley
84 1989 Zinfandel Dry Creek Valley
86 1988 Zinfandel Dry Creek Valley
83 1987 Zinfandel Dry Creek Valley

PRIDE MOUNTAIN VINEYARDS

83 1992 Cabernet Franc Napa Valley
92 1991 Cabernet Sauvignon Napa Valley
87 1993 Chardonnay Napa Valley Mountain Vineyards
88 1992 Chardonnay Napa Valley Mountain Vineyards
85 1991 Chardonnay Napa Valley Mountain Vineyards
85 1992 Merlot Napa Valley
88 1991 Merlot Napa Valley

QUADY WINERY

87 1993 Black Muscat California Elysium
82 1992 Black Muscat California Elysium
86 1990 Black Muscat California Elysium
83 1993 Orange Muscat California Electra
86 1992 Orange Muscat California Electra
84 1993 Orange Muscat California Essensia
73 1985 Orange Muscat California Essensia
87 1988 Port Amador County Starboard Batch 88 Rich Ruby
81 1987 Port Amador County Starboard
87 1989 Port Amador County Frank's Vineyard Starboard
81 1991 Port California LBV

QUAIL RIDGE CELLARS

85 1990 Cabernet Sauvignon Napa Valley
82 1989 Cabernet Sauvignon Napa Valley
80 1988 Cabernet Sauvignon Napa Valley
90 1987 Cabernet Sauvignon Napa Valley

87 1987 Cabernet Sauvignon Napa Valley Reserve

89 1986 Cabernet Sauvignon Napa Valley

80 1985 Cabernet Sauvignon Napa Valley

88 1984 Cabernet Sauvignon Napa Valley

84 1991 Chardonnay Napa Valley

81 1990 Merlot Napa Valley

79 1989 Merlot Napa Valley

82 1988 Merlot Napa Valley

86 1987 Merlot Napa Valley

88 1985 Merlot Napa Valley

85 1992 Sauvignon Blanc Napa Valley

QUIVIRA VINEYARDS

82 1991 Cabernet Blend Dry Creek Valley Cabernet Cuvée

87 1990 Cabernet Blend Dry Creek Valley Cabernet Cuvée

86 1989 Cabernet Blend Dry Creek Valley Cabernet Cuvée

84 1988 Cabernet Blend Dry Creek Valley Cabernet Cuvée

87 1987 Cabernet Blend Dry Creek Valley Cabernet Cuvée

84 1993 Rhône Blend Dry Creek Valley Dry Creek Cuvée

85 1992 Rhône Blend Dry Creek Valley Dry Creek Cuvée

85 1993 Sauvignon Blanc Dry Creek Valley

89 1992 Sauvignon Blanc Dry Creek Valley

84 1993 Sauvignon Blanc Dry Creek Valley Reserve

84 1992 Sauvignon Blanc Dry Creek Valley Reserve

89 1992 Zinfandel Dry Creek Valley

90 1991 Zinfandel Dry Creek Valley

90 1990 Zinfandel Dry Creek Valley

84 1989 Zinfandel Dry Creek Valley

88 1988 Zinfandel Dry Creek Valley

88 1987 Zinfandel Dry Creek Valley

88 1986 Zinfandel Dry Creek Valley

88 1984 Zinfandel Dry Creek Valley

QUPE CELLARS

90 1993 Chardonnay Santa Barbara County Sierra Madre Vineyard

88 1993 Chardonnay Santa Barbara County Sierra Madre Vineyard Reserve

91 1991 Marsanne Santa Barbara County Los Olivos Vineyard

85 1989 Rhône Blend Santa Barbara County Los Olivos Cuvée

90 1991 Syrah Central Coast

87 1989 Syrah Central Coast

90 1988 Syrah Central Coast

88 1987 Syrah Central Coast

92 1990 Syrah Santa Barbara County Bien Nacido Vineyard

89 1989 Syrah Santa Barbara County Bien Nacido Vineyard

83 1987 Syrah Santa Barbara County Bien Nacido Vineyard

RABBIT RIDGE VINEYARDS

86 1990 Cabernet Sauvignon Sonoma County Rabbit Ridge Ranch

77 1989 Cabernet Sauvignon Sonoma County Rabbit Ridge Ranch

89 1988 Cabernet Sauvignon Sonoma County Rabbit Ridge Ranch

88 1993 Chardonnay Russian River Valley Rabbit Ridge Ranch Reserve

89 1991 Chardonnay Russian River Valley Rabbit Ridge Ranch Reserve

80 1992 Chardonnay Sonoma County

84 1991 Chardonnay Sonoma County

86 1992 Merlot Carneros Sangiacomo Vineyard

80 1990 Petite Sirah Sonoma County

78 1990 Red Table Wine California Oddux Reserve Red

82 1991 Rhône Blend California Allure

83 1990 Rhône Blend California Allure

81 1989 Rhône Blend California Allure

84 1992 Sangiovese Dry Creek Valley Coniglio Selezione

85 1993 White Table Wine North Coast Mystique

90 1991 Zinfandel Sonoma County San Lorenzo Vineyard Reserve

85 1993 Zinfandel Dry Creek Valley

80 1992 Zinfandel Dry Creek Valley

87 1991 Zinfandel Dry Creek Valley

73 1990 Zinfandel Dry Creek Valley

86 1988 Zinfandel Russian River Valley Rabbit Ridge Ranch

86 1989 Zinfandel Sonoma County

RADANOVICH VINEYARDS & WINERY

77 1989 Cabernet Sauvignon Sierra Foothills Mariposa County

82 1991 Merlot Sierra Foothills

72 1989 Zinfandel Sierra Foothills Mariposa County

A. RAFANELLI WINERY

91 1991 Cabernet Sauvignon Dry Creek Valley

90 1990 Cabernet Sauvignon Dry Creek Valley

90 1988 Cabernet Sauvignon Dry Creek Valley

91 1987 Cabernet Sauvignon Dry Creek Valley

91 1986 Cabernet Sauvignon Dry Creek Valley

78 1985 Cabernet Sauvignon Dry Creek Valley

89 1992 Zinfandel Dry Creek Valley

89 1991 Zinfandel Dry Creek Valley

90 1990 Zinfandel Dry Creek Valley

85 1989 Zinfandel Dry Creek Valley

90 1988 Zinfandel Dry Creek Valley

84 1987 Zinfandel Dry Creek Valley

91 1986 Zinfandel Dry Creek Valley

RANCHO SISQUOC WINERY

88 1990 Cabernet Blend Santa Maria Valley Red Cellar Select

87 1989 Cabernet Blend Santa Maria Valley Red Cellar Select

84 1991 Cabernet Sauvignon Santa Maria Valley

76 1990 Cabernet Sauvignon Santa Maria Valley

85 1989 Cabernet Sauvignon Santa Maria Valley

73 1986 Cabernet Sauvignon Santa Maria Valley

81 1992 Chardonnay Santa Maria Valley

85 1991 Chardonnay Santa Maria Valley

80 1991 Merlot Santa Maria Valley

81 1992 Sauvignon Blanc Santa Maria Valley

KENT RASMUSSEN WINERY

83 1988 Cabernet Sauvignon Napa Valley

87 1992 Chardonnay Napa Valley

90 1991 Chardonnay Napa Valley

87 1992 Pinot Noir Carneros

88 1991 Pinot Noir Carneros

86 1990 Pinot Noir Carneros

84 1988 Pinot Noir Carneros

87 1992 Ramsay Merlot Napa Valley

88 1991 Ramsay Merlot Napa Valley

86 1989 Ramsay Merlot Napa Valley

82 1992 Ramsay Pinot Noir Carneros

81 1991 Ramsay Pinot Noir Carneros

82 1992 Ramsay Sangiovese California

RAVENSWOOD

84 1992 Cabernet Blend Sonoma County Mountain Claret

86 1992 Cabernet Blend Sonoma Mountain Pickberry Vineyard

83 1991 Cabernet Blend Sonoma Mountain Pickberry Vineyard

86 1990 Cabernet Blend Sonoma Mountain Pickberry Vineyard

89 1989 Cabernet Blend Sonoma Mountain Pickberry Vineyard

82 1988 Cabernet Blend Sonoma Mountain Pickberry Vineyard

87 1986 Cabernet Blend Sonoma Mountain Pickberry Vineyard

86 1992 Cabernet Sauvignon Sonoma County

84 1991 Cabernet Sauvignon Sonoma County

84 1989 Cabernet Sauvignon Sonoma County

89   1988 Cabernet Sauvignon Sonoma County

84   1987 Cabernet Sauvignon Sonoma County

86   1986 Cabernet Sauvignon Sonoma County

85   1985 Cabernet Sauvignon Sonoma County

84   1990 Cabernet Sauvignon Sonoma Valley Gregory Vineyard

85   1989 Cabernet Sauvignon Sonoma Valley Gregory Vineyard

80   1988 Cabernet Sauvignon Sonoma Valley Gregory Vineyard

84   1993 Chardonnay North Coast Vintners Blend

71   1991 Chardonnay Sonoma Valley

86   1992 Merlot Carneros Sangiacomo Vineyard

88   1990 Merlot Carneros Sangiacomo Vineyard

90   1989 Merlot Carneros Sangiacomo Vineyard

84   1992 Merlot North Coast Vintners Blend

85   1992 Merlot Sonoma County

85   1990 Merlot Sonoma County

86   1989 Merlot Sonoma County

87   1987 Merlot Sonoma County

80   1986 Merlot Sonoma County

91   1992 Zinfandel Napa Valley Dickerson Vineyard

87   1991 Zinfandel Napa Valley Dickerson Vineyard

92   1990 Zinfandel Napa Valley Dickerson Vineyard

87   1989 Zinfandel Napa Valley Dickerson Vineyard

84   1988 Zinfandel Napa Valley Dickerson Vineyard

86   1987 Zinfandel Napa Valley Dickerson Vineyard

88   1986 Zinfandel Napa Valley Dickerson Vineyard

87   1983 Zinfandel Napa Valley Dickerson Vineyard

85   1981 Zinfandel Napa Valley Dickerson Vineyard

83   1992 Zinfandel North Coast Vintners Blend

91   1992 Zinfandel Sonoma County

89   1990 Zinfandel Sonoma County

82   1989 Zinfandel Sonoma County

86   1988 Zinfandel Sonoma County

88   1987 Zinfandel Sonoma County

88   1986 Zinfandel Sonoma County

80   1985 Zinfandel Sonoma County

89   1992 Zinfandel Sonoma County Belloni

89   1991 Zinfandel Sonoma Valley Belloni

91   1992 Zinfandel Sonoma Valley Cooke

88   1991 Zinfandel Sonoma Valley Cooke

90   1990 Zinfandel Sonoma Valley Cooke

88   1987 Zinfandel Sonoma Valley Cooke

92   1992 Zinfandel Sonoma Valley Old Hill Vineyard

87   1991 Zinfandel Sonoma Valley Old Hill Vineyard

89   1990 Zinfandel Sonoma Valley Old Hill Vineyard

87   1987 Zinfandel Sonoma Valley Old Hill Vineyard

92   1986 Zinfandel Sonoma Valley Old Hill Vineyard

Martin Ray

91   1991 Cabernet Sauvignon Napa Valley

91   1992 Chardonnay California Mariage

Raymond Vineyard and Cellar

84   1991 Cabernet Sauvignon California Amberhill

85   1991 Cabernet Sauvignon Napa Valley

88   1990 Cabernet Sauvignon Napa Valley

87   1989 Cabernet Sauvignon Napa Valley

85   1988 Cabernet Sauvignon Napa Valley

83   1987 Cabernet Sauvignon Napa Valley

90   1986 Cabernet Sauvignon Napa Valley

84   1985 Cabernet Sauvignon Napa Valley

86   1978 Cabernet Sauvignon Napa Valley

88   1990 Cabernet Sauvignon Napa Valley Private Reserve

88   1988 Cabernet Sauvignon Napa Valley Private Reserve

88   1986 Cabernet Sauvignon Napa Valley Private Reserve

88   1985 Cabernet Sauvignon Napa Valley Private Reserve

88   1984 Cabernet Sauvignon Napa Valley Private Reserve

84   1983 Cabernet Sauvignon Napa Valley Private Reserve

86   1982 Cabernet Sauvignon Napa Valley Private Reserve

87   1981 Cabernet Sauvignon Napa Valley Private Reserve

85   1980 Cabernet Sauvignon Napa Valley Private Reserve

83   1993 Chardonnay California Amberhill

84   1992 Chardonnay California Amberhill

83   1991 Chardonnay California Selection

85   1992 Chardonnay Napa Valley

85   1991 Chardonnay Napa Valley

87   1992 Chardonnay Napa Valley Private Reserve

89   1991 Chardonnay Napa Valley Private Reserve

89   1989 Meritage Red Napa Valley

90   1990 Meritage Red Napa Valley Private Reserve

83   1992 Pinot Noir Napa Valley

81   1993 Sauvignon Blanc Napa Valley

77   1992 Sauvignon Blanc Napa Valley

Renaissance Vineyard & Winery

81   1990 Cabernet Sauvignon North Yuba

85   1992 Riesling North Yuba Dry

83   1992 Sauvignon Blanc North Yuba

85   1991 Sauvignon Blanc North Yuba Select Late Harvest

Renwood Winery

82   1992 Barbera Amador County

86   1991 Barbera Amador County

85   1989 Port Shenandoah Valley Late Bottled Vintage

83   1991 Zinfandel Amador County

88   1992 Zinfandel Shenandoah Valley Grandpére Vineyard

86   1991 Zinfandel Shenandoah Valley Grandpére Vineyard

Richardson Vineyards

79   1992 Cabernet Sauvignon Sonoma Valley Horne Vineyard

89   1991 Cabernet Sauvignon Sonoma Valley Horne Vineyard

73   1990 Cabernet Sauvignon Sonoma Valley Horne Vineyard

78   1989 Cabernet Sauvignon Sonoma Valley Horne Vineyard

87   1992 Merlot Carneros

86   1991 Merlot Carneros Gregory Vineyard

89   1990 Merlot Carneros Gregory Vineyard

83   1989 Merlot Carneros Gregory Vineyard

82   1991 Merlot Carneros Sangiacomo & Gregory Vineyards

87   1990 Merlot Carneros Sangiacomo Vineyard

80   1991 Pinot Noir Carneros Sangiacomo Vineyard

83   1990 Pinot Noir Carneros Sangiacomo Vineyard

86   1989 Pinot Noir Carneros Sangiacomo Vineyard

88   1987 Pinot Noir Carneros Sangiacomo Vineyard

85   1986 Pinot Noir Carneros Sangiacomo Vineyard

89   1992 Zinfandel Sonoma Valley Nora's Vineyard

Ridge Vineyards

84   1991 Cabernet Sauvignon Napa County York Creek

88   1990 Cabernet Sauvignon Napa County York Creek

85   1987 Cabernet Sauvignon Napa County York Creek

88   1986 Cabernet Sauvignon Napa County York Creek

86   1985 Cabernet Sauvignon Napa County York Creek

85   1984 Cabernet Sauvignon Napa County York Creek

73   1983 Cabernet Sauvignon Napa County York Creek

73   1982 Cabernet Sauvignon Napa County York Creek

74   1981 Cabernet Sauvignon Napa County York Creek

85   1980 Cabernet Sauvignon Napa County York Creek

86   1979 Cabernet Sauvignon Napa County York Creek

87   1978 Cabernet Sauvignon Napa County York Creek

88   1977 Cabernet Sauvignon Napa County York Creek

68   1976 Cabernet Sauvignon Napa County York Creek

87   1975 Cabernet Sauvignon Napa County York Creek

85   1974 Cabernet Sauvignon Napa County York Creek

89   1992 Cabernet Sauvignon Santa Cruz Mountains

89   1991 Cabernet Sauvignon Santa Cruz Mountains

85   1990 Cabernet Sauvignon Santa Cruz Mountains

82   1989 Cabernet Sauvignon Santa Cruz Mountains

68   1986 Cabernet Sauvignon Santa Cruz Mountains

64   1985 Cabernet Sauvignon Santa Cruz Mountains

84   1983 Cabernet Sauvignon Santa Cruz Mountains

91 1991 Cabernet Sauvignon Santa Cruz Mountains Monte Bello

92 1990 Cabernet Sauvignon Santa Cruz Mountains Monte Bello

90 1989 Cabernet Sauvignon Santa Cruz Mountains Monte Bello

82 1988 Cabernet Sauvignon Santa Cruz Mountains Monte Bello

88 1987 Cabernet Sauvignon Santa Cruz Mountains Monte Bello

85 1986 Cabernet Sauvignon Santa Cruz Mountains Monte Bello

95 1985 Cabernet Sauvignon Santa Cruz Mountains Monte Bello

88 1984 Cabernet Sauvignon Santa Cruz Mountains Monte Bello

75 1982 Cabernet Sauvignon Santa Cruz Mountains Monte Bello

89 1981 Cabernet Sauvignon Santa Cruz Mountains Monte Bello

80 1980 Cabernet Sauvignon Santa Cruz Mountains Monte Bello

92 1978 Cabernet Sauvignon Santa Cruz Mountains Monte Bello

92 1977 Cabernet Sauvignon Santa Cruz Mountains Monte Bello

83 1976 Cabernet Sauvignon Santa Cruz Mountains Monte Bello

88 1975 Cabernet Sauvignon Santa Cruz Mountains Monte Bello

94 1974 Cabernet Sauvignon Santa Cruz Mountains Monte Bello

87 1973 Cabernet Sauvignon Santa Cruz Mountains Monte Bello

82 1972 Cabernet Sauvignon Santa Cruz Mountains Monte Bello

85 1971 Cabernet Sauvignon Santa Cruz Mountains Monte Bello

96 1970 Cabernet Sauvignon Santa Cruz Mountains Monte Bello

92 1969 Cabernet Sauvignon Santa Cruz Mountains Monte Bello

87 1968 Cabernet Sauvignon Santa Cruz Mountains Monte Bello

86 1965 Cabernet Sauvignon Santa Cruz Mountains Monte Bello

90 1964 Cabernet Sauvignon Santa Cruz Mountains Monte Bello

92 1992 Chardonnay Santa Cruz Mountains

92 1991 Chardonnay Santa Cruz Mountains

80 1991 Merlot Napa County York Creek

82 1990 Merlot Napa County York Creek

89 1990 Merlot Sonoma County Bradford Mountain Vineyard

82 1989 Merlot Sonoma County Bradford Mountain Vineyard

75 1987 Merlot Sonoma County Bradford Mountain Vineyard

72 1986 Merlot Sonoma County Bradford Mountain Vineyard

87 1991 Petite Sirah Napa County York Creek

76 1987 Petite Sirah Napa County York Creek

87 1985 Petite Sirah Napa County York Creek

73 1990 Rhône Blend California Evangelo Vineyards Mataro-Mourvèdre

91 1993 Zinfandel Dry Creek Valley Lytton Springs

91 1992 Zinfandel Dry Creek Valley Lytton Springs

91 1991 Zinfandel Dry Creek Valley Lytton Springs

89 1990 Zinfandel Dry Creek Valley Lytton Springs

82 1989 Zinfandel Dry Creek Valley Lytton Springs

82 1988 Zinfandel Dry Creek Valley Lytton Springs

91 1987 Zinfandel Dry Creek Valley Lytton Springs

88 1986 Zinfandel Dry Creek Valley Lytton Springs

83 1985 Zinfandel Dry Creek Valley Lytton Springs

83 1974 Zinfandel Dry Creek Valley Lytton Springs

80 1990 Zinfandel Howell Mountain

87 1989 Zinfandel Howell Mountain

82 1988 Zinfandel Howell Mountain

83 1987 Zinfandel Howell Mountain

88 1991 Zinfandel Napa County York Creek

90 1991 Zinfandel Paso Robles

84 1990 Zinfandel Paso Robles

84 1989 Zinfandel Paso Robles

85 1987 Zinfandel Paso Robles

81 1986 Zinfandel Paso Robles

90 1992 Zinfandel Paso Robles Dusi Ranch

86 1990 Zinfandel Sonoma County

80 1989 Zinfandel Sonoma County

88 1988 Zinfandel Sonoma County

86 1992 Zinfandel Sonoma County Geyserville

90 1991 Zinfandel Sonoma County Geyserville

87 1990 Zinfandel Sonoma County Geyserville

84 1989 Zinfandel Sonoma County Geyserville

90 1988 Zinfandel Sonoma County Geyserville

88 1987 Zinfandel Sonoma County Geyserville

79 1986 Zinfandel Sonoma County Geyserville

83 1985 Zinfandel Sonoma County Geyserville

93 1992 Zinfandel Sonoma Valley Pagani Ranch

89 1991 Zinfandel Sonoma Valley Pagani Ranch

RITCHIE CREEK VINEYARDS

91 1991 Cabernet Sauvignon Napa Valley

89 1990 Cabernet Sauvignon Napa Valley

87 1985 Cabernet Sauvignon Napa Valley

78 1978 Cabernet Sauvignon Napa Valley

ROCHE WINERY

85 1992 Chardonnay Carneros Barrel Select Reserve

85 1991 Chardonnay Carneros

83 1990 Pinot Noir Carneros

81 1989 Pinot Noir Carneros

80 1988 Pinot Noir Carneros

83 1990 Pinot Noir Carneros Reserve

84 1991 Pinot Noir Carneros Unfiltered

78 1989 Pinot Noir Carneros Unfiltered

J. ROCHIOLI VINEYARD & WINERY

86 1991 Cabernet Sauvignon Russian River Valley Neoma's Vineyard Private Reserve

87 1990 Cabernet Sauvignon Russian River Valley Neoma's Vineyard Private Reserve

84 1989 Cabernet Sauvignon Russian River Valley Neoma's Vineyard Private Reserve

81 1988 Cabernet Sauvignon Russian River Valley Neoma's Vineyard Private Reserve

84 1987 Cabernet Sauvignon Russian River Valley Neoma's Vineyard Private Reserve

83 1986 Cabernet Sauvignon Russian River Valley Neoma's Vineyard Private Reserve

83 1985 Cabernet Sauvignon Russian River Valley Neoma's Vineyard Private Reserve

82 1983 Cabernet Sauvignon Russian River Valley Neoma's Vineyard Private Reserve

80 1982 Cabernet Sauvignon Russian River Valley Neoma's Vineyard Private Reserve

85 1993 Chardonnay Russian River Valley

90 1992 Chardonnay Russian River Valley

90 1991 Chardonnay Russian River Valley

90 1993 Chardonnay Russian River Valley Reserve

93 1992 Chardonnay Russian River Valley Reserve

91 1991 Chardonnay Russian River Valley Reserve

90 1991 Pinot Noir Russian River Valley

88 1990 Pinot Noir Russian River Valley

84 1989 Pinot Noir Russian River Valley

86 1988 Pinot Noir Russian River Valley

85 1987 Pinot Noir Russian River Valley

90 1986 Pinot Noir Russian River Valley

88 1985 Pinot Noir Russian River Valley

84 1984 Pinot Noir Russian River Valley

85 1982 Pinot Noir Russian River Valley

92 1992 Pinot Noir Russian River Valley Reserve Western Block

93 1991 Pinot Noir Russian River Valley Reserve

92 1990 Pinot Noir Russian River Valley Reserve

85 1990 Pinot Noir Russian River Valley Reserve Lot 9

88 1989 Pinot Noir Russian River Valley Reserve

90 1988 Pinot Noir Russian River Valley Reserve

85 1986 Pinot Noir Russian River Valley Reserve

84   1994 Sauvignon Blanc Russian River Valley

87   1993 Sauvignon Blanc Russian River Valley

89   1990 Sauvignon Blanc Russian River Valley

88   1993 Sauvignon Blanc Russian River Valley Reserve

88   1992 Sauvignon Blanc Russian River Valley Reserve

91   1992 Zinfandel Russian River Valley Sodini Vineyard

Rocking Horse

84   1991 Cabernet Sauvignon Napa Valley Hillside Cuvée

87   1989 Cabernet Sauvignon Napa Valley Hillside Cuvée

86   1992 Cabernet Sauvignon Napa Valley Garvey Family Vineyard

85   1992 Cabernet Sauvignon Stags Leap District Robinson Vineyard

90   1991 Cabernet Sauvignon Stags Leap District Robinson Vineyard

91   1990 Cabernet Sauvignon Stags Leap District Robinson Vineyard

84   1986 Cabernet Sauvignon Stags Leap District Robinson Vineyard

88   1991 Zinfandel Howell Mountain Lamborn Family Vineyard

84   1990 Zinfandel Howell Mountain Lamborn Family Vineyard

84   1989 Zinfandel Howell Mountain Lamborn Family Vineyard

Roederer Estate

90   NV Sparkling Wine Anderson Valley Brut

92   1989 Sparkling Wine Anderson Valley Brut L'Ermitage Prestige Cuvée

Rolling Hills Vineyards

86   1987 Cabernet Sauvignon California

77   1985 Pinot Noir Santa Maria Valley

Rombauer Vineyards

85   1990 Cabernet Franc Napa Valley

86   1990 Cabernet Sauvignon Napa Valley

78   1989 Cabernet Sauvignon Napa Valley

85   1987 Cabernet Sauvignon Napa Valley

88   1986 Cabernet Sauvignon Napa Valley

85   1985 Cabernet Sauvignon Napa Valley

84   1984 Cabernet Sauvignon Napa Valley

83   1987 Cabernet Sauvignon Napa Valley Le Meilleur du Chai

89   1986 Cabernet Sauvignon Napa Valley Le Meilleur du Chai

89   1985 Cabernet Sauvignon Napa Valley Le Meilleur du Chai

88   1984 Cabernet Sauvignon Napa Valley Le Meilleur du Chai

85   1983 Cabernet Sauvignon Napa Valley Le Meilleur du Chai

92   1993 Chardonnay Carneros

88   1992 Chardonnay Carneros

91   1991 Chardonnay Carneros

82   1991 Merlot Napa Valley

84   1990 Merlot Napa Valley

84   1989 Merlot Napa Valley

87   1987 Merlot Napa Valley

78   1986 Merlot Napa Valley

88   1993 Zinfandel Napa Valley

Rosenblum Cellars

85   1992 Cabernet Blend Napa Valley Holbrook Mitchell Vineyard Trio

86   1991 Cabernet Blend Napa Valley Holbrook Mitchell Vineyard Trio

87   1990 Cabernet Blend Napa Valley Holbrook Mitchell Vineyard Trio

88   1991 Cabernet Sauvignon Napa Valley George Hendry Vineyard Reserve

84   1990 Cabernet Sauvignon Napa Valley George Hendry Vineyard

80   1989 Merlot Napa Valley Holbrook Mitchell Vineyard

85   1989 Merlot Russian River Valley

81   1990 Merlot Russian River Valley Lone Oak Vineyard

73   1990 Pinot Noir Napa Valley George Hendry Vineyard

80   1991 Pinot Noir Russian River Valley Ellis Ranch

83   1992 Zinfandel Contra Costa County

90   1991 Zinfandel Contra Costa County

87   1990 Zinfandel Contra Costa County

86   1992 Zinfandel Mount Veeder Brandlin Ranch

88   1991 Zinfandel Mount Veeder Brandlin Ranch

86   1990 Zinfandel Napa Valley George Hendry Vineyard

84   1989 Zinfandel Napa Valley George Hendry Vineyard

77   1987 Zinfandel Napa Valley George Hendry Vineyard

86   1992 Zinfandel Napa Valley George Hendry Vineyard Reserve

89   1990 Zinfandel Napa Valley George Hendry Vineyard Reserve

84   1988 Zinfandel Napa Valley George Hendry Vineyard Reserve

87   1992 Zinfandel Paso Robles Richard Sauret Vineyard

88   1991 Zinfandel Paso Robles Richard Sauret Vineyard

87   1990 Zinfandel Paso Robles Richard Sauret Vineyard

84   1992 Zinfandel Sonoma County

86   1991 Zinfandel Sonoma County

88   1990 Zinfandel Sonoma County

89   1992 Zinfandel Sonoma Valley Samsel Vineyard Maggie's Reserve

91   1991 Zinfandel Sonoma Valley Samsel Vineyard Maggie's Reserve

90   1990 Zinfandel Sonoma Valley Smasel Vineyard Maggie's Reserve

Rosenthal – The Malibu Estate

91   1991 Cabernet Sauvignon California

Roudon-Smith Winery

77   1991 Cabernet Sauvignon California

70   1989 Pinot Noir Santa Cruz Mountains

82   1989 Pinot Noir Santa Cruz Mountains Cox Vineyard

84   1987 Pinot Noir Santa Cruz Mountains Cox Vineyard

Round Hill Winery

80   1991 Cabernet Sauvignon California

84   1990 Cabernet Sauvignon Napa Valley Reserve

83   1989 Cabernet Sauvignon Napa Valley Reserve

86   1993 Chardonnay California

81   1992 Chardonnay California

82   1993 Chardonnay Napa Valley Reserve

81   1991 Chardonnay Napa Valley Reserve

83   1993 Chardonnay Napa Valley Van Asperen Reserve

81   1992 Chardonnay Napa Valley Van Asperen Reserve

85   1993 Fumé Blanc Napa Valley

77   1992 Merlot California

83   1991 Merlot Napa Valley Reserve

85   1990 Zinfandel Napa Valley

89   1988 Zinfandel Napa Valley

87   1993 Rutherford Ranch Chardonnay Napa Valley

86   1992 Rutherford Ranch Chardonnay Napa Valley

82   1992 Rutherford Ranch Merlot Napa Valley

82   1990 Rutherford Ranch Merlot Napa Valley

85   1993 Rutherford Ranch Sauvignon Blanc Napa Valley

Royce Vineyards

77   1989 Cabernet Sauvignon Napa Valley

80   1987 Cabernet Sauvignon Sonoma County

78   1991 Chardonnay California

81   1990 Merlot Napa Valley Reserve

85   1991 Merlot Sonoma County

Rubissow-Sargent

85   1990 Cabernet Blend Mount Veeder Les Trompettes

79   1989 Cabernet Blend Mount Veeder Les Trompettes

84   1990 Cabernet Sauvignon Mount Veeder
85   1988 Cabernet Sauvignon Mount Veeder
86   1990 Merlot Mount Veeder

RUTHERFORD HILL WINERY

81   1991 Cabernet Sauvignon Napa Valley
82   1987 Cabernet Sauvignon Napa Valley
86   1987 Cabernet Sauvignon Napa Valley XVS
68   1986 Cabernet Sauvignon Napa Valley
82   1985 Cabernet Sauvignon Napa Valley
84   1984 Cabernet Sauvignon Napa Valley
83   1992 Chardonnay Napa Valley XVS Reserve
83   1991 Chardonnay Napa Valley XVS Reserve
82   1992 Chardonnay Napa Valley Jaeger Vineyards
85   1992 Merlot Napa Valley XVS Reserve
82   1991 Merlot Napa Valley XVS Reserve

SADDLEBACK CELLARS

90   1991 Cabernet Sauvignon Napa Valley
73   1988 Cabernet Sauvignon Napa Valley
83   1989 Cabernet Sauvignon Napa Valley Family Reserve
78   1988 Cabernet Sauvignon Napa Valley Family Reserve
81   1993 Chardonnay Napa Valley
73   1992 Chardonnay Napa Valley
78   1991 Chardonnay Napa Valley
82   1990 Pinot Blanc Napa Valley

ST. ANDREW'S WINERY

85   1986 Cabernet Sauvignon Napa Valley
82   1993 Chardonnay Napa Valley
83   1992 Chardonnay Napa Valley

ST. CLEMENT VINEYARDS

95   1992 Cabernet Blend Napa Valley Oroppas
94   1991 Cabernet Blend Napa Valley Oroppas
90   1991 Cabernet Sauvignon Napa Valley
90   1990 Cabernet Sauvignon Napa Valley
84   1989 Cabernet Sauvignon Napa Valley
86   1988 Cabernet Sauvignon Napa Valley
90   1987 Cabernet Sauvignon Napa Valley
90   1986 Cabernet Sauvignon Napa Valley
90   1985 Cabernet Sauvignon Napa Valley
87   1984 Cabernet Sauvignon Napa Valley
85   1983 Cabernet Sauvignon Napa Valley
87   1982 Cabernet Sauvignon Napa Valley
85   1981 Cabernet Sauvignon Napa Valley
82   1980 Cabernet Sauvignon Napa Valley
87   1979 Cabernet Sauvignon Napa Valley
88   1978 Cabernet Sauvignon Napa Valley
85   1977 Cabernet Sauvignon Napa Valley
84   NV Cabernet Sauvignon Napa Valley

84   1993 Chardonnay Carneros Abbott's Vineyard
91   1992 Chardonnay Carneros Abbott's Vineyard
90   1991 Chardonnay Carneros Abbott's Vineyard
86   1991 Chardonnay Napa Valley
89   1992 Merlot Napa Valley
83   1991 Merlot Napa Valley
87   1990 Merlot Napa Valley
86   1989 Merlot Napa Valley
90   1987 Merlot Napa Valley
79   1986 Merlot Napa Valley
88   1985 Merlot Napa Valley
81   1983 Merlot Napa Valley
87   1994 Sauvignon Blanc Napa Valley
84   1993 Sauvignon Blanc Napa Valley

ST. FRANCIS WINERY

83   1989 Cabernet Franc Sonoma Valley
85   1992 Cabernet Sauvignon Sonoma County
84   1991 Cabernet Sauvignon Sonoma County
89   1990 Cabernet Sauvignon Sonoma County
84   1989 Cabernet Sauvignon Sonoma County
89   1988 Cabernet Sauvignon Sonoma County
89   1986 Cabernet Sauvignon Sonoma County
88   1991 Cabernet Sauvignon Sonoma County Reserve
92   1990 Cabernet Sauvignon Sonoma Valley
89   1989 Cabernet Sauvignon Sonoma Valley
89   1987 Cabernet Sauvignon Sonoma Valley
86   1986 Cabernet Sauvignon Sonoma Valley
89   1989 Cabernet Sauvignon Sonoma Valley Reserve
87   1988 Cabernet Sauvignon Sonoma Valley Reserve
94   1986 Cabernet Sauvignon Sonoma Valley Reserve
82   1993 Chardonnay Sonoma County
84   1992 Chardonnay Sonoma County
84   1991 Chardonnay Sonoma County
90   1993 Chardonnay Sonoma Valley Reserve
91   1992 Chardonnay Sonoma Valley Reserve
85   1991 Chardonnay Sonoma Valley Reserve
73   1992 Gewürztraminer Sonoma County
86   1991 Merlot Sonoma Valley
88   1990 Merlot Sonoma Valley
79   1989 Merlot Sonoma Valley
82   1988 Merlot Sonoma Valley
80   1987 Merlot Sonoma Valley
85   1986 Merlot Sonoma Valley
93   1992 Merlot Sonoma Valley Reserve
89   1991 Merlot Sonoma Valley Reserve
91   1990 Merlot Sonoma Valley Reserve
90   1989 Merlot Sonoma Valley Reserve
82   1988 Merlot Sonoma Valley Reserve
91   1986 Merlot Sonoma Valley Reserve
87   1992 Zinfandel Sonoma Valley Old Vines

88   1990 Zinfandel Sonoma Valley Old Vines
85   1989 Zinfandel Sonoma Valley Old Vines

ST. SUPÉRY VINEYARD & WINERY

86   1990 Cabernet Sauvignon Napa Valley Dollarhide Ranch
85   1989 Cabernet Sauvignon Napa Valley Dollarhide Ranch
88   1989 Cabernet Sauvignon Napa Valley Dollarhide Ranch Limited Edition
85   1988 Cabernet Sauvignon Napa Valley Dollarhide Ranch
86   1987 Cabernet Sauvignon Napa Valley Dollarhide Ranch
81   1993 Chardonnay Napa Valley Dollarhide Ranch
83   1992 Chardonnay Napa Valley Dollarhide Ranch
86   1991 Chardonnay Napa Valley Dollarhide Ranch
80   1992 Merlot Napa Valley Dollarhide Ranch
85   1991 Merlot Napa Valley Dollarhide Ranch
86   1990 Merlot Napa Valley Dollarhide Ranch
87   1989 Merlot Napa Valley Dollarhide Ranch
76   1992 Muscat California
84   1992 Sauvignon Blanc Napa Valley Dollarhide Ranch
83   1991 Bonverre Cabernet Sauvignon California Lot Number 9
78   1992 Bonverre Chardonnay California Lot Number 14
76   1992 Bonverre Merlot California Lot Number 11
77   1992 Bonverre Sauvignon Blanc Napa Valley Lot Number 10

SAINTSBURY

85   1993 Chardonnay Carneros
85   1992 Chardonnay Carneros
87   1991 Chardonnay Carneros
89   1993 Chardonnay Carneros Reserve
91   1992 Chardonnay Carneros Reserve
92   1991 Chardonnay Carneros Reserve
85   1992 Pinot Noir Carneros
87   1991 Pinot Noir Carneros
90   1990 Pinot Noir Carneros
85   1989 Pinot Noir Carneros
91   1988 Pinot Noir Carneros
87   1987 Pinot Noir Carneros
92   1986 Pinot Noir Carneros
87   1985 Pinot Noir Carneros
86   1993 Pinot Noir Carneros Garnet
84   1992 Pinot Noir Carneros Garnet
88   1991 Pinot Noir Carneros Garnet
89   1992 Pinot Noir Carneros Reserve
89   1991 Pinot Noir Carneros Reserve
92   1990 Pinot Noir Carneros Reserve

SALMON CREEK

85 1993 Chardonnay Carneros

SAN SABA VINEYARD

88 1990 Cabernet Sauvignon Monterey County

70 1990 Bocage Cabernet Sauvignon Monterey County Proprietor's Cuvée

84 1990 Bocage Merlot Monterey County Proprietor's Cuvée

74 1989 Bocage Merlot Monterey County Proprietor's Cuvée

SANFORD WINERY

84 1991 Blush Santa Barbara County Vin Gris

90 1993 Chardonnay Santa Barbara County

88 1992 Chardonnay Santa Barbara County

91 1991 Chardonnay Santa Barbara County

90 1992 Chardonnay Santa Barbara County Barrel Select

91 1991 Chardonnay Santa Barbara County Barrel Select

86 1993 Chardonnay Santa Ynez Valley

88 1992 Chardonnay Santa Ynez Valley

88 1992 Pinot Noir Santa Barbara County

87 1991 Pinot Noir Santa Barbara County

89 1990 Pinot Noir Santa Barbara County

93 1989 Pinot Noir Santa Barbara County

91 1988 Pinot Noir Santa Barbara County

80 1987 Pinot Noir Santa Barbara County

87 1986 Pinot Noir Santa Barbara County

83 1985 Pinot Noir Santa Barbara County

73 1982 Pinot Noir Santa Barbara County

89 1979 Pinot Noir Santa Barbara County

88 1992 Pinot Noir Santa Barbara County Sanford & Benedict Vineyard Barrel Select

88 1991 Pinot Noir Santa Barbara County Sanford & Benedict Vineyard Barrel Select

94 1990 Pinot Noir Santa Barbara County Sanford & Benedict Vineyard Barrel Select

95 1989 Pinot Noir Santa Barbara County Sanford & Benedict Vineyard Barrel Select

92 1986 Pinot Noir Santa Barbara County Sanford & Benedict Vineyard Barrel Select

79 1985 Pinot Noir Santa Barbara County Sanford & Benedict Vineyard Barrel Select

92 1984 Pinot Noir Santa Barbara County Sanford & Benedict Vineyard Barrel Select

85 1984 Pinot Noir Central Coast

86 1983 Pinot Noir Central Coast

92 1984 Pinot Noir Santa Ynez Valley

70 1980 Pinot Noir Santa Ynez Valley

76 1977 Pinot Noir Santa Ynez Valley

89 1976 Pinot Noir Santa Ynez Valley

94 1975 Pinot Noir Santa Ynez Valley

82 1993 Sauvignon Blanc Santa Barbara County

85 1991 Sauvignon Blanc Santa Barbara County

SANTA BARBARA WINERY

75 1991 Cabernet Sauvignon Santa Ynez Valley

83 1990 Cabernet Sauvignon Santa Ynez Valley

79 1989 Cabernet Sauvignon Santa Ynez Valley

83 1988 Cabernet Sauvignon Santa Ynez Valley

84 1991 Cabernet Sauvignon Santa Ynez Valley Reserve

83 1990 Cabernet Sauvignon Santa Ynez Valley Reserve

82 1989 Cabernet Sauvignon Santa Ynez Valley Reserve

83 1988 Cabernet Sauvignon Santa Ynez Valley Reserve

84 1992 Chardonnay Santa Ynez Valley

89 1992 Chardonnay Santa Ynez Valley Lafond Vineyard

88 1991 Chardonnay Santa Ynez Valley Lafond Vineyard

89 1993 Chardonnay Santa Ynez Valley Reserve

89 1992 Chardonnay Santa Ynez Valley Reserve

86 1991 Chardonnay Santa Ynez Valley Reserve

82 1992 Johannisberg Riesling Santa Barbara County

71 1990 Johannisberg Riesling Santa Barbara County

76 1988 Johannisberg Riesling Santa Barbara County

84 1987 Johannisberg Riesling Santa Barbara County

82 1991 Pinot Noir Santa Barbara County

87 1990 Pinot Noir Santa Barbara County

84 1989 Pinot Noir Santa Barbara County

80 1986 Pinot Noir Santa Barbara County

79 1991 Pinot Noir Santa Barbara County Reserve

83 1990 Pinot Noir Santa Barbara County Reserve

87 1989 Pinot Noir Santa Barbara County Reserve

89 1987 Pinot Noir Santa Ynez Valley Reserve

83 1993 Sauvignon Blanc Santa Ynez Valley

80 1993 Sauvignon Blanc Santa Ynez Valley Reserve

85 1992 Sauvignon Blanc Santa Ynez Valley Reserve

68 1987 Sauvignon Blanc Santa Ynez Valley Reserve

72 1987 Sauvignon Blanc Santa Ynez Valley Valley View Vineyards

82 1994 Zinfandel Santa Ynez Valley Beaujour

84 1993 Zinfandel Santa Ynez Valley Beaujour

80 1992 Zinfandel Santa Ynez Valley Beaujour

84 1991 Zinfandel Santa Ynez Valley Beaujour

82 1987 Zinfandel Santa Ynez Valley Beaujour

85 1992 Zinfandel Santa Ynez Valley Lafond Vineyard

83 1991 Zinfandel Santa Ynez Valley Lafond Vineyard

84 1990 Zinfandel San Luis Obispo County Saucelito Canyon Vineyard

82 1989 Zinfandel San Luis Obispo County Saucelito Canyon Vineyard

87 1993 Zinfandel Santa Ynez Valley Late Harvest Essence

SANTA CRUZ MOUNTAIN VINEYARD

71 1989 Cabernet Sauvignon Santa Cruz Mountains Bates Ranch

87 1988 Cabernet Sauvignon Santa Cruz Mountains Bates Ranch

91 1987 Cabernet Sauvignon Santa Cruz Mountains Bates Ranch

89 1986 Cabernet Sauvignon Santa Cruz Mountains Bates Ranch

92 1985 Cabernet Sauvignon Santa Cruz Mountains Bates Ranch

87 1984 Cabernet Sauvignon Santa Cruz Mountains Bates Ranch

84 1983 Cabernet Sauvignon Santa Cruz Mountains Bates Ranch

75 1982 Cabernet Sauvignon Santa Cruz Mountains Bates Ranch

80 1981 Cabernet Sauvignon Santa Cruz Mountains Bates Ranch

86 1980 Cabernet Sauvignon Santa Cruz Mountains Bates Ranch

81 1979 Cabernet Sauvignon Santa Cruz Mountains Bates Ranch

88 1978 Cabernet Sauvignon Santa Cruz Mountains Bates Ranch

89 1991 Merlot California

83 1989 Merlot California

81 1990 Pinot Noir Santa Cruz Mountains

90 1989 Pinot Noir Santa Cruz Mountains

92 1988 Pinot Noir Santa Cruz Mountains

90 1987 Pinot Noir Santa Cruz Mountains

89 1985 Pinot Noir Santa Cruz Mountains

87 1990 Pinot Noir Santa Cruz Mountains Matteson Vineyard

87 1989 Pinot Noir Santa Cruz Mountains Matteson Vineyard

SANTA YNEZ WINERY

72 1987 Cabernet Blend Santa Barbara County Cabernet Merlot

62 1987 Pinot Noir Santa Maria Valley

84 1987 Zinfandel Paso Robles

SARAH'S VINEYARD

89 1993 Chardonnay Santa Clara County

89 1992 Chardonnay Santa Clara County

88 1992 Chardonnay Santa Clara County Lot II

V. SATTUI WINERY

87 1991 Cabernet Sauvignon Napa Valley Preston Vineyard

86 1988 Cabernet Sauvignon Napa Valley Preston Vineyard

88 1986 Cabernet Sauvignon Napa Valley Preston Vineyard

87 1985 Cabernet Sauvignon Napa Valley Preston Vineyard

86 1984 Cabernet Sauvignon Napa Valley Preston Vineyard

90 1991 Cabernet Sauvignon Napa Valley Preston Reserve Stock

87 1988 Cabernet Sauvignon Napa Valley Preston Vineyard Reserve Stock

86 1987 Cabernet Sauvignon Napa Valley Preston Vineyard Reserve Stock

86 1991 Cabernet Sauvignon Napa Valley Suzanne's Vineyard

81 1989 Cabernet Sauvignon Napa Valley Suzanne's Vineyard

82 1992 Chardonnay Napa Valley

88 1993 Chardonnay Napa Valley Carsi Vineyard Barrel Fermented

87 1992 Chardonnay Napa Valley Carsi Vineyard Barrel Fermented

86 1991 Chardonnay Napa Valley Carsi Vineyard Barrel Fermented

80 1989 Merlot Napa Valley

82 1993 Sauvignon Blanc Napa Valley

86 1991 Zinfandel Howell Mountain

SAUCELITO CANYON VINEYARD

87 1992 Zinfandel Arroyo Grande Valley

88 1991 Zinfandel Arroyo Grande Valley

85 1990 Zinfandel Arroyo Grande Valley

89 1989 Zinfandel Arroyo Grande Valley

87 1986 Zinfandel San Luis Obispo County

SAUSAL WINERY

84 1988 Cabernet Sauvignon Alexander Valley

88 1993 Zinfandel Alexander Valley

89 1992 Zinfandel Alexander Valley

85 1990 Zinfandel Alexander Valley

79 1989 Zinfandel Alexander Valley

82 1988 Zinfandel Alexander Valley

83 1987 Zinfandel Alexander Valley

87 1992 Zinfandel Alexander Valley Private Reserve

87 1991 Zinfandel Alexander Valley Private Reserve

88 1988 Zinfandel Alexander Valley Private Reserve

SCHARFFENBERGER CELLARS

89 1989 Sparkling Wine Mendocino County Blanc de Blancs

87 1989 Sparkling Wine Mendocino County Brut

86 NV Sparkling Wine Mendocino County Brut

88 NV Sparkling Wine Mendocino County Brut Rosé

87 NV Sparkling Wine Mendocino County Cremant Extra Dry

F. SCHERRER WINES

87 1993 Zinfandel Alexander Valley Old Vines

90 1992 Zinfandel Alexander Valley Old Vines

87 1991 Zinfandel Alexander Valley Old Vines Unfiltered

SCHOOL HOUSE

85 1992 Pinot Noir Napa Valley

84 1976 Pinot Noir Napa Valley

SCHRAMSBERG VINEYARDS

87 1989 Sparkling Wine Napa Valley Brut

87 1990 Sparkling Wine Napa Valley Brut Rosé Cuvée de Pinot

87 1989 Sparkling Wine Napa Valley Cremant Demi-Sec

90 1989 Sparkling Wine Napa Valley J. Schram

90 1988 Sparkling Wine Napa Valley J. Schram

SCHUETZ-OLES

82 1993 Chardonnay Napa Valley Chappell Vineyard

89 1992 Zinfandel Napa Valley Korte Ranch

SCHUG CARNEROS ESTATE

86 1992 Cabernet Sauvignon Sonoma Valley Heritage Reserve

78 1993 Chardonnay Carneros

80 1992 Chardonnay Carneros Barrel Fermented

83 1993 Chardonnay Sonoma Valley

82 1992 Chardonnay Sonoma Valley

86 1993 Pinot Noir Carneros

78 1992 Pinot Noir Carneros

83 1991 Pinot Noir Carneros

84 1991 Pinot Noir Carneros Heritage Reserve

78 1990 Pinot Noir Carneros

80 1990 Pinot Noir Carneros Beckstoffer Vineyard

74 1989 Pinot Noir Carneros Beckstoffer Vineyard

79 1988 Pinot Noir Carneros Beckstoffer Vineyard

81 1987 Pinot Noir Carneros Beckstoffer Vineyard

85 1986 Pinot Noir Carneros Beckstoffer Vineyard

78 1989 Pinot Noir Napa Valley Heinemann Vineyard Reserve

83 1985 Pinot Noir Napa Valley Heinemann Vineyard Reserve

73 1993 Sauvignon Blanc Sonoma Valley

SEA RIDGE WINERY

84 1989 Merlot Sonoma Coast Occidental Vineyard

82 1990 Pinot Noir Sonoma Coast Hirsch Vineyard

81 1989 Pinot Noir Sonoma Coast Hirsch Vineyard

82 1991 Zinfandel Sonoma Coast Occidental Vineyard

80 1990 Zinfandel Sonoma Coast Occidental Vineyard

SEAVEY VINEYARD

90 1991 Cabernet Sauvignon Napa Valley

89 1990 Cabernet Sauvignon Napa Valley

87 1992 Chardonnay Napa Valley

SEBASTIANI VINEYARDS

86 1992 Barbera

82 1989 Barbera

85 1988 Barbera

86 1987 Barbera

86 1989 Cabernet Franc Sonoma County

85 1991 Cabernet Sauvignon

80 1990 Cabernet Sauvignon

82 1989 Cabernet Sauvignon

77 1988 Cabernet Sauvignon

83 1988 Cabernet Sauvignon Reserve

87 1987 Cabernet Sauvignon Reserve

85 1986 Cabernet Sauvignon Reserve

85 1985 Cabernet Sauvignon Reserve

83 1978 Cabernet Sauvignon Reserve

88 1991 Cabernet Sauvignon Sonoma Valley Cherryblock Old Vines

82 1989 Cabernet Sauvignon Sonoma Valley Cherryblock Old Vines

84 1987 Cabernet Sauvignon Cherryblock

90 1993 Chardonnay Russian River Valley Dutton Ranch

87 1993 Chardonnay Sonoma Valley

83 1992 Chardonnay Sonoma Valley

84 1991 Chardonnay Sonoma Valley

86 1991 Chardonnay Sonoma Valley Reserve

82 1992 Merlot Sonoma Valley Sonoma Series

84 1991 Merlot Sonoma Valley Sonoma Series

82 1990 Merlot Sonoma Valley Sonoma Series

84 1989 Merlot Sonoma Valley Sonoma Series

86 1992 Syrah Sonoma County Sonoma Series

83 1991 Zinfandel Sonoma County Sonoma Series

85 1989 Zinfandel Sonoma County Sonoma Series

84 1988 Zinfandel Sonoma Valley Sonoma Series

88 1985 Zinfandel Sonoma County Family Selection

88 1991 Richard Cuneo Sparkling Wine Sonoma County Brut Cuvée de Chardonnay

SEGHESIO WINERY

84 1992 Cabernet Sauvignon Sonoma County

83 1991 Cabernet Sauvignon Sonoma County

84 1992 Carignane Alexander Valley Old Vines

82 1993 Chardonnay Sonoma County

85 1992 Chardonnay Sonoma County

83 1991 Chardonnay Sonoma County

81 1991 Pinot Noir Russian River Valley

78 1990 Pinot Noir Russian River Valley

83 1988 Pinot Noir Russian River Valley

84 1987 Pinot Noir Russian River Valley

83 1987 Pinot Noir Russian River Valley Reserve

83 1993 Pinot Noir Sonoma County

86 1990 Sangiovese Alexander Valley Chianti Station Old Vine

87 1991 Sangiovese Alexander Valley Vitigno Toscano

85 1993 Sauvignon Blanc Sonoma County

83 1990 Zinfandel Alexander Valley Old Vine Reserve

88 1988 Zinfandel Alexander Valley Reserve

80 1986 Zinfandel Alexander Valley Reserve

85 1987 Zinfandel Northern Sonoma

80 1986 Zinfandel Northern Sonoma

88 1992 Zinfandel Sonoma County

84 1991 Zinfandel Sonoma County

85 1990 Zinfandel Sonoma County

84 1989 Zinfandel Sonoma County

86 1988 Zinfandel Sonoma County

SELENE WINES

88 1991 Merlot Napa Valley

86 1993 Sauvignon Blanc Carneros Hyde Vineyard

90 1992 Sauvignon Blanc Carneros Hyde Vineyard

SEQUOIA GROVE VINEYARDS

90 1992 Cabernet Sauvignon Napa Valley

88 1991 Cabernet Sauvignon Napa Valley

90 1990 Cabernet Sauvignon Napa Valley

80 1989 Cabernet Sauvignon Napa Valley

87 1988 Cabernet Sauvignon Napa Valley

87 1987 Cabernet Sauvignon Napa Valley

86 1986 Cabernet Sauvignon Napa Valley

86 1985 Cabernet Sauvignon Napa Valley

85 1984 Cabernet Sauvignon Napa Valley

75 1983 Cabernet Sauvignon Napa Valley

82 1982 Cabernet Sauvignon Napa Valley

78 1981 Cabernet Sauvignon Napa Valley

89 1992 Cabernet Sauvignon Napa Valley Estate Reserve

91 1991 Cabernet Sauvignon Napa Valley Estate Reserve

91 1990 Cabernet Sauvignon Napa Valley Estate Reserve

90 1989 Cabernet Sauvignon Napa Valley Estate Reserve

83 1993 Chardonnay Carneros

86 1992 Chardonnay Carneros

82 1991 Chardonnay Carneros

82 1993 Chardonnay Napa Valley Estate Reserve

88 1992 Chardonnay Napa Valley Estate Reserve

82 1991 Chardonnay Napa Valley Estate Reserve

SHAFER VINEYARDS

90 1991 Cabernet Sauvignon Stags Leap District

90 1990 Cabernet Sauvignon Stags Leap District

86 1989 Cabernet Sauvignon Stags Leap District

88 1988 Cabernet Sauvignon Stags Leap District

92 1987 Cabernet Sauvignon Stags Leap District

93 1986 Cabernet Sauvignon Stags Leap District

91 1985 Cabernet Sauvignon Stags Leap District

91 1984 Cabernet Sauvignon Stags Leap District

87 1983 Cabernet Sauvignon Stags Leap District

88 1982 Cabernet Sauvignon Stags Leap District

82 1980 Cabernet Sauvignon Stags Leap District

88 1979 Cabernet Sauvignon Stags Leap District

94 1978 Cabernet Sauvignon Stags Leap District

93 1991 Cabernet Sauvignon Stags Leap District Hillside Select

94 1990 Cabernet Sauvignon Stags Leap District Hillside Select

88 1989 Cabernet Sauvignon Stags Leap District Hillside Select

85 1988 Cabernet Sauvignon Stags Leap District Hillside Select

92 1987 Cabernet Sauvignon Stags Leap District Hillside Select

89 1986 Cabernet Sauvignon Stags Leap District Hillside Select

94 1985 Cabernet Sauvignon Stags Leap District Hillside Select

90 1984 Cabernet Sauvignon Stags Leap District Hillside Select

86 1983 Cabernet Sauvignon Stags Leap District Hillside Select

88 1992 Chardonnay Napa Valley

88 1993 Chardonnay Napa Valley Barrel Select

85 1992 Chardonnay Napa Valley Barrel Select

91 1991 Chardonnay Napa Valley Barrel Select

88 1992 Merlot Napa Valley

89 1991 Merlot Napa Valley

91 1990 Merlot Napa Valley

87 1989 Merlot Napa Valley

83 1988 Merlot Napa Valley

92 1987 Merlot Napa Valley

91 1986 Merlot Napa Valley

87 1992 Sangiovese Stags Leap District Firebreak

84 1991 Sangiovese Stags Leap District Firebreak

SHENANDOAH VINEYARDS

85 1989 Cabernet Franc Amador County Varietal Adventure Series

88 1992 Cabernet Sauvignon Amador County

79 1991 Cabernet Sauvignon Amador County

84 1992 Orange Muscat Amador County

82 1993 Sauvignon Blanc Amador County

83 1992 Zinfandel Amador County Special Reserve

76 1991 Zinfandel Amador County Special Reserve

77 1993 Zinfandel Blend Amador County Zingiovese

81 1991 Zinfandel Blend Sierra Foothills Zinfandel/Sirah

SIERRA VISTA

76 1989 Cabernet Sauvignon El Dorado County

84 1988 Cabernet Sauvignon El Dorado County

84 1991 Cabernet Sauvignon El Dorado County Five Star Reserve

SIGNORELLO VINEYARDS

87 1991 Cabernet Sauvignon Napa Valley

90 1990 Cabernet Sauvignon Napa Valley

90 1992 Cabernet Sauvignon Napa Valley Founder's Reserve

90 1991 Cabernet Sauvignon Napa Valley Founder's Reserve

92 1990 Cabernet Sauvignon Napa Valley Founder's Reserve

85 1989 Cabernet Sauvignon Napa Valley Founder's Reserve

90 1988 Cabernet Sauvignon Napa Valley Founder's Reserve

88 1993 Chardonnay Napa Valley

91 1992 Chardonnay Napa Valley

91 1991 Chardonnay Napa Valley

90 1993 Chardonnay Napa Valley Founder's Reserve

88 1992 Chardonnay Napa Valley Founder's Reserve

86 1990 Merlot Napa Valley

91 1990 Petite Sirah Napa Valley

87 1991 Pinot Noir North Coast Founder's Reserve

82 1990 Pinot Noir North Coast Founder's Reserve

78 1989 Pinot Noir North Coast Founder's Reserve

85 1988 Pinot Noir North Coast Founder's Reserve

86 1991 Red Table Wine Napa Valley Il Taglio

91 1993 Sauvignon Blanc Napa Valley

87 1992 Sauvignon Blanc Napa Valley

86 1993 Sémillon Napa Valley Barrel Fermented

89 1992 Sémillon Napa Valley Barrel Fermented

81 1991 White Table Wine Napa Valley Il Taglio

86 1993 Zinfandel Napa Valley Unfined Unfiltered

75 1990 Zinfandel Napa Valley Unfined Unfiltered

SILVER MOUNTAIN VINEYARDS

84 1991 Chardonnay Monterey County

SILVER OAK CELLARS

89 1990 Cabernet Sauvignon Alexander Valley

82 1989 Cabernet Sauvignon Alexander Valley

90 1988 Cabernet Sauvignon Alexander Valley

89 1987 Cabernet Sauvignon Alexander Valley

93 1986 Cabernet Sauvignon Alexander Valley

95 1985 Cabernet Sauvignon Alexander Valley

89 1984 Cabernet Sauvignon Alexander Valley

85	1983 Cabernet Sauvignon Alexander Valley
88	1982 Cabernet Sauvignon Alexander Valley
86	1981 Cabernet Sauvignon Alexander Valley
88	1980 Cabernet Sauvignon Alexander Valley
85	1979 Cabernet Sauvignon Alexander Valley
91	1978 Cabernet Sauvignon Alexander Valley
88	1977 Cabernet Sauvignon Alexander Valley
84	1976 Cabernet Sauvignon Alexander Valley
88	1975 Cabernet Sauvignon Alexander Valley
84	1974 Cabernet Sauvignon Alexander Valley
80	1973 Cabernet Sauvignon Alexander Valley
83	1972 Cabernet Sauvignon Alexander Valley
91	1990 Cabernet Sauvignon Napa Valley
86	1989 Cabernet Sauvignon Napa Valley
88	1988 Cabernet Sauvignon Napa Valley
89	1987 Cabernet Sauvignon Napa Valley
92	1986 Cabernet Sauvignon Napa Valley
88	1985 Cabernet Sauvignon Napa Valley
87	1984 Cabernet Sauvignon Napa Valley
74	1983 Cabernet Sauvignon Napa Valley
86	1982 Cabernet Sauvignon Napa Valley
79	1981 Cabernet Sauvignon Napa Valley
73	1980 Cabernet Sauvignon Napa Valley
81	1979 Cabernet Sauvignon Napa Valley
88	1987 Cabernet Sauvignon Napa Valley Bonny's Vineyard
88	1986 Cabernet Sauvignon Napa Valley Bonny's Vineyard
90	1985 Cabernet Sauvignon Napa Valley Bonny's Vineyard
84	1984 Cabernet Sauvignon Napa Valley Bonny's Vineyard
82	1983 Cabernet Sauvignon Napa Valley Bonny's Vineyard
77	1981 Cabernet Sauvignon Napa Valley Bonny's Vineyard
73	1980 Cabernet Sauvignon Napa Valley Bonny's Vineyard
72	1979 Cabernet Sauvignon Napa Valley Bonny's Vineyard

SILVERADO HILL CELLARS

82	1993 Chardonnay Napa Valley
87	1992 Chardonnay Napa Valley
83	1993 Chardonnay Napa Valley Winemaker's Traditional Methode

SILVERADO VINEYARDS

90	1992 Cabernet Sauvignon Stags Leap District
93	1991 Cabernet Sauvignon Stags Leap District
90	1990 Cabernet Sauvignon Stags Leap District
81	1989 Cabernet Sauvignon Stags Leap District
86	1988 Cabernet Sauvignon Stags Leap District

92	1987 Cabernet Sauvignon Stags Leap District
90	1986 Cabernet Sauvignon Stags Leap District
92	1985 Cabernet Sauvignon Stags Leap District
91	1984 Cabernet Sauvignon Stags Leap District
88	1983 Cabernet Sauvignon Stags Leap District
88	1982 Cabernet Sauvignon Stags Leap District
90	1981 Cabernet Sauvignon Stags Leap District
97	1990 Cabernet Sauvignon Stags Leap District Limited Reserve
95	1987 Cabernet Sauvignon Stags Leap District Limited Reserve
96	1986 Cabernet Sauvignon Stags Leap District Limited Reserve
87	1993 Chardonnay Napa Valley
87	1992 Chardonnay Napa Valley
89	1991 Chardonnay Napa Valley
92	1992 Chardonnay Napa Valley Limited Reserve
93	NV Dessert Napa Valley
85	1992 Merlot Napa Valley
88	1991 Merlot Stags Leap District
87	1990 Merlot Stags Leap District
85	1989 Merlot Stags Leap District
85	1988 Merlot Stags Leap District
90	1987 Merlot Stags Leap District
89	1986 Merlot Stags Leap District
84	1993 Sauvignon Blanc Napa Valley
90	1992 Sauvignon Blanc Napa Valley

SIMI WINERY

77	1989 Cabernet Sauvignon Alexander Valley
84	1988 Cabernet Sauvignon Alexander Valley
89	1987 Cabernet Sauvignon Alexander Valley
85	1986 Cabernet Sauvignon Alexander Valley
91	1985 Cabernet Sauvignon Alexander Valley
86	1984 Cabernet Sauvignon Alexander Valley
92	1991 Cabernet Sauvignon Alexander Valley Reserve
84	1990 Cabernet Sauvignon Sonoma County Centennial Edition
87	1988 Cabernet Sauvignon Alexander Valley Reserve
88	1987 Cabernet Sauvignon Alexander Valley Reserve
89	1986 Cabernet Sauvignon Alexander Valley Reserve
90	1985 Cabernet Sauvignon Alexander Valley Reserve
88	1984 Cabernet Sauvignon Alexander Valley Reserve
85	1982 Cabernet Sauvignon Sonoma-Napa Counties Reserve
86	1981 Cabernet Sauvignon Alexander Valley Reserve
80	1980 Cabernet Sauvignon Alexander Valley Reserve
84	1979 Cabernet Sauvignon Alexander Valley Reserve
82	1974 Cabernet Sauvignon Alexander Valley Special Reserve
85	1991 Chardonnay Sonoma County
82	1989 Chardonnay Sonoma County Reserve

89	1988 Chardonnay Sonoma County Reserve
92	1987 Chardonnay Sonoma County Reserve
92	1986 Chardonnay Sonoma County Reserve
91	1985 Chardonnay Sonoma County Reserve
84	1992 Meritage White Sonoma County Sendal
88	1991 Meritage White Sonoma County Sendal
78	1992 Red Table Wine North Coast Altaire
84	1993 Sauvignon Blanc Sonoma County

ROBERT SINSKEY VINEYARDS

88	1989 Cabernet Sauvignon Stags Leap District
87	1993 Chardonnay Carneros
87	1992 Chardonnay Carneros
88	1991 Chardonnay Carneros
87	1990 Meritage Red Carneros RSV Claret Reserve
85	1989 Meritage Red Carneros RSV Claret Reserve
83	1988 Meritage Red Carneros RSV Claret Reserve
88	1991 Meritage Red Stags Leap District RSV Claret Reserve
86	1990 Merlot Carneros
82	1989 Merlot Carneros
88	1987 Merlot Napa Valley
83	1986 Merlot Napa Valley
83	1992 Pinot Noir Carneros
82	1991 Pinot Noir Carneros
89	1990 Pinot Noir Carneros
81	1988 Pinot Noir Carneros
86	1987 Pinot Noir Carneros
80	1990 Pinot Noir Carneros RSV Reserve
87	1990 Aries Cabernet Sauvignon Napa Valley
86	1989 Aries Merlot Carneros
85	1992 Aries Pinot Noir Carneros
84	1991 Aries Pinot Noir Carneros
70	1989 Aries Pinot Noir Carneros Cuvée Vivace

SKY VINEYARDS

88	1990 Zinfandel Mount Veeder
87	1989 Zinfandel Mount Veeder
78	1988 Zinfandel Napa Valley
90	1987 Zinfandel Napa Valley
88	1985 Zinfandel Napa Valley

SMITH AND HOOK

86	1991 Cabernet Sauvignon Santa Lucia Highlands
87	1990 Cabernet Sauvignon Santa Lucia Highlands
80	1988 Cabernet Sauvignon Santa Lucia Highlands
85	1992 Merlot Santa Lucia Highlands
74	1991 Merlot Santa Lucia Highlands
81	1990 Merlot Santa Lucia Highlands
70	1989 Merlot Santa Lucia Highlands
80	1988 Merlot Santa Lucia Highlands
83	1987 Merlot Santa Lucia Highlands

86 1986 Merlot Santa Lucia Highlands

79 1992 Lone Oak Cabernet Sauvignon Monterey County

SMITH-MADRONE VINEYARD

80 1985 Cabernet Sauvignon Napa Valley

85 1984 Cabernet Sauvignon Napa Valley

79 1983 Cabernet Sauvignon Napa Valley

SMOTHERS BROTHERS WINES

84 1990 Cabernet Sauvignon Sonoma Valley Remick Ridge Ranch

82 1989 Cabernet Sauvignon Sonoma Valley Remick Ridge Ranch

SOBON ESTATE

81 1990 Cabernet Franc Shenandoah Valley

86 1992 Rhône Blend Shenandoah Valley Rhône Rouge

82 1994 Rhône Blend Shenandoah Valley Rose

82 1991 Syrah Shenandoah Valley

86 1990 Syrah Shenandoah Valley

84 1993 Viognier Shenandoah Valley

82 1992 Zinfandel Fiddletown Lubenko

81 1992 Zinfandel Shenandoah Valley

88 1988 Zinfandel Shenandoah Valley

78 1990 Zinfandel Shenandoah Valley Old Vines Sobon Estate

82 1992 Zinfandel Shenandoah Valley Rocky Top

81 1990 Zinfandel Sierra Foothills

86 1989 Zinfandel Sierra Foothills

SODA CANYON VINEYARDS

83 1992 Chardonnay Napa Valley 14th Leaf

85 1991 Chardonnay Napa Valley 13th Leaf

SOLIS WINERY

85 1991 Chardonnay Santa Clara County Barrel Fermented

81 1991 Merlot Santa Clara County

78 1988 Pinot Noir Santa Clara County

79 1991 Zinfandel Blend Santa Clara County Old Vines Seducente

SOLITUDE WINES

90 1993 Chardonnay Carneros Sangiacomo Vineyard

89 1991 Chardonnay Carneros Sangiacomo Vineyard

84 1992 Pinot Noir Sonoma County

75 1991 Pinot Noir Sonoma County

SONOMA CREEK WINERY

84 1991 Cabernet Sauvignon Sonoma Valley Reserve

74 1988 Cabernet Sauvignon Sonoma Valley Reserve

84 1993 Chardonnay Carneros

70 1992 Chardonnay Carneros Barrel Fermented

87 1992 Chardonnay Carneros Estate Bottled Organically Grown

85 1992 Merlot Sonoma Valley Sangiacomo Vineyard

77 1992 Pinot Noir Carneros

78 1992 Zinfandel Sonoma County

78 1990 Zinfandel Sonoma County

SONOMA-CUTRER VINEYARDS

88 1992 Chardonnay Sonoma Coast Cutrer Vineyard

88 1991 Chardonnay Sonoma Coast Cutrer Vineyard

87 1990 Chardonnay Sonoma Coast Cutrer Vineyard

88 1991 Chardonnay Sonoma Coast Les Pierres

87 1990 Chardonnay Sonoma Coast Les Pierres

86 1989 Chardonnay Sonoma Coast Les Pierres

93 1988 Chardonnay Sonoma Valley Les Pierres

90 1987 Chardonnay Sonoma Valley Les Pierres

84 1993 Chardonnay Sonoma Coast Russian River Ranches

83 1992 Chardonnay Russian River Valley Russian River Ranches

84 1991 Chardonnay Russian River Valley Russian River Ranches

86 1990 Chardonnay Russian River Valley Russian River Ranches

82 1989 Chardonnay Russian River Valley Russian River Ranches

88 1988 Chardonnay Russian River Valley Russian River Ranches

SONOMA-LOEB

89 1993 Chardonnay Sonoma County Ambassador John L. Loeb Jr.'s Private Reserve

89 1992 Chardonnay Sonoma County Ambassador John L. Loeb Jr.'s Private Reserve

90 1991 Chardonnay Sonoma County Ambassador John L. Loeb Jr.'s Private Reserve

89 1991 Chardonnay Sonoma County Private Reserve

SOQUEL VINEYARDS

86 1991 Cabernet Sauvignon Santa Cruz Mountains

88 1990 Cabernet Sauvignon Santa Cruz Mountains

84 1989 Cabernet Sauvignon Santa Cruz Mountains Special Reserve

83 1991 Cabernet Sauvignon Stags Leap District

85 1990 Cabernet Sauvignon Stags Leap District

83 1989 Cabernet Sauvignon Stags Leap District

75 1991 Chardonnay Santa Cruz Mountains

80 1991 Pinot Noir Santa Cruz Mountains

86 1990 Pinot Noir Santa Cruz Mountains

79 1991 Zinfandel Alexander Valley

SPOTTSWOODE WINERY

93 1991 Cabernet Sauvignon Napa Valley

91 1990 Cabernet Sauvignon Napa Valley

89 1989 Cabernet Sauvignon Napa Valley

90 1988 Cabernet Sauvignon Napa Valley

96 1987 Cabernet Sauvignon Napa Valley

96 1986 Cabernet Sauvignon Napa Valley

95 1985 Cabernet Sauvignon Napa Valley

90 1984 Cabernet Sauvignon Napa Valley

88 1983 Cabernet Sauvignon Napa Valley

88 1982 Cabernet Sauvignon Napa Valley

87 1994 Sauvignon Blanc Napa Valley

85 1993 Sauvignon Blanc Napa Valley

SPRING MOUNTAIN VINEYARDS

90 1986 Cabernet Sauvignon Napa Valley

83 1985 Cabernet Sauvignon Napa Valley

85 1984 Cabernet Sauvignon Napa Valley

78 1983 Cabernet Sauvignon Napa Valley

83 NV Cabernet Sauvignon Napa Valley Lot H 68-69

STAGLIN FAMILY VINEYARD

88 1991 Cabernet Sauvignon Napa Valley

88 1990 Cabernet Sauvignon Napa Valley

87 1989 Cabernet Sauvignon Napa Valley

88 1993 Sangiovese Napa Valley Stagliano

STAG'S LEAP WINE CELLARS

92 1991 Cabernet Blend Napa Valley Cask 23

94 1990 Cabernet Blend Napa Valley Cask 23

80 1987 Cabernet Blend Napa Valley Cask 23

82 1986 Cabernet Blend Napa Valley Cask 23

98 1985 Cabernet Blend Napa Valley Cask 23

89 1984 Cabernet Blend Napa Valley Cask 23

86 1983 Cabernet Blend Napa Valley Cask 23

88 1979 Cabernet Blend Napa Valley Cask 23

92 1978 Cabernet Blend Napa Valley Cask 23

89 1977 Cabernet Blend Napa Valley Cask 23

94 1974 Cabernet Blend Napa Valley Cask 23

87 1991 Cabernet Sauvignon Napa Valley

89 1990 Cabernet Sauvignon Napa Valley

83 1989 Cabernet Sauvignon Napa Valley

87 1988 Cabernet Sauvignon Napa Valley

88 1991 Cabernet Sauvignon Napa Valley Fay Vineyard

90 1990 Cabernet Sauvignon Napa Valley Fay Vineyard

84 1989 Cabernet Sauvignon Napa Valley Fay Vineyard

80 1989 Cabernet Sauvignon Napa Valley SLV/Fay Vineyard Blend

90 1990 Cabernet Sauvignon Stags Leap District SLV

87 1988 Cabernet Sauvignon Stags Leap District SLV

77 1987 Cabernet Sauvignon Stags Leap District SLV

89 1986 Cabernet Sauvignon Stags Leap District SLV

94 1985 Cabernet Sauvignon Stags Leap District SLV

89 1984 Cabernet Sauvignon Stags Leap District SLV

88	1981 Cabernet Sauvignon Stags Leap District Stag's Leap Vineyard
89	1978 Cabernet Sauvignon Stags Leap District Stag's Leap Vineyard
88	1978 Cabernet Sauvignon Stags Leap District Stag's Leap Vineyard Lot 2
85	1977 Cabernet Sauvignon Stags Leap District Stag's Leap Vineyard
88	1977 Cabernet Sauvignon Stags Leap District Stag's Leap Vineyard Lot 2
87	1974 Cabernet Sauvignon Stags Leap District Stag's Leap Vineyard
86	1973 Cabernet Sauvignon Stags Leap District Stag's Leap Vineyard
70	1972 Cabernet Sauvignon Stags Leap District Stag's Leap Vineyard
88	1993 Chardonnay Napa Valley
88	1992 Chardonnay Napa Valley
89	1993 Chardonnay Napa Valley Reserve
90	1992 Chardonnay Napa Valley Reserve
91	1991 Chardonnay Napa Valley Reserve
87	1991 Merlot Napa Valley
87	1990 Merlot Napa Valley
86	1985 Merlot Napa Valley
85	1991 Petite Sirah Napa Valley
87	1987 Petite Sirah Napa Valley
85	1985 Petite Sirah Napa Valley
77	1993 Sauvignon Blanc Napa Valley Rancho Chimiles
82	1992 Sauvignon Blanc Napa Valley Rancho Chimiles
86	1992 White Riesling Napa Valley
79	1993 Hawk Crest Sauvignon Blanc California

STAGS' LEAP WINERY

85	1991 Cabernet Sauvignon Napa Valley
86	1989 Cabernet Sauvignon Napa Valley
88	1987 Cabernet Sauvignon Stags Leap District
88	1986 Cabernet Sauvignon Stags Leap District
85	1985 Cabernet Sauvignon Stags Leap District
87	1984 Cabernet Sauvignon Stags Leap District
78	1990 Merlot Napa Valley
87	1989 Merlot Napa Valley
85	1987 Merlot Napa Valley
84	1986 Merlot Napa Valley
91	1990 Petite Sirah Napa Valley
84	1989 Petite Sirah Napa Valley
86	1988 Petite Sirah Napa Valley
86	1988 Petite Sirah Napa Valley Reserve
83	1987 Petite Sirah Napa Valley
82	1987 Petite Sirah Napa Valley Petite Syrah
87	1986 Petite Sirah Napa Valley
84	1985 Petite Sirah Napa Valley

85	1984 Petite Sirah Napa Valley
82	1983 Petite Sirah Napa Valley
86	1982 Petite Sirah Napa Valley
80	1981 Petite Sirah Napa Valley
80	1980 Petite Sirah Napa Valley
79	1979 Petite Sirah Napa Valley
89	1978 Petite Sirah Napa Valley
83	1977 Petite Sirah Napa Valley
89	1976 Petite Sirah Napa Valley
84	1975 Petite Sirah Napa Valley
87	1974 Petite Sirah Napa Valley
88	1973 Petite Sirah Napa Valley
91	1972 Petite Sirah Napa Valley

P. AND M. STAIGER

83	1993 Chardonnay Santa Cruz Mountains
80	1992 Chardonnay Santa Cruz Mountains

STAR HILL WINES

82	1990 Cabernet Sauvignon Napa Valley Bartolucci Vineyard Doc's Reserve
87	1987 Cabernet Sauvignon Napa Valley Bartolucci Vineyard Doc's Reserve
82	1988 Pinot Noir Napa Valley Doc's Reserve
87	1987 Pinot Noir Napa Valley Doc's Reserve

STEELE WINES

86	1993 Chardonnay California
90	1992 Chardonnay California
87	1991 Chardonnay California
90	1992 Chardonnay Carneros Sangiocomo Vineyard
90	1991 Chardonnay Carneros Sangiocomo Vineyard
89	1992 Chardonnay Mendocino County Dennison Vineyard
91	1993 Chardonnay Mendocino County DuPratt Vineyard
86	1992 Chardonnay Mendocino County DuPratt Vineyard
92	1991 Chardonnay Mendocino County DuPratt Vineyard
90	1993 Chardonnay Mendocino County Lolonis Vineyard
92	1992 Chardonnay Mendocino County Lolonis Vineyard
91	1991 Chardonnay Mendocino County Lolonis Vineyard
89	1993 Chardonnay Santa Barbara County Bien Nacido Vineyard
90	1992 Chardonnay Santa Barbara County Bien Nacido Vineyard
92	1992 Chardonnay Sonoma Valley Durell Vineyard
89	1993 Pinot Blanc Santa Barbara County Bien Nacido Vineyard

91	1992 Pinot Blanc Santa Barbara County Bien Nacido Vineyard
90	1993 Pinot Noir Carneros
88	1992 Pinot Noir Carneros
90	1991 Pinot Noir Carneros
88	1993 Pinot Noir Sonoma Valley Durell Vineyard
87	1992 Pinot Noir Sonoma Valley Durell Vineyard
88	1993 Pinot Noir Carneros Sangiacomo Vineyard
90	1991 Pinot Noir Carneros Sangiacomo Vineyard
86	1992 Pinot Noir Mendocino County DuPratt Vineyard
86	1993 Pinot Noir Santa Barbara County Bien Nacido Vineyard
89	1993 Zinfandel Clear Lake Catfish Vineyard
90	1992 Zinfandel Clear Lake Catfish Vineyard
90	1991 Zinfandel Clear Lake Catfish Vineyard
87	1993 Zinfandel Mendocino County Pacini Vineyard
84	1992 Zinfandel Mendocino County Pacini Vineyard
87	1991 Zinfandel Mendocino County Pacini Vineyard
78	1994 Shooting Star Blush Mendocino County Pacini Vineyard Zin Gris
83	1992 Shooting Star Cabernet Franc Clear Lake
88	1991 Shooting Star Cabernet Franc Lake County
82	1993 Shooting Star Chardonnay Mendocino County
87	1992 Shooting Star Merlot Clear Lake
88	1991 Shooting Star Merlot Lake County
86	1993 Shooting Star Pinot Noir Mendocino County
87	1993 Shooting Star Zinfandel Clear Lake
87	1993 Shooting Star Zinfandel Lake County

STELTZNER VINEYARDS

84	1992 Cabernet Blend Stags Leap District Claret
84	1991 Cabernet Blend Stags Leap District Claret
87	1990 Cabernet Blend Stags Leap District Claret
85	1991 Cabernet Sauvignon Stags Leap District
85	1991 Cabernet Sauvignon Stags Leap District Commemorative
87	1990 Cabernet Sauvignon Stags Leap District
82	1988 Cabernet Sauvignon Stags Leap District
85	1987 Cabernet Sauvignon Stags Leap District
88	1986 Cabernet Sauvignon Stags Leap District
88	1985 Cabernet Sauvignon Stags Leap District
87	1984 Cabernet Sauvignon Stags Leap District
90	1983 Cabernet Sauvignon Stags Leap District
84	1981 Cabernet Sauvignon Stags Leap District
85	1980 Cabernet Sauvignon Stags Leap District
88	1978 Cabernet Sauvignon Stags Leap District
82	1977 Cabernet Sauvignon Stags Leap District
82	1992 Merlot Stags Leap District
83	1991 Merlot Stags Leap District
84	1990 Merlot Stags Leap District
84	1989 Merlot Stags Leap District

81 1991 Sauvignon Blanc Napa Valley Oak Knoll Ranch

ROBERT STEMMLER WINERY

78 1991 Pinot Noir Sonoma County

80 1990 Pinot Noir Sonoma County

71 1989 Pinot Noir Sonoma County

71 1988 Pinot Noir Sonoma County

82 1987 Pinot Noir Sonoma County

STERLING VINEYARDS

90 1991 Cabernet Blend Napa Valley Reserve

87 1990 Cabernet Blend Napa Valley Reserve

88 1989 Cabernet Blend Napa Valley Reserve

85 1988 Cabernet Blend Napa Valley Reserve

90 1987 Cabernet Blend Napa Valley Reserve

93 1986 Cabernet Blend Napa Valley Reserve

96 1985 Cabernet Blend Napa Valley Reserve

90 1984 Cabernet Blend Napa Valley Reserve

82 1983 Cabernet Blend Napa Valley Reserve

75 1982 Cabernet Blend Napa Valley Reserve

83 1981 Cabernet Blend Napa Valley Reserve

88 1980 Cabernet Blend Napa Valley Reserve

77 1979 Cabernet Blend Napa Valley Reserve

90 1978 Cabernet Blend Napa Valley Reserve

83 1974 Cabernet Blend Napa Valley Reserve

85 1973 Cabernet Blend Napa Valley Reserve

86 1991 Cabernet Blend Napa Valley Three Palms Vineyard

85 1988 Cabernet Blend Napa Valley Three Palms Vineyard

87 1987 Cabernet Blend Napa Valley Three Palms Vineyard

85 1986 Cabernet Blend Napa Valley Three Palms Vineyard

89 1985 Cabernet Blend Napa Valley Three Palms Vineyard

82 1991 Cabernet Sauvignon Napa Valley

83 1990 Cabernet Sauvignon Napa Valley

83 1989 Cabernet Sauvignon Napa Valley

80 1988 Cabernet Sauvignon Napa Valley

85 1987 Cabernet Sauvignon Napa Valley

87 1986 Cabernet Sauvignon Napa Valley

89 1985 Cabernet Sauvignon Napa Valley

83 1991 Cabernet Sauvignon Napa Valley Diamond Mountain Ranch

81 1990 Cabernet Sauvignon Napa Valley Diamond Mountain Ranch

79 1989 Cabernet Sauvignon Napa Valley Diamond Mountain Ranch

86 1987 Cabernet Sauvignon Napa Valley Diamond Mountain Ranch

87 1986 Cabernet Sauvignon Napa Valley Diamond Mountain Ranch

85 1985 Cabernet Sauvignon Napa Valley Diamond Mountain Ranch

84 1984 Cabernet Sauvignon Napa Valley Diamond Mountain Ranch

78 1993 Chardonnay Carneros Winery Lake Vineyard

67 1992 Chardonnay Carneros Winery Lake Vineyard

81 1991 Chardonnay Carneros Winery Lake Vineyard

82 1993 Chardonnay Napa Valley

85 1993 Chardonnay Napa Valley Sterling Collections Z Lot

81 1992 Chardonnay Napa Valley

78 1991 Chardonnay Napa Valley

84 1992 Chardonnay Napa Valley Diamond Mountain Ranch

81 1991 Chardonnay Napa Valley Diamond Mountain Ranch

79 1991 Merlot Napa Valley

82 1990 Merlot Napa Valley

82 1990 Merlot Napa Valley Three Palms Vineyard

82 1989 Merlot Napa Valley

83 1988 Merlot Napa Valley

83 1987 Merlot Napa Valley

84 1986 Merlot Napa Valley

83 1985 Merlot Napa Valley

73 1992 Pinot Noir Carneros Winery Lake Vineyard

78 1991 Pinot Noir Carneros Winery Lake Vineyard

73 1990 Pinot Noir Carneros Winery Lake Vineyard

83 1989 Pinot Noir Carneros Winery Lake Vineyard

83 1988 Pinot Noir Carneros Winery Lake Vineyard

81 1987 Pinot Noir Carneros Winery Lake Vineyard

87 1986 Pinot Noir Carneros Winery Lake Vineyard

80 1993 Sauvignon Blanc Napa Valley

72 1992 Sauvignon Blanc Napa Valley

STEVENOT WINERY

83 1988 Cabernet Sauvignon Amador County Grand Reserve

82 1987 Cabernet Sauvignon Calaveras County Grand Reserve

82 1992 Cabernet Sauvignon Calaveras County Reserve

84 1991 Cabernet Sauvignon Calaveras County Reserve

84 1990 Cabernet Sauvignon Calaveras County Reserve

83 1991 Cabernet Sauvignon California

74 1992 Chardonnay Calaveras County Barrel Fermented

82 1993 Chardonnay Calaveras County Reserve

79 1992 Chardonnay California

82 1993 Chardonnay Sierra Foothills

75 1991 Merlot North Coast Reserve

STONEGATE WINERY

81 1990 Cabernet Franc Napa Valley

81 1990 Cabernet Sauvignon Napa Valley

80 1989 Cabernet Sauvignon Napa Valley

84 1988 Cabernet Sauvignon Napa Valley

82 1987 Cabernet Sauvignon Napa Valley

86 1986 Cabernet Sauvignon Napa Valley

87 1978 Cabernet Sauvignon Napa Valley

83 1991 Chardonnay Sonoma County Bella Vista Vineyard

83 1988 Meritage Red Napa Valley Reserve

83 1987 Meritage Red Napa Valley Reserve

86 1989 Merlot Napa Valley

81 1988 Merlot Napa Valley

83 1987 Merlot Napa Valley Pershing Vineyard

85 1987 Merlot Napa Valley Spaulding Vineyard

82 1986 Merlot Napa Valley

STONESTREET

91 1991 Cabernet Blend Alexander Valley Legacy

86 1990 Cabernet Blend Alexander Valley Legacy

87 1991 Cabernet Sauvignon Alexander Valley

82 1989 Cabernet Sauvignon Alexander Valley

82 1988 Cabernet Sauvignon Alexander Valley

92 1993 Chardonnay Sonoma County

90 1992 Chardonnay Sonoma County

88 1991 Chardonnay Sonoma County

85 1993 Gewürztraminer Anderson Valley

78 1991 Gewürztraminer Sonoma County

89 1992 Merlot Alexander Valley

87 1991 Merlot Alexander Valley

82 1990 Merlot Alexander Valley

88 1989 Merlot Alexander Valley

83 1990 Pinot Noir Russian River Valley

85 1992 Pinot Noir Sonoma County

89 1991 Pinot Noir Sonoma County

STONY HILL VINEYARD

83 1992 Chardonnay Napa Valley

88 1991 Chardonnay Napa Valley

88 1990 Chardonnay Napa Valley

90 1988 Chardonnay Napa Valley

87 1986 Chardonnay Napa Valley

92 1985 Chardonnay Napa Valley

90 1984 Chardonnay Napa Valley

85 1982 Chardonnay Napa Valley

86 1981 Chardonnay Napa Valley

86 1980 Chardonnay Napa Valley

81 1979 Chardonnay Napa Valley

85 1978 Chardonnay Napa Valley

91 1977 Chardonnay Napa Valley

88	1976 Chardonnay Napa Valley
75	1975 Chardonnay Napa Valley
73	1974 Chardonnay Napa Valley
79	1973 Chardonnay Napa Valley
83	1972 Chardonnay Napa Valley
80	1971 Chardonnay Napa Valley
92	1970 Chardonnay Napa Valley
93	1968 Chardonnay Napa Valley
90	1965 Chardonnay Napa Valley
98	1964 Chardonnay Napa Valley
96	1962 Chardonnay Napa Valley
88	1960 Chardonnay Napa Valley
86	1993 Chardonnay Napa Valley SHV

STONY RIDGE WINERY

78	1989 Cabernet Sauvignon California
78	1989 Cabernet Sauvignon Napa Valley Limited Release
85	1991 Merlot North Coast Limited Release
82	1990 Merlot North Coast Limited Release

STORRS WINERY

85	1993 Chardonnay Santa Cruz Mountains Christie Vineyard Mountain Vineyard Collection
86	1993 Chardonnay Santa Cruz Mountains Vanumanutagi Vineyards
82	1990 Zinfandel California Beauregard Ranch Ben Lomond Mountain

STORY VINEYARD

86	1991 Zinfandel Shenandoah Valley
83	1990 Zinfandel Shenandoah Valley

STORYBOOK MOUNTAIN VINEYARDS

87	1991 Zinfandel Howell Mountain
83	1990 Zinfandel Howell Mountain
80	1989 Zinfandel Howell Mountain
79	1988 Zinfandel Howell Mountain
88	1987 Zinfandel Howell Mountain
88	1986 Zinfandel Howell Mountain
84	1991 Zinfandel Napa Valley Reserve
71	1989 Zinfandel Napa Valley Reserve
86	1988 Zinfandel Napa Valley Reserve
89	1987 Zinfandel Napa Valley Reserve
82	1986 Zinfandel Napa Valley Reserve
88	1985 Zinfandel Napa Valley Reserve
88	1984 Zinfandel Napa Valley Reserve

STRATFORD WINERY

81	1990 Cabernet Sauvignon California
82	1991 Chardonnay California
84	1991 Merlot California
85	1991 Sauvignon Blanc California Partners' Reserve
83	1991 Zinfandel California

STRAUS VINEYARDS

85	1991 Merlot Napa Valley
85	1990 Merlot Napa Valley
81	1989 Merlot Napa Valley
82	1988 Merlot Napa Valley
87	1987 Merlot Napa Valley
89	1986 Merlot Napa Valley

RODNEY STRONG VINEYARDS

90	1990 Cabernet Sauvignon Northern Sonoma Reserve
84	1988 Cabernet Sauvignon Northern Sonoma Reserve
90	1987 Cabernet Sauvignon Northern Sonoma Reserve
86	1990 Cabernet Sauvignon Northern Sonoma Alexander's Crown
91	1988 Cabernet Sauvignon Northern Sonoma Alexander's Crown
89	1987 Cabernet Sauvignon Alexander Valley Alexander's Crown
83	1985 Cabernet Sauvignon Alexander Valley Alexander's Crown
82	1984 Cabernet Sauvignon Alexander Valley Alexander's Crown
84	1979 Cabernet Sauvignon Sonoma County Alexander's Crown Sonoma Vineyards
77	1978 Cabernet Sauvignon Sonoma County Alexander's Crown Sonoma Vineyards
73	1977 Cabernet Sauvignon Sonoma County Alexander's Crown Sonoma Vineyards
87	1976 Cabernet Sauvignon Sonoma County Alexander's Crown Sonoma Vineyards
83	1975 Cabernet Sauvignon Sonoma County Alexander's Crown Sonoma Vineyards
83	1974 Cabernet Sauvignon Sonoma County Alexander's Crown Sonoma Vineyards
83	1992 Cabernet Sauvignon Sonoma Coast
82	1991 Cabernet Sauvignon Sonoma County
81	1990 Cabernet Sauvignon Sonoma County
85	1993 Chardonnay Chalk Hill Chalk Hill Vineyard
87	1992 Chardonnay Chalk Hill Chalk Hill Vineyard
74	1991 Chardonnay Chalk Hill Chalk Hill Vineyard
83	1993 Chardonnay Sonoma County
82	1992 Chardonnay Sonoma County
84	1992 Merlot Sonoma County
83	1992 Pinot Noir Russian River Valley River East Vineyard
87	1991 Pinot Noir Russian River Valley River East Vineyard
82	1990 Pinot Noir Russian River Valley River East Vineyard
83	1985 Pinot Noir Russian River Valley River East Vineyard
84	1994 Sauvignon Blanc Northern Sonoma Charlotte's Home Vineyard

85	1993 Sauvignon Blanc Northern Sonoma Charlotte's Home Vineyard
86	1992 Zinfandel Russian River Valley River West Vineyard Old Vines
82	1991 Zinfandel Russian River Valley River West Vineyard Old Vines
86	1990 Zinfandel Russian River Valley River West Vineyard Old Vines
89	1988 Zinfandel Russian River Valley River West Vineyard Old Vines
82	1987 Zinfandel Russian River Valley River West Vineyard Old Vines

SULLIVAN VINEYARDS WINERY

88	1992 Cabernet Sauvignon Napa Valley
78	1991 Cabernet Sauvignon Napa Valley
87	1990 Cabernet Sauvignon Napa Valley
84	1989 Cabernet Sauvignon Napa Valley
87	1984 Cabernet Sauvignon Napa Valley
84	1991 Cabernet Sauvignon Napa Valley Private Reserve
88	1990 Cabernet Sauvignon Napa Valley Private Reserve
86	1989 Cabernet Sauvignon Napa Valley Private Reserve
83	1988 Cabernet Sauvignon Napa Valley Private Reserve
88	1992 Merlot Napa Valley
84	1991 Merlot Napa Valley
84	1990 Merlot Napa Valley
86	1989 Merlot Napa Valley
88	1987 Merlot Napa Valley

SUMMIT LAKE VINEYARDS & WINERY

84	1989 Zinfandel Howell Mountain
82	1988 Zinfandel Howell Mountain
87	1987 Zinfandel Howell Mountain
84	1986 Zinfandel Howell Mountain
86	1985 Zinfandel Howell Mountain

SUTTER HOME WINERY

84	1991 Cabernet Sauvignon Napa Valley Reserve
87	1990 Cabernet Sauvignon Napa Valley Centennial Selection Reserve
74	1993 Chardonnay California
79	1992 Chardonnay California
79	1993 Chenin Blanc California
79	1992 Merlot California
79	1992 Sauvignon Blanc California
75	1992 Zinfandel California
84	1990 Zinfandel Amador County Centennial Selection

JOSEPH SWAN VINEYARDS

—	1990 Cabernet Sauvignon Sonoma Mountain Steiner Vineyard

83   1991 Pinot Noir Russian River Valley

88   1990 Pinot Noir Russian River Valley

79   1988 Pinot Noir Sonoma Coast

87   1985 Pinot Noir Sonoma Coast

84   1993 Pinot Noir Sonoma Mountain Steiner Vineyard

88   1992 Pinot Noir Sonoma Mountain Steiner Vineyard

86   1992 Pinot Noir Sonoma Mountain Wolfspierre Vineyard

88   1991 Red Table Wine Russian River Valley Cotes du Rosa

92   1992 Zinfandel Russian River Valley Frati Ranch

92   1992 Zinfandel Russian River Valley V.H.S.R. Vineyard

80   1989 Zinfandel Sonoma County

82   1988 Zinfandel Sonoma County

86   1987 Zinfandel Sonoma County

89   1986 Zinfandel Sonoma County

77   1992 Zinfandel Sonoma Valley Stellwagen Vineyard

80   1989 Zinfandel Sonoma Valley Stellwagen Vineyard

86   1987 Zinfandel Sonoma Valley Stellwagen Vineyard

86   1987 Zinfandel Sonoma County Ziegler Vineyard

SWANSON VINEYARDS

90   1991 Cabernet Sauvignon Napa Valley

89   1990 Cabernet Sauvignon Napa Valley

82   1988 Cabernet Sauvignon Napa Valley

90   1987 Cabernet Sauvignon Napa Valley

88   1993 Chardonnay Carneros

89   1992 Chardonnay Carneros

87   1991 Chardonnay Carneros

90   1990 Chardonnay Napa Valley Reserve

86   1992 Merlot Napa Valley

89   1991 Merlot Napa Valley

82   1990 Merlot Napa Valley

91   1992 Sangiovese Napa Valley

88   1991 Sangiovese Napa Valley

88   1991 Sémillon Napa Valley Late Harvest

80   1988 Sémillon Napa Valley Late Harvest

89   1992 Syrah Napa Valley

85   1988 Zinfandel Napa Valley

TAFT STREET WINERY

86   1993 Chardonnay Sonoma County

77   1993 Sauvignon Blanc Sonoma County

ROBERT TALBOTT VINEYARDS

91   1992 Chardonnay Monterey County

90   1991 Chardonnay Monterey County Diamond T Estate

84   1993 Logan Winery Chardonnay Monterey County

84   1992 Logan Winery Chardonnay Monterey County

84   1991 Logan Winery Chardonnay Monterey County

TALLEY VINEYARDS

88   1993 Chardonnay Arroyo Grande Valley

81   1991 Chardonnay Arroyo Grande Valley

82   1992 Pinot Noir Arroyo Grande Valley

87   1990 Pinot Noir Arroyo Grande Valley

75   1989 Pinot Noir Arroyo Grande Valley

IVAN TAMAS WINERY

77   1991 Cabernet Sauvignon Livermore Valley Le Clan des Quatre Vineyards

84   1993 Chardonnay Livermore Valley Hayes Ranch

82   1992 Chardonnay Livermore Valley Hayes Ranch

82   1992 Sauvignon Blanc Livermore Valley Figoni Ranch

LANE TANNER

84   1992 Pinot Noir Santa Barbara County

79   1991 Pinot Noir Santa Barbara County

85   1990 Pinot Noir Santa Barbara County Sierra Madre Vineyard

81   1987 Pinot Noir Santa Barbara County Sierra Madre Vineyard Hitching Post

82   1992 Pinot Noir Santa Ynez Valley Sanford & Benedict Vineyard

88   1991 Pinot Noir Santa Ynez Valley Sanford & Benedict Vineyard

85   1989 Pinot Noir Santa Ynez Valley Sanford & Benedict Vineyard

THE TERRACES

86   1990 Cabernet Sauvignon Napa Valley

88   1989 Cabernet Sauvignon Napa Valley

88   1988 Cabernet Sauvignon Napa Valley

92   1987 Cabernet Sauvignon Napa Valley

91   1986 Cabernet Sauvignon Napa Valley

87   1991 Zinfandel Napa Valley

88   1990 Zinfandel Napa Valley

88   1989 Zinfandel Napa Valley

86   1988 Zinfandel Napa Valley

89   1987 Zinfandel Napa Valley

87   1985 Zinfandel Napa Valley Hogue Vineyard

SEAN H. THACKREY & CO.

83   1990 Syrah Napa Valley Orion

90   1989 Syrah Napa Valley Orion

89   1988 Syrah Napa Valley Orion

92   1987 Syrah Napa Valley Orion

89   1986 Syrah Napa Valley Orion

TOBIN JAMES

84   1990 Cabernet Sauvignon Paso Robles Private Stash

88   1989 Cabernet Sauvignon Paso Robles Private Stash

86   1991 Cabernet Sauvignon San Luis Obispo County Twilight

89   1991 Chardonnay Paso Robles

86   1991 Merlot Paso Robles Full Moon

84   1992 Merlot San Luis Obispo County Made in the Shade

84   1992 Pinot Noir Santa Barbara County Black Tie

88   1990 Pinot Noir Santa Barbara County Sunshine

88   1990 Zinfandel Paso Robles Big Shot

82   1991 Zinfandel Paso Robles Big Time

84   1991 Zinfandel Paso Robles Blue Moon Reserve

84   1990 Zinfandel Paso Robles Blue Moon Reserve

84   1992 Zinfandel Paso Robles Solar Flair

87   1991 Zinfandel Paso Robles Solar Flair

86   1991 Zinfandel Paso Robles Sure Fire

PHILIP TOGNI VINEYARD

91   1992 Cabernet Sauvignon Napa Valley

90   1991 Cabernet Sauvignon Napa Valley

92   1990 Cabernet Sauvignon Napa Valley

84   1989 Cabernet Sauvignon Napa Valley

90   1988 Cabernet Sauvignon Napa Valley

94   1987 Cabernet Sauvignon Napa Valley

90   1986 Cabernet Sauvignon Napa Valley

89   1985 Cabernet Sauvignon Napa Valley

85   1984 Cabernet Sauvignon Napa Valley

84   1983 Cabernet Sauvignon Napa Valley

87   1992 Sauvignon Blanc Napa Valley

TOPAZ

82   1990 Cabernet Blend Napa Valley Rouge de Trois

TOPOLOS

79   1991 Cabernet Blend Sonoma County Riserva

83   1992 Cabernet Sauvignon Sonoma County

79   1992 Chardonnay Sonoma County Dry Farmed Old Vines Barrel Fermented

79   1992 Pinot Noir Sonoma Mountain Dry Farmed

84   1992 Zinfandel Sonoma County

81   1991 Zinfandel Sonoma County

83   1992 Zinfandel Sonoma County Ultimo

84   1991 Zinfandel Sonoma County Ultimo

77   1988 Zinfandel Sonoma County Ultimo

78   1992 Zinfandel Sonoma County Rossi Ranch

85   1991 Zinfandel Sonoma County Rossi Ranch

84   1990 Zinfandel Sonoma County Rossi Ranch

84   1989 Zinfandel Sonoma County Rossi Ranch

MARIMAR TORRES ESTATE

91   1992 Chardonnay Green Valley-Sonoma Don Miguel Vineyard

90   1991 Chardonnay Green Valley-Sonoma Don Miguel Vineyard

86 1992 Pinot Noir Green Valley-Sonoma Don Miguel Vineyard

TREFETHEN VINEYARDS

84 1989 Cabernet Sauvignon Napa Valley

82 1988 Cabernet Sauvignon Napa Valley

86 1987 Cabernet Sauvignon Napa Valley

84 1986 Cabernet Sauvignon Napa Valley

86 1989 Cabernet Sauvignon Napa Valley Reserve

82 1986 Cabernet Sauvignon Napa Valley Reserve

86 1993 Chardonnay Napa Valley

83 1992 Chardonnay Napa Valley

TRENTADUE WINERY

77 1989 Cabernet Sauvignon Dry Creek Valley

78 1992 Chardonnay Alexander Valley

85 1991 Sangiovese Alexander Valley

88 1992 Zinfandel Sonoma County

TRUCHARD VINEYARDS

87 1991 Cabernet Sauvignon Carneros

86 1990 Cabernet Sauvignon Carneros

85 1989 Cabernet Sauvignon Carneros

89 1993 Chardonnay Carneros

90 1992 Chardonnay Carneros

90 1991 Chardonnay Carneros

82 1990 Chardonnay Carneros

85 1991 Merlot Carneros

85 1990 Merlot Carneros

81 1989 Merlot Carneros

84 1992 Pinot Noir Carneros

82 1991 Pinot Noir Carneros

86 1990 Pinot Noir Carneros

88 1989 Pinot Noir Carneros

93 1993 Syrah Carneros

89 1992 Syrah Carneros

TUDAL WINERY

88 1990 Cabernet Sauvignon Napa Valley

74 1989 Cabernet Sauvignon Napa Valley

80 1988 Cabernet Sauvignon Napa Valley

87 1986 Cabernet Sauvignon Napa Valley

87 1985 Cabernet Sauvignon Napa Valley

89 1984 Cabernet Sauvignon Napa Valley

TULOCAY WINERY

85 1991 Cabernet Sauvignon Napa Valley Cliff Vineyard

74 1990 Cabernet Sauvignon Napa Valley Cliff Vineyard

87 1991 Cabernet Sauvignon Napa Valley DeCelles Vineyard

84 1988 Cabernet Sauvignon Napa Valley Egan Vineyard

74 1987 Cabernet Sauvignon Napa Valley Egan Vineyard

83 1993 Chardonnay Napa Valley DeCelles Vineyard

87 1991 Chardonnay Napa Valley DeCelles Vineyard

76 1989 Pinot Noir Napa Valley Haynes Vineyard

75 1988 Pinot Noir Napa Valley Haynes Vineyard

TURLEY WINE CELLARS

93 1993 Zinfandel Napa Valley Aida Vineyard

95 1993 Zinfandel Napa Valley Haynes Vineyard

88 1993 Zinfandel Napa Valley Moore Vineyard

TURNBULL WINE CELLARS

88 1991 Cabernet Sauvignon Napa Valley

80 1990 Cabernet Sauvignon Napa Valley

85 1989 Cabernet Sauvignon Napa Valley

84 1988 Cabernet Sauvignon Napa Valley

86 1985 Cabernet Sauvignon Napa Valley

85 1984 Cabernet Sauvignon Napa Valley

85 1983 Cabernet Sauvignon Napa Valley

81 1982 Cabernet Sauvignon Napa Valley

87 1981 Cabernet Sauvignon Napa Valley

84 1980 Cabernet Sauvignon Napa Valley

83 1979 Cabernet Sauvignon Napa Valley

87 1990 Cabernet Sauvignon Napa Valley Vineyard Selection 67

85 1989 Cabernet Sauvignon Napa Valley Vineyard Selection 67

86 1988 Cabernet Sauvignon Napa Valley Vineyard Selection 67

88 1987 Cabernet Sauvignon Napa Valley Vineyard Selection 67

86 1986 Cabernet Sauvignon Napa Valley Vineyard Selection 67

89 1986 Cabernet Sauvignon Napa Valley Vineyard Selection 82

T VINE

83 1992 Zinfandel Napa Valley

TWIN HILLS WINERY

72 1991 Cabernet Sauvignon Paso Robles

80 1992 Chardonnay Paso Robles Reserve

80 1991 Zinfandel Paso Robles

VALLEY OF THE MOON WINERY

80 1990 Zinfandel Sonoma Valley Reserve

VAN DER HEYDEN VINEYARD

80 1987 Cabernet Sauvignon Alexander Valley

75 1991 Chardonnay Napa Valley

78 1989 Chardonnay Napa Valley Private Reserve

VENTANA VINEYARDS

88 1992 Chardonnay Monterey County Gold Stripe Selection

88 1991 Chardonnay Monterey County Gold Stripe Selection

87 1989 Chardonnay Monterey County Gold Stripe Selection

81 1993 Chenin Blanc Monterey County

84 1993 Johannisberg Riesling Monterey County

82 1992 Johannisberg Riesling Monterey County

89 1993 Sauvignon Blanc Monterey County

77 1991 Sauvignon Blanc Monterey County

VIADER VINEYARDS

88 1992 Cabernet Blend Napa Valley

91 1991 Cabernet Blend Napa Valley

91 1990 Cabernet Blend Napa Valley

89 1989 Cabernet Blend Napa Valley

VIANO VINEYARDS

81 1988 Cabernet Sauvignon California Reserve Selection

86 1988 Dessert Contra Costa County Reserve Selection

80 1991 Zinfandel Contra Costa County Sand Rock Hill Vineyard Reserve

81 1989 Zinfandel Contra Costa County Sand Rock Hill Vineyard Reserve

VIANSA WINERY

85 1987 Cabernet Blend Napa-Sonoma Counties Obsidian

80 1989 Cabernet Blend Napa-Sonoma Counties Riserva Anatra Rosso

76 1988 Cabernet Sauvignon Napa-Sonoma Counties

78 1988 Cabernet Sauvignon Napa-Sonoma Counties Reserve

81 1990 Nebbiolo California Nebbiolo

83 1990 Red Table Wine Napa County Thalia

80 1991 Zinfandel Blend Sonoma Valley Prindelo

VICHON WINERY

84 1992 Cabernet Sauvignon California Coastal Selection

82 1991 Cabernet Sauvignon California Coastal Selection

84 1991 Cabernet Sauvignon Napa Valley

88 1990 Cabernet Sauvignon Napa Valley

89 1989 Cabernet Sauvignon Napa Valley

84 1988 Cabernet Sauvignon Napa Valley

91 1990 Cabernet Sauvignon Stags Leap District SLD

88 1989 Cabernet Sauvignon Stags Leap District SLD

88 1988 Cabernet Sauvignon Stags Leap District SLD

87 1987 Cabernet Sauvignon Stags Leap District SLD

88	1986 Cabernet Sauvignon Stags Leap District SLD
90	1985 Cabernet Sauvignon Stags Leap District SLD
82	1993 Chardonnay California Coastal Selection
83	1993 Chardonnay Napa Valley
88	1992 Chardonnay Napa Valley
89	1991 Chardonnay Napa Valley
83	1992 Merlot California Coastal Selection
82	1991 Merlot Napa Valley
89	1990 Merlot Napa Valley
87	1989 Merlot Napa Valley
81	1988 Merlot Napa Valley
89	1987 Merlot Napa Valley
86	1986 Merlot Napa Valley
85	1993 Sauvignon Blend Napa Valley Chevrignon

VILLA HELENA WINERY

71	1990 Cabernet Sauvignon Napa Valley Baron von Kees Vineyard
87	1992 Viognier Napa Valley

VILLA MT. EDEN

82	1991 Cabernet Sauvignon California Cellar Select
86	1990 Cabernet Sauvignon Napa Valley
88	1987 Cabernet Sauvignon Napa Valley
84	1986 Cabernet Sauvignon Napa Valley
85	1978 Cabernet Sauvignon Napa Valley
90	1974 Cabernet Sauvignon Napa Valley
83	1991 Cabernet Sauvignon Napa Valley Grand Reserve
87	1990 Cabernet Sauvignon Napa Valley Grand Reserve
84	1989 Cabernet Sauvignon Napa Valley Grand Reserve
86	1988 Cabernet Sauvignon Napa Valley Grand Reserve
92	1992 Cabernet Sauvignon Mendocino County Signature Series
85	1993 Chardonnay California Cellar Select
83	1992 Chardonnay California Cellar Select
91	1993 Chardonnay Carneros Grand Reserve
88	1992 Chardonnay Carneros Grand Reserve
87	1991 Chardonnay Carneros Grand Reserve
93	1993 Chardonnay Santa Barbara County Signature Series
85	1991 Merlot Napa Valley Grand Reserve
88	1990 Merlot Napa Valley Grand Reserve
88	1993 Pinot Blanc Santa Maria Valley Bien Nacido Vineyard Grand Reserve
83	1993 Pinot Noir California Cellar Select
84	1991 Pinot Noir Carneros Grand Reserve
82	1988 Pinot Noir Napa Valley
84	1993 Pinot Noir Santa Maria Valley Bien Nacido Vineyard Grand Reserve

84	1992 Zinfandel California Cellar Select
86	1991 Zinfandel California Cellar Select
84	1990 Zinfandel California Cellar Select
86	1989 Zinfandel California Cellar Select

VINE CLIFF CELLARS

88	1991 Cabernet Sauvignon Napa Valley
87	1990 Cabernet Sauvignon Napa Valley
89	1993 Chardonnay Napa Valley Proprietress Reserve

VITA NOVA

87	1986 Cabernet Blend Santa Barbara County Reservatum

VON STRASSER VINEYARDS

88	1992 Cabernet Sauvignon Diamond Mountain
88	1991 Cabernet Sauvignon Diamond Mountain
89	1990 Cabernet Sauvignon Diamond Mountain

VOSS

83	1992 Chardonnay Napa Valley
85	1991 Chardonnay Napa Valley
83	1992 Merlot Napa Valley
75	1991 Merlot Napa Valley
88	1993 Sauvignon Blanc Napa Valley
77	1992 Zinfandel Alexander Valley

WELLINGTON VINEYARDS

83	1991 Cabernet Sauvignon Mount Veeder Random Ridge Vineyard
86	1990 Cabernet Sauvignon Mount Veeder Random Ridge Vineyard
86	1989 Cabernet Sauvignon Mount Veeder Random Ridge Vineyard
85	1991 Cabernet Sauvignon Sonoma County Mohrhardt Ridge Vineyard
83	1990 Cabernet Sauvignon Sonoma County Mohrhardt Ridge Vineyard
85	1989 Cabernet Sauvignon Sonoma County Mohrhardt Ridge Vineyard
84	1993 Chardonnay Sonoma Valley Barrel Fermented
81	1993 Chardonnay Sonoma County Barrel Fermented Lot 2
70	1992 Chardonnay Sonoma Valley Barrel Fermented
88	1991 Chardonnay Sonoma Valley Barrel Fermented
84	1991 Merlot Sonoma County
85	1991 Red Table Wine Sonoma Valley Criolla Old Vines
85	1990 Red Table Wine Sonoma Valley Criolla Old Vines
87	1992 Zinfandel Sonoma Valley 100 Year Old Vines
84	1992 Zinfandel Sonoma Valley Casa Santinamaria

WENTE BROS.

82	1991 Cabernet Sauvignon Livermore Valley Charles Wetmore Vineyard Estate Reserve
86	1990 Cabernet Sauvignon Livermore Valley Charles Wetmore Vineyard Estate Reserve
84	1989 Cabernet Sauvignon Livermore Valley Charles Wetmore Vineyard Estate Reserve
86	1987 Cabernet Sauvignon Livermore Valley Charles Wetmore Vineyard Estate Reserve
82	1986 Cabernet Sauvignon Livermore Valley Charles Wetmore Vineyard Estate Reserve
85	1992 Chardonnay Arroyo Seco Riva Ranch
87	1991 Chardonnay Arroyo Seco Riva Ranch
85	1993 Chardonnay Central Coast Wente Family Estate Selection
84	1992 Chardonnay Central Coast Wente Family Estate Selection
88	1991 Chardonnay Livermore Valley Herman Wente Vineyard Reserve
84	1991 Merlot Livermore Valley Crane Ridge
84	1990 Merlot Livermore Valley Crane Ridge
85	1993 Sauvignon Blanc Livermore Valley Wente Family Estate Selection
83	1992 Sauvignon Blanc Livermore Valley Wente Family Estate Selection

WHALER VINEYARD

84	1992 Zinfandel Mendocino County
84	1991 Zinfandel Mendocino County
81	1990 Zinfandel Mendocino County
83	1989 Zinfandel Mendocino County
87	1992 Zinfandel Mendocino County Flagship
87	1991 Zinfandel Mendocino County Flagship
85	1990 Zinfandel Mendocino County Flagship

WHEELER WINERY

84	1991 Cabernet Sauvignon Dry Creek Valley Norse Vineyard
81	1989 Cabernet Sauvignon Dry Creek Valley Norse Vineyard
83	1988 Cabernet Sauvignon Dry Creek Valley Norse Vineyard
84	1987 Cabernet Sauvignon Dry Creek Valley Norse Vineyard
83	1986 Cabernet Sauvignon Dry Creek Valley Norse Vineyard
84	1993 Chardonnay Sonoma County
87	1992 Chardonnay Sonoma County
91	1991 Chardonnay Sonoma County
79	1992 Merlot Dry Creek Valley
76	1990 Red Table Wine California Quintet
86	1992 Sauvignon Blanc Sonoma County
87	1992 Zinfandel Dry Creek Valley
80	1991 Zinfandel Dry Creek Valley

WHITCRAFT WINERY

89 1993 Chardonnay Santa Maria Valley Bien Nacido Vineyard

88 1992 Chardonnay Santa Maria Valley Bien Nacido Vineyard

90 1992 Pinot Noir Russian River Valley Olivet Lane Vineyard

88 1991 Pinot Noir Russian River Valley Olivet Lane Vineyard

88 1993 Pinot Noir Santa Maria Valley Bien Nacido Vineyard

90 1993 Pinot Noir Santa Maria Valley Bien Nacido Vineyard Q Block

88 1992 Pinot Noir Santa Maria Valley Bien Nacido Vineyard

87 1991 Pinot Noir Santa Maria Valley Bien Nacido Vineyard

88 1990 Pinot Noir Santa Maria Valley Bien Nacido Vineyard

WHITE OAK VINEYARDS & WINERY

84 1992 Cabernet Franc Alexander Valley

84 1989 Cabernet Franc Alexander Valley

82 1991 Cabernet Sauvignon Alexander Valley

84 1990 Cabernet Sauvignon Alexander Valley

85 1988 Cabernet Sauvignon Alexander Valley

84 1985 Cabernet Sauvignon Alexander Valley Myers Limited Reserve

85 1987 Cabernet Sauvignon Sonoma County

82 1993 Chardonnay Russian River Valley Poplar Ranch Private Reserve

83 1993 Chardonnay Sonoma County

80 1991 Chardonnay Sonoma County

87 1991 Chardonnay Sonoma County Myers Limited Reserve

87 1993 Chenin Blanc California

83 1993 Sauvignon Blanc Sonoma County

80 1992 Zinfandel Alexander Valley Church Vineyard

73 1990 Zinfandel Alexander Valley Church Vineyard

84 1992 Zinfandel Dry Creek Valley Saunders Vineyard

90 1990 Zinfandel Dry Creek Valley Saunders Vineyard

85 1992 Zinfandel Sonoma County

87 1991 Zinfandel Sonoma County

85 1989 Zinfandel Sonoma County

86 1992 Zinfandel Sonoma County Limited Reserve

88 1991 Zinfandel Sonoma County Limited Reserve

WHITE ROCK VINEYARDS

87 1992 Chardonnay Napa Valley

88 1991 Chardonnay Napa Valley

88 1990 Meritage Red Napa Valley Claret

83 1989 Meritage Red Napa Valley Claret

84 1988 Meritage Red Napa Valley Claret

80 1986 Meritage Red Napa Valley Claret

WHITEHALL LANE WINERY

86 1990 Cabernet Franc Napa Valley

79 1989 Cabernet Franc Napa Valley

86 1988 Cabernet Franc Napa Valley

87 1991 Cabernet Sauvignon Napa Valley

87 1990 Cabernet Sauvignon Napa Valley

85 1988 Cabernet Sauvignon Napa Valley

83 1987 Cabernet Sauvignon Napa Valley

87 1986 Cabernet Sauvignon Napa Valley

88 1985 Cabernet Sauvignon Napa Valley

89 1991 Cabernet Sauvignon Napa Valley Reserve

89 1990 Cabernet Sauvignon Napa Valley Reserve

87 1989 Cabernet Sauvignon Napa Valley Reserve

86 1988 Cabernet Sauvignon Napa Valley Reserve

90 1987 Cabernet Sauvignon Napa Valley Reserve

88 1991 Cabernet Sauvignon Napa Valley Morisoli Vineyard

87 1990 Cabernet Sauvignon Napa Valley Morisoli Vineyard

82 1993 Chardonnay Napa Valley

89 1992 Chardonnay Napa Valley

85 1991 Meritage Red Napa Valley

88 1992 Merlot Knights Valley

86 1991 Merlot Knights Valley

86 1990 Merlot Knights Valley

84 1989 Merlot Knights Valley

82 1988 Merlot Knights Valley

77 1987 Merlot Knights Valley

82 1990 Pinot Noir Alexander Valley

82 1988 Pinot Noir Alexander Valley

87 1987 Pinot Noir Napa Valley

82 1985 Pinot Noir Napa Valley

81 1993 Sauvignon Blanc Napa Valley Barrel Fermented

WILD HORSE WINERY

88 1987 Cabernet Sauvignon Paso Robles

86 1986 Cabernet Sauvignon Paso Robles

85 1987 Cabernet Sauvignon Paso Robles Cheval Sauvage

70 1985 Cabernet Sauvignon Paso Robles Wild Horse Vineyards

87 1992 Cabernet Sauvignon San Luis Obispo County

84 1993 Chardonnay Central Coast

87 1992 Chardonnay Central Coast

86 1993 Malvasia Bianca Monterey County

89 1990 Merlot Central Coast Cheval Sauvage

85 1991 Merlot San Luis Obispo County

84 1989 Merlot Central Coast

85 1988 Merlot Central Coast

80 1987 Merlot Central Coast

87 1986 Merlot Central Coast

83 1993 Pinot Blanc Monterey County

90 1993 Pinot Blanc Santa Barbara County Bien Nacido Vineyard

85 1993 Pinot Noir Central Coast

82 1992 Pinot Noir Central Coast

87 1991 Pinot Noir Central Coast

91 1990 Pinot Noir Paso Robles Cheval Sauvage

86 1990 Pinot Noir Santa Barbara County

87 1989 Pinot Noir Santa Barbara County

87 1988 Pinot Noir Santa Barbara County

86 1987 Pinot Noir Santa Barbara County

85 1986 Pinot Noir Santa Barbara County

82 1985 Pinot Noir Santa Barbara County

85 1989 Pinot Noir Santa Barbara County Cheval Sauvage

88 1984 Pinot Noir Santa Maria Valley

84 1986 Pinot Noir Santa Maria Valley Sierra Madre Vineyard

90 1983 Pinot Noir Santa Maria Valley Sierra Madre Vineyard

85 1992 Red Table Wine Cienega Valley Negrette

85 1989 Zinfandel Paso Robles

88 1990 Zinfandel Paso Robles Unbridled

WILDCAT

74 1989 Merlot Sonoma Valley

78 1988 Merlot Sonoma Valley

WILDHURST VINEYARDS

76 1991 Cabernet Sauvignon Clear Lake

85 1993 Chardonnay California

80 1991 Chardonnay Sonoma County

85 1993 Chardonnay Sonoma County Reserve

89 1991 Chardonnay Sonoma County Reserve

84 1993 Fumé Blanc Clear Lake Reserve

84 1991 Merlot Clear Lake

84 1992 Merlot Lake County Reserve

87 1991 Merlot Lake County Reserve

74 1992 Pinot Noir Mendocino County

82 1991 Riesling Clear Lake Dry

80 1992 Zinfandel Clear Lake

86 1991 Zinfandel Clear Lake

85 1990 Zinfandel Clear Lake

WILLIAMS & SELYEM WINERY

91 1993 Chardonnay Russian River Valley Allen Vineyard

90 1992 Chardonnay Russian River Valley Allen Vineyard

92 1992 Pinot Noir Anderson Valley Ferrington Vineyard

85 1993 Pinot Noir Russian River Valley

90 1992 Pinot Noir Russian River Valley

93 1991 Pinot Noir Russian River Valley

93 1990 Pinot Noir Russian River Valley

83 1993 Pinot Noir Sonoma Coast

87 1989 Pinot Noir Sonoma Coast

92 1988 Pinot Noir Sonoma Coast

91 1986 Pinot Noir Sonoma County

84 1985 Pinot Noir Sonoma County

89 1982 Pinot Noir Sonoma County

91 1992 Pinot Noir Russian River Valley Allen Vineyard

93 1991 Pinot Noir Russian River Valley Allen Vineyard

93 1990 Pinot Noir Russian River Valley Allen Vineyard

88 1989 Pinot Noir Russian River Valley Allen Vineyard

94 1988 Pinot Noir Russian River Valley Allen Vineyard

92 1987 Pinot Noir Russian River Valley Allen Vineyard

85 1993 Pinot Noir Russian River Valley Cohn Vineyard

85 1993 Pinot Noir Russian River Valley Olivet Lane Vineyard

89 1992 Pinot Noir Russian River Valley Olivet Lane Vineyard

92 1991 Pinot Noir Russian River Valley Olivet Lane Vineyard

84 1990 Pinot Noir Russian River Valley Olivet Lane Vineyard

90 1989 Pinot Noir Russian River Valley Olivet Lane Vineyard

95 1992 Pinot Noir Russian River Valley Rochioli Vineyard

95 1991 Pinot Noir Russian River Valley Rochioli Vineyard

91 1990 Pinot Noir Russian River Valley Rochioli Vineyard

88 1989 Pinot Noir Russian River Valley Rochioli Vineyard

94 1988 Pinot Noir Russian River Valley Rochioli Vineyard

92 1987 Pinot Noir Russian River Valley Rochioli Vineyard

93 1986 Pinot Noir Russian River Valley Rochioli Vineyard

89 1985 Pinot Noir Russian River Valley Rochioli Vineyard

95 1991 Pinot Noir Sonoma Coast Summa Vineyard

84 1988 Pinot Noir Sonoma Coast Summa Vineyard

91 1992 Zinfandel Russian River Valley Leno Martinelli Vineyard

92 1991 Zinfandel Russian River Valley Leno Martinelli Vineyard

92 1990 Zinfandel Russian River Valley Leno Martinelli Vineyard

89 1989 Zinfandel Russian River Valley Leno Martinelli Vineyard

89 1988 Zinfandel Russian River Valley Leno Martinelli Vineyard

90 1987 Zinfandel Russian River Valley Leno Martinelli Vineyard

88 1986 Zinfandel Russian River Valley Leno Martinelli Vineyard

87 1985 Zinfandel Russian River Valley Leno Martinelli Vineyard

88 1984 Zinfandel Russian River Valley Leno Martinelli Vineyard

86 1983 Zinfandel Russian River Valley Leno Martinelli Vineyard

84 1982 Zinfandel Sonoma County

88 1981 Zinfandel Sonoma County

Windemere

83 1989 Cabernet Sauvignon Napa Valley

88 1990 Cabernet Sauvignon Napa Valley Diamond Mountain

84 1992 Chardonnay Edna Valley Mac Gregor Vineyard

77 1991 Chardonnay Edna Valley MacGregor Vineyard

York Mountain Winery

71 1989 Cabernet Sauvignon San Luis Obispo County

84 1993 Chardonnay San Luis Obispo County

80 1992 Chardonnay San Luis Obispo County

79 1991 Merlot San Luis Obispo County

82 1990 Pinot Noir San Luis Obispo County

82 1990 Zinfandel San Luis Obispo County

Zaca Mesa Winery

86 1991 Chardonnay Santa Barbara County

90 1992 Chardonnay Santa Barbara County Alumni Winemaker Series James A. Clendenen

85 1992 Chardonnay Santa Barbara County Chapel Vineyard

85 1993 Chardonnay Santa Barbara County Zaca Vineyards

85 1989 Pinot Noir Santa Barbara County

74 1990 Pinot Noir Santa Barbara County Reserve

73 1989 Pinot Noir Santa Barbara County Reserve

85 1988 Pinot Noir Santa Barbara County Reserve

82 1987 Pinot Noir Santa Barbara County Reserve

82 1990 Pinot Noir Santa Barbara County Sierra Madre Vineyard

85 1993 Rhône Blend Santa Barbara County Cuvée Z

78 1992 Rhône Blend Santa Barbara County Cuvée Z

82 1990 Syrah Santa Barbara County

83 1989 Syrah Santa Barbara County

89 1992 Syrah Santa Barbara County Alumni Winemaker Series Bob Lindquist

85 1992 Syrah Santa Barbara County Chapel Vineyard

ZD Wines

88 1990 Cabernet Sauvignon Napa Valley

78 1989 Cabernet Sauvignon Napa Valley

86 1988 Cabernet Sauvignon Napa Valley

88 1987 Cabernet Sauvignon Napa Valley

89 1987 Cabernet Sauvignon Napa Valley Reserve

85 1986 Cabernet Sauvignon Napa Valley

87 1985 Cabernet Sauvignon Napa Valley

85 1984 Cabernet Sauvignon Napa Valley

84 1983 Cabernet Sauvignon Napa Valley

83 1982 Cabernet Sauvignon Napa Valley

82 1981 Cabernet Sauvignon Napa Valley

84 1980 Cabernet Sauvignon Napa Valley

85 1993 Chardonnay California 25th Anniversary Vintage

87 1991 Chardonnay California

78 1991 Pinot Noir Carneros

86 1990 Pinot Noir Carneros

82 1989 Pinot Noir Carneros

82 1988 Pinot Noir Carneros

79 1985 Pinot Noir Carneros

WINERY STAR RATINGS

❖

5 STAR ★★★★★

Araujo Estate Wines
Au Bon Climat
Beringer Vineyards
Caymus Vineyards
Dalla Valle Vineyards
Diamond Creek Vineyards
Dominus Estate
Dunn Vineyards
El Molino
Gary Farrell Wines
Forman Vineyard
Grace Family Vineyards
Kistler Vineyards
Marcassin Winery
Matanzas Creek Winery
Robert Mondavi Winery
Opus One
Patz & Hall Wine Co.
Ridge Vineyards
J. Rochioli Vineyard & Winery
Sanford Winery
Spottswoode Winery
Williams & Selyem Winery

4 STAR ★★★★

Anderson's Conn Valley Vineyards
Arrowood Vineyards & Winery
Robert Biale Vineyards
David Bruce Winery
Byron Vineyards & Winery

Cain Cellars
Calera Wine Co.
Cambria Winery & Vineyard
Chalone Vineyard
Chateau Montelena Winery
Chateau Potelle
Chateau St. Jean
Cuvaison Winery
Dehlinger Winery
Dickerson Vineyard
Duckhorn Vineyards
Étude Wines
Far Niente Winery
Ferrari-Carano Winery
Flora Springs Wine Co.
E. & J. Gallo Winery
Geyser Peak Winery
Groth Vineyards & Winery
Guenoc Winery
Hanzell Vineyards
Harlan Estate
Hartwell Vineyards
The Hess Collection Winery
Laurel Glen Vineyard
Livingston Wines
Lytton Springs Winery
Markham Vineyards
Mayacamas Vineyards
Mer et Soleil
Peter Michael Winery
Mount Eden Vineyards
Nalle Winery
Navarro Vineyards
Niebaum-Coppola Estate Winery

Oakville Ranch Vineyards
Joseph Phelps Vineyards
Qupe Cellars
A. Rafanelli Winery
Ravenswood
Roederer Estate
St. Clement Vineyards
St. Francis Winery
Saintsbury
Shafer Vineyards
Signorello Vineyards
Silver Oak Cellars
Silverado Vineyards
Simi Winery
Sky Vineyards
Stag's Leap Wine Cellars
Steele Wines
Stony Hill Vineyard
Robert Talbott Vineyards
Philip Togni Vineyard
Marimar Torres Estate
Turley Wine Cellars
Viader Vineyards

3 STAR ★★★

Abreu Vineyards
Acacia Winery
Adelaida Cellars
Alexander Valley Vineyards
Altamura Winery and Vineyards
S. Anderson Vineyard
Vincent Arroyo Winery

Atlas Peak Vineyards

Azalea Springs

Bancroft Vineyards

Bannister Winery

Barnett Vineyards

Beaulieu Vineyard

Belvedere Winery

Benziger Family Winery

Bernardus Vineyards & Winery

Blockheadia Ringnosii

Bonny Doon Vineyard

Bouchaine Vineyards

The Brander Vineyard

Burgess Cellars

Cafaro Cellars

Cakebread Cellars

Cale Cellars

Camelot

Canepa Cellars

Carmenet Vineyard

Carneros Creek Winery

Chalk Hill Winery

Chamisal Vineyard

Chappellet Vineyard

Chateau Souverain

Chateau Woltner

Chauffe-eau Cellars

Cinnabar Vineyard & Winery

Cline Cellars

Clos du Bois

Clos Du Val

Clos La Chance

Clos Pegase

Codorniu Napa

B. R. Cohn Winery

Colgin

Concannon Vineyard

Conn Creek Winery

Corison

Cornerstone Cellars

Cosentino Winery

Cronin Vineyards

Cutler Cellars

De Loach Vineyards

Domain Hill & Mayes

Domaine Carneros

Domaine Chandon

Dry Creek Vineyard

Eberle Winery

Tom Eddy

Edmeades Winery

Edmunds St. John

Edna Valley Vineyard

Elizabeth Vineyards

Elyse Vineyards

Estancia

Gloria Ferrer Champagne Caves

Fetzer Vineyards

Fiddlehead Cellars

Fife Vineyards

Firestone Vineyard

Fisher Vineyards

Foxen Vineyard

Franciscan Vineyards

Franus Winery

Freemark Abbey Winery

Frog's Leap Winery

The Gainey Vineyards

Georis Winery

Girard Winery

Green and Red Vineyard

Greenwood Ridge Vineyards

Grgich Hills Cellar

Gundlach Bundschu Winery

Harrison Vineyards

Havens Wine Cellars

Heitz Wine Cellars

Hidden Cellars Winery

William Hill Winery

Hitching Post Winery

Paul Hobbs Cellars

Hop Kiln Winery

Husch Vineyards

Iron Horse Vineyards

Jade Mountain Winery

Jarvis

Jordan Vineyard and Winery

Judd's Hill

Justin Vineyards & Winery

Kalin Cellars

Kendall-Jackson

Kathryn Kennedy Winery

Kenwood Vineyards

Charles Krug Winery

Kunde Estate Winery

La Crema

La Jota Vineyard Co.

Lakewood

Landmark Vineyards

Laurier

Lewis Cellars

J. Lohr Winery

Long Vineyards

Lyeth

Macrostie Winery

Maison Deutz Winery

Louis M. Martini Winery

Meridian Vineyards

Merryvale Vineyards

Monticello Cellars

Moondance Cellars

Z Moore Winery

Moraga

Morgan Winery

Mount Veeder Winery

Mumm Napa Valley

Murphy-Goode Estate Winery

Murrieta's Well

Napa Ridge

Newlan Vineyards and Winery

Newton Vineyard

Norman Vineyards

Oakford Vineyards

The Ojai Vineyard

Optima

Pahlmeyer

Paradigm

Fess Parker Winery

Peachy Canyon Winery

Robert Pecota Winery

Peju Province Winery

Robert Pepi Winery

Pine Ridge Winery

Piper Sonoma Cellars

Bernard Pradel Cellars

Preston Vineyards

Pride Mountain Vineyards

Quady Winery

Quivira Vineyards

Kent Rasmussen Winery

Martin Ray Winery

Raymond Vineyard and Cellar

Renwood Winery

Richardson Vineyards

Ritchie Creek Vineyards

Rocking Horse

Rombauer Vineyards

Rosenblum Cellars

Rosenthal – The Malibu Estate

St. Supéry Vineyard & Winery

Santa Barbara Winery

Santa Cruz Mountain Vineyard

Sarah's Vineyard

V. Sattui Winery

Saucelito Canyon Vineyard

Sausal Winery

Scharffenberger Cellars

F. Scherrer Wines

Schramsberg Vineyards

Schuetz-Oles

Seavey Vineyard

Sebastiani Vineyards

Selene Wines

Sequoia Grove Vineyards

Robert Sinskey Vineyards

Sonoma-Cutrer Vineyards

Sonoma-Loeb

Staglin Family Vineyard

Stags' Leap Winery

Steltzner Vineyards

Sterling Vineyards

Stonestreet

Storybook Mountain Vineyards

Straus Vineyards

Rodney Strong Vineyards

Sullivan Vineyards Winery

Joseph Swan Vineyards

Swanson Vineyards

The Terraces

Sean H. Thackrey & Co.

Thomas-Hsi

Tobin James

Trefethen Vineyards

Truchard Vineyards

Tudal Winery

Turnbull Wine Cellars

Vichon Winery

Villa Mt. Eden

Vine Cliff Cellars

Vita Nova

von Strasser Vineyards

Wente Bros.

Whitcraft Winery

White Oak Vineyards & Winery

White Rock Vineyards

Whitehall Lane Winery

Wild Horse Winery

Zaca Mesa Winery

ZD Wines

2 STAR ★★

Adler Fels

Alban Vineyards

Alderbrook Winery

Amador Foothill Winery

Arciero Winery

Armida Winery

David Arthur Vineyards

Babcock Vineyards

Baileyana

Bandiera Winery

Bargetto Winery

Bayview Cellars

Beaucanon Winery

Bellerose Vineyard

Bergfeld Winery

Black Mountain

Black Sheep Vintners

Blue Heron Lake Winery

Boeger Winery

Bogle Vineyards

Brandborg Cellars

Braren Pauli Winery

Briceland Vineyards

Brindiamo

Brutocao Cellars

Buehler Vineyards

Buena Vista Winery

Byington Winery & Vineyards

Davis Bynum Winery

Callaway Vineyard and Winery

Carey Cellars

Castle Rock

Castoro Cellars

Cedar Mountain Winery

Chateau Chevre Winery

Chateau de Baun

Chateau de Leu Winery

Chateau Julien Winery

Chatom Vineyards

Chimère Winery

Chimney Rock Winery

Christophe

Christopher Creek Winery

Claiborne & Churchill

Claudia Springs Winery

Cloninger Cellars

R. & J. Cook

Corbett Canyon Vineyards

Cottonwood Canyon

H. Coturri and Sons

Thomas Coyne Winery

Robert Craig Wine Cellars

Creston Vineyards & Winery

Crichton Hall

Culbertson Winery

De Lorimier Winery

Deer Park Winery

DeMoor Winery

Deux Amis Winery

Domaine Napa Winery

Domaine Saint Gregory

Domaine St. George Winery

Duncan Peak Vineyards

Dunnewood Vineyards

Durney Vineyard

Duxoup

Elkhorn Peak Cellars

Elliston Vineyards

Estate William Baccala

Estrella River Winery

Evensen Vineyards & Winery

Fallenleaf Vineyard

Farella-Park Vineyards

Fenestra Winery

Ficklin Vineyard

Field Stone Winery

Fieldbrook Valley Winery

Thomas Fogarty Winery

Folie à Deux Winery

Foppiano Vineyards

Forest Glen

Forest Hill Vineyard

Fortino Winery

Fremont Creek Winery

Frey Winery

Frick Winery

J. Fritz Cellars

Gabrielli Winery

Gan Eden

Daniel Gehrs

Glen Ellen Winery

Golden Creek Vineyard

Goosecross Cellars

Graeser Winery

Grand Cru Vineyards

Granite Springs Winery

Greenstone Winery

Guilliams Vineyards

Hacienda Wine Cellars

Hagafen Cellars

Hahn Estates

Hallcrest Vineyards

Handley Cellars

Hanna Winery

Harmony Cellars

Hart Winery

Haywood Winery

Homewood Winery

Louis Honig Cellars

Hope Farms

Robert Hunter Winery

Indian Springs Vineyards

Inglenook-Napa Valley

Innisfree

Jackson Valley Vineyards

Jaeger Family Wine Co.

Jekel Vineyards

Jepson Vineyards

Jory Winery

Joullian Vineyards

Joya Winery

Karly Wines

Robert Keenan Winery

J. Kerr Wines

Klein

Konrad Estate

Korbel Champagne Cellars

Lakespring Winery

Lambert Bridge

Lamborn Family Vineyards

Lava Cap Winery

Lazy Creek Vineyards

Leeward Winery

Limerick Lane

Limur Winery

Liparita Cellars

Lockwood

Lolonis Winery

Richard Longoria Wines

The Lucas Winery

Madrona Vineyards

Manzanita

Marietta Cellars

Mark West Vineyards

Martin Brothers Winery

Martinelli Winery

Mastantuono

Mazzocco Vineyards

Peter McCoy Vineyards

McDowell Valley Vineyards

McHenry Vineyard

The Meeker Vineyard

Mendocino Hill

Michel-Schlumberger

Mietz Cellars

Milano Winery

Milat Vineyards

Mill Creek Vineyards

Mirassou Vineyards

Mission View Vineyards & Winery

Mont St. John Cellars

Monte Volpe

Monterey Peninsula Winery

The Monterey Vineyard

Montevina Wines

Moshin Vineyards

Mount Konocti Winery

Mount Palomar Winery

Robert Mueller Cellars

Nelson Estate

Nevada City Winery

Neyers

Nichelini Winery

Obester Winery

Octopus Mountain

Olivet Lane Estate

Page Mill Winery

Paraiso Springs Vineyards

Parducci Wine Cellars

J. Pedroncelli Winery

Pellegrini Winery

Mario Perelli-Minetti Winery

Peterson Winery

R. H. Phillips Vineyard

Plam Vineyards & Winery

Prager Winery & Port Works

Quail Ridge Cellars

Rabbit Ridge Vineyards

Rancho Sisquoc Winery

Renaissance Vineyard & Winery

Roche Winery

Rolling Hills Vineyards

Roudon-Smith Winery

Round Hill Winery

Royce Vineyards

Rubissow-Sargent

Rustridge Vineyards & Winery

Rutherford Hill Winery

Saddleback Cellars

St. Andrews Winery

Salmon Creek

San Saba Vineyard

Santa Ynez Winery

School House

Schug Carneros Estate

Sea Ridge Winery

Seghesio Winery

Shenandoah Vineyards

Sierra Vista

Silver Mountain Vineyards

Silverado Hill Cellars

Smith and Hook

Smith-Madrone Vineyard

Smothers Brothers Wines

Sobon Estate

Soda Canyon Vineyards

Solis Winery

Solitude Wines

Sonoma Creek Winery

Soquel Vineyards

P. and M. Staiger

Star Hill Wines

Stevenot Winery

Stonegate Winery

Storrs Winery

Story Winery

Stratford Winery

Summit Lake Vineyards & Winery

Sutter Home Winery

Taft Street Winery

Talley Vineyards

Ivan Tamas Winery

Lane Tanner

Topaz

Topolos

Trentadue Winery

Tulocay Winery

T Vine

Van der Heyden Vineyard

Ventana Vineyards

Viano Vineyards

Viansa Winery

Voss Vineyards

Weibel Vineyards

Wellington Vineyards

Whaler Vineyard

Wheeler Winery

Wild Hog Hill Vineyard

Wildhurst Vineyards

Windemere

1 STAR ★

Ahlgren Vineyard

Alexander Valley Fruit & Trading Co.

Antelope Valley Winery

Austin Cellars

Baldinelli Vineyards

Maurice Carrie Vineyards and Winery

Cecchetti Sebastiani Cellars

Chansa Cellars

Chateau Diana

Cilurzo Vineyard and Winery

Devlin Wine Cellars

J. Filippi Vintage Co.

Grove Street Winery

Emilio Guglielmo Winery

Harbor Winery

Lake Sonoma Winery

Las Vinas Winery

Melim Vineyard and Winery

Montpellier

Pacheco Ranch Winery

Pepperwood Springs Vineyards

Radanovich Vineyards & Winery

Retzlaff Vineyards

Robert Stemmler Winery

Stony Ridge Winery

Villa Helena Winery

Wermuth Winery

Wildcat

Christine Woods Winery

York Mountain Winery

——— N R ———

Beaucastel Estate

Beauregard Ranch

Bella Luna Winery

Bryant Family Vineyard

Cache Cellars

Christian Brothers

DeNatale Vineyards

Dion

Eagle Ridge Winery

Fellom Ranch Vineyards

Fitzpatrick Winery

Gerwer Winery

Gold Hill Vineyard

Hafner Vineyard

Houtz Vineyards

Keegan Cellars

Johnson's Alexander Valley Wines

Juliana Vineyards

Las Montanas Winery

Livermore Valley Cellars

Martz Vineyards

Merry Vintners

Charles B. Mitchell Vineyards

Mosby Winery

Porter Creek Vineyards

River Road Vineyards

River Run Vintners

Salamandre Wine Cellars

Sonora Winery & Port Works

Spring Mountain Vineyards

St. Amant Winery

Sunrise Winery

Sycamore Creek Vineyards

Tiffany Hill

Twin Hills Winery

Valley of the Moon Winery

Weinstock Cellars

Westwood Winery

Wing Canyon

Woodside Vineyards

Young's Vineyard

Zayante Vineyards

WINE STAR RATINGS

❖

ALEATICO

NR   Montevina Wines Amador County

BARBERA

★★★   Konrad Estate Amador County

★★★   La Famiglia di Robert Mondavi California

★★★   Monte Volpe Mendocino County

★★★   Preston Vineyards Dry Creek Valley

★★★   Renwood Winery Amador County

★★★   Boeger Winery El Dorado County

★★★   Louis M. Martini Winery California

★★★   Montevina Wines Amador County Reserve

★★   Pellegrini Family Sonoma Valley Old Vines

★★   Sebastiani Vineyards Sonoma County Sonoma Series

NR   Hallcrest Vineyards El Dorado County Ritchie Vineyard

NR   Monterey Peninsula Winery California Vineyard View Pleasant Hill

NR   Westwood Winery El Dorado County Ritchie Vineyard

BLACK MUSCAT

★★★★   Philip Togni Vineyard Napa Valley

★★★   Quady Winery California Elysium

★★   Gan Eden San Joaquin County

NR   Shenandoah Vineyards Amador County Blush

★★★   Étude Wines Carneros Pinot Noir Rose

★★   Bonny Doon Vineyard California Vin Gris de Cigare

★★   Navarro Vineyards Anderson Valley Pinot Gris

★★   Sanford Winery Santa Barbara County Vin Gris

NR   Gerwer Winery El Dorado County White Zinfandel

NR   Johnson's Alexander Valley Wines Alexander Valley White Zinfandel

NR   Shooting Star Mendocino County Pacini Vineyard Zin Gris

NR   Stevenot Winery Calaveras County White Zinfandel

NR   Weinstock Cellars White Zinfandel

CABERNET BLEND

★★★★★   Dalla Valle Vineyards Napa Valley Maya

★★★★★   Opus One Napa Valley

★★★★★   Joseph Phelps Vineyards Napa Valley Insignia

★★★★★   St. Clement Vineyards Napa Valley Oroppas

★★★★★   Stag's Leap Wine Cellars Napa Valley Cask 23

★★★★   Niebaum-Coppola Estate Winery Napa Valley Rubicon

★★★★   Pahlmeyer Napa Valley

★★★★   Sterling Vineyards Napa Valley Reserve

★★★   Benziger Family Winery Sonoma Mountain A Tribute

★★★   Conn Creek Winery Napa Valley Anthology

★★★   Dickerson Vineyard Napa Valley Ruby Cabernet Limited Reserve

★★★   Duckhorn Vineyards Howell Mountain

★★★   Iron Horse Vineyards Alexander Valley T-T Vineyards Cabernets

★★★   Justin Vineyards & Winery San Luis Obispo County Isosceles Reserve

★★★   Justin Vineyards & Winery San Luis Obispo County Justification

★★★   Kathryn Kennedy Winery California Lateral

★★★ Lyeth Alexander Valley

★★★ Murrieta's Well Livermore Valley Vendimia

★★★ Quivira Vineyards Dry Creek Valley Cabernet Cuvée

★★★ Ravenswood Sonoma Mountain Pickberry Vineyard

★★★ Sterling Vineyards Napa Valley Three Palms Vineyard

★★★ Stonestreet Alexander Valley Legacy

★★ Bellerose Vineyard Sonoma County Cuvée Bellerose

★★ Cain Cellars Napa Valley Cuvée

★★ Castoro Cellars Paso Robles Dieci Anni

★★ Clos Pegase Napa Valley Hommage

★★ Cronin Vineyards California Joe's Cuvée

★★ Cronin Vineyards Stags Leap District Robinson Vineyard Concerto

★★ Elliston Vineyards Napa Valley Captain's Claret

★★ Hope Farms Paso Robles Claret

★★ Mazzocco Vineyards Sonoma County Matrix

★★ Rancho Sisquoc Winery Santa Maria Valley Red Cellar Select

★★ Ravenswood Sonoma County Mountain Claret

★★ Rosenblum Cellars Napa Valley Holbrook Mitchell Vineyard Trio

★★ Rubissow-Sargent Mount Veeder Les Trompettes

★★ Steltzner Vineyards Stags Leap District Claret

★★ Vita Nova Santa Barbara County Reservatum

★ The Brander Vineyard Santa Ynez Valley Bouchet Tête de Cuvée

★ Concannon Vineyard Livermore Valley Assemblage

★ Topolos Sonoma County Riserva

NR Edmunds St. John Napa Valley Les Fleurs du Chaparral

NR Fenestra Winery Livermore Valley

NR Golden Creek Vineyard Sonoma County Caberlot Reserve

NR Santa Ynez Winery Santa Barbara County Cabernet Merlot

NR Sierra Vista El Dorado County Lynelle

NR Topaz Napa Valley Rouge de Trois

CABERNET FRANC

★★★ The Gainey Vineyard Santa Ynez Valley Limited Selection

★★★ Guenoc Winery Lake County

★★★ Gundlach Bundschu Winery Sonoma Valley Rhinefarm Vineyards

★★★ Justin Vineyards & Winery San Luis Obispo County

★★★ La Jota Vineyard Co. Howell Mountain

★★★ Mount Konocti Winery Lake County Kelsey

★★★ Shooting Star Clear Lake

★★ Benziger Family Winery Alexander Valley Blue Rock Vineyard Imagery Series

★★ Bouchaine Vineyards Sonoma Valley Limited Release

★★ Clos du Bois Alexander Valley Reserve L'Étranger

★★ Cosentino Winery North Coast

★★ Dry Creek Vineyard Dry Creek Valley

★★ Indian Springs Vineyards Nevada County

★★ Jarvis Napa Valley

★★ Jekel Vineyards Monterey County

★★ Kendall-Jackson California Vintner's Reserve

★★ Nelson Estate Sonoma County

★★ Niebaum-Coppola Estate Winery Napa Valley Francis Coppola Family Wines

★★ Parducci Wine Cellars Mendocino County

★★ Pride Mountain Vineyards Napa Valley

★★ Sebastiani Vineyards Sonoma Valley Sonoma Series

★★ White Oak Vineyards & Winery Alexander Valley

★ Dehlinger Winery Russian River Valley

NR Rombauer Vineyards Napa Valley

NR St. Francis Winery Sonoma Valley

NR Sobon Estate Shenandoah Valley

NR Stonegate Winery Napa Valley

NR Wing Canyon Mount Veeder

CABERNET SAUVIGNON

★★★★★ Araujo Estate Wines Napa Valley Eisele Vineyard

★★★★★ Beaulieu Vineyard Napa Valley Georges de Latour Private Reserve

★★★★★ Beringer Vineyards Napa Valley Private Reserve

★★★★★ Beringer Vineyards Napa Valley Chabot Vineyard

★★★★★ Caymus Vineyards Napa Valley Special Selection

★★★★★ Chateau Montelena Winery Napa Valley The Montelena Estate

★★★★★ Dalla Valle Vineyards Napa Valley

★★★★★ Diamond Creek Vineyards Napa Valley Gravelly Meadow

★★★★★ Diamond Creek Vineyards Napa Valley Gravelly Meadow Lake Blend

★★★★★ Diamond Creek Vineyards Napa Valley Lake Vineyard

★★★★★ Diamond Creek Vineyards Napa Valley Red Rock Terrace

★★★★★ Diamond Creek Vineyards Napa Valley Volcanic Hill

★★★★★ Dominus Estate Napa Valley

★★★★★ Duckhorn Vineyards Napa Valley

★★★★★ Dunn Vineyards Howell Mountain

★★★★★ Forman Vineyard Napa Valley

★★★★★ Flora Springs Wine Co. Napa Valley Reserve

★★★★★ Grace Family Vineyards Napa Valley

★★★★★ Groth Vineyards & Winery Napa Valley Reserve

★★★★★ Heitz Wine Cellars Napa Valley Martha's Vineyard

★★★★★ The Hess Collection Winery Mount Veeder

★★★★★ The Hess Collection Winery Mount Veeder Reserve

★★★★★ Robert Mondavi Winery Napa Valley Reserve

★★★★★ Ridge Vineyards Santa Cruz Mountains Monte Bello

★★★★★ Shafer Vineyards Stags Leap District Hillside Select

★★★★★ Silverado Vineyards Stags Leap District Limited Reserve

★★★★★ Spottswoode Winery Napa Valley

★★★★ S. Anderson Vineyard Stags Leap District Richard Chambers Vineyard

★★★★ Anderson's Conn Valley Vineyards Napa Valley Estate Reserve

★★★★ Arrowood Vineyards & Winery Sonoma County

★★★★ Caymus Vineyards Napa Valley

★★★★ Chateau Potelle Mount Veeder V.G.S.

★★★★ Chateau St. Jean Sonoma County Reserve

★★★★ Clos Du Val Stags Leap District Reserve

★★★★ B. R. Cohn Winery Sonoma Valley Olive Hill Vineyard

★★★★ Dunn Vineyards Napa Valley

★★★★ Étude Wines Napa Valley

★★★★ Far Niente Winery Napa Valley

★★★★ Freemark Abbey Winery Napa Valley Bosche

★★★★ E. & J. Gallo Winery Northern Sonoma

★★★★ Geyser Peak Winery Alexander Valley Estate Reserve

★★★★ Groth Vineyards & Winery Napa Valley

★★★★ Guenoc Winery Napa Valley Beckstoffer Vineyard Reserve

★★★★ Harlan Estate Napa Valley

★★★★ Hartwell Vineyards Stags Leap District

★★★★ Kenwood Vineyards Sonoma Valley Artist Series

★★★★ Laurel Glen Vineyard Sonoma Mountain

★★★★ Livingston Wines Napa Valley Moffett Vineyard

★★★★ Mayacamas Vineyards Napa Valley

★★★★ Robert Mondavi Winery Napa Valley

★★★★ Oakville Ranch Vineyards Napa Valley

★★★★ Oakville Ranch Vineyards Napa Valley Lewis Select

★★★★ Oakville Ranch Vineyards Napa Valley Reserve

★★★★ Joseph Phelps Vineyards Napa Valley Backus Vineyard

★★★★ Joseph Phelps Vineyards Napa Valley Eisele Vineyard

★★★★   A. Rafanelli Winery Dry Creek Valley

★★★★   St. Clement Vineyards Napa Valley

★★★★   Sequoia Grove Vineyards Napa Valley Estate Reserve

★★★★   Shafer Vineyards Stags Leap District

★★★★   Signorello Vineyards Napa Valley Founder's Reserve

★★★★   Silver Oak Cellars Alexander Valley

★★★★   Silver Oak Cellars Napa Valley

★★★★   Silver Oak Cellars Napa Valley Bonny's Vineyard

★★★★   Silverado Vineyards Stags Leap District

★★★★   Simi Winery Alexander Valley Reserve

★★★★   Stag's Leap Wine Cellars Napa Valley Fay Vineyard

★★★★   Stag's Leap Wine Cellars Stags Leap District SLV

★★★★   Philip Togni Vineyard Napa Valley

★★★★   Villa Mt. Eden Mendocino County Signature Series

★★★   Abreu Vineyards Napa Valley

★★★   Adelaida Cellars Paso Robles

★★★   Alexander Valley Vineyards Alexander Valley

★★★   Alexander Valley Vineyards Alexander Valley Wetzel Family Estate

★★★   Altamura Winery and Vineyards Napa Valley

★★★   Arrowood Vineyards & Winery Sonoma County Reserve Speciale

★★★   Vincent Arroyo Winery Napa Valley

★★★   Atlas Peak Vineyards Napa Valley

★★★   Barnett Vineyards Spring Mountain Rattlesnake Hill

★★★   Benziger Family Winery Sonoma County

★★★   Beringer Vineyards Knights Valley

★★★   Buehler Vineyards Napa Valley Reserve

★★★   Burgess Cellars Napa Valley Vintage Selection

★★★   Cafaro Cellars Napa Valley

★★★   Cakebread Cellars Napa Valley

★★★   Carmenet Vineyard Sonoma County Dynamite Cabernet

★★★   Carmenet Vineyard Sonoma Valley Moon Mountain Estate Vineyard

★★★   Chalk Hill Winery Chalk Hill

★★★   Chappellet Vineyard Napa Valley

★★★   Chappellet Vineyard Napa Valley Pritchard Hill Estates

★★★   Chateau Montelena Winery Napa Valley Calistoga Cuvée

★★★   Chateau Potelle Napa Valley Cuvée 95

★★★   Chateau Souverain Alexander Valley

★★★   Chateau Souverain Alexander Valley Winemaker's Reserve

★★★   Chateau St. Jean Sonoma County Cinq Cépages

★★★   Clos du Bois Alexander Valley Winemaker's Reserve

★★★   Clos du Bois Alexander Valley Briarcrest Vineyard

★★★   Clos du Bois Alexander Valley Marlstone Vineyard

★★★   Clos Du Val Napa Valley

★★★   Clos Du Val Stags Leap District

★★★   Clos La Chance Santa Cruz Mountains

★★★   Clos Pegase Napa Valley

★★★   Colgin Napa Valley

★★★   Corison Napa Valley

★★★   Cornerstone Cellars Howell Mountain

★★★   Counterpoint Sonoma Mountain

★★★   Cronin Vineyards Stags Leap District Robinson Vineyard

★★★   Cutler Cellars Sonoma Valley Batto Ranch

★★★   Cuvaison Winery Napa Valley

★★★   Diamond Creek Vineyards Napa Valley Three Vineyard Blend

★★★   Domain Hill & Mayes Napa Valley Clos Fontaine du Mont Reserve

★★★   Dry Creek Vineyard Dry Creek Valley

★★★   Dry Creek Vineyard Dry Creek Valley Reserve

★★★   Dry Creek Vineyard Sonoma County

★★★   Tom Eddy Napa Valley

★★★ Gary Farrell Wines Sonoma County Ladi's Vineyard

★★★ Ferrari-Carano Winery Sonoma County

★★★ Ferrari-Carano Winery Sonoma County Reserve

★★★ Fetzer Vineyards Sonoma County Reserve

★★★ Fisher Vineyards Napa Valley Coach Insignia

★★★ Fisher Vineyards Sonoma County Wedding Vineyard

★★★ Flora Springs Wine Co. Napa Valley

★★★ Folie à Deux Winery Napa Valley

★★★ Foxen Vineyard Santa Barbara County

★★★ Franciscan Vineyards Napa Valley Oakville Estate

★★★ Franciscan Vineyards Napa Valley Oakville Estate Reserve

★★★ Freemark Abbey Winery Napa Valley Sycamore Vineyard

★★★ Frog's Leap Winery Napa Valley

★★★ E. & J. Gallo Winery Sonoma County Gallo Sonoma

★★★ Girard Winery Napa Valley

★★★ Girard Winery Napa Valley Reserve

★★★ Grgich Hills Cellar Napa Valley

★★★ Gundlach Bundschu Winery Sonoma Valley Rhinefarm Vineyards

★★★ Gundlach Bundschu Winery Sonoma Valley Rhinefarm Vineyards Vintage Reserve

★★★ Hanna Winery Alexander Valley

★★★ Harrison Vineyards Napa Valley

★★★ Harrison Vineyards Napa Valley Reserve

★★★ Heitz Wine Cellars Napa Valley

★★★ Heitz Wine Cellars Napa Valley Bella Oaks Vineyard

★★★ Heitz Wine Cellars Napa Valley Trailside Vineyard

★★★ William Hill Winery Napa Valley Gold Label Reserve

★★★ Paul Hobbs Cellars Carneros Hyde Vineyard

★★★ Husch Vineyards Mendocino County La Ribera Ranch

★★★ Inglenook-Napa Valley Napa Valley Reserve Cask

★★★ Inglenook-Napa Valley Napa Valley Reunion

★★★ Jarvis Napa Valley

★★★ Jordan Vineyard and Winery Alexander Valley

★★★ Judd's Hill Napa Valley

★★★ Justin Vineyards & Winery San Luis Obispo County

★★★ Justin Vineyards & Winery San Luis Obispo County Society Reserve

★★★ Kendall-Jackson California Grand Reserve

★★★ Kathryn Kennedy Winery Santa Cruz Mountains

★★★ Kenwood Vineyards Sonoma Valley

★★★ Kenwood Vineyards Sonoma Valley Jack London Vineyard

★★★ Kistler Vineyards Sonoma Valley Kistler Estate Vineyard

★★★ Charles Krug Winery Napa Valley Vintage Selection

★★★ Kunde Estate Winery Sonoma Valley

★★★ La Jota Vineyard Co. Howell Mountain

★★★ Liparita Cellars Howell Mountain

★★★ J. Lohr Winery Paso Robles Seven Oaks

★★★ Long Vineyards Napa Valley

★★★ Lyeth Alexander Valley

★★★ Markham Vineyards Napa Valley

★★★ Louis M. Martini Winery Napa Valley Reserve

★★★ Louis M. Martini Winery Sonoma Valley Monte Rosso

★★★ Meridian Vineyards Paso Robles

★★★ Merryvale Vineyards Napa Valley

★★★ Peter Michael Winery Knights Valley Les Pavots

★★★ Monticello Cellars Napa Valley Corley Reserve

★★★ Monticello Cellars Napa Valley Jefferson Cuvée

★★★ Moraga Bel Air

★★★ Morgan Winery Carmel Valley

★★★ Mount Eden Vineyards Santa Cruz Mountains

★★★ Mount Eden Vineyards Santa Cruz Mountains Old Vine Reserve

★★★   Mount Eden Vineyards Santa Cruz Mountains Lathweisen Ridge

★★★   Mount Veeder Winery Napa Valley

★★★   Murphy-Goode Estate Winery Alexander Valley

★★★   Murphy-Goode Estate Winery Alexander Valley Murphy Ranch

★★★   Nalle Winery Dry Creek Valley

★★★   Navarro Vineyards Mendocino County

★★★   Newlan Vineyards and Winery Napa Valley

★★★   Newton Vineyard Napa Valley

★★★   Norman Vineyards Paso Robles

★★★   Oakford Vineyards Napa Valley

★★★   Optima Alexander Valley

★★★   Paradigm Napa Valley

★★★   Peachy Canyon Winery Central Coast

★★★   Peachy Canyon Winery Paso Robles

★★★   Robert Pecota Winery Napa Valley Kara's Vineyard

★★★   Peju Province Winery Napa Valley

★★★   Peju Province Winery Napa Valley HB Vineyard

★★★   Robert Pepi Winery Napa Valley Vine Hill Ranch

★★★   Joseph Phelps Vineyards Napa Valley

★★★   Pine Ridge Winery Napa Valley Andrus Reserve

★★★   Pine Ridge Winery Stags Leap District

★★★   Preston Vineyards Dry Creek Valley

★★★   Pride Mountain Vineyards Napa Valley

★★★   Martin Ray Winery Napa Valley

★★★   Raymond Vineyard and Cellar Napa Valley

★★★   Raymond Vineyard and Cellar Napa Valley Private Reserve

★★★   Ridge Vineyards Santa Cruz Mountains

★★★   Ritchie Creek Vineyards Napa Valley

★★★   Rocking Horse Napa Valley Hillside Cuvée

★★★   Rocking Horse Napa Valley Garvey Family Vineyard

★★★   Rocking Horse Stags Leap District Robinson Vineyard

★★★   Rombauer Vineyards Napa Valley Le Meilleur du Chai

★★★   Rosenblum Cellars Napa Valley George Hendry Vineyard

★★★   Rosenthal – The Malibu Estate California

★★★   Round Hill Winery Napa Valley Reserve

★★★   St. Francis Winery Sonoma County

★★★   St. Francis Winery Sonoma Valley Reserve

★★★   St. Supéry Vineyard & Winery Napa Valley Dollarhide Ranch

★★★   Santa Cruz Mountain Vineyard Santa Cruz Mountains Bates Ranch

★★★   V. Sattui Winery Napa Valley

★★★   V. Sattui Winery Napa Valley Preston Vineyard Reserve Stock

★★★   V. Sattui Winery Napa Valley Suzanne's Vineyard

★★★   Seavey Vineyard Napa Valley

★★★   Sebastiani Vineyards Sonoma Valley Sonoma Series

★★★   Sebastiani Vineyards Sonoma Valley Cherryblock Old Vines

★★★   Sequoia Grove Vineyards Napa Valley

★★★   Signorello Vineyards Napa Valley

★★★   Simi Winery Alexander Valley

★★★   Stag's Leap Wine Cellars Napa Valley

★★★   Staglin Family Vineyard Napa Valley

★★★   Steltzner Vineyards Stags Leap District

★★★   Stonestreet Alexander Valley

★★★   Rodney Strong Vineyards Northern Sonoma Reserve

★★★   Rodney Strong Vineyards Northern Sonoma Alexander's Crown

★★★   Sullivan Vineyards Winery Napa Valley

★★★   Sullivan Vineyards Winery Napa Valley Private Reserve

★★★   Swanson Vineyards Napa Valley

★★★   Terra Rosa Napa Valley

★★★   The Terraces Napa Valley

★★★   Trefethen Vineyards Napa Valley Reserve

★★★   Truchard Vineyards Carneros

★★★   Tudal Winery Napa Valley

★★★ Turnbull Wine Cellars Napa Valley

★★★ Vichon Winery Stags Leap District SLD

★★★ Vine Cliff Cellars Napa Valley

★★★ von Strasser Vineyards Diamond Mountain

★★★ Whitehall Lane Winery Napa Valley

★★★ Whitehall Lane Winery Napa Valley Reserve

★★★ Whitehall Lane Winery Napa Valley Morisoli Vineyard

★★★ Wild Horse Winery Paso Robles Cheval Sauvage

★★★ Wild Horse Winery San Luis Obispo County

★★★ ZD Wines Napa Valley

★★ Aries Napa Valley

★★ Bandiera Winery Napa Valley

★★ Bayview Cellars Napa Valley

★★ Beaucanon Winery Napa Valley

★★ Beaulieu Vineyard Napa Valley Beau Tour

★★ Beaulieu Vineyard Napa Valley Rutherford

★★ Belvedere Winery Sonoma County

★★ Benziger Family Winery Knights Valley

★★ Bergfeld Winery Napa Valley

★★ Black Mountain Alexander Valley Fat Cat

★★ Bocage Monterey County Proprietor's Cuvée

★★ Boeger Winery El Dorado County

★★ Bogle Vineyards California

★★ Bon Marché Napa Valley

★★ Braren Pauli Winery Dry Creek Valley

★★ Brutocao Cellars Mendocino County Proprietor's Special Reserve

★★ Brutocao Cellars Mendocino County Albert Vineyard

★★ Buehler Vineyards Napa Valley

★★ Buena Vista Winery Carneros

★★ Buena Vista Winery Carneros Grand Reserve

★★ Byington Winery & Vineyards Napa Valley

★★ Byron Vineyards & Winery Santa Barbara County

★★ Camelot Central Coast

★★ Castoro Cellars Paso Robles Reserve

★★ Castoro Cellars Paso Robles The Wine

★★ Cedar Mountain Winery Livermore Valley Blanches Vineyard

★★ Chateau St. Jean Sonoma County

★★ Chatom Vineyards Calaveras County

★★ Chauffe-eau Cellars Alexander Valley

★★ Chestnut Hill Winery California Coastal Cuvée

★★ Chimney Rock Winery Stags Leap District

★★ Christophe Napa Valley

★★ Cinnabar Vineyard & Winery Santa Cruz Mountains

★★ Cloninger Cellars Monterey County

★★ Clos du Bois Alexander Valley

★★ Cloverdale Ranch Alexander Valley Estate Cuvée

★★ B. R. Cohn Winery Napa County Silver Label

★★ Conn Creek Winery Napa Valley Barrel Select

★★ Conn Creek Winery Napa Valley Limited Release

★★ Corbett Canyon Vineyards California Coastal Classic

★★ Corbett Canyon Vineyards Napa Valley Reserve

★★ Cosentino Winery Napa Valley

★★ Cosentino Winery Napa Valley Punched Cap Fermented Unfined

★★ Côtes de Sonoma Sonoma County

★★ Creston Vineyards & Winery Paso Robles

★★ Creston Vineyards & Winery Paso Robles Winemaker's Selection

★★ Creston Vineyards & Winery San Luis Obispo County

★★ Cronin Vineyards San Mateo County Shaw & Cronin Cuvée

★★ Cronin Vineyards Santa Cruz Mountains

★★ De Loach Vineyards Russian River Valley

★★ Deer Park Winery Howell Mountain Beatty Ranch Reserve

★★ Dehlinger Winery Russian River Valley

★★ DeMoor Winery Napa Valley

★★ Deux Amis Winery Dry Creek Valley

★★   Domaine du Grand Archer Sonoma County

★★   Domaine St. George Winery California Vintage Reserve

★★   Domaine St. George Winery Sonoma County Premier Cuvée Reserve

★★   Duncan Peak Vineyards Mendocino County

★★   Dunnewood Vineyards North Coast Barrel Select

★★   Durney Vineyard Carmel Valley

★★   Durney Vineyard Carmel Valley Reserve

★★   Eberle Winery Paso Robles

★★   Eberle Winery Paso Robles Reserve

★★   Estancia Alexander Valley

★★   Farella-Park Vineyards Napa Valley

★★   Fetzer Vineyards California Valley Oaks

★★   Fetzer Vineyards North Coast Barrel Select

★★   Field Stone Winery Alexander Valley

★★   Field Stone Winery Alexander Valley Staten Family Reserve

★★   Field Stone Winery Alexander Valley Vineyard Blend

★★   Field Stone Winery Alexander Valley Hoot Owl Creek Vineyards

★★   Field Stone Winery Alexander Valley Hoot Owl Creek Vineyards Reserve

★★   Field Stone Winery Alexander Valley Turkey Hill Vineyard

★★   Firestone Vineyard Santa Ynez Valley

★★   Firestone Vineyard Santa Ynez Valley Vintage Reserve

★★   Forest Glen Sonoma County

★★   Forest Glen Sonoma County Barrel Select

★★   Foss Creek Sonoma County

★★   Fox Mountain Sonoma County Reserve

★★   Foxen Vineyard Santa Maria Valley

★★   Freemark Abbey Winery Napa Valley

★★   Fremont Creek Winery

★★   The Gainey Vineyard Santa Barbara County Limited Selection

★★   Gan Eden Alexander Valley

★★   Geyser Peak Winery Sonoma County

★★   Glass Mountain Quarry California

★★   Graeser Winery Napa Valley

★★   Greenwood Ridge Vineyards Anderson Valley

★★   Greenwood Ridge Vineyards Anderson Valley Estate Reserve

★★   Greenwood Ridge Vineyards Mendocino County

★★   Guenoc Winery Lake County

★★   Guenoc Winery North Coast

★★   Guilliams Vineyards Spring Mountain

★★   Hacienda Winery California Clair de Lune

★★   Hagafen Cellars Napa Valley

★★   Hagafen Cellars Napa Valley Reserve

★★   Hahn Estates Santa Lucia Highlands

★★   Hallcrest Vineyards El Dorado County Covington Vineyard

★★   Hallcrest Vineyards El Dorado County De Cascabel Vineyard Proprietors Reserve

★★   Hallcrest Vineyards Santa Cruz Mountains Beauregard Ranch Proprietors Reserve

★★   Hanzell Vineyards Sonoma Valley

★★   Harmony Cellars Paso Robles

★★   Haywood Winery California Vintner's Select

★★   Haywood Winery Sonoma Valley Los Chamizal Vineyard

★★   Hess Select California

★★   William Hill Winery Napa Valley Silver Label

★★   Louis Honig Cellars Napa Valley

★★   Hop Kiln Winery Russian River Valley

★★   Husch Vineyards Mendocino County North Field Select

★★   Indian Springs Vineyards Nevada County

★★   Inglenook-Napa Valley Napa Valley

★★   Innisfree Napa Valley

★★   Jekel Vineyards Arroyo Seco

★★   Kalin Cellars Sonoma County Reserve

★★   Karly Wines El Dorado County Stromberg Carpenter Vineyard

★★   Robert Keenan Winery Napa Valley

★★   Kendall-Jackson California Vintner's Reserve

★★   Klein Santa Cruz Mountains

★★   Charles Krug Winery Napa Valley

★★ Lakespring Winery Napa Valley

★★ Lakespring Winery Napa Valley Reserve Selection

★★ Lakespring Winery Napa Valley Vintage Selection

★★ Lambert Bridge Sonoma County

★★ Laurent Cellars Napa Valley Reserve

★★ Lava Cap Winery El Dorado County

★★ Liberty School California Vintner Select Series Three

★★ Livingston Wines Napa Valley Stanley's Selection

★★ Lockwood Monterey County

★★ Lockwood Monterey County Partners' Reserve

★★ J. Lohr Winery California Cypress

★★ Lolonis Winery Mendocino County Private Reserve

★★ Lone Oak Monterey County

★★ Longoria Wine Cellars Santa Ynez Valley

★★ Lytton Springs Winery Mendocino County Private Reserve

★★ Madrona Vineyards El Dorado County

★★ Louis M. Martini Winery North Coast

★★ Mazzocco Vineyards Sonoma County

★★ McDowell Valley Vineyards Mendocino County

★★ The Meeker Vineyard Dry Creek Valley

★★ The Meeker Vineyard Dry Creek Valley Gold Leaf Cuvée

★★ The Meeker Vineyard Dry Creek Valley Scharf Family Vineyard

★★ Mendocino Hill Mendocino County

★★ Michel-Schlumberger Dry Creek Valley

★★ Mill Creek Vineyards Dry Creek Valley

★★ Mirassou Vineyards Monterey County Family Selection

★★ Mirassou Vineyards Monterey County Harvest Reserve Limited Bottling

★★ Mission View Vineyards & Winery Paso Robles

★★ Robert Mondavi-Woodbridge California

★★ Mont St. John Cellars Napa Valley

★★ Monterey Peninsula Winery Monterey County

★★ The Monterey Vineyard Monterey County Limited Release

★★ Moondance Napa Valley

★★ Mount Konocti Winery Lake County Kelsey

★★ Napa Ridge Central Coast

★★ Napa Ridge Central Coast Oak Barrel

★★ Napa Ridge Napa Valley Coastal Reserve

★★ Napa Ridge North Coast Coastal

★★ Napa Ridge North Coast Coastal Oak Barrel

★★ Napa Ridge North Coast Coastal Reserve

★★ Napa Ridge North Coast North Coast Reserve

★★ Nevada City Winery Sierra Foothills

★★ Neyers Napa Valley

★★ Nichelini Winery Napa Valley Joseph A. Nichelini Vineyards

★★ Octopus Mountain Anderson Valley Dennison Vineyard

★★ Page Mill Winery Napa Valley V. & L. Eisele Vineyard

★★ Parducci Wine Cellars Mendocino County

★★ J. Pedroncelli Winery Dry Creek Valley

★★ J. Pedroncelli Winery Dry Creek Valley Reserve

★★ Mario Perelli-Minetti Winery Napa Valley

★★ Peterson Winery Dry Creek Valley

★★ R.H. Phillips Vineyard California

★★ Pine Ridge Winery Diamond Mountain

★★ Pine Ridge Winery Napa Valley Rutherford Cuvée

★★ Plam Vineyards & Winery California

★★ Plam Vineyards & Winery Napa Valley

★★ Bernard Pradel Cellars Napa Valley Limited Barrel Selection

★★ Bernard Pradel Cellars Napa Valley Howell Mountain Ranch

★★ Prager Winery & Port Works Napa Valley Port

★★ Quail Ridge Cellars Napa Valley

★★ Rabbit Ridge Vineyards Sonoma County Rabbit Ridge Ranch Estate Reserve

★★ Rancho Sisquoc Winery Santa Maria Valley

★★ Kent Rasmussen Winery Napa Valley

★★ Ravenswood Sonoma County

★★ Ravenswood Sonoma Valley Gregory Vineyard

★★ Raymond Vineyard and Cellar California Amberhill

★★ Richardson Vineyards Sonoma Valley Horne Vineyard

★★ Ridge Vineyards Napa County York Creek

★★ J. Rochioli Vineyard & Winery Russian River Valley Neoma's Vineyard Private Reserve

★★ Rombauer Vineyards Napa Valley

★★ Round Hill Winery California

★★ Rubissow-Sargent Mount Veeder

★★ Rutherford Hill Winery Napa Valley

★★ Rutherford Hill Winery Napa Valley XVS

★★ Saddleback Cellars Napa Valley

★★ St. Andrews Winery Napa Valley

★★ San Saba Vineyard Monterey County

★★ Santa Barbara Winery Santa Ynez Valley

★★ Santa Barbara Winery Santa Ynez Valley Reserve

★★ Sausal Winery Alexander Valley

★★ Seghesio Winery Sonoma County

★★ Shenandoah Vineyards Amador County

★★ Sierra Vista El Dorado County

★★ Sierra Vista El Dorado County Five Star Reserve

★★ Smith and Hook Santa Lucia Highlands

★★ Smith-Madrone Vineyard Napa Valley

★★ Smothers Brothers Wines Sonoma Valley Remick Ridge Ranch

★★ Soquel Vineyards Santa Cruz Mountains

★★ Soquel Vineyards Stags Leap District

★★ Stags' Leap Winery Napa Valley

★★ P. and M. Staiger Santa Cruz Mountains

★★ Star Hill Wines Napa Valley Bartolucci Vineyard Doc's Reserve

★★ Sterling Vineyards Napa Valley

★★ Sterling Vineyards Napa Valley Diamond Mountain Ranch

★★ Stevenot Winery Calaveras County Reserve

★★ Stevenot Winery California

★★ Stonegate Winery Napa Valley

★★ Stratford Winery California

★★ Rodney Strong Vineyards Sonoma Coast

★★ Sutter Home Winery Napa Valley Reserve

★★ Tobin James Paso Robles Private Stash

★★ Tobin James San Luis Obispo County Twilight

★★ Trefethen Vineyards Napa Valley

★★ Tulocay Winery Napa Valley Cliff Vineyard

★★ Tulocay Winery Napa Valley DeCelles Vineyard

★★ Van der Heyden Vineyard Alexander Valley

★★ Viano Vineyards Contra Costa County

★★ Viansa Winery Napa-Sonoma Counties

★★ Viansa Winery Napa-Sonoma Counties Reserve

★★ Vichon Winery California Coastal Selection

★★ Vichon Winery Napa Valley

★★ Villa Mt. Eden California Cellar Select

★★ Villa Mt. Eden Napa Valley

★★ Villa Mt. Eden Napa Valley Grand Reserve

★★ Weibel Vineyards

★★ Wellington Vineyards Mount Veeder Random Ridge Vineyard

★★ Wellington Vineyards Sonoma County Mohrhardt Ridge Vineyard

★★ Wente Bros. Livermore Valley Charles Wetmore Vineyard Estate Reserve

★★ Wheeler Winery Dry Creek Valley Norse Vineyard Private Reserve

★★ White Oak Vineyards & Winery Alexander Valley Myers Limited Reserve

★★ Windemere Napa Valley

★ Ahlgren Vineyard Santa Cruz Mountains Bates Ranch

★ Arciero Winery Paso Robles

★ Austin Cellars Santa Barbara County Mille Délices

★ Austin Cellars Santa Barbara County Perry's Reserve

★ Brindiamo California Limited Bottling

★ Davis Bynum Winery Sonoma County

★ Callaway Vineyard and Winery California Hawk Watch

★ Cecchetti Sebastiani Cellars Alexander Valley

★ Concannon Vineyard Central Coast Selected Vineyards

★ Devlin Wine Cellars Santa Cruz Mountains Beauregard Ranch

★ Foppiano Vineyards Russian River Valley

★ The Gainey Vineyard Santa Maria Valley

★ The Gainey Vineyard Santa Ynez Valley

★ La Crosse Napa Valley

★ La Vieille Montagne Napa Valley

★ Leeward Winery Alexander Valley

★ Maacama Creek Alexander Valley Reserve

★ Maacama Creek Alexander Valley Melim Vineyard

★ Maacama Creek Alexander Valley Melim Vineyard Reserve

★ Montevina Wines California

★ Mount Palomar Winery Temecula

★ Nichelini Winery Napa Valley

★ Pacheco Ranch Winery Marin County

★ Pepperwood Grove California

★ Radanovich Vineyards & Winery Sierra Foothills Mariposa County

★ Sonoma Creek Winery Sonoma Valley Reserve

★ Stony Ridge Winery California

★ Stony Ridge Winery Napa Valley Limited Release

★ Ivan Tamas Winery Livermore Valley Le Clan des Quatre Vineyards

★ Topolos Sonoma County

★ Trentadue Winery Dry Creek Valley

★ Tulocay Winery Napa Valley Egan Vineyard

★ Villa Helena Winery Napa Valley Baron von Kees Vineyard

★ York Mountain Winery San Luis Obispo County

★ Stephen Zellerbach California

NR Baldinelli Vineyards Amador County

NR Beaulieu Vineyard Napa Valley Claret Special Release

NR Bonverre California Lot Number 9

NR Crystal Valley Cellars Napa Valley Unfined

NR Fellom Ranch Vineyards Santa Cruz Mountains

NR Fenestra Winery Livermore Valley

NR Fenestra Winery Monterey County Smith and Hook Vineyard

NR Fitzpatrick Winery Coloma Canyon

NR Golden Creek Vineyard Sonoma County

NR Goode & Ready Alexander Valley Goode-Ready The Second Cabernet

NR Grove Street Winery California Vineyard Select

NR Hafner Alexander Valley

NR Hart Winery Temecula Hansen Vineyard

NR Houtz Vineyards Santa Ynez Valley

NR Johnson's Alexander Valley Wines Alexander Valley

NR Joullian Vineyards Carmel Valley

NR Korbel Champagne Cellars Alexander Valley

NR Las Montanas Winery Sonoma Valley

NR Las Viñas Winery California Private Reserve

NR Livermore Valley Cellars Livermore Valley

NR Martz Vineyards Mendocino County

NR Milano Winery Mendocino County Sanel Valley Vineyard

NR Milat Vineyards Napa Valley

NR Charles B. Mitchell Vineyards El Dorado County

NR Monte Verde California Proprietor's Reserve

NR Gustave Niebaum Napa Valley Reference

NR Gustave Niebaum Napa Valley Mast Vineyard

NR Gustave Niebaum Napa Valley Tench Vineyard

NR Norman Vineyards Paso Robles No Nonsense Red

NR Renaissance Vineyard & Winery North Yuba

NR Retzlaff Vineyards Livermore Valley

NR River Road Vineyard

NR River Run Vintners

NR   Rolling Hills Vineyards California

NR   Roudon-Smith Winery California

NR   Royce Vineyards Napa Valley

NR   Royce Vineyards Sonoma County

NR   Rustridge Vineyards & Winery Napa Valley

NR   Schug Carneros Estate Sonoma Valley
       Heritage Reserve

NR   Robert Sinskey Vineyards Napa Valley

NR   Spring Mountain Vineyards Napa Valley

NR   Sunrise Winery Santa Cruz Mountains Arata
       Vineyard

NR   Joseph Swan Vineyards Sonoma Mountain
       Steiner Vineyard

NR   Sycamore Creek Vineyards

NR   Twin Hills Winery Paso Robles

NR   Valley of the Moon Winery Sonoma Valley

NR   Voss Vineyards

NR   Wild Hog Hill Vineyard

NR   Wildhurst Vineyards Clear Lake

NR   Wing Canyon Mount Veeder

NR   Woodside Vineyards Santa Cruz Mountains

NR   Young's Vineyard Amador County

CARIGNANE

★★   Cline Cellars Contra Costa County

★★   Seghesio Winery Alexander Valley Old Vines

CHARBONO

★★   Duxoup Napa Valley

★★   Konrad Estate Mendocino County

CHARDONNAY

★★★★★   Arrowood Vineyards & Winery Sonoma
        County Réserve Spéciale

★★★★★   Au Bon Climat Santa Barbara County Le
        Bouge D'à Côté

★★★★★   Au Bon Climat Santa Barbara County
        Reserve

★★★★★   Beringer Vineyards Napa Valley Private
        Reserve

★★★★★   Beringer Vineyards Napa Valley Sbragia
        Limited Release

★★★★★   Chalone Vineyard Chalone

★★★★★   Chalone Vineyard Chalone Reserve

★★★★★   Chateau St. Jean Alexander Valley Robert
        Young Vineyard

★★★★★   Chateau St. Jean Alexander Valley Robert
        Young Vineyard Reserve

★★★★★   De Loach Vineyards Russian River Valley
        O.F.S.

★★★★★   El Molino Napa Valley

★★★★★   Gary Farrell Wines Russian River Valley
        Allen Vineyard

★★★★★   Ferrari-Carano Winery Alexander Valley

★★★★★   Ferrari-Carano Winery California Reserve

★★★★★   Ferrari-Carano Winery Napa-Sonoma
        Counties Reserve

★★★★★   Flora Springs Wine Co. Napa Valley Barrel
        Fermented

★★★★★   Forman Vineyard Napa Valley

★★★★★   Grgich Hills Cellar Napa Valley

★★★★★   Hanzell Vineyards Sonoma Valley

★★★★★   Kistler Vineyards Russian River Valley
        Dutton Ranch

★★★★★   Kistler Vineyards Russian River Valley Vine
        Hill Road Vineyard

★★★★★   Kistler Vineyards Sonoma Coast

★★★★★   Kistler Vineyards Sonoma County

★★★★★   Kistler Vineyards Sonoma County Cuvée
        Cathleen

★★★★★   Kistler Vineyards Sonoma Mountain McCrea
        Vineyard

★★★★★   Kistler Vineyards Sonoma Valley Durell
        Vineyard

★★★★★   Kistler Vineyards Sonoma Valley Kistler
        Estate Vineyard

★★★★★   Long Vineyards Napa Valley

★★★★★   Marcassin Winery Alexander Valley Gauer
        Ranch Upper Barn

★★★★★   Marcassin Winery Carneros Hudson Vineyard

★★★★★   Marcassin Winery Sonoma County Lorenzo
        Vineyard

★★★★★   Matanzas Creek Winery Sonoma Valley

★★★★★ Matanzas Creek Winery Sonoma Valley Journey

★★★★★ Merryvale Vineyards Napa Valley Reserve

★★★★★ Peter Michael Winery Napa County Clos du Ciel

★★★★★ Peter Michael Winery Napa Valley Cuvée Indigene

★★★★★ Peter Michael Winery Sonoma County Mon Plaisir

★★★★★ Robert Mondavi Winery Carneros

★★★★★ Robert Mondavi Winery Napa Valley Reserve

★★★★★ Patz & Hall Wine Co. Napa Valley

★★★★★ J. Rochioli Vineyard & Winery Russian River Valley Reserve

★★★★★ Sanford Winery Santa Barbara County Barrel Select

★★★★★ Silverado Vineyards Napa Valley Limited Reserve

★★★★★ Simi Winery Sonoma County Reserve

★★★★★ Stony Hill Vineyard Napa Valley

★★★★★ Williams & Selyem Winery Russian River Valley Allen Vineyard

★★★★ Arrowood Vineyards & Winery Sonoma County

★★★★ Arrowood Vineyards & Winery Sonoma County Cuvée Michel Berthoud

★★★★ Au Bon Climat Arroyo Grande Valley Talley Reserve

★★★★ Au Bon Climat Santa Barbara County

★★★★ Au Bon Climat Santa Barbara County Bien Nacido Vineyard Reserve

★★★★ Byron Vineyards & Winery Santa Barbara County

★★★★ Byron Vineyards & Winery Santa Barbara County Reserve

★★★★ Byron Vineyards & Winery Santa Maria Valley

★★★★ Cambria Winery & Vineyard Santa Maria Valley Reserve

★★★★ Cambria Winery & Vineyard Santa Maria Valley Katherine's Vineyard Reserve

★★★★ Chateau Montelena Winery Napa Valley

★★★★ Chateau Potelle Mount Veeder V.G.S.

★★★★ Chateau Souverain Russian River Valley Allen Vineyard

★★★★ Chateau St. Jean Alexander Valley Belle Terre Vineyard

★★★★ Chateau St. Jean Alexander Valley Belle Terre Vineyard Reserve

★★★★ Cronin Vineyards Santa Cruz Mountains

★★★★ Cuvaison Winery Carneros

★★★★ Cuvaison Winery Carneros Reserve

★★★★ De Loach Vineyards Russian River Valley

★★★★ Dehlinger Winery Russian River Valley Montrachet Cuvée

★★★★ Far Niente Winery Napa Valley

★★★★ Gary Farrell Wines Russian River Valley

★★★★ Gary Farrell Wines Russian River Valley Westside Farms

★★★★ Gloria Ferrer Champagne Caves Carneros

★★★★ Fisher Vineyards Sonoma County Whitney's Vineyard

★★★★ Franciscan Vineyards Napa Valley Oakville Estate Cuvée Sauvage

★★★★ The Gainey Vineyard Santa Ynez Valley Limited Selection

★★★★ E. & J. Gallo Winery Northern Sonoma

★★★★ Geyser Peak Winery Alexander Valley Reserve

★★★★ Girard Winery Napa Valley

★★★★ Girard Winery Napa Valley Reserve

★★★★ Grgich Hills Cellar Carneros Carneros Selection

★★★★ Guenoc Winery Guenoc Valley Genevieve Magoon Vineyard Reserve

★★★★ Paul Hobbs Cellars Sonoma Mountain Richard Dinner Vineyard

★★★★ Markham Vineyards Napa Valley Barrel Fermented

★★★★ Mayacamas Vineyards Napa Valley

★★★★ Monticello Cellars Napa Valley Corley Reserve

★★★★ Mount Eden Vineyards Santa Cruz Mountains

★★★★ Navarro Vineyards Anderson Valley Premiere Reserve

★★★★ Ridge Vineyards Santa Cruz Mountains

★★★★ J. Rochioli Vineyard & Winery Russian River Valley

★★★★ St. Clement Vineyards Carneros Abbott's Vineyard

★★★★ St. Francis Winery Sonoma Valley Reserve

★★★★ Saintsbury Carneros Reserve

★★★★ Sanford Winery Santa Barbara County

★★★★ Sanford Winery Santa Ynez Valley

★★★★ Signorello Vineyards Napa Valley Founder's Reserve

★★★★ Stag's Leap Wine Cellars Napa Valley Reserve

★★★★ Steele Wines Carneros Sangiacomo Vineyard

★★★★ Steele Wines Mendocino County DuPratt Vineyard

★★★★ Steele Wines Mendocino County Lolonis Vineyard

★★★★ Steele Wines Santa Barbara County Bien Nacido Vineyard

★★★★ Steele Wines Sonoma Valley Durell Vineyard

★★★★ Stonestreet Sonoma County

★★★★ Swanson Vineyards Napa Valley Reserve

★★★★ Robert Talbott Vineyards Monterey County

★★★★ Robert Talbott Vineyards Monterey County Diamond T Estate

★★★★ Marimar Torres Estate Green Valley-Sonoma Don Miguel Vineyard

★★★★ Truchard Vineyards Carneros

★★★★ Villa Mt. Eden Santa Barbara County Signature Series

★★★ Acacia Winery Carneros

★★★ Acacia Winery Carneros Reserve

★★★ Adelaida Cellars San Luis Obispo County

★★★ Adelaida Cellars San Luis Obispo County Reserve

★★★ Altamura Winery and Vineyards Napa Valley

★★★ S. Anderson Vineyard Carneros

★★★ S. Anderson Vineyard Stags Leap District

★★★ S. Anderson Vineyard Stags Leap District Proprietor's Reserve

★★★ Atlas Peak Vineyards Atlas Peak

★★★ Bancroft Vineyards Howell Mountain

★★★ Bannister Winery Russian River Valley Allen Vineyard

★★★ Beaulieu Vineyard Carneros Carneros Reserve

★★★ Belvedere Winery Sonoma County Preferred Stock

★★★ Benziger Family Winery Carneros Premiere Vineyard

★★★ Beringer Vineyards Napa Valley

★★★ Beringer Vineyards Napa Valley Proprietor Grown

★★★ Bernardus Vineyards & Winery Monterey County

★★★ Bouchaine Vineyards Carneros Estate Reserve

★★★ David Bruce Winery Santa Cruz Mountains Estate Reserve

★★★ David Bruce Winery Santa Cruz Mountains Meyley Vineyard

★★★ David Bruce Winery Santa Cruz Mountains Split Rail Vineyard

★★★ Burgess Cellars Napa Valley Debourbage Barrel Fermented

★★★ Burgess Cellars Napa Valley Triere Vineyard

★★★ Byington Winery & Vineyards Santa Cruz Mountains

★★★ Cakebread Cellars Napa Valley

★★★ Cakebread Cellars Napa Valley Reserve

★★★ Cale Cellars Carneros Sangiacomo Vineyard

★★★ Calera Wine Co. Central Coast

★★★ Calera Wine Co. Mount Harlan

★★★ Camelot Santa Barbara County

★★★ Canepa Cellars Alexander Valley

★★★ Carneros Creek Winery Carneros

★★★ Chalk Hill Winery Chalk Hill

★★★ Chamisal Vineyard Edna Valley

★★★ Chappellet Vineyard Napa Valley

★★★ Chateau Souverain Russian River Valley Allen Vineyard Reserve

★★★ Chateau Souverain Russian River Valley Rochioli Vineyard Reserve

★★★ Chateau Souverain Sonoma County Barrel Fermented

★★★ Chateau Woltner Howell Mountain Estate Reserve

★★★ Chateau Woltner Howell Mountain Frederique Vineyard

★★★ Chateau Woltner Howell Mountain St. Thomas Vineyard

★★★ Chateau Woltner Howell Mountain Titus Vineyard

★★★ Chauffe-eau Cellars Carneros Sangiacomo Vineyard Sans Filtrage

★★★ Chauffe-eau Cellars Russian River Valley Dutton Ranch Sans Filtrage

★★★ Cinnabar Vineyard & Winery Santa Cruz Mountains

★★★ Cinnabar Vineyard & Winery Santa Cruz Mountains Saratoga Estate

★★★ Clos du Bois Dry Creek Valley Calcaire Vineyard

★★★ Clos du Bois Dry Creek Valley Flintwood Vineyard

★★★ Clos Du Val Carneros Carneros Estate

★★★ Clos La Chance Santa Cruz Mountains

★★★ Clos Pegase Carneros

★★★ B. R. Cohn Winery Carneros

★★★ Cosentino Winery Napa Valley The Sculptor

★★★ Cronin Vineyards Alexander Valley Stuhlmuller Vineyard

★★★ Cronin Vineyards Napa Valley

★★★ Dehlinger Winery Russian River Valley

★★★ Domain Hill & Mayes Napa Valley Clos Fontaine du Mont

★★★ Edmeades Winery Anderson Valley Dennison Vineyard

★★★ Edna Valley Vineyard Edna Valley

★★★ Edna Valley Vineyard Edna Valley Paragon Vineyard Reserve

★★★ Estancia Monterey County

★★★ Estancia Monterey County Reserve

★★★ Fetzer Vineyards Mendocino County Reserve

★★★ Firestone Vineyard Santa Ynez Valley Barrel Fermented

★★★ Fisher Vineyards Sonoma County Coach Insignia

★★★ Forest Hill Vineyard Napa Valley Private Reserve

★★★ Foxen Vineyard Santa Maria Valley Tinaquaic Vineyard

★★★ Franciscan Vineyards Napa Valley Oakville Estate Barrel Fermented

★★★ Freemark Abbey Winery Napa Valley

★★★ Freemark Abbey Winery Napa Valley Carpy Ranch

★★★ Frog's Leap Winery Carneros

★★★ E. & J. Gallo Winery Sonoma County Gallo Sonoma

★★★ Guenoc Winery Guenoc Valley

★★★ Hacienda Winery California Clair de Lune

★★★ Harrison Vineyards Napa Valley

★★★ The Hess Collection Winery Mount Veeder

★★★ The Hess Collection Winery Napa Valley

★★★ Hidden Cellars Winery Mendocino County

★★★ Hidden Cellars Winery Mendocino County Reserve

★★★ William Hill Winery Napa Valley

★★★ Hop Kiln Winery Russian River Valley M. Griffin Vineyards

★★★ Husch Vineyards Anderson Valley Special Reserve

★★★ Husch Vineyards Mendocino County

★★★ Iron Horse Vineyards Green Valley-Sonoma

★★★ Iron Horse Vineyards Sonoma County Cuvée Joy

★★★ Jarvis Napa Valley

★★★ Justin Vineyards & Winery Central Coast Barrel Fermented

★★★ Justin Vineyards & Winery San Luis Obispo County

★★★ Kalin Cellars Livermore Valley Cuvée W

★★★ Kalin Cellars Potter Valley Cuvée BL

★★★ Kalin Cellars Sonoma County Cuvée CH

★★★ Kalin Cellars Sonoma County Cuvée DD

★★★ Kalin Cellars Sonoma County Cuvée LD

★★★ Kalin Cellars Sonoma County Cuvée LR

★★★ Kalin Cellars Sonoma County Cuvée LV

★★★ Kendall-Jackson California Grand Reserve

★★★ Kendall-Jackson Santa Maria Valley Camelot Vineyard

★★★ Kendall-Jackson Sonoma Valley Durell Vineyard

★★★ Kenwood Vineyards Sonoma Valley Reserve

★★★ Kenwood Vineyards Sonoma Valley Beltane Ranch

★★★ Kenwood Vineyards Sonoma Valley Yulupa Vineyard

★★★ Charles Krug Winery Carneros Carneros Reserve

★★★ Kunde Estate Winery Sonoma Valley

★★★ Kunde Estate Winery Sonoma Valley Estate Reserve

★★★ Kunde Estate Winery Sonoma Valley Kinneybrook Vineyard

★★★ Kunde Estate Winery Sonoma Valley Wildwood Vineyard

★★★ La Crema California

★★★ La Crema California Reserve

★★★ Landmark Vineyards Alexander Valley Damaris Reserve

★★★ Landmark Vineyards Sonoma Valley Two Williams Vineyard

★★★ Laurent Cellars Napa Valley

★★★ Laurier Sonoma County

★★★ Lewis Cellars Napa Valley Oakville Ranch Reserve

★★★ J. Lohr Winery California Cypress

★★★ J. Lohr Winery Monterey County Riverstone

★★★ Macrostie Winery Carneros

★★★ Louis M. Martini Winery Napa Valley

★★★ Louis M. Martini Winery Napa Valley Reserve

★★★ Meridian Vineyards Edna Valley

★★★ Meridian Vineyards Santa Barbara County

★★★ Meridian Vineyards Santa Barbara County Reserve

★★★ Merryvale Vineyards Napa Valley Starmont

★★★ Robert Mondavi Winery Napa Valley

★★★ Morgan Winery Monterey County Reserve

★★★ Mount Eden Vineyards Edna Valley MacGregor Vineyard

★★★ Mount Eden Vineyards Santa Barbara County

★★★ Mount Konocti Winery California Grand Reserve

★★★ Mount Veeder Winery Napa Valley

★★★ Robert Mueller Cellars Russian River Valley LB Barrel Fermented

★★★ Murphy-Goode Estate Winery Alexander Valley

★★★ Murphy-Goode Estate Winery Alexander Valley Reserve

★★★ Murphy-Goode Estate Winery Alexander Valley Murphy Ranch

★★★ Murphy-Goode Estate Winery Russian River Valley J & K Murphy Vineyard

★★★ Murphy-Goode Estate Winery Russian River Valley J & K Murphy Vineyard Reserve

★★★ Napa Ridge Central Coast

★★★ Napa Ridge Central Coast Coastal Vines

★★★ Napa Ridge Central Coast Special Select

★★★ Napa Ridge Napa Valley Coastal Reserve

★★★ Napa Ridge Napa Valley Frisinger Vineyard

★★★ Napa Ridge North Coast

★★★ Napa Ridge North Coast Coastal Reserve

★★★ Navarro Vineyards Anderson Valley

★★★ Newton Vineyard Napa Valley

★★★ Oakville Ranch Vineyards Napa Valley ORV

★★★ Oakville Ranch Vineyards Napa Valley Vista Vineyard

★★★ The Ojai Vineyard Arroyo Grande Valley

★★★ The Ojai Vineyard Arroyo Grande Valley Reserve

★★★ The Ojai Vineyard Santa Barbara County

★★★ The Ojai Vineyard Santa Barbara County Reserve

★★★ Optima Sonoma County

★★★ Pahlmeyer Napa Valley

★★★ Fess Parker Winery Santa Barbara County

★★★ Fess Parker Winery Santa Barbara County American Tradition Reserve

★★★ Joseph Phelps Vineyards Carneros

★★★ Pine Ridge Winery Napa Valley Knollside Cuvée

★★★ Pine Ridge Winery Stags Leap District

★★★ Pine Ridge Winery Stags Leap District Vieille Vigne

★★★ Pinnacles Monterey County

★★★ Pride Mountain Vineyards Napa Valley Mountain Vineyards

★★★ Qupe Cellars Santa Barbara County Sierra Madre Vineyard

★★★ Rabbit Ridge Vineyards Russian River Valley Rabbit Ridge Ranch

★★★ Kent Rasmussen Winery Napa Valley

★★★ Martin Ray Winery California Mariage

★★★ Raymond Vineyard and Cellar Napa Valley

★★★ Raymond Vineyard and Cellar Napa Valley Private Reserve

★★★ Rombauer Vineyards Carneros

★★★ Saintsbury Carneros

★★★ Santa Barbara Winery Santa Ynez Valley Reserve

★★★ Santa Barbara Winery Santa Ynez Valley Lafond Vineyard

★★★ Sarah's Vineyard Santa Clara County

★★★ Sarah's Vineyard Santa Clara County Lot II

★★★ V. Sattui Winery Napa Valley

★★★ V. Sattui Winery Napa Valley Carsi Vineyard Barrel Fermented

★★★ Seavey Vineyard Napa Valley

★★★ Sebastiani Vineyards Russian River Valley Dutton Ranch

★★★ Sebastiani Vineyards Sonoma County Reserve

★★★ Sequoia Grove Vineyards Napa Valley Estate Reserve

★★★ Shafer Vineyards Napa Valley

★★★ Shafer Vineyards Napa Valley Barrel Select

★★★ Signorello Vineyards Napa Valley

★★★ Silverado Vineyards Napa Valley

★★★ Simi Winery Sonoma County

★★★ Robert Sinskey Vineyards Carneros

★★★ Smith-Madrone Vineyard Napa Valley

★★★ Solitude Wines Carneros Sangiacomo Vineyard

★★★ Sonoma-Cutrer Vineyards Sonoma Coast Cutrer Vineyard

★★★ Sonoma-Cutrer Vineyards Sonoma Coast Les Pierres

★★★ Sonoma-Cutrer Vineyards Sonoma Coast Russian River Ranches

★★★ Sonoma-Loeb Sonoma County

★★★ Sonoma-Loeb Sonoma County Ambassador John L. Loeb Jr.'s Private Reserve

★★★ Sonoma-Loeb Sonoma County Private Reserve

★★★ Stag's Leap Wine Cellars Napa Valley

★★★ Steele Wines California

★★★ Steele Wines Mendocino County Dennison Vineyard

★★★ Stony Hill Vineyard Napa Valley SHV

★★★ Swanson Vineyards Carneros

★★★ Thomas-Hsi Napa Valley

★★★ Tobin James Paso Robles

★★★ Trefethen Vineyards Napa Valley

★★★ Ventana Vineyards Monterey County Gold Stripe Selection

★★★ Vichon Winery Napa Valley

★★★ Villa Mt. Eden Carneros Grand Reserve

★★★ Vine Cliff Cellars Napa Valley Proprietress Reserve

★★★ Vita Nova Santa Barbara County

★★★ Wente Bros. Arroyo Seco Riva Ranch

★★★ Wente Bros. Central Coast Wente Family Estate Selection

★★★ Wente Bros. Livermore Valley Herman Wente Vineyard Reserve

★★★ Wheeler Winery Sonoma County

★★★ Whitcraft Winery Santa Maria Valley Bien Nacido Vineyard

★★★ White Oak Vineyards & Winery Russian River Valley Poplar Ranch Private Reserve

★★★ White Oak Vineyards & Winery Sonoma County

★★★ White Oak Vineyards & Winery Sonoma County Myers Limited Reserve

★★★ White Rock Vineyards Napa Valley

★★★ Whitehall Lane Winery Napa Valley

★★★ Wild Horse Winery Central Coast

★★★ Zaca Mesa Winery Santa Barbara County

★★★ Zaca Mesa Winery Santa Barbara County Chapel Vineyard

★★★ Zaca Mesa Winery Santa Barbara County Zaca Vineyards

★★★ ZD Wines California

★★ Adler Fels Sonoma County

★★ Adler Fels Sonoma County Coleman Reserve

★★ Alderbrook Winery Dry Creek Valley

★★ Alexander Valley Vineyards Alexander Valley

★★ Alexander Valley Vineyards Alexander Valley Wetzel Family Estate

★★ Arciero Winery Paso Robles

★★ Armida Winery Russian River Valley

★★ David Arthur Vineyards Napa Valley

★★ Babcock Vineyards Santa Barbara County

★★ Babcock Vineyards Santa Ynez Valley Mt. Carmel Vineyard

★★ Baileyana Edna Valley Paragon Vineyard

★★ Bandiera Winery Napa Valley

★★ Bargetto Winery Central Coast Cypress

★★ Bargetto Winery Santa Cruz Mountains

★★ Bayview Cellars Carneros

★★ Beaucanon Winery Napa Valley

★★ Beaulieu Vineyard Carneros

★★ Beaulieu Vineyard Napa Valley Beau Tour

★★ Beaulieu Vineyard Napa Valley Beaufort

★★ Belvedere Winery Alexander Valley

★★ Benziger Family Winery Sonoma County

★★ Black Mountain Alexander Valley Douglass Hill

★★ Black Mountain Alexander Valley Gravel Bar

★★ Blue Heron Lake Winery Wild Horse Valley

★★ Boeger Winery El Dorado County

★★ Bogle Vineyards California

★★ Bogle Vineyards California Reserve

★★ Bouchaine Vineyards Carneros

★★ The Brander Vineyard Santa Ynez Valley Bouchet Tête de Cuvée

★★ Brindiamo California

★★ Brutocao Cellars Mendocino County

★★ Brutocao Cellars Mendocino County Bliss Vineyard

★★ Buehler Vineyards Russian River Valley

★★ Buena Vista Winery Carneros

★★ Buena Vista Winery Carneros Grand Reserve

★★ Byington Winery & Vineyards Mount Veeder

★★ Byington Winery & Vineyards Napa Valley

★★ Byington Winery & Vineyards Santa Cruz Mountains Redwood Hill Vineyard

★★ Davis Bynum Winery Russian River Valley Allen-Griffin Vineyards Limited Release

★★ Davis Bynum Winery Sonoma County

★★ Calistoga Vineyards Napa Valley

★★ Callaway Vineyard and Winery Temecula Hawk Watch Calla-Lees

★★ Canyon Road California

★★ Carmenet Vineyard Carneros Sangiacomo Vineyard

★★ Carneros Creek Winery California Fleur de Carneros

★★ Castle Rock Napa Valley Barrel Fermented

★★ Castoro Cellars Paso Robles Reserve

★★ Castoro Cellars San Luis Obispo County

★★ Castoro Cellars San Luis Obispo County The Wine

★★ Cedar Mountain Winery Livermore Valley Blanches Vineyard

★★ Chateau Chevre Winery Napa Valley

★★ Chateau de Baun Russian River Valley

★★ Chateau de Leu Winery Green Valley-Solano

★★ Chateau Julien Winery Monterey County Barrel Fermented

★★ Chateau Julien Winery Monterey County Private Reserve

★★ Chateau Potelle Napa Valley

★★ Chateau St. Jean Sonoma County

★★ Chateau Woltner Howell Mountain

★★ Chatom Vineyards Calaveras County

★★ Chestnut Hill Winery California

★★ Chestnut Hill Winery California

★★ Chimere Winery Edna Valley

★★ Chimney Rock Winery Carneros

★★ Christophe Napa County

★★ Claiborne & Churchill Edna Valley MacGregor Vineyard

★★ Claudia Springs Winery Anderson Valley

★★ Cloninger Cellars Monterey County

★★ Clos du Bois Alexander Valley Barrel Fermented

★★ B. R. Cohn Winery Carneros Joseph Herman Vineyard Reserve

★★ B. R. Cohn Winery Napa Valley Silver Label

★★ Concannon Vineyard Central Coast Selected Vineyards

★★ Concannon Vineyard Livermore Valley Reserve

★★ Corbett Canyon Vineyards Santa Barbara County Reserve

★★ Cosentino Winery Napa Valley

★★ Côtes de Sonoma Sonoma County

★★ Cottonwood Canyon Santa Barbara County

★★ Cottonwood Canyon Santa Barbara County Barrel Select

★★ Crichton Hall Napa Valley

★★ Cronin Vineyards Monterey County Ventana Vineyard

★★ De Loach Vineyards Sonoma County Sonoma Cuvée

★★ De Lorimier Winery Alexander Valley Clonal Select

★★ De Lorimier Winery Alexander Valley Prism

★★ DeMoor Winery Napa Valley

★★ Domaine Napa Winery Napa Valley

★★ Domaine Saint Gregory Mendocino County

★★ Dry Creek Vineyard Sonoma County

★★ Dry Creek Vineyard Sonoma County Barrel Fermented

★★ Dunnewood Vineyards Carneros Gold Label Select

★★ Dunnewood Vineyards North Coast Barrel Select

★★ Durney Vineyard Carmel Valley

★★ Eberle Winery Paso Robles

★★ Edmeades Winery Mendocino County

★★ Elkhorn Peak Cellars Napa Valley Fagan Creek Vineyards

★★ Elliston Vineyards Central Coast Sunol Valley Vineyard

★★ Estate William Baccala Sonoma County

★★ Estrella River Winery California Proprietor's Reserve

★★ Fallenleaf Vineyard Carneros

★★ Farella-Park Vineyards Napa Valley Barrel Fermented

★★ Fetzer Vineyards California Sundial

★★ Fetzer Vineyards Mendocino County Barrel Select

★★ Fetzer Vineyards Mendocino County Bonterra Organically Grown

★★ Fetzer Vineyards North Coast Barrel Select

★★ Field Stone Winery Sonoma County

★★ Fieldbrook Valley Winery Mendocino County Redwood Valley Vineyard

★★ Thomas Fogarty Winery Santa Cruz Mountains

★★ Folie à Deux Winery Napa Valley

★★ Forest Glen Sonoma County

★★ Forest Glen Sonoma County Barrel Fermented

★★ Foss Creek Central Coast Barrel Fermented

★★ Foss Creek Sonoma County 85% Barrel Fermented

★★ Foxen Vineyard Santa Maria Valley

★★ Fremont Creek Winery

★★ J. Fritz Cellars Dry Creek Valley

★★ J. Fritz Cellars Russian River Valley Barrel Select

★★ J. Fritz Cellars Sonoma County

★★ Gabrielli Winery Mendocino County

★★ Gabrielli Winery Mendocino County Reserve

★★ The Gainey Vineyard Santa Barbara County

★★ Gan Eden Sonoma County

★★ Gavilan Vineyards Chalone

★★ Daniel Gehrs Monterey County

★★ Geyser Peak Winery Sonoma County

★★ Glass Mountain Quarry California

★★ Glen Ellen Winery California Proprietor's Reserve

★★ Goosecross Cellars Napa Valley

★★ Graeser Winery Napa Valley Silverado Summers Vineyard

★★ Green and Red Vineyard Napa Valley Catacula Vineyard

★★ Greenwood Ridge Vineyards Anderson Valley Du Pratt Vineyard

★★ Greenwood Ridge Vineyards Mendocino County

★★ Groth Vineyards & Winery Napa Valley

★★ Gundlach Bundschu Winery Sonoma Valley

★★ Gundlach Bundschu Winery Sonoma Valley Sangiacomo Ranch Special Selection

★★ Hagafen Cellars Napa Valley

★★ Hagafen Cellars Napa Valley Reserve

★★ Hahn Estates Monterey County

★★ Handley Cellars Anderson Valley

★★ Handley Cellars Dry Creek Valley

★★ Hanna Winery Russian River Valley Reserve

★★ Hanna Winery Sonoma County

★★ Harmony Cellars Paso Robles

★★ Haywood Winery California Vintner's Select

★★ Heitz Wine Cellars Napa Valley

★★ Hess Select California

★★ Hidden Cellars Winery Mendocino County Organically Grown Grapes

★★ Jekel Vineyards Arroyo Seco Gravelstone Vineyard

★★ Jepson Vineyards Mendocino County

★★ Jordan Vineyard and Winery Alexander Valley

★★ Jory Winery Santa Clara County Selected Clone

★★ Joullian Vineyards Monterey County

★★ Joullian Vineyards Monterey County Family Reserve

★★ Karly Wines Edna Valley MacGregor Vineyard

★★ Robert Keenan Winery Napa Valley

★★ Kendall-Jackson California Vintner's Reserve

★★ Kenwood Vineyards Sonoma County

★★ Kenwood Vineyards Sonoma Valley

★★ J. Kerr Wines Santa Barbara County

★★ Konrad Estate Mendocino County

★★ Korbel Champagne Cellars Russian River Valley

★★ Charles Krug Winery Napa Valley

★★ Lakespring Winery Napa Valley

★★ Lambert Bridge Sonoma County

★★ Landmark Vineyards Sonoma County Overlook

★★ Lazy Creek Vineyards Anderson Valley

★★ Leeward Winery Central Coast

★★ Limur Winery Napa Valley

★★ Liparita Cellars Howell Mountain

★★ Lockwood Monterey County

★★ Lockwood Monterey County Partners' Reserve

★★ Logan Winery Monterey County

★★ Lolonis Winery Mendocino County Estate Reserve

★★ Longoria Wine Cellars Santa Barbara County

★★ Longoria Wine Cellars Santa Ynez Valley Huber Vineyard

★★ Lyeth Sonoma County

★★ Madrona Vineyards El Dorado County

★★ Mark West Vineyards Russian River Valley Barrel Fermented

★★ Martinelli Winery Russian River Valley

★★ Mazzocco Vineyards Alexander Valley River Lane Vineyard

★★ Peter McCoy Vineyards Knights Valley Clos des Pierres

★★ McDowell Valley Vineyards Mendocino County

★★ McHenry Vineyard Santa Cruz Mountains

★★ Michel-Schlumberger Dry Creek Valley

★★ Mill Creek Vineyards Dry Creek Valley

★★ Mirassou Vineyards Monterey County Family Selection

★★ Mirassou Vineyards Monterey County Harvest Reserve

★★ Mirassou Vineyards Santa Clara County 140th Anniversary Selection

★★ Robert Mondavi-Woodbridge California

★★ Mont St. John Cellars Carneros Organically Grown Grapes

★★ Mont St. John Cellars Carneros Madonna Vineyards

★★ Monticello Cellars Napa Valley

★★ Morgan Winery Monterey County

★★ Mount Konocti Winery California Kelsey

★★ Mount Palomar Winery Temecula Reserve

★★ Nevada City Winery Nevada County Barrel Fermented

★★ Newlan Vineyards and Winery Napa Valley Reserve

★★ Neyers Carneros

★★ Obester Winery Mendocino County

★★ Octopus Mountain Anderson Valley Dennison Vineyard

★★ Olivet Lane Estate Russian River Valley

★★ Page Mill Winery California Cuvée Select

★★ Page Mill Winery Santa Barbara County Bien Nacido Vineyard

★★ Page Mill Winery Santa Clara County Elizabeth Garbett Vineyard

★★ Paraiso Springs Vineyards Santa Lucia Highlands Barrel Fermented

★★ Parducci Wine Cellars Mendocino County

★★ J. Pedroncelli Winery Dry Creek Valley

★★ Peju Province Winery Napa Valley

★★ Peju Province Winery Napa Valley HB Vineyard Barrel Fermented

★★ Robert Pepi Winery Napa Valley Puncheon Fermented

★★ Peterson Winery Anderson Valley

★★ R.H. Phillips Vineyard Dunnigan Hills Barrel Cuvée

★★ Plam Vineyards & Winery Napa Valley

★★ Q.C. Fly California

★★ Quail Ridge Cellars Napa Valley

★★ Rabbit Ridge Vineyards Sonoma County

★★ Rancho Sisquoc Winery Santa Maria Valley

★★ Ravenswood North Coast Vintners Blend

★★ Ravenswood Sonoma Valley

★★ Raymond Vineyard and Cellar California Amberhill

★★ Raymond Vineyard and Cellar California Selection

★★ Roche Winery Carneros

★★ Round Hill Winery California

★★ Round Hill Winery Napa Valley Reserve

★★ Round Hill Winery Napa Valley Van Asperen Reserve

★★ Rutherford Hill Winery Napa Valley XVS Reserve

★★ Rutherford Hill Winery Napa Valley Jaeger Vineyards

★★ Rutherford Ranch Napa Valley

★★ St. Andrews Winery Napa Valley

★★ St. Francis Winery Sonoma County

★★ St. Supéry Vineyard & Winery Napa Valley Dollarhide Ranch

★★ Salmon Creek Carneros

★★ Santa Barbara Winery Santa Ynez Valley

★★ Schuetz-Oles Napa Valley Chappell Vineyard

★★ Schug Carneros Estate Carneros

★★ Schug Carneros Estate Sonoma Valley

★★ Sebastiani Vineyards Sonoma Valley Sonoma Series

★★ Seghesio Winery Sonoma County

★★ Sequoia Grove Vineyards Carneros

★★ Shooting Star Mendocino County

★★ Silver Mountain Vineyards Monterey County

★★ Silverado Hill Cellars Napa Valley

★★ Soda Canyon Vineyards Napa Valley

★★ Solis Winery Santa Clara County Barrel Fermented

★★ Sonoma Creek Winery Carneros

★★ P. and M. Staiger Santa Cruz Mountains

★★ Star Hill Wines Napa Valley

★★ Sterling Vineyards Carneros Winery Lake Vineyard

★★ Sterling Vineyards Napa Valley

★★ Sterling Vineyards Napa Valley Diamond Mountain Ranch

★★ Stonegate Winery Sonoma County Bella Vista Vineyard

★★ Storrs Winery Santa Cruz Mountains Christie Vineyard Mountain Vineyard Collection

★★ Storrs Winery Santa Cruz Mountains Vanumanutagi Vineyards Mountain Vineyard Collection

★★ Stratford Winery California

★★ Rodney Strong Vineyards Chalk Hill Chalk Hill Vineyard

★★ Rodney Strong Vineyards Sonoma County

★★ Sutter Home Winery California

★★ Taft Street Winery Sonoma County

★★ Talley Vineyards Arroyo Grande Valley

★★ Ivan Tamas Winery Livermore Valley Hayes Ranch

★★ Tulocay Winery Napa Valley DeCelles Vineyard

★★ M. G. Vallejo California Harvest Select

★★ Viansa Winery Sonoma Valley

★★ Vichon Winery California Coastal Selection

★★ Villa Mt. Eden California Cellar Select

★★ Voss Vineyards Napa Valley

★★ Weibel Vineyards

★★ Wellington Vineyards Sonoma Valley Barrel Fermented

★★ Wildhurst Vineyards California

★★ Windemere Edna Valley MacGregor Vineyard

★★ York Mountain Winery San Luis Obispo County

★★ Stephen Zellerbach California

★ Ahlgren Vineyard Santa Cruz Mountains Buerge Vineyard

★ Ahlgren Vineyard Santa Cruz Mountains Mayers Vineyard

★ Antelope Valley Winery Central Coast

★ Bergfeld Winery Napa Valley

★ Bon Marché Sonoma County

★ Maurice Carrie Vineyards and Winery Temecula

★ Maurice Carrie Vineyards and Winery Temecula Private Reserve

★ Chansa Cellars Santa Barbara County

★ Cilurzo Vineyard and Winery Temecula Barrel Fermented Reserve

★ Corbett Canyon Vineyards Central Coast Coastal Classic

★ Creston Vineyards & Winery Paso Robles

★ Devlin Wine Cellars Santa Cruz Mountains Meyley Vineyard

★ Domaine St. George Winery California Vintage Reserve

★ Fenestra Winery Livermore Valley Toy Vineyard

★ La Crosse Napa Valley

★ Leeward Winery Edna Valley Reserve

★ Leeward Winery Edna Valley Paragon Vineyard Reserve

★ Maacama Creek Alexander Valley Melim Vineyard Reserve

★ The Meeker Vineyard Dry Creek Valley

★ Mission View Vineyards & Winery San Luis Obispo County

★ The Monterey Vineyard Monterey County Classic

★ The Monterey Vineyard Monterey County Limited Release

★ Montpellier California

★ Mount Palomar Winery Temecula

★ Obester Winery Mendocino County Barrel Fermented

★ Pepperwood Grove California

★ Saddleback Cellars Napa Valley

★ Soquel Vineyards Santa Cruz Mountains

★ Stevenot Winery Calaveras County Reserve

★ Stevenot Winery Sierra Foothills

★ Topolos Sonoma County Dry Farmed Old Vines Barrel Fermented

★ Trentadue Winery Alexander Valley

★ Van der Heyden Vineyard Napa Valley

★ Van der Heyden Vineyard Napa Valley Private Reserve

★ Christine Woods Winery Anderson Valley

NR	Au Bon Climat Santa Maria Valley Gold Coast Vineyard
NR	Bel Arbors California Founder's Selection
NR	Bonverre California Lot Number 14
NR	Cache Cellars Napa Valley
NR	Cronin Vineyards California Nancy's Cuvée
NR	Dion Sonoma Valley
NR	Evensen Vineyards & Winery Napa Valley
NR	Joseph Filippi Vintage Co. Monterey County Limited Release Winemaker's Reserve
NR	Greenwood Ridge Vineyards Anderson Valley Late Harvest
NR	Grove Street Winery Sonoma County
NR	Grove Street Winery Sonoma County Vintage Select
NR	Grove Street Winery Sonoma County Healdsburg Vineyard Select
NR	Emilio Guglielmo Winery Monterey County
NR	Hafner Alexander Valley
NR	Hallcrest Vineyards California Fortuyn Cuvée
NR	Hallcrest Vineyards Santa Cruz Mountains Meyley Vineyard
NR	Houtz Vineyards Santa Ynez Valley
NR	Johnson's Alexander Valley Wines Alexander Valley
NR	Jory Winery California White Zeppelin Blimp de Blanc
NR	Kendall-Jackson California Late Harvest Select
NR	Leeward Winery Monterey County
NR	Leeward Winery Ventura County
NR	Livermore Valley Cellars Livermore Valley
NR	Milat Vineyards Napa Valley
NR	Monte Verde Central Coast Proprietor's Reserve
NR	Monterey Peninsula Winery Monterey County Sleepy Hollow Vineyard
NR	Gustave Niebaum Napa Valley Reference
NR	Organic Wine Works Mendocino County Redwood Valley Vineyards
NR	Porter Creek Vineyards Russian River Valley
NR	River Road Vineyard

NR	River Run Vintners
NR	Roudon-Smith Winery Central Coast
NR	Roudon-Smith Winery Santa Cruz Mountains
NR	Royce Vineyards California
NR	Rustridge Vineyards & Winery Napa Valley
NR	Salamandre Wine Cellars
NR	Santa Cruz Mountain Vineyard Santa Cruz Mountains
NR	Sierra Vista El Dorado County
NR	Staglin Family Vineyard Napa Valley
NR	Sunrise Winery Livermore Valley Beyers Ranch
NR	Sycamore Creek Vineyards
NR	Tiffany Hill Edna Valley
NR	Twin Hills Winery Paso Robles Reserve
NR	Viano Vineyards Contra Costa County
NR	Villa Helena Winery Napa Valley
NR	Weinstock Cellars
NR	Wing Canyon Mount Veeder
NR	Woodside Vineyards Santa Cruz Mountains
NR	Zayante Vineyards Santa Cruz Mountains

CHENIN BLANC

★★★★	Chappellet Vineyard Napa Valley Dry
★★★	Callaway Vineyard and Winery Temecula Sweet Nancy Late Harvest
★★★	Chalone Vineyard Chalone
★★★	Foxen Vineyard Santa Barbara County
★★★	Preston Vineyards Dry Creek Valley Barrel Aged
★★	Dry Creek Vineyard California Dry
★★	Durney Vineyard Carmel Valley
★★	Folie à Deux Winery Napa Valley
★★	Daniel Gehrs Monterey County Le Chenay
★★	Daniel Gehrs Santa Barbara County Le Cheniere
★★	Girard Winery Napa Valley Dry
★★	Husch Vineyards Mendocino County La Ribera Ranch
★★	Kendall-Jackson California Vintner's Reserve
★★	La Petite Vigne Napa Valley

★★ Mirassou Vineyards Monterey County Family Selection Dry

★★ Ventana Vineyards Monterey County

★★ Weibel Vineyards

★★ White Oak Vineyards & Winery California

NR Bonny Doon Vineyard California Pacific Rim

NR Houtz Vineyards Santa Ynez Valley

NR Milat Vineyards Napa Valley

NR Sutter Home Winery California

CINSAULT

NR Lake Sonoma Winery Dry Creek Valley Vintner's Reserve

CORTESE

★★ Castelletto Temecula

DESSERT

NR Alexander Valley Fruit & Trading Co. Alexander Valley

NR Silverado Vineyards Napa Valley

NR Viano Vineyards Contra Costa County

FRENCH COLOMBARD

NR Livermore Valley Cellars Livermore Valley

NR Wermuth Winery Napa Valley

NR Woodside Vineyards

FUMÉ BLANC (*SEE ALSO* SAUVIGNON BLANC)

★★★ Chateau St. Jean Russian River Valley La Petite Étoile

★★★ Ferrari-Carano Winery Sonoma County

★★★ Ferrari-Carano Winery Sonoma County Reserve

★★★ Grgich Hills Cellar Napa Valley

★★★ Iron Horse Vineyards Alexander Valley T-T Vineyards

★★★ Robert Mondavi Winery Napa Valley

★★★ Robert Mondavi Winery Napa Valley To-Kalon Vineyard Reserve

★★★ Murphy-Goode Estate Winery Alexander Valley

★★★ Murphy-Goode Estate Winery Alexander Valley Reserve

★★ Bandiera Winery Napa Valley

★★ Benziger Family Winery Sonoma County

★★ Beringer Vineyards Napa Valley

★★ Bogle Vineyards Lake County Dry

★★ Davis Bynum Winery Russian River Valley Shone Farm

★★ Chateau St. Jean Sonoma County Dry

★★ Chimney Rock Winery Napa Valley

★★ De Loach Vineyards Russian River Valley

★★ Dry Creek Vineyard Dry Creek Valley Barrel Fermented Reserve

★★ Dry Creek Vineyard Dry Creek Valley Reserve

★★ Dry Creek Vineyard Sonoma County

★★ Fetzer Vineyards Mendocino County

★★ J. Lohr Winery California Cypress

★★ Mount Konocti Winery Lake County

★★ Mount Konocti Winery Lake County Grand Reserve

★★ J. Pedroncelli Winery Dry Creek Valley

★ Lambert Bridge Sonoma County

NR Organic Wine Works Napa Valley

NR Round Hill Winery Napa Valley

NR Sierra Vista El Dorado County

NR Wildhurst Vineyards Clear Lake Reserve

GAMAY

★★ Duxoup Dry Creek Valley

NR Weinstock Cellars

NR Wermuth Winery Napa Valley

GAMAY BEAUJOLAIS

★★★ Beringer Vineyards North Coast Nouveau

★★★ Preston Vineyards Dry Creek Valley

NR Pepperwood Grove California Nouveau

GEWÜRZTRAMINER

★★★★ Navarro Vineyards North Coast Late Harvest Sweet

★★★ De Loach Vineyards Russian River Valley Late Harvest

★★★ Firestone Vineyard California

★★★ Husch Vineyards Anderson Valley Late Harvest

★★★ Z Moore Winery Russian River Valley Barrel Fermented

★★★ Z Moore Winery Russian River Valley McIlroy/Martinelli Barrel Fermented Puncheon Select

★★★ Navarro Vineyards Anderson Valley Dry

★★★ Joseph Phelps Vineyards California

★★★ Stonestreet Anderson Valley

★★★ Stony Hill Vineyard Napa Valley

★★ Adler Fels Sonoma County

★★ Alexander Valley Vineyards Alexander Valley

★★ Bayview Cellars Napa Valley

★★ Bouchaine Vineyards Russian River Valley Dry

★★ Buena Vista Winery Carneros

★★ Davis Bynum Winery Russian River Valley

★★ Chateau St. Jean Sonoma County

★★ Claiborne & Churchill Central Coast Dry Alsatian Style

★★ Clos du Bois Alexander Valley Early Harvest

★★ De Loach Vineyards Russian River Valley Early Harvest

★★ Fetzer Vineyards California

★★ Gan Eden Monterey County Late Harvest

★★ Geyser Peak Winery Sonoma County

★★ Gundlach Bundschu Winery Sonoma Valley Rhinefarm Vineyards

★★ Hop Kiln Winery Russian River Valley M. Griffin Vineyards

★★ Kendall-Jackson California Vintner's Reserve

★★ Mark West Vineyards Russian River Valley

★★ Louis M. Martini Winery Russian River Valley

★★ Mill Creek Vineyards Dry Creek Valley

★★ Obester Winery Anderson Valley

★★ Paraiso Springs Vineyards Santa Lucia Highlands

★★ St. Francis Winery Sonoma County

★★ Storrs Winery Monterey County

★ Field Stone Winery Sonoma County

NR Bargetto Winery Monterey County

NR Evensen Vineyards & Winery Napa Valley

NR Grand Cru Vineyards California Premium Selection

GRENACHE

★★★ Bonny Doon Vineyard California Clos de Gilroy

★★★ Joseph Phelps Vineyards California Vin du Mistral Rosé

NR Edmunds St. John El Dorado County Marchini Bianco

ITALIAN BLEND

★★★★ Ferrari-Carano Winery Sonoma County Siena

★★ Atlas Peak Vineyards Atlas Peak Consenso

★★ Martin Brothers Winery Paso Robles Etrusco

★★ Monte Volpe Mendocino County Pinot Bianco

NR Sarah's Vineyard Santa Clara County Innocence

JOHANNISBERG RIESLING (*SEE ALSO* RIESLING, WHITE RIESLING)

★★★★★ Chateau St. Jean Alexander Valley Hoot Owl Creek Vineyards Late Harvest Special Select

★★★★ Freemark Abbey Winery Napa Valley Edelwein Gold

★★★★ Geyser Peak Winery Mendocino County Late Harvest Selected Dried Berry

★★★ Fetzer Vineyards Sonoma County Late Harvest Reserve

★★★ Firestone Vineyard Santa Barbara County Selected Harvest

★★★ Freemark Abbey Winery Napa Valley

★★★ Grgich Hills Cellar Napa Valley Late Harvest

★★★ Kendall-Jackson California Late Harvest Select

★★★ Long Vineyards Napa Valley

★★★ Long Vineyards Napa Valley Botrytis

★★★ Newlan Vineyards and Winery Napa Valley Late Harvest

★★★ Smith-Madrone Vineyard Napa Valley

★★★ Stony Hill Vineyard Napa Valley

★★ Chateau Montelena Winery Napa Valley

★★ Fetzer Vineyards California

★★ Hagafen Cellars Napa Valley

★★ Hidden Cellars Winery Mendocino County

★★ Hop Kiln Winery Russian River Valley M. Griffin Vineyards

★★ Kendall-Jackson California Vintner's Reserve

★★ Mirassou Vineyards Monterey County Select Late Harvest Reserve

★★ Paraiso Springs Vineyards Santa Lucia Highlands Late Harvest Hand Selected

★★ Fess Parker Winery Santa Barbara County

★★ Joseph Phelps Vineyards Napa Valley

★★ Santa Barbara Winery Santa Barbara County

★★ Ventana Vineyards Monterey County

★ Robert Mondavi Winery Napa Valley

NR Boeger Winery El Dorado County

NR Grand Cru Vineyards California Premium Selection

NR Sycamore Creek Vineyards

MALBEC

★★ Clos du Bois Alexander Valley Reserve L'Ètranger

★★ Geyser Peak Winery Alexander Valley

NR Jekel Vineyards Arroyo Seco The Sanctuary Estate

MALVASIA BIANCA

★★★ La Famiglia di Robert Mondavi California

NR Wild Horse Winery Monterey County

MARSANNE

★★★★ Qupe Cellars Santa Barbara County Los Olivos Vineyard

★★★ Preston Vineyards Dry Creek Valley Organically Grown Grapes

MERITAGE RED

★★★★ Cain Cellars Napa Valley Cain Five

★★★★ Flora Springs Wine Co. Napa Valley Trilogy

★★★★ Kendall-Jackson California Cardinale

★★★ Beringer Vineyards Knights Valley

★★★ Carmenet Vineyard Sonoma Valley

★★★ Chimney Rock Winery Stags Leap District Èlevage

★★★ Cosentino Winery Napa Valley M. Coz

★★★ Cutler Cellars Sonoma Valley Satyre

★★★ Dry Creek Vineyard Dry Creek Valley

★★★ Estancia Alexander Valley

★★★ Franciscan Vineyards Napa Valley Magnificat

★★★ Geyser Peak Winery Alexander Valley Reserve Alexandre

★★★ Guenoc Winery California Langtry Estate

★★★ Kunde Estate Winery Sonoma Valley Louis Kunde Founder's Reserve

★★★ Merryvale Vineyards Napa Valley Profile

★★★ Mount Veeder Winery Napa Valley

★★★ Mount Veeder Winery Napa Valley Reserve

★★★ Newton Vineyard Napa Valley Claret

★★★ Raymond Vineyard and Cellar Napa Valley Private Reserve

★★★ Robert Sinskey Vineyards Carneros RSV Claret Reserve

★★★ Robert Sinskey Vineyards Stags Leap District RSV Claret

★★★ White Rock Vineyards Napa Valley Claret

★★ Beaulieu Vineyard Napa Valley

★★ Cosentino Winery California The Poet

★★ Cronin Vineyards Stags Leap District Robinson Vineyard Concerto

★★ De Lorimier Winery Alexander Valley Mosaic

★★ Gundlach Bundschu Winery Sonoma Valley Bearitage

★★ Jekel Vineyards Arroyo Seco The Sanctuary Estate Symmetry

★★ Konrad Estate Mendocino County Mélange à Trois

★★ Mount Konocti Winery Clear Lake

★★ Nevada City Winery Nevada County Claret The Director's Reserve

★★ Stonegate Winery Napa Valley Reserve

NR Boeger Winery El Dorado County

NR Cache Cellars Napa Valley

NR Hacienda Winery Sonoma County Antares

NR Peju Province Winery Napa Valley

NR Whitehall Lane Winery Napa Valley

MERITAGE WHITE

★★★ Estancia Monterey County

★★★ Guenoc Winery Guenoc Valley Langtry Estate

★★★ Hidden Cellars Winery Mendocino County Alchemy

★★★ Kendall-Jackson California Royale

★★★ Merryvale Vineyards Napa Valley

★★★ Simi Winery Sonoma County Sendal

★★ Alderbrook Winery Dry Creek Valley Duet

★★ Beringer Vineyards Knights Valley

★★ Carmenet Vineyard Edna Valley Paragon Vineyard

★★ De Lorimier Winery Alexander Valley Spectrum

MERLOT

★★★★★ Beringer Vineyards Howell Mountain Bancroft Ranch

★★★★★ Duckhorn Vineyards Napa Valley

★★★★★ Matanzas Creek Winery Sonoma Valley

★★★★ Arrowood Vineyards & Winery Sonoma County

★★★★ Dickerson Vineyard Napa Valley Limited Reserve

★★★★ Markham Vineyards Napa Valley

★★★★ Shafer Vineyards Stags Leap District

★★★★ St. Francis Winery Sonoma Valley Reserve

★★★ Alexander Valley Vineyards Alexander Valley

★★★ Azalea Springs Napa Valley

★★★ Cafaro Cellars Napa Valley

★★★ Chateau Souverain Alexander Valley

★★★ Clos du Bois Sonoma County

★★★ Clos Du Val Stags Leap District

★★★ Cosentino Winery Napa Valley

★★★ Cuvaison Winery Carneros

★★★ De Loach Vineyards Russian River Valley

★★★ Duckhorn Vineyards Napa Valley Three Palms Vineyard

★★★ Duckhorn Vineyards Napa Valley Vine Hill Ranch

★★★ Estancia Alexander Valley

★★★ Estate William Baccala Napa Valley

★★★ Gary Farrell Wines Sonoma County Ladi's Vineyard

★★★ Ferrari-Carano Winery Alexander Valley

★★★ Foxen Vineyard Santa Barbara County

★★★ Franciscan Vineyards Napa Valley Oakville Estate

★★★ Franciscan Vineyards Napa Valley Oakville Estate Reserve

★★★ Georis Winery Carmel Valley

★★★ Geyser Peak Winery Alexander Valley

★★★ Gundlach Bundschu Winery Sonoma Valley

★★★ Gundlach Bundschu Winery Sonoma Valley Rhinefarm Vineyards

★★★ Havens Wine Cellars Carneros Truchard Vineyard Reserve

★★★ Havens Wine Cellars Napa Valley

★★★ The Hess Collection Winery Napa Valley

★★★ Kendall-Jackson Alexander Valley

★★★ Kendall-Jackson California Grand Reserve

★★★ Kenwood Vineyards Sonoma Valley Jack London Vineyard

★★★ Kenwood Vineyards Sonoma Valley Massara Vineyards

★★★ Louis M. Martini Winery Russian River Valley Los Vinedos del Rio Vineyard Selection

★★★ Robert Mondavi Winery Napa Valley

★★★ Monticello Cellars Napa Valley

★★★ Moondance Napa Valley

★★★ Newton Vineyard Napa Valley

★★★ Peachy Canyon Winery Paso Robles

★★★ Robert Pecota Winery Napa Valley Steven Andre Vineyard

★★★ Joseph Phelps Vineyards Napa Valley

★★★ Pride Mountain Vineyards Napa Valley

★★★ Ramsey Napa Valley

★★★ Ravenswood Carneros Sangiacomo Vineyard

★★★ Richardson Vineyards Carneros

★★★ St. Clement Vineyards Napa Valley

★★★ St. Francis Winery Sonoma Valley

★★★ St. Supéry Vineyard & Winery Napa Valley Dollarhide Ranch

★★★ Selene Wines Napa Valley

★★★ Shooting Star Clear Lake

★★★ Signorello Vineyards Napa Valley

★★★ Silverado Vineyards Stags Leap District

★★★ Robert Sinskey Vineyards Carneros

★★★ Stag's Leap Wine Cellars Napa Valley

★★★ Stonestreet Alexander Valley

★★★ Straus Vineyards Napa Valley

★★★ Sullivan Vineyards Winery Napa Valley

★★★ Swanson Vineyards Napa Valley

★★★ Vichon Winery Napa Valley

★★★ Villa Mt. Eden Napa Valley Grand Reserve

★★★ Wild Horse Winery San Luis Obispo County

★★ Alexander Valley Vineyards Alexander Valley Wetzel Family Estate

★★ Aries Carneros

★★ Armida Winery Russian River Valley

★★ Beaulieu Vineyard Napa Valley Beau Tour

★★ Bellerose Vineyard Sonoma County

★★ Belvedere Winery Sonoma County

★★ Benziger Family Winery Sonoma County

★★ Bergfeld Winery Napa Valley

★★ Boeger Winery El Dorado County

★★ Bogle Vineyards California

★★ Braren Pauli Winery Alexander Valley

★★ Brutocao Cellars Mendocino County

★★ Buena Vista Winery Carneros

★★ Buena Vista Winery Carneros Grand Reserve

★★ Byington Winery & Vineyards Sonoma County Bradford Mountain Vineyard

★★ Chappellet Vineyard Napa Valley

★★ Chateau Chevre Winery Napa Valley

★★ Chateau Julien Winery Monterey County

★★ Chateau Julien Winery Monterey County Private Reserve

★★ Chateau St. Jean Sonoma County

★★ Chatom Vineyards Calaveras County

★★ Chimère Winery Santa Barbara County

★★ Clos Pegase Napa Valley

★★ B. R. Cohn Winery Napa Valley Silver Label

★★ B. R. Cohn Winery Napa-Sonoma Counties

★★ Conn Creek Winery Napa Valley Barrel Select

★★ Thomas Coyne Winery El Dorado County Quartz Hill Vineyard

★★ Thomas Coyne Winery Sonoma County

★★ Creston Vineyards & Winery Paso Robles

★★ Domaine du Grand Archer Sonoma County

★★ Domaine Napa Winery Napa Valley

★★ Dry Creek Vineyard Dry Creek Valley

★★ Dry Creek Vineyard Dry Creek Valley Reserve

★★ Dry Creek Vineyard Dry Creek Valley Bullock House Vineyard

★★ Dunnewood Vineyards North Coast Barrel Select

★★ Farella-Park Vineyards Napa Valley

★★ Fenestra Winery Livermore Valley

★★ Fieldbrook Valley Winery Napa Valley Frediani Vineyard

★★ Firestone Vineyard Santa Ynez Valley

★★ Fisher Vineyards Napa Valley

★★ Foppiano Vineyards Russian River Valley

★★ Freemark Abbey Winery Napa Valley

★★ Frog's Leap Winery Napa Valley

★★ The Gainey Vineyard Santa Ynez Valley Limited Selection

★★ E. & J. Gallo Winery Dry Creek Valley Frei Ranch Vineyard

★★ Golden Creek Vineyard Sonoma County Reserve

★★ Greenwood Ridge Vineyards Anderson Valley

★★ Groth Vineyards & Winery Napa Valley

★★ Hacienda Winery California Clair de Lune

★★ Hahn Estates Monterey County

★★ Hallcrest Vineyards El Dorado County De Cascabel Vineyard

★★ Hallcrest Vineyards El Dorado County De Cascabel Vineyards Proprietors Reserve

★★ Hanna Winery Alexander Valley

★★ William Hill Winery Napa Valley

★★ Indian Springs Vineyards Nevada County

★★ Inglenook-Napa Valley Napa Valley Reserve

★★ Jaeger Family Wine Co. Napa Valley Inglewood Vineyard

★★ Jekel Vineyards Arroyo Seco The Sanctuary Estate

★★ Robert Keenan Winery Napa Valley

★★ Kenwood Vineyards Sonoma County

★★ Charles Krug Winery Napa Valley

★★ Lake Sonoma Winery Dry Creek Valley Yoakim Bridge Ranch

★★ Lakespring Winery Napa Valley Yount Mill Vineyard

★★ Lambert Bridge Sonoma County

★★ Lava Cap Winery El Dorado County

★★ Leeward Winery Napa Valley

★★ Lockwood Monterey County

★★ J. Lohr Winery California Cypress

★★ Longoria Wine Cellars Santa Ynez Valley

★★ Macrostie Winery Carneros

★★ Louis M. Martini Winery North Coast

★★ Merryvale Vineyards Napa Valley

★★ Michel-Schlumberger Dry Creek Valley

★★ Mietz Cellars Sonoma County

★★ Mill Creek Vineyards Dry Creek Valley

★★ Mirassou Vineyards Central Coast Family Selection

★★ Mount Konocti Winery Lake County

★★ Murphy-Goode Estate Winery Alexander Valley

★★ Murphy-Goode Estate Winery Alexander Valley Murphy Ranch

★★ Napa Ridge North Coast Coastal

★★ Neyers Napa Valley

★★ Niebaum-Coppola Estate Winery Napa Valley Francis Coppola Family Wines

★★ Pahlmeyer Napa Valley Caldwell Vineyard

★★ Parducci Wine Cellars North Coast

★★ Pine Ridge Winery Carneros

★★ Pine Ridge Winery Napa Valley Selected Cuvée

★★ Plam Vineyards & Winery Napa Valley

★★ Poppy Hill Napa Valley Founder's Selection

★★ Quail Ridge Cellars Napa Valley

★★ Rabbit Ridge Vineyards Carneros Sangiacomo Vineyard

★★ Rancho Sisquoc Winery Santa Maria Valley

★★ Ravenswood North Coast Vintners Blend

★★ Ravenswood Sonoma County

★★ Ridge Vineyards Napa County York Creek

★★ Ridge Vineyards Sonoma County Bradford Mountain Vineyard

★★ Rombauer Vineyards Napa Valley

★★ Rosenblum Cellars Napa Valley Holbrook Mitchell Vineyard

★★ Rosenblum Cellars Russian River Valley

★★ Rosenblum Cellars Russian River Valley Lone Oak Vineyard

★★ Round Hill Winery California

★★ Round Hill Winery Napa Valley Reserve

★★ Royce Vineyards Napa Valley Reserve

★★ Royce Vineyards Sonoma County

★★ Rubissow-Sargent Mount Veeder

★★ Rutherford Hill Winery Napa Valley XVS Reserve

★★ Rutherford Ranch Napa Valley

★★ Santa Cruz Mountain Vineyard California

★★ V. Sattui Winery Napa Valley

★★ Sebastiani Vineyards Sonoma Valley Sonoma Series

★★ Smith and Hook Santa Lucia Highlands

★★ Solis Winery Santa Clara County

★★ Stags' Leap Winery Napa Valley

★★ Steltzner Vineyards Stags Leap District

★★ Sterling Vineyards Napa Valley

★★ Stonegate Winery Napa Valley

★★ Stony Ridge Winery North Coast Limited Release

★★ Storrs Winery Santa Clara County San Ysidro Vineyard

★★ Stratford Winery California

★★ Rodney Strong Vineyards Sonoma County

★★ Sutter Home Winery California

★★ Tobin James Paso Robles Full Moon

★★ Tobin James San Luis Obispo County Made in the Shade

★★ Truchard Vineyards Carneros

★★ Vichon Winery California Coastal Selection

★★ Voss Vineyards Napa Valley

★★ Wente Bros. Livermore Valley Crane Ridge

★★ Whitehall Lane Winery Knights Valley

★★ Wildhurst Vineyards Clear Lake

★ Antelope Valley Winery California Bien Nacido Vineyards

★ Beaucanon Winery Napa Valley

★ Bocage Monterey County Proprietor's Cuvée

★ Chestnut Hill Winery North Coast Coastal Cuvée

★ Cline Cellars California

★ Chesnut Hill Winery North Coast Coastal Cuvée

★ Corbett Canyon Vineyards California Coastal Classic

★ Kunde Estate Winery Sonoma Valley

★ La Crosse Napa Valley

★ Mazzocco Vineyards Dry Creek Valley

★ Mission View Vineyards & Winery Paso Robles Limited Release

★ Montpellier California

★ J. Pedroncelli Winery Dry Creek Valley

★ Radanovich Vineyards & Winery Sierra Foothills

★ Wildcat Sonoma Valley

★ York Mountain Winery San Luis Obispo County

NR Bargetto Winery Central Coast

NR Bonverre California Lot Number 11

NR The Brander Vineyard Santa Ynez Valley Three Flags

NR Davis Bynum Winery Russian River Valley Laureles Vineyard

NR Cache Cellars Napa Valley

NR Fetzer Vineyards California Eagle Peak

NR Gold Hill Vineyard El Dorado County

NR Grand Cru Vineyards California Premium Selection

NR Guenoc Winery Lake-Napa Counties

NR Emilio Guglielmo Winery Napa Valley

NR Harbor Winery Napa Valley Narsai David Vineyard

NR Hart Winery Temecula

NR Liparita Cellars Howell Mountain

NR Gustave Niebaum Napa Valley Reference

NR Organic Wine Works Butte County

NR River Run Vintners

NR Salamandre Wine Cellars

NR Sarah's Vineyard Santa Clara County

NR Sea Ridge Winery Sonoma Coast Occidental Vineyard

NR Sonoma Creek Winery Sonoma Valley Sangiacomo Vineyard

NR Stevenot Winery North Coast Reserve

NR Ventana Vineyards

NR Wellington Vineyards Sonoma County

NR Wheeler Winery Dry Creek Valley

NR Wing Canyon Mount Veeder

MOURVÈDRE

★★★ Bonny Doon Vineyard California Old Telegram

★★★ Cline Cellars Contra Costa County

★★★ Cline Cellars Contra Costa County Reserve

★★ Jade Mountain Winery California Unfiltered

★★ R.H. Phillips Vineyard California EXP

NR Chateau St. Jean Sonoma Valley

NR Edmunds St. John California

NR Sebastiani Vineyards Sonoma County Sonoma Series

MUSCAT

★★★	Robert Pecota Winery Napa Valley Muscato di Andrea
★★★	Robert Pecota Winery Napa Valley Sweet Andrea Select
★★	Monte Volpe Mendocino County
★	Cline Cellars Contra Costa County
NR	Ca' del Solo Monterey County Moscato del Solo
NR	Robert Mondavi Winery Napa Valley Moscato d'Oro
NR	St. Supéry Vineyard & Winery California

MUSCAT CANELLI

★★★★	Bonny Doon Vineyard Monterey County Vin de Glaciere
★★	Eberle Winery Paso Robles
NR	Belvedere Winery Alexander Valley Late Harvest

NEBBIOLO

★★	Arciero Winery Paso Robles
★★	Viansa Winery California Nebbiolo
NR	Mosby Winery Santa Barbara County Rosso di Nebbiolo

ORANGE MUSCAT

★★★	Quady Winery California Electra
★★★	Quady Winery California Essensia
NR	Shenandoah Vineyards Amador County

PETITE SIRAH

★★★★	Stags' Leap Winery Napa Valley
★★★	Concannon Vineyard Central Coast
★★★	Concannon Vineyard Central Coast Selected Vineyards
★★★	Fife Vineyards Napa Valley Les Vieilles Vignes
★★★	Foppiano Vineyards Napa Valley La Grande Petite
★★★	Foppiano Vineyards Russian River Valley
★★★	Foppiano Vineyards Russian River Valley Reserve Le Grande Petite
★★★	Foppiano Vineyards Sonoma County
★★★	Guenoc Winery North Coast
★★★	Signorello Vineyards Napa Valley
★★★	Stag's Leap Wine Cellars Napa Valley
★★	Bogle Vineyards California
★★	Deer Park Winery Howell Mountain
★★	Fetzer Vineyards Mendocino County Reserve
★★	Field Stone Winery Alexander Valley
★★	Fife Vineyards Napa Valley
★★	Hop Kiln Winery Russian River Valley M. Griffin Vineyards
★★	Hop Kiln Winery Sonoma County
★★	Karly Wines Amador County Not So Petite Sirah
★★	Konrad Estate Mendocino County
★★	Mirassou Vineyards Monterey County Family Selection
★★	Parducci Wine Cellars Mendocino County
★★	Prager Winery & Port Works Napa Valley Port
★★	Rabbit Ridge Vineyards Sonoma County
★★	Ridge Vineyards Napa County York Creek
★	Black Mountain Alexander Valley Bosun Crest
NR	Gerwer Winery El Dorado County
NR	Geyser Peak Winery Alexander Valley
NR	La Jota Vineyard Co. Howell Mountain
NR	Roudon-Smith Winery San Luis Obispo County
NR	Santa Cruz Mountain Vineyard Santa Cruz Mountains

PETITE VERDOT

★★	Geyser Peak Winery Alexander Valley

PINOT BLANC

★★★★	Chalone Vineyard Chalone
★★★★	Steele Wines Santa Barbara County Bien Nacido Vineyard
★★★	Au Bon Climat Santa Barbara County
★★★	Byron Vineyards & Winery Santa Barbara County
★★★	Étude Wines Napa Valley

★★★ Villa Mt. Eden Santa Maria Valley Bien
Nacido Vineyard Grand Reserve

★★★ Wild Horse Winery Monterey County

★★★ Wild Horse Winery Santa Barbara County
Bien Nacido Vineyard

★★ Benziger Family Winery Sonoma Mountain
Skinner Vineyard Imagery Series

★★ Elliston Vineyards Central Coast Sunol Valley
Vineyard

★★ Gavilan Vineyards Chalone

★★ Daniel Gehrs Monterey County

★★ Joya Winery Napa Valley

★★ Meridian Vineyards Santa Barbara County

★★ Mirassou Vineyards Monterey County Family
Selection White Burgundy

★★ Mirassou Vineyards Monterey County
Harvest Reserve

★★ Monte Volpe Mendocino County

★★ Murphy-Goode Estate Winery Alexander
Valley

★★ Paraiso Springs Vineyards Monterey County

★★ Saddleback Cellars Napa Valley

★ Chimére Winery Santa Barbara County

NR Crystal Valley Cellars Napa Valley

NR Sunrise Winery Santa Cruz Mountains St.
Charles Vineyard

NR Ventana Vineyards

PINOT GRIGIO

★★ Long Vineyards Napa Valley

NR Edmunds St. John El Dorado County

PINOT NOIR

★★★★★ Calera Wine Co. Mount Harlan Jensen

★★★★★ Gary Farrell Wines Russian River Valley
Allen Vineyard

★★★★★ Robert Mondavi Winery Napa Valley Reserve

★★★★★ J. Rochioli Vineyard & Winery Russian River
Valley Reserve

★★★★★ Sanford Winery Santa Barbara County
Sanford & Benedict Vineyard Barrel Select

★★★★★ Williams & Selyem Winery Russian River
Valley Allen Vineyard

★★★★★ Williams & Selyem Winery Russian River
Valley Rochioli Vineyard

★★★★ Au Bon Climat Santa Barbara County Bien
Nacido Vineyard La Bauge Au-Dessus

★★★★ Au Bon Climat Santa Maria Valley Rancho
Vinedo Vineyard

★★★★ Au Bon Climat Santa Ynez Valley Sanford &
Benedict Vineyard

★★★★ David Bruce Winery Santa Cruz Mountains

★★★★ David Bruce Winery Santa Cruz Mountains
Estate Reserve

★★★★ Calera Wine Co. Mount Harlan Mills

★★★★ Calera Wine Co. Mount Harlan Selleck

★★★★ Dehlinger Winery Russian River Valley
Reserve

★★★★ El Molino Napa Valley

★★★★ Gary Farrell Wines Russian River Valley

★★★★ Gary Farrell Wines Santa Barbara County
Bien Nacido Vineyard

★★★★ J. Rochioli Vineyard & Winery Russian River
Valley

★★★★ Saintsbury Carneros Reserve

★★★★ Sanford Winery Santa Barbara County

★★★★ Santa Cruz Mountain Vineyard Santa Cruz
Mountains

★★★★ Steele Wines Carneros Sangiacomo Vineyard

★★★★ Williams & Selyem Winery Anderson Valley
Ferrington Vineyard

★★★★ Williams & Selyem Winery Russian River
Valley

★★★★ Williams & Selyem Winery Russian River
Valley Cohn Vineyard

★★★★ Williams & Selyem Winery Russian River
Valley Olivet Lane Vineyard

★★★★ Williams & Selyem Winery Sonoma Coast

★★★★ Williams & Selyem Winery Sonoma Coast
Summa Vineyard

★★★ Acacia Winery Carneros St. Clair Vineyard
Reserve

★★★ Beaulieu Vineyard Carneros Carneros
Reserve

★★★ Bouchaine Vineyards Carneros Reserve

★★★ Byron Vineyards & Winery Santa Barbara County

★★★ Byron Vineyards & Winery Santa Barbara County Reserve

★★★ Calera Wine Co. Mount Harlan Reed

★★★ Cambria Winery & Vineyard Santa Maria Valley Reserve

★★★ Cambria Winery & Vineyard Santa Maria Valley Julia's Vineyard

★★★ Camelot Central Coast

★★★ Carneros Creek Winery Carneros

★★★ Carneros Creek Winery Carneros Signature Reserve

★★★ Caymus Vineyards Napa Valley Special Selection

★★★ Chalone Vineyard Chalone

★★★ Chalone Vineyard Chalone Reserve

★★★ Cuvaison Winery Carneros

★★★ Dehlinger Winery Russian River Valley

★★★ Edmeades Winery Anderson Valley Dennison Vineyard

★★★ Étude Wines Carneros

★★★ Fiddlehead Cellars Santa Maria Valley

★★★ Foxen Vineyard Santa Maria Valley

★★★ Foxen Vineyard Santa Ynez Valley Sanford & Benedict Vineyard

★★★ The Gainey Vineyard Santa Ynez Valley Limited Selection

★★★ Greenwood Ridge Vineyards Anderson Valley

★★★ Greenwood Ridge Vineyards Anderson Valley Roederer Estate Vineyards

★★★ Greenwood Ridge Vineyards Mendocino County

★★★ Hanzell Vineyards Sonoma Valley

★★★ Hitching Post Winery Santa Maria Valley

★★★ Hitching Post Winery Santa Ynez Valley Sanford & Benedict Vineyard

★★★ Paul Hobbs Cellars Carneros Hyde Vineyard

★★★ Iron Horse Vineyards Green Valley-Sonoma

★★★ Kendall-Jackson California Grand Reserve

★★★ Kistler Vineyards Russian River Valley Cuvée Catherine

★★★ Kistler Vineyards Russian River Valley Dutton Ranch

★★★ Kistler Vineyards Sonoma Mountain McCrea Vineyard

★★★ La Crema California

★★★ La Crema California Reserve

★★★ Lazy Creek Vineyards Anderson Valley

★★★ Longoria Wine Cellars Santa Maria Valley Bien Nacido Vineyard

★★★ Mahoney Estate Carneros Las Piedras Vineyard

★★★ Robert Mondavi Winery Carneros

★★★ Robert Mondavi Winery Napa Valley

★★★ Monticello Cellars Napa Valley

★★★ Monticello Cellars Napa Valley Corley Family Vineyards

★★★ Morgan Winery Carneros Reserve

★★★ Morgan Winery Monterey County Reserve

★★★ Mount Eden Vineyards Edna Valley

★★★ Mount Eden Vineyards Santa Cruz Mountains

★★★ Navarro Vineyards Anderson Valley Méthode l'Ancienne

★★★ Kent Rasmussen Winery Carneros

★★★ Richardson Vineyards Carneros Sangiacomo Vineyard

★★★ Saintsbury Carneros

★★★ Saintsbury Carneros Garnet

★★★ Santa Barbara Winery Santa Barbara County Reserve

★★★ Santa Cruz Mountain Vineyard Santa Cruz Mountains Matteson Vineyard

★★★ Shooting Star Mendocino County

★★★ Signorello Vineyards North Coast Founder's Reserve

★★★ Robert Sinskey Vineyards Carneros

★★★ Steele Wines Carneros

★★★ Steele Wines Mendocino County DuPratt Vineyard

★★★ Steele Wines Santa Barbara County Bien Nacido Vineyard

★★★ Steele Wines Sonoma Valley Durell Vineyard

★★★ Stonestreet Sonoma County

★★★ Marimar Torres Estate Green Valley-Sonoma Don Miguel Vineyard

★★★ Truchard Vineyards Carneros

★★★ Whitcraft Winery Russian River Valley Olivet Lane Vineyard

★★★ Whitcraft Winery Santa Maria Valley Bien Nacido Vineyard

★★★ Wild Horse Winery Central Coast

★★ Acacia Winery Carneros

★★ Alexander Valley Vineyards Alexander Valley

★★ Alexander Valley Vineyards Alexander Valley Wetzel Family Estate

★★ Anderson's Conn Valley Vineyards Napa Valley

★★ Anderson's Conn Valley Vineyards Napa Valley Valhalla Vineyards

★★ Aries Carneros

★★ Aries Carneros Cuvée Vivace

★★ Babcock Vineyards Santa Ynez Valley

★★ Babcock Vineyards Santa Ynez Valley Sanford & Benedict Vineyard

★★ Beaulieu Vineyard Carneros

★★ Beaulieu Vineyard Napa Valley Beau Tour

★★ Benziger Family Winery Sonoma County

★★ Bernardus Vineyards & Winery Santa Barbara County Bien Nacido Vineyard

★★ Bouchaine Vineyards Carneros

★★ Brandborg Cellars Santa Maria Valley Bien Nacido Vineyard

★★ Briceland Vineyards Humboldt County

★★ Buena Vista Winery Carneros

★★ Buena Vista Winery Carneros Grand Reserve

★★ Davis Bynum Winery Russian River Valley Limited Release

★★ Calera Wine Co. Central Coast

★★ Carneros Creek Winery Carneros Fleur de Carneros

★★ Chateau de Baun Sonoma County

★★ Chateau La Grande Roche Napa Valley

★★ Chateau Souverain Carneros Winemaker's Reserve

★★ Chateau St. Jean Sonoma County

★★ Claiborne & Churchill Edna Valley MacGregor Vineyard

★★ Claudia Springs Winery Anderson Valley

★★ Clos du Bois Sonoma County

★★ Clos Du Val Carneros

★★ Cosentino Winery Carneros

★★ Cosentino Winery Carneros Punched Cap Fermented

★★ Cottonwood Canyon Santa Barbara County

★★ Cottonwood Canyon Santa Barbara County Barrel Select

★★ Cronin Vineyards Santa Cruz Mountains Peter Martin Ray Vineyard

★★ De Loach Vineyards Russian River Valley

★★ De Loach Vineyards Russian River Valley O.F.S.

★★ Domaine Saint Gregory Mendocino County

★★ Durney Vineyard Carmel Valley

★★ Edna Valley Vineyard Edna Valley

★★ Edna Valley Vineyard Edna Valley Paragon Vineyard Reserve

★★ Estancia Monterey County

★★ Gloria Ferrer Champagne Caves Carneros

★★ Fetzer Vineyards California

★★ Fetzer Vineyards North Coast Barrel Select

★★ Fetzer Vineyards Santa Barbara County Bien Nacido Vineyards

★★ Fetzer Vineyards Sonoma County Olivet Lane Vineyard

★★ Fieldbrook Valley Winery Napa Valley Beard Vineyard

★★ Thomas Fogarty Winery Napa Valley

★★ Thomas Fogarty Winery Santa Cruz Mountains

★★ The Gainey Vineyard Santa Barbara County

★★ The Gainey Vineyard Santa Maria Valley

★★ Gavilan Vineyards Chalone

★★ Gundlach Bundschu Winery Sonoma Valley Rhinefarm Vineyards

★★ Hacienda Winery Sonoma Valley Estate Reserve

★★ Handley Cellars Anderson Valley

★★ Harmony Cellars Paso Robles

★★ Hess Select California

★★ Hess Select Santa Maria Valley Bien Nacido Vineyard

★★ Husch Vineyards Anderson Valley

★★ Jekel Vineyards Arroyo Seco

★★ Kalin Cellars Sonoma County

★★ Keltie Brook Carneros Unfiltered

★★ Kendall-Jackson California Vintner's Reserve

★★ Kenwood Vineyards Sonoma Valley Jack London Vineyard

★★ J. Kerr Wines Santa Barbara County

★★ Charles Krug Winery Carneros

★★ Macrostie Winery Carneros

★★ Mark West Vineyards Russian River Valley

★★ Louis M. Martini Winery Carneros

★★ McHenry Vineyard Santa Cruz Mountains

★★ Meridian Vineyards Edna Valley Reserve

★★ Meridian Vineyards Santa Barbara County

★★ Meridian Vineyards Santa Barbara County Reserve

★★ Mont St. John Cellars Carneros

★★ Monterey Peninsula Winery Monterey County Sleepy Hollow Vineyard

★★ Morgan Winery California

★★ Morgan Winery Monterey County

★★ Moshin Vineyards Russian River Valley

★★ Napa Ridge North Coast Coastal

★★ Navarro Vineyards Anderson Valley

★★ Newlan Vineyards and Winery Napa Valley

★★ Newlan Vineyards and Winery Napa Valley Napa-Villages

★★ Newlan Vineyards and Winery Napa Valley Reserve

★★ Newlan Vineyards and Winery Napa Valley School House Vieilles Vignes

★★ Newlan Vineyards and Winery Napa Valley Vieilles Vignes

★★ Octopus Mountain Anderson Valley Dennison Vineyard

★★ The Ojai Vineyard Santa Barbara County

★★ Olivet Lane Estate Russian River Valley

★★ Page Mill Winery Santa Barbara County Bien Nacido Vineyard

★★ Parducci Wine Cellars Mendocino County

★★ Fess Parker Winery Santa Barbara County

★★ Pepperwood Grove California

★★ Pinnacles Monterey County Pinnacles Vineyard

★★ Prager Winery & Port Works Napa Valley Port

★★ Q.C. Fly California

★★ Ramsey Carneros

★★ Raymond Vineyard and Cellar Napa Valley

★★ Roche Winery Carneros

★★ Rosenblum Cellars Napa Valley George Hendry Vineyard

★★ Rosenblum Cellars Russian River Valley Ellis Ranch

★★ Roudon-Smith Winery Santa Cruz Mountains

★★ Roudon-Smith Winery Santa Cruz Mountains Cox Vineyard

★★ Santa Barbara Winery Santa Barbara County

★★ School House Napa Valley

★★ Schug Carneros Estate Carneros

★★ Schug Carneros Estate Carneros Heritage Reserve

★★ Sea Ridge Winery Sonoma Coast Hirsch Vineyard

★★ Seghesio Winery Russian River Valley

★★ Seghesio Winery Sonoma County

★★ Solitude Wines Sonoma County

★★ Soquel Vineyards Santa Cruz Mountains

★★ Star Hill Wines Napa Valley Doc's Reserve

★★ Rodney Strong Vineyards Russian River Valley River East Vineyard

★★ Joseph Swan Vineyards Russian River Valley

★★ Joseph Swan Vineyards Sonoma Mountain Steiner Vineyard

★★ Talley Vineyards Arroyo Grande Valley

★★ Lane Tanner Santa Barbara County

★★ Lane Tanner Santa Ynez Valley Sanford & Benedict Vineyard

★★ Tobin James Santa Barbara County Black Tie

★★ Tobin James Santa Barbara County Sunshine

★★ Villa Mt. Eden California Cellar Select

★★ Villa Mt. Eden Carneros Grand Reserve

★★ Villa Mt. Eden Santa Maria Valley Bien Nacido Vineyard Grand Reserve

★★ Whitehall Lane Winery Alexander Valley

★★ Zaca Mesa Winery Santa Barbara County Sierra Madre Vineyard

★★ ZD Wines Carneros

★ Armida Winery Russian River Valley

★ Austin Cellars Santa Barbara County Reserve

★ Bearboat Russian River Valley

★ Bon Marché Sonoma County

★ Brindiamo Santa Barbara County Santa Maria Hills Vineyard Limited Bottling

★ Byington Winery & Vineyards Santa Barbara County Bien Nacido Vineyard

★ Davis Bynum Winery Russian River Valley

★ Maurice Carrie Vineyards and Winery Santa Barbara County

★ Castoro Cellars Santa Barbara County

★ Chateau de Leu Winery Napa Valley

★ Christophe Carneros

★ Corbett Canyon Vineyards Santa Barbara County Reserve

★ Creston Vineyards & Winery Paso Robles

★ Elkhorn Peak Cellars Napa Valley Fagan Creek Vineyards

★ Jory Winery California San Ysidro Vineyard

★ Leeward Winery Santa Barbara County

★ Mayacamas Vineyards Napa Valley

★ Mirassou Vineyards Monterey County Family Selection

★ Mirassou Vineyards Monterey County Harvest Selection Limited Bottling

★ The Monterey Vineyard Monterey County Classic

★ Paraiso Springs Vineyards Carneros

★ J. Pedroncelli Winery Dry Creek Valley

★ Pepperwood Springs Vineyards Anderson Valley

★ Pepperwood Springs Vineyards Mendocino County Vidmar Vineyard

★ Solis Winery Santa Clara County

★ Robert Stemmler Winery Sonoma County

★ Sterling Vineyards Carneros Winery Lake Vineyard

★ Topolos Sonoma Mountain Dry Farmed

★ Trefethen Vineyards Napa Valley

★ Tulocay Winery Napa Valley Haynes Vineyard

★ Weibel Vineyards

★ Christine Woods Winery Anderson Valley Estate Reserve

★ York Mountain Winery San Luis Obispo County

NR Au Bon Climat Arroyo Grande Valley Talley and Paragon Vineyards

NR Bargetto Winery Santa Cruz Mountains

NR Buehler Vineyards Central Coast

NR DeNatale Vineyards Russian River Valley

NR Ferrari-Carano Winery Napa-Sonoma Counties Rhonda's Reserve

NR Emilio Guglielmo Winery Santa Clara Valley Private Reserve

NR Hagafen Cellars Napa Valley

NR Hanna Winery Russian River Valley

NR Innisfree California

NR Johnson's Alexander Valley Wines Alexander Valley

NR Obester Winery Anderson Valley

NR Organic Wine Works Mendocino County

NR Porter Creek Vineyards Russian River Valley

NR Rolling Hills Vineyards Santa Maria Valley

NR Salamandre Wine Cellars

NR Santa Ynez Winery Santa Maria Valley

NR Sonoma Creek Winery Carneros

NR Weinstock Cellars

NR Wild Hog Hill Vineyard Sonoma County

NR Wildhurst Vineyards Mendocino County

PORT

★★★ Geyser Peak Winery Alexander Valley Henry's Reserve Vintage Port

★★ Ficklin Vineyard California Special Bottling No. 5

★★ Ficklin Vineyard California Tinta

★★ Guenoc Winery California

★★ Justin Vineyards & Winery San Luis Obispo County Obtuse

★★ Marietta Cellars Alexander Valley

★★ Quady Winery Amador County Starboard

★★ Quady Winery California LBV

★★ Renwood Winery Shenandoah Valley Late Bottled Vintage

NR Konrad Estate Mendocino County Petite Sirah Port Admiral's Quinta

NR Rutherford Hill Winery Napa Valley Zinfandel Port

NR St. Amant Amador County Vintage Port

NR St. Amant Amador County Zinfandel Port

NR Sonora Winery & Port Works Amador County

RED TABLE WINE

★★★ Elyse Vineyards Napa Valley Nero Misto

★★★ Z Moore Winery Mendocino County Danato

★★★ Signorello Vineyards Napa Valley Il Taglio

★★ Brindiamo South Coast Gioveto Limited Bottling

★★ Côtes de Sonoma Sonoma County Deux Cépages

★★ Fetzer Vineyards Mendocino County Bonterra Organically Grown Grapes

★★ Hop Kiln Winery Russian River Valley M. Griffin Vineyards Valdiguie

★★ Hop Kiln Winery Sonoma County Marty Griffin's Big Red

★★ Jory Winery California Black Hand Mano Nero

★★ Jory Winery California Red Zeppelin Bon Jory Red

★★ Marietta Cellars Sonoma County Old Vine Red Lot 14

★★ Parducci Wine Cellars Mendocino County Bono-Sirah

★★ Viansa Winery Napa County Thalia

★★ Wellington Vineyards Sonoma Valley Criolla Old Vines

NR Bonny Doon Vineyard California Le Gaucher

NR Emilio Guglielmo Winery Santa Clara County Claret 13th Limited Bottling

NR Mastantuono California Carminello

NR Montevina Wines Amador County Montanaro

NR Navarro Vineyards Mendocino County Petits Villages

NR Organic Wine Works California A Notre Terre

NR J. Pedroncelli Winery Sonoma County Primitivo Misto

NR Rabbit Ridge Vineyards California Oddux Reserve Red

NR St. Amant Amador County

NR Simi Winery North Coast Altaire

NR Joseph Swan Vineyards Russian River Valley Cotes du Rosa

NR Wheeler Winery California Quintet

NR Wild Horse Winery Cienega Valley Negrette

RHÔNE BLEND

★★★ Bonny Doon Vineyard California Le Cigare Volant

★★★ Bonny Doon Vineyard Santa Cruz Mountains Le Sophiste

★★★ Cline Cellars Contra Costa County Oakley Cuvée

★★★ Edmunds St. John California Les Côtes Sauvages

★★★ Joseph Phelps Vineyards California Vin du Mistral Le Mistral

★★★ R.H. Phillips Vineyard California Alliance

★★★ Preston Vineyards Dry Creek Valley Faux

★★★ Preston Vineyards Dry Creek Valley Sirah-Syrah

★★★ Qupe Cellars Santa Barbara County Los Olivos Cuvée

★★ Brindiamo South Coast Rosso Vecchio Limited Bottling

★★ Ca' del Solo California Big House Red

★★ Cline Cellars Contra Costa County Côtes d'Oakley

★★ Jade Mountain Winery California La Provençale

★★ Jory Winery California Red Zeppelin II The Emperor's Reserve

★★ McDowell Valley Vineyards McDowell Valley Les Vieux Cépages

★★ Quivira Vineyards Dry Creek Valley Dry Creek Cuvée

★★ Rabbit Ridge Vineyards California Allure

★★ Zaca Mesa Winery Santa Barbara County Cuvée Z

NR Ca' del Solo American Il Pescatore

NR Edmunds St. John California El Nino

NR Edmunds St. John California Port O'Call New World Red Table Wine

NR Edmunds St. John Napa Valley Cuvée Wahluke

NR Ridge Vineyards California Evangelo Vineyards Mataro-Mourvèdre

NR Sierra Vista El Dorado County Fleur de Montagne

NR Sobon Estate Shenandoah Valley Rhône Rouge

NR Sobon Estate Shenandoah Valley Rosé

RIESLING (*SEE ALSO* JOHANNISBERG RIESLING, WHITE RIESLING)

★★ Alexander Valley Vineyards Alexander Valley

★★ Claiborne & Churchill Central Coast Dry Alsatian Style

★★ The Gainey Vineyard Santa Ynez Valley

★★ Greenwood Ridge Vineyards Anderson Valley

NR Geyser Peak Winery Sonoma County Trione Vineyards Late Harvest Reserve

NR Renaissance Vineyard & Winery North Yuba Dry

NR Wildhurst Vineyards Clear Lake Dry

ROUSSANNE

★★ Alban Vineyards San Luis Obispo County

SANGIOVESE

★★★ Atlas Peak Vineyards Atlas Peak Reserve

★★★ Cambria Winery & Vineyard Santa Maria Valley Tepusquet Vineyard

★★★ Ferrari-Carano Winery Alexander Valley

★★★ Flora Springs Wine Co. Napa Valley

★★★ La Famiglia di Robert Mondavi California

★★★ Swanson Vineyards Napa Valley

★★ Atlas Peak Vineyards Atlas Peak

★★ Chatom Vineyards Calaveras County

★★ Estancia Alexander Valley

★★ Indian Springs Vineyards Nevada County

★★ Monte Volpe Mendocino County

★★ Obester Winery Mendocino County

★★ Robert Pepi Winery Napa Valley Colline di Sassi

★★ Rabbit Ridge Vineyards Dry Creek Valley Coniglio Selezione

★★ Ramsey California

★★ Seghesio Winery Alexander Valley Chianti Station Old Vine

★★ Seghesio Winery Alexander Valley Vitigno Toscano

★★ Shafer Vineyards Stags Leap District Firebreak

★★ Trentadue Winery Alexander Valley

★ Castelletto Temecula

NR Montevina Wines Amador County

NR Mosby Winery Santa Barbara County Vigna Della Casa Vecchia

NR Silverado Vineyards Napa Valley

NR Staglin Family Vineyard Napa Valley Stagliano

SAUVIGNON BLANC (*SEE ALSO* FUMÉ BLANC)

★★★★ Caymus Vineyards Napa Valley Barrel Fermented

★★★★ Gary Farrell Wines Russian River Valley Rochioli Vineyard

★★★★ Matanzas Creek Winery Sonoma County

★★★★ J. Rochioli Vineyard & Winery Russian River Valley Reserve

★★★ Babcock Vineyards Santa Ynez Valley 11 Oaks Ranch

★★★ Bernardus Vineyards & Winery Monterey County

★★★ The Brander Vineyard Santa Ynez Valley

★★★ The Brander Vineyard Santa Ynez Valley Cuvée Nicolas

★★★ Brutocao Cellars Mendocino County

★★★ Buena Vista Winery Lake County

★★★ Byron Vineyards & Winery Santa Barbara County

★★★ Cakebread Cellars Napa Valley

★★★ Chalk Hill Winery Chalk Hill

★★★ Chateau Souverain Alexander Valley Barrel Fermented

★★★ Clos du Bois Sonoma County

★★★ Duckhorn Vineyards Napa Valley

★★★ Ferrari-Carano Winery Sonoma County Eldorado Gold

★★★ Field Stone Winery Mendocino County Quillen Vineyard

★★★ Flora Springs Wine Co. Napa Valley Soliloquy

★★★ Guenoc Winery Guenoc Valley

★★★ Hanna Winery Sonoma County

★★★ Hidden Cellars Winery Mendocino County

★★★ Hidden Cellars Winery Mendocino County Organically Grown Grapes

★★★ Husch Vineyards Mendocino County

★★★ Husch Vineyards Mendocino County La Ribera Ranch

★★★ Kendall-Jackson California Grand Reserve

★★★ Kenwood Vineyards Sonoma County

★★★ Lockwood Monterey County

★★★ Markham Vineyards Napa Valley

★★★ Mayacamas Vineyards Napa Valley

★★★ Merryvale Vineyards Napa Valley

★★★ Morgan Winery Sonoma County

★★★ Murphy-Goode Estate Winery Alexander Valley Dry

★★★ Navarro Vineyards Mendocino County Cuvée 128

★★★ Robert Pecota Winery Napa Valley

★★★ Robert Pepi Winery Napa Valley Reserve Selection

★★★ Robert Pepi Winery Napa Valley Two-Heart Canopy

★★★ Quivira Vineyards Dry Creek Valley

★★★ Quivira Vineyards Dry Creek Valley Reserve

★★★ J. Rochioli Vineyard & Winery Russian River Valley

★★★ St. Clement Vineyards Napa Valley

★★★ Sanford Winery Santa Barbara County

★★★ Selene Wines Carneros Hyde Vineyard

★★★ Signorello Vineyards Napa Valley

★★★ Silverado Vineyards Napa Valley

★★★ Simi Winery Sonoma County

★★★ Spottswoode Winery Napa Valley

★★★ Rodney Strong Vineyards Northern Sonoma Charlotte's Home Vineyard

★★★ Philip Togni Vineyard Napa Valley

★★★ Voss Vineyards Napa Valley

★★ Alderbrook Winery Dry Creek Valley

★★ Beaulieu Vineyard California Beau Tour

★★ Beaulieu Vineyard Napa Valley Dry

★★ Boeger Winery El Dorado County

★★ Briceland Vineyards Humboldt County

★★ Byington Winery & Vineyards San Luis Obispo County French Camp Vineyard Dry

★★ Cain Cellars Monterey County Musque

★★ Callaway Vineyard and Winery Temecula

★★ Canyon Road California

★★ Chateau Potelle Napa Valley

★★ Chatom Vineyards Calaveras County

★★ Clos Pegase Napa Valley

★★ Concannon Vineyard Livermore Valley

★★ Cotes de Sonoma Sonoma County

★★ De Loach Vineyards Russian River Valley Dry

★★ DeMoor Winery Napa Valley

★★ Estancia Monterey County

★★ Fallenleaf Vineyard Sonoma Valley

★★ Fetzer Vineyards Mendocino County Barrel Select

★★ Fieldbrook Valley Winery California Meredith Vineyard

★★ Fieldbrook Valley Winery Mendocino County Webb Vineyard

★★ Foppiano Vineyards Dry Creek Valley

★★ Fremont Creek Winery

★★ J. Fritz Cellars Dry Creek Valley

★★ Frog's Leap Winery Napa Valley

★★ The Gainey Vineyard Santa Ynez Valley Limited Selection

★★ Gan Eden Sonoma County

★★ Daniel Gehrs Monterey County Fumé En Vogue

★★ Geyser Peak Winery Sonoma County

★★ Greenwood Ridge Vineyards Anderson Valley

★★ Groth Vineyards & Winery Napa Valley

★★ Handley Cellars Dry Creek Valley

★★ Hawk Crest California

★★ William Hill Winery Napa Valley

★★ Louis Honig Cellars Napa Valley

★★ Jepson Vineyards Mendocino County

★★ Joullian Vineyards Carmel Valley

★★ Joullian Vineyards Carmel Valley Family Reserve

★★ Karly Wines Amador County

★★ Kendall-Jackson California Vintner's Reserve

★★ Lakespring Winery Napa Valley Yount Mill Vineyard

★★ Lakewood Clear Lake

★★ Mark West Vineyards Russian River Valley

★★ The Meeker Vineyard Dry Creek Valley Gold Leaf Cuvée

★★ Meridian Vineyards California

★★ Mill Creek Vineyards Dry Creek Valley

★★ Mirassou Vineyards California

★★ Robert Mondavi-Woodbridge California

★★ Montpellier California

★★ Mount Palomar Winery Temecula Reserve

★★ Napa Ridge North Coast Coastal

★★ Obester Winery Mendocino County

★★ Parducci Wine Cellars North Coast

★★ Peju Province Winery Napa Valley Late Harvest Special Select

★★ Joseph Phelps Vineyards Napa Valley

★★ R.H. Phillips Vineyard California Night Harvest

★★ Preston Vineyards Dry Creek Valley Cuvée de Fume

★★ Quail Ridge Cellars Napa Valley

★★ Rancho Sisquoc Winery Santa Maria Valley

★★ Raymond Vineyard and Cellar Napa Valley

★★ Renaissance Vineyard & Winery North Yuba

★★ Renaissance Vineyard & Winery North Yuba Select Late Harvest

★★ Rutherford Ranch Napa Valley

★★ St. Supéry Vineyard & Winery Napa Valley Dollarhide Ranch

★★ V. Sattui Winery Napa Valley

★★ Seghesio Winery Sonoma County

★★ Stag's Leap Wine Cellars Napa Valley Rancho Chimiles

★★ Steltzner Vineyards Napa Valley Oak Knoll Ranch

★★ Sterling Vineyards Napa Valley

★★ Stratford Winery California Partners' Reserve

★★ Sutter Home Winery California

★★ Taft Street Winery Sonoma County

★★ Ivan Tamas Winery Livermore Valley Figoni Ranch

★★ M. G. Vallejo California

★★ Ventana Vineyards Monterey County

★★ Wente Bros. Livermore Valley Wente Family Estate Selection

★★ Wheeler Winery Sonoma County

★★ White Oak Vineyards & Winery Sonoma County

★★ Whitehall Lane Winery Napa Valley Barrel Fermented

★ Adler Fels Sonoma County

★ Amador Foothill Winery Shenandoah Valley Amador Fume

★ Austin Cellars Santa Barbara County Reserve

★ Austin Cellars Santa Barbara County Lucas Vineyard

★ Corbett Canyon Vineyards Central Coast Coastal Classic

★ Domaine Napa Winery Napa Valley Michel A. Perret

★ Dunnewood Vineyards North Coast Barrel Select

★ Estrella River Winery California Proprietor's Reserve

★ Farella-Park Vineyards Napa Valley

★ Firestone Vineyard Santa Ynez Valley

★ Limerick Lane Russian River Valley Collins Vineyard

★ Mission View Vineyards & Winery San Luis Obispo County

★ Mount Palomar Winery Temecula

★ Santa Barbara Winery Santa Ynez Valley

★ Santa Barbara Winery Santa Ynez Valley Reserve

★ Stephen Zellerbach California

NR Bellerose Vineyard Dry Creek Valley Barrel Fermented Reserve

NR Bonverre Napa Valley Lot Number 10

NR Callaway Vineyard and Winery Temecula Hawk Watch

NR Crystal Valley Cellars Napa Valley

NR Dry Creek Vineyard Sonoma County Late Harvest Soleil

NR Joseph Filippi Vintage Co. Monterey County Limited Release Winemaker's Reserve

NR Fitzpatrick Winery El Dorado County

NR Gerwer Winery El Dorado County

NR Hart Winery Temecula

NR Kunde Estate Winery Sonoma Valley Magnolia Lane

NR Martinelli Winery Russian River Valley

NR Charles B. Mitchell Vineyards El Dorado County

NR Nichelini Winery Napa Valley Joseph A. Nichelini Vineyards

NR Schug Carneros Estate Sonoma Valley

NR Shenandoah Vineyards Amador County

SAUVIGNON BLEND

★★★★★ Beringer Vineyards Napa Valley Nightingale

★★★ Benziger Family Winery Sonoma Mountain A Tribute

★★★ The Brander Vineyard Santa Ynez Valley Cuvée Natalie

★★★ Cronin Vineyards Napa Valley

★★★ Lakewood Clear Lake Chevriot

★★★ Vita Nova Santa Barbara County Reservatum

★★ Concannon Vineyard Livermore Valley Assemblage

★★ Cosentino Winery Napa Valley The Novelist

★★ Murrieta's Well Livermore Valley Vendimia

★★ Vichon Winery Napa Valley Chevrignon

SCHEUREBE

★★★★ Joseph Phelps Vineyards Napa Valley Special Select

SÉMILLON

★★★★★ Dolce California Dolce

★★★ Chalk Hill Winery Chalk Hill

★★★ Joseph Phelps Vineyards Napa Valley Délice du Sémillon

★★★ Signorello Vineyards Napa Valley Barrel Fermented

★★ Alderbrook Winery Dry Creek Valley

★★ Benziger Family Winery Sonoma Mountain

★★ Chatom Vineyards Calaveras County

★★ Cline Cellars California Barrel Fermented

★★ Clos Du Val Stags Leap District

★★ Fenestra Winery Livermore Valley

★★ Gan Eden Sonoma County

★★ Lakewood Clear Lake

★★ Swanson Vineyards Napa Valley Late Harvest

NR Organic Wine Works Napa Valley

SPARKLING WINE

★★★★ Domaine Chandon Napa-Sonoma Counties Brut Reserve

★★★★ Iron Horse Vineyards Green Valley-Sonoma Blanc de Blancs

★★★★ Mumm Napa Valley Napa Valley DVX

★★★★ Roederer Estate Anderson Valley Brut L'Ermitage

★★★★ Schramsberg Napa Valley J. Schram

★★★ S. Anderson Vineyard Napa Valley

★★★ Chateau St. Jean Sonoma County

★★★ Codorniu Napa Napa Valley

★★★ Richard Cuneo Sonoma County Brut Cuvée de Chardonnay

★★★ Domaine Carneros Carneros Brut

★★★ Domaine Carneros Carneros Brut Blanc de Blancs

★★★ Domaine Carneros Carneros Taittinger

★★★ Domaine Chandon Carneros Blanc de Noirs

★★★ Domaine Chandon Napa County Brut Cuvée

★★★ Gloria Ferrer Champagne Caves Carneros Late Disgorged Cuvée

★★★ Gloria Ferrer Champagne Caves Sonoma County

★★★ Iron Horse Vineyards Green Valley-Sonoma Brut Late Disgorged

★★★ Iron Horse Vineyards Green Valley-Sonoma Brut Rosé

★★★ Iron Horse Vineyards Green Valley-Sonoma Brut Vrais Amis

★★★ Iron Horse Vineyards Green Valley-Sonoma Demi-Sec

★★★ Iron Horse Vineyards Green Valley-Sonoma Wedding Cuvée

★★★ J Sonoma County Brut

★★★ Maison Deutz Winery San Luis Obispo County Brut Rosé

★★★ Maison Deutz Winery San Luis Obispo County Reserve

★★★ Mumm Napa Valley Carneros Winery Lake Vineyard Brut

★★★ Mumm Napa Valley Napa Valley Blanc de Blancs

★★★ Mumm Napa Valley Napa Valley Blanc de Noirs

★★★ Mumm Napa Valley Napa Valley Cuvée Napa Brut

★★★ Mumm Napa Valley Napa Valley Cuvée Napa Brut Reserve

★★★ Mumm Napa Valley Napa Valley Prestige Cuvée Brut

★★★ Piper Sonoma Cellars Sonoma County Blanc de Noirs

★★★ Piper Sonoma Cellars Sonoma County Brut

★★★ Piper Sonoma Cellars Sonoma County Tête de Cuvée

★★★ Roederer Estate Anderson Valley Brut

★★★ Scharffenberger Cellars Mendocino County Blanc de Blancs

★★★ Scharffenberger Cellars Mendocino County Brut

★★★ Scharffenberger Cellars Mendocino County Brut Rosé

★★★ Scharffenberger Cellars Mendocino County Extra Dry

★★★ Schramsberg Vineyards Napa Valley Blanc de Blancs

★★★ Schramsberg Vineyards Napa Valley Blanc de Noirs

★★★ Schramsberg Vineyards Napa Valley Brut

★★★ Schramsberg Vineyards Napa Valley Brut Rosé Cuvée de Pinot

★★★ Schramsberg Vineyards Napa Valley Cremant Demi-Sec

★★ Culbertson Winery California Artist Series Cuvée de Frontignan

★★ Robert Hunter Sonoma Valley Brut de Noirs

★★ Jepson Vineyards Mendocino County

★★ Jepson Vineyards Mendocino County Blanc de Blancs

★★ Martin Brothers Winery California Moscato Allegro

★★ Korbel Champagne Cellars California Natural

★★ Maison Deutz Winery San Luis Obispo County Blanc de Noir

★★ Maison Deutz Winery San Luis Obispo County Brut Cuvée

★★ Mirassou Vineyards Monterey County

★★ Navarro Vineyards Anderson Valley Brut

★ Korbel Champagne Cellars California Blanc de Blancs

★	Korbel Champagne Cellars California Blanc de Noirs Cuvée Master's Reserve
★	Korbel Champagne Cellars California Brut
★	Korbel Champagne Cellars California Rosé
NR	Bargetto Winery Santa Maria Valley Blanc de Noir 60th Anniversary 1933-1993
NR	Benziger Family Winery Carneros Brut Imagery Series
NR	Bonny Doon Vineyard California Le Canard Froid Pinot Meunier
NR	Chateau de Baun Sonoma County Brut
NR	Folie à Deux Winery Napa Valley

SYMPHONY

★★★	Chateau de Baun Russian River Valley Finale Late Harvest
NR	Martz Vineyards Mendocino County

SYRAH

★★★★	Dehlinger Winery Russian River Valley
★★★★	Edmunds St. John Sonoma Valley Durell Vineyard
★★★★	Geyser Peak Winery Alexander Valley
★★★★	Geyser Peak Winery Alexander Valley Reserve
★★★★	Jade Mountain Winery Napa Valley
★★★★	Qupe Cellars Central Coast
★★★★	Qupe Cellars Santa Barbara County Bien Nacido Vineyard
★★★★	Truchard Vineyards Carneros
★★★	Cambria Winery & Vineyard Santa Maria Valley Tepusquet Vineyard
★★★	Eberle Winery Paso Robles Fralich Vineyard
★★★	Edmunds St. John Sonoma Valley
★★★	Kendall-Jackson California Grand Reserve
★★★	Kendall-Jackson California Vintner's Reserve
★★★	Kendall-Jackson Sonoma Valley Durell Vineyard
★★★	Meridian Vineyards Paso Robles
★★★	The Ojai Vineyard California
★★★	Joseph Phelps Vineyards Napa Valley Vin du Mistral
★★★	R.H. Phillips Vineyard California EXP

★★★	Preston Vineyards Dry Creek Valley
★★★	Swanson Vineyards Napa Valley
★★★	Sean H. Thackrey & Co. Napa Valley Orion
★★	Benziger Family Winery Paso Robles
★★	Christopher Creek Russian River Valley
★★	Cline Cellars Contra Costa County
★★	Duxoup Dry Creek Valley
★★	Indian Springs Vineyards Nevada County
★★	Karly Wines Amador County
★★	McDowell Valley Vineyards Mendocino County
★★	Fess Parker Winery Santa Barbara County
★★	Sobon Estate Shenandoah Valley
★★	Zaca Mesa Winery Santa Barbara County
★★	Zaca Mesa Winery Santa Barbara County Chapel Vineyard
NR	River Run Vintners
NR	Sebastiani Vineyards Sonoma County Sonoma Series
NR	Sierra Vista El Dorado County
NR	Ventana Vineyards

TOCAI FRULIANI

★★★	La Famiglia di Robert Mondavi California

VIOGNIER

★★★★	Joseph Phelps Vineyards Napa Valley Vin du Mistral
★★★★	Qupe Cellars Santa Barbara County
★★★	Arrowood Vineyards & Winery Russian River Valley Saralee's Vineyard
★★★	Beringer Vineyards Napa Valley Hudson Vineyard
★★★	Edmunds St. John Knights Valley
★★★	Kunde Estate Winery Sonoma Valley
★★★	La Jota Vineyard Co. Howell Mountain
★★★	Preston Vineyards Dry Creek Valley
★★	Alban Vineyards San Luis Obispo County
★★	Callaway Vineyard and Winery Temecula
★★	McDowell Valley Vineyards Mendocino County
★★	R.H. Phillips Vineyard Dunnigan Hills EXP

★★ Villa Helena Winery Napa Valley

NR Eberle Winery Paso Robles Fralich Vineyard

NR La Jota Vineyard Co. Howell Mountain Sweet

NR Sierra Vista El Dorado County

NR Sobon Estate Shenandoah Valley

White Riesling (*see also* Johannisberg Riesling, Riesling)

★★★★ Arrowood Vineyards & Winery Russian River Valley Oak Meadow Vineyard Select Late Harvest

★★★ Greenwood Ridge Vineyards Mendocino County Late Harvest

★★★ Jekel Vineyards Arroyo Seco

★★ Gundlach Bundschu Winery Sonoma Valley Dresel's Sonoma Riesling

★★ Navarro Vineyards Anderson Valley

★★ Stag's Leap Wine Cellars Napa Valley

★★ Trefethen Vineyards Napa Valley

★ Callaway Vineyard and Winery Temecula

NR Bonny Doon Vineyard California Pacific Rim

NR Monterey Peninsula Winery Monterey County Sleepy Hollow Vineyard Late Harvest

White Table Wine

★★★★ Caymus Vineyards California Conundrum

★★ Ca' del Solo Monterey County Malvasia Bianca

★★ Creston Vineyards & Winery Paso Robles Chevrier Blanc

★★ Gabrielli Winery Mendocino County Ascenza

★★ Daniel Gehrs Monterey County Muscadet

★★ Geyser Peak Winery California Semchard

★★ Liberty School California Three Valley Select

★★ Rabbit Ridge Vineyards North Coast Mystique

NR Ca' del Solo California Il Pescatore

NR Fenestra Winery Livermore Valley Semonnay

NR Moshin Vineyards Russian River Valley Blanc de Noir Barrel Fermented

NR Mount Konocti Winery Lake County Sémillon-Chardonnay

NR Navarro Vineyards Mendocino County Edelzwicker

NR Signorello Vineyards Napa Valley Il Taglio

Zinfandel

★★★★★ Dickerson Vineyard Napa Valley Limited Reserve

★★★★★ Lytton Springs Winery Sonoma County

★★★★★ Ravenswood Napa Valley Dickerson Vineyard

★★★★★ Ridge Vineyards Dry Creek Valley Lytton Springs

★★★★★ Williams & Selyem Winery Russian River Valley Leno Martinelli Vineyard

★★★★ Robert Biale Vineyards Napa Valley Aldo's Vineyard

★★★★ Chateau Potelle Mount Veeder V.G.S.

★★★★ Gary Farrell Wines Russian River Valley

★★★★ Ferrari-Carano Winery Dry Creek Valley

★★★★ Franus Winery Napa Valley Hendry Vineyard

★★★★ E. & J. Gallo Winery Dry Creek Valley Frei Ranch Vineyard

★★★★ Robert Mondavi Winery Napa Valley

★★★★ Nalle Winery Dry Creek Valley

★★★★ Quivira Vineyards Dry Creek Valley

★★★★ Rabbit Ridge Vineyards Sonoma County San Lorenzo Vineyard Reserve

★★★★ A. Rafanelli Winery Dry Creek Valley

★★★★ Ravenswood Sonoma County

★★★★ Ravenswood Sonoma Valley Belloni

★★★★ Ravenswood Sonoma Valley Cooke

★★★★ Ravenswood Sonoma Valley Old Hill Vineyard

★★★★ Ridge Vineyards Paso Robles

★★★★ Ridge Vineyards Paso Robles Dusi Ranch

★★★★ Ridge Vineyards Sonoma County Geyserville

★★★★ Ridge Vineyards Sonoma Valley Pagani Ranch

★★★★ J. Rochioli Vineyard & Winery Russian River Valley Sodini Vineyard

★★★★ Rosenblum Cellars Sonoma Valley Samsel Vineyard Maggie's Reserve

★★★★ Sky Vineyards Mount Veeder

★★★★ Steele Wines Clear Lake Catfish Vineyard

★★★★ Turley Wine Cellars Napa Valley Aida Vineyard

★★★★ Turley Wine Cellars Napa Valley Haynes Vineyard

★★★★ Turley Wine Cellars Napa Valley Moore Vineyard

★★★ Adelaida Cellars San Luis Obispo County

★★★ Benziger Family Winery Dry Creek Valley Mayo Family & Carreras Vineyard Imagery Series Zinfandel Port

★★★ Beringer Vineyards Napa Valley

★★★ Blockheadia Ringnosii Napa Valley

★★★ Boeger Winery El Dorado County Walker Vineyard

★★★ David Bruce Winery San Luis Obispo County

★★★ Burgess Cellars Napa Valley

★★★ Cakebread Cellars Howell Mountain

★★★ Castoro Cellars Paso Robles The Wine

★★★ Caviste Napa Valley

★★★ Caymus Vineyards Napa Valley

★★★ Chateau Souverain Dry Creek Valley

★★★ Cline Cellars Contra Costa County

★★★ Cline Cellars Contra Costa County Big Break

★★★ Cline Cellars Contra Costa County Bridgehead

★★★ Cline Cellars Contra Costa County Reserve

★★★ Clos du Bois Sonoma County

★★★ Clos Du Val Stags Leap District

★★★ Cosentino Winery Sonoma County The Zin

★★★ De Loach Vineyards Russian River Valley

★★★ De Loach Vineyards Russian River Valley Barbieri Ranch

★★★ De Loach Vineyards Russian River Valley Papera Ranch

★★★ De Loach Vineyards Russian River Valley Pelletti Ranch

★★★ Dry Creek Vineyard Dry Creek Valley

★★★ Dry Creek Vineyard Dry Creek Valley Old Vines

★★★ Dry Creek Vineyard Dry Creek Valley Reserve

★★★ Dry Creek Vineyard Sonoma County Old Vines

★★★ Eberle Winery Paso Robles Sauret Vineyard

★★★ Edmeades Winery Mendocino County Ciapusci Vineyard

★★★ Edmeades Winery Mendocino County Zeni Vineyard

★★★ Edmeades Winery North Coast

★★★ Edmunds St. John California

★★★ Edmunds St. John Mount Veeder

★★★ Elizabeth Vineyards Mendocino County

★★★ Elyse Vineyards Howell Mountain

★★★ Elyse Vineyards Napa Valley Coeur du Val

★★★ Elyse Vineyards Napa Valley Morisoli Vineyard

★★★ Fetzer Vineyards Mendocino County Reserve

★★★ Fife Vineyards Napa Valley

★★★ Fife Vineyards Napa Valley Les Vieilles Vignes

★★★ Franciscan Vineyards Napa Valley Oakville Estate

★★★ Franus Winery Mount Veeder Brandlin Vineyard

★★★ Green and Red Vineyard Napa Valley Chiles Mill Vineyard

★★★ Greenwood Ridge Vineyards Sonoma County

★★★ Greenwood Ridge Vineyards Sonoma County Scherrer Vineyards

★★★ Gundlach Bundschu Winery Sonoma Valley

★★★ Gundlach Bundschu Winery Sonoma Valley Rhinefarm Vineyards

★★★ Haywood Winery Sonoma Valley

★★★ Haywood Winery Sonoma Valley Los Chamizal Vineyard

★★★ Haywood Winery Sonoma Valley Rocky Terrace

★★★ Hidden Cellars Winery Mendocino County

★★★ Hidden Cellars Winery Mendocino County McAdams Vineyard

★★★ Hidden Cellars Winery Mendocino County Pacini Vineyard

★★★ Hop Kiln Winery Russian River Valley

★★★ Hop Kiln Winery Russian River Valley Primitivo

★★★ Kendall-Jackson Anderson Valley Ciapusci Vineyard

★★★ Kendall-Jackson Anderson Valley DuPratt Vineyard

★★★ Kendall-Jackson California Grand Reserve

★★★ Kendall-Jackson Mendocino County

★★★ Kendall-Jackson Mendocino County Zeni Vineyard

★★★ Kenwood Vineyards Sonoma Valley

★★★ Kenwood Vineyards Sonoma Valley Barricia Estate Vineyard

★★★ Kenwood Vineyards Sonoma Valley Jack London Vineyard

★★★ Limerick Lane Russian River Valley

★★★ Martinelli Winery Russian River Valley Jackass Vineyard

★★★ Mazzocco Vineyards Sonoma County

★★★ The Meeker Vineyard Dry Creek Valley Gold Leaf Cuvée

★★★ Moondance Sonoma Valley

★★★ Murrieta's Well Livermore Valley

★★★ Navarro Vineyards Mendocino County

★★★ Newlan Vineyards and Winery Napa Valley

★★★ Niebaum-Coppola Estate Winery Napa Valley Edizione Pennino

★★★ Norman Vineyards Paso Robles

★★★ Peachy Canyon Winery Paso Robles

★★★ Peachy Canyon Winery Paso Robles Especial

★★★ Peachy Canyon Winery Paso Robles Westside

★★★ Peachy Canyon Winery Paso Robles Dusi Ranch

★★★ Joseph Phelps Vineyards Alexander Valley

★★★ Preston Vineyards Dry Creek Valley

★★★ Renwood Winery Amador County

★★★ Renwood Winery Shenandoah Valley Grandpère Vineyard

★★★ Richardson Vineyards Sonoma Valley Nora's Vineyard

★★★ Ridge Vineyards Sonoma County

★★★ Rocking Horse Howell Mountain Lamborn Family Vineyard

★★★ Rosenblum Cellars Contra Costa County

★★★ Rosenblum Cellars Mount Veeder Brandlin Ranch

★★★ Rosenblum Cellars Napa Valley George Hendry Vineyard

★★★ Rosenblum Cellars Paso Robles Richard Sauret Vineyard

★★★ Rosenblum Cellars Sonoma County

★★★ Round Hill Winery Napa Valley

★★★ St. Francis Winery Sonoma Valley Old Vines

★★★ V. Sattui Winery Howell Mountain

★★★ V. Sattui Winery Napa Valley Suzanne's Vineyard

★★★ Saucelito Canyon Vineyard Arroyo Grande Valley

★★★ Sausal Winery Alexander Valley

★★★ Sausal Winery Alexander Valley Private Reserve

★★★ F. Scherrer Wines Alexander Valley Old Vines

★★★ Schuetz-Oles Napa Valley Korte Ranch

★★★ Shooting Star Clear Lake

★★★ Shooting Star Lake County

★★★ Steele Wines Mendocino County Pacini Vineyard

★★★ Storybook Mountain Vineyards Howell Mountain

★★★ Storybook Mountain Vineyards Napa Valley Reserve

★★★ Rodney Strong Vineyards Russian River Valley River West Vineyard Old Vines

★★★ Joseph Swan Vineyards Russian River Valley Frati Ranch

★★★ Joseph Swan Vineyards Russian River Valley V.H.S.R. Vineyard

★★★ The Terraces Napa Valley

★★★ Tobin James Paso Robles Solar Flair

★★★ Tobin James Paso Robles Sure Fire

★★★ Whaler Vineyard Mendocino County Flagship

★★★ White Oak Vineyards & Winery Alexander Valley Church Vineyard

★★★ White Oak Vineyards & Winery Dry Creek Valley Saunders Vineyard

★★★ White Oak Vineyards & Winery Sonoma County

★★★ White Oak Vineyards & Winery Sonoma County Limited Reserve

★★★ Wild Horse Winery Paso Robles Unbridled

★★ Alderbrook Winery Dry Creek Valley

★★ Amador Foothill Winery Fiddletown Eschen Vineyard

★★ Arciero Winery Paso Robles

★★ Bannister Winery Dry Creek Valley

★★ Belvedere Winery Dry Creek Valley

★★ Benziger Family Winery Sonoma County

★★ Black Sheep Vintners Sierra Foothills

★★ Boeger Winery El Dorado County

★★ Bogle Vineyards California

★★ Brandborg Cellars Napa Valley

★★ Brutocao Cellars Mendocino County

★★ Brutocao Cellars Mendocino County Hopland Ranch

★★ Buehler Vineyards Napa Valley

★★ Byington Winery & Vineyards Santa Clara County Calle Cielo Vineyard

★★ Davis Bynum Winery Russian River Valley

★★ Chateau Montelena Winery Napa Valley

★★ Chatom Vineyards Calaveras County

★★ Claudia Springs Winery Mendocino County

★★ H. Coturri and Sons Sonoma Valley Chauvet Vineyards

★★ Creston Vineyards & Winery Paso Robles

★★ Deer Park Winery Howell Mountain Beatty Ranch

★★ Deer Park Winery Howell Mountain Beatty Ranch Reserve

★★ DeMoor Winery Napa Valley

★★ Fenestra Winery Livermore Valley

★★ Fetzer Vineyards Mendocino County Barrel Select

★★ Fieldbrook Valley Winery Mendocino County Pacini Vineyard

★★ Foppiano Vineyards Dry Creek Valley

★★ Frey Winery Mendocino County

★★ Frick Winery Dry Creek Valley

★★ J. Fritz Cellars Dry Creek Valley 80-Year-Old Vines

★★ Frog's Leap Winery Napa Valley

★★ Gabrielli Winery Mendocino County

★★ Gabrielli Winery Mendocino County Reserve

★★ Granite Springs Winery El Dorado County

★★ Greenstone Winery Amador County

★★ Greenstone Winery Amador County Special Release

★★ Grgich Hills Cellar Sonoma County

★★ Guenoc Winery California

★★ Hallcrest Vineyards California Doe Mill Vineyard

★★ Homewood Winery Dry Creek Valley Quinn Vineyard

★★ Homewood Winery Sonoma Valley 110-Year-Old Vines

★★ Jackson Valley Vineyards Amador County

★★ Jory Winery California Old Barrister Cuvée 91

★★ Joya Winery Napa Valley

★★ Karly Wines Amador County

★★ Karly Wines Amador County Pokerville

★★ Karly Wines Amador County Sadie Upton Vineyard

★★ Kendall-Jackson California Vintner's Reserve

★★ Konrad Estate Mendocino County

★★ Konrad Estate Mendocino County Ricetti Vineyard

★★ Charles Krug Winery Napa Valley

★★ Kunde Estate Winery Sonoma Valley The Shaw Vineyard

★★ Lambert Bridge Dry Creek Valley

★★ Lamborn Family Vineyards Howell Mountain

★★ Lolonis Winery Mendocino County

★★ Lolonis Winery Mendocino County Private Reserve

★★ Lolonis Winery Mendocino County Lolonis Vineyard Private Reserve

★★ Lucas Winery

★★ Manzanita Alexander Valley

★★   Marietta Cellars Sonoma County

★★   Martin Brothers Winery Paso Robles Primitiva

★★   McDowell Valley Vineyards McDowell Valley

★★   The Meeker Vineyard Dry Creek Valley

★★   The Meeker Vineyard Sonoma County Sonoma Cuvée

★★   Meridian Vineyards Paso Robles

★★   Milano Winery Mendocino County Sanel Valley Vineyard

★★   Robert Mondavi-Woodbridge California

★★   Monterey Peninsula Winery Amador County Ferrero Ranch

★★   Montevina Wines Amador County

★★   Montevina Wines Amador County Reserve

★★   Morgan Winery Sonoma County

★★   Nevada City Winery Sierra Foothills

★★   Organic Wine Works Napa County

★★   Parducci Wine Cellars Mendocino County

★★   J. Pedroncelli Winery Dry Creek Valley

★★   Pellegrini Family Sonoma County Old Vines

★★   Peterson Winery Dry Creek Valley

★★   Rabbit Ridge Vineyards Dry Creek Valley

★★   Ravenswood North Coast Vintners Blend

★★   Ridge Vineyards Howell Mountain

★★   Rombauer Vineyards Napa Valley

★★   Santa Barbara Winery San Luis Obispo County Saucelito Canyon Vineyard

★★   Santa Barbara Winery Santa Ynez Valley Beaujour

★★   Santa Barbara Winery Santa Ynez Valley Lafond Vineyard

★★   Sea Ridge Winery Sonoma Coast Occidental Vineyard

★★   Sebastiani Vineyards Sonoma County Sonoma Series

★★   Seghesio Winery Alexander Valley Old Vine Reserve

★★   Seghesio Winery Sonoma County

★★   Shenandoah Vineyards Amador County

★★   Shenandoah Vineyards Amador County Special Reserve

★★   Signorello Vineyards Napa Valley Unfined Unfiltered

★★   Sobon Estate Fiddletown Lubenko

★★   Sobon Estate Shenandoah Valley

★★   Sobon Estate Sierra Foothills

★★   Storrs Winery California Beauregard Ranch Ben Lomond Mountain

★★   Story Vineyard Shenandoah Valley

★★   Stratford Winery California

★★   Summit Lake Vineyards & Winery Howell Mountain

★★   Sutter Home Winery California

★★   Joseph Swan Vineyards Sonoma Valley Stellwagen Vineyard

★★   Tobin James Paso Robles Big Shot

★★   Tobin James Paso Robles Big Time

★★   Tobin James Paso Robles Blue Moon Reserve

★★   Topolos Sonoma County

★★   Topolos Sonoma County Ultimo

★★   Topolos Sonoma County Rossi Ranch

★★   Trentadue Winery Sonoma County

★★   Tulocay Winery Napa Valley Casanova Vineyards

★★   T Vine Napa Valley

★★   Viano Vineyards Contra Costa County

★★   Villa Mt. Eden California Cellar Select

★★   Wellington Vineyards Sonoma Valley 100-Year-Old Vines

★★   Wellington Vineyards Sonoma Valley Casa Santinamaria

★★   Whaler Vineyard Mendocino County

★★   Wheeler Winery Dry Creek Valley

★★   Wildhurst Vineyards Clear Lake

★★   York Mountain Winery San Luis Obispo County

★   Alexander Valley Vineyards Alexander Valley Sin Zin

★   Amador Foothill Winery Shenandoah Valley Ferrero Vineyard

★   Amador Foothill Winery Shenandoah Valley Grandpere Vineyard

★ Black Mountain Alexander Valley Cramer Ridge

★ Dunnewood Vineyards Sonoma Valley Barrel Select

★ Heitz Wine Cellars Napa Valley Heitz Vineyard

★ Kunde Estate Winery Sonoma Valley Century Vines

★ Lake Sonoma Winery Dry Creek Valley

★ Lava Cap Winery El Dorado County

★ Mirassou Vineyards Central Coast Family Selection

★ Mirassou Vineyards Santa Clara Valley Harvest Reserve

★ Montevina Wines Amador County Brioso

★ Radanovich Vineyards & Winery Sierra Foothills Mariposa County

★ Sonoma Creek Winery Sonoma County

★ Voss Vineyards Alexander Valley

NR Alexander Valley Fruit & Trading Co. Dry Creek Valley

NR Baldinelli Vineyards Shenandoah Valley

NR Dion Sonoma Valley

NR Eagle Ridge Winery Amador County Grandpère Vineyard

NR Fellom Ranch Vineyards Santa Clara County

NR Fitzpatrick Winery Shenandoah Valley

NR Folie à Deux Winery Napa Valley

NR Emilio Guglielmo Winery Santa Clara Valley Private Reserve

NR La Jota Vineyard Co. Howell Mountain

NR Las Montanas Winery Sonoma Valley

NR Livermore Valley Cellars Livermore Valley

NR Louis M. Martini Winery Sonoma Valley

NR Martz Vineyards Mendocino County

NR Milat Vineyards Napa Valley

NR Napa Ridge Central Coast Coastal

NR Obester Winery Mendocino County

NR Ridge Vineyards Napa County York Creek

NR River Run Vintners

NR Roudon-Smith Winery San Luis Obispo County

NR Rustridge Vineyards & Winery Napa Valley

NR Rutherford Hill Winery Napa Valley

NR Santa Barbara Winery Santa Ynez Valley Late Harvest Essence

NR Santa Ynez Winery Paso Robles

NR Sierra Vista El Dorado County

NR Sonora Winery & Port Works Sonoma County

NR Soquel Vineyards Alexander Valley

NR Stevenot Winery Calaveras County

NR Sunrise Winery Santa Cruz Mountains Picchetti Ranch

NR Swanson Vineyards Napa Valley

NR Twin Hills Winery Paso Robles

NR Valley of the Moon Winery Sonoma Valley Reserve

NR Wermuth Winery Napa Valley

NR Wild Hog Hill Vineyard

NR Windemere Paso Robles

NR Woodside Vineyards

NR Young's Vineyard Amador County

NR Zayante Vineyards Santa Cruz Mountains

ZINFANDEL BLEND

★★ Shenandoah Vineyards Amador County Zingiovese

★★ Viansa Winery Sonoma Valley Prindelo

★ Solis Winery Santa Clara County Old Vines Seducente

NR Rustridge Vineyards & Winery Napa Valley Cabernet Zinfandel

NR Shenandoah Vineyards Sierra Foothills Zinfandel/Sirah

APPENDIX 4

CALIFORNIA VINTAGE CHART: 1933 TO 1994

1. RECENT VINTAGES

VINTAGE	OVERALL	CABERNET SAUVIGNON	CHARDONNAY	MERLOT	PINOT NOIR	ZINFANDEL
1994	★★★★	★★★★★	★★★★	★★★	★★★★	★★★★
1993	★★★	★★★	★★★★	★★★	★★★	★★★
1992	★★★★★	★★★★★	★★★★★	★★★★	★★★★	★★★★
1991	★★★★★	★★★★★	★★★★★	★★★★	★★★★	★★★★★
1990	★★★★★	★★★★★	★★★★★	★★★★	★★★★★	★★★★★
1989	★★	★★	★★★	★★★	★★	★★
1988	★★	★★	★★★★	★★	★★	★★
1987	★★★★	★★★★	★★★★	★★★★	★★	★★★★
1986	★★★★★	★★★★★	★★★★★	★★★	★★★★	★★★★
1985	★★★★★	★★★★★	★★★★★	★★★★	★★★★	★★★★★
1984	★★★★	★★★★★	★★★★	★★★	★★★★	★★★★
1983	★★	★★	★★	★★★★	★★	★★★
1982	★★	★★	★★	★★★	★★	★★★
1981	★★★	★★★	★★★★	★★★	★★★	★★
1980	★★	★★	★★★	★★	★★★	★★

KEY:

★★★★★ Outstanding   ★★★★ Excellent   ★★★ Good to Very Good   ★★ Average   ★ Poor

2. OLDER VINTAGES

1970s		1960s		1950s	
VINTAGE	OVERALL	VINTAGE	OVERALL	VINTAGE	OVERALL
1979	★★★★	1969	★★★★	1959	★★★
1978	★★★★★	1968	★★★★★	1958	★★★★★
1977	★★★	1967	★★	1957	★★
1976	★★	1966	★★★★	1956	★★★
1975	★★★★	1965	★★★	1955	★★★
1974	★★★★★	1964	★★★★	1954	★★★
1973	★★★	1963	★	1953	★
1972	★	1962	★	1952	★★★
1971	★	1961	★★	1951	★★★★★
1970	★★★★★	1960	★★★	1950	★★★★

1940s		1930s	
VINTAGE	OVERALL	VINTAGE	OVERALL
1949	★★★	1939	★★★
1948	★	1938	★★
1947	★★★	1937	★★★
1946	★★★★	1936	★★★★
1945	★★★★	1935	★★
1944	★★	1934	★★★
1943	★★	1933	★★★
1942	★★★		
1941	★★★★		
1940	★★★★		

KEY:

★★★★★ Outstanding   ★★★★ Excellent   ★★★ Good to Very Good   ★★ Average   ★ Poor

Appendix 5
Vineyard Directory

❖

Vineyard	Appellation	Owner	Varieties	Wineries Using Vineyard
Abbott's	Carneros	St. Clement Vineyards	Chardonnay	St. Clement Vineyards
Aida	Napa Valley	Aïda Brownell	Zinfandel, Petite Sirah	Turley Wine Cellars
Albert	Anderson Valley	Brutocao	Cabernet Sauvignon	Brutocao Cellars
Aldo's	Napa Valley	Aldo Biale	Zinfandel	Robert Biale Vineyards
Alegria	Russian River Valley	Bill Nachbaur	Syrah	Wellington Winery
Alexander's Crown	Alexander Valley	Klein Family Vintners	Cabernet Sauvignon	Rodney Strong Vineyards
Allen	Russian River Valley	Howard Allen	Chardonnay, Pinot Noir	Chateau Souverain, Bannister Winery, Williams & Selyem Winery, Gary Farrell Wines
Amaya Ridge	Santa Cruz Mountains	Don Curry	Pinot Noir	McHenry Vineyard
American Canyon Ranch	Napa Valley	Jaeger Vineyards	Chardonnay	Rutherford Hill Winery
Anderson Crest	Anderson Valley	Kendall-Jackson	Chardonnay, Pinot Noir	Edmeades Winery
Andre, Steven	Napa Valley	Robert Pecota Winery	Merlot	Robert Pecota Winery
Andrus	Rutherford	Gary & Nancy Andrus	Cabernet Sauvignon, Cabernet Franc, Merlot, Petit Verdot, Malbec	Pine Ridge Winery
Aquarius Ranch	Russian River Valley	McIlroy Family	Chardonnay	Gary Farrell Wines
Arata	Santa Cruz Mountains	Mrs. David Arata	Cabernet Sauvignon	Sunrise Winery
Arrastra	El Dorado County	Doug & Marian Laisz	Charbono, Merlot	Westwood Winery
Arrendell	Green Valley	Kendall-Jackson	Pinot Noir, Chardonnay	Hartford Court
Backus	Napa Valley	Marian W. Backus	Cabernet Sauvignon	Joseph Phelps Vineyards
Bancroft Ranch	Howell Mountain	Jim Bancroft	Merlot	Beringer Vineyard
Barbieri Ranch	Russian River Valley	De Loach Vineyards	Zinfandel	De Loach Vineyards
Baron Von Kees	Napa Valley	Walter Von Kees	Cabernet Sauvignon	Villa Helena
Barricia	Sonoma Valley	Pat Herron	Zinfandel	Kenwood Vineyards
Bartolucci	Napa Valley	Bartolucci Family	Cabernet Sauvignon	Star Hill Wines
Bates Ranch	Santa Cruz Mountains	John B. Bates	Cabernet Sauvignon, Cabernet Franc	Ahlgren Vineyard, Bargetto, Byington, Devlin, Santa Cruz Mountain Vineyards
Battuello	Napa Valley	Craig Battuello	Cabernet Sauvignon	Van Der Heyden Vineyard
Bay View (Toad Hall)	Carneros	J. & C. Komes	Chardonnay, Pinot Noir	Flora Springs Wine Co.
Beard	Napa Valley	Ed Beard	Pinot Noir	Fieldbrook Valley Winery
Beatty Ranch	Howell Mountain	M. Beatty	Zinfandel	Deer Park Winery
Beauregard Ranch	Ben Lomond Mountain	Jim Beauregard	Chardonnay, Zinfandel	Devlin, Hallcrest, Storrs Winery
Beckstoffer	Carneros	Andrew Beckstoffer	Pinot Noir, Chardonnay	Fremont Creek, Schug Winery
Beckstoffer IV	Rutherford	Andrew Beckstoffer	Cabernet Sauvignon, Chardonnay	Carneros, Fremont Creek Estate, Stag's Leap Wine Cellars, Guenoc Winery
Beckwith	San Luis Obispo	Bob Beckwith	Zinfandel	Roudon-Smith Winery

VINEYARD	APPELLATION	OWNER	VARIETIES	WINERIES USING VINEYARD
Bella Oaks	Napa Valley	Barney & Belle Rhodes	Cabernet	Heitz Wine Cellars
Bella Vista	Sonoma County	Bod & Jackie Hayes	Chardonnay	Stonegate Winery
Belle Terre	Alexander Valley	Henry & Ron Dick	Chardonnay	Chateau St. Jean
Belloni	Russian River Valley	Ricardo Belloni	Zinfandel	Ravenswood Winery
Beltane Ranch	Sonoma Valley	Alexa Wood	Chardonnay	Kenwood Vineyards
Besson	Santa Clara Valley	George Besson	Cabernet Sauvignon, Zinfandel	Ahlgren Vineyard
Beyers Ranch	Livermore Valley	Wente Bros.	Chardonnay	Sunrise Winery
Bien Nacido	Santa Maria Valley	Thornhill Ranches	Cabernet Sauvignon, Chardonnay, Merlot, Pinot Noir, Pinot Blanc, Syrah	Au Bon Climat, Brandborg Cellars, Caparone, Chansa Cellars, Gary Farrell, Fetzer Vineyards, Hitching Post, Lane Tanner, Longoria, Page Mill, Qupe, Steele Wines, Whitcraft
Bingham	Mount Veeder	Bingham Family	Cabernet Sauvignon	Domain Hill & Mayes
Black, Michael	Napa Valley	Michael Black	Merlot	Paul Hobbs Winery
Blackberry Ranch	Russian River Valley	Klein Family Vintners	Zinfandel	Windsor Vineyards
Blanches	Livermore Valley	Earl & Linda Ault	Cabernet Sauvignon, Chardonnay	Cedar Mountain Winery
Bliss	Anderson Valley	Brutocao Cellars	Chardonnay	Brutocao Cellars
Blue Rock	Alexander Valley	Ken Kahn	Cabernet Franc, Malbec, Petit Verdot	Benziger Family Winery
Bonny's	Napa Valley	Justin & Bonny Meyer	Cabernet Sauvignon	Silver Oak Wine Cellars
Bosche	Napa Valley	Bosche Family	Cabernet Sauvignon	Freemark Abbey Winery
Bradford Mountain	Dry Creek Valley	Bill Hambrecht	Cabernet Sauvignon, Zinfandel	Peterson Winery, Bannister Winery
Brandlin Ranch	Mount Veeder	Brandlin Family	Zinfandel	Rosenblum Cellars
Briarcrest	Alexander Valley	Clos du Bois	Cabernet Sauvignon	Clos du Bois
Burr	Dry Creek Valley	Robert Benevidas	Cabernet Sauvignon	J. Pedroncelli Winery
Bush	El Dorado County	Dick Bush	Riesling	Domaine de la Terre Rouge
Butow	Mendocino County	Butow Family	Syrah	Frey Winery
Buttonwood Farms	Santa Barbara County	Betty Williams	Sauvignon Blanc	The Ojai Vineyard
Calcaire	Alexander Valley	Clos du Bois	Chardonnay	Clos du Bois
Caldwell	Napa Valley	John Caldwell	Merlot	Jade Mountain
Camp Meeting Ridge	Sonoma Coast	Walt & Joan Flowers	Chardonnay, Pinot Noir	Kistler Vineyards
Carmel	Monterey County	In Vino Veritas	Chenin Blanc, Pinot Blanc	Daniel Gehrs
Carpy Ranch	Napa Valley	Chuck Carpy	Chardonnay	Freemark Abbey Winery
Carr	Mount Veeder	Norman Carr	Chardonnay	Patz & Hall Wine Co.
Carrari	Santa Barbara County	Joe Carrari	Muscat Canneli	John Kerr
Carsi	Napa Valley	V. Sattui Winery	Chardonnay	V. Sattui Winery
Casa Cassara	Santa Ynez Valley	Ben & Mary Cassara	Pinot Noir	Babcock Vineyards
Casa Santinamaria	Sonoma Valley	Bill Hawley	Zinfandel	Wellington Winery
Casanova	Napa Valley	Frank Casanova	Zinfandel	Tulocay Winery
Catacula	Napa Valley	Jay Heminway	Chardonnay	Green and Red Vineyard
Catfish	Clear Lake	Howard Strickler	Zinfandel	Steele Wines
Cedolini	Cienaga	Cedolini Family	Zinfandel	Cienaga Valley Vineyards & Winery
Chabot	Napa Valley	Suzanne Boqueraz	Cabernet Sauvignon	Beringer Vineyard
Chalk Hill	Chalk Hill	Klein Family Vintners	Chardonnay	Rodney Strong Vineyards
Chambers, Richard	Stags Leap District	Richard Chambers	Cabernet Sauvignon, Merlot, Cabernet Franc	S. Anderson Vineyard
Chapel	Santa Barbara County	John C. Cushman	Chardonnay, Syrah	York Mountain, Zaca Mesa Winery
Chappell	Napa Valley	Russ Oles	Chardonnay	Schuetz-Oles
Chappellet	Napa Valley	Chappellet	Cabernet Sauvignon	Moondance Cellars
Charles Wetmore	Livermore Valley	Wente Bros.	Cabernet Sauvignon	Wente Bros. Estate Winery
Charlotte's Home	Northern Sonoma	Rodney Strong Vineyards	Sauvignon Blanc	Rodney Strong Vineyards

VINEYARD	APPELLATION	OWNER	VARIETIES	WINERIES USING VINEYARD
Chateau Margarite	Napa	Mike Loftus & Margarite Davit	Cabernet Sauvignon, Cabernet Franc, Merlot, Malbec, Petit Verdot	Vigil Vineyard
Cherry Block	Sonoma Valley	Sebastiani Vineyards	Cabernet Sauvignon	Sebastiani Vineyards
Chiles Mill	Napa Valley	Jay Heminway	Zinfandel	Green and Red Vineyard
Christie	Santa Cruz Mountains	Christie Family	Chardonnay	Storrs Winery
Ciapusci	Anderson Valley	Nick Ciapusci Family	Zinfandel	Edmeades Winery
Clarkspring	Sierra Foothills	Frank Alviso	Orange Muscat	Concannon Vineyard
Cliff	Napa Valley	Ron Cliff	Cabernet Sauvignon	Tulocay Winery
Clockspring	Amador County	N/A	Zinfandel, Chardonnay, Sauvignon Blanc	Orleans Hill
Coastlands	Sonoma Coast	David & Diane Cobb	Pinot Noir	Williams & Selyem Winery
Cobblestone	Arroyo Seco	Sal Levine	Pinot Blanc	Monterey Cellars Monterey Peninsula
Collins	Russian River Valley	Collins Family	Zinfandel	Gary Farrell Wines
Coloma Canyon	El Dorado County	Sid Davis	Cabernet Sauvignon	Fitzpatrick Winery
Concannon, James	Livermore Valley	Concannon Vineyard	Sauvignon Blanc	Concannon Vineyard
Cooke	Sonoma Valley	Charles Cooke	Zinfandel	Ravenswood Winery
Corley Family	Napa Valley	Corley Family	Cabernet Sauvignon, Chardonnay, Merlot, Pinot Noir	Monticello Cellars
Côtes du Rosa	Russian River Valley	Frank Mancini	Carignane	Joseph Swan Vineyards
Covington	El Dorado County	Woody Covington	Cabernet Sauvignon	Hallcrest Vineyards
Cowan, Robert	Amador County	Robert Cowan	Zinfandel	Fitzpatrick Winery
Cox	Santa Cruz Mountains	Ralph Cox	Pinot Noir	Roudon-Smith Winery
Cox	Mendocino County	Jack Cox	Chardonnay	Konrad Estate
Crane Creek	Dry Creek Valley	Lambert Bridge	Cabernet Sauvignon	Lambert Bridge
Crane Ridge	Livermore Valley	Wente Bros.	Merlot	Wente Bros. Estate Winery
Creek Side	Russian River Valley	Porter Creek	Pinot Noir	Porter Creek Vineyards
Creekside	Russian River Valley	Chateau de Baun	Chardonnay	Chateau de Baun
Crossroads Ranch	Oakville	Komes & Garvey Families	Chardonnay, Sauvignon Blanc, Merlot	Flora Springs Wine Co.
Cuneo/Saini	Dry Creek Valley	Saini Farms Inc.	Zinfandel	Mazzocco Vineyards
Cutrer	Sonoma Coast	Sonoma-Cutrer Vineyards	Chardonnay	Sonoma-Cutrer Vineyards
Cypress Ranch	Napa Valley	J.W. Komes	Sauvignon Blanc, Cabernet Sauvignon, Zinfandel	Flora Springs Wine Co.
Damaris	Alexander Valley	Landmark Vineyards	Chardonnay	Landmark Vineyards
David, Narsai	Napa Valley	Narsai David	Merlot	Harbor Winery
De Cascabel	El Dorado County	John De Cascabel	Merlot, Cabernet Sauvignon	Hallcrest Vineyards
DeCelles	Napa Valley	Joe DeCelles	Chardonnay	Tulocay Winery
Dennison	Anderson Valley	Dennison Brothers	Chardonnay, Riesling, Pinot Noir	Briceland Vineyards, Edmeades Winery, Steele Wines
Diamond Mountain	Napa Valley	Sterling Vineyards	Cabernet Franc, Cabernet Sauvignon, Chardonnay, Merlot	Sterling Vineyards
Diamond T Estate	Monterey County	Robert Talbott Vineyards	Chardonnay	Robert Talbott Vineyards
Dicicco Terrace	Santa Cruz County	Doug & Gene Dicicco	Gewürztraminer	Roudon-Smith Winery
Dickerson	Napa Valley	William Dickerson	Zinfandel	Ravenswood Winery
Dinner, Richard	Sonoma Mountain	Richard Dinner	Chardonnay	Paul Hobbs Winery
Dirk	Santa Cruz Mountains	Dirk Reed	Chardonnay	Storrs Winery
Doe Mill	Placer County	Paul Peterson	Zinfandel, Syrah	Hallcrest Vineyards
Dollarhide Ranch	Napa Valley	St. Supéry Vineyards	Cabernet Sauvignon, Cabernet Franc, Merlot	St. Supéry Vineyards & Winery
Don Miguel	Sonoma County Green Valley	Torres Family	Chardonnay, Pinot Noir	Marimar Torres Estate
DuPratt	Anderson Valley	Tom Krig	Chardonnay, Pinot Noir, Zinfandel	Greenwood Ridge Vineyards, Steele Wines

VINEYARD	APPELLATION	OWNER	VARIETIES	WINERIES USING VINEYARD
Dunn	Howell Mountain	Randy Dunn	Petite Sirah	Deer Park Winery, Dunn Vineyards
Durell	Carneros	Ed Durell	Syrah, Chardonnay, Pinot Noir	Edmunds St. John, Steele Wines, Kistler Vineyards
Dusi Ranch	Paso Robles	Benito Dusi	Zinfandel	Peachy Canyon Winery
Dutton Ranch	Russian River Valley	Warren Dutton	Chardonnay	Kistler Vineyards
Dyer's Farm	Napa Valley	Don Dyer	Zinfandel, Refosco	Robert Biale Vineyards
Eisele	Napa Valley	Araujo Estate Wines	Cabernet Sauvignon, Sauvignon Blanc	Araujo Estate Wines
Eisele, V. & L.	Napa Valley	V. & L. Eisele	Cabernet Sauvignon	Quail Ridge Cellars, Page Mill Winery
11 Oaks Ranch	Santa Ynez Valley	Paul Albrecht	Sauvignon Blanc, Sangiovese	Babcock Vineyards
Eschen	Fiddletown	Chester Eschen	Zinfandel	Amador Foothill Winery, Santino Wines
Fagan Creek	Napa Valley	Elkhorn Peak Cellars	Chardonnay, Pinot Noir	Elkhorn Peak Cellars
Fay	Stags Leap District	Winiarski Family	Cabernet Sauvignon	Stag's Leap Wine Cellars
Fay	Alexander Valley	John Fay	Cabernet Sauvignon	J. Pedroncelli Winery
Ferrero Ranch	Shenendoah Valley	John Ferrero	Zinfandel	Amador Foothill Winery, Monterey Peninsula Winery
Ferrington	Anderson Valley	Richard Ferrington	Sauvignon Blanc, Pinot Noir	Greenwood Ridge Vineyards, Williams & Selyem Winery
Figoni Ranch	Livermore Valley	Wente Bros.	Sauvignon Blanc	Ivan Tamas
Fralich	Paso Robles	Harry Fralich	Syrah, Viognier	Eberle Winery
Frati Ranch	Russian River Valley	Angelo Frati	Zinfandel	Joseph Swan Vineyards
French Camp	Paso Robles	Hank Ashby	Chardonnay, Sauvignon Blanc	Pesenti Winery, Page Mill Winery
Frisinger	Napa Valley	Jim Frisinger	Chardonnay	Napa Ridge
Gambogi Ranch	Russian River Valley	De Loach Vineyards	Zinfandel	De Loach Vineyards
Garbett, Elizabeth	Santa Clara County	Elizabeth Garbett	Chardonnay	Page Mill Winery
Garvey Family	Rutherford	Pat & Julie Garvey	Cabernet Sauvignon	Rocking Horse, Flora Springs Wine Co.
Gauer Ranch	Alexander Valley	Kendall-Jackson Winery	Chardonnay	Peter Michael Winery, Marcassin
Gennie's	Carneros	Pat & Julie Garvey	Chardonnay	Flora Springs Wine Co.
Geyserville	Alexander Valley	Leo & Evelyn Trentadue	Zinfandel, Carignane, Petite Sirah	Ridge Vineyards
Giles	Sonoma Valley	Gina Giles	Cabernet Franc	Richardson Vineyards
God Speed	Mount Veeder	Larry Stricker	Cabernet Sauvignon, Chardonnay	Domain Hill & Mayes
Graham	Livermore Valley	Bob Graham	Zinfandel	Livermore Valley Cellars
Grandpère	Shenandoah Valley	Scott Harvey	Zinfandel	Santino Wines
Gravelly Meadow	Napa Valley	Diamond Creek Vineyards	Cabernet Sauvignon	Diamond Creek Vineyards
Greer	Temecula	Bruce & Gail Greer	Chardonnay, Muscat	Baily Vineyard & Winery
Gregory	Carneros	Dick & Joey Gregory	Cabernet Sauvignon	Ravenswood Winery
Griffin, M.	Russian River Valley	Marty Griffin	Cabernet Sauvignon, Chardonnay	Hop Kiln Winery
Hafner	Alexander Valley	Hafner Vineyard	Chardonnay, Cabernet Sauvignon	Hafner
Hambrecht	Dry Creek Valley	Bill Hambrecht	Cabernet Sauvignon	Peterson Winery
Harris	Sonoma	Rosenblum Cellars	Cabernet Sauvignon	Audubon Cellars
Hartwell	Stags Leap District	Bob Hartwell	Cabernet Sauvignon	Hartwell Vineyards
Hayes Ranch	Livermore Valley	Wente Bros.	Chardonnay	Ivan Tamas
Hayne	Napa Valley	Hayne Family	Zinfandel, Petite Sirah	Turley Wine Cellars
Haynes	Napa Valley	Duncan Haynes	Pinot Noir	Tulocay Winery, Westwood Winery
HB	Napa Valley	Peju Province	Cabernet Sauvignon, Chardonnay	Peju Province Winery
Hedin	Russian River Valley	Roger Hedin	Cabernet Sauvignon	Davis Bynum Winery
Hendry, George	Napa Valley	George Hendry	Zinfandel, Cabernet Sauvignon	Rosenblum Cellars
Herbert	El Dorado County	Beverly Herbert	Sauvignon Blanc, Zinfandel	Sierra Vista
Herman Wente	Livermore Valley	Wente Bros.	Chardonnay	Wente Bros. Estate Winery

VINEYARD	APPELLATION	OWNER	VARIETIES	WINERIES USING VINEYARD
Hidden Valley	San Benito	Stewart O'Brien	Chardonnay	River Run Vintners
Hillside	Russian River Valley	Porter Creek	Pinot Noir	Porter Creek Vineyards
Hirsch	Sonoma Coast	David Hirsch	Pinot Noir	Sea Ridge Winery
Horne	Sonoma Valley	R. & B. Horne	Cabernet Sauvignon	Richardson Vineyards
Howell Mountain Ranch	Howell Mountain	Bernard Pradel Cellars	Cabernet Sauvignon	Bernard Pradel Cellars
Hudson	Carneros	Lee Hudson	Syrah, Chardonnay, Cabernet Franc, Merlot, Pinot Noir	Havens Wine Cellars, Jade Mountain, Marcassin
Hyde	Carneros	Larry & Richard Hyde	Cabernet Sauvignon, Pinot Noir, Sauvignon Blanc	Paul Hobbs Winery, Selene Wines
Inglewood	Napa Valley	Jaeger Vineyards	Merlot	Jaeger Inglewood Vineyard
J.K.	Santa Barbara County	Joe Kalina	Chardonnay, Merlot, Syrah	John Kerr
Jacoboni	Carneros	J & D Jacoboni	Pinot Noir	Crane Canyon Cellars
Jaeger	Napa Valley	Jaeger Vineyards	Chardonnay	Rutherford Hill Winery
Jennifer's	Russian River Valley	Jackson Hartford Family	Zinfandel	Hartford Court
Jensen	Mt. Harlan	Calera Wine Co.	Pinot Noir	Calera Wine Co.
Joullian Estate	Carmel Valley	Joullian Vineyard Ltd.	Cabernet Sauvignon, Sauvignon Blanc	Joullian Vineyards
Julia's	Santa Maria Valley	Barbara Banke	Pinot Noir	Cambria Winery & Vineyard
Juliana	Napa Valley	Tucker Catlin	Sauvignon Blanc	N/A
Kalthoff	Livermore Valley	Steve Kalthoff	Cabernet Sauvignon	Thomas Coyne Winery
Kara's	Napa Valley	Robert Pecota	Cabernet Sauvignon	Robert Pecota Winery
Katherine's	Santa Maria Valley	Barbara Banke	Chardonnay	Cambria Winery & Vineyard
Kinneybrook	Sonoma Valley	Kunde Family	Chardonnay	Kunde Estate Winery
Knights Valley	Knights Valley	Wine World Estates	Sauvignon Blanc, Cabernet Franc, Merlot, Cabernet Sauvignon, Sémillon	Beringer Vineyard
Knollside	Napa Valley	Pine Ridge Winery	Chardonnay	Pine Ridge Winery
Komes Ranch	Rutherford	J.W. Komes	Cabernet Sauvignon, Merlot, Petit Verdot, Cabernet Franc, Sangiovese	Flora Springs Wine Co.
Korte Ranch	Napa Valley	Hal Pagendarm	Zinfandel	Schuetz Oles
Kunde Estate	Sonoma Valley	Kunde Family	Merlot, Cabernet Franc	Kunde Estate Wines
La Cuesta	Santa Ynez Valley	Carey Cellars	Cabernet Sauvignon, Merlot	Carey Cellars, Cache Cellars
La Dolce De Vita	Napa Valley	Rich De Vita	Cabernet Sauvignon	Pope Valley Cellars
La Petite Étoile	Russian River Valley	Chateau St. Jean	Sauvignon Blanc	Chateau St. Jean
La Ribera	Mendocino County	H.A. Oswald Family	Sauvignon Blanc, Cabernet Sauvignon, Chenin Blanc	Husch Vineyards
La Rocha	Butte County	Phil La Rocha	Zinfandel	Hallcrest Vineyards
Ladi's	Sonoma County	Ladi Danielik	Cabernet Sauvignon, Merlot	Gary Farrell Wines
Lafond	Santa Ynez Valley	Pierre Lafond	Chardonnay, Pinot Noir, Zinfandel, Sauvignon Blanc	Santa Barbara Winery
Laguna Ridge	Russian River Valley	Byron Craighead	Zinfandel	Joseph Swan Vineyards
Lake	Napa Valley	Diamond Creek Vineyards	Cabernet Sauvignon	Diamond Creek Vineyards
Lamb	Napa Valley	Lamb Family	Cabernet Sauvignon	Fisher Vineyards
Lamborn	Howell Mountain	Mike Lamborn	Zinfandel	Rocking Horse
Laureles	Russian River Valley	Davis Bynum Winery	Merlot	Davis Bynum Winery
LeBaron Estate	Russian River Valley	Klein Family Vintners	Riesling	Windsor Vineyards
Leonardini	St. Helena	Leonardini Family	Cabernet Sauvignon, Merlot, Zinfandel	Whitehall Lane Winery
Les Pavot	Knights Valley	Peter Michael Winery	Cabernet Sauvignon	Peter Michael Winery
Les Pierres	Sonoma Coast	Sonoma-Cutrer Vineyards	Chardonnay	Sonoma-Cutrer Vineyards
Linsteadt	Amador County	Don Linsteadt	Barbera	Santino Wines
Liparita	Howell Mountain	Robert Burrows	Cabernet Sauvignon	Paul Hobbs Winery
Lolonis	Mendocino County	Lolonis Family	Chardonnay	Steele Wines
London Ranch, Jack	Sonoma Valley	Milo Shepard	Cabernet Sauvignon, Zinfandel, Pinot Noir, Merlot	Kenwood Vineyards

VINEYARD	APPELLATION	OWNER	VARIETIES	WINERIES USING VINEYARD
Lorenzo	Sonoma Coast	N/A	Chardonnay	Marcassin
Los Chamizal	Sonoma Valley	Peter Haywood	Zinfandel	Haywood Winery
Los Vinedos del Rio	Russian River Valley	Louis M. Martini Winery	Merlot	Louis M. Martini Winery
Lucas Vineyard	Santa Barbara County	Louis Lucas	Sauvignon Blanc, Chenin Blanc	Austin Cellars
Lytton Springs	Dry Creek Valley	Ridge Vineyards	Zinfandel, Petite Sirah, Grenache	Ridge Vineyards
MacGregor	Edna Valley	Andy MacGregor	Chardonnay, Pinot Noir	Mount Eden Vineyards, Morgan Winery, Piedra Creek Winery, Claiborne & Churchill
Madonna	Carneros	Buck Bartolucci	Chardonnay, Pinot Noir	Mont St. John Cellars
Magoon, Genevieve	Guenoc Valley	Guenoc Winery	Chardonnay	Guenoc Winery
Mannstand	Santa Clara County	Mannstand Family	Riesling	Hallcrest Vineyards
Marlstone	Alexander Valley	Clos du Bois	Cabernet Sauvignon, Merlot, Malbec, Petit Verdot	Clos du Bois
Martha's	Napa Valley	Tom & Martha May	Cabernet Sauvignon	Heitz Wine Cellars
Martinelli	Russian River Valley	Lee Martinelli	Gewürztraminer	Z. Moore Winery
Massara	Sonoma Valley	Sal Massara	Merlot	Kenwood Vineyards
Massaro	Carneros	Ray & Shirley Massaro	Pinot Noir	McHenry Vineyard
Matteson	Santa Cruz Mountains	Mike Matteson	Chardonnay, Pinot Noir	Santa Cruz Mountain Vineyard
Mauritson	Alexander Valley	Tom Mauritson	Cabernet Sauvignon, Merlot	Braren Pauli
Maya	Napa Valley	Dalla Valle Vineyards	Cabernet Sauvignon	Dalla Valle Vineyards
Mayers	Santa Cruz Mountains	Ed & Barbara Mayers	Chardonnay	Ahlgren Vineyard
McCrea	Sonoma Mountain	Kistler Vineyards	Chardonnay	Kistler Vineyards
Meeker Ranch, Martin	Paso Robles	Martin Meeker	Merlot	Roudon-Smith Winery
Melim	Alexander Valley	Clifford Melim	Cabernet Sauvignon, Cabernet Franc, Merlot, Chardonnay	Melim Vineyard & Winery
Meredith	Trinity County	Randall Meredith	Merlot	Fieldbrook Valley Winery
Meyley	Santa Cruz Mountains	Redtree Properties	Chardonnay	David Bruce Winery, Hallcrest Vineyards, Storrs Winery
Miller	Cienaga	Miller Family	Zinfandel	Cienaga Valley Vineyards & Winery
Miller, S.	Santa Cruz Mountains	S. Miller	Chardonnay	Santa Cruz Mountain Vineyard
Mills	Mt. Harlan	Calera Wine Co.	Pinot Noir	Calera Wine Co.
Mitchell, Holbrook	Napa Valley	Holbrook Mitchell	Cabernet Sauvignon	Rosenblum Cellars
Moffett	Rutherford Bench	John & Diane Livingston	Cabernet Sauvignon, Merlot, Cabernet Franc	Livingston Wines
Monmartre	Santa Cruz Mountains	Mariani Vineyards	Chardonnay, Zinfandel	Mariani Vineyards
Monte Bello	Santa Cruz Mountains	Ridge Vineyards Inc.	Cabernet Sauvignon, Merlot, Petit Verdot	Ridge Vineyards
Monte Rosso	Sonoma Valley	Louis M. Martini Winery	Cabernet Sauvignon, Zinfandel	Louis M. Martini Winery, Ravenswood Winery
Moore	Napa Valley	N/A	Zinfandel	Turley Wine Cellars
Morisoli	Rutherford	Gary Morisoli	Cabernet Sauvignon, Zinfandel	Whitehall Lane Winery, Elyse Vineyards
Mother's	Temecula	Baily Vineyards & Winery	Riesling	Baily Vineyard & Winery
Mountanos	Redwood Valley	Mark Mountanos	Cabernet Sauvignon	River Run Vintners
Mourhardt Ridge	Sonoma County	Phil Mourhardt	Cabernet Sauvignon	Wellington Winery
Mt. Carmel	Santa Ynez Valley	Carmelite Convent	Chardonnay, Pinot Noir	Babcock Vineyards
Murphy Ranch	Alexander Valley	Murphy Ranch	Merlot, Cabernet Sauvignon, Chardonnay	Murphy-Goode Estate Winery, Windsor Vineyards
Nichelini	Napa Valley	Joseph A. Nichelini	Zinfandel, Cabernet Sauvignon	Boeger Winery
Nora's	Sonoma Valley	Jack Baritau	Zinfandel	Richardson Vineyards

VINEYARD	APPELLATION	OWNER	VARIETIES	WINERIES USING VINEYARD
Norman	Paso Robles	Art Norman	Barbera	Eberle Winery
Norse	Dry Creek Valley	Boisset Wines USA	Cabernet Sauvignon	Wheeler Winery
Oak Meadow	Russian River Valley	Vino Farms	Riesling	Arrowood Vineyards & Winery
Oakville Ranch	Oakville	Miner Family	Chardonnay, Cabernet Sauvignon	Lewis Cellars
Obermeyer	Paso Robles	John Obermeyer	Zinfandel	Hitching Post/Hartley Ostini
Occidental	Sonoma Coast	Rober von Weidlich	Zinfandel, Merlot	Sea Ridge Winery
Old Hill	Sonoma Valley	Otto Teller	Zinfandel	Ravenswood Winery
Old Vines River West	Russian River Valley	Syar Industries	Zinfandel	Rodney Strong Vineyards
Olive Grove	Napa Valley	Van Aspern	Cabernet Sauvignon	Round Hill Winery
Olive Hill	Sonoma Valley	Bruce Cohn	Cabernet Sauvignon	B.R. Cohn Winery
Oliver	El Dorado County	Gene Oliver	Muscat Canelli	Lava Cap Winery
Olivet Lane	Russian River Valley	Robert Pellegrini	Pinot Noir	Williams & Selyem Winery, Fetzer Vineyards, Whitcraft Winery
P. & J.	Napa Valley	Pat & Julie Garvey	Chardonnay, Sauvignon Blanc	Flora Springs Wine Co.
Pacini	Mendocino County	Larry Pacini	Zinfandel	Fieldbrook Valley Winery, Steele Wines
Pagani Ranch	Sonoma Valley	Pagani Family	Zinfandel, Mataro, Petite Sirah	Ridge Vineyards
Palomares	North Central	Chouinard	Chardonnay	Chouinard Vineyards
Papera Ranch	Russian River Valley	De Loach Vineyards	Zinfandel	De Loach Vineyards
Paragon	Edna Valley	Niven Family	Sémillon	Carmenet Vineyard
Passalacqua	Sonoma County	EMK Passalacqua	Zinfandel	Sonora Winery & Port Works
Peirano Estate	Lodi	Lance & Cornelia Randolph	Zinfandel	Peirano Estate Vineyards
Pelletti Ranch	Russian River Valley	De Loach Vineyards	Zinfandel	De Loach Vineyards
Picchetti Ranch	Santa Cruz Mountains	Midpeninsula Regional Open Space District	Zinfandel	Sunrise Winery
Pickberry	Sonoma Mountain	Chris & Lorna Strotz	Cabernet Sauvignon, Cabernet Franc, Merlot	Ravenswood Winery
Picnic Hill	Shenandoah Valley	Bruce & Jan Tichenor	Zinfandel	Story Winery
Polson	Dry Creek Valley	Bob Polson	Zinfandel	Lake Sonoma Winery
Poplar Ranch	Russian River Valley	Kent Richik	Chardonnay	White Oak Vineyards & Winery
Porter Bass	Russian River Valley	Sue & Dirk Bass	Zinfandel	Wild Hog Vineryard
Posert & Sons	Napa Valley	Harvey Posert	Cabernet Sauvignon	Robert Biale Vineyards
Potter	Shenendoah Valley	Don Potter	Zinfandel	Amador Foothill Winery
Preston Ranch	Russian River Valley	Vino Farms	Chardonnay	Windsor Vineyards
Preston	Rutherford	Dick Preston	Cabernet Sauvignon	V. Sattui Winery
Quail Haven	Mt. Veeder	Bing & Ronnie Bingham	Chardonnay	Thomas-Hsi
Quail Hill	Russian River Valley	Daniel Moore	Chardonnay, Pinot Noir	Lynmar
Quartz Hill	El Dorado County	Bob Scharpf	Merlot	Thomas Coyne Winery
R.W.L.	Rutherford	Robert Long	Cabernet Sauvignon	David Arthur Vineyards
Rancho Chimiles	Napa Valley	Terry Wilson	Sauvignon Blanc	Stag's Leap Wine Cellars
Rancho Vinedo	Santa Maria Valley	Edwin Newhall Woods Family	Pinot Noir	Au Bon Climat
Randle Hill	Mendocino County	Yorkville Cellars	Sauvignon Blanc	Yorkville Cellars
Random Ridge	Mt. Veeder	Bill Hawley	Cabernet Sauvignon, Cabernet Franc	Wellington Winery
Rattle Snake Hill	Napa Valley	Barnett Vineyards	Cabernet	Barnett Vineyards
Rattlesnake Acres	Napa Valley	Roy Enderlin	Petite Sirah	Schuetz-Oles
RCF	Napa Valley	Fisher Vineyards	Merlot	Fisher Vineyards
Red Rock Terrace	Napa Valley	Diamond Creek Vineyards	Cabernet Sauvignon	Diamond Creek Vineyards
Redwood Hill	Santa Cruz Mountains	Joanne Barber	Chardonnay	Byington Winery & Vineyards
Reed	Mt. Harlan	Calera Wine Co.	Pinot Noir	Calera Wine Co.

VINEYARD	APPELLATION	OWNER	VARIETIES	WINERIES USING VINEYARD
Reeves	El Dorado County	Enid MacCready Reeves	Zinfandel	Sierra Vista
Remick Ridge	Sonoma Valley	Thomas B. Smothers	Chardonnay, Merlot, Cabernet Sauvignon	Smothers Brothers Wines
Renata's	Mt. Veeder	Renata Wright	Pinot Noir	Star Hill Wines
Rhinefarm	Sonoma Valley	Jim Bundschu	Cabernet Sauvignon, Cabernet Franc, Gewürztraminer, Merlot, Pinot Noir, Zinfandel	Gundlach Bundschu Winery
Rio San Lucas	Monterey County	Naraghi Farms	Cabernet Franc	Concannon Vineyard
Ritchie	El Dorado County	George Ritchie	Barbera	Hallcrest Vineyards
Riva Ranch	Arroyo Seco	Wente Bros.	Chardonnay	Wente Bros. Estate Winery
River East	Russian River Valley	Klein Family Vintners	Pinot Noir	Rodney Strong Vineyards
River West Estate	Russian River Valley	Klein Family Vintners	Cabernet Sauvignon, Merlot	Windsor Vineyards
Robinson	Stags Leap District	Norm & Helen Robinson	Cabernet Sauvignon	Rocking Horse, Cronin Vineyards
RobinWood	Napa Valley	Bob Kreider	Zinfandel	Round Hill Winery
Rochioli	Russian River Valley	Joe Rochioli	Zinfandel, Sauvignon Blanc, Pinot Noir	Bannister Winery, Gary Farrell Wines, Williams & Selyem Winery, Solitude
Roederer Estate	Anderson Valley	Roederer Estate	Pinot Noir	Greenwood Ridge Vineyards
Rogers	Carneros	Bob & Miriel Rogers	Pinot Noir	Westwood Winery
Rogers	Dry Creek Valley	Harry & Ann Rogers	Zinfandel	J. Fritz Cellars
Rossi Ranch	Sonoma County	Val Rossi	Zinfandel	Topolos at Russian River Vineyards
Russian River Ranches	Sonoma Coast	Sonoma-Cutrer Vineyards	Chardonnay	Sonoma-Cutrer Vineyards
St. Andrew's	Napa Valley	Clos Du Val	Chardonnay	St. Andrew's Winery
St. Charles	Santa Cruz Mountains	Hong Kong Metro Realty	Pinot Blanc, Pinot Noir, Sémillon	Byington Winery & Vineyards
San Bernabe	Monterey County	Delicato Vineyards	Chardonnay	Chouinard Vineyards
San Ysidro	San Ysidro	San Ysidro Corp.	Merlot	Storrs Winery
Sanctuary Estate	Arroyo Seco	Jekel Vineyards	Cabernet Sauvignon, Merlot	Jekel Vineyards
Sanel Valley	Mendocino County	Frank & Jim Milone	Chardonnay, Zinfandel, Cabernet Sauvignon	Milano Winery
Sanford & Benedict	Santa Ynez Valley	Robert Atkins & Richard Sanford	Pinot Noir	Babcock Vineyards, Au Bon Climat, Lane Tanner, Foxen Vineyard, Post, Sanford Winery
Sangiacomo	Carneros	Angelo Sangiacomo	Chardonnay, Merlot, Pinot Noir, Sauvignon Blanc	Cale Cellars, Carmenet, Joseph Phelps Vineyards, Solitude Wines, Gundlach Bundschu Winery, Chateau Souverain, Chappell Family, Ravenswood, Richardson, Steele Wines, Sonoma Creek Winery
Sansel	Sonoma	William Samsel	Zinfandel	Rosenblum Cellars
Santa Gertrude's	Temecula	Baily Vineyards & Winery	Cabernet Sauvignon	Baily Vineyard & Winery
Saralee's	Russian River Valley	Rich & Saralee Kunde	Pinot Blanc, Viognier	Arrowood Vineyards & Winery
Saratoga	Santa Clara	Harry Bellicitti	Zinfandel	Fellom Ranch Vineyards
Saratoga	Santa Cruz Mountains	Tom Mudd	Chardonnay	Cinnabar Vineyards & Winery
Saunders	Dry Creek Valley	Roy Saunders	Zinfandel	White Oak Vineyards & Winery
Sauret, Richard	Paso Robles	Richard Sauret	Zinfandel	Eberle Winery, Au Bon Climat, Rosenblum
Saviez	Napa Valley	Paul Saviez	French Colombard	Carmenet Vineyard
Scharf Family	Dry Creek Valley	Stephen Scharf	Cabernet Sauvignon	The Meeker Vineyard
Scherrer	Alexander Valley	Ed Scherrer	Zinfandel	Greenwood Ridge Vineyards
Selleck	Mt. Harlan	Calera Wine Co.	Pinot Noir	Calera Wine Co.
Seven Arches	Alexander Valley	Kernit Rankin	Cabernet Sauvignon	Dunnewood Vineyards
Shandon Valley	Paso Robles	Bill Danley	Riesling	Pesenti Winery
Shell Creek	Paso Robles	Sinton	Gamay	Castoro Cellars

VINEYARD	APPELLATION	OWNER	VARIETIES	WINERIES USING VINEYARD
Shiloh Hill	Russian River Valley	Howard Bracker	Syrah	Alderbrook Winery
Shone Farm	Russian River Valley	Santa Rosa Junior College	Sauvignon Blanc	Davis Bynum Winery
Shypoke	Napa Valley	Ginny & Gary Heitz	Charbono	Bayview Cellars
Sierra Madre	Santa Barbara County	Sierra Madre Vineyard Inc.	Pinot Noir, Chardonnay, Syrah	York Mountain, Zaca Mesa Winery
Silverado Summers	Napa Valley	Herb Haufman	Chardonnay	Graeser Winery
Skinner	Sonoma County	Dr. Lee Skinner	Pinot Blanc	Benziger Family Winery
Sleepy Hollow	Monterey County	Robert Talbott	Riesling, Pinot Noir, Chardonnay	Monterey Peninsula Winery
Smith & Hook	Santa Lucia Highlands	N. Hahn	Cabernet Sauvignon	Fenestra Winery
Smith-Reichle	Alexander Valley	Chuck Reichle	Cabernet Sauvignon	Byington Winery & Vineyards, Chauffe-eau Cellars
Split Rail	Santa Cruz Mountains	Thomasen	Chardonnay, Pinot Noir	David Bruce Winery
Staglin Family	Rutherford	Staglin Family	Cabernet Sauvignon	Staglin Family Vineyard
Star Hill Estate	Napa Valley	Jacob Goldenberg	Pinot Noir	Star Hill Wines
Steiner	Sonoma Mountain	Dave Steiner	Pinot Noir, Cabernet Sauvignon	Joseph Swan Vineyards
Stuhlmuller	Alexander Valley	Roger Stuhlmuller	Chardonnay	Cronin Vineyards
Summa	Sonoma Coast	Scott & Joan Zeller	Pinot Noir	Williams & Selyem Winery
Summers Ranch	Knights Valley	Jim & Beth Summers	Merlot	Judd's Hill
Sunny Oak	El Dorado County	Al & Teddy Wolterbeck	Syrah	Westwood Winery
Suzanne's	Napa Valley	V. Sattui Winery	Zinfandel, Cabernet Sauvignon	V. Sattui Winery
Sycamore	Napa Valley	John Bryan	Cabernet Sauvignon	Freemark Abbey Winery
Talley	Arroyo Grande	Brian Talley	Chardonnay, Pinot Noir	Babcock Vineyards, Au Bon Climat, The Ojai Vineyard
TC Vineyard	Amador County	Chuck Sisney	Zinfandel	Sonora Winery & Port Works
Terra Vin	Napa Valley	James Pawlak	Zinfandel, Refosco, Cabernet Sauvignon	
Three Palms	Napa Valley	John & Joan Upton	Merlot	Duckhorn Vineyards, Sterling Vineyards
Tichenor	Shenandoah Valley	Bruce Tichenor & Story Winery	Zinfandel	Domaine de la Terre Rouge
Tinaquaic	Santa Maria Valley	Foxen Vineyard Inc.	Chardonnay, Cabernet Sauvignon	Foxen Vineyard
To-Kalon	Oakville	Robert Mondavi Winery	Sauvignon Blanc	Robert Mondavi Winery
Toy	Livermore Valley	Art Toy	Chardonnay, Cabernet Sauvignon	Fenestra Winery, Livermore Valley Cellars
Trailside	Napa Valley	Heitz Wine Cellars	Cabernet Sauvignon	Heitz Wine Cellars
Triere	Napa Valley	Tom Burgess	Chardonnay	Burgess Cellars
Turnbull	Napa Valley	Turnbull	Cabernet Franc	Moondance Cellars
Twin Rivers	El Dorado County	Lang Wines	Zinfandel	Lang Wines
Two Williams	Sonoma County	Landmark Winery	Chardonnay	Landmark Winery
V.H.S.R.	Russian River Valley	Pat Bohn	Zinfandel	Joseph Swan Vineyards
Vahalla	Napa Valley	Arthur Anderson	Pinot Noir	Anderson's Conn Valley Vineyards
Vanomanutagi	Santa Cruz Mountains	Leonard Ware	Chardonnay	Storrs Winery
Ventana	Monterey County	Doug Meador	Chardonnay, Gewürztraminer, Syrah, Riesling	Chouinard Vineyards, Ahlgren Vineyard, Thomas Fogarty Winery, River Run Vintners
Venturi	Mendocino County	Larry Venturi	Charbono	Konrad Estate
Vigna Bella	Shenandoah Valley	Amador Foothill Winery	Sangiovese	Amador Foothill Winery
Vine Hill Ranch	Napa Valley	Bob Phillips	Cabernet Sauvignon	Robert Pepi Winery
Vine Hill	Russian River Valley	Kistler Vineyards	Chardonnay	Kistler Vineyards
Vineyard View	Pleasant Hill	Al Lippencott	Barbara	Monterey Cellars Monterey Peninsula
Vista	Napa Valley	Oakville Ranch Vineyards	Chardonnay	Oakville Ranch Vineyards
Volcanic Hill	Napa Valley	Diamond Creek Vineyards	Cabernet Sauvignon	Diamond Creek Vineyards
Walker	El Dorado County	Lloyd Walker	Zinfandel	Boeger Winery

VINEYARD	APPELLATION	OWNER	VARIETIES	WINERIES USING VINEYARD
Webb	Mendocino County	Roger Webb	Sauvignon Blanc	Fieldbrook Valley Winery
Wedding	Sonoma County	Juelle & Fred Fisher	Cabernet Sauvignon	Fisher Vineyards
Whitney's	Sonoma County	Juelle & Fred Fisher	Chardonnay	Fisher Vineyards
Whittington	El Dorado County	Dave Whittington	Pinot Noir	Wheeler Winery
Wildwood	Sonoma Valley	Kunde Family	Chardonnay	Kunde Estate Winery
Winery Lake	Carneros	Seagram Classics Wine Co.	Chardonnay, Pinot Noir	Mumm Napa Valley, Sterling
Yoakim Bridge Ranch	Dry Creek Valley	Jerry Petersen	Merlot	Lake Sonoma Winery
York Creek	Spring Mountain	Fritz Maytag	Zinfandel, Petite Sirah	Ridge Vineyards
Young, Robert	Alexander Valley	Robert Young	Chardonnay, Pinot Blanc	Chateau St. Jean
Yountville Ranch	Napa Valley	Bernard Pradel Cellars	Cabernet Sauvignon	Bernard Pradel Cellars
Yulupa	Sonoma Valley	Kenwood Vineyards	Chardonnay	Kenwood Vineyards
Zeigler	Russian River Valley	Kirt Zeigler	Zinfandel	Joseph Swan Vineyards
Zeni	Anderson Valley	George Zeni	Zinfandel	Edmeades Winery

GRAPE ACREAGE BY COUNTY

CABERNET SAUVIGNON

NUMBER OF ACRES

COUNTY	1980	1985	Percent Change 1980-85	1990	Percent Change 1980-90	1993	Percent Change 1990-93	1994	Percent Change 1990-94
Alameda	39	56	44%	205	426%	223	9%	222	8%
Amador	45	49	9%	46	2%	36	-22%	26	-43%
Butte	171	85	-50%	72	-58%	65	-10%	65	-10%
Calaveras	9	18	100%	17	89%	28	65%	15	-12%
Colusa	0	0	0%	10	100%	30	200%	30	200%
Contra Costa	0	0	0%	9	100%	9	0%	16	78%
El Dorado	22	37	68%	57	159%	61	7%	82	44%
Fresno	59	0	-100%	0	-100%	35	100%	35	100%
Glenn	0	0	0%	0	0%	0	0%	0	0%
Humboldt	0	1	100%	0	0%	0	0%	0	0%
Kern	853	520	-39%	603	-29%	900	49%	954	58%
Kings	0	0	0%	0	0%	37	100%	37	100%
Lake	1,080	1,155	7%	954	-12%	859	-10%	942	-1%
Los Angeles	0	0	0%	0	0%	0	0%	0	0%
Madera	56	35	-38%	61	9%	119	95%	119	95%
Marin	14	11	-21%	8	-43%	10	25%	9	13%
Mariposa	0	0	0%	1	100%	1	0%	5	400%
Mendocino	920	896	-3%	1,108	20%	1,301	17%	1,285	16%
Merced	112	99	-12%	101	-10%	254	151%	253	150%
Monterey	4,364	2,757	-37%	2,741	-37%	3,603	31%	3,582	31%
Napa	5,051	6,027	19%	7,067	40%	8,669	23%	8,850	25%
Nevada	3	7	133%	24	700%	20	-17%	24	0%
Orange	15	0	-100%	0	-100%	0	0%	0	0%
Placer	3	2	-33%	0	-100%	0	0%	0	0%
Riverside	235	152	-35%	116	-51%	83	-28%	89	-23%
Sacramento	520	527	1%	659	27%	1,060	61%	1,138	73%
San Benito	508	378	-26%	307	-40%	277	-10%	277	-10%
San Bernardino	0	0	0%	0	0%	0	0%	0	0%
San Diego	0	6	100%	4	100%	1	-75%	1	-75%
San Joaquin	573	582	2%	1,355	136%	3,336	146%	3,439	154%

Cabernet Sauvignon *continued*

COUNTY	1980	1985	Percent Change 1980-85	1990	Percent Change 1980-90	1993	Percent Change 1990-93	1994	Percent Change 1990-94
San Luis Obispo	926	849	-8%	1,395	51%	2,533	82%	2,596	86%
San Mateo	4	3	-25%	12	200%	12	0%	10	-17%
Santa Barbara	1,079	776	-28%	825	-24%	732	-11%	569	-31%
Santa Clara	182	188	3%	146	-20%	147	1%	151	3%
Santa Cruz	12	10	-17%	4	-67%	4	0%	4	0%
Shasta	5	5	0%	5	0%	5	0%	5	0%
Solano	235	199	-15%	165	-30%	218	32%	219	33%
Sonoma	4,359	4,600	6%	5,431	25%	5,924	9%	6,357	17%
Stanislaus	187	157	-16%	210	12%	418	99%	455	117%
Tehama	34	37	9%	30	-12%	25	-17%	25	-17%
Trinity	0	0	0%	0	0%	0	0%	0	0%
Tulare	43	0	-100%	53	23%	308	481%	306	477%
Tuolumne	0	0	0%	0	0%	0	0%	0	0%
Ventura	1	0	-100%	0	-100%	0	0%	0	0%
Yolo	30	31	3%	160	433%	153	-4%	249	56%
Yuba	10	175	1,650%	154	1,440%	154	0%	154	0%
TOTAL CABERNET	**21,759**	**20,430**	**-6%**	**24,115**	**11%**	**31,650**	**31%**	**32,595**	**35%**

CHARDONNAY

NUMBER OF ACRES

COUNTY	1980	1985	Percent Change 1980-85	1990	Percent Change 1980-90	1993	Percent Change 1990-93	1994	Percent Change 1990-94
Alameda	122	183	50%	540	343%	670	24%	668	24%
Amador	0	25	100%	32	100%	29	-9%	6	-81%
Butte	7	0	-100%	0	-100%	0	0%	0	0%
Calaveras	0	22	100%	24	100%	49	104%	45	88%
Colusa	0	0	0%	9	100%	68	656%	73	711%
Contra Costa	0	0	0%	0	0%	8	100%	8	100%
El Dorado	15	40	167%	52	247%	58	12%	56	8%
Fresno	80	209	161%	269	236%	260	-3%	265	-1%
Glenn	0	0	0%	0	0%	0	0%	0	0%
Humboldt	0	0	0%	0	0%	0	0%	0	0%

Chardonnay *continued*

NUMBER OF ACRES

COUNTY	1980	1985	Percent Change 1980-85	1990	Percent Change 1980-90	1993	Percent Change 1990-93	1994	Percent Change 1990-94
Kern	12	12	0%	89	642%	405	355%	405	355%
Kings	0	0	0%	0	0%	0	0%	0	0%
Lake	5	201	3,920%	268	5,260%	560	109%	614	129%
Los Angeles	0	0	0%	0	0%	0	0%	0	0%
Madera	110	127	15%	166	51%	310	87%	317	91%
Marin	0	0	0%	0	0%	0	0%	3	100%
Mariposa	0	0	0%	1	100%	7	600%	7	600%
Mendocino	574	1,250	118%	2,668	365%	3,405	28%	3,921	47%
Merced	12	20	67%	24	100%	783	3,163%	925	3,754%
Monterey	2,699	4,000	48%	5,558	106%	9,396	69%	9,859	77%
Napa	2,965	6,095	106%	7,997	170%	8,906	11%	8,591	7%
Nevada	0	14	100%	60	100%	55	-8%	55	-8%
Orange	0	0	0%	0	0%	0	0%	0	0%
Placer	1	1	0%	1	0%	0	-100%	0	-100%
Riverside	172	491	185%	1,052	512%	1,128	7%	1,227	17%
Sacramento	17	43	153%	313	1,741%	1,271	306%	1,408	350%
San Benito	883	397	-55%	429	-51%	346	-19%	376	-12%
San Bernardino	0	0	0%	0	0%	0	0%	4	100%
San Diego	0	3	100%	22	100%	25	-14%	18	-18%
San Joaquin	19	178	837%	2,428	12,679%	4,754	96%	5,281	118%
San Luis Obispo	411	653	59%	1,973	380%	2,664	35%	3,013	53%
San Mateo	2	16	700%	27	1,250%	27	0%	24	-11%
Santa Barbara	931	2,117	127%	3,585	285%	5,040	41%	5,300	48%
Santa Clara	53	97	83%	227	328%	268	18%	319	41%
Santa Cruz	20	19	-5%	39	95%	31	-21%	76	95%
Shasta	0	0	0%	0	0%	0	0%	11	100%
Solano	3	28	833%	239	7,867%	403	69%	385	61%
Sonoma	3,049	6,489	113%	8,701	185%	10,872	25%	11,308	30%
Stanislaus	0	10	100%	31	100%	615	1,884%	666	2,048%
Tehama	39	78	100%	77	97%	76	-1%	76	-1%
Trinity	0	0	0%	2	100%	2	0%	0	-100%
Tulare	43	0	-100%	0	-100%	127	100%	127	100%
Tuolumne	0	0	0%	0	0%	0	0%	0	0%
Ventura	1	0	-100%	0	-100%	0	0%	0	0%
Yolo	0	16	100%	251	100%	670	167%	797	218%
Yuba	0	13	100%	20	100%	21	5%	21	5%
TOTAL CHARDONNAY	**12,245**	**22,847**	**87%**	**37,174**	**204%**	**53,309**	**43%**	**56,255**	**51%**

MERLOT

NUMBER OF ACRES

COUNTY	1980	1985	Percent Change 1980-85	1990	Percent Change 1980-90	1993	Percent Change 1990-93	1994	Percent Change 1990-94
Alameda	2	2	0%	56	2,700%	67	20%	79	41%
Amador	6	0	-100%	0	-100%	1	100%	3	100%
Butte	1	1	0%	5	400%	9	80%	9	80%
Calaveras	0	1	100%	4	100%	7	75%	17	325%
Colusa	0	0	0%	0	0%	0	0%	0	0%
Contra Costa	0	0	0%	0	0%	0	0%	0	0%
El Dorado	5	7	40%	9	80%	15	67%	35	289%
Fresno	0	0	0%	0	0%	27	100%	27	100%
Glenn	6	0	-100%	0	-100%	0	0%	0	0%
Humboldt	0	0	0%	0	0%	0	0%	0	0%
Kern	0	0	0%	39	100%	70	79%	70	79%
Kings	0	0	0%	0	0%	0	0%	0	0%
Lake	51	68	33%	101	98%	114	13%	165	63%
Los Angeles	0	0	0%	0	0%	0	0%	0	0%
Madera	28	28	0%	28	0%	169	504%	169	504%
Marin	0	0	0%	0	0%	0	0%	0	0%
Mariposa	0	0	0%	7	100%	7	0%	8	14%
Mendocino	100	50	-50%	80	-20%	297	271%	364	355%
Merced	13	0	-100%	0	-100%	161	100%	182	100%
Monterey	632	256	-59%	412	-35%	751	82%	833	102%
Napa	639	711	11%	1,511	136%	2,421	60%	2,721	80%
Nevada	0	0	0%	10	100%	10	0%	20	100%
Orange	0	0	0%	0	0%	0	0%	0	0%
Placer	0	0	0%	0	0%	0	0%	0	0%
Riverside	0	4	100%	7	100%	14	100%	8	14%
Sacramento	98	132	35%	198	102%	351	77%	461	133%
San Benito	0	0	0%	48	100%	40	-17%	60	25%
San Bernardino	0	0	0%	0	0%	0	0%	0	0%
San Diego	0	0	0%	4	100%	4	0%	10	150%
San Joaquin	72	42	-42%	10	-86%	735	7,250%	893	8,830%
San Luis Obispo	166	21	-87%	125	-25%	222	78%	353	182%
San Mateo	0	0	0%	0	0%	0	0%	0	0%
Santa Barbara	272	156	-43%	217	-20%	203	-6%	214	-1%
Santa Clara	0	2	100%	21	100%	42	100%	83	295%
Santa Cruz	0	0	0%	0	0%	0	0%	0	0%

Merlot *continued*

				NUMBER OF ACRES					
COUNTY	1980	1985	Percent Change 1980-85	1990	Percent Change 1980-90	1993	Percent Change 1990-93	1994	Percent Change 1990-94
Shasta	0	0	0%	0	0%	0	0%	0	0%
Solano	0	0	0%	0	0%	25	100%	44	100%
Sonoma	501	464	-7%	1,052	110%	2,012	91%	2,530	140%
Stanislaus	0	0	0%	0	0%	0	0%	10	100%
Tehama	0	0	0%	0	0%	0	0%	0	0%
Trinity	0	0	0%	0	0%	0	0%	0	0%
Tulare	0	0	0%	0	0%	3	100%	3	100%
Tuolumne	0	0	0%	0	0%	0	0%	0	0%
Ventura	0	0	0%	0	0%	0	0%	0	0%
Yolo	0	10	100%	66	100%	158	139%	225	241%
Yuba	0	0	0%	0	0%	9	100%	9	100%
TOTAL MERLOT	**2,592**	**1,955**	**-25%**	**4,010**	**55%**	**7,944**	**98%**	**9,605**	**140%**

PINOT NOIR

				NUMBER OF ACRES					
COUNTY	1980	1985	Percent Change 1980-85	1990	Percent Change 1980-90	1993	Percent Change 1990-93	1994	Percent Change 1990-94
Alameda	76	76	0%	20	-74%	0	-100%	14	-30%
Amador	0	0	0%	0	0%	0	0%	0	0%
Butte	4	0	-100%	0	-100%	0	0%	0	0%
Calaveras	0	0	0%	0	0%	0	0%	0	0%
Colusa	0	0	0%	0	0%	0	0%	0	0%
Contra Costa	0	0	0%	0	0%	0	0%	0	0%
El Dorado	0	2	100%	0	0%	0	0%	3	100%
Fresno	40	0	-100%	0	-100%	0	0%	0	0%
Glenn	0	0	0%	0	0%	0	0%	0	0%
Humboldt	0	0	0%	0	0%	0	0%	0	0%
Kern	0	0	0%	0	0%	10	100%	10	100%
Kings	0	0	0%	0	0%	0	0%	0	0%
Lake	7	7	0%	0	-100%	0	0%	0	0%
Los Angeles	0	0	0%	0	0%	0	0%	0	0%
Madera	0	15	100%	15	100%	5	-67%	5	-67%

Pinot Noir *continued*

NUMBER OF ACRES

COUNTY	1980	1985	Percent Change 1980-85	1990	Percent Change 1980-90	1993	Percent Change 1990-93	1994	Percent Change 1990-94
Marin	0	0	0%	0	0%	0	0%	3	100%
Mariposa	0	0	0%	0	0%	0	0%	0	0%
Mendocino	317	295	-7%	668	111%	548	-18%	689	3%
Merced	0	0	0%	0	0%	0	0%	0	0%
Monterey	1,971	1,291	-35%	1,550	-21%	1,444	-7%	1,369	-12%
Napa	2,340	2,144	-8%	2,458	5%	2,383	-3%	2,464	0%
Nevada	3	5	67%	3	0%	2	-33%	2	-33%
Orange	0	0	0%	0	0%	0	0%	0	0%
Placer	0	0	0%	0	0%	0	0%	0	0%
Riverside	4	0	-100%	0	-100%	0	0%	0	0%
Sacramento	0	0	0%	0	0%	0	0%	0	0%
San Benito	764	331	-57%	236	-69%	179	-24%	189	-20%
San Bernardino	0	17	100%	0	0%	0	0%	0	0%
San Diego	0	0	0%	0	0%	0	0%	0	0%
San Joaquin	0	0	0%	0	0%	0	0%	0	0%
San Luis Obispo	96	81	-16%	169	76%	186	10%	220	30%
San Mateo	0	1	100%	6	100%	6	0%	6	0%
Santa Barbara	693	589	-15%	699	1%	773	11%	759	9%
Santa Clara	94	70	-26%	52	-45%	48	-8%	54	4%
Santa Cruz	22	25	14%	30	36%	24	-20%	14	-53%
Shasta	0	0	0%	0	0%	0	0%	0	0%
Solano	25	22	-12%	16	-36%	25	56%	20	25%
Sonoma	2,768	2,458	-11%	2,632	-5%	2,944	12%	2,905	10%
Stanislaus	0	0	0%	0	0%	0	0%	0	0%
Tehama	0	0	0%	0	0%	0	0%	0	0%
Trinity	0	0	0%	0	0%	1	100%	1	100%
Tulare	0	0	0%	0	0%	0	0%	0	0%
Tuolumne	0	0	0%	0	0%	0	0%	0	0%
Ventura	0	0	0%	0	0%	0	0%	0	0%
Yolo	0	0	0%	0	0%	0	0%	0	0%
Yuba	0	0	0%	0	0%	0	0%	0	0%
TOTAL PINOT NOIR	**9,224**	**7,429**	**-19%**	**8,554**	**-7%**	**8,578**	**0%**	**8,727**	**2%**

SAUVIGNON BLANC

NUMBER OF ACRES

COUNTY	1980	1985	Percent Change 1980-85	1990	Percent Change 1980-90	1993	Percent Change 1990-93	1994	Percent Change 1990-94
Alameda	130	162	25%	172	32%	161	-6%	162	-6%
Amador	9	281	3,022%	232	2,478%	143	-38%	103	-56%
Butte	0	0	0%	0	0%	0	0%	0	0%
Calaveras	0	30	100%	8	100%	45	463%	44	450%
Colusa	0	0	0%	0	0%	0	0%	0	0%
Contra Costa	0	0	0%	0	0%	0	0%	0	0%
El Dorado	5	98	1,860%	92	1,740%	86	-7%	66	-28%
Fresno	0	3	100%	3	100%	3	0%	3	0%
Glenn	0	0	0%	0	0%	0	0%	0	0%
Humboldt	0	0	0%	0	0%	0	0%	0	0%
Kern	0	20	100%	76	100%	76	0%	76	0%
Kings	0	0	0%	0	0%	0	0%	0	0%
Lake	194	590	204%	517	166%	641	24%	645	25%
Los Angeles	0	0	0%	0	0%	0	0%	0	0%
Madera	40	70	75%	92	130%	118	28%	118	28%
Marin	0	0	0%	0	0%	0	0%	0	0%
Mariposa	0	0	0%	6	100%	6	0%	6	0%
Mendocino	117	631	439%	863	638%	813	-6%	954	11%
Merced	317	704	122%	778	145%	623	-20%	583	-25%
Monterey	1,041	1,549	49%	1,453	40%	1,443	-1%	1,403	-3%
Napa	730	3,347	358%	2,782	281%	2,391	-14%	2,165	-22%
Nevada	0	7	100%	7	100%	0	-100%	0	-100%
Orange	0	0	0%	0	0%	0	0%	0	0%
Placer	5	7	40%	5	0%	0	-100%	0	-100%
Riverside	127	698	450%	258	103%	207	-20%	163	-37%
Sacramento	138	341	147%	355	157%	251	-29%	214	-40%
San Benito	14	12	-14%	1	-93%	1	0%	0	-100%
San Bernardino	0	4	100%	4	100%	4	0%	4	0%
San Diego	21	4	-81%	2	-90%	2	0%	5	150%
San Joaquin	159	1,059	566%	1,176	640%	1,434	22%	1,289	10%
San Luis Obispo	379	893	136%	650	72%	693	7%	651	0%
San Mateo	0	0	0%	0	0%	0	0%	0	0%
Santa Barbara	97	410	323%	443	357%	345	-22%	250	-44%
Santa Clara	8	24	200%	11	38%	10	-9%	10	-9%
Santa Cruz	1	0	-100%	0	-100%	0	0%	0	0%

Sauvignon Blanc *continued*

NUMBER OF ACRES

COUNTY	1980	1985	Percent Change 1980-85	1990	Percent Change 1980-90	1993	Percent Change 1990-93	1994	Percent Change 1990-94
Shasta	11	31	182%	31	182%	0	-100%	0	-100%
Solano	4	114	2,750%	189	4,625%	196	4%	196	4%
Sonoma	423	1,601	278%	1,563	270%	1,408	-10%	1,418	-9%
Stanislaus	191	319	67%	502	163%	461	-8%	456	-9%
Tehama	0	0	0%	0	0%	0	0%	0	0%
Trinity	0	0	0%	0	0%	0	0%	0	0%
Tulare	0	99	100%	0	0%	23	100%	23	100%
Tuolumne	0	0	0%	0	0%	0	0%	0	0%
Ventura	0	0	0%	0	0%	0	0%	0	0%
Yolo	0	127	100%	259	100%	268	3%	270	4%
Yuba	10	64	540%	67	570%	68	1%	68	1%
TOTAL SAUVIGNON BLANC	**4,171**	**13,299**	**219%**	**12,597**	**202%**	**11,920**	**-5%**	**11,345**	**-10%**

ZINFANDEL

NUMBER OF ACRES

COUNTY	1980	1985	Percent Change 1980-85	1990	Percent Change 1980-90	1993	Percent Change 1990-93	1994	Percent Change 1990-94
Alameda	74	56	-24%	56	-24%	56	0%	56	0%
Amador	697	1,008	45%	1,094	57%	1,198	10%	1,200	10%
Butte	85	18	-79%	0	-100%	0	0%	0	0%
Calaveras	43	39	-9%	47	9%	40	-15%	45	-4%
Colusa	0	0	0%	37	100%	1,035	2,697%	1,035	2,697%
Contra Costa	390	367	-6%	293	-25%	242	-17%	241	-18%
El Dorado	59	136	131%	142	141%	143	1%	148	4%
Fresno	196	141	-28%	346	77%	601	74%	600	73%
Glenn	9	9	0%	9	0%	300	3,233%	300	3,233%
Humboldt	0	0	0%	0	0%	0	0%	0	0%
Kern	86	62	-28%	649	655%	1,071	65%	1,184	82%
Kings	0	0	0%	68	100%	145	113%	145	113%
Lake	305	329	8%	251	-18%	304	21%	321	28%
Los Angeles	0	0	0%	0	0%	0	0%	2	100%
Madera	79	86	9%	629	696%	1,046	66%	1,058	68%

Zinfandel *continued*

NUMBER OF ACRES

COUNTY	1980	1985	Percent Change 1980-85	1990	Percent Change 1980-90	1993	Percent Change 1990-93	1994	Percent Change 1990-94
Marin	0	0	0%	0	0%	0	0%	0	0%
Mariposa	0	0	0%	12	100%	6	-50%	6	-50%
Mendocino	1,238	1,346	9%	1,643	33%	1,744	6%	1,715	4%
Merced	143	99	-31%	544	280%	903	66%	894	64%
Monterey	2,364	1,795	-24%	1,868	-21%	1,465	-22%	1,420	-24%
Napa	1,886	1,940	3%	1,844	-2%	2,032	10%	1,989	8%
Nevada	3	5	67%	2	-33%	2	0%	2	0%
Orange	0	0	0%	0	0%	0	0%	0	0%
Placer	33	23	-30%	20	-39%	20	0%	19	-5%
Riverside	133	97	-27%	106	-20%	80	-25%	81	-24%
Sacramento	449	361	-20%	356	-21%	348	-2%	288	-19%
San Benito	204	25	-88%	30	-85%	24	-20%	23	-23%
San Bernardino	2,280	1,214	-47%	642	-72%	552	-14%	480	-25%
San Diego	20	9	-55%	9	-55%	0	-100%	0	-100%
San Joaquin	10,978	9,912	-10%	10,977	0%	12,439	13%	12,523	14%
San Luis Obispo	963	977	1%	1,260	31%	1,204	-4%	1,173	-7%
San Mateo	0	0	0%	0	0%	0	0%	0	0%
Santa Barbara	62	43	-31%	24	-61%	16	-33%	16	-33%
Santa Clara	122	109	-11%	89	-27%	71	-20%	71	-20%
Santa Cruz	7	6	-14%	4	-43%	4	0%	4	0%
Shasta	0	0	0%	0	0%	0	0%	0	0%
Solano	26	33	27%	73	181%	102	40%	99	36%
Sonoma	4,118	4,221	3%	3,924	-5%	3,701	-6%	3,769	-4%
Stanislaus	540	254	-53%	489	-9%	1,020	109%	1,060	117%
Tehama	11	0	-100%	0	-100%	0	0%	0	0%
Trinity	0	0	0%	0	0%	0	0%	0	0%
Tulare	0	0	0%	369	100%	733	99%	657	78%
Tuolumne	0	0	0%	0	0%	0	0%	0	0%
Ventura	0	0	0%	0	0%	0	0%	0	0%
Yolo	46	55	20%	83	80%	82	-1%	80	-4%
Yuba	3	0	-100%	0	-100%	0	0%	0	0%
TOTAL ZINFANDEL	**27,652**	**24,775**	**-10%**	**27,989**	**1%**	**32,729**	**17%**	**32,704**	**17%**

SOURCE: CALIFORNIA AGRICULTURAL STATISTICS SERVICE

GLOSSARY

❖

ACETIC ACID: All wines contain acetic acid, or vinegar, but usually the amount is quite small—from 0.03% to 0.06%—and not perceptible to smell or taste. Once table wines reach 0.07% or above, a sweet/sour vinegary smell and taste becomes evident. At low levels, acetic acid can enhance the character of a wine, but at higher levels (over 0.1%), it can become the dominant flavor and is considered a major flaw. A related substance, ethyl acetate, contributes a nail polish-like smell.

ACID: A compound present in all grapes and an essential component of wine that preserves it, enlivens and shapes its flavors and helps prolong its aftertaste. There are four major kinds of acids—tartaric, malic, lactic and citric—found in wine. Acid is identifiable by the crisp, sharp character it imparts to a wine.

ACIDIC: Used to describe wines whose total acid is so high that they taste tart or sour and have a sharp edge on the palate.

ACIDITY: The acidity of a balanced dry table wine is in the range of 0.6% to 0.75% of the wine's volume. It is legal in California to correct deficient acidity by adding acid, although it is often overdone, leading to unusually sharp, acidic wines.

ACRID: Describes a harsh or bitter taste or pungent smell that is due to excess sulfur.

AERATION: The process of letting a wine "breathe" in the open air, or swirling wine in a glass. It's debatable whether aerating bottled wines (mostly reds) improves their quality. Aeration can soften young, tannic wines; it can also fatigue older ones.

AFTERTASTE: The taste or flavors that linger in the mouth after the wine is tasted, spit or swallowed. The aftertaste or "finish" is the most important factor in judging a wine's character and quality. Great wines have rich, long, complex aftertastes.

AGGRESSIVE: Unpleasantly harsh in taste or texture, usually due to a high level of tannin or acid.

ALCOHOL: Ethyl alcohol, a chemical compound formed by the action of natural or added yeast on the sugar content of grapes during fermentation.

ALCOHOL BY VOLUME: As required by law, wineries must state the alcohol level of a wine on its label. This is usually expressed as a numerical percentage of the volume. For table wines the law allows a 1.5% variation above or below the stated percentage as long as the alcohol does not exceed 14%. Thus, wineries may legally avoid revealing the actual alcohol content of their wines by labeling them as "table wine."

ALCOHOLIC: Used to describe a wine that has too much alcohol for its body and weight, making it unbalanced. A wine with too much alcohol will taste uncharacteristically heavy or hot as a result. This quality is noticeable in aroma and aftertaste.

AMERICAN OAK: Increasingly popular as an alternative to French oak for aging barrels, as quality improves and vintners learn how to treat the wood to meet their needs. Marked by strong vanilla, dill and cedary notes, it is used primarily for aging Cabernet, Merlot and Zinfandel, for which it is the preferred oak. It's less desirable, although used occasionally, for Chardonnay or Pinot Noir. Many wineries use American oak, yet claim

731

to use French oak because of its more prestigious image. American oak barrels sell in the $250 range, compared to more than $500 for the French ones.

AMERICAN VITICULTURAL AREA (AVA): A delimited, geographical grape-growing area that has officially been given appellation status by the Bureau of Alcohol, Tobacco and Firearms. Two examples are Napa Valley and Sonoma Valley. See also VITICULTURAL AREA.

AMPELOGRAPHY: The study of grape varieties.

APPEARANCE: Refers to a wine's clarity, not color.

APPELLATION: Defines the area where a wine's grapes were grown, such as Alexander Valley or Russian River Valley. In order to use an appellation on a California wine label, 85% of the grapes used to make the wine must be grown in the specified district.

AROMA: Traditionally defined as the smell that wine acquires from the grapes and from fermentation. Now it more commonly means the wine's total smell, including changes that resulted from oak aging or that occurred in the bottle—good or bad. "Bouquet" has a similar meaning.

ASTRINGENT: Describes a rough, harsh, puckery feel in the mouth, usually from tannin or high acidity, that red wines (and a few whites) have. When the harshness stands out, the wine is astringent.

AUSTERE: Used to describe relatively hard, high acid wines that lack depth and roundness. Usually said of young wines that need time to soften, or wines that lack richness and body.

AWKWARD: Describes a wine that has poor structure, is clumsy or is out of balance.

BACKBONE: Used to denote those wines that are full-bodied, well-structured and balanced by a desirable level of acidity.

BACKWARD: Used to describe a young wine that is less developed than others of its type and class from the same vintage.

BALANCE: A wine has balance when its elements are harmonious and no single element dominates.

BALTHAZAR: An oversized bottle which holds the equivalent of 12 to 16 standard bottles.

BARREL FERMENTED: Denotes wine that has been fermented in small casks (usually 55-gallon oak barrels) instead of larger tanks. Advocates believe that barrel fermentation contributes greater harmony between the oak and the wine, increases body and adds complexity, texture and flavor. Its liabilities are that more labor is required and greater risks are involved. It is being used increasingly with California Chardonnay.

BITE: A marked degree of acidity or tannin. An acid grip in the finish should be more like a zestful tang and is tolerable only in a rich, full-bodied wine.

BITTER: Describes one of the four basic tastes (along with sour, salty and sweet). Some grapes—notably Gewürztraminer and Muscat—often have a noticeable bitter edge to their flavors. Another source of bitterness is tannin or stems. If the bitter quality dominates the wine's flavor or aftertaste, it is considered a fault. In sweet wines a trace of bitterness may complement the flavors. In young red wines it can be a warning signal, as bitterness doesn't always dissipate with age. Normally, a fine, mature wine should not be bitter on the palate.

BLANC DE BLANCS: "White of whites," meaning a white wine made of white grapes, such as Champagne made of Chardonnay.

BLANC DE NOIRS: White wine made of red or black grapes, where the juice is squeezed from the grapes and fermented without skin contact. The wines can have a pale pink hue.

BLUNT: Strong in flavor and often alcoholic, but lacking in aromatic interest and development on the palate.

BODY: The impression of weight or fullness on the palate; usually the result of a combination of glycerin, alcohol and sugar. Commonly expressed as full-bodied, medium-bodied or medium-weight, or light-bodied.

BOTRYTIS CINEREA: Called the "Noble Rot." A beneficial and often highly desirable mold or fungus that attacks grapes under certain climatic conditions and causes them to shrivel, deeply concentrating the flavors, sugar and acid.

BOTTLE SICKNESS: A temporary condition characterized by muted or disjointed fruit flavors. It often occurs immediately after bottling or when wines (usually fragile wines) are shaken in travel. Also called bottle shock. A few days of rest is the cure.

BOTTLED BY: Means the wine could have been purchased ready-made and simply bottled by the brand owner, or made under contract by another winery. When the label reads "produced and bottled by" or "made and bottled by" it means the winery produced the wine from start to finish.

BOUQUET: The smell that a wine develops after it has been bottled and aged. Most appropriate for mature wines that have developed complex flavors beyond basic young fruit and oak aromas.

BRAWNY: Used to describe wines that are hard, intense, tannic and that have raw, woody flavors. The opposite of elegant.

BRIARY: Describes young wines with an earthy or stemmy wild berry character.

BRIGHT: Used for fresh, ripe, zesty, lively young wines with vivid, focused flavors.

BRILLIANT: Describes the appearance of very clear wines with absolutely no visible suspended or particulate matter. Not always a plus, as it can indicate a highly filtered wine.

BRIX: A measurement of the sugar content of grapes, must and wine, indicating the degree of the grapes' ripeness (meaning sugar level) at harvest. Most table-wine grapes are harvested at between 21 and 25 Brix . To get an alcohol conversion level, multiply the stated Brix by .55.

BROWNING: Describes a wine's color, and is a sign that a wine is mature and may be faded. A bad sign in young red (or white) wines, but less significant in older wines. Wines 20 to 30 years old may have a brownish edge yet still be enjoyable.

BRUT: A general term used to designate a relatively dry-finished Champagne or sparkling wine, often the driest wine made by the producer.

BURNT: Describes wines that have an overdone, smoky, toasty or singed edge. Also used to describe overripe grapes.

BUTTERY: Indicates the smell of melted butter or toasty oak. Also a reference to texture, as in "a rich, buttery Chardonnay."

CARBONIC MACERATION: Fermentation of whole, uncrushed grapes in a carbon dioxide atmosphere. In practice, the weight of the upper layers of grapes in a vat will break the skins of the lowest layer; the resultant wine is partly a product of carbonic maceration and partly of traditional fermentation of juice.

CASK NUMBER: A meaningless term sometimes used for special wines, as in Stag's Leap Wine Cellars Cask 23, but often applied to ordinary wines.

CEDARY: Denotes the smell of cedar wood associated with mature Cabernet Sauvignon and Cabernet blends aged in French or American oak.

CELLARED BY: Means the wine was not produced at the winery where it was bottled. It usually indicates that the wine was purchased from another source.

CHAPTALIZATION: The addition of sugar to juice before fermentation, used to boost sugar levels in under-ripe grapes. Illegal in California.

CHARMAT: Mass production method for sparkling wine. Indicates the wines are fermented in large stainless steel tanks and later drawn off into the bottle under pressure. Also known as the "bulk process."

CHEWY: Describes rich, heavy, tannic wines that are full-bodied.

CIGAR BOX: Another descriptor for a cedary aroma.

CLEAN: Fresh on the palate and free of any off-taste. Does not necessarily imply good quality.

CLONE: A group of vines originating from a single, individual plant propagated asexually from a single source. Clones are selected for the unique qualities of the grapes and wines they yield, such as flavor, productivity and adaptability to growing conditions.

CLOSED: Describes wines that are concentrated and have character, yet are shy in intensity.

CLOUDINESS: Lack of clarity to the eye. Fine for old wines with sediment, but it can be a warning signal of protein instability, yeast spoilage or re-fermentation in the bottle in younger wines.

CLOYING: Describes ultra-sweet or sugary wines that lack the balance provided by acid, alcohol, bitterness or intense flavor.

COARSE: Usually refers to texture, and in particular, excessive tannin or oak. Also used to describe harsh bubbles in sparkling wines.

COLD STABILIZATION: A clarification technique in which a wine's temperature is lowered to 32 degrees F, causing the tartrates and other insoluble solids to precipitate.

COMPLEXITY: An element in all great wines and many very good ones; a combination of richness, depth, flavor intensity, focus, balance, harmony and finesse.

CORKED: Describes a wine having the off-putting, musty, molding-newspaper flavor and aroma and dry aftertaste caused by a tainted cork.

CRUSH: Harvest season when the grapes are picked and crushed.

CUVÉE: A blend or special lot of wine.

DECANTING: A process for separating the sediment from a wine before drinking. Accomplished by slowly and carefully pouring the wine from its bottle into another container.

DELICATE: Used to describe light- to medium-weight wines with good flavors. A desirable quality in wines such as Pinot Noir or Riesling.

DEMI-SEC: In the language of Champagne, a term relating to sweetness. It can be misleading; although demi-sec means half-dry, demi-sec sparkling wines are usually slightly sweet to medium sweet.

DENSE: Describes a wine that has concentrated aromas on the nose and palate. A good sign in young wines.

DEPTH: Describes the complexity and concentration of flavors in a wine, as in a wine with excellent or uncommon depth. Opposite of shallow.

DIRTY: Covers any and all foul, rank, off-putting smells that can occur in a wine, including those caused by bad barrels or corks. A sign of poor winemaking.

DOSAGE: In bottle-fermented sparkling wines, a small amount of wine (usually sweet) that is added back to the bottle once the yeast sediment that collects in the neck of the bottle is removed.

DRY: Having no perceptible taste of sugar. Most wine tasters begin to perceive sugar at levels of 0.5% to 0.7%. For my purposes, I describe as dry any wine with residual sugar of 0.5% or less.

DRYING OUT: Losing fruit (or sweetness in sweet wines) to the extent that acid, alcohol or tannin dominate the taste. At this stage the wine will not improve.

DUMB: Describes a phase young wines undergo when their flavors and aromas are undeveloped. A synonym of closed.

EARLY HARVEST: Denotes a wine made from early-harvested grapes, usually lower than average in alcoholic content or sweetness.

EARTHY: Used to describe both positive and negative attributes in wine. At its best, a pleasant, clean quality that adds complexity to aroma and flavors. The flip side is a funky, barnyardy character that borders on or crosses into dirtiness.

ELEGANT: Used to describe wines of grace, balance and beauty.

EMPTY: Similar to hollow; devoid of flavor and interest.

ENOLOGY: The science and study of winemaking. Also spelled oenology.

ESTATE BOTTLED: A term once used by producers for those wines made from vineyards that they owned and that were contiguous to the winery "estate." Today it indicates the winery either owns the vineyard or has a long-term lease to purchase the grapes.

ETHYL ACETATE: A sweet, vinegary smell that often accompanies acetic acid. It exists to some extent in all wines and in small doses can be a plus. When it is strong and smells like nail polish, it's a defect.

EXTRA DRY: A common Champagne term not to be taken literally. Most Champagnes so labeled are sweet.

EXTRACT: Richness and depth of concentration of fruit in a wine. Usually a positive quality, although high extract wine can also be highly tannic.

FADING: Describes a wine that is losing color, fruit or flavor, usually as a result of age.

FAT: Full-bodied, high alcohol wines low in acidity give a "fat" impression on the palate. Can be a plus with bold, ripe, rich flavors; can also suggest the wine's structure is suspect.

FERMENTATION: The process by which yeast converts sugar into alcohol and carbon dioxide; turns grape juice into wine.

FIELD BLEND: When a vineyard is planted to several different varieties, the grapes being harvested together to produce a single wine, the wine called a field blend.

FILTERING: The process of removing particles from wine after fermentation. Most wines unless otherwise labeled are filtered for both clarity and stability.

FINING: A technique for clarifying wine using agents such as bentonite (powdered clay), gelatin or egg whites, which combine with sediment particles and cause them to settle to the bottom, where they can be easily removed.

FINISH: The key to judging a wine's quality is finish, also called aftertaste—a measure of the taste or flavors that linger in the mouth after the wine is tasted. Great wines have rich, long, complex finishes.

FLABBY: Soft, feeble, lacking acidity on the palate.

FLAT: Having low acidity; the next stage after flabby. Can also refer to a sparkling wine that has lost its bubbles.

FLESHY: Soft and smooth in texture, with very little tannin.

FLINTY: A descriptor for extremely dry white wines such as Sauvignon Blanc, whose bouquet is reminiscent of flint struck against steel.

FLORAL (also FLOWERY): Literally, having the characteristic aromas of flowers. Mostly associated with white wines.

FORTIFIED: Denotes a wine whose alcohol content has been increased by the addition of brandy or neutral spirits.

FOXY: A term used to describe the unique musky and grapey character of many native American *labrusca* varieties.

FREE-RUN JUICE: The juice that escapes after the grape skins are crushed or squeezed prior to fermentation.

FRESH: Having a lively, clean and fruity character. An essential for young wines.

FRUITY: Having the aroma and taste of fruit or fruits.

GRACEFUL: Describes a wine that is harmonious and pleasing in a subtle way.

GRAPEY: Characterized by simple flavors and aromas associated with fresh table grapes; distinct from the more complex fruit flavors (currant, black cherry, fig or apricot) found in fine wines.

GRASSY: A signature descriptor for Sauvignon Blanc and a pleasant one unless overbearing and pungent.

GREEN: Tasting of unripe fruit. Wines made from unripe grapes will often possess this quality. Pleasant in Riesling and Gewürztraminer.

GRIP: A welcome firmness of texture, usually from tannin, which helps give definition to wines such as Cabernet and Port.

GROWN, PRODUCED AND BOTTLED: Means the winery handled each aspect of wine growing.

HALF-BOTTLE: Holds 375 milliliters or 3/8 liter.

HARD: Firm; a quality that usually results from high acidity or tannins. Often a descriptor for young red wines.

HARMONIOUS: Well balanced, with no component obtrusive or lacking.

HARSH: Used to describe astringent wines that are tannic or high in alcohol.

HAZY: Used to describe a wine that has small amounts of visible matter. A good quality if a wine is unfined and unfiltered.

HEARTY: Used to describe the full, warm, sometimes rustic qualities found in red wines with high alcohol.

HEADY: Describes high-alcohol wines.

HERBACEOUS: Denotes the taste and smell of herbs in a wine. A plus in many wines such as Sauvignon Blanc, and to a lesser extent Merlot and Cabernet. Herbal is a synonym.

HOLLOW: Lacking in flavor. Describes a wine that has a first taste and a short finish, and lacks depth at mid-palate.

HOT: High alcohol, unbalanced wines that tend to burn with "heat" on the finish are called hot. Acceptable in Port-style wines.

IMPERIAL: An oversized bottle holding four to six liters; the equivalent of eight standard bottles.

JEROBOAM: An oversized bottle the equivalent of six bottles; also called a double magnum.

LATE HARVEST: On labels, indicates that a wine was made from grapes picked later than normal and at a higher sugar (Brix) level than normal. Usually associated with botrytized and dessert-style wines.

LEAFY: Describes the slightly herbaceous, vegetal quality reminiscent of leaves. Can be a positive or a negative, depending on whether it adds to or detracts from a wine's flavor.

LEAN: A not necessarily critical term used to describe wines made in an austere style. When used as a term of criticism, it indicates a wine is lacking in fruit.

LEES: Sediment remaining in a barrel or tank during and after fermentation. Often used as in *sur lie* aging, which indicates a wine is aged "on its lees."

LEGS: The viscous droplets that form and ease down the sides of the glass when the wine is swirled.

LENGTH: The amount of time the sensations of taste and aroma persist after swallowing. The longer the better.

LIMOUSIN: A type of oak cask from Limoges, France.

LINGERING: Used to describe the flavor and persistence of flavor in a wine after tasting. When the aftertaste remains on the palate for several seconds, it is said to be lingering.

LIVELY: Describes wines that are fresh and fruity, bright and vivacious.

LUSH: Wines that are high in residual sugar and taste soft or viscous are called lush.

MACERATION: During fermentation, the steeping of the grape skins and solids in the wine, where alcohol acts as a solvent to extract color, tannin and aroma from the skins.

MADE AND BOTTLED BY: Indicates only that the winery crushed, fermented and bottled a minimum of 10% of the wine in the bottle. Very misleading.

MADERIZED: Describes the brownish color and slightly sweet, somewhat carmelized and often nutty character found in mature dessert-style wines.

MAGNUM: An oversized bottle that holds 1.5 liters.

MALIC: Describes the green applelike flavor found in young grapes which diminishes as they ripen and mature.

MALOLACTIC FERMENTATION: A secondary fermentation occurring in most wines, this natural process converts malic acid into softer lactic acid and carbon dioxide, thus reducing the wine's total acidity. Adds complexity to whites such as Chardonnay and softens reds such as Cabernet and Merlot.

MATURE: Ready to drink.

MEATY: Describes red wines that show plenty of concentration and a chewy quality. They may even have an aroma of cooked meat.

MERCAPTANS: An unpleasant, rubbery smell of old sulfur; encountered mainly in very old white wines.

MERITAGE: An invented term, used by California wineries, for Bordeaux-style red and white blended wines. Combines "merit" with "heritage." The term arose out of the need to name wines that didn't meet minimal labeling requirements for varietals (i.e., 75% of the named grape variety). For reds, the grapes allowed are Cabernet Sauvignon, Merlot, Cabernet Franc, Petite Verdot and Malbec; for whites, Sauvignon Blanc and Sémillon. Joseph Phelps Insignia and Flora Springs Trilogy are examples of wines whose blends vary each year, with no one grape dominating.

MÉTHODE CHAMPENOISE: The labor-intensive and costly process whereby wine undergoes a secondary fermentation inside the bottle, creating bubbles.

METHUSELAH: An extra-large bottle holding 6 liters; the equivalent of eight standard bottles.

MURKY: More than deeply colored; lacking brightness, turbid and sometimes a bit swampy. Mainly a fault of red wines.

MUST: The unfermented juice of grapes extracted by crushing or pressing; grape juice in the cask or vat before it is converted into wine.

MUSTY: Having an off-putting moldy or mildewy smell. The result of a wine being made from moldy grapes, stored in improperly cleaned tanks and barrels, or contaminated by a poor cork.

NEBUCHADNEZZAR: A giant wine bottle holding 15 liters; the equivalent of 20 standard bottles.

NOBLE ROT: See BOTRYTIS CINEREA.

NOSE: The character of a wine as determined by the olfactory sense. Also called aroma; includes bouquet.

NOUVEAU: A style of light, fruity, youthful red wine bottled and sold as soon as possible. Applies mostly to Beaujolais.

NUTTY: Used to describe oxidized wines. Often a flaw, but when it's close to an oaky flavor it can be a plus.

OAKY: Describes the aroma or taste quality imparted to a wine by the oak barrels or casks in which it was aged. Can be either positive or negative. The terms toasty, vanilla, dill, cedary and smoky indicate the desirable qualities of oak; charred, burnt, green cedar, lumber and plywood describe its unpleasant side.

OFF-DRY: Indicates a slightly sweet wine in which the residual sugar is barely perceptible—0.6% to 1.4%.

OXIDIZED: Describes wine that has been exposed too long to air and taken on a brownish color, losing its freshness and perhaps beginning to smell and taste like Sherry or old apples. Oxidized wines are also called maderized or sherrified.

PEAK: The time when a wine tastes its best—very subjective.

PERFUMED: Describes the strong, usually sweet and floral aromas of some white wines.

PH: A chemical measurement of acidity/alkalinity; the higher the pH the weaker the acid. Used by some wineries as a measurement of ripeness in relation to acidity. Low pH wines taste tart and crisp; higher pH wines are more susceptible to bacterial growth. A range of 3.0 to 3.4 is desirable for white wines, while 3.3 to 3.6 is best for reds.

PHYLLOXERA: Tiny aphids or root lice that attack *Vitus vinifera* roots. The disease was widespread in both Europe and California during the late 19th century, and returned to California in the 1980s.

POTENT: Intense and powerful.

PRESS WINE (or PRESSING): The juice extracted under pressure after pressing for white wines and after fermentation for reds. Press wine has more flavor and aroma, deeper color and often more tannins than free-run juice. Wineries often blend a portion of press wine back into the main cuvée for added backbone.

PRIVATE RESERVE: This description, along with Reserve, once stood for the best wines a winery produced, but lacking a legal definition many wineries use it or a spin-off (Proprietor's Reserve) for rather ordinary wines. Depending upon the producer, it may still signify excellent quality.

PRODUCED AND BOTTLED BY: Indicates that the winery crushed, fermented and bottled at least 75% of the wine in the bottle.

PRUNY: Having the flavor of overripe, dried-out grapes. Can add complexity in the right dose.

PUCKERY: Describes highly tannic and very dry wines.

PUNGENT: Having a powerful, assertive smell linked to a high level of volatile acidity.

RACKING: The practice of moving wine by hose from one container to another, leaving sediment behind. For aeration or clarification.

RAISINY: Having the taste of raisins from ultra-ripe or overripe grapes. Can be pleasant in small doses in some wines.

RAW: Young and undeveloped. A good descriptor of barrel samples of red wine. Raw wines are often tannic and high in alcohol or acidity.

REDUCED: Commonly used to describe a wine that has not been exposed to air.

REHOBOAM: Oversized bottle equivalent to 4.5 liters or six regular bottles.

RESIDUAL SUGAR: Unfermented grape sugar in a finished wine.

RICH: Wines with generous, full, pleasant flavors, usually sweet and round in nature, are described as rich. In dry wines, richness may be supplied by high alcohol and glycerin, by complex flavors and by an oaky vanilla character. Decidedly sweet wines are also described as rich when the sweetness is backed up by fruity, ripe flavors.

ROBUST: Means full-bodied, intense and vigorous, perhaps a bit overblown.

ROUND: Describes a texture that is smooth, not coarse or tannic.

RUSTIC: Describes wines made by old-fashioned methods or tasting like wines made in an earlier era. Can be a positive quality in distinctive wines that require aging. Can also be a negative quality when used to describe a young, earthy wine that should be fresh and fruity.

SALMANAZAR: An oversized bottle holding 9 liters, the equivalent of 12 regular bottles.

SMOKY: Usually an oak barrel byproduct, a smoky quality can add flavor and aromatic complexity to wines.

SOFT: Describes wines low in acid or tannin (sometimes both), making for easy drinking. Opposite of hard.

SPICY: A descriptor for many wines, indicating the presence of spice flavors such as anise, cinnamon, cloves, mint and pepper which are often present in complex wines.

STALE: Wines that have lost their fresh, youthful qualities are called stale. Opposite of fresh.

STALKY: Smells and tastes of grape stems or has leaf- or hay-like aromas.

STEMMY: Wines fermented too long with the grape stems may develop this quality: an unpleasant and often dominant stemmy aroma and green astringency.

STRUCTURE: The interaction of elements such as acid, tannin, glycerin, alcohol and body as it relates to a wine's texture and mouthfeel. Usually preceded by a modifier, as in "firm structure" or "lacking in structure".

SUBTLE: Describes delicate wines with finesse, or flavors that are understated rather than full-blown and overt. A positive characteristic.

SUPPLE: Describes texture, mostly with reds, as it relates to tannin, body and oak. A positive characteristic.

SUR LIE: Wines aged *sur lie* are kept in contact with the dead yeast cells and are not racked or otherwise filtered. Adds complexity to Chardonnay and Sauvignon Blanc; can occasionally be overdone and lead to a leesy flavor that is off-putting.

TANKY: Describes dull, dank qualities that show up in wines aged too long in tanks.

TANNIN: The mouth-puckering substance—found mostly in red wines—that is derived primarily from grape skins, seeds and stems, but also from oak barrels. Tannin acts as a natural preservative that helps wine age and develop.

TART: Sharp-tasting because of acidity. Occasionally used as a synonym for acidic.

TARTARIC ACID: The principal acid in wine.

TARTRATES: Harmless crystals of potassium bitartrate that may form in cask or bottle (often on the cork) from the tartaric acid naturally present in wine.

THIN: Lacking body and depth.

TIGHT: Describes a wine's structure, concentration and body, as in a "tightly wound" wine. Closed or compact are similar terms.

TINNY: Metallic tasting.

TIRED: Limp, feeble, lackluster.

TOASTY: Describes a flavor derived from the oak barrels in which wines are aged. Also, a character that sometimes develops in sparkling wines.

VEGETAL: Some wines contain elements in their smell and taste which are reminiscent of plants and vegetables. In Cabernet Sauvignon a small amount of this vegetal quality is said to be part of varietal character. But when the vegetal element takes over, or when it shows up in wines in which it does not belong, those wines are considered flawed. Wine scientists have been able to identify the chemical constituent that makes wines smell like asparagus and bell peppers, but are not sure why it occurs more often in Central Coast vineyards than in others.

VELVETY: Having rich flavor and a silky, sumptuous texture.

VINICULTURE: The science or study of grape production for wine and the making of wine.

VINOUS: Literally means "winelike" and is usually applied to dull wines lacking in distinct varietal character.

VINTAGE DATE: Indicates the year that a wine was made. In order to carry a vintage date, a wine must come from grapes that are be at least 95% from the stated calendar year.

VINTED BY: Largely meaningless phrase that means the winery purchased the wine in bulk from another winery and bottled it.

VINTNER: Translates as wine merchant, but generally indicates a wine producer/or winery proprietor.

VINTNER-GROWN: Means wine from a winery-owned vineyard situated outside the winery's delimited viticultural area.

VITICULTURAL AREA: Defines a legal grape-growing area distinguished by geographical features based on climate, soil, elevation, history and other definable boundaries. In the U.S., a wine must be 85% from grapes grown within the viticultural area to carry the appellation name. For varietal bottling, a minimum of 75% of that wine must be made from the designated grape variety.

VITICULTURE: The cultivation, science and study of grapes.

VOLATILE (Or Volatile Acidity): Describes an excessive and undesirable amount of acidity, which gives a wine a slightly sour, vinegary edge. At very low levels (0.1%), it is largely undetectable; at higher levels it is considered a major defect.

YEAST: Micro-organisms that produce the enzymes which convert sugar to alcohol. Necessary for the fermentation of grape juice into wine.

Index